BUSINESS LAW

WEST
ACADEMIC
PUBLISHING

© 2017 LEG, Inc. d/b/a West Academic
    444 Cedar Street, Suite 700
    St. Paul, MN 55101
    1-877-888-1330

Printed in the United States of America

ISBN: 978-1-68328-641-7

PREFACE

No business topic is complete without an examination of legal and compliance issues. Whether it is accounting, management, human resources, or marketing, the law permeates business subjects. Learning and understanding relevant business laws can be challenging for even mid-career business students. This book addresses that challenge by emphasizing the most significant legal issues for each topic, explaining and clarifying the important aspects of applicable laws, and providing insight by discussing the laws in a comprehensive manner.

This text brings business law to life for students. Each chapter starts with a clear statement of the Key Objectives to orient students to the general goals of the material to follow and to alert them to the topics they will be mastering in each chapter. Following the Key Objectives is a Chapter Overview that provides a general description of the topic and an Introduction that includes more detail and discusses any relevant societal, governmental, or legal considerations. Each chapter then breaks the material into practical pieces, integrating the law with the relevant business activity.

The text effectively covers the content for each chapter, while providing an accessible and approachable resource. The book describes legal methods such as legal research, writing, and logic. Relevant terms that may be new to the students are highlighted and defined in each chapter. Sidebars, examples, and graphics reinforce the key points. In addition, each chapter contains content features to promote student learning and classroom engagement. These features include the following:

CASES AND BRIEFS

This book uses both case briefs and excerpts from decisions to aid student understanding. Using the High Court Case Summaries model, the briefs in the text focus on the lesson to be learned from each decision.

Each brief starts with a headline-style statement of the rule of the case, the name and citation, and an identification of the parties procedurally and practically. In *National Federation of Independent Business v. Sebelius* (Chapter 1), for instance, Sebelius is identified as the defendant and as Secretary of Health and Human Services and the National Federation of Independent Business is identified as the plaintiff and as a business interest group. Each time a party is referenced in the brief, the party is clearly flagged as plaintiff (P) or defendant (D) in the original case. Students then receive an overview with an "instant facts" description, the black-letter rule, and the procedural basis.

With that grounding, the student proceeds to a lengthier version of the facts, the issue phrased as a yes/no question, and the court's decision. Pertinent legal concepts are presented and described using common English, with legal terminology clearly defined. Some briefs also include a short analysis and a glossary.

Exerpts from other cases are also included. These items include forward matter and formatting similar to the briefs, but allow students to tackle the actual text of real-life decisions. This process demonstrates legal risks experienced by businesses.

Case briefs and fuller excerpts appear throughout the text. To promote full understanding of the model and of case analysis, Chapter 1 discusses case briefing and shows how to brief a case. In this way, students are attuned to the model and may apply it themselves.

REVIEW QUESTIONS

Each chapter includes Review Questions for students to prepare individually or work through in class with instructor guidance.

DISCUSSION QUESTIONS

Discussion Questions range from hypotheticals to ethics dilemmas. They include variations on legal themes found in each chapter, and address common issues faced by business people. They are suitable for group work or instructor-led conversations.

VOCABULARY

Legal terminology is defined repeatedly to avoid confusion. Case briefs include short glossaries where new terms are introduced. The main text highlights legal references by bolding the word or phrase. The term is then defined in the text, and added to a glossary at the end of the chapter. Finally, for overall reference, all the terms in the book are gathered in a master glossary in the appendix.

ELECTRONIC RESOURCES

Supporting materials, including presentations, test banks, and hand-outs, are available at legalenvironmentofbusiness.com.

In addition to the features described above, this text includes:

- a broad selection of topics, including foundational issues, business formation, types of law, contracting, employment, and regulatory issues;

- numerous examples, case excerpts, sidebars, review materials, and exercises, with a focus on practical applications;

- several useful appendices, including those addressing primary law, key terms, and other aids;

- an accessible but non-patronizing language and tone aimed at undergraduates;

- newer cases and examples, while still including the seminal decisions found in most other business law texts; and

- graphics included throughout the text wherever appropriate or helpful.

This text's features stand out when compared to other introductory business law texts. As a textbook that focuses on clarifying and describing the implications of relevant laws and cases without over-simplification, it is an invaluable tool to provide the foundation for a business-law education and to act as a springboard for classroom discussions.

ACKNOWLEDGEMENTS

We owe a great debt of gratitude to the following professors and scholars who reviewed this text and provided insights, edits, additions, and critiques. Their combined experience hammered, shaped, and finally polished this text into its current form. Their work was essential to the finished product.

Charlotte Alexander
Assistant Professor of Legal Studies
Department of Risk Management and Insurance
Georgia State University

Elizabeth Brown
Assistant Professor
Law, Taxation and Financial Planning
Bentley University

Brian Elzweig, J.D., LL.M.
Instructor of Business Law
Department of Accounting and Finance
University of West Florida

Dr. Michelle Evans
Associate Professor
Department of Political Science
Texas State University

Ryan C. Grelecki, J.D.
Clinical Assistant Professor of Legal Studies
Department of Risk Management & Insurance
J. Mack Robinson College of Business
Georgia State University

Lydie Louis
Professor of Finance
Hult International Business School

Susan Marsnik
Professor, Ethics and Business Law
College of Arts and Sciences
University of St. Thomas

Karen E. Maull
Instructor
Smeal College of Business
Penn State University

David Orozco, J.D.
Associate Professor of Legal Studies
Dean's Emerging Scholar
College of Business
Florida State University

Alan Roline
Director of the MBA Program and Associate Professor of Business Law
Labovitz School of Business and Economics
University of Minnesota, Duluth

Kurt M. Saunders, J.D., LL.M.
Acting Chair & Professor
Department of Business Law
California State University, Northridge

Cindy Schipani
Merwin H. Waterman Collegiate Professor of
Business Administration
Professor of Business Law
Ross School of Business
University of Michigan

Dr. Laura L. Sullivan
Associate Professor
College of Business
Sam Houston State University

James Cahoy
Senior Acquisitions Editor
West Academic

Elizabeth Eisenhart
Acquisitions Editor
West Academic

Stacey Supina
Adjunct Professor
University of St. Thomas

Randall Holbrook
Senior Attorney
Legal Research Center, Inc.

A NOTE TO STUDENTS

Every business topic involves legal issues, from financial filings required by the Securities and Exchange Commission to rules covering advertising claims. Studying business law as an independent subject places these topic-specific regimes into context.

This book is designed to provide that perspective. As a businessperson, your career will involve many decisions about business formation, operations, and cooperation. Each chapter in this book covers an area of major business decisions, and addresses the major legal issues raised by that concern. Learning how the law impacts business choices now will help you make informed decisions when they arise later.

The following features will help guide your reading:

- Key Objectives at the beginning of each chapter define the major concepts you should absorb from the text.

- The Chapter Overview sets the stage for detailed discussions that follow.

- Legal vocabulary is highlighted and defined as it appears, making ideas clearer.

- Practical examples show how the rules work in real life.

- Graphics and tables summarize critical information.

- Review questions help test whether you achieved the chapter's objectives.

- Discussion questions offer new ways to apply the chapter's lessons.

In addition, each chapter includes both summaries of significant legal decisions and longer exerpts from other court rulings. These items enhance your understanding and prepare you for classroom discussions. The case summaries are in the form of case briefs. Case briefs are how attorneys and law students outline decisions. They simplify legal terminology and cut to the core of the ruling.

The briefs used in this text focus on the lesson to be learned from each decision. Each brief starts with a headline-style statement of the rule of the case, the name and citation, and an identification of the parties in the case. Identifying the parties makes it easier to keep track of them and their role in the dispute. Each brief points out the central issue resolved by the court, how that issue was decided, and the court's reasoning for its decision. This model helps walk through a complex (and often lengthy) document to absorb its core message.

The case excerpts also include the rule of the case and other orienting information at the beginning. Unlike case briefs, though, these excerpts allow you to read the actual text published by the appellate court and draw independent conclusions about the outcome. This process accelerates complete comprehension of the subject matter as it plays out in the courts.

With your instructor's guidance, this textbook will give you a solid grounding in key business law concepts, and an understanding of legal risk

We gratefully acknowledge the permission to reprint the Uniform Commercial Code from the Permanent Editorial Board of the Uniform Commercial Code. Copyright held by the American Law Institute and the National Conference of Commissioners on Uniform State Laws. We also gratefully acknowledge the assistance of JAMS Alternative Dispute Resolution in granting permission to reprint Comprehensive Arbitration Rules and Procedures.

TABLE OF CONTENTS

BUSINESS LAW

1

INTRODUCTION TO LAW

KEY OBJECTIVES:

▶ Understand the various sources of laws regulating business and business transactions.

▶ Understand how to read important legal case decisions, and how they affect business dealings.

▶ Gain familiarity with the ethical standards governing business transactions.

CHAPTER OVERVIEW

Before you can meaningfully engage in the study of business, you must understand the laws that govern business activities and relationships. This chapter gives you a broad overview of the United States legal system and its impact on business transactions. This will serve as a foundation to the rest of the chapters in this book.

INTRODUCTION

When Lao Tzu philosophized that "a journey of a thousand miles begins with a single step," he certainly did not have the United States legal system in mind. But the quote is as applicable to the U.S. legal system as it was to any facet of ancient Chinese culture.

The journey to the American legal system as we know it today began with the implementation of the English common law by the 13 original colonies. It continued with the ratification of the United States Constitution in 1789. Ratification of the Constitution put our legal system on the path to where we are today. And while the path includes many twists and turns, the beginning of that path is our Constitution.

The U.S. Constitution is divided into seven articles. Articles I, II, and III establish three branches of the federal government: the legislative, executive, and judicial branches. Each branch is powerful in its own way, but power is checked by the other branches. This system helps prevent one person or branch of government from dominating the American people, and allows each branch of government to operate as a balance on the powers of the others. This concept is referred to as the separation of powers. Next, in Articles IV and V, the Constitution identifies specific matters over which the federal government has exclusive control,

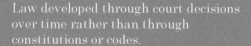

COMMON LAW:
Law developed through court decisions over time rather than through constitutions or codes.

SEPARATION OF POWERS:
Giving legislative, executive, and judicial powers of government to separate bodies of the government.

FEDERALISM:
Governmental system that shares power between national and state governments.

leaving all other matters to the discretion of the individual state governments. Dividing power between the national and state governments is a concept referred to as federalism. But the U.S. Constitution makes clear in Article VI that federal law is superior to state law, in what is referred to as the "Supremacy Clause."

While the U.S. Constitution is helpful for understanding the structure of the federal government, it is important to note that each state has its own governmental structure. While many state structures are similar to the federal structure, there are differences from state-to-state. The differences are often minor. The overview in this chapter pertains in largest part to the federal government structure.

ENUMERATED POWERS:

Specific identified powers reserved only for the federal government.

I. The United States Legal Structure

The United States is governed through the cooperation of three distinct branches: the legislative branch, which makes the laws; the executive branch, which enforces the laws; and the judicial branch, which interprets the laws. These are, of course, very broad descriptions. Each branch is discussed in more detail below.

Legislative Branch

Article I of the Constitution grants legislative powers to Congress, and lists the specific matters over which Congress can legislate. These enumerated powers include matters that pertain to the United States as a whole, such as issuing money, collecting tax, spending for the general welfare, regulating trade between states and between the U.S. and foreign countries, issuing patents and copyrights, and immigration.

While Congress makes liberal use of its power over these matters, the taxing and spending clause is used often. The following case brief, National Association of Independent Business v. Sebelius, focuses on the Affordable Care Act, commonly called Obamacare. In this summary of the longer case, you will see that the Court determined that the law is permitted under the taxation clause of the U.S. Constitution.

The United States Legislature, or Congress, has 535 members and numerous additional employees who provide support services to the members. Congress is divided into two parts, the Senate and the House of Representatives.

Each state elects two senators; thus, the Senate has 100 members. The number of senators changes only if a new state is added or one is removed. Senators are elected to six-year terms, in even years, with approximately one-third of Senate seats up for election in any even year. There is no limit to the number of six-year terms a senator may serve.

The House of Representatives currently has 435 voting members and six non-voting members

THE PATIENT PROTECTION AND AFFORDABLE CARE ACT'S INDIVIDUAL MANDATE IS CONSTITUTIONAL, BUT THE MEDICAID EXPANSION IS NOT.

National Federation of Independent Business v. Sebelius
(Business Group) v. (Secretary of Health and Human Services)
131 S. Ct. 2566 (2012)

INSTANT FACTS:

The National Federation of Independent Business (P) brought suit against Sebelius (D) as a representative of the government, claiming that (1) the mandate in the Patient Protection and Affordable Care Act that individuals purchase health insurance exceeded Congress's power under the Constitution, and (2) the requirement that states expand their Medicaid programs or lose all federal funding was also unconstitutional. The Act was enacted under the Spending Clause of the Constitution

BLACK LETTER RULE:

The legitimacy of Spending Clause legislation depends on whether a state voluntarily and knowingly accepts the terms of such programs, and when Congress threatens to terminate other grants as a means of pressuring the states to accept a Spending Clause program, the legislation runs counter to this nation's system of federalism.

PROCEDURAL BASIS:

Appeal from an order of the Eleventh Circuit Court of Appeals holding the Patient Protection and Affordable Care Act unconstitutional in part.

FACTS:

Congress enacted the Patient Protection and Affordable Care Act in 2010. The Act aimed to increase the number of Americans covered by health insurance and decrease the cost of health care. The mandate of the Act requires most Americans to maintain at least minimal health care coverage or be charged a penalty—a "shared responsibility" payment. The Act also expanded the scope of the Medicaid program, increasing the number of low-income individuals to whom states must provide health insurance coverage. A consortium of businesses took legal action against the government opposing these provisions.

ISSUE:

Did Congress have the power under the Constitution to enact the challenged provisions of the Patient Protection and Affordable Care Act of 2010?

DECISION AND RATIONALE:

(Roberts, C.J.) Yes and no. With regard to the individual mandate, the power of Congress to regulate interstate commerce does not include the power to compel individuals to become active in commerce by purchasing a product. In our system, Congress has limited powers, and other powers are reserved to the states. The facets of governing that touch on citizens' daily lives are normally administered by the states. The Constitution authorizes Congress to "regulate Commerce with foreign Nations, and among the several States, and with the Indian Tribes." This Congressional power to regulate commerce presupposes the existence of some commercial activity to be regulated. Cases dealing with Commerce Clause powers have always described those powers as reaching an "activity."

The individual mandate does not regulate existing activity; instead, it compels individuals to become active in commerce by purchasing a product. Construing the Commerce Clause to permit Congress to regulate individuals precisely because they are doing nothing would open a new and potentially vast domain to congressional authority. The Government (D) argues that sickness and injury are unpredictable but unavoidable, and so the uninsured as a class are active in the market for health care. The mandate merely regulates how individuals pay for that active participation. The phrase "active in the market for health care" has no constitutional significance. An individual who bought a car two years ago and who may buy another in the future is not "active in the car market."

The Government (D) also argues that Congress has the power under the Necessary and Proper

Clause to enact the individual mandate because it is an integral part of a comprehensive scheme of economic regulation. The Necessary and Proper Clause gives Congress the power to enact provisions incidental to an enumerated power, and conducive to its beneficial exercise. The Clause is merely a declaration that the means of carrying into execution the enumerated powers of Congress are included in the grant. We have been very deferential to Congress's determination that a regulation is "necessary." But we have also carried out our responsibility to declare unconstitutional those laws that undermine the structure of government established by the Constitution.

Applying these principles, the individual mandate cannot be sustained under the Necessary and Proper Clause as an essential component of the insurance reforms. Each of our prior cases upholding laws under that Clause involved exercises of authority derived from a granted power. The individual mandate vests Congress with the extraordinary ability to create the necessary predicate to the exercise of an enumerated power. Such a conception of the Necessary and Proper Clause would allow Congress to reach beyond the natural limit of its authority and draw within its regulatory scope those who otherwise would be outside of it.

Having concluded that the individual mandate is invalid under the Commerce Clause, we must next consider the Government's (D) argument that the individual mandate is a valid exercise of Congress's taxing powers. Here, we agree with the Government (D). Congress has broad authority to levy taxes, and there is no constitutional basis to hold that an individual is exempt from taxation due to his or her inactivity. Although the Commerce Clause does not give Congress the authority to regulate inactivity that burdens commerce, the Constitution does not provide the same guarantee with regard to taxation.

The power to tax is limited to the power to require an individual to pay money into the Federal Treasury. The shared responsibility payment has the functional characteristics of a tax, rather than a penalty. For most Americans, the amount that will be due will be far less than the price of insurance. The payment is collected by the Internal Revenue Service through the normal means of collecting revenue, except that the Service may not use criminal prosecutions to collect payments. The payments here will collect revenue, but they are also intended to influence conduct, by expanding health insurance coverage. Taxes that encourage conduct are nothing new. Every tax is in some measure regulatory, in that a tax interposes an economic impediment to the activity taxed. The fact that the law requiring the payments seeks to shape decisions about whether to buy health insurance does not mean that it cannot be a valid exercise of the taxing power.

Turning to the Medicaid issue, the legitimacy of Spending Clause legislation depends on whether a state voluntarily and knowingly accepts the terms of such programs. When Congress threatens to terminate other grants as a means of pressuring the states to accept a Spending Clause program, the legislation runs counter to this nation's system of federalism. The Medicaid expansion fails to pass muster under this principle.

Congress may use its spending power to create incentives for States to act in accordance with federal policies, but when pressure turns into compulsion the legislation runs contrary to our system of federalism. Permitting the federal government (D) to force the states to implement a federal program threatens the political accountability key to our federal system. State officials will bear the brunt of public disapproval, while the federal officials who devised the program may remain insulated from the ramifications of their decision. This is not a danger when a State has a legitimate choice whether to accept the federal conditions in exchange for federal funds.

The federal government (D) claims that the Medicaid expansion is merely a modification of the existing program because the states agreed that Congress could change the terms of Medicaid when they signed on in the first place. Although Congress's power to legislate under the Spending Clause is broad, it does not include surprising participating states with post-acceptance or "retroactive" conditions. We have no need to fix a line where persuasion gives way to coercion. It is enough that wherever that line may be, the Act is surely beyond it.

Affirmed in part, reversed in part.

ANALYSIS:

The Commerce Clause portion of this opinion generated much debate about its implications for Congress's legislative authority. Some commentators see it as a substantial limitation, if not a rollback, of Congressional authority. Others have noted that the Court ultimately upheld this unusual method of regulating the market, albeit on other grounds.

The shared responsibility payments are called "penalties" in the Act. It is not clear why Congress, which so carefully framed the payments to have the attributes of a tax, refused to call them a tax. It has been suggested that this was a failure of political courage. Congress simply did not want to open itself to the criticism that it was levying new taxes.

The dissenters (not included here) argued that the payments cannot be upheld as a tax because Congress did not "frame" them as such. This argument says that the law must be struck down even if the Constitution permitted Congress to enact it, because Congress used the wrong labels.

CASE VOCABULARY:

CAPITATION:
A tax levy that is a fixed sum per person, without regard to any other factors.

MEDICAID:
A federal-state cooperative program providing medical care to low-income individuals. The program is administered by the states in compliance with federal criteria, and is funded jointly by the state and federal governments.

QUESTIONS FOR DISCUSSION:
Why would legislators use words other than "tax" in legislation? Do you agree with the dissent that labels are critical to understanding and applying the law?

(non-voting members are from the District of Columbia and U.S. territories). The number of members is based on population, with roughly one representative seat for every 710,000 individuals. Therefore, states have differing numbers of representatives in the House. For example, California, with a population of nearly 38 million, has 53 members representing it in the House. North Dakota, in contrast, has only one member representing it in the House, due to its population of roughly 723,000. Representatives are elected to two-year terms, in even years. This means that the composition of the House can change drastically during each even-year election, as every seat is up for election. There is no limit to the number of terms a representative may serve.

The Legislature's primary duty is to make laws, but it has additional powers. For example, declarations of war must be passed in both the House and Senate. Congress determines how many seats there are in the United States Supreme Court. Presidential appointments of federal judges must be confirmed through a simple majority vote of the Senate.

Another important congressional power is its implicit power to conduct investigations. Although investigatory powers are not set out explicitly in the Constitution, Congress has regarded investigations as a part of its general governmental oversight powers. The courts have generally not interfered with investigations, saying that Congress may investigate if "clear legislation" could result from the investigation. Since the first congressional investigation in 1792, Congress has looked into interstate commerce, Ku Klux Klan activities, the sinking of the R.M.S. *Titanic*, Wall Street banking practices, organized crime, the sale of cotton, the Vietnam War, presidential campaign practices, and television game shows.

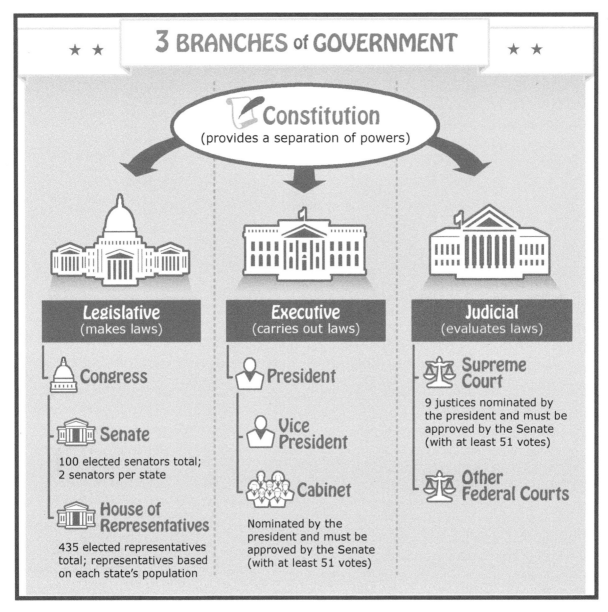

With so much power over laws resting with the legislative branch, it is easy to understand why corporations and lobby groups representing business and industry interact so closely with elected members. While corporations and unions are banned from contributing directly to candidates for federal office, many corporations find individuals within the organization to donate and then present those donations together through "bundling." Meanwhile, lobbyists are often active in forming political action committees (PACs) to contribute to the campaigns of candidates they favor and in coordinating fundraisers where like-minded individual donors are assembled.

While lobbyists are, rightly or wrongly, blamed for much of what is wrong with government today, proposals to limit lobbying raise constitutional issues. The First Amendment protects the "right of the people to . . . petition the Government for the redress of grievances." Lobbying is considered a form of "petitioning." While some restrictions may be placed on lobbying activities (for example, lobbyists may be required to register), an outright ban on lobbying probably would be unconstitutional.

Executive Branch

Article II of the Constitution calls for a president to serve as chief executive for the country and to enforce the laws passed by Congress. The president is elected every four years in even years. The president is limited to two full terms in office. The Constitution requires the president to be at least 35 years old, to be a natural born citizen of the United States, and to have resided in the United States for at least 14 years.

The Constitution leaves great discretion to the president to assemble a team, or cabinet, to assist in enforcing the laws of the land. In general terms, that cabinet includes the vice president and the heads of 15 executive departments:

- Secretary of Agriculture
- Secretary of Commerce
- Secretary of Defense
- Secretary of Education

- Secretary of Energy
- Secretary of Health and Human Services
- Secretary of Homeland Security
- Secretary of Housing and Urban Development
- Secretary of the Interior
- Secretary of Labor
- Secretary of State
- Secretary of Transportation
- Secretary of Treasury
- Secretary of Veterans Affairs
- Attorney General

Over the years, this team has grown to include large executive departments, agencies, boards, commissions, and committees. As a result, there are now more than four million employees working under the executive branch. These governmental representatives are charged with enforcing laws on a day-to-day basis.

Lest it appear that the president, then, is only an administrator working for Congress to carry out their laws, remember that the president also holds a very important veto power. The president has ten days to sign or veto any bill passed in the Legislature. However, to prevent the president from using the veto power to effectively "take over" the government, Congress may override presidential vetoes with a two-thirds majority vote from both the House and the Senate. The presidential veto and legislative override are just two examples of the checks and balances built into the Constitution.

CABINET:

The most senior appointed officers of the executive branch of government, nominated by the President and confirmed by the Senate.

Another presidential power is the power to recognize (or not recognize) foreign governments. The president can enter into agreements with foreign governments through official treaties that require Senate approval or through executive orders. An executive order is an order issued by the president, or by an official acting on his behalf, to direct executive agencies, or to set policy for the executive branch. Because they are not approved through the Senate, executive orders are inferior to treaties.

This power to manage relations with foreign power is reserved to the federal government. Thinking broadly, giving the president and the federal government the power to manage relations with foreign powers, rather than allowing individual states to strike international deals, helps to protect secrets and strategies involved in managing foreign relations.

Foreign relations are also best handled at the federal level because of their impact on national security, the national economy, and other national concerns. For example, in 1996, Massachusetts adopted a law that barred state entities from buying goods or services from entities on a "restricted purchase list." The list was made up of those who did business with the government of Myanmar, or those who were headquartered in Myanmar. Three months later, the U.S. Congress passed a law imposing economic sanctions on Myanmar. One provision of the federal law stated that the President was authorized to issue an order barring new investment in that country by "United States persons" if certain events happened. The President issued such an order a few months Congress passed the law. The U.S. Supreme Court held that the federal law pre-empted the Massachusetts law. The Massachusetts law undermined the President's capacity for effective diplomacy, and "compromise[d] the very capacity of the President to speak for the Nation with one voice in dealing with foreign governments." This is just one example how foreign relations are left in the hands of the federal government.

Judicial Branch

Article III of the Constitution establishes a Supreme Court of the United States and allows Congress to establish lower federal courts. Each federal (and state) court has its own specific jurisdiction. Jurisdiction is the legal power to hear a case.

JURISDICTION:
The legal power of a court to hear a case.

FEDERAL QUESTION JURISDICTION:
Case with alleged violations of the U.S. Constitution, federal laws, or federal treaties.

CONSTITUTIONALITY:
Whether a law or government action agrees with the Constitution.

As one example of an executive order, on August 12, 2016, President Obama signed Executive Order 13735, setting out who would serve as acting Secretary of the Treasury if the Secretary and Deputy Secretary were unable to serve.

CONSTITUTION

LEGISLATIVE BRANCH

CONGRESS

Senate   House of Representatives

Architect of the Capitol
United States Botanic Garden
Government Accountability Office
Government Printing Office
Library of Congress
Congressional Budget Office

EXECUTIVE BRANCH

PRESIDENT   VICE PRESIDENT

EXECUTIVE OFFICE OF THE PRESIDENT

White House Office
Office of the Vice President
Council of Economic Advisers
Council on Environmental Quality
National Security Council
Office of Management And Budget
Office of National Drug Control Policy
Office of Policy Development
Office of Science And Technology Policy

JUDICIAL BRANCH

SUPREME COURT

United States Courts of Appeals
United States District Courts
Territorial Courts
United States Court of International Trade
United States Court of Federal Claims
United States Court of Appeals for the Armed Forces
United States Tax Court
United States Court of Appeals for Veterans Claims
Administrative Office of the United States Courts
Federal Judicial Center
United States Sentencing Commission

EXECUTIVE CABINET

- Department of Agriculture
- Department of Commerce
- Department of Defense
- Department of Education
- Department of Energy
- Department of Health and Human Services
- Department of Homeland Security
- Department of Housing and Urban Development
- Department of the Interior
- Department of Justice
- Department of Labor
- Department of State
- Department of Transportation
- Department of the Treasury
- Department of Veterans Affairs

INDEPENDENT AGENCIES

African Development Foundation
Central Intelligence Agency
Commodity Futures Trading Commission
Consumer Product Safety Commission
Corporation For National and Community Service
Defense Nuclear Facilities Safety Board
Environmental Protection Agency
Equal Employment Opportunity Commission
Export-import Bank of the United States
Farm Credit Administration
Federal Communications Commission
Federal Deposit Insurance Corporation
Federal Election Commission
Federal Housing Finance Agency
Federal Labor Relations Authority
Federal Maritime Commission
Federal Mediation and Conciliation Service
Federal Mine Safety and Health Review Commission
Federal Reserve System
Federal Retirement Thrift Investment Board
Federal Trade Commission
General Services Administration
Inter-american Foundation
Merit Systems Protection Board
National Aeronautics and Space Administration
National Archives and Records Administration
National Capital Planning Commission
National Credit Union Administration
National Foundation On the Arts and the Humanities
National Labor Relations Board
National Mediation Board
National Railroad Passenger Corporation (Amtrak)
National Science Foundation
National Transportation Safety Board
Nuclear Regulatory Commission
Occupational Safety and Health Review Commission
Office of Government Ethics
Office of Personnel Management
Office Of Special Counsel
Peace Corps
Pension Benefit Guaranty Corporation
Postal Regulatory Commission
National Railroad Retirement Board
Selective Service System
Small Business Administration
Social Security Administration
Tennessee Valley Authority
Trade And Development Agency
United States Agency for International Development
United States Commission on Civil Rights
United States International Trade Commission
United States Postal Service

The Supreme Court and federal courts have jurisdiction over disputes between citizens of different states and disputes involving non-U.S. citizens. The federal courts also decide cases where a party claims their Constitutional rights or protections have been withheld. These matters are said to involve a federal question.

In addition to these issues, the Supreme Court established another important power early in its history. In Marbury v. Madison, a landmark case from 1803, the Supreme Court established that it held the power to decide the constitutionality of newer laws.

Initially, this decision appears to limit the Supreme Court's power by stating the Court cannot order a government official to take a specific action. However, looking forward, the decision made the Supreme Court more powerful. The decision established that the Court has the power to determine what laws mean and to eliminate laws that conflict with the U.S. Constitution.

Federal judges are appointed by the president, and confirmed with a simple majority vote of the Senate. A federal judge enjoys a life-long appointment, which generally ends only on the judge's death or retirement. But Congress may also impeach and remove a federal judge in extreme circumstances.

In addition to the courts established under Article III, Congress has established other tribunals that have some judicial functions.

These tribunals, known as Article I courts after the Article of the Constitution setting out the authority of Congress, have a circumscribed authority. They are sometimes set up to review federal agency decisions. They may also be ancillary courts, attached to federal district courts. Judges or judicial officers of Article I courts do not have life tenure, and their salaries may be reduced during their terms of office. Decisions of an Article I court that may deprive a person of life, liberty, or a property interest are subject to review by an Article III court.

Examples of Article I tribunals include:

- Bankruptcy Courts

- Court of Appeals for the Armed Forces

- Court of Appeals for Veterans Claims

- Court of Federal Claims

- U.S. Tax Court

II. Sources of Law

Laws come from constitutions, statutes, treaties, regulations, and court decisions. There are federal and state versions of each, except that treaties are found only at the federal level. Constitutions, statutes, treaties, and regulations form a body of enacted laws, while court decisions either interpret enacted laws or create new laws. Each type of law carries weight based on its source.

THE COURTS MAY OVERTURN LEGISLATION THAT IS UNCONSTITUTIONAL

Marbury v. Madison
(Appointee) vs. (Secretary of State)
5 U.S. (1 Cranch) 137, 2 L. Ed. 60 (1803)

At the December term 1801, William Marbury, Dennis Ramsay, Robert Townsend Hooe, and William Harper, by their counsel severally moved the court for a rule to James Madison, secretary of state of the United States, to show cause why a mandamus should not issue commanding him to cause to be delivered to them respectively their several commissions as justices of the peace in the district of Columbia.

This motion was supported by affidavits of the following facts: that notice of this motion had been given to Mr. Madison; that Mr. Adams, the late president of the United States, nominated the applicants to the senate for their advice and consent to be appointed justices of the peace of the district of Columbia; that the senate advised and consented to the appointments; that commissions in due form were signed by the said president appointing them justices, &c. and that the seal of the United States was in due form affixed to the said commissions by the secretary of state; that the applicants have requested Mr. Madison to deliver them their said commissions, who has not complied with that request; and that their said commissions are withheld from them; that the applicants have made application to Mr. Madison as secretary of state of the United States at his office, for information whether the commissions were signed and sealed as aforesaid; that explicit and satisfactory information has not been given in answer to that inquiry, either by the secretary of state, or any officer in the department of state; that application has been made to the secretary of the senate for a certificate of the nomination of the applicants, and of the advice and consent of the senate, who has declined giving such a certificate; whereupon a rule was made to show cause on the fourth day of this term.

[...]

The questions argued by the counsel for the relators were, 1. Whether the supreme court can award the writ of mandamus in any case. 2. Whether it will lie to a secretary of state, in any case whatever. 3. Whether in the present case the court may award a mandamus to James Madison, secretary of state.

[...]

The act to establish the judicial courts of the United States authorizes the supreme court 'to issue writs of mandamus, in cases warranted by the principles and usages of law, to any courts appointed, or persons holding office, under the authority of the United States.'

The secretary of state, being a person, holding an office under the authority of the United States, is precisely within the letter of the description; and if this court is not authorized to issue a writ of mandamus to such an officer, it must be because the law is unconstitutional, and therefore absolutely incapable of conferring the authority, and assigning the duties which its words purport to confer and assign.

The constitution vests the whole judicial power of the United States in one supreme court, and such inferior courts as congress shall, from time to time, ordain and establish. This power is expressly extended to all cases arising under the laws of the United States; and consequently, in some form, may be exercised over the present case; because the right claimed is given by a law of the United States.

In the distribution of this power it is declared that 'the supreme court shall have original jurisdiction in all cases affecting ambassadors, other public ministers and consuls, and those in which a state shall be a party. In all other cases, the supreme court shall have appellate jurisdiction.'

It has been insisted at the bar, that as the original grant of jurisdiction to the supreme and inferior courts is general, and the clause, assigning original jurisdiction to the supreme court, contains no negative or restrictive words; the power remains to the legislature to assign original jurisdiction to that court in other cases than those specified in the article which has been recited; provided those cases belong to the judicial power of the United States.

If it had been intended to leave it in the discretion of the legislature to apportion the judicial power between the supreme and inferior courts according to the will of that body, it would certainly have been useless to have proceeded further than to have defined the judicial power, and the tribunals in which it should be vested. The subsequent part of the section is mere surplusage, is entirely without meaning, if such is to be the construction. If congress remains at liberty to give this court appellate jurisdiction, where the constitution has declared their jurisdiction shall be original; and original jurisdiction where the constitution has declared it shall be appellate; the distribution of jurisdiction made in the constitution, is form without substance.

Affirmative words are often, in their operation, negative of other objects than those affirmed; and in this case, a negative or exclusive sense must be given to them or they have no operation at all.

It cannot be presumed that any clause in the constitution is intended to be without effect; and therefore such construction is inadmissible, unless the words require it. If the solicitude of the convention, respecting our peace with foreign powers, induced a provision that the supreme court should take original jurisdiction in cases which might be supposed to affect them; yet the clause would have proceeded no further than to provide for such cases, if no further restriction on the powers of congress had been intended. That they should have appellate jurisdiction in all other cases, with such exceptions as congress might make, is no restriction; unless the words be deemed exclusive of original jurisdiction.

When an instrument organizing fundamentally a judicial system, divides it into one supreme, and so many inferior courts as the legislature may ordain and establish; then enumerates its powers, and proceeds so far to distribute them, as to define the jurisdiction of the supreme court by declaring the cases in which it shall take original jurisdiction, and that in others it shall take appellate jurisdiction, the plain import of the words seems to be, that in one class of cases its jurisdiction is original, and not appellate; in the other it is appellate, and not original. If any other construction would render the clause inoperative, that is an additional reason for rejecting such other construction, and for adhering to the obvious meaning.

To enable this court then to issue a mandamus, it must be shown to be an exercise of appellate jurisdiction, or to be necessary to enable them to exercise appellate jurisdiction.

It has been stated at the bar that the appellate jurisdiction may be exercised in a variety of forms, and that if it be the will of the legislature that a mandamus should be used for that purpose, that will must be obeyed. This is true; yet the jurisdiction must be appellate, not original.

It is the essential criterion of appellate jurisdiction, that it revises and corrects the proceedings in a cause already instituted, and does not create that case. Although, therefore, a mandamus may be directed to courts, yet to issue such a writ to an officer for the delivery of a paper, is in effect the same as to sustain an original action for that paper, and therefore seems not to belong to appellate, but to original jurisdiction. Neither is it necessary in such a case as this, to enable the court to exercise its appellate jurisdiction.

The authority, therefore, given to the supreme court, by the act establishing the judicial courts of the United States, to issue writs of mandamus to public officers, appears not to be warranted by the constitution; and it becomes necessary to inquire whether a jurisdiction, so conferred, can be exercised.

The question, whether an act, repugnant to the constitution, can become the law of the land, is a question deeply interesting to the United States; but, happily, not of an intricacy proportioned to its interest. It seems only necessary to recognise certain principles, supposed to have been long and well established, to decide it.

That the people have an original right to establish, for their future government, such principles as, in their opinion, shall most conduce to their own happiness, is the basis on which the whole American fabric has been erected. The exercise of this original right is a very great exertion; nor can it nor ought it to be frequently repeated. The principles, therefore, so established are deemed fundamental. And as the authority, from which they proceed, is supreme, and can seldom act, they are designed to be permanent.

This original and supreme will organizes the government, and assigns to different departments their respective powers. It may either stop here; or establish certain limits not to be transcended by those departments.

The government of the United States is of the latter description. The powers of the legislature are defined and limited; and that those limits may not be mistaken or forgotten, the constitution is written. To what purpose are powers limited, and to what purpose is that limitation committed to writing; if these limits may, at any time, be passed by those intended to be restrained? The distinction between a government with limited and unlimited powers is abolished, if those limits do not confine the persons on whom they are imposed, and if acts prohibited and acts allowed are of equal obligation. It is a proposition too plain to be contested, that the constitution controls any legislative act repugnant to it; or, that the legislature may alter the constitution by an ordinary act.

Between these alternatives there is no middle ground. The constitution is either a superior, paramount law, unchangeable by ordinary means, or it is on a level with ordinary legislative acts, and like other acts, is alterable when the legislature shall please to alter it.

If the former part of the alternative be true, then a legislative act contrary to the constitution is not law: if the latter part be true, then written constitutions are absurd attempts, on the part of the people, to limit a power in its own nature illimitable.

Certainly all those who have framed written constitutions contemplate them as forming the fundamental and paramount law of the nation, and consequently the theory of every such government must be, that an act of the legislature repugnant to the constitution is void.

This theory is essentially attached to a written constitution, and is consequently to be considered by this court as one of the fundamental principles of our society. It is not therefore to be lost sight of in the further consideration of this subject.

If an act of the legislature, repugnant to the constitution, is void, does it, notwithstanding its invalidity, bind the courts and oblige them to give it effect? Or, in other words, though it be not law, does it constitute a rule as operative as if it was a law? This would be to overthrow in fact what was established in theory; and would seem, at first view, an absurdity too gross to be insisted on. It shall, however, receive a more attentive consideration.

It is emphatically the province and duty of the judicial department to say what the law is. Those who apply the rule to particular cases, must of necessity expound and interpret that rule. If two laws conflict with each other, the courts must decide on the operation of each. So if a law be in opposition to the constitution: if both the law and the constitution apply to a particular case, so that the court must either decide that case conformably to the law, disregarding the constitution; or conformably to the constitution, disregarding the law: the court must determine which of these conflicting rules governs the case. This is of the very essence of judicial duty.

If then the courts are to regard the constitution; and he constitution is superior to any ordinary act of the legislature; the constitution, and not such ordinary act, must govern the case to which they both apply.

Those then who controvert the principle that the constitution is to be considered, in court, as a paramount law, are reduced to the necessity of maintaining that courts must close their eyes on the constitution, and see only the law.

This doctrine would subvert the very foundation of all written constitutions. It would declare that an act, which, according to the principles and theory of our government, is entirely void, is yet, in practice, completely obligatory. It would declare, that if the legislature shall do what is expressly forbidden, such act, notwithstanding the express prohibition, is in reality effectual. It would be giving to the legislature a practical and real omnipotence with the same breath which professes to restrict their powers within narrow limits. It is prescribing limits, and declaring that those limits may be passed at pleasure.

That it thus reduces to nothing what we have deemed the greatest improvement on political institutions-a written constitution, would of itself be sufficient, in America where written constitutions have been viewed with so much reverence, for rejecting the construction. But the peculiar expressions of the constitution of the United States furnish additional arguments in favour of its rejection.

The judicial power of the United States is extended to all cases arising under the constitution. Could it be the intention of those who gave this power, to say that, in using it, the constitution should not be looked into? That a case arising under the constitution should be decided without examining the instrument under which it arises?

This is too extravagant to be maintained.

In some cases then, the constitution must be looked into by the judges. And if they can open it at all, what part of it are they forbidden to read, or to obey?

There are many other parts of the constitution which serve to illustrate this subject.

It is declared that 'no tax or duty shall be laid on articles exported from any state.' Suppose a duty on the export of cotton, of tobacco, or of flour; and a suit instituted to recover it. Ought judgment to be rendered in such a case? ought the judges to close their eyes on the constitution, and only see the law.

The constitution declares that 'no bill of attainder or ex post facto law shall be passed.'

If, however, such a bill should be passed and a person should be prosecuted under it, must the court condemn to death those victims whom the constitution endeavours to preserve?

'No person,' says the constitution, 'shall be convicted of treason unless on the testimony of two witnesses to the same overt act, or on confession in open court.'

Here the language of the constitution is addressed especially to the courts. It prescribes, directly for them, a rule of evidence not to be departed from. If the legislature should change that rule, and declare one witness, or a confession out of court, sufficient for conviction, must the constitutional principle yield to the legislative act?

From these and many other selections which might be made, it is apparent, that the framers of the constitution contemplated that instrument as a rule for the government of courts, as well as of the legislature.

Why otherwise does it direct the judges to take an oath to support it? This oath certainly applies, in an especial manner, to their conduct in their official character. How immoral to impose it on them, if they were to be used as the instruments, and the knowing instruments, for violating what they swear to support!

The oath of office, too, imposed by the legislature, is completely demonstrative of the legislative opinion on this subject. It is in these words: 'I do solemnly swear that I will administer justice without respect to persons, and do equal right to the poor and to the rich; and that I will faithfully and impartially discharge all the duties incumbent on me as according to the best of my abilities and understanding, agreeably to the constitution and laws of the United States.'

Why does a judge swear to discharge his duties agreeably to the constitution of the United States, if that constitution forms no rule for his government? if it is closed upon him and cannot be inspected by him.

If such be the real state of things, this is worse than solemn mockery. To prescribe, or to take this oath, becomes equally a crime.

It is also not entirely unworthy of observation, that in declaring what shall be the supreme law of the land, the constitution itself is first mentioned; and not the laws of the United States generally, but those only which shall be made in pursuance of the constitution, have that rank.

Thus, the particular phraseology of the constitution of the United States confirms and strengthens the principle, supposed to be essential to all written constitutions, that a law repugnant to the constitution is void, and that courts, as well as other departments, are bound by that instrument.

The rule must be discharged.

VESTED RIGHT:
A right that is unconditional, that cannot be taken away from a party.

WRIT OF MANDAMUS:
A writ requiring a lower court or government official to perform some duty or act.

COMMENT:

Although Marbury is said to have established the idea of judicial review in the United States, the practice was not unknown before that case, and was well-established in state courts. Marbury is significant as being the first time the Supreme Court struck down an act of Congress as unconstitutional. The Court first ruled on the constitutionality of a federal statute seven years earlier, when it held that a tax on carriages was not unconstitutional. Hylton v. U.S., 3 U.S. 171 (1796). The Court did not strike down another statute as unconstitutional until the infamous case of Dred Scott v. Sanford, 60 U.S. 393 (1857), in which the Missouri Compromise was declared to be unconstitutional.

QUESTIONS FOR DISCUSSION:

The law struck down in Marbury was passed by a majority of votes in Congress, and duly approved by President Adams. Does the practice of judicial review violate democratic principles? Or does the refinement of laws through judicial review improve the law over time?

Constitution

Article VI of the Constitution establishes that the U.S. Constitution is the supreme law of the land. This means that the laws stemming from it carry the most weight. Moreover, no other law, regardless the source, may conflict with the U.S. Constitution.

ENACTED LAWS:

Laws adopted by a legislative or administrative body.

The Constitution not only provides laws regarding the federal government's structure and powers, it also lists specific rights for individuals. These rights were introduced through the Bill of Rights, which was added to the U.S. Constitution in 1791. The Bill of Rights includes 10 amendments that, among other protections, guarantee freedom of speech and religion, the right to peacefully assemble, the right to bear arms, protection from unreasonable searches and seizures, and the right to fair proceedings in civil and criminal cases. Later amendments added more rights and protections. The Fourteenth Amendment, for example, provides equal protection under the law. When a person, group, or even a corporation believes constitutional

The Hierarchy of Laws:

Sometimes different laws are in conflict. In those cases, laws generally give way to more fundamental provisions. This list starts with the Constitution as the supreme law of the land, and continues through to state common law, which usually applies only to matters within that state.

- U.S. Constitution
- Federal statutes and treaties
- Federal administrative agency regulations
- Federal common law
- State constitutions
- State statutes
- State agency regulations
- State common law

rights or protections have been denied, a claim may be filed in a federal district court.

Each state has its own constitution as well. Most state constitutions establish the structure of the state's government, but they vary greatly beyond that starting point. State constitutions may deal with the matters that the U.S. Constitution has left for states to regulate. State constitutions may also include provisions similar to those in the U.S. Constitution. But because the U.S. Constitution is the supreme law of the land, the state constitutions cannot conflict with it.

Statutes

Statutes are laws passed by federal or state legislatures. At the federal level, members of the House or Senate begin the legislative process by introducing a proposed law as a bill. The bill is assigned to a committee, which discusses and studies the bill. If the committee finds the proposed law viable, they send it to the rest of the House or Senate, depending on where the bill started. The House or Senate debates and votes on the bill. The version voted upon may be far different than the originally proposed bill due to amendments the committee and House or Senate make.

If a simple majority of representatives or senators vote for the bill, it is passed and is sent to the other branch of Congress, where it is put

through the same process of committee study, debate, amendment, and vote. Here again, a simple majority voting in favor passes the bill. Because the bill is amended separately by the House and Senate, the final versions that are passed may be different. Therefore, the two versions are sent to a committee with both House and Senate members to create a final version. The final version is again voted on by both the House and Senate, requiring a simple majority vote from each.

The Constitution requires only a majority in both houses of Congress to pass legislation. As a practical matter, however, passage of a bill in the Senate (with some exceptions) requires 60 votes in favor. Legislation in the Senate may be delayed or stopped by a procedural device known as the filibuster. The filibuster dates from 1806, and is based on a ruling by then-Vice President, and President of the Senate, Aaron Burr that the rule that allowed debate on legislation to be cut off by a simple majority vote be deleted (the Constitution grants each house of Congress the power to make its own rules). More than a century later, the Senate adopted rules for cloture, or a vote to end debate. Cloture rules require a supermajority vote to end debate.

STATUTES:
Written laws passed by a legislative body.

State constitutions may, however, give their residents additional rights and protections, beyond those guaranteed by the federal Constitution. For example, some state constitutions provide a right to education within the state—a right that does not appear in the supreme law of the land.

The traditional image of the filibuster is of a few Senators taking to the floor of the Senate chamber and talking at great length. The modern-day filibuster is nowhere near that dramatic. Instead of lengthy speeches, a filibuster now consists of offering numerous amendments to legislation, and demanding a time-consuming roll-call vote on each one.

Once Congress has approved a bill, the president has ten days to either approve the bill or veto it. The process is time-consuming, and often spills from one election cycle to the next, where a previously passed bill may not win final approval due to changes in members.

States pass laws using procedures that are usually defined in the state constitution and are often similar to the federal procedures for passing laws. In addition, counties, cities, towns, and villages enact laws. These laws are generally called ordinances, and they carry less weight than any federal or state law. Local governments derive their authority to pass ordinances from state law.

As previously discussed, neither federal nor state statutes may conflict with the U.S. Constitution. State statutes cannot conflict with federal statutes, either. But that still leaves plenty for state statutes to cover. States develop their own criminal laws for activities not regulated at the federal level. Additionally, state statutes can enhance protections offered by federal statutes, just as state constitutions can offer more protection than the U.S. Constitution.

One example of this can be seen by comparing the United States Civil Rights Act of 1964 with similar state statutes. The federal Civil Rights Act makes it illegal to discriminate against someone based on race, color, religion, national origin, or sex. But in 1976, for example, Michigan passed the Elliott-Larsen Civil Rights Act, which prohibits discrimination based on religion, race, color, national origin, sex, age, height, weight, or marital status. Thus, Michigan is just one state that guarantees protection for all the groups protected by the federal law, plus additional groups based on age, height, weight, and marital status.

Regulations

At the federal level, it is up to the executive, the president, to uphold the laws. Because the president cannot personally enforce the thousands of laws enacted by Congress, the president relies, in part, on administrative agencies to enforce laws. For example, if Congress passes a new law limiting the amount of pollution manufacturing plants can put into the air, then the Environmental Protection Agency (EPA) generally acts on the president's behalf to enforce the law. To do so, the EPA has been given the power to write procedures and guidelines for enforcing

Question: If a Michigan employee believes he was discriminated against at work because of his weight, does he sue based on the U.S. Civil Rights Act or the Michigan Civil Rights Act? **Answer:** Michigan.

Question: If the employee believes he was discriminated against based on religion, does he sue based on the federal or state act? **Answer:** Both!

the law, so long as they do not conflict with the law. For example, the EPA may set a schedule for routine testing that the manufacturing plants must follow, and the EPA may determine that suspected violators will be tried first in an administrative hearing rather than in a federal district court. The case of Chevron v. Natural Resources Defense Council, Inc., provides an excellent example.

State regulatory agencies work in much the same way. Building on the previous example, California may enact even stricter air pollution limits. In other words, all states must follow the federal law, but each state is free to give its citizens more protection than the federal law. In our example, the chief executive of California (the governor) will likely task California's state environmental protection agency with developing procedures and guidelines to enforce the state's air pollution restrictions.

Administrative agencies do not have unlimited discretion when making regulations. Congress may not delegate its legislative authority to an executive branch agency. When an agency is directed to make regulations, Congress must give the agency an "intelligible principle" on which to base the regulations. This standard is applied loosely, and it is rare that a regulation is struck down because does not follow an agency's intelligible principle.

Common/Case Law

Courts have a dual role in creating the law: creating and interpreting common law, and

---

SUPREME COURT DEMANDS DEFERENCE TO AGENCIES' STATUTORY CONSTRUCTION

Chevron v. Natural Resources Defense Council
(Environmental Protection Agency [and Polluters]) v. (Environmentalists)
467 U.S. 837, 104 S. Ct. 2778, 81 L. Ed. 2d 694 (1984)

INSTANT FACTS:
When the EPA interpreted the Clean Air Act to allow polluting factories to add new equipment while keeping pollution levels constant, environmentalists claim the Act should be interpreted to reduce pollution.

BLACK LETTER RULE:
If an agency's interpretation of its enabling statute is challenged, (i) reviewing courts must first independently determine if the statute clearly requires or forbids the agency's interpretation, then, (ii) if the statute is ambiguous, courts must uphold the agency's interpretation if it is a permissible construction of the statute.

PROCEDURAL BASIS:
In suit challenging agency's interpretation of statute, appeal from declaration for plaintiffs.

FACTS:
The Clean Air Act's (CAA) 1977 Amendments required polluters to obtain a state permit before constructing any "new or modified stationary sources" of air pollution. Obtaining the permit required abating new pollution stringently. The Environmental Protection Agency (EPA) (D) promulgated a rule interpreting the statutory phrase "stationary source" to include all polluting devices within a single plant. Thus, under EPA's (D) "bubble policy," factories could add a new pollutant, or increase emissions from an existing one, without obtaining a permit, if the addition/

increase did not increase the factory's total emissions, e.g., by replacing a broken polluting machine with a new one, or increasing emissions from one machine but reducing emissions from another.

Environmental lobby Natural Resources Defense Council (NRDC) (P) challenged EPA's (D) interpretation as unlawful, contending "source" means each polluting device. At trial, the Court of Appeals held for NRDC (P), finding the CAA indicated no Congressional opinion about the EPA's (D) "bubble policy," and finding NRDC's (P) interpretation served the CAA's goals better. EPA (D) appealed.

ISSUE:

If an agency's statutory mandate is ambiguous, may a court overturn the agency's construction of that statute upon finding it is not the best interpretation?

DECISION AND RATIONALE:

(Stevens, J.) No. If an agency's interpretation of its enabling statute is challenged, (i) reviewing courts must first independently determine if the statute clearly requires or forbids the agency's interpretation. Then, (ii) if the statute is ambiguous, courts must uphold the agency's interpretation if it is a permissible construction of the statute.

When courts review an agency's construction of the statute it administers, they must do so in two stages. First, if the court determines Congress spoke directly on the precise issue, then it must follow Congress' intent. But if the court determines the statute is silent or ambiguous on the issue, then it must determine whether the agency's interpretation is a permissible construction of the statute. If so, the court must uphold that interpretation, even if the court feels the agency's interpretation is not the only one, or not the best one.

Courts, upon finding Congressional ambiguity, cannot simply impose their own construction of the statute. Congress delegated to agencies the right to interpret the statutes they administer, and courts must give considerable deference to agencies' interpretation. This is because (i) judges are not experts, (ii) statutes' language often reflects a political choice or compromise, which courts should not upset, and (iii) when Congress delegates policymaking to Executive agencies, that is a political choice by elected officials, which should not be disturbed by the (unelected) judiciary.

Here, the Court of Appeals erred. First, it found, correctly, that the statutory language was ambiguous and the legislative history was unilluminating. Next, however, it failed to consider whether the EPA's (D) construction was permissible, and instead improperly imposed its own reading. Reversed.

ANALYSIS:

In Chevron, the Supreme Court sets the standard for courts' review of agencies' interpretations of their enabling statutes. It is a landmark case, and the most-cited decision in administrative law. Chevron requires courts to analyze agencies' statutory interpretations very deferentially; not surprisingly, in practice agencies prevail seventy-one percent of the time.

Chevron reconciles the longstanding Marbury v. Madison doctrine—that courts are the final interpreters of statutes—with more recent concerns about judges trampling Congress's delegation and overriding administrators' expertise, by its "Chevron two-step" approach. First, the courts may interpret the statute using their independent judgment, to decide whether the statute clearly demands one construction. But if the court decides it does not, then it must review the agency's interpretation with great deference.

CASE VOCABULARY:

ABATEMENT:

Reduction.

QUESTIONS FOR DISCUSSION:

How far should courts go in deferring to agency decisions? Many regulations involve complex scientific or technical principles. Does that make deference more or less appropriate?

interpreting and applying enacted, or codified, laws. Common law is law developed only through court decisions. It is said to be uncodified, meaning there is no statute or code that formally establishes the law.

The doctrine of stare decisis means that lower courts must apply the law decided by higher courts of appeal or the Supreme Court. Once a legal principle is established in a court decision, it is said to be a precedent. Courts generally follow or build on their own precedents in later cases involving the same types of issues, as well as following precedents set by higher courts.

Stare decisis is not an absolute rule, however. Courts may overturn their own precedents (although not those of higher courts). This will happen for many reasons. A court may determine that a rule set out in an older case no longer serves a purpose, or society has changed so much that a rule no longer makes sense. For example, the traditional common law rule

regarding leases of residential property was that a landlord had no obligation to maintain the rented premises, or ensure that the property was fit for habitation. A lease was regarded as being akin to a sale of the property, with the difference between the two being that the landlord would, eventually, be allowed to retake possession of the leased premises. Courts began to revisit that rule in the 1960s and 1970s. It

COMMON LAW:
Judicial decisions that create a body of law over time.

UNCODIFIED LAW:
Rules taken from custom and precedent rather than statutes.

STARE DECISIS:
Legal principle that directs courts to follow precedents.

PRECEDENT:
An earlier court decision regarded as a guide to be considered in similar, subsequent cases.

When first learning about the common law, some people dismiss it as "made up." But many of our most well-known legal rules were developed through court decisions. For example, if you were arrested, you would expect that the police would "read" your rights, starting with "You have the right to remain silent. Anything you say can and will be used against you in a court of law." The rights that the police recite when they arrest a suspect are granted by the Constitution, but the requirement that an arrested person is informed of those rights was set by the U.S. Supreme Court in a 1966 case entitled Miranda v. Arizona, 384 U.S. 436. The case name is used when people refer to "Miranda warnings" or ask if a person was "Mirandized"— meaning that they were told their rights. While Miranda rights are widely recognized because of film and television (or personal experience), the common law also includes much older legal standards, such as contract interpretation rules and business liabilities. Some of today's common law has its origins in court decisions from hundreds of years in the past.

was noted by those courts that the common law rule was developed at a time when a lease of real property was a lease of agricultural property for a term that could stretch out for many years. The modern residential lease, on the other hand, is typically for an apartment or a house only—no agricultural or commercial property is involved. Given the change in the purpose of the transaction, it made sense for courts to begin requiring landlords to keep their premises in a habitable condition.

Over the decades, most common law rules have been codified. In other words, legislatures have enacted statutes to either take the place of common law or supplement it in some way. But even where common law has been codified, courts will still use it as a resource in interpreting those codes.

Constitutions and legal codes, by their very nature, can often be vague or incomplete. This is even desirable, as no one can predict every situation that might come up in the future. For example, the U.S. Constitution guarantees free speech. But does that mean individuals may say anything? May you claim a product you sell will cure cancer if it does not really cure cancer? May you publish an article stating that your neighbor is a murderer if she has not murdered anyone? The answer, of course, is no. Those statements go too far, and may injure others. But who decides exactly what you may say, and which statements go too far?

Sometimes constitutional provisions or statutes are further defined by regulatory agencies or by other statutes, for example, and this helps. But other times, the codes remain unclear to some extent or another. This lack of clarity may be intentional. For example, "fair use" of a copyrighted work is not an exception to infringement, even though it involves using another person's work without their permission. The term "fair use" is not defined in the law. This omission was by design: when Congress amended the Copyright Act to include the common law created doctrine of an explicit statement about fair use, there was concern that a precise definition of the term would be too restrictive, and would hamper the way the law responds to new, unforeseen uses. In such instances, a case can be filed in court so the court can determine precisely what the legislature intended or what the law should be concerning new technology or uses.

When a court decides these issues, it sets a standard for future, similar cases. This standard is called precedent. If the decision is made in a federal appeals court, for example, then the trial courts in that district must apply the law as set out in that decision when hearing future

In 1976, the U.S. Supreme Court decided that the Fair Labor Standards Act could not apply to state or local government employers. *National League of Cities v. Usery*, 426 U.S. 833. The Act established a minimum wage, among other protections, so state and local governments were exempted from those rules. Nine years later, the Supreme Court reversed its position in *Garcia v. San Antonio Metropolitan Transit Authority*, 469 U.S. 528. The Court set forth sound reasons for the departure from precedent (too long to set forth here), but a reversal in such a short timeframe is still unusual.

cases. Likewise, if the U.S. Supreme Court decides a matter, then all federal courts below it must follow that decision when deciding future cases (as well as state courts that need to apply federal law). Because they help to define the enacted laws, these types of decisions carry the same weight as the laws they define.

Treaties and International Law

Treaties are agreements with foreign nations. Only the federal government may enter into treaties. Official treaties are proposed by the president and confirmed by a vote of two thirds of the Senate. The Constitution provides that treaties hold the same weight as federal statutes.

When we talk about international law, we are typically referring to public international law. This refers to rules that govern the relationships between countries; certain international organizations, such as the European Union, that have the legal authority to act at an international level; and the rules governing the relationships between countries, organizations, and individuals. Generally, countries voluntarily agree to the rules, which are spelled out in treaties adopted by those countries. There is also a large body of international law that is made up of general practices, or customs, that are accepted by most nations. While international law typically applies to how governments act, some public international law significantly impacts international business.

International law is compromised in large part of public international law and supranational law. Common public international law topics are admiralty law, international criminal law, and humanitarian law. Businesses are interested in laws concerning trade and intellectual property rights. Supranational law refers to regional agreements, such as the European Union. The rules in those agreements can carry more weight than the nation's own laws.

A good example of international law that impacts international business is the International Maritime Organization (IMO). Organized by the United Nations, the IMO regulates shipping, focusing on safety, environmental impact, cooperation, and security. Currently 171 nations participate. Participating countries follow the rules in the treaty known as the Convention on the International Maritime Organization. The IMO rules affect the processes and costs of transporting goods overseas.

International law tends to be reactionary, and is often developed in response to world events. For example, the United Nations organizes many of the largest international law programs. The IMO branch of the United Nations proposed additional rules in 1967, following the Torrey Canyon Oil Spill. These rules, which finally took effect in 1983, address pollution by ships at sea, another example of international law significantly affecting business practices. On the other hand, regional trade agreements, intellectual property treaties, and other systems that have a large impact on multinational businesses tend to refine obligations and relationships to take place in the future.

Not all international law is reactionary, though. Many international agreements seek to facilitate international business. The Convention on

Contracts for the International Sale of Goods, for instance, helps businesses gain predictability and fair outcomes in their international transactions.

Civil and Criminal Law

As you can tell, the U.S. legal system is large and complex, and includes many smaller and more specialized units. Here again we break down our study of the legal system into two parts, civil and criminal law. Civil law deals with disputes between private parties, such as contract matters or personal injury cases. The government uses criminal law to punish individuals who commit crimes.

Civil and criminal cases are heard in both federal and state courts. They are similar in some ways, but there are important differences between the two.

Civil claims start when a party called the plaintiff, which can be a person, group, corporation, or government body, believes another party has injured them or will injure them in the future. The injury can be physical, financial, or even emotional in some cases. The party with the injury, usually through a lawyer, starts the process by filing a claim in court, called a complaint. This is the first step in a lawsuit. Throughout the process, parties must follow a rather extensive set of rules, called the Federal Rules of Civil Procedure (FRCP), if the complaint is filed in the federal courts. Each state court system has a similar set of rules governing how cases will proceed through the state court system. State court rules are fairly similar to the federal rules in major respects.

BURDEN OF PROOF:
Amount of proof needed to prove one's case.

CIVIL CLAIMS:
Lawsuit to remedy a private wrong.

PARTY:
Plaintiff or defendant in a court case.

Remember that the same behavior or activity can lead to civil claims, criminal claims, or both. Take, for example, the criminal case of the People of the State of California vs. Orenthal James (O.J.) Simpson. On October 3, 1995, a jury found then-famous football player O.J. Simpson not guilty for the murders of his ex-wife, Nicole Brown Simpson, and her friend, Ronald Goldman. Later, the victims' families brought civil claims against Mr. Simpson for wrongful death, a state tort action. In February 1997, long after the not-guilty criminal verdict, jurors concluded that Mr. Simpson should pay the victims' families victims $33.5 million for causing the deaths. It is unusual to have such different outcomes in civil and criminal cases based on the same activity, but it is possible. This is due, in part, to the different burden, or degree of proof, needed to win a civil case rather than a criminal case. A criminal case must be proved "beyond a reasonable doubt" while a civil matter is decided by a "preponderance of the evidence"—a much lower bar.

Under the FRCP, the complaint must include two things:

1. An explanation for why the court has the authority to decide the case, and

2. A short description telling why the injured party deserves to win.

The short description included in the original complaint must name a cause of action for the claim. A cause of action is a fact or set of facts that gives a party the legal right to seek judgment against another party. There are far too many civil causes of action to list here, but some common ones include:

• Breach of Contract

• Negligence

• Defamation

• Patent Infringement

• Trespass

A complaint may include more than one cause of action. The facts may support more than one legal theory. Suppose a company hires a marketer, and makes that person responsible for writing brochures for the business; the employment agreement includes a non-compete clause. If the marketer were to quit and go to work across town for the company's main competitor, the company might bring an action to enforce the non-compete clause. If the marketer copied the text and logos that he created for the company and re-used them in the competitor's marketing materials upon taking his new job, the original company could also sue for the marketer's

violation of the company's intellectual property rights in the same lawsuit.

There is another way that a complaint could include multiple causes of action: alternative pleading. Alternative pleading means that different types of claims are listed in the same complaint, even if those claims are logically inconsistent or legally contradictory. For example, an action claiming that a defendant negligently struck the plaintiff may include another claim that the defendant struck the plaintiff intentionally, even though the defendant could only have done one or the other. This is known as alternative pleading. Different types of claims are allowed, even if they are logically inconsistent or contradictory.

There are several reasons for using alternative pleading. An event could have happened for several reasons, and the actual reason may become apparent only after further investigation and discovery. There may also be pragmatic concerns for the recovery of damages. In the previous example, the damages for a negligent act might be covered by insurance, making it more likely that a successful plaintiff would be able to recover damages or reach a satisfactory settlement. On the other hand, the damages from an intentional act would not be dischargeable in bankruptcy.

When a complaint is filed, the filing party becomes the plaintiff. The party against whom the complaint was filed is the defendant. Each cause of action has a set of elements that the plaintiff must prove to win. The elements are like pieces of a puzzle, and all of the pieces must be proven for the plaintiff to win. The burden is on the plaintiff, who must prove each element by a preponderance of the evidence. Loosely, this means the plaintiff must show that it is more likely than not that the defendant is responsible. Essentially, 51 percent of the evidence must support the plaintiff.

Once a complaint is filed and served, the case is assigned to an impartial judge who has no personal interest in the outcome of the case. The complaint is served by handing a copy of it to the defendant, by handing it to someone designated by the defendant, or by handing it to a person living at the defendant's address. If the defendant cannot be found, court rules provide that service may be made by publishing notice in a newspaper for a period of time. The defendant has 20 days after the complaint is served to respond. Defendants, usually through a lawyer, may ask that the case be dismissed because the complaint did not adequately state a cause of action. This is referred to as filing a motion to dismiss. Or defendants might respond by stating the reasons they do not believe the plaintiff should win. This is called filing an answer.

When filing an answer, a defendant's response may also include a counterclaim, or a third-party complaint. A counterclaim alleges that the plaintiff is liable to the defendant for something that arose out of the same occurrence or trans-

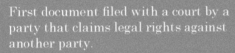

COMPLAINT:
First document filed with a court by a party that claims legal rights against another party.

CAUSE OF ACTION:
Fact(s) that enable a party to bring legal action against another party.

PLAINTIFF:
Party starting legal action against another party.

DEFENDANT:
Party accused in a legal action.

ELEMENTS:
Parts of a crime or legal action that each must be proven.

PREPONDERANCE OF THE EVIDENCE:
More than half of the evidence.

MOTION TO DISMISS:
Party's request to end a legal action.

Alternative pleading is allowed in a response to a complaint. The classic example is of a hypothetical answer to a complaint alleging the plaintiff was injured when the defendant's dog bit her. Alternative pleading would allow the defendant to argue:

1. His dog doesn't bite;

2. The dog was tied up that night;

3. The plaintiff was never bitten; and

4. The defendant does not own a dog.

While this list may appear bizarre, the defenses would all be valid individually. As the lawsuit proceeds, evidence may obviate one or more of these defenses, or bolster them. Providing the possible alternative defenses in the defendant's answer preserves them for consideration down the line.

action as set out in plaintiff's complaint. For example, a person who is sued by a contractor for non-payment may make a counterclaim that the work was performed negligently. A third-party complaint alleges that someone other than the defendant is liable for the plaintiff's damages. The contractor who is sued for negligently performing construction work may allege that the damage was caused by faulty materials made or sold by a third -party not named as a defendant in the plaintiff's original complaint. Unlike a complaint, a counterclaim or third-party complaint does not have to acknowledge that the plaintiff sustained any damage, or that any damage was even partially the fault of the defendant.

Note that a counterclaim or third-party complaint does not have to acknowledge that the plaintiff sustained any damage, or that any damage was even partially the fault of the defendant.

ANSWER:
Response to a complaint.

DISCOVERY PROCESS:
The process by which the parties to a lawsuit obtain information from each other and from witnesses.

INJUNCTION:
Court order for a party to do or not to do a specific thing.

DIRECT EXAMINATION:
Examination of a witness by the party that called the witness to testify.

No two lawsuits are the same. Each side can file motions for a variety of reasons. A motion is simply a formal request to the court. For example, the defendant might think the injury was someone else's fault, and file a motion asking that another defendant be added to the case. Or one party might think the other party is not complying with the court's orders and may file a motion to "compel" compliance. This type of motion requests that the court demand the other party follow a request, such as producing documents or other evidence. The court controls this part of the process through a scheduling order, which tells the parties when certain parts of the case must be completed, including a deadline for filing motions.

An important part of the schedule is the discovery process. This is a time when the two sides can ask each other to turn over or share records and other possible evidence. For example, suppose a woman injured in a car accident sues the driver of the car that hit her vehicle. The other driver might think the accident was the woman's fault, because she was not paying attention. The driver might want to ask the woman to provide her cell phone record for that day, to see if she might have been talking on the phone or texting at the time of the accident. The driver's lawyer would make a discovery request for those records. Discovery is also the time when the two sides might interview witnesses, and even each other.

While this process sounds simple, there are often disputes over whether one side should have to provide all the things the other side is asking for. These disputes often cause delays and might require a hearing with the judge to iron out disputes. By the end of the discovery process, it is possible that the information collected can lead the parties to want to settle their dispute. If not, the parties prepare for trial.

Whether there is a jury involved in the trial depends on what the plaintiff seeks to achieve. A plaintiff seeking money is generally entitled to a jury trial. But when a plaintiff asks for an injunction, for example, which is an order requiring the defendant to stop doing something, the judge decides the case without a jury.

Trials typically begin with the plaintiff, and then the defendant, giving opening statements. These statements are designed to set the stage for trial, in an effort to prepare the judge or jury to hear the evidence as it fits into the big picture.

Plaintiffs must then call witnesses and present evidence to prove the elements of their cases. After the plaintiff questions a witness, called direct examination, the defendant may ask follow-up questions, called cross-examination. This process might go back and forth, with the plaintiff asking additional questions (re-direct) and the defendant following up (re-cross).

When the plaintiff has called all witnesses, it is the defendant's turn to call witnesses and present evidence that supports his version of events or legal theories. The process is repeated, with defendant conducting direct examination of the witnesses and plaintiff conducting cross-examination.

When each side is done presenting evidence and testimony, each makes closing arguments, starting with the plaintiff. The case is then turned over to the judge or jury to decide. When the judge or jury gives its decision, it is deciding in favor of one party or the other.

If either party is not satisfied with the decision in the case, she may start the appeal process. In an appeal, a party is claiming that an error of law took place in the trial court. Some common reasons for appeals are that judges did not allow evidence that could have helped that party, or that the jury was given the wrong instructions for deciding the case.

Appeals are heard by appellate courts. Since appeals deal only with questions of law, there are no juries in appellate courts. In the federal court system, trials are generally held in one of the many federal district courts, and those decisions may be appealed to the circuit court of appeals. If either party remains dissatisfied after the appeal, she may ask the United States Supreme Court to correct the claimed errors. Most state court systems largely follow the same process, with a trial court and two levels of appellate courts.

With all these steps and variables, it is easy to understand why it often takes years before a lawsuit is finally over. It is also easy to under-

CROSS EXAMINATION:
Examination of a witness that has already testified in a court proceeding, conducted by the other side.

PROSECUTOR:
Public official who starts legal proceedings against another, usually for a crime.

CONVICTION:
Declaration of guilt for a criminal charge.

stand why judges tend to encourage parties to settle their disputes without a trial.

The criminal law system is similar to the civil law system in many ways, but there are also important differences:

- The party who starts a criminal proceeding is a prosecutor, not a plaintiff. The prosecutor works for the local, state, or federal government and represents the people served by that government. Crimes are wrongs against the nation, state, or municipality and its people. Civil cases involve wrongs against or between private parties. The party being charged with a crime is still called the defendant.

> The trial court makes factual determinations about the case. Appeals are based on the factual record as established at the trial court level; an appeals court does not re-open factual questions. Instead, the appeals court examines how the law was applied at the trial court, and whether any errors were made in that process. The reason that only trial courts rule on the facts is that the trial court (and the jury, if a jury trial) has the benefit of directly reviewing the evidence. Witnesses are only seen at the trial and questioned through the adversarial process that is designed to reveal what actually happened. The appeals court does not have that access, and therefore does not challenge the factual record.

- When a defendant loses a criminal case, the defendant is convicted while a losing party in a civil case is ordered to pay monetary damages.

- Convictions in criminal cases can result in loss of freedom, voting privileges, and other rights, depending on the crime. Civil liability is not punishment, and carries no consequences beyond being ordered to pay money or do something the person was already responsible for doing.

- Lawyers are sometimes provided free of charge for criminal defendants, unlike in most civil cases.

- In a criminal case, the defendant cannot be forced to testify in any way that might help the prosecutor prove the case.

- The burden of proof for a criminal conviction is proof beyond a reasonable doubt, which is much more difficult to prove than the civil preponderance-of-the-evidence burden. Judges and attorneys have struggled for generations to explain reasonable doubt clearly.

Crimes are divided into misdemeanors and felonies based on how serious the possible punishment can be. Misdemeanors are crimes where the worst possible penalties are fines or up to one year in jail. Felonies are crimes with maximum possible penalties of more than a year in prison.

Usually, the criminal process starts when police or federal agents arrest a suspected criminal and accuse the suspect of committing a specific crime. Prosecutors review the police report and evidence, decide if there is enough evidence to charge the suspect, and decide what crime or crimes the evidence supports. If charges are filed, the defendant hears the charges at a first court appearance, called an arraignment. During the arraignment, the defendant enters a plea of guilty or not guilty.

If the plea is not guilty, the judge decides whether to keep the defendant in jail while awaiting trial or let the defendant remain free while awaiting trial. The judge may decide the defendant can remain free without paying anything, or the judge might require the defendant to pay an amount of money before being released. The idea behind collecting a fee is to ensure that the defendant returns for the trial. The money paid is forfeited if the defendant does not do so. The defendant may also request a free lawyer during the arraignment.

The next step in the criminal process is a preliminary hearing. In some cases, a grand jury might be asked to listen to the prosecutor's evidence and determine whether there is enough to continue with the case. In other cases, a judge will hear the prosecutor's evidence and determine whether the case should continue. If the

judge or grand jury permits it, the case moves forward and is set for a trial date. Time is given for the defendant, usually through a lawyer, to review the evidence against the defendant. The defense may interview witnesses and collect evidence that tends to show it is less likely that the defendant committed the crime. This process is very similar to discovery in civil cases, with the exception that the defendant never has to speak to the prosecutor about the case.

Another similarity to civil cases is that criminal cases often settle at this stage. In criminal cases, this is called reaching a plea agreement. If an agreement is reached, the defendant will change the plea to guilty for the crime charged or for a less serious crime if the defendant and prosecutor agree. The defendant then accepts a penalty that both sides have agreed on. The judge must approve the plea agreement and make sure the defendant understands the rights he is giving up by pleading guilty.

MISDEMEANOR:
Minor wrong-doing.

FELONY:
A crime more serious than a misdemeanor, usually punishable by more than one year's imprisonment.

ARRAIGNMENT:
Court proceeding calling a party to court to answer a criminal charge.

A common understanding of "beyond a reasonable doubt" is that the prosecution's evidence must show that no other logical explanation can be concluded from the facts except that the defendant committed the crime, thereby overcoming the presumption that a person is innocent until proven guilty. A better definition of "beyond a reasonable doubt" is that it is the evidence presented by the prosecutor in a criminal trial proves the defendant's guilt to such a degree that no reasonable doubt could exist in the mind of a rational, reasonable person.

If the case proceeds to trial, the process is similar in many ways to a civil trial. The prosecutor gives the first opening statement, followed by the defense. The prosecutor calls witnesses and presents evidence to prove each element of the alleged crime. The defense can cross-examine the witnesses and challenge the evidence the prosecutor wants to present. The defense may then call its own witnesses and offer evidence that tends to show it is less likely the defendant committed the crime, or that there were circumstances that justified the defendant's actions, such as self-defense.

The defendant may or may not take the stand to testify. In other words, a defendant is not obligated to say anything in her own defense, and the jury is instructed that this silence may not be held against the defendant. In fact, a defendant is not required to present any evidence or witnesses at his trial. The burden is completely on the prosecutor to prove that the defendant committed the crime. The jury must presume the defendant is innocent unless the prosecutor proves every element of the crime beyond a reasonable doubt.

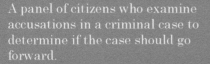

GRAND JURY:

A panel of citizens who examine accusations in a criminal case to determine if the case should go forward.

PLEA AGREEMENT:

Agreement in a criminal case between prosecutor and defendant by which defendant agrees to plead guilty to a particular charge in return for some deal from the prosecutor.

When both sides are done presenting evidence, the prosecutor and then the defense counsel give closing arguments. The judge then gives jurors instructions about the elements of the crime and the burden of proof the prosecutor must meet (beyond a reasonable doubt). The jury then discusses the case privately and comes to a decision. If the defendant has declined the right to a jury, the judge decides whether the prosecutor has proven the case.

If the defendant is found guilty, the judge will later impose a sentence, which may include jail or prison time, and usually requires the defendant to pay a variety of costs and penalties, as well. A defendant may appeal a criminal conviction or sentence using much the same procedure as in civil cases. But with rare exceptions, a prosecutor may not appeal if the defendant is found not guilty.

As a business student, you may feel that the civil legal process is the only one that will impact your career. That is not true. Corporations can break the law, and officers or employees can be charged criminally.

III. Federal and State Court Systems

Earlier in this chapter, you learned that there are both federal and state court systems. You read that only some claims can be heard in federal courts, while others must be heard in state courts. You also saw that states may structure their court systems in a way that best meets the state's needs, although many states use structures quite similar to the federal court structure. We will now look more closely at those federal and state court systems.

Federal Court System

The U.S. Constitution only created the U.S. Supreme Court. Congress was given the authority to create lower federal courts as needed. Today, the U.S. Supreme Court is assisted by 13 federal appellate courts and 94 federal district courts.

Cases based on federal causes of action are first filed in federal district courts. Some cases based on federal law may be filed in state courts, and proceed through the state court system. A federal lawsuit filed in state court may be removed to federal court at the option of the defendant. They may be appealed in the corresponding federal appellate court. As a last resort, the matter can be appealed again, by writ of certiorari (see sidebar) to the U.S. Supreme Court. But the U.S. Supreme Court accepts very few cases. The Court is allowed to choose which cases it will hear. It hears arguments in approximately 80 cases per year, and decides an additional 50 without hearing arguments. In an average year, 7,000 petitions are filed with the Court. Some factors that may influence whether the Supreme Court accepts a case include whether the case raises an important constitutional issue and whether the issue pertains to important current events in the country. A U.S. Supreme Court decision is the final word on the matter.

State and Federal Jurisdiction

Plaintiffs in civil actions are faced with a decision when they file a complaint: where to file the action. Most claims can be filed in state courts. But sometimes a plaintiff may prefer to file in a federal court. This decision may be because the issues are primarily based on federal law, or a plaintiff may feel he will have a better outcome in federal court.

A party who wants the Supreme Court to hear a case submits a petition for certiorari to the Court. The petition is a request for the Court to take the matter. If the Supreme Court agrees to review the case, it grants a writ of certiorari. Some state supreme courts also use certiorari to manage the cases they accept. Federal circuit courts or appeal and some state appeals courts take appeals "as a matter of right," meaning that they do not screen out cases prior to reviewing their merits.

Other times, a plaintiff may file in state court, but the defendant might want the case to be heard in a federal court instead. In those circumstances, the defendant may ask the state court to transfer the case. But only certain claims can be heard in federal court. When bringing a claim in federal court, the plaintiff must show that the federal court has both subject matter jurisdiction over the legal claim and personal jurisdiction over the parties .

Subject matter jurisdiction is the power to hear cases only involving particular issues. A family court could hear a divorce or custody case, for instance, but could not preside over a business-to-business contract dispute. Federal courts may hear cases only if they are based on diversity jurisdiction or a federal question, including questions involving the U.S. Constitution. Diversity jurisdiction applies when the two parties to a lawsuit are from different states, or when one party is from another country and the amount in controversy exceeds $75,000. There must be complete diversity of the parties. All of the defendants must be located in states different from the plaintiff's state when the lawsuit is filed. Federal questions are those that claim federal rights or protections are being withheld. These may include claims that challenge whether a law conflicts with the U.S. Constitution. In most cases not involving diversity or federal questions, state courts may be used. Federal courts have exclusive jurisdiction over areas such as bankruptcy, patents, or claims against the U.S. government.

Personal jurisdiction means that a court has the power to make a ruling against a particular person or organization. Personal jurisdiction is usually easy to show for individual people. Any federal court in the state where a person resides has personal jurisdiction over that person. For cases involving a corporation as the defendant, there are two ways to show personal jurisdiction: (1) the business was incorporated in the state where the court is located; or (2) the corporation's primary place of business, or headquarters, is in the state where the court is located. But there are other ways to show personal jurisdiction over a defendant, as well. Laws known as "long-arm statutes" may also grant jurisdiction over a non-resident of a state who is being sued for actions related to contacts he has with that state.

CONTINUOUS, SYSTEMATIC CONTACTS WITH A STATE SUBJECT A DEFENDANT TO JURISDICTION.

International Shoe Co. v. Washington
(Delaware Corporation) v. (State Taxing Authority)
326 U.S. 310, 66 S. Ct. 154, 90 L. Ed. 95 (1945)

INSTANT FACTS:
The State of Washington (P) sought to recover unemployment compensation fund contributions from International Shoe Co. (D). Even though it employed salespeople in Washington, International Shoe (D) argued that it was not subject to jurisdiction in Washington.

BLACK LETTER RULE:
A corporation is subject to jurisdiction in any state with which it has "minimum contacts," so that the exercise of jurisdiction is consistent with notions of "fair play and substantial justice."

PROCEDURAL BASIS:
Certiorari to review a decision of the Washington Supreme Court upholding jurisdiction over International Shoe (D).

FACTS:
International Shoe (D), a manufacturer and seller of shoes, was a Delaware corporation with its principal place of business in St. Louis, Missouri. International Shoe (D) had no office in Washington and made no contracts for sale or purchase of merchandise there. At one point, International

Shoe (D) employed eleven to thirteen salesmen who resided in Washington (P) but reported to sales managers in St. Louis. The salesmen solicited orders from prospective buyers, which orders were transmitted to St. Louis, where they were processed and the products were shipped.

The State of Washington (P) required employers to contribute a certain percentage of wages to its unemployment compensation fund. Because International Shoe (D) did not pay into the fund, the State (P) issued a notice of assessment. International Shoe (D) moved to set aside the assessment because it was not a Washington corporation. The workers' compensation appeal tribunal denied the motion and ruled that the Commissioner was entitled to recover unpaid workers' compensation contributions. After subsequent appeals, the decision was affirmed by the Washington Supreme Court, which held that the continuous solicitation of orders in Washington by the defendant's in-state salesmen sufficiently demonstrated that International Shoe (D) did business in the state.

ISSUE:

Is it consistent with due process to subject a nonresident defendant to jurisdiction in a state where the defendant is not present, but with which it has minimum contacts?

DECISION AND RATIONALE:

(Stone, C.J.) Yes. No longer is a party's physical presence in a state necessary to establish personal jurisdiction. Instead, a defendant may fairly be subject to personal jurisdiction, even if it is not physically present in a particular state, if it has certain "minimum contacts" with the state.

Determining whether jurisdiction is proper depends on the nature and quality of the defendant's contacts with the forum state. A defendant's single or isolated activity in a state is not enough to subject it to suits that are not connected with those activities. Conversely, if a defendant's conduct in a state is continuous and systematic, the defendant is subject to suits that are not related to those activities. To the extent a defendant exercises the privilege of conducting activities within a state, the defendant enjoys the benefits and protections of the law of that state and must accept the potential for suits to arise against them.

In this case, International Shoe's (D) activities in Washington (P) were neither irregular nor casual. They were systematic, continuous, and gave rise to a large volume of interstate business. The obligation to pay into the unemployment compensation fund arose directly from International Shoe's (D) activities in the state. These activities created sufficient ties with Washington (P) so as to make it reasonable to subject International Shoe (D) to jurisdiction there. Affirmed.

CASE VOCABULARY:

LONG-ARM STATUTE:

A statute providing for jurisdiction over a nonresident defendant who has had contacts with the territory in which the statute is in effect.

MINIMUM CONTACTS:

A nonresident defendant's forum-state connections, such as business activity or actions foreseeably leading to business activity, that are substantial enough to bring the defendant within the forum-state court's personal jurisdiction without offending traditional notions of fair play and substantial justice.

QUESTIONS FOR DISCUSSION:

Businesses depend less and less on "things." Paper records and files are nearly obsolete, and communications technology makes it possible for a person to do business in multiple locations without being physically present in any of them. Should this alter the way we consider minimum contacts for due process?

A pivotal case, International Shoe Co. v. State of Washington Office of Unemployment Compensation and Placement, introduces the concept of sufficient contacts. This is the idea that a corporation that knowingly does a great deal of business in a specific state may be sued in the federal courts in that state.

To show personal jurisdiction over a defendant, the plaintiff must show that the defendant has contact with the place where the federal court is

CERTIORARI:

A higher court's acceptance of a case from a lower court for review.

PERSONAL JURISDICTION:

Power of a court over the defendant in a case.

SUBJECT MATTER JURISDICTION:

Authority of a court to decide a case of a particular type.

SUFFICIENT CONTACTS:

Enough connection between a non-resident defendant with the location where a legal case is filed to give a court there personal jurisdiction over that defendant.

located. Contact with the forum is not enough. The court must also determine whether it is fair to require the defendant to appear in a court in that location. In Asahi Metal Industry Co., Ltd. v. Superior Court of California, Solano County, the U.S. Supreme Court determined that asking the defendant, a Japanese manufacturer, to appear in a California federal court was unreasonably inconvenient for the defendant, and that other, less burdensome options were available.

Venue

After a plaintiff has shown both personal and subject matter jurisdiction, she must show that the specific federal court is the correct venue for the case. Although the concepts are similar, they are treated separately by the courts, and they have different purposes, as well. Jurisdiction refers to a court's legal authority over parties to a lawsuit. It would not be fair for a court to

---

SELLING A PRODUCT INTO THE STREAM OF COMMERCE IS NOT ENOUGH TO IMPOSE JURISDICTION OVER A MANUFACTURER.

Asahi Metal Industry Co. v. Superior Court
(Japanese Manufacturer) v. (California Trial Court)
480 U.S. 102, 107 S. Ct. 1026 (1987)

INSTANT FACTS:
Victim of motorcycle accident brought suit in California court against Taiwanese tire tube maker, who cross-claimed against Japanese manufacturer of the tire tube valve assembly.

BLACK LETTER RULE:
The defendant must purposefully avail himself of the forum by more than just putting a product into the stream of commerce with the expectation that it will reach the forum state; however, such conduct is enough to satisfy the minimum contacts requirement.

PROCEDURAL BASIS:
Writ of Certiorari to the Supreme Court of California for its reversal of the Court of Appeal's writ of mandate directing the Superior Court to quash service of summons on cross-complaint for indemnification in action for damages for negligence.

FACTS:
In September 1978, Gary Zurcher and his wife, Ruth Ann Moreno, were in a serious motorcycle accident that left Ruth dead and Gary seriously injured. He claimed that the accident had been

caused when the rear wheel of his motorcycle suddenly lost air and exploded, sending the motorcycle out of control and into a tractor. Zurcher filed suit in Solano County, California, where the accident had occurred, alleging that the tire, tube, and sealant of his motorcycle were defective. He named as one of the defendants Cheng Shin Rubber Industrial Co., Ltd., the tire tube's Taiwanese manufacturer. Cheng Shin in turn filed a cross-claim—for indemnification in the event it was found liable—against Asahi Metal Industry Co., Ltd. (D), the Japanese manufacturer of the tire tube's valve assembly.

Zurcher eventually settled out of court with Cheng Shin, leaving Cheng Shin's cross-claim against Asahi (D) as the sole remaining issue to be tried. Asahi (D) argued that California could not exert jurisdiction over it, since Asahi lacked sufficient contacts with the state. Asahi (D) did not do business in California and did not import any products into California itself. Rather, it sold its valve assemblies to Cheng Shin and various other tire manufacturers. The sales to Cheng Shin took place in Taiwan, and the valve assemblies were shipped to Taiwan. Cheng Shin bought valve assemblies from other manufacturers as well. Sales to Cheng Shin accounted for a very small fraction of Asahi's (D) annual income—usually less than 1–2%.

Asahi (D) claimed that it had never contemplated that it might be subject to suit in California because of sales to Cheng Shin in Taiwan, but Cheng Shin claimed that Asahi (D) had been told and definitely knew that its products were being sold in California.

The trial court found that Asahi (D) could be subjected to California's jurisdiction. The Court of Appeal disagreed. Unfortunately for Asahi (D), the Supreme Court of California overruled the Court of Appeal, finding that Asahi's (D) intentional act of putting its products into the "stream of commerce" with the awareness that they might wind up in California was enough to justify California's exercise of jurisdiction. Asahi (D) proceeded to the U.S. Supreme Court.

ISSUE:

To establish minimum contacts with a state, is it enough to put a product into the stream of commerce, with the expectation that it will reach the forum state?

DECISION AND RATIONALE:

(O'Connor, joined by Rehnquist, Powell, and Scalia) No. It is not sufficient, for purposes of establishing that the defendant has minimum contacts with the forum state, to show that the defendant has intentionally placed its products into the stream of commerce—even if the defendant had the expectation in doing so that its products would reach the forum state. Something more, in addition to placing products in the stream of commerce, is necessary to establish minimum contacts between the defendant and the forum state.

Foreseeability alone is insufficient as a basis for jurisdiction. It is not enough that Asahi (D) might have been able to guess that some one or more of its products might eventually find its way into the state of California. Asahi (D) must have performed some act showing that it deliberately intended to take advantage of that state's market or laws. This does not mean that Asahi (D) could only invoke California's jurisdiction by importing its products directly. Cheng Shin's actions in importing Asahi's (D) products could qualify, provided that Asahi (D) took additional actions indicating its intent, such as, for instance, advertising or marketing its product in California, or deliberately designing its product to conform to regulations or laws unique to California, or providing a means for California users of its products to receive technical help or advice.

Since Asahi (D) has done nothing to indicate a deliberate wish on its part to see its products in California or to exploit the California market, it cannot be said to have the requisite minimum contacts with the state.

The minimum contacts analysis is not the only reason why California cannot exercise jurisdiction. There is still the matter of "traditional notions of fair play and substantial justice." Even if minimum contacts existed between Asahi (D) and California, it would be fundamentally unfair to require Asahi (D) to defend itself there. California's interest in this matter—the welfare of its citizens—was put to rest, for the most part, when Zurcher settled. The dispute is not just between two non-residents of California, but two nonresidents of the U.S. Given the rather extreme inconvenience necessitated by defending a suit in a distant forum and a foreign legal system, it would be unreasonable and unfair for California to exercise jurisdiction over Asahi (D) in this matter. Reversed and remanded.

ANALYSIS:
The Court unanimously held in this case that the California state court could not constitutionally exercise jurisdiction over Asahi (D). The Court followed a two-step analysis it had developed in its previous decisions. First, inquiry was made into the sufficiency of Asahi's (D) contacts with the forum state, and then those contacts were examined in light of fairness considerations to determine if the exercise of jurisdiction would be reasonable. Asahi's (D) mere awareness that the valve assemblies it sold to Cheng Shin eventually would end up in California was not sufficiently purposeful to establish minimum contacts.

CASE VOCABULARY:
INDEMNIFICATION:
Reimbursing another party for financial losses or damages, or an agreement to indemnify against losses or damages.

QUESTIONS FOR DISCUSSION:
The Court notes that jurisdictional requirements are not satisfied by placing an article in the stream of commerce even with the expectation the product will end up in a given state. Further actions, such as advertising or marketing, or designing a product to conform to unique requirements, would be necessary. Does that allow manufacturers to escape liability? If a manufacturer knows that a product will be sold and used in a particular state without any special targeting of that state, should she be allowed to claim that there is no jurisdiction?

impose liability on a party who had absolutely no connection to the geographic area where the court sits. For such parties, the court has no personal jurisdiction.

Venue, on the other hand, refers to a set of rules that considers the convenience of one court over another. Generally, a case is in the proper venue if it is filed in a federal district court where either (1) the defendant resides, or (2) most of the events that led to the lawsuit took place. If neither is true, venue is proper in any district court that has personal jurisdiction over the defendant. Parties have more discretion in selecting the venue for a lawsuit than in deciding which court has jurisdiction. While parties may agree that a dispute be heard in a particular court, the court will make its own determination of its jurisdiction. A court has no authority to hear a case without jurisdiction even if the parties agree that a court may hear it.

Foreign Legal Systems

In addition to the legal systems that we have already discussed, three others are important to business students, especially considering today's international business climate. Many countries use components of more than one system. Because today's business students will interact in global markets, it is important for you to recognize that other countries have their own way of doing business. You may be accountable under another country's legal system and the domestic laws of that country if you choose to do business there.

DIVERSITY JURISDICTION:
Court case with parties from different states or with a foreign party.

VENUE:
Residence of defendant or place where most events leading to a legal claim took place.

Civil Law

Civil law is a system where formal statutory codes are the primary source of law used by judges to decide cases. (In this context, "civil law" describes a legal system in a foreign country; it has a different meaning than "civil law" disputes between private parties in the U.S. system.) Foreign civil law systems rely on comprehensive codes, as well as constitutions, as their legal authority. Customary law and opinions of other courts are secondary sources, or evidence of what the law is, but they are not binding authority. This system grew from ancient Roman law, and forms the basis for legal systems in Continental Europe, such as France, Spain, and Portugal, and areas once colonized by those countries, such as Louisiana, Mexico and Quebec.

Civil law systems are also often found in countries with historical or current socialist or communist ties. Legal codes in those countries have been revised to include principles associated with Socialism and Communism. Some examples include Russia and the Ukraine China and Japan also have civil law systems. And unlike the rest of the United States, the Louisiana legal system is based on civil law.

The primary difference between civil law and common law systems is the role of the courts. Under the common law, rules are developed in court cases in the absence of legislation. If there is legislation, a court's interpretation of the rule will affect how other courts apply that legislative rule in different cases. The different roles for the courts lead to practical differences the roles that lawyers and judges play In common law and civil law systems. In common-law countries like our own, for example, lawyers serve as advocates, building a case and presenting it to a judge, who serves as more of a referee or arbiter between legal positions. In civil law systems, judges have a more active, investigative role than judges in common law jurisdictions, but they are limited in how much they may interpret the law.

Bijuridical Systems

Some countries have legal systems that include more than one category. The Canadian system, for example, stems from English common law concepts. But Quebec uses a French civil law system in most civil matters. Therefore, Canada is referred to as a bijuridical system. In the United States, Louisiana also follows a French civil law model. India's legal system, too, is based primarily on common law, but some parts of the country use a system based on Portuguese civil law. South Africa is another significant country with a bijuridical system.

Islamic Law

Approximately 1.3 billion people practice Islam. For non-Muslims, there is a great deal of confusion around the concept of Sharia law. Sharia is a traditional legal model derived from Islamic texts and authorities. Sharia also incorporates rules that stem from scholarly interpretations of the texts, and from community consensus or custom. Sharia, which means "the path," covers daily routines, family relations, financial matters, and criminal justice.

But how much Sharia is incorporated into formal government codes varies. In some countries, there is a constitution-level bar against laws that oppose Islamic writings. Such a prohibition leaves ample room for development of a complete legal system facilitating business, contracts, and finance. In other nations, such as Nigeria, Kenya, and Tanzania, Sharia is used mainly for personal and family issues for Islamic households.

Generally speaking, however, the overall legal system in Islamic countries is usually either common law or civil law. For example, Pakistan has a strong common law system served by highly trained attorneys, while Egypt uses a civil law model. (Saudi Arabia is one example of a country that uses neither common nor civil law.)

Even though Sharia may not formally be part of the legal system, it may impact business practices and transactions. One example is the prohibition against unearned interest (riba). Turkey is constitutionally a secular nation, but if you are doing business there, you may need to plan transactions to avoid interest payments. This requirement may not be part of the national law, but it may be a requirement of your Turkish business partner.

IV. Legal Analysis

Because court decisions are so important to understanding the finer points of how businesses must operate, business people must be comfortable reading court decisions. Those decisions, however, often use challenging language and specialized terminology to present complex discussions. This section will help decode decisions.

Case Format

A court decision contains certain important parts that you should be able to recognize as you read. Although case format differs slightly from court to court, the parts are essentially the same.

Heading: The case citation (where the case is published), the name of the case, the court that issued the decision, and the date of the decision.

Syllabus: The syllabus, when it is included, gives a short summary of the case, focusing on the legal issues in dispute and how the court resolved those issues.

Procedural History: The significant steps that have happened with the case so far: which courts have heard the case and what decisions did they make? This information may be missing if the decision is from a trial court where the case started.

Facts: A summary of what happened between the parties to lead to the lawsuit; the back-story of the case. This can be very short, or it can be very complex, going on for several pages.

Issues: While many things happened, each case usually comes down to one or a few matters that are truly in dispute; the legal question the court needs to decide.

Holding: The court's answer to the issue.

Judgment: The action that must be taken, based on the court's judgment.

Rule: What the decision means for the cases that come after it.

Cases written in recent years tend to be written more clearly than cases from several decades ago. Regardless, the parts identified above provide an organizational structure to reading cases.

Reading the Law

Reading the law is not like other types of reading. Learning to read cases will help you to develop your critical thinking skills while studying the court's opinion. When you read a court's opinion, you should be looking for very specific things. Of course, you will need to determine the rule in the case, but you must examine every aspect of the case to fully understand the rule. What role do the specific facts play in the court's decision? If the facts change, will the outcome be the same? What reasons (referred to as "rationale") did the court use in reaching its decision? What statutes, if any, did the court use to support its decision? How do previous cases fit into the court's analysis?

Let's use a simple example unrelated to the law: a teenager asks her parents for permission to travel out of state with friends for the weekend. Along with their answer (especially if the answer is no), the parents are likely to give a list of reasons supporting that decision, for example, these friends have been in trouble at school, the daughter regularly ignores house rules designed to keep her safe, the daughter violated her parents' trust the last time she was allowed to travel with these friends, etc. From this very basic rationale, we can formulate a rule: A teenager may not travel out of state with friends where past experience indi-cates an unreasonable risk of harm. And from this rule, we can start to predict the outcome of future cases. What will the outcome be, for example, if the next request involves a different set of friends?

Cases, much like a parenting decision, are simply written explanations that help us understand the law better. It would be impossible for the legislature to draft statutes that covered every single possible situation that might arise in the future. So when each new situation arises, and the people involved disagree about what the law requires or allows, courts are asked to intervene. In this way, each case is part of a much bigger picture. And although each case is very important to the parties, it is even more important to the rest of us. In a common law system, each case in which the judge interprets law builds on previous cases. The judges consider more than just the parties to a lawsuit, as each case builds on the ones before it in defining the law.

When reading cases, then, you need to keep the bigger picture in mind: how does this case help shape the law considering everything else we know about the law?

An efficient and effective way to read cases includes writing a case brief. This is a standardized way of summarizing the most important parts of the case. So let's look at an actual court decision, identify the parts of the decision, and examine the case brief. In fact, the cases in this book are presented in the form of case briefs. You should look at some of the actual opinions, though, to gain practice in reading cases effectively.

The somewhat humorous case of Mayo v Satan includes a short discussion of a concept we covered earlier in this chapter, personal jurisdiction, as well as some other legal issues. Read the case below, and then return to this discussion.

So, what happened here? The plaintiff, Mr. Gerald Mayo, attempted to sue Satan (and his "staff") for putting obstacles in the plaintiff's way and causing him problems. In this case, though, the court was not asked to decide whether the defendant had actually done what Mayo alleged. Instead, the case addressed a preliminary procedural matter: was Mayo allowed to bring the suit at all?

Many courts include a syllabus in their decisions. And in many other cases, the publisher will include a syllabus even when the court does not. The syllabus can be an excellent starting point when reading a case because it summarizes very briefly the key issues and holdings in the case. Having this information before reading the case gives you an advantage: you know what to look for. You can read the case with an eye toward understanding the basis for the court's holding, and understanding the nuances of the court's reasoning.

The syllabus in the Mayo case does a nice job of summarizing the most relevant parts of the case: Mr. Mayo wants to bring a civil-rights suit against the devil; the court said no, for three reasons: personal jurisdiction, problems with a class-action suit, and no way to notify Satan about the suit. Now read the syllabus carefully, with this summary in mind. Do you see how this will help you as you read the rest of the case?

Moving on to the opinion itself, you can see that the court states the legal issue in the first sentence of the opinion: "Plaintiff . . . prays for leave to file a complaint . . ." Plaintiff is asking the court's permission (or "leave") to sue Satan. Unfortunately, not all courts make it this easy to find the issue! The first sentence also identifies some of the statutes that are relevant to whether the court has jurisdiction.

The rest of the first paragraph, along with the second paragraph, gives background facts. The court could have gone into detail about the specific ways in which Satan allegedly interfered with the plaintiff's life, but those details are not relevant to whether the plaintiff should be allowed to sue. Courts will often include legally irrelevant detail anyway, though, so this is something to watch out for.

In the third paragraph, the court states its holding: Mr. Mayo's request is denied. It is helpful when a court starts with the conclusion like this, but you can also skip ahead to see how the court resolved the issue. Here, of course, you already knew the answer because the syllabus provided it. Reading a case can be a bit like putting a jigsaw puzzle together. It is far easier if you can see a picture of the final product while you're working on the puzzle. In the same way, if you know the court's holding, the rest of the decision can be easier to understand.

At this point, you may be wondering what "in forma pauperis" means. The law is filled with Latin terms that lawyers have become used to and that some would call "legalese." Regardless, it is important to stop when you come across a term you do not understand and look the term

54 F.R.D. 282

United States District Court, W. D. Pennsylvania.

UNITED STATES ex rel. Gerald MAYO

v.

SATAN AND HIS STAFF.

Misc. No. 5357.

Dec. 3, 1971.

Civil rights action against Satan and his servants who allegedly placed deliberate obstacles in plaintiff's path and caused his downfall, wherein plaintiff prayed for leave to proceed in forma pauperis. The District Court, Weber, J., held that plaintiff would not be granted leave to proceed in forma pauperis who in view of questions of personal jurisdiction over defendant, propriety of class action, and plaintiff's failure to include instructions for directions as to service of process.

Prayer denied.

Opinion

MEMORANDUM ORDER

WEBER, District Judge.

Plaintiff, alleging jurisdiction under 18 U.S.C. § 241, 28 U.S.C. § 1343, and 42 U.S.C. § 1983 prays for leave to file a complaint for violation of his civil rights in forma pauperis. He alleges that Satan has on numerous occasions caused plaintiff misery and unwarranted threats, against the will of plaintiff, that Satan has placed deliberate obstacles in his path and has caused plaintiff's downfall.

Plaintiff alleges that by reason of these acts Satan has deprived him of his constitutional rights.

We feel that the application to file and proceed in forma pauperis must be denied. Even if plaintiff's complaint reveals a prima facie recital of the infringement of the civil rights of a citizen of the United States, the Court has serious doubts that the complaint reveals a cause of action upon which relief can be granted by the court. We question whether plaintiff may obtain personal jurisdiction over the defendant in this judicial district. The complaint contains no allegation of residence in this district. While the official reports disclose no case where this defendant has appeared as defendant there is an unofficial account of a trial in New Hampshire where this defendant filed an action of mortgage foreclosure as plaintiff. The defendant in that action was represented by the preeminent advocate of that day, and raised the defense that the plaintiff was a foreign prince with no standing to sue in an American Court. This defense was overcome by overwhelming evidence to the contrary. Whether or not this would raise an estoppel in the present case we are unable to determine at this time.

If such action were to be allowed we would also face the question of whether it may be maintained as a class action. It appears to meet the requirements of Fed. R. of Civ. P. 23 that the class is so numerous that joinder of all members is impracticable, there are questions of law and fact common to the class, and the claims of the representative party is typical of the claims of the class. We cannot now determine if the representative party will fairly protect the interests of the class.

We note that the plaintiff has failed to include with his complaint the required form of instructions for the United States Marshal for directions as to service of process.

For the foregoing reasons we must exercise our discretion to refuse the prayer of plaintiff to proceed in forma pauperis.

It is ordered that the complaint be given a miscellaneous docket number and leave to proceed in forma pauperis be denied.

up. In forma pauperis mean "in the manner of a pauper." Practically speaking, it means that Mr. Mayo wants the court to waive the costs of filing his lawsuit. Although interesting, it is not relevant to the legal issue: whether Mr. Mayo will be allowed to sue.

The third paragraph next identifies and then explains the court's first reason for denying Mr. Mayo's request: even if Satan has violated Mr. Mayo's civil rights, the court cannot tell if it has personal jurisdiction over Satan. (You may want to go back and quickly review personal jurisdiction.) The court gives three reasons. First, Mr. Mayo did not include an address for Satan. Second, the court could not find any other cases in the district where Satan was a party, so that too suggests he does not live in the jurisdiction. Third, the court found an "unofficial account" of a New Hampshire case where Satan was a plaintiff (a reference to Steven Vincent Benét's short story, *The Devil and Daniel Webster*), which could affect this case. In other words, Mr. Mayo did not give the court enough information to allow it to conclude that it has personal jurisdiction over Satan.

In the next paragraph, the court theorizes that even if the court allows Mr. Mayo to file the suit, there are so many potential plaintiffs with the same claims against Satan, that the case might have to be tried as a class-action suit. The court even goes through the requirements for a class-action suit. But the last sentence of the paragraph explains why this is a problem: a class action requires someone to represent everyone else who has similar claims against the same defendant. The court does not have enough information to decide whether Mr. Mayo

could do this. This is the second reason the court will not allow Mr. Mayo to file the suit.

Finally, in the fifth paragraph of the opinion, the court notes that Mr. Mayo was required to include instructions to the U.S. Marshal to be able to deliver the complaint to the defendant. He failed to include those instructions. This is the third reason the court will not allow him to file the suit.

What is the "Rule"?

Unfortunately, you will not usually find a sentence in court decision that starts with, "The rule is . . ." It often takes careful reading to find, and then to understand, the rule from a case. The rule from the case is not the same as the holding, although they are closely connected. The holding is the answer to the issue. Will Mr. Mayo be allowed to sue? No.

The rule is what judges and lawyers can take from the case to help guide future decisions and future representation of clients. Here, we can formulate a rule from the court's holding and reasoning.

The court here held that Mr. Mayo could not file suit for three reasons. It is difficult to tell, though, whether a future plaintiff could sue Satan if, for example, he overcame one of the three reasons. Consider this: what if Mr. Mayo's application to the court had made clear that he would be an excellent class-action representative? Would the other two reasons be enough to preclude that next plaintiff from filing suit? Probably, but this is the sort of question that might be argued later.

First, presume that any one of the court's reasons was enough. In that case, we could formulate three rules:

1. A plaintiff may not file a lawsuit where the record lacks enough information for the court to determine whether it has personal jurisdiction over the defendant.

2. A plaintiff may not file a lawsuit where the suit will likely be a class action and the court cannot determine whether the plaintiff will fairly represent the interests of the class.

3. A plaintiff may not file a lawsuit where the complaint does not include service-of-process instruction to the U.S. Marshall, as required.

Alternatively, we might identify a single rule: A plaintiff may not file suit where the court cannot determine whether it has personal jurisdiction over the defendant, where the suit is likely to result in a class action and the court cannot determine whether the plaintiff will adequately represent the class, and where the plaintiff fails to include the required instructions to the U.S. Marshal in his complaint.

The rule, then, helps guide the legal community, including future plaintiffs. And if Mr. Mayo wants to try again, he will need to overcome at least the three obstacles listed by the court.

Now that we have identified the important parts of the *Mayo v. Satan* case, you can see how the parts come together in the case brief. In practice, writing the case brief is an ongoing process. You will understand the case better as you try to reduce its parts to writing. As you gain a better understanding, you will be able to refine the case brief.

Is it Good Law?

A critical question when reading cases is whether the case is "good law." In other words, does anyone need to follow this case? It has been said that the law is a living, breathing thing. And while the courts try to achieve stability in

---

A PLAINTIFF MAY NOT PROCEED IF THE COURT CANNOT DETERMINE WHETHER IT HAS PERSONAL JURISDICTION OVER THE DEFENDANT, WHETHER THE PLAINTIFF CAN ADEQUATELY REPRESENT THE INTERESTS OF THE CLASS, AND HOW THE DEFENDANT IS TO BE SERVED.

Mayo v. Satan
(Private Individual) v. (Evil Entity)
54 F.R.D. 282 (1971)

INSTANT FACTS:
Mayo (P) attempted to sue Satan (D) for violating Mayo's (P) civil rights by interfering with his life.

BLACK LETTER RULE:
A court must have personal jurisdiction to hear a case.

PROCEDURAL BASIS:
Civil rights action

FACTS:

Mayo (P) attempted to file a civil-rights action, in forma pauperis, against Satan and his staff (D) for causing Mayo (P) misery, making threats against Mayo (P), deliberately placing obstacles in Mayo's (P) path, and causing Mayo's (P) downfall.

ISSUE:

May the court hear a case against Satan?

DECISION AND RATIONALE:

(Weber, District Judge) No. (1) A plaintiff may not proceed in a lawsuit if the court does not have personal jurisdiction over the defendant. The court noted that Mayo (P) had not provided an address for Saturn (D), and that the court was unable to find any other case in the jurisdiction in which Saturn (D) was a party. (2) A plaintiff may not proceed in a lawsuit if that suit is likely to become a class action, and the court cannot determine whether the plaintiff can adequately represent the interests of the entire class. (3) A plaintiff may not proceed in a lawsuit if he fails to give instructions in his complaint that would allow the U.S. Marshal to serve the defendant. Application denied.

CASE VOCABULARY:

IN FORMA PAUPERIS:

"In the manner of a pauper"; being excused from paying court costs and fees.

QUESTIONS FOR DISCUSSION:

Should courts be required to consider all lawsuits, however frivolous or outlandish they may seem? Attorneys are required by rules of professional ethics, as well as by statutes and court rules, to act as "gatekeepers" and to decline to bring clearly meritless claims. Who fills that role when the plaintiff is unrepresented, as Mr. Mayo was here?

In 2007, Nebraska State Senator Ernie Chambers filed a lawsuit against God, seeking an injunction against "plagues and terroristic threats." Sen. Chambers, a member of the Legislative Judiciary Committee, said he was filing his suit in protest of the requirement that even frivolous lawsuits be considered by the courts. Sen. Chambers's suit was dismissed for failure to include an address for service of process on the defendant. What do you think of this outcome in light of the Mayo case?

---

the law, each new case still clarifies the law a bit. A new case may expand or limit the reach of the law, create an exception, create or change the way a word or phrase is defined, or overturn the existing law all together.

Because of this, it does no good to thoroughly understand a case, only to find out that later cases (or later statutes or rules) have changed the law, and that your case no longer carries any weight.

The methods of determining whether a case is still good law are outside the scope of this book. But you should be aware of this important detail when reading cases in the future.

The common-law practice that dictates that courts follow rules set out in earlier cases is the rule of *stare decisis*. Under the doctrine of *stare decisis*, when a court has set out a principle of law, it will adhere to that principle and apply it to all future cases with facts that are substantially the same. The doctrine ensures that similarly situated individuals are treated alike, instead of in accordance with the personal view of a judge. Rules may be changed, or even abolished, when there has been a significant change in circumstances since the adoption of the legal rule, or when the legal reasoning behind a rule is faulty. Absent those circumstances, like cases should be decided alike. *Stare decisis* aims to ensure stability and predictability in court decisions.

Law and Ethics

What are ethics? Ethics are standards of behavior determining how we respond in specific situations. Simply put, ethics are a code of conduct. In business, ethics are the legal, fair, and thoughtful ways businesses interact with stakeholders.

Where do ethics come from? Just like individuals have a lot of choice in how they conduct themselves, so do businesses. Both individuals and businesses are regulated by laws. The laws create the "ground floor" for individual and business conduct. If the basic responsibilities are not met, civil or criminal legal action can follow.

You probably strive to conduct yourself somewhat better than the minimum required by law. You may try to be kind to others or to "give back" to the community. There is no law saying you must speak pleasantly, volunteer in your community, or donate to charity, but you may choose to do so. This may be because you like being nice. It might be because you hope your good behavior will cause others to like you, be nice to you, respect you, or even hire you. It may be because you have a sense of obligation to do your part for the greater good.

Businesses are also encouraged to operate with principles above the minimum required by law. Businesses may choose to offer excellent customer service, pollute less than the law allows, pay above the minimum wage, or donate a portion of profits to good causes. Some business leaders are driven toward good behavior by a sense of social responsibility, while other businesses try to appeal to investors, customers, and

other stakeholders by having a track record of ethical behavior. Many ethics topics are covered in detail in the chapters that follow. This section provides a general overview of required ethical standards.

Business Ethics

In October 2001, a very large energy corporation, Enron, was caught hiding billions of dollars in business losses and debt from shareholders. After the world found out about Enron's poor financial health, the company declared bankruptcy within two months. Shareholders lost enormous amounts of money. Aside from the loss of 20,000 jobs and over $63 billion of investor money within Enron, the scandal also bankrupted Enron's auditing firm, Arthur Andersen LLP. The Enron scandal was a collection of ethical, as well as legal, failings. It was a very public and far-reaching example of the harm that can be done when a company breaks the law and is unethical in its dealing with stakeholders. Of course, Enron also violated the law.

Stakeholders: The word "stakeholders" in this context is just want it sounds like: those who hold a stake in a business's successes, failures, and conduct. Obviously, the owners and investors hold a financial stake, but a business has many other stakeholders as well. Its customers and employees stand to benefit or gain from the business's performance, and so do its suppliers and others it does business with. On a larger scale, the communities where the business conducts its trade are also stakeholders in the business's performance, not only in terms of profits (or losses), but also in the way it conducts business.

Imagine, on a small scale, a business that owns and leases commercial property. If that business is known for its high ethical standards, it is likely to attract tenants with similar values. On the other hand, if this commercial landlord has low ethical standards, it will, over time, develop a reputation in the community and will attract tenants that may, along with the landlord, have a negative impact on the community and the surrounding businesses.

As you work through this section, consider other ways a business's ethics might impact its community, in either a positive or negative way. For example, might an ethical business hire and keep different types of employees than an unethical business? What about the businesses who buy from or sell to an ethical versus unethical business? Can you think of other contexts where a business's ethics might impact the community?

Ethical Frameworks: In response to the Enron and Arthur Andersen scandals, as well as other similar scandals that quickly followed, Congress passed a federal act to improve the state of business ethics in the United States. The act is most commonly called the Sarbanes-Oxley Act of 2002 (SOX). By legislative standards, this act was drafted, passed, and enacted very quickly, on July 30, 2002. Here are the highlights:

1. Auditors must be wholly independent and federally registered, and must use approved standards in auditing. This provision protects investors and shareholders by making sure they get accurate information about a company's financial health.

2. Senior executives are personally responsible for providing accurate financial reports. Before this provision, bad business practices did not make people worry about jail sentences because businesses could not be sent to jail. With this provision, senior executives pay close attention to following the rules because they can go to jail if they do not.

3. Corporate officers and executives must disclose stock transactions to prevent insider trading. The Securities Exchange Commission (SEC) has the power to regulate these disclosure, investigate suspected violations, and to punish violators.

4. Market analysts must disclose any conflicts or financial interests. People invest based in part on analysts' recommendations. Investors should know if the analyst stands to make money by convincing people to invest in a specific company.

5. Companies and employees face penalties if they destroy records in the face of an investigation.

6. Whistleblowers, that is, employees who report their employers of suspected SOX violations, are protected from retaliation.

SOX had a huge impact on many aspects of business ethics. You will learn more about additional legal guidelines in the following chapters. Some of those laws cover truth in advertising and labelling; respecting the copyright, trademark, and patent materials of others; consumer protection; and embezzlement.

There is no law dictating how companies carry out their ethical obligations. Rather, companies comply in various ways based on a number of factors. Federal Sentencing Guidelines for corporations give a basis for determining if a compliance program will be effective, and whether that program should be a factor in mitigating a corporation's sentence for a crime. Many industries are heavily regulated. Businesses involved in those industries may have staff, or entire departments, specifically assigned to ensure the company follows the rules. These employees may be compliance officers, general counselors, or staff attorneys. Smaller companies may use consultants to monitor their business activities. And very small businesses may leave it up to officers or managers to ensure the rules are followed.

International Business Ethics: Individuals and businesses in the United States conduct business routinely with foreign companies and countries. It is common to order products on the Internet and buy products and supplies locally that originated or contain parts from other countries.

Just like the United States has the Sarbanes-Oxley Act, many countries have business ethics policies and laws. But the provisions are often very different, because each country has its own needs, issues, and values reflected in its ethics policies. There are also many countries with little or no regulation on business practices.

For a number of reasons, it would be nice to have universal business standards in place. Businesses and consumers around the world would know what to expect when they enter into a business transaction with a foreign company. Companies would be in similar competitive positions if they were all following the same standards. But there are two major obstacles to creating such a universal code: (1) Acceptable behavior varies greatly from country to country. No one could agree on what the standards should be. (2) No country can punish another country for violating the standards. The standards would be unenforceable.

Consider these two examples of topics that often arise when a universal business-ethics code is discussed.

1. *Employment Laws*: As recently as the 1800's, the United States exported goods that stemmed from slave labor. By that time, many other countries had banned slavery. That aspect of our business ethics offended many. Today, the United States and many other countries have labor standards related to safety, minimum wages, child labor, and work hour limits. But in other countries, the minimum pay a worker can expect can be significantly lower or higher than here, and the age when individuals might need to enter the work force might be significantly lower. Moreover, a typical work environment in another country might seem unsafe here. What could a universal code require for workplace safety in a country where few areas have running water or building codes?

2. *Bribery*: In the United States, it is illegal to bribe a government official to get business contracts with the government. Elsewhere, an offering to a public official is seen as polite. And in some countries, bribes are considered a customary part of doing business; they are expected. Historically, United States businesses have set up in foreign countries and paid bribes, as is the custom there, in an effort to be competitive. It was hard to prosecute them for activities they engaged in elsewhere, when the activities were legal in those countries, so Congress passed the Foreign Corrupt Practices Act (FCPA) in 1977. The FCPA outlaws paying bribes to foreign officials The FCPA is sometimes criticized for putting U.S. companies at a competitive disadvantage

> Ethical questions relating to sourcing are a matter of ongoing debate, especially in the retail apparel industry. Garment factories in countries that produce clothes for export, such as Bangladesh, are often unsafe for workers. In response, many retailers have said that it is difficult, if not impossible, for them to monitor the conditions in factories that produce their products.

Three notable attempts to find universal standards include the United Nations International Labour Organization, the Foreign Corrupt Practices Act of 1977, and the Organisation for Economic Co-Operation and Development Anti-Bribery Convention.

First, in 1919, the United Nations (UN) launched the International Labour Organization (ILO) to promote the rights of workers by encouraging living wages, employment opportunities, social protections, protection of workers in foreign countries, and job training. Membership is open to UN member countries that accept the invitation to join the ILO. To date, 187 countries participate, which is all but six of the UN member countries.

The ILO has a constitution and passes declarations regarding ethical employment practices. The problem the ILO faces is enforcement. Each country participates voluntarily, and can withdraw anytime. Additionally, each country can choose to adopt or reject each declaration the ILO passes. Even when a country accepts a declaration, the ILO has little power to discipline the country if it fails to follow the guidelines in the declaration. Because enforcement is difficult, the ILO is not considered a truly effective solution to the problem of exploited workers.

In the United States, Congress was concerned that U.S. companies with foreign operations were bribing government officials to gain an unfair advantage in competing for government contracts. In response to these concerns, Congress passed the Foreign Corrupt Practices Act of 1977 (FCPA). That act gave the Securities Exchange Commission and the Department of Justice the power to prosecute U.S. businesses engaged in bribery.

The FCPA was heavily criticized. Business leaders feared it made them less competitive against foreign companies that could, and often were expected to, use bribes to land business deals. This again led to discussions on the need for a universal solution.

The result was the Organisation for Economic Co-operation and Development (OECD) Anti-Bribery Convention, which took effect in 1999. Countries that joined the Convention agreed to pass legislation that outlawed bribery among businesses headquartered in their countries. To date, 41 countries have joined. But because only 20% of the countries around the world are members, the OECD Convention is not yet considered a universal solution to bribery.

Ethics Online

Compared to other technological advancements, the internet has changed the lives of average citizens in record time. In a country where legislation can take years to pass, this creates a problem for protecting internet users in the U.S. from privacy risks, scams, and having their ideas and their work used inappropriately. To a very large extent, we all use the internet at our own risk. In an ideal world, people would use the same ethical standards online that they use in other aspects of their lives. Civil society dictates we should not use hate speech, or use private information without permission. But feeling anonymous tempts some into behaving badly. Thus, the internet has created many hazards that legislators are scrambling to fix.

Among the most pressing issues related to online ethics are acceptable use and privacy concerns. Here, we examine federal attempts to protect users from these risks. You may recall reading earlier in this chapter that states may create laws that offer greater protection than federal laws provide. To that end, some states have introduced stricter laws than those discussed here.

Acceptable Use of Online Resources:
Every day millions of bits of copyrighted material are used inappropriately and without permission. These ideas and work products are protected by copyright laws, but the internet makes it easy for the materials to be "lifted," and difficult for the offenders to be caught. In the United States, federal protection of these electronic materials generally falls under the Digital Millennium Copyright Act of 1998. The act serves many purposes, including (1) criminalizing the production and distribution of technologies intended to steal or use copyrighted material, (2) making "hacking" into protected material illegal, (3) imposing strict penalties for internet copyright infringement, and (4) exempting internet service providers from being prosecuted for content their customers post or distribute. Among other features, this act requires internet service providers to immediately remove material when someone claims that material is copyrighted protected.

Privacy Concerns:
People are right to worry about their personal correspondence being viewed by others, including the government. One research agency estimated that in 2015, internet users around the world sent an average of 205 billion emails a day. While many of those messages go directly to trash or junk folders, many others contain the kind of personal correspondence that was once reserved for letters or notes slid across school desks. And while letters and notes in your home are protected from the prying eyes of the government through criminal

codes and constitutional rights to privacy, email in general, but particularly those in employment and personal settings are less protected.

One reason email is less protected is that the primary rules in place for protecting email correspondence were adopted in 1986, long before we used email as widely as we do today. The Electronic Communications Privacy Act of 1986, and with it the Stored Communications Act, have remained largely unchanged for 30 years. The acts require a search warrant to access email, just like the government would need to search your home. But the search-warrant requirement applies only to email that has been created in the previous 180 days. Older emails are considered abandoned, and can be accessed by the government with mere subpoenas. Therefore, emails older than six months are less protected from government searches than the letters you keep in your home.

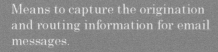

TRAP AND TRACE DEVICE:
Means to capture the origination and routing information for email messages.

Following the discovery of widespread terrorist activity within the United States in 2001, the American Patriot Act of 2001 was passed. Some parts were reauthorized in 2005. Later, in 2015, the U.S.A. Freedom Act renewed many of the Patriot Act's provisions. Relevant here, the Patriot Act authorized the government to collect certain information from online communications using trap and trace devices. This

information could be collected in the interest of national security when terrorist activity was suspected. The devices used to collect the information did not look at the message itself, but only the contact information of the senders and recipients.

In 2013, evidence was released that raised concerns about whether the government was overstepping its power by collecting bulk electronic records without specific suspicions of terrorist activity. Therefore, the 2015 Freedom Act reformed the law by requiring the government to specifically name the parties to be tracked.

Workplace Issues: Many employers take a keen interest in the online lives of employees and potential employees. Doing an internet search on a job candidate before deciding whether to interview her is common-place. Most employers report that they have declined to hire a job candidate based on what they have seen about a candidate online. This type of screening typically looks only at a person's public information. Employers make an initial judgment based on the way a person is willing to present himself to the world.

Consider the difference between what the government can do with regard to emails and what an employer can do. An individual is protected from government action by the search-warrant and subpoena requirements. An employee's emails on the employer's system, however, are generally searchable by the employer without notice or permission.

Some employers attempt to go beyond screening public information. Many employers have asked, or demanded, that employees tell them their passwords or other log-in information for social networking sites. While this is a violation of the terms of service for most sites, it is a rule that is difficult to enforce unless someone reports it. While several states have adopted laws that prohibit employers from asking for log-in information, it is a legal practice in many states. Efforts at enacting federal legislation to ban the practice have been unsuccessful.

Voluntary Standards

There have been many efforts to regulate ethics, but it remains largely a voluntary endeavor. The government would be hard-pressed to enforce mandatory community service on businesses, for example. In many instances, there is a fine line between unethical behavior and shrewd, even admirable, business dealings.

CHAPTER SUMMARY

It is crucial for everyone who engages in business to have some understanding of the law. Law and business complement each other. Business activities take place within a framework of laws. Likewise, many aspects of our legal system are put in place to reflect our business culture.

The American legal system is the product of many different factors. It is based on English common law, reflecting the early heritage of the United States. The authority of the government—and the division of powers between states and the federal government—reflects a historic commitment to federalism. Our constitutional government exists as a guard against unchecked, arbitrary power. New laws and regulations are made, and old ones repealed, reflecting changing social and political concerns. As the country and the business environment change, changes, so too will our laws change.

Review Questions

Review question 1.
What is the difference between ethics and law? If ethics are not required, why should businesses be concerned about them? Describe a scenario where ethics and law are both important to a business.

Review question 2.
What are the three branches of government in the United States? What are their different roles? Which branch does the president belong to? Which branch do government agencies belong to? The police?

Review question 3.
Is there an automatic right of appeal to the Supreme Court? To any other appellate court? What are the three levels of federal courts?

Review question 4.
How did the case of Marbury v. Madison change constitutional law in the United States?

Review question 5.
What are the parts of a court decision? What information is contained in each part?

Review question 6.
What is the difference between a bill and a law? Describe the legislative process of creating a statute.

Review question 7.
What is a plaintiff? A defendant? A prosecutor?

Review question 8.
What are the Federal Rules of Civil Procedure? When do they apply? What do they help regulate?

Review question 9.
When may a party present alternative legal theories? What is the purpose of "pleading in the alternative"?

Review question 10.
What is the difference between the holding and the rule in a published case? How can you tell the difference?

Questions for Discussion

Discussion question 1.

The following is an excerpt from a U.S. Supreme Court decision (citations are omitted). Brief the case. Does the decision raise any issues for private businesses that manage properties, such as shopping malls?

Board of Airport Commissioners v. Jews for Jesus, Inc.

482 U.S. 569 (1987)

O'CONNOR, J., delivered the opinion for a unanimous Court.

The issue presented in this case is whether a resolution banning all "First Amendment activities" at Los Angeles International Airport (LAX) violates the First Amendment.

On July 13, 1983, the Board of Airport Commissioners (Board) adopted Resolution No. 13787, which provides, in pertinent part:

NOW, THEREFORE, BE IT RESOLVED by the Board of Airport Commissioners that the Central Terminal Area at Los Angeles International Airport is not open for First Amendment activities by any individual and/or entity[.]

Respondent Jews for Jesus, Inc., is a nonprofit religious corporation. On July 6, 1984, Alan Howard Snyder, a minister of the Gospel for Jews for Jesus, was stopped by a Department of Airports peace officer while distributing free religious literature . . . The officer warned Snyder that the city would take legal action against him if he refused to leave as requested. Snyder stopped distributing the leaflets and left the airport terminal.

Jews for Jesus and Snyder then filed this action in the District Court for the Central District of California[.] First, respondents contended that the resolution was facially unconstitutional under Art. I, § 2, of the California Constitution and the First Amendment to the United States Constitution because it bans all speech in a public forum. . . . [T]he Court of Appeals concluded . . . . the resolution was unconstitutional on its face under the Federal Constitution. We granted certiorari[.] . . .

Under the First Amendment overbreadth doctrine, an individual whose own speech or conduct may be prohibited is permitted to challenge a statute on its face because it also threatens others not before the court -- those who desire to engage in legally protected expression but who may refrain from doing so rather than risk prosecution or undertake to have the law declared partially invalid. A statute may be invalidated on its face, however, only if the overbreadth is "substantial." The requirement that the overbreadth be substantial arose from our recognition that application of the overbreadth doctrine is, "manifestly, strong medicine," and that there must be a realistic danger that the statute itself will significantly compromise recognized First Amendment protections of parties not before the Court for it to be facially challenged on overbreadth grounds.

On its face, the resolution at issue in this case reaches the universe of expressive activity, and, by prohibiting all protected expression, purports to create a virtual "First Amendment Free Zone" at LAX. The resolution does not merely regulate expressive activity in the Central Terminal Area that might create problems such as congestion or the disruption of the activities of those who use LAX. Instead, the resolution expansively states that LAX "is not open for First Amendment activities by any individual and/or entity" . . . The resolution therefore does not merely reach the activity of respondents at LAX; it prohibits even talking and reading, or the wearing of campaign buttons or symbolic clothing. Under such a sweeping ban, virtually every individual who enters LAX may be found to violate the resolution . . . We think it obvious that such a ban cannot be justified . . . because no conceivable governmental interest would justify such an absolute prohibition of speech.

The petitioners suggest that the resolution is not substantially overbroad, because it is intended to reach only expressive activity unrelated to airport-related purposes. Such a limiting construction, however, is of little assistance in substantially reducing the overbreadth of the resolution. Much nondisruptive speech—such as the wearing of a T-shirt or button that contains a political message—may not be "airport-related," but is still protected speech[.] . . . We conclude that the resolution is substantially overbroad, and is not fairly subject to a limiting construction. Accordingly, we hold that the resolution violates the First Amendment.

Discussion question 2.

You are a U.S. Representative. Together with partners across the aisle, you have drafted a bill to provide grocery vouchers to college students who are spending more than 50% of their individual or family income on tuition, fees, books, and school materials. The so-called "Brain Food" bill has passed the House of Representatives and is headed to the Senate. The president held a press conference today saying that he does not like the idea. "Where's the food for newly returned veterans?" he says. You understand that some senators are echoing those comments with their constituents.

> What could happen to the bill in the Senate? What must happen there for the bill to move on to the next step?
>
> What if the Senate makes amendments to the bill that are inconsistent with your original goals for the legislation?
>
> How could the bill be blocked even if the Senate passes it?
>
> If the bill becomes law, how will the provisions be put into action? How can the law be challenged? Is it possible for the challenges to kill the law?
>
> What do you think of this process? Is it too cumbersome? Too much red tape? A good way to incorporate everyone's input?
>
> What do you think of the zero-sum game argument that the president uses against the bill in this scenario?

Discussion question 3.

The U.S. court system is adversarial. The idea is that having each side represented by an attorney who will contest and challenge the position of the other side, with a neutral judge making rulings, will tend to reveal the true state of affairs and lead to a fair resolution. By contrast, alternative dispute resolution techniques tend to focus on cooperation and reaching consensus between parties in dispute. What do you think of the adversarial court system? Would a collaborative model be preferable? Why or why not?

Discussion question 4.

Larry lives in Minnesota, but works in Wisconsin. He drives to Wisconsin every day he works. One morning after he has crossed into Wisconsin, he is distracted and collides with a Wisconsin-registered vehicle, injuring Betty, the driver. Her damages in medical expenses and other costs are $48,000. Larry does not have car insurance.

> Where can Betty sue Larry?
>
> Should she sue in state or federal court? In which level of court in the state or federal level?
>
> Betty hears about higher damages awards being granted by juries in Iowa to car crash victims. Iowa borders both Minnesota and Wisconsin. Should Betty be able to move her case to Iowa? Why or why not?
>
> After the litigation starts, Betty's attorney tells her that it will take over a year to go through the process and that the legal bills will be substantial. What are Betty's options if she does not want to continue the lawsuit?

Discussion question 5.

In Chaplinsky v. New Hampshire, 315 U.S. 568 (1942), a man was arrested for loudly insulting religion and a public official in the street. The law barred intentionally insulting speech from being used in a public place. The man challenged the constitutionality of the state law under which he was arrested, arguing that it harmed the right to free speech. While noting the importance of free speech, the U.S. Supreme Court upheld the law, saying that "fighting words"—those words that tend to incite an immediate breach of the peace—are not protected by the First Amendment. They add no value to public discourse, the Court said, and any benefit they do have is outweighed by the state's interest in public order.

> The Westboro Baptist Church is known nationally for its offensive protests at the funerals of soldiers and other public events. Their signs claim that "God hates" U.S. troops, Jews, Muslims, and LGBTQ people, among others. The signs also make other inflammatory claims. Are these protest signs "fighting words"? Should local communities enforce or even enact laws against that type of speech?
>
> Charlotte is walking on the sidewalk and accidentally cuts off Bill. Bill tells her to watch where she's going. Charlotte says, "Wow, you are a major jerk!" As she walks away, Bill hits Charlotte in the back of the head. Bill says

that Charlotte's comment amounted to fighting words, so he was justified in hitting Charlotte. Is he correct? Was Charlotte's statement protected by the First Amendment?

Discussion question 6.

One oft-stated advantage of common law systems is that they are adaptable, with decisions being based or crafted according to the situations of the parties. It is also said that civil law systems, relying on written codes, have the advantage of predictability. Do you regard predictability as more important than flexibility? Is there a way of balancing the two interests?

Discussion question 7.

The following scenario applies to questions 7 through 9. Ethical questions relating to sourcing are a matter of ongoing debate. The retail apparel industry is one sector that often confronts ethical issues around sourcing. Garment factories in countries that produce clothes for export, such as Bangladesh, often do not meet American safety standards. Some facilities are actively unsafe for workers. In response, many retailers have said that it is difficult, if not impossible, for them to monitor the conditions in factories that produce their products. Moreover, many factories may be in compliance with local and national laws, regardless of ongoing risk.

> If you were a buyer with a U.S. retailer, would you take these issues into consideration when sourcing? What standard would you use for deciding which producers to buy from? Would your answer change if you were unable to travel to each facility to look for yourself?

Discussion question 8.

Garment imports from the developing world allow for retailers to make higher profits on sales. The cheaper cost also makes clothes more affordable for less affluent buyers in the United States. If strict production safety rules were always applied, clothing might well become more expensive, and prices might rise beyond the ability of many consumers to pay.

> Does affordability for disadvantaged customers deserve consideration in your analysis? Does the retailer's profit margin?

Discussion question 9.

While some textile production facilities pose risks to workers, the workers need the jobs. Enhanced safety standards might result in closures of some production locations, which would displace workers.

> Does the workers' interest in continued local employment deserve to be considered? What about if children are employed at a garment maker, but their families need the children's income to survive?

> Are there ways that the retailer can use moral imagination to resolve any or all of these issues?

2

DISPUTE RESOLUTION

KEY OBJECTIVES:

▶ Learn the process through which a dispute is resolved in the court system.

▶ Understand the key features, advantages, and disadvantages of various methods of alternative dispute resolution.

▶ Understand the ways in which commercial parties attempt to avoid or plan for future business disputes.

CHAPTER OVERVIEW

In this chapter, we examine the available options for resolving disputes between business parties. We first walk through the formal process of resolving a dispute through the court system. After that, we review a number of methods of alternative dispute resolution. In addition to learning about the key features of each method of dispute resolution, we consider the advantages, disadvantages, and reasons why a business party might choose a particular method. We also look at several ways in which a commercial player can attempt to avoid, or at least minimize, potential business disputes. Finally, we discuss contract provisions commonly used by business parties to address dispute resolution issues before a dispute even arises.

ALTERNATIVE DISPUTE RESOLUTION:

Any means of settling disputes outside litigation.

INTRODUCTION

Although parties often have high expectations and the best of intentions, many business deals and relationships do not work out as the parties had hoped. A business may disagree with another company regarding the terms of the agreement between them. A company may have a dispute with a customer or employee. A corporation may need to file a lawsuit to protect its interest in proprietary information. Any number of circumstances may lead to a dispute.

When a business dispute arises, the parties may pursue a resolution in several ways. One way to resolve disputes is through the court system. This form of resolution is often slow, time-consuming, and expensive. In some circumstances, though, it may be the best option for parties to protect their interests. Other times, it may be the only option available. Sometimes, parties may prefer to use the court system because they want a formal, enforceable decision issued by a court of law. A formal decision may influence other cases or have more effect on the parties' behavior going forward.

Often, however, the parties are looking for a faster, more cost-effective way to resolve disputes. In that situation, the parties may look to **Alternative Dispute Resolution**, also known as **ADR**. There are several types of ADR, and each has its own advantages and disadvantages.

In this chapter, we examine formal dispute resolution through the court system as well as the various methods of alternative dispute resolution. We also consider ways in which a party can attempt to avoid disputes, and how parties might address the dispute resolution process through their business agreements before a dispute arises.

I. Litigation

Litigation is the process of resolving a dispute through a lawsuit in the court system. In litigation, the parties (plaintiff and defendant) present their claims, arguments, and evidence to a judge or jury. After the jury (or sometimes the judge) decides the case, the court issues a binding decision on the parties. Procedural rules control how the process works, and different rules apply to state and federal courts.

In the United States, litigation is an adversarial process. The plaintiff and the defendant are represented by attorneys advocating for their respective positions. Each side presents its best case, and each side has an opportunity to point out problems with the version presented by the other side, then the jury or judge must determine whose side they believe represents the truth. The goal of the process is to reach a decision in favor of one of the parties (*i.e.*, is the defendant liable to the plaintiff or not and, if so, how much money does the defendant owe the plaintiff?). Reaching a compromise solution is not typically a goal of litigation.

Pleadings

In a standard lawsuit, the initial documents filed by the plaintiff or defendant with a court are called the **pleadings**. The first pleading is the **complaint**, which starts the litigation process. The complaint is a document explaining why the court has the power to hear the case, the alleged facts of the case, the legal claims against the

LITIGATION:
The process of resolving a dispute through a lawsuit initiated in the court system.

PLEADINGS:
Documents filed with the court by the parties to a lawsuit. Pleadings include the complaint, answer, and counterclaims.

COMPLAINT:
A document filed by the party initiating a lawsuit (plaintiff) which contains a brief summary of the alleged facts of the case, the claims the party is alleging, and a statement of the relief desired from the other party (defendant).

PLAINTIFF:
The party who files a complaint to initiate a lawsuit against another party (defendant).

DEFENDANT:
The party who is being sued in a litigation.

In the American court system, except in special circumstances, each party must pay their own attorneys' fees and costs in litigation, even if they win the case. Under the "English rule," however, the losing party pays for the winner's fees in addition to its own. The English rule is a compelling approach, but it might discourage plaintiffs with modest means or those with a serious grievance who might have trouble finding the necessary evidence. Of course, the sheer cost of fees is its own disincentive under the American model.

other party, and the relief sought against the other party. The person who files the complaint is called the **plaintiff**. The party being sued is called the **defendant**.

After filing the complaint with the court, the plaintiff must serve the defendant by causing a copy of the complaint and a summons to be hand-delivered to the defendant. The summons informs the defendant of the lawsuit. The summons also tells the defendant that she must respond to the complaint within a certain number of days.

DISMISSAL IS APPROPRIATE ONLY IF NO SET OF FACTS CAN SUPPORT A CLAIM.

Conley v. Gibson
(Black Employees) v. (Union Officers)
355 U.S. 41, 78 S. Ct. 99 (1957)

INSTANT FACTS:
Black employees brought a class action against a union and its officers for not representing them or protecting their labor contract job and seniority rights.

BLACK LETTER RULE:
A complaint should not be dismissed for failure to state a claim unless it appears beyond doubt that the plaintiff can prove no set of supporting facts that would entitle him or her to relief.

PROCEDURAL BASIS:
Certiorari to review a dismissal of the complaint.

FACTS:
Conley and other black employees (P) brought a class action against a union, its local, and its officers, alleging federal Railway Labor Act violations. The complaint alleged that the plaintiffs were employees of the Texas and New Orleans Railroad in Houston and members of Local 28 of the Brotherhood of Railway and Steamship Clerks. A collective bargaining contract between the railroad and the union gave the members seniority and job rights. The railroad purported to abolish the jobs of the black employees, but, in reality, white employees filled most of the jobs and the few black employees hired back lost seniority. Despite the plaintiffs' requests, the union did not protect them against the discharges and refused to give them protection comparable to that given to white employees, thereby violating the union's duty of fair representation under the Railway Labor Act. Gibson and other union officers (D) moved to dismiss on the grounds that the National Railroad Adjustment Board had exclusive jurisdiction over the claims, that the railroad had not been joined as an indispensable party, and that the complaint failed to state a claim upon which relief could be granted. The trial court dismissed on the exclusive jurisdiction ground and the Fifth Circuit Court of Appeals affirmed.

ISSUE:

Should a complaint be dismissed for failure to state a claim upon which relief may be granted only if the plaintiff cannot prove a set of facts that would entitle him or her to relief?

DECISION AND RATIONALE:

(Black, J.) Yes. A complaint should be dismissed only if there is no doubt that the plaintiff cannot prove a set of facts entitling him to relief. Here, the complaint alleged that the plaintiffs were wrongfully discharged by the railroad and that the union refused to protect their jobs or to help them with their grievances because they were black. If proven, these allegations constitute a manifest breach of the union's statutory duty to represent fairly and without discrimination all bargaining unit members. Once a bargaining agent undertakes to represent a bargaining unit, it must represent in good faith and without discrimination all employees in the unit. The Federal Rules of Civil Procedure do not require a complaint to set forth specific facts to support general allegations of discrimination; the rules require only a "short and plain statement of the claim" that will give the defendant fair notice of the claim and the grounds upon which it rests. Following the simple guide of Rule 8(f) that "all pleadings shall be so construed as to do substantial justice," the complaint adequately sets forth a claim and gives the defendants fair notice of its basis. Pleading is not a game of skill in which one misstep of counsel may be decisive. Reversed.

ANALYSIS:

Conley is the leading case on pleading requirements under the Federal Rules of Civil Procedure. In *Conley*, the Supreme Court clearly demonstrates the liberality with which the Federal Rules of Civil Procedure approach pleading. The Court rejects two distinct arguments raised by the defendants: that no cause of action exists under the Railway Labor Act and that the complaint contains insufficient factual detail. In reaching its conclusion, the Court also dismissed the defendants' contention that the National Railroad Adjustment Board had exclusive jurisdiction and that the railroad was an indispensable party.

CASE VOCABULARY:

CLASS ACTION:

A lawsuit in which a single person or a small group of people represents the interests of a larger group.

QUESTIONS FOR DISCUSSION:

In employment lawsuits, the employees usually lack access to critical evidence that will prove their case. This evidence is gathered after the complaint through a process called "discovery." Do you think this decision was driven by the inability of the plaintiffs to complete their factual case until discovery? If so, is that a valid consideration? Compare this outcome with the result in the *Sanchez* case later in the chapter. What are the major differences?

THE SUPREME COURT TWEAKS A LONGSTANDING PLEADING STANDARD.

Bell Atl. Corp. v. Twombley
(Telephone Company) v. (Telephone Subscriber)
550 U.S. 544, 127 S. Ct. 1955 (2007)

INSTANT FACTS:

AT&T was broken up into local telephone service companies that did not provide long-distance services. Congress passed a law to allow the local telephone companies to re-enter the long-distance market. The law also allowed other companies to sell phone services to consumers. Twombley (P) and others sued, claiming that the local companies were working together to prevent other companies from selling to consumers in violation of the Sherman Act.

BLACK LETTER RULE:

A complaint alleging a violation of the Sherman Act must include facts that support a conspiracy theory, rather than facts that show independent similar conduct.

FACTS:

In 1984, AT&T was divested into a system of regional local telephone service monopolies, called "Incumbent Local Exchange Carriers" (ILECs), which were excluded from a separate, competitive market for long-distance service. That arrangement changed when Congress enacted the Telecommunications Act of 1996. The Act restructured local telephone markets so as to promote competition and established conditions for ILECs to reenter the competitive long-distance market, including sharing their network with "competitive local exchange carriers" (CLECs). The CLECs would use ILEC networks to purchase telephone services at wholesale rates for resale to consumers, lease elements of the network at bundled rates, or interconnect their facilities with ILEC facilities.

Twombley (P) represents a class of local telephone and high-speed internet subscribers charging the ILECs with violating § 1 of the Sherman Act, which prohibits any "contract, combination, . . . or conspiracy, in restraint of trade or commerce." Specifically, the complaint alleged that by engaging in a "parallel course of conduct" to prevent competition from CLECs within their respective local telephone service markets, the ILECs entered into a contract, combination, or conspiracy to prevent entry into their markets.

The district court dismissed the complaint for failure to state a claim for which relief can be granted. The court reasoned that, while parallel conduct may be alleged in support of a Sherman Act claim, the complaint must also allege additional facts that exclude independent action as an explanation for that parallel conduct. On appeal, the Second Circuit reversed, holding that no such additional facts need be pleaded to withstand a motion to dismiss.

PROCEDURAL BASIS:

The U.S. Supreme Court granted certiorari to review the Second Circuit decision.

ISSUE:

Can a complaint alleging a violation of the Sherman Act survive a motion to dismiss without some factual context suggesting coordination in violation of the Act?

DECISION AND RATIONALE:

(Souter, J.) No. Stating a claim under § 1 of the Sherman Act requires a complaint with enough factual matter, taken as true, to plausibly suggest that an agreement in restraint of trade or commerce was made. Simply stated, to violate the Sherman Act, a complaint must allege sufficient factual assertions that the defendants engaged in something more than independent parallel conduct; facts supporting a conspiracy must be alleged. While Federal Rule of Civil Procedure 8(a)(2) requires only that a pleading provide "a short and plain statement of the claim showing that the pleader is entitled to relief" and fair notice of the grounds upon which the complaint rests, the plaintiff must provide more than labels, conclusions, and formulaic recitations of the elements of the cause of action.

For a Sherman Act case, the pleader must provide plausible factual grounds to create a reasonable expectation that discovery will produce evidence of the existence of an illegal agreement. Facts showing parallel conduct, while relevant, do not allow an inference of a conspiracy by themselves. They merely suggest a possibility of conspiracy without the requisite plausibility.

Litigation, and discovery particularly, is an expensive and time-consuming process. To minimize the cost and burden, only plausible claims should be allowed to proceed. Otherwise, well-funded plaintiffs could force less fortunate defendants into ill-advised settlements to avoid mounting defense costs. Plaintiffs should not be allowed to engage in fishing expeditions in hopes of uncovering incriminating evidence they have no reason to know exists.

Here, the Complaint leaves no doubt that the plaintiffs' conspiracy claims rest on the parallel conduct of the ILECs. The factual resistance to the new CLEC presence in their respective markets was nothing more than a natural business reaction to new competition in a previously dominated market. Each ILEC, on its own, had reason to take business action to protect its territory. That does not necessarily indicate that there was a conspiracy among ILECs to coordinate those actions.

Evidence pointing to collusion or collaboration is needed to establish a conspiracy. The plaintiff suggests there was a conspiracy because each ILEC stayed within its own geographic region without invading another ILEC market. Without factual support for the claim, however, the alternative explanation for such self-limitation is that monopoly has been and is the norm in telecommunications. The ILECs were created to eliminate the nationwide AT&T monopoly and resulted in smaller regional monopolies. It is easily believed that the ILECs simply practiced what they knew. The facts in the complaint fail to take the plaintiffs' claims from conceivable to plausible. Reversed.

DISSENT:

(Stevens, J.) The complaint alleges that the defendants entered into an agreement to restrict competitive entry into the local telephone and internet services market, and supported that allegation with assertions that the individual defendants intentionally avoided infringing upon one another's markets and limited access to their networks for competitive reasons. In further support of these assertions, the complaint attributes a quote to a former CEO of one of the defendants that infringing upon a neighboring territory "might be a good way to turn a quick dollar but that doesn't make it right," and claimed that the individual defendants had an opportunity to communicate about maintaining territorial lines on numerous occasions.

While the defendants' parallel conduct may indeed suggest nothing more than sound economic practice, it may just as well be a product of an illegal agreement among the defendants. Yet, rather than compel the defendants to themselves explain the innocent meanings of these assertions through discovery and deposition testimony, the majority accepts the assurances of the defendants' lawyers that no conspiracy exists.

Any risks borne by allowing this case to proceed into pretrial discovery and beyond—such as increased litigation expense and juror confusion—can be minimized through careful case management and jury instructions.

The Federal Rules of Civil Procedure were not designed to keep litigants out of court but rather to keep them in. Nowhere in Rule 8's requirement of "a short and plain statement of the claim showing that the pleader is entitled to relief" is there a requirement of facts or evidence or conclusions. Rather, those requirements are left to pretrial discovery to determine whether a claim is sufficient to proceed to trial.

A complaint must set forth enough support for its claims to allow it to proceed to the pretrial phase. The plausibility standard created by the majority's decision is perfectly in line with a Rule 56 motion for summary judgment, but is irreconcilable with the requirements of Rule 8.

Finally, even accepting the majority's plausibility requirement, the complaint meets the standard. In alleging that the defendants' parallel conduct was a result of an illegal agreement, the facts of the complaint establish their claims as plausible. The facts alleged show that the defendants had numerous opportunities over many years to meet and discuss such an agreement, and attributed a public statement to a former CEO that suggests that these discussion in fact occurred. One plausible explanation for the CEO's comment was that he and his competitors had agreed not to infringe upon one another's territories. While such agreement may not in fact exist, the complaint certainly raises a plausible question worth of pretrial discovery. The complaint should not have been dismissed.

ANALYSIS:

The *Twombley* decision is perhaps one of the more controversial decisions (at least among lawyers) to have come from the Supreme Court in recent years. The Federal Rules of Civil Procedure were adopted in large part to change civil procedure from code pleading to notice pleading, leaving pretrial discovery to ferret out the truth and ensure justice. Rule 11 already required counsel to conduct some pre-filing investigation to be sure that his or her client's claims had sufficient factual support. Yet, after *Twombley*, that support appears to withstand dismissal only if it is sufficiently known, as opposed to discoverable, when the complaint is filed.

CASE VOCABULARY:

DIVESTITURE:

A court order to a defendant to rid itself of property, securities, or other assets to prevent a monopoly or restraint of trade.

MOTION TO DISMISS:
A request that the court dismiss the case because of settlement, voluntary withdrawal, or a procedural defect. Under the Federal Rules of Civil Procedure, a plaintiff may voluntarily dismiss the case (under Rule 41(a)) or the defendant may ask the court to dismiss the case, usually based on one of the defenses listed in Rule 12(b). These defenses include lack of personal or subject-matter jurisdiction, improper venue, insufficiency of process, the plaintiff's failure to state a claim on which relief can be granted, and the failure to join an indispensable party. A defendant will frequently file a motion to dismiss for failure to state a claim, which is governed by Rule 12(b)(6), claiming that even if all the plaintiff's allegations are true, they would not be legally sufficient to state a claim on which relief might be granted.

SHERMAN ACT:
A federal statute, passed in 1890, that prohibits direct or indirect interference with the freely competitive interstate production and distribution of goods. This Act was amended by the Clayton Act in 1914.

WELL-PLEADED COMPLAINT:
An original or initial pleading that sufficiently sets forth a claim for relief—by including the grounds for the court's jurisdiction, the basis for the relief claimed, and a demand for judgment—so that a defendant may draft an answer that is responsive to the issues presented. A well-pleaded complaint must raise a controlling issue of federal law for a federal court to have federal-question jurisdiction over the lawsuit.

QUESTIONS FOR DISCUSSION:
How does this case fit with *Conley v. Gibson*? Do you agree more with the majority opinion or the dissent? Why?

The defendant may respond to the complaint in several ways.

- In most cases, the defendant files a pleading called an **answer**. In the answer, the defendant admits or denies the facts alleged in the complaint. The answer also states the legal defenses upon which the defendant will rely.

- The defendant may also file a **counterclaim**. A counterclaim is a related lawsuit involving the same basic facts that is brought by the defendant against the plaintiff. For example, if Pinnacle Company sues Radd Inc. for breach of contract, Radd Inc. may file a counterclaim against Pinnacle arguing that Pinnacle breached the implied covenant of good faith and fair dealing. A counterclaim is typically filed along with the defendant's answer.

- As another option, the defendant may file a motion to dismiss. A motion to dismiss asks the court to dismiss the case outright. Motions to dismiss typically argue that the complaint does not state a valid legal claim that the court can resolve on any set of proven facts, that the court lacks the power to hear the case, or that the defendant was not properly served with the complaint. If the court grants the motion, the plaintiff may be allowed to file an amended complaint to fix whatever deficiency existed in the original complaint. If the court denies the motion, the defendant must then file an answer.

> **Example:**
>
> CP Productions sued Glover for copyright violation, claiming that Glover had downloaded CP Productions' copyrighted work via torrent. Glover did not respond to the lawsuit. The federal district court entered a default judgment against Glover for the maximum amount allowed by law for copyright violations ($150,000), plus attorney fees, and court costs. *CP Productions Inc. v. Glover*, 1:12-cv-0080-JMS-DML (S.D. Ind. March 26, 2013).

What happens if the defendant does not respond in one of these ways? For defendants, doing nothing is a poor choice. If a defendant does not respond after receiving valid notice of the lawsuit, the court will enter a **default judgment** against the defendant. A default judgment is a binding ruling in favor of the plaintiff. The default judgment grants the plaintiff the damages sought against the defendant. When served with a lawsuit, an individual or company should act quickly to avoid defaulting. Still, procedural rules exist which allow a defendant to remove a case from default under certain circumstances.

ANSWER:

A written pleading filed by a defendant to respond to a complaint filed by a plaintiff in a lawsuit.

COUNTERCLAIM:

A claim asserted by the defendant against the plaintiff in a lawsuit.

DEFAULT JUDGMENT:

A binding judgment entered by a court if the defendant does not respond to the plaintiff's complaint.

Discovery

If the complaint makes a valid claim and the case continues, the parties will engage in **discovery**. Discovery is the process by which the parties in a lawsuit obtain information from each other and from any witnesses prior to trial. In discovery, each party requests information, documents, records, and testimony from the opposing party. Each party must respond to the requests for information and documents, locate the requested information, and produce relevant documents and other information to the other side. The parties' attorneys rely upon depositions, interrogatories, requests for admission, and document requests to obtain information during discovery. The purpose of discovery is to allow the parties to obtain evidence that helps their case, to make the parties aware of evidence in favor of the opposing party's position, and to narrow the questions to be decided during trial.

Special court rules apply to the discovery process. The rules define the types of information that may be requested and limit the information that must be produced. The discovery rules also govern the conduct of the parties and their attorneys during discovery. Only information relevant to the case, or likely to lead to the discovery of relevant information, must be

UNITED STATES DISTRICT COURT
SOUTHERN DISTRICT OF INDIANA
INDIANAPOLIS DIVISION

CP PRODUCTIONS INC., *Plaintiff*,	)))	
vs.	))	1:12-cv-00808-JMS-DML
GERALD L. GLOVER, III, *Defendant*.	)))	

FINAL JUDGMENT

For the reasons set forth in the Court's contemporaneously entered Order, the Court now

enters **FINAL JUDGMENT** in favor of Plaintiff and against Defendant and taxes costs in favor

of Plaintiff and against Defendant for a total amount of **$151,425**. This figure includes:

1. Statutory damages of $150,000;

2. Attorneys' fees of $1,000; and

3. Costs of $425.

03/26/2013

Hon. Jane Magnus-Stinson, Judge
United States District Court
Southern District of Indiana

Distribution via ECF only:

Matthew Edward Dumas
HOSTETTER & O'HARA
matt@hostetter-ohara.com

Distribution via U.S. Mail:

Gerald L. Glover, III
5846 Hartle Drive
Indianapolis, IN 46216

produced to an opposing party. If a party believes that requested information is not relevant or is beyond the scope of the case, his attorney may object to the request and ask the court to deny the request. A party may also deny a request if that information sought is privileged, meaning it is protected from discovery because it is a communication between a party and his attorney or is work product created by or at the request of the attorney. If the court deems the information relevant or not protected by privilege, the party must produce it. If the party still refuses to do so, the requesting party's attorney may ask the court to compel the other party to produce the information.

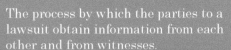

DISCOVERY:
The process by which the parties to a lawsuit obtain information from each other and from witnesses.

DEPOSITION:
The process of receiving and recording the sworn testimony of a party or witness during discovery.

Depositions: During discovery, a party may request to take the **deposition** of a party or witness who has information relevant to the case. A deposition is the process of taking the sworn testimony of a party or witness. A deposition is similar to providing testimony at trial. At the deposition, the party or witness provides answers to questions asked by the attorneys for both sides in the case. The party's or witness's answers are given under oath, and a court reporter takes down everything that is said.

The attorneys use depositions to obtain information for the case and to see how witnesses would perform if they were required to testify in court.

Interrogatories: The parties may also seek information through **interrogatories**. Interrogatories are written questions sent to the other party. The responding party must prepare written answers to the questions under oath. Interrogatories may only be directed to parties. Unlike a deposition request, interrogatories may not be issued to witnesses who are not parties in the case.

The written answers to interrogatories are usually prepared by the party's attorney. The attorneys may try to reveal as little information as possible in the answers. The attorneys preparing the answers also try to avoid wording that could be interpreted against the answering party. But they must be careful, because the court may penalize a party who fails to answer interrogatories.

DISCOVERY AND COURTROOM PROCEEDINGS ARE TRANSCRIBED BY A COURT REPORTER.

COURTESY OF GETTY IMAGES

One party might issue the following interrogatories to the other party:

> INTERROGATORY NO. 1: Describe in detail the nature of Defendant's business.
>
> INTERROGATORY NO. 2: Identify all agreements and/or contracts between Plaintiff and Defendant.
>
> INTERROGATORY NO. 3: Describe the transactions covered by the first contract between Plaintiff and Defendant.

The full list of interrogatories may go on for many pages, depending on the complexity of the case.

Requests for Admission: Parties may also issue **requests for admission**. Requests for admission ask the opposing party to admit or deny facts about the case. The purpose of requests for admission is to determine a set of facts upon which the parties agree and to avoid spending time trying to prove those facts in the courtroom.

Document Requests: Document requests are another tool used in discovery. Document requests seek the review of records and documents relevant to the case that are in the care, custody, and control of the other party. Any relevant material, including electronically stored information, may be requested in a document request.

In a breach of contract dispute, the plaintiff might send the following requests for admission to the defendant:

> REQUEST NO. 1: Admit that Defendant and Plaintiff entered into the Contract for Services on May 19, 2005.
>
> REQUEST NO. 2: Admit that Defendant failed or refused to pay all of the invoices issued by the Plaintiff for services provided under the Contract.

As with interrogatories, there may be many requests issued to a party.

Document requests are a different type of litigation tool, but they look very similar. A party seeking documents or records might make the following requests to the other party:

> REQUEST No.1: Provide any and all agreements/contracts between Plaintiff and Defendant dated May 19, 2005.
>
> REQUEST No. 2: Provide all documents, including electronic documents, relating to or discussing the May 19, 2005 agreement.

INTERROGATORIES:

A written set of questions served by a party to a lawsuit to an opposing party during discovery. The responding party prepares written answers under oath.

REQUESTS FOR ADMISSION:

A written set of questions or statements served by a party to a lawsuit on an opposing party or witness during discovery in an effort to determine agreed-upon facts. The responding party must deny or admit each statement in writing.

Electronic evidence includes all electronic documents, emails, voice mails, tweets, blogs, social media posts, files, and records. Computers and other electronic devices record a lot of information about electronic files (referred to as metadata), such as who created a file and when it was created, modified, or accessed. This metadata may be very relevant to the dispute. This electronic evidence and the related metadata are often referred to as **electronically stored information (ESI)**. Parties often find the information in and about the files, such as when a document was created or viewed, provides information useful to their case. Discovery rules require the parties to preserve documents and electronically stored information that may be relevant to the lawsuit if they reasonably anticipate litigation.

Several other types of information may be added to the process through discovery. Many of these items have no prior connection to the parties or to the dispute. For instance, scientific publications or expert reports created by third parties may provide critical data relevant to the case. Police records or reports may be important to the plaintiff or the defendant, even though the case is not a criminal matter. In short, any information relevant to the case may be part of the discovery process—including information gathered or created after the original complaint was filed. If necessary, parties can rely on the subpoena power of the court to compel non-parties to produce documents, provide deposition testimony, or appear in court in order to obtain relevant information.

Discovery takes time and costs money. The parties' attorneys may spend substantial billable time dealing with discovery requests and conducting depositions. It may also take a long time to locate, retrieve, and review documents requested by the other party. Attorney fees are not the only costs, as the parties may need to hire a specialist to assist them in retrieving, reconstructing, and reviewing electronically stored information. Depending on the circumstances, hundreds of thousands, if not millions, of electronic files from multiple locations around the country may need to be reviewed for a single case.

DOCUMENT REQUESTS:

A written request for documents, electronically stored information, or other items issued during discovery to an opposing party.

METADATA:

Information about electronic files describing how, when, and by whom a particular set of data was collected, and how the data is formatted.

ELECTRONICALLY STORED INFORMATION (ESI):

Data or information that is stored in electronic format, including documents, emails, voice mails, tweets, blogs, social media posts, files, and other records.

Motion Practice

Throughout litigation, the parties may file motions. A **motion** is a request to the judge to make a decision about some issue in the case. Some types of motions are frequently mentioned in legal dramas, such as:

Discovery Tools	
Tool	*Description*
Depositions	The process of receiving and recording sworn testimony of a party or witness. Attorneys for all parties in the case may ask questions of the deponent.
Interrogatories	Written questions submitted to the other party. The responding party must provide written answers under oath.
Requests for Admission	Written statements submitted to the other party in an effort to determine agreed-upon facts. The responding party must admit or deny each statement.
Document Requests	Written requests for records, documents, and other information, including electronically stored information, to be produced by the opposing party.

- A motion to treat a witness as hostile (if granted, the attorney has greater leeway in the format of questions to the witness).

- A motion to suppress evidence (an attorney may argue that certain evidence does not tend to prove a point, or that it is more inflammatory than relevant so that it might overly influence a jury).

- A motion to subpoena a witness (a party may ask the court to require that an absent witness appear in court for questioning by issuing an enforceable legal order—a subpoena—for the witness's presence).

As noted in a previous section, the defendant may file a motion to dismiss the case. Motions are also frequently filed during the discovery process. The parties may disagree on whether certain documents or information are relevant to the case and must be produced, whether documents may be withheld because of attorney-client privilege, or whether a party has completely responded to discovery requests. When such a dispute arises, a party may file a motion with the court asking the judge to resolve the issue.

Motion for Summary Judgment: After the conclusion of the discovery period, a party might also file a motion for summary judgment. In a motion for **summary judgment**, the party

MOTION:
A request to the judge to make a decision on an issue in a lawsuit.

is asking the court to decide the case without a trial. The court may consider the evidence gathered to that point, including sworn statements and documents obtained during discovery. Summary judgment may only be granted if there are no undisputed factual questions; if so, the judge determines how the law applies to those settled facts and decides the case, or some part of the case, without a trial.

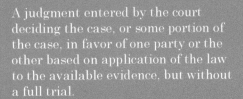

SUMMARY JUDGMENT:

A judgment entered by the court deciding the case, or some portion of the case, in favor of one party or the other based on application of the law to the available evidence, but without a full trial.

VOIR DIRE:

The process of questioning potential jurors to determine if they are qualified to serve on the jury.

DIRECTED VERDICT:

A ruling in a lawsuit entered by the trial judge after a determination that a reasonable jury could not reach a different conclusion.

Trial

If a case goes to trial, the parties present their arguments, evidence, and witnesses to the finder of fact. The finder of fact is either a jury or the judge. On television, trials are almost always heard by a jury. The jurors attend the trial and make decisions about the facts of the case. For instance, in a negligence lawsuit before a jury, the jurors determine whether the defendant failed to act with reasonable care in the

circumstances. The judge is responsible for the legal decisions in the case, including whether or not to grant motions. The judge also issues the decision in the case based on the jury's findings of fact.

Attorneys "move" for interim judicial decisions at all stages of litigation. For example, during a deposition, an attorney may object to the opposition's questions to a party, even though a judge is not present for these sessions. Despite the objection, the person being questioned must generally respond during the deposition. So what good is moving for an objection? Motions preserve all the issues that might be raised in a later appeals case, and recall that everything said during a deposition, by the deponent or the attorneys present, is taken down by the court reporter. If problems with the process are not put on the record when they arise, it is almost impossible to raise those issues in a later proceeding. It's a matter of "speak now or forever hold your peace!" In the case of depositions, the judge looks at the objections later when deciding whether deposition testimony can be admitted in court.

Despite the popularity of juries on television, juries hear relatively few cases. If the parties consent, civil cases can be heard by the judge acting as the finder of fact in a bench trial. The judge will also make legal determinations in the case. Using the judge as the finder of fact expedites the process because no jury needs to be selected for the trial. There is also no need for

> *Example:*
>
> Parties to lawsuits often find that the opposing party is not eager to comply with discovery requests. A motion to compel discovery in a hypothetical case looks something like the example below; it would be up to the court to grant or deny the motion.
>
> The Plaintiff, Aza Inc., by its attorney, Hugh Hugherson, moves for an Order compelling the Defendant, Bizz Corp., to promptly produce all outstanding discovery, and states grounds as follows:
>
> 1. That discovery in the form of Interrogatories and Request for Production of Documents was served on Defendant in this case on December 15, 2015.
>
> 2. That on April 1, 2016, Plaintiff requested by letter to Defendant's counsel that Answers to the Interrogatories and Requested Documents be promptly supplied.
>
> 3. That on September 1, 2016, Plaintiff requested by letter to Defendant's counsel that Answers to the Interrogatories and Requested Documents be promptly supplied.
>
> 4. That to this date, Plaintiff has not received either Answers to the Interrogatories or Requested Documents from Defendant in this matter.
>
> Wherefore, the Plaintiff moves for an Order compelling the Defendant to produce complete Answers and all of the Requested Documents within 15 days.
>
> Hugh Hugherson, Esq.

lengthy deliberations among jurors regarding the facts.

In a jury trial, the parties will engage in *voir dire*. *Voir dire* is the process of questioning potential jurors in order to determine who will serve on the jury. The purpose of *voir dire* is to ask prospective jurors questions that might expose conflicts of interest or bias for or against the plaintiff or defendant. Out of the pool of potential jurors, lawyers for each side will eliminate individuals whom they believe cannot fairly judge the facts of the case. When the pool is narrowed down to enough individuals to make up the jury, or when the attorneys have used all their opportunities to eliminate potential jurors, the remaining candidates are sworn in as the jury.

Once the jury is sworn in, the plaintiff presents his case first. During the plaintiff's case, the defendant may object to the evidence presented.

The defendant may also cross-examine the plaintiff's witnesses.

After the plaintiff's case, outside the presence of the jury, the defendant may make a motion for a **directed verdict**, also referred to as a motion for judgment as a matter of law in federal courts. This motion asks the judge to issue a verdict in favor of the defendant because the plaintiff has not presented enough evidence to justify a decision in the plaintiff's favor. If the judge denies the motion, the defendant then presents its evidence, to which the plaintiff's attorney can object, and its witnesses, whom the plaintiff's attorney can cross-examine. At end of the defendant's case, the attorneys present closing arguments.

JUDGMENT NOTWITHSTANDING THE VERDICT:

A judgment entered by the trial judge which reverses a jury verdict because the judge finds that there was no factual basis for the verdict or it was contrary to law.

APPEAL:

Review of a trial court decision by a higher court.

APPELLANT:

The party who files an appeal of a court decision.

APPELLEE:

The party responding to an appeal filed by the other party (appellant).

After closing arguments, the judge provides instructions to the jury regarding the law applicable to the case. The jurors then go to the jury room to deliberate and reach a verdict in favor of one of the parties. The jury may also need to decide on the amount of damages if they find one of the parties liable. After the jury has left the courtroom, either side can also move the court for a directed verdict.

Post-Trial Motions

After the jury issues a verdict, the parties may file post-trial motions. One type of post-trial motion is a motion for **judgment notwithstanding the verdict (JNOV)**. In a motion for JNOV, the requesting party asks the court to set aside the jury's verdict and enter judgment in her favor. If the judge believes the jury's verdict was incorrect based on the evidence presented at trial, the motion is granted. This outcome is rare.

A party may also file a motion for a new trial. In this motion, the party is asking the judge to set aside the jury verdict and hold a new trial. A motion for a new trial may be granted for a number of reasons. If the judge believes the jury made a mistake or returned an excessive verdict, if new evidence that could not have been discovered previously was brought forward, if an attorney or jurors behaved improperly, if the judge made a mistake when instructing the jury, or if other errors occurred, the motion may be granted, and the litigation process would begin again.

Appeal

Either party may **appeal** the jury's verdict or the judge's decision on any motions filed during the case. In order to appeal, a party must have legal grounds to challenge the outcome. In other words, the appealing party must show that there was a legal error. If a party decides to appeal, that party must file the appeal within a specified number of days. The appealing party must file a notice of appeal with the trial court where the case was decided. The appealing party is called the **appellant** or petitioner. The opposing party is called the **appellee** or respondent.

The appeal is filed with the appropriate appellate court. Appellate courts at the state level can include courts of appeal and state supreme courts.

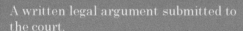

BRIEF:
A written legal argument submitted to the court.

ORAL ARGUMENT:
Spoken presentation of arguments to a court by attorneys for the parties appearing in person.

Most states call their top appellate court the state's supreme court, but New York and Maryland's top appellate courts are both called the Court of Appeals.

On appeal, the case is presented to a judge or a panel of judges. There is no jury at the appellate level. The appellant must provide the appellate court with a copy of the trial court record of the case. The record includes a copy of the trial transcript, all documents and motions filed in the trial court, and orders issued by the trial court. The appellate court may only consider evidence contained within the record. The appellant also files a **brief**. A brief is a party's written legal argument. The brief summarizes of the facts of the case, the issues being appealed, the applicable law, and the reasons that the trial court decision should be reversed. The appellee files an answering brief setting forth its opposing arguments.

After the parties have filed their briefs, the court reviews the documents and hears **oral argument**. At the oral argument, the attorneys present their cases orally to the appellate judges. The attorneys also answer questions from the judges. After oral argument, the appellate judges confer and then issue a written opinion. The appellate court may take one of the following actions: affirm (uphold) or reverse the trial court decision in whole or in part, modify the decision, or **remand** (send back) the case to the trial court to re-hear the case taking into account the appellate court's decision.

The losing party on appeal may petition to the highest state or federal court. The highest court of a state is usually called the **supreme court** (although both New York and Maryland call this court the "Court of Appeals"). The petition asks the supreme court to review the case. The supreme court decides which cases it will review. A party does not have the right to have its case

REMAND:
The result when an appellate court sends a case back to the trial court for further proceedings.

SUPREME COURT:
The highest appellate court in a jurisdiction.

WRIT OF CERTIORARI:
Permission to have a case heard by the U.S. Supreme Court that is given by the Court in response to a petition by the appealing party.

If a petition for review is granted, the parties must file new briefs. The parties also present oral arguments before the supreme court panel. The supreme court may affirm, reverse, modify, or remand the decision.

For federal cases, appeals from federal trial courts are heard by the federal circuit courts. If a party wishes further review after losing at the state supreme court or the federal circuit court, the party must file a petition for a **writ of certiorari** with the U.S. Supreme Court. The U.S. Supreme Court only hears cases after (1) all other appellate options for the issue have been exhausted, and (2) the Court grants a writ of certiorari meaning that it will hear the case. Although some say that they will "take it all the way to the Supreme Court," the U.S. Supreme Court only hears cases that it chooses to review.

heard by the supreme court. In fact, only a small percentage of petitions are granted by state supreme courts (or by the U.S. Supreme Court).

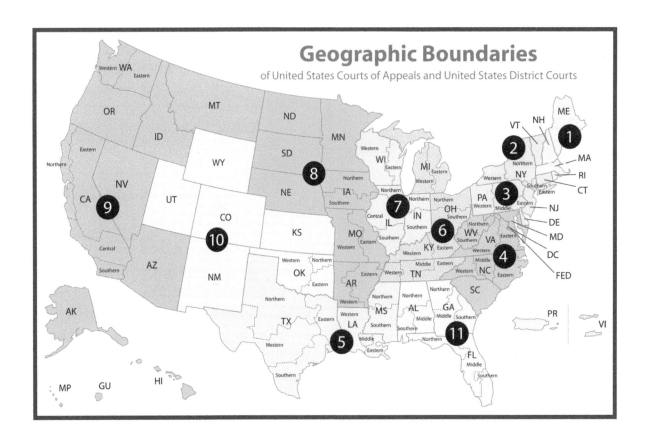

Geographic Boundaries
of United States Courts of Appeals and United States District Courts

The Litigation Process
• Plaintiff initiates lawsuit by filing a complaint with the court
• Defendant responds by filing an answer, counterclaim, or motion to dismiss
• The parties engage in discovery process
• The parties may file motions related to discovery or other issues
• The parties engage in voir dire process to determine jurors for trial
• Plaintiff's attorney gives his opening statement to the jury
• Defendant's attorney gives her opening statement to the jury
• Plaintiff's attorney presents his case to the jury; defendant cross-examines witnesses
• Defendant may move for a directed verdict
• Defendant's attorney presents her case to the jury; plaintiff cross-examines witnesses
• Parties present closing arguments
• Jury deliberates and returns verdict
• Judge may consider post-trial motions filed by the parties, such as a motion for a new trial, or motion for judgment notwithstanding the verdict
• Losing party may appeal if there are legal grounds to be decided on appeal
• If appealed, the parties must submit briefs to the appellate court

For most parties, there is no right to be heard by the Supreme Court.

Once all of these avenues for appeal have been exhausted, or petitions denied, the case is concluded.

II. Alternative Dispute Resolution

The entire litigation process can go on for several years. Each separate part of the process can take many months. The process can also be slow because the courts must work through a heavy load of cases. For this and other reasons, parties are increasingly using Alternative

Dispute Resolution ("ADR") to resolve business disputes. ADR may provide time and cost savings. ADR also gives the parties more control over the process, allows for creative solutions, and may help preserve the parties' relationship. We now look at the various types of alternative dispute resolution available to business entities and individuals.

Negotiation and Settlement

At any point during the litigation process, or even before litigation has begun, the parties may decide to deal with the case outside of court. The parties will discuss the issues to determine whether there is a way to resolve the problem. The process of informal dispute resolution between the parties is called **negotiation**. The goal of negotiation is to **settle** the case. Although not a formal type of alternative dispute resolution, negotiation leading to settlement is a very common alternative to litigation. Negotiations can take place at a meeting of the parties, or

by phone or email or other means. The parties' attorneys may not even be involved in these conversations. If the negotiations are successful, the parties will agree to a settlement. In a settlement, the defendant generally will agree to pay a sum of money to the plaintiff in exchange for the plaintiff's agreement to dismiss the court case.

Sometimes, the parties may even agree to settle after a verdict, if one party plans to appeal the trial court's judgment. In that situation, the parties may agree to a payment in exchange for agreeing not to file an appeal. A settlement may take many forms, depending on the circumstances and remedies sought by the parties.

The parties typically sign a written settlement agreement stating the terms agreed to between them. After the parties have signed the agreement, it becomes a legally binding contract. In many settlement agreements, the parties agree not to disclose the terms to which they have agreed.

A large majority of lawsuits today end in settlement. Parties choose settlement for a variety of reasons. Parties may wish to resolve the dispute quickly, rather than waiting years for litigation to conclude. Extended litigation may require corporate employees or business owners to spend a lot of time dealing with a case. If so, the lawsuit may distract the owner and employees from the ongoing work of the business. The parties may also wish to avoid the expense and uncertainty of trial.

Reputation may be another reason to settle. The parties may prefer settlement to avoid the public nature of litigation. Documents or other evidence may reveal embarrassing details or

NEGOTIATION:
A method of alternative dispute resolution in which the parties, either with or without their attorneys, work to reach a resolution.

SETTLE/SETTLEMENT:
Agreed final resolution of a dispute outside of court.

MEDIATION:
A method of alternative dispute resolution in which the parties work with a neutral third party, a mediator, in an attempt to reach a settlement.

facts about the parties, or may otherwise harm a party's public image. Furthermore, the adversarial nature of litigation often permanently damages the relationship between the parties. For all of these reasons and others, negotiation and settlement is a popular option for many parties involved in business disputes.

Mediation

In **mediation**, the parties to a lawsuit work with a neutral third party, or mediator, to help them reach a resolution. Typically, mediation is scheduled to occur on certain date and time, during which the mediator meets with the parties jointly and then meets with each party separately. Each party usually presents to the mediator a brief summary of the facts, evidence, and argument in support of their position. The mediator is likely to explain to each party what he views as the strengths and weaknesses of each side's position. The mediator tries to help the parties find common ground and a resolution to which both parties can agree.

The mediator does not issue a decision regarding the case, and the parties are not required to settle the case (although they may agree to be bound by the mediator's recommendation). Generally, therefore, mediation is less adversarial and contentious than litigation. As such, mediation is particularly useful in disputes between parties in long-term business relationships, such as business partners.

If the parties agree to the process, they may voluntarily attempt mediation at any time. In some instances, a court may require the parties to attempt mediation during the pre-trial stages of litigation. Although the parties are not required to reach a settlement in court-mandated mediation, they must cooperate in good faith with the mediation process. Some disputes are resolved through online mediation. In online mediation, the process is completed through the internet and electronic technologies, such as video-conferencing.

Typically, the parties will share the cost of mediator fees. In some circumstances, such as where one party has more resources than the other, one party may agree to pay all mediation fees. The parties may agree to any related details about the mediation, including, but not limited to, who the mediator will be and where the mediation will take place.

Arbitration

Arbitration is another form of alternative dispute resolution. In arbitration, the parties present their case to a neutral third party, the arbitrator, who issues a decision in the case. The parties may also agree to use a panel of arbitrators rather than a single decision maker. The arbitrator's decision is called an **award**. Arbitration is similar to litigation because the parties often engage in discovery and submit the case for a final decision. Typically, the parties agree to be bound by the arbitrator's decision. The parties may, however, agree to engage in nonbinding arbitration.

A party may appeal an arbitration award, but court review of an arbitration award is more limited than review of a court decision. An arbitration award will only be set aside for a few reasons, such as if the arbitrator engaged in misconduct or exceeded his authority, or if the award violates public policy. Because arbitration is voluntary and outside the public sphere, there are fewer ways to attack the outcome.

In an arbitration, the parties usually give opening statements and present evidence and witnesses to the arbitrator, as they could in a trial. But arbitration is usually less formal than a court proceeding. The procedural and evidence rules are often more relaxed during arbitration than in court. Certain types of evidence that may not be allowed in a court proceeding may be permitted in an arbitration. The discovery process in arbitration is usually limited and less burdensome than in litigation.

Parties generally choose arbitration because the process is faster and less expensive than trial. Often, the finality of the decision is seen as a benefit. Parties may also prefer that arbitration is a private proceeding. Another possible advantage of arbitration is that the parties typically select the arbitrator or panel who will decide the case. In some circumstances, the parties may prefer litigation to arbitration because they prefer to have a jury decide the case, they wish to have a public record of the case, or they want the ability to formally appeal the decision.

Arbitration providers have different systems for conducting their cases. The rules for JAMS Alternative Dispute Resolution are provided in the Appendix. Another provider of arbitration services is the American Arbitration Association. AAA's website, www.adr.org, includes information on the Association's rules and forms.

There are several situations where a company might prefer to proceed with arbitration in private rather than with litigation in public. If the dispute involves a trade secret, the details of that trade secret might be less exposed in arbitration. Or a business might choose private arbitration if the dispute has high potential for negative publicity. Attorneys should consider the private, confidential, or sensitive nature of client information during litigation as well. An attorney may move that sensitive information be considered by the court "under seal." If a piece of evidence is under seal, the court may consider it, but it does not become part of the case's public record. Keep in mind that a court is more likely to grant this protection for trade secrets or other information essential to a business than for details that will embarrass the company.

ARBITRATION:

A method of alternative dispute resolution in which the parties present their case to one or more neutral parties, called arbitrators, who issue a binding decision on the parties.

AWARD:

The final decision of the arbitrator in an arbitration proceeding.

Sample Arbitration Clause

Any controversy or claim arising out of or relating to this contract, or the breach thereof, shall be settled by arbitration administered by the American Arbitration Association in accordance with its Commercial Arbitration Rules. The arbitration hearing shall take place in _____, before a single arbitrator.

ARBITRATION CLAUSE:

A clause in a written agreement requiring the parties to resolve disputes between them through the arbitration process.

JUDICIAL ARBITRATION:

Arbitration that is required by a statute, court, court rule, or regulation, but is not binding on the parties.

Parties may agree to arbitrate a dispute after the dispute arises. In many instances, though, the parties agree to arbitrate any future disputes between them before any dispute occurs. Commercial contracts often include an **arbitration clause**. An arbitration clause states that if a dispute arises, the parties will resolve the dispute through arbitration and often prohibits the parties from initiating litigation until the dispute is submitted to arbitration. This type of arbitration, agreed to by the parties in a contract, is often referred to as private arbitration.

Arbitration clauses tend to be enforced under state statutes and laws. Some arbitration clauses limit arbitration to only certain types of disputes between the parties. For instance, an arbitration clause might state that "all employment disputes" must be submitted to arbitration. The parties could disagree regarding whether a dispute was an employment dispute or not. This leads to a question as to whether a particular dispute must be arbitrated or not. In such a situation, one party may file a lawsuit in court to compel the opposing party to use arbitration to

ARBITRATION CLAUSES ARE ENFORCEABLE IN EMPLOYMENT CONTRACTS.

Sanchez v. Nitro-Lift Technologies, L.L.C.
(Employee) v. (Employer)
762 F.3d 1139 (10th Cir. 2014)

This appeal involves a dispute concerning the scope of an arbitration clause between Nitro-Lift Technologies, L.L.C. ("Nitro-Lift"), and three of its former employees, Miguel Sanchez, Shane Schneider, and Eddie Howard (collectively, "plaintiffs"). Plaintiffs filed suit against Nitro-Lift, claiming it failed to pay overtime wages in violation of both the Fair Labor Standards Act ("FLSA"), 29 U.S.C. § 201 et seq., and the Oklahoma Protection of Labor Act ("OPLA"), Okla. Stat. tit. 40, § 165.1 et seq. Nitro-Lift appeals from two district court orders denying its motions to dismiss and compel arbitration, or in the alternative to stay the proceeding pending arbitration, arguing plaintiffs' wage disputes fall within the scope of the arbitration clause. We reverse.

[...]

At the beginning of their employment relationship with Nitro-Lift, each plaintiff signed an identical document labeled "Confidentiality/Non-Compete Agreement," which contains the arbitration clause at issue in this case. As the title of the agreement suggests, the language is generally limited to matters involving confidentiality and competition. Section 1 of the agreement adds the phrase "corporate property" to its subheading, and thereafter all the rights, obligations, and duties set forth in section 1 concern confidentiality, competition, and the return of corporate documents.

This is the only agreement between the parties and despite its title, Nitro-Lift claims it is an employment agreement because it was "essential" to plaintiffs' "relationship[] with Nitro-Lift," that "Nitro-Lift would not have hired Plaintiffs without their consent to the Agreements," and that "Plaintiffs would not have executed the Agreements without the assurance of employment by Nitro-Lift." Aplt. Br. at 6. But the only language in the contract that discusses compensation states in section 1(k) that "[i]n consideration of the receipt of Confidential Information during employment, the receipt of compensation, each element of compensation being hereby acknowledged by the Employee as adequate," the employee agrees not to compete. Aplt. App. at 238. Other than that specific clause, section 1 contains no language dealing with wages, hours, overtime compensation, or other rights, duties, and responsibilities regarding wages generally found in an employment contract.

[...]

Section 2 of the agreement contains the arbitration clause at issue and states in pertinent part in 2(a):

Any dispute, difference or unresolved question between Nitro-Lift and the Employee (collectively, the Disputing Parties) shall be settled by arbitration by a single arbitrator mutually agreeable to the Disputing Parties in an arbitration proceeding conducted in Houston, Texas in accordance with the rules existing at the date hereof of the American Arbitration Association ... and the costs (including, without limitation, reasonable fees and expenses of counsel and experts for the Disputing Parties) of such arbitration (including the costs to enforce or preserve the rights awarded in the arbitration) shall be borne by the Disputing Party whom the decision of the arbitrator is against. If the decision of the arbitrator is not clearly against one of the Disputing Parties or the decision of the arbitrator is against more than one Disputing Party on one or more issues, the costs of such arbitration shall be borne equally by the Disputing Parties.

[...]

In sworn affidavits, plaintiffs claim that when they were required to sign the contract, it was presented to them as an agreement specifically about confidentiality and competition. They contend Nitro-Lift did not explain the arbitration provision, did not allow them to read the document or the arbitration clause it contained, and did not allow them to ask questions or consult an attorney before signing the document. . . . Plaintiffs allege that almost every week they worked for Nitro-Lift, they each worked in excess of forty hours per week and Nitro-Lift refused to pay them "overtime compensation for the hours they worked in excess of forty," in violation of the FLSA.

[...]

In response, Nitro-Lift filed a motion to dismiss and compel arbitration, or alternatively to stay the proceeding pending arbitration. It argued that the arbitration clause contained in the agreement contractually obligated plaintiffs to submit their FLSA claims to arbitration under the Federal Arbitration Act ("FAA") and the Oklahoma Uniform Arbitration Act ("OUAA"), citing the liberal federal policy favoring arbitration, and the strong presumption in favor of arbitration under Oklahoma law. Nitro-Lift asserted the wage disputes are clearly within the scope of the arbitration clause, which mandates that "any dispute" be submitted to arbitration under the rules of the American Arbitration Association ("AAA").

[...]

The central issue raised on appeal is whether plaintiffs' statutory wage disputes fall within the scope of an arbitration clause contained in a contract labeled Confidentiality/Non-Compete Agreement, that is, whether plaintiffs agreed to submit their FLSA wage disputes to binding arbitration by signing the agreement at issue. Nitro-Lift contends, as it did below, that the language in the arbitration clause is broad and covers any disputes between it and plaintiffs, including their current wage claims. Plaintiffs counter that because the contract relates solely to issues of confidentiality and competition and was presented to them as such, the arbitration clause covers only disputes relating to the subject matter of the contract. They contend they never agreed to arbitrate wage disputes and to force them to do so would be contrary to the FAA and Supreme Court precedent. Our task is therefore to determine the scope of the arbitration clause at issue and whether plaintiffs' FLSA "claims fall within its scope." *Nat'l Am. Ins. Co. v. SCOR Reinsurance Co.*, 362 F.3d 1288, 1290 (10th Cir.2004). To do so, we first turn to the purpose of the FAA and the basic principles underlying arbitration.

Congress enacted the FAA "in response to widespread judicial hostility to arbitration." *Am. Express Co. v. Italian Colors Rest.*, ___ U.S. ___, 133 S.Ct. 2304, 2308-09, 186 L.Ed.2d 417 (2013). As is relevant here, section 2 of the FAA provides that arbitration agreements "shall be valid, irrevocable, and enforceable, save upon such grounds as exist at law or in equity for the revocation of any contract." 9 U.S.C. § 2. The Supreme Court has described "this provision as reflecting both a liberal federal policy favoring arbitration and the fundamental principle that arbitration is a matter of contract." *AT & T Mobility LLC v. Concepcion*, ___ U.S. ___, 131 S.Ct. 1740, 1745, 179 L.Ed.2d 742 (2011) (internal quotation marks and citations omitted). Consistent with these principles, the Court has stated that "courts must place arbitration agreements on equal footing with other contracts," *id.*, and "'rigorously enforce' arbitration agreements according to their terms." *Italian Colors*, 133 S.Ct. at 2309 (quoting *Dean Witter Reynolds, Inc. v. Byrd*, 470 U.S. 213, 221, 105 S.Ct. 1238, 84 L.Ed.2d 158 (1985)).

In line with its liberal policy favoring arbitration, the Court has noted that "any doubts concerning the scope of arbitrable issues should be resolved in favor of arbitration, whether the problem at hand is the construction of the contract language itself or an allegation of waiver, delay, or a like defense to arbitrability." [citations omitted]

[...]

Nevertheless, because "arbitration is a matter of contract" and the authority of an arbitrator arises only from the parties agreement to that forum in advance, "a party cannot be required to submit to arbitration any dispute which [it] has not agreed so to submit." *AT & T Techs., Inc. v. Commc'ns Workers of Am.*, 475 U.S. 643, 648-49, 106 S.Ct. 1415, 89 L.Ed.2d 648 (1986) (internal quotation marks and citations omitted). Federal law "simply requires courts to enforce privately negotiated agreements to arbitrate, like other contracts, in accordance with their terms." *Volt Info. Sciences, Inc. v. Bd. of Trs. of Leland Stanford Junior Univ.*, 489 U.S. 468, 478, 109 S.Ct. 1248, 103 L.Ed.2d 488 (1989).

Our circuit applies a three-part test when determining whether an issue falls within the scope of an arbitration clause. *Cummings*, 404 F.3d at 1261.

First, recognizing there is some range in the breadth of arbitration clauses, a court should classify the particular clause as either broad or narrow. Next, if reviewing a narrow clause, the court must determine whether the dispute is over an issue that is on its face within the purview of the clause, or over a collateral issue that is somehow connected to the main agreement that contains the arbitration clause. Where the arbitration clause is narrow, a collateral matter will generally be ruled beyond its purview. Where the arbitration clause is broad, there arises a presumption of arbitrability and arbitration of even a collateral matter will be ordered if the claim alleged implicates issues of contract construction or the parties' rights and obligations under it. [citations omitted]

Applying *Cummings'* first step, we agree with the district court that the arbitration clause at issue here is broad. In fact, we have not found any case with an arbitration clause as broad as this, stating that "*[a]ny dispute, difference or unresolved question* between" the parties must be arbitrated. Aplt. App. at 239 (emphasis added). This clause contains no limiting language, either restricting arbitration to any specific disputes or to the agreement itself.

[...]

We are not as convinced as the district court that the narrow context of the contract rebuts the presumption of arbitrability because "the strong presumption in favor of arbitrability applies with even greater force when such a broad arbitration clause is at issue." P & P Indus., 179 F.3d at 871 (internal quotation marks and citation omitted). In Cummings, we examined an arbitration clause that covered only "acts to terminate this Agreement," 404 F.3d at 1260, and explained that "the parties clearly manifested an intent to narrowly limit arbitration to specific disputes regarding the termination of the Operating Agreement," id. at 1262. Here, there is no manifestation of an intent to limit the arbitration agreement.

Even so, a contract "must be considered as a whole so as to give effect to all of its provisions without narrowly concentrating upon some clause or language taken out of context." *Eureka Water Co. v. Nestle Waters N. Am., Inc.*, 690 F.3d 1139, 1151 (10th Cir.2012) (quoting *Mercury Inv. Co. v. F.W. Woolworth Co.*, 706 P.2d 523, 529 (Okla.1985)). Plaintiffs contend we cannot ignore the narrow context of the agreement in which the arbitration clause is found and urge us not to read the broad arbitration clause in isolation. Although we agree with plaintiffs' argument, at best this contention makes the arbitration clause ambiguous. A contract "is ambiguous if it is reasonably susceptible to at least two different constructions," and to determine whether a contract is ambiguous "we look to the language of the entire agreement." *Id.* at 1149 (internal quotation marks omitted). In our view, when the broad arbitration clause is considered together with the entire language of the narrow contract, two reasonable constructions emerge — either the parties agreed to arbitrate all disputes arising between them, or they agreed to arbitrate all disputes concerning only those issues covered in the agreement.

We need not decide this difficult question, for we have stated that "to acknowledge the ambiguity is to resolve the issue, because all ambiguities must be resolved *in favor* of arbitrability." *Armijo*, 72 F.3d at 798. . . . We therefore hold that plaintiffs' FLSA wage disputes fall within the scope of the arbitration clause.

[...]

This does not end the matter, however. Notwithstanding the "liberal federal policy favoring arbitration agreements," *Moses*, 460 U.S. at 24, 103 S.Ct. 927, agreements which require the arbitration of statutory claims are only enforceable under the FAA so "long as the prospective litigant effectively may vindicate [his or her] statutory cause of action in the arbitral forum," *Gilmer*, 500 U.S. at 28, 111 S.Ct. 1647 (alteration in original). The Court in *Gilmer* reasoned that by submitting statutory claims to arbitration, a plaintiff does not lose the protection of the substantive rights afforded by the statute, but rather submits their resolution to an alternative forum. *Id.* at 26, 111 S.Ct. 1647.

Plaintiffs contend the arbitration provision here does exactly what Gilmer forbids, that is, it denies them the substantive rights afforded by the FLSA because it specifically provides that "the costs (including, without limitation, reasonable fees and expenses of counsel and experts for the Disputing Parties) of such arbitration... shall be borne by [the losing party]," or, at a minimum, requires the parties to split the costs of arbitration. Aplt. App. at 239. Contrary to the arbitration provision, the FLSA provides: "The court in such action shall, in addition to any judgment awarded to the plaintiff or plaintiffs, allow a reasonable attorney's fee to be paid by the defendant, and costs of the action." 29 U.S.C. § 216(b).

[...]

In response to Nitro-Lift's motion to compel arbitration, plaintiffs filed affidavits claiming inability to pay the arbitration costs and fees. The district court did not address this issue, however, because it determined that the FLSA claim was not within the arbitration provision. Given our reversal of the district court, it will need to determine on remand the effect of the cost-shifting provision in the arbitration clause[.]

[Footnotes omitted]

ANALYSIS:

Although courts were originally skeptical of and disfavored arbitration, this decision demonstrates the courts' significant change in attitude toward arbitration following passage of the Federal Arbitration Act. Even though the parties were not of equal bargaining power, the clause was contained in a Confidentiality Agreement, and the employees claimed not to have read the clause, they were still bound to its terms by signing the agreement. This case is also important because it shows how the interplay with other contract provisions may affect the enforceability of an arbitration clause. Here, the provision regarding attorneys' fees, which might seem to be an independent issue, could render the arbitration clause unenforceable with respect to this claim.

QUESTIONS FOR DISCUSSION:

While arbitration (and policies approving arbitration) often make sense for businesses in contractual relationships with other businesses, the balance of bargaining power is very different in this case. In this case, the employees were hourly workers, and it is easy to imagine that the contracts offered to them without an opportunity to renegotiate specific terms. When one side does not have an opportunity to fully negotiate, does it make sense to require terms such as arbitration clauses?

The Fair Labor Standards Act is designed to protect workers. Since an arbitrator does not have an obligation to follow the law, does this arbitration clause largely negate the protections of the FLSA for workers with arbitration agreements? In the wake of this decision, are companies more likely to include arbitration clauses in their employment agreements? Why or why not? On the other hand, the Federal Arbitration Act does not carve out exceptions for specific types of disputes. Do you think that it should?

MINI-TRIAL:

A method of alternative dispute resolution in which the parties present their arguments to a third party who issues an advisory opinion.

BINDING MEDIATION:

A method of alternative dispute resolution in which the parties attempt mediation, but if they do not reach an agreement, they agree to follow a binding decision issued by the mediator.

MEDIATION-ARBITRATION:

A method of alternative dispute resolution in which the parties attempt to mediate the case, and if they do not resolve the dispute, the dispute is then submitted to arbitration.

SUMMARY JURY TRIAL:

A method of alternative dispute resolution in which the parties engage in a short mock trial and a jury issues a non-binding verdict. The purpose is to encourage the parties to settle the case based on the verdict result.

resolve the dispute. The arbitration clause may indicate that the parties split the cost of arbitration, or state that the losing party pays the costs.

In a few types of cases, state statutes may require the parties to use arbitration to resolve disputes. This type of arbitration is called **judicial arbitration**. In judicial arbitration, the decision is not binding on the parties unless a party fails to reject the decision within a certain amount of time.

Other Kinds of ADR

Although negotiation, mediation, and arbitration are the traditional forms of ADR, a number of other types of ADR may also be used. In a **mini-trial**, the parties present their arguments to a third party who issues an advisory opinion setting forth the third party's conclusion as to how a court would decide the case.

Many of these other types of ADR are a combination of the three main forms of ADR. For example, in **binding mediation**, the parties attempt mediation. If the parties cannot reach agreement, they must follow a binding decision issued by the mediator. Similarly, in

Summary of Alternative Dispute Resolution Methods	
Type of ADR	**Key Features**
Negotiation	• Parties work together to resolve dispute • Attorneys may or may not be involved • Purpose is to reach a settlement
Mediation	• Third party neutral works with parties • Purpose is to reach a settlement
Arbitration	• Parties present evidence, witnesses, and arguments to arbitrator(s) • Arbitrator is neutral third party • Arbitrator(s) issue a binding award • Limited ability to appeal the decision
Mini-Trial	• Parties present evidence, witnesses, and arguments to a third party • Third party issues advisory opinion
Summary Jury Trial	• Parties present evidence, witnesses, and arguments to a jury • Jury issues nonbinding verdict • Parties must attempt mediation

mediation-arbitration, the parties attempt to mediate the case. If they cannot resolve the dispute, the dispute is then submitted to arbitration.

In some federal courts, the courts are using **summary jury trials** as another type of alternative dispute resolution. The summary jury trial is essentially a mock trial in which the parties present their case to a jury. The jury issues a verdict, but the verdict is not binding on the parties. The parties are required to attend negotiations following the summary jury trial.

III. Avoiding Disputes

Even for the most prepared business parties, disputes among entities, partners, customers, employees, and individuals are inevitable. Dispute resolution, in any form, can be a difficult, expensive, and unpleasant experience. Thus, many commercial parties look for ways to avoid, or at least minimize, potential disputes in their business relationships.

Contract Negotiation

Most business relationships are governed by contracts setting forth the actions to be taken or avoided by both parties. Through the process of negotiation, the parties propose contract terms and agree to or reject terms proposed by the other party. The parties modify the terms until both parties agree on the final contract. Business parties must take care in preparing commercial agreements. The agreement should be in writing and clearly state, in detail, what each party is expected to do. Disputes often arise when agreements do not clearly describe expectations and consequences. To avoid future misunderstandings or disagreements, the contract should avoid vague or confusing terms that are subject to multiple interpretations.

It is often difficult for the parties to imagine the need to end a business relationship when it is just beginning. A well-written contract will provide terms regarding termination of the relationship. Circumstances change and businesses frequently need to modify their business relationships. A clear and thorough contract can help make business transactions and transitions proceed smoothly.

The parties must also consider areas of possible conflict. Although it is impossible to anticipate every potential scenario, the contract should address how the parties will handle common situations that might arise. For example, the contract might state what happens if one party fails to pay an invoice on time, which is a common and foreseeable occurrence.

Business contracts frequently include terms relating to dispute resolution between the parties. One common contract term is the arbitration clause, in which the parties agree to resolve disputes through arbitration. Arbitration clauses might specify rules governing the

> Although popular culture often portrays deal-makers as "my way or the highway" types, the best negotiators seek win-win outcomes. Good contracts are sustainable and build strong business relationships. An unbalanced agreement is not a positive long-term solution for either party.

Example: Bruce owns a fruit supplier. His contract with a well-established restaurant states that the agreement is invalid if the restaurant is even a day late paying an invoice. During a busy week, the restaurant manager fails to put Bruce's regular payment in the mail, even though he has always been on time before. If Bruce throws the contract out, the restaurant will need to scramble to find a different supplier. Meanwhile, Bruce is stuck with perishable goods otherwise earmarked for the restaurant. If the contract (and Bruce) were more reasonable, the relationship would continue to be fruitful (so to speak).

arbitration, or indicate the arbitrator or organization who would handle the process. For instance, business entities often select JAMS or National Arbitration and Mediation to handle domestic disputes. The International Chamber of Commerce is a popular choice for handling international business disputes.

Other frequently used contract terms provide guidance should litigation occur. The parties might agree to attempt mediation before one of them may file a lawsuit. Or the parties might agree that the laws of a particular state will govern lawsuits between them. The contract can also specify the jurisdiction in which a lawsuit must be filed. Another common contract provision requires the lawsuit to be filed in the jurisdiction where the defendant has its principal place of business. This type of contract term discourages litigation because it requires the party who initiates the litigation to travel. Many contracts also include a provision that requires the party who loses in a lawsuit or arbitration to pay the attorneys' fees and costs of the winning party.

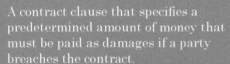

LIQUIDATED DAMAGES:

A contract clause that specifies a predetermined amount of money that must be paid as damages if a party breaches the contract.

LIMITATION OF LIABILITY:

A contract clause which restricts the amount of damages a party may recover from the other party in the event of a lawsuit.

Liquidated Damages

Another way business parties frequently address future dispute resolution is through the use of **liquidated damages** clauses. A liquidated damages clause states a predetermined amount of money that must be paid as damages if a party breaches the contract. The purpose of a liquidated damages clause is to provide a pre-agreed measure of damages if one party breaches the contract. The amount stated in the clause also gives the parties the opportunity to agree on an amount of damages at the time of the contract, which may foster settlement of a dispute later on. Liquidated damages clauses may not penalize the party who breaches the contract. The amount specified in the damages clause must be a reasonable approximation of the amount of damages the parties believe would result from a breach of the contract. The court may require some evidence that the damages are uncertain or would be difficult to prove in order to enforce a liquidated damages clause.

Limitation of Liability

Many business contracts contain a **limitation of liability** clause. A limitation of liability clause restricts the amount a party may recover against the other party, even if the party is able to prove damages above the amount stated in the clause. In other words, a limitation of liability clause can "cap" the amount of potential damages for which a business entity may be liable. Although somewhat similar to a liquidated damages clause, a limitation of liability clause is different. Liquidated damages must be based on a rough estimate of damages resulting from a breach of contract. A limitation of liability clause, however, generally does not require any relationship to the actual damages. If the parties negotiated and willingly agreed to the clause, it is likely to be enforced. If the term is included in a standardized form contract and is not specifically agreed to by the other party, the clause might not be enforced by the courts. The outcome in that case depends on whether the court feels that the parties both fully understood the limitation.

Maintaining Business Relationships

Although it may seem obvious, many business parties overlook the importance of maintaining a good working relationship after a deal is in place. In addition to other benefits, maintaining strong business relationships with partners and associates can address issues before they become full-blown disputes. Parties may wish to hold regular status or "check-in" meetings to address any issues that have arisen during the course of doing business. Although these meetings could be relatively informal, sometimes parties require status meetings on a regular schedule. A schedule for such meetings could be included in the agreement. The purpose of these meetings is to keep the lines of communication open and to work through small issues. The goal is to avoid large-scale disputes that require expensive or extensive dispute resolution efforts.

Cultural Issues

In today's world, business is a global enterprise. Businesses engage in commercial activity with business entities, partners, suppliers, vendors, employees, and customers in all parts of the globe. This means that commercial entities routinely work with people from all different cultures. The difference in cultural norms and expectations across the world can lead to misun-

The perception of time and its value vary widely from culture to culture. American businesspeople are often interested in "getting to work" when negotiating in other countries. But their negotiating partners may value the time learning about negotiating partners and their businesses. In Japan, the relationship is critical to a business deal, and an American urge to skip social events to focus on business may scupper the deal.

In some cultures, the need for consensus may slow the settlement process. For instance, Chinese companies tend to involve more team members in decisions, and may bring more people than expected to meetings. Because consensus is an important aspect of decision-making in China, reaching an acceptable solution for all parties is critical. Other cultures might bring multiple negotiators, but have one leader who can make faster decisions. It is essential to allow all parties the decision-making process they need.

Even physical norms can cause problems. In much of the Western world, eye contact conveys sincerity and attention. In Nigeria, however, prolonged eye contact may be considered rude, or even aggressive.

derstandings and disputes between business parties. For instance, in some cultures, a party may say "yes" to indicate acknowledgement or understanding. In other cultures, "yes" indicates agreement or acceptance. Likewise, some cultures tend to use unwritten handshake agreements in their business dealings. They may be suspicious of exhaustive written agreements. In other places, the parties prefer a written agreement detailing the business relationship.

When conducting business with parties in a different country, it is useful to gain a basic understanding of the culture there. On some occasions, commercial entities hire an advisor who has knowledge and experience working in a particular country to assist them with their business relationships. In the event of a dispute, cultural differences may become very important. If the parties decide to use a method of ADR involving a third party, such as a mediator or arbitrator, the parties may achieve best results by selecting a third party who has an understanding of the parties' cultural backgrounds.

CHAPTER SUMMARY

Engaging in business is not a solo activity. It necessarily involves communication, collaboration, and competition with other businesses and individuals. This constant interaction with others presents many opportunities for disputes to arise. An understanding of the available methods of dispute resolution is therefore critical for everyone in the business world.

When a dispute happens, business parties have many options to consider. In some circumstances, the parties may choose the formal litigation process to resolve a dispute. Increasingly, however, parties are looking for alternatives to the often lengthy and expensive litigation process. Several methods of alternative dispute resolution, including negotiation, mediation, and arbitration are frequently used by business parties to address disputes outside of the courtroom. Depending on the circumstances, these ADR methods may be less expensive, provide a quicker result, preserve the business relationship, and allow the parties more control over the resolution process.

Review Questions

Review question 1.
What are the different ways that a case may end up at the U.S. Supreme Court? How does a party bring a case before the Court? What are the Court's responsibilities to parties appealing a case?

Review question 2.
A plaintiff starts a lawsuit by filing a complaint. How may the defendant respond? What do the different types of responses achieve? What is the outcome if the defendant does not take action when served with a lawsuit? Would this result change if the defendant said that she had not received notice of the lawsuit?

Review question 3.
What are some reasons that a party might make a motion to the court? What are some different types of motions, and what are their desired outcomes? Which types of motions might occur in discovery or pre-trial? Which motions might be made at trial? How can a granted motion end a lawsuit?

Review question 4.
What happens during the discovery process? What tools can the parties use? How could one party use discovery strategically to force settlement? How could the court control discovery requests?

Review question 5.
What are the main types of alternative dispute resolution? What are the advantages of each? The disadvantages? Which appeals to you most and why?

Review question 6.
What issues relating to dispute resolution do business parties often address in their business contracts? Why is it smart to consider dispute resolution when drafting contracts? Do you think dispute resolution choices could be a negotiating point when drafting a contract? Why or why not?

Review question 7.
What are some of the ways that parties to a contract can control the costs should a dispute arise? What clauses do they need to include in their agreements?

After litigation, who pays the attorneys? How do other parts of the world handle this issue? Which model do you prefer and why?

Questions for Discussion

Discussion question 1.

Bigg Company is in the business of making processors for electronic devices. Hypo Corporation purchases one million processors from Bigg Company each year for use in Hypo Corporation's cell phones. The parties negotiate and sign an agreement governing this deal. This is one of many deals between the two companies, which have been doing business together for 10 years.

Last year, a dispute arose between the two companies. Bigg Company claims that Hypo Corporation did not pay for 10,000 of the processors, and Hypo claims that it did not pay because that batch of processors was defective.

Is litigation a good option for the parties to resolve this dispute? Why or why not?

What other dispute resolution methods might the parties consider? What are the advantages and disadvantages of other methods?

Discussion question 2.

Assume that under the terms of the contract in the prior question, the parties agreed to resolve all disputes through binding arbitration. Earlier this year, this dispute was decided through arbitration, with an award issued in favor of Bigg Company.

Hypo Corporation is unhappy with the arbitrator's decision. Can Hypo Corporation appeal the award? Does the corporation have any other recourse?

Discussion question 3.

Proprietor Pete owns a coffee shop in a small town. He hires two employees to work at the shop. One day, a customer trips over a rug on the shop floor and suffers second degree burns from spilling coffee on himself in the process. The customer believes Pete is at fault for the burn and threatens to sue him.

Two weeks prior, a different customer, Ferlin, who is the father of Pete's best friend, also tripped over the rug. Ferlin emailed Pete to make him aware of the hazard, but Ferlin was not injured and does not plan to make a claim against Pete. Pete forwarded that email to one of his employees, including a disparaging comment about Ferlin's clumsiness. That employee was working at the time of the burn incident.

Should Pete consider resolving the dispute before the customer files a complaint? Why or why not?

If so, what type of dispute resolution methods might Pete prefer? Which one might the customer want? Why?

What are the risks to Pete's business for each dispute resolution type in this scenario?

Discussion question 4.

Large Bank provides savings and checking accounts, debit cards, credit cards, and counseling services to its customers. Large Bank's customer agreement, signed by all customers who use any of the services listed above, contains an arbitration clause requiring "all disputes between the parties be submitted to arbitration."

Large Bank's sales associates were tasked with selling additional accounts to Large Bank's existing customers. Sales associates were required to meet rigorous sales quotas for the additional accounts. To meet those quotas, many sales associates began creating accounts in a customer's name, even though the customer was unaware of the account and did not agree to the additional account.

After learning about the fraudulent accounts, a number of customers sued Large Bank in court. Large Bank brought a motion to compel, arguing that the customers were bound by the arbitration clause in the customer agreement signed by the customers when they originally agreed to services provided by Large Bank.

Does the dispute have to be decided by arbitration?

Is it better for the customers to litigate the case through the court system or to agree to arbitration even if they are not bound by the clause? What about Large Bank?

What other options can the parties consider for resolving the dispute?

Discussion question 5.

Wiser and Bayer had a personal and business relationship for 15 years. After they broke up, Wiser changed the locks to a townhouse that Wiser owned but that Bayer lived in while Bayer was in town.

Bayer sued Wiser and two of Wiser's employees; she prepared the complaint without an attorney in order to save money. Her complaint alleged that Wiser promised her the townhouse and financial support indefinitely, even if their relationship ended. She also claimed that some of her property had been removed from the townhouse. Her complaint included seven different claims, including fraud, conversion, and breach of contract. The document is long and rambling, and isn't formatted like a legal complaint.

You are Wiser's attorney. Wiser visits your office and says that he can't tell which defendant Bayer intended for which of her seven claims. He also says there was no financial support agreement. Wiser thinks the complaint is "bogus" and unprofessional, and he doesn't think he needs to respond to it.

What options are open to Wiser? What course of action do you recommend?

Discussion question 6.
You are a new attorney. What would you advise in each of the following situations?

1. A friend brings in an employee agreement that he is considering. He is uncomfortable with the arbitration clause, because he is not sure what it means.

2. A small business owner shows you a licensing agreement drafted by a large company. It includes an arbitration clause. The small business will be working with some of the large company's trade secrets.

3. A building owner wants advice on a contract from a potential remodeling contractor. The contract includes a liquidated damages clause to cover any issues. The liquidated damages clause holds the contractor's liability to $5,000.

3

BUSINESS FORMS

KEY OBJECTIVES:

▶ Learn the different forms of business organization.

▶ Become familiar with the advantages and disadvantages of each form.

▶ Understand the requirements for operating and maintaining different types of businesses.

CHAPTER OVERVIEW

This chapter covers business forms. The term "business forms" refers to the different ownership structures businesses have. It also deals with the operations of each of these structures.

In this chapter, we will look at the various types of business forms. Each form has its own rules for its formation, as well as rules regarding the rights and obligations of business owners. We will look at these rules, and at the advantages and disadvantages of each form. There is no perfect business form for all purposes, but knowing about every form will help you make informed decisions about the best form for a particular situation.

INTRODUCTION

Choosing the form of a business is one of the most important decisions to be made when starting a business. The business form chosen will affect a business's taxes and its liability for debts and injuries. It will even affect the ability of the business to continue operating if any of the owners leave the business.

In any situation, the answer to the question, "What form of business should I choose?" will be, "It depends." There is no ideal business form that will meet all of a business's needs. Every form has its advantages and disadvantages. Selecting a form is a matter of deciding which one best meets the greatest concerns of the owners, while presenting the most tolerable disadvantages.

I. Unincorporated Forms

An unincorporated business may seem like the ultimate in simplicity. No incorporation means less paperwork and fewer formalities to deal with. There does not have to be a lot of effort put into creating the unincorporated business. In fact, it is probably safe to say that there are a lot of unincorporated businesses that are owned by people who do not realize they are operating an unincorporated business. They have chosen the business form by *not* choosing a form.

Sole Proprietorship

A **sole proprietorship** is the simplest form of business. Sole proprietorships are owned by one person (the proprietor). The proprietor owns not only the business, but also owns all of the assets personally. A sole proprietorship has no identity separate from the proprietor. The proprietor, therefore, is not only the personal owner of all of the business's assets, but is also personally responsible for all of the business's debts. All income or losses of the business are reported on the proprietor's individual income tax return.

The personal liability for business debts is the main reason most businesspeople will not choose a sole proprietorship as their business form. Even if a debt or obligation is incurred in the course of the proprietor's business, she is still personally responsible. All of her personal assets are at risk, as with any personal debt.

While many become sole proprietors just by doing business on their own and not bothering to incorporate, others are attracted to the form because of its simplicity. There is no registration required, no internal agreements to prepare, and all decisions are made by the proprietor. In theory, a sole proprietorship can conduct any

kind of business. A sole proprietor may not have co-owners, but there may be employees.

> Employee wages would be a personal business expense of the proprietor.

There is very little to be done when forming a sole proprietorship. The proprietor must obtain any licenses or permits for the type of business he intends to conduct. If the proprietor will be doing business under any name other than her legal name, most states require an assumed name certificate.

> An assumed name certificate is sometimes referred to as a "d.b.a.," which stands for "doing business as." The assumed name certificate may require publication of notice in a newspaper.

> For example, a person who plays as a musician at weddings for a fee, or a writer who is paid for articles from a number of publications (a freelance writer), could both be considered sole proprietors.

Once those minimal formalities are accomplished, the person will be considered a sole proprietor.

Ending a sole proprietorship is even simpler: the proprietor just stops doing business. Since all debts are the personal responsibility of the proprietor, and since all assets already belong to her, there is no formal "winding up" process to dissolve a sole proprietorship.

Filing federal income taxes is straightforward because sole proprietorships are considered

SOLE PROPRIETORSHIP:
An unincorporated business owned entirely by one person. The business is operated in the personal capacity of the owner, and the owner is personally liable for all debts and liabilities incurred in doing business.

> *Example:* Tanya works for a large corporation. She goes to school part-time and gets her CPA license. While she is looking for an accounting job, she decides to earn some extra money by doing tax returns and general accounting work for neighbors and small businesses. Tanya has business cards printed and sets up a website for her accounting business, but she does not incorporate. She gives one of her clients some bad advice about deducting medical expenses, and the client has to pay a substantial penalty to the IRS. The client sues Tanya for malpractice, and obtains a judgment. Tanya does not have malpractice insurance, so her (former) client garnishes her wages from her corporate job. Since Tanya is a sole proprietor, her personal wages are subject to garnishment.

> A sole proprietorship closes when the sole proprietor ceases to do business, regardless of how that happens. If the sole proprietor dies, the business also closes because it was not a separate entity. If a sole proprietor wishes to establish a family business that can be handed on to the next generation, she should look into other business forms and business succession planning.

"pass-through" entities. Being a pass-through entity means that the profits and losses are passed directly through the business to the proprietor and are taxed on the proprietor's individual tax returns. Unlike other forms of business, the proprietor is not required to file a separate business tax report. Instead, the proprietor will list business information on Schedule C of his individual tax return. The ability to report business earnings on the individual tax return allows the proprietor to avoid double taxation at the corporate and individual level, also saving additional costs on accounting and filing. This also means the business will be taxed at the rates applied to personal income, not corporate tax rates. It is for this reason that the overall tax rate of sole proprietorships is very low compared to other business entities.

The drawback of being a pass-through entity, however, is that there is no legal separation between the proprietor and the business. The means the proprietor is personally responsible for all liabilities, including business debts. If a business creditor seeks repayment from the sole proprietorship, the proprietor's personal assets such as personal bank accounts, home, and other personal property may be at risk.

Partnership

A **partnership** is an unincorporated business association made up of two or more owners who associate to do business. The partnership is created by the association of the partners. A partnership is a separate legal entity, but the partners and the partnership are not completely separated from one another.

> **Example:** Ken started teaching survival techniques, calling the classes "Worst Thing That Could Happen" training. He did not incorporate. Ken dug a deep hole to use in training students how to climb out of a hole with sheer sides. One student fell while climbing out, and cut his foot badly. The foot became infected and had to be removed. The same week, a wilderness training camp using the servicemark "Prepare for the Worst Thing That Could Happen" sued Ken for infringing on the camp's mark. The following week, Ken seriously injured a jogger with his car while taking students to a climbing gym, and the IRS sent a letter about why he wasn't reporting his training income on his individual tax returns. The various claims add up to millions of dollars. If Ken had been properly incorporated, these claims would be against his company, and recovery would be limited by the company's assets and insurance policies. Unincorporated, these claims proceed against Ken (and his modest assets) as an individual.

The lack of separation from the partners has two consequences. First, the partnership is not subject to federal income taxes. Like sole proprietorships, partnerships are considered pass-through entities, where profits and losses flow to the individual partner. Each partner is taxed on her share of partnership income, and each partner is allowed to claim a share of partnership losses as a deduction, but the partnership itself pays no federal income tax. Therefore, the partnership is often subject to a lower tax rate than corporations. The partnership does retain income-tax related responsibilities, however. The partnership is required to file an informational return that sets out each partner's distributive share of income and losses. The shares are determined by the agreement of the partners, but the allocation must reflect the economic reality of the partnership.

PARTNERSHIP:
An association of two or more persons who jointly own and carry on a business for profit.

> Partners must pay tax on their share of partnership income even if they do not actually receive any money from the partnership.

> The discussion in this section is about general partnerships. Other types of more formal partnership models are dealt with separately later in this chapter.

Remember that this exemption from income taxation refers only to federal income taxes. Partnerships are subject to other taxes, including sales and property taxes. Some states and communi-

> **Example:** Jonas and Willie are partners in a maritime consulting business. While on his way to a meeting with a client, Jonas, who is alone and driving his own car, drives through a traffic light and hits another vehicle. Willie and Jonas are both liable for any injuries caused.

> New York City levies a tax of 4% on the income of an unincorporated business.

ties also have business activity taxes that apply to unincorporated entities, and that are calculated on the receipts from business income.

The other consequence of having no separation from the partners is that partners are person-

JOINT AND SEVERAL LIABILITY:

Liability that applies both to a group and to the individual members of the group personally. Each member of the group is individually responsible for the entire amount of the liability, but the party who pays may have the right to recover from the liable parties who do not pay.

ally liable for all the debts and liabilities of the partnership. This liability is called **joint and several liability**, meaning that all members of the partnership of liable for the partnership debts. The partnership provides no legal protection. If a debt or liability is incurred in the scope of the partnership's business, each individual partner is liable. Likewise, this liability for partnership debt extends to all partners, even if the debt arose from the actions of a single partner.

The personal liability of partners is a significant drawback of the partnership form. Many businesses start as partnerships but are incorporated later, when the business begins to develop.

Forming a partnership is a simple matter. All that is required is for two or more people to associate to carry on a business for profit as co-owners. There is no requirement that there be a complex agreement, or even that there

> **Example:** Wren and Sven operate a convenience store as a partnership. Sven meets with a salesperson when Wren is out sick. The salesperson contracts with Sven to buy all the store's soft drinks from the salesperson's company. The contract requires pre-payment for the first six months of delivery. When Wren returns, she objects to the contract because she did not sign it, and tells Sven that they can't afford to make the up-front payment. Sven says he has no money in his personal accounts for the expense. Wren's objection does not release her from the contract because Sven may bind the partnership. Further, if she can't re-negotiate the soft-drink contract and Sven cannot contribute, she will be personally responsible for the payments in full.

sions apply to partnerships that have not made a different agreement.

In the absence of any other agreement, the UPA provides for equality between the partners. Each partner has an equal say in the management of the partnership, and each partner has

> Apple, Google, and Microsoft all started as partnerships, but incorporated soon after starting to do business.

Example: Maggie is a web designer. Although she is good at the visual aspects of web design, she is not confident of her ability to write the copy on the site. She asks her friend Kayla to join her in her business. "We work together, and just split everything 50-50." Kayla agrees. Maggie and Kayla have formed a partnership.

> The "people" forming a partnership may be individuals, corporations or limited liability companies, or any other type of business entity.

the right to an equal share of the partnership profits. Each partner also has the legal right to make contracts that will bind the partnership.

If partners do not want strict equality between themselves in any area, their partnership agreement may divide things up according to the partners' wishes. Partners generally have the right to operate the partnership according to their own preferences. A partnership agreement can be drafted to reflect those preferences.

should be a written agreement. The partners do not have to use the term "partnership," and it is not necessary that a partnership is intended. A legally sufficient partnership agreement can just be a few words between the partners.

Many partnerships operate without having a formal partnership agreement in place. Others will have formal agreements that do not cover many situations that will come up during the course of a partnership's operation. In that situation, a law known as the Uniform Partnership Act (UPA) comes into play. The UPA was first adopted in 1914, and modernized in 1997, 2011, and 2013. The UPA is the default law regarding partnerships. Most of the law's provi-

> The original version of the UPA was enacted in every state except Louisiana. As of November 2016, the 1997 version has been adopted by all but 11 U.S. jurisdictions (the 2011 and 2013 amendments are mostly technical changes to some language).

DETERMINING EXISTENCE OF PARTNERSHIP LOOKS AT CONDUCT OF PARTIES.

Carlson v. Brabham
(Girlfriend) v. (Boyfriend)
199 So.3d 735 (Miss. App. 2016)

1. Linda Carlson sued Larry Brabham for equitable division of partnership assets amounting to $167,762.06. The Amite County Chancery Court granted Brabham's motion for a directed verdict. Carlson appeals and asserts the chancellor improperly granted Brabham's motion. We find no error and affirm.

2. Brabham and Carlson began living together in 2004. At the time, Brabham worked in the logging industry, and Carlson worked full-time for Telepak Networks. Carlson and Brabham were both married when they became romantically involved. Brabham divorced his wife shortly after the start of his relationship with Carlson. Carlson, however, remained married to her husband for the duration of her relationship with Brabham.

3. Before their relationship, Brabham owned and operated Brabham Logging. When Brabham started seeing Carlson, she encouraged him to incorporate the business and change the name to Longhorn Logging. Carlson set up a meeting with an attorney for the purpose of incorporating the business. The incorporation papers listed Brabham as the president of the business, and Carlson as the secretary, treasurer, and agent for service of process.

4. After Longhorn Logging had operated for several years, the Mississippi Secretary of State administratively dissolved it for failing to file articles of incorporation and issue stock. The Longhorn Logging profit and loss detail statement showed that Longhorn Logging ceased operations as a viable business after September 2007. However, Longhorn Logging maintained an active bank account until March 16, 2009.

5. In addition to Longhorn Logging, Brabham owned a parcel of land on Amazing Grace Lane in Amite County. Brabham received the parcel as part of the divorce settlement with his ex-wife. Brabham intended to build a house on the property and began construction a year after starting his relationship with Carlson. The construction funds came out of the Longhorn Logging checking account, which Brabham used as both his business and personal bank account. Brabham completed the majority of the work himself, while Carlson did minor labor and selected the light fixtures and some of the furniture. When the house was completed, Carlson knew the house and land were in Brabham's name.

6. After two years at Amazing Grace Lane, Brabham's ex-wife offered to sell him their former home located on East Fork Road. Brabham sold the house on Amazing Grace Lane for $385,916. He used the proceeds to pay off the remaining land note of $97,479.22 on Amazing Grace Lane and purchase the house on East Fork Road for $250,000. Just as with the Amazing Grace Lane house, Brabham did not put Carlson's name on the deed to the house on East Fork Road. Though Carlson confronted Brabham about leaving her name off of the deed, Brabham did not change the deed, but instead purchased a life-insurance policy worth $250,000, which named Carlson as the beneficiary.

7. When Carlson and Brabham ended their relationship, Carlson removed her personal property from the East Fork Road home. However, Carlson also wanted a share of Longhorn Logging and the East Fork Road property. Carlson filed her original complaint for an equitable distribution of the properties on May 12, 2011. Both parties filed motions for summary judgement, which the chancellor denied, and the case proceeded to trial on March 7, 2013.

8. Brabham filed a motion for a directed verdict after Carlson presented her case-in-chief. The chancellor requested both parties submit proposed findings of fact and conclusions of law. After reviewing both parties' submissions, the chancellor adopted Brabham's findings of fact and conclusions of law in toto and entered a judgment in favor of Brabham.

[...]

II. Whether Brabham and Carlson formed a partnership.

16. Carlson claims she has a partnership interest in Longhorn Logging. Carlson further claims that she is entitled to an equitable division of Brabham's property at East Fork Road because she contributed to the house, and Brabham purchased it using funds from the Longhorn Logging checking account.

17. Mississippi Code Annotated section 79-13-202(a) (Rev.2013) defines a partnership as "the association of two or more persons to carry on as co-owners [of] a business for profit[.]" "The three main questions that are considered in partnership determination are (1) the intent of the parties, (2) the control question, and (3) profit sharing." Smith v. Redd, 593 So.2d 989, 994 (Miss.1991). The intent required to form a partnership may be implied. Id. However, profit sharing may be the most important factor. Century 21 Deep S. Props., Ltd. v. Keys, 652 So.2d 707, 715 (Miss.1995). "A person who receives a share of the profits of a business is presumed to be a partner in the business, unless the profits were received in payment... of wages or other compensation to an employee." Miss.Code Ann. § 79-13-202(c)(3)(iii).

A. Intent

18. We first look to intent to determine if the parties formed a partnership in Longhorn Logging. Brabham and Carlson agree that Carlson arranged to incorporate the business under Longhorn Logging, but Brabham contends this only changed the name of the business. Brabham disputes that he and Carlson intended to form a partnership with Longhorn Logging. "[W]hen parties dispute intent, it may only be proved by objective manifestations such as writings, conduct, or other such circumstances." Crowe v. Smith, 603 So.2d 301, 305 (Miss.1992). However, Brabham and Carlson did not enter into any written agreement to form a partnership. Therefore, when there is no written partnership agreement, the chancellor must look at the circumstances surrounding the relationship to determine intent. Summers v. A-1 Cash Inc.,911 So.2d 975, 979 (¶ 12) (Miss.Ct.App.2005). ¶ i) Carlson submitted evidence of her own testimony and that of close friends and relatives stating that Brabham said he and Carlson were partners in the logging company and "in it together." Brabham testified in his deposition that Longhorn Logging operated the same way as Brabham Logging, which existed prior to the relationship. Brabham, however, stated he gave Carlson check-writing authority and bookkeeping responsibilities. Nonetheless, Carlson completed multiple state forms naming Brabham as the sole owner of Longhorn Logging. As such, the chancellor agreed with Brabham's findings that Carlson did not prove that the parties intended to enter into a partnership agreement for Longhorn Logging.

19. Carlson also claims a partnership interest in the house at East Fork Road because Brabham purchased it with funds from the sale of the house at Amazing Grace Lane. But Brabham received the land at Amazing Grace Lane from his divorce settlement. Carlson failed to prove the amount of the sale price that came from the house or from the land. Carlson could only show that the proceeds from the Amazing Grace Lane house were placed into the Longhorn Logging account, and the proceeds were then used to purchase the East Fork Road house. However, because Carlson failed to prove the intent factor for a partnership in Longhorn Logging, she cannot claim the parties entered a partnership with the East Fork Road house based on its association with Longhorn Logging.

20. Carlson also claims she contributed $32,287.62 in personal funds to the Amazing Grace Lane house, but she fails to show why she should be entitled to a reimbursement. Carlson stated that she paid for some construction materials, supplied some fixtures, and bought some furniture for the house. However, there was testimony that Carlson repossessed her personal items, including the furniture. Carlson further failed to show that Brabham intended to form a partnership with Carlson for the house. Brabham owned the land and paid the note owed on the land, though Carlson argues she also paid some on the note. Additionally, only Brabham's name appeared on the deeds to the house and land. Similar to her Longhorn Logging argument, Carlson failed to demonstrate that she and Brabham intended to form a partnership regarding the house.

21. After weighing the testimony against the facts of the case, the chancellor found the parties lacked any intent to form a business partnership. Therefore, this Court finds Carlson failed to prove the intent requirement.

B. Control

22. Intent, however, is only one of the factors required to form a partnership. The second factor is control, and "[p]articipation in the control of the business is indicative of whether a partnership exists." Smith, 593 So.2d at 994. But "[w]hile control is indicative of the existence of a partnership, control by itself is not the exclusive indicator of partnership. Partner-like control may or may not be found depending on the surrounding circumstances, because the circumstances will vary from relationship to relationship." Summers, 911 So.2d at 980 (¶ 15) (internal quotations and citation omitted).

23. The day-to-day operation of the business involved Brabham working with the logging crew and operating Longhorn Logging. Brabham negotiated and signed the timber contracts, managed the timber crew, hired and fired employees, and negotiated for the purchase of new logging equipment. Carlson worked at Telepak full-time, but also did the bookkeeping for the logging business. Outside of the book-

keeping and finances, Carlson did not control any aspect of the business. Occasionally, Brabham would leave instructions with her to give to the timber crews or have her pick up a part for a piece of equipment. Carlson asserts that she hired Jeannette Sullivan, a friend of hers, to perform filing for the business along with general housekeeping duties, which demonstrated her control of the company.

24. Nonetheless, the chancellor found this evidence unpersuasive and ruled against Carlson on this factor. We agree. Carlson failed to prove she controlled the day-to-day operations or the direction of the business. Brabham was responsible for the business transactions, the operations, and the profits. Therefore, the control factor weighs against Carlson.

C. Profit Sharing

25. Of the three factors, profit sharing is the most important one in determining whether a partnership exists. Summers, 911 So.2d at 979 (¶ 11). The chancellor found that Carlson met the profit-sharing factor because Brabham used his income from Longhorn Logging for the couple's expenses. The Smith court ruled that occasionally splitting profits did not meet the requirements of partnership profit sharing. Smith, 593 So.2d at 995. Mississippi Code Annotated section 79-13-202(c)(3)(ii) imposes a presumption of partnership when profit sharing is proven, unless the share of the profits is received through wages. According to Longhorn Logging's 2007 profit and loss detail, Carlson received checks for bookkeeping services. Only Brabham received dividends, even though Longhorn Logging did not properly issue dividends. However, while not conclusive, this distinction strongly implies that Longhorn Logging did not consider Carlson a partner in the business.

26. The chancellor found that Carlson could prove only profit sharing. Although we find that the facts do not support this finding, this Court will not reverse the chancellor's decision as to this factor. The chancellor's overall determination that Brabham and Carlson were not partners was correct. Therefore, the chancellor did not abuse his discretion in finding no partnership existed between the parties. This issue is without merit.

III. Whether Brabham and Carlson formed a joint venture.

27. Carlson also asserts that the houses and business were a joint venture between the parties. Carlson further claims that she is entitled to an equitable distribution of the property that she and Brabham jointly accumulated as part of a joint venture. The chancellor dismissed Carlson's joint-venture claim due to the running of the statute of limitations. We agree. Additionally, we find the evidence did not support Carlson's joint-venture claim.

28. A partnership and a joint venture are identical "except the latter has limited and circumscribed boundaries." Hults v. Tillman, 480 So.2d 1134, 1141 (Miss.1985). "A joint venture is a form of contract, and [is] governed by contract law." Id. at 1143. The first question to determining the existence of a joint venture is whether the parties intended to form a joint venture. Id. The supreme court has stated:

We [have] broadly defined a joint venture as an association of persons to carry out a single business enterprise for profit, for which purpose they combine their property, money, efforts, skill[,] and knowledge. We said it exists when two or more persons combine in a joint business enterprise for their mutual benefit with an understanding that they are to share in profits or losses and ... have a voice in its management. We noted a condition precedent for its existence was a joint proprietary interest in the enterprise and right of mutual control.

Pittman v. Weber Energy Corp., 790 So.2d 823, 826 (¶ 10) (Miss.2001) (quoting Hults, 480 So.2d at 1143).

29. Further, mutual obligations and division of the proceeds alone do not constitute a joint venture. Hults, 480 So.2d at 1144. "[T]he existence of a joint venture may be inferred from the facts, circumstances, and conduct of the parties." Pennebaker v. Gray, 924 So.2d 611, 618 (¶ 24) (Miss.Ct.App.2006) (citation omitted). "The absence of any discussion or agreement about paying the expenses of the venture may support the conclusion that no joint venture exists." Id. at (¶ 22) (quoting Hults, 480 So.2d at 1147).

30. The parties did not have an agreement recognizing the existence of a joint venture, written or otherwise. There was no indication that Carlson and Brabham built the Amazing Grace Lane house or purchased the East Fork Road house solely for the purpose of making a profit. Carlson claimed she contributed $32,287.62 in personal funds to the Amazing Grace Lane house, but she did not prove that the parties intended to sell the house to make a profit. Brabham only sold the Amazing Grace Lane house when his ex-wife offered to sell their former home on East Fork Road.

31. Further, Brabham did not sell the East Fork Road house, but continued to live in it. This contradicts Carlson's assertion that the two acquired the East Fork Road house as a joint venture. "[A]

ctual intent to form a joint venture is essential." Hults, 480 So.2d at 1143. Because the evidence was insufficient to show actual intent, Carlson failed to prove the parties formed a joint venture for either the Amazing Grace Lane or the East Fork Road houses.

32. Nonetheless, Carlson claims that the business was part of a joint effort. Carlson testified she loaned money to Brabham for logging equipment to show their intent to form a joint venture. Carlson testified she paid $4,000 for a trailer, $4,000 for a dozer, and $7,000 for equipment. Carlson also argued she spent $13,000 on other equipment.

33. However, other evidence showed that Carlson received either a full or partial reimbursement for the equipment expenses. "If money, loaned to another for use in the enterprise, is to be repaid by the borrower, whether the venture succeeds or fails, the contract is ordinarily construed as one of lending and borrowing and not of [a] joint adventure." Boxwell v. Champagne, 229 Miss. 355, 366, 91 So.2d 256, 261 (1956). Though "the relationship of parties in a transaction may be that of joint adventurers rather than that of debtor and creditor," this occurs when the parties possess the intent to form a joint-venture agreement, unlike in this case. Id. Therefore, we determine that the evidence defeats a claim of a joint venture. Further, we agree with the chancellor that the statute of limitations precludes this claim. This issue is meritless.

[...]

ANALYSIS:

The original intent of the parties seems to have been creation of a corporation. A partnership was never intended or attempted. In hindsight, Carlson (P) could best have protected herself by making sure that stock in Longhorn was issued to her.

CASE VOCABULARY:

CHANCELLOR:

The judge presiding over a court of chancery, or equity.

QUESTIONS FOR DISCUSSION:

The court says that Carlson did not engage in the management of the enterprise, except for performing administrative functions. In a small enterprise like this one, how is the line drawn between management functions and administrative functions? Is that line drawn differently in a larger enterprise? In hindsight, how could Carlson have protected herself?

Example: Norma and Max are architects who have formed a partnership. Their agreement does not limit either partner's authority to make contracts. One day, Norma tells Max that she thinks they have all the business they can handle right now, and they should focus on their existing work. The next day, without Norma's knowledge, Max commits the partnership to design indoor swimming pools for a chain of hotels. The partnership is obligated to honor this agreement.

Example: Norma and Max have written a partnership agreement that does not provide for a way of calculating the division of partnership income. The partnership is paid $10,000 for the work done to design one indoor swimming pool. Norma's role in the project was limited to reviewing Max's final design. Because there is no agreement saying how income is to be divided, Norma and Max each receive $5,000.

A comprehensive partnership agreement may include the following:

- Name of the partnership,

- Contributions of cash, property, or services required of each partner,

- How profits and losses are to be allocated,

- How partnership authority is delegated,

- How new partners are admitted to the partnership, and

- What happens when one partner wants to withdraw, or is incapable of continuing in the business.

II. Limited Liability Forms

For most businesspeople, the main reason not to do business as an unincorporated entity is the personal liability of the business owners. Every business is going to be liable for something, whether it is a contract, a personal injury, or taxes. Shielding oneself from personal liability is an important concern when deciding which business form to choose.

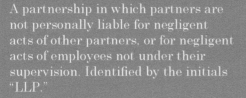

LIMITED LIABILITY PARTNERSHIP:

A partnership in which partners are not personally liable for negligent acts of other partners, or for negligent acts of employees not under their supervision. Identified by the initials "LLP."

Limited Liability Partnerships

A **limited liability partnership** (LLP) removes one of the main drawbacks of doing business in a partnership, namely, the personal liability of the partners. An LLP functions in the same way as a general partnership, but the personal liability of the partners is either limited or eliminated.

In most states, there are no special requirements to be met before an LLP may be formed. The partnership merely files a declaration or statement with either state or local authorities. The declaration states that, as of the date of the filing, the partnership will be a limited liability partnership. After that filing, most states require that an LLP include the initials "LLP" as a part of its name. While some states limit the partnerships that may become LLPs to partnerships of professionals such as lawyers, architects, or accountants, most states allow any partnership to file an LLP declaration.

The limitation on liability will also vary from state to state. Under the UPA provisions regarding LLPs, partners are not liable for any partnership obligations or liabilities. Most states have adopted this limitation. Some states, however, have a more restrictive liability limitation. In those states, partners are shielded from liability only for negligence claims. There

Professional limited liability partnerships use the initials "PLLP" at the ends of their names.

States that limit how LLP partners are protected from liability are called "partial shield" jurisdictions. In Nevada, for instance, the partial shield would limit a partner's liability for injuries negligently caused to a customer who tripped on a wet floor in the partnership's office. Damages would be limited to the organization's assets. If the partnership breached a contract, though, the damages arising from the breach could be enforced against the individual partners. Fortunately for LLPs, the legal trend is toward full-shield protection.

is no shield from liability for contract claims, or claims for intentional acts.

A partnership's status as an LLP does not make any difference to how the partnership is treated for income tax purposes. Income and losses still "pass through" to the partners who then report this information on their individual tax returns. The only significant difference between an LLP and a general partnership is the limitation of liability.

Limited Partnerships

All businesses need money. They need money to start up, and they need money to operate. A potential business person who does not

GENERAL PARTNERS LIABLE FOR BREACHES OF PARTNER OBLIGATIONS.

Ederer v. Gursky
(Nonequity Partner) v. (General Partner)
9 N.Y.3d 514, 881 N.E.2d 204, 851 N.Y.S.2d 108 (N.Y. 2007)

READ, J.

This appeal calls upon us to explore the nature and scope of Partnership Law § 26 (b). We hold that this provision does not shield a general partner in a registered limited liability partnership from personal liability for breaches of the partnership's or partners' obligations to each other.

I.

The relationship that deteriorated into this acrimonious dispute began promisingly enough in 1998 when plaintiff Louis Ederer affiliated with the law firm of Gursky & Associates, PC., which promptly changed its name to Gursky & Ederer, P.C. (the PC). Ederer joined the PC as a salaried, nonequity contract partner, but he had an understanding with defendant Steven R. Gursky, the PC's sole shareholder, that if their practice developed as anticipated, he would become a full equity partner in about two years' time.

Right on schedule, in May 2000 Gursky orally agreed to increase Ederer's annual compensation by about 17% and to make him a 30% shareholder in the PC as of July 1, the beginning of the PC's fiscal year.

In February 2001, the PC became a registered limited liability partnership known as Gursky & Ederer, LLP (the LLP). Significantly, there was no written partnership agreement. The LLP began billing all new legal services, while the PC billed and collected work-in-process and preexisting accounts receivable, and loaned money to the LLP to fund its start-up. In July 2001, the LLP admitted three new partners, defendants Mitchell B. Stern, Martin Feinberg and Michael A. Levine. They collectively acquired a 15% interest in the LLP, leaving Gursky with a 55% interest while Ederer retained his 30% interest.

[...]

In June 2003, Ederer advised Gursky that he was withdrawing as a partner in the LLP and a shareholder in the PC. Ederer chalks up his decision to a severe falling out with Gursky in early 2003 over the representation of a firm client. Gursky retorts that Ederer left because the LLP was cash-strapped and unprofitable, and blames him in no small part for this purported state of affairs.

On June 26, 2003, Ederer entered into a withdrawal agreement with the PC and the LLP, which Gursky signed as president of the PC and a partner in the LLP. Under this agreement, Ederer agreed to remain a partner in the LLP so as to serve as lead counsel for a trial scheduled to commence in Georgia on June 30, 2003, although he was not obligated to delay his withdrawal from the LLP beyond July 8. In exchange, the LLP agreed to "continue to pay [Ederer his] regular draw and other compensation through the date of [his] withdrawal from the [LLP]"; to have files on which he was working transferred to his new firm upon the client's request; to give him the opportunity to review his clients' bills before the LLP asked for payment; and to allow him and/or his representatives (including accountants) access to the LLP's and PC's books and records after his withdrawal from the LLP.

The PC was dissolved on June 30, 2003, although formal dissolution papers were not filed with the Secretary of State until March 2004. Ederer withdrew from the LLP on or about July 4, 2003 after having helped secure a $2 million verdict in the Georgia trial, which generated a $600,000 contingency fee for the LLP. After Ederer's departure, the LLP continued in business under the name Gursky & Partners, LLP until March 1, 2005, when it ceased operations.

In December 2003, Ederer commenced this action against the PC, the LLP, Gursky & Partners, LLP, and Gursky, Stern, Feinberg and Levine, seeking an accounting and asserting breach of the withdrawal agreement. In his amended verified complaint dated November 1, 2005, Ederer sought an accounting of his interest in the PC (the first cause of action) and the LLP (the second cause of action), and asserted causes of action for breach of contract relating to Gursky's May 2000 oral agreement to pay him 30% of the PC's profits (the third cause of action), the June 2003 written agreement to pay him for the two weeks he tried the Georgia case for the LLP (the fourth cause of action), and the unpaid portion of his loan to the PC in 2002 (the fifth cause of action).

In their verified answer dated November 7, 2005, defendants denied the gravamen of Ederer's complaint; and interposed numerous affirmative defenses as well as counterclaims sounding in breach of fiduciary duty, conversion, tortious interference with contractual relations, fraud and deceit and fraudulent inducement, breach of contract, and unjust enrichment. Defendants also counterclaimed for a declaration that the withdrawal agreement was void because entered into under the duress of Ederer's alleged threat not to try the case in Georgia.

[...]

Supreme Court determined that Ederer was entitled to an accounting against all defendants because Partnership Law § 26, which places limits on the personal liability of partners in an LLP, applies "to debts of the partnership or the partners to third parties" and "has nothing to do with a partner's fiduciary obligation to account to his partners for the assets of the partnership." The trial court also rejected defendants' argument that "an accounting of Ederer's interest in [the PC] should not be allowed both because [he] was not a shareholder in the P.C., and because the P.C. had effectively transferred all of its remaining assets to the LLP as of the date of [his] withdrawal from the firm, rendering the accounting of the P.C. duplicative." The court determined that, "[b]ecause of confusion of the location of the firm's assets at the time Ederer left the firm, in order for the accounting of [his] interest to be complete, it must necessarily include an accounting of the firm's assets taken by Gursky from the P.C., as well as an accounting of Ederer's partnership in the LLP."

[...]

II.

This appeal comes down to a dispute over the effect of the Legislature's 1994 amendments to section 26 of the Partnership Law (L 1994, ch 576, § 8). As originally adopted by the Legislature in 1919 (L 1919, ch 408), section 26 was identical to section 15 of the Uniform Partnership Act (UPA), which was drafted by the National Conference of Commissioners on Uniform State Laws and approved by the Conference in 1914. Prior to its amendment in 1994, section 26 provided that "[a]ll partners are liable

"1. Jointly and severally for everything chargeable to the partnership under sections twenty-four and twenty-five.

"2. Jointly for all other debts and obligations of the partnership; but any partner may enter into a separate obligation to perform a partnership contract."

Section 24 specifies that

"[w]here, by any wrongful act or omission of any partner acting in the ordinary course of the business of the partnership, or with the authority of his copartners, loss or injury is caused to any person, not being a partner in the partnership, or any penalty is incurred, the partnership is liable therefor to the same extent as the partner so acting or omitting to act."

Section 25 binds the partnership to "make good the loss"

"1. Where one partner acting within the scope of his apparent authority receives money or property of a third person and misapplies it; and

"2. Where the partnership in the course of its business receives money or property of a third person and the money or property so received is misapplied by any partner while it is in the custody of the partnership."

Partnership Law § 26, as originally enacted, and its prototype, section 15 of the UPA, have always been understood to mean what they plainly say: general partners are jointly and severally liable to nonpartner creditors for all wrongful acts and breaches of trust committed by their partners in carrying out the partnership's business, and jointly liable for all other debts to third parties. This proposition follows naturally from the very nature of a partnership, which is based on the law of principal and agent. Just as a principal is liable for the acts of its agents, each partner is personally responsible for the acts of other partners in the ordinary course of the partnership's business. In addition to this vicarious liability to nonpartner creditors, each partner concomitantly has an obligation to share or bear the losses of the partnership through contribution and indemnification in the context of an ongoing partnership . . . ; and contribution upon dissolution and winding up[.]

[...]

In New York, the Legislature enacted limited liability partnership legislation as a rider to the New York Limited Liability Company Law . . . Specifically, new section 26 (b) creates an exception to the vicarious liability otherwise applicable by virtue of section 26 (a) (original section 26 [section 15 of the UPA]), by providing that

"[e]xcept as provided by subdivisions (c) and (d) of this section, no partner of a partnership which is a registered limited liability partnership is liable or accountable, directly or indirectly (including by way of indemnification, contribution or otherwise), for any debts, obligations or liabilities of, or chargeable to, the registered limited liability partnership or each other, whether arising in tort, contract or otherwise, which are incurred, created or assumed by such partnership while such partnership is a registered limited liability partnership, solely by reason of being such a partner."

Section 26 (c) excludes from section 26 (b)'s liability shield "any negligent or wrongful act or misconduct committed by [a partner] or by any person under his or her direct supervision and control while rendering professional services on behalf of [the] registered limited liability partnership." Section 26 (d) allows partners to opt out from or reduce the reach of section 26 (b)'s protection from vicarious liability.

[...]

Defendants point out that section 26 (b) eliminates the liability of a partner in a limited liability partnership for "any debts" without distinguishing between debts owed to a third party or to the partnership or each other. As a result, they contend, the Legislature did not "leave open to conjecture whether § 26 (b) was intended to cover debts which may be owed by the [limited liability partnership] (or one partner) to other partners." This argument ignores, however, that the phrase "any debts" is part of a provision (section 26) that has always governed only a partner's liability to third parties, and, in fact, is part of article 3 of the Partnership Law ("Relations of Partners to Persons Dealing with the Partnership"), not article 4 ("Relations of Partners to One Another"). The logical inference, therefore, is that "any debts" refers to any debts owed a third party, absent very clear legislative direction to the contrary.

Defendants also note that chapter 576's legislative history illustrates the desire to enact liability protection for partners in limited liability partnerships that is "the same as that accorded to shareholders of a professional corporation organized under the [Business Corporation Law] [and] as that accorded to members of a professional LLC" (Senate Introducer Mem in Support, Bill Jacket, L 1994, ch 576). They point out that "the legislative history of the LLP Act plainly indicates that the Legislature intended to provide an even greater shield of individual liability to partners in LLPs than that enacted by other states as of the date of the legislation."

These observations are correct, but do not advance defendants' cause. Chapter 576 does, in fact, afford limited liability partners the same protection from third-party claims as New York law provides shareholders in professional corporations or professional limited liability companies. And unlike New York, most states "have adopted a partial liability shield protecting the partners only from vicarious personal liability for all partnership obligations arising from negligence, wrongful acts or misconduct, whether characterized as tort, contract or otherwise, committed while the partnership is an LLP" (see Prefatory Note Addendum to Uniform Partnership Act [1997] [explaining that RUPA, by contrast, "provid(es) for a corporate-styled liability shield which protects partners from vicarious personal liability for all partnership obligations incurred while a partnership is a limited liability partnership"]; see also Walker § 14:5, at 346 ["The type of LLP generally permitted by the states (other than Minnesota and New York) ... offers less insulation against personal liability than many other types of organization"]). Nowhere in the voluminous commentary on limited liability partnerships has anyone suggested that New York (or any other state) has adopted a statute expanding the concept of limited liability in the way asserted by defendants.

Next, defendants make two arguments in their attempt to reconcile their interpretation of section 26 (b) with Partnership Law § 74, which gives a partner "[t]he right to an account of his interest ... as against the winding up partners or the surviving partners or the person or partnership continuing the business, at the date of dissolution, in the absence of agreement to the contrary" . . . First, they argue that their fiduciary duty as partners to account to one another "is not the same as personal liability for the debts disclosed by the accounting." But the remedy of accounting is restitutionary by definition (see Eichengrun, Remedying the Remedy of Accounting, 60 Ind LJ 463, 463 [1984-1985] [in an accounting, "(t)he plaintiff must establish some basis for the obligation to account, the defendant is ordered to account, and the plaintiff then gets an order directing payment of the sum of money found due"]; see also Belsheim, The Old Action of Account, 45 Harv L Rev 466 [1931-1932]). Second, defendants claim that a partner is only personally liable for debts disclosed in an accounting which are attributable to that partner's own torts or wrongful conduct or *526 supervisory lapses, as excluded by Partnership Law § 26 (c) from the protection of section 26 (b). If the Legislature had intended to qualify section 74 in this manner, however, it surely would have explicitly made section 74 subject to sections 26 (b) and/or 26 (c). It did not do so for the same reason that defendants' arguments fail generally: section 26 (b) only addresses a partner's vicarious liability for partnership obligations.

In closing, we emphasize that the law of partnerships contemplates a written agreement among partners specifying the terms of their relationship. The Partnership Law's provisions are, for the most part, default requirements that come into play in the absence of an agreement. For example, the right to an accounting exists, "absen[t an] agreement to the contrary" (Partnership Law § 74). Partners might agree, as among themselves, to limit the right to contribution or indemnification or to exclude it altogether. In this case, however, there was no written partnership agreement; therefore, the provisions of the Partnership Law govern.

Accordingly, the order of the Appellate Division, insofar as appealed from, should be affirmed, with costs, and the certified question should be answered in the affirmative.

[Footnotes omitted]

QUESTIONS FOR DISCUSSION:

Suppose you and some business associates are planning on starting a business, and you are debating which form to choose. How important is being protected from liability for debts to your associates in choosing a type of business?

> **Example:** Alice, Jimmy, and Harriet are partners in a real estate brokerage that is set up as an LLP. Alice has been skimming profits from real estate sales by altering the figures on real estate documents. In most states, Jimmy and Harriet are not personally liable for Alice's thefts. In states that provide limited liability only for negligent acts, Alice and Jimmy, as well as Harriet, are liable for Harriet's thefts.

have money of her own may seek investors to contribute money and to share in the profits of the new business. Investors, however, will often have a say in how the business is operated. To limit the role of the investor of the operation of a business, a **limited partnership** (LP) may be formed.

An LP is similar to a general partnership, in that it is an association for the purpose of doing business. As with a general partnership, there is no income taxation of the LP. Distributions are taxed individually to each partner. The difference lies in the functions of the partners.

There are two sets of partners in a limited partnership: the general partner, and the limited partner. There must be at least one of each type of partner, although it is most common for an LP to have one general partner, and several **limited partners**. The **general partner** is responsible for the operation of the business of the LP. A general partner may be an individual, a corporation, or any other type of entity. The general partner also has unlimited personal liability for the debts and liabilities of the LP.

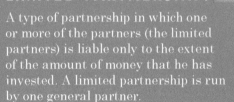

LIMITED PARTNERSHIP:

A type of partnership in which one or more of the partners (the limited partners) is liable only to the extent of the amount of money that he has invested. A limited partnership is run by one general partner.

LIMITED PARTNERS:

A partner in a limited partnership who receives a share of the profits, but whose personally liability for partnership debts is limited to her investment in the limited partnership.

GENERAL PARTNER:

In a limited partnership, the party who operates the business. A general partner is personally liable for the debts and obligations of the limited partnership.

As another layer of liability protection for the limited partners, the general partner may be a corporation. The corporate form further limits liability for the general partner's role in the organization. For instance, a corporation's debts belong to the corporation, and generally are not enforced against the people who started the corporation. If a corporate general partner faces debts for the partnership, collection may be limited to the resources held by that corporation.

> *Example:* Max, a theatrical producer, forms an LP to finance his next production. He is the general partner, and he finds 10 investors who are willing to be limited partners. Max raises $250,000 from the limited partners. The costs of the production are more than Max anticipated, so he gets a $150,000 loan from a bank to cover the remaining costs. Unfortunately, the production is a flop, and closes after six days. The limited partners have lost their contributions, but that is the only amount they have lost. Max is personally liable for the $150,000 loan.

The limited partners usually do not take any part in the operation of the business; in fact, in many states, limited partners are barred from active participation in the business. The limited partner invests money, and shares in any profits or losses of the LP. The liability of a limited partner for partnership debts is limited to the amount of the limited partner's contribution or investment. Most states require LPs to register with the state authorities.

One potential problem with a limited partnership is how to proceed if a partner withdraws from the organization. If the general partner withdraws (or dies), the limited partner faces the issue of replacing that management role. If a limited partner starts participating in the management of the limited partnership, then he becomes liable as a general partner, which might not be desirable. The fewer individuals there are, the more difficult the loss of a partner becomes. It is advisable to prepare a careful partnership agreement that specifies what should happen if a general or limited partner leaves.

As with other types of partnerships, limited partnerships are considered pass-through entities requiring that all partners individually report and pay taxes on their share of the profits. The limited partners, however, do not have to pay self-employment taxes, because they are not active in the business. For this reason, their share of partnership income is not considered "earned income" under the self-employment tax. Because the general partner is actively involved with the partnership, the general partner's share of partnership income is considered earned income subject to the self-employment tax.

There are many similarities between LLCs and LLPs. Both offer the advantage of pass-through taxation of profits. LLCs and LLPs also provide members or partners with protection from liability for business debts. The members of an LLC, however, are not protected from personal liability for the tortious acts of other members. The partners in an LLP, however, are protected from liability for their partners' negligence. Another key difference is who may be an owner. Many state laws limit who may be a partner In an LLP (especially one formed for professional purposes) to partners who are actually involved in the business. An LLC, however, may allow passive members who take on active part in the business.

Corporations

While terms such as "partnership," or even "company," are often used to describe different types of personal associations, a **corporation** is most properly thought of as a type of business form.

CORPORATION:

A separate legal entity formed under the laws of a state to do business. A corporation is distinct from its owners, and the owners are generally shielded from liability for the debts of the corporation.

SHAREHOLDER:

The owner of all or part of a corporation. Shareholders elect the directors of a corporation, and approve organic changes In the corporation's existence, but do not have any role in the day-to-day management of the corporation.

SHARE:

One of a number of equal parts into which the stock of a corporation is divided.

STOCK:

A proportional part of the capital of a corporation. Stock grants its owner the right to vote on the management of the corporation.

DIVIDENDS:

The distribution of profits to shareholders or members.

Corporations are creatures of state law. For many purposes, they are regarded as legal "persons." Although they have a legal existence, there is no physical "thing" that one can point to and say it is the corporation. The only tangible parts of a corporation are the property that it owns, and the people who own it or who work for it.

A corporation is owned by its **shareholders**. You may also see the older term "stockholder," which means the same thing. Shareholders measure their ownership interest according to the number of **shares** they own of a corporation's **stock**. Stock is the representation of the proportion of ownership. Every corporation must have at least one shareholder.

Ownership of stock usually gives shareholders the right to vote on the management of the corporation. Stock may be divided into different classes with different voting rights. For example, preferred stock gives its owner a superior right to **dividends** from the corporation, but the owner has no voting rights. Corporations have also issued stock with superior voting rights to fight takeover attempts.

The laws of each state determine when a corporation comes into being. In some states, a corpo-

Most state corporation laws are modeled on the Delaware General Corporation Law. Delaware has a reputation for having corporation-friendly laws and a thriving business environment. Selections from the Delaware General Corporation Law are included in the Appendix.

> **Example:** Outside investors have launched a bid to take over the Veruko Corporation. The directors of Veruko fight the takeover attempt by issuing 10,000 shares of Class B stock. Each share of Class B stock has three votes, while the pre-existing stock has only one vote per share. The extra votes give management enough control to defeat the takeover attempt.

ration exists when **articles of incorporation** are filed with the appropriate authority. In other states, a corporation does not exist until property or cash is exchanged for shares of stock.

One of the main features of a corporation, and one of the reasons it has historically been attractive to businesspeople, is the limitation of liability for shareholders. Because a corporation is its own entity, shareholders have limited personal liability for the debts or liabilities of the corporation. If a corporation is run properly, and all

ARTICLES OF INCORPORATION:
The document filed with the state for the formation of a corporation.

NON-PROFIT CORPORATION:
A business organization formed to serve some public purpose, rather than to make a profit for investors.

Corporations have a perpetual existence, unless the articles of incorporation say that the corporation will exist for only a limited time. A corporation will continue to exist, and continue to be

A shareholder may be personally liable if she participated in a wrongful act, or personally signed a contract. In those cases, the shareholder is personally liable because of actions she took as an individual. The corporation is liable only if she was acting as an agent of the corporation.

The oldest existing corporation in the United States is the Caswell-Massey Company, a personal-care products company founded in 1752. Some of the company's more renowned early customers include George Washington, the Marquis de Lafayette, and Lewis and Clark.

of the formalities of running a corporation are followed, the personal liability of shareholders is limited to the value of their investments in the corporation. Other assets of the shareholder are not at risk.

able to do business, as long as formalities are followed and the required filings are made. In theory, a corporation could last forever.

C Corporations

A significant disadvantage of a corporation is that corporations are subject to federal income tax, unless they are able to take advantage of an exception. A C corporation (named for Subchapter C of the Internal Revenue Code)

C CORPORATION:

A corporation that is subject to the federal corporate income tax. All for-profit corporations are C corporations, unless they qualify as an S corporation.

tax on the same profits. This is referred to as double-taxation, and C corporation tax rules causes many companies to choose a different corporate form.

C corporations do have substantial advantages. This business form features flexibility on ownership and management structure, and does not limit the potential number or type of shareholders. Most venture capital firms prefer C corporations for these reasons, but also because the national stock exchanges typically require C corporation status for a business to be publicly traded. If the company wishes to re-invest in the business to prompt growth or tackle a new

> **Example:** Lonnie is the CEO and sole shareholder of Subrido, Inc., a C corporation. In 2014, Subrido earned a profit of $50,000, all of which is to be paid to Lonnie. Subrido must pay federal income tax on the profit, and Lonnie must pay income tax when he receives the dividend.

> **Example:** In 2015, Subrido earned a profit of $75,000. Lonnie decides not to pay himself a dividend, but to put the profits towards building a new building for Subrido's headquarters. Subrido must pay corporate income tax on the profits. Lonnie did not receive any income, so he does not have to pay income tax on the profits.

is subject to corporate income tax. All corporations are C corporations unless they qualify as S corporations (discussed below).

Shareholders in C corporations are required to pay income tax on any dividends received from the corporation. These dividends are taxable even though the corporation has also paid

market, those re-investments receive a favorable tax treatment. The choice of a C corporation may have some disadvantages, but for a large or growing business, the form's pros may outweigh its cons.

> *Example:* Roberto owns 60% of the stock in Gelkis Manufacturing Co., and Diego owns the remaining 40%. Gelkis is an S corporation. In 2014, Gelkis makes a profit of $100,000. Only one-quarter of the profits are distributed, and the remainder is to be retained to keep up the company's cash reserves. Roberto receives $15,000, and must pay federal income tax on $60,000. Diego receives $10,000, and must pay tax on $40,000. Because Gelkis is an S corporation, shareholders are taxed on their proportionate share of the company's profits, even if some or all of that share is not paid to the shareholders.

S Corporations

Some corporations may take advantage of a provision in the federal income tax laws that allow the pass-through of corporate profits. Most states that have corporate income tax laws have similar provisions. The corporation pays no income tax, but shareholders pay on their proportional share of the company's income. The corporation is taxed like a partnership, but still has the limited liability of a corporation. Such a corporation is known as an **S corporation.**

A corporation will not be treated as an S corporation unless the corporation qualifies for a Subchapter S election. In order to qualify, the corporation must:

- Be incorporated in the United States,

- Have only individuals who are U.S. citizens or resident aliens as shareholders,

- Have no more than 100 shareholders,

S CORPORATION:

A corporation that meets certain qualifications regarding the number of shareholders and that issues only one class of stock and that has chosen to be taxed as a partnership.

LIMITED LIABILITY COMPANY:

A hybrid business organization that combines the liability protection for owners of a corporation, and management by its members, with the pass-through taxation of a partnership. Identified by the initials "LLC."

Another advantage of the S corporation form is it avoids self-employment tax. The self-employment tax is a Social Security and Medicare tax primarily for individuals who work for themselves. It is similar to the Social Security and Medicare taxes that employers withhold from the pay of employees. An employee of a properly incorporated S corporation does not have to pay the self-employment tax. For this reason, many individuals who work as consultants or contractors form S corporations and ask customers to pay that business rather than paying the individual personally.

> **Example:** Carla works as an ergonomics consultant for a variety of businesses. She completes all the work herself. To avoid self-employment taxes, Carla forms an S corporation in her name: Carla Karlsen, Inc. When she invoices her customers, she asks for payment to Carla Karlsen, Inc. The payments go directly to the business, and Carla may withdraw money from that account to pay herself individually. Her compensation is still subject to regular income tax at the federal and state levels, but it is not subject to the self-employment tax.

- Have only one class of stock, and

- File an election with the IRS that says the corporation will be an S corporation.

Financial institutions, insurance companies, and domestic international sales corporations may not be S corporations.

Shareholders of S corporations pay income tax on a proportionate share of the profits, even if those profits are not paid out to them. On the other hand, though, the company's income is not taxed twice as it would be for a C corporation. Further, if the S corporation suffers a loss, the shareholders may claim that loss on their personal tax return.

Because of the low shareholder limit and pass-through taxation, S corporations are popular with family businesses. The form also simplifies passing the business on to other family members when older shareholders wish to retire, because shares are easier to transfer than partnership interests. A family-owned S corporation can also execute stock transactions that would not happen in other business forms, such as "selling" shares to a family member in exchange for property rather than money.

III. Professional Forms

Businesses formed to practice a profession are normally governed by the same rules as businesses formed for any other purpose. There are a few exceptions. In California, for example, an LLC may not be formed by licensed professionals. The nature of practicing a profession, however, adds certain practical considerations to the choice of a business form.

Partnership

Traditionally, a partnership has been the business form of professionals who are joining together to practice a profession. A partnership of professionals operates under the same legal rules as any other partnership. Professionals, however, have the additional concern of malpractice. If a partner commits a negligent act in the course of his professional practice, all of the partners are liable. It does not matter if none of the other partners participated in the negligence, or that the negligent partner was working on his own. The nature of the partnership is that all of the partners are liable for all liabilities of the partnership.

The possibility of malpractice liability leads many professionals to choose an LLP (or, depending on the state, a "professional" LLP, signified by "PLLP"). The LLP allows the partners to keep the benefits of a partnership, but individual partners are shielded from liability for acts they did not commit.

Professional Limited Liability Companies

Some states allow professionals to form limited liability companies for their specific type of work. A "PLLC" may be formed if the state allows the form and the profession is included in the state statute.

> TJ earns her chiropractic license and sets up a clinic in Seattle, Washington. She sets up the business as a professional limited liability company, TJ Chiropractic PLLC. TJ is not a great businessperson, and she forgets to pay many of her vendors. They bring claims against the clinic in small claims court and win. The vendors can only recover financial damages from the business itself. One of the vendors, CJ, is also a patient. TJ fails to review CJ's file thoroughly, and makes an inappropriate adjustment, permanently damaging nerves in CJ's neck. If CJ sues for malpractice for this negligence and wins, TJ will be personally responsible for CJ's damages, a burden she may offset by maintaining malpractice insurance. A professional has personal liability for their own negligence regardless of the business form chosen.

> If a partner is found to have committed professional misconduct, the responsibility will remain with the guilty partner. The other partners will not be disciplined unless they participated in the misconduct.

The advantage of a professional limited liability company is the same as that for a normal LLC: the new entity protects the members from personal liability. The PLLC form makes an exception to the LLC's limited liability advantage, however. Individual members of the PLLC are not protected from personal liability for their own malpractice. Most professionals carry malpractice insurance in order to take care of possible financial liabilities related to malpractice claims.

Professional Corporations

A professional corporation (PC) is a special type of business form. It allows professionals to associate in a corporation to practice their professions. All of the shareholders in a PC must be authorized to practice their profession. In some states and for some professions, the board that

> Ethical rules for some professionals, such as lawyers, hold that corporations other than professional corporations may not be formed to practice that profession.

A group of experienced attorneys form a professional corporation in Ames, Iowa. Each attorney specializes in a different area of law, which means they can collectively handle more types of clients than they could individually, and they can offer more services to those clients. One attorney handles real estate issues for Kenji, and another prepares Kenji's estate plan. When Kenji is arrested for drunk driving, a third attorney at the firm agrees to defend Kenji against the charge. If the criminal lawyer fails to show up for Kenji's court date without explanation, that attorney is personally responsible for professional negligence (malpractice). The other two attorneys who represent Kenji on other matters are not responsible for the criminal lawyer's malpractice, because each attorney is responsible for her own torts.

licenses a profession must approve the formation of a PC.

Professional corporations allow shareholders to limit their liability for malpractice of other

FRANCHISE:

A franchise is a type of agreement that lets one party have access to another's proprietary knowledge, processes, and trademarks in order to sell a product or provide a service. The person who is granted the franchise (the franchisee) usually has the sole right to engage in the business in a given area.

shareholders. They may also qualify for Subchapter S status.

IV. Franchises

A **franchise** is not, strictly speaking, a separate business form. Instead, it is a licensing agreement. The agreement grants one person (the franchisee) the right to operate a business using a trademark owned by another person (the franchisor).

The largest franchise company, by number of locations, is Subway, with over 42,000 locations. The largest in terms of revenue is McDonald's.

Franchises offer several advantages for both parties. The franchisor gets the ability to operate his business in multiple locations without having to be directly involved in the day-to-day operation of each location. The franchisee gets the opportunity to run a business with some degree of independence, with the added advantage of being able to rely on the franchisor's goodwill and marketing efforts. In addition, some franchisors offer a high degree of support in the operation of the franchised business.

Franchising is regulated largely by the federal government, through the Federal Trade Commission. While the terms of a franchise agreement are left to negotiation between the franchisor and franchisee, FTC rules regulate the disclosures that must be provided to a prospective franchisee. The franchisee must be provided with a Franchise Disclosure Document before signing the franchise agreement, or before paying any money.

> The federal and state regulation of franchising provides important protections to aspiring franchisees. Most franchisors are large businesses with substantial legal departments and financial resources, while most franchisees are individuals or small business owners. The bargaining power is very uneven, so the law attempts to level the playing field by requiring clear information, full disclosures, and complete identification of the franchisor should any issues arise.

The Franchise Disclosure Document requires franchisors to provide audited financial statements. In addition, the Disclosure must include information about other franchisees in the territory, an estimate of franchise revenues, and an estimate of the franchisor's profitability. State law may also require additional disclosures.

The franchise agreement itself will set out the terms of the relationship between the franchisor

> Trademark law provides for the cancellation of a trademark if the owner licenses its use without adequate quality control. Since franchise contracts typically involve licensing the franchisor's trademarks, the franchisor should carefully police franchisee trademark use.

and franchisee. An agreement may provide for a high degree of supervision by the franchisor, calling for regular inspections. Franchise agreements commonly limit the products that may be offered by a franchisee, and some even restrict a franchisee's operating hours (for example, stating that the franchisee may not be open for business on Sundays).

V. Business Formation

Deciding which business form to use is the first step. It is also surprisingly difficult, with all the different factors that go into the decision. The next step, forming the business, is not always as difficult as it may seem.

As noted above, forming a sole proprietorship is very simple. Starting a sole proprietorship scarcely counts as "business formation" at all. A sole proprietor just starts doing business without forming a partnership, and without incorporating.

A partnership is also simple to form, but it can be difficult to form one well. It is easy to agree to associate as partners, thus meeting the legal definition of a "partnership." Without a well-crafted partnership agreement, however, virtually all partnerships are certain to run into problems in the course of doing business. Disputes will arise about everything from sharing the expenses of starting up, to what happens when a partner leaves the business.

Corporations and LLCs are somewhat more complicated to form, although it is not as complex as one might think. Since both types of businesses are formed by making a filing with the state, it is important to pay attention to all of the legal requirements, and be sure that they are followed exactly. On the other hand, the formalities are not difficult to learn and follow. Virtually every state allows online filing to form corporations and LLCs,

Corporate Promoters

A **corporate promoter** is a person who develops and organizes a new business venture. He may be promoting his own business, or he may be engaged in promoting business ventures for others. Promoters handle matters related to a corporation or LLC before it is formed, although their activities, such as soliciting investors, may continue after the company is formed.

CORPORATE PROMOTER:

A person who solicits investors for a corporation before it is formed.

FIDUCIARY:

A person who has the duty to act for another with total good faith, trust, and honesty. Corporate directors are fiduciaries, and are obligated to exercise a high degree of care when making corporate decisions.

The promoter's personal liability could lead to a harsh outcome if the business does not proceed to formation. For instance, a promoter who rents office space is personally responsible for the lease if the business never actually gets off the ground. But the promoter role is less and less common as business formation becomes more accessible through online filing and quicker business services from the government. A would-be promoter may now benefit from acting on behalf of an established legal entity with limited liability, rather than putting his personal assets on the line.

A promoter may make contracts for a company before the company is formed. A promoter who makes a contract like that is personally liable on the contract, unless otherwise agreed. If the company adopts the contract after the company is formed, the company is also liable. The promoter remains personally liable unless the company makes a new contract. Companies are usually not liable to promoters for payment for services rendered, or for reimbursement for expenses incurred unless the company expressly agrees after it is formed.

A corporate promoter stands in a **fiduciary** relationship to both the new company and its present and prospective owners. This fiduciary relationship continues until the promotion plan

DE FACTO CORPORATION MAY SHIELD OWNERS FROM PERSONAL LIABILITY.

GS Petroleum, Inc. v. R and S Fuel, Inc.
(Gas Station Seller) v. (Gas Station Buyer)
Delaware Superior Court. No. 07C-09-023 RRC (2009)

On or about March 13, 2006, GS Petroleum, Inc. ("Plaintiff") entered into a one page contract entitled "Agreement of Sale of Inventory and Business" ("Agreement"), which purported to sell a Shell gas station located at 2503 Concord Pike, New Castle County, Delaware, its inventory, and good will. The Agreement stated that it was "entered by and between R and S Fuel, Inc., a Delaware Corporation ... and GS Petroleum, Inc., a Delaware Corporation." However, R and S Fuel did not incorporate until March 27, 2006, two weeks after the Agreement was signed.

[...]

Pursuant to the terms of the Agreement, R and S Fuel took over operation of the gas station on April 15, 2006. Prior to operating the gas station, R and S Fuel filed its certificate of incorporation on March 27, 2006, obtained a temporary business license from the State of Delaware Division of Revenue on April 3, 2006, opened a corporate bank account on or before April 2, 2006, and filed a merchant change of ownership form on April 14, 2006. Shortly after taking over operation of the gas station, R and S Fuel wrote checks from its corporate bank account and insured the gas station in the corporation's name.

Plaintiff filed suit on September 5, 2007 alleging that R and S Fuel, Ms. Stamm, and Mr. Simpson are jointly and severally liable for failure to make payment pursuant to the Agreement in the amount of $123,744.89. [footnotes omitted]

II. THE PARTIES' CONTENTIONS

Defendants first contend that Susan Stamm and Richard Simpson are not personally liable because R and S Fuel was a de facto corporation at the time the Agreement was signed. Defendants also contend that Susan Stamm cannot be personally liable because she did not sign the Agreement. Pursuant to the Court's request for supplemental briefing on the issue of promoter's liability for preincorporation agreements, Defendants further maintain that Ms. Stamm and Mr. Simpson, as promoters of R and S Fuel, were released from liability by R and S Fuel's acceptance of the Agreement because it was clear from the Agreement that Ms. Stamm's and Mr. Simpson's liability was not intended.

In response, Plaintiff first contends that R and S Fuel did not exist on March 13, 2006, and thus it could not have been a party to the agreement; nor was R and S Fuel a de facto corporation because it did not make a bona fide attempt to organize as a corporation until after the Agreement was signed. Plaintiff also maintains, but without citation to any authority, that Mr. Simpson had "apparent agency" to bind Ms. Stamm to the Agreement. Pursuant to the Court's request for supplemental briefing, Plaintiff maintains that it is not clear from the Agreement that Ms. Stamm's and Mr. Simpson's liability was not intended.

[...]

IV. DISCUSSION

The issue before this Court is whether Ms. Stamm and Mr. Simpson were released from liability where the Agreement stated that it was "entered by and between R and S Fuel, Inc., a Delaware Corporation (herein referred to as "Buyer") and GS Petroleum, Inc., a Delaware Corporation (herein referred to as "Seller)," where R and S Fuel subsequently properly incorporated before taking over operation of the gas station, and R and S Fuel accepted the benefits of the Agreement. In essence, Defendants contend that Ms. Stamm and Mr. Simpson were promoters of a preincorporation agreement and that their personal liability was extinguished by R and S Fuel's adoption of the Agreement (and its acts in conformity therewith) and the clear intent of the Agreement to hold R and S Fuel alone liable. A promoter's liability in connection with a preincorporation agreement is an issue of apparent first impression in Delaware.

In American Legacy Foundation v. Lorillard Tobacco Company, the Court of Chancery applied the doctrine of adoption to preincorporation agreements. Citing Fletcher Cyclopedia of the Law of Corporations, which the Court of Chancery characterized as a "leading treatise," the American Legacy Foundation Court noted:

> American courts generally hold that promoters' contracts made on the corporation's behalf may be adopted, accepted or ratified by the corporation when organized, and that the corporation is then liable, both at law and equity, on the contract itself and not merely for the benefits which it has received. Accordingly, if the corporation accepts the contract's benefits, the corporation will be required to perform its obligations.[7]

The Court of Chancery concluded that "[u]nder Delaware law, if the subsequently formed corporation expressly adopts the preincorporation agreement or implicitly adopts it by accepting its benefits with knowledge of its terms, the corporation is bound by it .

In the instant case, R and S Fuel accepted the benefits of the Agreement. It is undisputed that R and S Fuel may be held liable for a breach of the Agreement. This Court must decide whether Ms. Stamm and Mr. Simpson may also be held liable.

Fletcher Cyclopedia of the Law of Corporations squarely addresses this issue:

> It is the general rule that adoption, acceptance or ratification creating corporate liability on a preincorporation contract is insufficient, standing alone, to release promoters from liability under the contract. Subsequent to the corporation's adoption or ratification, promoters may be released, however, where it is clear that the promoter's liability was not intended, the contract or other agreement releases the promoters, or there is a novation. The exact theory upon which this principle is rested varies among authorities. Moreover, language in some opinions suggests that in some jurisdictions, mere adoption by the corporation may relieve a promoter from liability. In any case, formation of the corporation is a prerequisite to a promoter's release. If there was no adoption or succession in liability, the promoters remain liable under the contract.

In this case, there was no subsequent agreement releasing the promoters, nor was there a novation. The remaining inquiry is whether it was clear from the Agreement that the promoters' liability was not intended.

The first paragraph of the Agreement identified the parties to the Agreement:

> This agreement made this 13th day of March, 2006, entered by and between R And S Fuel inc., [sic] a Delaware Corporation, (herein referred to as "Buyer") and GS Petroleum, inc. [sic] a Delaware Corporation (Herein referred to as "Seller").

It is notable that the term "Buyer" is in the singular and that nowhere in the body of the Agreement does Ms. Stamm's or Mr. Simpson's names appear.

The signature lines also suggest that the Agreement was between R and S Fuel and GS Petroleum.

[...]

The Agreement, taken as a whole, evidences an intent to bind R and S Fuel and GS Petroleum to its terms. While Ms. Stamm's and Mr. Simpson's names were not followed by a corporate title, it is nonetheless clear that Mr. Simpson was signing on behalf of R and S Fuel, just as Mr. Kumar was signing on behalf of GS Petroleum.

The Court also takes note of the fact that while R and S Fuel was not a corporate entity on March 13, 2006, the date the Agreement was signed, R and S Fuel properly incorporated on March 27, 2006, more than two weeks before it took over operation of the gas station on April 15, 2006. There is no indication (nor any suggestion by the parties) that R and S Fuel was a sham corporation. Prior to taking over operation of the gas station, R and S Fuel obtained a temporary business license from the State of Delaware Division of Revenue, opened a bank account, and filed a merchant change of ownership form on April 14, 2006. Shortly after taking over operation of the gas station, R and S Fuel wrote checks from its corporate bank account and insured the gas station in the corporation's name. The Court concludes that Ms. Stamm's and Mr. Simpson's liability was not intended and therefore R and S Fuel alone may be held liable for any alleged breach of the Agreement.

[Footnotes omitted]

has been accomplished. Usually, this will be when the company has been established and an independent board takes charge. As a fiduciary, a promoter must act with the utmost good faith. She must fully disclose to them all material facts involved in the promotion. She may not benefit by any secret profit or advantage gained at the expense of the company or its owners.

Filing Obligations

The formation of a corporation is similar to the formation of an LLC. In both cases, articles are filed with the state corporate authority. Usually, this is the secretary of state's office. The articles are normally a simple form, asking for basic information, such as the company's name, address, and the name and address of the person doing the filing. The name of the company must be distinct from others in the state. Articles may be filed online, or a hard copy may be filed.

> The name of a corporation must end in "Co.," "Corp.," "Ltd.," or some other word or abbreviation that shows the company is a corporation. The name of an LLC must end in the initials "LLC."

Filing articles of organization or incorporation is not the end of the filing requirements. Most states require periodic filings. These filings are usually made annually. Their sole purpose is to show that the corporation still exists.

If the required filings are not made, a company will lose its status as a company "in good standing." The consequences of losing good standing will vary from state-to-state. In general, it means that the company no longer exists. It will not be able to bring lawsuits in court, and it probably will lose the right to its **tradename**. In addition, the shareholders or members of the former company could be held personally liable for business liabilities.

Tax Obligations

Corporations and LLCs have tax filing obligations, even if the company itself does not have to pay any tax. This may seem counter-intuitive, since pass-through treatment may mean that the company has very little substance from a tax perspective. Business returns provide documentation of the source of individual's income from such pass-throughs, though, and maintain the distinction between the individual and the corporate entity.

> **Example:**
> A non-profit corporation is formed to operate a hospital. After a few years, the hospital corporation opens an elementary school for children in the neighborhood. The formation of the school is *ultra vires*.

TRADENAME:

A name, style, or symbol under which a business operates. The tradename identifies the business, and distinguishes it from others.

A C corporation must file an annual return. A return must be filed even though the corporation had no income to be taxed. Of course, the corporation must pay any tax that is due.

An S corporation is not liable for federal income tax, but must file a return. An LLC is liable for taxes only if it chooses to be taxed as a C corporation. The company still must make a filing with the Internal Revenue Service, even if it makes an S election. The filing summarizes each shareholder's or member's shares of the company's income or deductions and credits. The form may be as detailed as a regular income tax return, or much longer.

> In 2011, General Electric filed a corporate tax return estimated to be 57,000 pages long. Many of those pages were very important: GE did not have to pay tax on its profits for the year, which were in the billions of dollars.

Shareholders and LLC members are likewise required to file their own personal income tax returns. Establishing a business does not eliminate personal income tax responsibilities.

VI. Corporate Powers

Corporations and LLCs exist by virtue of state laws. These laws may limit the activities and powers of a company. Modern corporate law imposes some limits on the activities of companies. A corporation may not engage in banking business without special permission from state or federal regulators, for instance. Apart from limitations such as these, a company is free to decide on the business it will conduct.

A company will seldom make a formal declaration of the business it will engage in. At one time, corporations were required to state in the articles of incorporation what business they would engage in. Most incorporators met this requirement by saying that the corporation was being formed to conduct "any lawful business." A corporation that did something outside of its powers was said to be acting *ultra vires*.

State corporate and LLC laws now provide that a company is being organized for any lawful purpose unless the articles provide otherwise. The prohibition against acting *ultra vires* is largely obsolete. It has relevance only for non-profit or charitable corporations.

VII. Ongoing Management

Businesses don't run themselves. After a company is formed, there are two aspects to the ongoing management of the business. The first aspect is doing business; that is, doing whatever the business does to make money. The second is following all of the legal requirements for operating the type of business form chosen.

In order for a corporation to exist, certain formalities must be observed. Unless an exception applies, all corporations, of whatever size, must follow the same formalities.

While state law sets out the outline of the formalities to be followed, the corporation is usually given some leeway to decide the mechanics of those formalities. These mechanics are set out in the corporate by-laws. In an LLC, the comparable document is the operating agreement. By-laws are the internal rules of a corporation. Usually, state laws do not require a corporation to file its by-laws with the state, or even to have by-laws in place. It is, however, virtually impossible to run a corporation without by-laws.

By-laws address many topics. If there are special qualifications for being a director, those qualifications need to be in the by-laws. If there is no limitation, anyone can be a director of a corporation. Some corporations, however, may want to place a limit on who may be a director. The limitation may be that the director must be a shareholder. Corporate by-laws may include such a limitation.

By-laws may also include a buy-sell agreement. A buy-sell agreement is a limitation on how stock is disposed of, or sold. The agreement may provide that, before stock is sold, the shareholder must offer it to the other shareholders at the same price. This prevents ownership of a small corporation from being too widely dispersed.

The main corporate formality addressed by by-laws is the requirement that a company have

ULTRA VIRES:
An action outside the legal ability of an entity to perform.

BY-LAWS:
The rules and regulations adopted to govern the operation of a corporation.

OPERATING AGREEMENT:
The rules and regulations adopted to govern the operation of a limited liability company.

BOARD OF DIRECTORS:
Individuals elected by the shareholders to act as their representatives of shareholders to establish corporate policies and to make decisions on issues facing the company.

Corporations must hold shareholder meetings at least annually. The usual business of a shareholder meeting is to elect or re-elect the board of directors. Shareholders may also vote on amendments to the corporate by-laws, and must also approve organic changes to the corporation's existence, such as a merger with another corporation, or dissolution.

regular meetings. Shareholders and the **board of directors** must meet regularly. These meetings are typically separate, even if the directors and the shareholders are the same person. The by-laws will set out when a shareholders' meeting must be held. It will say when and where the directors' meeting is held. Provisions will often be made for special meetings, held in between regular meetings. Other topics, such as the quorum required for a shareholders' or directors' meeting, or the notice required for a special meeting, will also be included.

Many states have recognized that all of these formalities are a burden on smaller corporations. All of the formalities are required of all corporations, of whatever size, so a one-person corporation would be required to hold two annual meetings of herself: one as shareholder, one as director. Instead of requiring smaller corporations to go through this ritual, states have allowed some corporations, called closely-held or close corporations, to have one combined shareholders' and directors' meeting.

The states that allow corporations to combine meetings have different criteria for the corporations that will qualify. The most common qualifications are:

- The directors and the shareholders are the same people,

- The corporation is the only business of the shareholders (it is not an investment, but the shareholders are active employees of the corporation), and

- There is no ready market for stock in the corporation.

Corporate Finance

Corporate finance is a term used to describe all of the financial aspects of running a business. Corporate finance relates to maximizing shareholder value. This includes capital investments, as well as the strategies for managing assets.

Decisions regarding corporate finance are left to the discretion of the board of directors. As long as their decisions are permitted by law,

Example: Simio, Ltd. operates child-care centers. Simio wants to expand its operations into a new area. Corwin, a director of Simio, owns property in that area that would be suitable for the company's purposes. Corwin tells the other directors about his interest in the property, and offers it to Simio for sale. Corwin has not breached his duty of loyalty.

Example: Corwin learns of Simio's expansion plans. His cousin owns a property in the area that would be suitable. Corwin buys a half-interest in the property from his cousin at a steeply discounted price. The cousin, pretending to act on his own, negotiates a sale of the property to Simio, giving Corwin a healthy profit. Corwin has breached his duty of loyalty.

shareholders have very little say in these decisions, even though they are supposed to be made on their behalf, and to benefit them. The only remedy of an aggrieved shareholder is to seek to have the directors replaced at an election.

Board of Directors

The board of directors is responsible for managing the corporation. The board acts through meetings. Depending on the corporate by-laws, these meetings may be in person, in writing, or by phone.

Directors have a duty of loyalty to the corporation. This means that they must act in the best interests of the corporation. A director may not take unfair advantage of her position as a director. If she does business with the corporation, she must disclose her interest to the other directors.

Directors are also expected to be informed about the corporation's business. While they are not expected to be masters of every detail, they must at least have a general idea of what is going on with the business. Directors should also seek outside advice, such as legal or financial advice, as needed.

If a director makes a mistake, however, there is little that a shareholder can do. The business judgment rule says that, as a general matter, courts will not second-guess directors' decisions. Directors are given broad leeway, and are not subject to court supervision. The business judgment rule presumes that directors' actions were motivated by a regard for the best interests of the corporation if the directors acted:

- In good faith,

- On an informed basis, and

- In the honest belief that the actions taken were in the best interests of the corporation.

If the business judgment rule applies, directors are shielded from personal liability for their actions as directors. The shareholders' only remedy is to vote the incompetent director out of office.

Directors of publicly-traded corporations have additional requirements. These requirements are imposed by the Sarbanes-Oxley Act. The Act says that directors certify the accuracy of financial reports. Directors must also put internal controls to ensure compliance into place. The Sarbanes-Oxley Act is covered in detail in another chapter.

Publicly-traded companies must also comply with any Securities and Exchanges Commission (SEC) regulations. Compliance with SEC regulations and reporting requirements is mandatory for all public companies. Any company that does not meet these requirements may be fined heavily, disqualified from public trading, and even face an enforcement action by SEC.

It is common for corporations to designate a person to act as corporate secretary, to keep charge of corporate records and to maintain the minutes of corporate meetings. The secretary may or may not be an employee of the corporation.

A CORPORATE OFFICER MUST GIVE BUSINESS OPPORTUNITIES TO THE CORPORATION.

Guth v. Loft, Inc.
(Officer) v. (Corporation)
5 A.2d 503 (Del. Ch. 1939).

INSTANT FACTS:
Guth took a business opportunity for his family's business rather than give it to the company he served as president. The companies handled similar products.

BLACK LETTER RULE:
If a business opportunity is presented to a corporate officer or

director in his representative capacity, the law will not permit him to take the opportunity for himself.

FACTS:
Guth (D) was an officer of Loft, Inc. (P), a candy and syrup company. Loft (P) was primarily a retail operation, but also ran a wholesale business. Guth (D) and his family owned Grace Company, a manufacturer of soft drink syrups. Guth (D) was unhappy at the prices Loft (P) was paying for Coca-Cola syrups, and wanted to negotiate with Pepsi instead. Pepsi was declared bankrupt in 1931, but a representative made an agreement with Guth (D) to secure Pepsi's secret formula and trademarks from the bankruptcy court and to form a new company to manufacture Pepsi Cola. Guth (D) proceeded with this plan, and did not offer the opportunity to Luft (P). Loft (P) assisted in the endeavor and was repaid; however, Loft (P) did not own any shares in the new company. Guth's (D) private plan was to unseat Coca-Cola in Loft (P) retail outlets.

ISSUE:
May a corporate officer take a business opportunity for personal gain rather than give it to the corporation?

DECISION AND RATIONALE:
No. When an officer or director is acting in a representative capacity for the corporation, he may not take the opportunity for himself, assuming:

- The corporation is financially able to undertake it;
- The opportunity is in the line of the corporation's business and is of practical advantage to it; and
- The opportunity is one in which the corporation has an interest or a reasonable expectancy.

In this case, Loft (P) was financially capable of undertaking the opportunity. The Pepsi product was in line with Loft's (P) business, and the company had a reasonable expectation that the opportunity would be presented to it by Guth (D).

ANALYSIS:
The so-called "Guth Corollary" states that if an officer or director is in his individual capacity, he may take the opportunity as long as he does not steal corporate assets in the effort. The opportunity must not be essential to the corporation or be one that the corporation has an interest in. The difficult factual question is whether an officer or director is acting in his representative or individual capacity in any given case.

QUESTIONS FOR REVIEW:
A director may not take an opportunity for herself if the corporation has a reasonable expectancy of having an interest in it. How far should that expectancy extend? While most would agree that directors should not be allowed to compete with the corporation, should they be held liable for failing to predict a new corporate interest?

Many corporations have outside directors on the board. These directors are not employees of the corporation, and are often employed in different industries, but corporations value their detached perspective. Does the rule in this case put unfair restrictions on outside directors?

Corporate Officers

Corporate officers are agents or employees of the corporation. They have specific authority, delegated to them by the Board of Directors. For most corporations, officers are not legally required.

Corporate officers are usually appointed, not elected, although corporate by-laws could provide for election. They are the ones who handle the day-to-day operations that do not require action by the directors. As agents of the corporation, they are subject to the control of the board of directors.

Shareholders are the owners of the corporation. They act by voting at meetings. Shareholders generally may delegate their voting to a substitute or proxy. Shareholders may agree among themselves on how to vote, and a shareholder agreement may be enforced by petitioning a court for specific performance.

Shareholders have three functions:

- To elect the board of directors,

- To approve corporate by-laws, and

- To approve organic changes, such as a merger or dissolution of the corporation.

A shareholder has no direct management role, unless she is also an officer or director. Shareholders express their opinions about the management of a corporation through the directors they elect.

> The term "piercing the corporate veil" refers also to piercing the liability protection of an LLC. Generally, the same rules are followed.

Piercing the Corporate Veil

One of the main reasons for forming a corporation or an LLC is the liability protection for the owners. Shareholders or members are not liable for actions of their companies, even if there is only one shareholder or member, and even if that one shareholder or member is the sole director or governor, and the sole employee, of the company. That protection, however, has its limits. The liability protection may be set aside in the situation known as **piercing the corporate veil**.

Piercing the corporate veil will happen when the owners do not treat a company as a separate entity. In that case, the company is simply an alter ego of the owners, rather than a separate entity with its own liabilities. The most common reasons courts will allow the veil to be pierced are:

- *Failure to follow corporate formalities:* Failing to hold annual shareholder

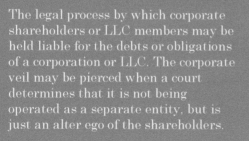

PIERCING THE CORPORATE VEIL:

The legal process by which corporate shareholders or LLC members may be held liable for the debts or obligations of a corporation or LLC. The corporate veil may be pierced when a court determines that it is not being operated as a separate entity, but is just an alter ego of the shareholders.

Wayne and Wanda start an S corporation to run an auto repair shop: W&W Auto Body, Inc. Wayne says he will take care of the bookkeeping, but does not do so. Instead of having customers pay W&W, he often has them write checks to him personally. He also takes money out of the cash register if he needs extra cash for personal purchases. Wanda buys a car to serve as a "courtesy car" for customers, but she likes it more than her car, so she uses it as her personal vehicle. She also pays a contractor working on her house with checks drawn on the W&W account. Both Wayne and Wanda are using W&W as an "alter ego" rather than running it as an entity separate from their personal lives. In such a case, a court might pierce the corporate veil, and hold Wayne and Wanda personally responsible for debts of the so-called business.

or directors' meetings, or neglecting to keep adequate records, makes it appear as though the owners themselves have disregarded the corporate form. While by-laws are not a legal requirement in most states, they provide the best plan for making sure corporate formalities are followed.

- *Continuous undercapitalization:* If a corporation does not have enough funds to operate, that means it is not a stand-alone enterprise. It is the alter ego of the owners.

- *Commingling funds:* This is perhaps the most common reason a corporate veil will be pierced. Business owners do not pay themselves a salary, but just help themselves to money as they need it. There is no separate business bank account, and company funds are used to pay personal expenses of the owners. The company is the alter ego of the owners, and its legal existence can be ignored.

PIERCING THE CORPORATE VEIL REQUIRES MORE THAN AN ALLEGATION OF FRAUD.

Doberstein v. G–P Industries, Inc.
(Homeowner) v. (Contractor)
2015 WL 6606484 (Del. Ch. 2015)

In October 2012, Doberstein entered into a contract with G–P (the "Agreement"), under which G–P agreed to serve as the general contractor on a significant home renovation project at Doberstein's Wilmington residence (the "Project"). On October 17, 2012, Greenplate, on behalf of G–P, prepared the Project's estimates and the Agreement. He estimated that the Project would cost Doberstein a total of $494,498. Under the terms of the Agreement, Doberstein was to provide advance deposits for subcontractors performing work on the basement as well as for the building permit. Otherwise, the Agreement did not contemplate Doberstein paying for any renovations before they were completed or paying subcontractors directly. Instead, G–P was to pay all subcontractors and to seek reimbursement through its invoices to Doberstein. In addition, G–P agreed to invoice Doberstein on the first of each month—with the exception of major material purchases, which were to be invoiced immediately—and to provide a three percent discount on labor charges when Doberstein paid in cash. G–P began work on the Project in November 2012. Defendants repeatedly assured Doberstein that the Project would be completed by the end of 2013.

Doberstein, who lives and works in Switzerland, began making monthly payments while abroad. On March 14, 2013, G–P sent Doberstein a $1,520 invoice for cabinet grade plywood. G–P had not yet begun construction on the portions of the Project that required the plywood, but purchased the plywood early because it was concerned that the cost would increase. Doberstein paid G–P to purchase the plywood in advance and store it until needed. Further, in that March 14 invoice and in an April 10, 2013 invoice, G–P offered Doberstein a three percent reduction on labor if she paid in cash directly to Greenplate. Doberstein paid a total amount of $33,950 in cash directly to Greenplate based on those two invoices.

[...]

In May 2013, Doberstein traveled from Switzerland to visit the Project site. Upon arrival, she discovered that little work had been completed, despite the fact that she had paid Defendants $127,820.10. After Doberstein returned to Switzerland, her interior designer, Matthew Pearson, spoke with Greenplate about the lack of progress. Greenplate explained that the Project had been delayed due to a lack of manpower, delays on other projects, and shuffling employees. He assured Pearson, however, that the Project still would be completed by the end of 2013.

On or about July 25 and 27, 2013, a neighbor, who also served as the president of the neighborhood homeowners' association, contacted Doberstein regarding the unkempt state of her property. The neighbor informed Doberstein that little progress had been made on the Project in the past several months, even after the meetings Doberstein and Pearson had with Greenplate. Doberstein contacted Greenplate, demanding action. On August 9, 2013, Greenplate sent a letter to Doberstein's neighbors, explaining that the Project had been delayed due to weather and manpower issues and stating that "we did stop working there in early May...." Despite halting work on the Project, G–P had sent Doberstein invoices from May through August for a total amount of $49,500.

Later in August 2013, Pearson began meeting weekly at the Project site with Greenplate and insisted that G–P prepare a schedule of the work to be done. During those weekly meetings, Pearson observed three to six workers on the Project at any given time. Doberstein and Pearson later discovered that the Project was unmanned most of the week and that the number of workers was increased on days when Greenplate would meet with one of them.

[...]

In September 2013, Doberstein learned that, contrary to her explicit instructions, Pearson had not been copied on the invoices sent to her by G–P and Greenplate. Doberstein reiterated her request for Pearson to be copied on all invoices. Later that month, during one of their weekly meetings, Greenplate revealed to Pearson that the Project would not be completed until the end of January 2014. Doberstein did not respond well to this news. To ameliorate her displeasure, Greenplate told Doberstein that the Project would be substantially complete by the end of 2013, such that Doberstein could move in her things. Throughout the rest of 2013, G–P's invoicing accelerated in amount and frequency. By the end of December 2013, Doberstein had paid a total of $314,434.68 to G–P and Greenplate since the Project's inception, representing fifty-eight percent of the total $542,159 due under the Agreement, though the Project was nowhere near complete.

In January 2014, Pearson informed Greenplate that the Project had to be completed by March 1, because Doberstein's builders' risk insurance policy would expire on that date. After multiple requests from Pearson, Greenplate finally submitted a completion schedule, which contemplated a March 1 completion date. Greenplate then told Doberstein that G–P would need to bill every two weeks rather than monthly. As a result, Doberstein set up direct wire transfers from her bank account to G–P's account. Between January 1 and February 21, 2014, Doberstein paid an additional $146,930.34 via wire transfers to G–P. The Project's final invoice was issued to Doberstein on February 17, 2014 and was followed by G–P's urgent requests for payment over the following few days.

[...]

On February 22, 2014, Doberstein, Pearson, Greenplate, and the flooring subcontractor met to discuss the Project. During the meeting, Greenplate admitted he would not have the Project complete by March 1, but promised Doberstein it would be complete by the end of April. Three days later, however, Greenplate fired G–P's employees and sent a letter to Doberstein and at least one other customer informing them that G–P would be abandoning their renovations, because financially, it was unable to continue in business. The letter stated that G–P's financial troubles were due, in part, to its underbidding of the Project, late payments by customers, and increased costs. In March, Greenplate and G–P abandoned the Project altogether. In April, Todd Breck, A.I.A., P.E., of Breckstone Architecture, inspected the Project and estimated that, at the time, the value of the work in place was approximately $298,272.98. To date, Doberstein has paid Defendants a total of $461,365.02.

[...]

Doberstein asserts six remaining counts against Defendants. In Count I, she seeks to pierce G–P's corporate veil and hold Greenplate personally liable for his fraudulent statements and misrepresentations to her. In Count II, Doberstein avers that Greenplate and G–P fraudulently concealed their plan to abandon the Project after she had paid in full under the Agreement. In Count III, Doberstein alleges Greenplate and G–P intentionally misrepresented the amount due under various invoices in order to extract unwarranted payments from her. In Count IV, Doberstein avers that Greenplate and G–P negligently misrepresented information regarding the status, completion, and billing of the Project. Count V asserts a claim against G–P for breach of an express contract, which Defendants do not contest in their motion. Finally, in Count VI, Doberstein alleges that Greenplate and G–P have been unjustly enriched by the amount they received from her for work they did not perform on the Project.

[...]

Doberstein claims that, despite Greenplate's otherwise limited liability, I should pierce G–P's corporate veil and hold him individually liable for his allegedly fraudulent conduct. "To state a 'veil-piercing claim,' the plaintiff must plead facts supporting an inference that the corporation, through its alter-ego, has created a sham entity designed to defraud investors and creditors."[12] Specific facts a court may consider when being asked to disregard the corporate form include: "(1) whether the company was adequately capitalized for the undertaking; (2) whether the company was solvent; (3) whether corporate formalities were observed; (4) whether the dominant shareholder siphoned company funds; and (5) whether, in general, the company simply functioned as a facade for the dominant shareholder." The decision to disregard the corporate entity "generally results not from a single factor, but rather some combination of them, and 'an overall element of injustice or unfairness must always be present, as well.'" Most importantly, "because Delaware public policy does not lightly disregard the separate legal existence of corporations, a plaintiff must do more than plead that one corporation is the alter ego of another in conclusory fashion in order for the Court to disregard their separate legal existence."

Doberstein contends that her claim for veil-piercing is supported by her allegations that Greenplate repeatedly communicated false statements to her concerning the work being done at her property and that she relied on those statements to her detriment. She alleges that Greenplate and G–P increased the frequency and the amount of their billing during the last six weeks of the Project, despite the fact that they knew they shortly were going to abandon it and cease doing business. According to Doberstein, because all the requisite elements of fraud are present, she has alleged a sufficient basis for disregarding the corporate identity of G–P and holding Greenplate personally liable. I disagree.

The case law governing veil-piercing requires me to consider whether the individual defendant—i.e., Greenplate—abused the corporate form and, through that abuse, perpetrated fraud on an innocent third party—i.e., Doberstein. It is not enough to allege, as Doberstein does, that Greenplate made fraudulent statements about his progress toward completing his contractual obligations. Those types of allegations may or may not support a claim for fraud, but Greenplate's wrongful acts must be tied to the manipulation of the corporate form in order to make veil-piercing justifiable on grounds of equity. No such nexus is alleged here.

The Complaint alleges that Greenplate knew that G–P was going out of business and, therefore, induced Doberstein to make accelerated payments from January 1 to February 21, 2014, to extract as much money from her as possible. Doberstein has not pled, however, that Greenplate siphoned funds from G–P to himself during those last six weeks and thereby used the corporate form to shield those funds and himself from liability once G–P went out of business. Absent such allegations, the Complaint states, at most, a claim for fraud against G–P due to actions taken by Greenplate on its behalf. Because Doberstein failed to allege that Greenplate utilized G–P as a sham entity to defraud her, Count I must be dismissed for failure to state a claim.

[...]

Doberstein contends that because she contracted with G–P to complete renovation work at her property while she was living abroad, she was "relying" on Defendants in a special way and, therefore, can bring this claim for equitable fraud. I do not find this argument persuasive. Sophisticated contractual parties who bargain at arm's length generally do not qualify for the kind of equitable protection that the negligent misrepresentation doctrine envisions in this regard . . .The obligations owed to Doberstein, therefore, were contractual in nature, and her remedy for breaches of those obligations can be obtained through an action sounding in contract. As a result, the Complaint fails to state a claim for negligent misrepresentation.

[...]

"A claim for unjust enrichment is not available if there is a contract that governs the relationship between parties that gives rise to the unjust enrichment claim." Doberstein has not identified any factual basis for her unjust enrichment claim independent of the allegations relating to her breach of contract claim . . .Thus, Doberstein's unjust enrichment claim also must be dismissed under Rule 12(b)(6).

[...]

[Footnotes omitted]

ANALYSIS:

Piercing the corporate veil is a difficult proposition. It is especially hard when all of the required corporate forms are observed. Businesspeople who manage to keep corporate funds separate from personal funds, and who keep all of the required records, are usually safe from veil-piercing claims.

QUESTIONS FOR DISCUSSION:

Should strict observance of corporate formalities be enough to defeat a claim for piercing the corporate veil?

Does the shield from liability offered by the corporate form encourage businesspeople to engage in fraudulent practices? Would Greenplate have acted differently if he knew he could be held personally liable for his actions?

There is a strong presumption against piercing the corporate veil. In order to allow it, courts require proof of very serious misconduct.

VIII. Voluntary Dissolution

Although a corporation or LLC could, in theory, exist forever, most will eventually come to an end. By one estimate, the average "lifespan" of a corporation is 45 years. The end may come voluntarily, as a result of a decision by the owners. The end may also be involuntary.

State laws provide for the orderly termination of corporations and LLCs. These laws set out the procedure to be followed before a corporation may be officially considered to have ended. The chief concern of these laws is protection of creditors. If a corporation goes out of business with unpaid debts, the creditors (most of whom will have had nothing to do with the corporation going out of business) will have no one left who is obligated to pay the debts.

Under most state laws, the procedure for the voluntary dissolution of a corporation or LLC is as follows:

Shareholder/member vote. The shareholders or members of the company must vote in favor of dissolution. The vote to dissolve must have been on the agenda for the meeting before the meeting takes place.

Notice of intent to dissolve. The notice must be filed with the state authority that is in charge of business registrations.

Stop doing business. While existing contracts may be fulfilled, the dissolving company must refrain from soliciting or accepting new business.

Collect assets. The assets of the company are used to pay creditors. Anything remaining is distributed to shareholders. All of the assets of the company need to be collected before the company may officially dissolve.

Pay creditors. Creditors are given notice of the dissolution, and given a time within which they may make a claim for payment. The notice may be written and sent directly to creditors, or published in a newspaper. Once all claims are paid, the company certifies that the debts are paid.

Distribute assets. Any remaining assets are distributed to the shareholders, in proportion to their ownership.

Succession Planning

Succession planning looks at what will be done if a key shareholder or member withdraws from the business. The withdrawal may be voluntary (retirement or accepting a new job) or involuntary (death or disability). Smaller, closely-held companies are especially vulnerable to disruption when a key member or shareholder leaves. Succession planning allows the business to stay in operation after such a departure.

Succession planning can take many forms, depending on the company. Many companies, large and small, have life insurance policies on key employees. Those policies, of course, pay only on the death of the employee. They do not cover the company in the event the employee just decides to leave.

Another option is the buy-sell agreement. A buy-sell agreement usually says that a shareholder who wants to sell her stock must first offer it to the other shareholders at the same price. Many agreements also provide for a buy-out in the event a shareholder dies, or is otherwise forced to leave the company.

> The by-laws of the Yokai Corp. provide that the stock of a deceased shareholder may be repurchased by the corporation at the directors' option. Shareholder Jane dies, leaving as her sole heirs her wife Cynthia and their son Roger. Cynthia has no interest in joining the business, and Roger is only twelve years old. The other shareholders of Yokai secure an appraisal of Jane's shares, and purchase the stock for that price from Jane's estate.

> **Example:** The Flechette Group is interested in acquiring the Anderson Department Store Co. Flechette makes an offer to the board of Anderson, but the offer is refused. Flechette then offers Anderson shareholders the chance to sell their stock for $15 per share. The current market price fluctuates between $12 and $13.50 per share. Flechette has made a tender offer.

> **Example:** Instead of buying Anderson stock from shareholders, Flechette buys stock on the open market. The principals of Flechette soon accumulate 30% of the stock. Along with some dissident shareholders, Flechette is able to vote in new directors on the board of Anderson. The new directors approve the takeover by Flechette.

Mergers and Acquisitions

Mergers and acquisitions are transactions that involve some combination of two or more companies.

A **merger** involves two or more companies combining into one company. In practice, there is usually one company that "survives" the merger. The management of the survivor company is installed as the management of the new company. In many cases, the new company may operate under the survivor's name.

Most state laws provide that a merger must be approved by a majority of the shareholders.

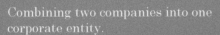

MERGER:
Combining two companies into one corporate entity.

ACQUISITION:
The purchase of a corporation by another entity or group of investors.

By-laws may provide that a larger majority must approve a merger.

An **acquisition** is when one company, or a group of investors, buys all or nearly all of the assets or stock of a corporation. Sometimes, these are "friendly" takeovers. A friendly takeover is one that has been approved by the management of the corporation being acquired. Management should approve a takeover when it is in the best interests of the shareholders.

A hostile takeover is one that does not have the approval of management. In a hostile takeover, the acquiring party may have made an offer for a friendly takeover that was refused. There are two types of hostile takeovers. With a tender offer takeover, shareholders are offered a price for their stock that is higher than the current market price. The board of directors must evaluate the offer, and then make a recommendation to the shareholders as to whether the offer should be accepted. It is then up to individual shareholders to decide whether to accept or reject this offer.

The other type of hostile takeover is a proxy fight. In a proxy fight, the acquiring party purchases enough stock to vote to replace the management of the board with one receptive to a takeover.

Mergers and acquisitions may raise antitrust concerns, if the companies involved are large.

IX. Involuntary Dissolution

Not all corporations end voluntarily. Involuntary dissolution can happen for a number of reasons. A corporation may neglect to make the required filings, and lose its status as a corporation in good standing, for example.

In some states, shareholders may bring a court action to force dissolution of a corporation. An action for dissolution is allowed when the board of directors is deadlocked. A deadlock renders the corporation legally incapable of doing anything. Some states also allow an action for dissolution when the majority of shareholders are taking actions that are harmful to the rest of the shareholders.

Bankruptcy

Bankruptcy is not always the death knell for a corporation. A Chapter 11 bankruptcy, for example, is meant to restructure the company and put it in good (or, at least better) financial shape. Chapter 11 contemplates the continuation of the business. A Chapter 7 bankruptcy, however, will result in the end of the business. The business is liquidated, and any assets are sold off.

In some circumstances, creditors may petition for an involuntary bankruptcy of a company. The petition may request either a Chapter 7 or Chapter 11. A petition for an involuntary bankruptcy may be brought if:

- There are unsecured claims of more than $15,775 (as of April 2016, through April 2019), or secured claims of at least $15,775 more than the value of the collateral securing them,

- These claims are undisputed,

- The company is generally not paying its debts, and

- The petition is brought by three creditors, if there are 12 or more creditors, having undisputed claims totaling more than $15,775. If there are fewer than 12 creditors, one creditor with claims totaling more than $15,775 may bring the petition.

An involuntary bankruptcy petition does not automatically result in a bankruptcy. The court is asked to declare that the company should be in bankruptcy. Until the court makes such an order, the company may continue to function normally.

Under the original version of the Uniform Partnership Act, a partnership dissolved on the death or withdrawal of a partner unless the partnership agreement provided otherwise.

Death of Key Member or Partner

Many small businesses depend on one or two key people for the bulk of their income. A company may in fact consist of only one key person. If that person dies, the business will likely stop.

Succession planning, as discussed above, may help to keep a business afloat if a key person dies. However, that may not be the case, especially if the key person was the only person involved. In that case, it will be necessary to take steps to dissolve the business.

CHAPTER SUMMARY

There is no "ideal" business organization. Each type presents distinct advantages and disadvantages. Choosing one type over another is a matter of deciding which advantages are most important, and which disadvantages can be tolerated. A good choice means understanding the pros and cons, and knowing how you can work with them.

A sole proprietorship is the most informal type of business. While it requires no formalities to start or operate, it is also the type of business that carries the greatest risk of personal liability. A general partnership is also simple, depending as it does on the agreement between the partners. The partners, however, continue to bear the risk of personal liability for business debts or obligations. Limited liability partnerships will generally take away this risk. Limited liability companies and corporations also protect the owners of the business from personal liability. There are formalities associated with corporate business models that must be followed in order to benefit from liability protections.

Choosing a business form is an ongoing obligation, and observing the requirements of each form is an essential responsibility for businesspeople.

Review Questions

Review question 1.

Define "limited partnership." How does a limited partnership vary from other partnership forms? Who runs the business of a limited partnership? Why would a business choose a partnership form over a limited liability company or other corporate form?

Review question 2.

What is the minimum number of directors a corporation must have? What is the role of the board of directors? What is the difference between a director and a shareholder? What do shareholders of a corporation do?

Review question 3.

What is a limited liability company? Why is it a popular business form? What are its advantages and disadvantages?

Review question 4.

What is the difference between a C corporation and an S corporation? What types of businesses are more likely to choose one or the other? What are the advantages and disadvantages of each forms? What elements would disqualify a business from being an S corporation?

Review question 5.

What documents are generally required to start a corporation? What is the process? What actions must a business take to remain an active corporation?

Review question 6.

What is a corporate promoter? What are the promoter's responsibilities? What does the corporation owe to the promoter? Under what circumstances could the promoter become personally responsible for money spent promoting the business?

Review question 7.

What is piercing the corporate veil? What are the consequences of piercing the veil? How can businesses avoid the problem?

Review question 8.

What is the difference between a Chapter 7 bankruptcy and a Chapter 11 bankruptcy? When does it make sense for a business to choose bankruptcy? What are the consequences, if any, for the business owners?

Review question 9.

What are corporate formalities? Why are they important? What relation do corporate formalities have to piercing the corporate veil?

Review question 10.

How do professional business forms protect the individuals who form those businesses? What are the limits to that protection? How can those risks be managed?

Questions for Discussion

Discussion question 1.

Tariq and Levi are physicians. They decide to combine their medical practices and form a partnership. A partnership agreement is prepared. One clause in the agreement calls for each partner to contribute $10,000 towards the initial start-up costs of the partnership. Tariq and Levi both sign the agreement, but paying the money cannot happen until the next day, when they will be able to open a partnership bank account. The next day, before he has a chance to pay the money, Levi performs a minor surgical procedure on a patient he has been treating for several years. He overlooks a notation in the patient's record that she cannot be given a certain anesthetic, and that anesthetic is ordered. The patient suffers a severe reaction and is permanently injured.

If the patient sued for malpractice, would Tariq be liable for Levi's malpractice? Why or why not?

What additional legal factor could change the answer to the first question?

Discussion question 2.

Arthur is the CEO and sole member of an LLC. The company has moved out of its offices and relocated to Arthur's home, while owing four months' rent on its former offices. The company is doing business only sporadically, as Arthur is, as he puts it, "practicing for retirement." The little money that does come in to the company is deposited into Arthur's personal checking account, as the company bank account was closed three months ago. Some favored suppliers of the company are paid occasionally by Arthur's personal check. Charlie, the former landlord of the company, threatens to sue the company for unpaid rent. Arthur tells him to go ahead, because "there's no money there for you to get."

> What is the legal doctrine that allows members to be held liable for unpaid LLC debts?

> In this case, can Charlie hold Arthur personally liable for the unpaid rent? Why or why not?

Suppose Charlie sues both Arthur and his LLC. Documents produced during discovery show that Arthur has held regular meetings of the board of governors, and has documented all of those meetings. Does this fact affect Charlie's ability to hold Arthur personally liable? Why or why not?

Discussion question 3.

You and two colleagues have decided to go into business together. You will have no other employees at first. You have been friends since you were children.

> What business form would you choose? Why would you choose that one?

> Explain the steps involved in creating that business form.

> What are the main disadvantages of that business form?

> What concerns do you have about starting a business with friends? How can you deal with those concerns?

Discussion question 4.

Sue decides to work as a distributor for a vitamin and supplement company. The company takes orders online and sends the orders in Sue's area to her. She packages and hand-delivers or mails the pills. She decides to work as a sole proprietorship because she is the whole business and she does not intend to add employees.

> Sue is driving to deliver an order. She uses the family car. She hits a pedestrian in a crosswalk when she was checking her text messages. What is Sue's liability to the pedestrian?

One of Sue's customers has an extreme allergic reaction to one of the supplements and ends up in a vegetative state. Sue does not do anything with the supplements other than deliver them. What is Sue's liability to the customer?

It is tax season. What are Sue's tax obligations for her business venture?

Discussion question 5.

The Takei family runs a jewelry shop. It is a true "mom and pop" business, started by Mr. and Mrs. Takei 40 years ago. Their only child, Glen, does the bookkeeping for the business in his spare time. The company is organized as an LLC with the couple as owners. Mrs. Takei is the jewelry maker, and Mr. Takei is the salesman and manager. They have some part-time employees, who are mostly unrelated college students.

Mrs. Takei dies, leaving the shop with nothing to sell when the stock runs out. What should Mr. Takei do?

Mr. Takei dies. Glen quits his day job and becomes the salesperson. What happens to the business when Mrs. Takei dies?

Mr. and Mrs. Takei decide to divorce. Mr. Takei wants to cash out the business. Mrs. Takei wants to keep going. Glen wants to take over the business when Mrs. Takei retires. How can these issues be resolved? What advance planning would have been helpful?

Discussion question 6.

Suzanne is a semi-retired sales executive. Her insight into the market and sales techniques are in high demand. Suzanne wants to increase her consulting work, but doesn't want to put her retirement savings in jeopardy. She also wants to avoid double taxation.

What business forms might Suzanne consider? What are the pros and cons of each?

Suzanne has been working as a sole proprietor to this point. If she continues in that way, are there issues she should consider or risks she should manage in advance?

Assume that instead of being a sales executive, Suzanne is a cosmetic dentist. What other forms might she consider? What risks might she face?

Discussion question 7.

Modern corporate law holds that directors have a fiduciary duty to the corporation. The late economist Milton Friedman disagreed with this rule, and argued that the duty of a director is to maximize value for the shareholders of the corporation.

Are the two rules different? If so, how?

In your opinion, should a director's loyalty be to the shareholders or to the corporation?

Discussion question 8.

Loren is the owner of several small commercial buildings. He would like to expand his business into a different part of the state, but he lacks the capital. David, an acquaintance, tells him that he will find investors who will put money into a corporation Loren forms to build apartments in a neighboring city. Loren agrees, and forms the corporation. David presents Loren with five investors, each of whom is willing to put up money for a large block of stock in the corporation. The stock purchases are completed. Loren knows that the investors are foreign nationals. He does not know, however, that they are all government officials and military officers who are using their investment to hide money that they have looted from their country's treasury.

Was the corporation formed for a fraudulent purpose? Does it matter whether David knew of the source of the funds?

Are there grounds for piercing the corporate veil?

4 CONTRACTS

KEY OBJECTIVES:

▶ Learn the rules for formation of a contract.

▶ Understand the consequences of a breach of contract.

▶ Become familiar with contract damages and remedies.

CHAPTER OVERVIEW

Contracts are a fundamental part of all business relationships and transactions. In this chapter, we will look at the laws regarding the formation and performance of contracts. We will review the remedies for breach of contract. Finally, we will look at a few of the special issues that relate to online contracts.

INTRODUCTION

Contracts are fundamental to business. Every transaction, every deal, every relationship in business hinges on some kind of contract. It has been said that the greatest privilege we have in business is the "right" to be sued over a contract. That right is the assurance that the contract will be performed or, if it is not performed, that there is a remedy for the party who suffers a loss. The ability to make contracts, and the confidence that the contract will be enforced, is an essential part of our economy.

What is a contract? Ask that question of five people, and you will get six different answers. Most of those answers will be at least partially true. We all have some intuitive understanding of what a contract is, even if we don't know the complete legal definition.

The most common answer you will hear when you ask what a contract is will probably say that a contract is some kind of promise. You may also hear that a contract is an agreement. While those answers are not entirely wrong, they are also not entirely correct. All contracts are promises, and all contracts are agreements, but not all promises or agreements are contracts. The full answer to the question goes a little further, and says that a contract is a promise or agreement that has some legal consequences if the promise is not kept, or the agreement is not followed.

What is special about a contract? What turns a promise into something that could be the subject of a lawsuit? It has nothing to do with the subject of the contract, or the value of the transaction. In most cases, it does not even hinge on whether the promise was written down. Instead, a contract is a promise that contains certain elements. If all of these elements are present, the promise becomes a contract.

I.   Contract Elements

Contracts can be very complex undertakings, involving millions of dollars and taking years to perform. They can also be extraordinarily simple: if you bought a cup of coffee this morning, you made and performed a contract. No matter how simple or complex, every **contract** is made up of the same five elements: offer; acceptance; consideration; capacity; and legality. All of these elements must be present, or the promise or agreement is not a promise and cannot be enforced.

> Note that certain types of contracts are subject to additional rules. For instance, sales contracts under the Uniform Commercial Code (covered in the next chapter) must follow statutory rules. This discussion covers general contract law.

Offer

An **offer** is a proposal. It invites another party to make a contract on certain terms. The offer is a promise to do, or to refrain from doing, some specified thing.

An offer is a proposal to make a contract. It person who receives the offer (the **offeree**) the ability to make a contract by accepting the offer. The formal legal requirements for an offer are fairly simple. The offer must give the offeree a

clear idea of what the terms of the contract will be. She must be given a chance to evaluate what her obligations will be, what the benefit of the contract to her will be, and what her potential responsibility will be if she does not perform the contract as promised. While the offer will probably not explicitly include all of this information, there should be enough clues for the offeree to deduce all of these consequences.

Note that all of the terms or details of the potential contract do not need to be communicated in the offer. It is enough that the essential terms that make up the bargain are communicated. The omitted details can be learned from other sources.

In order to be effective, an offer must be understood by the offeree to be an offer. The offeree must say or do something that manifests his intention to enter into a contract. Mere statements of intention, or a general willingness to do something, will not be an offer. Offers to negotiate or solicitations of bids are likewise not offers to make a contract. They are instead requests for a party to make an offer.

The way the offer is made, or the circumstances under which it is made, must lead a reasonable person to believe that accepting the offer will lead to a valid contract. Whether a statement is a serious effort at making an offer is usually

CONTRACT:
A legally enforceable promise.

OFFER:
A proposal to make a contract.

OFFEREE:
The person to whom an offer is made.

> A solicitation of bids for a large project is a request for offers. The responses sent in by potential vendors are the offers, which the soliciting company can choose to accept or not.

> *Example:* Ruth mentions to her friend Bo that she is planning on looking for a new apartment. Bo replies "Don't bother looking. I have a great apartment in a building I own. It's yours if you want it." Bo does not mention the address of the apartment, or how much rent he would expect Ruth to pay. Bo has not made an offer to Ruth.

> *Example:* Bo tells Ruth he has a one-bedroom apartment available in his building at 5691 Second Avenue, and the rent is $900/month. He says he is willing to give her a one-year lease that he will write up. The written lease form contains additional terms that oblige the tenant to pay all of her own utilities. Bo has made an offer to Ruth, even though all of the terms of the lease were not stated in the offer.

clear from the context. The test is an objective one: would a reasonable person understand that an offer had been made?

> Advertisements are subject to regulation to ensure that they are not unfair or misleading in terms of information about the product or service advertised. Ads are almost never considered to be contractual offers.

Normally, advertisements are not offers. There is an exception to this rule for advertisements that are clear and definite, and that make an explicit offer of a specific type of performance. For example, public announcements of a reward for information leading to the capture of a criminal suspect have been held to be offers. Such an announcement is an offer to make a unilateral contract, in which specific action is promised in exchange for another party's action or forbearance from taking action. An advertisement makes an offer if it leaves nothing open

> *Example:* Matt owns a neighborhood tavern. He has the habit of complaining constantly about how miserable he is running the bar, and how he wishes he could get out of the business. One day, during one of his complaining sessions, he concludes with the statement, "And the next person who gives me $5 has bought himself a bar!" The context of the statement shows that Matt is not making a serious offer.

> **Example:** Matt has decided to retire from operating the bar, and concentrate on another business he owns. He wants to turn the bar over to his son Bob. Matt does not want to give him the business, because he thinks it would sound better for Bob to have purchased the bar "for an undisclosed amount." Matt offers to sell it to him for $1. Matt has made a valid offer. The low price for the sale, in the context in which it was offered, makes it a serious offer.

> **Example:** A department store runs an advertisement in a newspaper saying that it will sell a black lapin (rabbit fur) stole worth $139.50 for $1 to the first customer in line on Saturday morning. The advertisement was an offer. *Lefkowitz v. Great Minneapolis Surplus Store, Inc.*, 251 Minn. 188, 86 N.W.2d 689 (1957).

for negotiation, or is not a solicitation for more offers (such as, an offer to buy a product).

Unless the offer says otherwise, an offer will remain open for a "reasonable time." The definition of a reasonable period of time depends on the circumstances of the offer. It may also depend upon the usages of the trade or community in which the offer was made. As a rule, an offer may be revoked at any time before it is accepted. Revocation occurs when the person making the offer (the **offeror**) tells the offeree that she no longer intends to make a contract. Alternately, an offer is revoked when the offeror does something inconsistent with an intention to enter into the contract. This could include making a second, or additional, offer that is inconsistent

ADVERTISEMENTS ARE NOT OFFERS.

Leonard v. Pepsico, Inc.
(High School Student) v. (Soft Drink Company)
88 F. Supp. 2d 116 (S.D.N.Y. 1999)

INSTANT FACTS:
Leonard (P) claimed that an advertisement was an offer for a sale of a fighter jet.

BLACK LETTER RULE:
An advertisement is not transformed into an enforceable offer merely by a potential offeree's expression of willingness to accept the offer.

FACTS:
Pepsico (D) ran a promotion that offered branded merchandise in exchange for "Pepsi Points." The points were obtained by buying Pepsi products, or the points could be purchased directly for $0.10 each. Leonard (P) saw a television commercial advertising the promotion. The commercial showed various items of merchandise, along with the number of points needed to obtain the item ("T-Shirt 75 Pepsi Points," or "Shades 175 Pepsi Points"). The commercial also showed a teenager riding to school in a Harrier fighter jet. The caption on that part of the advertisement read "Harrier Fighter

7,000,000 Pepsi Points." The commercial also said to see Pepsico's (D) printed catalog for further details. The catalog did not list a Harrier jet as being available under the promotion.

Leonard (P) raised $700,000 to buy the 7 million Pepsi Points. When he submitted his points to Pepsico (D) and said that he expected to receive a Harrier jet, Pepsico (D) turned him down. Leonard (P) sued for breach of contract, and Pepsico (D) moved for summary judgment

ISSUE:

Did the television commercial constitute a valid offer?

DECISION AND RATIONALE:

(Wood, J.) No. An advertisement is not transformed into an enforceable offer merely by a potential offeree's expression of willingness to accept the offer. While a "clear and definite" advertisement that leaves nothing for negotiation may be an offer, there are several reasons why the advertisement in this case does not meet the criteria for an offer.

First, the commercial cannot be regarded in itself as sufficiently definite, because it specifically reserved the details of the offer to the catalog. Second, even if the catalog had included a Harrier Jet among the items that could be obtained, the advertisement merely urged consumers to accumulate Pepsi Points and to refer to the catalog to determine how they could redeem them. The commercial sought a reciprocal promise

The court finds that no objective person could reasonably have concluded that the commercial actually offered consumers a Harrier Jet. If it is clear that an offer was not serious, then no offer has been made: In light of the obvious absurdity of the commercial, the court rejects Leonard's (P) argument that the commercial was not clearly in jest. Summary judgment for Pepsico (D) granted.

ANALYSIS:

This case did not put an end to the use of the Harrier jet in the Pepsi Points promotion. Pepsico (D) updated the commercial to say that the price would be 700 million Pepsi Points.

A Harrier jet is a fighter that can take off and land vertically. At the time of this case, a Harrier cost around $23 million. Federal law would have required stripping a jet of its ability to take off and land vertically before it could have been sold to a civilian.

QUESTIONS FOR DISCUSSION:

Do you think Leonard was serious in his belief he could receive the jet?

Suppose a business runs a point system that is so popular that the business suffers financially from giving away incentives. What may the business do in such a case?

with the terms of the first offer. Revocation is effective when the offeree receives it.

If the terms of the offer state that it will remain open for a specified time, it cannot be revoked before that time. Such an offer is called an option. Some courts and commentators use the terms "option" and "option contract" interchangeably. An option contract, however, must include all of the elements of a contract. It is thus more than just an offer that states it will not be revoked for a period of time.

The power to accept an offer is terminated by:

- Rejecting the offer,

- Making a **counteroffer**,

- Lapse of time,

- Revocation of the offer, or

- Death or incapacity of either the offeror or offeree.

The power to accept is also terminated if a condition of acceptance does not happen. For example, an offer of a reward for being the first person to make a solo ascent of a particular mountain is terminated as soon as someone does it. After that person makes the first ascent, it is no longer possible to be the first one to do it.

Acceptance

Acceptance is the second component of a contract. Without acceptance, there is no contract because there has been no agreement. Acceptance changes an offer into a statement of the terms of a contract. The power to revoke an offer comes to an end when the offer is accepted.

OFFEROR:
The person who makes an offer.

OPTION CONTRACT:
Agreement that allows a party to buy something for a given price at a later date.

COUNTEROFFER:
A response to an offer that proposes different or additional terms.

ACCEPTANCE:
Agreeing to the terms of an offer.

In order to be effective, the acceptance ordinarily must be communicated to the offeror. The unspoken or uncommunicated intention to accept has no effect. The offeree must at least make an attempt to communicate the acceptance.

If the offer does not set a time limit for acceptance, the acceptance must be conveyed within a reasonable time. "Reasonable" is determined according to the circumstances of each situation. Every situation will be different. A good rule of thumb used by many courts is that a reasonable time is the time that a reasonable person in the exact position of the offeree would believe to be satisfactory to the offeror. The purpose of the offeror in making and potentially performing the contract will affect the time allowed for acceptance, if the offeree knows or should know that purpose. A late acceptance is considered a counteroffer.

As a general rule, the acceptance must be an exact acceptance of the terms of the offer. This is known as the "mirror image" rule: the offer and acceptance must be expressions of assent to the same things. To put it another way, an acceptance must do no more than say "yes" to the offer. It must say "yes" unequivocally, and without added conditions. A qualified accep-

Example: The Flugel Street Business Association wants to sponsor an Independence Day fireworks display for the community. On May 15, a representative of the Association contacts the Susquehanna Pyrotechnic Company, asking for a quote. The next day, the Company responds with an offer to put on the show for $5,000. The Association does not make a decision until July 3, when they phone the Pyrotechnic Company to say that the offer is accepted. The acceptance was not communicated in a reasonable time, so it is ineffective as an acceptance.

> *Example:*
> Kris is interested in hiring someone to dig drainage ditches on her property. Fred submits an offer to do the job for $10,000. Fred has a number of other jobs pending, so he needs to be very certain of his commitments. His offer therefore says that "your acceptance of this offer must be received in writing in my office no later than September 10." On September 9, Kris telephones Fred saying that she intends to accept his bid, but would like to know when he will be able to start. Fred tells her that he will be able to start the next week. Kris says that's fine, but sends no additional communication to Fred. Kris has not accepted the offer.

> *Example:*
> Instead of saying that written acceptance "must be received," Fred's offer says "please send your acceptance to me no later than September 10." Kris's phone call on September 9 would probably be a valid acceptance.

tance is a rejection of the offer. The rejected offer cannot then be accepted unconditionally unless the offeror restates that offer.

A counteroffer starts the process all over again. The original offeror becomes the new offeree, and her acceptance is needed to form a contract. No contract is formed if the acceptance includes additional terms, although merely inquiring whether additional or different terms may be included does not constitute a rejection. If the offer is not withdrawn, the offer may still be accepted on its original terms. Similarly, an acceptance is not invalidated if the offeree requests different terms or concessions after accepting the offer. The contract is formed on the basis of the original offer. Note that the Uniform Commercial Code has changed this rule for acceptances of offers for the sale of goods, which will be discussed in the following chapter.

Courts have held that additional terms that are "collateral" to the contract do not turn an acceptance into a counteroffer. The definition of "collateral" will vary, according to the purpose of the contract. In one case, the court held that the request of a purchaser of real estate that the deed be executed in favor of someone other than

> *Example:*
> Lenny, a professional land surveyor, offers to do a survey of George's property for $1,000. George sends Lenny an e-mail that accepts the offer, adding that all work is to be done "competently, to the professional standards of land surveyors in the community." The additional terms were implied in Lenny's original offer, so restating them in the acceptance will not constitute a counteroffer.

RELEASE OF CLAIMS DRAFTED IN RESPONSE TO OFFER TO SETTLE MUST MIRROR THAT OFFER.

Pena v. Fox
(Injured Motorist) v. (Insured Motorist)
198 So.3d 61 (Fla. App. 2015)

Lucas, Judge.

Diana Pena appeals the circuit court's order dismissing her complaint against Matthew Fox with prejudice. Because the circuit court erroneously construed a settlement agreement between the parties where none had been made, we reverse the court's order.

This case invokes a hornbook tenet of contract law: the symmetry needed between an offer and an acceptance to establish an enforceable agreement. Ms. Pena and Mr. Fox were involved in an automobile accident on July 4, 2013, in which Ms. Pena allegedly sustained injuries. Prior to filing a lawsuit, Ms. Pena's counsel delivered a settlement offer to Mr. Fox's insurer, USAA Casualty Insurance Company. In her offer, Ms. Pena requested the policy limits from USAA in exchange for her release of all claims against Mr. Fox relating to the accident. The settlement offer contemplated that USAA would provide a proposed release form for Ms. Pena to execute, but it imposed certain conditions to that form which Ms. Pena's attorney addressed in detail in the offer letter:

> If USAA provides us all the information and funds requested above my [client] will sign a general release releasing all claims .... [M]y clients will sign a general release releasing all claims of my clients only. My clients will not accept, nor will they sign, a release containing a hold harmless nor an indemnity agreement, nor will my client release any claim other than your insured's claim; nor will my client release anyone's claim other than my client's claims [...]

After receiving the offer, USAA tendered a settlement check along with a proposed release to Ms. Pena's counsel. The release prepared by USAA included a prefatory paragraph by which Ms. Pena would acknowledge receipt of the settlement funds and would "release, acquit, and forever discharge Matthew R Fox his/her heirs, executors and assigns, from any liability." USAA's proposed release went on to state the following terms concerning Ms. Pena's release:

> I/We further state that while I/we hereby release all claims against Releasee(s), its agents, and employees, the payment hereunder does not satisfy all of my/our damages resulting from the accident .... I/We further reserve my/our right to pursue and recover all unpaid damages from any person, firm, or organization who may be responsible for payment of such damages, including first party health and automobile insurance coverage, but such reservation does not include the Releasee(s), its agents, and employees ....

Deeming the language "Releasee(s), its agents, and employees" as an attempt to expand the release to include USAA, Ms. Pena considered her prior offer rejected and proceeded to file a lawsuit against Mr. Fox. Mr. Fox responded by filing a Motion to Enforce Settlement, arguing Ms. Pena's complaint should be dismissed because it was barred by a settlement agreement.

[...]

Settlement agreements are governed by contract law. Like any contract, a settlement agreement is formed when there is mutual assent and a "meeting of the minds" between the parties—a condition that requires an offer and an acceptance supported by valid consideration. Florida law further requires that "an acceptance of an offer must be absolute and unconditional, identical with the terms of the offer." That is, the acceptance must be a "mirror image" of the offer in all material respects, or else it will be considered a counteroffer that rejects the original offer. An attempted acceptance can become a counteroffer "either by adding additional terms or not meeting the terms of the original offer."

The release USAA delivered appears to have done both: it added parties beyond those Ms. Pena roposed to release in her original offer, and it materially deviated from the limitation Ms. Pena's offer clearly expressed. The proposed release specifically releases Mr. Fox, his heirs, executors, and assigns in its first paragraph but then in another inexplicably shifts its reference to "Releasee(s)," a term that is nowhere defined within the document. Assuming, as the parties have, that Mr. Fox, his heirs, executors, and assigns, and "Releasees" are all one and the same, USAA's release goes on to expand the latter term to include Mr. Fox's "agents and employees," who are also left undefined and otherwise unidentified within the release. Presumably, the release's inclusion of "agents and employees" meant someone other than the "Releasee(s)" or Matthew R. Fox. Although the incongruity in terms may have been nothing more than boilerplate migrating across computer-generated files, nevertheless, "agents and employees" was a new term, and it was a part of USAA's response to Ms. Pena's offer. And that offer had been explicit: Ms. Pena would not agree to release any party other than Mr. Fox.

While we share the circuit court's view that the inclusion of Mr. Fox's agents and employees within the release was not the product of nefarious motives, USAA's intention when it drafted this document, whatever it might have been, was irrelevant to the issue at hand. Mr. Fox's proposed acceptance would release additional parties, Mr. Fox's agents and employees, which Ms. Pena's offer would not. His acceptance did not mirror her offer.

Reading Ms. Pena's offer and Mr. Fox's acceptance together, we conclude there was no meeting of the minds between these parties, and, thus, there was no settlement agreement that barred Ms. Pena's claims. Accordingly, we reverse the order dismissing the complaint and remand this case for further proceedings.

[Citations and footnotes omitted.]

QUESTIONS FOR DISCUSSION:

In context, what is meant by "boilerplate"? Can you provide other examples of boilerplate?

Do you agree that the insurance company behaved innocently here?

---

the offeree was "collateral," in that the identity of the new owner of the property was immaterial to the seller (*Wallerius v. Hare,* 200 Kan. 578, 438 P.2d 65 (1968)). An acceptance that recites implied terms not set out in the offer is not regarded as adding additional terms to a contract.

If an offer is silent on the subject, acceptance may be communicated in any reasonable way that allows the offeror to infer acceptance. In this context, a "reasonable" manner is one that is customary in similar transactions. An acceptance is also "reasonable" if it is communicated in the same manner as the offer. Acceptance sent via e-mail is reasonable if the offer was sent by e-mail, or if e-mail is commonly used for the type of transaction involved. There is no obligation to respond to an acceptance.

It is not unusual, however, for an offer to limit the manner in which it may be accepted. The offeror has the control over the terms of the offer, so she may set out the time, place, or manner of acceptance. If the offer includes requirements for the acceptance, those requirements must be

---

Example: A newspaper offers home delivery for $10 per week, and Ivan takes out a subscription. The price increases to $11 per week the next year, and Ivan continues to pay. In late November of this year, the newspaper sends a note to subscribers saying that the subscription price will increase on January 1. If Ivan does not cancel his subscription, the newspaper is justified in assuming that he has accepted the offer for the higher price.

> **Example:** After a heavy snowfall, Brian texts his neighbor Tommy to ask if Tommy can shovel the snow from his sidewalk. Brian says he will pay Tommy $15 if he does this job. Tommy does not reply to the text, but goes outside and shovels the walk. Tommy has accepted Brian's offer.

> **Example:** Tommy is outside shoveling his own sidewalk when Brian sends his text. He does not see the text, because he has left his phone inside. Tommy decides to shovel Brian's sidewalk anyway, as a neighborly gesture. Tommy has not accepted Brian's offer.

followed. If the requirements are not followed, the offer is deemed rejected. The question of whether an offer states a requirement for a method of acceptance, or merely a preference or suggestion, is sometimes open to interpretation. If the terms of the offer are clear and definite, then those terms must be followed. If there is any room for interpretation, courts will ask if the acceptance was reasonable.

In most cases, silence will not be construed as an acceptance. There are four exceptions to this general rule:

- Where goods are delivered or services performed under circumstances that make it clear they are not sent as a gift, and the goods are not rejected even though the recipient has the opportunity to do so,

- When the offeree takes or retains offered property, or acts in a way inconsistent with the offeror's ownership,

- When the offeror says that silence or inaction will be acceptance, and the offeree is silent, or fails to act, intending to accept the offer, or

- When the prior dealings of the parties make it clear that the offeree intends for silence to be acceptance.

Acceptance may also be made by performing the contract. It must be clear that the offer invites acceptance by performance, or that acceptance by performance is allowed. The performance must be in a way that shows it is intended as acceptance of the offer. Notification of the acceptance is not necessary unless the offeree has reason to know that the offeror has no convenient way of ascertaining that performance has taken place. In most cases in which acceptance may be by performance, the offeror will know of the acceptance when it happens, or shortly after it happens.

Consideration

Consideration is the ingredient that must be added to an offer and acceptance to make a contract. Without consideration, a contract is just an unenforceable promise to make a gift.

Consideration is explained in many different ways. It can best be thought of as something that

Example: A radio station stages a promotional event during halftime at a basketball game. The station offers $100 to anyone present at the game who can sink three free-throws in a row. Amanda steps up and sinks three consecutive free-throws. She has accepted the offer by her performance, and she is not obligated to give formal notification of her performance.

Example: Gertrude's Natural Pet Remedies offers $10,000 to anyone who cat has a hair ball after being dosed with Gertrude's Cat Tonic for three months. Shirley starts dosing her cat Ziggy with the tonic as directed on the bottle it comes in. Shirley has started her performance, and has accepted Gertrude's offer. She is not obligated to notify Gertrude's unless Ziggy has a hair ball.

CONSIDERATION:
A bargained for exchange; a legal detriment entered into as an exchange.

A statute in California defines consideration as a "benefit conferred, or agreed to be conferred, upon the promisor, by any other person, to which the promisor is not lawfully entitled, or any prejudice suffered, or agreed to be suffered, by such person, other than such as he is at the time of consent lawfully bound to suffer, as an inducement to the promisor . . ." Cal. Civ. Code § 1605.

you bargain for and that you give in return for something else. It is the reason, or the motive, for entering into the contract. Something of value has to flow from each party to the other.

The things exchanged do not have to have monetary value. Mutual promises may be consideration, as long as the promises are something that is possible for each party to do. The creation or termination of a legal relation may be consideration. Actually doing something that a person is not otherwise required to do may be consideration, if that behavior was induced by the contract.

Similarly, not doing something that a person has the right to do may also be consideration. This type of consideration is referred to as a legal detriment. The detriment does not mean

Example: Lou goes into a grocery store and takes a can of lima beans off the shelf. He gives the cashier $1.50 (the price marked on the can) and takes the lima beans out of the store. There was a contract to sell the lima beans. The consideration was the payment of $1.50 in exchange for the beans.

> **Example:** Eric tells his nephew Nick that he will pay him $1,000 if he gets a "decent" haircut and has his beard trimmed. Nick goes immediately to his barber and has his beard trimmed to a half-inch. He also has his man-bun cut off. Nick's haircut and beard trim are legal detriments, and are Nick's consideration for a contract with his uncle.

> **Example:** Eric never tires of telling Nick how much he disapproves of his appearance. Nick goes for a haircut and beard trim, hoping that Eric will be favorably impressed and offer him a job at the business he owns. The haircut and beard trim are not consideration, since they are not in exchange for any promise by Eric.

that a person's promise is harmful or disadvantageous to them. The "detriment" could, in fact, be something helpful or beneficial. It is also not important that the person receiving the performance gets no benefit from the doing or not-doing of the action. The detriment is just something that would not have happened in the absence of the agreement. The key requirement

FORBEARANCE OR GIVING UP SOME LEGAL RIGHT IS GOOD CONSIDERATION TO SUPPORT A PROMISE.

Hamer v. Sidway
(Assignee of Right of Nephew) v. (Executor of Uncle)
124 N.Y. 538, 27 N.E. 256 (1891)

INSTANT FACTS:
William E. Story Sr. (D) promised his nephew, William E. Story Jr. (P), that he would pay William Jr. $5,000 if William Jr. would refrain from drinking, using tobacco, swearing, and gambling, until William Jr. was 21 years of age, which William Jr. did.

BLACK LETTER RULE:
The party who abandons some legal right in the present or limits his legal freedom of action in the future as an inducement for a promise, gives sufficient consideration to create a legally binding contract.

PROCEDURAL BASIS:
An appeal from the Supreme Court reversing the trial court judgment that awarded judgment for Hamer (P), the assignee, against Sidway (D), the executor.

FACTS:
On March 20, 1869, William E. Story, Sr. (D) promised William E. Story, Jr. (P) that if William Jr. would refrain from drinking, using tobacco, swearing, and playing cards or billiards for money until William Jr. became 21 years of age, William Sr. would pay him $5,000. On January 31, 1875, after William Jr. (P) had become 21 years old, William Jr. wrote his uncle, William Sr. (D), and informed him that he had performed his part of the agreement and was entitled to the $5,000. William Sr. (D) wrote his nephew back and stated that "I have no doubt but you have, for which you shall have five thousand dollars as I promised you." However, William Sr. insisted that William Sr. continue to

keep the money in the bank for William Jr. until William Jr. was capable of making good decisions about the use of the money, when he would then receive the $5,000 with interest. William Jr. (P) agreed to these terms. On January 29, 1887, William Sr. (D) died without having paid William Jr. (P) the $5,000 and interest. William Jr.'s right was subsequently assigned to Hamer, the plaintiff, who sued William Sr.'s executor, Sidway, the defendant in this action.

ISSUE:
Is forbearance to do that for which one has a legal right to do sufficient consideration to support a promise made to induce the forbearance?

DECISION AND RATIONALE:
(Parker) Yes. A valuable consideration in the sense of the law may consist either in some right interest, profit, or benefit accruing to the one party, or some forbearance, detriment, loss, or responsibility given, suffered, or undertaken by the other. The forbearance does not have to benefit the promises or a third party, or have any substantial value to anyone. It is enough that something is promised, done, forborne, or suffered by the party to whom the promise is made as consideration for the promise made to him. William Jr. (P) used tobacco, occasionally drank liquor, and he had a legal right to do so. He abandoned these rights for a period of years upon the strength of William Sr.'s (D) promise that for such forbearance William Sr. would give him $5,000. It is not of any legal importance whether or not the forbearance benefitted William Sr. (D). The judgment of the Supreme Court is reversed and the special term judgment for plaintiff, Hamer, is affirmed.

ANALYSIS:
The waiver of the legal right in this case was clearly induced by the promise of the uncle. The court pointed out that the consideration given may in fact have benefitted the nephew even more than the uncle. However, the degree of benefit is not measured by the court to determine the validity of a contract. The determining factor is that William Sr. (D) "bargained" for the surrender of William Jr.'s (P) legal right to drink alcohol, use tobacco, and gamble. The abandonment of these rights may have saved William Jr. (P) money or contributed to his health; nevertheless, this same abandonment, when bargained for, is sufficient consideration to uphold the promise.

is that what is done, or not done, is an exchange for something.

A "moral obligation," meaning a promise to do something because it is the right thing to do, is not consideration. A moral obligation does not involve an exchange, and the person who is morally obligated does not receive anything in return for her performance. Promising to do something that is already required is also not consideration. There is no legal detriment in doing something a person is already required to do. If there is a dispute about a person's legal obligations, however, doing what would be required under that obligation may be consideration. In those cases, the legal detriment is not in doing the act, but in refraining from contesting the obligation to do it. Agreements to settle a lawsuit frequently state that there is no admission of fault by either party, so there is

Example: When Khalid and Marta get divorced, the final decree orders Khalid to sign ownership of their house to Marta within 90 days. In return, Marta is to transfer some mutual funds owned by the parties to Khalid. When Marta asks Khalid for the deed to the house, Khalid requests an additional $5,000. In return, he will sign over the house. Khalid's promise to sign over the house is not consideration for an agreement for Marta to pay any additional money.

Example:

After 90 days, Khalid learns that Marta liquidated some of the mutual fund shares to pay for her divorce lawyer. Khalid claims he is no longer obligated to sign he house over, but says he will do it if Marta pays him $5,000 as compensation for the shares she liquidated. Khalid's consideration is his agreement to refrain from contesting his obligation to sign over the house.

GOOD FAITH FORBEARANCE OF A CLAIM MAY SERVE AS CONSIDERATION.

Dyer v. National By-products, Inc.
(Former Employee) v. (Employer)
380 N.W.2d 732 (Iowa 1986)

SCHULTZ, Justice.

The determinative issue in this appeal is whether good faith forbearance to litigate a claim, which proves to be invalid and unfounded, is sufficient consideration to uphold a contract of settlement.

On October 29, 1981, Dale Dyer, an employee of National By-Products, lost his right foot in a job-related accident. Thereafter, the employer placed Dyer on a leave of absence at full pay from the date of his injury until August 16, 1982. At that time he returned to work as a foreman, the job he held prior to his injury. On March 11, 1983, the employer indefinitely laid off Dyer.

Dyer then filed the present lawsuit against his employer claiming that his discharge was a breach of an oral contract. He alleged that he in good faith believed that he had a valid claim against his employer for his personal injury. Further, Dyer claimed that his forbearance from litigating his claim was made in exchange for a promise from his employer that he would have lifetime employment. The employer specifically denied that it had offered a lifetime job to Dyer after his injury.

Preliminarily, we observe that the law favors the adjustment and settlement of controversies without resorting to court action. . . . The more difficult problem is whether the settlement of an unfounded claim asserted in good faith is consideration for a contract of settlement. Professor Corbin presents a view favorable to Dyer's argument when he states:

> [F]orbearance to press a claim, or a promise of such forbearance, may be a sufficient consideration even though the claim is wholly ill-founded. It may be ill-founded because the facts are not what he supposes them to be, or because the existing facts do not have the legal operation that he supposes them to have. In either case, his forbearance may be a sufficient consideration, although under certain circumstances it is not. The fact that the claim is ill-founded is not in itself enough to prevent forbearance from being a sufficient consideration for a promise.

Further, in the same section, it is noted that:

> The most generally prevailing, and probably the most satisfactory view is that forbearance is sufficient if there is any reasonable ground for the claimant's belief that it is just to try to enforce his claim. He must be asserting his claim "in good faith"; but this does not mean he must believe that his suit can be won. It means that he must not be making his claim or threatening suit for purposes of vexation, or in order to realize on its "nuisance value."

The Restatement (Second) of Contracts . . . supports the Corbin view and states:

Settlement of Claims

(1) Forbearance to assert or the surrender of a claim or defense which proves to be invalid is not consideration unless

(a) the claim or defense is in fact doubtful because of uncertainty as to the facts or the law, or

(b) the forbearing or surrendering party believes that the claim or defense may be fairly determined to be valid.

Comment: Requirement of good faith. The policy favoring compromise of disputed claims is clearest, perhaps, where a claim is surrendered at a time when it is uncertain whether it is valid or not. Even though the invalidity later becomes clear, the bargain is to be judged as it appeared to the parties at the time; if the claim was then doubtful, no inquiry is necessary as to their good faith. Even though the invalidity should have been clear at the time, the settlement of an honest dispute is upheld. But a mere assertion or denial of liability does not make a claim doubtful, and the fact that invalidity is obvious may indicate that it was known. [Such cases require] a showing of good faith.

However, not all jurisdictions adhere to this view. Some courts require that the claim forborne must have some merit in fact or at law before it can provide consideration and these jurisdictions reject those claims that are obviously invalid. . . . In fact, we find language in our own case law that supports the view which is favorable to the employer in this case. . . . Additionally, Professor Williston notes that:

While there is a great divergence of opinion respecting the kind of forbearance which will constitute consideration, the weight of authority holds that although forbearance from suit on a clearly invalid claim is insufficient consideration for a promise, forbearance from suit on a claim of doubtful validity is sufficient consideration for a promise if there is a sincere belief in the validity of the claim.

We believe, however, that the better reasoned approach is that expressed in the Restatement (Second) of Contracts[.] Even the above statement from Williston, although it may have been the state of the law in 1957, is a questionable assessment of the current law. . . . As noted before, as a matter of policy the law favors compromise and such policy would be defeated if a party could second guess his settlement and litigate the validity of the compromise. The requirement that the forbearing party assert the claim in good faith sufficiently protects the policy of law that favors the settlement of controversies. [...]

In the present case, the invalidity of Dyer's claim against the employer does not foreclose him, as a matter of law, from asserting that his forbearance was consideration for the alleged contract of settlement. However, the issue of Dyer's good faith must still be examined. In so doing, the issue of the validity of Dyer's claim should not be entirely overlooked:

. . . [T]here must generally be reasonable grounds for a belief in order for the court to be convinced that the belief was honestly entertained by the person who asserted it. Sufficient consideration requires more than the bald assertion by a claimant who has a claim, and to the extent that the validity or invalidity of a claim has a bearing upon whether there were reasonable grounds for believing in its possible validity, evidence of the validity or invalidity of a claim may be relevant to the issue of good faith.

[...]

Under the present state of the record, there remains a material fact as to whether Dyer's forbearance to assert his claim was in good faith . . . the case is reversed and remanded for further proceedings consistent with this opinion.

[Citations and footnotes omitted.]

ANALYSIS:

This decision provides a good example of how judges evaluate the status of the common law. The professors that the court cites are cited from "hornbooks" that discuss how the law has been applied on various issues by a large number of courts. The Restatement is written by the American Law Institute. There are a number of Restatements on different topics, including contracts. These books "restate" legal rules on the topic. Here, the court was more persuaded by the Restatement's explanation of the law on consideration in similar circumstances. Omitted portions of the decision showed that there were Iowa rulings that came down on separate sides of the argument; the state supreme court expressly overruled the cases that did not follow the Restatement view.

QUESTIONS FOR DISCUSSION:

How could the hornbooks and the Restatement reach different conclusions?

If Dyer had a potential claim, how would he know if he would succeed or not? Is that relevant to agreeing not to proceed with the claim? What do you think the court means by "good faith" in this decision?

How do you prove an oral contract?

no pre-existing legal obligation to do whatever the agreement requires. The legal detriment comes from doing what is not already an obligation, in exchange for giving up the legal right to continue to pursue a claim.

If there is an exchange, the adequacy of the consideration is not important. As long as there is an exchange, it does not matter that the value of one party's performance is disproportionate to the value of the other party's.

This is referred to as the "peppercorn" theory of consideration. Under this theory, even a single peppercorn will be valid consideration for a contract. Written contracts often are drafted to recite some nominal consideration, even though the actual price to be paid is much higher. This may be done to conceal the true price paid, or to create a binding contract when the parties are not concerned about the value of the exchange. An option contract, for example, may recite that "for $1 and other good and valuable consideration" a seller agrees to allow a buyer to make a formal offer to purchase property at a later

> Disproportionate values may be evidence of some other defect in the contract, such as fraud. There is some truth in the phrase "too good to be true."

There is a distinction made between the "adequacy" of consideration and the "sufficiency" of consideration. "Adequacy" refers to the question of whether the amount of consideration is a fair exchange. As noted, the adequacy of the consideration is not important.

The "sufficiency" of consideration is different from the adequacy. Sufficiency is the question of whether the consideration was in fact delivered as promised. If the consideration is not paid, or a promise is not performed, this is a "failure" of consideration. A failure of consideration means that the consideration was, for some reason, not transferred. If there has been a failure of consideration, there has been a breach of contract. Some courts have held that a written contract that says that consideration was paid creates a

> **Example:** Leo and Molly own a house that they rent to tenants. When their son Stephen graduates from college, they want to let him have the house. In order to avoid gift tax liability, Leo and Molly sell him the house for $10. The $10 is sufficient consideration for the sale.

date. In return, the seller agrees not to solicit or accept any other offers to purchase the property unless the buyer does not purchase it within the agreed-upon time period. The value of the property, and perhaps the value of the option, is almost always far more than $1.

> Consideration that is not a fair exchange will not, by itself, render a contract unenforceable. It may, however, be evidence of some other wrongdoing or defect that could make a contract voidable, such as fraud or undue influence.

presumption that it was in fact paid. The statement of consideration may be a simple recitation of the words "for value received." Unless there is contrary proof, the court will say that consideration was paid and not consider the issue further.

While consideration is bargained for, and is essential to every contract, it is not necessarily the same thing as the motive or inducement for a

PROMISSORY ESTOPPEL:

Legal doctrine converting a promise to a contract if injustice would otherwise result.

contract. A person may be induced or motivated to sell property by the hope of making a profit on the transaction. If she should, for whatever reason, agree to sell the property for a price that

means she only breaks even, the transaction is still supported by consideration.

Promissory Estoppel: There is an exception to the rule that a contract requires an exchange of consideration. That exception is known as **promissory estoppel** (also called "detrimental reliance" in some courts). Promissory estoppel lets a promise not made as a part of an exchange substitute for an exchange of consideration. It arises in contexts where there is traditionally no bargain made for performance.

Promissory estoppel will make a promise legally binding when:

- There is a promise,

- The promise is of a type that would induce a person to do something, or not to do something,

- The promise does induce that action or inaction, and

Example: An agreement to buy a house says that the promise is made "for $1 and other good and valuable consideration." Unless the seller can show that there was no real payment of consideration beyond the recitation, a court will acknowledge that there was consideration paid.

Example: Martin, a wealthy businessman, announces that he is making a $1 million gift to the local opera company. He makes this announcement at a press conference at which he shares the stage with the opera's director and two of its star performers. The opera company decides that the promised gift will allow it to commission a new work, so it arranges to pay a well-known composer $500,000 for two new operas. Martin, however, does not follow through on his gift. The opera company may be able to enforce his promise on the basis of promissory estoppel.

- It is necessary to enforce the promise in order to avoid an injustice.

Promissory estoppel can make a promise enforceable even when there is no explicit agreement. However, some courts have held that promissory estoppel applies only in cases in which the promised performance was requested. In order for promissory estoppel to apply, the promise must have been expected to induce action or inaction of a definite type.

Contracts Under Seal: At common law, a contract "under seal" did not have to be supported by consideration. The seal may have been some substance affixed to the document. In the few jurisdictions that recognize the effect of a seal, it may be a written or printed word or symbol.

The effect of the seal was to make a document's validity as a contract indisputable. An agreement was a binding contract if it:

- Was in writing,
- Had a seal affixed,
- Was delivered, and
- Named or identified the parties to the transaction.

The legal effect of the seal has been abolished in most jurisdictions, either by court decision or by statute.

Capacity

Capacity refers to a person's legal ability to make a contract. If a person does not have capacity, they are legally incapable of making a binding agreement. Any contract entered into by a person without legal capacity will be void.

There are several reasons for concluding that a person does not have legal capacity. One is mental defect or illness. If a person has a mental defect that prevents them from understanding the nature and consequences of their actions, a contract they enter into will be voidable. This is a different matter from saying that a person is not very intelligent, or that they are old or in ill health. Similarly, a lack of education or even illiteracy will not constitute a lack of mental capacity. The mental defect must be a substantial one that prevents understanding. It does not matter that the other party to the contract does not know of the mental defect.

CAPACITY:
The legal ability to make a contract.

Example: Rhea is in a car accident and suffers severe head trauma. The trauma has affected her mentally, so that her doctor has concluded that she has the mental abilities of a 10-year-old child. Billy, an aspiring filmmaker, has Rhea sign an agreement that allows Billy to make an "inspiring" documentary about Rhea and how she has managed her injuries. Rhea probably does not have the capacity to make such an agreement.

There is a presumption that every person has the mental capacity to make a contract. A lack of capacity must be proven by the party claiming a lack of capacity. The proof must show that the allegedly incompetent person was incapable of transacting the business involved in the contract. Appointment of a guardian over a person will usually be the same as a court finding that a person lacked mental capacity.

A person who is voluntarily intoxicated may also be found to lack capacity. The intoxication must be such that the person is incapable of knowing what he was doing, or of understanding the consequences of his acts. In those cases, a contract will be voidable only if the other party either caused the intoxication, or knew or had reason to know of the extent of the inability to act reasonably. This test applies only to voluntary intoxication, or people who are impaired after taking "recreational" drugs. A person who was intoxicated involuntarily, or who is taking medication that affects their thought processes, are treated as having a mental impairment.

It is assumed that an adult will have legal capacity, unless proven otherwise. A minor, defined as a person under the age of majority (generally 18), does not have capacity, however intelligent or sophisticated she may be. The minor's lack of capacity is different from other forms of incapacity. Contracts made by minors are unenforceable against the minor at the minor's option. This is true even if the minor misrepresented his age when making the contract. The minor or the minor's guardian, on the other hand, may enforce the contract against the other party. Minors may also be obligated to pay for necessities of life (food, shelter, or clothing) that are sold to them.

If a minor disaffirms a contract, or declares that he will no longer be bound by it, any property sold to him under the contract is returned to the seller. If the contract is for services, or if property sold cannot be returned, some courts have held that the minor must pay the reasonable value of the property or services received. The reasonable value is not necessarily the same amount that would be awarded as damages in a suit for breach of contract. Since a contract with a minor is voidable, the minor may in effect declare that there was no contract, and that he therefore cannot be in breach. Payment is awarded to the party who rendered performance on a theory of *quantum meruit* ("as much as she has deserved").

The rules regarding incapacity of minors applies only to unemancipated minors. Roughly half of the states provide for a judicial procedure for minors to have themselves declared emanci-

Example:	Reggie is 17 years old, and lives in a state where the age of majority is 18. He wants to throw a birthday party for his girlfriend, so he tells a caterer he is 18, and hires the caterer to supply food for the party. After the party, Reggie does not pay, and the caterer tries to collect from him. Reggie may disaffirm the contract, and avoid paying the full price, but he still may be liable for the value of the food supplied.

> **Example:**
> Kenneth offers Dana 10 grams of cocaine if she will do some electrical work on his house. Dana agrees. Since cocaine is an illegal drug, this contract is not legally enforceable.

> **Example:**
> Tura lives in a state in which the legal age for buying liquor is 18. When she turns 18, she orders several cases of wine for a party she intends to give in three months. A month after Tura places her order, the state legislature meets and raises the legal drinking age to 20. The contract to buy the wine is now illegal and may not be enforced.

pated. In the remaining states, a minor is automatically emancipated if he marries or joins the Armed Forces. An emancipated minor is treated for most purposes as an adult. He has the legal capacity to enter into contracts, and those contracts are not voidable due to age.

Legality

One of the basic principles of contract law is the idea of freedom of contract. This idea holds that we are free to make any contract that we want. This freedom is subject to the limitation that the subject of the contract must be legal. A contract that calls for someone to do something illegal is not enforceable. Illegality does not always mean that the contract calls for the commission of a crime. In many states, usury laws make it unlawful for a lender to charge interest over a certain amount to some borrowers. A contract that does charge an excessive rate of interest is

> An agreement to engage in illegal activity is a conspiracy.

often made void, but the charging of the interest is not in itself a crime.

Illegality does not automatically make a contract illegal and unenforceable. Most courts will look at the benefits of enforcing the contract, compared with the value of deterring the conduct that is prohibited. If the contract calls for actions that are not in themselves wrong or immoral, but are unlawful only because a statute or regulation makes them unlawful (*malum prohibitum*). In those cases, courts will generally allow recovery under the contract unless the law proscribing the unlawful contract states that such contracts will be unenforceable.

A number of courts have held that the rule against enforcement of illegal contracts applies only when both parties are at fault.

There are many statutes that do not prohibit certain activities, but that say that contracts made in violation of some of the terms of the statute will be unenforceable. For example, in most jurisdictions, a license is required to do heating and air conditioning work. The licensing statute may state that a contract to do such work

> *Example:* Federal agricultural regulations stated that contracts for the sale of peanuts to a processor must include a final price, and that price could not be changed. A contract that did not contain those terms was enforceable against the processor was enforceable, because the law allowed contracts to sell peanuts, and the federal laws and regulations did not make agreements without a final price term unenforceable. *Golden Peanut Co. v. Bass,* 275 Ga. 145, 563 S.E.2d 116 (2002).

by a person who is unlicensed is not enforceable. The heating and air conditioning work is not illegal, but doing it without a license is.

It is possible that the performance of a contract could become illegal after the agreement was made. In that case, performance of the contract may be excused. The contract was legal when made, but may not be enforced because performance would now be illegal. The U.S. Constitution, however, prohibits states from passing laws "impairing the Obligation of Contracts". The original purpose of this clause (Article I, section 10, clause 1) was to prohibit states from passing "private relief" laws that excused certain individuals from performing contracts. The U.S. Supreme Court held that a state law that retroactively impairs a contractual obligation is constitutional if the state has a "significant and legitimate public purpose" for the regulation. The purpose may include dealing with a social or economic problem. A law that enacts a general requirement, such as a criminal statute, will not be a violation of the Constitution.

Unconscionability:

The principle of freedom of contract generally allows adults to enter into any type of contract they choose. If one of those parties makes a bad deal, she is stuck with it. Courts have, however, often refused to enforce agreements deemed unconscionable.

There is no clear, all-purpose definition of unconscionability. The question is determined on a case-by-case basis. When considering whether a contract is unconscionable, the courts will look at:

- The relative benefit of the bargain to the parties when the contract was made,

- The methods used to negotiate the contract, and

- The relative bargaining power of the parties.

An unconscionability analysis is made up of two parts: substantive unconscionability, and procedural unconscionability. Both types of unconscionability must be present before a court will decline to enforce a contract.

Substantive unconscionability relates to the content of the contract. The issue is whether the contract terms are so unfair and unreasonable as to be unconscionable. A substantively unconscionable contract may have a clause or term that is totally one-sided or overly harsh, so that it oppresses or unfairly surprises an innocent party. Such a clause or term will create an overall imbalance in the obligations and rights under the agreement. The contract may also include a significant cost-price disparity, meaning that the price paid for the benefit of the agreement is significantly higher than the cost of providing that benefit. A contract term may also be held substantively unconscionable if it reallocates the risks of the bargain in an objectively unreasonable or unexpected way.

Procedural unconscionability looks at the relative bargaining power of the contracting parties, and the manner in which the agreement was reached. Courts will analyze the respective bargaining power of the contracting parties, and the ability of the particular contracting party. Factors that will be considered include a party's ability to understand the terms of the contract. Other factors that are considered include the use of high pressure tactics, the sophistication or wealth of the parties, the relative scarcity of the subject matter of the contract, the age of the parties, who drafted the contract, whether the terms were explained to the weaker party, and whether a pre-printed contract could be altered. Procedural unconscionability exists when the weaker party has no realistic alternative except to accept the term in question. If a party was free to accept or reject the term, there was no procedural unconscionability.

Despite these factors, courts are generally unwilling to find that a contract is unconscionable. The circumstances surrounding the agreement must be balanced against the freedom to enter into contracts. As a result, rulings of unconscionability are relatively rare.

II. Contract Formation

The elements of a contract are like the ingredients of a recipe. They are what you need to make it, but there remains the question of how all of the ingredients or elements go together. In contracts, if not in cooking, the answer to the question should be an easy one: the offer tells everyone involved what they are supposed to do. The idea is to give effect to the intent behind the making of the contract. When there are disputes about who is to do what, or when they are supposed to do it, the courts look for some evidence from which the intent of the parties can be deduced.

Written v. Oral

One of the common misunderstandings that people have about contract law is that a contract is not valid if it is not in writing. This simply is not true. Your purchase of a cup of coffee in the morning is a valid contract, yet it is not in writing. An oral agreement that has all of the elements of offer, acceptance, consideration, capacity, and legality will, with some exceptions, be a valid and binding contract.

Oral agreements that involve any type of transaction except the simplest ones face the inherent problem of proof. The proof problem is the basic one of proving that an agreement ever existed in the first place. It also involves the more complex one of proving what the terms of that agreement are. The terms of the agreement need to be proven with reasonable certainty, and in enough detail to determine the rights and obligations of each party and the conditions of performance. Oral agreements, by their very nature, invite

> *Example:* In 1984, a jury in Cook County, Illinois, found that the McDonald's Corporation breached a "handshake" non-written agreement with the Central Ice Cream Co. to distribute Central's "Triple Ripple" ice cream cones for 20 years. The jury awarded damages of $52 million. The case later settled for $15.5 million.

disputes about the meanings of terms, especially when one party will be considered to have performed his obligations.

There are exceptions to the general rule that a contract need not be in writing. Unless a contract falls into one of these exceptions, an oral contract is still valid and enforceable.

Note that, while some contracts are not enforceable unless they are in writing, the reverse is not true. There is no species of contract that is unenforceable if it is in writing. Even if a particular transaction does not require one, a written contract has the advantage of making it easier to prove what the parties intended to accomplish by their agreement.

STATUTE OF FRAUDS:
A law that states that certain types of contract are not enforceable unless they are in writing.

ANTENUPTIAL AGREEMENTS:
A pre-marital contract in which the parties agree on issues like the disposition of property after death or dissolution of the marriage

Statute of Frauds

There are some exceptions the general rule that non-written contracts are valid. Some types of contracts must be in writing or they are unenforceable. The main exception is known as the **Statute of Frauds**. The Statute of Frauds says that certain types of contracts will not be enforced unless there is a writing memorializing the contract.

As it now exists, the Statute of Frauds has little, if anything, to do with fraud. The original version of the Statute was enacted in England, in the 17th century. Before that time, testimony in contract lawsuits was given by hired experts who had no connection with the case except as a witness in court. These experts would testify to whatever the party hired them wanted to hear, regardless of whether it was true. In order to prevent this type of fraud on the courts, the Statute was enacted to require written evidence of the terms of certain types of contracts. The Statute, or variations on the Statute, has been adopted in almost every U.S. jurisdiction.

The traditional formulation of the Statute of Frauds provides that the following types of contracts may not be enforced unless there is some writing that evidences the agreement:

- Contracts in consideration of marriage, such as **antenuptial agreements**,

- Contracts that, by their terms, cannot be performed within one year,

- Contracts to sell an interest in land,

- Contracts by an executor or personal representative of an estate to pay an estate debt with her own money,

> Promises to marry are now generally legally unenforceable.

- Contracts for the sale of goods (not services) for $500 or more, and

- Contracts to answer for or guarantee another person's debts.

Several other statutes or regulations may require a written agreement in order to be effective. For example, a transfer of a copyright must be in writing, regardless of the price or value of the transfer.

The definitions of contracts that fall under the requirements of the Statute are read strictly. For example, a contract that will probably take more than one year to perform are not required to be in writing as "contracts that, by their terms, cannot be performed within one year." If there is any way possible for a contract to be performed in less than one year, the agreement will not come within this provision.

The Statute does not require an exhaustive, integrated statement of the agreement in writing. All that is necessary is a sufficient statement to establish that there in fact was an agreement and that the party charged with performance should be bound by it. The writing must have been signed by the party against whom the contract is being enforced. The signature can be any symbol intended to show agreement. It

Example: Hector, who is 65 years old and in generally good health, tells his niece Ana that he will pay her $15,000 per year, plus all of her living expenses, if she agrees to be his full-time caregiver for the rest of his life. Although it is likely that Hector will live for more than one year, it is possible that he could die before that. Ana's obligations under the contract could be fully performed in less than one year.

Example: In order to clear the title to some property owned by their family, Delta is willing to transfer her interest in the property to her brother Billy. She sends him a letter that says "I agree to sell you my interest in the property our parents owned at 123 Sycamore Street, Hometown City, for $1." She signs the letter with her full name. The letter meets the requirements of the Statute of Frauds.

Fuld, J.

In September of 1947, Nate Crabtree entered into preliminary negotiations with Elizabeth Arden Sales Corporation, manufacturers and sellers of cosmetics, looking toward his employment as sales manager. . . . Crabtree requested a three-year contract at $25,000 a year. . . . And he repeated his desire for a contract for three years to Miss Elizabeth Arden, the corporation's president. When Miss Arden finally indicated that she was prepared to offer a two-year contract, based on an annual salary of $20,000 for the first six months, $25,000 for the second six months and $30,000 for the second year, plus expenses of $5,000 a year for each of those years, Crabtree replied that that offer was "interesting". Miss Arden thereupon had her personal secretary make this memorandum on a telephone order blank that happened to be at hand:

"EMPLOYMENT AGREEMENT WITH NATE CRABTREE Date Sept 26-1947 At 681 — 5th Ave 6: PM * * * Begin 20000. 6 months 25000. 6 " 30000. 5000. — per year Expense money [2 years to make good] Arrangement with Mr Crabtree By Miss Arden Present Miss Arden Mr John Mr Crabtree Miss OLeary"

A few days later, Crabtree 'phoned Mr. Johns and telegraphed Miss Arden; he accepted the "invitation to join the Arden organization", and Miss Arden wired back her "welcome". When he reported for work, a "pay-roll change" card was made up and initialed by Mr. Johns, and then forwarded to the payroll department. Reciting that it was prepared on September 30, 1947, and was to be effective as of October 22d, it specified the names of the parties, Crabtree's "Job Classification" and, in addition, contained the notation that "This employee is to be paid as follows:

"First six months of employment $20,000. per annum

Next six months of employment   25,000. "   "

After one year of employment   30,000. "   "

Approved by   RPJ [initialed]"

After six months of employment, Crabtree received the scheduled increase from $20,000 to $25,000, but the further specified increase at the end of the year was not paid. Both Mr. Johns and the comptroller of the corporation, Mr. Carstens, told Crabtree that they would attempt to straighten out the matter with Miss Arden, and, with that in mind, the comptroller prepared another "pay-roll change" card, to which his signature is appended, noting that there was to be a "Salary increase" from $25,000 to $30,000 a year, "per contractual arrangements with Miss Arden". The latter, however, refused to approve the increase and, after further fruitless discussion, plaintiff left defendant's employ and commenced this action for breach of contract.

At the ensuing trial, defendant denied the existence of any agreement to employ plaintiff for two years, and further contended that, even if one had been made, the statute of frauds barred its enforcement. [...]

Each of the two payroll cards — the one initialed by defendant's general manager, the other signed by its comptroller — unquestionably constitutes a memorandum under the statute. That they were not prepared or signed with the intention of evidencing the contract, or that they came into existence subsequent to its execution, is of no consequence; it is enough, to meet the statute's demands, that they were signed with intent to authenticate the information contained therein and that such information does evidence the terms of the contract. Those two writings contain all of the essential terms of the contract — the parties to it, the position that plaintiff was to assume, the salary that he was to receive — except that relating to the duration of plaintiff's employment. Accordingly, we must consider whether that item, the length of the contract, may be supplied by reference to the earlier unsigned office memorandum, and, if so, whether its notation, "2 years to make good", sufficiently designates a period of employment.

The statute of frauds does not require the "memorandum * * * to be in one document. It may be pieced together out of separate writings, connected with one another either expressly or by the internal evidence of subject matter and occasion". Where each of the separate writings has been subscribed by the party to be charged, little if any difficulty is encountered. Where, however, some writings have been signed, and others have not — as in the case before us — there is basic disagreement as to what constitutes a sufficient connection permitting the unsigned papers to be considered as part of the statutory memorandum. The courts of some jurisdictions insist that there be a reference, of varying degrees of specificity, in the signed writing to that unsigned, and, if there is no such reference, they refuse to permit consideration of the latter in determining whether the memorandum satisfies the statute. That conclusion is based upon a construction of the statute which requires that the connection between the writings and defendant's acknowledgment of the one not subscribed, appear from examination of the papers alone, without the aid of parol evidence. The other position — which has gained increasing support over the years — is that a sufficient connection between the papers is established simply by a reference in them to the same subject matter or transaction. The statute is not pressed "to the extreme of a literal and rigid logic", and oral testimony is admitted to show the connection between the documents and to establish the acquiescence, of the party to be charged, to the contents of the one unsigned.

The view last expressed impresses us as the more sound, and . . . this court has on a number of occasions approved the rule, and we now definitively adopt it, permitting the signed and unsigned writings to be read together, provided that they clearly refer to the same subject matter or transaction.

The language of the statute — "Every agreement * * * is void, unless * * * some note or memorandum thereof be in writing, and subscribed by the party to be charged' does not impose the requirement that the signed acknowledgment of the contract must appear from the writings alone, unaided by oral testimony. The danger of fraud and perjury, generally attendant upon the admission of parol evidence, is at a minimum in a case such as this. None of the terms of the contract are supplied by parol. All of them must be set out in the various writings presented to the court, and at least one writing, the one establishing a contractual relationship between the parties, must bear the signature of the party to be charged, while the unsigned document must on its face refer to the same transaction as that set forth in the one that was signed. Parol evidence — to portray the circumstances surrounding the making of the memorandum — serves only to connect the separate documents and to show that there was assent, by the party to be charged, to the contents of the one unsigned. If that testimony does not convincingly connect the papers, or does not show assent to the unsigned paper, it is within the province of the judge to conclude, as a matter of law, that the statute has not been satisfied. [...]

Turning to the writings in the case before us — the unsigned office memo, the payroll change form initialed by the general manager Johns, and the paper signed by the comptroller Carstens — it is apparent, and most patently, that all three refer on their face to the same transaction. The parties, the position to be filled by plaintiff, the salary to be paid him, are all identically set forth; it is hardly possible that such detailed information could refer to another or a different agreement. . . . . The corroborative evidence of defendant's assent to the contents of the unsigned office memorandum is also convincing. . . . . [T]he evidence as to the conduct of the parties at the time it was prepared persuasively demonstrates defendant's assent to its terms. Under such circumstances, the courts below were fully justified in finding that the three papers constituted the "memorandum" of their agreement within the meaning of the statute.

Nor can there be any doubt that the memorandum contains all of the essential terms of the contract. Only one term, the length of the employment, is in dispute. . . . Quite obviously, as the courts below decided, the phrase signifies that the parties agreed to a term, a certain and definite term, of two years, after which, if plaintiff did not "make good", he would be subject to discharge. . . . Having in mind the relations of the parties, the course of the negotiations and plaintiff's insistence upon security of employment, the purpose of the phrase — or so the trier of the facts was warranted in finding — was to grant plaintiff the tenure he desired. . . . The judgment should be affirmed[.]

[Citations omitted.]

QUESTIONS FOR DISCUSSION:

1. Why didn't Crabtree insist on a formal written agreement in the first place?

2. Do you think the court was right to allow parol evidence here?

> *Example:* Quan places a telephone order for 1,000 reams of printer paper for his office. The paper costs $8/ream. It is to be shipped in two equal lots of 500 reams each. After the first ream is delivered, Quan concludes he ordered too much paper. He tells the seller he will not take any more, and because there was no written contract, he is not bound to pay for the paper that was delivered. There has been part performance, so Quan must pay for the paper delivered.

does not need to be handwritten. In other words, a plaintiff in a contract lawsuit may only sue parties who actually signed the contract. The "signature" or symbol shows that the person assented to the contract. In addition to being signed, the contract must:

- Reasonably identify the subject matter of the contract,

- Have sufficient indication that a contract was made, and

- Set out the essential terms with reasonable certainty.

A writing that shows that the parties are still negotiating a contract does not satisfy the writing requirement. Likewise, an "agreement to agree" is unenforceable under the Statute. If the writing does not contain language that can reasonably be construed as words of promise or agreement, the writing does not meet the requirements of the Statute of Frauds.

A written contract is only evidence of an agreement. It is not the agreement itself. The Statute of Frauds has the effect of allowing someone who may be a party to a contract to avoid her obligations under it due to a lack of evidence. Courts have created exceptions to the requirements of the Statute of Frauds. If a party agrees that a contract was formed, she may not claim that the Statute bars enforcement due to the lack of a writing. Acknowledgment of the existence of an agreement is evidence of an agreement, and it would be inconsistent for a party to acknowledge an agreement but claim it was unenforceable due to a lack of additional evidence of the agreement.

Partial performance of an oral agreement will also take the contract outside the Statute of Frauds. The reasoning behind this exception is that the party who receives the partial performance has often received the benefit that she was supposed to receive under the oral agreement. It would be unjust for that party to receive the benefit without having to perform her obligations.

A contract will also be taken outside the Statute of Frauds if there has been reliance on a verbal promise. The reliance must have been reasonable, meaning the promise relied upon must have been the kind that would be expected to induce a person to act, or not to act, in a certain manner. Enforcement of the promise will be granted only to avoid injustice. In deciding if enforcement is necessary to avoid injustice, courts look at:

- The availability and adequacy of other remedies,

- The nature of the action or inaction in relation to the remedy sought,

- The extent to which the action or inaction corroborates the evidence that a promise was made,

- The reasonableness of the action or inaction, and

- The extent to which the inaction or action was foreseeable.

The proof necessary to show reliance is difficult. Courts are reluctant to find reliance that justifies the enforcement of an oral contract, out of fear that such a finding could make the Statute of Frauds meaningless.

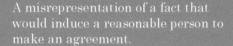

MATERIAL MISREPRESENTATION:

A misrepresentation of a fact that would induce a reasonable person to make an agreement.

Contract Performance and Enforcement

The contract is all put together. Now what? Formation of a contract is not the last stage. Now, the contract must be performed. If it is not performed, it must be enforced.

Enforceability

It is possible that the elements of a contract may appear to be in place, and all the appropriate rules on formation appear to have been followed, but there still is not an enforceable contract. The key here is that everything "appears" to be in place. There could be something present that negates one of the elements of the contract that would render the agreement unenforceable.

Fraud/Misrepresentation: A genuine agreement happens when both parties know what they have bargained for, and have an expectation that they will get it. When there is a misrepresentation in a contract, one party is not getting what he bargained for. A party has made an agreement, but it is not the agree-

Example: Jean operates an antique store. She has a set of dishes for sale. The dishes are actually inexpensive dishes made to have what the manufacturer considers a "retro" look, but Jean tells two potential buyers that these dishes were featured in a photo shoot in the November 1965 issue of an interior design magazine. The first buyer, Pedro, is just interested in buying dishes that match his dining room's color scheme. The misrepresentation is not material. The second buyer, Jasmine, has told Jean that she is looking for authentic dishes for a recreation of a mid-1960s home she is doing for a television program. The misrepresentation is material as to Jasmine.

ment that he thinks he has made. Fraudulent or material misrepresentation can render a contract voidable.

For purposes of deciding if a contract is voidable there are two types of misrepresentation: *material misrepresentation* and *fraudulent misrepresentation*. The two types of misrepresentation work in different ways. In general, a **material misrepresentation** is a misrepresentation of fact that would induce a reasonable person to make an agreement. The key term in this context is "fact," as distinct from opinion. Facts are statements that can be determined to be true or false.

A *material misrepresentation* is one that induced reliance. A misrepresentation may also be regarded as material if the person making the misrepresentation knows or should know that the person to whom the misrepresentation is being made is likely to be induced by that misrepresentation. Note that the intent to induce reliance is not an issue for a material misrepresentation. The question is whether a person relied on the statement, or whether the person making the statement knew that reliance was likely.

A material misrepresentation will make a contract voidable even though the person making it did not know it was false.

A *fraudulent misrepresentation* is also a false statement of fact, but it is one that was made with the intention of inducing reliance. Intention is more than knowing that the reliance was foreseeable. It is an expectation that the person hearing the statement will rely on it. Intention also means that the person who made the false statement either made it directly to the person hearing it, or made the statement to someone who would repeat it to the person. The intention is to induce reliance by a particular person.

The person making the statement must have made it with the knowledge that it was false, or without knowing whether it was false. Although the definition does not explicitly require that the misrepresentation be material, since there must have been an intention to induce reliance the

Example: Arvid is a professor of art history at a university. He is a well-known expert on 20th century American painting. His neighbor Margot is thinking of buying a painting he owns. Arvid tells her it is an original Jackson Pollack. In fact, the painting is just a student's effort to make a painting that looks like a Pollack. Margot buys the painting. Her reliance on Arvid's misrepresentation was reasonable.

Example: Instead of being an art history professor, Arvid is an engineer who knows nothing about art, and does not claim to know anything. When Margot asks if the painting is a Pollack, he shrugs and says "Sure, I guess so." Margot's reliance on that statement would not be reasonable.

fraudulent misrepresentation will usually also be a material misrepresentation.

Reliance is required in order to void a contract based on a misrepresentation. The reliance must have been somehow harmful to the person seeking to avoid the contract. This is a logical requirement, since a person who is not disadvantaged by a misrepresentation will be unlikely to try to avoid the contract. If there was no reliance on the false statement, the person to whom the false statement was made was not injured by that statement.

The reliance must also have been reasonable, or justifiable. The reasonableness of reliance looks at a number of factors. The relative ages of the parties is cponsidered, along with education and experience. Reliance is more likely to be deemed reasonable if the person making the false statement has some expertise in the field. If a statement appears reasonable on its face, and the person hearing it has no reason to believe it is not true, reliance is likely to be reasonable. A statement of opinion ("This is the finest car on the market today") will generally not be considered a misrepresentation. There are exceptions to this rule. If the opinion has, or purportedly has, some factual basis, or the person expressing the opinion has, or claims to have, superior knowledge, reliance on the opinion may be found justified. A statement of opinion may also constitute fraud if the statement was made with the intent of preventing the person who hears the statement from making her own investigation of the facts. Opinions will also constitute misrepresentations when the

COMPETITION IS NOT TORTIOUS INTERFERENCE OR FRAUD.

Speakers of Sport, Inc. v. ProServ, Inc.
(Sports Agency) v. (Sports Agency)
178 F.3d 862 (7th Cir. 1999)

Posner, Chief Judge

The plaintiff, Speakers of Sport, appeals from the grant of summary judgment to the defendant, ProServ, in a diversity suit in which one sports agency has charged another with tortious interference with a business relationship and related violations of Illinois law. . . . Ivan Rodriguez, a highly successful catcher with the Texas Rangers baseball team, in 1991 signed the first of several one-year contracts making Speakers his agent. ProServ wanted to expand its representation of baseball players and to this end invited Rodriguez to its office in Washington and there promised that it would get him between $2 and $4 million in endorsements if he signed with ProServ—which he did, terminating his contract (which was terminable at will) with Speakers. . . . ProServ failed to obtain significant endorsement for Rodriguez and after just one year he switched to another agent[.] Speakers brought this suit a few months later, charging that the promise of endorsements that ProServ had made to Rodriguez was fraudulent and had induced him to terminate his contract with Speakers.

[...]

There is in general nothing wrong with one sports agent trying to take a client from another if this can be done without precipitating a breach of contract. That is the process known as competition, which though painful, fierce, frequently ruthless, sometimes Darwinian in its pitilessness, is the cornerstone of our highly successful economic system. Competition is not a tort, but on the contrary provides a defense (the "competitor's privilege") to the tort of improper interference. It does not privilege inducing a breach of contract, but it does privilege inducing the lawful termination of a contract that is terminable at will. Sellers (including agents, who are sellers of services) do not "own" their customers[.]

There would be few more effective inhibitors of the competitive process than making it a tort for an agent to promise the client of another agent to do better by him, which is pretty much what this case comes down to. It is true that Speakers argues only that the competitor may not make a promise that he knows he cannot fulfill, may not, that is, compete by fraud. Because the competitor's privilege does not include a right to get business from a competitor by means of fraud, it is hard to quarrel with this position in the abstract, but the practicalities are different. If the argument were accepted and the new agent made a promise that was not fulfilled, the old agent would have a shot at convincing a jury that the new agent had known from the start that he couldn't deliver on the promise. Once a case gets to the jury, all bets are off. The practical consequence of Speakers' approach, therefore, would be that a sports agent who lured away the client of another agent with a promise to do better by him would be running a grave legal risk.

This threat to the competitive process is blocked by the principle . . . that promissory fraud is not actionable unless it is part of a scheme to defraud, that is, unless it is one element of a pattern of fraudulent acts. By requiring that the plaintiff show a pattern, by thus not letting him rest on proving a single promise, the law reduces the likelihood of a spurious suit[.]

The promise of endorsements was puffing not in the most common sense of a cascade of extravagant adjectives but in the equally valid sense of a sales pitch that is intended, and that a reasonable person in the position of the "promisee" would understand, to be aspirational rather than enforceable-an expression of hope rather than a commitment. It is not as if ProServ proposed to employ Rodriguez and pay him $2 million a year. That would be the kind of promise that could found an enforceable obligation. . . . The only reasonable meaning to attach to ProServ's so-called promise is that ProServ would try to get as many endorsements as possible for Rodriguez and that it was optimistic that it could get him at least $2 million worth of them. So understood, the "promise" was not a promise at all. But even if it was a promise (or a warranty), it cannot be the basis for a finding of fraud because it was not part of a scheme to defraud[.]

It can be argued, however, that competition can be tortious even if it does not involve an actionable fraud (which in Illinois would not include a fraudulent promise) or other independently tortious act, such as defamation, or trademark or patent infringement, or a theft of a trade secret; that competitors should not be allowed to use "unfair" tactics; and that a promise known by the promisor when made to be unfulfillable is such a tactic, especially when used on a relatively unsophisticated, albeit very well to do, baseball player. Considerable support for this view can be found in the case law. But the Illinois courts have not as yet embraced the doctrine, and we are not alone in thinking it pernicious. The doctrine's conception of wrongful competition is vague[.] Worse, the established standards of a trade or profession in regard to competition, and its ideas of unethical competitive conduct, are likely to reflect a desire to limit competition for reasons related to the self-interest of the trade or profession rather than to the welfare of its customers or clients. . . . [T]he tort of interference with business relationships should be confined to cases in which the defendant employed unlawful means to stiff a competitor[.]

[...]

It remains to consider Speakers' claim that ProServ violated the Illinois Consumer Fraud and Deceptive Business Practices Act. Speakers is not a consumer, and while a competitor is permitted to bring suit under the Act as a representative of the consumer interest (an example would be a case in which a multitude of consumers had been deceived by a competitor and their individual losses were too small to warrant the costs of suit), he must "prove, by clear and convincing evidence, how the complained-of conduct implicates consumer protection concerns." No effort at proving this was made here. . . . The seller can be hurt even if the customer is not; but to allow the seller to obtain damages from a competitor when no consumer has been hurt is unlikely to advance the consumer interest. Allowing Speakers to prevail would hurt consumers by reducing the vigor of competition between sports agents. The Rodriguezes of this world would be disserved, as Rodriguez himself, a most reluctant witness, appears to believe. Anyway, we don't think that the kind of puffing in which ProServ engaged amounts to an unfair method of competition or an unfair act or practice. [...]

[E]ven if Speakers could establish liability under either the common law of torts or the deceptive practices act, its suit would fail because it cannot possibly establish, as it seeks to do, a damages entitlement (the only relief it seeks) to the agent's fee on Rodriguez's $42 million contract. That contract was negotiated years after he left Speakers, and by another agent. Since Rodriguez had only a year-to-year contract with Speakers--terminable at will, moreover--and since obviously he was dissatisfied with Speakers at least to the extent of switching to ProServ . . . the likelihood that Speakers would have retained him had ProServ not lured him away is too slight to ground an award of such damages. Such an award would be the best example yet of puffing in the pie-in the-sky sense.

Affirmed.

[Citations omitted.]

QUESTIONS FOR DISCUSSION:

Could Rodriguez have sued ProServ for failing to secure $2 million in endorsements? Why or why not?

Could Speakers have sued Rodriguez? Why or why not?

---

person stating the opinion knows of facts that make the opinion unwarranted.

Another situation in which an opinion may constitute a fraudulent misrepresentation is when the parties are in a relationship of trust and confidence with each other. This is not necessarily a formal fiduciary relationship, but may be any type of relationship in which a person is held out as having superior knowledge or abilities. The opinions of a person in that type of relationship are given greater weight by the person who hears them. This trust obligates a speaker to be truthful in his opinions.

The term "statement" implies some active communication. The failure to speak or communicate may constitute a "false statement" in some circumstances. As a general rule, there is no obligation to speak up when a person is acting under a misapprehension. If there is a relationship of trust and confidence, there is an obligation to speak. Concealment or non-disclosure of critical facts may be a false statement. A statement will also be regarded as false if the falsity is implied or inferable from the surrounding circumstances.

Mistake

We all make mistakes. Some mistakes can affect the validity of a contract.

The type of mistake that will affect a contract is a mistake of fact. The mistake is not necessarily the result of a misrepresentation. It is a mistaken belief that is not in accord with the facts as they exist at the time of making the contract. This is not the same as an error in judgment (for example, deciding that goods are

Example: Ed has owned horses for several years. His niece Jodi wants to buy one of his horses. He tells her that one particular horse is a nice choice for a beginner, because he is gentle and docile. The horse is actually spirited and hard for Jodi to handle. Ed's opinion that the horse was a "nice choice" was a misrepresentation on which Jodi reasonably relied.

worth the price being charged). It is also not a prediction that does not come true (for example, artwork that does not appreciate in value as predicted). It is, instead, a mistake about fundamental assumptions that were held when the contract was made. If these assumptions are not true, the parties did not enter into the agreement they thought they were making. Finding that there was a mistake of fact can make a contract void. It can also be the basis for **reforming**, or rewriting, the contract.

Mutual Mistake: A mutual mistake of facts can make a contract voidable by the party to the contract who is adversely affected. It is not a trivial mistake, but one that is material to the agreement. There are four conditions that must be met before a contract is voidable for mutual mistake:

- The mistake must relate to the facts in existence at the time the contract was made. Mistakes of future facts, such as unexpected occurrences, will not make a contract void,

- The mistake relates to a basic assumption both parties made at the time of making the contract. This would include such things as the identity of the other party to the contract, or the existence of the subject of the contract,

- The mistake has a material effect on the contract, so that the contract is severely unfair and enforcement would be unjust, and

- The party who is asking to void the contract did not assume the risk of mistake. (Assuming the risk of mistake means not investigating the facts when given the opportunity or obligation to do so, or acting with the knowledge that the party does not know the essential facts.)

Contracts are voidable for mutual mistake when a decision to accept one party's interpretation over the other's would be arbitrary. Thus, a mistake of fact will not make a contract void unless it was a reasonable mistake under the circumstances. An "unreasonable" mistake, such as interpreting a term in a way that makes no sense in the context of the agreement, cannot be used to defeat an agreement. Unreasonable interpretations are not favored. Likewise, both parties must be equally at fault for the mistake. If one party bears more of the responsibility for the mistake, it is unfair to allow her to escape responsibility based on her fault.

If a contract has been partially performed, the court will not automatically declare it to be void on proof of a mutual mistake. That would have the effect of allowing a party to receive some

> *Example:* Ivy meets with Bjorn to finalize an agreement to sell a painting. The painting is being stored at Ivy's vacation home. While the discussion is going on, the vacation home and the painting are destroyed by fire. Neither Ivy not Bjorn know of this until after they sign the sales agreement. The contract may be voided for mutual mistake.

COURT VOIDS A CONTRACT THAT HINGED ON AN AMBIGUOUS TERM.

Raffles v. Wichelhaus
(Cotton Seller) v. (Cotton Buyer)
2 H. & C. 906, 159 Eng. Rep. 375 (Court of Exchequer 1864)

INSTANT FACTS:

Two parties to a cotton transaction disagree as to the exact identity of a ship named in their contract.

BLACK LETTER RULE:

A contract can be voided if it contains an ambiguous term which was, in fact, interpreted differently by the parties.

PROCEDURAL BASIS:

Decision of the Court of Exchequer on a breach of contract action.

FACTS:

Raffles (P) agreed to sell Wichelhaus (D) 125 bales of cotton which were supposed to arrive in England by ship. Wichelhaus (D) agreed to pay for the cotton after it arrived from Bombay on a ship called Peerless. Neither party to the contract knew it at the time, but there were two ships called Peerless which sailed from Bombay. One ship sailed in October. The second ship sailed in December. Unfortunately, each party had a different ship in mind for the transaction. Raffles (P) thought that the Peerless which sailed in December was the agreed upon ship. When that ship arrived in England, Raffles (P) attempted to complete the transaction. Wichelhaus (D), however, refused to accept delivery or to pay for the cotton since he had expected the other Peerless. Raffles (P) subsequently sued Wichelhaus (D) for breach of contract. Wlchelhaus's (D) plea followed and Raffles (P) demurred. The court then rendered its opinion.

ISSUE:

Can a specific contract term be interpreted according to a party's subjective interpretation of that term?

DECISION AND RATIONALE:

(Mellish) Yes. Raffles (P) and Wichelhaus (D) did not make it clear that the Peerless was a particular ship sailing on a particular date. When it turned out that there were actually two different ships named Peerless, a latent ambiguity was exposed in the contract. In that event, the court can hear parol evidence in order to establish that there was an actual subjective disagreement between the parties. Since there was no consensus ad litem, there is no contract. Since there is no contract, Raffles (P) has no right to sue for its breach. The action will be dismissed and judgement entered in favor of Wichelhaus (D).

ANALYSIS:

Note that the rule of law announced by the court is meant for the exceptional case. Usually, courts require the objective intent of the parties to govern the interpretation of a contract. Occasionally, though, a crucial term in the contract is subject to differing interpretations. If the parties actually interpreted an ambiguous term in different ways, the contract can be voided.

CASE VOCABULARY:

AD LITEM:

Ad litem means "for the purposes of the suit."

COURT OF EXCHEQUER:

A trial level court which existed until 1873. Its jurisdiction was subsequently turned over to the Exchequer Division and then the Queen's Bench Division of the High Court of Justice.

DEMURRER:

A demurrer is a means of attacking a party's pleading. In essence, the attacker argues that the pleading need not be answered because it is insufficient or defective in some manner. There are a variety of different demurrers, some of which are still recognized. The modem equivalent of a general demurrer is a request for dismissal under Federal Rule of Civil Procedure 12 (b) (6). A request under 12 (b) (6) alleges that the opposing party fails to state a claim for which relief can be granted.

PAROL EVIDENCE:
Oral or verbal evidence. In contract law, "parol evidence" refers to evidence of agreements outside of the written agreement. Parol evidence is generally not admissible when it would alter or contradict the terms of a written agreement.

or all of the benefit of the other's performance without any obligation on their part. Instead, the court will devise a remedy to avoid an injustice. The remedy may include protection of reliance interests, by requiring payment for the value of the performance rendered. Courts have also supplied "missing" terms to contracts.

Unilateral Mistake: If only one party is mistaken about a fact, it may be possible to void a contract. Relief for a unilateral mistake will be granted if the non-mistaken party first shows:

- The mistake relates to the facts in existence at the time the contract was made,

- The mistake relates to a basic assumption both parties made at the time of making the contract,

- The mistake has a material effect on the contract, so that the contract is severely unfair and enforcement would be unjust, and

- The party who is asking to void the contract did not assume the risk of mistake.

In addition, the non-mistaken party must also show either:

- The other party knew or had reason to know of the mistake, or

A unilateral mistake of fact could be the result of misrepresentation.

- The mistake makes the contract unconscionable. (A bad deal for the mistaken party does not mean that enforcement would be unconscionable.)

Declaring a contract void due to a unilateral mistake is done only in the most exceptional of circumstances. There must be some showing of misconduct, such as fraud or misrepresentation. The mistaken party must also have been reason-

Example: A contract for the sale of land would not be rendered void for unilateral mistake about the suitability of a house on the property for FHA financing. The deficiencies in the construction could be remedied for a relatively small amount in relation to the total cost of the land. The deficiencies were therefore not material to the transaction. *Mostrong v. Jackson,* 866 P.2d 573 (Utah App. 1993).

> **Example:**
> Virgil is visiting his friend Pete, and sees what looks like an expensive guitar. Virgil tells Pete that the guitar is a collector's item, and offers $1,000 for it. Pete knows that the guitar is an inexpensive knock-off he bought the week before, but accepts the offer of $1,000. He does not tell Virgil that the guitar is a recent copy, but he also has not told him that it is a collector's item. The contract is voidable for unilateral mistake.

> **Example:**
> Emma agrees to sell her house to Jaynie. The negotiations for the sale were done in a series of e-mails, all referring to the house at 70 Willow Street, and the sale price as $350,000. When the final purchase agreement is written up and signed, the address of the property is given as 80 Willow Street, and the sale price as $359,000. The contract may be reformed to reflect the true agreement between Emma and Jaynie.

able or excusable. The failure to read a contract all the way through, or a failure to investigate when given the opportunity, does not constitute a reasonable mistake.

Scrivener's Error: There is many a slip between the negotiations and the final contract. The negotiations for a contract may consist of multiple messages and discussion that are ultimately put into a final agreement. There are occasionally mistakes made in putting everything together. These are referred to as scrivener's errors. They are not the product of a mistake of facts or misrepresentation.

A scrivener's error does not mean a contract can be voided. Instead, the written instrument will be reformed to reflect what the parties intended when they made the contract.

Undue Influence

Undue influence will make a contract voidable. Undue influence is found when improper persuasion causes a person to enter into an unfair contract. This persuasion causes a person to lose his free agency.

There are two types of undue influence. The first type involves a person taking advantage of someone else's weakened state of mind. The "weakened state of mind" is not necessarily the result of incapacity, but comes from circumstances that make a person unable to make sound decisions. The person who takes advantage of that weakness knows of the vulnerability, and exploits it to her advantage. The undue influence is more than merely asking a favor. It is coercing favorable terms from another party.

The other type of undue influence comes from a fiduciary relationship. When a person has placed

> *Example:* Jorge's wife has just died in childbirth, along with the baby she was carrying. Jorge is devastated with grief. Frieda, a neighbor who knows of Jorge's mental state, offers to buy some jewelry owned by Jorge's late wife for one-tenth of the actual value of the jewels. Jorge agrees, not paying much attention to Frieda's offer. The sale of the jewelry could be voided for undue influence.

> *Example:* Floyd maintained a life insurance policy that named his wife Donna and their three children as beneficiaries. Floyd began a relationship with Mary Ann, and a few months later, Floyd and Donna were divorced. Floyd became estranged from his children. A few years after his divorce, Floyd became seriously ill. He gave Mary Ann power of attorney over his affairs, and she changed Floyd's life insurance to make herself the primary beneficiary. Although Floyd was in a vulnerable position, and Mary Ann could have exercised undue influence, there was no proof that she did so. It would not have been unnatural for Floyd to make Mary Ann the primary beneficiary under the circumstances. *Goff v. Weeks*, 246 Neb. 163, 517 N.W.2d 387 (1994).

their trust and confidence in another person, and that person receives an unfair advantage from a contract with the person who trusts him, the contract may be set aside for undue influence. It is not necessary to show that the fiduciary tried to take advantage of the relationship. The party who has been influenced has been made to feel that the other party will act in his interests. The trusted party takes advantage of that trust to his advantage.

Not all influence is regarded as undue. If the influence does not involve fear or coercion, it is not undue. The influence that flows naturally from affection or personal regard for the other party is also not undue influence. Undue influence is deliberately sought out by the party that is able to exercise the influence.

There rarely is direct proof of undue influence. Courts look at all of the circumstances surrounding a transaction to determine whether there was undue influence. A bargain that is unfair is not necessarily the product of undue influence, although it may be evidence of such influence.

> *Example:* Carlos is getting out of the Army, and is looking for a house for himself and his family. His great-aunt Ana is interested in selling her house. Ana has always been fond of Carlos, and she is proud of his military service. She sells her house to Carlos for 10% less than the probable fair market value of the house. Carlos has not exercised undue influence on Ana.

> *Example:*
>
> Luci has been Marco's attorney for many years. She has been a close adviser on many business and personal legal matters. One day, during a casual conversation, Luci remarks that she might be interested in moving from her house to a condominium. Marco offers to sell her a condominium unit he owns for the same price that he paid for it 10 years ago. This is significantly less than the market value of the unit. Luci agrees to the purchase. The contract may be set aside for undue influence.

Genuineness of Assent/ Duress

When discussing the elements of a contract, it is assumed that all of the elements are "genuine." An offer will not make a contract unless it is a genuine proposal to make a contract. Similarly, the acceptance of a genuine offer must be a real acceptance. A person's assent or agreement must be genuine before a valid contract will be found to exist. If there is something that means a person's assent was not genuine, there is no valid contract.

A "JOKE" SALE STILL MAY BE ENFORCED.
Lucy v. Zehmer
(Farm Buyer) v. (Farm Seller)
196 Va. 493, 84 S.E.2d 516 (1954)

INSTANT FACTS:
Two drunks agree to a farm sale written on the back of a bar bill.

BLACK LETTER RULE:
A contract is enforceable despite one party's subjective belief that the parties are joking.

PROCEDURAL BASIS:
Appeal from a trial court judgement for the defendant in a breach of contract action.

FACTS:
W.O. Lucy (Lucy) (P) and A.H. Zehmer (Zehmer) (D) were drinking at a bar when Lucy (P) offered to buy Zehmer's (D) farm for $50,000. Zehmer (D) thought it was a joke. In fact, he said that he was "high as a Georgia Pine" at the time. Nonetheless, he wrote up an agreement of sale on the back of a bar bill. Zehmer (D) and his wife signed the agreement and left it on the bar. When Lucy (P) picked it up, Zehmer (D) assured him that it was a joke. Lucy (P) insisted that he had purchased the farm and then left the bar. Lucy (P) brought a breach of contract suit against Zehmer (D), asking that the court enforce the sale of the farm by ordering specific performance of the agreement. The trial court denied Lucy's (P) request and this appeal followed.

ISSUE:
Will a contract be enforced despite one party's subjective belief that the parties are joking?

DECISION AND RATIONALE:
(Buchanan) Yes. The objective intent of the parties is central to a determination of their desire to be bound. This rule will be disregarded only when one party is aware of the other party's subjective intent not to be bound. In this case, Lucy (P) and Zehmer (D) haggled over the price of the farm,

the wording of the agreement, and the need for a token payment to seal the deal. They appear to have dealt with each other as reasonable parties to a genuine transaction. Lucy (P) had no idea that Zehmer (D) was secretly joking and Zehmer's (D) behavior, judged objectively, gave no indication of this before the agreement was delivered. As a result, the contract is enforceable and specific performance will be ordered. Reversed and remanded.

ANALYSIS:

The meeting of the minds doctrine, which required that each party to a contract have a subjective desire to be bound, is no longer the litmus test for a valid contract. In this case, a contract predicated on a joke remained enforceable even though Zehmer (D) was subjectively disinterested in selling his farm. Several mistakes can lead to the rescission of a contract, including transcription mistakes, jokes, ambiguities, and other problems. According to the Restatement (Second) of Contracts, when there is a mistake of fact that goes to a basic assumption of the contract, the party seeking to be excused from performance must show that they ought not to bear the risk of loss from the mistake. The analysis in mistake cases frequently hinges on which party was best situated to avoid the mistake. In this case, Zehmer (D) was best situated to avoid the confusion, because he had not made it clear that he was joking. However, a modem court would be unlikely to enforce the agreement under these circumstances.

CASE VOCABULARY:

LAST CLEAR CHANCE:

A doctrine usually associated with negligence law which places liability for an injury on the person with the last opportunity to avoid the accident by exercising reasonable care; it is not applied in every jurisdiction.

SPECIFIC PERFORMANCE:

A contract remedy which provides for exact performance on the contract when money damages would not adequately compensate the injured party. It is most often available for the sale of real estate and for the sale of unique goods, but it is not a commonly ordered remedy.

We have already considered several factors that relate to the genuineness of assent. Misrepresentation or mistake shows that the parties thought they were making an agreement about something that did not exist. Undue influence means that a person's assent was not the product of their own free will.

There is also no genuine assent if the agreement was the product of **duress.** Duress traditionally meant inducing agreement by means of a threat of bodily or physical harm. In recent years, courts have expanded the definition of duress

DURESS:

Inducing agreement by means of a threat or wrongful act.

to include any wrongful or unlawful act. The wrongful or unlawful act must be a kind that leaves the threatened person no reasonable alternative but to comply. A threat combined with an unfair agreement may cause the contract to be voided. If the threat is one that is "shocking" by the court will be regarded as duress, even if the transaction that results is not unduly unfair to the threatened party.

The threatened wrongful or unlawful act does not need to be physical harm. Economic duress may also constitute the kind of threat that will justify voiding a contract. Economic duress is a doctrine that seeks to enforce some ethical standards in the business world. While tough negotiations are not disfavored in the business arena, unlawful or wrongful pressure is not acceptable.

> **Example:** Dale supplies heating oil to several businesses; she is the only local heating oil seller. One local business is a new restaurant owned by Shadi. While discussing a contract for heating fuel sales, Dale mentions that her son Jake has just opened a new bakery, and is looking for commercial accounts. Shadi says that he is satisfied with the bakery his restaurant uses now. Dale says "Yeah, that's okay. I just don't know how you're going to make it through the winter if you can't heat your place." Shadi takes the hint, and signs a contract to buy bread from Jake. The contract is the product of duress, and is voidable.

> **Example:** AVX used tantalum, a scarce metal, to manufacture capacitors for electronic products When demand for capacitors and the tantalum used to manufacture increased dramatically in late 2000, Cabot took advantage of what was then a seller's market to negotiate aggressively a multi-year deal to supply AVX with tantalum. Eighteen months after executing the contract, AVX brought suit claiming that it was the product of economic duress. There was no economic duress under the circumstances, but even if there had been, AVX ratified the contract by performing under it and accepting Cabot's performance for a year and a half. *Cabot Corp. v. AVX Corp.*, 448 Mass. 629, 863 N.E. 2d 503 (2007).

But economic duress can be difficult to prove. Driving a hard bargain with a party who is in a very unfortunate economic situation will not constitute duress.

A contract that was entered into under duress may still be valid if it is ratified by the party who was subject to the duress. Ratification will be found when the benefits under the contract are intentionally accepted, or if she remains silent about the duress or acquiesces in the contract for any considerable length of time after opportunity is afforded to avoid it or have it annulled. Ratification will also be found if the party who was influenced recognizes the validity of the contract by acting upon it.

III. Performance

An executed contract must be performed appropriately.

Duty of Good Faith

Once an enforceable contract is made, it is up to the parties to perform the contract. Every contract carries with it the duty of good faith. That duty has two parts. The first is to perform, or make reasonable efforts to perform, the

Example:	Alice signs a contract to buy a new car from Zippy Motors, if she can obtain financing. Alice has second thoughts after leaving the dealership, and decides she doesn't want the car after all. She does not apply for a loan. Alice has breached her duty of good faith.

Example:	Alice applies for a loan at a bank located out-of-state. She knows that the bank will not be willing to lend to someone so far away. Alice has breached her duty of good faith.

Example:	Alice applies for a car loan at her local bank. The Zippy Motors salesman is angry that she is not trying to arrange financing through him. When the bank calls to verify the car being purchased, the salesman says he has no record of Alice ever trying to buy a car from Zippy. Zippy has breached its duty of good faith.

contractual duties. The second is the duty not to interfere with the other party's performance.

Good faith means that each party to a contract will provide, or attempt to provide, the other party with the benefits of the agreement she made. The precise definition of what constitutes good faith is elusive. Instead of attempting to come up with an all-purpose definition, courts have preferred to follow a case-by-case approach. This approach is a recognition that a precise definition would be virtually impossible. It is also a way of expressing preference for flexibility over certainty in this context.

The working definition of good faith amounts to saying that "good faith" is the absence of "bad faith." Bad faith is defined by examples of particular acts constituting bad faith. Some examples of bad faith include:

- Interference with the other party's performance,

- Willfully rendering performance in a substandard or slipshod way, or

- Abuse of a power to specify terms, such as making excessive demands for a product where the other party has agreed to supply all of the requirements the other has for a particular product.

Good faith does not exist outside of the terms of the contract. The duty of good faith does not require a party to go beyond the terms of a contract, or to waive any of its rights under the contract. Negotiating favorable terms is also not a breach of the duty of good faith.

> *Example:* Life insurance contracts promise to pay the beneficiary a certain sum of money. They are obligated to do this only when the insured dies. The death of the insured is an express condition for payment to the beneficiary.

Conditions

Performance of a contract is often made subject to certain conditions. A condition is an event that will give rise to a contractual duty if it occurs, or if it does not occur. The happening or non-happening of a condition may also excuse performance. Conditions in a contract may be express, implied in fact, or constructive. Courts will not hold that an event is a condition unless it is clear that the parties intended for it to be a condition. The expression of the parties' intent must be clear and unambiguous, or there must be a clear implication as to what the mutual intent is.

An express condition is one that is stated explicitly in the contract. They are created by the language used by the parties in making their contract. *Express conditions* are agreed to and imposed by the parties themselves. There is no particular language required to create an express condition. If there is an express condition in a contract, courts will usually require that the condition fully occurs before any contract duty is created or excused.

Implied-in-fact conditions are not set out expressly. The contract terms make it clear that the parties intended that something must happen before a duty would arise. The absence of express language does not defeat the finding that there is a condition.

Constructive conditions are conditions that are supplied by the court. A court will supply a condition if the parties to a contract have omitted a term that is essential to determine the rights and duties of the parties. The term supplied must be reasonable in the circumstances. Constructive conditions are found when duties are not expressed as conditions, but it is evident that a condition was intended. The court will not make a new agreement for the parties,

> *Example:* Grace agrees to print 1,000 t-shirts for Louise. Louise is to give Grace a copy of the logo she wants printed on the shirts. There is a condition implied-in-fact that Louise must furnish the logo before Grace is obligated to perform.

> *Example:* At a newsstand, Lyle picks up a newspaper and approaches the cashier. The cashier looks at the newspaper, and says "a dollar twenty-five, please." Lyle pays him $1.25 and leaves with the newspaper. Payment of $1.25 was a constructive condition of Lyle getting possession of the newspaper.

> **Example:** A shopping center lease provides that the lease is void "in the event that the lessee files a petition for relief under the Bankruptcy Code." A condition subsequent has been created.

but will give effect to their intention by interpreting the agreement to include a condition.

All conditions, whether express, implied-in-fact, or constructive, fall into two additional categories. Any condition is either a condition precedent, or a condition subsequent. A "condition precedent" is something that must occur before a contract, or a duty to perform a contract, arises. It is a fact or event that must take place before there is a binding agreement. Whether a contract contains a condition precedent depends on the parties' intent. That intent is determined by the language of the contract, as considered in the light of all the surrounding circumstances. The words the parties chose are the best indicators of an intent to create a condition precedent.

Conditional language ("If this happens, then I agree to do that") is the best way to decide whether there is a condition precedent. It is not, however, the only thing courts look for. The task is to construe the entire agreement. The presence or absence of "magic words" in the contract will not always be decisive. Many contracts include express statements that a condition is to be construed as a condition precedent. If so, the parties' intent is clear and the language will be construed as creating a condition precedent.

A condition subsequent provides for the cancellation or termination of an agreement on the happening or nonoccurrence of a stipulated event or condition. If that even happens or does not happen, the contract is automatically terminated without further duties and obligations on any party.

No precise technical words are required to create a condition subsequent, but it must be created either by express terms or by clear implication. Remember, though, that conditions are not favored by the courts. They tend to be harsh in their operation. Accordingly, courts require either clear, express language or an unambiguous manifestation of intent before finding that a condition exists.

Interpretation

One of the touchstones of contract law is that the courts attempt to give effect to the intentions of the parties to the contract. In order to do this, courts just interpret the contract to learn what that intent is.

Interpreting a contract starts with the plain language of the agreement. It is presumed that the parties intended the words in their agreement to be given their ordinary, everyday meanings. The party who proposes that a term has some other meaning must prove that the other meaning was intended.

Contracts are interpreted as entire documents, or as entire agreements. Specific clauses are not read in isolation, but are considered as a part of

Example:

Bob signs an agreement with his former employer, Jeff, that Bob will not engage in the same business "within the boundaries of Fairfax County, Virginia," for two years, in exchange for payment of $100,000. Bob then opens an office in the City of Fairfax, which is legally not a part of Fairfax County. Jeff bears the burden of proof that the parties intended that the term "Fairfax County" was intended to include the City of Fairfax.

Example:

By the custom of the trade, gold and other precious metals are weighed in troy ounces, rather than the avoirdupois ounces used for most other purposes. A contract for the sale of "six ounces of gold" will be read as calling for the sale of six troy ounces (about 187 grams) of gold, rather than six avoirdupois ounces (about 170 grams).

GRANT OF OWNERSHIP RIGHTS TO RECORDINGS INCLUDED RIGHTS TO REPRODUCE USING FUTURE TECHNOLOGIES.

Greenfield v. Philles Records, Inc.
(Singer) v. (Record Producer)
780 N.E.2d 166 (N.Y. App. 2002)

Graffeo, J.

In this contract dispute between a singing group and their record producer, we must determine whether the artists' transfer of full ownership rights to the master recordings of musical performances carried with it the unconditional right of the producer to redistribute those performances in any technological format.

[In 1963, a three-member group called "The Ronettes" signed an exclusive five-year music recording contract with the defendant, in exchange for ownership rights in their recordings. The members only received one payment under the agreement.]

Defendants subsequently began to capitalize on a resurgence of public interest in 1960s music by making use of new recording technologies and licensing master recordings of the Ronettes' vocal performances for use in movie and television productions, a process known in entertainment industry parlance as "synchronization." The most notable example was defendants' licensing of "Be My Baby" in 1987 for use in the motion picture "Dirty Dancing." . . . While defendants earned considerable compensation from such licensing and sales, no royalties were paid to any of the plaintiffs.

As a result, plaintiffs commenced this breach of contract action in 1987, alleging that the 1963 agreement did not provide Philles Records with the right to license the master recordings for synchronization and domestic redistribution, and demanded royalties from the sales of compilation albums[.]

[...]

The agreement between the parties consists of a two-page document, which apparently was widely used in the 1960s by music producers signing new artists. Plaintiffs executed the contract without the benefit of counsel. . . . The ownership rights provision of the contract provides:

"All recordings made hereunder and all records and reproductions made therefrom together with the performances embodied therein, shall be entirely [Philles'] property, free of any claims whatsoever by you or any person deriving any rights of interest from you. Without limitation of the foregoing, [Philles] shall have the right to make phonograph records, tape recordings or other reproductions of the performances embodied in such recordings by any method now or hereafter known, and to sell and deal in the same under any trade mark or trade names or labels designated by us, or we may at our election refrain therefrom."

Plaintiffs concede that the contract unambiguously gives defendants unconditional ownership rights to the master recordings, but contend that the agreement does not bestow the right to exploit those recordings in new markets or mediums since the document is silent on those topics. Defendants counter that the absence of specific references to synchronization and domestic licensing is irrelevant[.]

Despite the technological innovations that continue to revolutionize the recording industry, long-settled common-law contract rules still govern the interpretation of agreements between artists and their record producers. The fundamental, neutral precept of contract interpretation is that agreements are construed in accord with the parties' intent. "The best evidence of what parties to a written agreement intend is what they say in their writing". Thus, a written agreement that is complete, clear and unambiguous on its face must be enforced according to the plain meaning of its terms.

Extrinsic evidence of the parties' intent may be considered only if the agreement is ambiguous, which is an issue of law for the courts to decide. A contract is unambiguous if the language it uses has "a definite and precise meaning, unattended by danger of misconception in the purport of the [agreement] itself, and concerning which there is no reasonable basis for a difference of opinion". Thus, if the agreement on its face is reasonably susceptible of only one meaning, a court is not free to alter the contract to reflect its personal notions of fairness and equity.

The pivotal issue in this case is whether defendants are prohibited from using the master recordings for synchronization, and whatever future formats evolve from new technologies, in the absence of explicit contract language authorizing such uses. . . . [B]ecause there is no ambiguity in the terms of the Ronettes agreement, defendants are entitled to exercise complete ownership rights, subject to payment of applicable royalties due plaintiffs.

[...]

In analogous contexts, other courts have recognized that broad contractual provisions, similar to those in the Ronettes agreement, convey virtually unfettered reproduction rights to license holders in absence of specific exceptions to the contrary. In [a 1998 case], the plaintiff granted distribution rights in foreign countries to Igor Stravinsky's musical composition "The Rite of Spring," including the "right, license, privilege and authority to record [the composition] in any manner, medium or form" for use in the motion picture "Fantasia" to the Walt Disney Company. After Disney reproduced the song in videocassette and laser disc versions for foreign distribution, the plaintiff sought breach of contract damages on the basis that the agreement did not explicitly provide for distribution in new technological mediums.

The United States Court of Appeals for the Second Circuit reiterated its precedent that "licensee[s] may properly pursue any uses which may reasonably be said to fall within the medium as described in the license". . . . [T]he Second Circuit concluded that the broad language employed in the contract granted Disney the authority to use the musical composition in the videocassette version of the movie in the absence of any contractual indication otherwise. Thus, the language of the contract was the controlling factor in interpreting the agreement[.]

We agree with these prevalent rules of contract construction—the unconditional transfer of ownership rights to a work of art includes the right to use the work in any manner unless those rights are specifically limited by the terms of the contract[.]

In this case, plaintiffs concede that defendants own the master recordings. Notably, the agreement explicitly refers to defendants' "right to make phonograph records, tape recordings or other reproductions of the performances embodied in such recordings by any method now or hereafter known, and to sell and deal in the same" (emphasis added). Plaintiffs contend that the breadth of the ownership provision is limited by the agreement's introductory paragraph, which states that defendants' purpose for purchasing plaintiffs' performances was to make "phonograph records and/or tape recordings and other similar devices." However, when read in conjunction with the ownership provision, a reasonable meaning emerges—the phrase "other similar devices" refers to defendants' right to reproduce the performances by any current or future technological methods.

[...]

We realize that our conclusion here effectively prevents plaintiffs from sharing in the profits that defendants have received from synchronization licensing. However sympathetic plaintiffs' plight, we cannot resolve the case on that ground under the guise of contract construction. Our guiding principle must be to neutrally apply the rules of contract interpretation because only in this way can we ensure stability in the law and provide guidance to parties weighing the risks and advantages of entering a binding agreement. . . . Accordingly, the order of the Appellate Division should be modified, without costs, and the case remitted to Supreme Court for further proceedings in accordance with this opinion and, as so modified, affirmed.

QUESTIONS FOR DISCUSSION:

In 1963, the Ronettes were in their late teens to very early twenties and did not have the experience or legal representation enjoyed by the defendant. Should that disparity play a bigger role in this case? Is there a legal theory that might fit this situation?

Future technologies cannot be anticipated for contract purposes. Is a broad claim of rights always appropriate, or might unintended uses arise from unforeseeable technologies?

an integrated whole. The intention of the parties is best determined by looking at their entire agreement, rather than at bits and pieces of it.

Technical terms, or terms of art for a particular field, are given effect. If a party wants to engage in a specialized line of business, she will be presumed to be using the same terminology as other practitioners of that business. There is normally no need for the parties to specify that the technical term was the one intended. The usage of the trade will dictate how the terms are read.

When interpreting a contract, absurd or unlawful results should be avoided.

Example: Judy is a passenger in a small plane operated by her friend Marshall. When the plane lands, Judy gets out, but she is disoriented and accidentally walks into the propeller of the plane. She is severely injured. Marshall has an insurance policy that covers "injuries arising out of the operation of an aircraft." The company argues that Judy's injuries were not caused by operating an aircraft, because she was no longer a passenger and was walking away. Marshall argues that he should be covered, because Judy would not have been where she was if she had not just been a passenger in his plane. The court may find that the term "arising out of the operation of an aircraft" is ambiguous in these circumstances, and order that the insurance company provide coverage.

Ambiguous Terms

While the words in contracts are to be read according to their ordinary meanings, what happens when a word in a contract term has more than one "ordinary meaning?" When this happens, the contract term is ambiguous. An ambiguity arises when a term has more than one meaning that is reasonable in the context in which it was used. Multiple meanings by themselves do not mean that a clause is ambiguous. The multiple meanings must be such that any one of them could be assigned to the term and be equally valid. For example, the noun "pump" can mean either a mechanism for moving fluids, or a low-cut shoe. It would be very difficult to argue that the use of "pump" created an ambiguous term, since it will more than likely be clear from the context which of the two definitions applies.

An ambiguous term does not make a contract void, unless it rises to the level of a mutual mistake. The ambiguous clause is not excised from the contract. Instead, the contract is interpreted in the way that is the least favorable to the party who drafted the contract.

Ambiguous clauses are found frequently in insurance contracts. Since the majority of insurance policies are drafted by the insurance company, courts read the policies in the way that is the least favorable to the insurer.

Parol Evidence Rule

The meaning of a contract is not always clear from the final document. A party may claim that it is necessary to resort to proof of facts from outside a writing to show what the parties really intended. This type of evidence, known as "parol evidence," is subject to special rules before a court will consider it. While construing a contract in a way that reflects the intentions of the parties is the overriding goal of contract interpretation, using outside evidence too readily will go against the importance that is placed on having a final, written agreement.

> "Parol" means "outside the contract." The rule is not limited to verbal evidence.

The parol-evidence rule is subject to numerous qualifications and exceptions. In its most basic form, the rule generally precludes the use of evidence outside of a written contract to vary or contradict the terms of an unambiguous and integrated contract. When the parties have concluded a valid integrated agreement regarding a particular subject, the parol-evidence rule precludes the enforcement of inconsistent prior or contemporaneous agreements. The rule is justified on the theory that a written document is more reliable and accurate than human memories. It is also justified as preventing fraud or perjury.

As noted, there are numerous exceptions to this blanket rule. First, since the application of the rule depends on the existence of a valid, written contract, parol evidence will be admitted to show that there was some legal defect in the agreement. A party's lack of capacity, for example, is something that typically is proven by parol evidence.

Second, the rule applies to "integrated" contracts. An integrated contract is one that has been adopted by the parties as the complete and exclusive statement of their agreement. There are no excluded terms, or terms left for later negotiation or decision. A contract that appears on its face to be a complete and unambiguous statement of the parties' contractual intent is presumed to be an integrated writing. Parol evidence may be necessary to determine if the document is integrated. There may be an express integration clause, saying that a document "represents the entire agreement of the parties, and no additional or supplemental agreements have been made." The absence of such a clause does not mean that a contract is not an integrated writing, and the presence of such a clause is not necessarily conclusive proof that the contract is an integrated agreement. Parol evidence may still be needed to show integration.

The parol-evidence rule generally forbids the use of parol evidence to vary or contradict the terms of a written contract. Parol evidence may be used to establish facts that do not vary, alter, or contradict the terms of the agreement or the legal effect of the terms used. Parol evidence of the intention of the parties in executing the instrument, or about the interpretation one party gives to a certain term, may also be admitted.

Parol evidence rule that varies or contradicts the written terms of an integrated contract may be admitted to explain an ambiguity in the document, or to prove an outside oral agreement that does not vary the terms of the written contract. It may also be used to add a missing term if the writing states on its face that it does not set forth the complete agreement, or to show mistake or fraud.

Parties

Who is bound by a contract? Every contract has two parties, or two sets of parties, involved. There will be at least one offeror, and at least one offeree. Each party will have responsibilities regarding performance, and will be held accountable if he does not fulfill those responsibilities.

There are many occasions when the offeror and offeree are not the only ones involved in a contract. In building and construction contracts, for example, it is generally understood that the party who made the original contract will rely on others, known as subcontractors, to fulfill her obligations. There are also situations when a contracting party's obligations are performed by another party entirely.

> In the context of construction contracts, subcontractors may be able to enforce their claims for non-payment directly against building owners by recording a mechanic's lien on the property. Mechanic's liens are statutory rights, and can exist without a contractual relationship

Subcontractors: Suppose the owner of a building hires a construction company to do a complete renovation of her building. The construction company does not have either the employees or expertise to do everything involved

> **Example:** In order to pay off a debt, Shaurya agrees to turn over to his brother all of the income he receives from a consulting project. He arranges for the job to be done by Riya, a colleague. Shaurya has assigned the income, and delegated the performance.

> **Example:** Greta is known as the foremost expert in the U.S. on contemporary Scandinavian theater. She is due to give a lecture on that subject at a local cultural symposium, but the driveway to her house has been blocked by snow. Greta calls her neighbor Bert, and offers him $10 to shovel her driveway. Bert agrees, and sends his daughter Gina out to do the job. Bert's delegation of his agreement with Greta was proper. Greta could not, however, delegate her obligation to lecture to someone else.

with the renovation, so it hires others with that expertise. For our example, let us say that the construction company hires an electrician to redo the wiring in the building. The electrician is a subcontractor. A subcontractor has a contractual relationship, but it is not the original contractual relationship between the initial offeror and offeree. Instead, there is a separate contract with the construction company. The building owner will look to the construction company to ensure performance of all of the work, including the work done by the electrician. If the electrician breaches the contract, the building owner would bring a breach of contract action against the construction company, not the electrician. The construction company, if appropriate, would bring its own action against the electrician, by filing a third-party complaint.

Assignment and delegation: When a subcontractor is involved, the original party to the agreement remains responsible for performance as originally promised. In cases involving assignment or delegation, one or more of the original parties is no longer involved in the agreement. Technically, assignment and delegation are two separate things. Assignment is the transfer of some right, such as the right to receive payment. Delegation is performance of a party's obligations by someone other than the original contracting party.

> In modern usage, it is common for "assignment" to refer to transactions where there has been both a delegation and an assignment.

Delegation, on the other hand, does not require consideration, and does not necessarily relieve the delegating party of his obligations under the contract. As a general rule, a party to a contract may freely delegate her obligations under the agreement. There are two exceptions to this general rule. The first, self-explanatory, exception, is that obligations under a contract may not be transferred if the agreement prohibits it, or requires the approval of the other party before the transfer is made.

The second exception is that performance may not be delegated when it involves personal skill or talent. While arguably all contracts involve some degree of skill or talent, there are some where the contracting party's personal skills were essential to the bargain. The agreement was for that person to provide a particular service, and the same actions done by another person would not be the same performance.

The question of whether performance may be delegated depends on the intention of the parties. Many courts and commentators say that a contract where performance is dominated by factors that can be measured objectively is less "personal," and it is more likely that performance can be delegated. A contract that could be performed by anyone, or where personal services will be rendered by a party who is explicitly not named in the contract, may be delegated. If the performance of the contract requires special confidence, however, performance is less likely to be able to be delegated. Courts have split on the question of whether an exclusive sales agency is a contract that may be assigned.

Delegation does not relieve the delegating party of her liabilities under the contract. This is because the party who is supposed to receive performance is not a party to the delegation agreement. Any failure of performance remains the responsibility of the delegating party. A party may agree to relieve the delegating party

Example: Beth is looking for a piano teacher for her son Tristan, and a friend recommends Philip, a teacher at the Pleasant Valley House of Music. While she is arranging for Tristan to take lessons with Philip, she sees a flier that says the House of Music offers ukulele lessons. Beth has long wanted to play the ukulele, so she signs up for lessons. The House of Music tells her they will arrange a teacher for her. The agreement for piano lessons was to have lessons from Philip, so that performance cannot be delegated. There was no ukulele teacher specified, so delegation of that performance probably would not be a problem.

Example: Deshawn wants to have his mother's house renovated, so he hires Kayla, a home remodeling contractor to do the job. Deshawn hears that his old school friend Gabe is out of work, so he tells Kayla to hire Gabe to do the painting. Deshawn's mother is an intended third party beneficiary, since the contract was made with the purpose of benefitting her. Gabe is an incidental beneficiary. He will benefit, but his benefit was not the purpose of the contract.

> **Example:** Deshawn is having his mother's house renovated as a gift. His mother is a donee beneficiary of his contract with Kayla. Deshawn made the contract with Kayla based in part on her agreement to do some repair work for Deshawn's former business partner Gino, to satisfy a debt Deshawn owes Gino. Gino is a creditor third party beneficiary.

> **Example:** If Kayla does not complete the renovation job. Deshawn's mother may sue her for breach of contract. If she does not perform the repair services for Gino, Gino may sue either Deshawn or Kayla.

from responsibility, but that would be making a new contract, not a delegation.

Third party beneficiaries: Not all contracts are made to benefit only the parties to the contract. There may be others, called third party beneficiaries, who are intended to receive the benefit from the agreement. A third party beneficiary has the right to enforce a contract even though he was not a formal party to it.

While many contracts will benefit non-parties to the agreement, not every person who stands to benefit may enforce a contract. Only intended beneficiaries may enforce the agreement. Intended beneficiaries are third parties for whose benefit the contract was made. Other beneficiaries, called incidental beneficiaries, may not enforce an agreement.

There are two principal types of intended beneficiaries. A *creditor beneficiary* is one who receives the benefit as consideration for another promise, or in satisfaction of a debt. A *donee beneficiary* receives the benefit as a gift, without consideration.

A donee beneficiary may enforce the contract against the party who was supposed to provide performance for her benefit. A creditor benefi-

> **Example:** Black Hawk County Commercial Bank wants to offer credit cards only to its customers in its part of Iowa. Iowa has a usury law that limits the amount of interest that can be charged on loans. South Dakota has no usury law, so Black Hawk incorporates Black Hawk Credit Services in Rapid City. All of the Black Hawk credit cards are issued from Rapid City, and that is also where payments are sent and processed. The credit card agreement with Black Hawk says that the agreement "will be construed in accordance with the terms of the laws of the State of South Dakota." Since Black Hawk's credit card operation is run entirely out of South Dakota, the choice of law clause probably will be upheld.

ciary may sue either party, but may recover only from one.

Choice of Law Clauses

The law of contracts is not uniform across the United States. While most states follow the same rules, there are local variances that can have an effect on a transaction. Choosing which state's law will apply to a given agreement is the subject of a complex body of law. Many contracts attempt to make the choice easier by stating what law will apply.

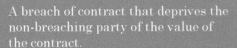

MATERIAL BREACH:
A breach of contract that deprives the non-breaching party of the value of the contract.

MINOR BREACH:
A breach of contract that allows the non-breaching party to have the benefits of the agreement.

Choice of law clauses state which jurisdiction's law will be used to interpret a contract. Many of them also state which court is the appropriate forum for hearing disputes. Courts will generally give effect to a choice of law clause as long as there is some connection between one of the parties and the jurisdiction chosen.

IV. Breach

Broadly speaking, a breach of contract is when one party to a contract does not perform their duties under the contract, or does not perform at the time or in the manner required. In order to bring a lawsuit for a breach of contract, a party must show the following facts:

- The existence of a valid contract,

- The complaining party's performance of the contract,

- The other party's failure to perform, and

- The failure to perform caused some injury.

Breaches are classified as either **material** or **minor**. The distinction between the two is important for deciding what the non-breaching party may do in response to the breach.

A *material breach* is one that goes to the very essence of the agreement. It deprives the non-breaching party of the benefits under the contract that she bargained for. A material breach will render the contract irreparably broken. The non-breaching party may declare the contract to be at an end, and sue the breaching party for damages. The non-breaching party has no further obligations under the contract.

It is possible that a breach of contract will not cause an injury. For example, a party may come out better from not having to incur the expenses of performance. In that case, he may not bring an action even though the contract was breached.

There is no precise definition of "material breach." Courts have said that a material breach is a failure to perform that defeats the essential purpose of the contract or makes it impossible

> *Example:*
>
> Rufus hires Daria to do an extensive remodeling job on his house. The contract requires that Daria install a new bathroom with a whirlpool bath. It also requires that Daria leave the premises in a "neat and clean" condition every day. The work is to be done by October 15, and Rufus will make payment in full.
>
> Unfortunately, Daria does not finish the bathroom by October 15; in fact, it looks like she has barely started the job. This is a major breach of the contract, and Rufus may declare the contract ended. He is not required to pay Daria, and may bring suit for damages.

> *Example:*
>
> Daria finishes the job on schedule. As Rufus inspects the job, he notices that Daria and her workers have left fast-food wrappers from their lunch under one of the bushes in his yard. This is a minor breach of the contract. Rufus may not cancel the contract, but he may recover damages for the cost of cleaning up.

for the other party to perform. A material breach goes to the root or essence of the agreement of the agreement and defeats the object of the parties in making the contract. It is sometimes said that the question is whether it is fairer to allow the non-breaching party to cancel than it would be to expect her to continue to perform. This lack of precision is deliberate. The goal is to make sure that each party is able to receive his expectations under the contract. Keeping the rule for deciding a material breach flexible allows for consideration of individual circumstances.

ANTICIPATORY BREACH:

Informing a party that a contract will be breached before the breach takes place.

The first party to a contract who commits a material breach is denied the right to enforce the contract. The non-breaching party is entitled to stop or cancel performance. One party's material breach is an excuse of the other party's performance.

A *minor breach* is one that still allows the non-breaching party to have the benefits of the agreement. Although there has not been strict compliance with every term of the contract, the non-breaching party may not declare the contract to be over. She must continue her obligations under the contract. This obligation to continue performance does not mean that she has no remedy for the other party's breach. The non-breaching party may still sue for damages caused by the breach.

When deciding if a breach is material or minor, courts look at the following factors:

- The benefit received by the non-breaching party,

- Whether the non-breaching party can be adequately compensated for the breach,

- The extent of the breaching party's performance,

- The hardship to the breaching party,

- The negligent or willful behavior of the breaching party, and

- The likelihood that the breaching party will complete the contract.

A breach of contract may occur before the performance was supposed to happen. This is known as an **anticipatory breach**. An anticipatory breach happens when a party notifies another that he will not be able to perform the contract. It may also happen when one party has reason to doubt that the contract will be performed, and asks for reassurance of performance but does not receive it.

> Performance will not be excused merely because performance is more difficult that originally believed.

When a contract is breached by anticipatory breach, the date of the breach is the time of the notification or failure to receive assurances. Determining the exact date of the breach is important for two reasons. One is that it tells the non-breaching party when he is obligated to act to mitigate his damages (see below). The second is that the date of the breach starts the time for bringing a lawsuit for breach of contract, and tells when the statute of limitations will bar any such lawsuit.

If a party does not perform his contractual obligations, his failure may still be excused. There may be defenses that can be raised to a claim of breach of contract. Some of these defenses,

Example: Franny's band is hired to play at a New Year's Eve Party given by Al. In early December, Al sees a report that two members of Franny's band have left, and that the band may not be performing any more. He writes to Franny, asking if she will in fact be able to play as agreed. If Franny does not reply, or is unable to say that the band will perform, Al may treat the contract as breached.

Example: Richard hires Joanna to sing at the opening of his new dinner theater. The night before the opening, a fault in the electrical wiring starts a fire, and the theater burns down. Performance of the contract is impossible, so Joanna's non-performance is excused.

> *Example:* Jack hires a minister to perform his wedding ceremony. The day before the ceremony, Jack's fiancé calls the wedding off and leaves town. The minister hears of this development and stays home that day. The purpose of the minister's performance has been frustrated, so her failure to appear at the time and place of the ceremony is excused.

> *Example:* Tina agrees to customize Graydon's car for $2,500. When the job is done, Graydon discovers that he does not have enough money to pay her. Tina agrees to take Graydon's valuable stamp collection instead of cash. Her acceptance of the stamp collection is an accord and satisfaction.

such as illegality, lack of capacity, mistake, or misrepresentation, have already been discussed. These defenses say, essentially, that no contract was truly made due to the circumstances, or the situation of the parties. There are other defenses that acknowledge the existence of a valid contract, but note that there is a reason why performance should be excused.

One such defense is impossibility. Impossibility may be raised when something happens after the making of the contract that makes the performance either pointless, or impossible. The thing that happens must not be the fault of the party seeking to be excused. Non-occurrence of

the event must have been a basic assumption when the contract was made.

A similar defense is the defense of frustration of purpose. When the purpose of a contract is frustrated, performance has not necessarily become impossible. Instead, it has become pointless. As with the defense of impossibility, an event occurs that was not anticipated. The non-occurrence of this event was a basic assumption of the parties at the time the contract was entered into. The event makes performance radically different from what was contemplated at the time of the agreement. Both parties knew of the purpose of the contract at the time it was made. While the defense of impossibility relates to the mechanics of performance as set out in the agreement, frustration of purpose relates to the underlying reason for entering into the contract.

Another defense is **accord and satisfaction**. Accord and satisfaction is when performance, or a substitute for performance, has been found adequate. This may be a compromise of a claim, or just an agreement to accept an alternate performance.

ACCORD AND SATISFACTION:
Accepting performance, or a substitute for performance, as adequate.

SPECIFIC PERFORMANCE:
An order from the court to do what the contract obligates the person to do.

V. Remedies

Remedies are the legal consequence for not keeping the promises of a contract. The term "remedy" is significant. The goal is to fix something that is wrong. They are not meant as a penalty, or as a deterrent to future misconduct.

The contract remedy that may seem the most intuitive is also the one that is awarded the least. **Specific performance** is an order from the court to do what the contract obligates you to do. It is ordered in cases in which an award of money will not be adequate compensation. In these cases, there is no amount of money that could put the non-breaching party in the same position as he would have been if the contract had not been breached. The most common cases in which specific performance will be ordered are:

- A contract for the sale of something unique. The non-breaching party cannot remedy her loss by buying an identical item from another seller.

- A contract for the sale of land. Every parcel of real estate is deemed unique.

- Shareholder voting agreements. It is hard, if not impossible, to calculate the monetary loss from such a breach.

There are a number of reasons specific performance is not ordered more frequently. One reason is custom: It just isn't done. A second reason is that courts do not want to be put in the

---

Example: Fred wants to buy a house as a graduation gift for his nephew Reginald. The farm Fred grew up on has been redeveloped into a residential community, Mitching Hill. Although all of the houses in Mitching Hill look identical, Fred identifies number 42 as being on the site of a fond memory from his childhood. He signs a contract to purchase number 42. The next day, the developer calls him and says he will not sell him number 42, as he wants to keep that house as a model. The developer says he can purchase number 41 or 43, instead. Numbers 41 and 43 are adjacent to number 42, and have the exact same layout and features. Fred refuses. A court may order specific performance of the contract to sell number 42.

Example: Jesse is hired to pave the parking lot at an office building owned by Noelle. The job is to be done on Saturday, and Jesse will be paid $10,000 for the job. On Wednesday, Noelle tells Jesse that she does not want the job done after all, and that Jesse should just forget it. Because he will not be doing the job, Jesse will not have to pay $5,000 for workers that day, and will not have to pay $2,500 for materials. In a breach of contract suit, Jesse's damages will be $2,500.

position of supervising a party's performance. When the contract is a sales contract, performance is easy and quick. If the contract requires more extensive performance, such as a construction contract, a court that ordered specific performance would have to go beyond ordering performance. There would be a continuing obligation to make sure performance was adequate.

A judgment ordering the payment of money, on the other hand, is easy to police. The money is either paid, or not paid. There is no opportunity for disputes about the quality of performance.

The typical remedy for breach of contract is an order to pay a sum of money to the non-breaching party. This is referred to as an award of **damages.** The award of damages is limited to the damages caused by the breach. Punitive or exemplary damages are rarely, if ever, allowed in contract cases. The only purpose of contract damages is compensation to the non-breaching party, to put that party in the same place as if the contract had not been breached. There are five types of contract damages.

Expectation damages equal the monetary amount of the benefit that would have been received if the contract had been performed as

DAMAGES:
A sum of money awarded as compensation for a breach of contract.

EXPECTATION DAMAGES:
The monetary value of the benefit that would have been received if the contract had been performed as agreed.

GENERAL DAMAGES:
The harm that normally flows form a breach of contract.

SPECIAL DAMAGES:
Damages that occur due to the special circumstances of a particular contract.

Expectation damages must be proven with a high degree of certainty. Courts do not permit an award speculative damages.

PARTY INJURED BY A BREACH OF CONTRACT CAN ONLY RECOVER THOSE DAMAGES THAT MAY REASONABLY BE CONSIDERED AS ARISING NATURALLY FROM THE BREACH, OR AS HAVING BEEN CONTEMPLATED BY THE PARTIES IN ADVANCE AS A LIKELY RESULT OF THE BREACH.

Hadley v. Baxendale
(Mill Operators) v. (Delivery Service)
9 Ex. 341, 156 Eng. Rep. 145 (1854)

INSTANT FACTS:
Baxendale failed to deliver a broken mill shaft for Hadley on time, and the delay prevented Hadley from reopening the mill on time.

BLACK LETTER RULE:
A party injured by another party's breach of contract can only recover those damages that may fairly and reasonably be considered either as arising naturally, or as may reasonably be supposed to

have been in the contemplation of both parties, at the time the contract was made, as the probable result of such a breach of the contract.

PROCEDURAL BASIS:
Rule nisi for new trial in action for damages for breach of contract of carriage.

FACTS:
The Hadleys (P) operated a mill in Gloucester. This mill had to be shut down on May 11, 1854, when the crankshaft of the steam engine which ran the mill became broken. The Hadleys (P) arranged to have the manufacturers of their (P) engine make a replacement one based on the pattern of the broken shaft. To accomplish this, a representative of the Hadleys (P) went to Baxendale (D) at Pickford & Co., a well-known carrier [delivery and transport] business, on May 13. This representative told the Baxendale's (D) clerk that the Hadleys' (P) mill was stopped, and that the shaft must be sent immediately to the manufacturers at Greenwich. The clerk assured the Hadleys' (P) servant that it could be delivered in a day.

The next morning, Baxendale (D) took the shaft and was paid to deliver it to Greenwich. This delivery was delayed by Baxendale's (D) neglect. As a result, the completion of repairs and the reopening of the mill were delayed by five days. In that time, the Hadleys (P) were compelled to pay wages. The Hadleys (P) claimed they (P) also lost wages totaling £300 [pounds] and sought judgment for that amount.

Baxendale (D) claimed these damages were too remote, and that liability should not be found. The jury awarded £25 in damages to the Hadleys (P). Baxendale (D) appealed.

ISSUE:
Should the measure of damages awarded to a party who is injured by a breach of contract be limited to only those damages that are not considered remote by the parties?

DECISION AND RATIONALE:
(Alderson) Yes. A party injured by another party's breach of contract can only recover those damages that may fairly and reasonably be considered either as arising naturally, or as may reasonably be supposed to have been in the contemplation of both parties, at the time the contract was made, as the probable result of such a breach of the contract. In other words, if the special circumstances under which a contract is made are described by one party to another, it follows that both sides are aware of these special circumstances. Thus, any damages caused by a breach would have been reasonably contemplated by the parties.

The measure of those damages would be the amount of injury which would ordinarily follow from such a breach under these circumstances. If, however, a party that breaches the contract did not know of these special circumstances, then he or she could only be presumed to have knowledge of the kind of injury that would result generally from a breach. This is because parties with knowledge of special circumstances regarding a contract could very well provide for them. It would be unfair for this advantage to be taken away from such parties by presuming otherwise.

Here, the Hadleys' (P) servant only told Baxendale's (D) clerk at the time the contract was made that the mill shaft was broken, and that the Hadleys (P) operated that mill. It is unclear how these circumstances could reasonably show that the mill's profits would be stopped if the delivery of the shaft to the manufacturer were unreasonably delayed. Baxendale (D) had no idea of whether the Hadleys (P) had an extra shaft at the mill, or whether the steam engine was otherwise defective. Ordinarily, a miller sending an engine shaft to a third person by a common carrier would not result in a loss of profits and a stopped mill.

The special circumstances here that would lead to such a situation were never communicated to Baxendale (D). Therefore, the loss of profits in this case cannot reasonably be considered such a consequence of the breach of the contract as could have been fairly and reasonably contemplated by both parties when they made this contract. The jury should not have taken the loss of profits into consideration when measuring damages. A new trial is necessary in this case. Rule absolute.

ANALYSIS:
Consequential damages are affected by the circumstances under which the contract was made, such as the amount of information provided by one party to another. The court here said the loss of profits for the mill could not have been in Baxendale's (D) "contemplation" because he (D) did not know if Hadley (P) had an extra mill shaft, if the mill engine was otherwise faulty, etc. This "contemplation" requirement imposed on the recovery of breach of contract damages was more severe than

the test for substantial or proximate cause used in actions for tort or breach of warranty. Shortly after the Hadley decision, it appeared that both English and American courts would transform this contemplation test into an even stricter one. Some courts supported the idea that a party could not be held liable for consequential damages unless that party had made a "tacit agreement" to assume that particular risk when making the contract. Fortunately, this restrictive test has not survived to this day, and is explicitly rejected in the comments to the UCC. The modern trend has been to define the test as one of "foreseeability." A party must only have been given notice of facts that made a loss foreseeable to be held liable.

CASE VOCABULARY:
COMMON CARRIER:
A business that offers its services to the public for transportation of people, goods, or messages.

NOLLE PROSEQUI:
A formal declaration that a prosecutor or plaintiff will "no longer prosecute" a particular case.

RULE ABSOLUTE:
A rule which commands that an order be forthwith enforced.

agreed. This amount is reduced by the amount that is saved by reason of the non-breaching party not being required to perform. The usual way of calculating expectation damages is to take the difference in value between the performance contracted for and the value of the performance that was given. The value of the contracted for performance may include the net profits that the non-breaching party was reasonably certain of receiving.

General damages are those that a contracting party would imagine being liable for if she breached the contract. They are the type of damages that would normally be anticipated to arise from the breach. In the example above, Noelle should realize that she would be liable for the monetary loss to Jesse. *Special damages* are not ones that would ordinarily be anticipated. They may be recovered only if the breaching party was aware that there were special facts or circumstances that would cause these damages.

When a contract has been breached, the non-breaching party must take reasonable steps to minimize, or mitigate, her damages.

Example: Noelle hires Jesse to pave the parking lot of her building for $10,000. Jesse does not show up to do the job as promised, and Noelle has to hire a different contractor for $12,000. The additional $2,000 is recoverable by Noelle as general damages. The cost of hiring a substitute should have been within Jesse's contemplation when he made the contract.

The substitute is not able to pave Noelle's parking lot until two weeks after Jesse was supposed to do it. This means that Noelle was not able to rent her parking lot to a visiting carnival, an event that would have paid her $5,000. Jesse is not liable for the additional $5,000 in special damages unless Noelle had made him aware of the carnival rental at the time the contract was made.

DAMAGES ARE LIMITED TO THE EXPENDITURES AND LOST PROFITS AT THE TIME AN EXECUTORY CONTRACT IS REPUDIATED.

Rockingham County v. Luten Bridge Co.
(County Commission) v. (Construction Company)
35 F.2d 301 (4th Cir. 1929)

Parker, Circuit Judge.

. . . The facts out of which the case arises, as shown by the affidavits and offers of proof appearing in the record, are as follows: On January 7, 1924, the board of commissioners of Rockingham county voted to award to plaintiff a contract for the construction of the bridge in controversy.

At . . . a regularly advertised called meeting . . . a resolution was unanimously adopted declaring that the contract for the building of the bridge was not legal and valid, and directing the clerk of the board to notify plaintiff that it refused to recognize same as a valid contract, and that plaintiff should proceed no further thereunder. . . . The clerk duly sent a certified copy of this resolution to plaintiff.

At the regular monthly meeting of the board on March 3d, a resolution was passed directing that plaintiff be notified that any work done on the bridge would be done by it at its own risk and hazard, that the board was of the opinion that the contract for the construction of the bridge was not valid and legal, and that, even if the board were mistaken as to this, it did not desire to construct the bridge, and would contest payment for same if constructed. A copy of this resolution was also sent to plaintiff. [...]

On November 24, 1924, plaintiff instituted this action against Rockingham county[.] Complaint was filed, setting forth the execution of the contract and the doing of work by plaintiff thereunder, and alleging that for work done up until November 3, 1924, the county was indebted in the sum of $18,301.07.

[...]

[T]he county now admits the execution and validity of the contract, and the breach on its part, the ultimate question in the case is one as to the measure of plaintiff's recovery [and] whether plaintiff . . . can recover under the contract for work done after [notices] were received, or is limited to the recovery of damages for breach of contract as of that date.

[...]

[A]s to the measure of plaintiff's recovery we do not think that, after the county had given notice, while the contract was still executory, that it did not desire the bridge built and would not pay for it, plaintiff could proceed to build it and recover the contract price. It is true that the county had no right to rescind the contract, and the notice given plaintiff amounted to a breach on its part; but, after plaintiff had received notice of the breach, it was its duty to do nothing to increase the damages flowing therefrom. If A enters into a binding contract to build a house for B, B, of course, has no right to rescind the contract without A's consent. But if, before the house is built, he decides that he does not want it, and notifies A to that effect, A has no right to proceed with the building and thus pile up damages. His remedy is to treat the contract as broken when he receives the notice, and sue for the recovery of such damages as he may have sustained from the breach, including any profit which he would have realized upon performance, as well as any other losses which may have resulted to him. In the case at bar, the county decided not to build the road of which the bridge was to be a part, and did not build it. The bridge, built in the midst of the forest, is of no value to the county because of this change of circumstances. When, therefore, the county gave notice to the plaintiff that it would not proceed with the project, plaintiff should have desisted from further work. It had no right thus to pile up damages by proceeding with the erection of a useless bridge.

[...]

[T]he rule as established by the great weight of authority in America is summed up in the following statement . . . :

"While a contract is executory a party has the power to stop performance on the other side by an explicit direction to that effect, subjecting himself to such damages as will compensate the other party for being stopped in the performance on his part at that stage in the execution of the contract. The party thus forbidden cannot afterwards go on, and thereby increase the damages, and then recover such damages from the other party. The legal right of either party to violate, abandon, or renounce his contract, on the usual terms of compensation to the other for the damages which the law recognizes and allows, subject to the jurisdiction of equity to decree specific performance in proper cases, is universally recognized and acted upon."

[...]

In the opinions in all of these some language was used which lends support to plaintiff's position, but in none of them was the point involved which is involved here, viz. whether, in application of the rule which requires that the party to a contract who is not in default do nothing to aggravate the damages arising from breach, he should not desist from performance of an executory contract for the erection of a structure when notified of the other party's repudiation, instead of piling up damages by proceeding with the work. As stated above, we think that reason and authority require that this question be answered in the affirmative. It follows that there was error in directing a verdict for plaintiff for the full amount of its claim. The measure of plaintiff's damage, upon its appearing that notice was duly given not to build the bridge, is an amount sufficient to compensate plaintiff for labor and materials expended and expense incurred in the part performance of the contract, prior to its repudiation, plus the profit which would have been realized if it had been carried out in accordance with its terms.

Reversed.

Example:

Cheryl agrees to remodel Del's house. Del agrees to pay for the work in stages. When the first payment is due, Del announces that she doesn't have the money to pay for the complete job. Cheryl should stop further work, and pursue Del for breach of contract. If she continues to work, she will not be able to recover damages for the work done after Del tells her the contract will not be fulfilled.

This may include stopping performance when the other party has breached the contract, or securing substitute performance.

Damages such as pain and suffering or emotional distress are usually not foreseeable, so are not recoverable in a contract action. In addition, a person's attorney's fees incurred in enforcing a contract are not recoverable unless the contract specifically provides.

There may be contracts where the expectation damages are too difficult to prove. The damages awarded in those cases will be **reliance** damages. Reliance damages are the amount that the non-breaching party spent to perform the contract, in reliance on the other party performing her obligations. They are reduced by any mitigation of damages the non-breaching

RELIANCE DAMAGES:

The amount that the non-breaching party spent to perform the contract, in reliance on the other party's performance.

Example:

Mavis has been hired as the manager of a new band. Her contract says that she will receive 10% of the receipts for each concert that she books. Mavis books concerts in four different cities, traveling to each one to inspect concert venues. She also spends money for internet and phone access, as well as on printing promotional materials. Before the first contract, the band members have a falling out and split up. Mavis does not know what the receipts from each concert could have been, because the band was new and an unknown quantity. Mavis may not recover her expectation damages, but she may recover what she spent to perform her contractual duties.

RESTITUTION DAMAGES:

Damages awarded when there was no legally enforceable contract.

Reliance damages are an alternative to expectation damages. Damages will be calculated under one rule or the other, not both. Reliance damages are sometimes referred to as a "second best" remedy, because there can be no recovery for loss of anticipated profits. If those anticipated profits could be proven with certainty, the non-breaching party would be able to bring an action for expectation damages.

party was able to accomplish. Reliance damages may not exceed the amount that would have been paid under the contract.

Example:

Meg makes a verbal agreement with Jo to buy $7,500 worth of yarn, to resell in Meg's craft shop. After half of the yarn is delivered, Meg says she doesn't want the rest. The contract is within the Statute of Frauds, so Jo may not sue for breach of contract. Jo may, however, sue for restitution for the value of the benefit conferred on Meg.

QUANTUM MERUIT IS AVAILABLE AS AN ALTERNATIVE TO BREACH OF CONTRACT.

U.S. for the use of Coastal Steel Erectors, Inc. v. Algernon Blair, Inc.
(Representative of Subcontractor) v. (Contractor)
479 F. 2d 638 (4th Cir. 1973)

INSTANT FACTS:
Coastal Steel (P) brought suit to recover the value of labor and equipment supplied, but the trial court denied recovery under the contract.

BLACK LETTER RULE:
When a contract is breached, the non-breaching party may sue for the value of the performance provided.

FACTS:

Blair (D) contracted with the U.S. Navy for the construction of a hospital. Blair (D) then contracted with Coastal (P) for services and to supply equipment for that contract. Coastal started to perform its obligations, supplying cranes for handling and placing steel. Blair (D) refused to pay for crane rental, maintaining that it was not obligated to do so under the subcontract. Coastal (P) then terminated its performance.

The district court found that the subcontract required Blair (D) to pay for crane use and that Blair's (D) refusal to do so justified Coastal's (P) termination of performance. The court then found that under the contract the amount due Coastal (P), less what had already been paid, totaled approximately $37,000. The court also found that Coastal (P) would have lost more than $37,000 if it had completed performance. Holding that any amount due Coastal (P) must be reduced by any loss it would have incurred by complete performance of the contract.

ISSUE:

Was Coastal (P) allowed to recover for the value of its services?

DECISION AND RATIONALE:

(Craven, J.) Yes. When a contract is breached, the non-breaching party may sue for the value of the performance provided. It is an accepted principle of contract law that the non-breaching party has the option to forego any suit on the contract and claim only the reasonable value of his performance. Coastal (P) has, at its own expense, provided Blair (D) with labor and the use of equipment. Blair (D) retained these benefits without having fully paid for them. On these facts, Coastal (P) is entitled to restitution in quantum meruit. The impact of quantum meruit is to allow a non-breaching party to recover the value of services provided to the defendant irrespective of whether he would have lost money on the contract and been unable to recover in a suit on the contract.

The measure of recovery for quantum meruit is the reasonable value of the performance. It is not diminished by any loss which would have been incurred by complete performance. The contract price may be evidence of reasonable value of the services, but it does not measure the value of the performance or limit recovery. The standard for measuring the reasonable value of the services rendered is the amount for which such services could have been purchased at the time and place the services were rendered. Reversed and remanded.

ANALYSIS:

Quantum meruit literally means "as much as he deserves." Coastal (P) may have come out better because of the breach of contract, because its recovery is measured by the value of services rendered, instead of considering the position it would have been in if the contract had not been breached . Coastal (P) may recover the value of its services, but the value is not measured by the contract price.

CASE VOCABULARY:

QUANTUM MERUIT:

An equitable doctrine that allows a party to recover the actual value of goods and services rendered, even in the absence of an enforceable contract. The goal is to prevent unjust enrichment of a party.

Note that a party may not recover reliance damages unless he would have earned some profit from his performance. If he would have broken even or sustained a loss, he was not damaged by the breach and so cannot bring an action. It is the obligation of the breaching party to prove that the contract would not have been profitable.

Restitution damages are awarded when there was no legal contract. The contract may have been voided for some reason, such as the incapacity of a party. There may be some other legal bar to enforcement of the contract, such as a

LIQUIDATED DAMAGES:

Damages fixed by the contract.

> **Example:** Stock photo licensing contracts call for the user of a picture to pay a flat fee to use a picture for a certain purpose. The contracts often have liquidated damages clauses that set damages at a certain multiple of the contract price, such as five times the price. Violating the terms of a photo license could cause substantial damages if, for example, the photo is used in a way that generates a large profit. It may also cause minimal damage. The probable damages cannot be estimated when the contract is made, so liquidated damages are included in the contract.

case in which there was no writing for a contract within the terms of the Statute of Frauds. They are appropriate in situations in which one party has partially performed his obligations, and the other party has received a benefit from that performance. Restitution damages for the value of the performance rendered are ordered to avoid unjust enrichment.

Liquidated damages are damages fixed by the contract. The limitation on liquidated damages is that they must be reasonable. Liquidated damages are used in cases where it is hard to know in advance what the damages for a breach of contract could be. It may be easy to ascertain the damage after the breach, but the crucial factor here is whether they could be estimated at the time the contract was entered into.

A liquidated damages clause will be upheld if the amount of damages called for is reasonable, and not punitive.

Interest damages will be awarded when the breach is the failure to pay a specific sum of money at a specific time. Interest is generally not awarded in other types of breach of contract cases.

> **Example:** Sonya owns a bar that buys its beer from Kipele Distributors. Her contract with Kipele runs until the end of the year. In July, Toshi, a sales representative for Tulala Wholesalers, visits Sonya's bar. He tells her that if she switches distributors now, he can save her 20% on the cost of beer. Sonya agrees, and cancels her contract with Kipele. Kipele may sue Sonya for breach of contract, and may also sue Tulala for interference with contract.

> **Example:** Sonya's contract with Kipele has a clause that says it may be renewed at the end of the year. Toshi tells her that if she doesn't renew, but switches to Tulala, she will save 20%. Sonya does not renew her contract with Kipele. Kipele may not sue for interference with contract.

VI. Contract Torts

The usual definition of a tort is a civil wrong that is not a breach of contract. This definition is not entirely correct. There are tort actions that involve a breach, or potential breach, of contract.

Interference with contract is the most important contract/tort action. In order to prove a claim of interference with contract, the aggrieved party must prove the following facts:

- The existence of a valid contract,

- The defendant knew of the existence of the contract,

- The defendant intentionally did something to interfere with the contract, and

- The aggrieved party was damaged by the defendant's actions.

It is essential for an action for interference that the defendant not only knew of the contract, and of the other parties' interests in it, but that he acted intentionally to interfere. An accidental or negligent interference will not be actionable. The action that interferes with contractual performance may be an inducement to breach the contract, but any type of interference that causes damage will support an action. The act of inducement does not necessarily involve threats or duress. Note that a lawsuit for interference with contract is not brought against the contracting party, although they may be independently liable for a breach of contract. The obligation not to interfere with another party's contractual obligations or rights is one imposed by law, not by mutual agreement. Note also that the tort does not prevent legitimate competition, provided existing contracts are respected. A refusal to bargain, including a refusal to extend an existing contract, is not interference.

An action related to the action for interference with a contract is an action for interference with a prospective contract. This type of interference induces or causes a third party not to enter into a prospective contract, or prevent a party from entering into a contract. In order to state a claim of tortious interference with prospective contractual relationship, the plaintiff must show:

- A prospective contractual relation,

- A reasonable likelihood that the anticipated contractual relation would take place,

- An action by the defendant to prevent the relation,

- The intent to harm the plaintiff by preventing the relation from occurring,

- The defendant acted without justification, and

- Actual damage from the defendant's conduct.

Blacklisting, or putting a person on a list of names to be boycotted or punished, is actionable only if there is some malicious purpose behind the blacklisting. If the reason a person

> Expectation damages must be proven with a high degree of certainty. Courts do not permit an award speculative damages.

> **Example:**
> Two stagehands were banned from working at city-owned facilities after a dispute about their work performance at a fund-raiser hosted by the mayor. The ban effectively prevent the stagehands from working, as there were few comparable venues that would hire them. The city's ban constituted interference with a prospective contract. *Minton v. Quintal*, 131 Haw. 167, 317 P.3d 1 (2013).

> **Example:**
> Seamen who were placed on a blacklist for making fraudulent claims for wages could not bring an action for interference with a prospective contract, even though the blacklist prevented them from finding work. The reasons for placing them on the blacklist were true, based on the seamen's actions. *Su v. M/V Southern Aster*, 978 F.2d 462 (9th Cir. 1992).

> **Example:**
> Jeffrey is accused of murdering his wife and children. He makes an agreement with Joe, a writer, that Joe write a book to prove Jeffrey's innocence. As Joe researches his book, he becomes convinced that Jeffrey is guilty. He writes the book in a way that details the arguments for Jeffrey's guilt. Jeffrey may sue Joe for breach of contract and fraud.

is put on a blacklist is true, the interference is not wrongful.

Some situations may support an action for tort and contract. When misrepresentation is involved, a party may bring a tort action for fraud, and may seek to declare the contract void. Contract claims have also been held to be the basis for claims under deceptive or unfair trade practice laws.

Online Contracts

Here's a news flash for you: more and more business is being done online. Electronic commerce has many advantages, but there are issues regarding contracting. The usual rules about contract formation contemplated people meeting face-to-face, or through representatives who met in person, and put the resulting agreement down on a piece of paper. When contracts are negotiated by electronic communications (e-mail, text) between people who may never meet in person, the old requirements of signed written agreements become problematic, to say the least.

Contract law has made some adaptation to electronic commerce. The adaptations do not change any substantive rules about the elements or requisites of a contract. Instead, the new rules set the parameters for contracts entered into online. The rules deal with the formalities of putting a written agreement together.

State contract laws generally provide that an exchange of e-mails will satisfy the requirement that a contract be in writing. Most states have also enacted the Electronic Signatures in Global and National Commerce Act (E-Sign Act). That Act provides that in most cases, a signature, contract, or other record relating to a transaction may not be denied legal effect solely because it is in electronic form. A contract is not invalid solely because an electronic signature or electronic record was used to form the contract. No specific form of electronic record is required. The term has been held to include tape recordings of conversations, as well as e-mails. With some exceptions, required consumer disclosures may also be made electronically if the consumer consents.

The E-Sign Act also provides, however, that acceptance of electronic signatures is not mandatory. While government agencies must accept electronic signatures, a private party may still require a physical signature on a piece of paper.

CHAPTER SUMMARY

A contract is a special type of promise. It is a promise that has five elements: offer, acceptance, consideration, capacity, and legality. The offer is a proposal to make a contract, and acceptance is agreeing to that proposal. Consideration is the exchange of something that makes the promise a contract, and not just an unenforceable promise to make a gift. Capacity is the legal ability to make a contract, while legality is the requirement that the promises made are to do something allowable under law. However simple or complex a promise may be, all five elements must be present in order to make it a contract.

Unlike most other promises we make ("I'll call you tomorrow"), there are consequences if a promise in a contract is not kept. These consequences are intended to put both contracting parties in the position they would have been in had the contract not been breached. The most common way of doing this is for a court to order the payment of damages sufficient to cover the loss caused by the breach. Alternately, the non-breaching party may be reimbursed for the cost of her performance, or for the value of her performance. The goal is to make the non-breaching party whole.

Review Questions

Review question 1.

Define "consideration." Why is consideration important to contracts? Consideration is usually monetary, but what are some other examples of valid consideration?

Review question 2.

When is silence acceptance of an offer? How else may an offer be accepted? What is a firm offer?

Review question 3.

What is "undue influence?" What is "duress?" How does the law address contracts that are the result of either undue influence or duress?

Review question 5.

What are liquidated damages? How would you measure them? What is the difference between liquidated damages and damages you might win in a lawsuit?

Review question 6.

What law requires certain contracts to be put in writing? What are some types of sales that must be in writing? Is there ever a good situation to conclude a contract without any written evidence?

Review question 7.

What is an accord and satisfaction? How does it differ from specific performance?

Review question 8.

What is the E-Sign Act? How does the Act improve online business transactions?

Questions for Discussion

Discussion question 1.

Beverly, a local newspaper publisher, has established a scholarship fund. The scholarship will pay for all of the expenses of the recipient's college education, including all of the student's living expenses. In return, the student who receives the scholarship must agree to work for Beverly's newspaper three years after earning a degree. After reviewing many applications, Beverly sends a letter to Kyle offering him the scholarship. Kyle responds by sending an e-mail that says only "Sounds great! Thanks!"

Is there a valid contract here? Why, or why not?

Assuming that there is a contract, is it the type of contract that has to be put into writing? Why, or why not?

After Kyle earns his degree, he gets a job offer from a local advertising agency. The ad agency would pay significantly more than the job with Beverly's newspaper. It would also offer more responsibility and chance for advancement. If Kyle were to accept the ad agency's offer, and he is found to have breached his contract with Beverly, what damages would he have to pay? Be specific.

Discussion question 2.
Pearl used to work for Ruth's company as a salesperson. She takes a different job, but remains friendly with Ruth. At a sales conference, Pearl and Ruth have lunch, during whichh Pearl gives Ruth some sales leads that she can't use but thinks would be good for Ruth's company. Ruth's new salesperson closes all the leads. Ruth sends Pearl a check for one percent of the revenue earned on the new accounts. When Pearl calls Ruth to ask why she got a check, Ruth says it was a "thank you" for the leads.

Is the check consideration for the leads? Why or why not?

Assume Pearl sends some more leads, and Ruth's company is just as successful with those. Ruth does not send a check, though. Is Ruth in breach of a contract?

Assume that after the first set of leads and the check, Pearl never calls Ruth about the check, but simply cashes it. Then she sends leads monthly for the next 18 months, while Ruth continues to send a check for one percent of the revenue on closed sales. If Ruth stops sending the checks at this point, is there a breach?

Discussion question 3.
Two local softball teams, the East Side Storks and the West Side Siroccos, have an intense, even bitter, rivalry. The rivalry has gone so far that the managers of the

teams have a "peace conference." At the conference, it is agreed that the Storks would not wear their team jackets on the west side of town (called "Sirocco territory"), and the Siroccos would not wear their team jackets on the east side of town.

Is there a valid contract? If so, what is the consideration for the contract?

Suppose a Stork were to wear his jacket while in Sirocco territory. If there were a valid contract between the Siroccos and the Storks, what damages would the Siroccos be able to claim?

Discussion question 4.

Helena has just opened a new business as a wedding planner. She hears that her cousin Chin is planning on getting married. Helena wants to establish a name for herself in the business, so she offers to do the job for half of the usual fee, which will almost cover Helena's expenses. Chin and his fiancée Alex accept the offer. Two days before the wedding, Chin calls Helena and tells her that she can stop work right now, and that Helena's services will not be used as planned.

Chin claims he does not need to pay, because the wedding planning was to be a gift, and that there was no consideration for a contract. Is this claim correct? Why or why not?

Suppose there is a valid contract, but Chin has cancelled it because he and Alex have decided to elope instead of having a formal wedding. What damages may Helena claim?

The wedding was cancelled because Alex is in the Army Reserve, and her unit was called up and sent overseas on active duty. Is Helena entitled to claim any damages? Why or why not?

Discussion question 5.

Denis is a consultant. He sees a request for proposals from a major company in a trade magazine. Denis wants the business, but does not think he can do it on his own. He contacts Polly about taking care of some of the work. They talk about the project, and Polly agrees that, if Denis gets the business, she will take care of half the work for $50/hour. Denis will pay Polly's fees to her out of the company's payments to him. Denis bids on the work. The company sends a letter saying that

Denis can have the project, but only if he reduces his bid by 20%. Denis accepts, and then tells Polly that he can only pay her $40/hour.

> Identify the offers, counter-offers, and acceptances in this scenario.

> If Polly is unwilling to work for the decreased rate, is her dispute with Denis or with the company? Why?

> What is a practical way that Denis can accept the business and satisfy Polly's rate requirement?

Discussion question 6.
Should economic duress be a way to avoid a contract? Why or why not? What level of economic pressure will constitute duress?

Discussion question 7.
Amos is in his mid-60s, and has never learned how to read. He relies on his son George for advice and assistance with any kind of documents. When Amos tells George he is interested in replacing some furniture, George refers him to his partner Luke, who runs a furniture store. Luke helps Amos select some furniture, and prepares an Installment sales contract for the transaction. George explains the contract to Amos, telling him that the monthly cost will be $65 per month. The written contract accurately sets out the number and amount of total payments that must be made, and also shows that the interest rate that Amos will end up paying is 40%. The agreement also gives Luke a security interest In Amos's car and other personal property that he has. George does not explain the interest rate or security agreement to Amos. Amos marks the contract, and George witnesses it as Amos's signature. The furniture is delivered. A few months later, George is away on an extended business trip, and fails to make sure payment is made. Luke repossesses all of Amos's furniture, as well as the other property subject to the security interest.

> Was the contract between Amos and Luke unconscionable? Why or why not?

> Was the contract the product of undue influence? Why or why not?

> Should the fact that Amos is illiterate make the contract voidable? What if no one was available to explain it to him?

5

UNIFORM COMMERCIAL CODE ARTICLE 2

KEY OBJECTIVES:

▶ Become familiar with sales contracts under the Uniform Commercial Code (UCC).

▶ Learn how the UCC differs from the common law of contracts.

▶ Understand when Article 2 of the Uniform Commercial Code applies to a contract.

CHAPTER OVERVIEW

This chapter discusses Article 2 of the Uniform Commercial Code, which establishes rules for the commercial sale of goods. Article 2 builds on the common law of contracts to set forth predicable and reasonable rules for goods contracts. This chapter will cover how Article 2 defines the major aspects of contracts, including formation, warranties, and damages.

INTRODUCTION

The most common type of contract is the contract for the sale of goods. It is a transaction we enter into almost every day. Any time we buy an item at our local store, we make that kind of contract. It is such a commonplace transaction that we seldom give it any thought.

A sale of goods is a contract, but the common law rules of contracts that you have already studied are not the entire picture. The law governing the sale of goods is Article 2 of the Uniform Commercial Code (UCC). Article 2 has been adopted in virtually every U.S. jurisdiction. It is meant to make the laws governing the sale of goods uniform across the nation. Most of the rules in Article 2 follow established common-law contract rules, with some adaptations.

The Uniform Commercial Code is not a federal law. Originally published in the 1950s, the UCC is a joint project of the National Conference of Commissioners on Uniform State Laws and the American Law Institute. The UCC itself is not binding, but it represents the best thinking and recommendations of policy-makers and legal scholars. The states can choose to adopt the entire UCC, or specific parts, or none at all. They may also change provisions in their own laws as they find appropriate.

> Louisiana has not officially adopted Article 2; however, the Civil Code provisions relating to sales have been revised to parallel Article 2.

Note that provisions from Article 2 are included in the appendix. You should refer to those materials as you review this chapter.

I. Sales of Goods

A "sale" is defined in Article 2 of the UCC as "the passing of title from the seller to the buyer for a price." The sale of goods means that legal

> **Example:**
>
> A contract for the sale of prefabricated modular housing units, each containing five motel rooms, was a contract for the sale of goods. The units were moveable, not permanently attached to the land at the time the contract was made, so they would be considered goods. *Cates v Morgan Portable Bldg. Corp.,* 591 F. 2d 17 (7th Cir. 1979).

ownership has passed from one party to another in exchange for some consideration.

The term "sale" does not include a temporary transfer of possession. That is a lease. Leases are governed by Article 2A of the UCC

Article 2 deals only with sales of goods. It does not cover the sale of real estate. It also does not cover the sale of services. Article 2 defines "goods" as

> all things (including specially manufactured goods) which are movable at the time of identification to the contract for sale other than the money in which the price is to be paid, investment securities . . . and **things in action.** "Goods" also includes the unborn young of animals and growing crops and other identified things attached to realty as described in the section on goods to be severed from realty.

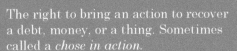

THING IN ACTION:

The right to bring an action to recover a debt, money, or a thing. Sometimes called a *chose in action.*

The distinction between goods and real estate, or realty, hinges largely on movability. Things that are not moveable, or that are permanently attached to land, are not "goods," even if they have been manufactured elsewhere. The characterization of whether an item is moveable, and therefore "goods," is made when the contract is formed. Goods may become realty once they are installed on land.

If the items being sold are permanently attached to the land, they are considered goods if the seller has agreed to sever them. Minerals or growing timber will be considered goods if they will be severed by the seller. If the buyer will sever them, as by extracting the minerals or cutting the timber, the contract is not for goods.

The sale of a business typically calls for the sale of all or most of the tangible assets of the business, such as inventory and equipment, thus making it a sale of goods. Sales of investment securities, such as corporate stock, are excluded from the definition of sales of goods. The sale may also include intangible assets, such as goodwill and intellectual property.

When a transaction involves both goods and other items, there may be a question as to whether Article 2 applies. Many courts use the predominant purpose test used for mixed sales of goods and services when reviewing a sale of

> *Example:*
>
> A contract between a programmer and a client for "computer programs and other services" that consisted of various customized software components was predominantly for the sale of goods. The services provided under the contract were not substantially different from those generally accompanying package sales of computer systems consisting of hardware and software, such as installation, training, and technical support. *Dealer Management Systems, Inc. v. Design Automotive Group, Inc.,* 355 Ill. App. 3d 416, 822 N.E. 2d 556 (2005).

> *Example:*
>
> A contract under which a financial management company converted its on-line data processing system to a new system provided by a different supplier was primarily for services and only incidentally for tangible items. The purchaser did not bargain for reels of tape containing computer data, but for the supplier's skill in putting the data on tapes for transfer to the subscriber's new data processing system. The reels of tape and similar tangible items were incidental to and "serendipitous spinoffs" of the supplier's expertise in the use of computers in the small loan business. *Liberty Financial Management Corp. v. Beneficial Data Processing Corp.,* 670 S.W. 2d 40 (Mo. App. 1984).

a business. Other courts use a test that looks at the reasonable totality of the circumstances surrounding the transaction. The two tests will often lead to similar results. The predominant purpose test asks whether the sale is predominantly a sale of goods, with non-goods incidentally involved. The totality of the circumstances test says that a transaction will be considered a sale of goods if the essential bulk of the assets sold qualify as goods.

SELLER OF EQUIPMENT AND SERVICES ENTITLED TO SEEK UCC REMEDIES.

Audio Visual Artistry v. Tanzer
(Designer-Installer of "Smart Home" Systems) v. (Homeowner)
403 S.W.3d 789 (Tenn. Ct. App. 2012)

INSTANT FACTS:
The parties contracted for the sale and installation of a "smart home" system, and the buyer refused to pay the final invoice.

BLACK LETTER RULE:
A "hybrid" sales contract, which sells both goods and services, is subject to UCC Article 2 if the sale of goods predominates over the sale of services.

FACTS:

Tanzer (D) hired Audio Visual Artistry (AVA) (P) to select and install equipment to incorporate into a then-unbuilt luxury home to make it "smart," that is, wired for a network to control televisions, telephones, music and computers, several independently controlled "zones" for music, whole-house lighting, and other features. The contract totaled over $78,000, of which $56,375 was allocated to equipment and $9880 was allocated to labor and programming services.

The contract acknowledged that Tanzer's (D) ideas of what his "smart home" should include would evolve over the course of the project, and specifically provided that "[v]erbal agreements throughout the life of the project may also be honored as part of this contract and will be documented by [Audio Visual Artistry (P)]." When Tanzer (D) and his family moved in about eighteen months later, the parties had agreed to numerous changes to the system.

The system had some bugs, and Tanzer (D) believed that debugging the system would take about three months. Fifteen months later, however, Tanzer (D) was still having significant trouble with the system. The ongoing bugs were exacerbated by a flood in the media room and a lightning strike that damaged a processor and Ethernet card. Even though "acts of God" were not covered under warranty, AVA (P) replaced the damaged components. Nevertheless, Tanzer (D) was dissatisfied and fired AVA (P), requesting a final billing.

The final billing brought the cost to an amount significantly higher than stated in the contract. Tanzer (D) disputed the final bill and AVA (P) sued for payment. After a second lightning strike, occurring after the action was filed, shut down the entire system, Tanzer (D) hired another contractor to make repairs. That contractor identified several significant problems with the installation.

The trial focused on damages and Tanzer's (D) remedies. A preliminary question, however, was whether the UCC and its remedies provisions applied to the contract. The trial court ruled that it did, because although the contract sold both goods and installation services, the purchase of goods predominated over the purchase of services.

ISSUE:

Did the UCC apply to a "hybrid" contract for the sale of both goods and services?

DECISION AND RATIONALE:

(Stafford, J.) Yes. A "hybrid" sales contract, which sells both goods and services, is subject to the UCC if the sale of goods predominates over the sale of services.

To answer the case's preliminary question, the appellate court conducted a detailed analysis of the UCC's scope. UCC Article 2 applies to sales of "goods," and will determine the available warranties and remedies to the seller and buyer, among other issues. To determine whether Article 2 will apply, courts apply the "predominant purpose" test. Simply stated, if the contract involves the sale of both goods and services, Article 2 will apply if the sale of goods predominates over the sale of services. To determine that question, courts examine the whole transaction to discover its "essence" or "main objective."

Whether goods predominate and labor is an incidental part of the transaction, or vice versa, is a question of fact. After examining two other cases, *Bonebrake v. Cox*, 499 F.2d 951 (8th Cir. 1974), and *Pass v. Shelby Aviation*, No. W1999-00018-COA-R9-CV, 2000 WL 388775 (Tenn. Ct. App. Apr. 13, 2000), the *Audio Visual Artistry* court set forth a four-factor test to determine the predominant purpose of a contract: "(1) the language of the contract; (2) the nature of the business of the supplier of goods and services; (3) the reason the parties entered into the contract; and (4) the amounts paid for the rendition of goods and services, respectively."

The wording of the contract may reveal how the parties describe their relationship, such as using "seller" and "purchaser" or "buyer," which tends to describe a sale of goods. The contract at issue in the case was called a "Systems Sale and Installation Contract," and Tanzer (D) was referred to as the "purchaser" of "equipment." "Equipment," in turn, is a term of art that denotes a sale of goods.

Tanzer (D) argued that, because the equipment was being incorporated into a house under construction, it became part of the completed building. In other words, the equipment was "fixtures" rather than "goods." The court rejected the argument, noting that if the items sold were identifiable as moveable goods before their installation, they would continue to be goods with respect to issues arising under the contract for their sale. The UCC's definition of goods is based on the concept of movability. *See* UCC § 2105.

The nature of AVA's (P) business also indicated that the predominant purpose of the contract was the sale of goods. AVA (P) did not manufacture equipment, but sold equipment made by others as part of an overall "design," which simply meant that AVA (P) determined which equipment would best meet a buyer's needs and would make the chosen equipment work together in an integrated system.

The court also considered the final product Tanzer (D) bargained to receive. At trial, Tanzer (D) *admitted* that he contracted for equipment and, in fact, he offered a spreadsheet itemizing specific equipment, including equipment he wanted to return, which supported AVA's (P) position that the equipment was moveable goods.

Finally, the court noted that the cost of the equipment set forth in the original agreement far exceeded the cost of the labor to install the equipment; goods constituted 82 percent of the contract prices.

Because all four factors supported the trial court's finding that the predominant purpose of the contract was the sale of goods, the appellate court affirmed the ruling that UCC Article 2 applied to the dispute.

ANALYSIS:

Are "smart homes" the wave of the future or a marketing strategy to entice consumers back into bricks-and-mortar stores? Major retailers like Best Buy and Home Depot suffer when consumers come into a store (think, high overhead) to see a product and shop, and then leave to buy the product over the internet. By offering to figure out what products the customer needs and see them installed, retailers may be able to keep the sale of goods in-house.

QUESTIONS FOR DISCUSSION:

On factor leading to the court's conclusion is that the cost allocated to the sale of goods was 82% of the total contract price. Suppose instead that the price for the goods was the same as the portion of the price allocated to installation. Would the result be the same?

The warranty of fitness for a particular purpose in UCC § 2-315 is based on the seller's "skill or judgment to select or furnish suitable goods." Does that language keep the "smart home" concept in Article 2?

Courts consider the same factors under either approach. The first factor is the contract itself. As with any contract, the language used by the parties is considered to determine their intent. The contract is reviewed to determine whether the parties intended to emphasize the goods or the non-goods part of their transaction.

The second factor is an examination of the reasons the parties entered into the transaction. If the sale of all of a business's assets lists only goods and not intangible property, Article 2 probably will govern. On the other hand, if a buyer acknowledges that she purchased all of the assets of a business in order to be able to use its patents, Article 2 did not apply, even though there were goods included in the transaction.

A third factor is the way the pricing of the contract is structured. If goods and non-goods are itemized separately, and priced separately, courts will often look at the ratio of the cost allocated to the goods to the overall price. The ratio is not necessarily determinative, but as a general rule, a contract that allocates most of the purchase price to the cost of the goods will be held to be governed by Article 2.

Finally, when there is litigation over the contract, courts will look at the parties' plead-

> **Example:** A contract for the sale of a grain company as an ongoing business provided for the sale of real estate, buildings, fixtures, furniture, equipment, personal property, goodwill, inventory, the business name, and other assets associated with the business. The largest part of the purchase price was allocated to the purchase of the non-goods. In addition, a large part of the goods in the sale were not itemized in the contract. An inventory of those goods was to take place on the day before the closing of the sale. Viewing the entire contract, the primary purpose was the sale of non-goods, and Article 2 did not apply. *MBH, Inc. v. John Otte Oil & Propane, Inc.,* 15 Neb. App. 341, 727 N.W. 2d 238 (2007).

ings, testimony, and other statements to see how they regard the contract. Admissions of the parties regarding their purpose for entering into the agreement are considered. The nature of the lawsuit over the transaction, and the relief requested, are also analyzed. This factor goes outside the transaction itself, and looks at the way the parties construe the agreement for the purposes of the particular dispute. It is possible that the same transaction could be regarded as either a sale of goods or a sale of non-goods, depending upon the nature of the dispute.

An alternate way of analyzing the sale of a business, or any other mixed or hybrid contract, is the "bifurcation approach." The bifurcation approach is used by a minority of courts. This approach splits the sales agreement into two contracts, one for the sale of goods, and one for the sale of non-goods. Bifurcation will not always be a practical way of looking at a given transaction. It works only when the contract is capable of neat division into goods and non-goods.

Merchants

Many of the rules in Article 2 apply only to transactions involving "**merchants**." A merchant is defined in Article 2 as

> a person who deals in goods of the kind or otherwise by his occupation holds himself out as having knowledge or skill peculiar to the practices or goods involved in the transaction or to whom such knowledge or skill may be attributed by his employment of an agent or broker or other intermediary

> **Example:** Article 2 did not apply in a suit over the sale of a business and all of its assets, when the suit alleged that the seller had fraudulently misstated the gross monthly income of the business. *D.G. Porter, Inc. v. Fridley,* 373 N.W. 2d 917 (N.D. 1985).

who by his occupation holds himself out as having such knowledge or skill.

The definition excludes casual or informal sales, such as a sale of used household items by an individual. It does not, however, include only full-time sellers or dealers. A person who has particular skill or expertise in the area relating to the goods sold could be considered a merchant.

MERCHANT:

Under Article 2 of the UCC, a person who regularly deals in goods of a kind.

II. Contract Formation and Performance

Article 2 does not alter most of the general rules of contract law. It does make some minor changes to promote clear and predictable contracting. Article 2 also provides "gap fillers" for terms that were not included in an agreement for whatever reason.

Example: A foundry was a merchant for purposes of the sale of a certain type of hardware even though the foundry had no experience manufacturing that product. By operating a foundry, the plaintiff held itself out as having skill in the practice of casting iron and in the selection of materials to be used. *Valley Iron & Steel Co. v. Thorin,* 278 Ore. 103, 562 P. 2d 1212 (1977).

PROCESSING GOODS DOES NOT MAKE THE PROCESSOR A MERCHANT.
Crestwood Membranes, Inc. (doing business as i2M) v. Constant Services, Inc.
(Pool Liner Sales Company) v. (Pool Liner Printer)
2017 WL 1088089 (M.D. Penn. 2017)

Robert D. Mariani, J.

CSI is a printing company that specializes in printing on flexible PVC plastics, such as vinyl pool liners. CSI's customers provide CSI with the material to print on and CSI applies ink to that material. CSI, however, does not manufacture any of the materials it prints on. i2M, one of CSI's customers, does manufactures pool liner vinyl. When a pool liner customer placed an order for vinyl from i2M, i2M would send vinyl to CSI and CSI would print patterns on it for i2M.

Eventually, end user customers complained that the pool liners' seams would separate and that patterns would fade. Christopher Hackett, i2M's owner, testified that the seam separation and fading issues were a result of CSI's printing practices. Despite this contention, there was a history of CSI complaining about the quality of vinyl that i2M provided for to it for printing.

[...]

CSI has moved for summary judgment on i2M's claims for breach of contract, breach of implied warranties, and negligent performance of a contract. Specifically, CSI argues that judgment should be entered in its favor on all of the claims because there are no genuine disputes of material fact for trial, the negligent performance of a contract claim is barred by the gist of the action doctrine, and the implied warranty claim fails because CSI is not a merchant or seller of goods.

C. Implied Warranty Claims

Lastly, CSI argues that i2M's implied warranty claims fail as a matter of law because CSI is not a "merchant" or a seller of "goods." The implied warranties of "merchantability and fitness for a particular purpose [ ] arise by operation of law under the Uniform Commercial Code (UCC), and serve to protect buyers from loss where goods purchased are below commercial standards or unfit for the buyer's purpose." Specifically, Article 2 of the Pennsylvania UCC provides that "a warranty that the goods shall be merchantable is implied in a contract for their sale if the seller is a merchant with respect to goods of that kind." Additionally,

[w]here the seller at the time of contracting has reason to know:

(1) any particular purpose for which the goods are required; and

(2) that the buyer is relying on the skill or judgment of the seller to select or furnish suitable goods;

there is ... an implied warranty that the goods shall be fit for such purpose.

Thus, "[u]nder a warranty of fitness for a particular use, the seller warrants that the goods sold are suitable for the special purpose of the buyer, while a warranty of merchantability is that the goods are reasonably fit for the general purposes for which they are sold."

Both warranties are only implied in contracts governed by Article 2 of the Pennsylvania UCC. "Article 2 of the UCC governs transactions involving products or 'goods,' thus before the protections of the warranties attach there must be a sale of goods." "'Goods' means all things (including specially manufactured goods) which are movable at the time of identification to the contract for sale other than the money in which the price is to be paid, investment securities ... and things in action." "Under this definition, 'goods' must be '(1) a thing, (2) existing, and (3) movable—'" "When the transaction involves predominantly the rendition of services, the fact that tangible movable goods may be involved in the performance of services does not bring the contract under the Code."

Additionally, the implied warranty of merchantability is only implied in a contract when "the seller is a merchant with respect to goods of that kind." The Pennsylvania USS defines "merchant" as

A person who:

(1) deals in goods of the kind; or

(2) otherwise by his occupation holds himself out as having knowledge or skill peculiar to the practices or goods involved in the transaction or to whom such knowledge or skill may be attributed by his employment of an agent or broker or other intermediary who by his occupation holds himself out as having such knowledge or skill.

CSI argues that it is neither a "merchant," nor a supplier of "goods," and therefore Article 2 of Pennsylvania's UCC does not apply and there is no implied warranty of merchantability or fitness for a particular purpose in its contracts with i2M. i2M's response, in full, is that "CSI's argument that i2M's implied warranty of merchantability/fitness claim fails because CSI is not a 'merchant' is a fact-intensive contention and is not subject to disposition on a motion for summary judgment."

There are several deficiencies with i2M's argument. First, i2M has offered no citation to any authority for its assertion that the determination of whether someone is a "merchant" cannot be decided as a matter of law on summary judgment. In fact, contrary to i2M's assertion, courts have previously found it appropriate to decide on summary judgment whether a party is a "merchant." Second, i2M does not offer any citation to facts in the record which indicate that CSI is a "merchant." Third, i2M's argument does not address CSI's second argument that CSI does not sell "goods."

Here, i2M has brought a cause of action based on breaches of implied warranties, not express warranties. Pennsylvania law, however, will only imply warranties of merchantability and fitness for a particular purpose into contracts if the contracts fall under the purview of Article 2 of Pennsylvania's UCC. The undisputed facts, however, show that CSI provided services to i2M, not goods, and, therefore, the transactions are not governed by the UCC. Specifically, the undisputed facts show that CSI is a printing company that specializes in printing on materials such as pool liners.

CSI does not manufacture any pool liners, but instead CSI's customers, such as i2M, provide CSI with the material to print on and CSI applies ink to that material.

i2M has not directed this Court to a single fact in the record from which this Court could infer that its contracts with CSI were for "goods" and not for printing services. . . . As CSI has established that it is undisputed that it provided printing services to i2M, and i2M has not shown any disputes of fact concerning whether its contracts with CSI were for "goods" as that term is defined in the UCC, i2M's warranty claims fail as a matter of law.

Accordingly, the Court will grant CSI's Motion for Summary Judgment as it pertains to i2M's warranty claims.

(Citations omitted.)

QUESTIONS FOR DISCUSSION:

Why did i2M try to show that CSI is a merchant?

Can you think of examples where a service provider might also be a merchant in the same goods? Is there a circumstance under which CSI could become a merchant?

Formation

A contract is created when an offer is accepted, and the agreement is supported by consideration. The terms "offer" and "acceptance" are not defined in Article 2, so the common law definitions are followed. A sales contract is made in any manner sufficient to show agreement. This may include conduct by both parties that recognizes the existence of a contract.

One of the features of Article 2 is that it defines default terms when the parties fail to include a term. Under the UCC, a contract may still be formed even if the time the contract was made remains undetermined, or if one or more contract terms have been left open. The essential facts are that the parties have intended to make a contract, and there is a reasonably certain basis for giving an appropriate remedy in the event the contract is breached.

Article 2 follows the common law rule that acceptance may be made by any reasonable means, unless the offer specifies otherwise. The rule regarding the requirements for the form of the acceptance is changed somewhat. Recall that, under the common law rules, acceptance must mirror the offer: it is just saying "yes" to the offer, with no additional terms or conditions. Under Article 2, however, an acceptance may be valid if it contains additional or different terms from those of the offer. The acceptance with additional or different terms is good unless the acceptance is expressly conditioned on accepting the additional or different terms.

If the acceptance contains terms different from the terms of the offer, Article 2 states that those terms do not become a part of the contract. If the contract is between merchants, additional terms become a part of the contract unless:

- The offer says expressly that acceptance must be limited to the terms of the offer,

- The additional terms materially alter the contract, or

- The offering party has given notification of her objection to the additional terms, or notice of her objections is given within a reasonable time.

Unless the offer says otherwise, acceptance may be made "in any manner and by any medium reasonable in the circumstances." This may include separate documents, meaning that the contract is effectively made up of multiple writings.

In business-to-business transactions, there are often multiple forms that make up the commercial contract. Not every routine contract can be minutely negotiated and drafted. Instead, the buyer may send off a purchase order, and depending on the terms, the seller may simply perform on that order (by shipping the goods ordered, for instance), or the seller may first send back a confirmation of the order.

If the terms contained on the purchase order and the confirmation do not match, then a question may arise as to which terms make up the agreement between the parties. If a purchase order says that any acceptance of the offer must be limited to its terms, then the purchase order controls. But if there is a discrepancy in the terms, that might create an issue.

When there is a minor discrepancy in the terms, then the last term on the matter wins. But if there is a material difference in terms, then there are two options.

Objection: The party that receives the materially different terms should object to those terms within a reasonable time. Then the parties can work together to clarify their understanding before performance begins (or decide not to proceed).

Article 2 on additional terms:

(1) A definite and seasonable expression of acceptance or a written confirmation which is sent within a reasonable time operates as an acceptance even though it states terms additional to or different from those offered or agreed upon, unless acceptance is expressly made conditional on assent to the additional or different terms.

(2) The additional terms are to be construed as proposals for addition to the contract. Between merchants such terms become part of the contract unless:

(a) the offer expressly limits acceptance to the terms of the offer;

(b) they materially alter it; or

(c) notification of objection to them has already been given or is given within a reasonable time after notice of them is received.

(3) Conduct by both parties which recognizes the existence of a contract is sufficient to establish a contract for sale although the writings of the parties do not otherwise establish a contract. In such case the terms of the particular contract consist of those terms on which the writings of the parties agree, together with any supplementary terms incorporated under any other provisions of this Act.

Exclusion: If neither party objects to terms that materially differ, then there is no agreement on those specific points. If performance takes place and a dispute later arises on one of those issues, a court may look to Article 2 for default provisions that could reasonably apply.

Article 2 also contains a version of the Statute of Frauds. The UCC version of the Statute says that contracts for the sale of goods for more than $500 must be in writing. There are exceptions to the writing requirement for the following:

- A written confirmation between merchants that is not objected to within 10 days after it is received,

- Contracts for specially manufactured goods not suitable for sale to others,

- Contracts for which payment for the goods has been made and accepted,

- Contracts for goods which have been received and accepted, and

- Admissions made in pleadings, testimony, or otherwise in court.

If an exception does not apply and the contract for sale of goods should have been written, then Article 2's provisions cannot be used when disputes arise. By expanding the Statute of Frauds with regard to sale-of-goods contracts, the UCC makes the point that a written agreement is better for all parties than an oral contract.

III. Performance

Performance of a sales contract under Article 2 follows rules similar to the common law rules for performance of a contract. The main difference between Article 2 and the common law is that a court construing a sales contract will supply "missing" terms for a contract. If the parties have neglected to include terms, the courts are allowed to add reasonable terms for:

> It may seem unlikely that material differences in terms would be allowed to stand in a transaction between businesses, but just as consumers rarely read the terms and conditions for their rental car agreements or cell phone contracts, departments managing a constant stream of orders and confirmations may well miss fine print. Unless there is a problem, the parties may never realize that there was a difference in their respective terms.

Example: George is a "village idiot" performer at various Renaissance-themed festivals. He could make more money if he were a knight, but the costume and weapons are expensive. George asks a vendor at one fair to outfit him for under $500. The vendor says, "I'll do it for $550" and George agrees on the spot. If George pays upon agreement, the contract would not need to be in writing to be enforceable under Article 2. If the vendor had agreed to supply George for $499, their contract also would not need to be written.

- Price of the goods, typically the market price,

- Time for delivery,

- Place for delivery (the seller's place of business), and

- Time for payment (when the buyer receives the goods).

These terms are just placeholders. The courts will not substitute terms in a contract if the parties have already included the terms.

Article 2 also contains a statement of the parol evidence rule. Terms of a written agreement intended by the parties to be the final expression of their agreement may not be contradicted by evidence of a prior agreement or of a contemporaneous oral agreement.

The terms of the writing may be explained or supplemented by evidence of the parties' course of performance, course of dealing, or usage. Course of performance refers to how the parties have been performing a contract that calls for repeated performance, such as a contract to make a delivery of fuel oil every month. Course of dealing refers to how the parties have performed other, similar agreements between them. Usage is the regular practice or method of dealing in an industry, or in a particular place. Usage has become so widespread that a person dealing in that industry or locality would be justified in assuming that the practice will be followed.

Terms may also be explained by evidence of consistent additional terms unless the court is a complete and exclusive statement of the terms of the agreement. As with other types of contracts, an integration clause ("This document constitutes the entire agreement of the parties relating to the sale of the goods identified herein.") will be evidence of a complete agreement.

IV. Warranties

Article 2 imposes requirements for warranties on goods sold by merchants. These warranties are valid unless they are effectively disclaimed.

Express Warranties: Express warranties are created by the seller, and communicated to the buyer. There is no need to use specific terms ("warranty" or "guarantee"). A warranty is created when the seller makes a statement of fact or promise about the goods to the buyer relating to the goods that becomes part of the basis of the bargain. Such a statement creates an express warranty that the goods will conform to the affirmation or promise. A description of the goods which is part of the basis of the bargain creates an express warranty that the goods conform to the description. Finally, a sample or model that is part of the basis of the bargain creates an express warranty that the goods will conform to the sample or model.

The term "basis of the bargain" is not defined in Article 2. Courts have held that any affirmation

Example: A golf ball manufacturer makes a claim in its advertising that its new golf ball will travel 15% further than the manufacturer's other models. An express warranty has been created.

of fact becomes part of the "basis of the bargain." Other courts have required some showing that the buyer relied on the statements before they can be said to be part of the basis of the bargain.

Statements of opinion, or "**puffery**," will not create a warranty.

PUFFERY:
Minor exaggeration of fact when selling goods.

Implied Warranties: Implied warranties are created by operation of law when a merchant sells goods. They are operative unless they are explicitly disclaimed. The warranties that are created are:

> Since express warranties are direct representations by the seller, they cannot be disclaimed. It would not make any sense for a seller to explicitly guarantee a level of quality or performance for a product, and then to say, "Oops, didn't mean that!" This logical inconsistency aside, sellers do sometimes attempt to disclaim express warranties.

- Merchantability – a warranty that the goods will pass without objection in the trade, or function as well as other goods of that type.

- Fitness for a particular purpose – if the seller has reason to know the buyer's particular purpose for buying the goods, and also knows that the buyer is relying upon the seller to select or recommend suitable goods for that purpose goods, the seller warrants that the goods will meet the particular purpose for which the buyer intends to use them.

- Non-infringement – a warranty that the goods will not infringe upon a rightful claim of any third party.

- Title – a warranty that the seller owns the goods and will transfer good title to the buyer.

- Freedom from Encumbrances – a warranty that the goods are free of any liens, security interests or other encumbrances.

Disclaiming Warranties: Implied warranties can be disclaimed, or excluded, by the parties. In order to disclaim the warranties of merchantability or fitness for a particular purpose, the disclaimer must be in a "conspicuous" writing. If the seller wants to disclaim

Example: A salesperson at an electronics store tells a customer that a certain home video system "will make you feel like you're sitting in the front row of your favorite movie theater." The statement is just puffery, so no warranty is created.

> **Example:** Fabulous Dress Company orders a variety of prom dresses from Sew-Sew, Inc. The contract states that the dresses will all conform to standard dress sizes and that the colors will match a pastel shoe line that Fabulous Dress Company carries. The Sew-Sew salesperson also told FDC's buyer that the dresses are "flattering to all shapes." When the dresses arrive, they are mis-sized and all black. Also, they look terrible on everyone who tries them on. Sew-Sew gave express warranties about the sizing and the colors, but the salesperson's statement about the dresses being flattering was puffery. When resolving the issue with FDC, Sew-Sew is responsible for the first two issues, but does not need to address the puffery (except, perhaps, from a customer service standpoint).

the warranty of merchantability specifically, the disclaimer must explicitly include the word "merchantability." Disclaimers that include words such as "as-is" or "with all faults" will usually disclaim all implied warranties.

V. International Sale of Goods Contracts

Article 2 represents an effort to harmonize the law of sales between the different states. This harmonization creates predictability in business transactions. When sales contracts cross international borders, the need for predictability is

the same, but choosing which country's law will apply to a transaction is often problematic. In order to make that decision less troublesome, a multilateral treaty, the United Nations Convention on Contracts for the International Sale of Goods (CISG, or the Vienna Convention) was signed. The United States became a party to the CISG effective January 1, 1988. Mexico ratified effective January 1, 1989, and Canada ratified effective May 1, 1992.

The CISG applies only to contracts for the sale of goods between private businesses who have their principal places of businesses in two different **contracting states**. There is an exception

> **Example:** A toaster purchased at an appliance store has an implied warranty that it will function as an acceptable toaster.

> **Example:** A designer goes to an electronics store to buy a computer to use in his design business. The salesperson listens to her questions, and recommends a particular model. There is an implied warranty that the computer is suitable for use in a design business.

to the requirement that the parties have their principal places of business in different CISG jurisdictions. If the business location with the closest connection to the contract is in another country, that location may be considered for purposes of deciding whether the CISG applies.

Like Article 2 of the UCC, the CISG applies only to the sales of goods, not services. Unlike

---

UCC WARRANTIES DO NOT APPLY TO SALES OF SERVICES.

Milau Associates, Inc. v. North Avenue Development Corp.
(Tenant) v. (Building Owner)
42 N.Y. 2d 482, 368 N.E. 2d 1247 (1977)

Wachtler, J.

A massive burst in an underground section of pipe, connecting a sprinkler system to the city water line, caused substantial water damage to bolts of textiles stored in a warehouse. The plaintiffs who were commercial tenants of the building sought recovery against both Milau Associates, the general contractor which built the warehouse, and Higgins Fire Protection, Inc., the subcontractor which designed and installed the sprinkler system. The suit was brought on the alternative theories of negligence and breach of implied warranty of fitness for a particular purpose.

Evidence adduced at the trial indicated that the break followed the occurrence of a phenomenon known as a "water hammer"--a sudden and unpredictable interruption in the flow from the city water main, followed by a back-surge and build-up of extreme internal pressure when the flow was again released. According to the plaintiffs' experts, this "hoop tension" caused a crack to develop at the root of a V-shaped notch discovered toward the end of the conduit; the fracture traveled along the length of the vulnerable section of pipe with a tearing action and the torrential result.

The "stress-raising" notch was alleged to have been produced by a dull tooth on the hydraulic squeeze cutter used by Higgins to cut sections of the commercially marketed pipe furnished by the subcontractor as specified in the work contract with Milau. Although the 400-foot-long connection had been carefully tested and had functioned properly in conjunction with the remainder of the system inside the building, only a few months in operation had caused enough rusting at the base of the notch, plaintiffs contended, to affect the integrity of the entire system. The defendants produced offsetting expert opinion that the pipe itself was neither defective as manufactured nor improperly installed.

The Trial Judge, having denied plaintiffs' request to charge that the contractors had impliedly warranted the fractured pipe to be fit for its intended purpose, submitted the case to the jury on the sole question of negligent installation. The jury returned a verdict in favor of the defendants, finding neither want of due care by Higgins nor negligent supervision by Milau.

The textile companies contest the trial court's restrictive rulings on the law of warranty. They assert that the V-shaped notch found in the ruptured section of pipe is adequate proof that this crucial component of the sprinkler system supplied by Higgins was defective. It is their contention that the jury would have been justified in finding a defect in the "goods" furnished under the hybrid sales-services contract without necessarily finding negligence on the part of either defendant. The plaintiffs argue that this defect made the pipe unfit for its intended purpose and that they were entitled to have the jury decide whether there was a breach of an implied warranty under section 2-315 of the Uniform Commercial Code or by application of common-law warranty principles.

The majority at the Appellate Division found the record to be "devoid of any evidence that the pipe installed by Higgins was unfit for its intended purpose," and concluded that neither the code nor the case law could be invoked to grant the extension of warranty protection sought by the plaintiffs .

The sales-services dichotomy has been recognized and developed from the days of the law merchant.* In a more contemporary formulation, this court in *Perlmutter v Beth David Hosp.* held that, "when service predominates, and transfer of personal property is but an incidental feature of the transaction", the exacting warranty standards for imposing liability without proof of fault will not be imported from the law of sales to cast purveyors of medical services in damages. In that case we held that this prohibition could not be circumvented by conceptually severing the sale of goods aspects of the transaction from the overriding service component so that a hospital's act of supplying and even separately charging for impure blood plasma could not in logic or common sense be separated from a physician's contribution in administering the plasma during the course of treatment. Viewed in its entirety, we held in *Perlmutter* that the transaction could not be characterized in part or in its underlying nature as one for the sale of goods, for Mrs. Perlmutter had checked into the hospital to restore her health, not to purchase blood.

[...]

As suggested in *Perlmutter,* those who hire experts for the predominant purpose of rendering services, relying on their special skills, cannot expect infallibility. Reasonable expectations, not perfect results in the face of any and all contingencies, will be ensured under a traditional negligence standard of conduct. In other words, unless the parties have contractually bound themselves to a higher standard of performance, reasonable care and competence owed generally by practitioners in the particular trade or profession defines the limits of an injured party's justifiable demands.

The parties to the contract underlying this action were perfectly free at the outset, although not after the fact, to adopt a higher standard of care to govern the contractors' performance. Indeed, under a subcontract in which Higgins undertook to design and put together a sprinkler system tailored to the needs of the commercial tenants, the subcontractor was obligated to "Furnish and install [a] wet pipe sprinkler system all in accordance with the requirements of the New York Fire Insurance Rating Organization, including *** One (1) 8" City water connection from pit at property line to inside of factory building". Additionally, by affixing its corporate signature to the standard form construction subcontract, the fire protection specialist "expressly warranted" that "all *** materials and equipment [which it] furnished and incorporated [would] be new" and that "all *Work* under this Subcontract shall be of good quality, free from faults and defects and in conformance with the Contract Documents. All *Work* not conforming to these standards may be considered defective" (emphasis added).

Section 2-313 of the Uniform Commercial Code requires that a "seller's" affirmation of fact to a "buyer" be made as part of the basis of the bargain, that is, the contract for the sale of goods. The express warranty section would therefore be no more applicable to a service contract than the code's implied warranty provisions. Of course, where the party rendering services can be shown to have expressly bound itself to the accomplishment of a particular result, the courts will enforce that promise.

[...]

Given the predominantly service-oriented character of the transaction, neither the code nor the common law of this State can be read to imply an undertaking to guard against economic loss stemming from the nonnegligent performance by a construction firm which has not contractually bound itself to provide perfect results. In fact, where courts in other jurisdictions have purported to apply an implied warranty of fitness to transactions which in essence contemplated the rendition of services, what was actually imposed was no more than a "warranty" that the performer would not act negligently, or a warranty of workmanlike performance imposing only the degree of care and skill that a reasonably prudent, skilled and qualified person would have exercised under the circumstances, or an implied warranty of competence and ability ordinarily possessed by those in the profession. The performance of Higgins and Milau was tested under precisely this standard and found free from any actionable departure.

[...]

Accordingly, the order of the Appellate Division should be affirmed.

[Citations omitted.]

QUESTIONS FOR DISCUSSION:

Should a breach of warranty depend on a showing of some kind of fault on the part of the one who breaches?

Does the obligation to perform services in a non-negligent manner imply an obligation to use products that conform to standards of merchantability?

UCC WARRANTIES APPLY TO SALES OF FOOD AND DRINK IN RESTAURANTS.

Shaffer v. Victoria Station, Inc.
(Restaurant Patron) v. (Restaurant)
91 Wash. 2d 295, 588 P.2d 233 (1978)

INSTANT FACTS:

Shaffer (P) sued for breach of warranty when a restaurant wine glass broke in his hand.

BLACK LETTER RULE:

The serving for value of food or drink to be consumed either on the premises or elsewhere is a sale, and Article 2 warranty provisions apply.

FACTS:

Shaffer (P) ordered a glass of wine at the Victoria Station restaurant (D). When he took his first or second sip, the wine glass broke in Shaffer's (P) hand. He alleged that this caused him permanent injury. Shaffer (P) brought suit against Victoria Station (D) based upon three theories: negligence, breach of implied warranty under the Uniform Commercial Code, and strict liability. Prior to trial, Shaffer's (P) attorney indicated that he could not prove negligence, and wished to submit the case to the jury on the grounds of breach of warranty and strict liability. The court ruled the case sounded in negligence alone, and granted Victoria Station's (D) motion for dismissal.

ISSUE:

Could Shaffer (P) bring suit for breach of warranty?

DECISION AND RATIONALE:

(Dolliver, J.) Yes. The serving for value of food or drink to be consumed either on the premises or elsewhere is a sale, and Article 2 warranty provisions apply. The UCC states that a warranty that goods shall be merchantable is implied in a contract for their sale if the seller is a merchant with respect to goods of that kind. It is our opinion that, when the Code states "the serving for value of food or drink to be consumed either on the premises or elsewhere is a sale" and that such food and drink must be "adequately contained, packaged, and labeled as the agreement may require", it covers entirely the situation in this case. Shaffer (P) ordered a glass of wine from Victoria Station (D). Victoria Station (D) sold and served the glass of wine to Shaffer (P) to be consumed by him on the premises. The wine could not be served as a drink nor could it be consumed without an adequate container. The drink sold includes the wine and the container both of which must be fit for the ordinary purpose for which used. Shaffer (P) alleges the drink sold wine in a glass was unfit and has, therefore, stated a cause of action. Reversed.

ANALYSIS:

The analysis in this case turns on the definition of what is being sold. The sale is not of the wine glass. Instead, the court says the sale is of wine contained in the glass. The defect was in the packaging of the wine, not in the wine itself.

QUESTIONS FOR DISCUSSION:

A restaurant patron orders a glass of wine. When she takes a sip, the patron learns that the wine has turned to vinegar. Is this a breach of warranty of merchantability?

Suppose that the glass had been set on the table empty, and it breaks when the patron lifts it to be filled by the server. Would the court's analysis hold up in that situation?

The major trading nations that have not ratified are Hong Kong, India, South Africa, and the United Kingdom. Taiwan, also a major global trader, is not eligible to sign United Nations treaties.

the UCC, the CISG does not apply to sales of goods "bought for personal, family or household use, unless the seller, at any time before or at the conclusion of the contract, neither knew nor ought to have known that the goods were bought for any such use."

CONTRACTING STATE:
A state that has signed and ratified the United Nations Convention on Contracts for the International Sale of Goods (CISG, or the Vienna Convention)

The CISG sets out rules for the formation of a sales contract. It provides that the contract is concluded by the exchange of offer and acceptance. The obligations of the parties to the contract are also set out. The sellers' obligations include delivering goods in conformity with the quantity and quality stipulated in the contract, and transferring the legal ownership of the goods. Obligations of the buyer include the obligation to pay the price and to take delivery of the goods. The CISG also sets out common remedies for breach of the contract. The aggrieved party may require performance, claim damages, or avoid the contract in case of fundamental breach.

One of the CISG's major purposes is to provide gap-filler provisions where the parties did not include a specific term. When negotiating internationally, it may be difficult to reach a full understanding or some issues might not be addressed or fully documented. In such a case, the CISG provides reasonable default terms for business-to-business transactions.

Domestic sales contracts are not affected by the CISG.

CHAPTER SUMMARY

Given the sheer volume of contracts for the sale of goods, it is little wonder that a uniform law was proposed to help fulfill the reasonable expecta-

Example: Bytor Corp. is located in Des Moines, Iowa, and has all its facilities in the state. Bytor executes a contract with Snow Dog Inc. to purchase wiring harnesses that Bytor will use in manufacturing. Snow Dog is a Canadian company, but the harnesses are produced in Taiwan. After the contract is signed, Bytor only deals with the Taiwanese facility and staff. The Convention will not apply because Taiwan is not a party to the CISG, even though the United States and Canada are. The same result would occur if the Snow Dog facility were in the United States instead of Taiwan.

Many U.S. businesses are more familiar with Article 2 than with the CISG. When the CISG might apply, the treaty allows parties to exempt themselves from its application by stating that it will not apply to the contract. Some businesses choose to nominate Article 2 as their choice of law in international agreements when exempting themselves from the CISG.

tions of the parties to those agreements. Article 2 of the Uniform Commercial Code provides helpful default provisions when the parties have not included all the terms they later find they need. Based on common-law contract principles, Article 2 offers brighter distinctions and more predictability for good contracts. Its warranty, writing, and performance provisions help make the marketplace more transparent and reliable for both parties.

Review Questions

Review question 1.

What does "UCC" stand for? How do state law and the UCC work together? What Article of the UCC deals with the sale of goods?

Review question 2.

According to Article 2, what types of contract must be in writing in order to be enforceable? What are the exceptions? Why does Article 2 differ from the common law on this issue?

Review question 3.

What warranties does Article 2 imply into sale-of-goods contracts? How can a seller disclaim those warranties?

Review question 4.

What is the difference between an express and an implied warranty under Article 2? Where does puffery fall on the spectrum?

Review question 5.

How does Article 2 resolve issues when the parties have failed to include a term in their agreement?

Review question 6.

What is the international equivalent of Article 2?

Questions for Discussion

Discussion question 1.

Jacob goes to a building supply store to buy a nail gun. He asks Leah, the salesperson, which one she recommends. Leah asks what Jacob wants the gun for, and he says he is building a new shed in his backyard. Leah tells him that the Nailz-it-Good 3000 will suit his needs. Jacob buys the nail gun and takes it home. The Nailz-it-Good 3000 is actually designed for light jobs for crafters, not for carpentry. It cannot drive nails into the wood Jacob is using, and it falls apart after an hour of attempted use.

> Is this a breach of the implied warranty of merchantability? Why or why not?

> Was there an implied warranty of fitness for particular purpose? Why or why not?

> If there were a warranty of fitness for a particular purpose, would there be a breach of that warranty here? Why or why not?

> Suppose Jacob takes the nail gun back to the store and demands a refund. An employee of the store looks in the box and finds a small piece of paper under one of the flaps. The piece of paper says "The Nailz-it-Good 3000 is sold AS IS, with no warranty." Is this enough to disclaim any warranties? Why or why not?

Discussion question 2.

Geri owns a land excavation business. She wants to replace some old equipment that she has, so she goes to see Melissa, a dealer in construction equipment. Melissa shows her the Prometheus 5000, a small bulldozer. Geri tests it, and decides it will be exactly what she needs. Melissa tells her that the model Geri saw has already been sold to another customer, but she can order another one from the factory and have it delivered by the end of next week. Geri says that will be fine, and that Melissa should send her a note with the charges. Melissa makes a note on her tablet computer, and Geri says "That looks cool. Do you know where I can buy one like it?" Melissa says she doesn't know, but she has another unused one just like it that Geri can have for $100. Geri agrees, and gives Melissa $100 in cash.

Three days later, Melissa sends Geri a note saying that the Prometheus 5000 will cost $25,000. Geri does not reply. She is unable to work, due to serious injuries to her hand. The injuries were caused when she plugged in the tablet she bought from Melissa in order to charge the battery. The battery exploded while Geri was holding the tablet.

The bulldozer is delivered to Geri's place of business, but because Geri can't work, no one is available to do anything about it.

> Is there a binding contract between Geri and Melissa? Why or why not?

> Is the note Melissa sent a sufficient writing for there to be an enforceable contract under the UCC? Why or why not?

> Did the exploding tablet breach an implied warranty of merchantability? Why or why not?

Discussion question 3.

Max opened a business holding himself out as a feng shui consultant. For a fee, he visits a client's home or office and gives them advice on the best way to arrange their space. As a part of his package of services, Max looks for the ideal furniture to maximize the flow of the chi in the room. The furniture Max selects is always from an inventory that he maintains in a warehouse, although he does make some effort at picking styles and colors the customer will appreciate.

Lydia hires Max to prepare her living room and dining room. Max assures her that he will find furniture that will be perfect for the room. "You will love it," he says. Lydia tell him that several of her friends are mobility-impaired, and Max needs to take that into account. Max assures her that the finished room and the furniture will accommodate everyone comfortably.

Max goes to his warehouse, selects a sofa, chairs, and some tables. He has them delivered to Lydia's house, where he arranges them into a pattern he regards as harmonious. When Lydia sees the results of Max's work, she is furious. She thinks the colors chosen are hideous, and the chairs are all too low to be used comfortably by someone who has difficulty walking. The furniture is also covered in a fabric treated with some substance that causes Lydia to have a serious allergic reaction. She is contacting her lawyer to see if there is legal action she can take against Max.

Is the transaction between Max and Lydia a sale of goods or services? Explain your answer.

Assume that the transaction was a sale of goods. Has there been a breach of the implied warranty of merchantability? Why or why not?

Still assuming this was a sale of goods, has there been a breach of warranty of fitness for a particular purpose? Why or why not?

Discussion question 4.

Alpha Co. manufactures bicycles. The company is creating a new bike for smaller children. Alpha's buyer looks through some trade catalogs and finds Zeta Corp., a Wyoming company that sells training wheel sets and tricycle wheels that appear to meet Alpha's design department's specifications. The buyer sends a purchase order to Zeta, and Zeta emails back a confirmation form. The purchase order specified that the products would meet the specifications Alpha needed, and that any disputes would be subject to arbitration. It also said that Alpha would pay on net 30 terms from the date of dispatch. The confirmation form includes fine print that says that purchases from Zeta must be paid in advance. It also disclaims all warranties, express or implied, and specifies that disputes will be heard in Wyoming trial court and decided under Wyoming law.

If performance proceeds with no further communication between the parties, what are the terms of the contract?

What Article 2 provisions would apply to this scenario? (Look in the appendix.)

What should Alpha's buyer do upon receiving the confirmation?

Discussion question 5.

What is your reaction to the idea of the Uniform Commercial Code? Does it add an additional layer of regulation that is unneeded over the common law, or does it make sense to promote predictability? Should state legislatures accept an independent body's recommendations or make their own law without regard to other states?

6

CREDITOR-DEBTOR ISSUES

KEY OBJECTIVES:
▶ Understand the main laws relating to debt collection.
▶ Gain familiarity with consumer lending laws.
▶ Understand the workings of bankruptcy and receivership.

CHAPTER OVERVIEW

This chapter covers debtor and creditor relations. The relations start when a **creditor** agrees to lend money or sell goods on credit to another. The person receiving credit or buying the goods is the **debtor.** This chapter will review the rules creditors are required to follow to make sure debtors know the terms of their agreement, and that debtors are treated fairly when they apply for credit.

We will also look at the laws that limit the ways a creditor may collect a debt or make collection more certain. Finally, the chapter will consider what happens when debts can't or won't be paid with a look at bankruptcy and receivership.

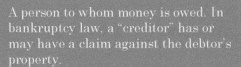

CREDITOR:

A person to whom money is owed. In bankruptcy law, a "creditor" has or may have a claim against the debtor's property.

DEBTOR:

A person who owes money. In bankruptcy law, the "debtor" is the person or entity that files a bankruptcy petition.

INTRODUCTION

It is no exaggeration to say that the modern economy runs on credit. Herbert Hoover called credit "the lifeblood of business, the lifeblood of prices and jobs." It is hard to see how any economy, other than the smallest and most basic, could function without credit. Credit is an efficient way of making sure payments are made and received as they are supposed to be.

Who gives credit to whom, and for what, is usually a matter for the parties involved to decide. There are some limits on this general rule. For example, lenders may not discriminate based on race or gender. There are also limits on how credit is extended. If you take out a loan to buy a car, the law doesn't say how much you may borrow. It does make sure that you know how much you're taking on. It also says that you should know how much it will cost you to repay the debt. If everyone knows what they are getting into, the details of the transaction are up to them.

The theory behind credit is one thing. In the real world, we know that credit is meaningless without payment. In order to make sure credit works, there must be a way of enforcing debts. When a person borrows to buy a car, the credit agreement probably said the car would be the collateral for the loan. The possibility of taking the car back was one way for the bank to know it would be paid. If you don't pay your credit card bills, or the mortgage on your house, there are ways set out in the law to collect those debts. But there is also the possibility that there just might not be enough money for all debts. Bankruptcy and receivership are mechanisms for protecting, as far as possible, the rights of everyone involved in a transaction.

I.   Creditor Protections

Enforcing debts is an issue for all creditors. There are no guarantees that any debtor will pay what she owes. A promise to pay a debt is only as good as the person who makes the promise. A lawsuit on a contract is a way to enforce a debt, but it can be time-consuming and expensive. In an ideal world, the problem would not arise at all. Unfortunately for creditors, the most the law can do for them is to provide ways for creditors to make payment more likely, or to minimize the loss caused by default. There are laws that offer certain creditors special protections beyond the possibility of a breach of contract suit. To benefit from these laws, however, a creditor must be careful to follow all the mandated steps.

Liens provide a mechanism to ensure payment by the debtor. The most common type of lien is a lien on real estate owned by the debtor. If the lien is filed correctly, it becomes part of the public record for the property, and the owner cannot sell (or, often, put other mortgages or obligations on the property) until the lien is challenged and removed or satisfied through payment.

Liens on real estate arise in a variety of ways. If a creditor wins a money judgment against a debtor and the debtor still does not pay, the court may place a lien on the debtor's real property. The creditor could then foreclose on the lien if the award remains unpaid. Other liens are based on work involving the encumbered property itself. These types of liens are considered below.

Mechanic's Liens: A "mechanic's lien" is a claim against real estate that an individual or company has worked on. Assuming the work is adequate, a contractor, subcontractor, painter, designer, electrician, plumber, or any other tradesperson who the homeowner contracts with to work on a property has a right to payment. In addition, any suppliers who provided materials for the work also require payment. If the homeowner does not pay a tradesperson or company that has worked on his house or supplied materials for that work, the worker or company may file a lien with the public records office against the property for the amount owed.

In order to enforce (demand payment or foreclose on) a lien, the lien must be "perfected." Within a fairly short period set out in state law (45 days, for instance), someone working on a property must fill out a form and send it to the homeowner. The form serves as notice that the person or company has a right to seek a lien. After work is complete and the worker or company is not

LIEN
A legal claim on a debtor's property in the amount of the debt owed.

> **Example:** Michelle hires a contractor to add a second story onto her home. To complete the job, the contractor orders lumber and sheetrock from a building supply company. The contractor also hires subcontractors to work on the floor finishes and an electrician to wire the new space. Michelle's contract with the contractor allows the contractor to make these arrangements. Michelle pays the contractor regularly, but the contractor finds that his costs are higher than expected. He does not pay the floor finisher or the electrician for their work, and he only settles half of the supply bill. Despite the fact that Michelle paid the contractor for the entire job, the subcontractors and the building supply company have the right to seek payment directly from Michelle, and they may place liens on her property to secure the debt.

> **Example:** Azure is a structural engineer who worked with a contractor on a remodel of a large home to ensure that a rooftop deck would be adequately supported and safe. The contractor's agreement with the homeowner specified structural engineering services, and Azure's final invoice was below her estimate. Nevertheless, the homeowner did not pay the contractor, so the contractor could not pay Azure. Azure went to the property office to file a lien, but because she could not show that she had provided notice of her lien rights to the homeowner, Azure was unable to file a lien.

paid, the lien is perfected by filing it with the correct property office.

When lien is perfected, it is connected to the property along with other obligations that the property secures. A house may serve as collateral for several financial obligations. These different obligations receive priority based on when they were filed. A higher priority (earlier) obligation must be satisfied before subordinate obligations can be paid.

Liens on Personal Property: While real estate liens provide excellent security, liens can also be created on **personal property**. Personal property is anything someone owns other than real estate. If someone works on personal property and the owner refuses to pay, the worker may legally refuse to release the item. This is a "possessory" lien, through which the customer is encouraged to pay for the work in order to receive the item back. This type of lien is simpler than a mechanic's lien; it only

PERSONAL PROPERTY:
Any property other than real estate. Also called "personalty."
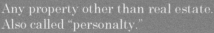

> **Example:**
>
> Bill has his house remodeled. At the time that he hired the contractor, Bill acted in good faith with every intention to pay for the work. Three subcontractors worked on the project. Bill received notice of lien rights from the contractor and two of the subcontractors within the specified period. Bill lost his job and had to seek expensive medical treatment, making him unable to pay for the remodel. The work stops, and the two subcontractors who gave Bill notice file their liens against the property within a few days of each other. The contractor fails to perfect a lien in time. Bill's house is subject to his original mortgage, a second mortgage, and an equity line of credit. The first subcontractor to the property office receives the fourth priority, and the second becomes fifth in line overall. The mortgages and the equity line must be satisfied before the first subcontractor can recover.

> **Example:**
>
> Mick owns a 1969 Dodge Charger, which is worth $10,000. He asks Muscle Car Madness to repaint the car. They agree on $2,500 for the work. MCM is busy and takes some time to get to Mick's car, but the eventual paint job is perfect. Mick refuses to pay because the work took so long. MCM may keep the car until Mick settles the bill. MCM must take care of the vehicle until the matter is settled.

requires possession. If the unpaid worker gives the item back, the lien is terminated.

Garnishment: Another way a creditor can recover money from an unwilling debtor is garnishment. If a creditor receives a court order showing that the debtor owes the creditor a specific amount, and the debtor does not pay, the creditor can be paid from the debtor's wages or bank accounts if a court grants permission. Under a court order, a bank holding an account for the debtor will pay out the debt. Alternatively, the creditor may garnish the debtor's wages. In that case, money will be taken directly from the debtor's pay before a check is issued. In both cases, there are limits to how much may be taken at a time, so if other creditors are already garnishing a particular debtor, later creditors may be out of luck.

Creditors are not the only parties who may garnish an individual's wages and accounts. The government may order garnishment following a court order that finds that an individual is in arrears on child support payments, for instance. Governmental garnishments may also be based on delinquent student loan accounts, unpaid taxes, and other obligations.

II. Truth in Lending

Most debts are incurred by agreement. It may be a loan agreement from a bank or a finance company, or it may be a credit card agreement. With some exceptions, business debts are governed by the law of contracts. Parties are free to negotiate terms, and it is up to each of them to safeguard their individual interests. Individuals who incur debt for their personal or household purposes (consumers) have more legal protections.

The Truth in Lending Act (TILA) is a federal law that applies to consumer finance. TILA is basically a disclosure law. Its goal is to protect consumers in credit transactions by making sure they know as much as possible before making an agreement. TILA does not say what the terms may be. It just says that those terms have to be set out clearly and conspicuously.

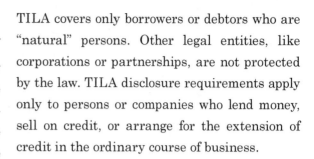

UNSECURED:

A debt is unsecured if there is no collateral guaranteeing the debt. Most credit cards are unsecured.

TILA covers only borrowers or debtors who are "natural" persons. Other legal entities, like corporations or partnerships, are not protected by the law. TILA disclosure requirements apply only to persons or companies who lend money, sell on credit, or arrange for the extension of credit in the ordinary course of business.

TILA applies to installment transactions that require four or more payments. It applies only to loans or extensions of credit that are primarily for personal, family, or household purposes. Since 2009, TILA has applied to student loans from private lenders. If credit is for a business or agricultural purpose, or for public utility service, TILA does not apply. TILA also does not apply to **unsecured** loans for over $50,000, or to credit extended by a securities broker.

The disclosures let borrowers shop around for the best terms. All lenders must use the same format to make the disclosures, so it is easier to compare terms.

The requirements for what a TILA disclosure says are set out in Regulation Z. Regulation Z was issued by the Federal Reserve Board, and is enforced jointly by the Federal Reserve and the Consumer Financial Protection Bureau (CFPB). The Federal Trade Commission (FTC)

Example: Rick's boss offers him a chance to buy a share of the restaurant he works at for $15,000. Rick gets a loan from his credit union for this amount. The loan documents do not have to include TILA disclosures, since the transaction is for a commercial purpose.

Instead of buying a share of the restaurant, Rick borrows $10,000 from his credit union for a family vacation in Africa. The loan is for a personal purpose, so the credit union will have to provide the TILA disclosures.

also enforces Regulation Z as it applies to non-bank lenders.

Regulation Z says that a TILA disclosure will include the following items:

- The Annual Percentage Rate (APR) of the loan.

- The amount financed, or how much is being borrowed.

- The finance charge, meaning the total dollar amount of interest and fees that will be charged if every payment is made on time.

- The total amount of all payments.

- The number of payments.

- The amount of each scheduled payment.

- The right of rescission (cancellation of the agreement).

- Late fees.

- Whether the borrower will have to pay a penalty if she repays all or part of the loan ahead of schedule.

A TILA disclosure should be given to the borrower before the loan agreement is final.

Other disclosures may be required, depending on the type of credit that is being extended. For example, a bank that issues a credit card has to give notice of changes in the interest rate it charges.

The right to **rescission** is the right to cancel the entire transaction. A borrower may rescind the agreement within three days of signing the agreement. Within that three-day window, a borrower may rescind for any reason. After three days, rescission is allowed only if the TILA disclosures were not correct. If the disclosures were not correct, the borrower has the right to rescind within three years of signing the contract. Rescission must be done by written notice. Note that rescission does not mean that the borrower gets to keep the money without

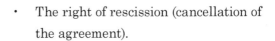

RESCISSION:

Cancellation of an agreement. The parties to the agreement are put back to where they were before the contract was made.

WRITTEN NOTICE OF INTENT TO RESCIND LOANS WITHIN THREE YEARS SATISFIES THE TRUTH-IN-LENDING ACT.

Jesinoski v. Countrywide Home Loans, Inc.
(Borrower) v. (Lender)
135 S. Ct. 790 (2015)

Scalia, J.

The Truth in Lending Act gives borrowers the right to rescind certain loans for up to three years after the transaction is consummated. The question presented is whether a borrower exercises this right by providing written notice to his lender, or whether he must also file a lawsuit before the 3–year period elapses.

On February 23, 2007, petitioners Larry and Cheryle Jesinoski refinanced the mortgage on their home by borrowing $611,000 from respondent Countrywide Home Loans, Inc. Exactly three years later, on February 23, 2010, the Jesinoskis mailed respondents a letter purporting to rescind the loan. Respondent Bank of America Home Loans replied on March 12, 2010, refusing to acknowledge the validity of the rescission. On February 24, 2011, the Jesinoskis filed suit in Federal District Court seeking a declaration of rescission and damages.

Respondents moved for judgment on the pleadings, which the District Court granted. The court concluded that the Act requires a borrower seeking rescission to file a lawsuit within three years of the transaction's consummation. Although the Jesinoskis notified respondents of their intention to rescind within that time, they did not file their first complaint until four years and one day after the loan's consummation. The Eighth Circuit affirmed. [citations omitted]

Congress passed the Truth in Lending Act to help consumers "avoid the uninformed use of credit, and to protect the consumer against inaccurate and unfair credit billing." 15 U.S.C. § 1601(a). To this end, the Act grants borrowers the right to rescind a loan "until midnight of the third business day following the consummation of the transaction or the delivery of the [disclosures required by the Act], whichever is later, by notifying the creditor, in accordance with regulations of the [Federal Reserve] Board, of his intention to do so." § 1635(a) (2006 ed.).* This regime grants borrowers an unconditional right to rescind for three days, after which they may rescind only if the lender failed to satisfy the Act's disclosure requirements. But this conditional right to rescind does not last forever. Even if a lender *never* makes the required disclosures, the "right of rescission shall expire three years after the date of consummation of the transaction or upon the sale of the property, whichever comes first." § 1635(f). The Eighth Circuit's affirmance in the present case rested upon its holding in *Keiran v. Home Capital, Inc.,* 720 F.3d 721, 727–728 (2013) that, unless a borrower has filed a suit for rescission within three years of the transaction's consummation, § 1635(f) extinguishes the right to rescind and bars relief.

That was error. Section 1635(a) explains in unequivocal terms how the right to rescind is to be exercised: It provides that a borrower "shall have the right to rescind ... *by notifying the creditor, in accordance with regulations of the Board, of his intention to do so* " (emphasis added). The language leaves no doubt that rescission is effected when the borrower notifies the creditor of his intention to rescind. It follows that, so long as the borrower notifies within three years after the transaction is consummated, his rescission is timely. The statute does not also require him to sue within three years.

Nothing in § 1635(f) changes this conclusion. Although § 1635(f) tells us *when* the right to rescind must be exercised, it says nothing about *how* that right is exercised. Our observation in *Beach v. Ocwen Fed. Bank,* 523 U.S. 410, 417, 118 S.Ct. 1408, 140 L.Ed.2d 566 (1998), that § 1635(f) "govern[s] the life of the underlying right" is beside the point. That case concerned a borrower's attempt to rescind in the course of a foreclosure proceeding initiated six years after the loan's consummation. We concluded only that there was "no federal right to rescind, defensively or otherwise, after the 3–year period of § 1635(f) has run," *id.,* at 419, 118 S.Ct. 1408, not that there was no rescission until a suit is filed.

Respondents do not dispute that § 1635(a) requires only written notice of rescission. Indeed, they concede that written notice suffices to rescind a loan within the first three days after the transaction is consummated. They further concede that written notice suffices after that period if the parties agree that the lender failed to make the required disclosures. Respondents argue, however, that if the parties dispute the adequacy of the disclosures—and thus the continued availability of the right to rescind—then written notice *does not* suffice.

Section 1635(a) nowhere suggests a distinction between disputed and undisputed rescissions, much less that a lawsuit would be required for the latter . . .The Act contemplates various situations in which the question of a lender's compliance with the Act's disclosure requirements may arise in a lawsuit—for example, a lender's foreclosure action in which the borrower raises inadequate disclosure as an affirmative defense. Section 1635(g) makes clear that a court may not only award rescission and thereby relieve the borrower of his financial obligation to the lender, but may also grant any of the remedies available under § 1640 (including statutory damages). It has no bearing upon whether and how borrower-rescission under § 1635(a) may occur.

Finally, respondents invoke the common law. It is true that rescission traditionally required either that the rescinding party return what he received before a rescission could be effected (rescission at law), or else that a court affirmatively decree rescission (rescission in equity). 2 D. Dobbs, Law of Remedies § 9.3(3), pp. 585–586 (2d ed. 1993). It is also true that the Act disclaims the common-law condition precedent to rescission at law that the borrower tender the proceeds received under the transaction. 15 U.S.C. § 1635(b). But the negation of rescission-at-law's tender requirement hardly implies that the Act codifies rescission in equity. Nothing in our jurisprudence, and no tool of statutory interpretation, requires that a congressional Act must be construed as implementing its closest common-law analogue . . . The clear import of § 1635(a) is that a borrower need only provide written notice to a lender in order to exercise his right to rescind. To the extent § 1635(b) alters the traditional process for unwinding such a unilaterally rescinded transaction, this is simply a case in which statutory law modifies common-law practice.

[...]

The Jesinoskis mailed respondents written notice of their intention to rescind within three years of their loan's consummation. Because this is all that a borrower must do in order to exercise his right to rescind under the Act, the court below erred in dismissing the complaint. Accordingly, we reverse the judgment of the Eighth Circuit and remand the case for further proceedings consistent with this opinion.

[Footnotes omitted]

QUESTIONS FOR DISCUSSION:

Countrywide attempts to draw a distinction between undisputed and disputed failures to make disclosures. The Court does not accept that argument. Should a different procedure be in place when there is a dispute as to whether required disclosures are made?

Is a three-year limitation period for rescission appropriate? Should it be shorter? Should it depend on the loan?

paying it back. Any money that was paid to the borrower must be returned.

Besides the disclosure provisions, there are several other important parts of TILA. A 1970 amendment to TILA prohibits credit card companies from sending customers unsolicited credit cards. There may be severe penalties for lenders who violate this rule. In September of 2016, Wells Fargo was penalized a total of $185 million for opening credit card and bank accounts without customers' knowledge or consent. Small amounts were transferred from customers' existing accounts, and the new, fraudulent account was closed right away. Although the amount of money charged to each customer may have been small, there were approximately 1.5 million bank accounts and 565,000 unauthorized credit card accounts opened. Wells Fargo agreed to refund $2.6 million in fees that were improperly charged.

TILA also says that customers may not be billed for unauthorized charges on unsolicited cards. Other provisions limit a customer's liability for unauthorized charges to $50 per card before she gives notice that a card was lost, and set out ways for resolving disputes between customers and credit card companies.

An important part of TILA is the Equal Credit Opportunity Act (ECOA). The ECOA says that a person may not be denied credit solely because of his race, religion, national origin, color, gender, marital status, age (provided he is of legal age, usually 18), or because he receives public assistance.

> While the ECOA does not ban discrimination based on sexual orientation or gender identity, a state's law may have such a ban.

A creditor may not consider those factors when a person applies for credit, although a creditor may ask about them as a way of helping to enforce anti-discrimination laws (lenders or applicants do not have to reveal that information unless they want to). Immigration status may be considered to decide if the person applying for credit will be allowed to stay in the U.S. long enough to repay the debt.

is necessary to take steps to collect a debt that is unpaid.

In most states, the law puts few limits about how a person working on his own can collect a debt owed to him personally. If a creditor can avoid criminal acts, such as making physical threats or harassing another person, how an individual creditor collects his own personal debts is mostly unregulated.

The same is true for business-to-business debts. In a commercial setting, the creditor and debtor are free to conduct and resolve their debts as they see fit.

Example: Jayesh was admitted to the United States with an H1-B visa. An H1-B visa allows a person to work in the United States for a fixed period of time, but does not authorize permanent or indefinite residence. If Jayesh applies for credit, the lender may consider the length of time he will be allowed to remain in the country in deciding whether to grant his application.

If a person meets a lender's standards for income and creditworthiness, she must be granted credit on the same terms as other qualifying customers. She may not be charged a higher interest rate, and a co-signer cannot be required if other customers would not be required to have one.

III. Fair Debt Collection Practices

Credit is always something of a gamble. Judging creditworthiness is really just calculating the odds that a person will pay a debt. Too often, it

Collection of debts is regulated strictly when the debt is a consumer debt. In that situation, collection is regulated by a federal law known as the Fair Debt Collection Practices Act (FDCPA). The FDCPA applies to debts primarily for personal, household, or family purposes. It also applies only in situations where the debt is being collected by a third-party. To fall within the Act, the third-party must be regularly engaged in attempting to collect debts. The third-party could be a collection agency or an attorney, but it does not include someone who is an employee of the creditor.

> **Example:**
>
> Nathan is the office manager for a dental office. Part of his job responsibilities is to contact patients regarding past-due payments. Nathan is not covered by the FDCPA, because he is an employee of the business collecting its own debts.
>
> Nathan leaves his job with the clinic and forms You Can't Handle the Tooth, LLC, a business that provides office management services for dental clinics. One of the services offered is collection of past-due accounts. Nathan is subject to the FDCPA, because he is collecting debts on behalf of someone other than his employer.

The FDCPA gives debt collectors three areas of compliance:

- Identification as a debt collector,

- Telling the debtor that she has the right to contest the debt, and

- Not harassing the debtor, and not making false statements or contacting others about the debt.

Identification means that the collector has to say that he is attempting to collect a debt. Communications from the collector are required to say that the contact is part of a debt collection effort.

IDENTIFICATION:

A collector must disclose that he is trying to collect a debt when contacting the debtor.

Telling the debtor of her right to contest the debt calls for sending a **validation notice**. The notice must be sent within five days of the collec-

tor's first contact with the debtor. The notice will say how much the debt is and name the party to whom the debt is owed. The notice will tell the debtor how to contest the debt in writing. The debtor will have 30 days to contest the debt. If she does not do so, it is assumed that the amount of the debt is not contested.

The final category of compliance is the one that is the subject of the most complaints under the FDCPA. Harassment includes contacting a debtor early in the morning, or late at night. It also includes calling a debtor at work if she has asked not to be contacted there, making threats, or using harsh or abusive language. Not making false statements includes misstating the amount of the debt, or trying to collect a debt the debtor is not liable for (for example, a debt that is over seven years old).

> According to the Consumer Financial Protection Bureau, 40% of the complaints against debt collectors in 2015 concerned attempts to collect a debt no longer owed.

FILING AN UNTIMELY PROOF OF CLAIM IS NOT A PRACTICE BARRED BY THE FAIR DEBT COLLECTION PRACTICES ACT.

Midland Funding, LLC v. Johnson
(Creditor) v. (Bankruptcy Filer)
_____ U.S. _____ (2017)

Breyer, J.

In March 2014, Aleida Johnson, the respondent, filed for personal bankruptcy under Chapter 13 of the Bankruptcy Code (or Code), 11 U. S. C. §1301 et seq, in the Federal District Court for the Southern District of Alabama. Two months later, Midland Funding, LLC, the petitioner, filed a "proof of claim," a written statement asserting that Johnson owed Midland a credit-card debt of $1,879.71. The statement added that the last time any charge appeared on Johnson's account was in May 2003, more than 10 years before Johnson filed for bankruptcy. The relevant statute of limitations is six years. See Ala. Code §6– 2–34 (2014). Johnson, represented by counsel, objected to the claim; Midland did not respond to the objection; and the Bankruptcy Court disallowed the claim.

Subsequently, Johnson brought this lawsuit against Midland seeking actual damages, statutory damages, attorney's fees, and costs for a violation of the Fair Debt Collection Practices Act. See 15 U. S. C. §1692k. The District Court decided that the Act did not apply and therefore dismissed the action. The Court of Appeals for the Eleventh Circuit disagreed and reversed the District Court. 823 F. 3d 1334 (2016). Midland filed a petition for certiorari, noting a division of opinion among the Courts of Appeals on the question whether the conduct at issue here is "false," "deceptive," "misleading," "unconscionable," or "unfair" within the meaning of the Act . . . We granted the petition. We now reverse the Court of Appeals.

Like the majority of Courts of Appeals that have considered the matter, we conclude that Midland's filing of a proof of claim that on its face indicates that the limitations period has run does not fall within the scope of any of the five relevant words of the Fair Debt Collection Practices Act. We believe it reasonably clear that Midland's proof of claim was not "false, deceptive, or misleading." Midland's proof of claim falls within the Bankruptcy Code's definition of the term "claim." A "claim" is a "right to payment." 11 U. S. C. §101(5)(A). State law usually determines whether a person has such a right . . . The relevant state law is the law of Alabama. And Alabama's law, like the law of many States, provides that a creditor has the right to payment of a debt even after the limitations period has expired . . .

Johnson argues that the Code's word "claim" means "enforceable claim." She notes that this Court once referred to a bankruptcy "claim" as "an enforceable obligation." And, she concludes, Midland's "proof of claim" was false (or deceptive or misleading) because its "claim" was not enforceable. But we do not find this argument convincing. The word "enforceable" does not appear in the Code's definition of "claim." . . . [I[t is difficult to square Johnson's interpretation with our later statement that "Congress intended . . . to adopt the broadest available definition of 'claim.'" [citations omitted]

[...]

Johnson looks for support to other provisions that govern bankruptcy proceedings, including §502(a) of the Bankruptcy Code, which states that a claim will be allowed in the absence of an objection, and Rule 3001(f) of the Federal Rules of Bankruptcy Procedure, which states that a properly filed "proof of claim . . . shall constitute prima facie evidence of the validity and amount of the claim." But these provisions do not discuss the scope of the term "claim." Rather, they restate the Bankruptcy Code's system for determining whether a claim will be allowed. Other provisions make clear that the running of a limitations period constitutes an affirmative defense, a defense that the debtor is to assert after a creditor makes a "claim." §§502, 558. The law has long treated unenforceability of a claim (due to the expiration of the limitations period) as an affirmative defense . . . And we see nothing misleading or deceptive in the filing of a proof of claim that, in effect, follows the Code's similar system . . . The audience in Chapter 13 bankruptcy cases includes a trustee, 11 U. S. C. §1302(a), who must examine proofs of claim and, where appropriate, pose an objection, §§704(a)(5), 1302(b)(1) (including any timeliness objection, §§502(b)(1), 558). And that trustee is likely to understand that, as the Code says, a proof of claim is a statement by the creditor that he or she has a right to payment subject to disallowance (including disallowance based upon, and following, the trustee's objection for untimeliness). §§101(5)(A), 502(b), 704(a)(5), 1302(b)(1). (We do not address the appropriate standard in ordinary civil litigation.)

[...]

Whether Midland's assertion of an obviously timebarred claim is "unfair" or "unconscionable" (within the terms of the Fair Debt Collection Practices Act) presents a closer question. First, Johnson points out that several lower courts have found or indicated that, in the context of an ordinary civil action to collect a debt, a debt collector's assertion of a claim known to be time barred is "unfair." We are not convinced, however, by this precedent. It considers a debt collector's assertion in a civil suit of a claim known to be stale. We assume, for argument's sake, that the precedent is correct in that context (a matter this Court itself has not decided and does not now decide). But the context of a civil suit differs significantly from the present context, that of a Chapter 13 bankruptcy proceeding. The lower courts rested their conclusions upon their concern that a consumer might unwittingly repay a timebarred debt. Thus the Seventh Circuit pointed out that "'few unsophisticated consumers would be aware that a statute of limitations could be used to defend against lawsuits based on stale debts.'" . . . Moreover, a consumer might pay a stale debt simply to avoid the cost and embarrassment of suit. 736 F. 3d, at 1079. These considerations have significantly diminished force in the context of a Chapter 13 bankruptcy. The consumer initiates such a proceeding, see 11 U. S. C. §§301, 303(a), and consequently the consumer is not likely to pay a stale claim just to avoid going to court. A knowledgeable trustee is available. See §1302(a). Procedural bankruptcy rules more directly guide the evaluation of claims. See Fed. Rule Bkrtcy. Proc. 3001(c)(3)(A); Advisory Committee's Notes on Rule 3001–2011 Amdt., 11 U. S. C. App., p. 678. And, as the Eighth Circuit Bankruptcy Appellate Panel put it, the claims resolution process is "generally a more streamlined and less unnerving prospect for a debtor than facing a collection lawsuit." In re Gatewood, 533 B. R. 905, 909 (2015); see also, e.g., 11 U. S. C. §502 (outlining generally the claims resolution process). These features of a Chapter 13 bankruptcy proceeding make it considerably more likely that an effort to collect upon a stale claim in bankruptcy will be met with resistance, objection, and disallowance.

Second, Johnson argues that the practice at least risks harm to the debtor and that there is not "a single legitimate reason" for allowing this kind of behavior. Would it not be obviously "unfair," she asks, for a debt collector to adopt a practice of buying up stale claims cheaply and asserting them in bankruptcy knowing they are stale and hoping for careless trustees? The United States, supporting Johnson, adds its view that the Federal Rules of Bankruptcy Procedure make the practice open to sanction, and argues that sanctionable conduct is unfair conduct . . . We are ultimately not persuaded by these arguments. The bankruptcy system, as we have already noted, treats untimeliness as an affirmative defense. The trustee normally bears the burden of investigating claims and pointing out that a claim is stale. Moreover, protections available in a Chapter 13 bankruptcy proceeding minimize the risk to the debtor. And, at least on occasion, the assertion of even a stale claim can benefit a debtor. Its filing and disallowance "discharge[s]" the debt. And that discharge means that the debt (even if unenforceable) will not remain on a credit report potentially affecting an individual's ability to borrow money, buy a home, and perhaps secure employment. . . . [citations omitted]

More importantly, a change in the simple affirmative defense approach, carving out an exception, itself would require defining the boundaries of the exception. Does it apply only where (as Johnson alleged in the complaint) a claim's staleness appears "on [the] face" of the proof of claim? Does it apply to other affirmative defenses or only to the running of a limitations period? At the same time, we do not find in either the Fair Debt Collection Practices Act or the Bankruptcy Code good reason to believe that Congress intended an ordinary civil court applying the Act to determine answers to these bankruptcy-related questions. The Act and the Code have different purposes and structural features. The Act seeks to help consumers, not necessarily by closing what Johnson and the United States characterize as a loophole in the Bankruptcy Code, but by preventing consumer bankruptcies in the first place. The Bankruptcy Code, by way of contrast, creates and maintains what we have called the "delicate balance of a debtor's protections and obligations." [citations omitted]

[...]

These circumstances, taken together, convince us that we cannot find the practice at issue here "unfair" or "unconscionable" within the terms of the Fair Debt Collection Practices Act.

[...]

Sotomayor, J. dissenting

Professional debt collectors have built a business out of buying stale debt, filing claims in bankruptcy proceedings to collect it, and hoping that no one notices that the debt is too old to be enforced by the courts. This practice is both "unfair" and "unconscionable." I respectfully dissent from the Court's conclusion to the contrary.

[...]

[S]tatutes of limitations have not deterred debt buyers. For years, they have filed suit in state courts—often in small-claims courts, where formal rules of evidence do not apply—to collect even debts too old to be enforced by those courts. Importantly, the debt buyers' only hope in these cases is that consumers will fail either to invoke the statute of limitations or to respond at all: In most States the statute of limitations is an affirmative defense, meaning that a consumer must appear in court and raise it in order to dismiss the suit. But consumers do fail to defend themselves in court—in fact, according to the FTC, over 90% fail to appear at all. The result is that debt buyers have won "billions of dollars in default judgments" simply by filing suit and betting that consumers will lack the resources to respond. The FDCPA's prohibitions on "misleading" and "unfair" conduct have largely beaten back this particular practice. Every court to have considered the question has held that a debt collector that knowingly files suit in court to collect a time-barred debt violates the FDCPA. In 2015, petitioner and its parent company entered into a consent decree with the Government prohibiting them from filing suit to collect timebarred debts and ordering them to pay $34 million in restitution. And the leading trade association has now adopted a resolution barring the practice. [citations omitted]

Stymied in state courts, the debt buyers have now turned to a new forum: bankruptcy courts. The same debt buyers that for years filed thousands of lawsuits in state courts across the country have begun to do the same thing in bankruptcy courts—specifically, in cases governed by Chapter 13 of the Bankruptcy Code, which allows consumers earning regular incomes to restructure their debts and repay as many as they can over a period of several years. As in ordinary civil cases, a debtor in a Chapter 13 bankruptcy proceeding is entitled to have dismissed any claim filed against his estate that is barred by a statute of limitations. As in ordinary civil cases, the statute of limitations is an affirmative defense, one that must be raised by either the debtor or the trustee of his estate before it is honored. And so—just as in ordinary civil cases—debt collectors may file claims in bankruptcy proceedings for stale debts and hope that no one notices that they are too old to be enforced. [citations omitted]

And that is exactly what the debt buyers have done. As a wide variety of courts and commentators have observed, debt buyers have "deluge[d]" the bankruptcy courts with claims "on debts deemed unenforceable under state statutes of limitations." This practice has become so widespread that the Government sued one debt buyer last year "to address [its] systemic abuse of the bankruptcy process"—including a "business model" of "knowingly and strategically" filing thousands of claims for time-barred debt. This practice, the Government explained, "manipulates the bankruptcy process by systematically shifting the burden" to trustees and debtors to object even to "frivolous claims"—especially given that filing an objection is costly, time consuming, and easy to overlook. [citations omitted]

[...]

The FDCPA prohibits professional debt collectors from engaging in "unfair" and "unconscionable" practices. 15 U. S. C. §1692f.4 Filing a claim in bankruptcy court for debt that a collector knows to be time barred—like filing a lawsuit in a court to collect such a debt—is just such a practice.

[Citations and footnotes omitted]

QUESTIONS FOR DISCUSSION:

The Court does not address the issue of whether the claim for the time-barred debt was in good faith, for a reason such as a mistaken calculation of the limitations period. Should that matter in these cases?

The Court puts the burden of enforcing compliance with the FDCPA in these situations on the trustee, and on counsel for the debtor. Is that fair? Does that defeat the purpose of the FDCPA?

Finally, collectors have only a limited right to contact a third-party about a debt. They may call another person only to verify an address or to locate a person.

VALIDATION NOTICE:

A notice to a debtor from a collector providing information on the debt, including the total and the creditor, as well as how to contest the debt.

STATUTORY DAMAGES:

Damages that are fixed by statute. They are awarded without considering what the actual loss was.

A collector who violates the FDCPA may be sued for damages. A debtor may recover actual damages caused by the violation, such as lost wages. The debtor may also collect **statutory damages** of up to $1,000. Statutory damages are fixed financial awards established by legislation.

IV. Fair Credit Reporting

Credit reports contain the information used to decide if a person should receive credit. They are also used for many other purposes, such as screening new employees or insurance underwriting. The agencies and bureaus that issue credit reports do not investigate, but only publish what information they receive from others. This relay system leads to the very real possibility that the important data in a credit report may be untrue. Inaccurate information in a credit report can have serious consequences. The Fair Credit Reporting Act (FCRA) is a federal law that protects consumers from inaccurate credit reporting. The FCRA also limits the use of credit reports.

A "credit score" is a number assigned to a person that is the result of a calculation designed to predict that person's creditworthiness. The specifics of the formula are proprietary trade secrets of the companies that develop them.

Example: Rhonda is interested in buying a house. She checks her credit score to learn what kind of interest rate she might be expected to pay. She is surprised to learn that her score is lower than she thought it would be. Rhonda obtains a copy of her credit report, and learns that the low score is due to a judgment entered against someone with her name. She contacts the attorney who obtained the judgment, and she tells Rhonda that the person who owed the judgment lived in another city, and there was no judgment against Rhonda. Rhonda informs the credit reporting agency, and the notation of the judgment is removed from Rhonda's credit file.

> ***Example:*** Maia applies for a mortgage to buy a house. Her credit score is 745. This high score indicates good credit, and Maia is offered a mortgage at a 3% annual percentage rate.
>
> Maia's brother Seth also applies for a mortgage. His credit is not as good as his sister's, and his score is only 625. He is able to get a mortgage, but the interest rate is 4.5%.

The FCRA says that consumers have the right to know what is in their credit files. While a company that makes credit reports is not required to tell a person if his credit is "good" or "bad," a consumer does have the right to see his credit score.

Consumers must also be told when their credit information has been used against them. For example, when a person is denied a new credit card because of the negative information in a credit report, that person has a right to be told. A person must also be told if she has been denied a job due to information in her credit file.

If there is inaccurate or outdated information in a consumer's file, he has the right to dispute that information. Inaccurate, incomplete, outdated, or unverified information must be removed. Note that information does not have to be removed if a consumer makes an untrue or distorted claim that the information is inaccurate.

A person who is the victim of an FCRA violation may bring a lawsuit for monetary damages. If the violation was willful, the victim may collect either his actual damages, or statutory damages between $100 and $1,000. If the violation was accidental or negligent, the victim may collect his actual damages only.

V. Article 9 Secured Transactions

While there is never any guarantee that a debt will be paid, there is an important step some creditors can take to protect themselves. A creditor who requires **collateral** (a right to property in exchange for the debt) is protecting herself in two ways. The first is that the fear of losing the collateral gives debtors an extra incentive to pay the debt. If that extra incentive doesn't work, the creditor can minimize her losses by taking the collateral and selling it.

Transactions that call for the giving of collateral are referred to as "secured transactions." Secured transactions are governed by Article 9 of the Uniform Commercial Code (UCC).

COLLATERAL: Property or goods used to guarantee payment of an obligation.

Article 9 of the UCC has been adopted in all 50 states, the District of Columbia, the U.S. Virgin Islands, and Puerto Rico.

Article 9 applies when the collateral is personal property, which is most property other than real estate. Under Article 9, a security interest will not attach to that collateral unless certain requirements are met.

First, value must be given. A security interest is not free. It is a form of contract, so something of value must be exchanged for the security interest.

Second, the person giving the security interest must have the legal right to use the property for collateral. This usually means that the person giving the security interest is the owner, or has the legal authority to act on behalf of the owner (for example, an officer of the corporation that owns the collateral). The owner of property may not always have the right to use it as collateral. There may be some contract restricting the right to give a security interest.

Third, a security agreement is authenticated. **Authentication** means that the agreement was signed, or there was some other proof of making the agreement. There must be some proof that the property was used as collateral as a part of an agreement. This agreement needs to identify the collateral that is being used.

The attachment of the security interest to the collateral is an agreement between the debtor and the creditor. Normally, this is all that is needed to secure the obligation. There will be situations when additional parties are involved. A debtor may want to use the same collateral to secure debts from other creditors. This is not necessarily illegal or fraudulent. It is often done when the collateral has a high value.

To protect the interests of secured creditors and potential secured creditors, Article 9 provides for **perfection** of security interests. As discussed above, perfection involves filing a security interest with a government office to make the interest a matter of public record.

Although perfection is a routine part of most secured transactions, it is not required in order to create a security interest. It is required in order to give anyone outside the original transaction notice that the property is collateral. Once a party has notice, it is up to her to decide how to proceed.

With limited exceptions, perfection requires the creditor to take certain steps. The most common exception is for **purchase money security interests** in consumer goods. A purchase money security interest is where the collateral was purchased with the money from the debt (for example, when the retailer finances the purchase of a large appliance). Those security interests attach and are perfected automatically.

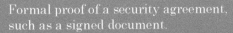

AUTHENTICATION:
Formal proof of a security agreement, such as a signed document.

PURCHASE MONEY SECURITY INTERESTS:
A security interest in property that is purchased by means of the debt, such as a car purchase loan secured by the car itself.

UNPERFECTED SECURITY INTERESTS DO NOT OVERRIDE OTHER CLAIMS.

Credit Bureau of Broken Bow, Inc. v. Moninger
(Lien Holder) v. (Truck Owner)
204 Neb. 679, 284 N.W. 2d 855 (1979)

INSTANT FACTS:
Moninger (D) told a deputy who was seizing his truck that the Bank (D) had a security interest in the truck.

BLACK LETTER RULE:
Verbal notice of an unperfected security interest does not prevent a prior creditor from seizing the collateral.

FACTS:
On October 20, 1977, the Credit Bureau of Broken Bow (P) won a default judgment against Moninger (D) for $1,518.27. On May 16, 1978, Moninger (D) renewed a loan he had with Broken Bow State Bank (D). Part of the collateral was to be a pickup truck Moninger (D) owned. There was no written security agreement.

On June 27, 1978, the Credit Bureau (D) obtained a writ of execution for the unpaid part of its judgment. The lien was given to the Sheriff for execution. A deputy looked at the motor vehicle records, and did not see any liens recorded on Moninger's (D) pickup. The deputy found Moninger (D), served him with the papers for execution, and told him that he was executing on the pickup. Moninger (D) the deputy that there was money borrowed from the Bank (D) against the pickup, and that the Bank (D) had title to the vehicle. The deputy then "grabbed ahold of the pickup." He then said "I execute on the pickup for the County of Custer." The deputy did not take possession of the truck, nor did he ask for the keys.

On July 10, the Bank (D) and Moninger (D) entered into a security agreement on the truck. The agreement was filed, and notation of the security interest was made on the truck's title. The truck was seized by deputies on July 13, and sold at a sheriff's sale. The sheriff asked the court to decide how the proceeds from the sale should be distributed. The court held that the Bank's (D) security interest was perfected on July 10, and that the sheriff had notice of the lien on July 7, 1978. The court also held that the Bank's (D) lien was prior to the Credit Bureau's (P) lien. The court ordered that the proceeds of the sheriff's sale should be paid to the Bank (D).

ISSUE:
Does verbal notice of a security interest make that interest prior to other liens?

DECISION AND RATIONALE:
(Brodkey, J.) No. Verbal notice of an unperfected security interest does not prevent a prior creditor from seizing the collateral. An unperfected security interest is subordinate to the rights of a lien creditor without knowledge of the security interest and before it is perfected. The Credit Bureau (P) became a lien creditor on July 7, 1978 when the sheriff levied on the vehicle. Notice by a debtor to the deputy was not sufficient. The Credit Bureau (P) was a lien creditor without knowledge of the security interest the Bank (D) claimed in the truck. The Bank (D) did not perfect its security interest in the vehicle until July 10, 1978, when it filed a security agreement entered into on that date. The Credit Bureau (P) thus has prior rights to the proceeds of the sheriff's sale.

The levy was valid, even though the deputy did not take physical possession of the truck. The deputy asserted his dominion over the truck, and exerted control over it. Reversed.

ANALYSIS:
If the court had held that telling the deputy that the Bank (D) had a security interest in the truck was sufficient notice, would the laws requiring recording of a security interest have any meaning? A security interest is recorded to give the public notice. It also leaves no room for doubt that notice was sufficient, instead of having a court dispute about who said what to whom, and when.

PERFECTION:

Filing of a security interest paperwork with the government to provide notice of the creditor's right to the security.

Other security interests require filing of documents. The basic document for perfection is the financing statement. Creditors will most often use a pre-printed version of this document called a "UCC-1," or even just "UCC." The UCC-1 asks for basic information, such as the names and addresses of the parties to the transaction. Getting the name of the debtor is very important. The records of perfected security interests are filed by the debtor's name. If the name listed on the statement is inaccurate or incomplete, future creditors could miss the statement.

The financing statement will also list the collateral that is covered by the statement. Note that the UCC does not require more than this infor-

mation. The financing statement does not have to list the amount of the debt that is secured.

The completed financing statement is filed with a public office. In many states, the Secretary of State is responsible for recording financing statements. In some states, there may also be an option to file the statement at the county level.

The purpose of perfecting a security interest is to give notice to potential creditors. The perfected interest is notice that there is another claim on the collateral. When there are multiple security interests, there may be a question of priority. Priority decides whose interest is taken care of first. Generally, security interests have priority according to the date of perfection. A security interest perfected on September 1 will have priority over an interest in the same collateral perfected on September 15. Both will have priority over an interest perfected on October 1.

Once a debt is paid, the debtor may request the creditor to give her a "termination statement." The termination statement says that there is

> A UCC Financing Statement allows creditors to formalize their agreements with debtors.

UCC FINANCING STATEMENT

FOLLOW INSTRUCTIONS

A. NAME & PHONE OF CONTACT AT FILER (optional)

B. E-MAIL CONTACT AT FILER (optional)

C. SEND ACKNOWLEDGMENT TO: (Name and Address)

THE ABOVE SPACE IS FOR FILING OFFICE USE ONLY

1. DEBTOR'S NAME: Provide only <u>one</u> Debtor name (1a or 1b) (use exact, full name; do not omit, modify, or abbreviate any part of the Debtor's name); if any part of the Individual Debtor's name will not fit in line 1b, leave all of item 1 blank, check here ☐ and provide the Individual Debtor information in item 10 of the Financing Statement Addendum (Form UCC1Ad)

1a. ORGANIZATION'S NAME			
OR 1b. INDIVIDUAL'S SURNAME	FIRST PERSONAL NAME	ADDITIONAL NAME(S)/INITIAL(S)	SUFFIX
1c. MAILING ADDRESS	CITY	STATE / POSTAL CODE	COUNTRY

2. DEBTOR'S NAME: Provide only <u>one</u> Debtor name (2a or 2b) (use exact, full name; do not omit, modify, or abbreviate any part of the Debtor's name); if any part of the Individual Debtor's name will not fit in line 2b, leave all of item 2 blank, check here ☐ and provide the Individual Debtor information in item 10 of the Financing Statement Addendum (Form UCC1Ad)

2a. ORGANIZATION'S NAME			
OR 2b. INDIVIDUAL'S SURNAME	FIRST PERSONAL NAME	ADDITIONAL NAME(S)/INITIAL(S)	SUFFIX
2c. MAILING ADDRESS	CITY	STATE / POSTAL CODE	COUNTRY

3. SECURED PARTY'S NAME (or NAME of ASSIGNEE of ASSIGNOR SECURED PARTY): Provide only <u>one</u> Secured Party name (3a or 3b)

3a. ORGANIZATION'S NAME			
OR 3b. INDIVIDUAL'S SURNAME	FIRST PERSONAL NAME	ADDITIONAL NAME(S)/INITIAL(S)	SUFFIX
3c. MAILING ADDRESS	CITY	STATE / POSTAL CODE	COUNTRY

4. COLLATERAL: This financing statement covers the following collateral:

5. Check <u>only</u> if applicable and check <u>only</u> one box: Collateral is ☐ held in a Trust (see UCC1Ad, item 17 and Instructions) ☐ being administered by a Decedent's Personal Representative

6a. Check <u>only</u> if applicable and check <u>only</u> one box:	**6b.** Check <u>only</u> if applicable and check <u>only</u> one box:
☐ Public-Finance Transaction ☐ Manufactured-Home Transaction ☐ A Debtor is a Transmitting Utility	☐ Agricultural Lien ☐ Non-UCC Filing

7. ALTERNATIVE DESIGNATION (if applicable): ☐ Lessee/Lessor ☐ Consignee/Consignor ☐ Seller/Buyer ☐ Bailee/Bailor ☐ Licensee/Licensor

8. OPTIONAL FILER REFERENCE DATA:

FILING OFFICE COPY — UCC FINANCING STATEMENT (Form UCC1) (Rev. 04/20/11)   International Association of Commercial Administrators (IACA)

> **Example:** Pete borrows $500 from Julie. He offers her his car as collateral, and the two fill out a financing statement. Julie does not get around to recording the statement that day. The next morning, Pete decides he needs more cash, so he asks Linc for a loan of $1,000. Pete also offers his car as collateral. Linc does a check for liens, and sees that none have been recorded against the car. Linc obtains a financing statement, and makes the loan. Linc takes the financing statement to the office of the state agency that administers security interests, and records the statement. Julie records hers the next day. Since Linc has perfected his security interest first, his interest has priority over Julie's.

no more security interest claimed on this collateral because of the security agreement. It is usually the debtor's responsibility to file the statement, to make the termination a matter of public record.

REPLEVIN:
A court order, or writ, deciding who is entitled to physical possession of particular personal property. Replevin does not decide who the legal owner of the property is, only who is entitled to possess it.

REAL ESTATE:
Land, structures permanently attached to land, and legal interests in land.

If the debt is not paid, the creditor's remedy is repossession. Repossession of the collateral must be done without breaching the peace. Most states bar a person doing a repossession from going on to private property without consent. Physical assault is likewise prohibited. If the person in possession of the collateral will not surrender it peacefully, the person doing the repossession may go to court and seek an order of **replevin.**

When the collateral is repossessed, it is sold in a "commercially reasonable manner." There is no firm definition of a "commercially reasonable" sale. It will depend on many circumstances, such as the nature of the collateral. Normally, a better price can be realized if a sale is widely advertised and potential buyers have time to reach the sale. On the other hand, it will cost money to store the collateral. While the cost of storing automobiles or construction equipment may be relatively low, perishable goods or livestock will come with high storage fees. It is best to sell that type of collateral quickly, both to minimize the storage fees or to avoid spoiling the collateral.

The proceeds of the sale are applied to the costs of conducting the sale, such as advertising or the fees of an auctioneer, and then to the debt. If there is anything remaining, it is paid to the debtor. If the proceeds of the sale aren't enough to pay the debt, the debtor is liable for the deficiency, which is the difference between

> *Example:*   Max is a car repossession specialist. Car dealers who sell cars on credit give him assignments when payments are not made. Max has three assignments this week. The first car is parked on a public street, and he is able to tow it without a problem. The second car is parked in a private driveway. Max asks the car buyer's husband, who is working outside, if he may come into the driveway. The husband reluctantly agrees, and Max repossesses the car. The third car is parked in a private, locked garage. Max cannot repossess the vehicle.

the amount of the proceeds and the amount of the debt.

VI. Mortgage Foreclosure

Article 9 applies only to agreements to use personal property as collateral. If **real estate** is the collateral for a debt, the transaction is called a mortgage. Real estate is land and the objects attached to the land, such as houses. Like an Article 9 secured transaction, a mortgage enforces a debt by giving the lender the right to retake the collateral.

A mortgage, or mortgage loan, is usually used to finance buying real estate, but the money raised through a mortgage can be used for any purpose. The loan is paid back in installments, usually over a period of several years. The regular payment includes principal and interest. The payments in the early years of a mortgage are typically credited to interest on the loan. The borrower is the legal owner of the title to the property. Her ownership is subject to the mortgage.

If a borrower defaults on a mortgage, the lender takes possession of the property by foreclosure. Foreclosure is governed by state law. While every state's laws will be slightly different, foreclosure usually follows a similar procedure.

> There were approximately 2.9 million foreclosure filings in 2010, the peak year for foreclosures.

Before a foreclosure may start, a lender often is required to give notice. The notice allows the borrower a period of time to cure the default, and bring the mortgage payments current. Some states may also require lenders and borrowers to try to come to an agreement to avoid foreclosure. These state laws require mediation between

> *Example:*   Colleen falls behind on her mortgage payments. Her mortgage lender sends a legal notice that the lender will seek foreclosure if the account is not corrected by a specific date. Colleen sells some stock and makes the late payments. Colleen has cured the default, and the foreclosure may not proceed.

lenders and borrowers for mortgages on residential property. If a settlement cannot be worked out, the foreclosure action will proceed.

A traditional mortgage is foreclosed through a judicial proceeding. A lawsuit is filed, and the borrower is served with a complaint. If the borrower does not answer or put in a defense, the lender will receive a default judgment.

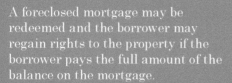

REDEEM/REDEMPTION: A foreclosed mortgage may be redeemed and the borrower may regain rights to the property if the borrower pays the full amount of the balance on the mortgage.

A judgment does not give the lender the right to immediate possession. Instead, the mortgaged property is sold at a public auction. Notice of the sale is published in a newspaper for a certain period of time. The borrower is also given a copy of the notice, or notice is posted on the property. Before the sale, the borrower may **redeem** the mortgage. The mortgage is redeemed if the borrower pays the full amount of the mortgage balance. Many states' laws also give the borrower a period of time to redeem the mortgage after the sale. Post-sale redemption requires paying the amount of the successful bid for the property.

Many states have an alternative to the traditional mortgage, known as the "deed of trust." With a deed of trust, the legal title to the property is held by a trustee. The biggest difference between a mortgage and a deed of trust comes up at foreclosure. A deed of trust is not foreclosed by a court action. Instead, it is foreclosed by sending a notice to the borrower.

As in a judicial foreclosure, the property is sold at a public sale. The borrower will have the right to redeem the property. Generally, the law provides for a shorter time for redemption of a deed of trust.

The winning bid at a foreclosure sale is often less than the amount due under the mortgage. The difference between the amount of the mortgage and the amount recovered is called a deficiency. In most states, a mortgage holder is allowed to pursue the mortgagee for the deficiency. Some states limit the right to pursue the deficiency to mortgages foreclosed through court action. Others impose restrictions on collecting the deficiency when the mortgage was on the mortgagee's principle residence. As a practical matter, many lenders may forego attempting to collect the deficiency. A mortgagee who has not

Example: Assume Colleen does not cure the default when her mortgage lender gave her notice that it would foreclose. Instead, she continued to fall behind. The bank foreclosed on Colleen's house, and prepared to sell the property. Colleen goes on a crowdfunding site and raises the money to pay off her mortgage. As long as she can pay the entire amount owed on the mortgage to the bank, Colleen will have redeemed the property and may take possession again.

made mortgage payments may not have enough assets to satisfy a judgment.

VII. Bankruptcy

Bankruptcy law has many purposes. For individuals and families, it is a way of getting a fresh start by being relieved from an unmanageable debt load. For businesses, bankruptcy can be a valuable tool for reorganizing and putting a business back on track. For local governments, bankruptcy can help avoid financial ruin.

Bankruptcy has a long, if checkered, history in American law. Before the Constitution was ratified, bankruptcy was left up to the states. Each state had the power to make (or not make) its own rules. This decentralized system caused problems for national commerce. As one commentator stated at the time, states could use "almost infinite" rules and standards. These differences could cause issues between states, including unfair variations in outcomes for similarly situated debtors in different jurisdictions.

When the Constitution was adopted in 1789, the drafters included a clause in Article I, section 8 that gave Congress the power to enact "uniform laws on the subject of bankruptcies throughout the United States." There seems to have been little debate or controversy about this clause. The drafters of the Constitution may have thought the reasoning was obvious. In Federalist Papers No. 42, James Madison said only that the "power of establishing uniform laws of bankruptcy is so intimately connected with the regulation of commerce, and will prevent so many frauds where the parties or their property may lie or be removed into different States, that

the expediency of it seems not likely to be drawn into question."

> States still have a hand in bankruptcy law. While bankruptcy itself is federal, states have different rules about what property may be exempted in a bankruptcy case. Some states allow the debtor to choose between their rules and the default federal exemptions, while others require that the debtor use state rules. Exemptions may include the debtor's "homestead" (the house where he lives), cars up to a certain value, and some types of bank accounts and benefits.

In the early days, Congress used its bankruptcy powers sparingly. Early bankruptcy laws were passed during bad economic times and were repealed, or allowed to expire. Congress enacted a bankruptcy law 1898 that was not set to expire. There has been a bankruptcy law in effect ever since.

The Bankruptcy Act today makes up Title 11 of the United States Code. Although bankruptcy is a federal law, there is no constitutional right to bring a bankruptcy action.

Bankruptcy courts are units of the U.S. district court. There is one in each federal judicial district. All bankruptcies are court proceedings, but they usually do not involve trials or lengthy hearings. The decisions a judge makes in a bankruptcy case may be appealed to the district court.

There is only one federal bankruptcy law, but there are six different types of bankruptcy cases. While each type of case involves different parties, and will accomplish different things, there are certain aspects that are common to each type of case.

The first is the terminology that is used. A person or company who starts a bankruptcy action, or who has a bankruptcy action started against them, is called the debtor. The debtor's property is called the estate, or the bankruptcy estate. The people who are owed money by the debtor, or who have some kind of monetary claim against the debtor, are the creditors. A bankruptcy case is administered by a **trustee**, or administrator. A trustee's role is to manage the estate for the protection of the creditors. Trustees are appointed by the Bankruptcy Court.

TRUSTEE:
A person appointed to hold or manage property for another. In bankruptcy law, a person appointed to oversee the case.

PETITION:
In bankruptcy law, the documents that ask the court for relief under the Bankruptcy Act

The second common thing is how a case starts. A case starts when a **petition** is filed with the clerk of bankruptcy court. A petition may be filed by a debtor or, in some cases, by a creditor.

When the petition is filed, the debtor must file additional documents:

- Schedules, or lists, of all assets and liabilities,
- Schedules of income and expenditures,
- Statement of financial affairs, and
- Statement of unexpired leases and **executory contracts** (a contract that has not been fully performed).

Different types of bankruptcy cases may call for additional documents to be filed.

The third common point is the stay. As soon as a petition is filed, an **automatic stay** goes into effect. The automatic stay is a legal stop on most efforts at collecting debts from the debtor. There are several exceptions to the stay:

- Child support or spousal support (alimony) collection,
- Criminal actions,
- Dissolution of marriage or divorce actions,

Example: Alan used his herd of dairy cattle as the collateral for a loan. He filed a bankruptcy petition. The bank became concerned that Alan would be unable or unwilling to take care of his cows. The bank may move the court for an order allowing it to repossess the herd.

- Domestic violence actions,

- Tax collection,

- Wage withholding to repay a loan from a retirement account, and

- Evictions, if the landlord already has a judgment against the tenant, or if the eviction is for endangerment or drug abuse.

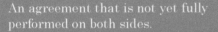

EXECUTORY CONTRACTS:

An agreement that is not yet fully performed on both sides.

AUTOMATIC STAY:

An order from the Bankruptcy Court that stops all collection efforts against a debtor. The automatic stay goes into effect as soon as a bankruptcy case is filed.

A creditor may ask the court to have the automatic stay lifted. A secured creditor may file a petition with the court for relief from the stay if the debt is not being paid. If a creditor stops making payments on her car loan, for instance, the lender may ask the court for permission to repossess the car. A secured creditor may also request the court to lift the stay if the creditor is not adequately protected. This means that the collateral for the debt is at risk of being damaged or destroyed and is not adequately insured.

Finally, in every bankruptcy case, the court holds a meeting of creditors. The debtor must attend this meeting. The debtor is placed under oath, and asked questions about her financial affairs. The trustee may ask the questions, but creditors may also speak. The meeting gives creditors a chance to get information directly from the debtor without having to make discovery requests.

Types of Bankruptcy

The different types of bankruptcy cases are referred to by chapter numbers that refer to portions of the federal bankruptcy statute. The chapter number tells you what kind of relief the debtor is asking for. A bankruptcy may close without payment to creditors. In another case, all or part of the creditors' claims will be repaid. It depends on which chapter of bankruptcy is used. It also depends on the facts of each individual case.

Example: Sadie files for bankruptcy, which triggers the automatic stay. One of Sadie's secured assets is a sailboat. She used to have it housed safely at a staffed marina, but when she started having money problems, she started storing it behind a rental house she owns in a rough neighborhood. She also stopped insuring the boat, in addition to stopping payments on the loan with which she bought it. The sailboat seller (the creditor) may ask for an exception to the automatic stay because the property is inadequately protected, putting the creditor's interest at risk.

Many people believe that if they are the creditor of someone who files bankruptcy, their debt is lost. That is true in many cases, but not in all. Creditors may file claims for payment after a bankruptcy is filed. Creditors in a Chapter 7 case will receive payment only if the estate has assets that are not **exempt** (protected from creditors by law). Creditors who file claims in Chapter 11, 12, or 13 cases will receive at least partial payment of their debts.

EXEMPT:

Protected from being taken by creditors, unless the owner agrees. State and federal law both list certain items of real and personal property that are exempt.

DISCHARGE:

A debt is discharged when the debtor is no longer liable for paying it.

Chapter 7

Chapter 7 is what most people think of when "bankruptcy" is mentioned. It is also referred to as a "liquidation," because the property of the estate that is not exempt is liquidated, or sold. The proceeds of the liquidation are paid to the creditors who have made claims. There is no other plan for repayment of creditors.

Chapter 7 bankruptcy may be filed by individuals, or a married couple may file a joint petition. Chapter 7 may also be filed by a business entity, such as a corporation, partnership, or an LLC. An entity that files Chapter 7 will be out of business afterwards, because all of its assets will be gone.

The end result of a successful Chapter 7 bankruptcy will be **discharge** of the debts. Discharge means that the debtor is no longer liable for that debt. The debt does not, technically, go away.

FEDERAL BANKRUPTCY EXEMPTIONS	
Description of Property	*Maximum Value (2016-2019)*
Real estate or a cooperative used as the debtor's residence, or a burial plot for the debtor or a dependent.	$23,675
One motor vehicle	$3,775
Household furnishings, household goods, wearing apparel, appliances, books, animals, crops, or musical instruments, held primarily for the personal, family, or household use of the debtor or a dependent	$600 per item; maximum aggregate value of $12,625
Jewelry held primarily for the personal, family, or household use of the debtor or a dependent.	$1,600

Any property selected by the debtor.	Aggregate value of $1,250, plus up to $11,850 of the unused amount of the exemption for real estate
Aggregate interest in any implements, professional books, or tools, of the trade of the debtor or of a dependent.	$2,375
Any unmatured life insurance contract owned by the debtor, other than a credit life insurance contract.	No limit
Life insurance policy with a loan value.	$12,625
Professionally prescribed health aids.	No limit
Public assistance, Social Security, disability, illness, unemployment, or veterans' benefits.	No limit
Alimony, support, separate maintenance, to the extent necessary for the support of the debtor and dependents.	No limit
Payments under a crime victims' reparation fund.	No limit
Wrongful death payment for a person on whom the debtor was dependent for support.	No limit
Life insurance payments for a person on whom the debtor was dependent.	No limit
Personal injury payments, except payments for pain and suffering or pecuniary loss.	$23,675
Payments for loss of future earnings.	No limit
Tax exempt retirement funds.	No limit
IRAs and Roth IRAs	$1,283,025
Amounts are subject to adjustment every three years. A married couple filing jointly may double the amount of the exemptions taken.	

Co-signers or guarantors of a debt will still be responsible. There are also several types of debts that cannot be discharged:

- Certain taxes or customs duties,
- Debts incurred through fraud or false statements,
- Debts from embezzlement or larceny,
- Alimony or child support,

- Damages for willful or malicious injury to another person,

- Fines or penalties owed to the government,

- Damages due to operating a vehicle while intoxicated, or

- Debts not listed on the debtor's schedules.

Student loan debts are not dischargeable unless not discharging the loan would cause an "undue hardship." Discharges of student loans due to undue hardship are very rare.

Discharge of even dischargeable debts will be denied if the debtor does not cooperate with the trustee, or fails to produce adequate records. Discharge will also be denied if the debtor makes false statements during the bankruptcy proceedings.

If there is doubt about whether a debt is dischargeable, a creditor may file an action in the bankruptcy court. The purpose of the action will be to decide if a debt is dischargeable. It is up to the creditor to prove that a particular debt

DEBTORS WHO DO NOT COOPERATE WITH THE TRUSTEE WILL BE DENIED A DISCHARGE.

Seror v. Lopez
(Trustee) v. (Bankruptcy Debtor)
532 B.R. 140 (2015)

INSTANT FACTS:
Seror (P) objected to Lopez's (D) Chapter 7 discharge for failure to provide financial records.

BLACK LETTER RULE:
A debtor's failure to turn over estate property and records will justify denying a Chapter 7 discharge.

FACTS:
Lopez was the debtor in a Chapter 7 proceeding. Lopez filed her schedules and statement of financial affairs ("SOFA"), but asserted her Fifth Amendment privilege against self-incrimination on some of the important questions in her SOFA. Lopez invoked her privilege with respect to questions about her income, and certain business losses. Lopez (D) also claimed the privilege about other business records, a gambling debt, and a claim she had against another person. She also claimed she was unable to turn over other books and records, because she had sold all of her electronic office equipment and could not reproduce them. An agreement was reached for her to turn over some records, but Lopez (D) failed to turn over any records. Seror (P) brought an action objecting to her discharge, saying that Lopez (D):

- Failed to keep or preserve records,
- Withheld records, and
- Failed to explain the loss of estate assets.

ISSUE:
Should Lopez (D) be denied a discharge?

DECISION AND RATIONALE:
(Tighe, J.) Yes. A debtor's failure to turn over estate property and records will justify denying a Chapter 7 discharge. A debtor must present sufficient written evidence to let creditors reasonably ascertain the debtor's present financial condition and to follow the debtor's business transactions for a reasonable period in the past. Although Lopez (D) eventually provided many records, she did it in a way that would slow the proceedings down and thwart any real understanding of her finances.

While Seror (P), as Trustee, has the duty to investigate Lopez's (D) financial affairs, the information about her assets must come primarily, if not entirely, from her. Seror (P) cannot conjure it out of thin air.

Lopez (D) correctly argues she cannot be denied a discharge for invoking her Fifth Amendment privilege against self-incrimination. But exercising her privilege against self-incrimination did not excuse Lopez (D) from cooperating with Seror (P) and does not protect Lopez (D) from being denied a discharge. Discharge denied.

ANALYSIS:

The reason for denying Lopez (D) a discharge is her failure to cooperate. It was not because her debts were non-dischargeable.

CASE VOCABULARY:

FIFTH AMENDMENT PRIVILEGE:

The rule set out in the Fifth Amendment to the U.S. Constitution that no person "shall be compelled in any criminal case to be a witness against himself." The privilege applies in any type of proceeding, so that a person may decline to answer questions if her answer could lead to criminal charges.

QUESTION FOR DISCUSSION:

Whose interests should a bankruptcy trustee protect?

---

cannot be discharged. Bankruptcy courts tend to resolve doubts in favor of debtors.

There is no minimum or maximum amount of debt to qualify for Chapter 7. The only limitation is that a Chapter 7 petition may not be an abuse of the bankruptcy system. Concerns that Chapter 7 was too easy to file, and let too many irresponsible debtors walk away from debt, led to new requirements for debtors.

Since 2005, debtors must pass a means test before they can file Chapter 7. Under the means test system, abuse of the system is presumed unless the debtor has a monthly income less than the median income for a household of her size in her state. The median monthly income is published by the U.S. Census Bureau. If a debtor has an income higher than the median, she can still file Chapter 7 if her monthly income after paying living expenses is not enough to pay off at least part of her unsecured debt. If she does have enough to pay, her case will be converted to a Chapter 13.

> It is estimated that 61% of consumer bankruptcies include medical debt. The average medical debt amount is over $9,300.

All Chapter 7 debtors, regardless of income, must certify that they have attended an approved credit counseling session.

Chapter 9

Chapter 9 is a financial reorganization for municipalities. A municipality is defined to include cities, towns, or villages. The term also includes counties, school districts, taxing districts, or publicly-owned utilities. A state is not a "municipality."

A municipality may not file a Chapter 9 petition unless state law gives it permission to do so. In addition, a municipality must be **insolvent** before it may file. A municipality is insolvent if it is not paying its debts. Insolvent can also mean that the municipality is unable to pay its debts as they come due.

INSOLVENT:
Unable to pay debts.

Reorganization may include delaying the time when a debt becomes due, reducing the principal or interest of a debt. It may also include getting a new loan to refinance a debt. The law does not require liquidation of any of a municipality's assets, but a voluntary sale of some assets may be part of a reorganization plan.

Bankruptcy courts usually do not take an active role in managing Chapter 9 cases. Courts will limit themselves to approving the petition, confirming a reorganization plan, and making sure the plan is put into effect.

In 2016, the U.S. Supreme Court ruled that cities and towns in Puerto Rico may not file for bankruptcy under Chapter 9, because Puerto Rico is not a state.

Sometimes, municipalities avoid bankruptcy by the thinnest of margins. In 1975, New York City came within hours of defaulting on its bills, and started the process for filing bankruptcy. A last-minute agreement by the city teachers' union to invest pension funds in city bonds made the filing unnecessary.

Chapter 11

Chapter 11 is a reorganization. Although individuals are allowed to file Chapter 11, it is mostly used by businesses. A Chapter 11 bankruptcy allows a business to restructure itself to become profitable. The restructuring can involve selling off part of the business, renegotiating debt, or rejecting executory contracts. The goal is continued survival, not liquidation. Unlike a Chapter 7 debtor, the debtor in a Chapter 11 case does not turn assets over to the trustee.

Chapter 11 bankruptcies use the same terminology as other types of bankruptcy, with one major exception. A debtor that files a Chapter 11 bankruptcy is officially known as the **debtor in possession**. The debtor in possession is responsible for keeping the business running during the Chapter 11 proceedings. The debtor in possession is required to perform most of the functions of a trustee. These duties include accounting

Example: The largest Chapter 9 bankruptcy, in terms of both the amount of money involved ($18-20 billion) and the size of the municipality (population 700,000), was the city of Detroit. The Emergency Financial Manager appointed by the state to oversee Detroit's finances filed a Chapter 9 petition on July 18, 2013. The city worked out a restructuring plan, and exited bankruptcy on December 10, 2014.

for property, examining and objecting to claims, and filing required reports. The debtor is also responsible for filing tax returns and reports that the court might require, such as a final accounting.

> ### DEBTOR IN POSSESSION:
> A Chapter 11 bankruptcy debtor over the term of the Chapter 11 process.

A company or person that files Chapter 11 files the same documents with the petition as other debtors would. In addition, the debtor must file a written disclosure statement and a plan of reorganization. The disclosure statement sets out information about the assets, liabilities, and business affairs of the debtor. In order for the case to move forward, the statement must be approved by the court after a hearing. The disclosure statement is the main source of information that creditors have to make an informed judgment about the reorganization plan.

Creditors may object to the disclosure statement. The most common objection is that the statement does not have enough detail to let creditors make an informed decision about the reorganization plan. Details that the courts expect to see include a listing of assets and liabilities, the circumstances that caused the debtor to file a bankruptcy petition, and the source for the information in the statement. The statement should also include a summary of the reorganization plan.

When the judge approves the disclosure statement, a date is set for voting on the plan of reorganization. The plan of reorganization, or just the "plan," is the debtor's proposal for restructuring the business and paying creditors. The debtor must file the plan within 120 days of filing the petition, or, if the debtor is a "small business," within 180 days.

> In Chapter 11 cases, a "small business" is a business that has less than $2 million in total debt.

If the plan is not filed within that time, any creditor may file a proposed plan. A plan will not go into effect unless it is approved by the court.

Chapter 11 is set up to encourage close participation by all creditors. Creditors have a say as to whether a plan will be approved, but their involvement goes deeper than just voting. It is common for creditors to get involved with the plan early. In many cases, creditors have negotiated a plan with the debtor before the petition is filed. After the petition is filed, the court will get

> **Example:** Interstate Stores operated several chains of discount stores. In the mid-1970s, the company filed Chapter 11 bankruptcy, and closed or sold its poorly performing units. The company then concentrated on its strongest component, the children's retailer Toys "R" Us.

input from creditors before taking or approving any action. Unsecured creditors may participate in the case through a creditor's committee appointed by the court. That committee is made up of the seven largest unsecured creditors. It participates in crafting the plan, but the committee also consults on the administration of the case, and investigates the debtor's operation of the business.

Every Chapter 11 plan is different, and is tailored to meet the circumstances and needs of each case. All claims of creditors must be classified according to the size of the claim, and the type of debt the claim is for. The plan will say how each classification will be treated. Each of the creditors in a classification must be treated the same.

> A collective bargaining agreement with an employees' union may be rejected only if the debtor has tried to negotiate with the union. The debtor may modify the agreement on its own terms if the modification is essential for the continuation of the business.

When creating a plan, debtors have some discretion in deciding how each classification of creditors will be treated. Employees may be terminated, and assets may be sold off. Contracts that have not been completed may be accepted as they are, rejected, or renegotiated.

Some creditors may receive less than full value for their claims. Others may have the value of their claim reduced. Claims that will not be paid in full are called "impaired" claims. Creditors with impaired claims are allowed to vote on the plan submitted by the debtor.

> Several U.S. airlines have gone through Chapter 11 reorganizations. Some analysts referred to these as "offensive" reorganizations, because the airlines used the process to achieve wage concessions from their highly paid staff in order to become more competitive.

After a vote is taken on the plan, the court will conduct a confirmation hearing to determine whether to confirm the plan. A plan may be approved if it is:

- Feasible,

- Proposed in good faith, and

- In compliance with all of the provisions of the Bankruptcy Code.

If the creditors vote down a plan that meets all of the legal requirements, the court may still approve the plan over their objections of the creditors. To do this, the court must find that the plan does not discriminate unfairly and is fair and equitable with respect to each dissenting class of impaired claims. This process is colorfully known as "cram down."

UNPERFECTED SECURITY INTERESTS DO NOT OVERRIDE OTHER CLAIMS.

In re: Arm Ventures, LLC
(Bankruptcy Debtor)
564 B.R. 77 (S.D. Fla. 2017)

Laurel M. Isicoff, Chief United States Bankruptcy Judge. The Debtor, Arm Ventures, LLC, filed its voluntary chapter 11 petition on October 4, 2016. The Debtor owns commercial property at 753–755 Arthur Godfrey Rd., Miami Beach, Florida 33140 (the "Commercial Property").

[...]

The state court set a foreclosure sale[.] The night before the sale, the Debtor removed the state court case to the United States District Court which removal cancelled the foreclosure sale. Soon thereafter, the case was remanded to the state court and a second foreclosure sale was set[.] The night before the second foreclosure sale, the Debtor removed the case to federal court again. The foreclosure sale was, again, automatically cancelled. . . . In the days leading up to the third sale, the Debtor filed multiple emergency motions in the state court to delay[.] The day before the third foreclosure sale, the Debtor filed this Chapter 11 case.

Shortly after the Debtor filed its petition, Ocean Bank filed this Motion arguing that the case should be dismissed for cause under 11 U.S.C. § 1112(b)(1) because the case was filed in bad faith. Ocean Bank argues that the Debtor's bad faith is evidenced by the Debtor's repeated attempts to stop the foreclosure sale by using procedures in both the state and federal court and using the bankruptcy court as a last resort when the prior procedures did not yield the Debtor's desired results. . . . [T]he Debtor acknowledged that the timing of the filing was unfortunate, but was really due to the fact that the Debtor was acting without advice of bankruptcy counsel when all those prior actions occurred. This argument is unpersuasive. The Debtor's principal is a lawyer, and also apparently the author of most, if not all, of the pleadings[.]

Nonetheless, the Debtor urges that it filed bankruptcy with the intention of reorganizing its business . . . Debtor filed a Plan of Reorganization [proposing] to rent space in the Commercial Property to a business that generates income from medical marijuana. . . . Ocean Bank pointed out that every court in the country that has dealt with a plan funded in whole or in part by the sale of marijuana has refused to confirm the plan.

1211 U.S.C. § 1112 lays out a non-exclusive list of reasons a court should consider dismissal of a chapter 11 case, including "for cause". "For cause" includes the filing of a bankruptcy case in bad faith. When determining whether a chapter 11 case should be dismissed as a bad faith filing, I must consider factors that evidence "an intent to abuse the judicial process and the purposes of the reorganization provisions". Thus I may consider factors such as "when there is no realistic possibility of an effective reorganization and it is evident that the debtor seeks merely to delay or frustrate the legitimate efforts of secured creditors to enforce their rights."

The Eleventh Circuit . . . listed a number of subjective factors in determining whether a dismissal for bad faith is appropriate. The factors include whether: (i) The Debtor only has one asset, ...; (ii) The Debtor has few unsecured creditors whose claims are small in relation to the claims of the Secured Creditors; (iii) The Debtor has few employees; (iv) The Property is the subject of a foreclosure action as a result of arrearages on the debt; (v) The Debtor's financial problems involve essentially a dispute between the Debtor and the Secured Creditors which can be resolved in the pending State Court Action; and (vi) The timing of the Debtor's filing evidences an intent to delay or frustrate the legitimate efforts of the Debtor's secured creditors to enforce their rights.

[...]

In determining whether dismissal is appropriate due to lack of good faith I may also consider whether the Debtor has the ability to reorganize itself. If after considering the economic realities of the Debtor's situation, I believe that there is no realistic chance for the Debtor to successfully reorganize, the case should be dismissed.

The Debtor argues that it will be able to prove feasibility at confirmation. Modern Pharmacy, the proposed tenant, has apparently applied for both state and federal approval to cultivate and sell marijuana; however, Modern Pharmacy has yet to have its applications granted. Ocean Bank argues that the Plan is unconfirmable because it is highly unlikely that Modern Pharmacy would be able to get both state and federal approval to manufacture and sell medical marijuana—especially since, according to Ocean Bank, the Commercial Property is in close proximity to a school and to a synagogue. However, it is not necessary for me to go into the details of where the Commercial Property is located, nor what is the status of the applications because the law is very clear—a bankruptcy plan that proposes to be funded through income generated by the sale of marijuana products cannot be confirmed unless the business generating the income is legal under both state law and federal law. Moreover, the conditions for feasibility are so speculative—both as to timing and authority—that any plan proposed by the Debtor based on the sale of marijuana is not confirmable, certainly not for the foreseeable future.

[...]

In each case where the court has denied confirmation or dismissed a case stemming from funding dependent in whole or in part from marijuana, the marijuana source of funding was legal under the relevant state law. The issue is whether Modern Pharmacy would be approved under Federal law to manufacture or sell marijuana. As of now, in all the years that marijuana has been explored as an option for treatment, only the University of Mississippi has ever received approval by the Federal government to grow, harvest, and store bulk marijuana and purified elements of marijuana for use by researchers. Thus it is highly unlikely, and at a minimum, at this juncture an extremely remote possibility, that the Debtor will receive approval from the Federal government.

In sum, in order to confirm the Amended Plan, the Debtor would face several hurdles including (a) proving by confirmation that Modern Pharmacy's business operation would be legal under both state and federal law and (b) proving that the income stream from the medical marijuana business would begin shortly after confirmation as opposed to years in the future.

It is not necessary to wait until a confirmation hearing. First, the Debtor cannot rid itself of the taint of the bad faith filing. Second, the Amended Plan is based on an enterprise illegal under Federal law, and therefore one that I cannot confirm because the Debtor cannot satisfy the requirements of 11 U.S.C. § 1129(a)(3). Third, the Amended Plan is highly speculative.

So, it is clear that this case is ripe for dismissal—both for subjective bad faith and objective bad faith; however, there is significant non-insider unsecured debt and I am not convinced at this juncture that dismissal is in the best interests of those creditors. It appears this case should remain in bankruptcy. . . . [but] due to the Debtor's bad faith in filing this case and the Debtor's inability or unwillingness to propose a confirmable plan, Ocean Bank is granted relief from stay subject to the conditions set forth below.

[Footnotes and citations omitted]

QUESTIONS FOR DISCUSSION:

Is it bad faith to use available legal remedies to halt a foreclosure sale? Why or why not?

Suppose Arm Ventures had an agreement with a tenant who had a valid state license for medical marijuana. Should that make a difference to the court's analysis of its plan?

Chapter 12

Chapter 12 bankruptcy allows debtors to make a plan to repay all or part of the debts of family farmers or commercial fishers. Chapter 12 debtors must have a regular income, and more than half of that income must come from farming or commercial fishing.

A Chapter 12 plan usually lasts from three to five years. It will not go into effect unless it is approved by the bankruptcy court. The court will approve a plan that is feasible. The plan must also meet the legal requirements for a Chapter 12 plan:

- Priority claims, defined above, must be paid in full, unless the priority creditor agrees otherwise; and

- Secured creditors must be paid at least as much as the value of their collateral.

If the original debt was scheduled to be paid off in more than three to five years, the debtor may continue with that schedule as long as any past due payments are made up during the plan.

Unsecured, non-priority debts will be discharged if the plan calls for all of the debtor's **disposable income** will be applied to plan payments, and if the creditors would receive at least as much as they would get in a Chapter 7 bankruptcy. Disposable income is any income not needed for the maintenance or support of the debtor or dependents, or for making payments needed to operate the debtor's business.

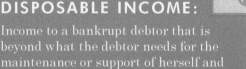

DISPOSABLE INCOME:
Income to a bankrupt debtor that is beyond what the debtor needs for the maintenance or support of herself and her dependents or for payments to operate her business.

Chapter 13

Chapter 13 bankruptcy is for individuals or married couples with mostly household or consumer debt. It is often called a "wage earn-er's plan," because it allows debtors with a regular income to repay all or part of their debts. Chapter 13 differs from a conventional repay-

ment plan, because the plan is always under the supervision of the Bankruptcy Court.

A Chapter 13 petition may be filed by an individual or a married couple. The petition includes the same documents as are filed in other bankruptcies, but the debtor must also file proof that he has received credit counseling, along with a copy of any debt repayment plan reached through credit counseling. The debtor must also file evidence of any payment from employers received within 60 days of filing, a statement of monthly net income, and a statement of any expected increase in income or expenses that may come up after the petition is filed. The court must also be informed of any interest the debtor has in federal or state qualified education or tuition accounts. Finally, the debtor must provide the trustee with a copy of his tax return for the most recent tax year, and tax returns filed after the petition is filed.

Chapter 13 has a special automatic stay provision for co-debtors. Unless the court says otherwise, a creditor may not try to collect a consumer debt from any individual who is liable along with the debtor. This special stay applies even if the co-debtor has not filed a petition.

The debtor must file a repayment plan no later than 14 days after the petition is filed. The plan must provide for payments of fixed amounts to the trustee on a regular basis. The trustee then distributes the funds to creditors who have filed valid claims according to the terms of the plan. Plans will stay in effect for three to five years after filing the petition. A Chapter 13 plan must pay priority claims in full unless a particular priority creditor agrees otherwise. If the claim is for a child or spousal support obligation, payment in full is required unless the debtor contributes all disposable income to a plan lasting five years.

For secured claims, the debtor may keep the collateral if the plan provides that the creditor will receive at least the value of the collateral. Unsecured claims do not have to be paid in full as long as the debtor will pay all her disposable income over the life of the plan, and as long as unsecured creditors receive at least as much under the plan as they would receive in a Chapter 7 liquidation.

A Chapter 13 plan must be approved by the Bankruptcy Court. The debtor must start making payments on the plan within 30 days after filing the petition, even if the plan has not yet been approved by the court. If the court confirms the plan, the trustee will start to distribute funds to creditors. If the plan is not approved, the debtor may file a modified plan, or convert the case to a Chapter 7 liquidation.

The Chapter 13 debtor is entitled to a discharge after all of the plan payments have been made if:

- All domestic support obligations have been paid,

- The debtor has not received a discharge in a prior case filed within a certain time, and

- The debtor has completed an approved course in financial management.

The discharge will release the debtor from all debts provided for by the plan.

Federal law strongly prefers that individuals who file bankruptcy file under Chapter 13, rather than Chapter 7.

Chapter 15

Chapter 15 deals with bankruptcies across international borders. It does not grant any different relief than any of the other chapters. Chapter 15 has two purposes. The first is to allow a trustee to act in a foreign country if a debtor has assets overseas. The second is to recognize a foreign bankruptcy proceeding for a debtor that has property in the United States. A representative appointed in a foreign proceeding would be allowed to handle the debtor's assets in the U.S.

Chapter 15 cases are very rare. In 2015, only 85 cases were filed under Chapter 15.

Example: Octaviar, an Australian company, was the subject of insolvency proceedings in Australia. Octaviar had legal claims against various parties in the U.S. It deposited a $10,000 retainer with a law firm to pursue those claims. The claims and the retainer met the legal requirement of property in the U.S. Octaviar was eligible for Chapter 15 relief recognizing the Australian proceeding. *In Re Octaviar Administration Pty. Ltd.,* 511 B.R. 361 (Bankr. S.D.N.Y. 2014).

Chapters of Bankruptcy		
Chapter	*Relief Granted*	*Eligible Debtors*
Seven	Liquidation of non-exempt property; discharge of debts	Individuals who qualify under the means test; business entities
Nine	Protection from creditors to allow the renegotiation and restructuring of debt	Municipalities
Eleven	Reorganization according to a plan	Individuals; business entities
Twelve	Reorganization and repayment of debts	Family farmers; individuals engaged in commercial fishing
Thirteen	Repayment of debts	Individuals with primarily personal and household debt
Fifteen	Recognition of a foreign bankruptcy or insolvency proceeding	Debtors who are party to a foreign proceeding and who have business interests or property in the United States

VIII. Receivership

In mid-2012, Zeek Rewards was flying high. The company ran an investment program that was based on an online auction service. For $1, a buyer got a chance to bid on heavily discounted items. Investors were then recruited to promote the auction site. An investor bought in at a set level. She would then, in theory, make money as she signed up more investors under her to promote the auctions. The auction profits were shared with all of the investors in the line.

Zeek Rewards did not last long. Federal regulators shut it down in August of 2012, right when it was at its peak. On August 27, 2012, the U.S. District Court for the Western District of North Carolina appointed a receiver to marshal and preserve all of the assets of Zeek Rewards. The receiver is using these assets to give refunds to those who lost money by investing in Zeek Rewards.

Receivers are appointed by a court to oversee a business. A receiver can be appointed for any one of a number of functions. He may be acting

RECEIVER:

A person appointed by a bankruptcy court to oversee a business.

solely to liquidate a business, as with Zeek Rewards. He may be working towards restructuring the business with an eye to making it profitable again. He may be attempting to stabilize it just long enough to find a buyer to take it over.

Receivership is different from bankruptcy in several ways. First, while bankruptcy is a federal matter, receivership can be either state or federal. Federal receivership typically is limited to federally-regulated businesses, such as banks or securities brokerages. Second, receivership is almost always involuntary. A receiver is appointed after or during a court case. Third, a company in receivership may not have the protections of bankruptcy law, unless the receiver is appointed as a part of a bankruptcy. This means that there is no automatic stay. It also means that debts are not discharged at the end of the case.

CHAPTER SUMMARY

Extending credit is a carefully regulated process. The decision about who gets credit is mostly left to the discretion of the creditor. That discretion must be exercised in a proper manner. At the same time, creditors are allowed to take steps to help ensure payment of debts. The most common step taken is obtaining a security interest in property as collateral. Security interests generally give the creditor the right to repossess and sell the collateral.

Bankruptcy is another facet of creditor-debtor relations. Bankruptcy could involve a liquidation and discharge of a debtor's obligations, or it could be a restructuring of a business. For individuals, bankruptcy could be a simple, court-supervised repayment plan. The goal of bankruptcy is a fresh start for the debtor, and protection for the creditors.

Review Questions

Review question 1.
Who enforces Regulation Z? What disclosure does the regulation govern? What is the goal of the disclosure, and why is it important for creditors and debtors?

Review question 2.
What is a foreclosure? How does a foreclosure differ from a repossession? What other way might a creditor seek compensation for an unpaid loan? How might a debtor stop a creditor from pursuing these remedies?

Review question 3.
What is a Chapter 12 bankruptcy? How does it differ from Chapter 13?

Review question 4.

What happens in a reorganization? Which chapter deals with reorganizations?

Review question 5.

What advantage does incorporation give to a business owner whose company holds bad debt? What are the consequences for business owners who do not incorporate but incur large debts for their companies? How does the concept of "piercing the corporate veil" apply to a business bankruptcy scenario?

Review question 6.

What steps should a creditor take to raise the likelihood of repayment? What actions should be taken prior to making a loan? What are the best remedies for non-payment?

Review question 7.

When there is more than one security interest on the same item of property, how is the priority of the interests determined?

Review question 8.

What do you suppose is the most common type of bankruptcy and why? What are the advantages and disadvantages of bankruptcy for a business? What is the automatic stay in bankruptcy?

Review question 9.

How is a security interest perfected? Why is it important to do that?

Questions for Discussion

Discussion question 1.

Jorge and Luis have decided to buy their uncle's restaurant supply business. Their father, who works as an engineer, agrees to lend them half of the money they will need. He has them sign an agreement to repay the loan in 12 monthly installments. He does not give them TILA disclosures. Four days after signing the agreement, Luis learns that his wife is pregnant. He decides it is a bad time for him to take on the financial risk of running a business, so he wants to get out of the loan agreement.

Under TILA, can the loan agreement be rescinded? Why or why not?

Suppose that, instead of borrowing the money from his father, Luis borrowed his share of the money from his credit union. Would your answer be the same? Why or why not?

Discussion question 2.

Andre and Caitlin go to their bank to apply for a loan to buy a new car. Andre has been married twice before, and this is Caitlin's second marriage. They meet their bank's credit and income requirements, but the loan officer who reviews the application has heard that spouses who have been married more than once before are at a higher risk of getting a divorce than other couples. A divorce could make it less likely that the loan would be repaid. Andre and Caitlin are approved for a loan, but have to pay 0.5% more interest than other borrowers.

Is this an ECOA violation? Why, or why not?

What if this were the first marriage for both, but Caitlin is a new immigrant to the United States and does not yet have a green card? Could the loan officer take that status into consideration?

Discussion question 3.

Howie runs a neighborhood bar. Although he does a good business, Howie is far from the most efficient manager around. He has neglected to pay state and federal income taxes for the past two years, and two different liquor wholesalers refuse to do business with him, due to unpaid bills. To stay open, Howie has taken to buying supplies at a local retail liquor store. This violates city ordinances, and the city is demanding he pay a penalty or his bar will be shut down. Howie is considering filing bankruptcy.

What chapters of bankruptcy can Howie file? Explain the differences between each chapter.

Suppose Howie is operating his bar as a sole proprietor, and he is personally liable for the bar's debts. If he files a Chapter 7 bankruptcy, would any of the debts be discharged? If so, which ones?

Discussion question 4.

Jasdeep is a 20-year-old college student who works as a department assistant. As compensation for this work, she receives an hourly wage and 10 percent rebate on her tuition for the semester. Due to an administrative error, Jasdeep receives a 20 percent rebate on her tuition. When the department discovers the error, it contacts Jasdeep at her permanent address to seek repayment. Jasdeep is on vacation when the letter arrives, and her mother calls the department to see what the problem is. The department secretary tells Jasdeep's mother that she has to make the repayment, because she is legally responsible for Jasdeep as long as she is a full-time student. Jasdeep's mother refuses to pay. Over the next three days, the secretary calls Jasdeep's mother 12 times at odd hours to pursue payment.

> Is Jasdeep's mother responsible for the debt?

> May the department secretary pursue Jasdeep's mother for the debt? May the secretary contact Jasdeep? Are there any limits on how the secretary may pursue either person? If so, why?

Discussion question 5.

Chang & Daughter LLC is a small business that earns most of its revenues through retail sales. Chang & Daughter sells its products at local craft fairs and farmer's markets. During the summer, their primary income is from the sale of fresh fruit and eggs that the company produces on a small farm plot it financed just outside of the city. The rest of the year, Chang & Daughter relies on sales of fragrant soaps, which accounts for just over half of the company's annual income. The soaps look handmade and contain dried herbs and flowers. Chang & Daughter import the soaps from China. After one of the better craft fairs loses its space, sales fall dramatically. Chang & Daughter start a website, which is starting to produce sales, but it is not yet keeping pace with payments on the farm plot. Chang & Daughter management starts considering a reorganization to stay in business.

> What chapter is most applicable to Chang & Daughter's needs?

> Is a reorganization a good idea, or should the company liquidate and start over? Does the company have another practical option?

7 TORTS

CHAPTER OVERVIEW

We live in a busy society with our fellow citizens. People are constantly engaged in personal and commercial activities. Through the course of those activities, people undertake a variety of actions. Some of those actions result in harm to others. The law attempts to balance the rights of citizens to go about their personal and commercial business with the rights of those who are harmed by another's actions. This balancing process is handled through tort law. A **tort** is a wrongful act resulting in harm to another person. Tort law attempts to provide compensation to persons who have been injured as a result of another's negligent, reckless, or intentional actions. Tort liability also influences behavior; the possibility of a lawsuit can deter harmful activity. The responsible party may be an individual or an organization.

In this chapter, we take a look at negligence claims and the elements that must be proven to hold a party liable for unintentional conduct. Next, we review the various intentional torts, with a focus on the intentional torts that are particularly relevant to business parties and entities. Finally, we discuss the ways in which a business party can be liable for defective products sold in the marketplace.

INTRODUCTION

In simple terms, a tort is a wrongful act that causes harm to another party. The person who was harmed, referred to as the **plaintiff**, may bring a lawsuit against the person who committed the wrongful conduct. The person who caused the harm is called the **tortfeasor**, or the **defendant**. A tort action seeks some compensation or other remedy for the party who was injured. Typically, the harmed party will seek money compensation, called **damages**.

PLAINTIFF:

The party who initiates a lawsuit; the injured party who seeks compensation from a tortfeasor.

TORTFEASOR:

An individual who commits a wrongful act that injures another person.

DEFENDANT:

The party who responds to a lawsuit initiated by another party; the defendant is the party whom the plaintiff alleges engaged in a tort.

DAMAGES:

Money compensation awarded to the injured party in a lawsuit.

A tort lawsuit is filed in civil court. Criminal penalties, such as imprisonment, are not available in civil court.

The law recognizes a variety of torts. These torts are based on the varying types of conduct that may cause harm to another party. To recover money or other remedies, the plaintiff must prove elements, or requirements, specific to each tort. Broadly speaking, torts can be divided into three categories: (1) negligence (non-intentional torts); (2) intentional torts; and (3) strict liability torts. We examine all three of these types of torts below. Furthermore, of particular interest in the business world, a business entity may be liable for any defective products it sells to consumers. **Products liability** is a specific type of tort that is based on the negligence and strict liability principles governing general tort law.

Generally speaking, a breach of contract between parties is not considered a tort. That may seem odd because a breach of a contract may cause harm to the other party. Nonetheless, the law of contracts, rather than torts, applies to cases that are strictly about a breach of contract. As noted in the chapter on contracts, there are contract torts, in which an outside party interferes with the performance of a contract, or induces another to breach a contract. In those cases, there could be two separate cases, based on different, if overlapping, sets of facts. The cases would be brought against different parties.

I.   Negligence

One of the most common types of torts is a **negligence** action. The law of negligence is based on the idea that in a society of many people, everyone must take care to avoid harm to others. A negligence tort results from a party's unintentional conduct. This means that the party did not intend or want to cause harm, but acted negligently. A party acts negligently when it fails to act the way an ordinary, reasonable person would act in the same circumstances. A party may act negligently in many different ways, and negligence lawsuits may arise from a variety of situations. Car accidents, slip and fall accidents, and medical malpractice claims are examples of negligence torts.

Businesses may be liable for negligence, just like individuals. A business owes a duty of care to its employees and its customers. A business entity is also responsible for the actions of its employees, who may be negligent in the performance of their work duties.

TORT:
A wrongful act resulting in harm to another person.

TORT CASE:
A lawsuit brought by an injured party seeking compensation from the wrongdoer.

PRODUCTS LIABILITY:
A manufacturer or seller's liability for a defective product created by the manufacturer and sold to the public.

NEGLIGENCE:
The failure to act as a reasonably prudent person would act in the same circumstances.

> **Example:** Consider a negligence lawsuit arising from a slip and fall accident. The customer was shopping in the produce section of a grocery store when he stepped on a strawberry that had fallen on the floor. The customer fell and hurt his shoulder. The strawberry had been on the ground for over two hours at the time the customer stepped on it. The customer sues the grocery store for negligence. The jury would consider whether a reasonable grocery store would have cleaned up the strawberry within two hours.

In a negligence lawsuit, the plaintiff must prove four elements: (1) a duty of reasonable care; (2) breach of that duty; (3) causation; and (4) resulting damages.

REASONABLE PERSON:
The legal standard by which a person's conduct is measured in a negligence action. A party must act as a reasonable person would act in the same circumstances.

Duty of Reasonable Care

The basic idea underlying a negligence tort is that each person owes a duty to society to exercise reasonable care in his actions. This standard does not require every person to be perfect at all times. Instead, each person is expected to act as a "**reasonable person**" would act in the same circumstances. The "reasonable person" is a fictitious concept. In a negligence case, the jury (or in some cases, the judge) must decide what a reasonable person would have done in the situation. The issue is how a reasonable person should act in the circumstances. The jury might consider customs in the local community or rules provided by statute to determine what is reasonable in a certain situation.

Because the standard depends on the circumstances, it varies for each situation. If the jury considers a claim against a developmentally disabled adult, for instance, the jury must consider what a reasonable person with that disability would do in the circumstances. If the case involves a claim for negligence against a professional, such as a doctor or attorney, the standard of care reflects that person's status as a professional. The professional must act as a reasonable person in that profession or trade

> **Example:** Many states have enacted statutes called dram shop acts. These laws make a bar owner or bartender liable if a customer becomes intoxicated and injures another person. The bar owner or bartender is liable because he provided the alcohol. Some states also hold social hosts liable if they provide alcohol to someone who injures another party.

> **Example:**
> Barbara was treated by two ophthalmologists for nearsightedness. She was fitted with contact lenses, and received treatment from the doctors over the course of several years. The doctors regarded Barbara's complaints about her vision as related to her contact lenses. After nine years, Barbara, who was 32 years old by then, was tested for glaucoma. At the time, it was not customary to test patients under 40 for glaucoma, because the disease was rare in younger patients. Barbara was found to have glaucoma, and one of her doctors acknowledged later that she probably had had it for ten years or more. The glaucoma pressure test was relatively inexpensive, and easily administered it. Failure to test Barbara for glaucoma was a breach of the duty of reasonable care. *Helling v. Carey,* 83 Wash. 2d 514, 519 P. 2d 981 (1974).

would act in that situation. The standard will also vary according to what the person is doing. A claim for negligence against a twelve-year-old child will consider how a reasonable twelve-year-old would act in the circumstances. If the child is engaged in a traditionally adult activity, such as driving a car or operating power tools, the child's actions will be judged according to the standards of any person engaged in those activities. The twelve-year-old who drives will be expected to act as a reasonable driver of a motor vehicle would, not just as a reasonable twelve-year-old driver.

Reasonable care is not necessarily "common care." Common care is doing what everyone else in the same situation does. A profession or industry may be slow to adopt new practices that could readily prevent some harm. While custom will be given weight in deciding what level of care is reasonable, courts will ultimately decide the question.

Although the precise definition of what actions or inactions constitute reasonable care will vary according to the situation, courts have developed criteria for judging reasonableness. Factors that are considered include:

- The recognition of the risk involved in the conduct,
- The realization of the unreasonable character of the risk, and
- The amount of care, skill, preparation, or warning the tortfeasor must provide.

Many courts emphasize foreseeability, or the recognition and realization of the risk, as the crucial factor. A failure to exercise ordinary care will be found when a person acts in a way that should reasonably cause him to foresee that he is subjecting himself or another to an unreasonable risk of harm. Risk is foreseeable if a reasonable person could foresee its occurrence, or if the person is on notice that the risk of danger is probable. If there is no foreseeable risk of harm caused by a person's actions, there is no failure to exercise reasonable care.

> **Example:** In the previous example, the failure to give Barbara a pressure test for glaucoma was a breach of the duty of reasonable care in part because Barbara complained of symptoms that were consistent with glaucoma. If she did not present those symptoms, failure to administer the test to her probably would not have been unreasonable, due to the fact that she was in an age group that had a low risk of developing glaucoma. The risk of harm posed by not administering the test would not have been foreseeable.

> **Example:** Margot is a newspaper reporter doing a story on an Ethiopian church that has just opened up in her city. The church does not receive many visitors, other than members of the congregation. She is looking for the office of the priest in charge when she sees a door with a notice written in an unfamiliar language. Margot opens the door and walks through. The notice warns that the floor in the room is not safe. Margot falls through the floor and is injured. Margot cannot claim that the risk of her actions was unforeseeable, even though she could not understand the notice. Margot should have asked someone what the notice meant, or not gone through the door without knowing what it said.

A person may not claim a lack of foreseeability if she was put on notice to investigate a situation, but fails to do so. Unfamiliar circumstances will give rise to an obligation to make some inquiries, to determine the existence of risk.

Breach of the Duty of Reasonable Care

A party breaches the duty of care when she fails to act as a reasonable person would in the same circumstances. The party may breach the standard of care through an action (placing a slippery plastic covering on the floor at a grocery store) or by failing to do something (failing to clean the floor at a store). In the strawberry example in the last section, assume that the jury concludes that a reasonable "person" (i.e., a reasonable grocery store) would clean up any fallen produce within two hours. If the jury also concludes that the grocery store did not clean up the strawberry for at least two hours on the day the customer slipped and fell, the defendant breached the duty of care.

A lack of reasonable care by itself will not constitute actionable negligence. A finding of negligence depends on the existence of a duty to another to act in a reasonable manner. There must be some relationship between the parties that gives rise to a duty. The duty itself is established by statutory or common law, or by contract. A moral or humane obligation will not obligate a person to act in any particular manner.

Causation

The plaintiff must prove that the defendant's actions were the cause of the plaintiff's injuries. Causation is usually discussed as two concepts: **cause-in-fact** ("but-for") causation and **proximate cause**. Both types of causation must be present for a defendant to be held responsible.

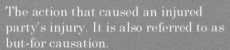

CAUSE-IN-FACT:
The action that caused an injured party's injury. It is also referred to as but-for causation.

PROXIMATE CAUSE:
The main or legal cause of an injury.

Under but-for causation, the defendant is only liable if the harm would not have occurred but for the defendant's actions. The issue is: "but for the defendant's actions, would the harm have occurred? Would the injury have occurred without the defendant's actions?"

Under the concept of proximate cause, the defendant is liable only if the type of harm that occurred was a foreseeable result of the defendant's actions. If the type of harm that occurred was not reasonably foreseeable, then the defendant cannot be responsible. The law finds it unfair to hold a person liable for risks that were unforeseeable.

There may be more than one cause for a negligent event. When two or more people act negligently but also act separately from each other, the acts are said to be concurrent causes of the injury. The concurrent acts do not necessarily occur simultaneously. A person whose negligent actions were a cause of the plaintiff's injury may be held liable. It does not matter that the person

Example:	Consider the strawberry slip and fall case again. To establish proximate causation, the customer must show that it was reasonably foreseeable that a customer might fall and be injured from a strawberry on the floor. If harm to the customer was a foreseeable result of the store's failure to clean up the strawberry, the customer can show proximate causation. If, however, some unpredictable chain of events occurs as a result of the strawberry on the floor, the proximate cause requirement would not be satisfied. For example, if a customer accidentally kicks the strawberry out into the parking lot, where a dog eats it and has an allergic reaction, leading it to bite a passing pedestrian, the pedestrian's injuries were not foreseeable from the store's failure to pick up the strawberry.

was not the sole cause of the injury. A defendant may be held liable even if his negligent act alone was not sufficient to cause the injury.

Intervening Event: In some cases, the defendant may be able to show an intervening event caused or contributed to the plaintiff's injury. This event may happen at the same time as the defendant's act, or may take place after the original incident. Sometimes, the defendant may be able to show that the intervening event breaks the chain of causation. If the intervening event is an unforeseeable event, that event may relieve the defendant of liability. In that situation, the event is called a superseding cause or intervening event. If the event is foreseeable, however, the defendant remains liable.

A DEFENDANT IS ONLY LIABLE FOR DAMAGES TO A PLAINTIFF TO WHOM THE DEFENDANT FORESEEABLY OWES THE DUTY OF CARE.

Palsgraf v. Long Island R.R. Co.
(Passenger) v. (Railroad)
248 N.Y. 339, 162 N.E. 99 (1928)

Cardozo, Ch. J.

Plaintiff was standing on a platform of defendant's railroad after buying a ticket to go to Rockaway Beach. A train stopped at the station, bound for another place. Two men ran forward to catch it. One of the men reached the platform of the car without mishap, though the train was already moving. The other man, carrying a package, jumped aboard the car, but seemed unsteady as if about to fall. A guard on the car, who had held the door open, reached forward to help him in, and another guard on the platform pushed him from behind. In this act, the package was dislodged, and fell upon the rails. It was a package of small size, about fifteen inches long, and was covered by a newspaper. In fact it contained fireworks, but there was nothing in its appearance to give notice of its contents. The fireworks when they fell exploded. The shock of the explosion threw down some scales at the other end of the platform, many feet away. The scales struck the plaintiff, causing injuries for which she sues. The conduct of the defendant's guard, if a wrong in its relation to the holder of the package, was not a wrong in its relation to the plaintiff, standing far away. Relatively to her it was not negligence at all. Nothing in the situation gave notice that the falling package had in it the potency of peril to persons thus removed. Negligence is not actionable unless it involves the invasion of a legally protected interest, the violation of a right. "Proof of negligence in the air, so to speak, will not do" [citations omitted] The plaintiff as she stood upon the platform of the station might claim to be protected against intentional invasion of her bodily security. Such invasion is not charged. She might claim to be protected against unintentional invasion by conduct involving in the thought of reasonable men an unreasonable hazard that such invasion would ensue. These, from the point of view of the law, were the bounds of her immunity, with perhaps some rare exceptions, survivals for the most part of ancient forms of liability, where conduct is held to be at the peril of the actor (Sullivan v. Dunham, 161 N. Y. 290). If no hazard was apparent to the eye of ordinary vigilance, an act innocent and harmless, at least to outward seeming, with reference to her, did not take to itself the quality of a tort because it happened to be a wrong, though apparently not one involving the risk of bodily insecurity, with reference to some one else. "In every instance, before negligence can be predicated of a given act, back of the act must be sought and found a duty to the individual complaining, the observance of which would have averted or avoided the injury" [citations omitted]

A different conclusion will involve us, and swiftly too, in a maze of contradictions. A guard stumbles over a package which has been left upon a platform. It seems to be a bundle of newspapers. It turns out to be a can of dynamite. To the eye of ordinary vigilance, the bundle is abandoned waste, which may be kicked or trod on with impunity. Is a passenger at the other end of the platform protected by the law against the unsuspected hazard concealed beneath the waste? If not, is the result to be any different, so far as the distant passenger is concerned, when the guard stumbles over a valise which a truckman or a porter has left upon the walk? The passenger far away, if the victim of a wrong at all, has a cause of action, not derivative, but original and primary. His claim to be protected against invasion of his bodily security is neither greater nor less because the act resulting in the invasion is a wrong to another far removed. In this case, the rights that are said to have been violated, the interests said to have been invaded, are not even of the same order. The man was not injured in his person nor even put in danger. The purpose of the act, as well as its effect, was to make his person safe. If there was a wrong to him at all, which may very well be doubted, it was a wrong to a property interest only, the safety of his package. Out of this wrong to property, which threatened injury to nothing else, there has passed, we are told, to the plaintiff by derivation or succession a right of action for the invasion of an interest of another order, the right to bodily security. The diversity of interests emphasizes the futility of the effort to build the plaintiff's right upon the basis of a wrong to some one else. The gain is one of emphasis, for a like result would follow if the interests were the same. Even then, the orbit of the danger as disclosed to the eye of reasonable vigilance would be the orbit of the duty. One who jostles one's neighbor in a crowd does not invade the rights of others standing at the outer fringe when the unintended contact casts a bomb upon the ground. The wrongdoer as to them is the man who carries the bomb, not the one who explodes it without suspicion of the danger. Life will have to be made over, and human nature transformed, before prevision so extravagant can be accepted as the norm of conduct, the customary standard to which behavior must conform.

The argument for the plaintiff is built upon the shifting meanings of such words as "wrong" and "wrongful," and shares their instability. What the plaintiff must show is "a wrong" to herself, i. e., a violation of her own right, and not merely a wrong to some one else, nor conduct "wrongful" because unsocial, but not "a wrong" to any one. We are told that one who drives at reckless speed through a crowded city street is guilty of a negligent act and, therefore, of a wrongful one irrespective of the consequences. Negligent the act is, and wrongful in the sense that it is unsocial, but wrongful and unsocial in relation to other travelers, only because the eye of vigilance perceives the risk of damage. If the same act were to be committed on a speedway or a race course, it would lose its wrongful quality. The risk reasonably to be perceived defines the duty to be obeyed, and risk imports relation; it is risk to another or to others within the range of apprehension (Seavey, Negligence, Subjective or Objective, 41 H. L. Rv. 6; Boronkay v. Robinson & Carpenter, 247 N. Y. 365). This does not mean, of course, that one who launches a destructive force is always relieved of liability if the force, though known to be destructive, pursues an unexpected path. . . . [W]rong is defined in terms of the natural or probable, at least when unintentional (Parrot v. Wells-Fargo Co. [The Nitro-Glycerine Case], 15 Wall. [U. S.] 524). The range of reasonable apprehension is at times a question for the court, and at times, if varying inferences are possible, a question for the jury. Here, by concession, there was nothing in the situation to suggest to the most cautious mind that the parcel wrapped in newspaper would spread wreckage through the station. If the guard had thrown it down knowingly and willfully, he would not have threatened the plaintiff's safety, so far as appearances could warn him. His conduct would not have involved, even then, an unreasonable probability of invasion of her bodily security. Liability can be no greater where the act is inadvertent.

Negligence, like risk, is thus a term of relation. Negligence in the abstract, apart from things related, is surely not a tort, if indeed it is understandable at all (BOWEN, L. J., in Thomas v. Quartermaine, 18 Q. B. D. 685, 694). Negligence is not a tort unless it results in the commission of a wrong, and the commission of a wrong imports the violation of a right, in this case, we are told, the right to be protected against interference with one's bodily security. But bodily security is protected, not against all forms of interference or aggression, but only against some. One who seeks redress at law does not make out a cause of action by showing without more that there has been damage to his person. If the harm was not willful, he must show that the act as to him had possibilities of danger so many and apparent as to entitle him to be protected against the doing of it though the harm was unintended. Affront to personality is still the keynote of the wrong. Confirmation of this view will be found in the history and development of the action on the case. Negligence as a basis of civil liability was unknown to mediaeval law (8 Holdsworth, History of English Law, p. 449; Street, Foundations of Legal Liability, vol. 1, = pp. 189, 190). For damage to the person, the sole remedy was trespass, and trespass did not lie in the absence of aggression, and that direct and personal (Holdsworth, op. cit. p. 453; Street, op. cit. vol. 3, pp. 258, 260, vol. 1, pp. 71, 74.) Liability for other damage, as where a servant without orders from the master does or omits something to the damage of another, is a plant of later growth (Holdsworth, op. cit. 450, 457; Wigmore, Responsibility for Tortious Acts, vol. 3, Essays in Anglo-American Legal History, 520, 523, 526, 533). When it emerged out of the legal soil, it was thought of as a variant of trespass, an offshoot of the parent stock. This appears in the form of action, which was known as trespass on the case (Holdsworth, op. cit. p. 449; cf. Scott v. Shepard, 2 Wm. Black. 892; Green, Rationale of Proximate Cause, p. 19). The victim does not sue derivatively, or by right of subrogation, to vindicate an interest invaded in the person of another. Thus to view his cause of action is to ignore the fundamental difference between tort and crime (Holland, Jurisprudence [12th ed.], p. 328). He sues for breach of a duty owing to himself.

The law of causation, remote or proximate, is thus foreign to the case before us. The question of liability is always anterior to the question of the measure of the consequences that go with liability. If there is no tort to be redressed, there is no occasion to consider what damage might be recovered if there were a finding of a tort. We may assume, without deciding, that negligence, not at large or in the abstract, but in relation to the plaintiff, would entail liability for any and all consequences, however novel or extraordinary. [citations omitted] There is room for argument that a distinction is to be drawn according to the diversity of interests invaded by the act, as where conduct negligent in that it threatens an insignificant invasion of an interest in property results in an unforseeable invasion of an interest of another order, as, e. g., one of bodily security. Perhaps other distinctions may be necessary. We do not go into the question now. The consequences to be followed must first be rooted in a wrong. The judgment of the Appellate Division and that of the Trial Term should be reversed, and the complaint dismissed, with costs in all courts.

DISSENT
Andrews, J.

Negligence may be defined roughly as an act or omission which unreasonably does or may affect the rights of others, or which unreasonably fails to protect oneself from the dangers resulting from such acts. Here I confine myself to the first branch of the definition. Nor do I comment on the word "unreasonable." For present purposes it sufficiently describes that average of conduct that society requires of its members.

There must be both the act or the omission, and the right. It is the act itself, not the intent of the actor, that is important . . .

[...]

[W]e are told that "there is no negligence unless there is in the particular case a legal duty to take care, and this duty must be one which is owed to the plaintiff himself and not merely to others." (Salmond Torts [6th ed.], 24.) This, I think too narrow a conception. Where there is the unreasonable act, and some right that may be affected there is negligence whether damage does or does not result. That is immaterial . . . Due care is a duty imposed on each one of us to protect society from unnecessary danger, not to protect A, B or C alone.

It may well be that there is no such thing as negligence in the abstract. "Proof of negligence in the air, so to speak, will not do." In an empty world negligence would not exist. It does involve a relationship between man and his fellows. But not merely a relationship between man and those whom he might reasonably expect his act would injure. Rather, a relationship between him and those whom he does in fact injure. If his act has a tendency to harm some one, it harms him a mile away as surely as it does those on the scene.

[...]

The proposition is this. Every one owes to the world at large the duty of refraining from those acts that may unreasonably threaten the safety of others. Such an act occurs. Not only is he wronged to whom harm might reasonably be expected to result, but he also who is in fact injured, even if he be outside what would generally be thought the danger zone. There needs be duty due the one complaining but this is not a duty to a particular individual because as to him harm might be expected . . . Unreasonable risk being taken, its consequences are not confined to those who might probably be hurt.

[...]

The right to recover damages rests on additional considerations. The plaintiff's rights must be injured, and this injury must be caused by the negligence . . . [W]hen injuries do result from our unlawful act we are liable for the consequences. It does not matter that they are unusual, unexpected, unforeseen and unforseeable. But there is one limitation. The damages must be so connected with the negligence that the latter may be said to be the proximate cause of the former.

[...]

There are some hints that may help us. The proximate cause, involved as it may be with many other causes, must be, at the least, something without which the event would not happen. The court must ask itself whether there was a natural and continuous sequence between cause and effect. Was the one a substantial factor in producing the other? Was there a direct connection between them, without too many intervening causes? Is the effect of cause on result not too attentuated? Is the cause likely, in the usual judgment of mankind, to produce the result? ... We draw an uncertain and wavering line, but draw it we must as best we can.

CASE VOCABULARY:

ATTENUATE:
To lessen or weaken.

CONFLAGRATION:
A great destructive burning or fire.

FORESEEABILITY:
The foreseeability of the consequences of a defendant's actions depend on the balancing between the likelihood of risk and the magnitude of damages flowing therefrom.

INVASION:
An encroachment upon the rights of another.

PROXIMATE CAUSE:
The type of cause which in the natural and continuous sequence unbroken by any new independent cause produces an event, and without which the injury would not have occurred.

QUESTIONS FOR DISCUSSION:

Do you agree more with the majority opinion or the dissent? If with the dissent, where would you draw the line for foreseeability? If with the majority, how do you square the possible unfairness to an uncompensated victim?

What if someone dropped firecrackers in a large store, and the explosion dislodged items on a shelf, which fell upon a customer. Does the result in this case make sense in that scenario? Why or why not?

Damages

In a negligence claim, the plaintiff must also show that he incurred some loss. There must be some harm to the plaintiff for a negligence action. Consider the strawberry slip and fall case discussed above. Imagine that the customer briefly slipped on the strawberry, but regained his footing and did not suffer any injury. In that circumstance, the plaintiff did not suffer any harm.

If a plaintiff proves the defendant breached the duty of care and caused harm, the plaintiff may receive money damages. Damages are provided to compensate the plaintiff for his losses. Depending on the case, damages may be awarded to compensate for physical injuries, damage to property, lost wages, medical expenses, pain and suffering, humiliation, and embarrassment.

Professional Malpractice Actions

As noted above, a lawsuit claiming negligence against a professional, such as a doctor or lawyer, is one type of negligence tort. A professional malpractice claim is similar to a standard claim for negligence. The plaintiff must prove the same basic elements: a duty, breach of duty, causation, and damages.

In this context, though, the professional must act as a reasonable person in that profession would act. The knowledge and expertise of a reasonable member of that profession is considered as part of the standard of care. A jury does not have expertise in every profession. Therefore, the jury will usually have to consider the testimony of experts who describe how a reasonable doctor, lawyer, or other professional would act. There is an exception for cases in which the negligence is so clear that the jury could determine for themselves whether actions are negligent.

> After a person has been injured, other individuals often stop to help the injured party. These individuals may be trained medical professionals, or simply concerned citizens who do not have any specialized knowledge. These individuals are sometimes referred to as Good Samaritans, based on a biblical story about people who are willing to stop and help others. What if the person who stops to help is negligent when helping and makes the injuries worse? In the past, the injured party could sue the individuals who had stopped to help. Society recognized that it was not good public policy. If an individual could be liable for stopping to help an injured person, Good Samaritans were discouraged from helping others. Thus, most states passed "Good Samaritan laws." These laws state that a person who is injured may not sue someone who stops to help them.

In recent years, many states have passed laws regarding medical malpractice claims. In some states, a plaintiff must follow certain procedures before they can file a medical malpractice lawsuit. For instance, a plaintiff might have to submit a claim to a panel of experts who review

> *Example:*
>
> Paula, a 75-year-old woman, went to see her doctor because she had a sore throat. She told the doctor the sore throat had persisted for three months. Paula's medical history form indicated that she has a daily smoking habit. The doctor looked in her throat and sent her home, believing it was only a virus that would clear up soon. After the sore throat continued for another five weeks, Paula went back to the doctor. This time, the doctor ran additional tests and discovered that Paula had throat cancer. By the time the cancer was detected, it was too late for Paula to undergo treatment and she died two months later. Paula's family sues the doctor for malpractice, claiming that he should have discovered the cancer when Paula first visited him. The jury will consider whether the doctor acted as reasonable doctor, with the skills and expertise of a medical professional, would have acted in the same situation. The parties will likely present the testimony of experts who understand the skills and knowledge of a doctor.

> *Example:*
>
> Hector, a surgeon, accidentally leaves a sponge inside of a patient after an operation. The court probably will hold that expert testimony is not needed to determine negligence.

> *Example:*
>
> Lisa's baby is two weeks overdue. Alice, her obstetrician, examines her but decides to wait three more days before she induces labor. The baby is born with severe birth defects that Lisa claims are caused by the delay in inducing labor. Expert testimony will be needed to determine whether the failure to induce in this situation was negligent.

the case before the plaintiff can file a lawsuit in court. A number of states also impose limits, or caps, on the amount of damages that a plaintiff may recover in a medical malpractice case.

Res Ipsa Loquitur

As stated above, in negligence cases, the plaintiff must typically show that the defendant's conduct was negligent. In some circumstances, the plaintiff is unable to show what the defen-

dant did. The plaintiff may not have any evidence to demonstrate what happened. In some unique situations, though, it is clear that the defendant must have caused the harm. If certain elements are met, negligence may be presumed under the doctrine of **res ipsa loquitur**. Res ipsa loquitur is a Latin phrase meaning "the thing speaks for itself." Negligence may be presumed where (1) the defendant had exclusive control of whatever caused the injury and (2) it is the type of accident that would not have happened without negligence. This concept is often best understood by looking at an example.

RES IPSA LOQUITUR:

Meaning "the thing speaks for itself," this legal principle allows negligence to be presumed when (1) a defendant had exclusive control of the circumstances under which someone was injured, and (2) the incident would not normally occur without negligence.

If the court finds that the case presents the type of situation to which res ipsa loquitur applies, then the defendant must prove he was not negligent.

Negligence Per Se

Sometimes, a party's conduct is considered negligent, without examining what a reasonable person would do. If someone violates a statute

Originally, a tort suit was only available to persons who had been injured. If a party died as a result of another party's action, the lawsuit died with the person. This discrepancy allowed a party to avoid liability where a party's injuries were severe enough to cause death of the victim. Eventually, the law recognized the unfairness of that doctrine. Today, all states have statutes recognizing wrongful death actions. A wrongful death suit is brought by the surviving family members of a person who has died. Wrongful death actions allow the family members to recover damages for the injuries they incur from the family member's death.

A closely related type of action is a survival action. Survival actions are brought for damages suffered by the victim between the time of the injury and the time of death. Damages in survival actions are not paid directly to the family members, but are paid to the victim's estate.

Example:	Big Building Co. is constructing a high rise building. A load of bricks is on the roof of the building. The load of bricks falls and injures Emilio, who was walking on the sidewalk below. The bricks were in Big Building's control and it is the type of accident that occurs only with negligence. Big Building is liable for Emilio's injury even though no one saw the load fall.

Example:	Sal was fishing in a boat at night. Another boat on the water collided with Sal's boat. Sal was thrown from the boat and drowned. Otto, the operator of the other boat, did not use running lights. A local regulation requires all watercraft to use running lights from sunset to sunrise. The regulation is designed to prevent collisions between boats at night. Otto's violation of the running light regulation could be considered negligence per se.

> **Example:** Klaus is making a delivery to a warehouse when he is struck and injured by a forklift that was backing up. Contrary to rules of the Occupational Safety and Health Administration (OSHA), the forklift was not making an audible signal (the repeated beeping) when it was backing up. Private actions under the occupational safety laws are not allowed, but Klaus may argue that the failure to have a beeping forklift was negligent.

or ordinance, that violation might be **negligence per se**. For negligence per se to apply, the statute must be designed to prevent the type of injury that occurred and set out clear rules of conduct.

NEGLIGENCE PER SE:

A doctrine under which negligence is proven through the defendant's violation of a statute or regulation designed to prevent the type of injury that occurred.

Not every violation of a statute will give rise to a tort action. Even if the statute is designed to prevent a given injury, an injured party may be barred from bringing an action that alleges only a violation of that statute. In many cases, however, the violation may be evidence of negligence. The distinction may be largely technical. It does, however, effect the presentation of proof at trial. It also allows the defendant to rebut the claim of negligence.

Defenses to Negligence Cases

Even if a defendant has engaged in a negligent act, the defendant might not always be liable for damages. In some circumstances, the defendant can show a defense exists. The defenses to negligence generally focus on the plaintiff's conduct. For instance, if a plaintiff is negligent himself, his negligence may reduce or prohibit the recovery of damages under the doctrine of comparative negligence. If a plaintiff assumes the risk of an activity, the plaintiff also may not recover against the defendant. Both of these defenses are discussed in detail later in this chapter.

II. Intentional Torts

An **intentional tort** occurs when the person who acts wrongly intends to perform the action. The person who performs the act does not need to intend the harm that resulted. The defendant only needs to intend his action. "Intentional"

> **Example:** Denny surprises his friend Jan by jumping out at him with a scary mask. Jan has a heart condition, and the scare causes Jan to have a heart attack. Denny committed an intentional tort, even though he did not intend for Jan to have a heart attack.

> *Example:*
>
> Tom is a defendant in a lawsuit brought against him by Wallace. During a deposition, Tom tells several lies while under oath. Ezra, Wallace's attorney, has proof that Tom is lying. While Tom has committed the crime of perjury, neither Wallace nor Ezra may bring a lawsuit against him for perjury. They may, however, be able to use Tom's false testimony to impeach his credibility at trial.

does not mean that the tortfeasor had any ill will or harmful motive.

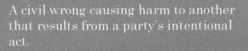

INTENTIONAL TORT:
A civil wrong causing harm to another that results from a party's intentional act.

There are many types of intentional torts. Assault, trespass, fraud, defamation, invasion of privacy, nuisance, and interference are all considered intentional torts. Several intentional torts are particularly relevant to business relations. These torts are discussed below.

There is some overlap between criminal law and the law of intentional torts. While many intentional torts are also crimes, not every criminal violation will be a tort. Some crimes are considered violations against the public order, and not just wrongs done to one party. No private action may be brought for that type of criminal violation.

Fraudulent Misrepresentation

A misrepresentation is a false or untrue statement. A **fraudulent misrepresentation** occurs when the party making the statement knew the statement was false, or made the statement recklessly without knowing whether it was true or not. To prove a fraud claim, a plaintiff must show that the defendant intentionally misrepresented a material fact, the plaintiff relied on the false statement, and the plaintiff was harmed by the misrepresentation. The defendant must intend for the plaintiff to rely on the false statement.

The false statement must relate to a material fact. A material fact is a fact that is important to the other party's decision.

The false statement must be a statement of fact. A party cannot be liable for a statement of

> *Example:*
>
> As part of its efforts to expand its business, ABC Company seeks a loan from National Bank. In its application, ABC Co. submits misleading financial statements to National Bank. Relying on those statements, National Bank provides the loan to ABC Co. ABC Co. defaults on the loan. National Bank may sue ABC Co. for fraud.

> **Example:**
> Business Inc. would like to engage in a transaction this quarter. Business Inc. tells its accountant, Amy Numbers, about the transaction, but does not ask her for any tax advice about the transaction. Based on a new IRS regulation, Amy knows that Business Inc. will owe a large tax bill for that transaction. Amy does not inform Business Inc. of the tax liability. Business Inc. may be able to sue Amy for failing to tell them about the tax liability.

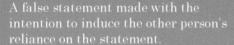

FRAUDULENT MISREPRESENTATION:
A false statement made with the intention to induce the other person's reliance on the statement.

In some circumstances, a party can also be liable for keeping quiet when they know a material fact that the other party does not know. If there is a special relationship of trust between the parties, one party has a duty to speak.

Interference with Contractual Relations

opinion or puffery. Puffery is an exaggerated statement about a product or service. Puffery is stated in vague, but complimentary terms. Puffery is considered to be the speaker's opinion and not a representation of fact about the product's actual qualities or capabilities. A statement that "this is the best car you'll ever drive" is puffery. It is not a statement of fact. However, the statement that "this car has passed all safety tests and contains anti-lock brakes" is a statement of fact. If the statement of fact is false, the speaker can be liable for misrepresentation.

Many business relationships involve a contract between two parties. If another party interferes with that contractual relationship, they may be liable for interference. The tort of **interference with contractual relations** allows a plaintiff to recover damages if a defendant causes one of the contracting parties to breach the contract. The elements of an intentional interference with contractual relations claim are (1) a valid contract between plaintiff and another party; (2) defendant knew about the contract; (3)

> **Example:**
> Company A and Company B entered an agreement. Company A will sell Company B 1,000 widgets for $10.00 per widget. Company C tells Company A that Company B is underpaying for the widgets. Company A breaches the contract with Company B by refusing to sell the widgets to Company B unless Company B pays $20.00 per widget. Company B might be liable to Company C for tortious interference with a contract, because Company C's conduct caused Company A to breach the contract.

Example: Company X would like to hire Best Band to perform at its annual employee appreciation party on June 10. Company X offers to pay Best Band $15,000 for its performance. Unbeknownst to Company X, Best Band had already agreed to perform at a different event on June 10. Best Band has a contract with Promotional Events, Inc., to perform at the other event for $5,000. In light of the higher amount of money offered by Company X, Best Band breaches the contract to perform at the other event. Promotional Events, Inc., does not have a claim for wrongful interference with contractual relations against Company X because Company X was unaware of Best Band's prior commitment.

Example: Bill owns a small accounting firm. His office has a contract to buy its office supplies from Paper Clips, Inc. Office Store Co. is a competitor of Paper Clips, Inc. Office Store Co. creates an aggressive new advertising campaign offering deep discounts on office supplies. Bill sees the advertising and decides to break his contract with Paper Clips and buy supplies from Office Store Co. Paper Clips, Inc., cannot sue Office Store Co. for interference because general advertising does not constitute wrongful interference.

defendant acted to interfere with the contract; (4) the contract was breached or disrupted; and (5) damage.

> To be liable, the defendant must have known about the contract.

INTENTIONAL INTERFERENCE WITH CONTRACTUAL RELATIONS:
The tort that occurs when a person intentionally harms the plaintiff's contractual or business relationship.

Furthermore, the interference must be the kind of conduct that falls outside the scope of fair competition. General advertising or marketing of products and services does not constitute interference.

Interference with Prospective Business Advantage

A party also may not interfere where two parties are currently in negotiations, but have not yet signed an agreement. This tort is called **interference with prospective business advantage**. To prove this claim, a plaintiff must show that (1) the plaintiff had an economic relationship with another party; (2) the defendant knew about the relationship; (3) the defen-

Example: Company XYZ rents office space from Larry Landlord. Company XYZ's lease with Larry Landlord will expire in two months. A new office building is being constructed by Barry Builder across the street. Larry Landlord knows that Company XYZ has been in negotiations with Barry Builder regarding a possible lease of office space in the new building. Larry does not want to lose Company XYZ as a tenant. Larry contacts a friend of his who works for the city permit office. Larry pays his friend to delay approval of the new building. Larry's friend interferes with the approval process so that the new building will not be available to lease for another eight months. Given the long delay until the building will be ready, Company XYZ decides to renew its lease in Larry's building. Barry Builder may sue Larry Landlord for interfering with the relationship between Barry Builder and Company XYZ.

Example: The only barber in a small town got into a lengthy dispute with the local banker. The banker rented a shop in town, and induced two barbers to start working there. The barbers paid no rent for the shop, and all of the profits were paid to the banker (who, in turn, paid the barbers a salary). The banker's sole purpose in opening the shop was to drive the first barber out of business. The banker has committed a prima facie tort. *Tuttle v. Buck*, 107 Minn. 146, 119 N.W. 946 (1911).

dant acted to disrupt the relationship; (4) the relationship was disrupted; and (5) the plaintiff incurred damages.

INTENTIONAL INTERFERENCE WITH PROSPECTIVE ECONOMIC ADVANTAGE:
The tort that occurs when a person intentionally harms the plaintiff's business relationship that was likely to have economic benefit for the plaintiff.

Prima Facie Tort

The prima facie tort covers injuries caused by wrongdoing that does not fit within the traditional types of tort actions. It is sometimes regarded as a type of interference with prospective business advantage, although the facts that may constitute a prima facie tort can go beyond the business context.

The prima facie tort is an intentional tort. It involves the infliction of harm by doing something that is otherwise lawful, but that is being done for the purpose of inflicting harm. The tortfeasor has no justification or excuse for committing the act.

> *Example:* Clara and Mary go to the Bde Maka Ska Casino to gamble. The casino has a sign at the entrance saying that photography on the gaming floor is strictly prohibited. After playing the slots for an hour, Clara takes a selfie with Mary, standing in front of a slot machine. A casino employee tells her that photography is prohibited, and they are ordered to leave. Clara and Mary are trespassing.

Trespass

Under common law rules of procedure, trespass was the name given to a broad category of intentional torts that caused injury to a person or property. Our modern understanding of the term is much narrower. Today, what we call the tort of trespass is defined as an intentional unlawful entry onto someone else's property. In some jurisdictions, it is required to show that the property was damaged even in a minimal amount. It is an interference with the right of a person who owns or possesses property to have the exclusive possession of the property.

The unlawful entry may be entering without permission. It may also include having the permission to come on the property, but staying after that permission is revoked. A person who refuses to leave after being ordered to do so commits a trespass even though she may have had permission to enter the property.

A trespass is a physical intrusion, but it is not necessarily an intrusion in which an unauthorized person is physically present on the property. Courts have held that the intrusion of objects, or even of particulate matter, can constitute a trespass.

Nuisance

Nuisance is related to trespass. In many cases, one intrusion can constitute both a trespass and a nuisance. Trespass, however, looks at a person's right to possess property. Nuisance is an interference with her right to use and enjoy the property. Nuisance is not an unlawful act by itself. Instead, the interference comes from the consequences of that act. In addition, while any minor damage can be the basis for a trespass action, a nuisance action requires the interference to be unreasonable and substantial. No physical entry on the land is required for a nuisance action.

While a landowner or occupant may bring an action for damages caused by a nuisance, she may also bring an action for an injunction against the continuation of the nuisance.

Defamation

In the United States, the Bill of Rights provides for freedom of speech. Although the right is broad, it is not well-understood by most people. Many are unaware that there are a number of restrictions on free speech. One such limit on that right is that a person may not make false statements about another person if that state-

> **Example:** During an interview with a large financial news publication, Ernie Executive, CFO of Company X, is asked about the company's poor performance. Ernie Executive states that "Company X's CEO is the worst CEO ever." That statement is opinion and cannot be defamatory.
>
> On the other hand, if Ernie Executive states that "Company X's CEO lied about the financial status of Company X during his press conference last week and falsified several documents submitted to the SEC." Here, the statement can be verified as true or false.

ment harms the other person's reputation. The tort of **defamation** holds the speaker liable for a false statement that damages a person's reputation. To hold a speaker liable, the statement must be a statement of fact, the statement must be published, and the false statement must harm another person's reputation. Written defamation is called **libel**. Spoken defamation is called **slander**.

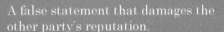

DEFAMATION:
A false statement that damages the other party's reputation.

LIBEL:
A written false statement that damages another person's reputation.

SLANDER:
A spoken false statement that damages another person's reputation.

Defamation law distinguishes between statements of fact and statements of opinion. In order to be defamatory, a statement must be a statement of fact, rather than an opinion. Because a statement of opinion cannot be deemed true or false, a party cannot be liable for an opinion.

Truth is a defense to defamation. If the statement is a true statement, the speaker cannot be liable.

To be published, a statement does not need to be written in a book or professionally published. In the law of defamation, publication means that the statement was communicated to another person. A statement is published if it is stated to a third party or otherwise made public. A statement may be published through magazines, television, email, blogs, websites, and social media, or verbal statements. Publication may be established even where someone overhears defamatory statements. A statement is published if the person making it is reasonably

> **Example:** Al writes a note to his co-worker Ken, falsely accusing Ken of embezzling from the company. If Al gives the note directly to Ken, there is no publication. If Al leaves the note on a table in the company break room where it can be seen by anyone coming in, there is publication.

> *Example:*
>
> After an argument with his co-worker John, Ryan goes to his desk and writes a letter to a local newspaper. In the letter, Ryan states that John, a high-ranking executive at the company, submitted false expense reports for reimbursement and lied during his deposition in a lawsuit against the company. Ryan saves the letter in his pocket, but does not send the letter. Several hours later, Ryan has second thoughts, rips up the letter, and throws it away. Because the statement was never communicated to a third party, the statement was not published.
>
> Assume instead that Ryan drafted an email making the same statements. Ryan sends the email to his girlfriend, with a message "I'm really tempted to send this to the newspapers, after what he's done to me." Ryan does not send the e-mail to anyone else, and his girlfriend deletes it after she reads it, but no one else sees it. This could be considered publication of the statement.

certain it will be seen or heard by a third party, even if it is not directly or explicitly transmitted to that third party.

A statement that is alleged to be defamatory must refer to an identifiable person. The identification does not have to be by the person's name if there are other facts or circumstances that would permit the identification of the person. The additional facts or circumstances must show that a person who heard the defamatory statement would understand that it was made about the plaintiff. If a statement is made about a group of people, it is not defamatory unless it singles out one or more members of the group. A person who is a member of a small group may be able to claim defamation if a reasonable listener would conclude that the statement was intended to refer to each individual member of the group.

A person claiming defamation must also show the statement damaged his reputation. As an example, the plaintiff might show that he lost his job, could not obtain work, or was rejected by social groups and family members. The damage may have little or no economic value. Some successful defamation plaintiffs are awarded nominal damages of $1. An award such as that is vindication for the plaintiff. She has proven that what the defendant said about her was false, even though there was no monetary loss for which she is compensated. If the plaintiff already had a negative reputation in the community, he may have a difficult time proving damage to his reputation from the defendant's statement.

It is possible that a statement would not appear defamatory on its face, but additional facts about the person about whom the statement is made make the statement defamatory. For example, a social media post that falsely congratulates Mike and Elaine on the birth of their child would not appear to be the kind of statement that would harm anyone's reputation. Mike, however, is married to Diane, and Elaine, his business partner, is married to Stan. The additional facts of the relationship could make a seemingly innocuous statement defamatory.

In a few circumstances, statements are "privileged" and cannot support a defamation claim, even if the statements are false statements of fact. For instance, witnesses who testify to a false statement in court cannot be sued for defamation. Likewise, legislators cannot be sued for defamation for statements made in the legislative chamber. Some jurisdictions recognize an employer privilege for statements made during an employee review. Good faith statements made by credit review agencies may also be privileged. If a statement would be protected by an evidentiary privilege, it will not support a defamation claim. For example, a person who falsely says that she and a co-worker deliberately planted a virus on her employer's computer system cannot be sued for defamation if she made her statement while confessing to her spiritual advisor.

Actual Malice

The law of defamation makes a distinction between public figures and private figures. Public figures must meet a higher standard to prove a defamation claim. Public officials and figures must prove the elements stated above, and that the defendant acted with **actual malice**. "Actual malice" means that the person who made the statement knew it was false, or was reckless about the truth and did not care if the statement was true or not. In other words, a public figure cannot sue for defamation where the speaker made an honest mistake about the facts.

> Actual malice is a difficult, but not impossible, standard to meet. In one recent case, Jesse Ventura, the former wrestler and governor of Minnesota, brought a defamation action against Chris Kyle. Chris Kyle, now deceased, was a former Navy SEAL and author of the book American Sniper, which was made into a movie. In the book, Kyle described an incident with Ventura. Kyle claimed Ventura made derogatory statements about Navy SEALs and the two engaged in a brawl. Ventura, a former SEAL himself, denied making the statements and the incident. Ventura argued the story ruined his reputation in the Navy SEAL community. Because Ventura is a public figure, he was required to show that Kyle acted with actual malice. The jury awarded $500,000 to Ventura on the defamation claim. On appeal, the court reversed the decision, but sent the case back to court for a new trial.

Example: A reporter for a large newspaper is writing a story about the governor. One of his sources tells him that the governor embezzled money from the company he worked for prior to running for office. The reporter has doubts about the truth of that statement because the source has provided false information in the past. The reporter did not check or try to verify the statement, but included it his story anyway. The reporter acted with actual malice.

Example:	Leigh is a prominent member of her business community, and she is also active in a number of civic and charitable organizations. Her business and community work has made her well-known in the area, and she is often mentioned for her work in the local media. Unfortunately, Leigh has been in a dispute with one of her neighbors for the past few months. The neighbor tells a business colleague who also knows her that "the inside of her house is a health hazard, what with all the dogs and cats who aren't housebroken wandering around. The place stinks to high heaven. She's also a hoarder—there is something wrong with that woman." The neighbor has never been in Leigh's house, but based his statement on some malicious gossip he heard from a former housekeeper. The neighbor's comment is defamation. Leigh does not have to prove actual malice, because the statement does not relate to her status as a public figure.

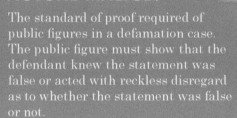

ACTUAL MALICE:
The standard of proof required of public figures in a defamation case. The public figure must show that the defendant knew the statement was false or acted with reckless disregard as to whether the statement was false or not.

The actual malice requirement originally applied only to statements about public officials. The purpose behind the requirement was to protect citizens' rights to criticize the people who govern. The actual malice requirement has now been extended to all public figures who have access to the media or have placed themselves in the public eye. Private persons do not need to prove actual malice. Private persons must show that the defendant was negligent in making the false statement.

The actual malice requirement only applies when there is some relationship between the false statement and the person's status as a public figure. A person may be a public figure for some purposes, but not necessarily a public figure for everything he does. A very few people may be "all purpose" public figures, such as the President of the United States, but most public figures have some part of their lives that is not open to public scrutiny.

Trade Libel/Product Disparagement

Trade libel is a type of defamation related to businesses. Trade libel is also referred to as product disparagement. Trade libel is a defamatory statement about the quality of a business's services or products. The purpose behind this tort is to maintain fair competition among businesses.

This type of defamation is similar to the general claim for defamation discussed above. In trade libel, the statement must state a fact about a business's services or products. Like the general

> **Example:** ABC Company and XYZ Corporation are competitors. Both companies produce and sell cameras. ABC Company recently stated that XYZ Corporation began installing poor quality lenses on its cameras without notifying customers. If untrue, ABC Company's statement could constitute product disparagement.

defamation claim, it must be a statement of fact and cannot be an opinion. As with other defamation claims, the statement must be published. Furthermore, the statement must damage the business's reputation. To show damage, the

Intentional Torts Relevant to Business Parties	
Intentional Tort	**Description**
Fraudulent Misrepresentation	• Defendant makes a false statement about a material fact relied upon by the plaintiff • Defendant knew the statement was false or was reckless about the truth • Statement must be a statement of fact, not opinion
Intentional Interference with Contractual Relations	• Defendant interferes with a contractual relationship between other parties • Defendant must know about the contract
Intentional Interference with Prospective Business Advantage	• Defendant interferes with a business relationship between other parties • No contract or formal agreement is in place • Defendant must know about the negotiations or prospective relationship
Prima Facie Tort	• Intentionally causing harm to another by lawful means • No justification
Trespass	• Intentionally entering onto the property of another without their permission
Nuisance	• Interfering with another person's use and enjoyment of their property

Defamation	• Defendant makes a false statement about the plaintiff that damages the plaintiff's reputation • Public officials and public figures need to prove the higher standard of actual malice
Trade Libel/Product Disparagement	• Defendant makes a false statement about the quality of a business's services or products
Intrusion Upon Seclusion	• Intentionally intruding upon someone's seclusion or private affairs, in a highly offensive manner
Publication of a Private Fact	• Giving widespread publicity to private information about another person in a highly offensive manner, and without their permission
Misappropriation of Likeness	• Using another person's image or name for one's own advantages, without the permission of that person
False Light	• Giving publicity to a false statement that presents another person in a false light

plaintiff must present proof that the statement resulted in lost business or profits.

TRADE LIBEL:

A defamatory statement about the quality of a business's services or products. It is also referred to as product disparagement.

Trade libel or product disparagement could also support other types of actions. Suits for false advertising, brought under the federal Lanham Act or similar state laws, may be based on false claims about the quality of a competitor's product. State laws regarding unfair trade practices may also allow an action to be brought against a person who falsely disparages the goods, services, or business of another by use of false or misleading representations of fact.

Example: XPLO Corp. provides fireworks shows for special events. Its driver was hauling a large truck of fireworks to Smallville for its Centennial celebration fireworks show. While the truck was parked in the parking lot of a restaurant during transit, several of the fireworks went off, causing the entire truckload to explode. Several restaurant patrons were injured from the blast. XPLO could be strictly liable for the patrons' injuries because the hauling of explosives is an inherently dangerous activity.

Negative or unfavorable statements, such as a comparison of two products, will not be actionable if they are accurate or true. For example, an advertisement that says a particular brand of chewing gum has eight sticks in a package while competing companies, whose product is shown in the advertisement, only sell seven sticks is not actionable if it is an accurate comparison.

III. Strict Liability

In a few limited circumstances, someone can be liable for a tort even though that person was not negligent or otherwise at fault. When a party is held liable without negligence or fault, it is called **strict liability**. Strict liability applies to a few situations where the party is engaging in an inherently dangerous or hazardous activity. If a party is engaging in an inherently dangerous activity, the party may be liable even if they took all reasonable steps to avoid injury to others.

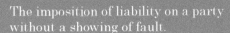

STRICT LIABILITY:
The imposition of liability on a party without a showing of fault.

An inherently dangerous activity is one that creates a foreseeable and highly significant risk of physical harm even when reasonable care is exercised by all actors, and that is not an activity of common usage. Examples of hazardous activities that might result in strict liability include keeping a wild animal, storage or transportation of flammable materials or explosives, blasting in a non-remote area, and emission of toxic fumes. Sometimes a court might consider

where the activity is taking place to determine if the activity is merely dangerous, or inherently dangerous. For instance, blasting that occurs in a remote, unpopulated area might not be considered inherently dangerous. However, because of the risk to people living and working in the area, blasting a building within a city is likely to be considered inherently dangerous.

Three elements must be established for a defendant to be strictly liable:

> 1. The defendant engaged in an inherently dangerous activity.
>
> 2. The inherently dangerous act caused something bad to happen to the plaintiff.
>
> 3. The plaintiff suffered harm from the resulting injury.

IV. Products Liability

Millions of products are bought and sold every day. Sometimes a product may harm a customer or another person. If a person is injured from a product with a defect, they may sue the parties responsible for the product. The entities involved in the supply chain of a product can all be liable for defective products. This includes the companies who manufacture, wholesale, and sell the product.

Each claim for products liability must describe the basis for liability on behalf of the company and the type of defect the product contains. In addition to showing the injury caused by a product, a plaintiff must show that (1) the manufacturer or other entity is liable for the product, (2) the product contained a defect, (3) the defect proximately caused the injury, and (4) the plaintiff suffered compensable damages.

There are several possible theories of liability by which a company may be responsible for a product. Like other tort actions, a products liability claim can be based on negligence or strict liability on behalf of the manufacturer or other entity. Products liability may also be based on breach of warranty. This means that a manufacturer or other party may be liable for a product if the business was negligent, if the entity created an unreasonably dangerous product, or if the manufacturer breached a warranty.

Negligence

As previously noted, a negligence claim may be brought in a number of different circumstances. A claim for products liability may be based on the manufacturer's negligence in making the product. The same elements required in a standard negligence action must also be shown in products liability cases. The standard of care in this instance is that of a reasonable manufacturer of similar products. In other words, a manufacturer must exercise a standard of care that is reasonable for those who manufacture similar products. The plaintiff must show that the manufacturer did not act like a reasonable manufacturer when it made the product.

Negligence liability may also be based on a manufacturer's or seller's advertising of a product. For example, an advertisement that says a certain brand of canned chicken is "ready to eat" implies that the bones have been removed from the meat. A warning or disclaimer in an advertisement ("Trained professional on a closed course") may negate negligence in advertising if it makes the reader aware of the risk posed by using the product.

The injured party must also show that they were injured and that the injury would not have happened without the manufacturer's negligence. In short, a claim for negligence with regard to products is the same as any other negligence claim. The same elements must be proved, with the only variation being the product's role in the injury.

Strict Liability

Under the law of torts, sometimes a party may also be liable even without negligence or proof of fault. As noted above, strict liability applies when a party engages in an inherently dangerous activity. Strict liability has been applied to products liability. If a manufacturer creates a product that is unreasonably dangerous, the manufacturer may be strictly liable for injuries resulting from the product. Thus, the manufacturer may be liable for a defective product even if the manufacturer was not negligent in making that product defective.

As the complexity of products has increased over time, it has often become difficult for injured parties to show that the manufacturer of a product had acted negligently. However, it did not seem fair to deny relief to people who were injured by products created by a manufacturer. Therefore, as a matter of public policy, the law holds that manufacturers may be strictly liable for the defective products they create. While a negligence claim focuses on the manufacturer's conduct, strict liability focuses on the product itself.

In order to recover in strict liability for a defective product, the plaintiff must show that:

- He was injured by the product,

- The injury occurred because the product was defective and unreasonably dangerous, and

- The defect existed when it left the hands of the manufacturer or seller.

Foreseeability may limit liability to injuries which can fairly be regarded as normal incidents of risks created by the product.

Evidence of due care by a manufacturer or seller is irrelevant in a products liability case. A manufacturer or seller may be strictly liable even if it used the utmost care. Similarly, a consumer's failure to exercise due care when using the product is not relevant to whether the product is unreasonably dangerous in the first place.

The doctrine of strict liability imposes liability for physical harm caused to the ultimate user or consumer of a dangerous and defective product, or to her property. The term "consumer" includes those who in fact consume a product, and also those who prepare it for consumption. The term "consumption" includes all of the uses for which a product is intended. "User" includes someone who is passively enjoying the benefit of a product. The terms "consumer" and "user" are to be construed broadly. Strict liability has been held to impose liability for injuries to those who purchase a product from an original purchaser, employees, users or consumers, passengers, and even innocent bystanders. Liability may be imposed even though the user or consumer has not bought the product from, or entered into any type of transaction with, the manufacturer or seller.

A **warranty** is a promise or guarantee to another party. In the commercial world, companies often provide a warranty about the products they make and sell. A warranty promises to

Types of Torts	
Type of Tort	**Key Features**
Negligence	• Defendant did not act as a reasonably prudent person in the circumstances
Intentional Torts	• Defendant intended his conduct, but not necessarily any harm • Does not require evil or harmful intent
Strict Liability	• No fault required on behalf of Defendant • Defendant engaged in inherently dangerous activity

ABESTOS IS A DEFECTIVE PRODUCT THAT RAISES MANUFACTURER LIABILITY FOR INJURIES CAUSED BY THE PRODUCT.

Arbogast v. A.W. Chesterton Co.
(Electrician) v. (Asbestos Products Manufacturer)
___, F. Supp. 3d ___, 2016 WL 3997292 (D. Md. 2016)

INSTANT FACTS:
Electrician sued manufacturers, distributors, and installers of products containing asbestos

BLACK LETTER RULE:
The manufacturer of a defective product may be liable for its negligence or in strict liability if the plaintiff can show the defective product caused the plaintiff's injury.

FACTS:
An electrician brought a products liability claim against the manufacturers of various products containing asbestos. The electrician claims he breathed in asbestos that was released into the air, causing his mesothelioma. The suit alleged liability on the basis of negligence and strict liability.

ISSUE:
Were manufacturers liable for asbestos in their products?

DECISION AND RATIONALE:
Yes. The court stated that a manufacturer may be strictly liable for a defect that existed when the product left the defendant's control and the defect makes the product unreasonably dangerous. The court noted that strict liability is essentially a version of negligence per se. Manufacturers may also be liable for failing to warn consumers about the dangers of asbestos. However, the electrician could not prove exposure to asbestos from many of the specific products. Thus, summary judgment was entered in favor of most of the defendants.

ANALYSIS:
This case focuses on the plaintiff's need to demonstrate causation. Even though it was clear that asbestos was dangerous, the plaintiff still needed to show he was exposed to the asbestos products. Without that showing, the plaintiff could not recover for the defective product, even if the product was dangerous.

QUESTIONS FOR DISCUSSION:
Should developing a disease strongly associated with asbestos establish causation? Assume that exposure to a certain type of laundry detergent caused serious illness over time. How would consumers prove that they had been exposed to the detergent years in the past?

Manufacturers were not aware that their product was hazardous when they first produced it; moreover, asbestos products undoubtedly saved many lives by preventing or stopping the spread of fires. Should manufacturers receive any credit for their good faith and the benefits of their products when products liability cases are brought?

the consumer that the product is of good quality, or that the product will operate safely for the purposes for which the product was intended. If a manufacturer provides a written statement of warranty, that is an express warranty.

If no express warranty is provided by the manufacturer, the law may find that a warranty is implied. That warranty is referred to as implied warranty. With respect to the sale of goods, the law implies a **warranty of merchantability**. This means that the manufacturer promises that the product is in good working order and can safely be used for the purposes stated on the label. If a product does not work as it is supposed to, the manufacturer may be liable for breach of warranty on the product.

WARRANTY:

A promise or guarantee to a consumer.

WARRANTY OF MERCHANTABILITY:

A promise from the manufacturer that the product is in good working order and can safely be used for the purposes stated on the label.

Types of Defects

A product may contain one of several types of defects. A problem in the manufacturing or design process, or the manner in which a product is packaged, might create a defective product. Furthermore, a manufacturer's failure to warn consumers about the dangers of a product can be a defect. There are four types of product defects: (1) a manufacturing defect; (2) a design defect; (3) a failure to warn (also known as a marketing defect); or (4) improper packaging.

Manufacturing Defects: A manufacturing defect is a defect that occurs in the manufacturing process. These defects may involve poor-quality materials or poor workmanship. A defect could also be due to a failure to follow the specifications of a product design. A product that fails or malfunctions under normal use may also be considered to have a manufacturing defect.

Design Defects: Design defects are defects in the product design. A product may be inherently dangerous or useless, even if manufactured properly, if the design is flawed. A product must meet ordinary consumer expectations for safe use. Design defects, unlike manufacturing defects, are caused by deliberate decisions. The

Although warranties may be thought of as a type of contract, many jurisdictions have done away with the doctrine that requires some kind of contractual relationship with a seller before a person may claim a breach of warranty. This doctrine, known as privity of contract, provided a defense to a breach of warranty claim brought by someone other than the purchaser of a product. Some jurisdictions have enacted statutes that provide a person may bring a claim for breach of warranty if she is a person whom the manufacturer, seller, or supplier might reasonably expect to use, consume, or be affected by the goods. This type of statute has been read as allowing recovery by bystanders who are injured by a product.

Example: Mike recently purchased a new coffee pot made by Sunrise Ventures. One morning, Mike brews a pot of coffee. When he goes to pour a cup of coffee, the handle separates from the pot and the coffee pot falls to the ground. The coffee pot shatters and hot coffee splashes on Mike, causing severe burns on his feet and legs. An expert examines the coffee pot and determines that one of the screws needed to securely attach the handle to the pot was not included. The missing screw is a manufacturing defect.

Example: Consider Mike and the coffee pot incident described above. Assume that the handle was originally attached with the intended screws. However, the expert determines that the handle was made of a lightweight plastic that cannot support the weight of the coffee pot when it is filled with coffee. The weak handle is a design defect.

Example: Rainbow Corp. manufactures aerosol paint cans. The aerosol cans are pressurized and contain highly flammable propellants. If the aerosol cans are exposed to flames or high temperatures, the cans can explode or create a fire. Rainbow Corp. knows about the flammability of its aerosol cans, but does not include a warning on its paint cans. Walt purchases a Rainbow aerosol can. Walt uses the paint can to paint a sign and then sets it down next to the space heater in the garage. After a few minutes, the can explodes, leaving Walt with serious injuries. Walt sues Rainbow for its failure to include a warning about the flammability of the aerosol cans.

manufacturer intended for the product to be marketed in the condition it was in.

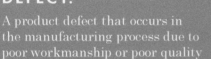

MANUFACTURING DEFECT:

A product defect that occurs in the manufacturing process due to poor workmanship or poor quality materials.

DESIGN DEFECT:

A defect in the design of the product that makes the product dangerous or useless.

Failure to Warn Defects: Some products contain inherent, but nonobvious dangers. These dangers exist due to the nature of the product, even if the product is carefully manufactured. Sometimes, the danger from these products can

be reduced by providing a warning to the user of the product. If a manufacturer fails to provide a warning about the dangers, it could be liable for its failure to warn consumers. A manufacturer does not owe a duty to warn about obvious risks. The duty to warn may include the duty to provide adequate instructions for the use of a product, although providing instructions will not take away the duty to warn of dangers.

Improper Packaging: The main function of packaging is to protect the contents from damage and to maintain freshness. Manufacturers must take care to use safe packaging for their products. A product may be considered defective if the package it comes in is not safe. The packaging includes plastic wrapping, boxes, cans, bottles, and other containers in which products are packaged and shipped. Some types of packaging can create an obvious risk, such as a glass bottle that may shatter, or an aluminum

LIABILITY FOR DEFECTIVE PRODUCT ONLY EXISTS IF THE DEFECT AROSE WHILE THE PRODUCT WAS IN THE DEFENDANT'S CONTROL.

Sheats v. The Kroger Company
(Shopper) v. (Grocery Store)
336 Ga. App. 307, 784 S.E.2d 442 (2016)

In this personal injury case, Brenda Sheats sued The Kroger Co. and Clayton Distributing Company, Inc. ("Clayton"), asserting claims based upon product liability, ordinary negligence, and res ipsa loquitur. Sheats also filed a motion for spoliation sanctions, asserting that Kroger destroyed evidence that was essential to her complaint.

In Case No. A15A2073, Sheats appeals from the trial court's order granting summary judgment to Clayton and denying her motion for spoliation sanctions against Kroger. In Case No. A15A2074, Sheats appeals from the grant of summary judgment to Kroger. For the reasons that follow, in Case No. A15A2073, we affirm the trial court's grant of summary judgment to Clayton, but vacate the trial court's denial of Sheats' motion for spoliation sanctions against Kroger, and we remand this case for further proceedings. In Case No. A15A2074, we affirm the trial court's grant of summary judgment to Kroger on Sheats' product liability and res ipsa loquitur claims, but reverse the grant of summary judgment to Kroger on Sheats' ordinary negligence claim.

"Summary judgment is proper when there is no genuine issue of material fact and the movant is entitled to judgment as a matter of law. OCGA § 9-11-56(c). We apply a de novo standard of review to an appeal from the grant of summary judgment, construing the evidence in the light most favorable to the nonmovant." (Citation and punctuation omitted.) Walker v. Gwinnett Hosp. System, 263 Ga.App. 554, 555, 588 S.E.2d 441 (2003).

Viewed in this light, the evidence shows that, on November 7, 2011, Sheats was shopping at a Kroger grocery store in Athens. Sheats took a cardboard package containing several glass bottles of Red Rock Golden Ginger Ale off of a shelf and placed it in her cart. Sheats then lifted a second pack off the shelf. As she did so, the bottom of the package opened up, all of the glass bottles fell to the floor, and they broke. At least one bottle struck Sheats' left foot, injuring her.

A store security guard was called to the aisle where the incident occurred. Upon arriving at the scene, the guard found Sheats standing among broken glass and spilled liquid and holding an empty cardboard package with a bottom that was "fully broken open[ ]." When Sheats told the security guard what happened, the guard asked Sheats to step away from the debris, and she asked for the package Sheats was holding. Sheats refused and told the guard that she

wanted to keep the package as evidence. The guard replied that she would keep the package as evidence instead. Sheats then complained to the guard about pain in her foot. The guard offered to call an ambulance, but Sheats declined, saying that she might go to a doctor later.

The guard escorted Sheats to the customer service counter at the front of the store, where Sheats told the store manager what happened. Sheats then told the manager that her left foot was hurting and she was going to the hospital. The manager completed a three-page "Customer Incident Report & Investigation Check List," which had the following statement printed on each page: "This report is being prepared in anticipation of litigation under the direction of legal counsel. It is confidential and is not to be released to any person unless approved by legal counsel and authorized by a member of Kroger management with such authority." The manager told Sheats that he would forward information about the incident to Kroger's headquarters, but he was not sure if Kroger's insurance would pay for treatment of the injury.

Shortly after the incident, the manager inspected the package and the shelf where it had been displayed and observed that both were dry. According to the manager, "[f]or some unknown reason, the glue on one side of the bottom of the package failed to stay glued to the other flap. I observed that one of the outside bottom flaps was cleanly separated from the other, inside bottom flap, and the glue was only stuck to one flap. It appeared to me that the glue didn't stick sufficiently to the other flap[.]" The manager then inspected all of the other Red Rock Ginger Ale packages on the shelf, but observed no similar problem. After inspecting the package, the manager recorded it, for inventory purposes, as a "lost" item due to breakage and put it with outgoing refuse to be discarded. The manager stated in his affidavit that, when he spoke to Sheats after the incident, he did not get the impression that Sheats would later file a lawsuit.

After leaving Kroger, Sheats went to a hospital emergency room. She was subsequently diagnosed with a blood clot in her left big toe and had to have surgery to remove the toenail. Sheats had to wear a protective shoe for two months after her surgery. Additionally, her toenail failed to grow back correctly, and she still had pain in her toe at the time of the summary judgment hearing.

Sheats filed this personal injury suit against Kroger and Clayton, setting forth product liability, ordinary negligence and res ipsa loquitur claims. Clayton filed a motion for summary judgment on the ground that Sheats had not provided any evidence to prove that the cardboard package had been defective. Kroger also filed a motion for summary judgment on the same basis. Sheats then filed a motion for spoliation sanctions against both defendants on the ground that Kroger had destroyed essential evidence, i.e., the package.

The trial court granted summary judgment to Clayton and Kroger on Sheat's product liability claims due to her failure to present evidence that the package was defective. It denied Sheats' motion for spoliation sanctions on the ground that she did not provide Kroger with actual notice that she was contemplating litigation at the time of the incident. The trial court also granted summary judgment to Kroger on Sheats' ordinary negligence and res ipsa loquitur claims. 1. Sheats argues that the trial court erred in denying her motion for spoliation sanctions because, at the time of the incident, Kroger should have reasonably anticipated that she was contemplating litigation. We agree.

(a) Spoliation sanctions against Kroger.

Spoliation is "the destruction or failure to preserve evidence" that is relevant to "contemplated or pending litigation." (Citation and punctuation omitted.) Phillips v. Harmon, 297 Ga. 386, 393(II), 774 S.E.2d 596 (2015). The destruction of evidence "may give rise to the rebuttable presumption that the evidence would have been harmful to the spoliator. However, in order for the injured party to pursue a remedy for spoliation, the spoliating party must have been under a duty to preserve the evidence at issue." Id. At 394(II), 774 S.E.2d 596. Moreover, a defendant's duty to preserve evidence, is not limited to situations where the plaintiff provides actual or express notice of litigation. Rather,

[n]otice that the plaintiff is contemplating litigation may also be derived from, ... other circumstances, such as the type and extent of the injury; the extent to which fault for the injury is clear; the potential financial exposure if faced with a finding of liability; the relationship and course of conduct between the parties, including past litigation or threatened litigation; and the frequency with which litigation occurs in similar circumstances.

Id. at 397(II), 774 S.E.2d 596. "Certainly a trial court has wide discretion in adjudicating spoliation issues, and such discretion will not be disturbed absent abuse. However, an appellate court cannot affirm a trial court's reasoning which is based upon an erroneous legal theory." (Citations omitted.) Id.

In this case, the trial court ruled that the uncontroverted evidence showed that Sheats failed to provide Kroger with actual notice that she was contemplating litigation at the time of her injury. In so ruling, the trial court relied solely on Sheats' deposition, wherein she was asked whether she was contemplating filing a lawsuit when she asked to keep the package, and Sheats answered "No." The trial court's ruling was based on the legally incorrect premise that Kroger's duty to preserve the evidence required actual notice of litigation from Sheats. Consequently, we vacate the denial of Sheats' spoliation motion as to Kroger and remand this case for the trial court to reconsider that motion in light of the correct legal analysis as set forth herein. See Phillips, supra, 297 Ga. at 397-398(II), 774 S.E.2d 596.

(b) Spoliation sanctions against Clayton.

Sanctions for spoliation cannot be applied against a party who did not destroy the evidence when there is no evidence to show that the destroying party was acting at the behest of the other party. Boswell v. Overhead Door Corp., 292 Ga.App. 234, 235-236, 664 S.E.2d 262 (2008). It follows that, because there is no evidence to show that Clayton directed Kroger to destroy the package or was even aware of the incident before it was destroyed, the trial court properly denied the motion for spoliation sanctions as to Clayton.

2. Sheats contends that the trial court erred in granting summary judgment to Clayton on her product liability claim on the basis that she failed to present evidence to prove that the package was defective. We disagree.

Regardless of whether the plaintiff proceeds under a theory of strict liability or negligence, the essence of a product liability claim is the presence of an actual defect in the product. Boswell, supra, 292 Ga.App. at 235, 664 S.E.2d 262. In order to prevail on such a claim, Sheats must prove that there was a defect in the product when it left the manufacturer, the defect was caused by the manufacturer's negligence, and the defect caused her injury. Id.; Miller v. Ford Motor Co., 287 Ga.App. 642, 644(1), 653 S.E.2d 82 (2007).

In this case, Sheats was unable to produce the package in order to prove a defect in the design or manufacturing because Kroger had discarded it. As noted above, however, no presumption of a product defect applies to Clayton as a result of such spoliation. See Division 1(b), supra. Further, although Sheats points to evidence about the condition of the package at the time she removed it from the store shelf, she is unable to prove that there was an original design or manufacturing defect that existed at the time it left Clayton's possession. Instead, it is just as likely that the problem that caused the package's bottom flap to open occurred because of something that was not related to its manufacture that occurred at some point after the package left Clayton's possession. See Miller, supra, 287 Ga.App. at 644(1), 653 S.E.2d 82; see also Jenkins v. Gen. Motors Corp., 240 Ga.App. 636, 637(1), 524 S.E.2d 324 (1999) (finding that there was evidence of several plausible explanations for the vehicle's brakes to fail other than a manufacturing defect). In fact, the evidence shows that none of the other packages of Red Rock Ginger Ale on Kroger's shelf had a problem similar to the one at issue here.

Consequently, Sheats cannot meet her burden of proving, by a preponderance of the evidence, that the package was defective when it left Clayton's possession. Thus, the trial court did not err in granting summary judgment to Clayton on her product liability claim.

3. To the extent Sheats argues that the trial court erred in ruling that she was required to present expert testimony on the issue of whether the package was defective, the trial court's order does not show that it issued such a ruling. Accordingly, this alleged error presents nothing for this Court to review. See Williamson v. Strickland & Smith, Inc., 296 Ga.App. 1, 6(7), 673 S.E.2d 858 (2009) (this Court will not consider issues that were not ruled upon by the trial court.).

4. Sheats argues that the trial court erred in granting summary judgment to Kroger on her res ipsa loquitur claim. In its order, the trial court ruled that Sheats had failed to establish an essential element of that claim, i.e., that the package had been under Kroger's exclusive control.

The elements of the doctrine of res ipsa loquitur are: (1) an injury which ordinarily does not occur in the absence of someone's negligence; (2) the injury must be caused by an agency or instrumentality within the defendant's exclusive control; and (3) the injury was not caused by any voluntary action or contribution on the part of the plaintiff. Aderhold v. Lowe's Home Ctrs., 284 Ga.App. 294, 295, 643 S.E.2d 811 (2007). "Res ipsa loquitur should be applied with caution and only in extreme cases, and is not applicable when there is an intermediary cause which could have produced the injury." (Citations and punctuation omitted.) Id.

Here, the trial court properly concluded that the package had not been in Kroger's exclusive control because the undisputed evidence showed that the package had been placed on a display shelf and was readily accessible to other customers. See Aderhold, supra, 284 Ga.App. at 296, 643 S.E.2d 811 (res ipsa loquitur doctrine did not apply when the undisputed evidence showed that the item at issue was stacked on a shelf within the reach of other customers). Accordingly, the trial court properly granted summary judgment to Kroger on Sheats' res ipsa loquitur claim.

5. Sheats contends that the trial court erred in granting summary judgment to Kroger on her product liability claim based upon a finding that she failed to present evidence to prove that the package was, in fact, defective. Sheats' product liability claim was based upon allegations that Kroger negligently sold a defective and unsafe product and failed to warn customers of the defect. Sheats presented evidence showing that the bottom of the package opened up when she lifted it

off the shelf. Sheats is unable to prove, however, that the package opened because of an original manufacturing defect, as opposed to some other cause, such as mishandling during delivery or while stocking the shelf. See Division 2, supra. Consequently, the trial court did not err in granting summary judgment to Kroger on Sheats' product liability claim. See Miller, supra, 287 Ga.App. at 645(1), 653 S.E.2d 82 (plaintiffs could not prevail on their failure to warn claim because that claim was predicated on the allegation that the product at issue had an original manufacturing defect).

6. Sheats contends that the trial court erred in granting summary judgment to Kroger on her ordinary negligence claim. She argues, inter alia, that jury issues remain regarding whether Kroger negligently failed to maintain a safe product display.

Pursuant to long-standing Georgia law, "[t]he situation of the retailer and consumer of packed products is properly governed by the rules of negligence law." (Citations and punctuation omitted.) Howard v. Jacobs' Pharmacy Co., 55 Ga.App. 163, 164, 189 S.E. 373 (1937). Accordingly, retailers owe consumers a duty "to supply goods packed by reliable manufacturers, [which] are without imperfections that may be discovered by an exercise of the care, skill, and experience of dealers in such products generally." (Citations and punctuation omitted.) Id.; see also Brock v. Simpson, 103 Ga.App. 800, 801(1), 120 S.E.2d 885 (1961); Fleetwood

Here, with regard to the allegedly defective package of Ginger Ale, Sheats presented evidence that the glue on one side of the bottom of the package failed to stay glued to the other flap, one of the outside bottom flaps was cleanly separated from the inside bottom flap, and the glue was stuck to only one flap. Because Kroger discarded the allegedly defective package, it cannot show that the alleged defect was not reasonably observable, and Sheats cannot show that it was. Consequently, the question of whether Kroger was or was not negligent, and whether Sheats' negligence claim is a jury issue, cannot be determined until the trial court first determines on remand whether spoliation occurred and, if so, which spoliation sanctions are appropriate.

In so holding, we note that, with regard to the spoliation issue, the trial court is authorized to craft a solution that fits the facts. For instance, the trial court may

(1) charge the jury that spoliation of evidence creates the rebuttable presumption that the evidence would have been harmful to the spoliator; (2) dismiss the case; or (3) exclude testimony about the evidence. This is not an exhaustive list of sanctions [that] a trial court may impose; rather, the trial court has wide latitude to fashion sanctions on a case-by-case basis, considering what is appropriate and fair under the circumstances.

ANALYSIS:

A manufacturer may be liable for defective packaging of a product. As in other products liability cases, the injured party must prove that the packaging contained a defect at the time it left the manufacturer's control.

QUESTIONS FOR DISCUSSION:

Parties to a lawsuit can be sanctioned for "spoliation," which refers to destruction or loss of evidence important to the case. Given that, why did the manager dispose of the packaging? Did the manager have any intent to deprive the customer of the evidence?

Should a manufacturer need to package for all eventualities when the product is out of the manufacturer's control? Why or why not?

can that can cut. Sometimes, packaging may be considered by some people to be too difficult to open. For example, if someone cuts himself or herself with a knife while trying to open a package that is difficult to open, they might claim the packaging was defective.

In cases involving improper packaging, the packaging is treated similarly to a product. Just like a product, the package may have a design flaw or become defective due to a problem in the manufacturing process. For instance, improper packaging may cause harm because it is not properly designed to safety transfer the prod-

Types of Defects	
Type of Defect	**Description**
Manufacturing Defect	• Product contains a defect from the manufacturing process • Product may have been poorly constructed or made out of subpar materials
Design Defect	• Product was not properly designed • The flaw in the design caused the product to be dangerous or useless
Failure to Warn	• The manufacturer failed to warn consumers about non-obvious risks of the product
Improper Packaging	• Packaging of a product was ineffective or caused injury to the plaintiff

ucts contained in the package. Likewise, something might happen during the manufacturing process, such as an improper seal, which makes the package defective.

In other situations, the packaging defect relates to labeling on the package. If the packaging is confusing or does not contain a warning about a danger from the product, the manufacturer may be liable for failing to warn about possible danger.

In some instances, packaging has been designed to make a product tamper-resistant. For example, manufacturers have created child-proof caps for medicine bottles. This type of packaging was created as a way to avoid possibly liability where a child obtains access to pills or other medicine that could be harmful to the child.

V. Defenses to Product Liability

Even where a manufacturer or other entity has been negligent or otherwise responsible for a defective product, the manufacturer may not be liable if a defense to liability applies. As shown below, the defenses in a products liability case typically focus on the behavior of the plaintiff.

Assumption of Risk

Assumption of the risk is one possible defense to tort actions. It is particularly useful in cases of products liability. Assumption of risk focuses on the plaintiff's conduct. In a products liability case, if a plaintiff assumes the risk posed by a product, the defendant is not liable for injury. To prove assumption of the risk, the defendant must show that the plaintiff actually knew of

Example:	Amir decides to go skydiving to celebrate his birthday. He signs up for a skydiving session with Sky High Co. Helpful Harnesses Inc. manufactures the parachute and harnesses used for skydiving, and provided to users by Sky High Co. At an orientation session, Sky High explains the risks of skydiving and tells the divers that Sky High Co. and Helpful Harnesses Inc. are not responsible for any equipment malfunctions. Amir chooses to go ahead with his skydiving session. It could be argued that Amir assumed the risk through his actions. He was aware of the risks, but decided to use the equipment anyway.

Now assume that Sky High Co. requires Amir to sign a waiver of liability before his skydiving session. The waiver states that skydiving has inherent dangers, and that Sky High Co. and Helpful Harnesses Inc. cannot guarantee safety. Amir agrees not to sue Sky High Co. or Helpful Harnesses Inc. if he is injured. By signing the waiver, Amir expressly assumes the risks of using the skydiving equipment.

A CONSUMER WHO KNOWS THE RISKS OF A PRODUCT CANNOT HOLD THE PRODUCT'S MANUFACTURER LIABLE.

Puckett v. The Plastics Group, Inc.
(Gasoline Container User) v. (Container Manufacturer)
561 Fed. Appx. 865 (2014)

Ralph James Puckett, III, appeals the District Court's grant of summary judgment in a product liability suit brought against The Plastics Group, Inc. For the reasons set forth below, we affirm the District Court's judgment.

In the early morning hours of January 16, 2010, Puckett tried to kindle a fire in his backyard. He struggled to get a big enough fire going, so, after eventually managing to produce a small flame, Puckett splashed some gasoline out of his gas can onto the open flame. The gas ignited and the vapors inside the can exploded. Puckett suffered severe burns over approximately half his body.

In April 2011 Puckett filed this action against The Plastics Group, the gas can's manufacturer, in the Northern District of Georgia. He asserted three claims under Georgia law: (1) defective design, because The Plastics Group did not include a safety device to prevent the vapors inside the can from igniting; (2) failure to warn, because the warning against exploding vapors was not conspicuous enough; and (3) negligence, based on the same claims of unreasonable design and insufficient warning.

After discovery, The Plastics Group filed a motion for summary judgment on all three claims. In considering the motion, the District Court accepted the following relevant facts as true: The gas can did not include a "flame arrestor"—a small mesh screen installed in the nozzle that is designed to reduce the risk of igniting vapors. A warning appeared on the side of the gas can that warned against the danger of exploding vapors. The warning was embossed on the side of the gas can—i.e., the letters were raised against the background—but the text was the same color as the background.

Puckett did not read the warning but was aware that gasoline is flammable and that splashing gasoline on the fire was dangerous; however, he was not aware of the possibility that the vapors inside the gas can could explode in the manner in which they did.

Taking these facts, the District Court held that Puckett assumed the risk of his injury when he splashed gasoline on the fire because he was aware of the danger he created by combining gasoline with an open flame . . . The court also held that the risk of injury from splashing gasoline on a fire is open and obvious, and so The Plastics Group did not have a duty to warn against that danger . . . And the court held that Puckett's conduct constituted contributory negligence, thus barring recovery on his negligence claim. See O.C.G.A. § 51–11–7 ("If the plaintiff by ordinary care could have avoided the consequences to himself caused by the defendant's negligence, he is not entitled to recover."). Accordingly, the District Court granted summary judgment in favor of The Plastics Group on all three of Puckett's claims.

[...]

Under Georgia law, assumption of risk bars recovery under all three of Puckett's claims. To prevail on an assumption of risk defense, a defendant must show that "the plaintiff (1) had actual knowledge of the danger; (2) understood and appreciated the risks associated with such danger; and (3) voluntarily exposed himself to those risks." Vaughn v. Pleasent, 266 Ga. 862, 864, 471 S.E.2d 866, 868 (1996). "The knowledge that a plaintiff who assumes the risk must subjectively possess is that of the specific, particular risk of harm associated with the activity or condition that proximately caused injury." Id.

All agree that Puckett knew gasoline was flammable (which is why he poured it on the fire) and that he appreciated the danger associated with pouring gasoline on an open flame. During his deposition, Puckett explained that he intentionally stood back a few feet, just in case the fire flared up, because "I didn't want to singe my eyebrows or anything." Puckett nonetheless contends that, even though he was aware of the risk of being burned while pouring gasoline on an open flame, he was not aware of the "drastically greater and qualitatively different" risk that his actions could cause the gas can to explode in his hand. While Georgia law requires knowledge of the "specific, particular risk of harm" that causes a plaintiff's injury, it does not recognize the distinction Puckett wishes to draw between knowledge of the danger and knowledge of the precise series of events that leads to the injury. The danger Puckett was aware of—that gas ignites when exposed to fire—caused his injuries. Puckett's expectation that he would, at worst, get singed eyebrows does not change the fact that he accepted the risk of being burned when he voluntarily poured gasoline onto a fire.

Therefore, we agree with the District Court that Puckett assumed the risk of his injuries. Because assumption of risk bars recovery under all of Puckett's claims, we need not address the remaining grounds for the District Court's grant of summary judgment.

AFFIRMED.

[Footnotes and citations omitted]

ANALYSIS:

This is an example of implied assumption of risk. The consumer's conduct, by exercising caution in using gasoline around the fire, showed that he appreciated a risk involved when using gasoline and fire. This case demonstrates that a general understanding of the risk involved in an activity is sufficient to assume the risk of the activity. Even though the product could have been designed to reduce the danger, the consumer's knowledge and acceptance of the risk prevented any liability by the manufacturer.

QUESTIONS FOR DISCUSSION:

As a matter of public policy, should the company be required to reduce the danger by adding a screen?

Can a consumer be said to assume the risks of an activity where, as here, the consumer does not actually know all the risks?

the hazard and continued to use the product anyway. It must be shown that the plaintiff had subjective knowledge of the risk. Assumption of risk will not apply if the plaintiff "should have known" of the risk, or if it was "reasonable to assume" that the plaintiff knew of it. It also must be shown that the plaintiff was aware of the specific risk that caused his injuries. A general awareness that a product could be dangerous in some way will not establish assumption of risk.

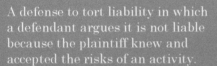

ASSUMPTION OF RISK:
A defense to tort liability in which a defendant argues it is not liable because the plaintiff knew and accepted the risks of an activity.

One can assume the risks of an activity expressly or impliedly. An express assumption of risk occurs when an individual signs an agreement or other document agreeing to assume the risks. Assumption of risk may also be implied from an individual's conduct. If the risk of a product is known to the individual, but she chooses to use the product anyway, assumption of risk is implied.

Comparative Fault

Everyone in society owes a duty to exercise reasonable care to avoid harm to others. This includes a duty to use reasonable care to avoid harm to oneself. In the past, most courts applied the doctrine of **contributory negligence**. Under this rule, if an injured party was at fault in any way for the incident causing harm, the injured party could not recover anything. The jury would consider the amount of fault of the injured party. If the jury determined that the injured party was only 1% at fault, the injured party could not recover anything.

Today, most jurisdictions apply the doctrine of **comparative negligence**. Comparative negligence considers the extent of fault of both parties. The jury allocates fault to both parties. For instance, the jury might determine that the plaintiff is 30% at fault and the defendant is 70% at fault. The defendant would be responsible for only 70% of the damages determined by the jury. Under a modified approach, some

Example: Troy was driving his ATV when he noticed the temperature light flashing. The ATV was manufactured by Outdoor Sports Co. The instruction manual stated that drivers should stop the vehicle and shut the engine off when the temperature light is blinking. The light came on because a hose in the engine was defective when the ATV was sold. Troy did not read the instruction manual and ignored the temperature light. Troy continued driving the vehicle. An electrical fire in the ATV caused Troy serious harm. Troy's failure to read the manual and his failure to deal with the flashing temperature light could be considered by the jury. If the jury finds Troy was 25% at fault, he may recover only 75% of his damages against Outdoor Sports Co.

STRICT LIABILITY CASES DO NOT REQUIRE CONSIDERATION OF COMPARATIVE NEGLIGENCE.

R.J. Reynolds Tobacco Co. v. Sury
(Tobacco Company) v. (Estate of Deceased Smoker)
118 So. 3d 849 (2013)

INSTANT FACTS:
The son of a smoker, as personal representative of the smoker's estate, brought a claim against tobacco companies.

BLACK LETTER RULE:
Comparative negligence does not apply to products liability claims based on strict liability and fraud.

FACTS:
The smoker died from lung cancer resulting from nicotine addiction. At trial, the jury concluded that the cigarette manufacturers were liable for placing a defective product, cigarettes, into the market. The jury determined the smoker was also contributorily negligent because of his decision to smoke the cigarettes. The smoker was found to be 60% negligent and each of the two tobacco companies was 20% negligent. The jury found the smoker's son suffered $1 million in damages.

ISSUE:
Should the products liability damage award be reduced based on the level of fault attributable to the plaintiff?

DECISION AND RATIONALE:
No. In this case, the plaintiff alleged negligence as well as several intentional torts (fraud, fraudulent concealment, and civil conspiracy) against the tobacco companies. The jury found the tobacco companies were negligent and strictly liable, and also engaged in fraud. The court held that comparative negligence did not apply because the action was based on intentional conduct in addition to negligence. Comparative negligence applies only to negligence actions.

ANALYSIS:
In this case, a large percentage of fault was attributable to the smoker himself. However, because the tobacco companies also engaged in intentional behavior, the companies were responsible for the entire damage award. The decision demonstrates that it is wise for a plaintiff to consider all possible theories of liability against a defendant. A plaintiff's claim may be vulnerable to a defense under one theory of liability that may not be available under other types of claims.

QUESTIONS FOR DISCUSSION:
Assume an individual dies from complications caused by extreme overeating. Is there a possible lawsuit against fast food companies that promote large servings? How would you craft the argument for the plaintiff? For the defendants?

Is it fair to attribute contributory negligence to an individual for using a product that has been scientifically shown to be addictive?

jurisdictions do not allow a plaintiff to recover damages if their fault is higher than the level of defendant's fault.

A product manufacturer or seller who relies on a defense of comparative fault has the burden of proving that the plaintiff acted negligently, and that her negligence was a part or the entire cause of her injuries. There is a presumption that a person exercised due care in the use of that product, but that presumption goes away on the introduction of any evidence to the contrary.

There is some similarity between the assumption of risk defense and comparative fault. The difference between the two lies in how close the actions are to the harm. Negligence may be found in actions that happen immediately before

Modification/Substantial Change

Modification is a potential defense if a product has been changed since it left the defendant's hands. In a products liability case, the plaintiff must show that the product was defective when it left the defendant's control. If the product was changed or modified before it injured the plaintiff, then the defendant may not be liable. A product can be changed in many ways. For instance, modification may be shown if safety guards are removed or if nonstandard parts are installed on the product.

To establish a modification defense, the defendant must prove the original design, how the product was changed, and that the change caused the plaintiff's injuries. The modification must be a substantial one that increases the likelihood of a malfunction, and the modification must have been the proximate cause of the plaintiff's injuries. The modification must also have been independent of the expected and intended use of the product. An alteration that was made to correct a manufacturing defect may not be used as a defense unless the manufacturer was not informed of the defect or the attempted correction.

CONTRIBUTORY NEGLIGENCE:
A doctrine under which a plaintiff may be barred from recovering damages because the plaintiff was partially at fault for the accident or injury.

COMPARATIVE NEGLIGENCE:
A doctrine under which a plaintiff's recovery of damages may be reduced by the amount of negligence attributed to the plaintiff.

an accident, while assumption of risk is putting oneself in a position to be harmed. In some jurisdictions, however, assumption of risk no longer exists as a separate defense. Instead, a party's actions in assuming a known risk are considered negligence, to be considered as a percentage of overall fault.

MODIFICATION:
A defense to products liability by which the defendant argues it should not be liable for the defective product because the plaintiff modified the product.

Example: Mark is using a table saw to cut wood for furniture he is making. The table saw was made by Woodchuck Inc. The saw came with a pre-installed blade guard to protect a user's hands. Mark removed the guard because he felt the guard made it hard for him to see the wood cuts. While cutting the wood for the furniture, Mark slices his finger and sues Woodchuck Inc. Woodchuck Inc. could argue the removal of the blade guard was a substantial change to the saw and that the removal of the guard caused Mark's injuries.

ALTERATIONS TO PRODUCTS MAY DEFEAT STRICT LIABILITY.

Rix v. General Motors
(Driver) v. (Car Manufacturer)
723 P.2d 195 (Mont. 1986)

INSTANT FACTS:
A driver was injured when his vehicle was hit from behind by a GMC vehicle.

BLACK LETTER RULE:
The manufacturer of a defective product may be strictly liable for a design defect or a manufacturing defect, unless the product was altered.

FACTS:
A man was injured when the vehicle he was driving was hit from behind by a GMC vehicle. The man sued GMC for products liability. The parties agreed that brake failure caused the accident. However, GMC claimed the product was altered after it left GMC's control, and the alteration relieved it of any liability.

ISSUE:
Did alteration of the vehicle prevent liability on behalf of the manufacturer for defective brakes?

DECISION AND RATIONALE:
Maybe. To establish strict liability, the plaintiff must show the vehicle's brake system was defective, the defect caused the injury, and the defect is traceable to the product. Slight alteration does not negate the manufacturer's liability for a design defect because wear and tear does not change the product's design. The availability of an alternative design is one of a number of factors considered in determining whether a design defect exists. In this case, the instructions to the jury were incorrect, and the case was remanded for a new trial.

ANALYSIS:
This case provides a clear description of the distinction between manufacturing and design defects. The court's discussion also demonstrates how the modification defense may apply differently to a design defect and a manufacturing defect. While alteration of the product may affect liability for manufacturing defects, insubstantial alterations do not affect design defects because the alterations do not change the product's original design. Design defects examine the design at the time the product left the defendant's control.

QUESTIONS FOR DISCUSSION:
Where does maintenance become alteration? Does a brake job using after-market parts rather than equipment supplied by the manufacturer constitute an alteration?

If your smart phone is hacked, and the hacker uses an app that you downloaded to the phone, was the download an alteration?

Failure to maintain a product properly may constitute an "alteration," and may operate as a defense. Similarly, inadequate or substandard work to maintain a product may be a defense.

Abnormal Uses/Product Misuse

A person may use a product to do something other than what the product was made to do. For example, a person may use an electric knife as a letter opener. If a person uses the product for a different purpose or in a way that it was not intended, the manufacturer may not be liable for product defects. This is referred to as product misuse.

Misuse is a defense only if the misuse was the proximate cause of the plaintiff's injuries. A manufacturer must expect or anticipate some misuse of its products. Product misuse is either foreseeable or unforeseeable. If a party misuses a product in a way that is reasonably foreseeable, the manufacturer may still be liable. On the other hand, if a party misuses a product in an unforeseeable manner, the manufacturer may have a defense to liability. In some states, product misuse is a complete defense. If the plaintiff misused the product, they cannot recover anything against the defendant. In other states, the plaintiff's misuse reduces the amount of compensation.

The foreseeability of misuse looks at several different factors. The normal environment in which a product is used is a factor, as well as a user's awareness of the dangers of the misuse.

> Most jurisdictions say that misuse of a product includes using it in a manner not intended by the manufacturer. If, however, the unintended misuse is foreseeable, the misuse defense probably will not be available.

If the defendant is aware of the misuse, through receipt of accident reports or complaints, the misuse may be regarded as having been foreseeable.

VI. Privacy Torts

Our lives are less private today than at any other time in history. Whenever you log on to the internet, or engage in even the most routine of transactions, you are making some aspect of your life available for inspection by anyone with the ability to find it. Although we may think

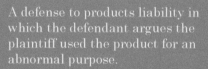

PRODUCT MISUSE:
A defense to products liability in which the defendant argues the plaintiff used the product for an abnormal purpose.

ABNORMAL USE:
A defense to products liability actions by which a defendant argues it is not responsible for harm caused by the product because the plaintiff used the product for an unforeseeable purpose.

Example: Tony is remodeling his home. He is replacing the tile flooring. He realizes he does not have a pry bar to lift up the old tiles. Tony decides to use a screwdriver to lift the old tiles. As Tony is lifting the tiles, the plastic handle on the screwdriver breaks and Tony is injured. The screwdriver was manufactured by ABC Tool Corp. At the time the screwdriver left ABC Tool Corp.'s control, the handle was defective because it was made from poor quality materials. If the use of a screwdriver as a pry bar is a foreseeable misuse of the screwdriver, ABC Tool Corp. may be liable for Tony's injuries. If Tony's use of the screwdriver is not foreseeable, that product misuse may reduce or prevent liability for ABC Tool Corp.

FORESEEABLE MISUSE OF A PRODUCT DOES NOT EXCLUDE MANUFACTURER LIABILITY.

Pitman v. Ameristep Corporation
(Hunting Guide) v. (Strap Manufacturer)
208 F. Supp. 3d 1053 (E.D. Mo. 2016)

INSTANT FACTS:
The manufacturer of ratchet straps claimed that a hunting guide's misuse of straps negated its liability for the guide's fall from a tree stand when the strap failed.

BLACK LETTER RULE:
Products liability depends on whether the product is dangerous during reasonably anticipated use of the product, which includes objectively foreseeable misuse.

FACTS:
A hunting guide fell from a tree stand after the ratchet straps he used to attach the stand to the tree failed. The guide had not read the warning label with the strap, but the experts agreed the strap was appropriate for use with tree stands. The guide originally installed the strap with a tree stand in September 2010, where he left it until January 2011. The strap was then stored indoors until inspected and re-installed. The guide installed the strap with the tree stand without wearing a safety harness. After installation, the strap failed and the guide fell from the tree. The guide claimed both design and manufacturing defects existed in the strap. The manufacturer claimed that leaving the strap attached to a tree stand outdoors for an extended period caused it to fail.

ISSUE:
Did the plaintiff's misuse of the product eliminate the ratchet strap manufacturer's liability for the product's failure?

DECISION AND RATIONALE:
Maybe. A design defect is one that makes the product unreasonably dangerous. When reviewing a design defect case, the focus should be on the reasonably anticipated use of the product rather than on the potential harm it could cause. Reasonably anticipated use includes objectively foreseeable misuse and abnormal use. A manufacturing defect exists when there is a problem during manufacturing of the specific item in question. This type of defect depends on whether the product is in its intended condition. In either circumstance, however, wear to the product over time is relevant, and excessive wear may be the true cause of the accident rather than a defect. The trial court will need to decide whether or not that was the case.

ANALYSIS:
The guide also brought a claim for failure to warn, arguing that the manufacturer had not adequately notified him of the dangers posed by the product during normal use. One issue was whether the warnings should have included how to inspect a ratchet strap to ensure it is still safe. What is a reasonable line to draw for product warnings?

QUESTIONS FOR DISCUSSION:
What are foreseeable misuses for a dining chair? A clothes iron? A bicycle? What misuses have you made of products?

If wear and tear is foreseeable, should product warnings include information on how to test a product for soundness on a regular basis? Are there any products that include such a warning?

our private lives are of little interest to anyone (including ourselves), there are many out there who will gladly pay money for the most mundane details that could possibly be monetized. This is why you will see so many internet ads for pet products after you buy a box of cat treats at your local store. It was no big deal to you, but to an advertiser, it's an opportunity.

Legal protection for our right to be left alone takes several forms. There are laws and regulations that limit what can be done with the information that others collect about us (for example, the Health Insurance Portability and Accountability Act, or HIPAA). There are also four types of tort action, commonly referred to as the "privacy torts," that represent attempts to protect our privacy. While courts nationwide have been slow to recognize all four of the privacy torts, most states now recognize a cause of action based on some of them.

> The loss of privacy in the modern world has long been a matter of concern. In 1890, Boston attorney Samuel Warren and Harvard Law School professor (later U.S. Supreme Court Justice) Louis Brandeis published an article in the Harvard Law Review titled "The Right to Privacy." The authors were concerned about the erosion of privacy for individuals, due to such innovations as instantaneous photography and gossipy newspapers. The article called for legal protections for the "right to be left alone."

The four privacy torts are:

- Intrusion upon seclusion,
- Publication of a private fact,
- Misappropriation of likeness, and
- False light.

Intrusion upon Seclusion: Intrusion upon seclusion is when a person intrudes, by physical means or otherwise, on the private affairs or concerns of another person. The intrusion must be intentional, and it must be the kind of intrusion that would be highly offensive to a reasonable person. The tort is complete once the intrusion is made. There is no requirement that the intruder publicize what he may have learned from the intrusion, or that the information reach the public. Similarly, there is no requirement that the victim suffer any damage as a result of the intrusion.

In order to bring an action for intrusion upon seclusion, it must be shown that the intrusion was offensive. The offensiveness of the intrusion is an objective one, and it will depend on the context. If a person consents to an intrusion, it will not be considered offensive. Giving someone a private letter to read for themselves, for example, will not constitute an actionable intrusion because the consent eliminates any claim that it was offensive. Observing or photographing someone in a public place will also not be regarded as offensive. Not taking any steps to keep information private will take away any offensiveness of an intrusion.

Example: During a meeting in his office with Rene, Louis excuses himself to get a file from another room. Rene sees that Louis has left his checkbook on his desk. She picks it up and looks through the check register. Rene never tells anyone what she saw in the register. She has intruded on Louis's seclusion.

In most jurisdictions, a physical intrusion such as a trespass is not required. Eavesdropping can be an intrusion if the person being listened to has a reasonable expectation of privacy when she is speaking. There must be an expectation that the conversation will be private, and that expectation must be a reasonable one.

The offensiveness of an intrusion may be mitigated by the public's interest in the information uncovered. While this mitigation has been applied to members of the traditional broadcast or print media, many courts have purposely ignored the distinction between professionals and amateurs, and provided protection for bystanders who record or photograph events of interest to the public. The protection from liability for news-gathering activities is broad, but it is not without its limits. Covering a story that is of public interest will not justify a truly offensive intrusion.

Publication of a Private Fact: The tort of publication of a private fact complements the tort of intrusion upon seclusion. Intrusion upon seclusion does not require that the private information seen be distributed or disseminated; publication of a private fact does not require that the person being held liable committed an intrusion. It is common for a given set of circumstances to give rise to both types of action: a person intrudes on the seclusion of another, and then publicizes what he learns as a result of the intrusion.

An action for publication of a private fact may be brought against a person who gives publicity to a matter concerning the private life of another. The publicity must have been highly offensive to a reasonable person, and the private fact must not be a matter of legitimate public interest. If there was consent to the publication, there is no violation.

Publication of a private fact is distinguishable from defamation for two main reasons. First, the publication that is required for defamation is very small. The defamatory statement

Example:	Megan works in a large office where all of the employees are in cubicles. She comes in late one day after a doctor's appointment, and immediately telephones her husband to tell him about the results of her physical. The connection is bad, so she needs to raise her voice so he can hear her. Devin, a co-worker sitting in the next cube, is able to overhear everything she says without trying to listen. Devin has not intruded on Megan's seclusion.

Example:	Instead of speaking to her husband at her desk, Megan uses her own phone and calls from an unused conference room. While she is speaking, Devin comes in the room looking for a chart that was used the day before. Megan lowers her voice while Devin is in the room, but he makes a point of walking by her so he can hear what she says. Devin has intruded on Megan's seclusion.

Example:	Andrew heard loud voices outside of his house that sounded like a fight was going on. When he went to his door to see what was happening, he saw an ambulance crew trying to put a man into the ambulance, apparently against his will. Andrew picked up his phone and started recording the incident. The incident was a matter of public interest that happened in plain view. Andrew has not intruded upon the man's seclusion.

Andrew goes up to the ambulance after the man is loaded in, but before it drives a way. Through one of the ambulance's windows, he can see a paramedic tending to the man. Andrew starts filming again, to record the aftermath of the previous incident. There was a reasonable expectation of privacy inside the ambulance, so Andrew was intruding upon the seclusion of those inside. |

must have been heard by only one other person. Publication of a private fact, however, requires a widespread publication. The private fact is made available to the public and is likely to become a matter of public knowledge. Publication to a large group of people will not be sufficient if that group is private. A private communication will not give rise to an action for publication.

Second, defamation requires a false statement. Publication of a private fact is the publication of a fact that is true. The offensiveness lies in the nature of the fact being disclosed. There are

Example:	Colleen suffers from a rare neurodegenerative disorder. Her doctor, Themi, has never treated this disorder before, but learns that there is an internet based group of physicians and scientists around the world who are researching the disorder. Membership in the group is restricted to professionals actively involved in the study or treatment of the disorder, and members are expected to share information about their patients only with other group members. Themi applies for membership, and is accepted. He shares the details of Colleen's condition with other group members. Although the disclosure of Colleen's private facts is made to a relatively large group, there is no publication of a private fact because the information is not disclosed to the public.

Themi's nurse Archie is very concerned about Colleen. He submits a prayer request for her at his church. Colleen's name and her condition are published in the church's bulletin. There are fewer than 100 members of the church, but anyone is welcome to come in and take a bulletin. The publication of the prayer request is a publication of a private fact |

many things about our lives that we try to keep private, even though they are true. A person's medical records, for example, contain private information that is accurate and truthful, but it is still information most of us would not want to have disclosed. Truth does not make the disclosure any less offensive.

The publication tort is based on the publication of facts that are private. They are facts that were reasonably expected to remain private. The "reasonableness" of that expectation is based on an objective standard: would the public at large expect that the type of facts disclosed would remain private? If the facts are public, their publication is not a violation of privacy rights, even if the facts were not widely known. The possibility of release to the public at some point in the future is enough to make a fact public.

There is an exception for the publication of private facts that are a matter of legitimate public concern. The public's interest in obtaining the information may outweigh the individual's privacy interest. The decision regarding the public's interest in a matter is made on a case-by-case basis. The nature of the information, and the person's interest in keeping it private, is balanced against the public's need to know.

Harold and Dorothy owned a business that did business with a school district. Dorothy was also a member of the school board. Due to controversy surrounding the contract, the board voted to end the contract with Harold and Dorothy. The local newspaper printed a story referring to termination of the "patronage" contract. The ending of the contract was a matter of legitimate public interest, and publication of the story did not violate Harold and Dorothy's right to privacy. *Rush v. Philadelphia Newspapers, Inc.*, 732 A. 2d 648 (Pa. Super. 1999).

Misappropriation of Likeness or Name: Misappropriation of likeness or name involves using someone else's identity, whether their image, their name, or some other part of their identity, without that person's permission and for one's own gain. Unlike intrusion upon seclusion or publication of a private fact, however, a plaintiff bringing an action of misappropriation of likeness must show that she was damaged by the misappropriation. Misappropriation involves more than just an incidental use of another person's identity. There must be a meaningful or purposeful use. A photographer who takes a picture of a street scene does not

Example: Peggy is running for County Treasurer. A local newspaper receives a tip, and learns that Peggy filed for bankruptcy seven years ago while living in a different state, and while she was going by the last name of her former husband. The newspaper prints a story about the bankruptcy. Peggy cannot claim publication of a private fact, since the records of the bankruptcy are public, even though they might be difficult to locate.

"misappropriate" the images of the people in the picture, unless he made a purposeful effort to get pictures of those particular people.

The tort of misappropriation requires that the taking be for the benefit of the person who does the taking. This benefit is usually a commercial benefit, such as using someone's picture in an advertisement. The misappropriation could also be for non-economic purposes, if that non-economic use causes economic harm. The interest protected is the interest in the exclusive use of identity.

Misappropriation of likeness is distinguishable from the tort of violation of the right of publicity. The right of publicity is the right of celebrities, whose name or likeness has some intrinsic economic value, to profit from their name or likeness. An action for violation of the right of publicity may not be brought unless the celebrity's identity is taken for financial purposes.

> William was the owner of an anti-abortion website. He posted blog posts that he falsely attributed to John, a prominent attorney and political commentator. He also registered an internet domain using John's nickname that directed traffic to William's site. William made no money from the use of the John's name or nickname. William was liable for misappropriation of John's name and nickname. *Faegere & Benson, LLP v. Purdy*, 367 F. Supp. 2d 1238 (D. Minn. 2005).

False Light: False light is perhaps the hardest of the privacy torts to define. It has not been adopted in every jurisdiction, as the facts needed to show false light are very close to those that would show defamation.

False light involves giving publicity to a matter that puts a person in a false light. The false light must be highly offensive to a reasonable person. The person who gave publicity to the matter must either have known that it was false, or acted in reckless disregard of the falsity.

> Tom is a singer with a distinctive voice. A snack food company created a series of advertisements in which an impersonator who did a very accurate mimicking of Tom's voice spoke lines that were said on the commercials by a cartoon cheetah. Tom's name was not mentioned on the commercials, and the cheetah was not drawn to look like Tom. The use of Tom's distinctive voice was a violation of his right of publicity. *Waits v. Frito-Lay, Inc.*, 978 F. 2d 1093 (9th Cir. 1992).

Many jurisdictions have declined to recognize an action for false light invasion of privacy on the grounds that it is too similar to defamation. There are three essential differences between the two torts. The first is that false light does not require the publication of a fact that is defamatory, or that tends to lower a person's reputation in the community. Instead, false light is based on a false portrayal that is highly offensive. Putting someone in a false light could involve showing that a person behaved in a cowardly manner in an emergency situation. While it is not defamatory to say that about a person, it is offensive to be portrayed that way falsely.

The second distinction is that false light requires widespread publicity. Showing someone in a false light is not actionable if only one person sees it. The false publicity must be to the public at large.

> Orlin was visiting an addiction treatment center's open house. While he was there, a newspaper photographer took a picture of the aversion treatment room while Orlin was standing in the room. The paper ran that picture, and Orlin claimed that it created the impression that he was a patient at the facility, not just a visitor. Orlin has stated a claim for false light. *Dean v. Guard Publishing Co.*, 73 Or. App. 656, 699 P. 2d 1158 (1985).

Finally, false light is meant to provide a remedy for a person's subjective suffering and humiliation. Defamation is meant to protect a person's reputation, but false light protects a person's individual feelings.

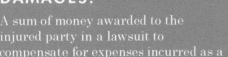

COMPENSATORY DAMAGES:
A sum of money awarded to the injured party in a lawsuit to compensate for expenses incurred as a result of the injuries.

VII. Damages

The purpose of a tort lawsuit is to recover compensation for the injuries resulting from the defendant's conduct. In some circumstances, however, a defendant may be required to pay other damages as punishment.

Compensatory Damages

In most tort lawsuits, the injured party is seeking money compensation, called damages. The damages meant to compensate the party for the injuries suffered are called **compensatory damages**. In most negligence-based tort suits, a successful party can recover compensatory damages only. Compensatory damages do not provide the injured party with a windfall. Rather, compensatory damages are designed to pay the party back for expenses incurred as a result of the party's injuries.

Compensatory damages may be awarded for expenses related to physical and emotional injuries. Depending on the case, a party might receive damages for pain and suffering, disfigurement, loss of reputation, medical expenses, and lost wages.

Punitive Damages

In some circumstances, a party may receive **punitive damages** in addition to compensatory damages. While compensatory damages take care of the plaintiff's monetary losses, punitive damages are meant to punish the wrongdoer. Punitive damages are available only in cases involving egregious conduct. Egregious

JURY-AWARDED COMPENSATORY DAMAGES WILL BE UPHELD IF REASONABLY SUPPORTED BY EVIDENCE.

Anderson v. Sears, Roebuck & Co.
(Burn Victims) v. (Heater Manufacturer)
377 F. Supp. 136 (E.D. La. 1974)

On April 23, 1970 the Britains' home was completely consumed by a fire which was ignited by a defective Sears' heater. Both Mildred Britain and her infant daughter, Helen Britain, were severely burned and Helen Britain suffered multiple permanent injuries. Thereafter, Mildred Britain and Harry Britain, individually and as administrator of the estate of Helen Britain, brought suit against Sears, Roebuck and Company, Preway, Inc., and Employers Mutual Liability Insurance Company of Wisconsin. Preway, Inc. and its insurer, Employers Mutual Liability Insurance Company of Wisconsin, third-partied Employers Liability Assurance Corporation, Ltd., the insurer of Controls Company of America, and plaintiffs then amended their complaint to add Employers Liability Assurance Corporation, Ltd. as an additional defendant. Plaintiffs ground their quest for recovery on two distinct theories. They allege that Sears was negligent in the installation, maintenance, and repair of the heater, and that Sears, Preway, and Employers Liability Assurance Corporation, the insurer of Controls Company of America, are liable as the manufacturers of the heater and its component parts.

[...]

The sole issue presently before the court is whether the damages awarded to Helen Britain were excessive.

Although the case defendants contend that the damages awarded to Helen Britain were excessive, none of them have referred me to any evidence which infers or establishes that the award was excessive, nor have they been able to establish that passion, prejudice or any other improper motive influenced the jury in making its award. Defendants ground their argument of excessiveness merely on the size of the verdict. The reasonableness of quantum, however, is not to be decided in a vacuum but rather is to be considered in light of the evidence as to the injuries and actual damages sustained and the future effects thereof. In this context, defendants have not offered any evidence at trial nor have they directed any cogent arguments in their briefs to sustain their burden of proving that the verdict was excessive.

The legal standard on which to gauge a jury verdict for remittitur purposes is the "maximum recovery rule," Gorsalitz v. Olin Mathieson Chemical Corp., 429 F.2d 1033 (5th Cir. 1970); Glazer v. Glazer, 278 F.Supp. 476 (E.D. La.1968). This rule directs the trial judge to determine whether the verdict of the jury exceeds the maximum amount which the jury could reasonably find and if it does, the trial judge may then reduce the verdict to the highest amount that the jury could properly have awarded. Functionally, the maximum recovery rule both preserves the constitutionally protected role of the jury as finder of facts and prevents the predilections of the judge from infecting the jury's determination. Thus, the court's task is to ascertain, by scrutinizing all of the evidence as to each element of damages, what amount would be the maximum the jury could have reasonably awarded. In this case there are five cardinal elements of damages: past physical and mental pain; future physical and mental pain; future medical expenses; loss of earning capacity and permanent disability and disfigurement.

PAST PHYSICAL AND MENTAL PAIN

The infant child Helen Britain, was almost burned to death in the tragic fire that swept her home. She was burned over forty per cent of her entire body; third degree burns cover eighty per cent of her scalp and second and third degree burns of the trunk and of her extremities account for the remainder. Helen Britain's immediate post-trauma treatment required hospitalization for twenty-eight days, during which time the child developed pneumonia, required numerous transfusions, suffered fever, vomiting, diarrhea, and infection, and underwent skin graft surgery, under general anesthesia, to her scalp, which was only partially successful. Keloid scarring caused webbing and ankylosis of the child's extremities and severely limited their motion. The child's fingers became adhered together; scarring bent the arm at the elbow in a burdensome, fixed position; and thick scarring on the thighs and on the side of and behind the knees impaired walking.

This child had to undergo subsequent hospitalizations for further major operations and treatment. The second major operation under general anesthesia was undertaken to graft new skin from the back and stomach to the remaining bare areas of the scalp. The third operation under general anesthesia was an attempt to relieve the deformity of her left hand caused by the webbing scars which bound down the fingers of that hand. A fourth operation under general anesthesia was performed to reduce scars which had grown back on the left hand again webbing the fingers. I cannot envisage the breadth and intensity of the pain experienced by Helen Britain throughout this ordeal.

The undisputed testimony reveals that one of the most tragic aspects of this case is that the horrible mental and emotional trauma caused to this child occurred at an age which medical experts maintain is crucial to a child's entire psyche and personality formation. Helen Britain's persistent emotional and mental disturbance is evidenced by bed wetting, nightmares, refusing to sleep alone, withdrawal, and speech impediments. Dr. Cyril Phillips, a psychiatrist, and Dr. Diamond both indicated that the child manifested to them, even at this early age, emotional illness and retarded mental growth.

The evidence reflects that an award of six hundred thousand dollars for this element of damages alone would not be unreasonable.

FUTURE PHYSICAL AND MENTAL PAIN

There is clear evidence that the stretching, pulling, and breaking down of scars inherent in growth will continue to cause severe pain and a crippling limitation of motion in varying degrees to all of Helen Britain's upper and lower extremities. Very little can be done to improve the condition of the scalp which will never be able to breathe, sweat or grow hair. There will be risks, trauma and pain, both physical and mental, with each of the recommended twenty-seven future operations which will extend over most of the child's adult life, if she is in fact fortunate enough to be able to risk undergoing these recommended surgeries. Furthermore, Helen Britain must vigilantly guard against irritation, infection and further injury to the damaged and abnormal skin, scars and grafts because any injury, however slight, can generate cancer in these adynamic areas.

The inherent stresses and tensions of each new phase of life will severely tax this little girl's debilitated and delicate mental and emotional capacity. Throughout her future life expectancy of seventy-five years, it is reasonable to expect, that she will be deprived of a normal social life and that she will never find a husband and raise a family. On top of this, Helen Britain will always be subjected to rejection, stares and tactless inquiries from children and adults.

The court concludes that an award of seven hundred fifty thousand dollars for this element of damages alone would not be excessive.

FUTURE MEDICAL EXPENSES

A large award for future medical expenses is justified. The uncontradicted testimony was that Helen Britain would need the guidance, treatment and counselling of a team of doctors, including plastic surgeons, psychiatrists and sociologists, throughout her lifetime. Add to this the cost of the twenty-seven recommended operations and the cost of private tutoring necessitated by the child's mental and emotional needs and the jury could justifiably award a figure of two hundred and fifty thousand dollars to cover these future expenses.

LOSS OF EARNING CAPACITY

The evidence of Helen Britain's disabilities both physical, mental and emotional was such that this court holds that the jury could properly find that these disabilities would prevent her from earning a living for the rest of her life. Not only do the physical impairments to her extremities disable her but her emotional limitations require avoiding stress and the combined effect is the permanent incapacity to maintain serious employment.

The jury was provided with actuarial figures which accurately calculated both the deduction of interest to be earned and the addition of an inflationary buffer, on any award made for future loss of earning capacity. In view of these incontrovertible projections at trial, it was within the province of the jury to award as much as $330,000.00 for the loss of earning capacity.

PERMANENT DISABILITY AND DISFIGUREMENT

The award for this element of damage must evaluate in monetary terms the compensation due this plaintiff for the permanent physical, mental and emotional disabilities and disfigurements proved by the evidence adduced at trial. A narration treating Miss Britain's permanent disabilities and disfigurements would be lengthy and redundant; therefore, I resort to listing.

1. The complete permanent loss of 80% of the scalp caused by the destruction of sweat glands, hair follicles and tissue — all of which effects a grotesque disfigurement and freakish appearance.

2. The permanent loss of the normal use of the legs.

3. The permanent impairment of the left fingers and hand caused by recurring webbing and resulting in limited motion.

4. The permanent impairment of the right hand caused by scars and webbing of the fingers.

5. The permanent injury to the left elbow and left arm with ankylosis and resulting in a crippling deformity.

6. The permanent destruction of 40% of the normal skin. As a result of this a large portion of the body is covered by "pigskin." Pigskin resembles the dry, cracked skin of an aged person and is highly susceptible to irritation from such ordinary things as temperature changes and washing.

7. Permanent scars over the majority of the body where skin donor sites were removed,

8. The permanent impairment of speech.

9. The loss of three years of formative and impressionable childhood.

10. Permanently reduced and impaired emotional capacity.

11. The permanent impairment of normal social, recreational and educational life.

12. The permanent imprint of her mother's hand on her stomach.

Considering each of the foregoing items, the court concludes that the jury had the prerogative of awarding up to one million, one hundred thousand dollars for this element of damages.

By totaling the estimated maximum recovery for each element of damages, the jury's actual award is placed in proper perspective. According to my calculations the maximum jury award supported by the evidence in this case could have been two million, nine hundred eighty thousand dollars. Obviously, the jury's two million dollar verdict is well within the periphery established by the maximum award test.

The defendants assert three other grounds for a remittitur. They contend that there was error in the verdict since the verdict exceeded the amount prayed for in the plaintiff's pleadings. This contention fails because the plaintiffs' pleadings were amended subsequent to the jury verdict to conform to the evidence and the verdict of the jury. This amendment was permitted by the court in accordance with law. [citations omitted]

Preway and its insurer argue that the introduction of photographs of the plaintiff was inflammatory. Since a part of plaintiff's claim for damages is for disfigurement and the humiliation and embarrassment resulting therefrom, I hold that these photographs were properly admitted to show the condition of the plaintiff as she appeared to others, at the time they were taken. [citations omitted]

The defendants suggest that the presence of the child in the courtroom and in the corridors of the courthouse in some way inflamed or prejudiced the jury. This allegation is unfounded; the defendants have not pointed out any wrongful conduct on the part of Helen Britain, her parents, or counsel for plaintiffs. Helen Britain was well behaved and quiet the entire time she was in the courtroom.

Accordingly I hold that there was not any bias, prejudice, or any other improper influence which motivated the jury in making its award.

QUESTIONS FOR DISCUSSION:

Large damage awards are designed to fund ongoing treatment over time through interest payments or investment. Assume the cost of treatment increases dramatically. Do you think a successful plaintiff should be able to revisit the award amount in such a case?

Assume that this accident occurred now and the same damages were awarded (In real dollar terms). Would a modern defendant challenge the damages? Why or why not?

conduct typically requires an intentional act by the defendant. Negligence cases typically do not involve intentional conduct on behalf of the defendant. Therefore, punitive damages are generally not available in negligence actions.

Where punitive damages are available, juries have occasionally granted extremely high figures. In one famous case, *Liebeck v. McDonald's Restaurants*, a customer spilled hot coffee on herself, and was injured badly enough to require skin grafts. In 1994, a New Mexico jury awarded the plaintiff $160,000 in compensatory damages, but $2.7 million in punitive damages against McDonald's. (An appeals court later reduced the award.) The case opened a national debate about punitive damages.

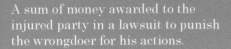

PUNITIVE DAMAGES:
A sum of money awarded to the injured party in a lawsuit to punish the wrongdoer for his actions.

The U.S. Supreme Court considered punitive damages in *State Farm Mutual Automobile Insurance Co. v. Campbell*, 538 U.S. 408 (2003). The Court held that the Due Process Clause of the Fourteenth Amendment prevents disproportionate punitive damage awards. The Court said it would be unfair for potential defendants to have no notice of the potential monetary penalty that would result from their actions. Punitive damages should be based on the egregiousness of the conduct, but generally should not be more than ten times the compensatory award.

Injunctive Relief: When a tort is a continuing wrongdoing, courts may order an injunction against the wrongful behavior. The injunction may be ordered in addition to an award of monetary damages. Examples of cases in which an injunction may be granted are cases involving nuisance or trespass (a continuing trespass, such as erecting a building that crosses a property line). Injunctions are ordered to stop behavior that is more than a one-time wrongful act. Injunctive relief eliminates the possibility of multiple cases being brought for the same sort of act and same sort of injury.

CHAPTER SUMMARY

Tort law provides a framework for injured parties to recover compensation from the parties who caused the injury. This applies to all actors in business just as it applies to individuals in their personal lives. In the business world, all entities and their employees must take care to act prudently in their actions with others. Furthermore, many commercial entities find that they may be liable, even without any negligence or fault, if a product they produce or sell contains a defect. Thus, it is important for all parties involved in business to understand the rules governing negligence, intentional torts, strict liability, and products liability. A thorough understanding of the principles guiding tort law recovery can help commercial entities to establish appropriate business practices and reduce organizational liability.

Review Questions

Review question 1.

What is the difference between negligent and intentional torts? What entities can commit a tort and be held liable for damages? How does an injured person seek tort damages?

Review question 2.

What is the reasonable person standard? How does it apply in negligence cases? How can the standard vary? What circumstances will be considered? Do a person's job or skills make any difference to the standard?

Review question 3.

What is the difference between slander and defamation? What is meant by the term "actual malice"? Is there a constitutional defense to either slander or defamation? Why or why not?

Review question 4.

What is an example of puffery? How is puffery different from fraud? How can you tell the difference?

Review question 5.

What are the different types of product defects? What defenses might a manufacturer assert in a products liability case?

Review question 6.

What are the elements of an interference with contract claim? How is this tort different from a breach of contract case? Why is there a difference in how the two issues are treated legally?

Review question 7.

If an employee commits a tort at work, is the employer liable? What information is needed to determine if an employer may be responsible for an employee's torts?

Review question 8.

What types of damages are available to parties who have been injured? What is the difference between compensatory and punitive damages? What are the goals of each type of damage award?

Review question 9.

What are the major privacy torts? How do the damages differ for the various claims?

Review question 10.

What is injunctive relief? When might a party seek injunctive relief?

Questions for Discussion

Discussion question 1.

Trina is competing in the Tri-City Triathlon. When she registered for the event, Trina signed a waiver. The waiver noted that participants assumed the risk of collisions with other participants. The organizer of the triathlon, Fun Sports, purchases a drone to use at the event. Earl, an employee of Fun Sports who has never used a drone before, uses the drone during the triathlon to take photos of the event for Fun Sports to post on their website for marketing. While Earl is operating the drone, the drone gets tangled in power lines. The blades of the drone sever one of the power lines. The line falls to the ground and hits Trina, who suffers severe burns. The incident also causes a power surge, which releases sparks and flames from a power line three blocks away. The sparks and flames burn a man, Pablo, walking below the power lines. Earl says the drone started acting erratically right before the incident.

   Does Trina have a tort claim against Fun Sports? If so, what type of tort?

   Does Pablo have a tort claim against Fun Sports?

   Can Fun Sports sue the drone manufacturer for a product defect?

Discussion question 2.

Coach Chris is a very popular basketball coach at Northeast Southwest College. He is under contract to coach at Northeast Southwest for the next three years. The terms of the contract were disclosed in a press release issued by the college. Coach Chris was approached by two men looking to establish a professional basketball team for the state of Hawaii, called the Hawaii Hornbills. Coach Chris has been discussing the possibility of leaving his job at Northeast Southwest to become the head coach of the Hornbills. Alfred, a friend of Coach Chris, overhears him talking about the Hornbills job offer to his wife. Alfred is a prominent business owner, and he is a huge supporter of the basketball team. Alfred and does not want Coach Chris to take the Hawaii job. That night, hoping to dissuade the Hornbills from hiring Coach Chris, Alfred posts on social media that he and his family vacationed in Hawaii several years ago with Coach Chris and his family. Alfred includes a video in which Coach Chris says he hates Hawaii. In the video, Coach Chris also says "the only good thing about Hawaii is that the people understand basketball better than the fans of Northeast Southwest." The video goes viral.

Upon seeing the video, the Hornbills tell Coach Chris that they will not hire him to coach the Hornbills. After public outrage, Northeast Southwest fires Coach Chris two weeks later. In response, Coach Chris conducts an interview in which he says "Alfred is not a friend. He is a traitor who does whatever he can to get what he wants. He has engaged in insider trading and his company defrauded the public. The government should conduct an investigation." Someone told Coach Chris that Alfred traded stocks based on inside information, but Coach Chris was not involved in the transaction.

> Could Alfred be liable for a tort? If so, which one(s)?
>
> Could Coach Chris be held liable for a tort? If so, which one(s)?

Discussion question 3.

Mika buys a new smart phone. The phone was designed and manufactured by Pyro Phones. One week after purchasing the phone, Mika drops the phone and cracks the screen. He purchases a replacement screen online and installs the screen on the phone. Two months later, Mika is using the phone when the battery overheats. The phone starts on fire and burns Mika's hands.

> Does Mika have a cause of action against Pyro Phones?
>
> Can Pyro Phones assert any defenses against Mika's claim?

Discussion question 4.

Bob works as a farm laborer. He is known for goofing around on the job to make people laugh. One day, while walking with his co-worker Patricia, Bob starts flapping his arms like a chicken to emphasize the punch line of a joke. Patricia moves to give Bob flapping room, and is hit by a swinging pulley that normally hangs above the door of the barn.

> Does Patricia have a tort claim against Bob? Against the farm? Against the pulley manufacturer? What type of claims?
>
> What elements are present for any identified tort claims?

Discussion question 5.

Kellogg USA has been sued several times because plaintiffs claim they were misled by the company. Specifically, the plaintiffs charge that they believed Froot Loops contained actual fruit. The cases are routinely dismissed.

> Why do courts dismiss these cases? Is the product name misleading?

> If a case went to trial, what defenses would make sense for Kellogg?

Discussion question 6.

Theresa is dining in a restaurant. A camera crew from a local television station comes into the restaurant and starts filming. Theresa asks them not to film her, but the crew films her anyway. The film is shown on the station's news program.

> Is this an intrusion upon Theresa's seclusion? Why or why not?

> Has the television station appropriated her likeness? Why or why not?

> What additional facts would you need to know in order to give a definitive answer, or to change your answer?

Discussion question 7.

Bob owns a flower shop located in a state that does not bar discrimination based on a person's sexual orientation. A group of citizens in Bill's city want to protest the U.S. Supreme Court's ruling in Obergefell v. Hodges, which struck down laws that prohibited same-sex marriage. The group approaches local businesspeople, including Bob, and asks them to sign a declaration that they will not provide services for same-sex weddings. Bob signs the declaration, and tells the group that it has its full support, and that "As a married father of four, I am 100% behind traditional, biblical marriage." Although Bob is indeed married and a father, he has been carrying on a secret romantic relationship with Jon for several years. Jon is deeply hurt by Bob's public remarks, and considers telling the local news media about his affair with Bob.

> If John tells about his relationship with Bob, has he committed any of the privacy torts? If so which ones?

> Does the public interest in this information outweigh Bob's privacy interests?

Discussion question 8.

Rhoda is a model for a major designer. She admitted to the hospital for treatment following a suicide attempt. A nurse leaks some information about her treatment to a television gossip program. When Rhoda recovers, she is outraged, and points out that the release of her health information was a violation of the Health Insurance Portability and Accountability Act. Her attorney tells her that while there was a HIPAA violation, there is no provision in the law for individuals to recover damages for unauthorized release of their health information.

> How can Rhoda claim damages without support in the health information law?

8 INTELLECTUAL PROPERTY

KEY OBJECTIVES:

▶ Understand the distinctions between copyright, trademarks, patents, and trade secrets.

▶ Learn about the need to protect intellectual property interests.

▶ Learn about how intellectual property owners may license their rights.

CHAPTER OVERVIEW

This chapter covers intellectual property. Intellectual property is a form of property that comes from an idea. It can come from an invention, a song, or an advertising slogan, but it is not a physical thing. Instead, intellectual property is a right, or a set of rights, to control how a creation is used.

In this chapter, we will look at the various types of intellectual property. We will learn how to protect an owner's rights in that property. Finally, the chapter will consider how to allow others to make use of intellectual property through licensing.

INTRODUCTION

Thousands, if not millions, of people have paid a fee to access the number one song on the Billboard Hot 100. Most of them probably added the song to a playlist on their mobile phones.

That everyday scenario involves three types of intellectual property. You have to pay money for access to the song because of the copyright in the song. The band's name, "Billboard," and "Hot 100" are all trademarks. The cell phone works because of technology that is or was patented. And if you're drinking a Coca Cola or Dr. Pepper as you listen to the song or read this book, a fourth type of intellectual property comes into play: the recipes for both drinks are trade secrets. The brand names "Coca Cola" and "Dr. Pepper" are also trademarks.

Intellectual property serves a number of purposes. In the U.S., copyrights, trademarks, and patents are commercial assets. Legal protection makes it profitable to create things. For many creators and inventors, their intellectual property is also a way of having their creative or inventive efforts recognized. Trade secret law recognizes the value of keeping business information confidential, either temporarily or permanently. Intellectual property covers a lot of different areas, and affects virtually every type of business.

Understanding intellectual property law is important not only for the protection and commercial development of your own ideas, but to make sure that you do not run afoul of someone else's rights.

There are four main types of intellectual property: copyrights, trademarks, patents, and trade secrets. Each type protects different interests.

I.   Copyright

Copyright law has a long history in the United States. The Constitution gives Congress the power to

> promote the Progress of Science and useful Arts, by securing for limited Times to Authors and Inventors the exclusive Right to their respective Writings and Discoveries.

The first federal copyright law was the Copyright Act of 1790, passed in the second session of Congress. The law was brief by today's standards, taking up less than a full page in the official publication. It allowed copyright protection for any "map, chart, book or books" authored by a U.S. citizen. Copyright protection was for 14 years, and could be extended for 14 more.

> U.S. copyright protection was not extended to works by foreign nationals until 1891.

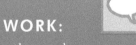

DERIVATIVE WORK:
A work based on another work. Examples of derivative works include adaptations or sequels.

Over time, the law has changed a great deal. The length of time copyright lasts has changed several times, and works by non-U.S. citizens are eligible for protection. The types of work that are eligible for protection have also been expanded dramatically, to include photographs, movies, sound recordings, and computer software. There have also been changes to adapt the law to new technology, and to the globalization of communication.

All of these changes are made within the same constitutional framework as the 1790 Act: securing exclusive rights to authors, for limited times. There are two important concepts contained in that sentence. First, copyright gives "exclusive" rights. When a person owns the copyright in a work, she is said to have a "bundle of rights." This bundle is made up of the right to do the following:

- Make copies of a work,

- Distribute copies,

- Create **derivative works**,

- Display the work publicly, if it is a visual work,

- Perform it publicly,

- Transmit the work by broadcast, webcast, or any other means, and

- Transmit the work by webcast.

Example: A photographer takes a picture of a statue in a cemetery. He has created an original work that is entitled to copyright protection. The photographer's right extends only to his photograph. The statue itself has its own copyright. *Leigh v. Warner Brothers*, 212 F.3d 1210 (11th Cir. 2000).

SAMPLING A SMALL AMOUNT OF RECORDED MUSIC IS NOT ACTIONABLE INFRINGEMENT.

VMG Salsoul, L.L.C. v. Ciccone
(Copyright Owner) v. (Singer)
824 F.3d 871 (9th Cir. 2016)

INSTANT FACTS:
Ciccone (D) recorded a song that included a short excerpt from another song, without getting the permission of VMG Salsoul (P), the copyright holder.

BLACK LETTER RULE:
Copying a small amount that cannot be recognized by the average audience is not copyright infringement.

FACTS:
Ciccone, known professionally as Madonna (D), and Pettibone (D) recorded the song "Vogue." The recording included a brief sample of sounds from the song "Love Break," that had been recorded some years earlier. The sample consisted of a "horn hit," a four-note chord that lasted 0.23 seconds. The hit was repeated in both "Love Break" and "Vogue" in similar patterns. There was testimony that Pettibone (D) directed the copying.

The District Court entered judgment for Ciccone (D) and Pettibone (D), saying that the sampling was de minimis, and therefore did not constitute infringement.

ISSUE:
Was the sampling infringement of the copyright in "Love Break?"

DECISION AND RATIONALE:
(Graber, J.) No. Copying a small amount that cannot be recognized by the average audience is not copyright infringement. Copyright law has long recognized that copying a trivial, or de minimis, amount of another work is not infringement. In order for copying to be infringement, the copying must be something which ordinary observations would cause to be recognized as having been taken from the work of another. After listening to the recordings in this case, we conclude that a reasonable jury could not conclude that an average audience would recognize the copying of the horn hit.

When Congress extended copyright protection to sound recordings, the intent was to treat sound recordings the same as any other copyrighted material. The de minimis exception applies to sound recordings. Affirmed.

ANALYSIS:
A de minimis exception is applied in many different areas of the law. Its purpose is to keep courts from spending time on petty or trivial disputes. The de minimis exception in copyright law is also a recognition that avoiding all copying is difficult, and small, unrecognizable instances of copying do not justify court action.

Sound recordings were not protected by U.S. copyright law until 1972.

CASE VOCABULARY:
DE MINIMIS:
Small, or trivial. From the Latin maxim de minimis non curat lex (the law does not concern itself with trifles)

QUESTION FOR DISCUSSION:
Assume a songwriter wrote a song using an identifiable portion of another song, but was not consciously aware of the other song. Is there a copyright infringement?

It is important to remember that these rights belong only to the owner of the copyright. She is the only one who may decide how, or whether, a work is used. It is not up to another party to decide that she would benefit from getting more or different exposure for the work. "Good publicity" or an expanded audience for a work does nothing to mitigate liability for copyright infringement.

The second concept is that the time of the exclusive rights is limited. All copyrights will expire after a period of time. The time of protection depends on when a work was created. Generally, if a work was created after 1978, copyright protection will last for the lifetime of the author, plus 70 years, with no renewal. The period may vary in some circumstances. The purpose of the limited time period is to allow the author ample opportunity to exploit her work, while still making sure that it is eventually available for unrestricted use by the public.

> In civil law countries, such as France, the copyright term also includes a time sufficient to protect the reputation of the author.

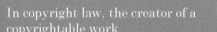

AUTHOR:

In copyright law, the creator of a copyrightable work.

WORK FOR HIRE:

A work that was either created by an employee within the scope of her employment, or that was commissioned for a special purpose with the written agreement that it would be work-for-hire. Copyright for a work-for-hire automatically vests in the employer or person who commissioned the work.

Automatic Copyright on Work Creation

Find the closest piece of paper. Draw any shape on it. Congratulations—you are now the **author** of a work that is protected by copyright!

Copyright is automatic when a work that is eligible for protection is created. There are no formalities necessary to have the copyright. You do not have to register, and you do not have to put any notice on your work, in order to have the copyright (although there are good reasons to do both of those things). Once it is created, the author is the owner of the copyright. The author may or may not be the owner of the work created. If you give the shape you drew a few minutes ago to a friend, you don't own the drawing any more, but you still own the copyright.

The only real limitation on this rule is that the work must qualify for copyright protection, or be copyrightable. A work qualifies for copyright protection if it is an

> original work[] of authorship fixed in any tangible medium of expression, now known or later developed, from which they can be perceived, reproduced, or otherwise communicated, either directly or with the aid of a machine or device.

An "original work" is one that has some new creative effort put into it. It does not mean that it is novel or even particularly unique. It just means that the work was created independently, and that there was some "spark" of creativity in it. The amount of creativity required is small, and the amount of effort required to make a work original is likewise small. Some commentators have suggested that even an accidental "spark of creativity," such as a deviation from a straight line caused by someone bumping a drafting table, is enough to make a work original. If there is anything that makes the work something other than an exact copy, there is originality.

While copyright protects entire works, there are some elements of a work that may not be protected. Using one of these elements without permission would not constitute copyright infringement. The non-copyrightable parts of a work include:

- Titles,

- Ideas,

- Facts,

- Processes and procedures,

- Quotations,

- Clichés and slogans,

- Natural elements, such as the coloring of a horse,

- Public domain material, or

- Scènes à faire, which are common elements or devices used in a particular type of work (for example, a handsome young vampire).

Since copyright does not protect individual or discrete elements of a work, the mere fact that one or more of these elements is used is not evidence of infringement. For example, a staple situation of holiday-themed comedies is the householder who decorates his house with an excessive number of Christmas lights. When the lights are plugged in, the entire neighborhood loses electricity. While the use of this situation may be evidence of a willingness to rely on a cliché for an easy laugh, it is not evidence of infringement.

Works that are based on another work, or derivative works, are considered original, and entitled to copyright protection. The creator of the original work has the exclusive right to create derivative works, but may authorize or license others to do so. The protection for the derivative works is separate from the protection given to the original work. The protection for the derivative work only applies to the new additions. It does not give the author of the derivative any copyright in the original work, if the original copyright is held by another person.

"Authorship" means that someone is responsible for the creation of the work. The work cannot be a naturally occurring phenomenon. The author of a work may be an individual, or there may be multiple authors. The author is almost always the owner of the copyright. If a work is **work for hire**, however, the "author" is the employer of the creators of the work, or the person who commissioned the work.

> A derivative work may infringe on the copyright of the original work, if it was created without the permission of the owner of the rights in the original work.

"Fixed in any tangible medium of expression" is a requirement that a work be physically recorded or memorialized by some means. This requirement serves two purposes. First, it allows the work to be recorded, so there is some way of knowing what is protected. For example, dance moves are creations, but they are not tangible. The choreography may, however, be protected by copyright if there is a diagram made of the moves. The second, and probably more important, purpose of the "fixed in any tangible medium of expression" requirement is to make clear that copyright protection will not be given to ideas. Instead, protection is given to the expression of those ideas. Many different authors may use the same basic idea for their works (think zombie apocalypse), but it is how that basic idea is expressed that gets the protection.

- Blank forms,

- Recipes,

- Mathematical proofs,

- Scientific theories,

- Historical facts, or

- Business methods.

Even if a type of work is not copyrightable, there may be expression attached to it, or closely associated with it that could be protected. Historical facts may not be copyrightable, but a novel based on those facts could be. While a mathematical formula cannot be copyrighted, computer software that makes use of that formula could be. Remember, however, that the copyright will not extend to the non-copyrightable parts of the work. The copyright protection given to

Example: In one of her cookbooks, the late Julia Child published a recipe for Caesar salad. She also told the story of how and where the salad was popularized (in Mexico, not Italy). The recipe is not copyrightable, but her telling of the story behind the recipe is.

Copyright protection can be extended to virtually any type of work. The only limitation set out in the law is that copyright cannot be granted to "any idea, procedure, process, system, method of operation, concept, principle, or discovery, regardless of the form in which it is described, explained, illustrated, or embodied in such work." This means that copyright expression cannot be extended to works such as:

the computer software does not mean that the mathematical formula now has protection independent of its inclusion in a copyrighted work.

Proving Copyright

It is very easy to get copyright in a work: copyright is automatic for creative expression. Proving that you have copyright is a different matter. The question of proof can come up in many different situations. Suppose you post a picture you have taken online, and then you learn that someone has used it without your permission. This could be an infringement of your copyright. In order to do anything about it, you first have to show that you own the copyright.

One of the best ways of proving copyright is the copyright notice. The copyright notice is not required for works published or created since March 1, 1989. An author will have good copyright without the notice, but the notice can help prove ownership.

Although the notice is not a legal requirement for valid copyright, it still is important. When notice is placed on a work, it tells anyone who sees the work that it is indeed protected by copyright. It also lets them know who the owner of the copyright is.

Notice is also important because it make it less likely that an infringer will be able to make a successful claim of innocent infringement. Innocent infringement is when a person who uses a work without permission is able to make a claim that she didn't know it was copyrighted work. An innocent infringer still must pay damages for copyright infringement, but the damages can be significantly less than what a non-innocent infringer would pay. If there is a good copyright notice on the work, a claim of innocent infringement will fail.

The copyright notice itself is very simple. It consists of:

- The letter "C" in a circle (©), the word "copyright," or the abbreviation "Copr.,"

- The year the work was first published, and

- The name of the owner of the copyright.

The notice must be placed on publicly distributed copies so that it can be visually perceived, directly, or with the aid of a device. It must be

---

A PERSON WHO CLAIMS INFRINGEMENT MUST PROVE OWNERSHIP OF THE COPYRIGHT.

Fleischer Studios, Inc. v. A.V.E.L.A., Inc.
(Copyright Licensor) v. (Competing Licensor)
654 F.3d 958 (9th Cir. 2011)

INSTANT FACTS:
Fleischer (P) claimed ownership in all the rights to the character Betty Boop.

BLACK LETTER RULE:
The plaintiff in an infringement action bears the burden of proving copyright ownership.

FACTS:
The character Betty Boop was developed in 1930, and all rights in the character and films were sold to Paramount. Paramount transferred its rights in the films only to UM & M, and the rights were resold multiple times, until Fleischer (P) purchased them. Fleischer (P) licensed the Betty Boop character for use in toys, dolls, and other merchandise. A.V.E.L.A (D) also licensed Betty Boop merchandise. The copyright under which A.V.E.L.A. (D) licensed its products is based on vintage posters featuring Betty Boop's image that A.V.E.L.A. (D) had restored. Fleischer (P) claimed that it owned the exclusive rights to the Betty Boop character. A.V.E.L.A. (D) claimed that Fleischer

(P) had not proven its exclusive ownership of the copyright. The district court entered judgment for A.V.E.L.A. (D).

ISSUE:
Was Fleischer (P) the holder of the entire copyright?

DECISION AND RATIONALE:
(Kagan, J.) No. The plaintiff in an infringement action bears the burden of proving copyright ownership. Fleischer has not met this burden. When Paramount sold copyrights to UM & M, the transfer included only the rights to the films. The rights to the character were excluded from the sale.

The licensee of a copyright work obtains only partial copyright privileges. Under the doctrine of indivisibility, a licensee of a copyright may not copyright a work in the licensee's name. Affirmed.

ANALYSIS:
The court and all of the parties agreed that the character Betty Boop was separately copyrightable. Fictional characters are protected by copyright apart from the works they appear in if the character is highly developed and distinctive. Stock characters are not protectable.

QUESTION FOR DISCUSSION:
Can you identify business opportunities where separate character rights would be important?

on the copy in a manner and location that gives reasonable notice of the claimed copyright.

Registering Copyrights

If an author has good copyright in a work without registering it, then why bother registering? After all, it takes time and costs money. What's the point?

Registration is not a legal requirement for having copyright, but it is still important. First, registration is evidence that you are the owner of the copyright in the work. It is evidence that can be rebutted, but if there is no other evidence introduced, the registration will be conclusive proof.

Second, the registration is public notice of who claims ownership. Copyright records are open to the public for searching, so the public at large is deemed to have notice of what is contained in those records. Once registration is completed, it is more difficult to claim ignorance of the true ownership in copyright. Records since 1978 are available online at http://cocatalog.loc.gov. They may be searched by name, title, keyword, registration number, or document number. Records for registrations before 1978 are only partially online, and a full search would have to be done in the federal Copyright Office in Washington, D.C.

> The Copyright Office is an agency of the Library of Congress.

Third, registration is a requirement for bringing a lawsuit against someone for infringing copyright. This sounds like a contradiction of the rule that copyright is automatic, but it isn't really. Copyright still exists as soon as a work is created, but the initial pleading in a lawsuit must say that a work was registered or registration has been submitted, even if registration was refused. An author or copyright owner may make a claim for infringement that took place before a work was registered, but before the suit

THE COPYRIGHT OFFICE'S SEARCH INTERFACE FOR COPYRIGHT RECORDS FROM 1978 TO PRESENT.

is filed, the work must be registered. It is not necessary that the application be acted upon before the suit is brought. It is sufficient if the plaintiff's complaint states that the application was submitted.

Registration is a very simple process. It may be done electronically (the preferred method), or by sending hard copies of the required documents to the U.S. Copyright Office in Washington, D.C. The process is also not as expensive as many might fear. As of 2017, the registration fees range from $35 to $55 for online registration, to $85 for paper registration. There are three steps for registering copyright: application, payment, and deposit of copies.

Application involves filling out a form. Typically, this form will be completed online. The form asks for information about the author of the work, and about the work itself. The applicant must give the title of the work, a description of the type of work that it is (for example, musical recording, audio-visual work, or one of several other options), and the name of the author. If

the work is based on another work, that information must be included in the application. The application form also asks if the work has been published.

Payment of the filing fee is required when the application is submitted. If the application is done online, it is much like making payment for any online purchase.

Deposit of copies means that two copies of the work are submitted. The copies may be sent electronically or by mail. Some works (for example, large works, or works that consist only of the original and no copies) may have photographs sent in as their deposit, instead of physical copies of the work.

After the application for registration is submitted, the Copyright Office examines the application. The examination is a simple process, especially when compared to the detailed examination for patent or trademark registrations. There are two facets to this examination. The first looks to see if all of the legal requirements for the application have been met. This is essentially a review to be sure the form is properly completed, and that the information submitted is accurate. An application will be denied if there is a "material omission" in the application, or if the information is inaccurate. The second part looks at whether the work is copyrightable. The inquiry is whether the work meets the minimal criteria of being an original work of authorship reduced to tangible form. The examination does *not* compare the work with other registered copyrights. If an application is submitted to register a work that infringes another, that infringement will not be noted by the Copyright Office.

If the application is denied, the applicant can ask for an internal review by the Copyright Office. After the review process, an applicant whose registration is still refused may bring a court action to compel registration. A person whose application is denied may bring an infringement action without appealing the refusal. In a case such as that, the court will ask the Copyright Office for an explanation as to why the application was denied.

PUBLIC DOMAIN:

Work that cannot be copyrighted. An old copyright may have expired, or the author or owner of the work has made an explicit designation that the work is public domain. The term also refers to U.S. Government works that cannot be copyrighted.

Protecting Copyrights

Putting the copyright notice on work and registering copyright are important protections. They are preventative measures and, as with all preventative measures, there will be times when they don't work. Other measures will have to be taken. The "other measures" take the form of a lawsuit for copyright infringement.

The law defines "infringement" as the "violation" of the exclusive rights of the owner of a copyright. "Violation" means exercising one of these rights without the permission of the owner. An infringement can be unintentional, as in cases where the infringer had a good faith belief that the work was **public domain**. A valid claim of infringement can be made even if the infringement did not cause any financial damage to the copyright owner, or even if the infringement can be seen as beneficial to the author.

The essence of an infringement lawsuit is a claim for unauthorized use, or copying, of the copyrighted work. A person cannot bring a copyright infringement lawsuit unless he registered, or tried to register, the copyright. He must also be the owner of the copyright when the suit is brought. The owner is either the author of the work, or a person who bought or licensed the copyright. While it is not conclusive proof, the listing of an owner's name on the registration certificate issued by the Copyright Office will be strong evidence of ownership.

Since an infringement lawsuit is a claim for unauthorized use of a copyrighted work, the suit will require proof that the material taken, or copied, was actually protected by copyright. If the part that was taken is public domain there is no infringement, even if there was copying.

A work enters the public domain in one of three ways. First, a work produced by the U.S. government is automatically in the public domain. There is no copyright in federal government publications or works, so those works may be reproduced freely, and derivative works may be prepared without restriction. The author of the derivative work has a copyright in whatever she added to the work.

> For many years, the National Oceanic and Atmospheric Administration (NOAA) has produced navigational maps or charts of U.S. waters. Chart No. 1 is a guide to all of the symbols on these charts. Private publishers have often reprinted all or part of Chart No. 1, sometimes altering the size of the publication, adding introductory or explanatory material, or omitting some of the content. These publishers may claim copyright protection for their selection and arrangement of the material, and for any additional material they create and add, but cannot claim copyright protection for the lists of symbols. The list is in the public domain as a federal government publication.

U.S. government publications are in the public domain only if produced by the U.S. government. It is possible for the federal government to obtain the copyright in a work produced by a private party. In that case, the government is

the copyright holder and the work is not in the public domain.

Second, an author or owner may dedicate the work to the public domain, by making an explicit statement that reserves no rights and has no limits on use. The statement must be unequivocal, and no rights may be reserved or limited. Many websites carry a notice that says that the writings on the site may be reproduced or redistributed only for educational and discussion purposes. This is not a dedication to the public domain, since some limitations are placed on the use of the work.

Third, the copyright to a work may have expired. Remember that the constitutional authorization for copyright laws says that authors are allowed protection of their work only "for limited Times." All copyrights will, eventually, expire. Work produced since 1978 is protected in the U.S. for 70 years after the death of the author. If the work is published anonymously or under a pseudonym, or if the author is a corporation (work-for-hire), copyright will last for 120 years from the date of creation. No renewals are allowed.

The time limits for copyright protection become more complicated for older works. All work published before 1923 is in the public domain, and work published between 1923 and 1963 is in the public domain if copyright was not renewed. It is possible to search the Copyright Office's online database to look for renewals, but that can sometimes be difficult. Multiple works by different authors may have the same title, and it may be hard to track the current status of an old copyright. If a work was published between 1923 and 1963, and copyright was renewed within 28 years of publication, the copyright runs for 95 years after the publication date. For work published with the proper copyright notice between 1964 and 1977, copyright extends from 95 years after the date of publication.

> Note that the copyright in part of a work may expire, while other elements may remain protected. For instance, a silent movie is probably in the public domain, but if new music is recorded to accompany it, the music is protected by copyright. The same is true for public domain books with new illustrations; the new work is copyrighted. And new recordings of public domain musical scores are copyrighted, because while the score itself is in the public domain, the new performance of that score is not.

Once the copyright in a work has expired, it normally enters the public domain for all time. There have been some limited exceptions to this rule. The most prominent of these has been the retroactive extension of copyright terms after the United States passed legislation in 1994 that restored the copyright for many works by foreign authors that had been regarded as being in the public domain. Some of the works that received protection again included early films by Alfred Hitchcock, novels by C.S. Lewis and Virginia Woolf, and Picasso's painting *Guernica*.

Prior to 1989, there was an additional way for work to be put in the public domain. At that time, if a work did not have a copyright notice or symbol on it, the work was not protected by copyright. The lack of notice is not an absolute guarantee that there is no copyright. If the work was published between 1978 and 1989 without a notice but the work was registered within five years of publication, it is not in the public domain.

RETROACTIVE EXTENSION OF COPYRIGHT TERM IS CONSTITUTIONAL.

Eldred v. Ashcroft
(Publisher) v. (U.S. Attorney General)
537 U.S. 186 (2003)

JUSTICE GINSBURG delivered the opinion of the Court.

This case concerns the authority the Constitution assigns to Congress to prescribe the duration of copyrights. The Copyright and Patent Clause of the Constitution, Art. I, § 8, cl. 8, provides as to copyrights: "Congress shall have Power ... [t]o promote the Progress of Science ... by securing [to Authors] for limited Times ... the exclusive Right to their . . . Writings." In 1998, in the measure here under inspection, Congress enlarged the duration of copyrights by 20 years. Copyright Term Extension Act (CTEA), Pub. L. 105-298, §§ 102(b) and (d), 112 Stat. 2827-2828 (amending 17 U.S.C. §§ 302, 304). As in the case of prior extensions, principally in 1831, 1909, and 1976, Congress provided for application of the enlarged terms to existing and future copyrights alike.

Petitioners are individuals and businesses whose products or services build on copyrighted works that have gone into the public domain. They seek a determination that the CTEA fails constitutional review under both the Copyright Clause's "limited Times" prescription and the First Amendment's free speech guarantee. Under the 1976 Copyright Act, copyright protection generally lasted from the work's creation until 50 years after the author's death. Pub. L. 94-553, § 302(a), 90 Stat. 2572 (1976 Act). Under the CTEA, most copyrights now run from creation until 70 years after the author's death. 17 U.S.C. § 302(a). Petitioners do not challenge the "life-plus-70-years" timespan itself. "Whether 50 years is enough, or 70 years too much," they acknowledge, "is not a judgment meet for this Court." Brief for Petitioners 14. Congress went awry, petitioners maintain, not with respect to newly created works, but in enlarging the term for published works with existing copyrights. The "limited Tim[e]" in effect when a copyright is secured, petitioners urge, becomes the constitutional boundary, a clear line beyond the power of Congress to extend. See *ibid.* As to the First Amendment, petitioners contend that the CTEA is a content-neutral regulation of speech that fails inspection under the heightened judicial scrutiny appropriate for such regulations.

In accord with the District Court and the Court of Appeals, we reject petitioners' challenges to the CTEA. In that 1998 legislation, as in all previous copyright term extensions, Congress placed existing and future copyrights in parity. In prescribing that alignment, we hold, Congress acted within its authority and did not transgress constitutional limitations.

[...]

We evaluate petitioners' challenge to the constitutionality of the CTEA against the backdrop of Congress' previous exercises of its authority under the Copyright Clause. The Nation's first copyright statute, enacted in 1790, provided a federal copyright term of 14 years from the date of publication, renewable for an additional 14 years if the author survived the first term. Act of May 31, 1790, ch. 15, § 1, 1 Stat. 124 (1790 Act). The 1790 Act's renewable 14-year term applied to existing works (*i. e.,* works already published and works created but not yet published) and future works alike. *Ibid.* Congress expanded the federal copyright term to 42 years in 1831 (28 years from publication, renewable for an additional 14 years), and to 56 years in 1909 (28 years from publication, renewable for an additional 28 years). Act of Feb. 3, 1831, ch. 16, §§ 1, 16, 4 Stat. 436, 439 (1831 Act); Act of Mar. 4, 1909, ch. 320, §§ 23-24, 35 Stat. 1080-1081 (1909 Act). Both times, Congress applied the new copyright term to existing and future works, 1831 Act §§ 1, 16; 1909 Act §§ 23-24; to qualify for the 1831 extension, an existing work had to be in its initial copyright term at the time the Act became effective, 1831 Act §§ 1, 16.

In 1976, Congress altered the method for computing federal copyright terms. 1976 Act §§ 302-304. For works created by identified natural persons, the 1976 Act provided that federal copyright protection would run from the work's creation, not—as in the 1790, 1831, and 1909 Acts—its publication; protection would last until 50 years after the author's death. § 302(a). In these respects, the 1976 Act aligned United States copyright terms with the then-dominant international standard adopted under the Berne Convention for the Protection of Literary and Artistic Works. See H. R. Rep. No. 94-1476, p. 135 (1976). For anonymous works, pseudonymous works, and works made for hire, the 1976 Act provided a term of 75 years from publication or 100 years from creation, whichever expired first. § 302(c).

These new copyright terms, the 1976 Act instructed, governed all works not published by its effective date of January 1, 1978, regardless of when the works were created. §§ 302-303. For published works with existing copyrights as of that date, the 1976 Act granted a copyright term of 75 years from the date of publication, §§ 304(a) and (b), a 19-year increase over the 56-year term applicable under the 1909 Act.

The measure at issue here, the CTEA, installed the fourth major duration extension of federal copyrights. Retaining the general structure of the 1976 Act, the CTEA enlarges the terms of all existing and future copyrights by 20 years. For works created by identified natural persons, the term now lasts from creation until 70 years after the author's death. 17 U.S.C. § 302(a). This standard harmonizes the baseline United States copyright term with the term adopted by the European Union in 1993. See Council Directive 93/98/EEC of 29 October 1993 Harmonizing the Term of Protection of Copyright and Certain Related Rights, 1993 Official J. Eur. Coms. (L 290), p. 9 (EU Council Directive 93/98). For anonymous works, pseudonymous works, and works made for hire, the term is 95 years from publication or 120 years from creation, whichever expires first. 17 U.S.C. § 302(c).

Paralleling the 1976 Act, the CTEA applies these new terms to all works not published by January

1, 1978. §§ 302(a), 303(a). For works published before 1978 with existing copyrights as of the CTEA's effective date, the CTEA extends the term to 95 years from publication. §§ 304(a) and (b). Thus, in common with the 1831, 1909, and 1976 Acts, the CTEA's new terms apply to both future and existing copyrights.

[...]

Petitioners' suit challenges the CTEA's constitutionality under both the Copyright Clause and the First Amendment. On cross-motions for judgment on the pleadings, the District Court entered judgment for the Attorney General (respondent here). The court held that the CTEA does not violate the "limited Times" restriction of the Copyright Clause because the CTEA's terms, though longer than the 1976 Act's terms, are still limited, not perpetual, and therefore fit within Congress' discretion. The court also held that "there are no First Amendment rights to use the copyrighted works of others."

The Court of Appeals for the District of Columbia Circuit affirmed . . .Copyright, the court reasoned, does not impermissibly restrict free speech, for it grants the author an exclusive right only to the specific form of expression; it does not shield any idea or fact contained in the copyrighted work, and it allows for "fair use" even of the expression itself.

A majority of the Court of Appeals also upheld the CTEA against petitioners' contention that the measure exceeds Congress' power under the Copyright Clause . . .

The appeals court found nothing in the constitutional text or its history to suggest that "a term of years for a copyright is not a 'limited Time' if it may later be extended for another 'limited Time.'" The court recounted that "the First Congress made the Copyright Act of 1790 applicable to subsisting copyrights arising under the copyright laws of the several states." That construction of Congress' authority under the Copyright Clause "by [those] contemporary with [the Constitution's] formation," the court said, merited "very great" and in this case "almost conclusive" weight. As early as [1843], the Court of Appeals added, this Court had made it "plain" that the same Clause permits Congress to "amplify the terms of an existing patent." The appeals court recognized that this Court has been similarly deferential to the judgment of Congress in the realm of copyright.

Concerning petitioners' assertion that Congress might evade the limitation on its authority by stringing together "an unlimited number of 'limited Times,'" the Court of Appeals stated that such legislative misbehavior "clearly is not the situation before us." Rather, the court noted, the CTEA "matches" the baseline term for "United States copyrights [with] the terms of copyrights granted by the European Union." "[I]n an era of multinational publishers and instantaneous electronic transmission," the court said, "harmonization in this regard has obvious practical benefits" and is "a 'necessary and proper' measure to meet contemporary circumstances rather than a step on the way to making copyrights perpetual."

[...]

We granted certiorari to address two questions: whether the CTEA's extension of existing copyrights exceeds Congress' power under the Copyright Clause; and whether the CTEA's extension of existing and future copyrights violates the First Amendment. We now answer those two questions in the negative and affirm.

[...]

We address first the determination of the courts below that Congress has authority under the Copyright Clause to extend the terms of existing copyrights. Text, history, and precedent, we conclude, confirm that the Copyright Clause empowers Congress to prescribe "limited Times" for copyright protection and to secure the same level and duration of protection for all copyright holders, present and future.

The CTEA's baseline term of life plus 70 years, petitioners concede, qualifies as a "limited Tim[e]" as applied to future copyrights. Petitioners contend, however, that existing copyrights extended to endure for that same term are not "limited." Petitioners' argument essentially reads into the text of the Copyright Clause the command that a time prescription, once set, becomes forever "fixed" or "inalterable." The word "limited," however, does not convey a meaning so constricted. At the time of the Framing, that word meant what it means today: "confine[d] within certain bounds," "restrain[ed]," or "circumscribe[d]." S. Johnson, A Dictionary of the English Language (7th ed. 1785); see T. Sheridan, A Complete Dictionary of the English Language (6th ed. 1796) ("confine[d] within certain bounds"); Webster's Third New International Dictionary 1312 (1976) ("confined within limits"; "restricted in extent, number, or duration"). Thus understood, a timespan appropriately "limited" as applied to future copyrights does not automatically cease to be "limited" when applied to existing copyrights. And as we observe, *infra,* at 209-210, there is no cause to suspect that a purpose to evade the "limited Times" prescription prompted Congress to adopt the CTEA.

To comprehend the scope of Congress' power under the Copyright Clause, "a page of history is worth a volume of logic." *New York Trust Co.* v. *Eisner,* 256 U.S. 345, 349 (1921) (Holmes, J.). History reveals an unbroken congressional practice of granting to authors of works with existing copyrights the benefit of term extensions so that all under copyright protection will be governed evenhandedly under the same regime. . . . [T]he First Congress accorded the protections of the Nation's first federal copyright statute to existing and future works alike. 1790 Act § 1. Since then, Congress has regularly applied duration extensions to both existing and future copyrights. 1831 Act §§ 1, 16; 1909 Act §§ 23-24; 1976 Act §§ 302-303; 17 U.S.C. §§ 302-304.

Because the Clause empowering Congress to confer copyrights also authorizes patents, congressional practice with respect to patents informs our inquiry. We count it significant that early Congresses extended the duration of numerous individual patents as well as copyrights. See, *e. g.,* Act of Jan. 7, 1808, ch. 6, 6 Stat. 70 (patent); Act of Mar. 3, 1809, ch. 35, 6 Stat. 80 (patent); Act of Feb. 7, 1815, ch. 36, 6 Stat. 147 (patent); Act of May 24, 1828, ch. 145, 6 Stat. 389 (copyright); Act of Feb. 11, 1830, ch. 13, 6 Stat. 403 (copyright) . . . The courts saw no "limited Times" impediment to such extensions; renewed or extended terms were upheld in the early days . . .

[...]

Congress' consistent historical practice of applying newly enacted copyright terms to future and existing copyrights reflects a judgment stated concisely by Representative Huntington at the time of the 1831 Act: "[J]ustice, policy, and equity alike forb[id]" that an "author who had sold his [work] a week ago, be placed in a worse situation than the author who should sell his work the day after the passing of [the] act." 7 Cong. Deb. 424 (1831); accord, Symposium, The Constitutionality of Copyright Term Extension, 18 Cardozo Arts & Ent. L. J. 651, 694 (2000) (Prof. Miller) ("[S]ince 1790, it has indeed been Congress's policy that the author of yesterday's work should not get a lesser reward than the author of tomorrow's work just because Congress passed a statute lengthening the term today."). The CTEA follows this historical practice by keeping the duration provisions of the 1976 Act largely in place and simply adding 20 years to each of them. Guided by text, history, and precedent, we cannot agree with petitioners' submission that extending the duration of existing copyrights is categorically beyond Congress' authority under the Copyright Clause.

Satisfied that the CTEA complies with the "limited Times" prescription, we turn now to whether it is a rational exercise of the legislative authority conferred by the Copyright Clause. On that point, we defer substantially to Congress . . .

The CTEA reflects judgments of a kind Congress typically makes, judgments we cannot dismiss as outside the Legislature's domain. . . . [A] key factor in the CTEA's passage was a 1993 European Union (EU) directive instructing EU members to establish a copyright term of life plus 70 years. EU Council Directive 93/98, Art. 1(1), p. 11; see 144 Cong. Rec. S12377-S12378 (daily ed. Oct. 12, 1998) (statement of Sen. Hatch). Consistent with the Berne Convention, the EU directed its members to deny this longer term to the works of any non-EU country whose laws did not secure the same extended term. See Berne Conv. Art. 7(8); P. Goldstein, International Copyright § 5.3, p. 239 (2001). By extending the baseline United States copyright term to life plus 70 years, Congress sought to ensure that American authors would receive the same copyright protection in Europe as their European counterparts. . . .

In addition to international concerns, Congress passed the CTEA in light of demographic, economic, and technological changes, and rationally credited projections that longer terms would encourage copyright holders to invest in the restoration and public distribution of their works.

In sum, we find that the CTEA is a rational enactment; we are not at liberty to second-guess congressional determinations and policy judgments of this order, however debatable or arguably unwise they may be. Accordingly, we cannot conclude that the CTEA — which continues the unbroken congressional practice of treating future and existing copyrights in parity for term extension purposes — is an impermissible exercise of Congress' power under the Copyright Clause.

[...]

Petitioners contend that even if the CTEA's 20-year term extension is literally a "limited Tim[e]," permitting Congress to extend existing copyrights allows it to evade the "limited Times" constraint by creating effectively perpetual copyrights through repeated extensions.

As the Court of Appeals observed, a regime of perpetual copyrights "clearly is not the situation before us." Nothing before this Court warrants construction of the CTEA's 20-year term extension as a congressional attempt to evade or override the "limited Times" constraint. Critically, we again emphasize, petitioners fail to show how the CTEA crosses a constitutionally significant threshold with respect to "limited Times" that the 1831, 1909, and 1976 Acts did not. . . . Those earlier Acts did not create perpetual copyrights, and neither does the CTEA.

[...]

More forcibly, petitioners contend that the CTEA's extension of existing copyrights does not "promote the Progress of Science" as contemplated by the preambular language of the Copyright Clause. Art. I, § 8, cl. 8. To sustain this objection, petitioners do not argue that the Clause's preamble is an independently enforceable limit on Congress' power. . . . Rather, they maintain that the preambular language identifies the sole end to which Congress may legislate; accordingly, they conclude, the meaning of "limited Times" must be "determined in light of that specified end." The CTEA's extension of existing copyrights categorically fails to "promote the Progress of Science," petitioners argue, because it does not stimulate the creation of new works but merely adds value to works already created.

As petitioners point out, we have described the Copyright Clause as "both a grant of power and a limitation," *Graham* v. *John Deere Co. of Kansas City,* 383 U.S. 1, 5 (1966), and have said that "[t]he primary objective of copyright" is "[t]o promote the Progress of Science." The "constitutional command," we have recognized, is that Congress, to the extent it enacts copyright laws at all, create a "system" that "promote[s] the Progress of Science."

We have also stressed, however, that it is generally for Congress, not the courts, to decide how best to pursue the Copyright Clause's objectives. . . .

On the issue of copyright duration, Congress, from the start, has routinely applied new definitions or adjustments of the copyright term to both future works and existing works not yet in the public domain. Such consistent congressional practice is entitled to "very great weight, and when it is remembered that the rights thus established have not been disputed during a period of [over two] centur[ies], it is almost conclusive." Indeed, "[t]his Court has repeatedly laid down the principle that a contemporaneous legislative exposition of the Constitution when the founders of our Government and framers of our Constitution were actively participating in public affairs, acquiesced in for a long term of years, fixes the construction to be given [the Constitution's] provisions." Congress' unbroken practice since the founding generation thus overwhelms petitioners' argument that the CTEA's extension of existing copyrights fails *per se* to "promote the Progress of Science."

[...]

For the several reasons stated, we find no Copyright Clause impediment to the CTEA's extension of existing copyrights.

[...]

Petitioners separately argue that the CTEA is a content-neutral regulation of speech that fails heightened judicial review under the First Amendment. We reject petitioners' plea for imposition of uncommonly strict scrutiny on a copyright scheme that incorporates its own speech-protective purposes and safeguards. The Copyright Clause and First Amendment were adopted close in time. This proximity indicates that, in the Framers' view, copyright's limited monopolies are compatible with free speech principles. Indeed, copyright's purpose is to *promote* the creation and publication of free expression. . . .

[...]

As we read the Framers' instruction, the Copyright Clause empowers Congress to determine the intellectual property regimes that, overall, in that body's judgment, will serve the ends of the Clause . . . The wisdom of Congress' action . . . is not within our province to second-guess. Satisfied that the legislation before us remains inside the domain the Constitution assigns to the First Branch, we affirm the judgment of the Court of Appeals.

It is so ordered.

JUSTICE STEVENS, dissenting.

The authority to issue copyrights stems from the same Clause in the Constitution that created the patent power. It provides:

"Congress shall have Power . . . To promote the Progress of Science and useful Arts, by securing for limited Times to Authors and Inventors the exclusive Right to their respective Writings and Discoveries." Art. I, § 8, cl. 8.

It is well settled that the Clause is "both a grant of power and a limitation" and that Congress "may not overreach the restraints imposed by the stated constitutional purpose." *Graham* v. *John Deere Co. of Kansas City,* 383 U. S. 1, 5-6 (1966). As we have made clear in the patent context, that purpose has two dimensions. Most obviously the grant of exclusive rights to their respective writings and discoveries is intended to encourage the creativity of "Authors and Inventors." But the requirement that those exclusive grants be for "limited Times" serves the ultimate purpose of promoting the "Progress of Science and useful Arts" by guaranteeing that those innovations will enter the public domain as soon as the period of exclusivity expires:

[...]

Neither the purpose of encouraging new inventions nor the overriding interest in advancing progress by adding knowledge to the public domain is served by retroactively increasing the inventor's compensation for a completed invention and frustrating the legitimate expectations of members of the public who want to make use of it in a free market. Because those twin purposes provide the only avenue for congressional action under the Copyright/Patent Clause of the Constitution, any other action is manifestly unconstitutional.

[...]

We have recognized that these twin purposes of encouraging new works and adding to the public domain apply to copyrights as well as patents. . . . And, as with patents, we have emphasized that the overriding purpose of providing a reward for authors' creative activity is to motivate that activity and "to allow the public access to the products of their genius after the limited period of exclusive control has expired." *Sony Corp. of America v. Universal City Studios, Inc.,* 464 U. S. 417, 429 (1984). *Ex post facto* extensions of copyrights result in a gratuitous transfer of wealth from the public to authors, publishers, and their successors in interest. Such retroactive extensions do not even arguably serve either of the purposes of the Copyright/Patent Clause . . .

[...]

The express grant of a perpetual copyright would unquestionably violate the textual requirement that the authors' exclusive rights be only "for limited Times." Whether the extraordinary length of the grants authorized by the 1998 Act are invalid because they are the functional equivalent of perpetual copyrights is a question that need not be answered in this case because the question presented by the certiorari petition merely challenges Congress' power to extend retroactively the terms of existing copyrights. Accordingly, there is no need to determine whether the deference that is normally given to congressional policy judgments may save from judicial review its decision respecting the appropriate length of the term. It is important to note, however, that a categorical rule prohibiting retroactive extensions would effectively preclude perpetual copyrights . . .

[...]

JUSTICE BREYER, dissenting.

The . . . statute before us, the 1998 Sonny Bono Copyright Term Extension Act, extends the term of most existing copyrights to 95 years and that of many new copyrights to 70 years after the author's death. The economic effect of this 20-year extension—the longest blanket extension since the

Nation's founding—is to make the copyright term not limited, but virtually perpetual. Its primary legal effect is to grant the extended term not to authors, but to their heirs, estates, or corporate successors. And most importantly, its practical effect is not to promote, but to inhibit, the progress of "Science" —by which word the Framers meant learning or knowledge . . .

The majority believes these conclusions rest upon practical judgments that at most suggest the statute is unwise, not that it is unconstitutional. Legal distinctions, however, are often matters of degree. And in this case the failings of degree are so serious that they amount to failings of constitutional kind. Although the Copyright Clause grants broad legislative power to Congress, that grant has limits. And in my view this statute falls outside them.

[…]

What copyright-related benefits might justify the statute's extension of copyright protection? First, no one could reasonably conclude that copyright's traditional economic rationale applies here. The extension will not act as an economic spur encouraging authors to create new works . . . No potential author can reasonably believe that he has more than a tiny chance of writing a classic that will survive commercially long enough for the copyright extension to matter . . .

[…]

[T]he Court relies heavily for justification upon international uniformity of terms. Although it can be helpful to look to international norms and legal experience in understanding American law, in this case the justification based upon foreign rules is surprisingly weak. Those who claim that significant copyright-related benefits flow from greater international uniformity of terms point to the fact that the nations of the European Union have adopted a system of copyright terms uniform among themselves. And the extension before this Court implements a term of life plus 70 years that appears to conform with the European standard. But how does "uniformity" help to justify this statute?

Despite appearances, the statute does *not* create a uniform American-European term with respect to the lion's share of the economically significant works that it affects—*all* works made "for hire" and *all* existing works created prior to 1978 . . .Neither does the statute create uniformity with respect to anonymous or pseudonymous works . . .

The statute does produce uniformity with respect to copyrights in new, post-1977 works attributed to natural persons. Compare 17 U. S. C. § 302(a) with EU Council Directive 93/98, Art. 1(1), p. 11. But these works constitute only a subset (likely a minority) of works that retain commercial value after 75 years . . . And the fact that uniformity comes so late, if at all, means that bringing American law into conformity with this particular aspect of European law will neither encourage creation nor benefit the long-dead author in any other important way.

[…]

In sum, the partial, future uniformity that the 1998 Act promises cannot reasonably be said to justify extension of the copyright term for new works. And concerns with uniformity cannot possibly justify the extension of the new term to older works, for the statute there creates no uniformity at all.

[Footnote references and citations omitted]

QUESTIONS FOR DISCUSSION:
Which justice made the strongest argument? Why?

Are copyright term lengths mainly serving media companies? What do you suppose will happen when major content providers start to reach the end of the copyright term for their most recognizable properties?

Fair Use

There is no part of copyright law that is more misunderstood than fair use. Everyone, it seems, "knows" what the rule is, and "knows" how it works. The internet is full of free advice on fair use, and what it is supposed to mean.

Fair use is a defense to a claim of copyright infringement. Much of the confusion surrounding it probably comes from the fact that it is not defined in copyright law. The vagueness was intentional: When Congress rewrote the copyright laws in 1976, it was decided to let fair use evolve, and adapt to new uses and new technologies that weren't foreseen at the time.

COPYING SOLELY FOR ELECTRONIC SEARCHING IS FAIR USE.
Authors Guild v. Google, Inc.
(Copyright Holders) v. (Search Engine)
803 F.3d 202 (2d Cir. 2015)

INSTANT FACTS:
Google (D) scanned copies of library books so they could be searched electronically, and claimed its copying was fair use.

BLACK LETTER RULE:
Making a digital copy of books for a search function is transformative, and is fair use of the copyrighted books.

FACTS:
In 2004, Google (D) started its library project. The project involved scanning books that were supplied by participating libraries, extracting a machine-readable text, and creating an index of the text of each book. Google (D) kept the original scan of each book, in part to improve accuracy as image-to-text conversion technologies improve. Some of the books include were protected by copyright, but Google (D) did not obtain the permission of the copyright holders (P) before scanning books. The search results display information about the book, as well as a limited amount of the text.

The Authors Guild (P) claimed that Google (D) was infringing copyrights. Google (D) claimed that the library project was fair use. The district court agreed.

ISSUE:
Was Google's (D) copying fair use?

DECISION AND RATIONALE:
(Leval, J.) Yes. Making a digital copy of books for a search function is transformative, and is fair use of the copyrighted books.

When a claim of fair use is made, the court considers all of the fair use factors: the purpose and nature of the copying, the nature of the copied work, the relative amount taken, and the effect on the market or potential market for the copied work. As applied to the copying in this case, the four factors work as follows:

The purpose of the copying was creating a copy of electronic searching. This is a transformative use, and transformative uses are more likely to be considered fair use.

The nature of the use is to provide information about the copied work, instead of just duplicating it. This factor favors fair use.

Entire works are copied, but the whole works are not displayed to the users of the search function. This factor also favors fair use.

The potential market for the copied books is not affected, because the search does not give users an effective substitute for the original. On average, no more than 16% of the copied book is displayed.

Considering all four factors leads to the conclusion that Google's (D) copying is fair use. Affirmed.

ANALYSIS:

When there is a claim of fair use, all four factors must be considered. In theory, no one factor is more important than any other. In practice, courts put a great deal of emphasis on looking for a transformative use, and on the harm to the potential market.

QUESTIONS FOR DISCUSSION:

What other purposes might Google have in mind for the scanned materials?

What intellectual property issues would be raised by those other purposes?

The Copyright Act says that the fair use of a copyrighted work is not infringement. Although fair use is not defined, the Act gives examples of the purposes of fair use:

- Criticism,

- Comment,

- News reporting,

- Teaching,

- Scholarship, and

- Research.

These purposes are only examples of the purposes of copying that will be fair use. Other purposes may also lead to a finding of fair use. Note, however, that courts have historically been more willing to find fair use when the purpose of the copying can be read as being one of the listed purposes.

Whether a particular use of someone else's work is fair use is decided on a case-by-case basis. There is no one thing that will lead a court to find fair use. Instead, courts look at a variety of factors, including:

- *The purpose of the copying.* Was the copying for one of the purposes listed as examples? If so, courts are more inclined to find fair use.

- *The degree of transformation.* Copying is more likely to be considered fair use if it was to create a new work, with a new expression, meaning, or message, rather than just duplicating another work.

- *The nature of the copyrighted work.* If the copyrighted work is a work of non-fiction, it is easier to make fair use of its contents (factual information).

Example: A rap group did a cover version of a well-known "golden oldie." Their cover added some lyrics that changed the tone of the song from a romantic ballad to a more cynical view of relationships. The Supreme Court held that the cover version created a new work that commented on the old, and could therefore be fair use. *Campbell v. Acuff-Rose Music,* 510 U.S. 569 (1994).

- *The relative amount taken.* Contrary to what you may have heard, there is no ratio, no fraction, and no maximum number of words that will guarantee that a particular use is still fair. Instead, the test is whether the amount taken was reasonable in relation to the purpose of the copying. Take no more of another work than is necessary.

- *The effect on the potential market for the original.* Copying is less likely to be fair use if it harms, or could harm, the market for the original. This question also looks at the harm to the market for derivative works. The court will want to determine whether the copier's use would replace or preempt the demand for the original.

Fair use is a defense to an infringement action. As with any defense to a legal claim, the party who claims it must be prepared to prove it to the satisfaction of the court or the jury. Cases that discuss fair use are excellent guidance for future situations, but it is important to bear in mind that every case is different, and there could be factors in any given situation that change the outcome.

TRADEMARK:
Something that is used to identify the source or origin of goods. Some of the things that may be a trademark include words, sounds, symbols, devices, logos, or phrases.

II. Trademark

Trademark and copyright are two entirely different things. While copyright protects creative expression in a work, **trademark** (or **servicemark**) is the way a business protects its brand by showing the source of the goods (or, in the case of servicemarks, services). For purposes of this discussion, references to "trademarks" will also imply a reference to "servicemarks."

Trademarks also do not have the same lengthy heritage as copyrights. The U.S. Constitution does not contain an explicit authorization for Congress to enact a trademark law. The first federal trademark law, the Trademark Act of 1870, stated that It was enacted pursuant to the power of Congress to legislate patents and copyrights. That law was struck down as unconstitutional in *The Trade Mark Cases,* 100 U.S. 82 (1879). A different trademark law, based on the power of Congress to regulate interstate commerce, was enacted in 1881 and amended substantially in 1902. The present trademark law, known as the Lanham Act, was enacted in 1946.

Trademarks serve three main functions:

- Protecting consumers from confusion about brands of products,

- Protecting the interest a business has in its goodwill, and

- Preserving honesty and fair dealing in commerce.

All three of these purposes are important. Protecting consumers from confusion is, however, the standard used when protecting a trademark from infringement. Infringement occurs when a person creates a "likelihood of confusion" regarding the source or origin of goods or services.

> State laws also provide trademark protection, either through statutory enactments, or through common-law principles. State-level trademarks are less expensive than a federal trademark, but the protection is limited to the state of registration.

Note that the standard is "likelihood." Actual confusion is not required to show infringement, but infringement will not be found if there is only a vague, theoretical possibility of confusion. Courts will consider many factors, but the overall idea is to determine if a reasonable consumer is likely to be confused.

A trademark can be almost anything. The main requirement for a trademark is that it be "distinctive." That means that it must distinguish goods from those coming from another source. A distinctive mark may not be too similar to another mark, and the distinction must be a real distinction, not a possibility or potentiality. This requirement points to an important difference between trademarks and other forms of intellectual property: the holder must use the mark in commerce to obtain rights. No other form of intellectual property has this requirement.

Examples of things that have been trademarks include:

- Words ("Xerox") or word strings,
- Slogans ("Float like a butterfly, sting like a bee"),
- Surnames ("Ford"),
- Letters or initials ("IBM"),
- Numbers ("4711"),
- Domain name ("Amazon.com"),
- Device (orange tab on pants),
- Shape (Coca Cola's bottle),
- Sign (golden arches),
- Non-functional product design or packaging (a round thermostat), or
- Color scheme.

Trademarks are distinctive to different degrees. While some marks may be distinctive when applied to any product, others will only be distinctive in some situations. The different levels of distinctiveness are:

Fanciful. A fanciful mark is one that is completely made up, and has no relation to any real thing. The brand "Xerox" is an example of a fanciful mark. There is no such thing as a "Xerox." Fanciful marks are inherently distinctive.

Arbitrary. An arbitrary mark is a real word that has no relation to its product. For example, apples have nothing to do with computers, so they are an arbitrary mark.

Suggestive. A suggestive mark calls to mind some aspect or quality of the product, but it requires some imagination. The name "Irish Spring" for soap asks you to make the asso- ciation between your image of springtime in Ireland and a bar of soap.

GENERIC MARKS NOT PROTECTED
Abercrombie & Fitch Co. v. Hunting World, Inc.
(Clothing Retailer) v. (Competitor)
537 F.2d 4 (2d Cir. 1999)

INSTANT FACTS:
Abercrombie & Fitch (P) claimed that Hunting World (D) infringed its trademark "Safari."

BLACK LETTER RULE:
In ascending order of the degree of protection given to a mark, the categories of trademarks are generic, descriptive, suggestive, and arbitrary or fanciful.

FACTS:
Abercrombie & Fitch's (A&F) (P) advertised and promoted products identified with its mark "Safari." The mark was used on clothing, hats, and shoes. Hunting World (D) operated a competing store near A&F's (P) main store. Hunting World (D) sold sporting apparel, including hats and shoes. Some of this apparel was identified by the use of the term "Safari" alone, or by expressions such as "Minisafari" and "Safariland."

A&F (P) sued Hunting World for trademark infringement. Hunting World (D) claimed that "safari" is an ordinary, common, descriptive, geographic, and generic word and was not eligible for protection as a trademark. Hunting World (D) asked the court to cancel all of A&F's (P) registrations that used the word "Safari" on the ground that A&F (P) had fraudulently failed to disclose the true nature of the term to the PTO. The district court entered judgment for Hunting World (D), saying that the term "Safari" was merely descriptive. The court also cancelled the registrations of all of A&F's (P) marks that used the word "Safari."

ISSUE:
Was the "Safari" mark merely descriptive?

DECISION AND RATIONALE:
(Friendly, J.) No. In ascending order of the degree of protection given to a mark, the categories of trademarks are generic, descriptive, suggestive, and arbitrary or fanciful. The distinctions between these categories are not always clear. A term that is in one category for a particular product may be in a different one for another. A term may shift categories through different usage through time, because a term may have one meaning to one group of users and a different one to others, or because the same term might be put to different uses for a single product.

A generic term is one that refers, or is understood to refer, to the genus of which the particular product is a species. A generic mark is not entitled to trademark protection. Applied to specific types of clothing, "Safari" has become a generic term. "Minisafari" may be used for a smaller brim hat. "Safari" has not become a generic term for boots or shoes. It is either "suggestive" or "merely descriptive." It is a valid trademark even if "merely descriptive" since it has become incontestable under the trademark laws. The trial court's cancellation of the "Safari" marks for some clothing is upheld. The remainder of the court's judgment is reversed.

ANALYSIS:
This case, which dates from the years A&F (P) was primarily a retailer of high-end outdoors equipment. It is the leading case that sets out the hierarchy of trademarks: generic, descriptive, suggestive, arbitrary, and fanciful. That hierarchy is commonly referred to as the "Abercrombie & Fitch hierarchy."

QUESTION FOR DISCUSSION:
At a later date, A&F trademarked the term "casual luxury." Where would you place that trademark on the hierarchy?

Descriptive. A descriptive mark says something directly about the product, or about the function of a product. No imagination is required to understand it, such as U-Haul Trucks. A descriptive mark is not regarded as distinctive, unless there is proof of a **secondary meaning** (a special meaning that attaches to a mark through use and advertising).

Generic. A generic mark is nothing more than the name of the product. It is not distinctive, and cannot be used as a trademark. Some generic marks, such as "laundromat," or "T.V. dinner," started as trademarks, but became generic.

SECONDARY MEANING:

A special meaning that attaches to a descriptive mark through use and advertising.

While most trademarks are identifying the manufacturer or seller of a product, there are some that are meant to identify some aspect of a product other than its source. A **certification mark** tells the consumer something about the product that is not necessarily unique to that product. It could say that a product comes from a certain place ("Florida orange juice"), or that it meets certain quality standards ("UL Listed"). It may also say that the product was produced under certain conditions ("Fair Trade" coffee). A **collective mark** is a mark that is used to identify a business as a member of a group, such as a trade association.

Different Marks

Two symbols are used to show that a mark is a trademark: TM, and ®. The two marks should not be confused, as there are important differences between them.

The capital letter "R" in a circle (®, called a "racol") shows that a trademark is registered with the U.S. Patent and Trademark Office (PTO). Registration means that the mark has passed an inspection, and meets the legal requirements for a trademark (including distinctiveness). A registered mark is also **incontestable** for five years after the registration date.

Using the racol for an unregistered mark is considered false advertising. If registration is applied for, the PTO could refuse registration, based on the unlawful use of the symbol.

"TM" means that a mark is not registered with the PTO, but is still claimed as a trademark. It may be unregistered because it does not meet the legal requirement that a mark be used in commerce before it can be registered. An unregistered mark does not get the same legal protection as a registered mark. The owner of an unregistered mark may claim common law protection for her mark. She may also be able to make a claim under state unfair trade practices or consumer protection laws for the unauthorized use of her mark.

The TM symbol may also be used if a mark is registered under state law, instead of federal law. State registration of a trademark does not protect a mark beyond the borders of the state.

It also does not make a mark eligible for protection under international law.

CERTIFICATION MARK:

A type of trademark that certifies some characteristic of a product, such as the place of origin, method of manufacture, quality, or material.

COLLECTIVE MARK:

A type of trademark that shows membership in a group, or that identifies the goods or services offered by the members of the group.

INCONTESTABLE:

A trademark that is immune from legal challenge to its validity.

An "intent to use" registration may be filed before the mark is actually used. The requirements for that registration are mostly the same as regular registration, except for showing that the mark has been used. Intent to use registration is optional.

Service Marks

A trademark is something that is used to identify the source or origin of goods. If a business is a seller or supplier of services, it would not use a trademark. Instead, it uses a service mark. A service mark is a mark that identifies the source or origin of services. For example, in 1996, the New York Times Company registered "All the News That's Fit to Print" as a service mark for "computer services, namely, providing databases featuring general news and information."

Service marks are subject to the same rules for registration and distinctiveness as trademarks.

Trademark Registration

Trademark protection is not automatic. A mark gets protection under federal law as a trademark only after it is registered. Registration of a trademark is also not automatic. The registration requirements are more stringent than those for copyright, and registration will be denied if a particular mark has unacceptable content.

Before registering, or even using, a trademark it is a good idea to conduct a search. The search will tell you if anyone else is using the same, or similar, mark. If someone else is using the same mark, you may still be able to register it for use with a different product. This is a good first step for both legal and business reasons. From the legal standpoint, the PTO will not register your mark if it is too much like another mark. Doing your own search before using the mark is no guarantee that the PTO will agree that your mark is distinct, but it can give you warning if there are in fact similar marks in use. From a business standpoint, it only makes sense that you would want to avoid using a mark that is too similar to one used by someone else.

If you are satisfied that the mark you want to use is distinctive, the next step is to start using the mark. Make note of the date the mark was first used in commerce. This is when you would use the "TM" designation, although it is not legally required. There is no minimum amount of time that a mark has to be used before an application is filed. The mark must be shown to have been used in interstate commerce, which basically means that the mark has been used in commercial transactions. The mark should be attached to the goods being provided. If you are registering a service mark, the mark should appear in any promotional or advertising materials.

The next step is to submit your application to the PTO, along with the filing fee. Applications may be done online. The application must include a specimen of how the mark is being used. The specimen is not just a drawing or diagram. It is often a tag or label, or a photograph that shows the mark on packaging. The mark must be shown on or in direct connection with the goods. For services, the specimen would be showing the mark in advertisements or promotional materials.

Once the application is submitted, it is first reviewed to make sure all of the requirements for an application are met (that is, all of the spaces on the application are filled in and the filing fee has been paid). If the minimum filing requirements are met, the application is assigned a serial number and forwarded to an examiner. The examiner reviews the application to decide if the mark meets the substantive legal standards for registering a trademark. The review will look at marks that have already been registered, as well as applications for registration. General business and news services will also be reviewed, all for the purpose of determining whether the mark is distinct from any mark currently in use, or that may be registered in the near future. This examination may take several months to complete. If the examiner decides that the mark should not be registered, the PTO issues an **office action** explaining the reasons for refusal. The office action gives the applicant a chance to respond, and possibly fix any deficiencies. The person applying for the trademark must respond to the office action within six months. If she does not, the application is declared abandoned.

If the refusal is based on technical requirements in the application, the PTO may informally advise the applicant of what she needs to do in order to bring the application up to the proper standards. An application may, however, be denied on substantive grounds. Substantive grounds for denying registration include:

> **Example:**   In 2015, the USPTO determined that there was no likelihood of confusion between Smart Ones® and Smart Balance® frozen meals. Although both marks used the word "smart," the USPTO decided that part of the mark was a descriptive term and therefore weak (as opposed to a fanciful or arbitrary term). The other halves of the marks (Ones and Balance) were different enough in form and in concept to remove the possibility of serious confusion. Even though the marks both referred to frozen meals, they were permitted to co-exist.

Example: In 2014, the USPTO cancelled the Washington Redskins' football team's trademarks on the grounds of offensiveness under contemporary standards. The USPTO determined that the issue of offense should focus on the described group rather than to the population as a whole. The ruling stated that "a preponderance of evidence that a substantial amount of Native Americans found the term Redskins to be disparaging when used in connection with professional football" was the relevant factor over "differing opinions" in the larger community. The team pursued an appeal that is pending as of this writing.

OFFICE ACTION:
An examiner's communication with the applicant for a trademark patent, usually giving reasons why the application is denied.

- *Likelihood of confusion.* The examiner does a search of existing trademarks and applications for registration to decide whether the marks are similar, and to related goods or services. The similarity could be visual, or it could be that the words in a mark sound alike. A mark does not have to be identical to another one for the registration to be refused. Similarly, a mark may be distinct from another, identical mark used in a different context. The same word may be used for different types of products, produced by different manufacturers.

- *Merely descriptive.* A mark that is merely descriptive just tells about some aspect of the product. A descriptive mark could still be registered if the applicant proves that a secondary meaning has been attached to the mark.

- *Deceptively descriptive.* This is a descriptive mark that is false. The quality or characteristic it describes is not associated with the product.

- *Geographically descriptive or misdescriptive.* This is a mark that has no significance as anything other than a geographic location. As with a descriptive mark, registration is allowed if a secondary meaning is shown.

- *Surname.* A family name cannot be registered as a trademark without proof of a secondary meaning.

- *Ornamentation.* Decoration on a product that does not serve to identify the product does not qualify as a trademark.

- *Immoral or scandalous matter.* This may include matter that is offensive or vulgar, according to contemporary standards. It is not necessarily obscene matter.

The objection that a mark is "merely descriptive" may be overcome by a showing that the mark has a secondary meaning. A secondary meaning is a descriptive mark that is distinct because the public has come to associate with a single product, or a product from only one source. A descriptive mark could be a name of a person, or a geographic place name. Colors that do not relate to the function of a product, or that are not required by some other law, such as pink for fiberglass building insulation, may be a descriptive mark in this context. Proof that a mark has a secondary meaning can take many forms. Surveys of consumers of the type of product allegedly associated with the mark may be used. Proof that the mark has been widely marketed, or that the mark has been used exclusively by one producer of goods, will also tend to show a secondary meaning.

If the examiner does not object to the application, or if the objections are corrected, the mark is approved for publication in the "Official Gazette," a weekly publication of the PTO. After publication, anyone who believes he may be damaged by the registration of the mark may file an opposition. This allows the PTO to consider objections to registration that may have been overlooked, or that were not apparent at the time of the original application. An opposition will result in a hearing before the Trademark Trial and Appeal Board.

If there is no opposition filed, or the opposition is unsuccessful, the mark is registered. The applicant receives a certificate of registration. The registration is for ten years, and may be renewed for additional ten-year periods. There is no limit to the number of times trademark registration may be renewed. In theory, a properly registered and renewed trademark could last forever, if the holder wanted to continue to use it commercially.

Trade Dress

A trademark is an identifiable thing. We can point to a slogan in an advertisement or a brand

> In the case of *Two Pesos, Inc. v. Taco Cabana, Inc.,* 505 U.S. 763 (1992), the Supreme Court held that the building design of a fast-food chain was protected trade dress. Taco Cabana's restaurants had a Mexican décor, described as "a festive eating atmosphere having interior dining and patio areas decorated with artifacts, bright colors, paintings and murals." Two Pesos had restaurant décor that was described as similar, but there was no claim that it was identical. Taco Cabana's trade dress was held inherently distinctive, and so was protected by trademark law even without proof that the dress had a secondary meaning. Do you perceive any issues with the trade dress as described that the Supreme Court may have missed?

Example: A bakery claimed that its design of a small apple pie was trade dress. The court held that a single piece of dough folded around fruit filling was functional, and not trade dress. *Sweet Street Desserts, Inc., v. Chudleigh's Ltd.,* 119 U.S.P.Q. 2d 1641(3d Cir. 2016).

name and know that it is a trademark. Many products, however, are identifiable by more than just a single word or image. There is an overall visual look and feel to the product that identifies it. That look and feel is called "trade dress."

Trade dress is the total image of a product. At one time, the term referred only to packaging. Now, the term has been expanded to include the size or shape of a product, its color or color combinations, the texture, and graphics. Trade dress may even include a flavor or taste.

A product's trade dress may be registered, just as a trademark is registered. In order to be registered, trade dress must be distinctive. Except for product packaging, most trade dress is not inherently distinctive. This is true even though the design is very unusual, such as a cocktail shaker shaped like a penguin. In order to be protected, the applicant for registration will have to show that dress that is not inherently distinctive has a secondary meaning associating it with a product. Consumers must be able to identify a product by the trade dress.

A product's look and feel may not be registered if it is merely functional. In this context, "functional" means that a feature is essential to the use or purpose of the product, or if it affects the cost or quality of the article. A seller of t-shirts might be able to claim that the color red is a part of her trade dress. A manufacturer of portable gasoline cans would not, since the red color is required for gasoline storage and therefore relates to the function of the product. The elements claimed to make up trade dress may serve no purpose other than identifying a product.

Although trade dress may be registered with the PTO, and acquire the same protection as a trademark, registration is not necessary for legal protection of a design. A suit may be brought against a person who copies a design or packaging. The suit would be brought on the grounds that the copying is likely to cause confusion among consumers.

Dilution

In the late 19th century, amateur photography was a newly-popular hobby. The hobby was dominated by the Eastman Kodak Company. Kodak sold almost all of the film and cameras on the market, so in all likelihood, a family photograph was taken with a Kodak camera, using Kodak film.

Kodak built a lot of goodwill and customer loyalty for itself. In 1897, an enterprising bicycle manufacturer decided to take advantage of that goodwill. He started making and selling "Kodak Bicycles." Since Eastman Kodak was not in the bicycle business, it was thought that this would not infringe on their trademark. There was no

> **Example:** A seafood wholesaler's use of the slogan "The Other Red Meat" to describe its salmon was held likely to dilute the slogan "The Other White Meat," used to describe pork. *National Pork Board v. Supreme Lobster & Seafood Co.*, 96 U.S.P.Q. 2d 1479 (T.T.A.B. 2010).

question that the use of "Kodak" to sell bicycles did not cause confusion among consumers, since the Eastman Kodak Company did not sell bicycles. The bicycles did not infringe, but it was dilution of the trademark. The court issued an injunction against making or selling Kodak Bicycles.

Trademark dilution is not trademark infringement. It is not necessary to show that there is a likelihood of confusion to bring an action for dilution. While the owner of any trademark may bring an action for infringement, dilution applies only to "famous" marks.

FIRST AMENDMENT MAY DEFEAT TRADEMARK CLAIMS.

Mattel, Inc. v. Walking Mountain Productions
(Toy Company) v. (Artist)
353 F. 3d 792 (9th Cir. 2003)

INSTANT FACTS:
Walking Mountain (D) sold photographs of a toy made by Mattel (P) in unusual situations, and Mattel (P) claimed trademark infringement.

BLACK LETTER RULE:
First Amendment concerns trump a trademark owner's right to control public discourse a mark has a meaning beyond its source-identifying function.

FACTS:
Walking Mountain (D) developed a series of 78 photographs that depicted Barbie dolls manufactured by Mattel (P) in various absurd and often sexualized positions. The word "Barbie" was used in some of the titles of the works. The photographs generally showed one or more nude Barbie dolls juxtaposed with vintage kitchen appliances. Walking Mountain (D) said that the photographs were an attempt to "critique [ ] the objectification of women associated with [Barbie], and . . . [to] lambast . . . the conventional beauty myth and the societal acceptance of women as objects because this is what Barbie embodies." Mattel (P) claimed trademark infringement. The district court entered judgment for Walking Mountain (D).

ISSUE:
Was the use of the Barbie dolls in the photographs trademark infringement?

DECISION AND RATIONALE:
(Pregerson, J.) No. First Amendment concerns trump a trademark owner's right to control public discourse a mark has a meaning beyond its source-identifying function. The purpose of trademark protection is to avoid confusion in marketplace, so consumers are not duped into buying a product they mistakenly believe is sponsored by a trademark owner. Walking Mountain's (D) use Mattel's (D) mark was relevant to Walking Mountain's (D) artistic work, and Walking Mountain (D) did not explicitly mislead as to Mattel's (P) sponsorship of the work. The public interest in free and artistic expression greatly outweighed Mattel's (P) concerns about potential consumer confusion.

Walking Mountain's (D) use of Mattel's (P) trade dress in parody photographs was noninfringing, nominative fair use. The trade dress was a necessary point of reference for Walking Mountain's (D) work, and only so much of the trade dress as was reasonably necessary was use. There was nothing to suggest Mattel's (P) sponsorship of the work. Affirmed.

ANALYSIS:
The irony of this case is that Mattel (P) may have been too successful with its mark. "Barbie" or "Barbie doll" has become such a common term that a reminder of its original product-identifying function is necessary.

QUESTION FOR DISCUSSION:
What business strategies other than intellectual property lawsuits may help companies protect their product's image?

Dilution will be found if the use of a mark is likely to:

- Blur or weaken the connection made in consumer's mind between the famous mark and the products or services it identifies, or

- Tarnish the famous mark, by using it in connection with inferior products, or by using it in an unwholesome or unsavory manner, such as in connection with sex or illegal drugs.

A mark may dilute another even if it is not identical or substantially similar to the famous mark. The two marks must only be sufficiently similar that consumers "conjure up" the famous mark when they see the second mark.

It is not necessary to prove economic damages in order to bring a successful dilution lawsuit.

Protecting Trademarks

Once a trademark is issued, it is up to the owner of the mark to protect it. The PTO is not an enforcement agency, so it is up to the trademark owner to enforce her rights in the mark. Trademark protection is an ongoing job. It must be done continuously and consistently.

The first step in protecting a trademark is to use it, and use it properly. A trademark registration will be cancelled if the mark does not continue to be used in commerce. Proper use includes spelling it properly, if it is a word, and always using the racol next to the mark. A trademark is a description, so it should always be used as an adjective, not a noun. The mark describes the thing. It is not the thing itself.

The second step is to monitor any use of the mark by third parties. If their usage of the mark is improper, it is appropriate to inform them that it is a registered trademark, and must be used appropriately. A trademark may be lost if third parties are allowed to use it improperly, so continuous monitoring is essential.

If these two methods of protecting a trademark are unsuccessful, a lawsuit may be necessary. A lawsuit to protect a trademark may be brought against a defendant who is acting in a way that is "likely to cause confusion, or to cause mistake, regarding the source, affiliation, connection, or sponsorship" of goods or services. This rule is generally expressed by the shorter term "likelihood of confusion."

Example: "Band-Aid" is a registered trademark. The advertising and promotional material for the product always refers to "Band-Aid Brand Adhesive Bandages."

Example: A magazine article reminiscing about life in a town in the 1960s mentions buying a "smooth cone" at a local establishment of that name. The president of Smooth Cone, Inc., writes to the magazine reminding it that "Smooth Cone" is a trademark, and must always be capitalized.

SAYING THE NAME OF A TRADEMARK IS NOT INFRINGEMENT.

New Kids on the Block v. News America Publishing, Inc.
(Boy Band) v. (Newspaper Publisher)
971 F.2d 302 (9th Cir. 1992)

INSTANT FACTS:
New Kids on the Block (NKB) (P) alleged that a newspaper's poll on the popularity of NKB (P) violated their trademark.

BLACK LETTER RULE:
Trademark fair use prevents a trademark owner from taking a descriptive term for exclusive use and preventing others from accurately describing the characteristics of the owner's product.

FACTS:
The New Kids on the Block (NKB) (P) were a popular musical group in the early 1990s. News America (D), the proprietor of two newspapers of national circulation, conducted separate polls of their readers. The polls sought an answer to a pressing question: Which one of the New Kids (P) was the most popular? NKB (P) claimed that the newspaper poll infringed on their trademark. The district court entered judgment for News America (D).

ISSUE:
Did the newspaper poll infringe on NKB's (P) trademark?

DECISION AND RATIONALE:
(Kozinski, J.) No. Trademark fair use prevents a trademark owner from taking a descriptive term for exclusive use and preventing others from accurately describing the characteristics of the owner's product. When someone other than the owner uses a trademark to describe the product of the owner, rather than the user's, the user is entitled to nominative fair use defense. In order for the defense to apply, the product or service in question must be one that is not really identifiable without the use of trademark, and only so much of the mark as is reasonably necessary to identify the product is used. There can be nothing to suggest sponsorship or endorsement by trademark holder.

There was nothing false or misleading about News America's (D) use of NKB's (P) mark. News America (D) referred to the trademark only as needed to identify the NKB (P) as the subject of the polls. Nothing suggested joint sponsorship or endorsement by the NKB (P). News America (D) was entitled to the nominative fair use defense to the infringement action. Affirmed.

ANALYSIS:
It is difficult to speak of popular entertainers without using their trademarks. In this case, the court noted that NKB's (P) trademark was on more than 500 products or services. The court referred to the situation as a "multi-media publicity blitzkrieg."

QUESTIONS FOR DISCUSSION:
Suppose a comedian with a controversial reputation started mentioning a product in his routines. What steps could the product's maker take to avoid a negative connotation for the product?

Why do you suppose that NKB brought this suit?

Genericide

"Genericide" refers to the process by which a trademark becomes the generic name for a product. The trademark no longer identifies goods as coming from one particular source. An example is "linoleum," the first trademark to become generic. A trademark owner may become so successful at promoting a product that other, similar products are not regarded as distinct.

The inquiry into whether a mark is generic has two parts:

- What is the genus of the goods or services at issue; and

- Is the term understood by the relevant public primarily as referring to the genus of goods or services?

The "genus" refers to the type of product. In the case of *Princeton Vanguard, LLC, v. Frito-Lay North America,* 786 F. 3d 960 (Fed. Cir. 2015), the product involved was called "Pretzel Crisps." The court agreed that the correct genus of the product was "pretzels," or "pretzel crackers."

The question of how the term is understood looks at how the mark as a whole is perceived. Evidence regarding this perception may come from any competent source. Dictionaries, newspapers, and other publications may be consulted. Consumer surveys are a standard method of proving what the perception is.

A trademark owner protects her trademark from becoming generic by using the mark properly, and by policing how the mark is used by others. A registered trademark should always be accompanied by a racol. It is important to remember that a trademark describes where a product comes from, so it should be used as an adjective, and not a noun. Thus, while it may sound stilted to hear a person on a television commercial ask for a "Kleenex brand tissue," that is the way of asking for the product that acknowledges the trademarks involved. Other steps to protect a mark include distinguishing it by capitalizing it, if appropriate, and by using it consistently in the same form as it was registered (not abbreviating it or shortening it).

Trademark owners can take preventive steps from having a mark become generic when the mark starts to be used as a generic term. Many manufacturers have resorted to extensive public advertising campaigns to reinforce in the public's mind the fact that a term that is starting to become generic is not the name of the genus of the product. For example, at one time, "Xerox" was often used as a synonym for both the noun and verb "photocopy." Attendees at meetings were handed "Xerox copies" of documents. A secretary's boss might have told him to "Xerox this for me," or "make a Xerox of this." The Xerox Corporation responded with an advertising campaign: "You can't Xerox a Xerox on a Xerox. But we don't mind at all if you copy a copy on a Xerox® copier." The campaign was successful, and it is far less common to hear of someone "Xeroxing" something than it was in the past.

> Most writing on the subject uses the full term "trademark fair use," to distinguish it from the more familiar type of fair use in copyright cases.

A mark that becomes generic is deemed abandoned. Once a mark has been deemed abandoned, it is possible that it could become a protected mark again. Some courts have allowed the "recapture" of a generic mark. A mark that has become generic can be recaptured by using a term consistently to market and advertise products. In 1896, the U.S. Supreme Court held that the term "Singer" had become the generic term for a certain type of sewing machine.

> **Example:**
> Describing the flavor of a beverage as "sweet-tart" was classic fair use, and did not infringe on the trademark of the candy "SweeTarts." "Sweet" and "tart" were being used by the beverage manufacturer as descriptive terms. *Sunmark, Inc. v. Ocean Spray Cranberries, Inc.*, 64 F. 3d 1055 (7th Cir. 1995).

> **Example:**
> The defendant in a trademark infringement case used the phrase "all in ONE" on a catalog. The plaintiff company had separately registered "ALL-IN-ONE" as a trademark. The court held that there was no infringement because the phrase was used for its descriptive, everyday meaning, and not to identify the source or origin of goods. *Marketquest Group, Inc. v. Bic Corp.*, 2015 WL 1757766 (S.D. Cal. 2015).

> **Example:**
> Toni operates an auto repair shop. On her webpage, she includes the statement that "We specialize in servicing late-model Volkswagens." There is no Volkswagen logo on the page, and Toni does not say that she is an "official" Volkswagen repair shop. Toni's use of the mark "Volkswagen" is nominative fair use.

Singer Mfg. Co. v. June Mfg. Co., 163 U.S. 169 (1896). Nearly sixty years later, the Fifth Circuit Court of Appeals held that the Singer Company had recaptured the mark by using the name on goods the company produced, and by advertising the goods continuously, and widely. The court found that Singer had done enough to change the public's perception of the term, and allowed it to reclaim the mark as its own. *Singer Mfg. Co. v. Briley*, 207 F. 2d 519 (5th Cir. 1953).

Recapture is a lengthy process, and it should be noted that not all courts have accepted that it can be effectively accomplished.

Fair Use

Fair use is a defense to a trademark infringement action. Trademark fair use lets a person use someone else's mark in some circumstances without liability for infringement, if certain conditions are met. Trademark fair use works differently from fair use in a copyright infringement action, largely because trademarks and copyrights protect different interests.

There are two types of trademark fair use. The first is "classic" fair use. Classic fair use is found when a descriptive trademark is used to describe the goods or services of another. The use must be done in good faith, and must not create a likelihood of confusion. Classic fair use comes into play when a trademark can have a descriptive meaning. It protects the use of common meanings of ordinary words.

The other type of trademark fair use is "nominative" fair use. Nominative fair use is when a trademark is used to refer to the goods or services of the trademark owner. Nominative fair use cannot imply any endorsement or sponsorship by the trademark holder. The use must be accurate, and not misleading. There must be no easier way to refer to the owner of the products. No more of the trademark than is necessary to identify the owner may be used (for example, a name may be used, but probably not a logo). The use must not create a likelihood of confusion.

III. Patents

Patents give protection to inventions. They prevent anyone else from making, selling, importing, or using the patented invention. While copyright protects the expression of an idea, a patent protects the functional item that comes from an idea.

A patent is a government-granted monopoly. If the invention meets certain legal criteria, a patent lets the patent holder, for a limited period of time, prevent anyone else from using her invention. In exchange for that monopoly, the inventor discloses the invention, and how it works, to the public.

ABSTRACT IDEAS MAY NOT BE PATENTED.

O'Reilly v. Morse
(Inventor) v. (Inventor of the Telegraph)
56 U.S. 62 (1854)

INSTANT FACTS:
Morse (P) received patents for his invention of the telegraph, and also received a patent on any method of transmitting messages electronically.

BLACK LETTER RULE:
Abstract ideas are not eligible for patent protection.

FACTS:
Morse (P) received patents for his invention of the telegraph. One of his claims was not limited to "specific machinery or parts of machinery." Instead, the claim was for "[t]he use of the motive power of the electric or galvanic current, which I call electro-magnetism, however developed for marking or printing intelligible characters, signs, or letters, at any distances." O'Reilly (D) claimed that this claim was too broad. The trial court agreed.

ISSUE:
Was Morse's (P) claim too broad?

DECISION AND RATIONALE:
(Taney, C.J.) Yes. Abstract ideas are not eligible for patent protection. Morse (P) did not discover that the electric or galvanic current will always print at a distance, no matter what may be the form of the machinery or mechanical contrivances through which it passes. Other persons may discover and disclose to the public other ways to use electromagnetic force to transmit messages. These other ways may be cheaper or work better. In effect, Morse (P) claims an exclusive right to use a manner and process which he has not described and that he has not invented. His claim is too broad, and not warranted by law. Affirmed.

ANALYSIS:
A patent is granted only for an invention that implements an idea. The general idea furthered by an invention, no matter how novel, does not receive protection. It should be noted that there were several other inventors who claimed to have invented telegraphy at around the same time, but the courts upheld Morse's (P) claim to be first.

QUESTIONS FOR DISCUSSION:
What type of intellectual property protection would Morse Code be entitled to?

Does the requirement that a patent implement an idea short-change innovators with useful concepts but no resources to put those concepts into practice?

U.S. Patent number 1 was issued in 1790 to Samuel Hopkins of Philadelphia. His invention was a process for making potash, an ingredient of fertilizer.

Patent protection is not automatic. An application must be approved after it is examined to see if the invention meets the legal qualifications for a patent. A patent is in force for 20 years after the application was filed, even though it may take two years or more to approve the application. Once the patent expires, the public is free to use the invention without the permission of the inventor.

Certain things are not patentable. Naturally occurring things, abstract ideas, and mathematical formulas are not subject to patents, even though these things may have commercial value. These "basic tools of scientific and technical work" are not available for patent.

Patent Requirements

In order to receive a patent, an invention must be new, useful, and non-obvious. *New* means that the invention was not patented, described

Example: John and Charles discovered that hot lead would form into a seamless mass when pressure was applied. By making some minor adjustments to an existing patented machine, this principle could be used to manufacture a better lead pipe. Allowing the new use to receive a patent would be tantamount to allowing a patent on the scientific principle discovered by John and Charles, so no patent could be issued. *Le Roy v. Tatham,* 55 U.S. (14 How.) 156 (1852).

Example: Rob invents a hat that is equipped with small propellers that spin when the wearer blinks. His invention is useful, for patent application purposes. His friend Teresa designs a perpetual motion machine that is supposed to power respirators. Her "invention" is not useful, because it cannot work.

> **Example:** Cayden receives a patent for a new type of juice extractor that has three speeds: high, medium, and low. Liam buys an extractor, and modifies it so that it has four speeds: high, medium high, medium low, and low. Liam cannot get a patent on his modified extractor because it is an obvious modification.

in a printed publication, in public use, on sale, available to the public, or described in another patent application. A new use for an old invention cannot result in a new patent.

Useful is another way of saying that the invention will actually function, and is not just a hypothetical idea. The bar for an invention being "useful" is a low one. "Useful" is just a requirement that the must produce some identifiable benefit, and be capable of use. There is no requirement that it accomplish some practical or profitable end. An invention for something purely recreational, or solely for amusement, may be considered "useful." Useful means only that the invention will in fact function.

Non-obvious means that an invention would not have been obvious to a person with ordinary skill in the general field of the invention. An invention is not non-obvious if it is just a trivial or obvious modification of the state of the art.

There are three types of patents: design patents, utility patents, and plant patents.

Design Patents

Design patents are for the ornamentation or decoration of a manufactured product. The patent is not for a stand-alone invention or creation. A design patent can only cover something that is affixed to another object. It may also be the design of the article itself (a toy figurine, for example). The distinction between design and utility patents is that a design patent is for how something looks, or for how it is ornamented. A utility patent is for how something works.

> **Example:** In 1982, U.S. Patent D265754 S was issued for "ornamental design for a toy figure." The toy represented Yoda from the *Star Wars* series of films.

> **Example:** Until a 2013 Supreme Court decision, portions of naturally occurring DNA could be patented. Myriad Genetics developed a process for identifying breast cancer genes based on isolated DNA material. The Court focused on the fact that the DNA occurred naturally, and held that just isolating a portion of DNA does not make that portion patentable. As a result of this decision, synthetic DNA is still patentable, but human DNA is not. *Association for Molecular Pathology v. Myriad Genetics, Inc.*, 569 U.S. ___ (2013).

HUMAN MATERIAL IS PATENTABLE.

Diamond v. Chakrabarty
(Commissioner of Patents and Trademarks) v. (Microbiologist)
447 U.S. 303 (1980)

CHIEF JUSTICE BURGER delivered the opinion of the Court.

We granted certiorari to determine whether a live, human-made micro-organism is patentable subject matter under 35 U.S.C. 101.

[...]

In 1972, respondent Chakrabarty, a microbiologist, filed a patent application, assigned to the General Electric Co. The application asserted 36 claims related to Chakrabarty's invention of "a bacterium from the genus Pseudomonas containing therein at least two stable energy-generating plasmids, each of said plasmids providing a separate hydrocarbon degradative pathway." This human-made, genetically engineered bacterium is capable of breaking down multiple components of crude oil. Because of this property, which is possessed by no naturally occurring bacteria, Chakrabarty's invention is believed to have significant value for the treatment of oil spills.

Chakrabarty's patent claims were of three types: first, process claims for the method of producing the bacteria; second, claims for an inoculum comprised of a carrier material floating on water, such as straw, and the new bacteria; and third, claims to the bacteria themselves. The patent examiner allowed the claims falling into the first two categories, but rejected claims for the bacteria. His decision rested on two grounds: (1) that micro-organisms are "products of nature," and (2) that as living things they are not patentable subject matter under 35 U.S.C. 101.

Chakrabarty appealed the rejection of these claims to the Patent Office Board of Appeals, and the Board affirmed the examiner on the second ground. Relying on the legislative history of the 1930 Plant Patent Act, in which Congress extended patent protection to certain asexually reproduced plants, the Board concluded that 101 was not intended to cover living things such as these laboratory created micro-organisms.

The Court of Customs and Patent Appeals, by a divided vote, reversed on the authority of its prior decision in *In re Bergy*, 563 F.2d 1031, 1038 (1977), which held that "the fact that microorganisms . . . are alive . . . [is] without legal significance" for purposes of the patent law . . .

[...]

The question before us in this case is a narrow one of statutory interpretation requiring us to construe 35 U.S.C. 101, which provides:

"Whoever invents or discovers any new and useful process, machine, manufacture, or composition of matter, or any new and useful improvement thereof, may obtain a patent therefor, subject to the conditions and requirements of this title."

Specifically, we must determine whether respondent's micro-organism constitutes a "manufacture" or "composition of matter" within the meaning of the statute.

[...]

In cases of statutory construction we begin, of course, with the language of the statute. And "unless otherwise defined, words will be interpreted as taking their ordinary, contemporary, common meaning." We have also cautioned that courts "should not read into the patent laws limitations and conditions which the legislature has not expressed."

Guided by these canons of construction, this Court has read the term "manufacture" in 101 in accordance with its dictionary definition to mean "the production of articles for use from raw or prepared materials by giving to these materials new forms, qualities, properties, or combinations, whether by hand-labor or by machinery." Similarly, "composition of matter" has been construed consistent with its common usage to include "all compositions of two or more substances and . . . all composite articles, whether they be the results of chemical union, or of mechanical mixture, or whether they be gases, fluids, powders or solids." In choosing such expansive terms as "manufacture" and "composition of matter," modified by the comprehensive "any," Congress plainly contemplated that the patent laws would be given wide scope.

The relevant legislative history also supports a broad construction. The Patent Act of 1793, authored by Thomas Jefferson, defined statutory subject matter as "any new and useful art, machine, manufacture, or composition of matter, or any new or useful improvement [thereof]." Act of Feb. 21, 1793, 1, 1 Stat. 319. The Act embodied Jefferson's philosophy that "ingenuity should receive a liberal encouragement." 5 Writings of Thomas Jefferson 75-76 (Washington ed. 1871). *See Graham v. John Deere Co.,* 383 U.S. 1, 7 -10 (1966). Subsequent patent statutes in 1836, 1870 and 1874 employed this same broad language. In 1952, when the patent laws were recodified, Congress replaced the word "art" with "process," but otherwise left Jefferson's language intact. The Committee Reports accompanying the 1952 Act inform us that Congress intended statutory subject matter to "include anything under the sun that is made by man." S. Rep. No. 1979, 82d Cong., 2d Sess., 5 (1952); H. R. Rep. No. 1923, 82d Cong., 2d Sess., 6 (1952).

This is not to suggest that 101 has no limits or that it embraces every discovery. The laws of nature, physical phenomena, and abstract ideas have been held not patentable. Thus, a new mineral discovered in the earth or a new plant found in the wild is not patentable subject matter. Likewise, Einstein could not patent his celebrated law that E=mc2; nor could Newton have patented the law of gravity. Such discoveries are "manifestations of . . . nature, free to all men and reserved exclusively to none."

Judged in this light, respondent's micro-organism plainly qualifies as patentable subject matter. His claim is not to a hitherto unknown natural phenomenon, but to a nonnaturally occurring manufacture or composition of matter - a product of human ingenuity "having a distinctive name, character [and] use." Hartranft v. Wiegmann, 121 U.S. 609, 615 (1887) . . .

[...]

Here, . . . the patentee has produced a new bacterium with markedly different characteristics from any found in nature and one having the potential for significant utility. His discovery is not nature's handiwork, but his own; accordingly it is patentable subject matter under 101.

[...]

The petitioner's second argument is that micro-organisms cannot qualify as patentable subject matter until Congress expressly authorizes such protection. His position rests on the fact that genetic technology was unforeseen when Congress enacted 101. From this it is argued that resolution of the patentability of inventions such as respondent's should be left to Congress . . .

It is, of course, correct that Congress, not the courts, must define the limits of patentability; but it is equally true that once Congress has spoken it is "the province and duty of the judicial department to say what the law is." Marbury v. Madison, 1 Cranch 137, 177 (1803). Congress has performed its constitutional role in defining patentable subject matter in 101; we perform ours in construing the language Congress has employed. In so doing, our obligation is to take statutes as we find them, guided, if ambiguity appears, by the legislative history and statutory purpose. Here, we perceive no ambiguity. The subject-matter provisions of the patent law have been cast in broad terms to fulfill the constitutional and statutory goal of promoting "the Progress of Science and the useful Arts" with all that means for the social and economic benefits envisioned by Jefferson. Broad general language is not necessarily ambiguous when congressional objectives require broad terms.

[...]

To buttress his argument, the petitioner, with the support of amicus, points to grave risks that may be generated by research endeavors such as respondent's. The briefs present a gruesome parade of horribles. Scientists, among them Nobel laureates, are quoted suggesting that genetic research may pose a serious threat to the human race, or, at the very least, that the dangers are far too substantial to permit such research to proceed apace at this time. We are told that genetic research and related technological developments may spread pollution and disease, that it may result in a loss of genetic diversity, and that its practice may tend to depreciate the value of human life. These arguments are forcefully, even passionately, presented; they remind us that, at times, human ingenuity seems unable to control fully the forces it creates - that, with Hamlet, it is sometimes better "to bear those ills we have than fly to others that we know not of."

It is argued that this Court should weigh these potential hazards in considering whether respondent's invention is patentable subject matter under 101. We disagree. The grant or denial of patents on micro-organisms is not likely to put an end to genetic research or to its attendant risks. The large amount of research that has already occurred when no researcher had sure knowledge that patent protection would be available suggests that legislative or judicial fiat as to patentability will not deter the scientific mind from probing into the unknown any more than Canute could command the tides. Whether respondent's claims are patentable may determine whether research efforts are accelerated by the hope of reward or slowed by want of incentives, but that is all.

What is more important is that we are without competence to entertain these arguments - either to brush them aside as fantasies generated by fear of the unknown, or to act on them. The choice we are urged to make is a matter of high policy for resolution within the legislative process after the kind of investigation, examination, and study that legislative bodies can provide and courts cannot. That process involves the balancing of competing values and interests, which in our democratic system is the business of elected representatives. Whatever their validity, the contentions now pressed on us should be addressed to the political branches of the Government, the Congress and the Executive, and not to the courts.

[...]

Accordingly, the judgment of the Court of Customs and Patent Appeals is

Affirmed.

MR. JUSTICE BRENNAN, with whom MR. JUSTICE WHITE, MR. JUSTICE MARSHALL, and MR. JUSTICE POWELL join, dissenting.

I agree with the Court that the question before us is a narrow one. Neither the future of scientific research, nor even the ability of respondent Chakrabarty to reap some monopoly profits from his pioneering work, is at stake. Patents on the processes by which he has produced and employed the new living organism are not contested. The only question we need decide is whether Congress, exercising its authority under Art. I, 8, of the Constitution, intended that he be able to secure a monopoly on the living organism itself, no matter how produced or how used. Because I believe the Court has misread the applicable legislation, I dissent.

[...]

In this case . . . we do not confront a complete legislative vacuum. The sweeping language of the Patent Act of 1793, as re-enacted in 1952, is not the last pronouncement Congress has made in this area. In 1930 Congress enacted the Plant Patent Act affording patent protection to developers of certain asexually reproduced plants. In 1970 Congress enacted the Plant Variety Protection Act to extend protection to certain new plant varieties capable of sexual reproduction. Thus, we are not dealing - as the Court would have it - with the routine problem of "unanticipated inventions." In these two Acts Congress has addressed the general problem of patenting animate inventions and has chosen carefully limited language granting protection to some kinds of discoveries, but specifically excluding others. These Acts strongly evidence a congressional limitation that excludes bacteria from patentability.

[...]

[Footnotes and citations omitted]

QUESTIONS FOR DISCUSSION:

1. Do you agree with the majority opinion or with the dissent? Why?

2. A patent on these types of materials offers an economic motive to pursue research. Some cases have looked at cells that were derived from human patients. In your view, is this the appropriate approach? What rights do the donors and families of biological material have? For further reading, please see *The Immortal Life of Henrietta Lacks* by Rebecca Skloot (Broadway Books 2011).

A patentable design may not be functional. This means that the design cannot be dictated by the function of the article. The design of a chair, for example, may be patented, but only if the design does not add a new function.

Design patents are also subject to the requirements that they be non-obvious and novel. A well-known person, or a naturally occurring object does not meet these requirements.

Utility Patents

A utility patent is the most common type of patent. According to the PTO, 90% of all patent applications are applications for a utility patent. Utility patents probably are what most people think of when they hear the word "patent."

Utility patents are issued for new inventions. The patent grants the holder the sole right to manufacture and sell the invention. The invention may be for a:

- New machine or manufactured device,

- Non-obvious improvement of an existing invention,

- Composition of matter, such as a new medication,

- Synthetic genetic sequence, or

- Business method.

Utility patents apply to the use or function of an invention. The appearance or decoration would be covered by a design patent.

Plant Patents

An inventor or discoverer of a new plant species may be awarded a plant patent. The new plant must be reproduced only asexually, and cannot be a tuber (such as a potato), or a plant that can be found in an uncultivated state. If the plant were "discovered," it must have been discovered in a cultivated area.

The term "plant" for purposes of patent law is given its ordinary meaning. There are limitations on what plants are eligible for a plant patent:

- A patent may be grated for a living plant organism that has a single, genetic makeup or genotype, and which can only be duplicated through asexual reproduction; that is, making an exact genetic copy of the plant through some means other than genetic seeds.

- Sports (a part of a plant, such as a bud or branch, that has a different form or structure from the rest of the plant), mutants, or hybrids are eligible.

- Algae and large (macro) fungi are patentable as plants, but bacteria are not.

Asexual reproduction must be proven. The PTO requires proof of reproduction to show that the plant is a stable, or continuing, species. The reproduction must have been performed with sufficient time to allow the evaluation of the offspring of the plant, to determine whether the new specimens retain the genetic characteristics of the original plant.

PATENT EXHAUSTION DOES NOT ALLOW COPYING.

Bowman v. Monsanto Co.
(Farmer) v. (Seed Maker)
133 S. Ct. 1761 (2013)

INSTANT FACTS:
Bowman (D) planted the progeny of soybeans grown from Monsanto's (P) patented seeds without permission.

BLACK LETTER RULE:
The doctrine of patent exhaustion says that the purchaser of a patented article is entitled to use or resell that article, but not to make copies of it.

FACTS:
Monsanto (P) invented and patented soybean seeds that were genetically altered to allow them to survive exposure to a certain herbicide. The seeds were sold subject to a licensing agreement that permitted farmers to plant the seed in one, and only one, growing season. Farmers may not save any of the harvested soybeans for replanting. Bowman (D) purchased soybeans intended for consumption from a grain elevator, planted them and treated them plants with herbicide. The plants without Monsanto's (P) genetic alteration died. Bowman (D) harvested the resulting soybeans that contained the alteration and saved some of these harvested seeds to use in the next season. Monsanto (P) sued Bowman (D) for patent infringement. Bowman raised the defense of patent exhaustion. The court entered judgment for Monsanto (P).

ISSUE:
Was Bowman's (D) planting of the soybeans protected by patent exhaustion?

DECISION AND RATIONALE:
(Kagan, J.) No. The doctrine of patent exhaustion says that the purchaser of a patented article is entitled to use or resell that article, but not to make copies of it. The doctrine restricts a patent holder's rights only as to the particular article" It does not affect the patent holder's ability to prevent a buyer from making new copies of the patented item. If the purchaser of that article could make and sell endless copies, the patent would effectively protect the invention for just a single sale. The exhaustion doctrine does not enable Bowman (D) to make additional patented soybeans without Monsanto's (P) permission, either express or implied. Affirmed.

ANALYSIS:
The Court was careful to note that its opinion applied only to the particular situation before it. Justice Kagan noted that self-replicating products "are becoming ever more prevalent, complex, and diverse." How patent exhaustion would apply to such an invention is not addressed in this opinion.

QUESTIONS FOR DISCUSSION:
What are your thoughts on how self-replicating products will be protected by patent in future?

A later Supreme Court decision reached an unexpected conclusion. *Impression Products, Inc. v. Lexmark International, Inc.*, 581 U.S. ___ (2017), dealt with whether patent law could restrict the re-sale of printer cartridges by companies that re-fill such cartridges with less expensive ink. The Court held that the exhaustion doctrine precluded Lexmark's patent-based claim against the re-sellers. As a matter of policy, should patent law be used so as to restrict an owner's use of an item? Is an expansion of the first sale doctrine for copyrights warranted?

A plant patent will only be granted if the invented or discovered plant meets the basis requirement that the plant be novel, non-obvious, and useful (that is, it must actually exist). Seeds, genes, and other newly invented elements of plant life may be patented, but the patent applied for would be a utility patent.

Securing a Patent

A patent is issued after an application is submitted by the inventor or someone to whom the invention has been assigned. The application must then be approved by the Patent and Trademark Office. The application process can be both complicated and time consuming.

> Patent searches are complex. While most experts say it is best to hire a professional to do the search, many also say that an inventor should do her own preliminary search as well. This will allow an inventor to familiarize herself with the prior art in the field.

The first step in applying for a patent is to do a patent search. Remember that patents are granted only for new inventions. A search is done to make sure that an invention is in fact novel. Patent searches may be done by the inventor, or she may hire a professional patent search firm. If an invention has already been disclosed to the public, it is not considered. A patent search should include foreign patents and technical literature, as well as existing patents and applications. A search done before an application is submitted will not be conclusive, as the PTO does its own search. It should, however, give the inventor a better idea as to whether someone else has come up with the same invention.

Patent searches are not mandatory. They can also be costly. Many inventors try to trim the costs involved in a patent application by skipping the examination. They may reason that there is no penalty for filing an application that

is ultimately rejected, provided that there is no willfully false statement in the application. This reasoning ignores the time and effort that goes into even an unsuccessful application. It also ignores the possibility that a patent search done early on, when the invention is first being developed, can save the time and expense of finalizing an invention that cannot be patented.

Patent Application

Once the search is completed, the application for a patent is submitted. The application consists of three parts: the written application, the claim, and the fee. The written application itself also contains three parts:

The specification and claim. A specification is a written description of the invention, and of the manner and process for manufacturing it. The specification has to be clear enough that a person with ordinary skill in the field that the invention is to work in could make and use it. The specification includes the following:

- The title of the invention;

- A cross-reference to related applications;

- A statement regarding federally-funded research, if the invention was developed under a federal contract, or if the research used to develop the invention was funded by a government grant;

- The background of the invention, emphasizing how the invention differs from the existing state of the art, and pointing out necessary improvements supplied by the invention;

- A summary of the invention, discussing topics such as the advantages of the invention, and how it fills the needs described in the background;

- Description of the drawings of the invention, if drawings are included; and

- A detailed description of the invention. This will include a general explanation of the invention and of how to use it. The description may also set out specific examples that can serve to illustrate how the invention may be used.

The specification also includes an abstract or summary.

A drawing. Drawings are required whenever the nature of the invention is such that a drawing is required to understand it. The drawing must show every feature of the invention (it is for this reason that multiple drawings, showing all different views of an invention, are often required). It must be clear enough to show how the invention will work. Photographs are allowed only if they are the only practicable method for illustrating the invention.

The oath or declaration. The oath states that the inventor swears that he "believes himself to be the original and first inventor of the process, machine, manufacture, or composition of matter, or improvement thereof, for which he solicits a patent; and shall state of what country he is a citizen."

The fee for filing a patent is in addition to the fee for the search and examination done by the PTO. The fees charged vary according to the type of patent application, and according to the size and income of the entity filing the application. As of 2017, the basic filing fee for just a utility patent application is $280, or $140 for a small entity (a non-profit organization, or an entity that has fewer than 500 employees), or $70 for a micro entity (a "small entity" that has not been named on more than four prior applications, and that has a gross income not more than three times the median household income). Search fees range from $30 for a design patent search for a micro entity, to $600 for a utility patent search for a non-small or micro entity. Examination fees range from $115 to $720.

After a complete application is submitted, it is referred to a PTO examiner. The examiner reviews the application to see if the invention meets the requirements for being patented. If the examiner decides that the invention does not meet the requirements for a patentable invention, she will explain her reasons. The inventor may either correct the application, or try to convince the examiner to change her mind. If the examiner does not change her mind, or corrections to the application are not made, the application is rejected. The inventor has the right to appeal.

If the application is granted, a patent is issued. A patent is good for 20 years after the date the application was filed (not the date the patent was issued). The inventor or owner of the patent must pay maintenance fees. A fee is paid 3 ½ years, 7 ½ years, and 11 ½ years after issuance. If the fee is not paid, the patent is abandoned and no longer exists for the invention. Maintenance fees increase for each successive fee, with the maximum fee as of 2017 set at $7,400. Many patents are abandoned because the maintenance fee is more than the value of the invention.

Protecting Patents

Protecting patents, like protecting copyrights or trademarks, is the responsibility of the owner. The PTO does not enforce patent rights. Instead, the owner of the patent must bring a patent infringement action in federal court.

A patent infringement action involves two steps: claim construction and comparison. The claims of an allegedly infringed patent are first reviewed to determine what the patent covers. Comparing the claims will involve examining the record created when the invention's patent application was considered. This examination will provide context for the claims, especially regarding the prior art. The two inventions are then directly compared. A patent is infringed if each and every element of one or more of an inventions claims is performed by the infringing device, or if or if the person accused of infringement actively encourages, sells, or offers to sell a component that leads to another person's infringement. If a patent infringement suit is successful, the damages may include royalties for the unauthorized use of the invention. The court may also order the payment of damages for lost profits, or price erosion.

Patent infringement is not the only reason a patent will need to be protected. Any person may request that a patent granted to another be re-examined. Such a request is based on the existence of a Subsequent New Question of Patentability (SNQ). An SNQ is established by an examination of prior patents and printed publications. The examination proves the existence of at least one new technological teaching affecting any claim of the patent that was not considered by the PTO in a prior proceeding involving the patent.

A re-examination could result in a patent being declared invalid. Note that there is a presumption that a patent granted by the PTO is valid.

IV. Trade Secrets

Copyrights, trademarks, and patents all protect different interests, but they share one thing in common: What they are protecting is public knowledge. A trademark is used in commerce, so will necessarily be seen by the public. The workings of an invention are included in the patent application and are also available for the public to inspect.

The lack of secrecy is one disadvantage of the three main forms of intellectual property. The other is that there are limits to the type of things that can be protected. These things still have value, but they do not fit into the categories of things that may be protected.

Information that is not to be disclosed to the public may be protected by the law of trade secrets. The Economic Espionage Act of 1996 criminalized some cases of theft or misappropriation of trade secrets. The theft or misappropriation of a trade secret is punishable by a fine of up to $500,000 per offense and a prison sentence of up to 15 years for individuals, or a fine of up to $10 million for an organization, if it is done intending to benefit a foreign government, instrumentality, or agent, or knowing that a foreign entity would benefit. The theft or misappropriation could include purchasing, receiving, or possessing a secret knowing that it was obtained without authorization. If the theft is of a trade secret that is related to or included in a product produced for or placed in interstate or foreign commerce, and is not done to benefit a foreign entity, but is done intending or knowing that the theft will injure any owner of that trade secret, the maximum sentence for an individual is a fine of $250,000, or imprisonment for not more than 10 years, or both. If an offense is committed by an organization, the maximum fine is $5 million.

Before 2016, trade secret protection was entirely a matter of state law. The Uniform Trade Secrets Act (UTSA), adopted by 48 states, was an effort to codify the existing common law regarding trade secrets, and the remedies for disclosing those secrets.

On May 11, 2016, President Obama signed into law the Defend Trade Secrets Act of 2016 (DTSA). The DTSA was effective immediately upon approval, and applies to all trade secret misappropriations occurring after that date. It makes trade secret protection a matter of federal law, but does not pre-empt state trade secret law. A lawsuit to protect trade secrets

> The UTSA does not explicitly include "intangible" information within the definition of a trade secret. Should intangible information be included? Why might it not be specifically provided for in the law?

could be brought in either state or federal court. In addition, unlike the UTSA, the DTSA does not pre-empt state common law tort remedies for misappropriating trade secrets.

The DTSA defines the term "trade secret" as information:

> In 2011, the only acknowledged copy of the recipe for Coca Cola was moved to a secure vault at the company's headquarters in Atlanta.

- That is secret, and

- That has economic value.

Further, the information that can be a trade secret includes information in any form, "whether

Example: The marketing department of a car company takes several weeks to prepare a report on highway miles driven by residents of each state. The report will be used to target advertising and marketing of cars, and will also be used to design new vehicles. The report is just a list of facts, so it cannot be copyrighted. It cannot be trademarked, because it is not being used to identify the source or origin of goods or services. It cannot be patented, because it is not an invention. But if it is kept secret at the company, the report is a trade secret that provides a competitive advantage.

tangible or intangible, stored, compiled, or memorialized physically, electronically, graphically, photographically, or in writing." The owner of the secret must have taken reasonable methods to preserve the secret.

The value of a trade secret is the competitive advantage that comes from knowing the information. If it is not known to others, then they obviously cannot use it. If a competitor would have to pay money to find or develop the information, it has economic value.

There is no limit on how long a trade secret can last. It may be a secret permanently. It may be revealed to the public at some time, as a new product that is kept secret until release. When it is revealed to the public, of course, it stops being a secret.

Protecting Trade Secrets

For information to be a legally protected trade secret, it is not enough that it not be generally known. The information must also be subject to reasonable efforts to maintain the secrecy. It is also not enough that the owner of the information wants it kept secret. The owner must take affirmative steps to keep it secret. These efforts can include non-disclosure agreements or strictly limiting the people who have access to the information.

The exact type of protection for trade secrets will vary, depending on the size of the company, and the nature of the secret. It may be sufficient to inform employees that they are not to disclose anything that goes on in the workplace. That blanket requirement does not, however, identify specific categories of information to be kept secret. It may be too broad to provide meaningful protection.

Confidentiality agreements with employees and non-employees are the most common means of protecting trade secrets. It is especially important that these agreements set out clearly what information, or what types of information, will be considered secret. Warning labels can be placed on documents or presentations, and employees should get periodic reminders of their obligations to keep secrets.

Confidentiality agreements from non-employees who may be exposed to confidential information are especially important. Employees may be subject to a company-wide confidentiality policy, which may count as a "reasonable effort" to maintain secrecy in a given situation. Outsiders, such as potential customers or contractors, will not be covered by an internal company secrecy policy.

While confidentiality agreements are important, most companies that work to keep trade secrets

Example: A restaurant has a signature cocktail that it advertises heavily as its own special creation. Whenever the restaurant hires a new bartender, she is told that one of the conditions of her employment is that she never reveal the recipe for the cocktail. The recipe is subject to reasonable efforts to maintain secrecy.

have adopted policies and practices that supplement confidentiality agreements. These policies can include such basic, and seemingly obvious, measures as making office computers password-protected. Employees are also given training on the obligation to preserve trade secrets.

If a trade secret is improperly revealed, litigation may be necessary. Generally, the goal of trade secret litigation is to prevent or minimize further disclosure of the secret.

V.   Location of Use

The type and extent of protection intellectual property depends partly on where the property is created and used. The location of the property determines what law will be applied. The type of intellectual property will also indictate the type and extent of protection granted.

Extent of Protection

Intellectual property is protected under federal and state law, depending on what type of property it is. Federal protection is nationwide. State law protection extends only as far as the state in which the property is created or used.

Patents are creatures of federal law. Copyrights, since 1978, are also governed solely by federal law. Any state common-law copyright protection has, in effect, been abolished. Actions to protect patents and copyrights are brought in federal courts.

Trade secrets, on the other hand, are governed by state and federal law. While most state trade secret laws follow the same general pattern, every state sets its own limitations on the creation and use of trade secrets. For example, the usual definition of trade secret says that the secret must be the subject of "reasonable efforts" to keep it a secret. What is reasonable in a given context may vary in different states. Lawsuits to protect trade secrets have traditionally been brought in state courts, although there will often be the option of bringing an action in federal court as well. The authority of state courts to enforce their orders and judgments does not extend beyond the borders of the state.

Trademarks can be either federal or state matters. Every state has its own trademark law.

> There are some key differences between federal and state trade secret litigation. For example, in many state courts, including California, a plaintiff in a trade secret action must describe the trade secrets at issue with reasonable particularity before engaging in discovery regarding the misappropriation claim. In other states, while the secret must be described early in the lawsuit, there is no bar to conducting discovery before the identification is made.

Most of these laws are similar to the federal trademark law, but as with trade secrets, any action to enforce a state-granted trademark must be brought in state court. The authority to enforce orders or judgment in a state court trademark infringement action stops at the state's borders.

A trademark registered with the PTO receives nationwide protection. Actions to enforce or protect a federal trademark are brought in federal court. Although federal registration of a trademark is often more complex than state registration, it may be worth the trouble to get nationwide protection for a trademark.

International Protection

> **CONVENTION:**
> In international law, an agreement among several nations.

There is no such thing as "international" intellectual property. Every type of intellectual property is created and recognized by the laws of each nation. International law does, however, provide for the protection of intellectual property.

> The U.S. became a party to the Berne Convention on March 1, 1989, when the Berne Convention Implementation Act of 1988 was enacted.

International coordination of intellectual property rights is governed by a series of treaties, or **conventions**. These conventions offer certain advantages to the owners of intellectual property in member nations. In order to allow the owners to get these advantages, the intellectual property laws of member nations must meet certain requirements. There are three principal conventions that relate to intellectual property:

- The Berne Convention, which governs copyright,

- The Paris Convention for the Protection of Industrial Property, which governs trademarks and patents, and

- The Agreement on Trade-Related Aspects of Intellectual Property Rights (TRIPS), which provides an alternative enforcement mechanism.

The United States is a signatory to each of these three conventions. Signatories must conform their national laws to the terms provided in each of the conventions.

While intellectual property protections remain a creature of national law, the international treaties are useful for a number of reasons. Berne and TRIPS create minimum standards

> *Example:* Until a 2013 Supreme Court decision, portions of naturally occurring DNA could be patented. Myriad Genetics developed a process for identifying breast cancer genes based on isolated DNA material. The Court focused on the fact that the DNA occurred naturally, and held that just isolating a portion of DNA does not make that portion patentable. As a result of this decision, synthetic DNA is still patentable, but human DNA is not. *Association for Molecular Pathology v. Myriad Genetics, Inc.*, 569 U.S. ___ (2013).

of intellectual property protection for signatory nations. The Paris Convention establishes priority rights that make securing protection in other countries much easier.

TRIPS, which was agreed to in 1994, incorporates the Berne and Paris Conventions. A nation that is a part of TRIPS also agrees that it will adopt those two conventions. The incentive for joining TRIPS is that it is a condition for joining the World Trade Organization (WTO). A state that is a member of the WTO may trade with other member states with fewer barriers, such as high tariffs. Most of the world's largest economies are WTO members, so the prospect of trade with those countries is a strong reason to agree to TRIPS.

The Berne Convention requires the copyright laws of member states to conform to certain requirements. The most important provisions of the Berne Convention are:

- Equal treatment of works from other member states. For instance, a Canadian work distributed in the United States is entitled to the protection of U.S. copyright law.

- No formalities may be required for protection. Registration may not be required in order for a work to be copyright protected.

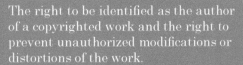
MORAL RIGHTS:
The right to be identified as the author of a copyrighted work and the right to prevent unauthorized modifications or distortions of the work.

- Fair use must be allowed.

- Copyright must last for a minimum of the life of the author plus 50 years. It may last longer, as it does in the United States and the European Union, but life plus 50 years is the minimum.

- **Moral rights** must be recognized. Moral rights are rights of an author of a copyrighted work that are recognized largely in European law. The rights are directed towards protecting the reputation of the author, and give the author the right to control what happens to their work.

The four principal moral rights are:

- Attribution, or the right to be identified publicly as the author of a work, and the right to prevent non-authors from claiming authorship;

- Integrity, or the right to prevent distortion, mutilation, or other modification of the work that would harm the author's reputation;

- Disclosure, meaning the sole right of the author to determine when a work is ready for display or publication; and

- Withdrawal, or the right to remove a work from circulation, upon payment of a fee.

Moral rights have not been fully adopted in the United States. The Visual Artists' Rights Act (VARA) grants the creators of fine art the rights of integrity and attribution. VARA has a limited application, in that it applies only to paintings, drawings, sculpture, prints, and still photographs produced for exhibition only and

MORAL RIGHTS ARE NOT RECOGNIZED UNDER U.S. LAW.

Gilliam v. American Broadcasting Companies, Inc.
(Writer) v. (Television Network)
538 F.2d 14 (2d Cir. 1980)

LUMBARD, Circuit Judge:

Plaintiffs, a group of British writers and performers known as "Monty Python," appeal from a denial by Judge Lasker in the Southern District of a preliminary injunction to restrain the American Broadcasting Company (ABC) from broadcasting edited versions of three separate programs originally written and performed by Monty Python for broadcast by the British Broadcasting Corporation (BBC). We agree with Judge Lasker that the appellants have demonstrated that the excising done for ABC impairs the integrity of the original work. We further find that the countervailing injuries that Judge Lasker found might have accrued to ABC as a result of an injunction at a prior date no longer exist. We therefore direct the issuance of a preliminary injunction by the district court.

Since its formation in 1969, the Monty Python group has gained popularity primarily through its thirty-minute television programs created for BBC as part of a comedy series entitled "Monty Python's Flying Circus." In accordance with an agreement between Monty Python and BBC, the group writes and delivers to BBC scripts for use in the television series. This scriptwriters' agreement recites in great detail the procedure to be followed when any alterations are to be made in the script prior to recording of the program.[2] The essence of this section of the agreement is that, while BBC retains final authority to make changes, appellants or their representatives exercise optimum control over the scripts consistent with BBC's authority and only minor changes may be made without prior consultation with the writers. Nothing in the scriptwriters' agreement entitles BBC to alter a program once it has been recorded. The agreement further provides that, subject to the terms therein, the group retains all rights in the script.

Under the agreement, BBC may license the transmission of recordings of the television programs in any overseas territory. The series has been broadcast in this country primarily on non-commercial public broadcasting television stations, although several of the programs have been broadcast on commercial stations in Texas and Nevada. In each instance, the thirty-minute programs have been broadcast as originally recorded and broadcast in England in their entirety and without commercial interruption.

In October 1973, Time-Life Films acquired the right to distribute in the United States certain BBC television programs, including the Monty Python series. Time-Life was permitted to edit the programs only "for insertion of commercials, applicable censorship or governmental . . . rules and regulations, and National Association of Broadcasters and time segment requirements." No similar clause was included in the scriptwriters' agreement between appellants and BBC. Prior to this time, ABC had sought to acquire the right to broadcast excerpts from various Monty Python programs in the spring of 1975, but the group rejected the proposal for such a disjoined format. Thereafter, in July 1975, ABC agreed with Time-Life to broadcast two ninety-minute specials each comprising three thirty-minute Monty Python programs that had not previously been shown in this country.

Correspondence between representatives of BBC and Monty Python reveals that these parties assumed that ABC would broadcast each of the Monty Python programs "in its entirety." On September 5, 1975, however, the group's British representative inquired of BBC how ABC planned to show the programs in their entirety if approximately 24 minutes of each 90 minute program were to be devoted to commercials. BBC replied on September 12, "we can only reassure you that ABC have decided to run the programmes 'back to back,' and that there is a firm undertaking not to segment them."

ABC broadcast the first of the specials on October 3, 1975. Appellants did not see a tape of the program until late November and were allegedly "appalled" at the discontinuity and "mutilation" that had resulted from the editing done by Time-Life for ABC. Twenty-four minutes of the original 90 minutes of recording had been omitted. Some of the editing had been done in order to make time for commercials; other material had been edited, according to ABC, because the original programs contained offensive or obscene matter.

In early December, Monty Python learned that ABC planned to broadcast the second special on December 26, 1975. The parties began negotiations concerning editing of that program and a delay of the broadcast until Monty Python could view it. These negotiations were futile, however, and on December 15 the group filed this action to enjoin the broadcast and for damages. . . .

Judge Lasker granted Monty Python's request for more limited relief by requiring ABC to broadcast a disclaimer during the December 26 special to the effect that the group dissociated itself from the program because of the editing. A panel of this court, however, granted a stay of that order until this appeal could be heard and permitted ABC to broadcast, at the beginning of the special, only the legend that the program had been edited by ABC. We heard argument on April 13 and, at that time, enjoined ABC from any further broadcast of edited Monty Python programs pending the decision of the court.

[. . .]

We then reach the question whether there is a likelihood that appellants will succeed on the merits. In concluding that there is a likelihood of infringement here, we rely especially on the fact that the editing was substantial, i. e., approximately 27 per cent of the original program was omitted, and the editing contravened contractual provisions that limited the right to edit Monty Python material. It should be emphasized that our discussion of these matters refers only to such facts as have been developed upon the hearing for a preliminary injunction. Modified or contrary findings may become appropriate after a plenary trial.

Judge Lasker denied the preliminary injunction in part because he was unsure of the ownership of the copyright in the recorded program. Appellants first contend that the question of ownership is irrelevant because the recorded program was merely a derivative work taken from the script in which they hold the uncontested copyright. Thus, even if BBC owned the copyright in the recorded program, its use of that work would be limited by the license granted to BBC by Monty Python for use of the underlying script. We agree.

[...]

It also seems likely that appellants will succeed on the theory that, regardless of the right ABC had to broadcast an edited program, the cuts made constituted an actionable mutilation of Monty Python's work. This cause of action, which seeks redress for deformation of an artist's work, finds its roots in the continental concept of droit moral, or moral right, which may generally be summarized as including the right of the artist to have his work attributed to him in the form in which he created it. American copyright law, as presently written, does not recognize moral rights or provide a cause of action for their violation, since the law seeks to vindicate the economic, rather than the personal, rights of authors. Nevertheless, the economic incentive for artistic and intellectual creation that serves as the foundation for American copyright law cannot be reconciled with the inability of artists to obtain relief for mutilation or misrepresentation of their work to the public on which the artists are financially dependent. Thus courts have long granted relief for misrepresentation of an artist's work by relying on theories outside the statutory law of copyright, such as contract law, or the tort of unfair competition. Although such decisions are clothed in terms of proprietary right in one's creation, they also properly vindicate the author's personal right to prevent the presentation of his work to the public in a distorted form.

Here, the appellants claim that the editing done for ABC mutilated the original work and that consequently the broadcast of those programs as the creation of Monty Python violated the Lanham Act s 43(a). This statute, the federal counterpart to state unfair competition laws, has been invoked to prevent misrepresentations that may injure plaintiff's business or personal reputation, even where no registered trademark is concerned. It is sufficient to violate the Act that a representation of a product, although technically true, creates a false impression of the product's origin.

These cases cannot be distinguished from the situation in which a television network broadcasts a program properly designated as having been written and performed by a group, but which has been edited, without the writer's consent, into a form that departs substantially from the original work. "To deform his work is to present him to the public as the creator of a work not his own, and thus makes him subject to criticism for work he has not done." In such a case, it is the writer or performer, rather than the network, who suffers the consequences of the mutilation, for the public will have only the final product by which to evaluate the work. Thus, an allegation that a defendant has presented to the public a "garbled," distorted version of plaintiff's work seeks to redress the very rights sought to be protected by the Lanham Act and should be recognized as stating a cause of action under that statute. . . .

During the hearing on the preliminary injunction, Judge Lasker viewed the edited version of the Monty Python program broadcast on December 26 and the original, unedited version. After hearing argument of this appeal, this panel also viewed and compared the two versions. We find that the truncated version at times omitted the climax of the skits to which appellants' rare brand of humor was leading and at other times deleted essential elements in the schematic development of a story line. We therefore agree with Judge Lasker's conclusion that the edited version broadcast by ABC impaired the integrity of appellants' work and represented to the public as the product of appellants what was actually a mere caricature of their talents. We believe that a valid cause of action for such distortion exists and that therefore a preliminary injunction may issue to prevent repetition of the broadcast prior to final determination of the issues.

[...]

For these reasons we direct that the district court issue the preliminary injunction sought by the appellants.

[Footnotes and citations omitted]

QUESTIONS FOR DISCUSSION:

What, if any, is the difference between an edited version of a filmed work and a derivative work?

Was it fair for the troup to assume that the works would be played in their entirety? Why or why not?

not for commercial or advertising purposes. The work must have been produced in an edition of 200 or fewer copies, signed and numbered by the author. In addition, California and New York have enacted laws giving visual artists some protection for moral rights. Some court decisions have also attempted to find moral rights in other existing U.S. laws.

> U.S. law does not provide for compulsory licensing for failure to work a patent. A patent will be cancelled if the maintenance fees are not paid.

The Paris Convention also sets out requirements that the laws of member states must follow. Those requirements include:

- *Independence of patents.* If one member state grants a patent, other members are not required to grant a patent. Refusal by one member to grant a patent does not obligate another member to refuse a patent for the same invention.

- *Right of priority.* If a patent or trademark application is filed in one member nation within a certain period of time after filing for protection in another, the application in the second nation is treated as if it had been filed on the same day as the first application. This gives the applicant priority over other applications for the same or similar mark or invention filed after the initial application, but before the second or subsequent applications.

- *Limits on compulsory licenses.* In some countries, a governmental authority has the authority to grant a license to use an invention if the owner of the patent does not "work" the invention sufficiently. The Paris Convention states that any compulsory license may be granted only if the request is filed within three years of the grating of the patent, or four years after the application. A compulsory license may not be granted if the patent holder has a legitimate reason to justify her inaction.

- *Trademark acceptance.* With some exceptions, a trademark registered in one member state must be accepted for registration in other member states.

- *Unfair competition laws.* Laws must provide for protection against unfair competition, or the false indication of the source of goods.

Both the Berne and Paris Conventions are administered by the World Intellectual Property Organization (WIPO), headquartered in Geneva, Switzerland.

VI. Protecting Intellectual Property

The owner of intellectual property is solely responsible for protecting that property. With limited exceptions, there is no law enforcement agency to prosecute the improper taking of intellectual property. It is up to the owner to deter or prevent that improper taking or use, and to pursue any wrongdoers.

Intellectual property has no physical existence. Except for trade secrets, it is also freely accessible to almost anyone. The objects protected by intellectual property are also easily duplicated. All of this presents special problems for the owner who tries to protect her property.

Revealing Information

Most intellectual property can be seen, if not used, by the public at large. That is just the nature of the beast. A trademark, for example, cannot identify a product unless it is attached to something that is being offered for sale.

The owner of intellectual property may still decide when that property is to be revealed to the public. Before that time, when the subject of the property is still being developed, it may be designated as a trade secret.

Confidentiality agreements with employees are the most common means of protecting trade secrets. These agreements should define what will be considered trade secrets. The trade secrets themselves should be safeguarded and revealed only to employees with confidentiality

Example: Earl is invited to bid on an advertising campaign for Heitor's limousine service. The campaign is to bring attention to a new fleet of specialty cars that will be made available. Before he shows Earl the details of the new service, Heitor requires him to sign an agreement that none of the information will be released until the advertising campaign starts.

agreements on a "need-to-know" basis. These employees should be reminded of their confidentiality obligation on a regular basis.

Non-employees are often allowed to learn confidential information. Confidentiality agreements should also be obtained from them. The non-employee's signature on a confidentiality agreement should be a condition of participating in whatever activity will or might bring that person into contact with the confidential information.

Every confidentiality agreement has at least three essential provisions:

- The definition of what will be regarded as confidential information, including what information is excluded from the definition;

- The obligations of the party who receives access to the confidential information; and

- The duration of the agreement.

The definitions can set out categories of information without being overly specific about the exact information covered. Too much specificity creates a risk that the information will be inadvertently disclosed in the agreement, or that the information can be deduced or pieced together from the description. If the limitation is too broad, it could include Information that is not legally regarded as a trade secret (such as, Information that has already been disclosed or that is generally known to the public). An example of a definition clause could read "Confidential Information includes all processes, testing results, surveys, and financial data regarding products not released for sale to the public. The term does not include data relating to products that have been offered for sale on or prior to the date of this agreement."

The party who receives confidential information is of course obligated to keep it confidential. An agreement might also require individual employees or contractors of the receiving party to sign confidentiality agreements.

The length of time an agreement will be in effect is a matter to be negotiated, depending on the purposes of the agreement. An employee who will learn a secret process or formula may be required to sign a lifetime confidentiality agreement. In some situations, a party may be barred from disclosure of a secret for a definite period, such as five years. Any time period should be long enough to allow the owner of the secret adequate time to profit economically from the continued secrecy.

Example: Grokster offered a peer-to-peer file sharing platform. The courts found that the primary use of Grokster (90%, by some estimates) was the unauthorized sharing and distribution of music and other files. Although Grokster did not do any of the copying itself, by offering the platform and not policing it for unlawful sharing, Grokster was indirectly infringing. *MGM Studios, Inc. v. Grokster, Ltd.,* 545 U.S. 913 (2005).

> **Example:** Independent vendors sold counterfeit recordings at a swap meet. The operator of the swap meet could be liable for vicarious infringement because he reserved the right to terminate vendors for any reason, and because he collected admission fees from customers, daily rental fees from vendors, and profited from concession stand sales and parking fees. *Fonovisa, Inc. v. Cherry Auction, Inc.*, 76 F.3d 259 (9th Cir. 1996).

Confidentiality agreements often include other provisions, such as an arbitration clause. It is also common for confidentiality agreements to contain a provision requiring the payment of the prevailing party's attorney's fees in the event of a dispute.

Standards for Infringement

Since each type of intellectual property protects something different, the standards for a finding that the owner's rights have been violated, or infringed, are different.

Copyright Infringement: Copyright infringement is usually defined as unauthorized copying of a protected work. This copying may be either direct or indirect. "Direct" means that the person named in the suit is the one doing the copying. "Indirect" is not actively copying, but it is doing something that assists another person's infringement.

There are two types of indirect infringement: contributory infringement, and vicarious infringement. Contributory infringement involves substantial participation in another person's infringement. This participation could be supplying a device that will let a person infringe, while promoting its use for copyright infringement. Contributory infringement also requires knowledge of the infringement. Vicarious infringement will be found when there is copyright infringement and the vicarious infringer benefits financially from the infringement, and was in a position to control the infringement.

Copying may be proven in a number of ways. There may be direct evidence of unauthorized copying, such as performing a song at a public event without getting permission first. Often, however, the proof of copying is indirect. Indirect proof (or circumstantial evidence) of copying is done by showing access to the copyrighted work, and a "substantial similarity" between the original work and the allegedly infringing work.

Access means that the alleged infringer had a reasonable opportunity to see or hear the original work. It does not mean a bare possibility that the infringer could have seen the work, or that it was theoretically possible. Access can be proven by showing that the original work was so widely distributed that it was likely the infringer knew about it. It can also be proven by showing that a third party connected with both the infringer and the author of the original had access. For example, access has been found when a composer's assistant sent copies of sheet music to a publisher who also published the work of the infringing songwriter. Finally, some courts have held that access may be inferred if the allegedly infringing work is so similar to the original that it is highly likely that the works were not created independently. In that situation, it must be shown that the two works are so similar as to negate any possibility of independent creation.

The definition of "substantial similarity" can be a hard one to nail down. If there has been verbatim copying, such as using a lengthy clip from a movie in another work, there is a substantial similarity if the clip was a "significant" clip from the earlier work. There is no clear definition for what a "significant" amount would be. This inquiry involves questions of fair use, so the amount that may be taken will depend on the purpose for which it is taken, as well as the potential effect on the market for the original work A clip from a popular television show inserted into an academic presentation on the development of contemporary fiction might be longer than a clip from the same show inserted into a mash-up for a music video.

If the copying were not verbatim, a substantial similarity may also be found if the overall look and feel of the first work were copied. Courts have developed several different tests for finding copying. The test that is used in any one case depends on the geographic area the case was brought in. The four tests are described as follows:

- *The "Ordinary Observer" test.* This test asks whether an ordinary observer would conclude that the alleged copy was appropriated from the original work. The question is whether the ordinary observer, unless he set out to detect the disparities, would be disposed to overlook the differences between the two works, and regard their aesthetic appeal as the same. In situations in which the copyrighted work contains protected and unprotected elements, the question is whether the ordinary observer, putting aside the unprotected elements, would still see a substantial similarity.

- *The "Extrinsic/Intrinsic" test.* This test asks two questions. The first question ("Extrinsic") is whether the two works are made up of similar elements, such as the theme of the work, the medium, or the materials used to put the work together. This part of the question is an objective analysis of the expression. Specific criteria are listed and analyzed to decide similarity at this stage. Expert testimony may be used to assist with the listing and comparison. Some courts have

Example: A costume store advertised for rental a costume called "Duffy the Dragon." Duffy was a purple "reptilian" costume. The court held that the substantial similarity between Duffy the Dragon and Barney the Dinosaur should be considered from the viewpoint of young children, the intended audience for both costumes. *Lyons Partnership, L.P. v. Morris Costumes, Inc.,* 243 F.3d 789 (4th Cir. 2001).

> **Example:** The word "Fender" is registered as a trademark by the Fender Musical Instruments Corporation, for products such as speakers, cell phone cases, and stringed musical instruments. The same word has been registered as a trademark by Jaguar Land Rover Ltd., for printed matter and toys. Although the word registered as a trademark is identical, the registration is for different types of products. The likelihood of confusion is small.

held that if there is strong proof of access, the amount of similarity required for a finding of infringement is lower. If there are similarities between the elements of the two works, the second question ("Intrinsic") looks at the reaction of the ordinary observer when the two works are compared. Expert testimony is not appropriate at this stage of the inquiry. The decision is a subjective one for the court or jury.

- *The "Abstraction/Filtration/Comparison" test.* The elements of the two works are analyzed in detail (abstraction). The non-copyrightable elements are taken out (filtration), and the remaining copyrightable elements are compared (comparison). This test is often referred to as the "discerning ordinary observer" test.

- *The "Intended Audience" test.* The court tries to compare the two works through the eyes of the intended audience (for example, children).

The defenses to an infringement action are limited. It is not a defense to show that the copyright owner sustained no harm, or even that the infringement was a good thing for her ("good exposure"). It is also not a defense to show that the copyright owner is not pursuing all infringers.

A defendant may prove that he did not have access to the work, or did not copy it. He may also show that his copying was fair use (see above). The defendant may also prove that the work was in the public domain.

Trademark Infringement: The test for trademark infringement is whether a defendant's actions are "likely to cause confusion, or to cause mistake, regarding the source, affiliation, connection, or sponsorship" of goods or services. The concern is not that two marks will be confused, but rather whether people will believe that the goods identified by the two marks come from the same source. This rule is generally expressed by the shorter term, "likelihood of confusion."

There is no litmus test for a likelihood of confusion. Actual confusion is not required, but if there is in fact evidence of confusion, that evidence will be used to show that there is such a likelihood. Some of the other evidence that is considered includes:

- *The similarity or dissimilarity of the marks.* The more closely two marks resemble each other, the more plausible is that there will be confusion.

> *Example:* A publisher did not act in bad faith in choosing the mark "O The Oprah Magazine" when the name of the magazine was associated with a prominent media personality, and the publisher did a trademark search and concluded that the title would not infringe on the trademark of "<<O>>" magazine. *Brockmeyer v. Hearst Corp.,* 248 F. Supp. 2d 281 (S.D.N.Y. 2003).

- *The similarity or dissimilarity of the goods involved.* If a similar mark is attached to two dissimilar products, there is less likelihood of confusion. This factor, along with the similarity or dissimilarity of the marks, is arguably the most significant factor. If two marks bear little resemblance to one another, it is less likely that buyers will think the goods identified by those marks are from the same seller. Similarly, different types of products are usually assumed to come from different manufacturers.

- *Trade channels.* How do the goods reach the consumer? If they are sold only through authorized sellers, there is less likelihood of confusion. Conversely, there is a greater likelihood of confusion when goods are sold in mass market retailers, where similar products from competing sellers are displayed in close proximity.

- *Conditions under which goods are sold.* Is the product usually an impulse buy, or is it an item that the average buyer will put a lot of thought into buying? If a product is the kind of thing that is just grabbed off of a retail display, consumers are making quick decisions, and not spending much time analyzing the marks. This could be evidence of a likelihood of confusion.

- *The relative strength of marks.* Are the marks inherently distinctive, or merely descriptive?

- *Fame of the marks.* If a mark is used only for a specialized, niche product, it is less likely to be confused with another type of product from another seller. A mark that is known only in a limited geographic area is less likely to be confused with one that has wider geographic range.

- *Intent of the alleged infringer.* It is possible to have a similar mark without intending to infringe on another owner's mark. Courts often consider intent when deciding if confusion is likely.

- *Likelihood of expansion.* If products are sold in different markets, there is less likelihood of confusion. If it is probable that one mark will be sold in the other market, the likelihood becomes stronger.

Note that identical marks are not necessarily infringing. The PTO shows 324 uses of the word "Catalina," registered to numerous different users, for products including bathing suits, software, and cookies.

Patent Infringement: A patent infringement action involves two steps: claim construction, and comparison.

Claim construction is the central part of a patent infringement lawsuit. It looks at what claims of the original patent are alleged to be infringed. The court tries to decide what the claim says that the invention is supposed to be.

Claims must be given their broadest reasonable interpretation. The first step in claim construction is consideration of the plain language of the claim. Terms in a claim are given the ordinary meaning a person skilled in the field of the patent would have given them at the time of the invention. If that is unclear, the court will look next at the patent specification. The specification may show that the patent holder gave some terms a special meaning. A possible meaning may also be disclaimed in the specification. Documents relating to the application for a patent (called the "prosecution history") may show how the inventor understood her invention.

If this evidence intrinsic to the patent application does not let the court understand the claim adequately, the court may look at other evidence. This extrinsic evidence includes evidence such as scientific and technical literature, or expert opinion. While extrinsic evidence is useful to the inquiry, most courts regard intrinsic evidence as more reliable. Intrinsic evidence relates to the specific patent at issue, while extrinsic evidence has a more general application. Extrinsic evidence is also often developed specifically for litigation.

The second step is comparison. The claims of the two inventions are compared. An invention infringes on the patent of another if it copies only one claim. The copying may be literal, meaning that every element of the claim is copied. Each and every element of the claim must be found in the infringing device. Copying may also be equivalent, meaning that the differences between the two would be regarded as insubstantial by a person skilled in the field. The equivalence is between elements in individual claims, not the invention as a whole.

There are two types of patent infringement: direct and indirect. *Direct infringement* is making, using, or selling a patented invention, or importing a patented invention into the U.S., without the permission of the owner of the patent. This type of infringement is strict liability, which means that the infringer may be held liable even if he did not have the intent to infringe on the patent.

Indirect infringement is either contributory infringement, or inducement. Both require a showing that the defendant knew of the existence of the patent. Contributory infringement is selling or importing into the U.S. a component of a patented invention without authorization when the only use of the component is in the patented product. The contributory infringer must have known that the component was either used to infringe the patent, or designed for infringing use. Inducement is shown when a person engaged in inducing or encouraging a third party to take actions that infringe on a patent, knowing that the induced acts comprise patent infringement. Both types of indirect infringement require proof that the patent was infringed.

Trade Secret Misappropriation: The DTSA defines misappropriation of a trade secret as:

"Patent trolling" is a pejorative firm, applied to litigants who purchase patents, often as a deep discount, without intending to manufacture or market the invention. The patent is used as the basis for infringement lawsuits that seek damages In excess of the actual value of the patent. A number of states have passed legislation, or taken administrative action, to fight patent trolls.

- Acquisition of a trade secret of another by a person who knows or has reason to know that the trade secret was acquired by improper means; or

- Disclosure or use of a trade secret of another without express or implied consent by a person who—

    - Used improper means to acquire knowledge of the trade secret; or

    - At the time of disclosure or use, knew or had reason to know that the trade secret was obtained from or through a person who used improper means to acquire the trade secret; or

    - Acquired under circumstances giving rise to a duty to maintain the secrecy or limit the use of the trade secret.

The term "improper means" includes theft, bribery, misrepresentation, breach, inducing a violation of a duty to maintain secrecy, or espionage. The term does not include reverse engineering or independent derivation, "or any other lawful means of acquisition."

Each act of taking, use, or disclosure of a trade secret is a separate misappropriation.

A "whistleblower" who reveals trade secret to a government agency to report a violation of the law is immune from liability under the DTSA.

Enforcing Intellectual Property

The remedies for improper use of the intellectual property of another include both money damages and injunctive relief against further infringement. The damages are to remedy the harm that has already been done. The injunction is to prevent the harm from continuing.

In a successful copyright infringement suit, the copyright owner may get an injunction against further infringement. The injunction may also include an order requiring destruction of any existing infringing materials, as well as destruction of the materials used to produce the infringing matter.

In addition to, or in place of, an injunction, a copyright owner may collect money damages. These damages may be the dollar amount of her actual loss, such as profits lost because of the infringement, or profits earned by the infringer. Instead of actual damages, the owner of an infringed copyright may elect to recover statutory damages. Statutory damages are set by the Copyright Act. They may be awarded without regard to any actual harm suffered. Statutory damages range from a low of $750 per infringement for innocent infringers, to a high of $30,000 per infringement. The amount to be awarded in a given case is an amount the court

LONG-TERM GOOD FAITH INFRINGER OF TRADEMARK MAY RECEIVE ADDITIONAL TIME TO COMPLY.

AMF, Inc. v. Sleekcraft Boats
(Boat Manufacturer) v. (Boat Manufacturer)
599 F.2d 341 (9th Cir. 1979)

J. BLAINE ANDERSON, Circuit Judge:

In this trademark infringement action, the district court, after a brief non-jury trial, found appellant AMF's trademark was valid, but not infringed, and denied AMF's request for injunctive relief.

AMF and appellee Nescher both manufacture recreational boats. AMF uses the mark Slickcraft, and Nescher uses Sleekcraft. The crux of this appeal is whether concurrent use of the two marks is likely to confuse the public. The district judge held that confusion was unlikely. We disagree and remand for entry of a limited injunction.

I. FACTS

AMF's predecessor used the name Slickcraft Boat Company from 1954 to 1969 when it became a division of AMF. The mark Slickcraft was federally registered on April 1, 1969, and has been continuously used since then as a trademark for this line of recreational boats.

Slickcraft boats are distributed and advertised nationally. AMF has authorized over one hundred retail outlets to sell the Slickcraft line. For the years 1966-1974, promotional expenditures for the Slickcraft line averaged approximately $200,000 annually. Gross sales for the same period approached $50,000,000.

After several years in the boat-building business, appellee Nescher organized a sole proprietorship, Nescher Boats, in 1962. This venture failed in 1967. In late 1968 Nescher began anew and adopted the name Sleekcraft. Since then Sleekcraft has been the Nescher trademark. The name Sleekcraft was selected without knowledge of appellant's use. After AMF notified him of the alleged trademark infringement, Nescher adopted a distinctive logo and added the identifying phrase "Boats by Nescher" on plaques affixed to the boat and in much of its advertising. The Sleekcraft mark still appears alone on some of appellee's stationery, signs, trucks, and advertisements.

The Sleekcraft venture succeeded. Expenditures for promotion increased from $6,800 in 1970 to $126,000 in 1974. Gross sales rose from $331,000 in 1970 to over $6,000,000 in 1975. Like AMF, Nescher sells his boats through authorized local dealers.

Slickcraft boats are advertised primarily in magazines of general circulation. Nescher advertises primarily in publications for boat racing enthusiasts. Both parties exhibit their product line at boat shows, sometimes the same show.

[...]

When the goods produced by the alleged infringer compete for sales with those of the trademark owner, infringement usually will be found if the marks are sufficiently similar that confusion can be expected. When the goods are related, but not competitive, several other factors are added to the calculus. If the goods are totally unrelated, there can be no infringement because confusion is unlikely.

AMF contends these boat lines are competitive. Both lines are comprised of sporty, fiberglass boats often used for water skiing; the sizes of the boats are similar as are the prices. Nescher contends his boats are not competitive with Slickcraft boats because his are true high performance boats intended for racing enthusiasts.

The district court found that although there was some overlap in potential customers for the two product lines, the boats "appeal to separate sub-markets." Slickcraft boats are for general family recreation, and Sleekcraft boats are for persons who want high speed recreation; thus, the district court concluded, competition between the lines is negligible . . . [A]fter careful review of all the exhibits introduced at trial, we are convinced the district court's finding was warranted by the evidence.

[...]

Accordingly, we must consider all the relevant circumstances in assessing the likelihood of confusion. [...]

In determining whether confusion between related goods is likely, the following factors are relevant:

1. strength of the mark;

2. proximity of the goods;

3. similarity of the marks;

4. evidence of actual confusion;

5. marketing channels used;

6. type of goods and the degree of care likely to be exercised by the purchaser;

7. defendant's intent in selecting the mark; and

8. likelihood of expansion of the product lines.

See, e. g., Sleeper Lounge Co. v. Bell Manufacturing Co., 253 F.2d at 722; Restatement of Torts s 731 (1938). We discuss each serially.

1. Strength of the mark

A strong mark is inherently distinctive, for example, an arbitrary or fanciful mark; it will be afforded the widest ambit of protection from infringing uses . . . A descriptive mark tells something about the product; it will be protected only when secondary meaning is shown. In between lie suggestive marks which subtly connote something about the products. Although less distinctive than an arbitrary or fanciful mark and therefore a comparatively weak mark, a suggestive mark will be protected without proof of secondary meaning.

Slickcraft is, AMF asserts, a fanciful mark and therefore entitled to wide protection. This assertion is incorrect. The issue, as we view it, is whether Slickcraft is descriptive or suggestive of appellant's boats.

The district court did not make any explicit finding regarding the strength of appellant's mark. Implicitly, however, the findings indicate the mark was viewed as suggestive: proof of secondary meaning was not offered or discussed, and yet the district court concluded that the mark Slickcraft was valid and deserved some protection from potential infringement.

Whether Slickcraft is suggestive or descriptive is a close question. The line separating the two is uncertain; extrapolating the line from precedent would be impossible.

Although the distinction between descriptive and suggestive marks may be inarticulable, several criteria offer guidance. The primary criterion is "the imaginativeness involved in the suggestion," that is, how immediate and direct is the thought process from the mark to the particular product. From the word Slickcraft one might readily conjure up the image of appellant's boats, yet a number of other images might also follow. A secondary criterion is whether granting the trademark owner a limited monopoly will in fact inhibit legitimate use of the mark by other sellers. There is no evidence here that others have used or desire to use Slickcraft in describing their goods. Another criterion is whether the mark is actually viewed by the public as an indication of the product's origin or as a self-serving description of it. We think buyers probably will understand that Slickcraft is a trademark, particularly since it is generally used in conjunction with the mark AMF. Based on the above criteria and our reading of the district court's findings, we hold that Slickcraft is a suggestive mark when applied to boats.

2. Proximity of the goods

For related goods, the danger presented is that the public will mistakenly assume there is an association between the producers of the related goods, though no such association exists. The more likely the public is to make such an association, the less similarity in the marks is requisite to a finding of likelihood of confusion. Thus, less similarity between the marks will suffice when the goods are complementary, the products are sold to the same class of purchasers, or the goods are similar in use and function.

Although these product lines are non-competing, they are extremely close in use and function. In fact, their uses overlap. Both are for recreational boating on bays and lakes. Both are designed for water skiing and speedy cruises. Their functional features, for the most part, are also similar: fiberglass bodies, outboard motors, and open seating for a handful of people. Although the Sleek-craft boat is for higher speed recreation and its refinements support the market distinction the district court made, they are so closely related that a diminished standard of similarity must be applied when comparing the two marks.

3. Similarity of the marks

The district court found that "the two marks are easily distinguishable in use either when written or spoken."

[...]

Similarity of the marks is tested on three levels: sight, sound, and meaning. Each must be considered as they are encountered in the marketplace. Although similarity is measured by the marks as entities, similarities weigh more heavily than differences. .

Standing alone the words Sleekcraft and Slickcraft are the same except for two inconspicuous letters in the middle of the first syllable . . . To the eye, the words are similar.

In support of the district court's finding, Nescher points out that the distinctive logo on his boats and brochures negates the similarity of the words. We agree: the names appear dissimilar when viewed in conjunction with the logo, but the logo is often absent. The exhibits show that the word Sleekcraft is frequently found alone in trade journals, company stationery, and various advertisements.

Nescher also points out that the Slickcraft name is usually accompanied by the additional trademark AMF. As a result of this consistent use, Nescher argues, AMF has become the salient part of the mark indicative of the product's origin.

Although the effect is negligible here even though AMF is a well-known house name for recreational equipment. The exhibits show that the AMF mark is down-played in the brochures and advertisements; the letters AMF are smaller and skewed to one side. Throughout the promotional materials, the emphasis is on the Slickcraft name. Accordingly, we find that Slickcraft is the more conspicuous mark and serves to indicate the source of origin to the public.

Another argument pressed by Nescher is that we should disregard the common suffix "craft" and compare Slick and Sleek alone. Although these are the salient parts of the two marks, we must consider the entire mark. Craft, a generic frequently used in trademarks on boats, is not itself protectible, yet the common endings do add to the marks' similarity. The difference between Slick and Sleek is insufficient to overcome the overall visual similarity.

Sound is also important because reputation is often conveyed word-of-mouth. We recognize that the two sounds can be distinguished, but the difference is only in a small part of one syllable. In *G. D. Searle & Co. v. Chas. Pfizer & Co.*, 265 F.2d 385 (CA 7 1959), *Cert. denied*, 361 U.S. 819, 80 S.Ct. 64, 4 L.Ed.2d 65 (1959), the court reversed the trial court's finding that Bonamine sounded "unlike" Dramamine, stating that: "Slight differences in the sound of trademarks will not protect the infringer." *Id.* at 387. The difference here is even slighter. In a case in which the difference in sound corresponds closely with the instant appeal, the Court of Customs and Patent Appeals held that the sounds Pediglo and Pechglo were similar. *Vanity Fair Mills, Inc. v. Pedigree Fabrics, Inc.*, 161 F.2d 226, 228, 34 C.C.P.A. 1043 (1947). In reversing the patent commissioner's decision allowing the Pediglo mark to be registered, the court said that the question was not a "close one." *Id. See also Celanese Corp. v. DuPont De Nemours & Co.*, 154 F.2d at 145, 33 C.C.P.A. 857 (Clarapel and Clarifoil "sound very nearly alike"); *David Sherman Corp. v. Heublein, Inc.*, 340 F.2d 377, 381 (CA 8 1965) (Smirnoff and Sarnoff "strikingly alike when spoken").

Neither expert testimony nor survey evidence was introduced below to support the trial court's finding that the marks were easily distinguishable to the eye and the ear . . . The district judge based his conclusion on a comparison of the marks. After making the same comparison, we are left with a definite and firm conviction that his conclusion is incorrect . . .

The final criterion reinforces our conclusion. Closeness in meaning can itself substantiate a claim of similarity of trademarks. *See, e. g., S. C. Johnson & Son, Inc. v. Drop Dead Co.*, 210 F.Supp.

816 (S.D.Cal.1962), Aff'd, 326 F.2d 87 (9 Cir. 1963) (Pledge and Promise). Nescher contends the words are sharply different in meaning. This contention is not convincing; the words are virtual synonyms. Webster's New World Dictionary of the American Language 1371 (1966).

Despite the trial court's findings, we hold that the marks are quite similar on all three levels.

4. Evidence of actual confusion

Evidence that use of the two marks has already led to confusion is persuasive proof that future confusion is likely. Proving actual confusion is difficult, however, and the courts have often discounted such evidence because it was unclear or insubstantial.

AMF introduced evidence that confusion had occurred both in the trade and in the mind of the buying public. A substantial showing of confusion among either group might have convinced the trial court that continued use would lead to further confusion.

The district judge found that in light of the number of sales and the extent of the parties' advertising, the amount of past confusion was negligible. We cannot say this finding is clearly erroneous though we might have viewed the evidence more generously.

Because of the difficulty in garnering such evidence, the failure to prove instances of actual confusion is not dispositive. Consequently, this factor is weighed heavily only when there is evidence of past confusion or, perhaps, when the particular circumstances indicate such evidence should have been available.

5. Marketing channels

Convergent marketing channels increase the likelihood of confusion. There is no evidence in the record that both lines were sold under the same roof except at boat shows; the normal marketing channels used by both AMF and Nescher are, however, parallel. Each sells through authorized retail dealers in diverse localities. The same sales methods are employed. The price ranges are almost identical. Each line is advertised extensively though different national magazines are used; the retail dealers also promote the lines, by participating in smaller boat shows and by advertising in local newspapers and classified telephone directories. Although different submarkets are involved, the general class of boat purchasers exposed to the products overlap.

6. Type of goods and purchaser care

Both parties produce high quality, expensive goods. According to the findings of fact, the boats "are purchased only after thoughtful, careful evaluation of the product and the performance the purchaser expects."

In assessing the likelihood of confusion to the public, the standard used by the courts is the typical buyer exercising ordinary caution. Although the wholly indifferent may be excluded, the standard includes the ignorant and the credulous. When the buyer has expertise in the field, a higher standard is proper though it will not preclude a finding that confusion is likely. Similarly, when the goods are expensive, the buyer can be expected to exercise greater care in his purchases; again, though, confusion may still be likely.

The parties vigorously dispute the validity of the trial court's finding on how discriminating the average buyer actually is. Although AMF presented expert testimony to the contrary, the court's finding is amply supported by the record. The care exercised by the typical purchaser, though it might virtually eliminate mistaken purchases, does not guarantee that confusion as to association or sponsorship is unlikely.

The district court also found that trademarks are unimportant to the average boat buyer. Common sense and the evidence indicate this is not the type of purchase made only on "general impressions." This inattention to trade symbols does reduce the possibilities for confusion.

The high quality of defendant's boats is also relevant in another way. The hallmark of a trademark owner's interest in preventing use of his mark on related goods is the threat such use poses to the reputation of his own goods. When the alleged infringer's goods are of equal quality, there is little harm to the reputation earned by the trademarked goods. Yet this is no defense, for present quality is no assurance of continued quality. The wrong inheres in involuntarily entrusting one's business reputation to another business; AMF, of course, cannot control the quality of Sleekcraft boats. In addition, what may be deemed a beneficial feature in a racing boat may be seen as a deficiency to a person seeking a craft for general-purpose recreation; the confused consumer may then decide, without even perusing one, that a Slickcraft boat will not suit his needs. Finally, equivalence in quality may actually contribute to the assumption of a common connection.

7. Intent

The district judge found that Nescher was unaware of appellant's use of the Slickcraft mark when he adopted the Sleekcraft name. There was no evidence that anyone attempted to palm off the latter boats for the former. And after notification of the purported infringement, Nescher designed a distinctive logo. We agree with the district judge: appellee's good faith cannot be questioned.

When the alleged infringer knowingly adopts a mark similar to another's, reviewing courts presume that the defendant can accomplish his purpose: that is, that the public will be deceived. Good faith is less probative of the likelihood of confusion, yet may be given considerable weight in fashioning a remedy.

8. Likelihood of expansion

Inasmuch as a trademark owner is afforded greater protection against competing goods, a "strong possibility" that either party may expand his business to compete with the other will weigh in favor of finding that the present use is infringing. When goods are closely related, any expansion is likely to result in direct competition. The evidence shows that both parties are diversifying their model lines. The potential that one or both of the parties will enter the other's submarket with a competing model is strong.

VI. REMEDY

Based on the preceding analysis, we hold that Nescher has infringed the Slickcraft mark. Since Nescher's use is continuing, an injunction should have been entered. Several considerations, however, convince us that a limited injunction will suffice.

Both parties have used their trademarks for over a decade. AMF has a substantial investment in the Slickcraft name, yet a complete prohibition against appellee's use of the Sleekcraft name is unnecessary to protect against encroachment of appellant's mark, or to eliminate public confusion. Appellee has also expended much effort and money to build and preserve the goodwill of its mark.

There is little doubt both parties honestly desire to avoid confusion of their products. Nescher adopted the Sleekcraft name in good faith and has subsequently taken steps to avoid confusion. Use of the Nescher logo in all facets of the business would ensure that confusion would not occur. The exhibits, particularly the yellow pages advertisements, convince us that this is not being done.

Thus, in "balancing the conflicting interests both parties have in the unimpaired continuation of their trade-mark use," and the interest the public and the trade have in avoiding confusion, we conclude that a limited mandatory injunction is warranted. Upon remand the district court should consider the above interests in structuring appropriate relief. At minimum, the logo should appear in all advertisements, signs, and promotional materials prepared either by appellee or by his retail dealers, and on all appellee's business forms except those intended for strictly internal use. A specific disclaimer of any association with AMF or the Slickcraft line seems unnecessary, nor do we think it necessary to enjoin Nescher from expanding his product line. In its discretion the district judge may allow appellee sufficient time to consume supplies at hand and to add the logo to more permanent assets, such as business signs.

REVERSED and REMANDED.

[Citations omitted]

QUESTIONS FOR DISCUSSION:

Is the value of a trademark similar to a leading mark worth the risk of an infringement claim? Do you think most such similar trademarks are intentional or unintentional?

Can you think of other examples of similar trademarks? Are the consumers for those goods likely to be confused by the similarities?

"considers just." If the copyright owner proves that the infringement was willful, the court may, in its discretion, increase the award of damages to a maximum of $150,000 per infringement. If the infringer "was not aware and had no reason to believe that his or her acts constituted an infringement of copyright," damages may be lowered to no less than $200.

> A copyright or trademark owner who prevails in his infringement suit may also collect his attorney's fees and court costs from the infringer.

In a successful suit for trademark infringement, the trademark owner may get an injunction against any further infringement. This injunction is meant to ensure that the trademark owner does not sustain any further damage to his mark, or his mark's reputation. The owner may also get damages for lost sales, lost good will, and lost income. If the infringement was willful, the damages may be tripled by the court.

In a trademark dilution suit, monetary damages are typically awarded only when the dilution was willful. If the dilution was not willful, the trademark owner is limited to obtaining an injunction against further dilution.

If a patent infringement suit is successful, the damages may include:

- A royalty, for use of the original invention, or

- Lost profits of the inventor or patent holder.

The inventor's lost profits may be measured by lost sales. This includes sales that the inventor was not able to make due to the infringement, but also sales made by the infringer that would have been made by the inventor but for the infringement. Lost profits may also include price erosion. Price erosion is a decrease in the price of the invention caused by the marketplace competition of the infringing article, or price increases that the inventor was forced to forego due to the infringement.

The remedy for revealing a trade secret without authorization is for the court to issue an injunction against further use or release of the secret. Money damages, including punitive damages, are also available. Punitive or exemplary damages may be up to twice the amount of the actual damages, but are awarded only if the owner of the secret notified employees in writing of the whistleblower immunity provisions of the DTSA. Misappropriated trade secrets may also

Example: Willie is an amateur motorcycle mechanic. He gets a patent for a new, very efficient hand brake. Willie cannot manufacture enough of his new brakes to be profitable, and he cannot get the financing to set himself up for manufacturing. He also has no idea how to bring his invention to market. The Yoash Company, a large manufacturer of motorcycle components, licenses the patent from Willie, and manufactures and sells the new brake.

> **Example:** Peter opens a restaurant in Philadelphia called "Mother's," and gives it a theme reminiscent of a nightclub in a *film noir* movie. Peter registers a trademark in the name and trade dress of the restaurant. Edie, a patron visiting Philadelphia from Houston, enjoys the restaurant and wants to open one just like it in Houston. Peter can license the trademark and trade dress to Edie.

> **Example:** In the example above, Edie is careless about hygiene standards at the Houston restaurant. There is an outbreak of salmonella among patrons who have eaten there. News of the outbreak reaches Philadelphia, and the business at Peter's restaurant drops off noticeably.

be seized by the owner. An order allowing seizure may be granted without notice to the defendant.

VII. Licensing

Licensing gives someone other than the owner permission to make some use of intellectual property. The original author of the property may retain some rights, or the license may turn over all rights in the property for a period of time. Licensing is a matter of contract between the parties. The legal requirements for a valid license are generally the same as those for any other contract. The specific terms of the licensing agreement are worked out by those involved in the agreement.

Pros and Cons

There are definite advantages and disadvantages to licensing intellectual property. Whether the good outweighs the bad depends on the people involved in the agreement, and the type of property being licensed.

Pros: The author of copyrighted material, or the inventor of a patented invention, usually is interested in trying to make money off of the material or invention. It is often the case that the author or inventor can't find a way to do that on her own. She may not have the resources, or she may not know how to do it. By licensing her rights to someone who can exploit the property, the author or inventor can share in the profits.

The advantage to the person who receives the license is getting access to new work or inventions without having to develop it on his own.

Licensing intellectual property may also expand the use of a work or invention into a new market. It may also give a new form to the licensed work, such as putting illustrations from a children's book on dishes or clothing. Licensing can expand the geographic reach of goods or services beyond their original territory.

Cons: Licensing intellectual property calls for a close examination, both of the property involved and the person who will receive the license. The person who receives the license wants to be sure that the property is worth her trouble to license. The person who is giving the license needs to make sure that the license will use his property to its best advantage.

Licensing also means giving up a certain amount of control over the use of the property. While a well-crafted licensing agreement will provide for adequate quality control, there is always the chance that mistakes will be made. These mistakes can damage the reputation of the property covered by the license. There is also the possibility that the person who receives the license is ineffective at the uses made of the property. The owner of intellectual property should do due diligence on any potential license holder, to make sure she is capable of a profitable use of the property.

Contractual Safeguards

Every licensing agreement is going to be different. The needs and interests of the parties are going to differ in each agreement, and it is important to make sure that the agreement meets those needs and interests. An "off the shelf" agreement will seldom be good enough.

While there are no standardized requirements for a licensing agreement, there are some contract provisions that should at least be considered.

Description of the property: This is a very basic term. The exact property to be licensed should be described clearly enough to get rid of any uncertainty about what the license covers. A clear description is especially important if the property being licensed is from a catalog or collection (for example, a set of stock photos offered for license on a website). If the licensed property is a patent, giving the number of the patent is sufficient.

Description of the uses: The owner of intellectual property may want to limit how it is used. He may want to grant licenses for different uses to different parties. He may want to make sure that the property is not used in a way that would hurt his reputation, or that would make it look like he is endorsing something he does not approve of. If the original owner of the property to be licensed wants to limit how the property will be used, the limits need to be set out in the licensing agreement.

Payment: Payment is the reason for most licensing agreements. The agreement should be very clear about how and when payment is made to the person granting the license. It should also say how much the payment is to be, or how

---

Example: An American candy maker's main product has a cinnamon taste that domestic consumers like. In Europe, though, the candy made under the same product name uses liquorice flavor because that taste is more appealing than cinnamon in that market. If a gray market importer brings the candy into the United States, consumers might dislike the liquorice flavor and stop buying the domestic product, not realizing that the candy was manufactured for a different market.

> **Example:** Supap, a student at a university in the U.S., had family members in Thailand buy textbooks that were identical to the ones sold in the U.S., and send them to them. He resold the books for a considerable profit. The first sale doctrine protected his right to import and resell textbooks, because they were purchased lawfully in Thailand. *Kirtsaeng v. John Wiley & Sons, Inc.,* 133 S. Ct. 1351 (2013).

payment is to be calculated, if royalties are to be paid.

Accounting: If payment is to take the form of royalties, there should be some provision for an accounting. This allows the person giving the license to make sure she is receiving the proper amount of royalties. If there is a possibility of renewing the license, it can also help her decide if she will renew the license with that same party, or if she will find someone else.

Dispute resolution: Disputes can arise under even the best-crafted agreement. Planning for those disputes by putting in a mechanism for resolving them (such as, mediation or arbitration) can let those disputes be resolved efficiently, without undue expense.

Potential Issues

Anytime anyone enters the marketplace, there are pitfalls that may or may not come up. Licensing involves entering the market, so there are issues that potentially arise during a transaction. It is not always possible to deal with these issues in advance in a licensing agreement. The issues will have to be dealt with as they arise.

Gray market sales: A gray market importer purchases a legitimate product outside the United States, then brings it into the country to compete with domestic versions of goods made by the same company. There is no copyright violation, but the foreign version of the product may undercut sales of the domestic version, or the quality or features may not appeal to consumers, negatively impacting the brand.

Gray market sales are treated differently under copyright, trademark, and patent law, although the patent issues have not been finally settled. The resale of imported items protected by copyright is allowed under U.S. law. Under the **first sale** doctrine, a person is allowed to resell the physical copy of a copyright protected item, provided she acquired the item lawfully. For example, you may resell your textbooks at the end of the term without violating the copy-

FIRST SALE:

A defense to an action for copyright and patent infringement. A person who lawfully acquires a copyright or patent protected item may resell that item without violating the copyright or patent.

right owner's right to distribute copies. For purposes of the first sale doctrine, it does not matter if those copies were purchased solely to resell them. It also does not matter if they were purchased outside the U.S. As long as an item was lawfully acquired, it may be resold.

Trademark law is more restrictive on first sale. Trademark laws generally prohibit gray market imports of genuine goods unless the first sale was by a seller under the trademark owner's control, such as a licensee. Even in that case, gray market goods sold by the trademark owner or its licensee may be excluded if there are material differences in the products. Material differences are those likely to cause consumer confusion.

The rule may be different for patented material. In February 2016, the Court of Appeals for the Federal Circuit ruled that gray market sales of patented goods are not protected by the first sale rule. The unauthorized import and resale of patented goods may be prevented by the patent holder. Note that this holding sets out a clear rule to be followed, but the case is currently being appealed to the U.S. Supreme Court.

Quality control: A trademark helps to protect the reputation of the owner. The owner of a trademark has a remedy for infringement, but also for tarnishment through trademark dilution, as well.

When a mark, or any other kind of intellectual property is licensed, however, the owner is putting his reputation in the hands of someone else. Quality control becomes an issue. The owner of intellectual property should be concerned that the property is being used in a way that, at least, does not harm its reputation.

A licensing agreement can be drafted to include quality control measures. What these measures are will vary, according to the type of property being licensed, the nature of the use of the license, and the preference of the parties. Some trademark owners, for example, will insist on setting out detailed specifications and requirements as a condition of getting a license to use the mark. Others may not want the added burden of continual monitoring of the use, so will leave the quality control issue to a general requirement that nothing be done to damage the reputation of the property.

Note that allowing use of a trademark without quality control may result in cancellation of the trademark.

Infringement. Licensing intellectual property opens up new possibilities for infringement. Since licensing will bring the property to more people, there are more potential copiers.

A licensing agreement should make it clear who is responsible for pursuing infringers. The original owner may wish to retain control over

Example: Chuck is interested in getting a license to open a "Mother's" restaurant in Baltimore. Peter is leery, after his experience with Edie. The license agreement includes a provision that Peter may inspect Chuck's restaurant at any time, without prior notice.

infringement actions. The person who obtains the license may feel that she has an equal, if not greater, interest in protecting the property, so the license agreement may give her the responsibility for protecting it. If the original owner has a minimal financial interest in exploiting the property, he may prefer to leave it to the license holder to enforce her rights.

VIII. Intellectual Property and Technology

Before the 24-hour news cycle became a feature of modern life, getting news from around the world was a challenge. The regular media outlets relied upon by most people were selective in their reporting. A person who wanted to hear from any other source had limited options. Today, of course, the situation has changed. The internet and cable television let us have instant, convenient, and inexpensive access to information from virtually everywhere in the world. Three-dimensional printing, robotics, virtual reality, and cloning technologies are creating new challenges for intellectual property law, and observers can expect some interesting developments as they become more widespread.

Technological changes present new challenges for intellectual property law. Patent law has adapted to new developments in biotechnology and medicine. Copyright law has had to adapt to the universal availability of devices that will copy other work. Trademark law must adapt to the single, global marketplace brought about by the internet.

In recent years, intellectual property law has managed to accommodate the new technologies. While it is tempting to try and predict what the future will bring, the past has shown us that any kind of prediction is apt to miss the mark.

Larger Reach of Intellectual Property

Where was your car built? Many of us would answer "in the United States." A more accurate answer for most of us might be "I'm not sure." The automotive industry, like virtually every other industry, has become globalized. Even cars that are assembled in the United States or that are sold under a traditionally American brand name are often built largely of components made in other countries.

This globalization extends to intellectual property law. While there is no authority to enforce U.S. law in foreign countries, courts have found ways to reach violations that take place overseas. There are two different factors that courts consider. First, has the offending use of intellectual property will cause some harm within

> **Example:** A cartoonist has developed a popular cartoon character. That character has been adopted, without the cartoonist's permission, as the symbol of a political ideology he opposes. Since he does not know who is responsible for the unpermitted use of his work, the cartoonist likewise does not know whom he would sue for infringement.

the United States? For a patent or trade secret, the harm occurs when the intellectual property is used to develop something that is imported into the United States. For trademarks, a major issue is whether the effect the foreign infringement will have on commerce in the U.S. greater than the effect in the foreign country.

The second factor is whether the infringement has some connection with the United States. For copyrights, the question is whether the infringer took some action in the U.S. to further the infringement. If an act that furthers the infringement takes place in the U.S., it does not matter that the actual infringement took place overseas.

Courts have a limited remedy in cases of overseas infringement. In most cases, courts will ban imports of the offending article.

Increased Enforcement Challenges

There are two essential features of the internet that have made intellectual property enforcement challenging. The first is the ease of use. The second is the possibility of anonymity.

The ease of use means that copying other work is easier than ever before. A video can be downloaded from the web, and uploaded to another site in a matter of minutes. The ease of use, and the ready availability of material, can lead to a lax attitude about protecting intellectual property, or respecting the property of others. For example, while most of us would not take the time to photocopy all the pages of a 300-page book, a lot of us would download an online version of that book for free, without giving it much thought.

The potential for anonymity makes it hard to know whom to pursue for intellectual property violations. It can also be hard to know where to look for them. Without having an identifiable person to pursue for infringement, it is virtually impossible to enforce intellectual property rights.

Protection of Technical Intellectual Property

Protection of new types of technology has often followed the popular perception of that technology. In 1972, the U.S. Supreme Court ruled that a software program was just a mathematical algorithm, and that algorithm could not be patented. Nearly ten years later, the Court backtracked somewhat, holding that, while the algorithm could not be patented, the use made of it could be a patentable invention. It was not until the mid-1990s, when computers had become commonplace, that software was recognized as a patentable invention and not a naturally occurring sequence of numbers.

New technology receives legal protection if it is able to fit into the existing categories of intellectual property. Thus, software can be protected by a patent because the courts have been able to characterize it as an invention. The essential scope of patent law did not change. Instead, what changed was the perception of the nature of software. Inventions and works of authorship will receive protection, and it is vital that any new technology be understood as an invention or work of authorship.

CHAPTER SUMMARY

Intellectual property law protects creations. A person who invents something receives a patent to protect that creation. A person who creates most other types of work—a book, a song, a picture—receives copyright protection. The creation of a mark to identify where something comes from is a trademark. If the creation is not something that is to be shared with the public, it is a trade secret.

Each type of intellectual property protects a different interest and serves a different policy goal. The main principle is that property is entitled to protection even if it is not physical property. The act of creation is encouraged by granting and recognizing this protection.

Review Questions

Review question 1.

How long does a patent last? May it be renewed? Is it possible to make a change to a patent and refile it as a new patent? If so, what changes would be adequate?

Review question 2.

What is a trade secret? In what circumstances might a company choose to protect its intellectual property this way rather than another means? What are the advantages of a trade secret? How are they protected? How long do they last?

Review question 3.

What is the legal definition of trademark infringement? If a trademark is infringed, how can the trademark holder seek compensation? Are there circumstances under which the use of a trademark or trade name by another is not an infringement?

Review question 4.

What is a derivative work? What effect does a derivative work have on an original copyright? Who may create a derivative work? How is a derivative work different from an idea in terms of copyright protection?

Review question 5.

What is a service mark? How are service marks protected? May they be infringed? How would you show that a service mark is registered with the government?

Review question 6.

What are moral rights? How do moral rights differ around the world?

Review question 7.

Is copyright registration always necessary? In what circumstances?

Review question 8.

How long does a trademark or servicemark last? A copyright? What happens to each after protection ends? What are the ways that intellectual property may enter the public domain?

Review question 9.

What are the major intellectual property treaties? What do they accomplish?

Review question 10.

What is licensing? What types of contractual provisions should a license include?

Questions for Discussion

Discussion question 1.

Kano and Dave have come up with a new machine for cleaning and smoothing cymbals. They call their new system the Toph 2016, and start to sell it under that name. To help promote the product, they enlist their friend Miriam, a drummer, to make a short video showing how she uses the Toph 2016. Kano starts working on some new promotional material. He shows it to Dave, and both agree that they will not reveal any of the new promotional material until next year.

Can anything in this situation may be protected by a patent? If so, what?

Is there anything that may be protected by copyright? If so, what?

Is the new promotional material a trade secret? Why, or why not?

Explain how Kano and Dave could get trademark protection for the name "Toph 2016."

Discussion question 2.

Jamal owns a childcare center. The center does not advertise outside of Jamal's neighborhood, and there is only one location. He calls his center "Jamal's Jym." One day, he receives a letter from an attorney representing "Jamal's Gym," an upscale fitness center. The letter says that Jamal is infringing on the trademark of the fitness center. Jamal's Gym does not advertise or do business in Jamal's area.

Is Jamal infringing on the fitness center's trademark? Why, or why not?

Discussion question 3.

Carlos and Betty own a coffee shop. Last Saturday, they staged the "World's Worst Karaoke" contest. Contestants were encouraged to sing along with recorded music, and sing as badly as they can. The recordings are not licensed for commercial use.

Is this copyright infringement? Why or why not?

Suppose Carlos and Betty claim that their event was fair use, as a commentary on the recorded songs. Would this defense succeed? Why or why not?

Discussion question 4.

Hannah devises a simple machine that lets her roll large quantities of meatballs. How would she get patent protection for her invention? What if she wanted patent protection in another country? How could Hannah grant a right to produce the machine to a manufacturer while retaining her patent?

Discussion question 5.

Olaf is an ice sculptor. His works have been featured in many bridal magazines, and his work is popular at conferences and restaurant openings. Olaf sees a photograph of one of his sculptures on the website of one of his competitors, Sven. The photograph was taken at a wedding reception by one of the guests, and Sven downloaded the picture from the guest's Facebook page. Sven is using the photo to advertise that he can create the same sculpture. Olaf angrily calls Sven, but Sven says, "An ice sculpture isn't exactly fixed in a permanent form, so you don't have a copyright!"

Who has a copyright in the sculpture in the photograph?

Who has a copyright to the photograph?

What potential copyright disputes are raised by this set of facts? Are there any defenses to those claims?

Discussion question 6.

Tillie and Albert moved into their home in 1953. Beginning in 1953, Tillie had Albert pose with their children pose for a photograph every year in front of their Christmas tree, which was always put in the same place in the living room. Tillie put these photos in a special album. She took a picture every year until she died in 2003. The photo album was put in a box of miscellaneous items donated to a thrift store. The album was purchased by Devin, an artist and musician. Devin rearranged the pictures on the pages, and wrote a song cycle to accompany his display of the pictures. The album and the songs were featured on Devin's website. Louise sees the pictures on Devin's site, and downloads copies. She writes insulting captions for them, and posts them on her own website, "Dorkiest Families of All Time."

Identify the copyrights each person might hold in any of the works here.

Identify any copyright infringement issues in this scenario.

If U.S. law recognized moral rights, whose moral rights would be violated?

9 AGENCY

KEY OBJECTIVES:
▶ Understand the operation of the law of agency.
▶ Understand the concept of vicarious liability.
▶ Learn the limits of the term "scope of authority."

CHAPTER OVERVIEW

This chapter covers the law of agency. Agency is a relationship that allows one person (the **agent**) to act on behalf of another person (the **principal**). Agency law governs the obligations and responsibilities involved when one person acts through another.

In this chapter, we will look at the law of agency. We will learn how the agency relationship is formed, and how it is ended. We will look at the limits of agency, and consider the extent of a principal's liability for what an agent does.

INTRODUCTION

Agency is a very basic legal relationship. Having someone act on your behalf is a common thing. In fact, there are some entities (corporations, LLCs) that have to have someone acting on their behalf. Agency law reflects the reality of acting through another.

There are some limits built into that relationship. While it seems logical to most of us that a principal would be liable for the acts of her agent, the inquiry has to start with deciding who is an agent. There is also the question of how far that relationship goes. It defies logic to say the principal is responsible for everything a person who happens to be his agent does. Agency has its boundaries, and knowing those boundaries is the key to understanding how it works.

The law of agency starts with four main points: (1) scope, (2) duties and liabilities, (3) apparent authority, and (4) termination.

I. Scope of the Relationship

Agency is a relationship that is created by contract. The relationship is defined by the agreement of both the principal and the agent. The agreement may be explicit, or it may be inferred, but it must be present. Without agreement, there is no agency relationship. Although much of the focus of agency law is on interactions with people who are not parties to any agreement, finding that an agreement exists

AGENT:

A person who is authorized to act for another person.

PRINCIPAL:

A person who authorizes another to act on her behalf.

is the first step in discussing the principal/agent relationship.

> The terms "agent" and "employee" are not interchangeable. Agents are not all employees, and an employee will not always be an agent.

An agency agreement may be written or verbal. An unwritten agency agreement can be shown by explicit language, or by conduct.

Many people quickly think of real estate agents as an everyday example of agency. A real estate agent acts on her principal's behalf to find a property, negotiate a purchase price, complete all necessary paperwork, and close the sale. The principal ultimately chooses the property to buy, and the agent acts under the principal's direction.

Another common type of agency agreement is the **power of attorney**. A power of attorney is an explicit grant of authority to act on behalf of another.

Example: Nick is helping his friend Tom fix his fence. Tom asks Nick to drive to the hardware store to buy nails and paint for the project. Nick is Tom's agent when he does that errand.

Example: James just received a job offer in a new city. He contacts Phil, a real estate agent in that city, and asks for help to find a new place to live. Phil sends over his standard agency agreement. Under the agreement, Phil will act as an exclusive agent for James for his real estate search. If James finds a property on his own or with a different agent while Phil is still James's exclusive agent, James will owe Phil a commission on that other property.

Whatever form an agency agreement takes, there must be an intention to create an agency relationship. The principal must intend that the agent will act for her, and the agent must intend to act on behalf of the principal. Both parties must also intend that the agent's actions be subject to the control of the principal.

The power of attorney may be a general power of attorney, giving the agent the broad authority to make virtually every type of financial or business decision. The power may also be a special power of attorney. A special power means that the agent's authority is limited to certain designated functions. For example, a person may give a power of attorney that gives only the power to sell her property.

An agent who has a power of attorney is called the "attorney in fact." No legal training or licensure is implied by that title. Instead, this use of "attorney" simply refers to a person acting on behalf of another person.

POWER OF ATTORNEY:

A document by which a principal gives an agent authority to perform specified acts on behalf of the principal.

HEALTH CARE POWER OF ATTORNEY:

A power of attorney that allows another to make health care decisions when the principal is unable to make those choices.

LIVING WILL:

A document that shows a person's choices for end-of-life care when he is unable to indicate those preferences.

DURABLE POWER OF ATTORNEY:

A power of attorney that remains effective even if the principal becomes incapacitated.

A person must be of sound mind before he can execute a power of attorney. As a general rule, the power is revoked if that situation changes. For example, if a person who grants a power of attorney is in an accident and is unconscious for an extended period, the power will be revoked.

The "sound mind" rule has two exceptions:

1. *Health Care Decisions:* Many states recognize a document known as a **health care power of attorney**. A health care power of attorney grants the authority to make decisions regarding another person's health care if that person cannot do so. Unlike a **living will**, a health care power of attorney does not apply only to end-of-life decision making. The health care power of attorney can go into effect if a person is temporarily unable to communicate his wishes.

2. *Durable Power of Attorney:* A **durable power of attorney** is one that states that it will remain in effect even if the person granting it becomes incapacitated. It is in full effect when the person granting it is of sound mind, but it does not end if that status changes. A durable power of attorney may cover the same power as any

| *Example:* | Min is in the reception area of Constanza's office, waiting for an appointment with Constanza. A man comes in and says he had called earlier about buying a computer from Constanza. The man gives Min a check for what he says was the purchase price, and takes the computer. When Constanza comes out, she sees that the computer is gone and that there is a check for the price she wanted. Constanza takes the check and thanks Min for taking care of the sale. Constanza has ratified Min's actions. |

> **Example:** Patrice is a talent agent representing The Amazing Paulo, a magician. Patrice goes to a venue to try to book a show for Paulo. Another magician is setting up for a show, and says he will hire her as an assistant for his act if she takes Paulo's booking elsewhere. Even though Patrice has always wanted to be a magician's lovely assistant, she cannot take the offer. Her responsibility is to The Amazing Paulo.

other power of attorney. It may relate to business and financial matters, to health care decisions, or to both.

A **springing power of attorney** is a type of durable power of attorney. A springing power of attorney only goes into effect when the person granting it becomes incapacitated. It has no effect when the person granting it is capable of conducting his affairs.

Note that neither the health care power of attorney nor the durable power of attorney change the requirement that the person granting

the power be of sound mind when signing the power of attorney document.

Agency agreements are not always made in advance. An agency agreement may be found if the principal **ratifies** the actions of another person. Ratification is when the deed is done, and the principal approves and accepts the benefits of it.

Some state laws also create an agency relationship even without an agreement between the parties. For example, in many states, a person who drives a car with the permission of the owner is the agent of the owner while driving the car.

II.   Duties and Liabilities

When a person agrees to act as the agent of another person, she agrees to take on certain duties. Likewise, the principal has certain duties and obligations to the agent. The specifics of these duties are governed primarily by the agreement between the principal and the agent. There are, however, also duties that are implied by law, even if they are not explicitly stated.

Agents owe a **fiduciary duty** to their principals. This duty encompasses several other responsibilities to the principal, including:

SPRINGING POWER OF ATTORNEY:

A power of attorney that becomes effective when the principal becomes incapacitated (it "springs" into effect).

RATIFY:

Accepting or confirming a prior act.

FIDUCIARY/FIDUCIARY DUTY:

A fiduciary is a person required to act for the benefit of another person. A fiduciary owes the other person the duties of good faith, trust, confidence, and candor.

- Duty of Loyalty—the agent must act for the benefit of the principal, above his own self-interest. The agent must avoid conflicts of interest with the principal, and may not take advantage of her position as agent to gain a personal benefit.

- Duty of Obedience—the agent must obey the principal's lawful instructions.

- Duty to Provide an Accounting—the agent must keep an account of any property or money that the agent handles for the principal, and provide those records to the principal if she asks for it.

- Duty of Reimbursement—the principal must reimburse the agent for necessary costs she incurs in the reasonable course of the agency relationship.

- Duty of Indemnification—the principal must compensate the agent for liabilities the agent incurs while the agent is lawfully taking care of authorized business for the principal.

- Duty of Cooperation—the principal must cooperate with and assist the agent so that she can perform her role.

> **Example:** Charles asks Ben to file a deed with the property office. Ben drives to the office, parks at a meter, pays for a half-hour of parking, and goes into the office. After 20 minutes, Ben is still in line, and is told that if he leaves, he will lose his place. Ben is five minutes late back to the car, but he has a ticket. Since he was acting as an agent for Charles, Ben is entitled to have Charles pay the parking ticket.

- Duty of Due Care—the agent has an implied duty to use reasonable skill and diligence in pursuit of the principal's goals.

- Duty of Notification—the agent must keep the principal informed of all developments in the matters the agent is handling on the principal's behalf.

On the other side of the equation, principals owe duties to their agents:

- Duty of Compensation—the principal must pay the agent for his services in a timely manner.

- Duty to Provide Safe Working Conditions—if he is providing workspace or equipment, the principal must make sure it is safe. He must also notify the agent if there are any safety issues.

When an agent acts on behalf of his principal, he is subject to the principal's control. The control is not necessarily minute-by-minute control, although a particular agreement may provide for that level of supervision. "Subject to the principal's control" normally means only that the agent must follow the principal's lawful instructions. There is no obligation to follow unlawful instructions. The general contract

> **Example:**
> Lucy is a fashion designer. She makes an agreement with Otis that Otis will receive half of the proceeds obtained from his efforts to market clothes designed by Lucy. Although the agreement does not say so explicitly, Otis has an obligation to act in good faith and to attempt to market Lucy's designs. *Wood v. Lucy, Lady Duff-Gordon,* 222 N.Y. 88, 118 N.E. 214 (1917).

duty to act in good faith requires that the agent make at least a reasonable effort to act on behalf of the principal.

> The duty of good faith and fair dealing also requires the principal not to interfere with the agent's performance of her duties.

The agent's duty to act also includes a duty to use the reasonable care and skill necessary in order to do the job. The level of care and skill necessary is the ordinary degree of care and skill that would be considered the reasonable standard for the job.

SCOPE OF AUTHORITY:
The amount of power granted to an agent under a specific agency agreement.

INDEMNIFY:
To insure or secure another party against a future loss or liability.

The agent's actions are limited by the principal's lawful instructions, and by the scope of the agent's authority. The **scope of authority** refers to the range of power delegated to an agent. Anything an agent does must be within the scope of his authority, or the principal will not be responsible for it.

The principal also takes on certain duties when making an agency agreement. There is the duty to act in good faith, and to follow the terms of the agency contract. If compensation is part of the agency agreement, there is a duty of the principal to pay as agreed. The principal is also responsible for reimbursing the agent for expenses and obligations the agent incurs, or payments that the agent makes, in the course of her duties.

In addition, the principal also must **indemnify** and protect the agent from any other claims or liabilities that come up in the course of the agent's performance.

If an agent breaches an agency agreement, that violation will often release the principal from any further obligations under the agreement.

> **Example:**
> Nick, from the first example, returns from the hardware store with the paint and nails requested by Tom. Nick paid for the supplies himself, so Tom is obligated to reimburse Nick.

The breach of the agreement must be the kind that would lead to a conclusion that the agent repudiates the agreement.

ACTUAL AUTHORITY:
The powers actually granted to an agent by the principal.

APPARENT AUTHORITY:
The reasonable assumption that an agent is allowed to act for a principal under given circumstances.

Apparent Authority

The question of whether an agency relationship exists is one that is important to third parties other than the principal and the agent. When negotiating a contract, for example, it is important to know if you are negotiating with someone who is an agent, and who therefore has the power to bind the principal. Powers a principal explicitly or impliedly grants to an agent are the agent's **actual authority**. Of course, few outsiders are going to know the extent of the actual authority granted by a particular agency relationship. Those outsiders will base their own judgment on whether there is agency on how the principal allows the supposed agent to act. This is known as relying on an agent's **apparent authority**.

Apparent authority comes from the actions of the principal. The principal acts in a way that makes her unable to deny the existence of agency. The principal's actions make it apparent to others that a specific person is the agent of that principal.

In order for apparent authority to exist, the principal's actions must be of a kind that would lead a reasonable person to conclude that there is an agency relationship. The reasonable person is one who is familiar with typical business practices and customs. If such a person would be justified in believing that an agency relationship exists, apparent authority, and an agency relationship, will be found.

Example: Ahmet lets his brother Caleb use his office for his own business. Caleb uses Ahmet's telephone and e-mail address for his business communication. Ahmet also lets Caleb order business supplies using Ahmet's business account. Shortly after Caleb places a large supply order, he leaves on an extended vacation. The supply seller looks to Ahmet for payment. Ahmet has allowed the creation of apparent authority, so Caleb was acting as his agent.

Example: Assume the same facts as in the prior example, except Ahmet does not know Caleb uses his office for business. He has never given him permission to do so. Caleb does not have apparent authority.

There are many agency cases related to high-value luxury goods, such as furs or jewelry. In these cases, a jeweler or other merchant serves as an agent for the actual owner of the goods. One such case involved a jeweler who loaned jewelry to an auction house "on memorandum." This meant that the jeweler sent pieces of jewelry to the auction house "for examination" with a memo stating that the jeweler continued to own the piece until the auction house gave notice to the jeweler that the auctioneer agreed to pay a stated price for the item, and the jeweler accepted the arrangement. Legally, the jeweler acted as principal, with the auction house as its agent to solicit offers for the piece.

This was a standard methodology in the jewelry trade, but on this occasion, the auction house sold the piece without notifying the jeweler, and went into bankruptcy shortly thereafter. Unpaid for the piece, the jeweler sought to recover it from the person who bought it at auction. The jeweler argued that selling the piece was outside the auctioneer's authority, but the court disagreed. The purchaser had no reason to know of the arrangement between the jeweler and the auctioneer. The jeweler allowed the auctioneer to display the piece without informing customers that it was "on memorandum." The court also noted that the jeweler had previously allowed other pieces to be sold without the formal notice requirement. Given these facts, the jeweler was responsible for the auctioneer's apparent authority to sell the piece, and could not roll back that apparent authority or the transaction. *See Zendman v. Harry Winston, Inc.*, 305 N.Y. 180, 111 N.E.2d 971 (1953).

A single, isolated act will seldom be sufficient to justify apparent authority. There is instead a pattern of behavior that justifies the authority.

Remember that it is the actions of the principal that create apparent authority. Actions of the agent alone are not sufficient.

III. Termination

Termination of agency means that the agent (or former agent) no longer has the authority to act for the principal. Whenever an agency relationship ends, it is the responsibility of the principal to make sure that others know that the relationship is over. In some instances, there is nothing that needs to be done, except to avoid any actions that could appear to be a continuation of apparent authority. For instance, if the agent used the principal's offices to work on the principal's behalf, the principal should not allow the agent to continue to work there while conducting other business. In other cases, such as in a business where the agent had ongoing relationships with customers, it may be necessary to inform the other parties directly. Some principals may find it advisable to publish a legal notice, saying the agency relationship has terminated.

An agency relationship may be terminated by lapse of time, act of the parties, or operation of law.

Lapse of Time

A principal and agent may agree that an agency relationship will last for a definite period of time. When that period of time expires, the agency terminates automatically. If no time for the expiration of the agreement is stated, the agency relationship could continue indefinitely.

Act of the Parties

Agency is based on an agreement. As with all agreements, the parties are allowed to end the agreement by mutual consent. The parties may agree to end their relationship at any time, even if the agreement said that the agency was to last for a certain period of time.

Either the principal or agent may terminate the relationship without the consent of the other party. If the agent terminates the agreement, it is called **renunciation**. If the principal ends the agreement, it is **revocation**.

If a party revokes or renounces the agency agreement, it is still possible that the party who acts to terminate the agreement may be in breach of contract. Whether there is a breach of contract will depend on the terms of the agreement. Many employment agreements are for employment at will, and may be terminated by either party at any time. On the other hand, an employer may not terminate the relationship for reasons that would constitute employment discrimination.

Operation of Law

Certain events may cause the termination of an agency agreement by "operation of law." Parties may agree in advance on what events

RENUNCIATION:
Termination of an agency agreement by the agent.

REVOCATION:
Termination of an agency agreement by the principal.

Example: Alan hires an African-American woman, Paula, to be his sales representative. Paula makes all her sales goals, but after a few months, Alan concludes that a white man would make even more sales in the same territory. Alan may not terminate Paula's employment for such a discriminatory reason.

Example: Alex is an independent consultant with no employees. His consulting practice is very busy, and he occasionally travels to client offices out of state. A client asks that he spend three weeks at a facility overseas. Alex asks his sister Maria to manage the office, take calls, and make bank deposits during his absence. When Alex returns from his business trip, Maria is no longer his agent.

> **Example:** Super Grocery Corp. hires Luis to find sales leads in a new market. As part of this work, Luis drives to various grocery stores and restaurants to talk to potential customers. One day before starting his rounds, Luis goes to a doctor's appointment. When leaving the doctor's office, he runs into another car in the parking lot. Super Grocery is not responsible for the damage in the parking lot because Luis was not working as an agent in attending a medical appointment. This result does not change even if Luis claims that he had to go to the doctor because of stress caused by his work for Super Grocery.

may or will cause the agreement to end. If or when that event happens, the relationship is terminated. An agency relationship also may be limited to a specific purpose. In those cases, the relationship will end when that purpose has been accomplished.

The bankruptcy of one party may terminate agency. A debtor in a Chapter 11 bankruptcy (a reorganization) may reject an ongoing agency agreement. Rejection could lead to renegotiation of the agreement, or just the termination of any relationship. For an example of bankruptcy terminating an agency relationship, see the example provided in the section on apparent authority, above.

An agency agreement is a type of contract. Any of the events that would terminate a contract will also make an agency agreement end. Events that make performance impossible, such as the goal of a contract becoming impossible or one of the parties dying, will bring the agency agreement to an end.

IV. Vicarious Liability

Vicarious liability allows the principal to be responsible, or liable, for the actions of the agent. The principal's liability is based on what the agent did while furthering the principal's interests.

> Vicarious liability is summed up by the Latin words respondeat superior, or "let the master respond."

Vicarious liability attaches to actions done by the agent within the scope of his authority as agent. In other words, the principal is responsible for the things that the agent does on his behalf, but not for other actions or failures to act.

An agent whose principal is vicariously liable is also liable for his or her wrongful acts. The principal retains the duty to indemnify the agent. (Note that this duty to indemnify does not apply to criminal actions.)

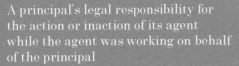

VICARIOUS LIABILITY:
A principal's legal responsibility for the action or inaction of its agent while the agent was working on behalf of the principal

Principals often argue that an agent's activities were beyond the scope of the express authority the principal granted. They may further claim that they had no idea of the methods or actions the agent was using in pursuing the principal's purposes, or that they would have repudiated the agent's actions if they had known what was happening. But if the principal willfully tried not to know what the agent was up to, the principal may still be liable. A principal cannot legally benefit from being deliberately ignorant of an agent's actions.

As an example, suppose that an importer is buying leather goods from overseas for retail in the United States. The country of origin for the product is under sanctions from the U.S. following an unsuccessful attempt to resolve a trade dispute. Under the sanctions, goods from the country are subject to high tariff rates. The importer is trying out a new customs broker for this piece of the business. The leather goods that the broker is processing do not seem to be subject to the high tariff rates that the importer had expected under the sanctions, resulting in higher profit margins for the importer. Despite being aware of the sanctions and their intended effect, the importer does not question the broker's work; rather, when copies of the broker's paperwork arrive, the importer just shreds them without reading.

It is later revealed that the broker misstated the origin of the leather goods, and stated that they were from a non-sanctioned country. The importer will also be liable for the broker's actions as the importer's agent. The importer had reason to know that the broker was doing something inappropriate, but chose not to look into it. Deliberate ignorance is legally the same as knowing of the agent's actions and doing nothing to stop them acting that way on the principal's behalf.

For the principal, vicarious liability has positive and negative aspects. The positive aspect is that being legally responsible for the acts of an agent enables principals to act through agents. Third parties who deal with agents do not have to concern themselves about who will be responsible for performance of a contract. Vicarious liability removes the uncertainty from dealing with others.

The negative aspect of vicarious liability is the same as the positive aspect: legal responsibility for the actions of an agent. If an agent does something wrong, the principal may be held liable.

EMPLOYER'S LIABILITY FOR DISCRIMINATION DEPENDS ON REASON-ABLENESS OF EMPLOYER'S CONDUCT.

Faragher v. City of Boca Raton
(Former Lifeguard) v. (Employer)
524 U.S. 775 (1998)

INSTANT FACTS:
Faragher (P) argues that Boca Raton (D) should be liable for sexual harassment by two of her immediate supervisors.

BLACK LETTER RULE:
An employer may be vicariously liable for sexual harassment by a supervisory employee.

FACTS:
Faragher (P) was a lifeguard for the City of Boca Raton (D). After she quit her job, she brought suit against Boca Raton (D) and Terry (D) and Silverman (D), her supervisors. She claimed that Terry (D) and Silverman (D) had created a "sexually hostile atmosphere" at work. Faragher (P) said that they had repeatedly subjected female lifeguards to offensive touching and lewd remarks. She also said that they talked about women in offensive ways.

The district court held that Boca Raton (D) could be held liable for the harassment by Terry (D) and Silverman (D). The court found that the harassment was pervasive enough to support an inference that Boca Raton (D) had knowledge or constructive knowledge of it. The court also found that Terry (D) and Silverman (D) were acting as Boca Raton's (D) agents when they harassed, and a third supervisor knew of the harassment but failed to report it. The Court of Appeals reversed. It held that Terry (D) and Silverman (D) were not acting within the scope of their employment, that their agency relationship with Boca Raton (D) did not facilitate the harassment. Boca Raton (D) could not be considered to have known about the harassment because of its pervasiveness or because the other supervisor knew about it.

ISSUE:
Could Boca Raton (D) be vicariously liable for the harassment by Terry (D) and Silverman (D)?

DECISION AND RATIONALE:
(Souter, J.) Yes. An employer may be vicariously liable for sexual harassment by a supervisory employee. The employment relationship makes it possible for supervisory employees to abuse their authority and subject the employees they supervise to sexual harassment. The victim may be reluctant to accept the risks of blowing the whistle on a superior. When a supervisor discriminates against employees, his actions necessarily draw upon his superior position. An employee generally cannot deal with a supervisor's abusive conduct the same way she might deal with abuse from a co-worker.

Vicarious liability for harassment is not automatic. If the victim could have avoided harm, an employer who took reasonable care to prevent the harm will not be liable. If damages could have been mitigated, there can be no award for what a victim's own efforts could have avoided. Reversed.

DISSENT:
(Thomas, J.) An employer should be held vicariously liable for hostile environment sexual harassment only if the employee suffers some adverse employment consequence.

ANALYSIS:
The holding in this case was limited 15 years later by the case of Vance v. Ball State Univ., 133 S. Ct. 2434 (2013). In that case, the Court refined the definition of "supervisor." For purposes of vicarious liability for harassment, a supervisor is defined as a person who can take "tangible actions" against employees, such as hiring or firing.

QUESTIONS FOR DISCUSSION:
Do you agree with the majority decision of the dissent? Why?

VICARIOUS LIABILITY: HOW FAR DOES IT GO?

A major federal case demonstrated the extent of vicarious liability. In *Castillo v. Case Farms of Ohio*, 96 F. Supp. 2d 578 (W.D. Tex. 1999), Case Farms, a chicken processing plant, needed help with staffing. Case Farms made an agreement with America's Tempcorps (ATC) to recruit workers in Texas for positions in Ohio. Case Farms would pay ATC for every hour an ATC worker worked at the processing plant; ATC paid the recruits.

ATC was able to recruit workers for the Case Farms contract, describing a comparatively rosy employment and living situation waiting for them in Ohio. The recruiter provided the workers with a phone number for an individual at Case (Alvaro Hernandez) to use on arrival. Hernandez worked for both Case and ATC. He arranged for housing for the ATC recruits, as well as daily transportation to the plant in a van owned by Case Farms.

The workers were housed in appalling conditions. Raw sewage and rat infestations were reported, and some housing lacked heat and electricity. Workers slept on the floor in overcrowded and unsafe units with no gender segregation. The Case Farm van that took workers to the plant was outfitted with concrete block-and-board benches rather than seats, and exhaust fumes vented into the vehicle.

The recruits sued Case Farms for a variety of claims, including vicarious liability as the principal for the actions of its agents, ATC and Hernandez. The court's lengthy decision included decisions on the agency arguments. As the court stated, "The fact that Congress has created a statutory framework of protections for migrant workers in no way exempts agricultural employers, recruiters, and overseers from common law agency principles." First, the court analyzed the scope of ATC's agency:

> Plaintiffs' supplementary theory of Case Farms liability is, therefore, based on traditional, pre-AWPA [Agricultural Worker Protection Act] common law tenets of agency. Plaintiffs argue that an agency relationship existed between ATC and Case Farms, and that the scope of that relationship included both the express authority to recruit and hire people to work at Case Farms' plant, and the implied authority to do all things proper, usual, and necessary to exercise that authority. Case Farms responds that to the extent any agency relationship existed between ATC and Case Farms, the scope of that agency was limited solely to informing recruits about the availability of work in Ohio at Case Farms' processing plant.

> The fundamental precepts of the law of agency are well settled. At common law, a principal may be held liable for the acts of its purported agent based on an actual agency relationship created by the principal's express or implied delegation of authority to the agent. Wells Fargo Business v. Ben Kozloff, Inc., 695 F.2d 940, 944-45 (5th Cir.1983); Esso Intern., Inc. v. S.S. Captain John, 443 F.2d 1144, 1146 (5th Cir.1971). Both forms of agency are at issue here. Express actual authority exists "where the principal has made it clear to the agent that he [or she] wants the act under scrutiny to be done." Pasant v. Jackson Nat'l Life Ins. Co., 52 F.3d 94, 97 (5th Cir.1995). Further, giving an agent express authority to undertake a certain act also includes the implied authority to do all things proper, usual, and necessary to exercise that express authority. Sheet Metal Workers Local Union 54 v. E.F. Etie Sheet Metal Co., 1 F.3d 1464, 1471 (5th Cir.1993); Mechanical Wholesale, Inc. v. Universal-Rundle Corp., 432 F.2d 228, 230-31 (5th Cir.1970) ("An agent has apparent or implied authority to do those things which are usual and proper to conduct business which he is employed to conduct.")

> Applying these principles, the plaintiffs assert that the scope of the agency relationship between Case Farms and ATC expressly authorized ATC to recruit and hire people to work at Case Farms' Ohio plant. Such a contention is certainly well-supported by the evidence. Former Case Farms' Director of Corporate Development, Andy Cilona, among others, testified that "the arrangement with ATC was for it to hire workers for Case Farms' production." Cilona Examination Tr. at 27-28; see Trial Tr. at 579, 598. Based on Case Farms' explicit agreement with ATC, it is found, by a preponderance of the evidence, that such an express agency relationship, the scope of which included recruiting and hiring migrant workers to perform jobs at Case Farms' plant, did exist between Case Farms and ATC.

> A principal is liable for the actions of an agent only if those actions are taken in the scope of the agent's employment. See, Entente Mineral Co., v. Parker, 956 F.2d 524, 526 (5th Cir.1992);

see also RESTATEMENT (SECOND) OF AGENCY § 228 (1958). While Case Farms acknowledges that ATC was expressly authorized to recruit and hire workers for its plant, the chicken processing company maintains that the scope of that relationship was extremely narrow, and that the vagueness of the plaintiffs' claim that ATC was Case Farms' agent glosses over the exact nature of the relationship between ATC and Case Farms. The plaintiffs, on the other hand, argue that the scope of ATC's express authority to recruit and hire people to work at Case Farms' plant included the implied authority to do all things proper, usual, and necessary to exercise that authority. See, Wells Fargo Business Credit v. Ben Kozloff, Inc., 695 F.2d 940, 945 (5th Cir.1983).

A preponderance of the evidence supports the plaintiffs' contention. Credible evidence, adduced at trial, reveals that housing and transportation issues were well within the class of activities proper, usual, and necessary to recruit and hire workers for Case Farms' Ohio processing plant. It is uncontested that the combination of its high turnover rate, and relative isolation from metropolitan areas, complicates Case Farms' recruitment process. For Case Farms, recruitment was, at all relevant times, an on-going, virtually nation-wide undertaking. The very fact that this Ohio chicken processing plant was recruiting workers in Florida and Texas attests to the difficulties it faces finding workers. Furthermore, once the workers arrived in Ohio, it was difficult for workers to find housing on their own because of language barriers, lack of personal transportation, and their unfamiliarity with the area. So, it was essential to the success of Case Farms' hiring practices to assist out-of-state workers with housing. [citation omitted] Case Farms, before any relationship with ATC, actually did assist incoming workers with housing and transportation in Ohio. Cilona Ex. Tr. at 28. Furthermore, it was clear from the evidence adduced at trial that Case Farms meant for ATC to perform these duties. [citation omitted] Thus, it is found that Case Farms knew that these duties were proper, usual, and necessary in order to recruit and retain a workforce primarily migrating from out-of-state.

Case Farms points out, and places much weight on the fact, that its representatives Cilona and Kohli both testified that ATC was not authorized to hire workers and make them full fledged "Case Farms" employees. [citation omitted] Rather, under the arrangement with ATC, the workers would supposedly remain "ATC employees," despite the fact that they worked in the Case Farms plant, doing the same work, at the same rate of pay, under the supervision of the same supervisors, as Case Farms workers.

Whether or not a plaintiff would become a "full-fledged" Case Farms employee, however, cannot be dispositive of the agency issue at hand. At issue in this civil action is precisely the question of whether superficial differences (such as which company's name appeared on a plaintiff's pay stub) somehow immunize the company that owns and operates the plant from liability. Given the fact that housing and transportation were necessary components of Case Farms' recruitment process, ATC's actions in those arenas were within the scope of its relationship as an agent of Case Farms.

For the foregoing reasons, it is found that the ATC defendants were clearly acting as Case Farms' agent in all of their actions relating to the recruitment and hiring of workers for Case Farms' chicken processing plant in Winesburg, Ohio.

The court then turned to Hernandez's role as an alleged agent for the chicken processor.

Another threshold issue, that should be resolved before the individual legal claims are considered, is whether Case Farms may be held responsible for the actions of Alvaro Hernandez. The evidence shows that Case Farms' own employee, Alvaro Hernandez, who also apparently worked for ATC, had express and implied authority to assist ATC workers with housing and transportation.

Alvaro Hernandez was a line leader supervisor at the Case Farms' plant. ATC provided recruits with Hernandez's phone number and instructed them to call him upon their arrival in Ohio. As an example of his role at the plant, credible evidence was presented that Alvaro Hernandez took plaintiffs Martin Hernandez and his sister, Esperanza Hernandez, to the plant on their first day of work, issued them their supplies, showed them how to punch in their time cards, and showed them where they would be working. [citation omitted] Alvaro Hernandez also assisted those two plaintiffs with obtaining a shift change, and with receiving their pay in cash.

Similarly, Case Farms employee Alvaro Hernandez took an active and prominent role in situating plaintiff (and "ATC employee") Michelle Galvan upon her arrival in Ohio. . . . When Hernandez arrived at the plant, he told Galvan that he would take Galvan and her companions to a trailer, but that it had no electricity. . . . Galvan told Hernandez that she and the others preferred to stay at the plant rather than be put in a place without heat or electricity. . . . Galvan understood from Hernandez that the housing he put her in was temporary and that he would find another house for her and the other women, but he never did. [citation omitted] Galvan also testified that she understood from Hernandez that the van in which he drove her and others to and from work belonged to Case Farms. [citation omitted] Galvan complained repeatedly to several Case Farms supervisors about the housing and the rides to work. . . . Case Farms' Human Resources Director, Andy Cilona, told her to speak to Hernandez about the problem [indicating] that Alvaro Hernandez was working as an agent of Case Farms.

As it did in with respect to ATC's role, Case Farms contends that the scope of Alvaro Hernandez's role was too limited to establish his role as an agent regarding these actions. . . . [.]

For the purposes of determining his status as an agent of Case Farms, it is necessary to examine the actual instances of instruction from his supervisors and actual actions taken by Hernandez, rather than his theoretical job description. The fact that an agent's action, directed and approved by a principal, is not included in the agent's descriptive job summary does not immunize the principal from liability. The alleged agent's actual conduct, rather than his official descriptive duties, can establish liability of a principal for its agent's actions. From his actions, it is determined that Alvaro Hernandez was, in fact, working as an agent of Case Farms, along with agent ATC.

Furthermore, Case Farms' proposition that Hernandez's daily transportation of ATC employees to and from work was performed as an ATC employee, not a Case Farms employee, begs the question of Hernandez's apparent authority to act on Case Farms' behalf. Whether he was working for ATC (an agent of Case Farms) or for Case Farms, his actions can, under common law agency principles, be attributed to Case Farms.

Based on the totality of the credible evidence adduced at trial, it is determined that Alvaro Hernandez was acting under the authorization and direction of Case Farms' employees, and that the functions he carried out with respect to the 1996 plaintiffs were done in his capacity as a Case Farms employee; thus, he was, perforce, an agent of Case Farms. In those instances where Hernandez may have acted on his own behalf for ATC, he would still be an agent of Case Farms via ATC. Case Farms may, therefore, be held responsible for Hernandez's housing and transportation activities in relation to the 1996 plaintiffs.

The court concluded that Case Farms could not escape liability as the principal for ATC and, by extension, Hernandez. Explicit authorization was not necessary to raise vicarious liability; Case Farms was responsible for the "necessary components" of the agency activity. In the circumstances, recruiting temporary labor necessarily raised housing and transportation issues.

Given this case, consider the following questions:

1. The ATC workers were relocated from Texas to Ohio by bus, so most arrived without their own transportation, and language and mobility issues complicated independent housing searches. Given this, the court held that transportation and housing services were a necessary part of the agency relationship. Do you agree? What if the area near the plant had good, affordable public transportation? What if ATC was recruiting English-speaking graduate students in Texas for a project in Ohio? For a project in Beijing?

2. Case Farms was aware of the local transportation problem (the unsafe van owned by the company). What was the company's ethical obligation for safe transportation of the ATC workers? Do you believe that Case Farms was wholly unaware of the related housing issues? If the company knew about the substandard housing, what was its ethical obligation with regard to housing for the ATC workers?

3. The court also decided that ATC's actions could be imputed to Case Farms on the issue of whether Case had complied with federal statutes concerning the treatment of migrant and temporary agricultural workers. As a matter of public policy, do you think it is a good idea to use an agent's actions to show that a principal violated a statute? Does the fact that Case and ATC had only an oral contract make a difference to your analysis?

4. Why did ATC, Hernandez, and Case Farms choose to behave in the way they did? What are the legal and ethical consequences for a principal's deliberate ignorance of an agent's action or inaction?

> *Example:* Inez is a salesperson at Rory's art gallery. She tells a customer that a painting in the gallery was done by a certain well-known artist. Inez knows that the painting was actually done by a local amateur painter who had learned to copy the artist's style. Rory is liable for Inez's misrepresentation.

Employer Liability for Malfeasance

"Malfeasance" is an unlawful or wrongful act. The term typically refers to an intentional or deliberate act, such as fraud, misrepresentation, or embezzlement. Malfeasance is distinct from negligent or unintentional acts.

Principals seldom, if ever, authorize agents to engage in intentional wrongdoing. A principal will still be liable for an agent's wrongdoing if it was committed within the scope of the agency. There are different tests for determining what is within the scope of employment. Most courts look at the agent's motivation. If the agent was motivated by a desire to further the employer's interests, the malfeasance will have been committed within the scope of the agency relationship. The principal will therefore be liable.

Vicarious liability does not apply to criminal acts committed by the agent, even if they are intended to benefit the principal. If an agent commits a crime in the course of his agency, it is the agent, rather than the principal, who is liable. If the principal participates in the crime, she may be liable as a co-conspirator or an accomplice, but the agent may not escape criminal liability.

Many activities fall short of criminal wrongdoing, however, and may still be imputed to a principal if undertaken by an agent. In the sidebar in the vicarious liability discussion above, the customs broker misstated the country of origin for the leather goods, meaning that the imports were subject to lower tariff rates. Misrepresenting the country of origin is against the law, but if unintentional, may not rise to the level of a crime. If the broker made the change intentionally, however, the principal in that scenario might be liable as a co-conspirator or accomplice, given the willingness to look the other way.

> *Example:* Abie is driving a delivery truck for Rose's Irish Bakery. He is looking for the address for his next delivery, and does not see a pedestrian crossing the street. Abie hits the pedestrian, injuring her severely. Rose's Irish Bakery is vicariously liable for the pedestrian's injuries.

NO HARD AND FAST RULE CAN BE APPLIED TO RESOLVE THE "SCOPE OF EMPLOYMENT" INQUIRY; RATHER, EACH CASE MUST BE DECIDED ON ITS OWN INDIVIDUAL FACTS.

Edgewater Motels, Inc. v. Gatzke
(Hotel) v. (Guest)
277 N.W.2d 11 (Minn. 1979)

This matter consists of two consolidated appeals from the post-trial orders of the St. Louis County District Court. Plaintiff Edgewater Motels, Inc., and defendant A. J. Gatzke contend that the trial judge erred by ordering judgment for defendant Walgreen Company notwithstanding a jury verdict which found that Gatzke, a Walgreen employee, negligently caused a fire in plaintiff's motel while he was in the scope of his employment. Plaintiff also claims that the trial judge erred in refusing to set aside a jury finding that plaintiff's negligence caused 40 percent of the damages sustained by Edgewater. We reverse in part and affirm in part.

The fire in question broke out on August 24, 1973, in a room at the Edgewater Motel in Duluth, Minnesota, occupied by Arlen Gatzke. In July 1973, Gatzke, a 31-year Walgreen employee and then district manager, spent approximately three weeks in Duluth supervising the opening of a new Walgreen's restaurant. . . . Gatzke thought of himself as a "24 hour a day man." He received calls from other Walgreen restaurants in his district when problems arose. He was allowed to call home at company expense. His laundry, living expenses, and entertainment were items of reimbursement. There were no constraints as to where he would perform his duties or at what time of day they would be performed.

On August 23, 1977, Gatzke worked on the restaurant premises for about seventeen hours. This was the seventh consecutive day that he put in such long hours. One of his responsibilities that day was to work with Curtis Hubbard, a Walgreen district manager from another territory who was in Duluth to observe a restaurant opening and learn the techniques employed. Gatzke's supervisor, B. J. Treet, a Walgreen's regional director, was also present.

Between 12:00 and 12:30 a. m., Gatzke, Hubbard, Treet, and a chef left the restaurant in a company-provided car. The chef was dropped off at his hotel, the Duluth Radisson, and the other three proceeded to the Edgewater, where they each had a room. Upon arrival at the Edgewater, Treet went to his room. Gatzke and Hubbard decided to walk across the street to the Bellows restaurant to have a drink.

In about an hour's time Gatzke consumed a total of four brandy Manhattans, three of which were "doubles." While at the Bellows, Gatzke and Hubbard spent part of the time discussing the operation of the newly-opened Walgreen restaurant. Additionally, Gatzke and the Bellows' bartender talked a little about the mixing and pricing of drinks. The testimony showed that Gatzke was interested in learning the bar business because the new Walgreen restaurant served liquor.

Between 1:15 and 1:30 a. m. Gatzke and Hubbard left the Bellows and walked back to the Edgewater. Witnesses testified that Gatzke acted normal and appeared sober. [...]

While Gatzke completed the expense account he "probably" smoked a cigarette. The record indicates that Gatzke smoked about two packages of cigarettes per day. A maid testified that the ash trays in Gatzke's room would generally be full of cigarette butts and ashes when she cleaned the room. She also noticed at times that the plastic wastebasket next to the desk contained cigarette butts.

After filling out the expense account Gatzke went to bed, and soon thereafter a fire broke out. Gatzke escaped from the burning room, but the fire spread rapidly and caused extensive damage to the motel. The amount of damages was stipulated by the parties at $330,360.

One of plaintiff's expert witnesses, Dr. Ordean Anderson, a fire reconstruction specialist, testified that the fire started in, or next to, the plastic wastebasket located to the side of the desk in Gatzke's room. He also stated that the fire was caused by a burning cigarette or match. [...]

The jury found that Gatzke's negligence was a direct cause of 60 percent of the damages sustained by Edgewater. The jury also determined that Gatzke's negligent act occurred within the scope of his employment with Walgreen's. Plaintiff was found to be negligent (apparently for providing a plastic wastebasket) and such negligence was determined to be responsible for 40 percent of the fire damage sustained by Edgewater. [...]

Thereafter, Walgreen's moved for judgment notwithstanding the jury findings and, in the alternative, a new trial. Plaintiff moved to set aside the jury's findings that Edgewater was negligent and that such negligence was a direct cause of the fire. The district court granted Walgreen's motion for judgment notwithstanding the verdict, ruling that Gatzke's negligence did not occur within the scope of his employment, and denied all other motions.

The following issues are presented in this case:

(1) Did the trial court err in setting aside the jury finding that Gatzke's negligent conduct occurred in the scope of his employment?

(2) Did the trial court err in refusing to set aside the jury's findings that Edgewater was contributorily negligent and that such negligence was a direct cause of the damages sustained by Edgewater?

1. The granting of a judgment notwithstanding a jury verdict is a pure question of law. Ford v. Stevens, 280 Minn. 16, 157 N.W.2d 510 (1968). In reviewing the trial court's decision we apply the same standard as the trial court did in passing upon the jury verdict.

[...]

It is reasonably inferable from the evidence, and not challenged by Walgreen's or Gatzke on appeal, that Gatzke's negligent smoking of a cigarette was a direct cause of the damages sustained by Edgewater. The question raised here is whether the facts of this case reasonably support the imposition of vicarious liability on Walgreen's for the conceded negligent act of its employee.

It is well settled that for an employer to be held vicariously liable for an employee's negligent conduct the employee's wrongful act must be committed within the scope of his employment. Seidl v. Trollhaugen, Inc., 305 Minn. 506, 232 N.W.2d 236 (1975); Nelson v. Nelson, 282 Minn. 487, 166 N.W.2d 70 (1969).

[...]

To support a finding that an employee's negligent act occurred within his scope of employment, it must be shown that his conduct was, to some degree, in furtherance of the interests of his employer. Lange v. National Biscuit Co., 297 Minn. 399, 211 N.W.2d 783 (1973); Laurie v. Mueller, supra. This principle is recognized by Restatement, Agency 2d, § 235, which states:

"An act of a servant is not within the scope of employment if it is done with no intention to perform it as a part of or incident to a service on account of which he is employed."

Other factors to be considered in the scope of employment determination are whether the conduct is of the kind that the employee is authorized to perform and whether the act occurs substantially within authorized time and space restrictions. Boland v. Morrill, 270 Minn. 86, 132 N.W.2d 711 (1965); Restatement, Agency 2d, § 228. No hard and fast rule can be applied to resolve the "scope of employment" inquiry. Rather, each case must be decided on its own individual facts. Seidl v. Trollhaugen, Inc., supra; Laurie v. Mueller, supra.

The initial question raised by the instant factual situation is whether an employee's smoking of a cigarette can constitute conduct within his scope of employment. This issue has not been dealt with by this court. The courts which have considered the question have not agreed on its resolution. See, Annot., 20 A.L.R.3d 893 (1968). A number of courts which have dealt with the instant issue have ruled that the act of smoking, even when done simultaneously with work-related activity, is not within the employee's scope of employment because it is a matter personal to the employee which is not done in furtherance of the employer's interests. [citations omitted]

Other courts which have considered the question have reasoned that the smoking of a cigarette, if done while engaged in the business of the employer, is within an employee's scope of employment because it is a minor deviation from the employee's work-related activities, and thus merely an act done incidental to general employment. [citations omitted]

For example, in Wood v. Saunders, supra, a gas station attendant negligently threw his lighted cigarette across an automobile's fuel tank opening while he was filling the vehicle with gasoline. The court, in finding this act to be within the employee's scope of employment, stated:

"In the case at bar, there was no abandonment by the employee of the master's purposes and business while the employee was smoking and carrying the lighted cigarette. There was merely a combining by the employee, with the carrying out of the master's purposes, of an incidental and contemporaneous carrying out of the employee's private purposes. * * *" 228 App.Div. 72, 238 N.Y.S. 574.

The question of whether smoking can be within an employee's scope of employment is a close one, but after careful consideration of the issue we are persuaded by the reasoning of the courts which hold that smoking can be an act within an employee's scope of employment. It seems only logical to conclude that an employee does not abandon his employment as a matter of law while temporarily acting for his personal comfort when such activities involve only slight deviations from work that are reasonable under the circumstances, such as eating, drinking, or smoking. As was stated by the court in De Mirjian v. Ideal Heating Corp., supra:

"A mere deviation by an employee from the strict course of his duty does not release his employer from liability. An employee does not cease to be acting within the course of his employment because of an incidental personal act, or by slight deflections for a personal or private purpose, if his main purpose is still to carry on the business of his employer. Such deviations which do not amount to a turning aside completely from the employer's business, so as to be inconsistent with its pursuit, are often reasonably expected and the employer's assent may be fairly assumed. In many instances they are the mingling of a personal purpose with the pursuit of the employer's business. In order to release an employer from liability, the deviation must be so material or substantial as to amount to an entire departure. * * *" 129 Cal. App.2d 765, 278 P.2d 118 (citation omitted).

We agree with this analysis and hereby hold that an employer can be held vicariously liable for his employee's negligent smoking of a cigarette he was otherwise acting in the scope of his employment at the time of the negligent act.

Thus, we must next determine whether Gatzke was otherwise in the scope of his employment at the time of his negligent act. In setting aside the jury's scope of employment determination, the trial court stated that:

"* * * it is difficult to discount the effect of four drinks — three of which were `double' — taken within the period of about 30 minutes. Had Gatzke gone immediately to his room, as did his supervisor, and then filled out his expense 17*17 account, there might be some validity to his claim that he was within the scope of his employment."

It appears that the district court felt that Gatzke was outside the scope of his employment while he was at the Bellows, and thus was similarly outside his scope of employment when he returned to his room to fill out his expense account. The record, however, contains a reasonable basis from which a jury could find that Gatzke was involved in serving his employer's interests at the time he was at the bar. Gatzke testified that, while at the Bellows, he discussed the operation of the newly-opened Walgreen's restaurant with Hubbard. Also, the bartender stated that on that night "[a] few times we [Gatzke and the bartender] would talk about his business and my business, how to make drinks, prices."

But more importantly, even assuming that Gatzke was outside the scope of his employment while he was at the bar, there is evidence from which a jury could reasonably find that Gatzke resumed his employment activities after he returned to his motel room and filled out his expense account. The expense account was, of course, completed so that Gatzke could be reimbursed by Walgreen's for his work-related expenses. In this sense, Gatzke is performing an act for his own personal benefit. However, the completion of the expense account also furthers the employer's business in that it provides detailed documentation of business expenses so that they are properly deductible for tax purposes. See, 26 U.S.C.A. § 274 (1978). In this light, the filling out of the expense form can be viewed as serving a dual purpose; that of furthering Gatzke's personal interests and promoting his employer's business purposes. According, it is reasonable for the jury to find that the completion of the expense account is an act done in furtherance of the employer's business purposes.

Additionally, the record indicates that Gatzke was an executive type of employee who had no set working hours. He considered himself a 24-hour-a-day man; his room at the Edgewater Motel was his "office away from home." It was therefore also reasonable for the jury to determine that the filling out of his expense account was done within authorized time and space limits of his employment.

In light of the above, we hold that it was reasonable for the jury to find that Gatzke was acting within the scope of his employment when he completed his expense account. Accordingly, we set aside the trial court's grant of judgment for Walgreen's and reinstate the jury's determination that Gatzke was working within the scope of his employment at the time of his negligent act.

2. Edgewater contends that the jury's findings relating to Edgewater's contributory negligence are not reasonably supported by the record. It first claims that it owed no duty to protect against its guests' negligence.

[…]

The record indicates that Edgewater had notice of its guests' practice of placing cigarette materials in their motel rooms' plastic wastebaskets. The Edgewater maid who regularly cleaned the room in which Gatzke was staying testified that she had seen cigarette butts in the wastebasket in Gatzke's room. She also stated that, in her experience, she had observed that many other motel residents would often "dump" ash trays and cigarettes in their motel rooms' plastic wastebaskets. She further testified that the head housekeeper had knowledge of the motel guests' habit of leaving cigarette butts in these plastic baskets. In light of these facts, and consistent with the principle articulated in Jacobs v. Draper, supra, it was reasonable for the jury to find that Edgewater had a duty to protect against the dangers which might flow from its guests' disposal of smoking materials in the motel rooms' wastebaskets.

Edgewater further contends that defendants failed to prove that the use of a plastic wastebasket in and of itself can amount to a breach of a duty of due care. Again, however, the record does not support this contention. Edgewater's own expert witness, Dr. Anderson, testified that the plastic material out of which the wastebasket was made "burns readily." In fact, he had no difficulty igniting the remains of the wastebasket with a common household match. Based on this alone, the jury could quite reasonably conclude that a motel owner, aware that smoking materials were often dumped into wastebaskets, breached a duty of due care by providing a highly combustible plastic wastebasket.

It is also argued by Edgewater that its use of plastic wastebaskets was not negligent because "the use of such wastebaskets is commonplace." Of course, there is no merit to this contention as it is basic horn-book law that "[e]ven an entire industry, by adopting such careless methods to save time, effort or money, cannot be permitted to set its own uncontrolled standard." Prosser, Torts (4 ed.), § 33 at 167. Edgewater's conduct must be compared to that of the reasonably prudent motel owner, not that of a similarly negligent one.

Edgewater finally claims that, even if its use of a plastic wastebasket was negligent, such negligence was not a proximate cause of the fire damage. This contention is premised on the theory that the evidence does not show that the fire originated in the wastebasket. Plaintiff's expert, Dr. Anderson, in reference to the origin of the fire, testified on direct examination as follows . . .

"Q Where, in your opinion, with reference to the wastebasket, did the fire originate, Doctor?
"A Basically in the wastebasket.["]

The above testimony, coupled with the reasonable inferences which may be drawn from the facts of this case (i. e., a person would presumably dispose of a cigarette in a wastebasket, rather than next to it), provides a reasonable basis from which the jury finding of proximate cause is supported.

The trial court's granting of judgment to Walgreen is hereby set aside, and the jury's verdict is hereby reinstated in its entirety.

CASE VOCABULARY

ISSUE OF FIRST IMPRESSION:
Refers to the first time a question of law is considered for determination by a court.

JUDGMENT N.O.V.:
Literally: notwithstanding the verdict. A judgment which reverses the determination of the jury, and is granted when a judge determines that the jury verdict had no reasonable support in fact or was contrary to law.

NEGLIGENCE:
Failure to exercise that degree of care which a reasonable person would exercise under the same circumstances.

REASONABLE PERSON:
A hypothetical person who exercises those qualities of attention, knowledge, intelligence and judgment which society requires of its members for the protection of their own interest and the interests of others.

SCOPE OF EMPLOYMENT:
An act of a servant done with the intention to perform it as a part of or incident to a service on account of which he is employed.

QUESTIONS FOR DISCUSSION:
Consider the facts that led to the court's decision. What changes to the facts would have changed the outcome? What is the smallest possible change to the facts you can identify that might have resulted in a different decision?

To what extent do changing cultural norms impact the "scope of employment" analysis? Would the smoking scenario described here support the same outcome today? What if the case took place today, but instead of smoking, Gatzke was watching cat videos on his work laptop, fell asleep, and the battery overheated, causing a fire? Would it matter if he were filling out an expense report on his phone while the cat videos played?

Employer Liability for Negligence

Negligence is defined as the failure to exercise the degree of care that a reasonably prudent person would have exercised in a given situation. Negligent acts will include everything from traffic accidents to professional malpractice. They are generally considered to be unintentional acts.

Principals are liable for the negligent acts of agents committed within the scope of the agent's authority. When a case involves a negligent act, the principal's liability is clearer than in cases involving an intentional act of the agent. A principal can make a strong claim that an agent's intentional wrongdoing was not authorized, but a lawful, authorized action may be done in a negligent way and cause injury.

Negligent Hiring and Retention

Vicarious liability depends on a finding that the agent was acting within the scope of his authority. If the agent was not within the scope of his authority, the principal is not vicariously liable. She still could be liable on the theory that the principal was negligent in hiring the agent, or negligent in keeping him on. This is not the same as vicarious liability: The principal is being held liable for her own negligence, not for the acts of her agent.

A claim for negligent hiring is based on the idea that an employer should not hire a person who has a background that would show that the person is untrustworthy or dangerous. The negligence lies in hiring such a person when the employer knew or should have known about the employee's background. If a person is being hired for a position that involves a lot of public contact, or that brings them into unsupervised contact with the property of others, the employer is obligated to look into the person's record.

> Many states have laws requiring criminal background checks when a person is hired for a certain type of position, such as a job involving working with children. Volunteer programs may also be required to perform checks on their volunteer staff.

Any negligence claim, including a negligent hiring claim, requires evidence that the employer's negligence caused the victim's injury. If the employer's negligence did not cause the harm, there is no liability. Causation may be shown by evidence that the employer put the employee in contact with the victim, and that the harm done by the employee was caused by the same type of conduct that would have been revealed in an investigation.

Negligent hiring claims depend on information about an employee's background that the employer knew or should have known. There are practical and legal limits to what can be learned from even a thorough background check. If the employer could not reasonably have found out about something in the employee's background, it is not negligence to hire that employee.

Negligent retention relates to situations in which the employer learned of an employee's dangerous tendencies after she was hired. Despite learning of these tendencies, if the employer still does not terminate the employee, it may be considered negligence. As with a negligent hiring claim, negligent retention looks at both the employer's knowledge, and whether the failure to act caused the victim's harm.

Scope of Authority

When discussing a principal's vicarious liability, it is always necessary to know what the scope of an agent's authority is. The **scope of authority** can be understood as a limitation on both the agent and the principal. The agent's actions on behalf of the principal are limited by her scope of authority, and the principal is not responsible for anything done by the agent outside the scope of authority.

Example: Matias has served two separate prison sentences for financial fraud. Hassan does not do a background check, but hires Matias to work as a personal banker. Matias uses his access to customer bank accounts to steal money from customers. Hassan could be liable for the negligent hiring of Matias.

Example: In the prior example, Matias had convictions for assault, not fraud. Hassan's negligence in not checking Matias's background did not cause the loss to customers (although Hassan could be vicariously liable for Matias's actions in a civil lawsuit for "conversion," a non-criminal taking of property).

> **Example:** When Claude was sixteen, he worked in a jewelry shop. He was arrested and convicted for stealing jewelry and watches left with his employer for repair. Because he was a juvenile, his record was sealed, and is not accessible to the public. Two years later, he goes to work for Jack, a jeweler in another city. Jack does a background check on Claude, but the records of his earlier thefts are not found. Claude once again steals property left by customers. Jack is not liable for negligent hiring, because he did not know, and could not have known, that there was a risk that Claude would steal.

> **Example:** Roger hires Nancy after a background check reveals nothing negative in her record. After Nancy has worked for Roger for a few months, Nancy is arrested for assault on three separate occasions. Roger learns of the arrests, but does not terminate Nancy. After her second arrest, Nancy gets in an argument with a person delivering furniture to the office, and she assaults the delivery person. Roger may be liable for negligent retention of Nancy.

A principal may grant an agent explicit permission to do certain actions, or to accomplish certain tasks. This is known as **express authority**. The scope of the express authority is defined by the agency agreement.

The grant of express authority will not always list every step the agent must take, or every individual thing the agent must do. This may be intentional, as it would be difficult to draft an agency agreement that could cover every conceivable situation that might arise. In appropriate situations, the agent will have the implied authority to act. **Implied authority** is the authority to do whatever is reasonably necessary to accomplish the task set out in the grant of express authority.

Implied authority also includes the authority to act in an emergency. This authority extends to protecting and preserving the property of the principal. It may include the authority to do things that would normally be outside the scope of the agent's authority.

The scope of the agent's authority is limited to those actions done to further the principal's interests. If the agent makes a major physical departure from performing his duties, he may be engaged in a **frolic.** The principal is not liable for the acts of the agent done during a frolic.

EXPRESS AUTHORITY:
Actions and tasks that the principal specifically assigns to an agent.

IMPLIED AUTHORITY:
The agent's power to do whatever is necessary to accomplish specific responsibilities assigned by the principal.

Example: Jodi is hired by Leo to open a branch of Leo's financial planning office in another city. Jodi rents an office, obtains office equipment, and purchases office supplies. Jodi has the implied authority for all of those transactions.

To decide if an agent is engaged in a frolic, courts will look at several factors, such as:

- How much time does the departure take?

A detour is a lesser departure. A principal could still be liable for an agent's actions during a detour.

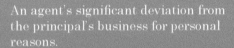

FROLIC:
An agent's significant deviation from the principal's business for personal reasons.

DETOUR:
An agent's minor deviation from the principal's business for personal reasons.

- Was this foreseeable? Has it happened in the past, or does it happen with other agents?

- Did this happen somewhere the agent would not be expected to be?

- Was the agent's motive to help the employer, or was it solely for her own benefit?

CHAPTER SUMMARY

Agency is how one person acts through another person. Some "persons," such as corporations, can act only through their agents. The rule of "respondeat superior" sums up agency law. When an agent acts for another person, or principal, the principal may be responsible for those actions. Acts done on behalf of the principal are the responsibility of the principal.

Example: Linh is a salesperson employed by Tatu, Inc. Linh has several sales calls to make during the day, but this afternoon, she has some unexpected extra time between calls. She decides to drive to a department store ten miles away to buy a baby gift for her sister. While on the way back from the store, she accidentally hits and injures a pedestrian. Linh was on a frolic, so the company would not be liable. But assume that instead of going shopping, Linh decides to kill time by stopping for coffee at a place across the street from her next call. While walking across the street, she accidentally bumps into another pedestrian, spilling hot coffee on the pedestrian, who is severely burned. Linh probably would not be considered to be engaged in a frolic, and Tatu would be vicariously liable.

Review Questions

Review question 1.
When is the term "respondeat superior" relevant? What does it mean, and why does it matter?

Review question 2.
What is negligent hiring? Negligent retention? What are some of the circumstances in which a principal would be considered not to be negligent in hiring or retaining a person, even though the person had a history of bad acts?

Review question 3.
When is a principal vicariously liable for the wrongful acts of an agent? Is a principal responsible for criminal activity by an agent? What if that activity was in furtherance of the principal's interests?

Review question 4.
Describe what a "fiduciary duty" is. What fiduciary duties does an agent owe to his principal?

Review question 5.
What does a "power of attorney" do? What are some of the different types of powers of attorney? Why would a person want to have one? What does a person need to have to be able to make a valid power of attorney appointment?

Review question 6.
What is the difference between a frolic and a detour? Why is it relevant in determining vicarious liability of a principal?

Review question 7.
Provide an example of express authority, then describe specific, related activities that could be said to also be authorized because they are necessary to completion of the primary task. Can you identify the limits of implied authority for the example you created?

Review question 8.
What is deliberate ignorance? If a principal is deliberately ignorant of an agent's actions, what is the effect on the principal's liability for those actions?

Questions for Discussion

Discussion question 1.

Nelson is a bouncer at a bar. One night, he forces Bob to leave the bar by picking him up by the back of his shirt collar, and tossing him out on the sidewalk. Bob lands face-first on the sidewalk, and loses three teeth.

> Bob is being ejected because he is very loud and unruly, trying to start fights with other patrons. Is the bar owner liable for Bob's injuries? Why or why not?

> Bob is being ejected because he and Nelson got into a heated, but non-disruptive and non-violent, political argument. Is the bar owner liable for Bob's injuries?

Discussion question 2.

Emin plans to take a six-week vacation from the clothing store he operates. He leaves his assistant Lamar in charge, telling him to keep the store running the usual hours, and in the usual way. A week after Emin leaves, a shipment of sweaters arrives. Lamar accepts the shipment, and signs for the delivery. A few days after that, one of the salespeople quits, and Lamar hires Henry to replace him. Two weeks before Emin is to return, a hurricane bears down on the city where the store is located. The Governor orders everyone to evacuate. Lamar boards up the windows, closes the store, and leaves town with the employees.

> What is the scope of Lamar's express authority here?

> Did Lamar have the authority to accept the shipment of sweaters? Why or why not?

> Did he have the authority to hire Henry? Why or why not?

> Did Lamar have the authority to close the store? Why or why not?

Discussion question 3.

When a business engages an agent to work on its behalf, what types of things should the business know about the agent? What types of background research would be advisable? Do you think it is important for an agent to be aligned with the business's culture and values? Why or why not?

Discussion question 4.

Givens Gifts employs John and Felicia. John works in IT and Felicia works in sales. John and Felicia become romantically involved and move in together. The relationship starts to sour, and John and Felicia argue, but never at work. During one fight at home, John punches Felicia, knocking her unconscious. He is convicted of assault and goes to prison. Felicia finds another job while John is in prison.

When John is released, he applies to be rehired by Givens Gifts. Two managers disagree about whether hiring John is a good idea. One manager says that John has a history of assaulting co-workers, so the hire would be negligent. The other says that John did not assault a co-worker but was involved in a domestic violence crime, and has paid his debt to society. This manager also argues that the proposed IT job keeps John out of contact with most of the remaining workforce. He also admits that he told John he could have his job back after prison.

> Which side do you agree with? Why?
>
> Is this a case of potential negligent hiring? Negligent retention?
>
> Do you think the manager was authorized to make promises to John about re-hire?
>
> Do any of your answers change if John was never officially terminated by Givens Gifts?

Discussion question 5.

Juno is living overseas. She grants her brother Drew a power of attorney to sell her house. Drew places the property with a real estate agent and keeps it tidy, but the house doesn't sell. On the advice of the real estate agent, Drew pays an exterminator to remove bats in the attic and a painter to freshen up the interior walls. The house still doesn't sell. Drew then pays a contractor to finish the basement. He also tells his neighbor that if the neighbor doesn't buy Juno's house, he will report the neighbor's son to the police for dealing drugs. The son is not a drug dealer. Juno is unaware of any of these actions beyond the house listing.

> Which of Drew's actions are within the scope of his authority under the power of attorney? For which items did he have apparent authority?

Is Juno vicariously liable for the debts to the contractor, painter, and exterminator? Why or why not?

Is Juno responsible to Drew's neighbor? Why or why not?

Discussion question 6.

Capitol City is starting a symphony orchestra. The city hired a famous conductor who was out of work because he has a terrible temper. At his last job, he threw his baton and then a book at the first trombone during rehearsal; the player was not seriously hurt, but the conductor was fired. He is known for belittling his musicians, especially women; however, his orchestras have always been top-rated. Several talent agencies send musicians to audition. The conductor hires a couple of musicians from his own network, but chooses most of the orchestra from the people sent by the talent agencies. At the first rehearsal, he calls a female player an unpublishable name and makes her stand on a chair for the entire session. At the second rehearsal, he makes the same player stand on a chair again, and throws a pencil at one of the clarinetists. Despite complaints about this and similar, later incidents, the conductor remains with the orchestra.

Did Capitol City negligently hire the conductor? Did it negligently retain him?

Do the musicians who are targeted by the conductor have any claims against the talent agencies that referred them to the orchestra?

Does your answer change if the conductor or the city council asked the talent agencies to recruit musicians from graduate schools or other orchestras? Why or why not?

10 EMPLOYMENT

CHAPTER OVERVIEW

This chapter examines the laws governing the employment relationship in the United States. Nearly all businesses, regardless of industry, hire workers on a temporary or ongoing basis. As a result, an understanding of the laws governing workers and employers is critical to everyone involved in business.

In this chapter, we first look at the difference between employees and independent contractors. Next, we review the benefits available to employees, and the obligations imposed on employers. We examine the issues raised by termination and consider the ways that foreign citizens may legally work in the United States. The text looks at anti-discrimination laws in detail, and finally, we examine the role of unions and collective bargaining in the workplace.

INTRODUCTION

The employee relationship is fundamental to business. Commercial entities need workers in order to successfully run their operations. Employment is equally important for the workers, who need employment to provide compensation and other benefits for themselves and their families. Employment has a significant impact on an individual's standard of living and quality of life, issues of health and safety, and access to health care. As such, it is fair to say that employment and employment-related issues touch on nearly all aspects of life. Therefore, the law attempts to strike a balance between the rights of employers and rights of workers.

Not all workers are treated the same under the law. Indeed, there is an important distinction between employees and non-employees. Once an employment relationship is established, the employer takes on a number of responsibilities with respect to its employees. Employees are entitled to benefits and protections not available to non-employee workers. Employers must provide certain wages, provide a safe workplace, and may not discriminate against employees on the basis of certain personal characteristics. In a unionized workplace, employers must take care to avoid violations with respect to union members. This very significant relationship, the employment relationship, is examined in detail in this chapter.

I.   Employment Relationship

When a person is hired for a wage, salary, or payment to perform work for an employer under a contract of employment, that person is generally—but not always—an **employee**. An employee provides services on a regular basis in exchange for compensation. An employee does not provide the services as part of an independent business. Employees generally work for continuous periods with no specified end date. An employee works under the instructions and training provided by the employer. The employer provides the tools or equipment needed to perform the job.

A key characteristic of an employment relationship is that the employer has substantial control over the manner in which the work is completed. The employer controls the worker's hours, the place where they work, and decides what tasks are to be done by the employee.

Being an employee gives a worker certain rights. The alternative is working as an independent contractor. Independent contractors do not have as many rights as employees, but they are subject to more freedom in how and where they perform the work. These distinctions will be discussed further in this section.

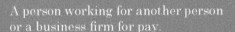

EMPLOYEE:
A person working for another person or a business firm for pay.

AT-WILL EMPLOYMENT:
An employment relationship under which the employer or employee may end the relationship at any time.

At-Will Employment

Today, most employees are **at-will employees**. At-will employment means that either the employer or employee may end the relationship at any time. Under at-will employment, an employer may fire the employee any time without cause. In other words, the employer does not need a reason to fire the employee.

Employee documents often indicate that an employee is hired at-will. For instance, the job application, employment agreement, and employee handbook may state that the employee is under an at-will employment relationship.

> The following is a sample at-will employment statement you might find in an employee handbook: "As an employee of the Company, you are employed at will. You may terminate your employment at any time, for any reason, with or without cause. Similarly, the Company may end the employment relationship with you at any time, for any reason, with or without cause."

These documents might also state that the employee can be "fired for any reason." A statement of that type establishes an at-will relationship. Generally, unless some documentation or action by the employer shows the employment is not at-will, the law assumes all employee relationships are at-will.

Some employees have a contract stating that the employee may only be fired for certain reasons. For instance, the employment contract might state the employee may only be fired for illegal or unethical behavior. In that situation, the employee is not an at-will employee. If an employer fires a non-at-will employee and does not do so for a reason stated in the agreement, the employee may sue the employer.

Even in at-will employment, the employer may not discriminate against employees on the basis of certain personal characteristics. The anti-discrimination laws applicable to employers are discussed later in this chapter.

Employers take on responsibilities for employees that do not apply for independent contractors. With respect to employees, employers must

---

EMPLOYEE MANUAL MAY CREATE A CONTRACTUAL RELATIONSHIP.

Pine River State Bank v. Mettille
(Bank) v. (Terminated Loan Officer)
333 N.W.2d 622 (Minn. 1983)

INSTANT FACTS:
Plaintiff employee claimed the employer was required to follow procedures identified in employee handbook in order to terminate his employment.

BLACK LETTER RULE:
An employee handbook creates a contract between the employee and employer.

FACTS:
The plaintiff was a loan officer at a bank. His employment was terminated due to poor performance. The employee sued, claiming that the bank did not comply with the terms of the employee handbook given to bank employees. The manual included provisions that required two reprimands before an employee could be suspended or discharged. Under the terms of the handbook, the employer could terminate employment only after a factual review performed according to certain procedures. Employees were to be given a chance to improve after a reprimand. The bank did not follow the procedures in the handbook before terminating the plaintiff's employment.

ISSUE:
Does an employee handbook create a contract between the employee and employer?

DECISION AND RATIONALE:
Yes. The Minnesota Supreme Court held that the employment handbook constituted a binding agreement. The bank's failure to follow the disciplinary provision of the handbook could be considered a breach of contract. The Court stated that the employer issued an offer of employment when it disseminated the handbook. By continuing to work for the employer after the handbook came out, the employee accepted the terms. The employer was then contractually obligated to follow the procedures specified in the handbook.

ANALYSIS:
This decision provided employees with significant rights. Prior to this ruling, employers could terminate at-will employees as they pleased. Many employers now skirt this holding by including a disclaimer in the employee handbook. For instance, the handbook may include a statement that it is subject to change and is not binding on the employer.

QUESTIONS FOR DISCUSSION:
Would an obligation to follow certain practices regarding an employer's relationship with employees be beneficial? If so, how? Would a business ever be in favor of such an obligation?

In the absence of an employee handbook, do consistent practices in the workplace create expectations for employees? Would it be fair to enforce those expectations legally?

withhold and pay Social Security and Medicare taxes. Employers also pay unemployment tax on wages paid to an employee. Generally, an employer does not withhold taxes for independent contractors.

Independent Contractor

Independent contractors are workers with a high level of independence who are not employees, but who are free to offer their services to the general public. Freelancers, contract or "gig" workers, and temporary workers are generally considered independent contractors.

If the parties intend to enter an independent contractor relationship, the employer and worker typically sign an agreement stating that the worker is an independent contractor. However, an agreement between the employer and worker does not definitively decide independent contractor status. To determine if a worker is an employee or an independent contractor, the law looks at all of the circumstances. No single issue is enough to decide the matter one way or the other.

Several factors are examined to determine if a person is working as an employee or an independent contractor, but no single element is enough on its own. All the factors must be considered in balance. Different factors may be considered,

There is a significant amount of commentary and controversy surrounding the "gig" economy, sometimes referred to as the sharing economy. In recent years, businesses based on a model utilizing independent contractors for short-term projects and tasks have boomed. These businesses use technology to match individuals who are willing to perform a requested task with persons looking for someone to provide a specific service. The work is done on a project by project basis with no expectation or promise of continuing employment. An example is the transportation network company Uber. A rider requests a ride by using a mobile app, and a driver nearby may accept or decline the request.

Proponents of the gig economy argue that this model brings more wage-earning opportunities to more people. Critics argue that this business model eliminates traditional, secure jobs and replaces them with part-time, low-paid work without employee benefits. Others note that the number of independent contractor workers was increasing well before the gig economy. The use of this model by businesses raises important questions about whether the individuals accepting the company's gigs are independent contractors or employees.

depending upon the purpose of the discussion. For purposes of deciding if a person is an independent contractor regarding their tax status, the factors applied by the IRS include:

INDEPENDENT CONTRACTORS:
Workers with a high level of independence who are in business for themselves.

> *Example:* Erin works for Marmco. Erin sits in a four-desk pod with three other workers. The other workers are all full time employees and do the exact same work as Erin. Marmco supplies a computer, a phone extension, and an email address. Erin is required to work 8:00 a.m. to 4:30 p.m. Monday through Friday. Under these facts, Erin is likely to be considered an employee.
>
> Assume instead that Erin is paid $1,200.00 per week to provide graphic design services for Marmco. Marmco provides a small desk for her use, but Erin is not required to work on-site. Erin provides her own computer and phone. Erin often works at home, from 6:00 a.m. to 3:00 p.m. Sometimes, she chooses to work from 8:00 a.m. to 4:30 p.m. instead. Based on these facts, Erin is likely to be considered an independent contractor.

- Does the worker or employer supply the equipment, materials and tools?

- Does the worker or employer control the hours of employment?

- Is the work temporary or permanent?

- Does the worker or employer control the tasks that are performed?

- Does the employer provide training?

- Does the worker complete tasks for more than one company?

- Is the worker's presence required at certain events?

Slightly different factors are used when deciding employment discrimination claims. In deciding whether a person is an employee, and thus protected by the laws against discrimination in employment, the Equal Opportunity Employment Commission (EEOC) considers whether:

- The employer can hire or fire the individual or set the rules and regulations of the individual's work,

- The organization supervises the individual's work, and, if so, to what extent,

- The individual reports to someone higher in the organization,

- The individual is able to influence the organization, and, if so, to what extent,

- The parties intended that the individual be an employee, as expressed in written agreements or contracts, and

- The individual shares in the profits, losses, and liabilities of the organization.

Many companies try to save money by classifying workers as independent contractors. Companies do not have to pay benefits or taxes on those workers, providing substantial savings. But it is important for employers to classify workers correctly as employees or independent contractors. The classification of a worker as an employee or contractor has consequences for the employer and the worker. The classification also affects the employer's responsibilities to withhold and pay certain taxes. Employment status may also provide certain employment benefits offered by the employer. Independent contractors do not receive the benefits afforded to employees.

The classification of workers is also significant with respect to the Affordable Care Act (ACA). The number of full-time employees working for an organization determines whether the organization must provide medical coverage to its employees. Likewise, the number of employees determines whether an organization is a "large employer" under the ACA. A large employer must offer minimal essential coverage to at least 95 percent of its full-time employees and their dependents.

Because there is no clear test to determine if a party is an employee or independent contractor, an employer may incorrectly classify a worker. It is usually cheaper for an employer if a worker is classified as an independent contractor. This creates an incentive for employers to classify workers as independent contractors. When discussing the **misclassification** of workers, then, the issue is whether an independent contractor should have been treated as an employee. Employers are subject to penalties for the misclassification of workers.

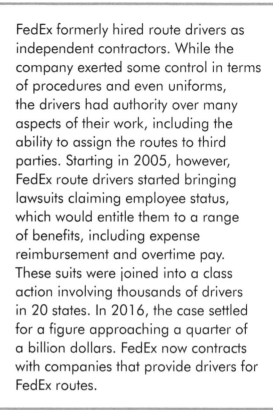

FedEx formerly hired route drivers as independent contractors. While the company exerted some control in terms of procedures and even uniforms, the drivers had authority over many aspects of their work, including the ability to assign the routes to third parties. Starting in 2005, however, FedEx route drivers started bringing lawsuits claiming employee status, which would entitle them to a range of benefits, including expense reimbursement and overtime pay. These suits were joined into a class action involving thousands of drivers in 20 states. In 2016, the case settled for a figure approaching a quarter of a billion dollars. FedEx now contracts with companies that provide drivers for FedEx routes.

An employer may unintentionally misclassify a worker as an independent contractor. If the employer makes an honest mistake about the worker's status, that is an unintentional misclassification. This error may occur if the employer fails to structure and document the independent contractor relationship to comply with the laws. The employer may be liable for unpaid taxes and tax withholdings, unpaid unemployment insurance taxes, unpaid workers' compensation premiums, unpaid overtime or minimum wages, and unpaid sick and vacation pay. In some circumstances, the employer may have to pay compensation for its failure to provide the workers with group health, disability, and life insurance coverage. An employer must also pay fines as a penalty for the misclassification.

MISCLASSIFICATION:

When an employer incorrectly classifies an employee as an independent contractor.

In recent years, the government has engaged in a concerted effort to fight worker misclassification. The U.S. Department of Labor awarded millions of dollars in grants to a number of states to combat the issue. Recent federal budget requests similarly sought funding to provide further grants. Numerous states have worked together to create inter-agency task forces to study the misclassification problem and coordinate enforcement efforts.

An employer may intentionally classify a worker as an independent contractor. An employer who intentionally misclassifies a worker must pay the unpaid taxes and withholdings, unpaid workers' compensation, unpaid overtime, unpaid minimum wages, and unpaid sick and vacation pay. In addition, if the employer intentionally misclassified workers, it is subject to monetary fines. An employer and its upper management may also face criminal penalties, such as fines and imprisonment.

THE EMPLOYER'S CONTROL OVER A WORKER IS THE MAIN FOCUS WHEN DETERMINING EMPLOYEE OR INDEPENDENT CONTRACTOR STATUS.

Clackamas Gastroenterology Associates, P.C. v. Wells
(Medical Group) v. (Disabled Employee)
538 U.S. 440 (2003)

The Americans with Disabilities Act of 1990 (ADA or Act), 104 Stat. 327, as amended, 42 U. S. C. § 12101 *et seq.,* like other federal antidiscrimination legislation, is inapplicable to very small businesses. Under the ADA an "employer" is not covered unless its work force includes "15 or more employees for each working day in each of 20 or more calendar weeks in the current or preceding calendar year." § 12111(5). The question in this case is whether four physicians actively engaged in medical practice as shareholders and directors of a professional corporation should be counted as "employees."

[...]

"We have often been asked to construe the meaning of 'employee' where the statute containing the term does not helpfully define it." *Nationwide Mut. Ins. Co.* v. *Darden,* 503 U. S. 318, 322 (1992). The definition of the term in the ADA simply states that an "employee" is "an individual employed by an employer." 42 U. S. C. § 12111(4). That surely qualifies as a mere "nominal definition" that is "completely circular and explains nothing." *Darden,* 503 U. S., at 323. As we explained in *Darden,* our cases construing similar language give us guidance on how best to fill the gap in the statutory text.

In *Darden* we were faced with the question whether an insurance salesman was an independent contractor or an "employee" covered by the Employee Retirement Income Security Act of 1974 (ERISA). Because ERISA's definition of "employee" was "completely circular," 503 U. S., at 323, we followed the same general approach that we had previously used in deciding whether a sculptor was an "employee" within the meaning of the Copyright Act of 1976, see *Community for Creative Non-Violence* v. Reid, 490 U. S. 730 (1989), and we adopted a common-law test for determining who qualifies as an "employee" under ERISA. Quoting Reid, 490 U. S., at 739-740, we explained that "'when Congress has used the term "employee" without defining it, we have concluded that Congress intended to describe the conventional master-servant relationship as understood by common-law agency doctrine.'" *Darden*, 503 U. S., at 322-323.

[...]

Darden described the common-law test for determining whether a hired party is an employee as follows:

"'[W]e consider the hiring party's right to control the manner and means by which the product is accomplished. Among the other factors relevant to this inquiry are the skill required; the source of the instrumentalities and tools; the location of the work; the duration of the relationship between the parties; whether the hiring party has the right to assign additional projects to the hired party; the extent of the hired party's discretion over when and how long to work; the method of payment; the hired party's role in hiring and paying assistants; whether the work is part of the regular business of the hiring party; whether the hiring party is in business; the provision of employee benefits; and the tax treatment of the hired party.'" 503 U. S., at 323-324 (quoting *Community for Creative Non-Violence v. Reid*, 490 U. S. 730, 751-752 (1989), and citing Restatement (Second) of Agency § 220(2) (1958)).

These particular factors are not directly applicable to this case because we are not faced with drawing a line between independent contractors and employees. Rather, our inquiry is whether a shareholder-director is an employee or, alternatively, the kind of person that the common law would consider an employer.

[...]

[T]he common law's definition of the master-servant relationship does provide helpful guidance. At common law the relevant factors defining the master-servant relationship focus on the master's control over the servant. The general definition of the term "servant" in the Restatement (Second) of Agency § 2(2) (1957), for example, refers to a person whose work is "controlled or is subject to the right to control by the master." See also *id.*, § 220(1) ("A servant is a person employed to perform services in the affairs of another and who with respect to the physical conduct in the performance of the services is subject to the other's control or right to control"). In addition, the Restatement's more specific definition of the term "servant" lists factors to be considered when distinguishing between servants and independent contractors, the first of which is "the extent of control" that one may exercise over the details of the work of the other. *id.*, § 220(2)(a). We think that the common-law element of control is the principal guidepost that should be followed in this case.

This is the position that is advocated by the Equal Employment Opportunity Commission (EEOC), the agency that has special enforcement responsibilities under the ADA and other federal statutes containing similar threshold issues for determining coverage. It argues that a court should examine "whether shareholder-directors operate independently and manage the business or instead are subject to the firm's control." According to the EEOC's view, "[i]f the shareholder-directors operate independently and manage the business, they are proprietors and not employees; if they are subject to the firm's control, they are employees." [citations omitted]

Specific EEOC guidelines discuss both the broad question of who is an "employee" and the narrower question of when partners, officers, members of boards of directors, and major shareholders qualify as employees. . . . With respect to the broad question, the guidelines list 16 factors-taken from *Darden* that may be relevant to "whether the employer controls the means and manner of the worker's work performance." The guidelines list six factors to be considered in answering the narrower question, which they frame as "whether the individual acts independently and participates in managing the organization, or whether the individual is subject to the organization's control." [citations omitted]

We are persuaded by the EEOC's focus on the common law touchstone of control, see *Skidmore v. Swift & Co.*, 323 U. S. 134, 140 (1944),9 and specifically by its submission that each of the following six factors is relevant to the inquiry whether a shareholder-director is an employee:

"Whether the organization can hire or fire the individual or set the rules and regulations of the individual's work

"Whether and, if so, to what extent the organization supervises the individual's work

"Whether the individual reports to someone higher in the organization

"Whether and, if so, to what extent the individual is able to influence the organization

"Whether the parties intended that the individual be an employee, as expressed in written agreements or contracts

"Whether the individual shares in the profits, losses, and liabilities of the organization." [citation omitted]

As the EEOC's standard reflects, an employer is the person, or group of persons, who owns and manages the enterprise. The employer can hire and fire employees, can assign tasks to employees and supervise their performance, and can decide how the profits and losses of the business are to be distributed. The mere fact that a person has a particular title-such as partner, director, or vice president-should not necessarily be used to determine whether he or she is an employee or a proprietor. . . . Nor should the mere existence of a document styled "employment agreement" lead inexorably to the conclusion that either party is an employee.

[...]

Some of the District Court's findings-when considered in light of the EEOC's standard-appear to weigh in favor of a conclusion that the four director-shareholder physicians in this case are not employees of the clinic. For example, they apparently control the operation of their clinic, they share the profits, and they are personally liable for malpractice claims. There may, however, be evidence in the record that would contradict those findings or support a contrary conclusion under the EEOC's standard that we endorse today. Accordingly, as we did in Darden, we reverse the judgment of the Court of Appeals and remand the case to that court for further proceedings consistent with this opinion.

QUESTIONS FOR DISCUSSION:

Anti-discrimination laws are based on employment status, but more and more people are working as independent contractors. How could or should the law adapt to deal with those types of work relationships?

Of the elements cited here, would you pick control as the primary aspect of an employment relationship?

II. Wages and Employee Benefits

Employee status comes with several significant benefits for the employee. An employee works for the employer for compensation. The employer and employee agree to the wage to be paid to the employee. The parties typically have great discretion to determine the amount of pay. However, minimum wage and overtime pay rules do impose some restrictions on the wage. Furthermore, in addition to various required benefits, employers may voluntarily offer other benefits to employees. **Employee benefits** refers to non-cash compensation and services provided to employees, including insurance programs, paid absences, pensions, stock ownership plans, or other services.

Minimum Wage

Most employers are subject to **minimum wage** laws. Minimum wage laws require employers to pay a minimum hourly wage to its workers. The national minimum wage is set by the federal Fair Labor Standards Act (FLSA). That law applies

EMPLOYEE BENEFITS:
Non-cash compensation and services provided to employees by employers.

> The original national minimum wage under the Fair Labor Standards Act was $0.25/hour in 1938. Other landmarks include $1.00 in 1956, $2.00 in 1974, $3.10 in 1980. At the beginning of the century, the minimum wage was $5.15.

to businesses that produce goods for interstate commerce and engage in interstate commerce.

MINIMUM WAGE:

The lowest wage permitted by law to be paid to workers.

Many states also have minimum wage laws, and some large cities have minimum wage ordinances. The "Fight for $15" movement seeks to move state and local wage thresholds to $15/hour. Several cities, including San Francisco and Seattle, have raised their wage levels to work towards $15/hour. California implemented a plan to raise wages over several years to achieve $15/hour by 2022.

Minimum wage laws do not require that an employee be paid for all of the time spent in connection with work. Generally, the FLSA covers employees when they are necessarily required to be on the employer's premises, on duty, or at a prescribed workplace. There is no coverage for any preliminary steps before starting work, or for steps the employee goes through when leaving the premises.

SECURITY SCREENING IS NOT PAID WORK TIME.

Integrity Staffing Solutions, Inc. v. Busk
(Warehouse Staffing Company) v. (Warehouse Workers)
574 U.S. _____, 135 S. Ct. 513 (2014)

Petitioner Integrity Staffing Solutions, Inc., provides warehouse staffing to Amazon.com throughout the United States. Respondents Jesse Busk and Laurie Castro worked as hourly employees of Integrity Staffing at warehouses in Las Vegas and Fenley, Nevada, respectively. As warehouse employees, they retrieved products from the shelves and packaged those products for delivery to Amazon customers.

Integrity Staffing required its employees to undergo a security screening before leaving the warehouse at the end of each day. During this screening, employees removed items such as wallets, keys, and belts from their persons and passed through metal detectors.

In 2010, Busk and Castro filed a putative class action against Integrity Staffing on behalf of similarly situated employees in the Nevada warehouses for alleged violations of the FLSA and Nevada labor laws. As relevant here, the employees alleged that they were entitled to compensation under the FLSA for the time spent waiting to undergo and actually undergoing the security screenings. They alleged that such time amounted to roughly 25 minutes each day and that it could have been reduced to a de minimis amount by adding more security screeners or by staggering the termination of shifts so that employees could flow through the checkpoint more quickly. They also alleged that the screenings were conducted "to prevent employee theft" and thus occurred "solely for the benefit of the employers and their customers." [citation omitted]

[...]

Enacted in 1938, the FLSA established a minimum wage and overtime compensation for each hour worked in excess of 40 hours in each workweek. §§ 6(a)(1), 7(a)(3), 52 Stat. 1062-1063. An employer who violated these provisions could be held civilly liable for backpay, liquidated damages, and attorney's fees. § 16, id., at 1069.

But the FLSA did not define "work" or "workweek," and this Court interpreted those terms broadly.

[...]

Congress responded swiftly. It found that the FLSA had "been interpreted judicially in disregard of long-established customs, practices, and contracts between employers and employees, thereby creating wholly unexpected liabilities, immense in amount and retroactive in operation, upon employers." 29 U.S.C. § 251(a). Declaring the situation to be an "emergency," Congress found that, if such interpretations "were permitted to stand, ... the payment of such liabilities would bring about financial ruin of many employers" and "employees would receive windfall payments ... for activities performed by them without any expectation of reward beyond that included in their agreed rates of pay." §§ 251(a)-(b).

Congress met this emergency with the Portal-to-Portal Act. The Portal-to-Portal Act exempted employers from liability for future claims based on two categories of work-related activities as follows:

"(a) Except as provided in subsection (b) [which covers work compensable by contract or custom], no employer shall be subject to any liability or punishment under the Fair Labor Standards Act of 1938, as amended, ... on account of the failure of such employer ... to pay an employee overtime compensation, for or on account of any of the following activities of such employee engaged in on or after the date of the enactment of this Act —

"(1) walking, riding, or traveling to and from the actual place of performance of the principal activity or activities which such employee is employed to perform, and

"(2) activities which are preliminary to or postliminary to said principal activity or activities,

"which occur either prior to the time on any particular workday at which such employee commences, or subsequent to the time on any particular workday at which he ceases, such principal activity or activities." § 4, 61 Stat. 86-87 (codified at 29 U.S.C. § 254(a)).

At issue here is the exemption for "activities which are preliminary to or postliminary to said principal activity or activities."

[...]

This Court has consistently interpreted "the term `principal activity or activities' [to] embrac[e] all activities which are an `integral and indispensable part of the principal activities.'" IBP, Inc. v. Alvarez, 546 U.S. 21, 29-30, 126 S. Ct. 514, 163 L.Ed.2d 288 (2005) (quoting Steiner v. Mitchell, 350 U.S. 247, 252-253, 76 S. Ct. 330, 100 L.Ed. 267 (1956)). Our prior opinions used those words in their ordinary sense. The word "integral" means "[b]elonging to or making up an integral whole; constituent, component; spec[ifically] necessary to the completeness or integrity of the whole; forming an intrinsic portion or element, as distinguished from an adjunct or appendage." 5 Oxford English Dictionary 366 (1933) (OED); accord, Brief for United States as Amicus Curiae 20 (Brief for United States); see also Webster's New International Dictionary 1290 (2d ed. 1954) (Webster's Second) ("[e]ssential to completeness; constituent, as a part"). And, when used to describe a duty, "indispensable" means a duty "[t]hat cannot be dispensed with, remitted, set aside, disregarded, or neglected." 5 OED 219; accord, Brief for United States 19; see also Webster's Second 1267 ("[n]ot capable of being dispensed with, set aside, neglected, or pronounced nonobligatory"). An activity is therefore integral and indispensable to the principal activities that an employee is employed to perform if it is an intrinsic element of those activities and one with which the employee cannot dispense if he is to perform his principal activities. As we describe below, this definition, as applied in these circumstances, is consistent with the Department of Labor's regulations.

[...]

The Department of Labor's regulations are consistent with this approach. See 29 CFR § 790.8(b) (2013) ("The term `principal activities' includes all activities which are an integral part of a principal activity"); § 790.8(c) ("Among the activities included as an integral part of a principal activity are those closely related activities which are indispensable to its performance"). As an illustration, those regulations explain that the time spent by an employee in a chemical plant changing clothes would be compensable if he "c[ould not] perform his principal activities without putting on certain clothes" but would not be compensable if "changing clothes [were] merely a convenience to the employee and not directly related to his principal activities." See § 790.8(c). As the regulations explain, "when performed under the conditions normally present," activities including "checking in and out and waiting in line to do so, changing clothes, washing up or showering, and waiting in line to receive pay checks" are "'preliminary'" or "'postliminary'" activities. § 790.7(g).

[...]

The security screenings at issue here are noncompensable postliminary activities. To begin with, the screenings were not the "principal activity or activities which [the] employee is employed to perform." 29 U.S.C. § 254(a)(1). Integrity Staffing did not employ its workers to undergo security screenings, but to retrieve products from warehouse shelves and package those products for shipment to Amazon customers.

The security screenings also were not "integral and indispensable" to the employees' duties as warehouse workers. As explained above, an activity is not integral and indispensable to an employee's principal activities unless it is an intrinsic element of those activities and one with which the employee cannot dispense if he is to perform those activities. The screenings were not an intrinsic element of retrieving products from warehouse shelves or packaging them for shipment. And Integrity Staffing could have eliminated the screenings altogether without impairing the employees' ability to complete their work.

[...]

If the test could be satisfied merely by the fact that an employer required an activity, it would sweep into "principal activities" the very activities that the Portal-to-Portal Act was designed to address . . . A test that turns on whether the activity is for the benefit of the employer is similarly overbroad. [citation omitted]

Finally, we reject the employees' argument that time spent waiting to undergo the security screenings is compensable under the FLSA because Integrity Staffing could have reduced that time to a de minimis amount. The fact that an employer could conceivably reduce the time spent by employees on any preliminary or postliminary activity does not change the nature of the activity or its relationship to the principal activities that an employee is employed to perform. These arguments are properly presented to the employer at the bargaining table, see 29 U.S.C. § 254(b)(1), not to a court in an FLSA claim.

* * *

We hold that an activity is integral and indispensable to the principal activities that an employee is employed to perform — and thus compensable under the FLSA — if it is an intrinsic element of those activities and one with which the employee cannot dispense if he is to perform his principal activities. Because the employees' time spent waiting to undergo and undergoing Integrity Staffing's security screenings does not meet these criteria, we reverse the judgment of the Court of Appeals.

ANALYSIS:
It is unclear how far this reasoning extends. Where the activity is closely aligned with the principal activity, time expended is likely to be compensable. For instance, a long line of precedent holds that the time spent putting on and taking off protective gear required for the job is compensable time. This decision did not alter that line of cases.

QUESTIONS FOR DISCUSSION:
What is your opinion on this decision? If employees could not have this job without the security check (in other words, they could not decline the check), does that make the check an integral part of the job?

If the security screening were paid, would it be difficult to draw a line for other work-related activities? Would walking to or from mass transit for work be compensable? How would you draw the line?

Certain groups of employees are exempt from the minimum wage laws. Salaried employees, including executive, administrative, and professional employees, some seasonal workers, and casual babysitters and companions to the elderly are all exempt from the minimum wage laws.

Overtime Pay

A regular workweek is considered 40 hours of work in a week. Employees are entitled to **overtime pay** for hours worked over 40 hours in one week. Employers must pay 1.5 times the worker's normal hourly wage for each hour worked over 40 hours in one week. The employees exempt from the minimum wage requirements and several other groups of employees are exempt from overtime rules.

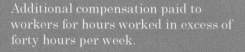

OVERTIME PAY:
Additional compensation paid to workers for hours worked in excess of forty hours per week.

FAMILY AND MEDICAL LEAVE:
An unpaid leave from work taken by an employee for family and medical reasons. Eligible employees of covered employers are authorized to take unpaid, job-protected leave for specified family and medical reasons. Group health insurance coverage continues under the same terms and conditions as if the employee had not taken leave

Mandated Benefits

Employers often provide a number of benefits to their employees. For example, employers might offer paid vacation time, tuition reimbursement, and retirement savings plans. These employee benefits are voluntarily provided by employers. A few other benefits are required by law. Employers must withhold Social Security, Medicare, and Federal Insurance Contributions Act (FICA) payments. Employers must also provide unemployment insurance and workers' compensation insurance (discussed below). Large employers must provide health insurance to employees. In addition, employees who leave a company that provided health insurance have the right to continue their health insurance coverage by assuming the premium payments. This continuation is often referred to as COBRA coverage, after the Consolidated Omnibus Budget Reconciliation Act of 1985 that established the right. Beyond health care coverage and other benefits, many employees are entitled to family and medical leave.

Family and Medical Leave

Under the Family and Medical Leave Act, employees may take up to 12 weeks of unpaid leave during a 12-month period for family and medical reasons. The Act applies to companies with 50 or more employees. A qualifying employee of a business with 50+ employees cannot be fired for taking **family and medical leave**. To qualify, the employee must work 1,250 hours for the employer in the twelve months prior to the leave. An employee may take family and medical leave after the birth or adoption of a child, to care for a family member (spouse, son, daughter, or parent) with a serious health condition, or if the employee is unable to perform her job because of a serious health condition.

The Family and Medical leave Act also provides for military caregiver leave. An eligible employee is allowed up to 26 weeks of unpaid leave during a 12 month period to care for a spouse, child, next-of-kin, or parent who is a covered service member with a serious injury or Illness. Covered active duty is defined as deployment to a foreign country.

MATERNITY LEAVE:

A period of absence from work for a female employee for the purpose of giving birth and taking care of an infant child, or for the adoption of a child.

PATERNITY LEAVE:

An absence from work provided to male employees upon the birth of a child, or for the adoption of a child.

SICK LEAVE:

An absence from work when an employee is sick.

Other Leaves

There are several other common leave types and rules for employers and employees to be aware of.

Paternity/Maternity Leave: Maternity leave is a period of absence from work for a female employee. The leave is provided for the purpose of giving birth and taking care of the infant child. **Paternity leave** is an absence from work provided to male employees upon the birth of a child. As noted above, the Family and Medical Leave Act provides 12 weeks of unpaid leave after an employee has had or adopted a child. Many states also require employers to provide maternity or paternity leave. Some employers voluntarily provide paid maternity and paternity leave for their employees. Employers may also provide more than 12 weeks of unpaid maternity or paternity leave as an employee benefit—12 weeks is only the legal threshold for larger employers.

Sick Leave: Employers are not required to provide paid **sick leave** for employees. Sick leave is time off of work when an employee is sick. However, many employers choose to offer a certain amount of paid sick leave for their employees.

In the past, companies would often provide separate amounts of time off for personal days, sick leave, and vacation time. Currently, many companies offer employees a certain number of hours of Paid Time Off, or PTO. Typical PTO policies combine sick leave, vacation leave, and floating holidays into a single amount of PTO. Employees may use PTO time as they wish, for vacation, sick time, appointments, or other reasons. Under many PTO policies, the employee accrues a specific number of PTO hours during each pay period.

Types of Leave	
Type of Leave	*Description*

Family and Medical Leave	• Unpaid leave, for up to 12 weeks during a 12-month period, for the following reasons:
	
	  • The birth, adoption, or foster placement of a child, and to care for the child within one year of the birth, adoption, or placement,
	
	  • To care for a spouse, child, or parent with a serious health condition,
	
	  • A serious health condition that makes the employee unable to perform the essential functions of her job, or
	
	  • A qualifying situation that arises out of the fat that the employee's spouse, child, or parent is a covered military member on active duty.
	
	• Required under federal law for employers with 50 or more employees within 75 miles. An employee is eligible if he has worked 1,250 hours during the 12 months prior to the star of the leave.

Military Care-giver Leave	An eligible employee may take up to 26 weeks of unpaid leave during a 12-month period to care for a spouse, child, next-of-kin, or parent who is a covered service member with a serious injury or illness. Covered active duty is defined as deployment to a foreign country.
Paternity/ Maternity Leave	• A period of absence from work for an employee for the purpose of birth or adoption and/or taking care of an infant child • Paid leave is not required by federal law.
Sick Leave	• Time off during illness • Not required by law in most jurisdictions
Vacation Leave	• Time off for vacation • Not required by law
Jury Leave	• Employees must be allowed to serve on a jury. • In many states, employer has the right to deduct juror's payment from the employee's paycheck.

Vacation Leave and Holidays: Employers are not required to provide paid vacation time to their employees. Many employers voluntarily offer some amount of vacation leave to employees. Many companies also provide a number of paid days off on certain holidays each year.

Jury Leave: Employees may be required to serve on a jury. When that happens, the employer cannot penalize the employee for serving on a jury. A few states do not allow employers to deduct pay for employee time spent on jury duty. In most states, though, an employer may deduct pay for jury duty service. Although not required, many employers choose to provide paid leave for jury duty.

III. Termination of Employment

When an employer chooses to end the employment relationship, the employer **terminates** the employee. Under at-will employment, an employer does not need to provide a specific notice period before terminating an employee. An employer must pay the employee for all time worked until termination. In most states, state laws require the employer to provide the employee's final paycheck within a specified amount of time.

The law provides certain rights to employees who have lost their job. Terminated employees have the right to continuing health insurance coverage. Under the law, employers with 20 or more employees must allow terminated employees to continue participation in the employer's health insurance plan. The employer does not pay for the health insurance. It is the employee's responsibility to pay the insurance premiums.

Unemployment Compensation

In some circumstances, terminated employees may qualify for **unemployment compensation**. Unemployment payments provide temporary financial assistance for workers who have lost a job. When qualified, an unemployed worker may receive unemployment compensation while searching for a new job. Unemployment compensation provides a percentage of the employee's regular pay for up to 26 weeks.

Unemployment is administered at the state level. Generally, however, to qualify for unemployment, the employee must be out of work through no fault of her own. The job loss might be a budget issue or other non-performance-based lay-off, such as when a product is discontinued and the employees supporting the product are no longer needed. In addition, to qualify under state law, an applicant must:

- Possess authorization to work in the United States,

TERMINATION:
When an employee is fired or laid off from his or her job.

UNEMPLOYMENT COMPENSATION:
Insurance benefits paid by the government to individuals who are out of work.

An employee who quits rather than being terminated might still qualify for unemployment benefits. If the employee suffered a "constructive discharge," she might receive unemployment payments following a review of the circumstances. Constructive discharge means that the employee really had no choice other than to resign; therefore, the resignation was forced by the employer to the extent that it amounts to a termination. Constructive discharge may result from intolerable working conditions that the employer did not remedy, such as dangerous conditions or persistent harassment. Employees may have difficulty proving that a situation was bad enough to qualify as "intolerable."

Another possibility follows the termination of an independent contractor. If the contractor was misclassified and should have been an employee, the contractor may seek unemployment. In such a case, the state will review the terms of the contractor's engagement to determine if the employer should have classified the contractor as an employee. If so, the applicant might receive unemployment benefits, and the employer may be responsible for back taxes and other penalties based on the misclassification.

- Have worked for a set period prior to applying, and

- Pursue an active job search while receiving payments.

Unemployment is usually not provided for employees who quit, or for those who are terminated following misconduct. In the case of misconduct other possible ineligibility, an employer may challenge the applicant's right to unemployment benefits. Employers fight unemployment claims because they must carry unemployment insurance, and their rates are based on how many benefits are paid out.

Another typical requirement for unemployment is that the recipient is available to work. If the worker left employment because of disability, for instance, unemployment might not be available to him. As with the other requirements, the specific rules vary by state.

WARN Act

The federal Worker Adjustment and Retraining Notification Act (the "WARN Act") requires employers to provide 60 days' notice before a plant closing or mass layoff. It applies to employers with 100 or more employees. With respect to plant closings, notice is required if the shutdown will result in loss of employment for 50 or more employees in a 30-day period. Notice is required for a mass layoff resulting in employment loss for 500 or more employees, or 50-499 employees if they make up at least 33% of the employer's active workforce.

Severance Agreements

Sometimes, the employer and employee enter a **severance agreement** following termination. Under a severance agreement, the employer agrees to give the employee a severance package in exchange for the employee's

SEVERANCE AGREEMENT:

A contract between an employer and employee detailing the rights and responsibilities of both parties after job termination.

agreement not to sue the employer. As part of the severance package, the employee typically receives a cash payment. The employer may also agree to pay for continued health insurance, training opportunities, or assistance in finding other employment.

Various state laws restrict the form and completion of a release as part of a severance agreement. Terminated employees may have an extended period to consider the agreement, or may be able to rescind their signatures if they sign before the end of that time. In addition, a federal law covers "older" workers to ensure they receive clear information. The Older Workers Benefit Protection Act of 1990 sets additional requirements for severance of workers aged 40 or older. Severance agreements for these employees must advise the employee to contact an attorney to review the agreement. The document must be written in clear and plain language, and the terminated employee must receive 21 days to consider whether to sign a release. The employer may not require that the employee release claims arising after he signs the document; in other words, the release only covers issues that came up prior to the execution of the severance agreement.

IV. Employee Protection Laws

State and federal laws set out protections for employees that bind employers to treat them according to specific standards.

Anti-Discrimination Laws

The law recognizes the importance of fairness in employment relationships. Federal and state laws prohibit employers from discriminating against employees based on race or skin color, national origin, genetic information (such as family medical history), gender or pregnancy, religion, disability, and age. These personal characteristics are referred to as **protected classes**. Some state anti-discrimination laws may prohibit discrimination on additional grounds, such as marital status, political affiliation, and sexual orientation. Employers are legally responsible for discrimination by managers, supervisors, or other employees.

Title VII

Title VII of the Civil Rights Act of 1964 is the main source of anti-discrimination law. Title VII applies to most businesses with 15 or more employees. It is illegal for employers to discriminate based upon race or skin color, national origin, genetic information (such as family medical history), gender or pregnancy, and religion in hiring, compensation, training, promotion, termination or any other terms or condition of employment.

Title VII does have a narrow exception. An employer may discriminate on the basis of reli-

PROTECTED CLASS:

A personal characteristic that cannot be targeted for discrimination.

TITLE VII:

A section of the Civil Rights Act of 1964 prohibiting employment discrimination on the basis of sex, race, color, national origin, and religion.

BONA FIDE OCCUPATIONAL QUALIFICATION:

An employment qualification, related to an essential job duty, that employers may consider in making decisions about hiring and retention of employees.

DISPARATE TREATMENT:

Intentional, unequal treatment of an employee on the basis of a protected class by an employer.

BFOQ discrimination is not allowed for race under Title VII or any other law. It is allowed for age under the federal Age Discrimination in Employment Act.

gion, sex, or national origin if that characteristic is a **bona fide occupational qualification**. A bona fide occupational qualification (often shortened to BFOQ) is a job qualification that is reasonably necessary to the normal operation of the business. For instance, it might be a bona fide occupational qualification for the president of a religious college to be a member of that religion. It is less likely that the groundskeeper at the college would need to share that faith. The courts view this exception very critically, so the organization must have a compelling case for the discrimination if it is challenged.

A Title VII violation may result from intentional conduct or conduct that appears to have been based on a discriminatory motive if it cannot be explained otherwise. **Disparate treatment** refers to employer actions that appear to be based directly on a discriminatory motivation.

Disparate treatment refers to any adverse employment action—failure to hire, failure to promote, demotions, unfavorable assignments, and so forth. Once an initial case is shown that there may have been disparate treatment, the

Example: Xeta Corporation is a large multinational corporation. The Global Accounts Business Group consists of 45 employees. The manager of the Global Accounts Group, who is also Caucasian, has hired five Caucasian employees in the past two years. Emily is an African-American applicant for a position at Xeta. She is fully qualified for the position, and the interview goes well. After the interview, the manager sends her a letter that Xeta is not proceeding with her application. Emily notices that the job continues to be advertised with the same requirements. Emily later hears that the job has been filled by an acquaintance who is white. Based on these facts, it appears that Xeta's failure to hire Emily may have been disparate treatment.

TITLE VII SEX DISCRIMINATION CLAIM THAT SEXUAL HARASSMENT HAS CREATED A HOSTILE WORK ENVIRONMENT IS NOT BARRED BECAUSE THE ALLEGED HARASSERS ARE THE SAME SEX AS PLAINTIFF.

Oncale v. Sundowner Offshore Services, Inc.
(Employee) v. (Employer)
523 U.S. 75 (1998)

In late October 1991, Oncale was working for respondent Sundowner Offshore Services, Inc., on a Chevron U. S. A., Inc., oil platform in the Gulf of Mexico. He was employed as a roustabout on an eight-man crew which included respondents John Lyons, Danny Pippen, and Brandon Johnson. Lyons, the crane operator, and Pippen, the driller, had supervisory authority. On several occasions, Oncale was forcibly subjected to sex-related, humiliating actions against him by Lyons, Pippen, and Johnson in the presence of the rest of the crew. Pippen and Lyons also physically assaulted Oncale in a sexual manner, and Lyons threatened him with rape. [citation omitted]

Oncale's complaints to supervisory personnel produced no remedial action; in fact, the company's Safety Compliance Clerk, Valent Hohen, told Oncale that Lyons and Pippen "picked [on] him all the time too," and called him a name suggesting homosexuality. Oncale eventually quit-asking that his pink slip reflect that he "voluntarily left due to sexual harassment and verbal abuse." When asked at his deposition why he left Sundowner, Oncale stated: "I felt that if I didn't leave my job, that I would be raped or forced to have sex." [citations omitted]

[...]

Title VII of the Civil Rights Act of 1964 provides, in relevant part, that "[i]t shall be an unlawful employment practice for an employer ... to discriminate against any individual with respect to his compensation, terms, conditions, or privileges of employment, because of such individual's race, color, religion, sex, or national origin." 78 Stat. 255, as amended, 42 U. S. C. § 2000e-2(a)(1). We have held that this not only covers "terms" and "conditions" in the narrow contractual sense, but "evinces a congressional intent to strike at the entire spectrum of disparate treatment of men and women in employment." *Meritor Savings Bank, FSB* v. *Vinson,* 477 U. S. 57, 64 (1986) (citations and internal quotation marks omitted). "When the workplace is permeated with discriminatory intimidation, ridicule, and insult that is sufficiently severe or pervasive to alter the conditions of the victim's employment and create an abusive working environment, Title VII is violated." *Harris* v. *Forklift Systems, Inc., 510* U. S. 17, 21 (1993) (citations and internal quotation marks omitted).

Title VII's prohibition of discrimination "because of ... sex" protects men as well as women, *Newport News Shipbuilding* & *Dry Dock Co.* v. *EEOC,* 462 U. S. 669, 682 (1983), and in the related context of racial discrimination in the workplace we have rejected any conclusive presumption that an employer will not discriminate against members of his own race. "Because of the many facets of human motivation, it would be unwise to presume as a matter of law that human beings of one definable group will not discriminate against other members of their group." *Castaneda* v. *Partida,* 430 U. S. 482, 499 (1977). See also *id.,* at 515-516, n. 6 (Powell, J., joined by Burger, C. J., and REHNQUIST, J., dissenting) . . . If our precedents leave any doubt on the question, we hold today that nothing in Title VII necessarily bars a claim of discrimination "because of ... sex" merely because the plaintiff and the defendant (or the person charged with acting on behalf of the defendant) are of the same sex.

Courts have had little trouble with that principle in cases like *Johnson,* where an employee claims to have been passed over for a job or promotion. But when the issue arises in the context of a "hostile environment" sexual harassment claim, the state and federal courts have taken a bewildering variety of stances. Some, like the Fifth Circuit in this case, have held that same-sex sexual harassment claims are never cognizable under Title VII. See also, *e. g., Goluszek* v. *H. P. Smith,* 697 F. Supp. 1452 (ND Ill. 1988). Other decisions say that such claims are actionable only if the plaintiff can prove that the harasser is homosexual (and thus presumably motivated by sexual desire). Compare *McWilliams* v. *Fairfax County Board of Supervisors,* 72 F.3d 1191 (CA4 1996), with *Wrightson* v. *Pizza Hut of America,* 99 F.3d 138 (CA4 1996). Still others suggest that workplace harassment that is sexual in content is always actionable, regardless of the harasser's sex, sexual orientation, or motivations. See *Doe* v. *Belleville,* 119 F.3d 563 (CA7 1997).

We see no justification in the statutory language or our precedents for a categorical rule excluding same-sex harassment claims from the coverage of Title VII. As some courts have observed, male-on-male sexual harassment in the workplace was assuredly not the principal evil Congress was concerned with when it enacted Title VII. But statutory prohibitions often go beyond the principal evil to cover reasonably comparable evils, and it is ultimately the provisions of our laws rather than the principal concerns of our legislators by which we are governed. Title VII prohibits "discrimi-nat[ion] ... because of ... sex" in the "terms" or "conditions" of employment. Our holding that this includes sexual harassment must extend to sexual harassment of any kind that meets the statutory requirements.

Respondents and their *amici* contend that recognizing liability for same-sex harassment will trans-form Title VII into a general civility code for the American workplace. But that risk is no greater for same-sex than for opposite-sex harassment, and is adequately met by careful attention to the requirements of the statute. Title VII does not prohibit all verbal or physical harassment in the workplace; it is directed only at *"discriminat[ion] ... because of ... sex."* We have never held that workplace harassment, even harassment between men and women, is automatically discrimination because of sex merely because the words used have sexual content or connotations. "The critical issue, Title VII's text indicates, is whether members of one sex are exposed to disadvantageous terms or conditions of employment to which members of the other sex are not exposed." *Harris, supra,* at 25 (GINSBURG, J., concurring).

[...]

And there is another requirement that prevents Title VII from expanding into a general civility code: As we emphasized in *Meritor* and *Harris,* the statute does not reach genuine but innocuous differences in the ways men and women routinely interact with members of the same sex and of the opposite sex. The prohibition of harassment on the basis of sex requires neither asexuality nor androgyny in the workplace; it forbids only behavior so objectively offensive as to alter the "condi-tions" of the victim's employment. "Conduct that is not severe or pervasive enough to create an objectively hostile or abusive work environment-an environment that a reasonable person would find hostile or abusive-is beyond Title VII's purview." *Harris,* 510 U. S., at 21, citing *Meritor,* 477 U. S., at 67. We have always regarded that requirement as crucial, and as sufficient to ensure that courts and juries do not mistake ordinary socializing in the workplace-such as male-on-male horse-play or intersexual flirtation-for discriminatory "conditions of employment."

We have emphasized, moreover, that the objective severity of harassment should be judged from the perspective of a reasonable person in the plaintiff's position, considering "all the circum-stances." *Harris, supra,* at 23. In same-sex (as in all) harassment cases, that inquiry requires careful consideration of the social context in which particular behavior occurs and is experienced by its target. A professional football player's working environment is not severely or pervasively abusive, for example, if the coach smacks him on the buttocks as he heads onto the field-even if the same behavior would reasonably be experienced as abusive by the coach's secretary (male or female) back at the office. The real social impact of workplace behavior often depends on a constel-lation of surrounding circumstances, expectations, and relationships which are not fully captured by a simple recitation of the words used or the physical acts performed. Common sense, and an appropriate sensitivity to social context, will enable courts and juries to distinguish between simple teasing or roughhousing among members of the same sex, and conduct which a reasonable person in the plaintiff's position would find severely hostile or abusive.

QUESTIONS FOR DISCUSSION:

A hostile environment claim is distinct from a "quid pro quo" claim, wherein the plaintiff is pres-sured into sexual contact or a relationship in an employment situation. Should there be a legal distinction between the two?

Oncale was the most junior worker on the rig. If he had been subjected to violent hazing without the sexual aspect, what claims could he have brought against Sundowner?

DISCRIMINATION CAN BE SHOWN BY CIRCUMSTANTIAL EVIDENCE.

Desert Palace, Inc. v. Costa
(Casino Development) v. (Equipment Operator)
539 U.S. 90 (2003)

INSTANT FACTS:

Female employee sued employer for sex discrimination based on circumstantial evidence of discrimination.

BLACK LETTER RULE:

Circumstantial evidence is sufficient to prove mixed motive discrimination.

FACTS:

A female employee who worked as a heavy equipment operator at Desert Palace Casino was terminated. She brought a sex discrimination lawsuit, claiming that she experienced sex discrimination as an employee. The employee presented evidence that she had been stalked by a supervisor, received harsher discipline than male employees for the same conduct, received less favorable treatment than men regarding overtime, and was subjected to sex-based slurs by her supervisors. At trial, the jury instructions stated that jurors were to rule for the employee if they determined that sex was a motivating factor in the firing. The jurors were to do so even if other legal factors were also present. The jury ruled in favor of the employee. Desert Palace appealed, arguing that the instructions incorrectly shifted the burden of proof to the defendant. A full panel of Eleventh Circuit judges upheld the jury verdict.

ISSUE:

Is a plaintiff required to show direct evidence of discrimination in order to prove mixed motive discrimination?

DECISION AND RATIONALE:

No. Circumstantial evidence of discrimination is sufficient to prove a claim for mixed motive discrimination. The Supreme Court found that a reasonable jury could conclude that the plaintiff's sex was a motivating factor in the employer's decision, based on the circumstantial evidence presented by the plaintiff. The Court upheld the jury verdict.

ANALYSIS:

Under the mixed-motive theory of discrimination, the plaintiff must show that both legitimate and illegitimate reasons motivated the employer's decision. Prior to this decision, the courts held that direct evidence of discrimination was necessary to prove mixed-motive discrimination. The direct evidence standard was considered a heightened standard of proof. This decision lowered the standard of proof for plaintiffs trying to prove discrimination claims.

QUESTIONS FOR DISCUSSION:

In an employment situation, the employer typically has superior control over any direct evidence about the employment relationship. Does a shift to the acceptance of circumstantial evidence help level the playing field, or should claimants meet a higher standard?

In a mixed-motive case, some of the motives behind an employer's decision are legitimate. Under a traditional at-will employment relationship, would one legitimate reason be adequate?

---

burden shifts to the employer to show that there was a legitimate and non-discriminatory reason for that treatment.

The other side may be able to show that the given reason is actually a pretext, and discrimination was the real motive. An employer may not use a job requirement as a pretext for discrimination based on a protected characteristic. Discrimination may occur when an employee is not promoted or provided other advancement or opportunities, is not hired, or is terminated because of the characteristic. State anti-discrimination laws may prohibit discrimination on additional grounds.

An employer may also violate Title VII through conduct that tends to disfavor a particular groups. A neutral employment policy may violate Title VII if the policy has a **disparate impact** on members of a protected class. A disparate impact policy is illegal if the employer cannot justify the policy as a job-related business necessity.

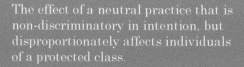

DISPARATE IMPACT:
The effect of a neutral practice that is non-discriminatory in intention, but disproportionately affects individuals of a protected class.

If an employee believes they have been discriminated against, they must file a Charge of Discrimination with the Equal Employment Opportunity Commission (EEOC). The EEOC will investigate the complaint. After the investigation, the EEOC may issue a Notice of Right to Sue. That notice gives the employee permission to file a lawsuit in a court of law.

Age Discrimination

The Age Discrimination in Employment Act (ADEA) forbids employment discrimination against anyone 40 years of age or older. The ADEA prohibits discrimination in hiring, promotion, compensation, or termination of employment and layoffs. In a slight difference from Title VII, the ADEA applies to employers with 20 or more employees.

Employers may not indicate an age preference or limit in job notices or advertisements. Employers also may not deny benefits to older employees. In a few exceptions, the employer may specify an age limit if age is a bona fide occupational qualification necessary to the job. For instance, age limits are appropriate for obvious situations (a young actor is necessary to play a young character in a movie). There is also a public safety exception. Thus, police and fire departments may use maximum hiring and mandatory retirement ages. An employer may favor an older employee over a younger one, even if the younger employee is 40 or more years old.

Many employers used to impose a mandatory retirement age that required workers to retire once they reached a certain age. Generally

Example: A lumber company requires applicants to lift and carry 125 pounds up three flights of stairs. The policy has a negative impact on female applicants. Lumber company employees need to lift heavy weight. The company did not intentionally mean to discriminate against female employees. The company would have to show that lifting that amount of weight for that distance is necessary and job-related. If the lumber company always uses cranes for loads over 50 pounds, then the requirement is too broad, and any disparate impact is discriminatory.

speaking, the ADEA does not allow the use of a mandatory retirement age policy. There is an exception for certain individuals. Employers may enforce a mandatory retirement age for bona fide executives and those who receive an annual payment of at least $44,000.

Disability Discrimination

The law prohibits discrimination in employment based on an employee's disability. The Americans with Disabilities Act (ADA) forbids discrimination in the hiring, promotion, compensation, training, and firing of disabled workers. Under the ADA, a person with a disability is someone who:

- Has a physical or mental impairment that substantially limits one or more major life activities,

- Has a record of such impairment, or

- Is perceived by others as having such an impairment.

The ADA requires employers to make a **reasonable accommodation** for a disabled worker unless the accommodation would cause "undue hardship" for the business. A reasonable accommodation is a modification or adjustment to enable people with disabilities to perform job duties.

Accommodations vary depending upon the individual employee. Depending on the circumstances, some examples of a reasonable accommodation by an employer might include:

- Modify facilities to make them accessible and usable by persons with disabilities.

- Restructure a position.

- Allow a modified work schedule.

- Obtain new equipment or devices.

- Provide readers or interpreters.

While many managers fear the costs of an accommodation, most are low-cost, or even free.

If an accommodation would cause an "undue hardship," then the employer can avoid taking action. An undue hardship exists where the accommodation would require significant difficulty or expense for the employer. Whether an accommodation creates an undue hardship depends on several factors, including the employer's size, financial resources, and the nature of its operation. An employer is not required to lower its quality standards to make an accommodation. Also, an employer does not need to provide personal items, such as glasses or hearing aids. Employers must ensure that employees understand ADA requirements and the need to provide reasonable accommodations.

In 2008, the ADA was augmented by the Americans with Disabilities Act Amendments Act. The Amendments Act rejected many interpretations of the ADA in the courts, and made it

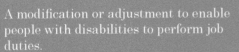

REASONABLE ACCOMMODATION:
A modification or adjustment to enable people with disabilities to perform job duties.

Example: In 2016, McDonald's Corporation settled a disability discrimination suit by the U.S. Equal Employment Opportunity Commission (EEOC). The EEOC alleged that McDonald's refused to interview a deaf job applicant once it learned of his disability. The applicant is unable to hear or speak, but had previously worked at a McDonald's in another state. The suit claimed that the restaurant manager canceled his job interview upon learning that he needed an interpreter. The applicant's sister offered to serve as an interpreter. The restaurant interviewed and hired new workers after the applicant tried to reschedule an interview. McDonalds agreed to pay $56,500 and provide training to its managers regarding ADA requirements.

Example: A salon manager refused an accommodation requested by a stylist employee. The employee suffered from claustrophobia and asked for an end station. The employee was originally given an end station, but the salon manager then moved the employee to a different station between two other stylists. The employee had a panic attack. The salon corporation agreed to pay $60,000 in damages and to provide ADA training to its managers at several salon locations in that state.

easier for claimants to prove that they have a disability that entitles them to ADA protection.

The Amendments Act's definition of disability is consistent with the ADA, but the Act updated how that definition should be read. Because Supreme Court and other judicial decisions had interpreted the ADA's requirements quite strictly, many people with "impairments that substantially limits one or more major life activities" were effectively excluded from the law's anti-discrimination protections. In response, the Amendments Act did the following:

- Specified that "disability" should be construed broadly to include more people,

- Required that mitigating measures (medications, for instance) be disregarded when evaluating whether substantial impairment exists,

- Broadened the concept of "major life activities," and

- Decreased the thresholds for proof of discrimination based on the "perception" of disability.

> A small mom-and-pop shop might not be able to accommodate an employee who cannot lift at least 25 pounds, but a large company has more options to reassign the employee to other duties or change other aspects of the work environment.

AMENDMENTS ACT EXPANDS THE PROTECTIONS OF THE ADA.

Cannon v. Jacobs Field Services North America, Inc.
(Job Applicant) v. (Employer)
No. 15–20127 (5th Cir Jan. 13, 2016)

JOLLY, HAYNES, and COSTA, Circuit Judges.

Cannon is a mechanical engineer with over twenty years of experience. In 2010, he had surgery to repair a torn rotator cuff in his right shoulder. The surgery was unsuccessful. As a result, Cannon can no longer raise his right arm above shoulder level, and is limited in his ability to push or pull with his right arm.

In 2011, Cannon applied for a job as a field engineer with JFS. JFS offered him the job. Cannon underwent a pre-employment physical. During the exam, Cannon told the doctor about his inoperable rotator cuff injury . . . The doctor cleared Cannon for the position so long as JFS offered the following accommodations for the rotator cuff injury: no driving company vehicles; no lifting, pushing, or pulling more than ten pounds; and no working with his hands above shoulder level.

JFS did not agree to the proposed accommodations. Instead, on July 18, the same day it received the "Medical Clearance" form with the list of accommodations, it determined that Cannon was physically incapable of performing the job. . . . [A supervisor] explained that the job required an employee "capable of driving, climbing, lifting, and walking" as the job site was located "in the mountains with rough/rocky terrain" and "spread over several miles."

A human resources representative contacted Cannon around this time. Not mentioning the seemingly unequivocal position taken by the manager that Cannon could not do the job, the HR representative informed Cannon only that JFS had concerns that he could not reach above his head with his right arm. Cannon asked whether he could contact someone to resolve the concerns and was told to call the Occupational Health Department. Cannon promptly did so and was told that JFS needed him to clarify whether (1) he could climb a ladder and (2) was still taking [prescription painkillers]. Again, there was no indication that the job offer had been rescinded, and Cannon took the requests for additional information to mean that satisfactory responses would eliminate the concerns. Cannon provided the requested information, submitting documentation from his doctor stating that he was "specifically cleared for climbing vertical ladders and maintaining 3–point contact with either arm" and was being weaned from [painkillers]. . . . Cannon continued to try to prove to JFS that he was capable of climbing a ladder in an effort to have his offer reinstated—sending a video of himself climbing a ladder while maintaining 3–point contact. JFS did not respond.

[...]

The district court granted summary judgment in favor of JFS. It found that Cannon's rotator cuff injury did not render him disabled under the ADA, and, even if he were disabled, he was not qualified for the field engineer position.

[...]

The ADA prohibits discrimination against on the basis of a disability. As with other antidiscrimination statutes in the employment context, a plaintiff trying to show a violation of the ADA using circumstantial evidence must satisfy the McDonnell Douglas burden-shifting framework. To make out his prima facie showing under that framework, Cannon must show that: (1) the plaintiff has a disability, or was regarded as disabled; (2) he was qualified for the job; and (3) he was subject to an adverse employment decision on account of his disability. If he makes that showing, a presumption of discrimination arises, and the employer must "articulate a legitimate non-discriminatory reason for the adverse employment action." The burden then shifts to the plaintiff to produce evidence from which a jury could conclude that the employer's articulated reason is pretextual.

Under the ADA, an individual suffers from a "disability," if that individual has "a physical impairment that substantially limits one or more major life activities." The district court concluded that Cannon was not disabled because his "injured shoulder did not substantially impair[ ] his daily functioning." Whatever merit that finding of no disability may have had under the original ADA, it is at odds with changes brought about by the ADA Amendments Act of 2008. Those amendments "make it easier for people with disabilities to obtain protection under the ADA." A principal way in which Congress accomplished that goal was to broaden the definition of "disability." Two features of that expanded concept of disability support a finding of disability in this case.

The first aspect of the 2008 Act that helps establish Cannon's injury as a disability is its clarification that the Supreme Court and EEOC had interpreted the "substantially limits" standard to be a more demanding one than Congress had intended. The 2008 Act thus provides "Rules of Construction Regarding the Definition of Disability," which focus on construing the "substantially limits" standard "in favor of broad coverage." EEOC regulations implementing the 2008 Amendments follow this command in concluding that "the threshold issue of whether an impairment 'substantially limits' a major life activity should not demand extensive analysis," and the term "shall be interpreted and applied to require a degree of functional limitation that is lower than the standard for 'substantially limits' applied" previously. The inquiry in this post-amendment case is thus whether Cannon's impairment substantially limits his ability "to perform a major life activity as compared to most people in the general population."

There is ample evidence to support a conclusion that Cannon's injury qualifies as a disability under the more relaxed standard. Although the district court concluded otherwise, the ADA includes "lifting" in its list of major life activities. . . . Given that lifting and reaching are "major life activities," Cannon's shoulder injury is a qualifying disability if it "substantially limits" his ability to perform such tasks. There is certainly evidence to that effect. [...]

JFS's belief that Cannon's injury resulted in substantial impairment—even if that view were mistaken—is the second reason why the 2008 amendments support a finding that Cannon was disabled. The ADA now covers not just someone who is disabled but also those subjected to discrimination because they are "regarded as having an actual or perceived physical or mental impairment whether or not the impairment limits or is perceived to limit a major life activity." The amended "regarded as" provision reflects the view that "unfounded concerns, mistaken beliefs, fears, myths, or prejudice about disabilities are just as disabling as actual impairments." It overrules "prior authority 'requiring a plaintiff to show that the employer regarded him or her as being substantially limited in a major life activity.'" . . . We thus conclude that evidence exists supporting a finding either that Cannon is disabled or was regarded as disabled.

That brings us the closer question of whether, despite Cannon's impairments, he was still qualified for the field engineer position. To be a qualified employee, Cannon must be able to show that he could either (1) "perform the essential functions of the job in spite of [his] disability," or (2) that "a reasonable accommodation of [his] disability would have enabled [him] to perform the essential functions of his job." . . . A function is "essential" if it bears "more than a marginal relationship" to the employee's job.

[...]

We first address driving, which the district court held was essential because of the vastness of the worksite and a function that Cannon could not perform because of his [painkiller] prescription. Assuming that driving is an essential function of the field engineer position, a conclusion that Cannon disputes, there is sufficient evidence from which a jury could conclude that Cannon was able to perform that duty. JFS cites an unwritten, though quite sensible, policy that "employees who are taking narcotics are not permitted to operate company vehicles." But there is a dispute about whether Cannon was still taking the medication or, at the least, could have stopped taking it once he started working. The painkiller was prescribed "as needed." Cannon asserts he stopped taking the medication prior to applying and informed JFS of that prior to being told that his offer had been revoked. . . . [T]he evidence creates a dispute that a jury should decide about whether Cannon could have avoided taking the medication while working for JFS.

[...]

The next essential function that JFS found disqualifying is climbing a ladder. This time Cannon agrees that the field engineer job requires the ability to climb a ladder. . . . But there is conflicting evidence about whether Cannon can climb the ladder with reasonable accommodation. Cannon's doctor submitted a medical release to JFS [clearing Cannon for ladder work] . . . [a]nd after learning that JFS rescinded his job offer based on its belief that the shoulder injury would prevent him from climbing a ladder, Cannon submitted a video of himself climbing a ladder while maintaining 3–point contact. . . . In light of the doctor's note and video, we are unable to conclude that there is no evidence supporting the view that Cannon can limb a ladder despite his impairment.

[...]

If JFS convinces a jury that Cannon cannot perform essential functions of the job because of the injury, then it has offered a lawful reason for its decision. But if the jury credits the evidence we have cited favoring Cannon and concludes he was disabled, yet still qualified to be a field engineer, then revoking Cannon's job offer based on his physical impairment would have constituted the discrimination that the ADA forbids.

[...]

We REVERSE the grant of summary judgment and REMAND this case.

[Citations and footnotes omitted]

QUESTIONS FOR DISCUSSION:

Suppose a job applicant tripped on her way in to a job interview, causing her to limp when walking around the office. If the interviewer observed the limp, what other things would need to be true for the applicant to have a disability discrimination claim?

Think of any job—one you've held or are otherwise familiar with. What are some of the essential functions of that job? How are essential functions distinct from qualifications?

Employee Safety

Employers must provide a safe workplace for their employees. The Occupational and Safety Health Act governs an employer's responsibilities for a safe workplace. The goal of the act is to protect employees from toxic chemicals, excessive noise, mechanical dangers, and unsanitary working conditions. The Occupational and Safety Health Administration administers the workplace safety laws. All employers are subject to **OSHA** requirements. Employers who violate OSHA standards are subject to fines.

To comply with OSHA requirements, employers must:

- Allow employees to access their medical records maintained by the employer.

OSHA:
The Occupational Safety and Health Administration, which implements and enforces workplace safety rules.

- Provide well-maintained tools and equipment.

- Provide employees with personal protective equipment to protect against hazards, such as helmets, eye protection, hearing protection, and hard-toed shoes.

- Train employers on how to handle hazardous materials.

- Report accidents to OSHA within eight hours of the accident.

- Keep records of work-related accidents, injuries, and illnesses.

Employees have the right to file an OSHA complaint without retaliation from the employer. Employees also have the right to participate in OSHA workplace inspections. Employees also have some responsibilities under OSHA. Employees must review employer-provided OSHA standards and requirements and attend safety training provided by employers.

> *Example:* A Dollar General store was cited for several safety violations, including blocking of an emergency exit door, blocked electrical panels, and failure to keep a clear path to an emergency exit door. OSHA proposed $215,578 in fines.

According to OSHA, the top 10 safety violations in 2016 were:

1. Lack of fall protection.
2. Hazard communication.
3. Scaffolds.
4. Lack of respiratory protection.
5. Lockout/tagout (failure to disable machinery during repair or maintenance).
6. Powered industrial trucks.
7. Ladders.
8. Machine guarding.
9. Electrical wiring.
10. Electrical, general requirements.

There are 22 state and territories known as "state plan" jurisdictions: Alaska, Arizona, California, Hawaii, Indiana, Iowa, Kentucky, Maryland, Michigan, Minnesota, Nevada, New Mexico, North Carolina, Oregon, Puerto Rico, South Carolina, Tennessee, Utah, Vermont, Virginia, Washington, and Wyoming. Another six states and territories have plans applying to government employees: Connecticut, Illinois, Maine, New Jersey, New York, and the U.S. Virgin Islands.

OSHA is a federal law. Before OSHA became law, a number of states already had workplace safety laws in place. At the time OSHA passed, each state had the option to submit an occupational safety and health plan to the Secretary of Labor. In states where the Secretary adopted the state plan, employers follow the state plan instead of the federal law.

Many state plans have standards identical to OSHA. State plans may address hazards that are not included in the federal OSHA rules. States may also impose fines and penalties that are stricter than those under federal law.

Workers' Compensation

Workers' compensation is a type of insurance providing benefits to employees who are injured on the job. State laws require most employers, depending on the number of employees, to have workers' compensation for their employees. Workers' compensation benefits are generally available without any finding of negligence or fault on the employer.

WORKERS' COMPENSATION:
A type of insurance providing benefits to employees who are injured on the job.

> *Example:*
>
> Arne works for Atlantic-Pacific Power Company. As part of their expansion efforts, the company is building a new cooling tower. Scaffolding was built for the construction workers working on the new tower. The scaffolding was built quickly and not up to code in order to allow the workers to achieve construction goals ahead of schedule. The platform of the scaffolding gave way and collapsed inward with Arne and 17 workers on it. Arne and the other workers suffered severe injuries. The workers would be entitled to workers' compensation for their injuries.
>
> Assume that Arne was managing the crew of workers on the platform. He knew that company policy was to limit the number of workers on the platform to only 15 employees, but he made the decision to allow three additional workers on the platform. Arne's violation of company policy might bar his recovery of benefits.

Each state has its own workers' compensation statute. To receive benefits, the employee's injury must occur in the course of employment. This means that the injury must take place while the employee is engaged in work duties. An employee may not receive benefits if the injury were self-inflicted, if the injury happened while committing a crime, or if the employee violated company policy.

The purpose of worker's compensation is to compensate workers for job-related injuries without the expense of litigation. Generally, the employee may recover compensation for loss of income and for medical expenses. Benefits are available for both temporary and permanent injuries. If a worker dies from his injuries, workers' compensation provides payment to the family. Employees agree to give up their right to sue the employer when they accept workers' compensation. It is illegal for an employer to fire, retaliate, or discriminate against an employee who files a worker's compensation claim.

Disability Insurance

Disability insurance is a program of the Social Security Administration. **Disability insurance** provides income protection to individuals who become disabled and cannot work for a long period of time. Social Security disability income insurance is available to employees who have made Federal Insurance Contributions Act (FICA) contributions. FICA requires employees to contribute part of their earnings to the program.

The purpose of disability insurance is to help disabled workers maintain their standard of

DISABILITY INSURANCE:

A type of insurance providing income protection to individuals who become disabled and cannot work for a long period of time.

> *Example:* Donna has worked for Albright Industries for the past 29 years. She is in charge of accounts payable for the company. Donna recently suffered a stroke, during which her brain lacked oxygen for several minutes. The stroke left Donna partially paralyzed and unable to concentrate for more than a few minutes at a time. She cannot perform her job duties. In light of her age and the severity of the condition, doctors do not expect her to recover her mental abilities. Donna is likely to be eligible for disability benefits.

living and pay their expenses during a period of disability. Disability insurance replaces only a portion of income; it does not provide full replacement income during the disability. Unlike workers' compensation, disability insurance coverage is provided even if the disability is not job-related.

Generally, a doctor's report is required to establish the disability. To qualify for the insurance, the employee must be unable to engage in any substantial activity because of a physical or mental impairment. The impairment must either be expected to last for at least 12 months or result in death. The amount of the disability payment is determined through a formula using the worker's earnings before he became disabled.

The Social Security Administration will consider the following five factors to determine if an individual is eligible for disability benefits.

- To be eligible for disability benefits, the individual generally cannot be working, or cannot make more than the base amount set by Social Security.

- The condition must significantly interfere with basic work activities.

- The disability must be on the Social Security Administration list of conditions, or of equal severity.

- The disability must interfere with the individual's ability to perform work they did previously.

- The worker must be unable to perform a different job that is less demanding, based on the individual's condition, age, and experience.

Some employers also offer private disability insurance options to employees. These insurance policies are not run by the Social Security Administration and may provide benefits under different circumstances.

Affirmative Action

Affirmative action refers to hiring and employment programs designed to remedy prior societal discrimination. Affirmative action programs take measures to increase minority and female representation in hiring. These programs are premised on the idea that past discrimination has left minorities at a disadvantage. Thus, affirmative action programs actively seek out minority and female candidates.

The government has adopted affirmative action program requirements. At the federal level, businesses that contract with the federal government must implement a written affirmative action policy to recruit and promote qualified minorities, women, persons with disabilities, and covered veterans. The affirmative actions might include training programs and outreach. Many states also require some sort of affirmative action for public employers or businesses working with the government. In recent years, however, a number of states have passed laws that prohibit government employers from giving preferential treatment based on race, national origin, or gender in employment.

Unless contracting with the government, private employers are not required to have an

UNIVERSITIES MAY CONSIDER RACE IN ADMISSIONS DECISIONS.

Fisher v. University of Texas
(College Applicant) v. (University)
___ US ___, 136 S. Ct. 2198 (2016)

INSTANT FACTS:
Caucasian university applicant challenged University's admission policy that considered race as one factor in the admissions process.

BLACK LETTER RULE:
University admissions policy may consider race as one factor in determining admission eligibility.

FACTS:
The University of Texas utilizes a two-part admissions policy. Under the first part, all students who graduated in the top ten percent of their high school class are admitted to the university. Under the second part of the policy, the University selects applicants to fill the remaining spots by considering a number of factors. Race is considered indirectly as part of an applicant's Personal Achievement Score, which encompasses race. A Caucasian applicant to the University, whose application was rejected, challenged the policy. The applicant claimed the second part of the policy violates the Equal Protection Clause. The trial court and Court of Appeals found in favor of the university.

ISSUE:
Can a university consider race in its admission policy?

DECISION AND RATIONALE:
Yes. A university may implement a race-conscious admissions policy to achieve the educational benefits of student diversity. The policy may not use specific numbers or goals. The university showed a compelling interest in achieving a diverse student body. None of the alternatives suggested by the plaintiff was feasible to achieve the university's interest.

ANALYSIS:
The decision affirmed the importance of diversity in society, but it does not open the door to all affirmative action policies. To be upheld, a policy must be based on concrete diversity goals. It must also further a university's compelling interest. The decision was not unanimous. Justice Alito issued a long dissent, joined by two other Justices. The dissent stated that the university did not demonstrate the need for a race-based policy. Affirmative action proponents consider the decision a significant development for diversity efforts.

QUESTIONS FOR DISCUSSION:
What are some other factors a university might consider other than student achievement? What compelling interests do these factors serve?

University of Texas offered Fisher the opportunity to start at a satellite campus and transfer to UT later. Does that sound like a reasonable offer to you? Is there ever a right to attend a specific university?

affirmative action program. As noted above, employers cannot discriminate against workers based on race, gender, or other protected characteristics. In addition, many private employers today choose to have a diversity program. Although not required to do so, many employers believe such policies are a good thing to do or feel a diverse workplace benefits the business. These policies often focus on outreach to minorities and promoting inclusion in the workplace. Employers must take care to ensure that race or gender is only one of many factors considered in an employment decision.

V. Immigration and Employment

In today's world, employers often look outside the United States to find workers with the skills and experience they require. However, United States immigration law imposes restrictions on the ability of foreign workers to take employment positions in the U.S. Generally, anyone who wishes to enter the United States must obtain a visa from the U.S. government. Nonimmigrant visas allow foreign visitors a temporary stay. An immigrant visa allows for permanent residence. A worker visa is required for those visitors who want to come to the United States for employment. All foreign workers must have authorization to work in the United States.

Employees must provide proof that they are legally able to work in the United States. Before hiring a new employee, all U.S. employers must request proof of immigration status or right to work through an Employment Authorization Document. Employers may be sanctioned for violating this rule.

Employers must use an I-9 form when hiring an employee, regardless of the employee's immigration status. The I-9 form requires the employee to produce documentation to show that he may work legally in the United States. Employers must make a reasonable effort to ensure that the documents provided are genuine.

Permanent Resident Status

Employers often wish to hire foreign citizens to fill certain positions in their company. This need may arise because specialized knowledge or experience is necessary for the position, or because there is a shortage of workers in the United States. Employers may sponsor employees for permanent resident status. The employer must complete and file an application with U.S. Citizenship and Immigration Services. By filing the petition, the employer is indicating its intent to hire the employee if the petition is approved.

To obtain permanent status, foreign workers must show that they have unique skills, or will not negatively affect U.S. workers. Generally, the employer needs to obtain a permanent **labor certification** from the Department of Labor before filing a petition to USCIS. The Depart-

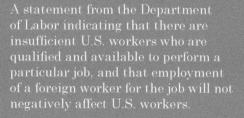

LABOR CERTIFICATION:
A statement from the Department of Labor indicating that there are insufficient U.S. workers who are qualified and available to perform a particular job, and that employment of a foreign worker for the job will not negatively affect U.S. workers.

Employment Eligibility Verification
Department of Homeland Security
U.S. Citizenship and Immigration Services

**USCIS
Form I-9**
OMB No. 1615-0047
Expires 08/31/2019

▶ **START HERE:** Read instructions carefully before completing this form. The instructions must be available, either in paper or electronically, during completion of this form. Employers are liable for errors in the completion of this form.

ANTI-DISCRIMINATION NOTICE: It is illegal to discriminate against work-authorized individuals. Employers **CANNOT** specify which document(s) an employee may present to establish employment authorization and identity. The refusal to hire or continue to employ an individual because the documentation presented has a future expiration date may also constitute illegal discrimination.

Section 1. Employee Information and Attestation *(Employees must complete and sign Section 1 of Form I-9 no later than the **first day of employment**, but not before accepting a job offer.)*

Last Name *(Family Name)*	First Name *(Given Name)*	Middle Initial	Other Last Names Used *(if any)*

Address *(Street Number and Name)*	Apt. Number	City or Town	State	ZIP Code

Date of Birth *(mm/dd/yyyy)*	U.S. Social Security Number	Employee's E-mail Address	Employee's Telephone Number
	☐☐☐ - ☐☐ - ☐☐☐☐		

I am aware that federal law provides for imprisonment and/or fines for false statements or use of false documents in connection with the completion of this form.

I attest, under penalty of perjury, that I am (check one of the following boxes):

☐ 1. A citizen of the United States

☐ 2. A noncitizen national of the United States *(See instructions)*

☐ 3. A lawful permanent resident   (Alien Registration Number/USCIS Number): _____

☐ 4. An alien authorized to work   until (expiration date, if applicable, mm/dd/yyyy): _____
        Some aliens may write "N/A" in the expiration date field. *(See instructions)*

Aliens authorized to work must provide only one of the following document numbers to complete Form I-9:
An Alien Registration Number/USCIS Number OR Form I-94 Admission Number OR Foreign Passport Number.

1. Alien Registration Number/USCIS Number: _____
            OR
2. Form I-94 Admission Number: _____
            OR
3. Foreign Passport Number: _____

    Country of Issuance: _____

QR Code - Section 1
Do Not Write In This Space

Signature of Employee	Today's Date *(mm/dd/yyyy)*

Preparer and/or Translator Certification (check one):
☐ I did not use a preparer or translator.   ☐ A preparer(s) and/or translator(s) assisted the employee in completing Section 1.
(Fields below must be completed and signed when preparers and/or translators assist an employee in completing Section 1.)

I attest, under penalty of perjury, that I have assisted in the completion of Section 1 of this form and that to the best of my knowledge the information is true and correct.

Signature of Preparer or Translator	Today's Date *(mm/dd/yyyy)*

Last Name *(Family Name)*	First Name *(Given Name)*

Address *(Street Number and Name)*	City or Town	State	ZIP Code

🛑 *Employer Completes Next Page* 🛑

Form I-9 11/14/2016 N   Page 1 of 3

Employment Eligibility Verification
Department of Homeland Security
U.S. Citizenship and Immigration Services

USCIS
Form I-9
OMB No. 1615-0047
Expires 08/31/2019

Section 2. Employer or Authorized Representative Review and Verification

(Employers or their authorized representative must complete and sign Section 2 within 3 business days of the employee's first day of employment. You must physically examine one document from List A OR a combination of one document from List B and one document from List C as listed on the "Lists of Acceptable Documents.")

Employee Info from Section 1	Last Name *(Family Name)*	First Name *(Given Name)*	M.I.	Citizenship/Immigration Status

List A Identity and Employment Authorization	**OR**	**List B** Identity	**AND**	**List C** Employment Authorization

List A
Document Title

Issuing Authority

Document Number

Expiration Date *(if any)(mm/dd/yyyy)*

Document Title

Issuing Authority

Document Number

Expiration Date *(if any)(mm/dd/yyyy)*

Document Title

Issuing Authority

Document Number

Expiration Date *(if any)(mm/dd/yyyy)*

List B
Document Title

Issuing Authority

Document Number

Expiration Date *(if any)(mm/dd/yyyy)*

List C
Document Title

Issuing Authority

Document Number

Expiration Date *(if any)(mm/dd/yyyy)*

Additional Information

QR Code - Sections 2 & 3
Do Not Write In This Space

Certification: I attest, under penalty of perjury, that (1) I have examined the document(s) presented by the above-named employee, (2) the above-listed document(s) appear to be genuine and to relate to the employee named, and (3) to the best of my knowledge the employee is authorized to work in the United States.

The employee's first day of employment *(mm/dd/yyyy)*: _____ *(See instructions for exemptions)*

Signature of Employer or Authorized Representative	Today's Date*(mm/dd/yyyy)*	Title of Employer or Authorized Representative
Last Name of Employer or Authorized Representative	First Name of Employer or Authorized Representative	Employer's Business or Organization Name

Employer's Business or Organization Address (Street Number and Name)	City or Town	State	ZIP Code

Section 3. Reverification and Rehires *(To be completed and signed by employer or authorized representative.)*

A. New Name *(if applicable)*			B. Date of Rehire *(if applicable)*
Last Name *(Family Name)*	First Name *(Given Name)*	Middle Initial	Date *(mm/dd/yyyy)*

C. If the employee's previous grant of employment authorization has expired, provide the information for the document or receipt that establishes continuing employment authorization in the space provided below.

Document Title	Document Number	Expiration Date *(if any) (mm/dd/yyyy)*

I attest, under penalty of perjury, that to the best of my knowledge, this employee is authorized to work in the United States, and if the employee presented document(s), the document(s) I have examined appear to be genuine and to relate to the individual.

Signature of Employer or Authorized Representative	Today's Date *(mm/dd/yyyy)*	Name of Employer or Authorized Representative

Form I-9 11/14/2016 N

LISTS OF ACCEPTABLE DOCUMENTS
All documents must be UNEXPIRED

Employees may present one selection from List A
or a combination of one selection from List B and one selection from List C.

LIST A Documents that Establish Both Identity and Employment Authorization	OR	LIST B Documents that Establish Identity	AND	LIST C Documents that Establish Employment Authorization
1. U.S. Passport or U.S. Passport Card		1. Driver's license or ID card issued by a State or outlying possession of the United States provided it contains a photograph or information such as name, date of birth, gender, height, eye color, and address		1. A Social Security Account Number card, unless the card includes one of the following restrictions: (1) NOT VALID FOR EMPLOYMENT (2) VALID FOR WORK ONLY WITH INS AUTHORIZATION (3) VALID FOR WORK ONLY WITH DHS AUTHORIZATION
2. Permanent Resident Card or Alien Registration Receipt Card (Form I-551)		2. ID card issued by federal, state or local government agencies or entities, provided it contains a photograph or information such as name, date of birth, gender, height, eye color, and address		2. Certification of Birth Abroad issued by the Department of State (Form FS-545)
3. Foreign passport that contains a temporary I-551 stamp or temporary I-551 printed notation on a machine-readable immigrant visa		3. School ID card with a photograph		3. Certification of Report of Birth issued by the Department of State (Form DS-1350)
4. Employment Authorization Document that contains a photograph (Form I-766)		4. Voter's registration card 5. U.S. Military card or draft record		4. Original or certified copy of birth certificate issued by a State, county, municipal authority, or territory of the United States bearing an official seal
5. For a nonimmigrant alien authorized to work for a specific employer because of his or her status: a. Foreign passport; and b. Form I-94 or Form I-94A that has the following: (1) The same name as the passport; and (2) An endorsement of the alien's nonimmigrant status as long as that period of endorsement has not yet expired and the proposed employment is not in conflict with any restrictions or limitations identified on the form.		6. Military dependent's ID card 7. U.S. Coast Guard Merchant Mariner Card 8. Native American tribal document 9. Driver's license issued by a Canadian government authority **For persons under age 18 who are unable to present a document listed above:**		5. Native American tribal document 6. U.S. Citizen ID Card (Form I-197) 7. Identification Card for Use of Resident Citizen in the United States (Form I-179)
6. Passport from the Federated States of Micronesia (FSM) or the Republic of the Marshall Islands (RMI) with Form I-94 or Form I-94A indicating nonimmigrant admission under the Compact of Free Association Between the United States and the FSM or RMI		10. School record or report card 11. Clinic, doctor, or hospital record 12. Day-care or nursery school record		8. Employment authorization document issued by the Department of Homeland Security

Examples of many of these documents appear in Part 8 of the Handbook for Employers (M-274).

Refer to the instructions for more information about acceptable receipts.

ment of Labor certifies that there are insufficient U.S. workers who are qualified and available to perform the job. The certification also indicates that employment of the foreign worker will not negatively affect U.S. workers. In order to obtain the certification, the employer must conduct a recruiting and hiring process to make sure no U.S. workers are qualified and willing to take the job.

WORK PERMIT:
Authorization from U.S. Citizenship and Immigration Services allowing individuals living in the United States under non-work visas to work in the U.S.

Temporary Work Visas

Temporary work visas are available to foreign workers who wish to enter the United States for temporary employment. Before an employee seeks a visa, the employer must file a petition with the U.S. Citizenship and Immigration Services. Some temporary worker categories have a limited number of petitions available each year. The employee must have an employment offer before a visa may be granted. There are different types of temporary work visas for various kinds of work.

Work Permits

Many foreign nationals live in the U.S. under various types of non-work visas. For instance, asylees, spouses of various visa holders, people with Temporary Protected Status, and students experiencing economic hardship are all examples of foreign nationals living in the U.S. under non-work visas. If individuals under a non-work visa wish to work in the United States, they must apply for a **work permit** from U.S. Citizenship and Immigration Services. If granted, USCIS will issue a photo identity card, called an Employment Authorization Document, to the worker. The Employment Authorization Document is similar to a driver's license and provides proof of the individual's right to work in the U.S.

Types of Permanent Worker Visas	
EB-1 – Priority Workers	Extraordinary professors and researchers, multinational executives and managers
EB-2 – Professionals With Advanced Degrees or Persons With Exceptional Ability	Exceptional ability in the sciences, arts, or business; will substantially benefit the economy or interests of the U.S.
EB-3 – Professional or Skilled Workers	Professionals with a college degree; capable of performing skilled or unskilled labor for which qualified workers are not available in the United States

Common Temporary Worker Visa Categories	
H-1B: Person in Specialty Occupation	To work in a specialty occupation; requires a higher education degree
H-2A: Temporary Agricultural Worker	Temporary or seasonal agricultural work
H-2B: Temporary Non-agricultural Worker	Temporary or seasonal non-agricultural work
H-3: Trainee or Special Education visitor	To receive training not available in the home country
L: Intracompany Transferee	To work at a branch, parent, affiliate, or subsidiary of the current employer; managerial or executive capacity, or with specialized knowledge
O: Individual with Extraordinary Ability or Achievement	Extraordinary ability in the sciences, arts, education, business, or athletics

VI. Labor Organization

A **labor union** is an organized association of workers in the same trade that is formed for the purpose of representing the members' interests regarding wages, benefits, and working conditions. Unions permit workers to act together to achieve more favorable terms of employment. All workers in the United States have the right to join a union. Employees also have the right to form unions in the workplace.

Employers may not interfere with union activities, discriminate against union employees, or retaliate against union organizing. Specifically, employers may not do any of the following:

- Threaten to shut the business down if workers form a union.

- Question workers about union matters, meetings, or supporters.

- Ask workers whether they belong to a union.

- Fire or punish workers for engaging in union activity.

- Retaliate through firing, reassignment, or layoffs against workers because of union activity.

The National Labor Relations Board (NLRB) provides a process for forming a union at a workplace. If 30% of the employees show interest in forming a union, the employees can petition the NLRB to hold a representative election. No managers or supervisors may vote for unionization. The NLRB will then hold an election. If a

> *Example:*   Aida Company manufactures electronic components. Its employees belong to a union. The employees requested a pay increase. Aida Company claims that it is financially unable to provide the increase. The union requested Aida Company's financial information to verify its argument. Aida Company will likely have to provide its financial information to the union.

majority of the employees vote for unionization, a union is established.

Collective Bargaining

Collective bargaining is the process through which unions negotiate terms of employment with employers on behalf of the employees. These terms of employment may include pay, health care, pensions, hours, health and safety policies, and other benefits. The union employees select a representative who negotiates on their behalf. The union members then vote to approve or reject the proposed contract terms.

LABOR UNION:

An organized association of workers in the same trade that is formed for the purpose of representing the members' interests regarding wages, benefits, and working conditions.

COLLECTIVE BARGAINING:

The process through which unions negotiate terms of employment with employers on behalf of the employees.

COLLECTIVE BARGAINING AGREEMENT:

The agreed-upon contract between union employees and the employer.

The agreed-upon contract is called a **collective bargaining agreement**.

Employees and employers must engage in good faith bargaining. The employer has a duty to provide some information to the union during the collective bargaining process. The union must show that the information is relevant to the employer/employee relationship. Generally, the employer must provide information about wages and benefits. Sometimes, the employer must produce additional information.

In some circumstances, the employer may withhold confidential information, such as highly personal information or trade secret information. The union must also produce relevant information requested by the employer.

If the union and cannot agree on contract terms, the union members may decide to **strike**. A strike occurs when all of the union workers refuse to come to work. The purpose of the strike is to disrupt the employer's business. Workers use a strike to persuade the employer to keep negotiating or to agree to their terms. Strikes are typically used as a last resort measure. The workers do not receive pay during the strike. The employer may hire replacement workers during the strike.

The National Labor Relations Act gives union employees the right to strike. However, the law also imposes restrictions on the right to strike. To be lawful, a strike must take place for a lawful purpose. Both economic strikers and unfair labor strikers are lawful. **Economic strikers** strike to obtain an economic benefit such as a higher wage or shorter hours. Economic strikers maintain their status as employees, but they can be permanently replaced by the employer. **Unfair labor practice strikers** protest an unfair labor practice by the employer. Unfair labor practice strikers cannot be discharged or permanently replaced. A strike may be considered unlawful if the workers strike to support an unfair union labor practice, the strike violates a no-strike provision of a contract, or the strikers engage in misconduct.

In contrast to a strike, a **lockout** is a temporary work stoppage started by the employer.

In a lockout, the employer typically refuses to allow employees on the premises. The purpose of the lockout is to persuade employees to accept the terms offered by the employer. During the lockout, the employer may hire temporary replacement workers. The employer must rehire the union employees after the lockout.

Right to Work Laws

Right to work laws hold that workers cannot be required or forced to join to a union. These laws prohibit union security agreements between employers and labor unions. Union security agreements may require employee membership in a union or the payment of union dues. The right to work laws allow non-union workers to work at unionized workplaces without having to join the union or pay union dues or fees. Currently 26 states have right to work statutes in place.

STRIKE:
A collective effort of union employees to refuse to work in order to persuade the employer to negotiate or accept contract terms.

ECONOMIC STRIKERS:
Striking union workers seeking to obtain an economic benefit for the workers.

UNFAIR LABOR PRACTICE STRIKERS:
Union workers who are striking to protest an unfair labor practice by the employer.

LOCKOUT:
A temporary work stoppage implemented by the employer.

In September 2016, Long Island University locked out all of its faculty members a few days before classes started. The faculty members were barred from campus and their email accounts. The faculty members are part of a union, and the contract with the University had recently expired. In a vote, the union members rejected the University's proposed contract terms. Recent negotiations between the University and the faculty union ended with a faculty strike, so the University decided to conduct a lockout to avoid another strike. The lockout ended after 12 days when the faculty union and University reached an agreement.

Right to work laws have been the subject of disagreement. Those in favor of the laws argue that forcing parties to join unions is unfair and violates the employees' right to freedom of association. Opponents of the laws argue that the laws undermine the union system by allowing workers a "free ride" to enjoy the benefits of union-negotiated terms of employment without contributing to the union.

RIGHT TO WORK LAWS:
Laws prohibiting agreements between employers and unions that require workers to join the union or pay union dues or fees.

CHAPTER SUMMARY

Regardless of the path chosen, nearly every individual and organization involved in business deals with employment issues. From the entry-level employee at a retail store to the CEO of a large corporation, employment law affects all workers. As a worker, one's status as an employee brings about certain benefits and protections not available to independent contractors. Noncompliance with the rules governing the employment relationship can be costly for commercial entities. Thus, as an employer, employment law imposes obligations that may affect business and organizational decisions beyond the basic working conditions and terms of employment. Whether as the employee or employer, both, or neither, the rules of employment will likely affect every businessperson's career or business operation.

Review Questions

Review question 1.

What is at-will employment? What are the limits on at-will employment? What are some of the employees and groups who are not at-will?

Review question 2.

What are the differences between employees and independent contractors? What is the most important distinction to determine? What are the pros and cons of hiring an employee or an independent contractor? What are the pros and cons of being an employee or an independent contractor?

Review question 3.

What benefits are employees entitled to? What bearing does the number of employees have on available benefits? What amount of time off is required for at-will employees?

Review question 4.

What types of leave are available to employees? For family leave, what are some of the qualifying relationships for which leave may be taken? For medical leave, what types of medical conditions support the right to take leave?

Review question 5.

What are the protected characteristics listed in Title VII? What other laws have expanded the scope of antidiscrimination laws at the federal level?

Review question 6.

What must an employer do to provide a safe workplace? Which agency oversees safety in the workplace? What is worker's compensation? Who is eligible for disability benefits?

Review question 7.

When can foreign citizens work in the United States? What are the employer's responsibilities when hiring a foreign citizen?

Review question 8.

What is collective bargaining? What is "right to work" and how does it impact union votes? How does a strike differ from a lockout?

Review question 9.

How is "disability" defined under the ADA? What is the employer's obligation to an employee with a disability?

Review question 10.

What protections do older workers receive under federal law? Are there any corresponding protections for younger employees?

Questions for Discussion

Discussion question 1.

Amy is a software programmer. Amy works for a company called Amazing Apps, Inc. She is paid for each app when she notifies the company that it is complete. Amazing Apps creates mobile phone apps. Customers submit an app idea to Amazing Apps, which then assigns the programming job to one of its programmers. Once an app project is assigned to Amy, she can work on it during whatever hours she chooses, as long as she works at least eight hours per day. She may work from home most days, but she is required to come to the office to work at least one day per week. She may work in the office every day, if she likes. Amazing Apps' workplace is set up with temporary desks for everyone. People may claim whichever workspace they want once they get to the office, and they must remove all of their materials from the workspace at the end of the day. Lockers are available for workers to keep their materials. Amazing Apps provided Amy with a cell phone and computer. Once the app is completed, Amy must demo the app to the customer. This is sometimes done in person, sometimes with internet technology, such as Skype. During these demos, the programmers are required to wear a shirt with the Amazing Apps logo provided by Amazing Apps.

Is Amy an employee of Amazing Apps or an independent contractor?

If Amy is an employee, what are the effects of employee status for Amy and Amazing Apps?

Assume Amazing Apps, Inc. classifies her as an independent contractor, but the EEOC later determines Amy was an employee. What consequences might happen to Amazing Apps?

Discussion question 2.

Lois is a black female employee of Energy Enterprises. Energy Enterprises has 267 employees. Lois is 48 years old, and has worked at the company for 25 years. Lois has received good work performance evaluations and has received several promotions over the years. She is currently a project manager. Last year, the company reorganized and restructured its business operations. As a result, Lois now has a new supervisor, Barry. Barry is a white male who is 55 years old. Lois overheard Barry telling another employee that "Lois is very attractive if you like that sort of thing," that "she is thinner than you'd expect" and a "cougar." Several months ago, Lois told Barry that she is suffering from migraines, which the doctors think may be caused by the new computer screens installed at the office. Barry told her there was nothing he could do about the screens because upper management really likes the new screens. Last week, Barry promoted one white male and one white female employee to Senior Project Managers. The male employee is 41 years old and has worked at the company for 10 years. The female employee is 35 years old and has worked at the company for eight years. The new Senior Project Managers received the same performance evaluation rating as Lois.

> Does Lois have a claim for discrimination against the employer? If so, on what grounds?

> Assume Lois has a claim for sex discrimination. Is it based on disparate treatment or disparate impact?

> Are there any reasonable accommodations that the employer might offer to Lois?

Discussion question 3.

Chris is a human resources manager for Bigg & Large Corp., a multinational corporation headquartered in Memphis. Bigg & Large manufacturers, distributes, and sells a variety of food products worldwide. The company employs 6,000 workers across the world, 5,000 of which work in Memphis. Tennessee is a right to work state. The workers are currently undergoing a unionization campaign. The head of the research division, Alberto Ienstien, would like to hire a worker from Italy to assist in research and development of some new Italian food products at the lab in Memphis. He has recruited an employee who is an Italian citizen and has a Ph.D. in food science.

How should Chris respond to these questions from Alberto?

What must Bigg & Large do to be able to hire the recruit to work in the United States?

The recruit has indicated an interest in voting in the unionization election, and has asked Alberto a lot of questions about it. If the vote takes place while the recruit is working there, is there anything that Alberto cannot say to him about unionization?

If the unionization campaign is successful, is the recruit required to join the union?

Discussion question 4.

Maher works at 4Q Manufacturing in assembly. When he started work, he received an employee handbook. The handbook contained a section about discipline. The section said that if an employee broke a rule, then he or she would receive an oral warning. If the employee broke a second rule, then he or she would receive a written warning. If the employee broke a third rule, then he or she would be terminated.

What are your thoughts on the following scenarios?

On his first day of work, Maher made a mistake when assembling a component. His supervisor said, "That's strike one, Maher!" A year later, Maher forgot to lock the storeroom door at the end of a shift, and he was written up. Ten years later, Maher had to leave early because of a family emergency, and failed to clock out. 4Q terminated him because he had broken a third rule.

Maher works for three years at the company without a problem, and then is caught on CCTV stealing office supplies. His supervisor says that Maher is fired, but Maher says that he should keep his job and just receive an oral warning.

Maher has a great record at 4Q. He works alongside Jill, who is the supervisor's niece. Jill is often late and ignores instructions, but is never given any warnings. Maher has a bad week where he is late twice and forgets to check safety gear once. Maher is terminated.

Discussion question 5.

Title VII prohibits discrimination on the basis of race, color, national origin, sex, or religion. Some state human rights laws add further protections, such as sexual orientation, gender identity, or "creed" (a subset of religion usually referring to how an individual legally pursues his or her religion). Do the following examples describe discrimination? What would you recommend in each case?

> James works for a restaurant. James recently converted to Sikhism and started wearing a turban. His manager fires him because he cannot wear the hat and hairnet that comes with his uniform when wearing the turban, which James will not remove.

> Denise is married to Val. Val is originally from Russia, but is a legal resident of the United States and is applying for citizenship. Denise works at a treatment center for alcohol and drug dependency. Denise's boss finds out that Val is Russian and starts checking Denise's work more thoroughly. When Denise asks if there is a problem, her boss says, "Well, you live with a Russian, and vodka is their national drink, so I have concerns about your commitment to the cause."

> Assume the same facts as above, only Val does not have legal residence status and Denise and Val are only engaged.

> Bertha was brought up Catholic, but does not attend mass any more. Her family is still Catholic. Bertha starts working as a teacher's assistant in a Christian grade school. Bertha is assigned to a teacher who immediately asks, "Are you Christian?" Bertha replies, "Well, I was brought up Catholic, but I'm not very religious now." The teacher does not reply, but later asks to have Bertha assigned elsewhere because "Catholics are not really Christians."

Discussion question 6.

Bobbi is an at-will employee of Hey There Sandwiches. Bobbi is a better-than-average worker, but often argues with her supervisor about priorities or workplace rules. Bobbi's supervisor becomes tired of the arguing during a busy lunch shift and fires Bobbi, even though that will leave the shop short-handed. Assume the supervisor does not actually have the authority to fire Bobbi, but that the owner ratifies the supervisor's decision, even though the owner believes Bobbi is a good worker and did not see any misconduct.

>May the owner fire Bobbi in these circumstances?

>Assume instead that Bobbi quit during the lunch rush. Is that acceptable for an at-will employee?

>What if the owner had orally promised Bobbi that she would have a job until "at least the end of the year"? Could the supervisor still fire Bobbi if the supervisor did not know of the promise? Does the promise change Bobbi's at-will status?

Discussion question 7.

Mary works for Mielobone Corporation in the company's headquarters building. The headquarters building is located in a high crime area, so Mielobone employees seldom leave the building during the work day. A parking ramp for employees' cars is attached to the building. Mary works late one night, and when she goes to her car, the ramp is mostly empty. David, a resident of the neighborhood, is in the ramp looking for things to steal from cars. He has no other connection with Mielobone, apart from living in the vicinity. David surprises Mary, and brutally assaults her. Mary makes a worker's compensation claim for her injuries.

>Do Mary's injuries arise out of her employment with Mielobone? Why or why not?

>Mary is carrying some papers that are blown out of her hand by a fluke breeze when she leaves the building. She steps out of the ramp to retrieve them, and is then assaulted by David. Do Mary's injuries arise out of her employment with Mielobone? Why or why not?

Discussion question 8.

The first step in screening candidates for employment, according to many employers, is to do a search for the applicants' social media profiles. Employers say they look for items of concern, such as alcohol or drug use, or disparaging comments about employers or co-workers. Some employers also say that they read postings to see if applicants have acceptable communications skills or basic etiquette online. Critics of the practice says that many people post on social media about the religion or ethnicity, leaving employers open to claims of discrimination. Others say that most postings are about lawful activities, such as political activities, that should not be a factor in hiring.

In your opinion, is it appropriate to consider a prospective employee's social media profile? Why or why not?

Suppose the profile reveals that the applicant for a job has strong political opinions. Political viewpoints are not protected under anti-discrimination laws, but It is lawful to have strong opinions. Is it appropriate for employers to refuse to hire an applicant who engages in lawful activity? Why or why not?

BUSINESS RELATIONSHIPS

CHAPTER OVERVIEW

This chapter covers business relationships. Businesses can have a range of relationships, from investors to landlords to vendors and customers. Companies even have important relationships with their direct competitors. Here, we've grouped some of the laws that have the greatest impact on relations between businesses.. We will consider investor relations in the context of corporate laws. We will look at laws relating to transactions between businesses, such as antitrust laws and tariff schedules. Finally, we will look at the law of real estate ownership and leasing.

INTRODUCTION

Most of the areas of the law covered in this textbook apply to businesses and individuals alike. For example, contract law, which is arguably the foundation of all business transactions, uses the same rules for individuals and business entities (with a very few exceptions, such as consumer protection laws). In most situations, there is not one law for business and another for individuals.

There are, however, laws that are unique to businesses. They deal with the operations of a business. While most legal rules (such as contracts and torts) will apply to these operations, some types of operations involve legal rules that are unique to the business world. Most of these rules are meant to ensure fair dealing. Examples of these rules are those involving investor relations, or the laws on antitrust. Others are geared more towards the mechanics of a business operation. These rules include those that relate to transportation terms, import tariff schedules, or real estate ownership.

I.   Investor Relations

Why does a corporation exist? With some exceptions and qualifications, the simplest answer is, "to make money." Make money for whom? The answer to that question is even simpler. The primary purpose of the existence of corporations is to make money for its owners, the shareholders. Maximizing shareholder value is an important goal of corporate directors and officers.

Maximizing value is not the end of the responsibilities directors and officers owe to shareholders. Directors in particular owe the duties of loyalty and care to the business and its shareholders. The duty of loyalty means that the director focuses his efforts on the company and does not take opportunities from the business.

While turning a profit is central to running a business, that does not mean that companies cannot have other goals. Directors' decisions are protected by the "business judgment rule"—a presumption that the directors acted in the best interests of the company. Those interests often go beyond generating revenue. Many businesses make substantial positive changes in their communities by donating to charities or sponsoring events. Companies may commit to being more environmentally friendly than the law requires, even if that commitment means that shareholders receive a lower return.

For instance, a director for a consulting company who hears of a consulting contract should refer that information to the company. She should not take the contract for herself personally or for her family. In short, a director should not personally take advantage of the company or leverage his position for personal gain. The company's interests should be ahead of the director's own.

Directors also owe a duty of care. The duty of care simply means that directors will act for the company in good faith, and will behave as a reasonably prudent person would in the circumstances. The duty of care means that directors may not act on a whim or take unreasonable risks for the company. They must be reasonably informed in their decision making, and act in good faith, with an honest belief that their decisions are in the best interest of the corporation. Directors are also obligated to oversee the operations of the corporation, to ensure that the applicable laws are obeyed.

In publicly-traded corporations, there is an added duty of transparency. This transparency extends to both shareholders and potential shareholders. Transparency is generally included within the broader category of investor relations. "Investor relations" refers to communication between a corporation and the investment community. These communications let investors make informed decisions about the value of a company's stock, and whether it is worth their while to invest in it. In many companies, investor relations are part of the duties of the public relations department.

The meaning of investor relations has undergone considerable expansion in recent years. The **Sarbanes-Oxley Act** gave increased importance to investor relations in publicly-traded companies. The Act places an increased emphasis on the accuracy of the information that is disclosed to the public. Sarbanes-Oxley also gave a new emphasis on internal controls for publicly-traded companies. The internal controls are ways a company ensures compliance and prevent violations of laws or rules. The effectiveness of these controls is also something that is disclosed to the investing public.

Important and effective federal laws already regulated securities prior to Sarbanes-Oxley. Federal securities laws, known as the Securities Act of 1933 and the Securities Exchange Act of

SARBANES-OXLEY ACT:
A federal law that protects investors from fraudulent accounting practices.

1934, established reporting requirements. The goal of these laws is to provide investors with the information needed to make sound investments. The Securities Act of 1933 (1933 Act) focused on the initial release of securities to the public from the issuer. The 1933 Act established the securities registration and prospectus publication requirements that public companies still follow. First, a Registration Statement is filed with the SEC. Then, the prospectus must be distributed to the buyers of the securities before they make their purchase. This allows the buyers to make an informed decision about making a purchase, and also helps to prevent fraud. A prospectus lists the securities to be offered for sale and described how the securities issuer (the company offering the stock, for instance) is managed. In addition, the prospectus provides independently certified financial statements. It includes the information in the Registration Statement that will be valuable to the public. The documents are filed, and are available to the public for review.

The 1934 Securities Exchange Act (1934 Act) created the Securities and Exchange Commission to enforce the federal law. While the 1933 Act covered issuance of new securities, this Act focused on regulation of the secondary market—how securities are traded and sold among investors, brokers, and others after the initial issuance. It contains substantial anti-fraud measures.

One of the most notable anti-fraud tools is SEC Rule 10b-5, which is authorized by the 1934 Act and which was adopted in 1942. Rule 10b-5 bars the use of "any manipulative or deceptive device or contrivance in contravention of such rules and regulations as the Commission may prescribe as necessary or appropriate in the public interest or for the protection of investors." In practice, the SEC uses Rule 10b-5 to pursue insider trading, price fixing, and fraudulent techniques to boost the price of specific securities. It can also be used to penalize failures to disclose pertinent information to would-be investors.

> Rule 10b-5 was adopted in response to reports that a company president was making pessimistic predictions about his company's performance, while simultaneously purchasing the company's stock for himself. The only comment about the rule prior to its adoption was by Commissioner Sumner Pike, who reportedly said "Well, we are against fraud, aren't we?"

The 1933 Act and the 1934 Act provided a sound basis for the market, and the laws proved equal to many challenges over the years. At the end of the last century, however, the market faced new regulatory issues. In the mid-1990s, the stock market surged. Stock prices rose to record high levels. New entrants in the market, especially those doing business through the then-new internet ("dot com" companies), drove much of this surge. The surge ended abruptly in 2000, and stock prices collapsed.

After-the-fact investigations showed that the surging market was accompanied by fraud and misdealing. The boom in stock prices made many corporate executives focus on short-term profits that would drive stock prices, rather than on strategies that would keep a company in business over the long-term. Several publicly-traded companies had disclosed false information in their required reports—an unlawful act under federal law. Some financial reports were also adjusted to show that goals for earnings were being met.

Investors who relied on the accuracy of the false reports lost billions of dollars. By some estimates, more individual investors lost money in the 2000 downturn than in the 1929 Wall Street crash, because more individual investors had money invested. Many companies, including established companies and new start-ups, collapsed. The collapse of these companies also made many investors lose faith in the integrity of U.S. securities markets.

Established companies brought down by the scandals included Enron, WorldCom, and Tyco International. Another company that failed because of the scandals was Arthur Andersen, a venerable accounting firm that was convicted of obstructing justice for trying to hide its role in Enron's false reporting. Note, though, that Enron and others were sanctioned under existing securities law, and not by Sarbanes-Oxley. Sarbanes-Oxley was a reaction to the crisis.

In response, the "Public Company Accounting Reform and Investor Protection Act" was enacted in 2002. This Act, usually referred to as "Sarbanes-Oxley," or "SOX," was the Congressional response to the scandals of the early 2000s. The goal of SOX is to protect investors and the public by improving the financial reporting landscape for publicly-held companies. Accountability standards for corporate insiders were tightened, and the oversight of accountants and auditors was strengthened. SOX includes both civil and criminal provisions, meaning that violators could be subject to both lawsuits and to criminal prosecution.

SOX passed by nearly unanimous votes in both houses of Congress.

Accountants and Auditors

The first sections of SOX relate to accountants and auditors. The law created a federal regulatory agency, the Public Company Accounting Oversight Board (PCAOB). All public accounting companies must register with the PCAOB. When they register, firms must provide:

- A list of their clients,
- The fees paid from each client,
- A complete financial disclosure,
- A statement of quality control, and
- A list of the accountants working for the firm.

The firm must also disclose all legal actions in which the firm is involved.

Reports of firm activity are submitted to the PCAOB annually. Accounting firms that provide services to 100 or more publicly-traded companies are subject to annual inspection by the PCAOB. Firms that provide services to fewer than 100 companies are subject to inspection every three years. Inspection reports are available to the public.

> No corporate officer or director, or any other person acting under their direction, may do anything that would fraudulently influence, coerce, manipulate, or mislead an accountant performing an audit of the financial statements of the company for the purpose of making those financial statements materially misleading.

Accounting firms also must develop a set of internal quality control standards. These standards must promote compliance with all securities laws and regulations of the PCAOB. If the PCAOB finds that these quality control standards are insufficient, it may send in advisors to assist and monitor the firm as it develops adequate standards.

The PCAOB may investigate any firm at its discretion. It may require any accountant at a firm, or at the client of the firm, to testify. A violation of accounting standards could subject an individual to a fine of up to $750,000 for each individual violation. Violators could also face permanent suspension of their accounting licenses.

In addition to accounting practices, SOX addresses auditing practices and the independence of auditors. Many of the dishonest accounting practices committed in the 1990s were undertaken by auditors who had close relationships with the management of the companies they were supposed to be auditing. Painting a favorable picture of a company's financial state was beneficial for the business of the accounting firm.

To help ensure independence of auditors, a public accounting firm may audit a company indefinitely, but must rotate the lead audit partner and the lead review partner every five years. This limitation removes an incentive for collaboration between the corporate board and the accountants.

Another requirement of Sarbanes-Oxley is that every public company must have an audit committee that is directly responsible for the appointment, compensation, and oversight of the work of an accounting firm. All services to be provided by an accounting firm must be pre-approved by the audit committee. Audit committee members are usually members of the board of directors.

The audit committee must also establish quality controls to ensure that audit reporting is accurate and complete. Audit committees are responsible for monitoring and receiving complaints from employees about questionable accounting practices or about ethics issues. Committees must allow complaints to be made anonymously.

SOX sets forth nine prohibited activities that public accounting firms may not provide when they are performing auditing services. The list of prohibited services helps prevent conflicts of interests by preventing accounting firms from auditing their own work. These prohibited services include:

1. Corporate management functions,

2. Legal or expert services,

3. Bookkeeping or services related to financial statements,

4. Appraisals or valuations,

5. Actuarial services,

6. Internal audit outsourcing,

7. Financial information systems design,

8. Broker-dealer, or investment banking services, and

9. Any other service prohibited by the Board.

Financial Reporting

Some of the most significant provisions of Sarbanes-Oxley relate to responsibility for financial reports. Reports filed with the Securities and Exchange Commission (SEC) are public information. The required disclosures made to the SEC must be certified as accurate by the officers of the corporation who sign those disclosures. The disclosure and certification requirements recognize that disclosure is meaningless unless the information that is being disclosed is accurate.

The certification must state that:

- The signing officer has reviewed the disclosure.

- To the best of the officer's knowledge, the disclosure does not contain any false statement of material fact, or an omission of a material fact.

- Based on the officer's knowledge, the financial information in the disclosure is a fair representation of the financial condition of the company.

The CEO and CFO of a publicly traded corporation must also disclose the company's "disclosure controls and procedures." Disclosure controls and procedures are the mechanisms that a corporation has in place to make sure that disclosures are made in a timely manner. Under Sarbanes-Oxley, this process includes certifying that these controls and procedures are working, and that their effectiveness has been evaluated. The officers must also certify that auditors have been informed of any deficiencies in the corporation's procedures for providing information to auditors. Any significant changes in internal controls, or any related factors that could have an impact on internal controls, must be reported.

Certification is not the only Sarbanes-Oxley requirement for financial statements. Certifications only cover items that the signing officer personally knows. In addition to the certification, the financial statements must actually be accurate. A certification that an officer knows some of the details is not an excuse for inaccurate statements. Accurate information may go beyond what the signing officer knows herself. All material information must be included, whether or not the signing officer knows about it.

There are a number of items that a signing officer may not know personally, but that are accurate about the company's finances. As one example, the financial disclosure cannot leave out "off-balance sheet" items. Off-balance sheet items are those that are not reported on a company's balance sheet. This requirement

> *Example:*
>
> A certain model airliner has a useful life of 25 years. TravelsOn Airlines leases one for five years. The rental payments for the plane are not included on TravelsOn's balance sheet as rental payments. Instead, they are deducted from the airline's profits as operating expenses. The lease payments are an off-balance sheet item. They must be disclosed on TravelsOn's financial reports.

was a response to the use of "special purpose entities" at Enron. These entities allowed Enron to increase its leverage and return on assets without having to report the debt on its balance sheet. Enron took the use of special purpose entities to extremes of complexity, and also used them as a kind of dumping ground for assets that were falling in value. Transferring these assets to special purpose entities meant their losses would be kept off Enron's books.

The SEC may file a civil action against officers who violate the disclosure requirements. Private civil lawsuits may also be brought by aggrieved investors.

Internal Controls

Section 404 of the Sarbanes-Oxley Act requires all annual financial reports to include an internal control report. This report affirms that management is responsible for having adequate internal control structures in place. "Adequate internal controls" provide reasonable assurance that:

- The financial reporting is reliable, and

- Financial statements have been prepared according to **generally accepted accounting principles**.

Management must assess the effectiveness of the control structure. Any shortcomings in the control structures must be reported. In addition, registered external auditors must verify the accuracy of management's report on the company's internal controls.

Criminal Penalties

SOX imposes criminal penalties for violations of some of its provisions. Criminal prosecutions under SOX are brought by the Department of Justice, rather than the SEC. A person who certifies a financial statement knowing that the periodic report that goes with the statement does not meet SOX's requirements may be fined up to $1 million, sentenced to prison for up to 10 years, or receive both a fine and a prison sentence. If the false certification is willful, the penalty is a fine of up to $5 million, imprison-

GENERALLY ACCEPTED ACCOUNTING PRINCIPLES (GAAP):

A common set of accounting principles, standards, and procedures that companies must follow when putting financial statements together. The Principles are issued by the Financial Accounting Standards Board, a private, non-profit organization.

> SOX does not define the distinction between "knowing" and "willful" certification. In other contexts, federal courts have concluded that "willful" could mean deliberately ignoring facts.

ment for up to 20 years, or both a fine and a prison term.

A person who alters, destroys, mutilates, conceals, or falsifies records, documents, or tangible objects with the intent to obstruct, impede, or influence a legal investigation may

> A fisherman actively threw undersized fish back into the ocean in order to avoid a fine. He was convicted under this provision, but his conviction was later reversed. The U.S. Supreme Court held that the "tangible objects" provision is meant to apply only to financial records. Yates v. U.S., 574 U.S. ____ (2015).

be fined a maximum of $5 million or sentenced to up to 20 years in prison.

SOX also places criminal penalties for retaliating against employees who report their employers' Sarbanes-Oxley violations. Any person who acts to hurt the livelihood of a whistleblower may be fined not more than $1 million, sentenced to prison for not more than 10 years, or receive both a fine and a prison sentence.

The requirements of the Sarbanes-Oxley Act have increased the expense and complexity of investor relations. At the same time, the knowledge that there are individuals who are personally accountable for the accuracy of financial information has benefitted the market by raising investor confidence.

II. Business to Business Issues

The traditional economic model of a business talks about how it does business with members of the public. While most people start businesses focused on serving customers, a significant part of daily operations involves interacting with other businesses. Every company needs to deal with other businesses as suppliers, vendors, and competitors.

Dealings with other businesses can take many forms. If the relationship is strictly that of a buyer to a seller, the dealing is probably a matter of contract. If the dealings bring businesses together too closely, there could be antitrust issues. When a business hires another to transport its goods, questions of tariffs and the rules for handling freight are involved.

> Outside the U.S., antitrust laws are referred to as "competition laws."

Antitrust Laws

Most businesspeople may think of other businesses only as competition. Even though competition in a given market, or a given industry, may be keen, there is much cooperation and joint effort among competitors. Even though businesses may be competitors, they still have many common interests that lead them to work together for a common end. Cooperation between competitors is not unlawful. That cooperation, however, may be taken too far.

Antitrust law deals with businesses who take their cooperation too far, and who have substituted cooperation for competition. Antitrust laws do not bar a business from growing if it does so by operating a better business. Instead, it prohibits the use of unfair tactics to take over or divide up a market.

It is generally held that the benefits of competition to consumers outweigh the negative effects competition may have on individual businesses. Antitrust laws do not bar a business from becoming big if it does that by operating a better business. Instead, it prohibits the use of unfair tactics.

CARTEL:

A combination of sellers or producers of a product who join together to control production or price.

There are two principal federal antitrust laws: the Sherman Antitrust Act and the Clayton Act.

> Somewhat unexpectedly, the Sherman Act does not define "trust."

Sherman Act: The Sherman Antitrust Act was passed in 1890, and has been amended several times since then. It was the first federal legislation against monopolies or **cartels**. The law was a reaction to popular sentiment against the growing economic power of big business.

There are two essential provisions of the Sherman Act. The foundational provisions contained in Section 1 of the Act declare that every "contract, combination in the form of trust or otherwise, or conspiracy, in restraint of trade or commerce among the several States, or with foreign nations" is illegal.

The prohibition is against agreements to restrain trade. If competition is limited through market forces, there is no violation.

Although the Sherman Act is clear that every contract or combination is unlawful, the Supreme Court has held that Section 1 prohibits only "unreasonable" restraints of trade. An unreasonable restraint is one that involves a blatant attempt to restrain trade. These blatant attempts are called per se violations. If a per se violation is proven, there is no defense or legal justification for the combination. The motive

Example: A small town has enough business to support only two gas stations. Neither station will sell gas at a higher price than the other station, but selling gas too cheaply would undercut a station's profit. Without agreeing to do so, both stations end up charging the same price for gas. There is no violation of the Sherman Act.

> **Example:** Ace Construction Co. and Expert Contracting, Ltd., agree with each other on a schedule of prices for certain common construction jobs. Each company agrees to charge no less than the price on the schedule for these jobs. Ace and Expert have committed a *per se* violation.

or intent of the parties to the agreement are not considered. Per se violations are always regarded as harmful to commerce.

> An agreement between competitors to fix prices or otherwise restrict trade is known as a "horizontal restraint."

Most alleged violations of Section 1 are not clearly blatant. In those more common cases, the courts use what is called the "rule of reason" to determine if a contract or combination is unreasonable, and therefore unlawful. The rule of reason approach looks at the totality of the circumstances before deciding if a practice is unlawful. A court will look at the reasons for taking an action before making a judgment. The

VERTICAL INTEGRATION VIOLATES THE SHERMAN ACT.

U.S. v. Paramount Pictures
(Government) v. (Motion Picture Company)
334 U.S. 131 (1948)

INSTANT FACTS:
The U.S. Government (P) claimed that the methods Paramount (D) and other companies used for distributing movies violated antitrust laws.

BLACK LETTER RULE:
A vertically integrated enterprise is a monopoly, which violates the Sherman Anti–Trust Act.

FACTS:
The U.S. Government (P) brought an antitrust action against Paramount (D) and other motion picture distributors. The U.S. (P) alleged that the distributors violated antitrust laws by implementing five practices for distributing movies:

- Scheduling movies so that they would be shown only at certain theaters, to avoid competing with another theater's showing ("clearances and runs"),
- The joint ownership of theaters by two competing movie studios ("Pooling"),
- Allocating profits among theaters that showed a particular film,
- Requiring theaters to take an entire group of films for showing ("Block booking"), which Paramount (D) and the other defendants argued was a legitimate exercise of their copyrights in their movies, and
- Discriminating against smaller theaters in favor of larger chains.

The District Court found that clearances and runs had a legitimate purpose, and were not a restraint of trade. The District Court found that the remaining practices were unlawful restraints, and issued an injunction ordering the practices stopped. The court also concluded that it did not have the authority to continue an arbitration mechanism set up in a previous case involving the same parties.

ISSUE:

Did the movie distribution practices constitute an unlawful restraint of trade?

DECISION AND RATIONALE:

(Douglas, J.) Yes. A vertically integrated enterprise is a monopoly, which violates the Sherman Anti–Trust Act. The enterprise is unlawful if there is a power to exclude competition, and a purpose or intent to do so. The evidence that the distribution practices are unlawful restraints of trade is incontestable.

The pooling agreements and joint ownership were just to substitute monopoly for competition. Block booking was an unlawful enlargement of the producer's copyright. The evidence supported the conclusion that smaller theaters were discriminated against. However, the District Court did have the authority to continue the arbitration mechanism. Affirmed in part, reversed in part.

DISSENT:

(Frankfurter, J.) The Supreme Court should have deferred to the District Court's determination that it did not have the power to continue the arbitration program.

ANALYSIS:

This case is often cited as bringing an end to the "golden age" of Hollywood. Motion picture studios were required to divest themselves of theaters, and new, independent film distributors were able to enter the market. The Court's decision in this case, coupled with other factors like the rise of television, put the film industry into a slump from which it did not recover until the early 1970s.

Note that acquisitions leading to a monopoly are not the only way to create an anti-competitive enterprise. Companies may also grow without acquiring other enterprises, and eventually occupy a market to the extent that regulators become involved.

QUESTIONS FOR DISCUSSION:

How might consumers (the movie-going public) have been harmed by the anti-competitive practices in this case?

What would be the best remedy for the anti-competitive practices here?

---

motives and intent of the actors is relevant. The court will also consider the economic benefits and costs of the action, to determine whether that action causes bad economic effects.

Section 2 of the Sherman Act prohibits monopolies. To prove a violation of Section 2 in court, it must be shown that the defendant:

- Has **monopoly** power in the relevant market, and

- That power was acquired or maintained willfully.

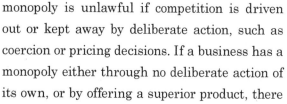

A monopoly is generally considered to excist when one business has between 70-90% of the market.

Section 2 does not prohibit all monopolies. A monopoly is unlawful if competition is driven out or kept away by deliberate action, such as coercion or pricing decisions. If a business has a monopoly either through no deliberate action of its own, or by offering a superior product, there is no violation of Section 2.

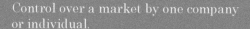

MONOPOLY:

Control over a market by one company or individual.

> **Example:** The manufacturers of audio compact discs and CD players agreed that CDs will meet certain technical standards. This agreement restrains trade, in that it limits the formats for recorded music. On the other hand, it allows standardization, so that consumers need to buy only one type of player or disc. Any disc can be played on any player. The agreement is reasonable, and not a violation of the Act.

> **Example:** Two daily newspapers, the Journal and the Gazette, were published in the same city. The Journal hired a new editor who expanded the coverage of the paper's internet site, and who started running new features sections. The Gazette did not change how it did business. The changes from the new publisher proved very popular, and the Journal started adding subscribers and advertisers. The Gazette lost too much income to continue, and went out of business. The Journal has a monopoly, but it did not attain that monopoly through unlawful means. There is no violation of Section 2.

Monopolies are unlawful if they come about through misconduct, such as an agreement to bar competition.

A violation of either provision of the Sherman Act is a felony. The maximum penalty is a fine of $100 million for a corporation and $1 million for an individual. An individual could also be sentenced to up to 10 years in prison. The maximum fine may be increased to twice the amount gained from the illegal acts or twice the money lost by the victims of the crime, if either of those amounts is over $100 million.

Clayton Act: The Clayton Act was passed in 1914. The purpose of the Act was to address anti-competitive practices that became popular after the Sherman Act was passed. For example, the Sherman Act prohibited cartels and combinations, but did not prevent companies merging to dominate markets. The Sherman Act was also used in ways that the sponsors of the law did not intend, such as breaking up unions.

The Clayton Act is enforced primarily through civil lawsuits. These lawsuits are brought either by private parties or the U.S. government.

A successful suit under the Clayton Act may result in a damage award that is three times the actual damages proven.

The Clayton Act makes certain enumerated types of activities unlawful. The four types of unlawful activities are:

- Price discrimination between different purchasers that substantially lessens competition or tends to create a monopoly,

> Approximately 90% of all Clayton Act lawsuits are brought by private parties.

- Sales conditioned on the buyer not dealing with competitors of the seller, or on the buyer also purchasing another different product if those requirements substantially lessen competition,

- **Mergers** and **acquisitions** that may substantially lessen competition, and

> **MERGER:**
> The combining or uniting of two companies.
>
> **ACQUISITION:**
> Gaining of possession or control over a company.

- Any person acting as a director of two or more competing corporations, if a merger of those corporations would violate the anti-trust laws by merging.

The prohibition against price discrimination prevents sellers from selling the same goods to different purchasers at different prices other than in specific contexts. To violate the prohibition, the goods must have been of a "like grade or quality." The sales to different customers must also have been made in the same general time period. Unlawful price discrimination includes practices such as:

- Below-cost sales in certain locations,

- Price differences that cannot be explained by cost savings, or the need to compete on price in one area, or

- Promotional allowances, such as special introductory prices.

Making sales conditioned on buying another product made by the seller tends to create a monopoly for the seller. There may be a justification for the condition, to ensure compliance with product standards. A violation is usually found when the products have no relation to one

Example: Instead of going out of business, the Gazette fights back. It reaches a secret agreement with prominent local merchants that they will advertise only in the Gazette. The loss of advertising revenue means that the Journal cannot pay for its expensive new improvements, so the paper closes. The Gazette attained its monopoly through unlawful means, and there is a Section 2 violation.

Example: A salt wholesaler advertised a quantity discount, but made the discount available only to five national grocery chains. The five chains were the only ones that bought sufficient quantities to qualify for the discount. The salt wholesaler was engaged in unlawful price discrimination. *Federal Trade Commission v. Morton Salt,* 334 U.S. 37 (1948).

> **Example:** A manufacturer of photocopiers tells customers that the warranty on its copiers will be voided if the customer does not buy toner cartridges and paper from the manufacturer. The toner cartridges are manufactured to detailed specifications relating to their function, but the paper sold by the manufacturer is no different than the paper sold by any other company. The toner cartridge requirement may not be unlawful, but the paper requirement probably is.

another, or when there is no technical reason why products from a different seller could not be used.

The most significant provisions of the Clayton Act relate to mergers. While some mergers can benefit competition and consumers by allowing greater efficiencies, other mergers damage the market by eliminating competition. This could result in higher prices and lower quality for consumers.

The Clayton Act prohibits mergers and acquisitions whose effect could be "substantially to lessen competition, or to tend to create a monopoly." Three kinds of mergers may have this effect: (1) horizontal mergers, which involve two competitors; (2) vertical mergers, which involve firms in a buyer-seller relationship; and (3) potential competition mergers. In a potential competition merger, one company is likely to enter the market and become a potential competitor of the other.

Horizontal mergers eliminate competitors. They may change the competitive environment so the remaining firms could coordinate on competitive practices, such as pricing. The surviving firm could also raise prices on its own without facing any competitive pressures.

Vertical mergers are between firms in a buyer-seller relationship. The manufacturer of a product might merge with a distributor, or with a company that sells a component of the product. Vertical mergers can lead to significant cost savings. They can also improve market efficiency, by improving the coordination between different companies in the supply chain. A vertical merger could also pose problems for competition. A competitor might be unable to gain access to an important component or to a channel of distribution.

A potential competition merger is where one competitor buying a company that is planning to enter its market to compete. That type of merger could prevent the increased competition that would result from a new entry into the market. It could also eliminate the effect that potential competitor could have. Companies already in the market would not be inclined to take competitive steps that might make it less attractive for a newcomer to enter the market.

The rules against anti-competitive mergers are applied before a merger occurs. The Federal Trade Commission and U.S. Department of Justice must be notified before certain large mergers may take place. The federal agencies are then given an opportunity to review the effect the proposed merger may have on competition. The merger may not take place if it is determined that the merger would have an adverse effect on U.S. commerce.

III. Sourcing and Transportation Issues

Many businesses center on producing tangible goods—that is, they make physical products rather than provide services. Transactions in goods leads inevitably to questions about the practicalities buying or selling them. It also leads to questions about getting them from the seller to the buyer.

> Inland waterways include navigable rivers, canal systems, and ship passages. The St. Lawrence Seaway System is a good example. Ocean vessels are able to navigate from the Atlantic Ocean through St. Lawrence System locks into the Great Lakes. Such ships can go as far inland as Duluth, Minnesota—over 1,600 miles by road.

Transporting goods costs money. Domestically, transport may be by truck, train, or air. Internationally, many shipments are also made via ocean or inland waterway.

Whatever way the goods are moved, the buyer and seller must agree who will pay for transport. There are also ways that buyers and sellers can split those costs. But the fees charged for shipping are not the only potential cost involved.

There is also the risk that the goods being shipped will be destroyed or damaged, or will otherwise not make it to their destination. If the goods are lost, the financial loss depends on which party was considered to have had responsibility or ownership for the goods at the time. Transportation Risk and Costs

Most consumer sales transactions are simple. We go into a store, make a selection, pay the price, and take our purchase with us. We own the item as soon as we pay for it. Our understanding of a sale as an exchange of money for goods is built around this model. When this model is altered by not making the change of possession immediate, or by requiring delivery to a different location, a new concern is raised. That concern is the "risk of loss."

The risk of loss deals with the question of who is responsible for goods that are damaged, lost, or destroyed. At some point in every sales transaction, that risk passes from the seller to the buyer. The parties may have agreed who bears the risk of loss, and that agreement will control. If one party breaches the shipping agreement, that party bears the risk of loss, even when the breach does not relate to the loss.

> Deciding who has the risk of loss will also affect a party's obligation or need to purchase insurance coverage. If a seller is responsible for insurance but does not purchase a policy, the seller may be financially responsible for the loss directly.

> *Example:* Allied Widget purchases three lathes from D & C Equipment Sales. The sales contract states that the lathes are to be delivered no later than November 16. Due to administrative errors at D & C, the lathes do not arrive at Allied until November 18. Two of the lathes are damaged when they are delivered. D & C has the risk of loss, and is responsible for the damage.

If there is no contract breach, Article 2 of the Uniform Commercial Code sets out rules for determining who has the risk of loss in a given situation. When the seller does not handle the delivery, but transfers goods to a common carrier for transport, the risk depends on the terms of the shipping contract. If the contract does not require the seller to deliver the goods to a particular address, but says that the seller is language that makes an agreement a destination contract.

To make shipping easier, trade terms provide a short-hand for common transport practices. These short codes define buyer and seller responsibilities in a few letters. For domestic shipments, businesses often use the Uniform Commercial Code trade terms, while the Inter-

> *Example:* Damon orders sound recording equipment from Euthyphro Acoustics. The contract says that Euthyphro will ship the equipment via common carrier. Euthyphro delivers the equipment to the North Western Railway for shipment. The risk of loss passes to Damon when equipment is delivered to the railway.

will deliver the goods to a carrier for shipment (a shipment contract), the risk passes to the buyer on delivery to the carrier.

A "destination" contract, which requires delivery of the goods, keeps the risk of loss with the seller until the buyer receives the goods. The seller is also obligated to pay the costs of shipping the goods to the destination.

A "shipment" contract puts the risk of loss on the buyer. The buyer is responsible for the costs of delivering the goods to the carrier for shipment, but has no obligation for further delivery costs. Shipment contracts are presumed, unless there

national Chamber of Commerce "Incoterms" are commonly used for international shipments. Since the terms vary, it is important to choose the correct one. The parties must also define where shipment or delivery takes place. That location is listed after the trade term in parentheses. The table shows just a few of the common terms from each system, and how they differ.

Harmonized Tariff Schedule

Many businesses import products or components, or export goods to buyers in other countries. In these cases, costs are different than

Comparison of Selected Trade Terms			
UCC Trade Term	*Meaning*	*Incoterm 2010*	*Meaning*
CIF (destination)	"Cost, Insurance, and Freight" • Buyer's cost for goods includes Seller's expense for shipment and for shipping insurance. • Seller must arrange shipping and insurance and provide documentation to Buyer. • Risk of loss passes to Buyer once the goods are loaded, but the insurance covers Buyer in case of loss. • Applies to any type of shipment.	CIF (destination port)	"Cost, Insurance, and Freight" • Buyer's cost for goods includes Seller's expense for shipment and for shipping insurance. • Seller must arrange shipping and insurance and provide documentation to Buyer. • Risk of loss passes to Buyer once goods are on board, but the insurance covers Buyer in case of loss. • Only applies to ocean and inland seaway shipments.
FOB (shipment location)	"Free on Board" • Seller places goods in the possession of shipper and supplies documentation to Buyer. • Seller pays expenses until the goods are provided to shipper; all remaining costs pass to Buyer. • Risk of loss passes to Buyer once the goods are put in shipper's possession. • Applies to any type of shipment.	FOB (shipment port)	"Free on Board" • Seller delivers goods to shipper at named port of shipment and provides documentation to Buyer; all remaining costs pass to Buyer. • Risk of loss passes when goods are on board; all remaining costs pass to Buyer. • Only applies to ocean and inland waterway shipments.

Comparison of Selected Trade Terms			
UCC Trade Term	Meaning	Incoterm 2010	Meaning
FOB (destination)	"Free on Board" • Seller must arrange and pay for transport of the goods to destination; all remaining costs pass to Buyer. • Risk of loss passes to Buyer once goods are delivered. • Applies to any type of shipment.	DDP (destination)	"Delivered Duty Paid" • Seller must arrange and pay for transport of goods to Buyer; Buyer's only cost is unloading. • Seller must arrange for import clearance formalities and payment of import fees and duties. • Risk of loss passes to Buyer when the goods are at Buyer's location. • Applies to any type of shipment.
Ex Ship (destination port, terminal, or airport)	"Ex[terior] of Ship" • Seller must arrange and pay for transport of the goods to destination transportation facility; all remaining costs pass to Buyer. • Risk of loss passes to Buyer once goods unloaded. • Applies to any type of shipment.	DAT (destination port, terminal, or airport)	"Delivered at Terminal" • Seller must arrange and pay for transport of the goods to destination transportation facility; all remaining costs pass to Buyer. • Risk of loss passes to Buyer when goods are available at the facility. • Applies to any type of shipment.

they would be for a domestic sale. Aside from shipment and documentation costs, customs duties may also be imposed. Sometimes, there are further customs fees covering services such as short-term warehousing or inspections.

CUSTOMS DUTY:

A tax paid on imported items based on the country of origin and the item's description.

> A customs duty is the tax paid on an import. It is based on the product's value or quantity, or a combination of value and quantity. A tariff is a list (or "schedule") of the customs duties. Despite the difference, businesspeople often refer to customs duties as "tariffs."

Customs duties are taxes applied to goods entering a country. Duties are used to control imports to achieve policy goals. For instance, a high duty rate on cigarettes discourages smoking by restricting the supply of imported cigarettes and by making the consumer cost higher. Duties may be lower for goods from friendly countries, and much higher for the same products from disfavored nations. Governments can also use customs duties to shield domestic producers from competition.

In order to make customs duties easy to understand, the United States developed the Harmonized Tariff Schedule (HTS). The HTS became effective in 1989. The schedule consists of numbered categories of possible imports that allow customs officials to identify an import accurately. Each numbered description is followed by applicable duty rates.

The customs duty on an import may vary depending on its country of origin. Most countries' imports will receive a standard duty rate. If a country is in a negotiated trade relationship with the United States, however, imports from that country may receive a lower rate. If there are trade sanctions on a country, imports will receive a high duty rate.

The graphic shows a page from the HTS. Heading 6911 covers plates; this is the first page for that heading. The excerpt shows the HTS's precision and the range of duties. Under Rates of Duty on the right, the "General" column shows the standard rate (6 to 26 percent, depending

Example: In 1930, Congress passed the Smoot-Hawley Tariff Act. The Act raised customs duties on thousands of items commonly imported into the United States. The Act's goal was to discourage imports of goods that U.S. companies produced at home. Congress believed that Smoot-Hawley would improve the economy. Instead, other countries retaliated by raising duties on American products, which reduced the markets for U.S. goods. Congress intended that the Act would improve the Great Depression, but the economy continued to decline. It is difficult to determine the extent of Smoot-Hawley's economic impact, but most economists agree that the Act at least contributed to the Depression.

Harmonized Tariff Schedule of the United States (2016) Supplement-1
Annotated for Statistical Reporting Purposes

XIII
69-8

Heading/ Subheading	Stat. Suf- fix	Article Description	Unit of Quantity	Rates of Duty		
				1		2
				General	Special	
6911		Tableware, kitchenware, other household articles and toilet articles, of porcelain or china:				
6911.10		Tableware and kitchenware:				
6911.10.10	00	Hotel or restaurant ware and other ware not household ware..	doz.pcs......	25%	Free (A+, AU, BH, CA, CL, CO, D, E, IL, JO, MA, MX, P, PA, PE, SG) 5% (OM) 12.5% (KR)	75%
		Other:				
		Of bone chinaware:				
6911.10.15	00	Valued not over $31.50 per dozen pieces......	doz.pcs......	8%	Free (A, AU, BH, CA, CL, CO, D, E, IL, JO, KR, MA, MX, OM, P, PA, PE, SG)	75%
6911.10.25	00	Other...............	doz.pcs......	6%	Free (A, AU, BH, CA, CL, CO, D, E, IL, JO, KR, MA, MX, OM, P, PA, PE, SG)	75%
		Other:				
		Available in specified sets:				
6911.10.35		In any pattern for which the aggregate value of the articles listed in additional U.S. note 6(b) of this chapter is not over $56....	....	26%	Free (A, AU, BH, CA, CL, CO, D, E, IL, JO, MA, MX, OM, P, PA, PE, SG) 13% (KR)	75%
	10	Plates not over 27.9 cm in maximum dimension; teacups and saucers; mugs; soups, fruits and cereals, the foregoing not over 22.9 cm in maximum dimension...........................	doz. pcs.			
	50	Other....................................	doz. pcs.			

on the product). The "Special" column shows the rates for specific trade agreements (free to 13 percent). The trade agreements are shown by short abbreviations. Column 2 shows rates applied to countries under sanction (75 percent). This is only the first page of four covering plates. The entire HTS is a very large document.

Buyers and sellers must pay close attention to HTS categories. If imports are not correctly categorized, there may be substantial fines and back duties to pay. U.S. Customs and Border Protection may conduct audits of import records to determine the extent of underpayment. And deliberate use of an inaccurate tariff category to avoid customs duties is a federal crime. U.S. Customs can help importers categorize products before they ship. Customs brokers, private businesspeople licensed by the Treasury Department, act as the agents of importers, assisting them with the technical requirements for importing goods into the United States. Likewise, freight

---

SUMMARY JUDGMENT NOT APROPRIATE IN DISPUTE OVER CLASSIFICATION OF ACTION FIGURES.

Toy Biz, Inc. v. U.S.
(Toy Importer) v. (Customs Authority)
24 C.I.T. 1351 (2000)

This is the fourth and final opinion for this Court in a case involving the tariff classification of dozens of action figures from various Marvel Comics series. . . . The legal issue presented in this case involves the construction of the "dolls" provision vis a vis the "other toys" provision.

Plaintiff Toy Biz, Inc. ("Toy Biz") brings this action to challenge the tariff classification by the United States Customs Service ("Customs" or "Defendant") of various items imported from China and entered at the ports of Seattle and Los Angeles in 1994. The items are action figures from various Marvel Comics series . . .. Customs classified the items as "Dolls representing only human beings and parts and accessories thereof: Dolls whether or not dressed: Other: Not over 33 cm in height," under subheading 9502.10.40 of the HTSUS (1994), dutiable at 12% ad valorem. Toy Biz contends that the action figures at issue are properly classifiable as "Toys representing animals or other non-human creatures (for example, robots and monsters) and parts and accessories thereof: Other," under subheading 9503.49.00, HTSUS (1994), dutiable at 6.8% ad valorem.

[...]

In its entirety, HTSUS (1994) subheading 9503.49.00 reads: "Other toys; reduced-size ("scale") models and similar recreational models, working or not; puzzles of all kinds; parts and accessories thereof: Toys representing animals or non-human creatures (for example, robots and monsters) and parts and accessories thereof: Other."

[...]

Here, Customs classified the items under HTSUS heading 9502, "Dolls representing only human beings and parts and accessories thereof." Basing its contention on the wording of HTSUS 9502, Toy Biz argues that to be classifiable as a "doll," the "item must represent only, i.e., exclusively, a human being." Toy Biz points to the tentacles, claws, wings or other non-human features that a number of the items at issue possesses. Toy Biz thus concludes that the items at issue are not classifiable as "dolls" because "the figures represent creatures other than humans, and possess features characteristic of non-humans."

Toy Biz next argues that the items are properly classifiable as "Toys representing animals or non-human creatures (for example, robots and monsters)" under subheading 9503.49.00, by virtue of possessing non-human features. Toy Biz observes that the Explanatory Note 95.03(A)(1) provides that "other toys" under heading 9503 include "[t]oys representing animals or non-human creatures even if possessing predominantly human physical characteristics (e.g. angels, robots, devils, monsters)."

[...]

The court first recognizes that the 9503 "other toys" provision of the HTSUS is a residual or a default provision. Both the 9502 "dolls" and the 9503 "other toys" provisions appear in Chapter 95 of the HTSUS, titled "Toys, Games and Sports Equipment; Parts and Accessories Thereof." The first heading, 9501, is reserved for "[w]heeled toys designed to be ridden by children;" heading 9502, for "dolls;" and heading 9503, for "other toys." The Explanatory Note 95.03 to heading 9503 explicitly states that the "other toys" provision includes all toys not included in 9501 and 9502. Thus, heading 9503 is a default provision intended to encompass all toys that are not "wheeled toys" or "dolls." Accordingly, when the choice is between the "dolls" and "other toys" provisions of the HTSUS, the construction of the provisions must start with that of "dolls." The construction of the "dolls" provision may not, however, render either the "other toys" provision or any other provision of the HTSUS meaningless and lead to ambiguous and contradictory results. It is therefore necessary to interpret the "dolls" provision in the context of the entire Chapter 95 and especially in relation to the "other toys" provision.

Moreover, the observation that the "other toys" provision is a residual provision compels the conclusion that the "dolls" and "other toys" classifications are mutually exclusive.

[...]

The task of the court is to ascertain which meaning the words "representing" and "only" were intended to carry in the phrase "dolls representing only human beings" in heading 9502 of the HTSUS. The question regarding the word "only" is answered more readily. The court agrees with Toy Biz that one of the primary meanings of the term "only" is "exclusively." . . . Therefore, the heading "dolls representing only human beings" can be read as "dolls representing human beings, as opposed to any other beings."

There is no definition for these terms in the HTSUS.

The meaning of the term "representing" in heading 9502 is harder to ascertain. Toy Biz urges that "to represent" in this context means more (or other) than "to resemble." The court agrees. The reason is multi-fold. First, consulting the OED, the court finds that "to resemble" is only one of the many possible meanings of "to represent." In the senses more pertinent to our purpose here, "to represent" may, for example, mean "to show, exhibit, or display to the eye," "to portray, depict, delineate," "to symbolize, to serve as a visible or concrete embodiment of," "to stand for or in place of," "to be the figure or image of," "to take or fill the place of," or "to serve as a specimen or example of" a person or a thing. Second, given the entire context of the HTSUS, "to represent" in "dolls representing only human beings" must mean something more than (or other than) "to resemble." In other words, one cannot read the "dolls" provision as meaning exclusively "dolls resembling human beings." This reading of the "dolls" provision would create ambiguity and conflict with the "other toys" provision of the HTSUS. One of the subheadings at issue here reads "Toys representing animals or non-human creatures (for example, robots and monsters)." The accompanying Explanatory Note 95.03, HTSUS, further explains that "[t]hese include: (1) Toys representing animals or nonhuman creatures even if possessing predominantly human physical characteristics"[.] Thus, the "other toys" provision clearly encompasses toys that possess predominantly human physical characteristics, i.e. resemble human beings. If "to represent" in "dolls representing only human beings" meant exclusively "to resemble," a toy that merely resembled a human being would be prima facie classifiable under both the "dolls" and "other toys" provisions. The HTSUS scheme, however, prevents this interpretation. As explained above, see supra note 19 and accompanying text, the "dolls" and the "other toys" provisions are mutually exclusive; and an item cannot be classified as both a "doll" and "other toy."

[...]

The court next considers what the effect these interpretations of "only" and "to represent" have on the "dolls" provision that reads "dolls representing only human beings." To be classified as a "doll" under the HTSUS, a toy needs to be an "embodiment" of a human being or to serve as an "example" of a human being. This condition is more restrictive than merely to resemble a human being. The word "only" further restricts the provision because it will not allow the representation of any being other than a human being to be classified as a "doll." The court thus concludes that by excluding toys that do not exclusively represent human beings (however much they resemble human beings), the HTSUS "dolls" provision has indeed narrowed the scope of what can be classified as "dolls" when compared with the TSUS "dolls" provision which simply read "Dolls, and parts of dolls including doll clothing," and was not restricted by any qualifiers.

[...]

The court next considers whether the items at issue here are properly classifiable as "dolls" under the HTSUS. The action figures at issue are organized by Toy Biz in various assortments. The figures . . . are five-inch poseable (or capable of standing erect with movable joints) plastic figures, collectively referred to "X-Men" action figures. [further description omitted]

[...]

Whatever the degree is to which they resemble human beings, the court finds that these action figures do not represent human beings and are therefore not properly classifiable as "dolls" under HTSUS heading 9502. The court bases its finding on at least three observations. First, most of the figures at issue exhibit at least one non-human characteristic. The court does not agree with Customs that the few non-human characteristics the figures possess, such as claws or robotic eyes, "fall far short of transforming [these figures] into something other than the human beings which they represent" because the issue under the HTSUS is not a straight headcount of the human features a figure may possess, rather the issue is whether the figure as a whole and in a wider context represents a human being. Moreover, under the more restrictive "dolls" provision of the HTSUS, even one non-human feature the figure possesses prohibits its classification as a "doll."

[...]

Second, these Marvel characters are known in popular culture as "mutants." That fact further informs their classification. . . . Third, the "X-Men" figures are marketed and packaged as "mutants" or "people born with `x-tra' power." [This] lends further credence to the assertion that they represent creatures other than (or more than) human beings. For all the foregoing reasons, the "X-Men" and "X-Force" figures considered are not properly classifiable as "dolls" under HTSUS heading 9502.

If these figures are not "dolls" . . . then they must fall into the category of "other toys" under HTSUS heading 9503. . . . Any toy not classifiable as a "doll" or a "wheeled toy" falls under the "other toys" category.

[Citations omitted]

CASE VOCABULARY:
SUMMARY JUDGMENT:
Judgment for a party rendered without a trial, granted when there is no genuine issue of material fact.

QUESTIONS FOR DISCUSSION:
Does the task of "casual observation" for non-human features seem onerous?

Importers may ask the Customs Service for a ruling on how an item should be classified. The government is bound by that decision, which adds predictability to the full import cost. Why would an importer choose to forego this guidance?

forwarders work with exporters of products to ensure their efficient transportation, and also compliance with U.S. export regulations.

Trading Areas

The Harmonized Tariff Schedule shows how trading relationships between countries can result in lower duty rates for businesses. There are many types of trade relationships that countries can create. Each relationship has its own unique benefits and responsibilities, supported by agreement between the countries. Trade agreements are primarily about economic issues, but often include clauses about other issues of concern. Including these conditions is one way that the United States builds alliances with other countries.

Many trade relationships are bilateral, meaning that they only involve two countries. The United States has several bilateral agreements of varying complexity. One example is the Peru Trade Promotion Agreement. That agreement eliminated the majority of duties on U.S. agricultural exports to Peru, and reduced or eliminated U.S. duties on imports of Peruvian products. The agreement also includes terms dealing with environmental and labor protections.

FREE TRADE AREA:
Countries that negotiate a free trade agreement to reduce or eliminate customs duties and other trade barriers between themselves.

CUSTOMS UNION:
A free trade area that also adopts a common external tariff.

COMMON MARKET:
A geographic group of countries that seek to eliminate trade barriers among themselves and promote free movement of capital and labor within the member countries.

Sometimes, a bilateral agreement may grow to involve more countries. An agreement between

the United States and Canada later became the basis for the North American Free Trade Agreement (NAFTA). The Canada-United States Free Trade Agreement dates to 1987. The negotiation of a three-party North American agreement among Mexico, Canada, and the United States followed. NAFTA was signed by the parties in 1992.

Trade relationships take several forms. The most common types are:

- Free trade areas.
- Customs unions.
- Common markets.

Free trade areas include countries that have signed a free trade agreement. The members of a free trade area reduce or eliminate duties and other limitations on each other's products in order to promote trade among the area's countries. NAFTA established a free trade area for the three member countries. The countries do not need to share a border to be considered a free trade area.

Customs unions are free trade areas with another level of economic coordination. In addition to reducing or eliminating duties on each other's products, customs union members also agree to use a consistent tariff schedule and customs duty rates for non-members. These rates are likely higher than the rates within the area, but they are still attractive rates. This "common external tariff" makes the customs union attractive to businesses outside the area. Businesses can export to any member and receive the same rates. With the rates inside the area at low levels or eliminated entirely, businesses have more flexibility for transportation and market development in a customs union.

Common markets use the customs union concept but with far more internal interaction and coordination among members. A common market involves a geographic area that eliminates duties and trade restrictions among the member countries. In addition, a common market strives to achieve free movement of capital and labor among members.

The European Union is one of the most complex trade areas. The European Union's founding documents define four freedoms as necessary to a common market:

- Free movement of capital.

- Free movement of goods.

- Free movement of services.

- Free movement of people.

> The East African Community (EAC) is a customs union that originally formed in 1967. The member countries include Burundi, Kenya, Rwanda, South Sudan, Tanzania, and Uganda. The EAC has an interesting history. It grew from an innovative earlier agreement in the 1940s, and was still ahead of its time in 1967. The union disbanded in the late 1970s, but reformed in 2000. The EAC is working to deepen its agreement while coordinating productively with other African trade blocs.

> The free movement of capital can only be fully achieved by a shared currency. A common currency (such as the Euro) eliminates the trade issue posed by fluctuating exchange rates and related fees. Some European Union members chose not to participate in the common currency when it was introduced. One of those countries, Great Britain, has since held a referendum to leave the European Union. The process of leaving is commonly known as "Brexit."

In a fully evolved common market, there would be unrestrained trade and movement among member countries, much as there is unrestrained trade and movement among states in the United States.

IV. Real Estate Leases and Ownership

Most businesses will have some involvement with real estate. This involvement is not necessarily developing or investing in real estate. It includes such simple, everyday transactions as leasing a space to work.

The term "real estate" or "real property" has expanded from its original meaning of "land." Real estate still refers to land, but it also refers to things attached to the land, such as buildings. If something on the land cannot be moved without damaging the land, that thing is included in the term "real estate."

The term also includes interests in land like **mortgages** or **reversionary interests.** A

MORTGAGE:

The use of real estate as collateral for a debt.

REVERSIONARY INTEREST:

An interest in real estate that will give the holder ownership of the property in the future, when a certain event happens.

mortgage uses real estate as collateral for a debt. The most well-known type of mortgages are those where a home buyer secures the loan for purchase of a home using the home as collateral. A reversionary interest means that someone will gain ownership of the property at some point in the future when a defined event occurs. These interests do not give any present right to own or possess real estate. Instead, they create a possibility that the owner of the interest could own or possess the land at some point in the future, if some event should happen.

Ownership

Ownership of land (also referred to as "title") comes into being after the land is transferred to that person. The transfer must be done in a writing. Transfers of real estate are evidenced by a document known as a **deed**, which says that the ownership has passed from one person or entity to another. Deeds must be signed by the person making the transfer (the **grantor**). They must also describe the property that is being transferred. Deeds are recorded with a local government office, to give the public notice of who owns or claims ownership of a particular piece of property.

A deed will also say what interest is being created in the person receiving the land (the **grantee**). For example, if the grantor is transferring ownership to two new owners, the deed will say "to A and B, as **tenants in common**," or "to A and B, as **joint tenants**." Even though "tenants" are associated with rental properties, it is also a legal term for types of ownership. Tenants in common are two or more co-owners of real estate who each have an interest in the property that can be sold without the permission of the other tenants in common. Their interest in the property is not ownership of a specific portion of the premises. Joint tenants also do not own a specific portion. The main difference between a tenancy in common and a joint tenancy is that joint tenants may not sell individual interests in the property without the permission of the other joint tenants. Joint tenancy are most commonly

Example: Ali's mother owns her home, where she lives with her boyfriend, Dale. In Ali's mother's will, she gives Dale the right to live in the house until he dies, should she die before he does. After she or Dale dies, the property goes to Ali or Ali's children. When Ali's mother dies, Dale receives the right to continue living in the home. He is responsible for paying utilities and for maintaining the property. When Dale dies, the interest in the property reverts to Ali.

used when a married couple owns real estate jointly. When one joint tenant dies, the other automatically inherits her interest, without regard to a will or any probate proceedings. In contrast, the interest of a tenant-in-common becomes part of the tenant's estate, and does not pass to the other tenants unless a will or other document directs.

A deed may also make certain promises about the right of the grantor to transfer the property. A promise that no one other than the grantor has any claim or interest in the property makes the deed a **general warranty deed**. A promise that says only that the grantor has done nothing to affect her ownership of the property is a **limited warranty deed**. Such a deed does not ensure that there are no other interests to the property, only that the grantor has not created any such interests. A deed that makes no promises, but that says only that the grantee takes whatever right the grantor has, is a **quitclaim deed**.

Ownership of land does not always require a sale of the land. In some limited circumstances, a party may gain ownership of property through a process known as **adverse possession**. Adverse possession allows a party to become the legal owner of property if she has been in continuous possession of real estate for a period of time. The possession must be open and notorious, meaning the adverse possessor may not attempt to conceal or deny her possession. Possession must be hostile to the title of the legal owner of the property, meaning it cannot be with the permission of the owner. The possession of the property must be open and hostile continuously, through the entire term set out by statute.

Some state laws include additional requirements, such as a requirement that the adverse possessor have started his possession

DEED:
A document that evidences a transfer of real estate. All transfers or conveyances of real estate must be in writing.

GRANTOR:
A person who transfer ownership of property to another.

TENANTS IN COMMON:
Two or more co-owners of real estate who take an undivided interest in the property. A tenant in common may sell her interest in the property without the permission of the other tenant.

JOINT TENANTS:
Two or more co-owners of real estate who take an undivided interest in the property. A joint tenant may not sell his interest in the property without the permission of the other joint tenant.

Real estate transactions—and some other types of agreements—must be documented in writing. This rule is referred to as the "Statute of Frauds," even though it is not a U.S. statute. The original Statute from which the rule takes its name was an English law from 1677 designed to prevent false witness testimony regarding a transaction.

GENERAL WARRANTY DEED:

A deed that guarantees that the grantor of real estate has good title to the property.

LIMITED WARRANTY DEED:

A deed that guarantees that nothing the grantor has done while she owned the property affects the title to the property.

QUITCLAIM DEED:

A deed that gives the grantee all of the grantor's interest in property. A quitclaim deed does not guarantee title.

intending to become the owner, or that the possessor have paid the property taxes on the property during his adverse possession.

Adverse possession laws are designed to make it difficult to gain title through adverse possession. The doctrine essentially rewards a trespasser who has the patience to continue his trespass for a period of time. He is allowed to gain

In some states, quitclaim deeds are not considered transfers of real estate, but are releases of claims. In other words, the person giving the quitclaim deed is only saying, "I release any ownership or other legal claims to this particular piece of property." The claims are not released in favor of a new owner, as they would be in a transfer.

ownership of property without compensating the original lawful owner.

Ownership of real estate may be limited by exceptions, or reservations. A grantor may want to retain the right to drill for oil on property that is being transferred, so a reservation in the deed would give her the right to start or continue drilling. Ownership may be subject to a mortgage, or a tenant may have leased all or part of the property.

Property ownership may also be limited by an **easement** over the property. An easement gives someone other than the owner of the property the right to use, but not possess, all or part of the property. Easements may be granted to allow a person to cross over another person's land in order to reach her own property. It may also include an agreement to restrict the location or height of buildings on a property, to ensure that the other property owner continues to have access to wind and sunlight.

Easements are created by express agreement, by implication, or by prescription. An agreement to create an easement must show clearly that an easement was intended. It is not enough that a deed to property say that the conveyance is "subject to an easement." The agreement or grant that creates an easement must be in writing. If the easement relates to a specific part of the property (for example, an easement to run electrical wires under the property), that part should be described with particularity.

Easements by implication are found to exist when it is proven that the parties to a real estate transaction intended that an easement exist, even though that intent was not stated explicitly.

> *Example:* Bela, Sam, and Pat are involved in a lawsuit over the ownership of real estate. Bela and Sam come to a settlement, and Bela pays Sam $50,000. In return, Sam gives Bela a quitclaim deed. Sam no longer has an interest in the property, but the quitclaim deed does not resolve Pat's claim. Bela does not yet have clear title.

Easements are often implied when a property owner sells part of her land. A property owner may lead a purchaser to believe that there will be an easement over the property she retains, and the purchaser may act in reliance on that representation. An easement by necessity will be implied when a parcel would otherwise have no other access to a public street or highway.

An easement may also arise by prescription. An easement by prescription is similar to gaining title by adverse possession, except that the result is an easement, rather than a transfer of title. To obtain an easement by prescription, the land must be subject to open and continuous use for a defined period of time.

Leases

EASEMENT:
The right to use or cross land, without the right to possess the land.

A **lease** gives a person or company (the **tenant**) the right to occupy real estate for a period of time. The right may be for a fixed period of time, or it may last indefinitely. It does not give

> *Example:* Jim and Billy own adjoining farms. Jim is also a dealer in second-hand farm implements. He notices that Billy is not using a strip of his property next to Jim's, so Jim stores his farm implement inventory there. Jim does not ask Billy for permission, but he makes no attempt to cover or conceal the implements he is storing. Billy sees the implements, but thinks the strip is not suited for cultivation, so he doesn't tell Jim to stop, Jim continues to store his inventory on the strip for twenty years, the term set out in the state's adverse possession statute. Jim becomes the owner of the strip of property.
>
> Same facts, except that the boundary between the two farms has always been uncertain. Jim thinks he is storing his inventory on his own land. Billy is negotiating to sell his farm, and has a survey done to determine the correct boundaries. Jim and Billy learn that the implements are on Billy's land only after the survey. Jim does not receive title by adverse possession, since his possession was not hostile to Billy's title.

> **Example:** Diana makes an agreement with Declan that says Declan can use a few feet of her property for a driveway. Declan has an easement over Diana's property.

> **Example:** Carolyn owns a large tract of land that is bounded on the south side by a public highway, and by a river on the north side. She sells the north one-half of her property to Bea, who wants to build her house on the river. The only access to a public road for Bea is across Carolyn's property. Bea has an easement by implication across Carolyn's property.

the **tenant** ownership rights in the property. Instead, the tenant has the exclusive right to possess and use the property during the term of the lease.

> At common law, the time period was 20 years. States have enacted different statutes regarding the time period, with some providing for a period as short as ten years.

All leases are subject to the requirements of the Statute of Frauds, which requires that contracts which cannot be performed in less than one year be put in writing. Apart from that requirement, there are different rules that govern leases of commercial real estate and leases of residential real estate. Residential leases are subject to legal requirements that the property be maintained to an appropriate standard, called a "warranty of habitability." This warranty means that the property is fit to live in, and will remain fit through the term of the lease.

Commercial leases, on the other hand, are open to negotiation. Unless the lease provides otherwise, a **landlord's** only obligation is to ensure the tenant's "quiet enjoyment" of the property. Quiet enjoyment means only that the landlord will not interfere with the tenant's use of the property. The tenant's only obligation is to pay rent as promised and not destroy the premises.

There are two essential categories of commercial real estate lease. The differences between the two center around what services are included in the tenant's base rental payment.

A gross lease calls for all expenses of the building to be paid by the landlord. These expenses include utilities, taxes, and custodial services. A

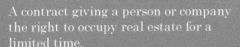

LEASE:
A contract giving a person or company the right to occupy real estate for a limited time.

TENANT:
A person who rents real estate from another.

LANDLORD:
A person who leases real estate to another.

VERBAL AGREEMENTS FOR SALE OR LONG-TERM LEASE OF LAND ARE NOT ENFORCEABLE.

Boone v. Coe
(Potential Tenant) v. (Farm Owner)
153 Ky. 233, 154 S.W. 900 (1913)

CLAY, C.

Plaintiffs, W. H. Boone and J. T. Coe, brought this action against defendant, J. F. Coe, to recover certain damages, alleged to have resulted from defendant's breach of a parol contract of lease for one year to commence at a future date. It appears from the petition that the defendant was the owner of a large and valuable farm in Ford county, Tex. Plaintiffs were farmers, and were living with their families in Monroe county, Ky. In the fall of 1909 defendant made a verbal contract with plaintiffs, whereby he rented to them his farm in Texas for a period of 12 months, to commence from the date of plaintiffs' arrival at defendant's farm. Defendant agreed that if plaintiffs would leave their said homes and businesses in Kentucky, and with their families, horses, and wagons, move to defendant's farm in Texas, and take charge of, manage, and cultivate same in wheat, corn, and cotton for the 12 months next following plaintiffs' arrival at said farm, the defendant would have a dwelling completed on said farm and ready for occupancy upon their arrival, which dwelling plaintiffs would occupy as a residence during the period of said tenancy. Defendant also agreed that he would furnish necessary material at a convenient place on said farm out of which to erect a good and commodious stock and grain barn, to be used by plaintiffs. The petition further alleges that plaintiffs were to cultivate certain portions of the farm, and were to receive certain portions of the crops raised, and that plaintiffs, in conformity with their said agreement, did move from Kentucky to the farm in Texas, and carried with them their families, wagons, horses, and camping outfit, and in going to Texas they traveled for a period of 55 days. It is also charged that defendant broke his contract, in that he failed to have ready and completed on the farm a dwelling house in which plaintiffs and their families could move, and also failed to furnish the necessary material for the erection of a suitable barn; that on December 6th defendant refused to permit plaintiffs to occupy the house and premises, and failed and refused to permit them to cultivate the land or any part thereof; that on the ___ day of December, 1909, they started for their home in Kentucky, and arrived there after traveling for a period of 4 days. It is charged that plaintiffs spent in going to Texas, in cash, the sum of $150; that the loss of time to plaintiffs and their teams in making the trip to Texas was reasonably worth $8 a day for a period of 55 days, or the sum of $440; that the loss of time to them and their teams during the period they remained in Texas was $8 a day for 22 days, or $176; that they paid out in actual cash for transportation for themselves, families, and teams from Texas to Kentucky the sum of $211.80; that the loss of time to them and their teams in making the last-named trip was reasonably worth the sum of $100; that in abandoning and giving up their homes and businesses in Kentucky they had been damaged in the sum of $150, making a total damage of $1,387.80, for which judgment was asked. Defendant's demurrer to the petition was sustained and the petition dismissed. Plaintiffs appeal.

Under the rule in force in this state the statute of frauds relates to the remedy or mode of procedure, and not to the validity of the contract. Though the land is located in Texas, the parol contract of lease was made here, and here it is sought to enforce it. If unenforceable under our statute, it cannot be enforced here . . .

The statute of frauds provides as follows: "No action shall be brought to charge any person: 6. Upon any contract for the sale of real estate, or any lease thereof, for longer term than one year; nor 7. Upon any agreement which is not to be performed within one year from the making thereof, unless the promise, contract, agreement, representation, assurance, or ratification, or some memorandum or note thereof, be in writing, and signed by the party to be charged therewith, or by his authorized agent; but the consideration need not be expressed in the writing; it may be proved when necessary, or disproved by parol or other evidence." A parol lease of land for one year, to commence at a future date, is within the statute.

The question sharply presented is: May plaintiffs recover for expenses incurred and time lost on the faith of a contract that is unenforceable under the statute of frauds?

[...]

CLAY, C.

Plaintiffs, W. H. Boone and J. T. Coe, brought this action against defendant, J. F. Coe, to recover certain damages, alleged to have resulted from defendant's breach of a parol contract of lease for one year to commence at a future date. It appears from the petition that the defendant was the owner of a large and valuable farm in Ford county, Tex. Plaintiffs were farmers, and were living with their families in Monroe county, Ky. In the fall of 1909 defendant made a verbal contract with plaintiffs, whereby he rented to them his farm in Texas for a period of 12 months, to commence from the date of plaintiffs' arrival at defendant's farm. Defendant agreed that if plaintiffs would leave their said homes and businesses in Kentucky, and with their families, horses, and wagons, move to defendant's farm in Texas, and take charge of, manage, and cultivate same in wheat, corn, and cotton for the 12 months next following plaintiffs' arrival at said farm, the defendant would have a dwelling completed on said farm and ready for occupancy upon their arrival, which dwelling plaintiffs would occupy as a residence during the period of said tenancy. Defendant also agreed that he would furnish necessary material at a convenient place on said farm out of which to erect a good and commodious stock and grain barn, to be used by plaintiffs. The petition further alleges that plaintiffs were to cultivate certain portions of the farm, and were to receive certain portions of the crops raised, and that plaintiffs, in conformity with their said agreement, did move from Kentucky to the farm in Texas, and carried with them their families, wagons, horses, and camping outfit, and in going to Texas they traveled for a period of 55 days. It is also charged that defendant broke his contract, in that he failed to have ready and completed on the farm a dwelling house in which plaintiffs and their families could move, and also failed to furnish the necessary material for the erection of a suitable barn; that on December 6th defendant refused to permit plaintiffs to occupy the house and premises, and failed and refused to permit them to cultivate the land or any part thereof; that on the ___ day of December, 1909, they started for their home in Kentucky, and arrived there after traveling for a period of 4 days. It is charged that plaintiffs spent in going to Texas, in cash, the sum of $150; that the loss of time to plaintiffs and their teams in making the trip to Texas was reasonably worth $8 a day for a period of 55 days, or the sum of $440; that the loss of time to them and their teams during the period they remained in Texas was $8 a day for 22 days, or $176; that they paid out in actual cash for transportation for themselves, families, and teams from Texas to Kentucky the sum of $211.80; that the loss of time to them and their teams in making the last-named trip was reasonably worth the sum of $100; that in abandoning and giving up their homes and businesses in Kentucky they had been damaged in the sum of $150, making a total damage of $1,387.80, for which judgment was asked. Defendant's demurrer to the petition was sustained and the petition dismissed. Plaintiffs appeal.

Under the rule in force in this state the statute of frauds relates to the remedy or mode of procedure, and not to the validity of the contract. Though the land is located in Texas, the parol contract of lease was made here, and here it is sought to enforce it. If unenforceable under our statute, it cannot be enforced here . . .

The statute of frauds provides as follows: "No action shall be brought to charge any person: 6. Upon any contract for the sale of real estate, or any lease thereof, for longer term than one year; nor 7. Upon any agreement which is not to be performed within one year from the making thereof, unless the promise, contract, agreement, representation, assurance, or ratification, or some memorandum or note thereof, be in writing, and signed by the party to be charged therewith, or by his authorized agent; but the consideration need not be expressed in the writing; it may be proved when necessary, or disproved by parol or other evidence." A parol lease of land for one year, to commence at a future date, is within the statute.

The question sharply presented is: May plaintiffs recover for expenses incurred and time lost on the faith of a contract that is unenforceable under the statute of frauds?

[...]

In Brown on Statute of Frauds, § 118a, the rule is announced in the following language: "The rule that, where one person pays money or performs services for another upon a contract void under the statute of frauds, he may recover the money upon a count for money paid, or recover for the services upon a quantum meruit, applies only to cases where the defendant has received and holds the money paid or the benefit of the services rendered. It does not apply to cases of money paid by the plaintiff to a third person in execution of a verbal contract between the plaintiff and defendant, such as by the statute of frauds must be in writing."

In the case under consideration the plaintiffs merely sustained a loss. Defendant received no benefit. Had he received a benefit, the law would imply an obligation to pay therefor. Having received no benefit, no obligation to pay is implied. The statute says that the contract of defendant made with plaintiffs is unenforceable. Defendant therefore had the legal right to decline to carry it out. To require him to pay plaintiffs for losses and expenses incurred on the faith of the contract, without any benefit accruing to him, would, in effect, uphold a contract upon which the statute expressly declares no action shall be brought. The statute was enacted for the purpose of preventing frauds and perjuries. That it is a valuable statute is shown by the fact that similar statutes are in force in practically all, if not all, of the states of the Union. Being a valuable statute, the purpose of the lawmakers in its enactment should not be defeated by permitting recoveries in cases to which its provisions were intended to apply.

Judgment affirmed.

QUESTIONS FOR DISCUSSION:

How could Boone have ensured that the agreement would be enforceable?

What do you think about the application of the Statute of Frauds in cases that arguably result in an injustice?

---

modified gross lease incorporates some or all of the expenses of the premises into the base rent.

A net lease calls for the tenant to pay a base rent plus some or all of the expenses of the premises. The tenant may pay a base rent, plus a pro-rata share of the property taxes levied on the premises (single net lease). The tenant may pay a pro-rata share of taxes and building maintenance expenses, along with the base rent (double net lease). The lease may call for the tenant to pay a share of the three major expenses: property taxes; common area maintenance, and insurance (triple net lease).

> Some local city housing codes impose detailed requirements on residential landlords that go beyond mere "habitability."

The terms of a commercial lease are for negotiation by the landlord and tenant. Some terms may be standard terms in a community. While those are customary, they may be altered by agreement. Common subjects for negotiation include:

- Maintenance, of the leased premises, and common areas of a building, and the exterior,

---

Example: Albert's farmhouse is on the corner of his property furthest away from the entrance to the land that opens onto a public road. It is, however, much closer to another road that is separated from Albert's property by an unused right-of-way owned by the North Western Railway. Albert and his family have driven or walked over the right-of-way, roughly along the same path, for over twenty years. Albert has an easement by prescription.

BUSINESS LAW

Example: Susan rented office space in a building that has a warehouse attached to it. George rented the office below hers, and also rented the adjacent warehouse space. George's business uses a forklift, and the fumes from the forklift give Susan headaches. The landlord is not operating the forklift, so there is no violation of the right to quiet enjoyment.

- Utilities, especially if the tenant is expected to pay a portion of the utilities for common or shared areas,

- Limiting the other tenants who may rent in the premises (for example, a retail tenant may stipulate that no competing business be allowed to rent in the same premises), and

- The calculation of rent.

Depending on community practice, rent is usually stated as a certain amount per square foot. The method for calculating each individual month's rent may vary, and the method for determining the square footage of space may vary. Some leases of retail space call for the tenant to pay a base rent plus a percentage of the tenant's income.

Unlawful Detainer: If a tenant does not comply with his obligations under the lease, the landlord may seek to have him evicted. This is done by an action known as an unlawful detainer. Unlawful detainer is the most common means for removing a tenant. An unlawful detainer action seeks a court order that the tenant no longer has a right to occupy the property. To remove a tenant, a landlord must use the court procedure. Most states outlaw self-help in the

Types of Leases	
Flat lease	• Single rent, for a definite period of time
Gross lease	• Single rent, tenant pays some building costs • An escalator clause may increase rent if expenses go up
Net lease	• Base rent plus percentage of expenses • Tenant may pay all or part of taxes
Step lease	• Rent varies over term by some amount • Example: ½ the monthly rent is paid in year one, full rent is paid in year two, 1 ½ rent is paid in year three
Percentage lease	• Fixed rent, and a percentage of the tenant's income
Cost-of-living lease	• Variable rent, adjusted according to the inflation rate

> *Example:*
>
> Vic and Cindy have rented space from Camp Knife Estates Mobile Home Park. They moved their home onto the space, paid their rent as scheduled, and complied with all other terms of their lease. A county inspector makes a routine visit to Camp Knife, and tells the management that Vic and Cindy's home is too large for the lot they have rented, according to county regulations. Camp Knife probably will not be able to bring an unlawful detainer action, but may be able to bring an action in ejectment to have Vic and Cindy removed.

form of physically removing a tenant without a court order.

Unlawful detainer actions are meant to be quick and simple. Hearings are scheduled to be held within a few days of the service of the summons and complaint. The only issue to be decided is who has the right to be in possession of the premises. Other issues, such as past-due rent, are dealt with separately, in other proceedings. The procedures set out for an unlawful detainer action must be followed exactly. The state law will also set out the valid reasons for bringing an action. Non-payment of rent and violation of the terms of the lease are some of the most common grounds for bringing an action. Other causes for eviction may include damage to the property beyond normal wear and tear, or holding over after the termination of a lease.

If an unlawful detainer action is successful, the tenant or occupant and her property are physically removed from the premises.

The alternative to an unlawful detainer is an action for **ejectment.** An ejectment action is brought by a person who owns property to remove a person who is in unlawful possession of that property. In most states, an ejectment action may be brought against a person who is not a tenant, such as a trespasser, or an adjoining property owner who has made an improvement that crosses the boundary line between the properties. In many states, an action for ejectment may be brought to remove a tenant or former tenant who is unlawfully in possession of the property, but whose unlawful occupancy is not grounds for bringing an unlawful detainer action.

Restrictions on the Use of Land

A land owner's right to use his or her property is not absolute. Various restrictions may be put on the use of property. Some of these restrictions arise by agreement. Others are imposed by law.

UNLAWFUL DETAINER:

A type of legal action claiming that a tenant no longer has the right to remain on a property.

EJECTMENT:

A common-law action to recover possession of land.

At one time, it was common for deeds of residential property to contain a covenant that the property would not be sold to a buyer of a particular race or religion. Those covenants were rule unlawful by the U.S. Supreme Court in 1948. *See, Shelley v. Kraemer,* 334 U.S. 1 (1948).

Covenants: When a restriction on the use of property arises by agreement, the agreement is typically referred to as a **covenant.** A covenant may be set out in the deed to real estate, or it may be the subject of a separate agreement. No specific language is needed to create a covenant. The only requirement is that the language used show clearly the intent to create a covenant.

There are two types of covenants: personal and real. A personal covenant is a personal obligation that does not immediately concern the land. It is binding only on the parties who make the agreement. A real covenant "runs with the land." It is concerned with the use and enjoyment of the property.

A covenant is a real covenant that runs with the land if:

- The parties making the covenant intended such an agreement,

- There is privity of estate between the person seeking to enforce the covenant and the person against whom enforcement is sought, and

- The covenant touches and concerns the land involved.

Privity of estate means that the parties to the covenant have or had some kind of interest in the property. A seller and purchaser of real estate will be said to have horizontal privity. When the buyer sells the property to another buyer, there will be vertical privity.

A covenant will touch and concern land if it bears upon the use and enjoyment of the property. It is the kind of agreement that can only be made by the owner of the property. Generally, a covenant touches and concerns the land if it calls for a party to do, or refrain from doing, some act on the land.

Zoning: Zoning is a local law or ordinance that limits the type of uses of property. Zoning regulates the use of land, and promotes orderly development. It will also protect property owners, by ensuring that nearby property is used in a compatible manner. Zoning may also help control the adverse effects of some uses of property, by concentrating that type of use in one particular area.

Example: Curt purchased a large suburban lot to build a house on. He decides that the property is much larger than he needs, so he sells half of the property to Tierney. As a condition of the sale, Curt and Tierney agree that they will only build one single-family home on their respective tracts. This is a covenant that touches and concerns the land.

> **Example:** The houses on Sheboygan Avenue were built in the early 1900s, to house employees at a nearby factory. They are all uniform in exterior appearance. The city has amended its zoning ordinance to create the "Sheboygan Avenue Historic District." Homeowners in the District may not make any structural changes that would alter the exterior appearance of their houses, although they are free to make any interior changes they wish. The zoning restriction probably would be upheld as reasonable.

The power to enact zoning ordinances is a part of the police power of a municipality. Ordinances are frequently challenged as unconstitutional takings of land for which compensation must be paid. Zoning ordinances will be upheld as long as they are reasonable, and do not deprive the property owner of any use of her land.

A zoning ordinance or law divides a municipality into different areas. Different property uses are permitted in each area. Many ordinances will also set limits on building or lot sizes within an area. If a property owner wishes to make use of her property in a way that would not be permitted by the zoning ordinance, she may apply for a variance to allow the use. Variances are largely left to the discretion of the authorities who enforce the zoning laws, although courts will not permit a zoning board to act in an arbitrary manner when it grants or denies applications for variances.

Eminent Domain

Property is often taken by a unit of government for some purpose. This is known as **eminent domain.** Under the Fifth Amendment to the U.S. Constitution, and comparable provisions in most state constitutions, the government may take private property for a public use, but just compensation must be paid.

> Eminent domain is usually thought of and discussed as relating to takings of real estate; however, the same rules apply to the taking of personal property, or even intangible property, for public use. The use of eminent domain over anything other than real estate is rare. In the 1980s, the City of Oakland, California, attempted unsuccessfully to use eminent domain to keep the city's NFL franchise from moving.

> **Example:** Leona owns a large home that is in an area zoned for single-family homes only. Since her home was built, streets and a nearby highway were re-routed, and the traffic in front of her hose makes it less desirable as a residence. Leona would like to renovate her home to allow her to operate a restaurant. Leona must apply for a variance.

The requirement of a "public use" was the subject of controversy in recent years. In the case of *Kelo v. City of New London,* 545 U.S. 469 (2005), the U.S. Supreme Court held that taking private property for a private business development could be a "public use," and so was not prohibited by the Fifth Amendment. Note that the Court did not say that all takings to benefit a private party would be a public use. The Court merely deferred to the judgment of the City of New London that the planned private development would be a public benefit.

PRIVATE DEVELOPMENT MAY BE PUBLIC USE.

Kelo v. City of New London
(Homeowner) v. (City)
545 U.S. 469 (2005)

(Stevens, J.) In 2000, the city of New London approved a development plan that, in the words of the Supreme Court of Connecticut, was "projected to create in excess of 1,000 jobs, to increase tax and other revenues, and to revitalize an economically distressed city, including its downtown and waterfront areas." In assembling the land needed for this project, the city's development agent has purchased property from willing sellers and proposes to use the power of eminent domain to acquire the remainder of the property from unwilling owners in exchange for just compensation. The question presented is whether the city's proposed disposition of this property qualifies as a "public use" within the meaning of the Takings Clause of the Fifth Amendment to the Constitution.

Petitioner Susette Kelo has lived in the Fort Trumbull area since 1997. She has made extensive improvements to her house, which she prizes for its water view . . . There is no allegation that any of [the condemned] properties is blighted or otherwise in poor condition; rather, they were condemned only because they happen to be located in the development area.

In December 2000, petitioners brought this action in the New London Superior Court. They claimed, among other things, that the taking of their properties would violate the "public use" restriction in the Fifth Amendment. After a 7-day bench trial, the Superior Court granted a permanent restraining order . . .

After the Superior Court ruled, both sides took appeals to the Supreme Court of Connecticut. That court held, over a dissent, that all of the City's proposed takings were valid. It began by upholding the lower court's determination that the takings were authorized by chapter 132, the State's municipal development statute . . . Next, relying on cases such as *Hawaii Housing Authority* v. *Midkiff,* 467 U.S. 229 (1984), and *Berman* v. *Parker,* 348 U.S. 26 (1954), the court held that such economic development qualified as a valid public use under both the Federal and State Constitutions . . .

Finally, adhering to its precedents, the court went on to determine, first, whether the takings of the particular properties at issue were "reasonably necessary" to achieving the City's intended public use, and, second, whether the takings were for "reasonably foreseeable needs" . . .

We granted certiorari to determine whether a city's decision to take property for the purpose of economic development satisfies the "public use" requirement of the Fifth Amendment. 542 U.S. ___ (2004).

[...]

Two polar propositions are perfectly clear. On the one hand, it has long been accepted that the sovereign may not take the property of *A* for the sole purpose of transferring it to another private party *B*, even though *A* is paid just compensation. On the other hand, it is equally clear that a State may transfer property from one private party to another if future "use by the public" is the purpose of the taking; the condemnation of land for a railroad with common-carrier duties is a familiar example. Neither of these propositions, however, determines the disposition of this case.

As for the first proposition, the City would no doubt be forbidden from taking petitioners' land for the purpose of conferring a private benefit on a particular private party. Nor would the City be allowed to take property under the mere pretext of a public purpose, when its actual purpose was to bestow a private benefit. The takings before us, however, would be executed pursuant to a "carefully considered" development plan. The trial judge and all the members of the Supreme Court of Connecticut agreed that there was no evidence of an illegitimate purpose in this case. Therefore, as was true of the statute challenged in *Midkiff,* the City's development plan was not adopted "to benefit a particular class of identifiable individuals."

On the other hand, this is not a case in which the City is planning to open the condemned land—at least not in its entirety—to use by the general public. Nor will the private lessees of the land in any sense be required to operate like common carriers, making their services available to all comers. But although such a projected use would be sufficient to satisfy the public use requirement, this "Court long ago rejected any literal requirement that condemned property be put into use for the general public." Indeed, while many state courts in the mid-19th century endorsed "use by the public" as the proper definition of public use, that narrow view steadily eroded over time. Not only was the "use by the public" test difficult to administer (*e.g.*, what proportion of the public need have access to the property? at what price?), but it proved to be impractical given the diverse and always evolving needs of society.⁸ Accordingly, when this Court began applying the Fifth Amendment to the States at the close of the 19th century, it embraced the broader and more natural interpretation of public use as "public purpose." Thus, in a case upholding a mining company's use of an aerial bucket line to transport ore over property it did not own, Justice Holmes' opinion for the Court stressed "the inadequacy of use by the general public as a universal test." We have repeatedly and consistently rejected that narrow test ever since.

The disposition of this case therefore turns on the question whether the City's development plan serves a "public purpose." Without exception, our cases have defined that concept broadly, reflecting our longstanding policy of deference to legislative judgments in this field.

In *Berman* v. *Parker,* 348 U.S. 26 (1954), this Court upheld a redevelopment plan targeting a blighted area of Washington, D. C., in which most of the housing for the area's 5,000 inhabitants was beyond repair. Under the plan, the area would be condemned and part of it utilized for the construction of streets, schools, and other public facilities. The remainder of the land would be leased or sold to private parties for the purpose of redevelopment, including the construction of low-cost housing.

[...]

"We do not sit to determine whether a particular housing project is or is not desirable. The concept of the public welfare is broad and inclusive... . The values it represents are spiritual as well as physical, aesthetic as well as monetary. It is within the power of the legislature to determine that the community should be beautiful as well as healthy, spacious as well as clean, well-balanced as well as carefully patrolled. In the present case, the Congress and its authorized agencies have made determinations that take into account a wide variety of values. It is not for us to reappraise them. If those who govern the District of Columbia decide that the Nation's Capital should be beautiful as well as sanitary, there is nothing in the Fifth Amendment that stands in the way."

In *Hawaii Housing Authority* v. *Midkiff,* 467 U.S. 229 (1984), the Court considered a Hawaii statute whereby fee title was taken from lessors and transferred to lessees (for just compensation) in order to reduce the concentration of land ownership. We unanimously upheld the statute and rejected the Ninth Circuit's view that it was "a naked attempt on the part of the state of Hawaii to take the property of A and transfer it to B solely for B's private use and benefit" . . . [W]e concluded that the State's purpose of eliminating the "social and economic evils of a land oligopoly" qualified as a valid public use. Our opinion also rejected the contention that the mere fact that the State immediately transferred the properties to private individuals upon condemnation somehow diminished the public character of the taking. "[I]t is only the taking's purpose, and not its mechanics," we explained, that matters in determining public use.

[...]

Viewed as a whole, our jurisprudence has recognized that the needs of society have varied between different parts of the Nation, just as they have evolved over time in response to changed circumstances. . .For more than a century, our public use jurisprudence has wisely eschewed rigid formulas and intrusive scrutiny in favor of affording legislatures broad latitude in determining what public needs justify the use of the takings power.

[...]

Those who govern the City were not confronted with the need to remove blight in the Fort Trumbull area, but their determination that the area was sufficiently distressed to justify a program of economic rejuvenation is entitled to our deference. The City has carefully formulated an economic development plan that it believes will provide appreciable benefits to the community, including–but by no means limited to–new jobs and increased tax revenue. As with other exercises in urban planning and development, the City is endeavoring to coordinate a variety of commercial, residential, and recreational uses of land, with the hope that they will form a whole greater than the sum of its parts. To effectuate this plan, the City has invoked a state statute that specifically authorizes the use of eminent domain to promote economic development. Given the comprehensive character of the plan, the thorough deliberation that preceded its adoption, and the limited scope of our review, it is appropriate for us, as it was in *Berman*, to resolve the challenges of the individual owners, not on a piecemeal basis, but rather in light of the entire plan. Because that plan unquestionably serves a public purpose, the takings challenged here satisfy the public use requirement of the Fifth Amendment.

[...]

Alternatively, petitioners maintain that for takings of this kind we should require a "reasonable certainty" that the expected public benefits will actually accrue. Such a rule, however, would represent an even greater departure from our precedent. "When the legislature's purpose is legitimate and its means are not irrational, our cases make clear that empirical debates over the wisdom of takings–no less than debates over the wisdom of other kinds of socioeconomic legislation–are not to be carried out in the federal courts" . . . A constitutional rule that required postponement of the judicial approval of every condemnation until the likelihood of success of the plan had been assured would unquestionably impose a significant impediment to the successful consummation of many such plans.

[...]

In affirming the City's authority to take petitioners' properties, we do not minimize the hardship that condemnations may entail, notwithstanding the payment of just compensation. We emphasize that nothing in our opinion precludes any State from placing further restrictions on its exercise of the takings power . . . As the submissions of the parties and their *amici* make clear, the necessity and wisdom of using eminent domain to promote economic development are certainly matters of legitimate public debate. This Court's authority, however, extends only to determining whether the City's proposed condemnations are for a "public use" within the meaning of the Fifth Amendment to the Federal Constitution. Because over a century of our case law interpreting that provision dictates an affirmative answer to that question, we may not grant petitioners the relief that they seek.

The judgment of the Supreme Court of Connecticut is affirmed.

It is so ordered.

[Citations and footnotes omitted]

QUESTIONS FOR DISCUSSION:

Is promoting private business to encourage economic development a public purpose?

In parts of the opinion not reproduced here, Justice Stevens made much of the fact that the City of New London had carefully planned a comprehensive development scheme. Should that make a difference to the determination that the taking here was for a public purpose? Suppose that, instead of formulating a comprehensive plan, the City had moved to take the property with the idea of tearing down any buildings on it and offering it for sale to any prospective developer. Would that still be a public purpose?

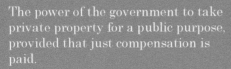

EMINENT DOMAIN:
The power of the government to take private property for a public purpose, provided that just compensation is paid.

The *Kelo* decision, as noted, set off a great deal of controversy. State legislatures across the country amended eminent domain laws to prohibit or severely limit eminent domain, especially regarding eminent domain takings for economic development purposes. The result is that most states now prohibit, with some exceptions, eminent domain takings to benefit private parties. Private property in most states may be taken only for a governmental purpose, such as a road or a public building, or to eradicate blight. "Blight" is also carefully defined to include an area of several properties, rather than merely targeting an individual property.

> In many states, private utility companies, pipelines, or railroads have some eminent domain powers.

If a unit of government plans to take property, and if the taking meets the criteria for "public use" under local law, the property owner is entitled to receive the fair market value of his property. "Fair market value" is the price a willing seller would receive from a willing buyer in an arm's length transaction, with the price freely negotiated by the parties. Many state laws provide for a formal appraisal process to determine the value. The goal is to award the property owner the same price that he would have received if he had sold the property on the open market.

The proceeding by which property is taken is known as a condemnation proceeding. The end result of a successful condemnation action is the transfer of title in the property to the condemning authority. In some jurisdictions, and in condemnation actions brought by the federal government, all other rights or claims to the property are extinguished.

CHAPTER SUMMARY

Businesses interact with the rest of the world on many levels, and not just with customers. Misleading a company's investors is prohibited by the Sarbanes-Oxley Act. Antitrust laws prohibited agreeing with other businesses to limit competition, or restrain trade. Rules on the risk of loss when goods are transported provide certainty about who is responsible when goods are damaged in shipment. Tariffs and trading areas regulate the ways business is transacted across national borders.

Every business—even one that does business only online—must have a physical location. Business relationships therefore include the ownership or rental of real estate. Rental involves making a lease agreement with a landlord, while ownership involves the proper documentation of the transaction.

Review Questions

Review question 1.
Define "F.O.B." How does F.O.B. differ under the UCC and Incoterms? What other information should be included with F.O.B. or other trade terms? What terms are most appropriate for domestic shipments? For international shipments?

Review question 2.
What is a "horizontal" merger? What is a "vertical" merger? How does the law treat each type of merger? What law requires government approval of large corporate mergers? Does federal law prohibit monopolies?

Review question 3.
Who is responsible for the accuracy of financial statements of publicly-traded corporations? What type of financial information must be disclosed?

Review question 4.
What is quiet enjoyment? To whom does quiet enjoyment apply? What types of actions (or failures to act) might violate quiet enjoyment?

Review question 5.
What is the Sarbanes-Oxley Act? How does it impact financial reporting? Are there businesses that do not need to adhere to the Act? Why or why not?

Review question 6.
What are the four freedoms and how do they work within a common market? What are the differences between a common market and a customs union? Between a customs union and a free trade area?

Review question 7.
What is the difference between tenants-in-common and joint tenants? Why might you choose one form over the other?

Review question 8.
What is eminent domain? When may a government exercise eminent domain? What are the limits on the practice?

Review question 9.

What did the Sherman Act and the Clayton Act achieve? What are the differences between the two laws? How are they applied?

Questions for Discussion

Discussion question 1.

Delish, O-So-Yummy, and Jim Norton are competing companies that operate chains of donut shops. They agree to form an association, the National Donut Association, to discuss and address common interests. At the Association's first meeting, discussions revolve around land use restrictions, environmental marketing, and food labeling requirements.

Is the Association an antitrust violation? Why or why not?

In many cities, the competing donut shops are very close to each other. Delish instructs shop managers to send employees every day to O-So-Yummy and Jim Norton to learn what prices are being charged and what promotions are being offered. Managers are directed to match prices, and run similar promotions. Is this an antitrust violation? Why or why not?

Discussion question 2.

A Jim Norton store is located in a suburban strip mall. There is an empty storefront at the opposite end of the mall. The mall's owner leases that space to O-So-Yummy.

Is this a violation of Jim Norton's right of quiet enjoyment? Why or why not?

Suppose the foot traffic to Jim Norton's drops by 40% in the first two months after the O-So-Yummy store opens. Does this violate the right to quiet enjoyment? Why or why not?

What terms could have been put into the lease to avoid this situation?

Discussion question 3.

A shoe manufacturer in Levelland, Texas ordered a shaping machine from a dealer in Cleveland, Ohio. When the machine arrives on June 23, it is damaged beyond repair. Explain which party bears the risk of loss in each of these situations.

The sales contract contained the term "F.O.B. Cleveland."

The sales contract contained the term "F.O.B. Levelland."

The sales contract was silent on risk of loss.

The sales contract was silent on risk of loss, but stated that the machine was to be delivered no later than June 19.

Discussion question 4.

The United States is a member of several bilateral trade agreements. It is also the member of the three-party North American Free Trade Area. Does the membership of NAFTA change the country's responsibilities under its various bilateral trade agreements? What if another NAFTA country started trade sanctions against one of the United States' bilateral trade partners? What impact would that have on the NAFTA agreement? On NAFTA relationships?

Discussion question 5.

Pravesh sells handmade wooden toys. He is looking for a retail location to sell the toys. He would like to be in a specific neighborhood near his home, but there is limited open retail space in that area. Denise owns a large apartment building adjacent to the main shopping area. She has a vacancy on the ground floor and offers it to Pravesh as a retail space. You are advising Pravesh on the lease. What is your response to each of the following scenarios? Are the requests legal? Are they fair?

Denise says she will only allow exterior signage for the shop if Pravesh agrees to pay for all exterior maintenance for the property.

Pravesh wants to be able to veto competing businesses if Denise chooses to lease other space in the building to retailers.

Denise says she is not certain if retail is "technically" allowed in the building, but she does not think it will be an issue.

Denise will give Pravesh a rent credit if he helps her remove delinquent tenants elsewhere in the building.

Pravesh asks for a reduction in rent if he has a bad sales month.

Discussion question 6.

Some economists have argued that antitrust laws reflect a misunderstanding of how markets work. They claim that this type of government interference in the market hurts competition by allowing businesses to use governmental authority and litigation to bring down competitors. This hurts consumers, who would benefit from genuine competition that is not protected by the antitrust laws. Do you agree with this analysis?

Discussion question 7.

The Metropolis & Smallville Railroad has a right-of-way about twenty feet wide with tracks on it running through a residential neighborhood of a city. Part of the right-of-way is used occasionally to park freight cars that are not being used at the time, but about a mile of the right-of-way is unused. The Railroad does not want to sell the part that it does not use, saying that it wants to "keep its options open." The city would like to get rid of the right-of-way, as it attracts litter, and is overgrown with weeds. The right-of-way is too narrow to build on.

> Would condemnation of the right-of-way be for a public purpose? Why or why not?

> How would the compensation for condemnation of the property be calculated?

Discussion question 8.

The City of New Middlemarch has a comprehensive zoning code. The northwest quarter of the city is zoned for residential uses only. Zoe, a real estate developer, has heard from several acquaintances who live in that part of town that they are tired of having to drive across the city to buy groceries. She buys three adjoining lots in the northwest quarter, and has asked the city Planning and Zoning Commission for a variance to build a small retail development there.

> You are a member of the Planning and Zoning Commission. What questions to you have for Zoe before you make up your mind on her application for a variance?

> What other information would you need to make a decision?

Discussion question 9.

Do the duties of corporate officers and directors imposed by Sarbanes-Oxley impose unfair obligations on the people who hold those offices? Will SOX discourage outsiders from becoming directors? Is this a bad thing for the corporations or their shareholders?

12 REGULATORY REGIMES

CHAPTER OVERVIEW

This chapter covers regulatory regimes. The term "regulatory regimes" refers to the body of law adopted by regulatory and administrative agencies. This law is made by specialized agencies, acting under authority delegated to them by law. Agencies exist at both the state and federal levels, with authority granted to them by legislation.

In this chapter, we will look at some of the major federal regulatory regimes that have the greatest impact on business. We will examine some of the law relating to advertising and marketing, including deceptive trade practices and consumer protection laws. We will consider the regulation of the securities marketplace, and review significant aspects of the law of environmental protection. While we will focus on federal regulations here, remember that there is an additional layer of regulation in each state.

INTRODUCTION

Much of the governmental regulation of business activity comes from administrative agencies or boards. These agencies are acting with authority granted to them by Congress or the state legislature. Although legislative action (statutes) is important, much of the day-to-day "street level" regulation of business is done by agency officials, making rules and regulations that have the same force as if they were a law passed by the legislative branch and approved by the executive.

To some people, the idea of unelected agency bureaucrats making laws may seem undemocratic. But Congress delegates authority to regulatory agencies to create these regulations. And regulatory agencies often deal with highly specialized or technical matters. The agencies and their staff have developed the expertise to address these issues in a knowledgeable way.

While the legislature gives agencies authority to act by passing specific laws, the agencies, boards, and other administrative bodies are part of the executive branch of government. The executive branch enforces the law. These administrative bodies make rules that give the laws practical effect, and then enforce those rules.

I. Administrative Procedure Act

The process of making administrative rules does not exclude participation by the public. Federal agencies make their rules according to the **Administrative Procedure Act** (APA). The APA sets standards for federal regulatory activity.

The purpose of the APA is to:

- Require agencies to keep the public informed of their organization, procedures and rules,

- Provide for public participation in the rulemaking process,

- Establish uniform standards for the conduct of formal rulemaking and **adjudication**, and

- Define the scope of **judicial review**.

Federal agencies act according to authority granted by Congress. When an agency identifies a need for a regulation that is within its existing authority, or when Congress mandates the adoption of a rule, the agency develops the rule based on broad guidelines established by Congress. Congress delegates authority to administrative bodies in this way not to avoid responsibility, but to have the most knowledgeable and experienced people apply the law to specific circumstances. The Environmental Protection Agency's staff includes environmental scientists, for instance, while the United State Department of Agriculture employs experts on soil, food safety, and crop yields, among a range of other issues.

When developing a rule, agencies are required to take into account the benefits and costs, both quantitative and qualitative. Once a rule is developed, the agency will then publish the proposed rule in the **Federal Register**. The notice will solicit comments from the public on the proposed rule, and tell the public when comments must be received. After the agency considers any public feedback and makes any appropriate changes, it then publishes a final rule in the Federal Register. In issuing a final rule, the agency must describe and respond to the public comments that were received. Agencies are not required to revise the rule to take into account such comments, but they often do.

ADMINISTRATIVE PROCEDURE ACT:

The federal law that establishes the procedure for rulemaking and adjudication by federal administrative agencies.

ADJUDICATION:

The exercise of judicial power by an administrative agency. Adjudication usually deals with disputes between the agency and individuals or business entities.

JUDICIAL REVIEW:

A court's review of an administrative agency's factual or legal findings.

FEDERAL REGISTER:

A daily publication containing documents and orders issued by Executive Branch agencies.

Many states have laws about the adoption of administrative regulations patterned after the APA.

> "Major rules" are defined as rules likely to have an annual effect on the national economy of $100 million or more; that will increase costs and prices for certain constituencies such as consumers or state and local governments; or that will have some other adverse effect on the economy.

The publication of a new rule will include the specific date when it becomes effective and enforceable. Major rules take effect 60 days after their final publication date.

Other rules go into effect 30 days after the final publication. The delay period allows Congress to review the rule and, if necessary, act to invalidate the regulation. If Congress disapproves of a new regulation, it may pass a joint resolution of disapproval. The joint resolution must be signed by the president. If signed, the rule will not take effect.

COURTS SHOULD YIELD TO MOST AGENCY ACTIONS.

Chevron U.S.A., Inc. v. Natural Resources Defense Council, Inc.
(Energy Company) v. (Public Interest Group)
467 U.S. 837 (1984)

STEVENS, J., Opinion of the Court

Congress enacted certain requirements applicable to States that had not achieved the national air quality standards established by the Environmental Protection Agency (EPA) pursuant to earlier legislation. The amended Clean Air Act required these "nonattainment" States to establish a permit program regulating "new or modified major stationary sources" of air pollution. Generally, a permit may not be issued for a new or modified major stationary source unless several stringent conditions are met. The EPA regulation promulgated to implement this permit requirement allows a State to adopt a plantwide definition of the term "stationary source." Under this definition, an existing plant that contains several pollution-emitting devices may install or modify one piece of equipment without meeting the permit conditions if the alteration will not increase the total emissions from the plant. The question presented by these cases is whether EPA's decision to allow States to treat all of the pollution-emitting devices within the same industrial grouping as though they were encased within a single "bubble" is based on a reasonable construction of the statutory term "stationary source." . . . [T]he relevant part of the amended Clean Air Act "does not explicitly define what Congress envisioned as a 'stationary source, to which the permit program . . . should apply[.]"

When a court reviews an agency's construction of the statute which it administers, it is confronted with two questions. First, always, is the question whether Congress has directly spoken to the precise question at issue. If the intent of Congress is clear, that is the end of the matter . . . . If, however, the court determines Congress has not directly addressed the precise question at issue, the court does not simply impose its own construction on the statute, as would be necessary in the absence of an administrative interpretation. Rather, if the statute is silent or ambiguous with respect to the specific issue, the question for the court is whether the agency's answer is based on a permissible constructions of the statute.

[...]

If Congress has explicitly left a gap for the agency to fill, there is an express delegation of authority to the agency to elucidate a specific provision of the statute by regulation. Such legislative regulations are given controlling weight unless they are arbitrary, capricious, or manifestly contrary to the statute. Sometimes the legislative delegation to an agency on a particular question is implicit, rather than explicit. In such a case, a court may not substitute its own construction of a statutory provision for a reasonable interpretation made by the administrator of an agency.

We have long recognized that considerable weight should be accorded to an executive department's construction of a statutory scheme it is entrusted to administer, and the principle of deference to administrative interpretations has been consistently followed by this Court whenever decision as to the meaning or reach of a statute has involved reconciling conflicting policies, and a full understanding of the force of the statutory policy in the given situation has depended upon more than ordinary knowledge respecting the matters subjected to agency regulations.

[...]

In light of these well-settled principles, it is clear that the Court of Appeals misconceived the nature of its role in reviewing the regulations at issue. Once it determined, after its own examination of the legislation, that Congress did not actually have an intent regarding the applicability of the bubble concept to the permit program, the question before it was not whether, in its view, the concept is "inappropriate" in the general context of a program designed to improve air quality, but whether the Administrator's view that it is appropriate in the context of this particular program is a reasonable one. Based on the examination of the legislation and its history which follows, we agree with the Court of Appeals that Congress did not have a specific intention on the applicability of the bubble concept in these cases, and conclude that the EPA's use of that concept here is a reasonable policy choice for the agency to make.

[...]

The [federal enabling law] contain[s] no specific reference to the "bubble concept." Nor do they contain a specific definition of the term "stationary source," though they did not disturb the definition of "stationary source" contained [elsewhere]. Section 302(j), however, defines the term "major stationary source" as follows:

(j) Except as otherwise expressly provided, the terms "major stationary source" and "major emitting facility" mean any stationary facility or source of air pollutants which directly emits, or has the potential to emit, one hundred tons per year or more of any air pollutant [... .]

The legislative history . . . does not contain any specific comment on the "bubble concept" or the question whether a plantwide definition of a stationary source is permissible under the permit program.

[...]

[T]he EPA [initially] adopted a dual definition of "source" for nonattainment areas that required a permit whenever a change in either the entire plant, or one of its components, would result in a significant increase in emissions even if the increase was completely offset by reductions elsewhere in the plant. The EPA expressed the opinion that this interpretation was "more consistent with congressional intent" than the plantwide definition because it "would bring in more sources or modifications for review," but its primary legal analysis was predicated on the two Court of Appeals decisions.

In 1981, a new administration took office and initiated a "Government-wide reexamination of regulatory burdens and complexities." In the context of that review, the EPA reevaluated the various arguments that had been advanced in connection with the proper definition of the term "source" and concluded that the term should be given the same definition in [all areas].

In explaining its conclusion, the EPA first noted that the definitional issue was not squarely addressed in either the statute or its legislative history, and therefore that the issue involved an agency "judgment as how to best carry out the Act." It then set forth several reasons for concluding that the plantwide definition was more appropriate. It pointed out that the dual definition "can act as a disincentive to new investment and modernization by discouraging modifications to existing facilities" and can actually retard progress in air pollution control by discouraging replacement of older, dirtier processes or pieces of equipment with new, cleaner ones. . . . Moreover, the new definition . . . would simplify EPA's rules[.] . . . Finally, the agency explained that additional requirements that remained in place would accomplish the fundamental purposes of achieving attainment . . . as expeditiously as possible.

[...]

We are not persuaded that parsing of general terms in the text of the statute will reveal an actual intent of Congress. We know full well that this language is not dispositive; the terms are overlapping, and the language is not precisely directed to the question of the applicability of a given term in the context of a larger operation. To the extent any congressional "intent" can be discerned from this language, it would appear that the listing of overlapping, illustrative terms was intended to enlarge, rather than to confine, the scope of the agency's power to regulate particular sources in order to effectuate the policies of the Act.

[The legislative] history plainly identifies the policy concerns that motivated the enactment; the plantwide definition is fully consistent with one of those concerns -- the allowance of reasonable economic growth -- and, whether or not we believe it most effectively implements the other, we must recognize that the EPA has advanced a reasonable explanation for its conclusion that the regulations serve the environmental objectives as well. Indeed, its reasoning is supported by the public record developed in the rulemaking process, as well as by certain private studies.

[...]

The fact that the agency has from time to time changed its interpretation of the term "source" does not, as respondents argue, lead us to conclude that no deference should be accorded the agency's interpretation of the statute. An initial agency interpretation is not instantly carved in stone. On the contrary, the agency, to engage in informed rulemaking, must consider varying interpretations and the wisdom of its policy on a continuing basis. Moreover, the fact that the agency has adopted different definitions in different contexts adds force to the argument that the definition itself is flexible, particularly since Congress has never indicated any disapproval of a flexible reading of the statute.
[...]

[T]he Administrator's interpretation represents a reasonable accommodation of manifestly competing interests, and is entitled to deference: the regulatory scheme is technical and complex, the agency considered the matter in a detailed and reasoned fashion, and the decision involves reconciling conflicting policies. Congress intended to accommodate both interests, but did not do so itself on the level of specificity presented by these cases. Perhaps that body consciously desired the Administrator to strike the balance at this level, thinking that those with great expertise and charged with responsibility for administering the provision would be in a better position to do so; perhaps it simply did not consider the question at this level; and perhaps Congress was unable to forge a coalition on either side of the question, and those on each side decided to take their chances with the scheme devised by the agency. For judicial purposes, it matters not which of these things occurred.

Judges are not experts in the field, and are not part of either political branch of the Government. Courts must, in some cases, reconcile competing political interests, but not on the basis of the judges' personal policy preferences. In contrast, an agency to which Congress has delegated policymaking responsibilities may, within the limits of that delegation, properly rely upon the incumbent administration's views of wise policy to inform its judgments. While agencies are not directly accountable to the people, the Chief Executive is, and it is entirely appropriate for this political branch of the Government to make such policy choices -- resolving the competing interests which Congress itself either inadvertently did not resolve, or intentionally left to be resolved by the agency charged with the administration of the statute in light of everyday realities.

When a challenge to an agency construction of a statutory provision, fairly conceptualized, really centers on the wisdom of the agency's policy, rather than whether it is a reasonable choice within a gap left open by Congress, the challenge must fail. In such a case, federal judges -- who have no constituency -- have a duty to respect legitimate policy choices made by those who do.

[...]

We hold that the EPA's definition of the term "source" is a permissible construction of the statute which seeks to accommodate progress in reducing air pollution with economic growth.

[Citations and footnotes omitted.]

Court Challenges

Final regulations may be challenged by court actions. These actions are initially brought against an agency by affected parties. A new rule will not be overturned by a court unless a high standard is met, as established in the APA:

5 U.S.C. § 706 - Scope of review

To the extent necessary to decision and when presented, the reviewing court shall decide all relevant questions of law, interpret constitutional and statutory provisions, and determine the meaning or applicability of the terms of an agency action. The reviewing court shall—

(1) compel agency action unlawfully withheld or unreasonably delayed; and

(2) hold unlawful and set aside agency action, findings, and conclusions found to be—

(A) arbitrary, capricious, an abuse of discretion, or otherwise not in accordance with law;

(B) contrary to constitutional right, power, privilege, or immunity;

(C) in excess of statutory jurisdiction, authority, or limitations, or short of statutory right;

(D) without observance of procedure required by law;

(E) unsupported by substantial evidence […]; or

(F) unwarranted by the facts […].

The "arbitrary and capricious" standard means that the courts will rarely overturn a regulation promulgated by an administrative body. An agency will almost always have a reasonably good rationale for the regulations it promulgates. Under the standard, even a *bad* reason is adequate for the court to leave a regulation in place, because a bad reason is still a reason, and not an arbitrary or capricious decision.

The arbitrary and capricious standard recognizes the administrative body's expertise and experience. It also promotes predictability and stability in administrative actions: if a regulation is well-known and well-established, then compliance requirements are also well-known and well-established. This position was bolstered in a famous Supreme Court decision.

"Chevron deference" is the legal shorthand for the Supreme Court's decision that courts should defer to agency determinations in most cases. The case established a test for whether deference was warranted:

1. When making the law that the agency is administering, did Congress speak directly to the precise question in dispute? If so, then that intent controls the outcome.

2. If Congress did not speak directly to the precise issue, the court may not impose its own interpretation on the law. In that case, all the court may decide is whether the agency's interpretation is based on a "permissible" reading of the law.

ADMINISTRATIVE AGENCIES HELP THE LEGISLATIVE, EXECUTIVE, AND JUDICIAL BRANCHES OF BOTH FEDERAL AND STATE GOVERNMENTS TO REGULATE CERTAIN INDUSTRIES AND ACTIVITIES.

Fund for Animals, Inc. v. Rice
(Environmental Conservation Group) v. (Not Stated)
85 F.3d 535 (11th Cir. 1996)

INSTANT FACTS:
An environmental group filed suit against the Army Corps of Engineers, the Fish and Wildlife Service, and the Environmental Protection Agency when those agencies approved the building of a landfill in an area that would allegedly harm two endangered species.

BLACK LETTER RULE:
Administrative agencies act on behalf of the three branches of government in making rules for the regulation of certain activities, enforcing those rules, and then adjudicating certain disputes that arise with respect to those rules.

PROCEDURAL BASIS:
Appeal to the Eleventh Circuit Court of Appeals of a federal district court decision approving of the actions of three administrative agencies with regard to the building of a landfill.

FACTS:
On November 22, 1989, Sarasota County, Florida, filed an application with the Army Corps of Engineers (the Corps) (D) for a permit to build a landfill on a 6,150 acre site in the county. The County was required to seek a permit from the Corps (D) because the proposed landfill affected some wetlands. Under federal law, the Corps (D) had to approve of any discharge of dredged or fill materials into the waters of the United States.

The plan received some opposition and had to be altered in various ways over the next few years. The original plan, which affected 120 acres of wetlands, was later modified so that only 74 acres would be affected. This modification was the result of Clean Water Act concerns expressed by the Environmental Protection Agency (EPA) (D). Concern was also expressed that the landfill would adversely affect two endangered species—the Florida panther and the Eastern Indigo Snake—though the Fish and Wildlife Service (FWS) (D) ultimately determined in two separate opinions that those species would not be injured by the plan.

Finally, on April 13, 1995, a permit for the building of the proposed landfill was given. Based on its view that the FWS (D) and the Corps (D) were incorrect in determining that the panther and the snake would not be adversely affected by the landfill, Fund For Animals, Inc. (P), an environmental group, filed suit in federal court against the Corps (D), the FWS (D), and the EPA (D), among others.

ISSUE:
Did the district court err in affirming the decisions of the Corps (D) and the FWS (D) with respect to the landfill and the endangered species?

DECISION AND RATIONALE:
(Dubina, J.) No. The judgment of the district court is affirmed.

ANALYSIS:
Fund for Animals is a good example of how our nation's administrative agency system works in a real-life situation.

Three separate administrative agencies play a role in the decision here. The first is the Army Corps of Engineers. As the opinion states, the Corps is charged with granting permits for the discharge of dredged or fill material into the "waters of the United States"—federal law prohibits any such discharge without permission from the Corps. Congress created the Corps, in part, to assist it and the executive branch in protecting our nation's waterways.

The second administrative agency involved in this case is the Environmental Protection Agency.

The EPA is charged with, among other things, reviewing "proposed permit issuances for consistency with" certain environmental guidelines that it has promulgated. In this sense, the EPA acts for Congress, the executive branch, and the judiciary in a number of ways. First, it has created guidelines for the issuance of permits by the Corps. In that sense, it engaged in (and continues to engage in) legislative activity—it is making rules that all citizens must follow. In reviewing proposed permit issuances for consistency, the EPA is adjudicating. It is determining which permits will be allowed to stand and which will not, much like a criminal or civil court determines whether a person's activities are or have been in conformance with the law. And finally, in enforcing its promulgated regulations, the EPA is performing executive activities. Congress, the president and the judiciary do not have the time or expertise to create detailed rules for the discharge of materials into waterways and to then enforce those rules as necessary. To assist them in doing so, the EPA was created.

The third administrative agency involved in this case is the Fish and Wildlife Service. As the opinion demonstrates, the FWS is charged with administering the Endangered Species Act. In doing so it issues opinions regarding the way in which individual endangered species will be affected by certain proposed activities. In performing these duties, it is assisting all three branches of government in carrying out their activities.

What's "permissible" for the agency? Any interpretation that is not arbitrary or capricious is permissible.

The Chevron decision is controversial. Many legal scholars argue that the Supreme Court's formulation of the rule hobbles the judiciary when reviewing administrative actions, reducing the effect of the separation of powers. Others criticize that the decision effectively makes policy-making priorities more important than legislation in administrative actions, because almost any administrative reading of the law would be "permissible." Proponents of Chevron deference point to the highly technical and specialized nature of current regulatory needs. Courts cannot be expected to have the technical knowledge necessary to second-guess a federal agency, and without that knowledge, the courts should not wield that power except in the most extreme cases.

II. Product Regulations

Many administrative agencies have been formed by Congress to regulate commercial endeavors, such as how a product is marketed. Regulations on advertising, packaging, labelling, and marketing must be followed as businesses produce and sell goods.

Advertising and Marketing

Advertising is an important part of American business. It is also closely regulated. One purpose of such regulation is to protect consumers, but it also serves to protect the integrity of the marketplace.

Any kind of government regulation of communication raises First Amendment concerns. The First Amendment to the U.S. Constitution guarantees the right to free speech, among other fundamental rights. For many years, the courts held that commercial or business advertising (referred to as "commercial speech")

was not entitled to any protections under the First Amendment.

That doctrine has changed over the years. The law now protects commercial speech from unwarranted governmental regulation. Suppose an advertisement is challenged by a governmental agency for violating a regulation, even though the ad relates to a lawful activity and is not misleading. In such a case, the courts look at the government's purpose in regulating the advertisement. The governmental interest to be served by the regulation must be important. Further, the regulation will be considered lawful by the courts only if the regulation directly advances that governmental interest. Even then, the regulation will only be upheld if it is no more extensive than necessary to serve that interest.

Under that test, courts have allowed numerous types of advertising regulations, including ads that:

- Are deceptive or fraudulent,

- Further criminal schemes (for example, ads promoting a **pyramid scheme**),

- Invade personal privacy (for example, ads that use someone's likeness without their permission),

- Otherwise infringe on the rights of others (for example, ads that infringe on a trademark),

- Are directed towards a captive audience, and

- Are for illegal goods or services.

There are two federal agencies that regulate advertising. The Food and Drug Administration (FDA), which is part of the Department of Health and Human Services, regulates certain aspects of the advertising for medications. The other agency, the Federal Trade Commission (FTC), is an independent agency that has been delegated the power to regulate most of the other types of advertising that we see.

Deceptive Trade Practices

The Federal Trade Commission has the power to enforce the federal laws against "unfair or deceptive acts in commerce." Because the FTC

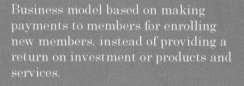

PYRAMID SCHEME:
Business model based on making payments to members for enrolling new members, instead of providing a return on investment or products and services.

Example: Lynn runs a travel company that specializes in trips to Las Vegas. She runs an ad for an "all-inclusive gambling junket" in a state that does not allow any type of gambling. The state may not restrict her advertisement. Lynn is advertising gambling that will take place in a state where it is legal. It is not illegal to travel to Las Vegas, so the ad does not advertise illegal goods or services, or further a criminal scheme.

has nationwide jurisdiction, its rules are especially important for businesses to follow.

The FTC has issued general guidelines that set out when an act or practice will be deemed deceptive. A practice will be considered deceptive if there is a "material" (meaning "essential" in this context) representation, omission, or practice that is likely to mislead a consumer.

If there is express or intentional deception by the advertiser, the FTC will presume the decep-

tion related to a material issue. Implied claims about health, safety, durability, or performance are also presumed to be material.

> According to the FTC, a representation is "material" if it is likely to affect a consumer's conduct or decision with regard to a product or service.

Example: A company sold a set of 40 games. The company advertised that training on these games for 10 to 15 minutes three or four times a week could help users achieve their "full potential in every aspect of life." The games were advertised as improving performance on everyday tasks, delaying age-related cognitive decline, and reducing cognitive impairment associated with health conditions. The company also advertised that scientific studies proved these benefits. In fact, there was no reliable scientific evidence supporting these claims. The advertisement was deceptive. *In the Matter of Lumos Lab, Inc.,* F.T.C. File No. 132 3212 (2016).

Example: A car company manufactures a hybrid gasoline/electric vehicle. The company claims in its ads that the car goes 150 miles on a single gallon of gasoline. The car did achieve that gas mileage on one occasion when driven by a professional driver on a closed track under ideal conditions. Actual mileage for the car is much lower, particularly when the temperature is below freezing. The advertising claim does not have a reasonable factual basis. It also omitted qualifying information, such as "your mileage may vary" depending on driving conditions and how the car is driven.

Example: A bakery advertised its "Dieter's Friend" bread as having "33% fewer calories per slice than our regular bread." The advertisements omit the fact that Dieter's Friend bread is the same as the bakery's regular bread, sliced 33% thinner. The ad is deceptive.

A demonstration or mock-up of how a product works is deceptive if the ad implies that it was actual proof of performance. For instance, a cut-away mock-up of a dishwasher with signs showing a specific water-saving feature could be deceptive if the cut-away misrepresents the water-saving technology actually used in the dishwasher.

An act may be deemed deceptive even if there is no proof of actual deception. The question is whether it is likely to mislead a consumer. Any factual claims in advertising must be supported by a reasonable factual basis at the time the claim was made. Qualifying information (such as "your mileage may vary" in an ad for a car boosting a high miles-per-gallon figure) may not be omitted.

Endorsements of products or services are deceptive if they do not reflect the honest opinions or beliefs of the endorsing party. "Endorsements" are defined as a message that consumers are likely to believe comes from someone other than the advertiser. Endorsements are often made by celebrities, but may also be made by product owners or users. Endorsements cannot make representations that would be deceptive if they were made directly by the sponsor. There must also be reason to believe that the endorser continues as a bona fide user of the product for as long as the advertisement is run.

Note that the definitions and examples of deceptive practices all relate to factual claims, as distinct from opinions. Factual claims can be proven or disproven, and will require substantiation. On the other hand, there is no way an opinion can be proven or disproven. As long as the opinion statement does not represent a false endorsement, it will not be considered deceptive.

Example: A tire company runs an advertisement that shows a picture of a small child in a toy car with the caption "The Best Tires for Today's Cars." There is no endorsement, as a consumer is not likely to believe that the opinion comes from the child pictured. The same caption runs under a picture of a well-known racing driver. There is an endorsement, even if the caption is not labeled as a quotation from the driver.

Example: An advertisement for Parolacxas Beer includes the line "The flavor, mmm! It's quite okay!" That is a statement of opinion, and not deceptive. Another ad for the same beer says "98% of all beer drinkers agree: Parolacxas Beer is quite okay!" If the 98% figure does not represent the results of a real survey, the ad is deceptive.

The FTC has issued guidance for advertisers in different industries, or for advertisers who want to make certain types of claims about their products. This guidance is not an official regulation, but is advice from the FTC on what it considers appropriate.

An example of advertiser guidance is the "Green Guide." The Green Guide was first issued in 1992, and has been supplemented and updated three times since. It is guidance for advertisers who wish to make environmental claims about their products or services. The Guide does not create any new rules. Instead, existing rules are placed in context. Advertisers who use terms such as "biodegradable," "recyclable," or "ozone safe" are told how the terms can and should be used in advertising. Advertisers are also cautioned not to use overly broad terms ("environmentally friendly" or "eco-friendly") that cannot be substantiated.

State Law

Most states also have laws regarding deceptive practices that apply within the state. These laws usually have a list of specific practices that will be regarded as deceptive. Although the list will vary from state-to-state, the prohibited practices typically fall into one of three general categories:

- Misrepresentations,

- False sponsorship, and

- Disparagement.

> Disparagement in this context means a false statement that the advertiser's product or service performs better than a competitor's product or service.

Common examples of deceptive trade practices prohibited by state regulations include:

- Falsely representing the source, sponsorship, approval, certification, accessories, characteristics, benefits, or quantities of a product or service,

- Representing goods as original or new when they are in fact reconditioned or used,

- Falsely stating that replacements or repairs are needed,

- Advertising goods or services not intending to sell them as advertised, or not having enough in stock to meet reasonably expected demand, and

Example: Maggie designs and markets a new type of pillow. She is allowed to give a presentation about her pillow to the National Insomnia Institute, an organization of sleep researchers. Maggie's advertising claims that the pillow is the "Official Pillow of the National Insomnia Institute," but the Institute has done nothing beyond allowing her to promote her pillow at its meeting. Maggie has committed a deceptive trade practice.

- Passing off goods or services as those of another (for example, mislabeling goods)

State deceptive trade practices laws are usually enforced by the state attorney general, who brings an action on behalf of all consumers in a state. However, it is possible that private lawsuits by individuals harmed by such practices can also be brought against a company. Again, the enforcement may vary depending on the individual state's laws.

Labelling and Packaging

Advertising is an important factor in influencing consumer buying choices, but it is not the only factor. Packaging and labeling are also important. The package that contains a product, or the label on that package, can be just as deceptive as a false advertisement. To ensure that consumer packaging does not deceive or mislead consumers, Congress enacted the Fair Packaging and Labeling Act (FPLA) in 1967.

The FPLA requires the FTC and the FDA to issue regulations for sellers and manufacturers

to follow when putting **consumer products** on the market. These regulations require all consumer commodities to be labeled to disclose:

- The net quantity of the contents of the package, in both metric and inch/pound units, as appropriate,

- The identity of commodity (that is, what is in the package), and

- The name and place of business of the product's manufacturer, packer, or distributor.

The agencies that administer the FPLA may also make additional regulations if necessary to prevent consumer deception (or to make it easier to compare value). These additional regulations may cover descriptions of ingredients, packaging requirements, the use of "cents-off" or lower price labeling, or the characterization of package sizes.

Some types of goods, such as alcoholic beverages, are exempt from the FPLA. Because of specific concerns about alcohol sales, the labelling and packaging of these products is regulated by a different federal law. In addition, manufacturers or sellers may request an exemption for a particular type of product. If granted, the exemption will often have different requirements that still allow consumers to know how much of a product they are purchasing. Many states also have laws that regulate the packaging and labelling of consumer goods. If there is a conflict between the state laws and the FPLA or regulations that implement the FPLA, federal law will control if the state laws are less stringent than or require information different from the requirements of

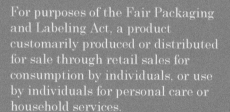

CONSUMER PRODUCT:

For purposes of the Fair Packaging and Labeling Act, a product customarily produced or distributed for sale through retail sales for consumption by individuals, or use by individuals for personal care or household services.

PREEMPTION:

The principle that federal law can supersede state law or regulation.

> **Example:** An FTC regulation provides that Christmas tree ornaments are exempt from the net quantity labelling rules. The package containing the ornaments must express the quantity "in terms of numerical count of the ornaments." The ornaments must also be packaged so that the ornaments are clearly visible to the purchaser at the time of purchase. 16 C.F.R. § 501.2.

> **Example:** The FPLA requires accurate labelling of the quantity of goods in a package. State law in California has a similar requirement. The regulations implementing the FPLA say that packages containing flour may lawfully vary from the weight on the label, to allow for variations in weight caused by loss of moisture. California law has no such allowance. Federal law supersedes the state law. *Jones v. Rath Packing Co.,* 430 U.S. 519 (1977).

the FPLA or its implementing regulations. This prioritization of federal law is referred to as the preemption doctrine.

The FPLA is not the only federal law dealing with packaging and labelling. Other laws deal with packaging of specific commodities. For example, the Federal Meat Inspection Act covers how meat may be packed for health and safety, while the Federal Insecticide, Fungicide, and Rodenticide Act deals with labelling for these potentially hazardous products. Packaging and labelling are also subject to the requirements that they not be deceptive or misleading.

III. Consumer Protection Laws

Consumer protection laws are an attempt to level the playing field in the business marketplace. Traditional free-market economics would enforce all business transactions freely negotiated between the parties, consumer protection laws recognize that there is a disparity between consumers and the companies that sell them products. The laws are an effort to equalize the bargaining power of consumers against the companies that sell goods and services to them.

Most consumer protection laws do not regulate what is sold (except for dangerous products), but instead regulate the way the sale is made. Companies must make specific disclosures to consumers about their products and services. The disclosure laws aim to give consumers enough accurate information to make an informed decision about what they are buying. Deciding what to buy is left to the consumer, provided the consumer has the facts she needs.

We have already considered some laws that protect consumers. The laws relating to advertising emphasize accuracy and truthfulness. The packaging and labelling laws also require accurate information to allow consumers to make meaningful comparisons between different products. Although there probably can never be complete equality of bargaining power in a consumer transaction, consumer protection laws are an important step to reducing the inherent inequality.

Consumer Sales

A "consumer sale" is a sale of goods to a buyer who plans to use the goods for personal or household (non-business) purposes. The sale of the goods takes place in the normal course of the seller's business. A sale of business goods or a casual sale by a non-business seller are not consumer sales.

State and federal laws regarding deceptive or unfair trade practices provide consumers basic protection when they buy goods. Accuracy in labelling and honesty in product descriptions are the overall goals.

The laws that call for accuracy and honesty are good starts, but they cannot provide complete protection. Deceptive trade practice laws can often seem too vague to give consumers meaningful protection in particular transactions. In addition, although the laws call for the presentation of accurate information, they do not always say how that information is to be presented. Often, the consumer is not given a way to test a seller's assurance that information is accurate.

To address these issues, a number of state and federal laws regulate how a sales transaction is made. These laws usually apply to specific types of transactions, or specific types of products. The intent is to focus on the real potential for abuse that exists that may not be covered by general admonitions not to do anything "deceptive."

Telemarketing: The federal Telephone Consumer Protection Act (TCPA) regulates telephone solicitations. The law authorizes the FTC and Federal Communications Commission (FCC) to make rules that require telemarketers to tell people they call that it is a sales call. The rules say that telemarketers are also required to provide:

- The telemarketer's name,
- The name of the entity for whom the call is made, and
- A telephone number or address at which this entity can be contacted.

Intentional misrepresentations are prohibited. Telemarketers must give a clear statement of the total cost of any goods or services offered. They must also set out the terms of the sale. Financial services must be paid for only after they have been performed or delivered.

"Cooling Off" Periods: Most sales contracts cannot be cancelled by the buyer. Once you have agreed to purchase a computer, a hair dryer, or a pair of jeans, the deal is final as soon as the contract is formed. In some cases, retailers (especially of consumer goods) may provide generous return policies that allow buyers to return goods. Most consumers do not realize that such policies are purely voluntary. Retailers generally have no legal obligation to allow returns after the sale is complete. However, both state and federal law make exceptions for some types of sales, or for sales made under certain circumstances.

Under FTC rules, a person who buys something worth $25 or more in a door-to-door consumer sales transaction has three business days to cancel the sale. Likewise, a person who purchases goods for $130 or more at a sale at a location away from the seller's usual place of business has three business days to cancel the transaction. The seller must tell the buyer about the right to cancel at the time of the sale, and give the buyer two copies of a cancellation form.

> Under FTC rules, a "business day" includes Saturday, but does not include Sunday or federal holidays.

Under such statutes, a buyer may generally cancel a sale for any reason. To cancel a sale, the buyer must mail a copy of the cancellation form to the seller. If the buyer does not have a cancellation form, he can write a cancellation letter. The letter or form must be post-marked before midnight of the third business day after the date of the sales contract. The seller then has 10 days to refund the money paid by the buyer. The seller must either pick up the items within 20 days or reimburse the buyer for mailing expenses to send back the items. The buyer must make any goods received available to the seller in the same condition as when they were received.

The federal rule does not apply to sales made at art or craft fairs. It also does not apply to motor vehicle sales if the dealer has at least one permanent place of business.

Plain Language Rules: A persistent complaint of many consumers is that they can't understand what a contract says. The information that is in the contract might be accurate, but that doesn't do much good for the consumer who can't understand it.

To address this problem, many states have enacted "plain English" or "readability" laws. These laws try to ensure that consumer contracts are easy to understand. Although some states have general requirements that contracts be clearly written and use ordinary words, some states have a more detailed list of requirements. For example, the Pennsylvania statute lists nine "language guidelines" and three "visual guidelines" that are looked at when deciding if a document meets readability requirements.

> State cooling-off laws are similar, but apply only to specific goods or services, such as gym memberships, timeshares, or dating services.

Note that violating the readability statutes will not make a contract void or unenforceable in most states. Some state statutes do, however, provide for a consumer's right to sue for violations of the law.

Example: An appliance store rents space for three days at a home remodeling show. Any sales of appliances it makes at the sale are subject to the buyer's right to cancel. If a customer agrees to purchase an appliance, but completes the transaction at the seller's regular store, the right to cancel does not apply.

IF A CONTRACT IS UNCONSCIONABLE WHEN MADE, IT IS UNENFORCEABLE.

Williams v. Walker-Thomas Furniture Co.
(Furniture Renter-Buyers) v. (Furniture Leasing Company)
350 F.2d 445 (D.C. Cir. 1965)

J. SKELLY WRIGHT, Circuit Judge

Appellee, Walker-Thomas Furniture Company, operates a retail furniture store in the District of Columbia. During the period from 1957 to 1962 each appellant in these cases purchased a number of household items from Walker-Thomas, for which payment was to be made in installments. The terms of each purchase were contained in a printed form contract which set forth the value of the purchased item and purported to lease the item to appellant for a stipulated monthly rent payment. The contract then provided, in substance, that title would remain in Walker-Thomas until the total of all the monthly payments made equaled the stated value of the item, at which time appellants could take title. In the event of a default in the payment of any monthly installment, Walker-Thomas could repossess the item.

The contract further provided that "the amount of each periodical installment payment to be made by [purchaser] to the Company under this present lease shall be inclusive of and not in addition to the amount of each installment payment to be made by [purchaser] under such prior leases, bills or accounts; and all payments now and hereafter made by [purchaser] shall be credited pro rata on all outstanding leases, bills and accounts due the Company by [purchaser] at the time each such payment is made." . . . The effect of this rather obscure provision was to keep a balance due on every item purchased until the balance due on all items, whenever purchased, was liquidated. As a result, the debt incurred at the time of purchase of each item was secured by the right to repossess all the items previously purchased by the same purchaser, and each new item purchased automatically became subject to a security interest arising out of the previous dealings.

On May 12, 1962, appellant Thorne purchased an item described as a Daveno, three tables, and two lamps, having total stated value of $391.10. Shortly thereafter, he defaulted on his monthly payments and appellee sought to replevy [reclaim] all the items purchased since the first transaction in 1958. Similarly, on April 17, 1962, appellant Williams bought a stereo set of stated value of $514.95. She too defaulted shortly thereafter, and appellee sought to replevy all the items purchased since December, 1957. The Court of General Sessions granted judgment for appellee. The District of Columbia Court of Appeals affirmed, and we granted appellants' motion for leave to appeal to this court.

At the time of this purchase her account showed a balance of $164 still owing from her prior purchases. The total of all the purchases made over the years in question came to $1,800. The total payments amounted to $1,400.

Appellants' principal contention, rejected by both the trial and the appellate courts below, is that these contracts, or at least some of them, are unconscionable and, hence, not enforceable. In its opinion in Williams v. Walker-Thomas Furniture Company, 198 A.2d 914, 916 (1964), the District of Columbia Court of Appeals explained its rejection of this contention as follows:

> "Appellant's second argument presents a more serious question. The record reveals that prior to the last purchase appellant had reduced the balance in her account to $164. The last purchase, a stereo set, raised the balance due to $678. Significantly, at the time of this and the preceding purchases, appellee was aware of appellant's financial position. The reverse side of the stereo contract listed the name of appellant's social worker and her $218 monthly stipend from the government. Nevertheless, with full knowledge that appellant had to feed, clothe and support both herself and seven children on this amount, appellee sold her a $514 stereo set.

> "We cannot condemn too strongly appellee's conduct. It raises serious questions of sharp practice and irresponsible business dealings. A review of the legislation in the District of Columbia affecting retail sales and the pertinent decisions of the highest court in this jurisdiction disclose, however, no ground upon which this court can declare the contracts in question contrary to public

policy. We note that were the Maryland Retail Installment Sales Act, Art. 83 §§ 128-153, or its equivalent, in force in the District of Columbia, we could grant appellant appropriate relief. We think Congress should consider corrective legislation to protect the public from such exploitive contracts as were utilized in the case at bar."

We do not agree that the court lacked the power to refuse enforcement to contracts found to be unconscionable. In other jurisdictions, it has been held as a matter of common law that unconscionable contracts are not enforceable.

[...]

Congress has recently enacted the Uniform Commercial Code, which specifically provides that the court may refuse to enforce a contract which it finds to be unconscionable at the time it was made. 28 D.C. CODE § 2-302 (Supp. IV 1965). The enactment of this section, which occurred subsequent to the contracts here in suit, does not mean that the common law of the District of Columbia was otherwise at the time of enactment, nor does it preclude the court from adopting a similar rule in the exercise of its powers to develop the common law for the District of Columbia. In fact, in view of the absence of prior authority on the point, we consider the congressional adoption of § 2-302 persuasive authority for following the rationale of the cases from which the section is explicitly derived.

Accordingly, we hold that where the element of unconscionability is present at the time a contract is made, the contract should not be enforced.

Unconscionability has generally been recognized to include an absence of meaningful choice on the part of one of the parties together with contract terms which are unreasonably favorable to the other party. Whether a meaningful choice is present in a particular case can only be determined by consideration of all the circumstances surrounding the transaction. In many cases the meaningfulness of the choice is negated by a gross inequality of bargaining power. The manner in which the contract was entered is also relevant to this consideration. Did each party to the contract, considering his obvious education or lack of it, have a reasonable opportunity to understand the terms of the contract, or were the important terms hidden in a maze of fine print and minimized by deceptive sales practices? Ordinarily, one who signs an agreement without full knowledge of its terms might be held to assume the risk that he has entered a one-sided bargain. But when a party of little bargaining power, and hence little real choice, signs a commercially unreasonable contract with little or no knowledge of its terms, it is hardly likely that his consent, or even an objective manifestation of his consent, was ever given to all the terms. In such a case the usual rule that the terms of the agreement are not to be questioned should be abandoned and the court should consider whether the terms of the contract are so unfair that enforcement should be withheld.

[...]

In determining reasonableness or fairness, the primary concern must be with the terms of the contract considered in light of the circumstances existing when the contract was made. The test is not simple, nor can it be mechanically applied. The terms are to be considered "in the light of the general commercial background and the commercial needs of the particular trade or case." Corbin suggests the test as being whether the terms are "so extreme as to appear unconscionable according to the mores and business practices of the time and place." We think this formulation correctly states the test to be applied in those cases where no meaningful choice was exercised upon entering the contract.

[Citations omitted.]

QUESTIONS FOR DISCUSSION:

If the consumers here were fully informed of the conditions of the transaction, do you think that it was an unconscionable contract?

How is responsibility apportioned in a consumer sales contract? Should the seller have more or less responsibility for the buyer's actions?

Unconscionability: Consumer sales contracts are subject to the rules on unconscionability. An unconscionable contract or clause may not be enforceable.

Consumer Safety

Dangerous products regularly make it into the marketplace. The traditional remedy for a consumer who is injured is to bring a lawsuit against the seller and/or the manufacturer for damages. This approach is unsatisfactory for several reasons. First, it is inefficient. A lawsuit for a defective or dangerous product can take years to resolve. Second, it is expensive. Manufacturers and sellers may have to pay large verdicts and settlements, and the lawsuits themselves are expensive to bring and to defend. Third, and perhaps most important, the whole system depends on a person or people being injured or killed before improvements are made.

> The CPSC does not deal with safety issues of motor vehicles. Those are within the jurisdiction of the National Highway Traffic Safety Administration.

Although it is impossible to ensure that no one is ever injured by a product, federal law does attempt to minimize the likelihood. The Consumer Product Safety Act created the Consumer Product Safety Commission (CPSC), an independent agency with the mission of promoting consumer safety. It is authorized to ban the sale of dangerous consumer products or to recall those previously sold in the marketplace.

It is also authorized to research and establish safety requirements, and to develop standards for product safety. These standards are often developed in cooperation with industry groups. The CPSC also makes rules about consumer products when it identifies a consumer product hazard that is not already addressed by a voluntary standard, or when Congress orders rulemaking. These rules may set out design requirements. They may also amount to a ban on a certain type of product. These rules may set out design requirements that must be met before a product can be sold, or may amount to a ban on the sale of certain products.

The recall authority of the CPSC allows it to order a seller to recall a product from the marketplace. Manufacturers are under an obligation to notify the CPSC if it obtains information that a product it sells:

- Fails to comply with an applicable consumer product safety rule or with a voluntary consumer product safety standard,

Example: In 2007, toys imported from China were found to contain lead-based paint. Lead in paint has been linked to serious health problems for children, including behavioral problems, learning disorders, and even death. U.S. manufacturers recalled over 10 million toys and other children's items, because of excessive amounts of lead.

- Fails to comply with any other rule, regulation, standard or ban under a law enforced by the CPSC,

- Contains a defect which could create a substantial product hazard, or

- Creates an unreasonable risk of serious injury or death.

The staff of the CPSC evaluates the report to determine the hazard posed by the product. An immediate recall will be ordered when the risk of death or grievous injury or illness is likely or very likely, or serious injury or illness is very likely. Lesser hazards are evaluated to decide what corrective action would be warranted.

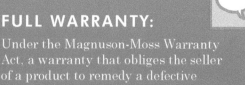

FULL WARRANTY:
Under the Magnuson-Moss Warranty Act, a warranty that obliges the seller of a product to remedy a defective product within a reasonable time. If the defect cannot be remedied after a reasonable number of attempts, the seller must replace it, or refund the price paid.

LIMITED WARRANTY:
Under the Magnuson-Moss Warranty Act, a warranty that does not meet the requirements of a full warranty. Such warranties must be clearly labeled as a limited warranty.

Warranties: A warranty is a promise that a product will perform in a certain manner. Article 2 of the Uniform Commercial Code (UCC) relates to express and implied warranties for goods. Although Article 2 sets out general require-

ments, the terms of these warranties are left to individual businesses in most cases. However, a federal law, the Magnuson-Moss Warranty Act, sets out detailed requirements for the terms of a warranty given in sales of consumer goods.

The Magnuson-Moss Warranty Act was passed in 1975. The purpose of the Act is to make warranties on consumer products more understandable and enforceable. The Act applies to consumers and consumer products, and gives the FTC further consumer protection authority. There is no requirement in the law that any product come with a warranty. If, however, the product is a consumer good and a warranty is given, it must comply with the Act. Failure to comply is considered an unfair trade practice.

Many states have similar warranty laws. They are generally referred to as "lemon laws."

The Act provides that a written warranty, if given, must disclose the terms and conditions of the warranty as required by rules of the Federal Trade Commission. The disclosure must be a full disclosure, and must be conspicuous. The disclosure must be written in simple and readily understood language and must also clearly state whether it is a **full warranty** or a **limited warranty**.

Magnuson-Moss is sometimes referred to as the "federal lemon law." A "lemon" is a new car with substantial operating problems that would not be anticipated on a new vehicle. States

SEMI-TRACTOR TRAILER IS NOT A CONSUMER GOOD.

Kwiatkowski V. Volvo Trucks North America, Inc.
(Semi Buyer) v. (Manufacturer and Seller)
500 F. Supp. 2d 875 (N.D. Ill. 2007)

Pallmeyer, District Judge.

Plaintiff, Wlodzimierz Kwiatkowski ("Kwiatkowski"), filed a three-count complaint against Defendant, Volvo Trucks North America ("Volvo"), alleging breach of a written warranty (Count I), and breach of the implied warranty of merchantability (Count II) and seeking to revoke his purchase of a 2007 Volvo semi-tractor trailer from a dealer in Ohio (Count III). Each claim is based on the Magnuson-Moss Warranty Act ("the Act"), 15 U.S.C. § 2301 *et. seq.,* which governs warranties on consumer products. Defendant Volvo has filed a motion to dismiss the complaint, arguing that the semi-tractor trailer purchased by Plaintiff is not a "consumer product" as defined in the Act. For the reasons set forth here, the motion is granted.

The Magnuson-Moss Act was adopted to make warranties on consumer products more readily understood and enforceable and to provide the Federal Trade Commission with means of better protecting consumers. The Act defines "consumer products" as "any personal property ... which is normally used for personal, family or household purposes ..." The implementing regulations explain that this definition encompasses all products commonly used for consumer purposes, regardless of their actual use by the individual purchaser. Products commonly used for both personal and commercial purposes are deemed consumer products, and any ambiguities in the definition are resolved in favor of coverage.

Despite the breadth of this definition, courts have identified certain commercial goods as outside the realm of "consumer product." *See, e.g., Mota,* 174 F.Supp.2d at 829 (fire sprinklers specifically used and installed in commercial buildings are nor "consumer products"); *Crume v. Ford Motor Co.,* 60 Or.App. 224, 653 P.2d 564 (1982) (holding a flatbed truck not to be a "consumer product" simply because the plaintiff occasionally used it for personal purposes); *Essex Insurance Co. v. Blount, Inc.,* 72 F.Supp.2d 722 (E.D.Tex.1999) (holding that, because a piece of heavy timber equipment was designed almost exclusively for commercial purposes, it was outside the definition of "consumer product" used in the Act); *Walsh v. Ford Motor Credit Co.,* 113 Misc.2d 546, 449 N.Y.S.2d 556 (N.Y.Sup.Ct.1982) (the Act does not apply to *"property such as a tractor trailer which is normally use for a commercial use of trucking"*) (emphasis added).

The Seventh Circuit addressed this issue tangentially in *Waypoint Aviation Services, Inc. v. Sandel Avionics, Inc.,* 469 F.3d 1071 (7th Cir.2006). Plaintiff in *Waypoint* brought a Magnuson-Moss action against the manufacturer of an airplane and the manufacturers of certain equipment in the airplane. The district court dismissed the case on the ground that an airplane cannot be a consumer product. . . . [T]he Court of Appeals disapproved of the district court's determination that "airplanes" could never be used for personal purposes and cautioned against any broad exclusion of categories of goods from the definition of "consumer product." For example, the court observed that, while most aircrafts are used only for commercial purposes, some nevertheless can be defined as "consumer products" if their principal function is personal recreation or transportation. . . . [T]he *Waypoint* court discouraged the exclusion of large categories of products from the definition, [but] it explicitly acknowledged that more narrow categories of motor vehicles—including, specifically, commercial tractor-trailers—may properly be excluded.

The court agrees with Defendant Volvo that a commercial tractor-trailer is not ordinarily used for personal, family, or household use. The normal and ordinary purpose for such trucks is to haul trailers in transport of goods and products over long distances for commercial benefit. Such a vehicle is not a "consumer product" and therefore beyond the reach of the Magnuson-Moss Act, on which each of Plaintiff's claims is based. . . . Defendant's motion to dismiss is granted.

[Citations omitted.]

QUESTIONS FOR DISCUSSION:

Based on this analysis, how would the court categorize a motorboat normally used for personal recreation, but actually used only for commercial boat tours?

Why does Magnuson-Moss only apply to warranties for consumer products? Is there a case to be made for it to apply to all warranties?

have individual lemon laws that provide remedies for consumers, however, while Magnuson-Moss primarily deals with clear disclosures to consumers.

IV. Investor Protection

The integrity of financial markets is of great importance to the U.S. economy. The U.S. government began regulating the markets for **securities** in the 1930s. The passage of the laws regulating securities trading was a reaction to the predatory trading practices that contributed in part to the stock market crash of 1929 and the Great Depression that followed.

One key aspect of federal securities regulation was the creation of the Securities and Exchange Commission (SEC). The SEC's mission is to:

- Protect investors,

- Maintain fair, orderly, and efficient markets, and

- Make it possible for companies to raise capital from investors.

SECURITY:

An instrument such as stocks (that evidences an ownership right), bonds (evidencing a debtor/creditor relationship), or an investment contract whereby a person invests in a common enterprise reasonably expecting profits derived primarily from the efforts of others.

PUBLICLY-TRADED COMPANIES:

A company whose stock is freely traded among members of the general public.

INSIDER TRADING:

The purchase or sale of securities on the basis of information that has not been made available to the public.

The SEC is governed by a board of five commissioners. No more than three commissioners may be of the same political party.

The SEC enforces the laws that require **publicly-traded companies** to submit periodic financial reports, and annual reports that describe the company's operations in the preceding year. These reports allow investors to make informed decisions when they buy and sell securities. The SEC also enforces the laws against insider trading and other fraudulent practices involving securities transactions, including **insider trading**.

Federal Securities Regulation

Federal securities regulation is based on eight principal laws. Each law has different objectives.

Securities Act of 1933: Many people call this Act the "Truth in Securities" law. It has two main objectives:

- Requiring that investors receive significant information about securities offered to the public, and

- Prohibiting deceit, misrepresentations, and other fraud in the sale of securities.

One of the ways the 1933 Act tries to accomplish these goals is by requiring the disclosure of important financial information when securities are offered for sale. This information lets investors make informed judgments about a company's securities. The information must be accurate, but the SEC does not guarantee its accuracy. The SEC also does not give an opinion on the safety or likely profitability of any security. Investors make their own decisions, based on the information that the SEC requires be made available to the public. The SEC makes no guarantee, nor does it insure against investors' losses.

Information is disclosed to investors through the registration of securities. In general, all securities sold in the U.S. must be registered with the SEC unless they are of an exempt type or part of an exempt transaction. All registration statements become public information after they are filed. The registration forms call for:

- A description of the company's business,

- A description of the security to be offered for sale,

- Information about the management of the company, and

- Certified financial statements prepared by independent accountants.

Securities Exchange Act of 1934: This law established the Securities and Exchange Commission and gave it oversight power over securities markets. The Act gives the SEC broad authority over virtually every aspect of the securities industry, and prohibits fraudulent activity in the sale and purchase of securities. This covers not only initial sale of securities, but also subsequent sales. The Act empowers the SEC to require periodic reporting of information by companies with publicly traded securities. Companies with more than $10 million in assets and whose securities are held by more than 500 owners must make these reports to the SEC. The SEC then makes the reports available to the public.

The 1934 Act authorized the SEC to create rules to regulate the securities markets. One of the SEC's resulting regulations is the insider trading rule known as Rule 10b-5. This broad rule prohibits fraud or deceit when buying or selling securities.

Trust Indenture Act: This Act applies to debt securities such as **bonds**, **debentures**, and **notes** offered for public sale.

AFFIRMATIVE FRAUD IS NOT REQUIRED TO ESTABLISH A RULE 10B-5 VIOLATION.

Affiliated Ute Citizens v. United States
(Citizens' Group) v. (Federal Government)
406 U.S. 128, 92 S. Ct. 1456, 31 L. Ed. 741 (1972)

INSTANT FACTS:
The defendants withheld material facts reasonably likely to influence stockholders' financial decisions.

BLACK LETTER RULE:
Facts are considered material if a reasonable investor might have considered them important in the making of an investment decision.

PROCEDURAL BASIS:
Certiorari to review an appellate decision.

FACTS:
Gale and Haslem worked for a bank representing members of a Native American tribe to assist with the sale of shares in a corporation (UDC) that had been formed to hold tribal assets. While representing their interests, Gale and Haslem induced mixed-blood stockholders to sell their shares, without informing them that their stock could sell at a higher price on the real estate market. By so doing, Gale and Haslem reaped financial benefits. The federal court of appeals held that no 10b–5 violation occurred, because there was no evidence of reliance on a material factual misrepresentation made by Gale and Haslem.

ISSUE:
Can the causation requirement under Rule 10b–5 be established by a failure to disclose a material fact?

DECISION AND RATIONALE:
(Blackmun, J.) Yes. The second subparagraph of Rule 10b–5 plainly specifies as securities violations the making of an untrue statement of material fact and the failure to state material facts. The defendants cannot withhold material facts from the stockholders and thereafter claim the stockholders did not rely upon their statements. "Under the circumstances of this case, involving primarily a failure to disclose, positive proof of reliance is not a prerequisite of recovery. All that is necessary is that the facts withheld be material in the sense that a reasonable investor might have considered them important in the making of this decision."

ANALYSIS:
In American Ute Citizens, Justice Blackmun indicated that facts are material if a reasonable investor "might" rely upon them. Whether semantic or not, the Supreme Court clarified this position in TSC Industries, Inc. v. Northway, Inc., 426 U.S. 438 (1976), where it stated that American Ute Citizens did not "articulate a precise definition of materiality, but only [gave] a 'sense' of the notion." The Court thereafter established that "[a]n omitted fact is material if there is a substantial likelihood that a reasonable shareholder would consider it important in deciding how to vote," explaining that if a reasonable investor would consider an omitted fact to alter the information available, the omitted fact is material.

CASE VOCABULARY:
CAUSATION:
The causing or producing of an effect.

CONCEALMENT:
The act of refraining from disclosure, especially an act by which one prevents or hinders the discovery of something.

MISREPRESENTATION:
The act of making a false or misleading statement about something, usually with the intent to deceive.

RELIANCE:
Dependence or trust by a person, especially when combined with action based on that dependence or trust.

QUESTIONS FOR DISCUSSION:
If no one relies on a misrepresentation, does it make sense for the misrepresentation to be illegal?

How would you prove reliance or non-reliance on a misrepresentation?

Investment Company Act: The Investment Company Act regulates companies, such as mutual funds, that engage primarily in investing and trading in securities, if their own securities are offered for sale to the public. The goal of this Act is to minimize the conflicts of interest that may arise in this type of operation.

Investment Advisers Act: This law requires some individuals or entities who advise others about securities investments to register with the SEC.

Sarbanes-Oxley Act: The Sarbanes-Oxley Act of 2002 put in place a number of reforms. These reforms are designed to enhance corporate responsibility, improve financial disclosures, and fight corporate and accounting fraud.

BOND:
A written promise to pay money. In securities law, long-term, interest bearing debt instruments, backed by the assets of the issuer.

DEBENTURE:
A bond backed only by the general credit and financial reputation of the company issuing the bond.

NOTE:
An unconditional written promise to pay money.

CEOs and principal financial officers of publicly-traded companies are required to certify the accuracy of financial reporting. The Act also created the "Public Company Accounting Oversight Board" to oversee corporate auditing. Sarbanes-Oxley also placed a renewed emphasis on corporate ethics. Publicly-traded companies are now required to disclose to the public whether they have a code of ethics.

Dodd-Frank Wall Street Reform and Consumer Protection Act: The Dodd-Frank Act is an effort to reshape the U.S. financial regulatory system. Some of these areas of reshaping include consumer protection, trading restrictions, credit ratings, regulation of financial products, corporate governance and disclosure, and transparency. Dodd-Frank, which was approved in 2010, has been called the most comprehensive financial regulatory reform since the Great Depression.

Jumpstart Our Business Startups Act (the "JOBS Act"): The JOBS Act minimizes SEC regulatory requirements for many companies. The goal is to make it easier for businesses to raise funds in public capital markets. The JOBS Act calls on the SEC to make rules to address **crowdfunding** investment solicitations, and to make them exempt from many of the more burdensome requirements of securities registration.

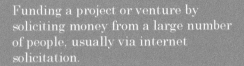

CROWDFUNDING:
Funding a project or venture by
soliciting money from a large number
of people, usually via internet
solicitation.

Consumer Financial Protection Bureau

The 2007-08 financial crisis saw the banking and finance industry shaken to its very core. The crisis revealed some of the fundamental weaknesses of the consumer finance industry, and also showed the ineffectiveness of the existing regulatory system. There was no single agency responsible or accountable for the protection of consumers in the financial industry. In 2010, as part of the Dodd-Frank Act, Congress established the Consumer Financial Protection Bureau (CFPB) to oversee consumer finance.

> Political disputes about the structure of the bureau meant that the first director was not confirmed by the Senate until July 2013.

The CFPB regulates traditional financial institutions, such as banks and credit unions, and also regulates payday lenders, foreclosure relief services, debt collectors, and mortgage servicers. The CFPB has made credit cards, mortgages, and student loans its priorities.

The CFPB enforces its rules through administrative proceedings and court actions. Enforcement actions are brought against companies that violate rules or defraud or discriminate against consumers. The CFPB pursues companies who take action against **whistleblowers** who report a company's violations. Successful enforcement actions usually result in some combination of a **civil penalty**, **restitution** for affected consumers, and an agreement to comply with CFPB regulations.

In addition to its enforcement activities, the CFPB conducts research about consumer financial markets and consumer behavior. This research helps identify potential problems and possible responses to those problems. The Bureau also has an extensive program of public outreach, to students, service members, and older Americans.

> *Example:*   A financial company that operated as an indirect auto lender allowed dealers who arranged financing through the company for car sales to charge a higher interest rate to African American, Hispanic, and Asian consumers. The CFPB ordered the company to pay $80 million in restitution to affected consumers. The company was also ordered to pay a civil penalty to the CFPB of $18 million, and to monitor the interest rates charged by dealers, to prevent discrimination. *In the Matter of Ally Financial Inc.*, 2013-CFPB-0010 (Dec. 20, 2013).

WHISTLEBLOWER:
An employee who reports her employer's wrongdoing to the government or to law enforcement.

CIVIL PENALTY:
A fine assessed for a violation of a statute or regulation. A civil penalty is not considered to be punishment for a crime.

RESTITUTION:
Payment to a victim in compensation for a loss. Restitution is usually ordered as a part of a civil or criminal penalty.

State Securities Law

Securities are regulated at the state level, as well as at the federal level. State securities laws are referred to as "Blue Sky Laws." The origin of the term is uncertain, but it may come from the first such law, passed in Kansas in 1911. The state's Banking Commissioner, arguing for passage of the law, inveighed against "blue sky merchants," who sold fraudulent investments backed by nothing but "the blue sky of Kansas."

Every state has a Blue Sky Law. Most Blue Sky Laws are modeled on the Uniform Securities Act (USA), but there is still little consistency in the laws. Despite these inconsistencies, state laws do have certain features in common:

- Registration of securities offered for sale in the state,

- Registration of broker-dealers, and

- Registration of securities firms.

Securities are required to be registered in every state in which they will be sold, unless they are exempt from state registration. In many cases, if a company must register its securities at the federal level, then states permit that registration to also satisfy their requirements.

States have limited authority to limit the sale of securities. Most regulation is done at the federal level, by the Securities and Exchange Commission. States also have the authority to conduct investigations and bring lawsuits for securities fraud; however, each state's authority to enforce its Blue Sky Laws is limited to securities sold within its borders. Before federal securities laws were passed, many traders openly advocated getting around Blue Sky Laws by selling securities through the mail, to customers in different states. The gaps in the ability to enforce securities laws were a strong motive for the passage of the federal legislation.

> Securities sold on national exchanges, such as NYSE or the NASDAQ/ National Market, are exempt.

V. Environmental Protection

Until the 1960s, environmental regulation in the United States was largely a matter for private lawsuits. There were very few environmental laws, so most complaints about air or water pollution were dealt with by tort litigation against an alleged polluter. Actions for torts such as **nuisance** or **trespass** were brought to seek either damages or injunctive relief against polluters.

Relying on tort litigation to insure clean air and water has its limitations. By nature, litigation is a piecemeal form of regulation, addressing problems only when and where a lawsuit is brought. In addition, litigation is remedial, not preventative. It does nothing to prevent new problems from arising in the future, with different parties.

Comprehensive environmental laws and regulations are intended to limit hazards before they become a problem. The advantage to the public is that there does not have to be any harm done before an environmental violation can be stopped. A system of statutes and regulations also provides certainty. Litigation is often unpredictable. The parties concerned can better predict outcomes if a rule is in place.

Federal and State Environmental Laws

Environmental laws have been enacted at both the state and federal levels. Many cities and counties also have environmental ordinances. The reasoning behind the adoption of these laws and regulations varies. The laws are usually justified as protecting the health and safety of the people. The power to regulate nuisances is another justification. Sometimes, environmental laws are justified under a theory of public trust: natural resources are regarded as being held in trust for the benefit of all people, and protecting that trust is a legitimate exercise of governmental authority. In some states, a clean environment is regarded as a fundamental right under the state's constitution.

State and federal environmental laws are often similar, or even identical. Unlike other areas in which federal and state laws overlap, there is little tension between the different layers of regulation. Enforcement of environmental

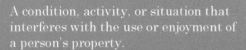

NUISANCE:

A condition, activity, or situation that interferes with the use or enjoyment of a person's property.

TRESPASS:

An unlawful act against the person or property of another. The term is usually used to mean entry onto another person's property without the permission of the owner.

Example: Bacon is affordable in the United States because of large-scale domestic hog farms. The problem is that an adult hog produces over 10 pounds of solid waste a day. To deal with that level of production, the waste may be kept in open "lagoons" that produce ammonia and methane gases. In recent years, dozens of federal lawsuits have been brought against hog farms in North Carolina, Missouri, and other states by people living and working near these operations. These lawsuits allege that the smell was a legal nuisance. The plaintiffs claim the smell and gases make their homes unlivable, and cause health problems. Several claims have already been successful, leading to efforts to limit damages in similar nuisance actions.

> *Example:*
>
> All persons are born free and have certain inalienable rights. They include the right to a clean and healthful environment and the rights of pursuing life's basic necessities, enjoying and defending their lives and liberties, acquiring, possessing and protecting property, and seeking their safety, health and happiness in all lawful ways. In enjoying these rights, all persons recognize corresponding responsibilities. *Mont. Const. Art. 2, § 3.*

laws is often done jointly, with federal and state regulators working together. This **cooperative federalism** is regarded by those who enforce environmental laws as "fundamental to the structure and effectiveness of environmental laws."

Air Quality

Federal air quality rules are based on the Clean Air Act. The Act requires the Environmental Protection Agency (EPA) to set rules for air pollutants. There are two principal types of air quality rules that relate to different types of air pollution, or different air quality concerns.

The first federal environmental law was the Rivers and Harbors Act of 1899, which prohibited discharging refuse into navigable waters without a permit.

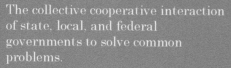

COOPERATIVE FEDERALISM:
The collective cooperative interaction of state, local, and federal governments to solve common problems.

The first set of rules, known as the National Ambient Air Quality Standards (NAAQS), sets limits for the quantities of known pollutants that may be in the air. There are two types of ambient air quality standards, labeled primary and secondary. Primary standards are for the protection of public health. This includes the protection of the health of sensitive populations, such as people with asthma, children, and the elderly. Secondary standards are limits that are set to protect the public welfare. The "public welfare" includes protection against decreased visibility, and damage to animals, crops, vegetation, and buildings.

In addition to setting ambient air quality standards, the Clean Air Act also authorizes the EPA to regulate hazardous air pollutants. Hazardous air pollutants are pollutants that are known or suspected to cause serious health effects or adverse environmental effects. The EPA has identified nearly 200 toxic air pollutants. Hazardous pollutant regulations are intended to reduce the air emissions of these pollutants to the environment.

EPA regulations address hazardous air pollutants from major sources, area sources, and mobile sources. "Major sources" are large industrial facilities. The Clean Air Act requires the EPA to regulate hazardous air pollutants from major sources in two phases. The first phase is "technology-based," with standards based on emissions levels that are already being achieved in an industry.

In the second phase, the EPA assesses the remaining health risks from each source category to determine whether the standards protect public health with an ample margin of safety, and also protect against adverse environmental effects. The EPA must determine whether more health-protective standards are necessary. The standards are also reviewed and revised, if necessary, to account for improvements in air

Individual area sources, such as gas stations and dry cleaners, usually have much lower emissions than major sources. These sources can, however, be numerous and widespread. They may also be located in heavily populated urban areas. The area source program includes a community support component. This recognizes that communities with disproportionate risks from hazardous air pollutants may be able to reduce some toxic sources more quickly and effectively through local initiatives. Mobile source regulations involve setting emissions standards for engines used for transportation.

NAVIGABLE WATERS:
A body of water used, or capable of being used, for commerce. The term includes the tributaries of such bodies of water.

pollution control or prevention. This is done within eight years of setting the original standards. "Area sources" are smaller sources, and "mobile sources" are motor vehicles, locomotives, and commercial marine vessels.

Water Quality

The EPA's regulation of water quality is based on the Clean Water Act. The purpose of the Clean Water Act is to restore and maintain the quality of the country's **navigable waters** with the goals of:

- Making the water safe for swimming,
- Protecting fish and wildlife, and
- Eliminating the discharge of pollutants into the water.

The Act is designed to achieve acceptable water quality standards, and it places restrictions on the discharge of pollutants. The Act also addresses the discharge into navigable waters of dredged or fill material, and of oil or hazardous substances.

The Act leaves much of the responsibility for protecting clean water to the states. A state or local government may adopt or enforce its own standards or limitations regarding water pollution, except that these standards may not be less stringent than the federal regulations.

The Clean Water Act requires the EPA to develop or revise criteria for water quality. These criteria are developed after consultation with state and other federal agencies, and with input from other interested persons. They must reflect the latest scientific knowledge on the effects of pollutants on health and welfare, the concentration and dispersal of pollutants and their byproducts, and the effects of pollutants on biological community diversity, productivity, and stability.

"WETLANDS" ARE NOT "NAVIGABLE WATERS."

Rapanos v. United States
(Shopping Mall Developer/Wetlands Owner) v. (Prosecuting Government)
547 U.S. 715, 126 S. Ct. 2208, 165 L. Ed. 2d 159 (2006)

INSTANT FACTS:

The plaintiffs discharged fill material into wetlands properties they owned in order to build a shopping mall and condominiums, and the government brought legal action against them because they did not obtain a permit before beginning development.

BLACK LETTER RULE:

The phrase "the waters of the United States," as used in the Clean Water Act, includes only those relatively permanent or continuously flowing bodies of water forming geographic features such as streams, oceans, rivers, and lakes, and does not include channels through which water intermittently flows or channels that provide periodic drainage for rainfall.

PROCEDURAL BASIS:

Supreme Court review of a federal circuit court decision affirming the district court's judgment in favor of the defendant.

FACTS:

The Clean Water Act makes it unlawful to discharge fill material into "navigable waters" without a permit, and it defines "navigable waters" to include "the waters of the United States." The Army Corps of Engineers, which issues permits for the discharge of fill material into navigable waters, interpreted "the waters of the United States" expansively to include not only traditional navigable waters, but also tributaries of such waters and wetlands "adjacent" to such waters and tributaries. The cases before the Court involved four Michigan wetlands lying near ditches or man-made drains that eventually emptied into traditional navigable waters. The United States brought civil enforcement proceedings against the petitioners, who had backfilled certain of these areas without a permit. The district court found federal jurisdiction over the wetlands because they were adjacent to "waters of the United States" or adjacent to "navigable waters." The Sixth Circuit affirmed.

ISSUE:

Did the courts below err in concluding that the wetlands in these cases constitute "navigable waters," such that the petitioners were required to obtain a permit under the Clean Water Act before discharging fill material into them?

DECISION AND RATIONALE:

(Scalia, J.) Yes. The phrase "the waters of the United States," as used in the Clean Water Act, includes only those relatively permanent or continuously flowing bodies of water forming geographic features such as streams, oceans, rivers, and lakes, and does not include channels through which water intermittently flows or channels that provide periodic drainage for rainfall.

We first addressed the meaning of "the waters of the United States," as used in the Clean Water Act, in U.S. v. Riverside Bayview Homes, Inc., 474 U.S. 121 (1985), in which we upheld the Corps' interpretation of this statutory phrase to include wetlands that abut traditional navigable waters. The petitioners contend here, however, that the waters must actually be navigable, or capable of navigation, to fall into the statutory category. Although the meaning of "navigable waters" as used in the Act is broader than the traditional dictionary definition, the Clean Water Act authorizes federal jurisdiction only over "waters," which connotes relatively permanent bodies of water, as opposed to ordinarily dry channels through which water occasionally flows. The Act's use of the phrase "navigable waters" also suggests that it confers jurisdiction only over relatively permanent bodies of water. Moreover, the Clean Water Act itself categorizes the channels that carry intermittent flows of water separately from "navigable waters."

Riverside Bayview rested on an ambiguity in defining where "water" ends and its abutting ("adjacent") wetlands begin, which allowed the Corps to rely in that case on ecological considerations to resolve the ambiguity in favor of treating all abutting wetlands as waters. But isolated ponds are not "waters of the United States" and present no boundary-drawing problem justifying reliance on ecological factors. Thus, we conclude that only those wetlands with a continuous surface connection to bodies that are "waters of the United States" in their own right, such that there is no clear demarcation between the two, are "adjacent" to such waters and covered by the Act. Because the Sixth Circuit applied an incorrect standard to determine whether the wetlands at issue are covered "waters," and because of the paucity of the record, the cases are remanded for further proceedings.

ANALYSIS:

In one of the cases before the Court here, Rapanos had filled 54 acres of wetlands with sand in preparation for the construction of a shopping mall, without filing for a permit. In another case, Carabell had actually proactively sought a permit to build condominiums on 19 acres of wetlands, but the request was denied. Neither of these parties prevailed in the lower courts.

QUESTIONS FOR DISCUSSION:

Some commentators believe that changes in the economy herald the end of the shopping mall. If large facilities such as malls become abandoned, what environmental laws might come into play?

If regulations cause a property to become less valuable, do you feel that the owner should be compensated? Why or why not?

States must adopt and review standards for water quality every three years. These standards are subject to EPA approval. Whenever a state revises or adopts a water quality standard, the standard must be submitted to the EPA for approval. Any new or revised state standard must be accompanied by a supporting analysis.

Waste Management and Toxic Substances

Governmental efforts to combat air and water pollution do not address the environmental hazards of the disposal of waste on land, or the use of toxic materials.

Waste Management: Although state and local governments have long regulated waste disposal by such measures as restricting landfills or junkyards, prohibiting households from burning trash, or making littering an offense, federal regulators generally did not get involved with solid waste. Garbage was considered a local matter.

Congress began federal involvement with the disposal of waste in 1976, when it enacted the Resource Conservation and Recovery Act (RCRA). RCRA governs the treatment, storage, and disposal of solid and hazardous waste. It deals only with active and future waste facilities, not abandoned or historical sites. RCRA

Example: In September 2016, the Washington State developed a rule that updates the state's water quality standards for certain toxic chemicals. The state rule sets standards for 97 chemicals, as opposed to 85 covered by federal rules. The Washington rule also sets standards for pollutants that were not formerly regulated.

puts in place a national framework for solid waste control.

RCRA explicitly recognizes that the collection and disposal of solid waste is primarily a matter of state, local, or regional control. The law thus gives states the principal role in managing nonhazardous solid waste disposal programs. The EPA regulations set out the general criteria for these programs. Solid waste must be used for resource recovery, or it must be disposed of in a sanitary manner. Open dumping of waste is not allowed.

Municipal and industrial waste disposal facilities must meet the EPA criteria for design, location restrictions, and assurances of financial viability. Facilities must also have a plan for corrective action, or cleanup of improperly handled waste, and there must be a plan for the eventual closure of the facility. A state may impose requirements that are more stringent than the federal requirements, but if a state does not develop a plan, the EPA rules will apply.

> "Resource recovery" is extracting materials from solid waste for a specific next use. It can include recycling, energy generation, or composting.

RCRA also authorizes the EPA to make regulations regarding hazardous waste. EPA regulations are intended to ensure the safe management of solid waste from the time it is gener-

ated until its final disposal ("cradle-to-grave" management). "Hazardous waste" is defined as solid waste that may:

- Cause, or significantly contribute to an increase in mortality or an increase in serious irreversible, or incapacitating reversible, illness; or

- Pose a substantial present or potential hazard to human health or the environment when improperly treated, stored, transported, or disposed of, or otherwise managed.

Hazardous waste regulation is also left primarily to the states. If a state does not have a hazardous waste program, the EPA will implement a program. EPA regulations set the criteria for hazardous waste generators, transporters, and for treatment, storage and disposal facilities. The EPA criteria include permitting requirements, enforcement, and corrective action or cleanup.

The cleanup of hazardous waste sites is regulated by the Comprehensive Environmental Response, Compensation, and Liability Act (CERCLA). CERCLA, also known as the "Superfund" law, provides for the prompt cleanup of hazardous waste sites. The costs of that cleanup are imposed on anyone who is determined to be potentially responsible for the contamination. Potentially responsible parties include:

- Those who generated the wastes disposed of at the site,

- Those who transported wastes to the site,

- Owners and operators of the site at the time of the disposal, and

- Current owners and operators of the site.

These costs are imposed even if the activity that generated the waste took place before CERCLA was enacted in 1980. If a former owner cannot be found or is insolvent, the costs may be covered by the government. Originally, the government costs were covered by a trust fund created through specific taxes. The formerly "super" fund has since been depleted, and the federal government's contributions are now made from general funds.

> Under CERCLA, responsibility for waste may include past owners of the property, even if they are no longer involved with the property, in addition to current owners who may have damaged the property.

In 1986, CERCLA was reinforced by the Superfund Amendments and Reauthorization Act (SARA). By the time SARA was drafted, the EPA had several years of experience in working with Superfund sites. The new law built on that experience to:

- Increase the funding amount allocated to Superfund project,

- Focus more closely on human health outcomes,

- Refine hazardous waste definitions for specific materials based on their impact on people's health,

- Add enforcement power and settlement options, and

- Prefer permanent site clean-ups rather than interim remedies.

Based on the substances and location of a site, it may be placed on the National Priority List. The list helps guide the EPA's response to problems by ranking the most dangerous locations in need of responsive action.

Toxic Substances: Not all hazardous substances are "waste." Industry often uses hazardous or toxic substances as a regular part of business. The Toxic Substances Control Act (TSCA) puts these substances under EPA regulation. The EPA has the authority to require

Example: From 1965 to 1974, a metal plating business disposed of some chemicals used in its business by dumping them in an unpaved lot behind the business's building. Only small amounts were disposed of at any given time, and no one responsible thought this posed any danger. The metal plating business moved to a new location in 1974, and other owners occupied the property. In 2010, a developer bought the property to develop it for housing. Tests showed that the soil was contaminated by hazardous waste. The metal plating business is responsible for some of the costs of cleanup.

reporting, record-keeping and testing requirements, and restrictions on chemical substances and/or mixtures. CERCLA also authorizes the EPA to respond to threatened or actual releases of hazardous substances.

The list of toxic substances includes more than 83,000 chemicals. If a person who manufactures, processes, or distributes a chemical substance obtains information supporting a conclusion that the substance presents a substantial risk of injury to health or the environment, she must immediately inform the EPA. The EPA must be notified before a new chemical substance is manufactured, and the EPA must be told of significant new uses of chemicals that could result in exposures to or releases of the chemical.

> The TSCA does not cover food, drugs, cosmetics, or pesticides. Food, drugs, and cosmetics are covered by the Food and Drug Administration. Pesticide rules are administered by the EPA.

One group of substances with well-known risks are those designed to control undesirable pests. The EPA regulates pesticides through the Federal Insecticide, Fungicide, and Rodenticide Act (FIFRA). FIFRA defines pesticides as any substance or mixture of substances intended for preventing, destroying, repelling, or mitigating any pest. That law prohibits the sale of unregistered pesticides. An application for registration must include a statement as to whether the pesticide is intended for general use, for use by anyone, or restricted use, meaning use only by certified applicators.

Any EPA rules on toxic substances will preempt state or local rules, unless the state or local rule bans the use of the toxic substance, or if the rule was adopted under the authority of a federal law (such as the Clean Air Act). State and local authorities may apply for permission to adopt more stringent requirements, but those requirements are generally regarded as frustrating the operation of a uniform national policy regarding toxic substances.

CHAPTER SUMMARY

Not all law is made by the legislative branch and signed by the executive. A significant body of law is made by governmental agencies. This law consists of administrative regulations that are usually related to specialized areas. These regulations are meant to implement or interpret laws passed by the legislative branch.

Examples of these regulations include rules on advertising, consumer protection, and unfair or deceptive trade practices. An extensive set of regulations deal with environmental subjects. Investor relations and publicly traded securities are also regulated by administrative law. Administrative regulations cover the fine details of complex topics, and compliance with these rules is critical to a successful business.

Review Questions

Review question 1.

What is the name of the federal law that sets out how administrative regulations are made? Describe the process for rule-making set out under that law. How does legislation interact with administrative regulations?

Review question 2.

What federal agencies regulate advertising? Does it matter what product is advertised? How do standards differ for various products?

Review question 3.

Where are new federal administrative regulations published? If a state and the federal government both regulate an issue, how does a business know which regulation applies? How can businesses and the public become involved in state and federal rule-making?

Review question 4.

According to the FTC, when is an advertisement considered deceptive?

Review question 5.

How are agencies created? What law created the Securities and Exchange Commission? How do agencies gain the power to create regulations? How does legislation act to limit or restrict administrative rulemaking?

Review question 6.

What are "Blue Sky" laws? How do they interact with other types of securities laws? Where are these laws enacted?

Review question 7.

What is the JOBS Act? What does it call on the SEC to accomplish? What does JOBS stand for?

Review question 8.

Describe Rule 10b-5 and its importance. How does the Sarbanes-Oxley Act modify the Securities Exchange Act of 1934?

Review question 9.

How are air and water quality regulated? What agency and laws are involved?

Review question 10.

What is a "Superfund" site? Which federal law deals with these sites? Which agency regulates how they are treated?

Questions for Discussion

Discussion question 1.

Bill opens a business selling bicycles. His inventory consists of bicycles he builds from parts of other bicycles. He advertises these as "New Handmade Bikes by Bill."

> Is Bill committing a deceptive trade practice? Why or why not?

> Is Bill's advertisement deceptive under FTC rules? Why or why not?

> A customer calls Bill on the phone and asks if Bill will fix a bike he sells if something goes wrong with it. Bill says, "Sure, I guess so." Under Magnuson-Moss, has Bill given a warranty? Why or why not?

Discussion question 2.

Acrylic acid is on the official list of toxic substances. Clarinda has obtained a quantity of acrylic acid. She operates a business that makes industrial adhesives, and she intends to use the acrylic acid to manufacture a specialty glue. Clarinda is concerned that the chemical is illegal for her to use. She lobbies the city council for help, and the city council passes an ordinance that allows the use of acrylic acid if the user obtains a city permit. The only criterion for a permit is paying a small fee.

> Is the city ordinance the only rule Clarinda needs to follow to use acrylic acid? Why or why not?

> Does the fact that acrylic acid is on the list of toxic substances mean Clarinda may not use it? Why or why not?

> If the acrylic acid is found to have leaked into the ground, is Clarinda liable for the cleanup costs? Why or why not?

Discussion question 3.

Shadi has come up with a recipe for a new beverage made from fruit and vegetable extracts. He starts to sell the beverage, advertising it as "Delicately Delicious." Unfortunately, the usual reaction of anyone who tries the drink is to spit it out because of its acrid taste. Shadi then decides to repurpose the drink. He starts to sell the drink as a nutritious weight loss supplement. Shadi has no reason to believe the drink helps lose weight, beyond his reasoning that dieters are advised to eat lots of fruit and vegetables. Shadi gives a supply of his drink to ten university professors with Ph.Ds in fields such as sociology and economics. Seven of them report losing weight after drinking the drink for several weeks, so Shadi notes in an advertisement that "a majority of the doctors surveyed report that their tests show" that the drink is effective for weight loss.

Is calling the drink "Delicately Delicious" deceptive advertising? Why or why not?

Is advertising the drink as a weight loss supplement deceptive advertising? Why or why not?

Is the claim about the survey of doctors deceptive advertising? Why or why not?

Discussion question 4.

Sunrise Dawn Farms is a small organic farm operation. The CEO does not use any mass-produced pesticides, but developed his own completely organic solution by soaking fresh garlic and coffee grounds in diluted orange juice. It does not eliminate all the insects that attack crops, but it does kill some and discourages others. The CEO starts the making the recipe on a larger scale and selling it in spray bottles as "Sunset for Bugs."

Does Sunrise Dawn Farms need to comply with any regulations when producing and selling Sunset for Bugs?

Is there a difference if Sunrise Dawn does not sell the product, but just makes enough for its own use? What if it requires its employees to apply it?

Does it matter that the product is completely organic? That it does not kill all the insects it is applied to?

Discussion question 5.

In which of the following cases would the consumer be granted a cooling off period? Are there situations where a cooling off period would make sense, even though the law does not allow for one?

Purchasing groceries at the local store.

Ordering a custom tailored suit.

Buying a vacation package on the phone.

Purchasing a vacuum cleaner from a door-to-door salesperson.

Buying kitchen gadgets at a home presentation hosted by a friend.

Buying furniture on a rent-to-own basis that results in paying more than the furniture is worth over time.

Discussion question 6.

Charles starts a business manufacturing biometric locks that only allow certain individuals to access the locked item. He receives funding from six private investors, and holds the company as the primary shareholder. The investors have the remaining shares in equal amounts. The company is fairly successful, and after the first year, it buys an additional $1 million worth of manufacturing equipment and production facilities worth $2.5 million. After five years, the shareholders decide to go public in order to raise funds for global locations. One thousand people buy shares. The following year, the company's assets are valued at $20 million.

At what point is the company obliged to make periodic reports to the SEC?

When must the company disclose financial information to the public?

13 CRIMINAL LAW

KEY OBJECTIVES:

▶ Understand the basic principles of criminal law.

▶ Become familiar with the elements of business-related crimes.

▶ Understand when a business may be held criminally liable.

CHAPTER OVERVIEW

This chapter covers criminal law, and particularly business-related crimes. Criminal law deals with wrongs done to the general public, or against the public order. While the primary victim of a given crime is typically an individual or a small group, the community as a whole is also a victim in a larger sense.

In this chapter, we will emphasize the aspects of criminal law that apply to the business world. We will learn the basic principles of criminal law. We will look at specific crimes that arise in the business context, and consider the circumstances in which directors, officers, and employees, or a corporation itself, may be convicted of a crime.

INTRODUCTION

Criminal law holds an endless fascination for us, as well as being the source of fear and disgust. Crime, criminals, victims, the circumstances in which the crimes arise, trials, and punishment have been staples of popular culture for as long as there has been a popular culture. It is also the material for endless political and social debates.

Most of the debates, and most of our interest, focus on violent crimes, or property crimes against individuals. This is understandable. The consequences of being assaulted or robbed are immediate and easy for the potential victim to comprehend. In recent years, however, there has been an increasing concern about business, or white collar crimes (named to reflect the white-collared shirts that the individuals who commit the crimes supposedly wear). Business crimes are non-violent offenses that are related to the business's activities. They include such crimes as fraud, embezzlement, and insider trading. While these crimes are less attention-grabbing than violent crime, their impact on the nation is powerful. According to the Federal Bureau of Investigation (FBI), business crimes cost the U.S. economy more than $300 billion per year. This figure includes the costs of prosecuting and punishing business criminals. It also encompasses the less immediate costs to the economy of failed businesses, lost jobs, and higher consumer prices. The monetary figure does not, however, attempt to quantify the intangible costs to society, including a loss of trust or confidence in our institutions and leaders. While the public's attention is focused on "crimes in the streets," the "crimes in the suites" are also doing substantial damage to the larger community as whole.

I. Basic Principles of Criminal Law

There are crimes that are easy for us to understand. Even if we don't know the precise legal terminology or elements, we have some idea of what is meant by crimes such as assault or burglary. There are other crimes that are more complex, and harder for most of us to conceptualize, such as insider trading. However simple or complex a crime may be, every crime is made up of two parts: **mens rea**, or guilty state of mind, and **actus reus**, the criminal act or acts. In order to obtain a conviction for a crime, the government prosecuting the crime must prove both of the elements of mens rea and actus reus **beyond a reasonable doubt**.

MENS REA:

Latin for "guilty mind." The mental state of a person committing the criminal act (actus reus).

ACTUS REUS:

Latin for "guilty act." Actions that constitute a crime when done with the appropriate state of mind (mens reus).

BEYOND A REASONABLE DOUBT:

Standard of proof for a criminal conviction. "Reasonable doubt" is when jurors are not convinced of the defendant's guilt, or when they believe there is a reasonable possibility that the defendant is not guilty.

STRICT LIABILITY:

A crime that does not have require proof of a guilty state of mind.

Mens Rea

Deciding the criminality of a person's actions depends upon deciding the state of her mind when she completed a series of actions that made up a crime. A lawful act may be criminal if it is done in a certain mental state (*mens rea*). The person's state of mind may also determine the degree of criminality with which the act was conducted. The critical issue is the person's intent, and whether the person's intent was deliberately against the law.

For most crimes, the *mens rea* will be either general intent or specific intent. The type of intent required to prove a particular crime depends on the legislation defining the crime. There are also some crimes that result from **strict liability**, which means that the person committing the crime is guilty regardless of his intent.

General Intent: General intent is the intent to do the physical actions that constitute a crime. The term refers only to a voluntary intentional act done by the person accused of breaking the law (defendant). It does not mean that the defendant intended to commit a crime, or to cause any harm, only that she voluntarily intentionally did the act that led to the harm that became the crime. An intent to cause harm is inferred from the fact that the defendant acted voluntarily and intentionally, which resulted in an injury to another person.

General intent means that a defendant's actions were deliberate, conscious, or purposeful. They were not done through accident, mistake, carelessness, or absent-mindedness. In most cases,

> ***Example:*** Daryl is upset that his partner Jesse refuses to clean up their house. One day as they are leaving the house, Daryl throws a lit cigarette on a stack of magazines. Daryl believes that this will do nothing more than create some smoke, which will scare Jesse into cleaning up. Unfortunately, the cigarette starts a fire, which destroys the house. Daryl has intentionally destroyed their house by fire.

showing that the defendant did the act which constitutes the crime is enough to show general intent of the *mens rea* to commit the crime. The intent is presumed from the defendant's actions.

A defendant will not be guilty of a general intent crime if she can prove that her actions were not voluntary (not done willingly). It is a defense to most crimes to prove that the criminal actions were done under **duress**, or out of **necessity**.

DURESS:
Threats of harm or other pressure that force a person to commit a criminal act against his will.

NECESSITY:
A defense to a criminal charge that says that the defendant acted in an emergency situation not of her own creation to prevent a harm greater than the harm caused by her actions.

TRANSFERRED INTENT:
Shifting intent from the crime the defendant originally intended to commit to the crime that actually was committed.

The duress and necessity defenses depend on either the actions of other parties (in the case of duress), or on circumstances outside of the defendant's control (necessity). Actions voluntarily taken by a defendant cannot negate her own general intent. For the defense of duress or necessity to apply, someone other than the defendant must have forced the defendant to take an action that resulted in a crime.

It is not a defense to a general intent crime to show that the injury caused was not the injury intended, or that the defendant intended to harm another victim. The doctrine of **transferred intent** will "shift" the intent so that the defendant is considered to have intended the harm that did result in the specific manner in which the injury occurred.

> Duress or necessity may not be used as a defense to a charge of **homicide**.

Intent must not be confused with motive. A defendant's motive is the inducement that tempts her to commit a crime. Intent is the mental state of the defendant once she decides to do it. Discerning the motive behind a criminal act may assist in the investigation of a crime, and in the identification of a suspect. A person without a discernable motive is unlikely to have formed the intent to commit a crime.

> **Example:** Lisa spends an evening at a bar drinking heavily. After she is asked to leave, she picks up a rock from the street and throws it through the front window of the bar. Lisa argues that she was too drunk to intend to throw the rock. She will still be held responsible. Her voluntary intoxication may not be used to attempt to prove that she did not have general intent to destroy the window, because no other person forced Lisa to drink. If Lisa were involuntarily intoxicated (for instance, by being forced to drink an intoxicating beverage), then there is a different result. In that case, if the intoxication against her will meant she was unable to understand that what she was doing was wrong, Lisa could successfully use duress as a defense.

> **Example:** Assume the same facts as in the prior example, except that Lisa argues that she did not throw the rock at the window, but at Kate, a former friend who was passing by. Kate ducked at the right moment, and the rock hit the window instead. Lisa still had the general intent to throw the rock at the window even though she was aiming at Kate. Lisa's intent to hit Kate is transferred to the window that she broke.

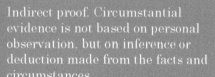

CIRCUMSTANTIAL EVIDENCE:

Indirect proof. Circumstantial evidence is not based on personal observation, but on inference or deduction made from the facts and circumstances.

HOMICIDE:

The taking of another person's life.

Evidence of a motive may also provide **circumstantial evidence** of an intent to commit a crime. Proof of a motive is not, however, essential to proving a defendant's guilt beyond a reasonable doubt.

Specific Intent: Specific intent is the intent to bring about a particular criminal result. In order to convict a person of a specific intent crime, the prosecutor must show that the defendant did some act voluntarily. The prosecutor must prove that the defendant took the specific action intending to cause harm. The crucial point is that a defendant has the subjective intention to cause harm regardless of the specific type of harm that results from his intention.

A crime is a specific intent crime if the description of the criminal act in the statute requires an intent to do some further act, or cause an additional consequence. For instance, in many states, burglary is defined as entering or remaining unlawfully in a building with the intent to commit a crime in the building. Burglary is a specific intent crime, because the

> *Example:* Charla hides at a library, intending to steal a valuable book after hours. While she waits, she starts reading a mystery, and becomes so involved in the story that she keeps reading through the night until the library opens the next morning. When she sees that the library is open, Charla goes home, leaving behind the book she intended to steal. Charla committed burglary because she stayed in the building with the specific intent to steal something, even though she did not go through with stealing the book.

crime requires intent to do something besides the original voluntary act of entering or remaining in a building. It also requires a further act to commit a crime while in the building.

> Automatism, or showing that a person had no control over her actions while sleepwalking or in a fugue state, is a defense in many states.

Specific intent relies on a defendant's subjective state of mind. The prosecution must allege and prove the defendant's particular purpose or intention in committing a criminal act. This proof often takes the form of circumstantial evidence. The facts and circumstances surrounding the defendant's criminal activity are considered. Motive, while not an element of a crime that must be proved, is often important to the question of specific intent.

It is a defense to show that the defendant did not, or could not, have the specific intent required to meet the *mens rea* element of a particular crime. The lack of specific intent may be due to the defendant's own actions, including a mistake of fact (an honest and reasonable mistake) that negates the *mens rea* element of a crime.

Strict Liability: Strict liability crimes do not require proof of a mental state. No *mens rea* needs to be proven by the prosecution. Strict liability is liability without fault. It applies to actions that, regardless of the care taken, are specifically not allowed by statute. Selling alcohol to a minor is a good example of a strict liability crime.

It is never presumed that a crime is a strict liability crime. Before a statute will be found to

> *Example:* After a night of heavy drinking, Bela tries to walk home. He is too drunk to recognize that the house he enters belongs to his next-door neighbors. Bela falls asleep on the living room couch. Since Bela did not intend to commit a crime in his neighbors' house, he is not guilty of burglary. Bela made an honest and reasonable mistake that negates the guilty mind element required to prove that crime (Bela may, however, be guilty of trespassing).

> **Example:** In most of the United States, it is legal to sell alcoholic beverages. It is, however, generally a crime to sell alcohol to a person under 21. A person who sells alcohol to a minor will be guilty even if she didn't know that the person was under 21.

create a strict liability crime, there must be a clear legislative intent not to require a particular mental state. Strict liability crimes are an exception to the general rule requiring proof of a mental state, and are not favored by the courts. Accordingly, courts require clear proof that an offense is in fact a strict liability crime.

To obtain a conviction for a strict liability crime, it is enough to show that the defendant did certain prohibited acts. It does not matter that she did not know that the acts were criminal, because *mens rea* is not required. As such, she is strictly liable for her acts, and the harm that results.

Strict liability and general intent crimes are not the same, even though both types of crimes require proof of certain acts being done. A strict liability crime requires proof of the defendant actually doing the prohibited criminal act. It is not necessary to prove that the defendant did not intend or did not know the act was legally prohibited. The defendant is still liable. Igno-rance of the law or of facts is not a defense. Except in rare cases, there is no defense to a strict liability crime. It will be a defense that the criminal acts were done involuntarily.

Most strict liability crimes call for relatively minor sentences.

Actus Reus

The *actus reus,* or guilty act, is a physical action that is criminal when done together with the appropriate *mens rea*. It is sometimes referred to as the external manifestation of the crime. A person cannot be convicted of a crime merely for having criminal thoughts. Some action besides thinking is required. A person's status (who they are, or a medical condition that the person possesses, for instance) cannot be a crime. Laws making it a crime merely to be a drug addict have been held to be unconstitutional, but the acts of selling or possessing illegal drugs are crimes, regardless of whether the seller or possessor is an addict.

> **Example:** Lars is watching a friend cutting down one tree out of a larger grove. He sees his ex-wife's new husband Evan walking nearby. He realizes that his friend cannot see Evan, and that Evan doesn't realize the tree is about to fall, or that it will probably fall on him. Lars thinks that outcome would be poetic justice, so he says nothing and gives no warning. Lars' voluntary failure to warn Evan or to stop his friend is *actus reus*.

> *Example:* Emil suffered a seizure while driving. He struck and killed a group of children. Prior to the accident, Emil had a long history of seizures. He noticed his hand jerking before losing control of his car, but he did not stop driving. Emil was guilty of criminal negligence. *People v. Decina,* 2 N.Y.2d 133, 138 N.E.2d 799 (1956).

An omission or failure to act may also be an *actus reus.* The reasoning is that there was a voluntary choice not to perform an act when action was required to be taken. The absence of an action is thus considered a voluntary "action." In order for an omission to be the *actus reus,* the criminal statute must clearly state that an omission is sufficient, and the law must impose a duty to take some action. Failure to file an income tax return is an omission that could also be a criminal offense, because the law imposes a duty to file.

A physical act will not be an *actus reus* if it was done involuntarily (accidentally). A reflex or convulsion, or a movement done while a person is asleep or unconscious, will not be an *actus reus.* But if a person knows that she is prone to an involuntary action (such as seizures) but acts despite knowing of the risk of her involuntary seizures, then she is liable for any harm resulting from her involuntary action.

WARRANT:
Written authority to conduct a search or to seize property or arrest a person.

II. Constitutional Limitations

Every criminal investigation and prosecution is subject to the Fifth Amendment to the U.S. Constitution. That Amendment provides, in relevant part, that no person shall be "deprived of life, liberty, or property, without due process of law." Due process is not something that can be defined with precision. The term does include, at the very least, notice of the charges that are being brought against the defendant, and an opportunity to mount a defense to those charges.

Due process also includes the rights guaranteed by the Fourth, Fifth, Sixth, and Eighth Amendments to the U.S. Constitution.

Search and Seizure

The law of search and seizure gives rise to more confusion and misunderstanding than just about any other area of criminal law. Search and seizure does not deal with acts that constitute a crime. Instead, it deals with the investigation and prosecution of crime. It is a procedural legal issue (the process of how a search was conducted), rather than a substantive legal issue (the application of individual rights to the person being searched).

The law of search and seizure is founded on the Fourth Amendment to the U.S. Constitu-

> **Example:** A police officer suspects that a man is using and selling drugs from his home. On garbage collection day in the man's neighborhood, the officer lifts full trash bags from the curb in front of the man's house. The bags are opaque and sealed, but the officer finds evidence of drug sales in the bags' content. While the man may complain that the police officer's rummage through his garbage bags required a warrant, the Supreme Court has ruled that there is no reasonable expectation of privacy in trash put out for collection. Bags put on the curb are "readily accessible to animals, children, scavengers, [and] snoops" as well as police officers. *California v. Greenwood*, 486 U.S. 35 (1988).

tion. The Amendment has two separate, but related provisions:

1. Protection against "unreasonable" searches and seizures; and

2. Rules limiting the issuance of search or arrest **warrants**.

The Amendment reads as follows:

> The right of the people to be secure in their persons, houses, papers, and effects, against unreasonable searches and seizures, shall not be violated, and no Warrants shall issue, but upon probable cause, supported by Oath or affirmation, and particularly describing the place to be searched, and the persons or things to be seized.

Most state constitutions contain provisions that echo the federal U.S. Constitution.

The first question for deciding Fourth Amendment issues is to ask if a search or a seizure occurred. The definition of "search" is not limited to a physical inspection or intrusion. The Fourth Amendment protects people, not places. The test for whether a search or a seizure has taken place looks at whether there was an intrusion on a person's reasonable expectation of privacy. Activities that violate the privacy upon which a person justifiably relied constitute a "search and seizure" under the Fourth Amendment However, if there were no intrusion, there was no search and no violation of the Fourth Amendment. Therefore, listening in on a conversation can be a search, even without a physical entry into a building. Likewise, attaching a location tracker to a person's car is considered a search, because the owner of the car has a reasonable expectation of privacy in the car. On the other hand, flying a helicopter 400 feet over a person's house to conduct surveillance is not a search, because the homeowner could not have any reasonable expectation of privacy in what could be seen from that altitude.

> If drugs are seen during the warranted search for weapons, the police may seize them. They may not conduct a search to look for drugs if they don't see them. Just being in a property does not grant the police the right to expand the scope of the warrant.

> *Example:* A warrant to search any building in Boston for smuggled goods would be a general warrant. It grants too much power to the warrant holder to decide where to search, and what to look for.

The Fourth Amendment prohibits only "unreasonable" searches and seizures. While there is no definition established for "reasonable" searches, there has long been a judicial preference for searches and seizures to be performed under warrant. A search or seizure without a warrant is not always unreasonable, but it is presumed that a legitimate warrant makes the search or seizure reasonable.

When the Constitution and the Bill of Rights were drafted, the Framers were mindful of the abuses of power by British authorities in the Colonies. One of these abuses was the "general warrant." A general warrant was an order that granted an official broad discretion to search unnamed premises, or arrest unnamed persons.

The Fourth Amendment bars general warrants, by requiring that the warrant specifically describe the place to be searched, or the persons or things to be seized. If the warrant says that the police may search "211 Pine Street, apartment 1" for illegal weapons, they may not also search apartment 2. They also may not search for drugs in apartment 1.

In addition, a warrant will be issued only "upon probable cause." **Probable cause** means that there are facts that support an objective belief

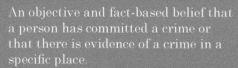

PROBABLE CAUSE:
An objective and fact-based belief that a person has committed a crime or that there is evidence of a crime in a specific place.

AFFIDAVIT:
A written statement of facts given under oath.

Probable cause is not the same as proof beyond a reasonable doubt. Probable cause is a lower bar that applies to issuance of warrants. "Beyond a reasonable doubt" is a standard that juries apply when determining whether a criminal defendant is guilty. The higher bar applies when a person's liberty is at stake.

> *Example:* Juanita, a narcotics officer, lives across the street from a house she believes is used for drug trafficking. Cars often drive up to the house, stay for a few minutes, and leave. Juanita has never spoken to the occupants of the house, and has never seen the inside of the house. Her neighbors tell her that they don't know what goes on in the house. Based only on these facts, Juanita does not have probable cause for a warrant.

that a person has committed a crime, or that there is evidence of a crime in the place to be searched. Facts are essential to probable cause; opinions or conclusions are inadequate to support a warrant. These facts are put into an **affidavit**, and presented to an official who is asked to issue a warrant. Probable cause does not require a mathematically measurable probability of a crime, but it must rely on more than a simple hunch or suspicion.

An additional requirement for warrants that is not found in the U.S. Constitution is that the warrant be issued by a neutral and detached official. Repeated court decisions over many years made this requirement a part of basic search and seizure law. The purpose of this part of search and seizure law is to include an objective party in the decision. Review of a warrant application by someone with no stake in the outcome of the case prevents corruption and abuse of power.

The official must be someone connected with the court system, although the official need not be a judge or a lawyer. The only requirement is that she be capable of deciding whether probable cause exists. If an official issues the warrant without adequate probable cause, the resulting search is lawful as long as the law enforcement officers who executed it acted under a good faith belief that the warrant was valid.

Searches performed without a warrant are presumed to be unreasonable. There are many exceptions to this rule, including but not limited to the following:

- *Consent.* A search is not unreasonable if the person gives his permission.

- *Lawful arrest.* If a person is lawfully arrested, either through an arrest warrant or on other probable cause, she may be searched.

- *Exigent circumstances.* If there is evidence or contraband that is in danger of being destroyed, a warrant is not required for a search and seizure.

- *Plain view.* Evidence that is in the plain sight of law enforcement officers where the officers have a right to be may be seized without a warrant.

- *Cars.* There are many circumstances that allow the warrantless search of a car. If there is probable cause to believe that a car contains evidence of criminal activity, for instance, an officer may lawfully

Example: A judge issues a warrant based on information furnished by law enforcement. Acting in reliance on the warrant, the police raid a house and seize a quantity of drugs. At a later hearing, a different judge concludes that there was no probable cause because the information used to apply for the warrant was stale. The U.S. Supreme Court held that, since the police relied in good faith on the validity of the warrant, a search pursuant to the warrant was lawful. *U.S. v. Leon,* 468 U.S. 897 (1984).

> *Example:* A police officer pulls over a red Camaro for running a traffic light. The car has a personalized license plate that reads "YUMM13." After going to the driver's window to issue a ticket, the officer receives a transmission that a bank was just robbed a few blocks away, and that the getaway car was a red sports car with a plate starting with a Y. Because there is probable cause to believe that the car was involved in the crime, the officer would be entitled to search any area of the car where the proceeds of a bank robbery could be stashed. (The officer would probably be justified in calling for back-up first.)

EXCLUSIONARY RULE:

A rule that prohibits illegally obtained evidence from being used in court.

search any area of the vehicle in which the evidence might be found.

If a search is unlawful, the evidence found as a result of the search usually may not be introduced into evidence in the criminal trial. This principle is known as the **exclusionary rule**. The purpose of the exclusionary rule is to deter misconduct by law enforcement. In cases where an unlawful search was done by a private party (for example, a security guard), the rule will not apply to the private party. The evidence may be introduced in court. The rule also does not apply if the evidence would have been found anyway (inevitable discovery).

> *Example:* A neighborhood watch member sneaks into a neighbor's house and looks in the kitchen drawer, where he sees stolen jewelry. This unlawful search would not exclude the evidence, because the search was performed by a private citizen.
>
> If a police officer looked in the drawer rather than a neighborhood watch member, the search would be illegal, and the jewelry could not be used as evidence. If another police officer arrived at the front door with a warrant to search for the jewelry while the first officer was looking at another area in the kitchen, though, the jewelry might be used as evidence. Even though the first officer's search was illegal, the discovery of the jewelry was inevitable by the second officer. The evidence may be admitted.

THE EXCLUSIONARY RULE IS APPLIED TO PROSECUTIONS IN STATE COURTS.

Mapp v. Ohio
(Homeowner) v. (State Government)
367 U.S. 643, 81 S. Ct. 1684 (1961)

INSTANT FACTS:

Mapp's (D) home was forcibly searched without a search warrant. Mapp (D) seeks to have the evidence seized therein suppressed under the Fourth Amendment's exclusionary rule.

BLACK LETTER RULE:

The exclusionary rule requiring evidence gathered in violation of the Fourth Amendment to be excluded from criminal proceedings applies equally to both the state and federal governments.

PROCEDURAL BASIS:

Certification to the U.S. Supreme Court after the State's highest appellate court affirmed the conviction and refused to apply the exclusionary rule.

FACTS:

On May 23, 1957, three police officers arrived at Mapp's (D) residence with information that someone was hiding out there and that evidence could be found in the home. Upon their arrival, the officers knocked and demanded entrance, but Mapp (D) refused to let them in without a warrant. Three hours later, when some additional officers arrived on the scene, Mapp (D) refused to answer the door. The officers then forced their way into the residence.

The officers conducted a widespread search and found obscene materials. No search warrant was ever produced, nor was this failure explained in any way. Mapp (D) was convicted on the strength of the evidence seized. The Ohio Supreme Court, after acknowledging that no warrant was ever produced, affirmed the conviction.

ISSUE:

Should the federal rule requiring the exclusion of evidence gathered in violation of the Fourth Amendment be applied to evidence used in state court proceedings as well?

DECISION AND RATIONALE:

(Clark, J.) Yes. Many states use the exclusionary rule, whereby evidence seized in violation of the Fourth Amendment cannot be used in a criminal trial. The highest court of California said it was "compelled" to adopt the exclusionary rule because other methods failed to secure compliance with the Constitution.

Since the Fourth Amendment's right of privacy has been declared enforceable against the states through the Due Process Clause of the Fourteenth Amendment, it is enforceable against them in the same way as against the federal government. Were it otherwise the Fourth Amendment would be largely meaningless. Presently, a federal prosecutor may make no use of evidence illegally seized, but a state's attorney across the street may, although he is supposedly operating under the enforceable prohibitions of the same constitutional Amendment.

There are those who say that the exclusionary rule allows criminals to go free when a police officer makes a mistake. This will no doubt be the case in some cases. But the criminal goes free, because it is the law that sets him free. Nothing can destroy a government more quickly than its failure to observe its own laws.

Nor can it be assumed that the exclusionary rule fetters law enforcement. Once we recognize that the right to privacy embodied in the Fourth Amendment is enforceable against the states, and that the right to be secure against invasions of privacy by state officers is constitutional in origin, we cannot permit that right to remain an empty promise. Our decision today gives to the individual no more than that which the Constitution guarantees, to the police officer no less than that to which honest law enforcement is entitled, and, to the courts, judicial integrity.

We therefore hold that all evidence obtained by searches and seizures in violation of the Constitution is, by that same authority, inadmissible in state court.

ANALYSIS:
Mapp is a judicial recognition of the state's failure to properly enforce the Fourth Amendment through means other than an exclusionary rule.

QUESTIONS FOR DISCUSSION:
Why didn't the officers just secure a warrant? The evidence was found in a drawer. If the police were seeking a fugitive, why did they look there?

Example:	Antoine was suspected of trafficking in illegal drugs. Narcotics agents secretly installed a GPS tracking device on his car. They did not have a valid warrant. The tracking device recorded Antoine's movements for several weeks. The data received from the device was used to obtain an indictment against Antoine for conspiracy to distribute cocaine. Attaching the tracking device to Antoine's car was a warrantless search, and the evidence obtained from it should not be admitted at trial. *U.S. v. Jones,* 565 U.S. 400 (2012).

Surveillance

The Fourth Amendment does not restrict many types of surveillance. A police office sitting outside a building watching who comes in and out does not need a warrant, because observing people in a public place is not a search. The activity being observed is in plain view. Electronic surveillance, such as wiretapping or bugging a room, constitutes a search for Fourth Amendment purposes. A warrant is required for most types of electronic surveillance, because the electronic surveillance involves matter that is not in the plain view of the public. There is a reasonable expectations that our telephone conversations and e-mail messages will be private.

Electronic surveillance is handled by the courts in much the same way as any other search. To obtain a warrant, law enforcement must make a showing of probable cause, and must describe in particularity the conversations to be intercepted. The description must set out a specific time period for the surveillance.

Federal law, the Communications Assistance for Law Enforcement Act requires telecommunication companies to cooperate with law enforcement agencies that engage in a wiretap. The company must give law enforcement access to the systems and facilities needed to track the communication of one subscriber without infringing on the privacy of other subscribers. The Act does not change the requirements for a search warrant, and does not pre-empt state laws regarding wiretapping.

These two acts do not preempt the numerous state statutes dealing with wiretapping and electronic surveillance.

The Fifth Amendment provides that "[n]o person shall be held to answer for a capital, or otherwise infamous crime, unless on a presentment or indictment of a Grand Jury . . ." All federal crimes must be charged by an indictment, but state laws vary on which crimes may or must be charged by a grand jury.

INDICTMENT:

A criminal accusation made by a grand jury upon a finding that there is probable cause that the defendant is guilty of a crime.

GRAND JURY:

A panel of qualified persons selected and organized to inquire into the commission of crimes in the jurisdiction from which the members are drawn.

Foreign Surveillance

In 1978, Congress passed the Foreign Intelligence Surveillance Act (FISA). The Act allows the President to order warrantless wiretapping in order to protect the United States against a potential grave attack, sabotage, or espionage. FISA also allows federal law enforcement to obtain a warrant for foreign intelligence taps from a special court (the Foreign Intelligence Surveillance Court) that hears applications for warrants in secret. Before a warrant is issued under FISA, the court must find probable cause to believe that the person to be tapped is a foreign power or the agent of a foreign power.

Grand Juries

In the federal system, and in many states, a criminal charge may be brought only after an **indictment** is issued by a **grand jury.** Grand juries are often granted broad authority to investigate, as well as charge, crimes.

The function of a grand jury is not to determine the guilt or innocence of a person charged with a crime. Instead, the grand jury considers whether there is sufficient evidence to bring a prosecution against the defendant. There are two questions a grand jury is supposed to answer: Was a crime committed? If so, did this particular person commit it?

The grand jury acts as a gatekeeper, approving only prosecutions that could result in a conviction. There is no constitutional requirement that a prosecutor present the grand jury with exculpatory evidence that may negate the defendant's guilt. U.S. Department of Justice guidelines, however, call for the introduction or presentment of "substantial" exculpatory evidence of which the prosecutor is "personally aware." The failure to present such evidence will not result in the dismissal of the indictment. Instead, the failure will be treated as a possible ethical infraction by the prosecutor

In the federal system, grand juries are convened by the District Court. They are made up of 16 to 23 jurors, depending on the district, and the jurors serve for varying terms of up to one year. The grand jury may meet only one or two days per week, and may meet only for a few hours on days that it is in session. Grand juries work closely with the prosecuting authorities.

Federal grand jury proceedings are secret. No one is allowed in the grand jury room while the grand jury is in session except the jurors, attorneys for the government, the witness being questioned, interpreters (if needed), and a court reporter or operator of a recording device. No one other than the jurors may be present during grand jury deliberations. Jurors and government attorneys are generally prohibited from disclosing what goes on in a grand jury proceeding.

A witness who is called to testify before a grand jury will not necessarily be informed in advance if she is the target of the grand jury investigation, or if she is merely being called to give testimony for the possible prosecution of another person. She may be represented by counsel, but the attorney may not be present when the witness gives her testimony. A witness may assert her Fifth Amendment privilege against self-incrimination by refusing to answer a question, but the witness may be compelled to testify after the prosecutor provides her with immunity. Immunity may be either **transactional immunity** or **use immunity**. Once a witness receives a grant of some type of immunity, she may be held in contempt for the duration of the grand jury term if she continues to refuse to testify.

While grand juries were intended as a protection against overzealous prosecutions, they are also the subject of much criticism. The proceedings are perceived as biased in favor of the prosecution. The secrecy of the proceedings also gives rise to much suspicion regarding the fairness of grand juries. Nevertheless, the grand jury is still seen as a gatekeeper, used to weed out meritless prosecutions, and to ensure that only cases that could realistically result in a conviction are prosecuted.

> Sol Wachtler, former Chief Judge of the New York Court of Appeals, once famously said that "If a district attorney wanted, a grand jury would indict a ham sandwich." In an ironic twist, a few years after making that statement, Judge Wachtler was indicted on charges of extortion, racketeering, and blackmail. He pleaded guilty to a harassment charge, and was sentenced to 15 months in federal prison.

TRANSACTIONAL IMMUNITY:

Immunity from prosecution for any criminal activity related to a witness's testimony.

USE IMMUNITY:

A grant of immunity that prohibits the government from using a witness's immunized testimony against her in a later prosecution, except for a prosecution for perjury, if the immunized testimony is false.

Right to Counsel

There are two constitutional rights to counsel in criminal proceedings. The first is based on the Fifth Amendment privilege against self-incrimination. The second is based on the explicit statement of the right to counsel in the Sixth Amendment.

In the famous decision in the famous case of *Miranda v. Arizona,* 384 U.S. 436 (1966), the U.S. Supreme Court established rules for law enforcement to follow when interrogating a person who is in custody. The Court's concern in that case is that a person who spoke to law enforcement while being questioned knew that they had the right not to speak, and that anything they did say was said after an informed waiver of the right not to speak. This is the origin of the *Miranda* warning. As the now-familiar warning was set out by the Court said:

> You have the right to remain silent. Anything you say can and will be used against you in a court of law. You have the right to speak to an attorney, and to have an attorney present during any questioning. If you cannot afford a lawyer, one will be appointed for you at government expense.

The requirement that a person in custody be informed of the right to an attorney was meant

Contrary to what you may have seen on television or in the movies, failure to give a *Miranda* warning does not mean that the arrest is invalid. It means that any statement or confession made may potentially be excluded from being introduced at trial.

to reduce the likelihood of a coerced confession, and to ensure that any statement given was accurate, and accurately reported at trial. A person may waive the right to have counsel present.

The Sixth Amendment to the U.S. Constitution provides that "In all criminal prosecutions, the accused shall enjoy the right . . . to have assistance of counsel for his defense." Courts have held that the Sixth Amendment right to counsel attaches when adversary judicial proceedings are started against the defendant. When the government initiates criminal charges against a defendant, whether by indictment, **arraignment,** or a complaint, the defendant has the right to have an attorney present. Questioning of a suspect after proceedings have been

Example: Alfred, a furnace repairman, is charged with stealing several items from a customer's home while he is repairing her furnace. He goes to court for his arraignment and is represented by an attorney. He is allowed to leave after the arraignment. After he leaves the courthouse, he walks over to the police station, where he sees Karen, the officer who investigated the incident. Alfred says he would like to "clear things up," and he proceeds to tell Karen the details of how and why he stole the items. Karen does not ask him if he wants his attorney present, and Alfred never asks for his attorney. Alfred has not made an explicit waiver of his right to counsel, so his statement may not be used as evidence against him.

ARRAIGNMENT:

The initial step of a criminal proceeding. In an arraignment, a defendant is brought before a judge to be informed of the charges, and to enter a plea.

FELONY:

A crime punishable by a sentence of more than one year, or by death.

MISDEMEANOR:

A crime punishable by a fine or imprisonment of no more than one year.

started must be done with his attorney present, or after the defendant has explicitly waived her right to have counsel present. It does not matter if the questioning is done when the defendant is in custody, or even if she volunteers to be questioned. The right to counsel may be waived. Any such waiver must be voluntary. The defendant must understand the consequences of her waiver. Waiver will not be presumed.

The right to counsel means the right to have adequate, effective representation. The standard is that the representation meet some minimal professional standards. It does not have to have been error free, or perfect. A conviction or a harsh sentence does not necessarily mean that representation was inadequate. Adequate, or competent, representation is representation that is within the range of competence generally demanded of criminal defense attorneys.

A criminal defendant has the right to represent herself. The court must allow a defen-dant to represent herself. Stand-by counsel may be appointed to assist or answer questions the defendant may have, by a defendant is not required to accept the services of an attorney.

III. Sentencing

A sentence is the consequence of a criminal conviction. It is ordered by the judge following the conviction of a defendant. The rationale behind criminal sentencing can vary. Many regard sentencing as an opportunity for vengeance or retribution, to be exacted by society. Others look at criminal sentences as a way of deterring other potential criminals. Some also believe that a criminal sentence should be used as an opportunity to rehabilitate a wrongdoer, or just a means to take him off the streets.

Criminal sentencing is limited by the Eighth Amendment to the U.S. Constitution. The Eighth Amendment prohibits imposing excessive fines or inflicting "cruel and unusual punishments." Courts have interpreted this limitation to mean that a criminal sentence must not be grossly disproportionate to the crime. Imposing a death sentence in a case that does not involve a homicide would generally be

> As a rule, a **felony** is a crime punishable by more than one year in prison, while a **misdemeanor** has a maximum penalty of one year or less. The focus is on the possibility of a year or more of punishment; a person convicted of a felony may serve less than a year in prison, but that does not change the felony conviction to a misdemeanor.

Example: Henry and Kenneth have been convicted of burglary. The law of their state imposes a maximum sentence of 10 years in prison for the level of burglary for which they were convicted. Henry has no prior criminal record, so the state's sentencing guidelines call for him to be placed on probation, and a **stayed sentence** a year and a day. Kenneth has four prior felony convictions, so the guidelines call for him to receive a sentence of 24 months in prison.

STAYED SENTENCE:

A sentence that the court imposes, but delays the requirement that the defendant comply with it immediately. For example, a stayed prison sentence will allow the defendant to remain free as long as he remains law abiding and complies with the conditions of probation.

PROBATION:

A criminal sentence in which the defendant is not imprisoned, but is allowed to remain free, subject to certain conditions.

SUSPENDED SENTENCE:

A criminal sentence that the defendant is not required to serve immediately.

considered grossly disproportionate. In cases not involving murder, prison sentences have rarely been found to be disproportionate. When considering if a sentence is disproportionate, courts consider several factors, including:

- The seriousness of the crime.

- The harm done to the victim.

- The defendant's involvement in the crime.

- The intent and motive in behind the crime.

- Sentences imposed on other defendants for the same or similar crime.

The statutes that define or create a crime will often set out the maximum possible sentence for that crime. The sentence may be incarceration, a monetary fine, or both. In many cases, a sentencing judge is authorized to sentence

Example: Albert has made a plan to burn down a vacant building that he owns in order to collect the insurance money. He goes to a gas station and buys a can of gas and some matches, then goes home and hides them in his garage. Albert is not guilty of attempted arson. Two nights later, he drives to the building and pries the door open, while carrying the gas and matches. A passer-by thinks Albert is a burglar, and grabs him before he can go into the building. Albert is guilty of attempted arson.

a defendant to **probation**, or to impose a **suspended sentence**.

Federal and state laws include a system of guidelines for **felony** sentencing. These guidelines were adopted to make sentences equivalent for similar defendants. Every defendant convicted for a certain crime would ideally receive a similar sentence, regardless of race, gender, or socio-economic status. The sentencing guidelines group offenses together according to severity, and then set the penalty as a function of the severity of the crime and the defendant's criminal history. Sentencing judges are allowed to consider certain aggravating or mitigating factors to increase or decrease a sentence, but they are usually required to give the reasons for these variations.

IV. Inchoate Crimes

"Inchoate" is another way of saying incomplete. Inchoate crimes are crimes that a person failed to complete. The act of taking steps towards the crime is deemed criminal even though no harm was done. Inchoate crimes include:

Example: Lavonne thinks that the watch she wants to buy from her friend Mack is stolen. In fact, Mack bought the watch at a retail store a year before. When Lavonne hands Mack $100 to buy the watch, Mack says that he changed his mind, and that the price is now $150. Lavonne does not have that much money with her, so she walks away to get the rest. Lavonne probably is not guilty of an attempt to purchase stolen property. Even though she thought the watch was stolen, it was not, so it was impossible for her to purchase a stolen watch in this transaction, only a used watch.

Example: Mazen and Greg work for the same company. Greg thinks of a way to create false invoices to put in for payment. He asks Mazen, who works in the accounting department, to process the invoices. Mazen refuses. Greg sends in the invoices himself, but they are determined to be fakes and are not paid. Greg is guilty of the inchoate crimes of soliciting another person to commit a crime, and of the attempt to commit embezzlement himself.

Example: Nestor plans to break into a store by smashing the front window. He gets a large hammer and swings at the window. The window is not glass; it is made out of an unbreakable plastic. The hammer bounces off, and the window does not break. Nestor is guilty of attempt, even though it is factually impossible for him to complete the crime as he planned.

- Attempts to commit a crime.

- Soliciting another person to commit a crime.

- Conspiring to commit a crime.

- Being an accessory or accomplice to a crime.

> If a crime is actually committed, the defendant may not be convicted of both attempt and the crime that was committed.

The underlying crime that was attempted, solicited, or conspired about is not always committed.

Inchoate crimes are punished for two main reasons. One reason is to prevent another crime. If a person is seen attempting a burglary, it is better to catch him before the burglary is complete. The second reason is deterrence. Punishing a person for attempting to commit a crime will discourage her from trying again and eventually completing the crime.

Inchoate crimes are "specific intent" crimes because there is an intent to commit the crime that was not completed.

Attempt

The crime of attempt involves more than planning or thinking about committing a crime. Attempt requires a substantial step towards the commission of a crime. The substantial step must be done with the intent or motive of committing a crime. The attempt is not necessarily an unlawful act on its own—the intent causes the unlawfulness. Once the act is done, the crime of attempt is complete.

Preparation is not the same as attempt. For an attempt, the defendant must come close to completing the crime, and there can be no reasonable doubt about the defendant's motive to commit that crime. In some states, a defendant will not be convicted of attempt unless he has completed all but the last step in committing the crime.

> If the person being solicited does not receive the communication, there is no solicitation.

> At common law, conspiracy required an agreement to commit a felony, but that rule has been changed by statute.

Example: Dion knows that if his building burns down, he would be a suspect. In order to create an alibi, he asks Dwayne to set a fire in the building while Dion is out of town on vacation. Dwayne hears Dion's request, but does not respond to it. Dion is guilty of solicitation.

Abandonment is a defense to attempt only if the defendant shows a complete withdrawal from the crime. Postponing or delaying the crime is not abandonment. In addition, the attempt must have been abandoned out of a change of heart, or remorse. It is not abandonment if the attempt is stopped because the crime became more difficult, or if the defendant decided it were more likely she would be caught.

In some jurisdictions, legal impossibility is a defense to attempt. Legal impossibility is when the defendant believes that what he is about to do is illegal when it in fact is legal.

There is a distinction between factual and legal impossibility. Factual impossibility means that an attempted crime cannot be completed because the facts are different than what the defendant thought they were. Factual impossibility is not a defense to an attempt charge.

Solicitation

Solicitation is the crime of asking or urging someone to commit a crime. It does not matter that the person solicited does not commit, attempt, or even agree to commit the crime. The crime of solicitation is complete when the request is made to, and received by, the person being solicited.

A conviction for solicitation requires proof that the defendant intended to promote or facilitate the commission of a crime. There must be evidence that strongly corroborates the defendant's specific intent to have a crime committed. Corroborating evidence includes evidence of the circumstances surrounding a defendant's conversations about the crime, as well as evidence of a defendant's discussions with other people. The evidence must show that the defendant was serious, and not just venting or complaining.

Example: Theo and Davi agree to rob a local bank. They plan the robbery down to the smallest detail. In jurisdictions that require an overt act, they are not guilty of conspiracy—planning itself is not an overt act in furtherance of the crime. If Theo goes to a car dealer and rents a car to use as the getaway car, however, that is an overt act. Upon the car rental, the crime of conspiracy is complete.

Example: Anya and Viktor devise a plan to smuggle heroin into the United States from Mexico. Anya travels to Mexico alone to pick up the drugs. While she is there, Viktor bribes a narcotics officer back in the United States to let Viktor know if there are suspicions about his and Anya's activities. Anya and Viktor are both guilty of bribery.

Conspiracy

A conspiracy is an agreement between two or more people to commit an unlawful act. In some states, a conspiracy may also be an agreement to commit a lawful act by unlawful means. The conspiracy is a crime distinct from the agreed-upon crime, and it may be punished separately, or in addition to that crime.

In most jurisdictions, the crime of conspiracy is not complete unless there is an overt act performed in furtherance of the conspiracy. In other words, the agreement alone is not enough. The overt act is apart from, and in addition to, the act of making an agreement to commit a crime. The act does not have to be unlawful, but it must be done to further the conspiracy. It may be something other than the crime that is agreed to be committed.

A person who is a part of a conspiracy is responsible for all acts done to further the conspiracy. This includes responsibility for all of the criminal actions agreed to, and also those outcomes that were not part of the agreement, but which were foreseeable as natural and probable consequences of the conspiracy. Co-conspirators are guilty even if they were not physically present at the time a criminal act was done, and even if they did not know about the participation of the conspirator who did the criminal act.

Conspiracy is different from solicitation. Solicitation does not require an agreement. Conspiracy also differs from attempt, in that the conspirators are guilty even though they did not take a substantial step towards commission of the crime. In jurisdictions that require an overt act to prove a conspiracy, any overt act separate from making the agreement will suffice. It does not have to be a substantial step as long as the act (no matter how small) furthers the commission of the crime.

PONZI SCHEME:

A fraudulent investment scheme in which money contributed by investors is used to pay people who made a prior investment. Usually, money is not invested in any revenue-producing enterprise, or if it is, the enterprise does not generate expected revenue.

Example: Nobusuke admires an antique sword that Roberta is selling. Roberta tells him that the sword was carried by a cavalry officer in the Civil War. In fact, Roberta knows that the sword was made by a local metalworking shop. Roberta says that she believes the sword can only increase in value. Roberta's claim that the sword was carried in the Civil War is fraudulent. Her remarks about the value increasing are only opinion, so they are not fraudulent.

Example:	Bruce, a college graduate who works in a bank, is visiting his cousin Phyllis. Phyllis has never finished high school, and does not read the news or follow business matters. While Bruce is visiting, Doug, an acquaintance of Phyllis's boss, stops by to tell them about an "exciting" new business opportunity that is "guaranteed" to double their investments in one month. The opportunity is a supposed resort development out-of-state. Doug knows that the plans for this development have already fallen through, but he is trying to raise money to pay off earlier investors (a classic **Ponzi scheme**). If Bruce were to invest, his reliance probably would be neither justified nor reasonable, since his education and experience should lead him to decline to rely on Doug's representations. Phyllis's reliance would probably be considered justifiable, since she is inexperienced and probably not knowledgeable about common business schemes.

V. Business-related Crimes

There are certain crimes that have special relevance in the business world. These crimes relate to the integrity of business relationships and transactions. Handling or misappropriating money is not required for all of these crimes, but each of the crimes will have a financial impact.

Fraud

The term "fraud" is used broadly by many people. It is often used to describe any type of deceit or dishonesty. More precisely, fraud is a misrepresentation of a fact that induces another person to act.

UNPAID TAXES ARE "PROPERTY" FOR PURPOSES OF FRAUD LAWS.
Fountain v. U.S.
(Convicted of Mail and Wire Fraud) v. (Prosecuting Government)
357 F.3d 250 (2d Cir. 2004)

INSTANT FACTS:
Fountain (P) was convicted of mail and wire fraud arising out of a scheme to circumvent Canadian tobacco taxes.

BLACK LETTER RULE:
The elements of mail or wire fraud violation are (1) a scheme to defraud, (2) money or property as the object of the scheme, and (3) use of the mails or wires to further the scheme.

FACTS:
Fountain (P) pled guilty to mail and wire fraud. The charges were based on his participation in a scheme to circumvent high Canadian taxes on tobacco products. The scheme involved using cashier's checks and wire transfers, and exchanging Canadian for U.S. currency. The currency was then used to transport cigarettes from Canada into the St. Regis Mohawk Reservation in New York, then back to Canada, to be sold on the black market.

Fountain (P) pled guilty to the charges, and was sentenced to 60 months in prison. He later brought a petition for habeas corpus relief. Fountain (P) claimed that his guilty plea was based on his participation in a scheme to defraud the Canadian government out of taxes. He argued that unpaid taxes are not "property" in the possession of a fraud victim, so the scheme could not constitute mail or wire fraud. Fountain (P) also argued that the "revenue rule," a common-law rule that says U.S. courts should not recognize foreign tax judgments. The District Court denied his petition.

ISSUE:

Was Fountain (P) guilty of mail and wire fraud?

DECISION AND RATIONALE:

(Katzmann, J.) Yes. The elements of mail or wire fraud violation are (1) a scheme to defraud, (2) money or property as the object of the scheme, and (3) use of the mails or wires to further the scheme. For purposes of the mail and wire fraud statutes, the thing obtained must be property in the hands of the victim. Taxes owed to the government are property in the hands of the government even if they have not yet been collected. Unless the law clearly states otherwise, the question of who properly has the right of use of the money owed the government for the period it is owed is answered in favor of the government. Because a government has a property right in tax revenues when they accrue, the tax revenues that would have been owed to Canadian governments are "property" for purposes of the mail and wire fraud statutes.

The common law revenue rule does not apply to this case. The mail and wire fraud statute do not preclude the prosecution of a defendant for participating in a scheme to defraud a foreign government of tax revenue. Affirmed.

ANALYSIS:

The revenue rule is a rule of international law that says courts should not hear suits to collect foreign taxes. The prosecution of Fountain (P) was not a suit to collect taxes, but a criminal prosecution for schemes to avoid those taxes. The result of the suit was incarceration upon a conviction, not an order to pay taxes.

CASE VOCABULARY:

HABEAS CORPUS:

A proceeding brought to challenge the legality of a person's confinement.

QUESTIONS FOR DISCUSSION:

Why wasn't this case decided in Canada?

Why should Fountain be able to challenge the outcome via habeas corpus when he pled guilty?

Example:

Gabriel sends a letter to Hailey through the mail, identifying himself as a physician working in an impoverished country. The letter says that Gabriel is soliciting funds to help build an urgently needed clinic. In fact, Gabriel lives in the United States, and has no involvement with any charitable or medical group. Gabriel has committed mail fraud.

Hailey sends Gabriel a monetary contribution. After he receives the contribution, Gabriel decides to go a little further. He calls Hailey on the telephone to thank her for her donation. He then asks if she can contribute more money to help train a nurse for the clinic. Hailey declines to send any further money. Gabriel is guilty of wire fraud because he used the telephone (an interstate activity) to contact Hailey.

> **Example:**
>
> Terry is a secretary and is in charge of the office's supply of petty cash. One day, she is short of lunch money, so she helps herself to $20 from the cash drawer, without getting permission. Technically, Terry is guilty of embezzlement.

> **Example:**
>
> Terry takes the $20 from petty cash, but plans to stop at an ATM after work in order to replace the $20 the next morning. In states that require proof of an intent to deprive the owner of property permanently, Terry may not be guilty of embezzlement.

Fraud may be either civil or criminal. In most jurisdictions, there is no single crime of fraud. Instead, acts done in certain contexts or with regard to certain transactions are crimes if they are done fraudulently. While every jurisdiction defines fraud or fraudulent acts differently, the usual elements of fraud are:

- A knowing and purposeful misrepresentation of a material fact.

- The intent to defraud (fool) the victim.

- Reasonable reliance by the victim on the misrepresentation.

- In many states, some damage to the victim due to the misrepresentation is required; however, federal law does not require any actual monetary damage to the victim.

Fraud requires a misrepresentation of fact, not an opinion. The defendant must also know that the statement was false when she made it. The fact misrepresented must have the natural

> **Example:**
>
> Hank owns a cattle feed lot. He is hired by Ben to feed and care for several head of cattle for a week before they are sent to auction. Towards the end of the week, Hank learns that Ben has filed for bankruptcy and will be going out of business. Hank calls Nicole, his accountant, to ask what he should do. She tells him that he may dispose of the cattle and keep the proceeds. Hank does so. Unfortunately, Nicole has misunderstood the situation. The cattle are actually to be turned over to the bankruptcy trustee. If Hank lives in a state that requires knowledge that conduct was unlawful, Hank may not be guilty of embezzlement. Depending on the state where he lives, though, Hank may be guilty of misappropriation, larceny, or theft, because the proceeds did not rightfully belong to Hank.

tendency to influence the person making a decision.

A misrepresentation is not fraudulent unless the person hearing it relied upon it. That reliance must be justifiable or reasonable. Reliance is not justifiable or reasonable if a person with intelligence, education, or experience similar to the victim's would not have relied on the misrepresentation.

There are many different types of fraud crime. Fraudulent acts are made criminal in several different contexts. Two of the most common fraud crimes are mail fraud and wire fraud. Mail fraud is the use of the U.S. Postal Service for fraudulent communications. Wire fraud uses the telephone or electronic communications for fraud. Both types of crimes cross state borders, which make the crimes interstate activities, and triggers federal laws.

Federal criminal law requires an intent to defraud. It does not require that the victim have sustained any actual monetary loss as a result of the fraud. Therefore, use of the mail or of telephones or electronic communication in furtherance of a fraudulent plan is a crime, even if no one falls for the message.

Embezzlement

"Embezzlement" conjures visions of some elaborate scheme to divert corporate funds to a secret offshore bank account. While that series of events probably would constitute embezzlement, the crime is typically much simpler.

Embezzlement is defined as the fraudulent taking of another person's property by one who is lawfully in possession of that property. The property is then used or applied to purposes other than the purpose for which it was originally held. The distinction between embezzlement and other types of theft is that the person who takes the other person's property is originally lawfully in possession of the property. The property is not taken from the owner. Instead, the embezzler has come into possession of the property lawfully, with the owner's express or implied consent. The intent to take the property may develop after the person comes into possession of it. If a person gains possession of property in good faith, but later changes his mind and acts in bad faith, he has committed embezzlement, regardless of whether the property is later returned.

> In addition to criminal liability, a person engaged in insider trading may be held liable in a civil lawsuit brought by the Securities and Exchange Commission, which regulates the securities trade.

In some states, embezzlement requires an intent to deprive the owner of the property permanently. In other states, the crime of embezzlement is complete when the property is taken or appropriated.

In some jurisdictions, a defendant will be guilty of embezzlement only if he acted knowingly, being aware that his act was unlawful. In other jurisdictions, there is no requirement that the defendant know the conduct is illegal.

> *Example:* Malik is an engineer with the National Transportation Safety Board. He is in charge of a safety investigation that may result in the recall of thousands of cars sold by Charon Motors. In his investigation, he works with Paolo, the chief safety engineer for Charon, and Liu, an attorney with an outside law firm representing Charon. Paolo makes regular reports on the progress of the investigation to Frank, the chief operating officer of Charon. Frank's secretary Ivan makes copies of Paolo's reports, and skims them before handing them to Frank. When the investigation is nearly complete, Malik comes home and tells his partner Logan that the NTSB is going to order a recall of virtually all cars manufactured by Charon for the past three years. Malik, Paolo, Liu, Frank, Ivan, and Logan are all insiders.

> *Example:* In the example above, Malik tells Logan that the recall of Charon Motors cars will be made in one week, on September 15. Logan calls his stock broker on September 13, and places an order to sell 5,000 shares of Charon stock immediately before the recall is announced. Liu owns 2,500 shares of Charon stock that she bought before her firm started representing the company. She sells her stock on September 16, the day after the recall is announced. Logan is guilty of insider trading; Liu is not.

> *Example:* Continuing with the facts from the prior example, Malik's recently-deceased mother owned 1,000 shares of Charon stock, as well as stock in several other companies. She left all of her stock to Malik. In order to settle a dispute with his siblings over their mother's estate, Malik agrees to sell the stock as soon as he receives permission from the probate court, and divide the proceeds with his siblings. The court grants its permission on September 12, and Malik sells all of the stock that day. Malik is not guilty of insider trading.

Insider Trading

The buying and selling of securities depends on the free flow of accurate information. Investors rely on this information to make informed decisions about their investments. Fairness demands that all investors have equal access to the same information, so that no one investor or group of investors is given an advantage. Securities laws therefore require that publicly-traded corporations make public any material (important) information that has the likelihood of affecting an investor's decision to invest in a company. While all important information must be presented to the public, there is an advantage to those who learn about it first. The first

GIVING INSIDE INFORMATION TO A RELATIVE VIOLATES SECURITIES LAWS.

Salman v. United States
(Trader using Inside Information) v. (Federal Government)
580 U.S. ___ (2016)

ALITO, J., delivered the opinion for a unanimous Court.

Section 10(b) of the Securities Exchange Act of 1934 and the Securities and Exchange Commission's Rule 10b-5 prohibit undisclosed trading on inside corporate information by individuals who are under a duty of trust and confidence that prohibits them from secretly using such information for their personal advantage.

These persons also may not tip inside information to others for trading. The tippee acquires the tipper's duty to disclose or abstain from trading if the tippee knows the information was disclosed in breach of the tipper's duty, and the tippee may commit securities fraud by trading in disregard of that knowledge. In Dirks v. SEC, 463 U. S. 646 (1983), this Court explained that a tippee's liability for trading on inside information hinges on whether the tipper breached a fiduciary duty by disclosing the information. A tipper breaches such a fiduciary duty, we held, when the tipper discloses the inside information for a personal benefit. And, we went on to say, a jury can infer a personal benefit--and thus a breach of the tipper's duty--where the tipper receives something of value in exchange for the tip or "makes a gift of confidential information to a trading relative or friend."

Petitioner Bassam Salman challenges his convictions for conspiracy and insider trading. Salman received lucrative trading tips from an extended family member, who had received the information from Salman's brother-in-law. Salman then traded on the information. He argues that he cannot be held liable as a tippee because the tipper (his brother-in-law) did not personally receive money or property in exchange for the tips and thus did not personally benefit from them.

Maher Kara was an investment banker in Citigroup's healthcare investment banking group. He dealt with highly confidential information about mergers and acquisitions involving Citigroup's clients. Maher enjoyed a close relationship with his older brother, [Michael]. . . . Michael began to trade on the information Maher shared with him. At first, Maher was unaware of his brother's trading activity, but eventually he began to suspect that it was taking place. . . . Ultimately, Maher began to assist Michael's trading by sharing inside information with his brother about pending mergers and acquisitions. . . . Without his younger brother's knowledge, Michael fed the information to others--including Salman, Michael's friend and Maher's brother-in-law. . . . Salman was indicted on one count of conspiracy to commit securities fraud, and four counts of securities fraud. . . . [B]oth Maher and Michael pleaded guilty and testified at Salman's trial.

[...] Maher testified that he shared inside information with his brother to benefit him and with the expectation that his brother would trade on it. . . . Michael told the jury that his brother's tips gave him "timely information that the average person does not have access to" and "access to stocks, options, and what have you, that I can capitalize on, that the average person would never have or dream of." Michael testified that he became friends with Salman when Maher was courting Salman's sister and later began sharing Maher's tips with Salman.

[...]

Salman contends that an insider's "gift of confidential information to a trading relative or friend," is not enough to establish securities fraud. Instead, Salman argues, a tipper does not personally benefit unless the tipper's goal in disclosing inside information is to obtain money, property, or something of tangible value. . . . The Government disagrees and argues that a gift of confidential information to anyone, not just a "trading relative or friend," is enough to prove securities fraud. . . . Under the Government's view, a tipper personally benefits whenever the tipper discloses confidential trading information for a noncorporate purpose. Accordingly, a gift to a friend, a family member, or anyone else would support the inference that the tipper exploited the trading value of inside information for personal purposes and thus personally benefited from the disclosure. . . .

The Government observes that, in order to establish a defendant's criminal liability as a tippee, it must prove beyond a reasonable doubt that the tipper expected that the information being disclosed would be used in securities trading. . . . The Government also notes that, to establish a defendant's criminal liability as a tippee, it must prove that the tippee knew that the tipper breached a duty--in other words, that the tippee knew that the tipper disclosed the information for a personal benefit and that the tipper expected trading to ensue.

[...]

In Dirks, we explained that a tippee is exposed to liability for trading on inside information only if the tippee participates in a breach of the tipper's fiduciary duty. Whether the tipper breached that duty depends "in large part on the purpose of the disclosure" to the tippee. . . . [The test] "is whether the insider personally will benefit, directly or indirectly, from his disclosure." Thus, the disclosure of confidential information without personal benefit is not enough. . . . This personal benefit can "often" be inferred "from objective facts and circumstances," we explained, such as "a relationship between the insider and the recipient that suggests a quid pro quo from the latter, or an intention to benefit the particular recipient." In particular, we held that "[t]he elements of fiduciary duty and exploitation of nonpublic information also exist when an insider makes a gift of confidential information to a trading relative or friend." [...]

Maher, the tipper, provided inside information to a close relative, his brother Michael. Dirks makes clear that a tipper breaches a fiduciary duty by making a gift of confidential information to "a trading relative," and that rule is sufficient to resolve the case at hand. As Salman's counsel acknowledged at oral argument, Maher would have breached his duty had he personally traded on the information here himself then given the proceeds as a gift to his brother. It is obvious that Maher would personally benefit in that situation. But Maher effectively achieved the same result by disclosing the information to Michael, and allowing him to trade on it. Dirks appropriately prohibits that approach . . . [that decision] specifies that when a tipper gives inside information to "a trading relative or friend," the jury can infer that the tipper meant to provide the equivalent of a cash gift. In such situations, the tipper benefits personally because giving a gift of trading information is the same thing as trading by the tipper followed by a gift of the proceeds. Here, by disclosing confidential information as a gift to his brother with the expectation that he would trade on it, Maher breached his duty of trust and confidence to Citigroup and its clients--a duty Salman acquired, and breached himself, by trading on the information with full knowledge that it had been improperly disclosed.

[...]

Dirks created a simple and clear "guiding principle" for determining tippee liability[.] . . . At most, Salman shows that in some factual circumstances assessing liability for gift-giving will be difficult. That alone cannot render "shapeless" a federal criminal prohibition[.] . . . Salman's jury was properly instructed that a personal benefit includes "the benefit one would obtain from simply making a gift of confidential information to a trading relative." [Conviction affirdmed.]

[Citations omitted.]

QUESTIONS FOR DISCUSSION:

How do you think insider trading is detected, especially where, as here, the trader is receiving information through an intermediary?

What do you think about insider trading? Is it as bad a crime as embezzlement? Should it be enforced as strictly?

investors to learn something important about their investments will be able to take advantage of it by buying or selling their stock before that information has a chance to make an impact on the market. By contrast, diligent investors who monitor news carefully and act quickly have an advantage, but it is a fair advantage. Any investor could take the same action if she took the time and effort.

There are, however, investors who will learn important news before it is made available to the public. These are insiders. They become aware of important information because of their positions within a company, performing work on behalf of the company, or information they obtained from someone within the company. Insiders include corporate officers, employees, directors, and outside professionals who have access to confidential information, government employees who have access to sensitive information, or people who receive this information from other insiders.

Insiders are allowed to buy and sell stock in their corporation, the same as any investor. Trades by insiders must be disclosed. Insider trading is criminal only when the insider makes a trade on information not available to the public.

The Securities and Exchange Commission (SEC), the federal agency responsible for regulating securities markets, takes the position that insider trading is not unlawful if a person is not aware of the non-public information. Insider trading is also not unlawful if the non-public information was not a factor in the decision to trade in the stock. Examples of trades where non-public information include trades made pursuant to a pre-existing plan or an agreement to trade that was made in good faith regardless of the non-public information.

VI. Corporate Criminal Liability

For many purposes, corporations are regarded as "persons." One aspect of that personhood is that a corporation may be convicted of a crime. Corporate criminal liability is based on the action or inaction of a company's directors, officers, employees, or agents that perform work on behalf of the company.

> As a general rule, an employee or agent is not subject to personal criminal liability for work undertaken for a business. Instead, the corporation is held liable. Higher-level officials may be held personally liable in some cases.

Example: Charon Motors' vice president in charge of manufacturing calculates that if the company reduces the quality of the material used to filter exhaust fumes by 20 percent, the cars will still pass initial government emissions tests. However, the exhaust filtration's effectiveness will deteriorate below environmental standards after three years on the road. At that point, it will not properly filter exhaust fumes. The vice president orders the change to save the company money. Charon Motors is criminally responsible for this officer's actions, because the decision to use the less effective filters was within the scope of the vice president's authority, and the decision benefitted the company.

A CORPORATION CAN BE CRIMINALLY LIABLE FOR THE ACTS OF ITS EMPLOYEES.

New York Central & Hudson River Railroad Co. v. United States
(Railroad Company) v. (Federal Government)
212 U.S. 481 (1909)

INSTANT FACTS:
An employee of a railroad company made a deal with a sugar refining company to pay the sugar company rebates in return for use of the railroad company lines, in violation of a federal statute.

BLACK LETTER RULE:
A corporation can be criminally liable for the acts of its employees.

PROCEDURAL BASIS:
Appeal of a federal circuit court decision finding the railroad company guilty of violating a federal statute against rebates.

FACTS:
An employee of the New York Central and Hudson River Railroad Company ("railroad company") (D) made a deal to pay rebates to the American Sugar Refining Company if they used the railroad company's (D) lines to ship its sugar. Under this [sweet deal], the railroad company (D) would ship the sugar between New York and Detroit at a rate of $0.18 per 100 lbs. instead of the published rate of $0.23—$0.21 per 100 lbs. Such rebates were illegal under federal law. The railroad company (D) and its assistant traffic manager were convicted under the statute for the payment of rebates to the sugar company and others. The railroad company (D) appealed the conviction arguing that the statute was unconstitutional because a corporation cannot be held criminally liable for the actions of its employees.

ISSUE:
Can a corporation be held criminally liable for the acts of its employees?

DECISION AND RATIONALE:
(Day, J.) Yes. The railroad company (D) argues that it is unconstitutional to hold a corporation liable to criminal prosecution because any punishment imposed would actually punish innocent stockholders and deprive them of their property in violation of due process. While earlier common law held that corporations were excluded from criminal liability, the modern rule accepts the capacity of corporations to commit crime.

It is an established rule that a corporation can be held responsible in tort for the damages caused by acts of one of its agents acting in the scope of his employment. Since a corporation acts by its officers and agents, their individual "purposes, motives, and intent" are part of the corporation. If a corporation can engage in conduct, it can intend to do such conduct. The officer or agent is acting to benefit the principal, which is, in this case, a corporation. If the conduct is criminal, the corporation must be held accountable for the acts.

The payment of rebates by its agents and officers benefited the corporation, and if only the agents and officers may be held liable, the statute against rebates could not be effectively enforced. There is "no valid objection in law, and every reason in public policy" why a corporation cannot be held liable for the actions and intent of its agents to whom the corporation has vested its authority in and whose actions and purposes are otherwise attributable to the corporation for whom they work. In modem times, a great majority of business transactions are conducted through corporations. To afford corporations immunity from all criminal punishment "would virtually take away the only means of effectually controlling the subject matter and correcting the abuses aimed at." Judgment affirmed.

ANALYSIS:
The underlying theory for imposing liability on a corporation is analogous to the doctrine of respondeat superior. Under respondeat superior, an employer can be held liable for torts committed by an employee during the scope of employment. Courts hold the employer or the corporation liable because they assume that the agent, when acting in the scope of her employment, is committing the

wrongdoing for the benefit of the employer or corporation. Thus, it seems logical to hold the superior actor liable for the actions of subordinates to whom the superior delegates authority.

Of course, a corporation cannot be held liable for crimes that cannot be committed by corporations in a practical sense. For example, an employee of the corporation may burglarize a competitor's home, but the act of breaking and entering can only be committed by an individual, not the corporation.

CASE VOCABULARY:
AMENDATORY:
Supplemental, additional.

WRIT OF ERROR:
An order by an appellate court directing the trial court to produce the record of the case it is reviewing.

QUESTIONS FOR DISCUSSION:
Does this outcome seem reasonable to you? Why or why not?

The railroad's shareholders were likely to be "punished" as the railroad argued. What role do the shareholders have in guiding corporate behavior? Is the railroad's argument any good?

Federal law under the corporate criminal liability doctrine permits a corporation to be criminally liable for crimes, if the crime was:

- Committed by the corporation's directors, officers, employees, or agents,

- Taken within the scope of authority of their employment,

- Done at least in part for the benefit of the corporation, and

- The act was imputed (attributed) to the corporation.

An activity falls within a person's scope of authority if that person takes the action on the corporation's behalf, and in performance of her general line of work. If this standard is met, the corporation will be liable even though it explicitly told the person not to commit the offense. A failure to take action to stop criminal activity may be considered as authorizing the crime. A corporation may have a formal policy against criminal activity, but the failure to enforce that policy may show that the criminal activity was authorized or tolerated.

Example: The Apophis Corporation operates a warehouse in a state where the crime of homicide includes negligently causing the death of another person. State law does not exclude a corporation from the definition of person. Max, the manager of the warehouse, decides he can increase the capacity of the warehouse, and thus increase revenue for Apophis, by moving temporary shelving units in front of an emergency exit. The next day, a fire breaks out, and three employees die because they are not able to reach an exit. Both Max and Apophis could be guilty of criminal homicide.

> *Example:* Curtis is the president of Curtis Fine Art Galleries, Inc. He hires Wolfgang, an accomplished but little-known painter, to make copies of paintings. An employee, Gladys, is put in charge of selling the paintings. She puts offers to sell them on the gallery's website, claiming that they are original paintings by named famous painters. Wolfgang has a brochure printed that repeats the claim made by Gladys, and sends a brochure through the U.S. mail. Curtis Fine Art Galleries could be guilty of wire fraud and mail fraud.

Many state criminal laws limit corporate criminal liability to misconduct by upper-level management officials (senior management such as directors and officers). The reasoning behind this limitation is that the intent of lower-level employees who commit the acts that constitute an offense may not properly be considered to be the intent of the corporation. The corporation will not be liable unless conduct was authorized by an officer or director. The motive to benefit the corporation must still be present. Additionally, under the responsible corporate officer doctrine, a court may assess criminal liability on a corporate executive or officer who did not engage in, direct, or know about a specific criminal violation. This liability is found when the corporate executive or officer is responsible for ensuring the company's compliance with the law, but fails to do so.

Both a corporation and the individuals who performed the criminal acts may be convicted of the same crime. If the individuals are acquitted, however, or never charged, the corporation may still be found guilty.

Specific Crimes

A corporation may be found guilty of almost any crime. While corporate crime is often thought of as encompassing only financial crimes, crimes of violence against a person may also be committed by a corporation. Criminal statutes refer to acts done by a "person," and the statutes are generally written so that "person" can include a corporation. As long as the test for determining whether a criminal act was done to benefit the corporation is met, the corporation may be held criminally liable.

A corporation may be criminally liable as long as all of the elements of the crime are committed by its directors, officers, agents, or employees. All of the actions constituting the crime do not have to be done by the same person.

Sentencing

Conviction of a crime leads to punishment. A corporation cannot be put in jail (although directors, officers, employees, and agents who committed the crime can be imprisoned). The range of punishments that may be given are different from those that would apply to a human being. The sentence against the company may include fines, restitution, probation, confiscation of property, or involuntary dissolution of the organization.

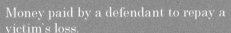

RESTITUTION:
Money paid by a defendant to repay a victim's loss.

Fines: Criminal statutes that provide for a monetary fine as punishment will set a maximum amount of that fine. The judge sentencing the corporation may be given a great deal of discretion in determining the exact amount of the fine. The Federal Sentencing Guidelines set general standards for corporate criminal fines, and the fine to be imposed is based on the severity of the offense. The money is paid to the government entity bringing the charges against the corporation.

The Federal Guidelines begin with the premise that a totally corrupt corporation should be fined out of existence, if possible. A corporation operated for criminal purposes should be fined so much that it is stripped of all of its assets. On the other hand, a judge is not required to impose a fine, if a fine would make it impossible to give full restitution to the victims of the crime.

Restitution: Monetary restitution (compensation) is ordered to pay the victims of a crime for the losses they have sustained. Unlike a fine, restitution is to go directly to the victims, rather than to the government. When it is imposed, restitution may be in addition to any fine or other penalty.

Probation: Probation may be imposed instead of, or in addition to, a fine or other penalty. Probation is designed to ensure that the corporation complies with all court orders and conditions of the sentence. Some of these conditions may include instituting a corporate compliance program, publicizing the conviction, undergoing regular audits, or engaging in community service. A term of probation may also include a prohibition against conducting certain types of business, or against contracting with the government.

Involuntary Dissolution: Involuntary dissolution can force a company to close its doors, and take away the company's ability operate. Companies are established at the state level. Dissolution occurs when the state Secretary of State believes sufficient reason exists to terminate a company's business operations. If the Secretary of State believes that a company's directors have abused their power, the state can force the company to close.

Example: TravelsOn Airways uses one of its aircraft to smuggle drugs into the U.S. The company is convicted of conspiracy and smuggling, and ordered to pay a fine. TravelsOn is also ordered to forfeit its airplane, and to forfeit all of the profits earned from smuggling drugs into the U.S.

CHAPTER SUMMARY

As an old radio program said, "The weed of crime bears bitter fruit." Criminal law is the government's way of protecting us from others. This protection takes the form of a threat of punishment when a crime is committed if the responsible party is apprehended.

Criminal law is not just about violent crime, or even about crimes committed by individuals. More and more, criminal law is about misconduct by businesses. A corporation that commits a crime is subject to punishment, even though that punishment may not take the same form as the punishment given to an individual.

The power to protect is not absolute. Constitutional limitations restrict what the government may do when investigating or punishing criminal activity. Criminal law thus protects us not just from criminals, but from those who would go too far in pursuing them.

Review Questions

Review question 1.

What is *mens rea*? What are the two types of intent and how do they differ? What types of crimes are related to each type of intent? Under what circumstances is intent irrelevant to criminal responsibility?

Review question 2.

How does *mens rea* differ from *actus reus*? How are both important to establishing criminal liability?

Review question 3.

What is an inchoate crime? Is there a difference between an inchoate crime and an attempted crime? What is necessary for a conspiracy to become a crime?

Review question 4.

Which constitutional amendment protects against cruel and unusual punishment? What is a grossly disproportionate penalty for a crime? What is the goal of sentencing guidelines? Why do judges have discretion in determining sentences for those convicted of crimes?

Review question 5.

What motivation is typical in corporate crimes? Do criminal sentences for corporations provide a complete remedy? Why is white collar crime so pervasive?

Review question 6.

When can a corporation be held criminally responsible? If only one person is responsible for a company's criminal act, did that person also act criminally? How does the legal system punish criminal wrongdoing by a corporation?

Review question 7.

What is embezzlement? How does it differ from other types of theft? Is it still embezzlement if the person taking the funds just "borrows" the money with the intent to replace it?

Review question 8.

When is insider trading unlawful? Who is an "insider"? When may an insider act despite having special knowledge about a company or transaction? Why does the law bar insider trading? At what point is information no longer considered "inside"?

Questions for Discussion

Discussion question 1.

Betty works as a bookkeeper for a corporation. One day, she tells her boss, Carlos, that she is short of money. Carlos says, "Just do what I used to do. Every now and then, cut yourself a company check. No one will care, as long as you don't make the checks too big." Betty starts writing herself a check for $25 each week.

Is Betty guilty of embezzlement? Why or why not?

Is there a conspiracy between Betty and Carlos? Why or why not?

Suppose Betty makes out the first check, but takes it home with her overnight because her bank is not open. Is Betty guilty of an attempted crime? Why or why not?

What if Betty takes home the first check, then has second thoughts and tears it up?

Discussion question 2.

Sheriff Omar believes that Edgar is using or trafficking in marijuana, but has been unable to find any proof, beyond smelling marijuana smoke whenever Edgar is nearby. Omar asks two of Edgar's neighbors if they know anything about his marijuana use. The neighbors say that they have seen marijuana plants growing in Edgar's basement, and that they bought marijuana from him. In reality, neither neighbor has ever been in Edgar's house, and they are just trying to get even with him for a property dispute. Omar puts the information from the neighbors in a search warrant application that he presents to Leigh, the county judge. Leigh approves the warrant. Omar then orders a team of his deputies to execute the warrant. The deputies go to Edgar's house and search it. They find a small amount of marijuana. One of the deputies sees two handguns on a coffee table. The deputy seizes those guns, and later learns that they were stolen from a gun shop.

> Is the search warrant valid? Why or why not?

> Will the exclusionary rule prevent using the marijuana as evidence at trial? Why or why not?

> Will the exclusionary rule prevent using the handguns as evidence at trial? Why or why not?

Discussion question 3.

Gil is a paralegal working for a publicly-traded corporation, and his girlfriend, Bertha, is a computer technician for the same company. Gil learns that the corporation they work for could be a target of a takeover attempt by a hedge fund. He and Bertha discuss the matter, and come to the conclusion that the value of the stock in their employer would increase dramatically if a takeover bid were made. They decide to buy stock in the company. In order to stay anonymous, Gil enlists his roommate Pete to make the purchases with money supplied by Gil and Bertha. Gil and Bertha do not tell him why they are buying the stock now. Pete puts the money in his bank account, planning to open an online brokerage account to make the purchase. After making the deposit, but before opening the account, Pete suffers a heart attack while sitting at his desk. He is taken to the hospital and does not make the purchases.

> Were Gil and Bertha insiders? Why or why not?

Was Pete an insider? Why or why not?

Was there a conspiracy? Why or why not? If this took place in a jurisdiction that requires an overt act for a conspiracy, identify the overt act.

Assume Gil and Bertha are insiders. Are they guilty of attempted insider trading? Why or why not?

Discussion question 4.

David does the accounting for his employer, Avaricia, Inc. Sheila, the CEO of Avaricia, tells him that the company needs to get a loan, but the bank does not feel that Avaricia has enough revenue coming in to make the payments. Sheila asks David to prepare a series of false invoices and receipts to present to the bank. David agrees, and prepares the false documents. Sheila then puts them in the mail to the bank, and also sends copies via fax. The bank approves the loan.

Identify the crimes that may have been committed in this scenario. Explain why you believe those crimes could have been committed.

Could Avaricia be held criminally liable in this situation? Why or why not?

Discussion question 5.

Carla is browsing in a clothing store. The only other person there is Emma, a sales clerk. Emma has a large stack of clothes that she is putting on the rack. She decides she likes one of the blouses she is hanging up, and puts in under her arm to take it home. Emma sees Carla watching her, and says "I have it coming. They treat me like dirt here. In fact, I quit! Help yourself to whatever you like," and walks out of the store with the blouse. Carla takes a few seconds to process what happened. She picks up a blouse from the rack and runs out the door with it, but drops it on her way out of the building.

Is Emma guilty of embezzlement? Why or why not?

Is Carla guilty of an attempted crime? Is she guilty of attempted embezzlement? Why or why not?

Unbeknownst to Carla, the owner of the store was giving away all of the inventory because she was about to close the business down. Is Carla guilty of an attempted theft? Why or why not?

Discussion question 6.

Courts in many states, and the federal system, sentence those convicted of crime according to guidelines. These guidelines consider the defendant's criminal record and a predetermined severity level of the crime to determine the presumptive sentence. Any sentence other than the presumptive sentence must be justified by the court. The purpose behind mandatory sentencing guidelines is to eliminate disparities in sentencing caused by racial or socioeconomic bias. Opponents of mandatory sentencing say that judges are not allowed to consider all of the factors that may mitigate a person's sentence.

What is your opinion regarding mandatory criminal sentences?

APPENDICES

1. Constitution of the United States

CONSTITUTION OF THE UNITED STATES

Preamble

We the People of the United States, in Order to form a more perfect Union, establish Justice, insure domestic Tranquility, provide for the common defense, promote the general Welfare, and secure the Blessings of Liberty to ourselves and our Posterity, do ordain and establish this Constitution for the United States of America.

Article I

SECTION 1. All legislative Powers herein granted shall be vested in a Congress of the United States, which shall consist of a Senate and House of Representatives.

SECTION 2. The House of Representatives shall be composed of Members chosen every second Year by the People of the several States, and the Electors in each State shall have the Qualifications requisite for Electors of the most numerous Branch of the State Legislature.

No Person shall be a Representative who shall not have attained to the Age of twenty five Years, and been seven Years a Citizen of the United States, and who shall not, when elected, be an Inhabitant of that State in which he shall be chosen.

Representatives and direct Taxes shall be apportioned among the several States which may be included within this Union, according to their respective Numbers, which shall be determined by adding to the whole Number of free Persons, including those bound to Service for a Term of Years, and excluding Indians not taxed, three fifths of all other Persons. The actual Enumeration shall be made within three Years after the first Meeting of the Congress of the United States, and within every subsequent Term of ten Years, in such Manner as they shall by Law direct. The Number of Representatives shall not exceed one for every thirty Thousand, but each State shall have at Least one Representative; and until such enumeration shall be made, the State of New Hampshire shall be entitled to chuse three, Massachusetts eight, Rhode-Island and Providence Plantations one, Connecticut five, New-York six, New Jersey four, Pennsylvania eight, Delaware one, Maryland six, Virginia ten, North Carolina five, South Carolina five, and Georgia three.

When vacancies happen in the Representation from any State, the Executive Authority thereof shall issue Writs of Election to fill such Vacancies.

The House of Representatives shall chuse their Speaker and other Officers; and shall have the sole Power of Impeachment.

SECTION 3. The Senate of the United States shall be composed of two Senators from each State, chosen by the Legislature thereof, for six Years; and each Senator shall have one Vote.

Immediately after they shall be assembled in Consequence of the first Election, they shall be divided as equally as may be into three Classes. The Seats of the Senators of the first Class shall be vacated at the Expiration of the second Year, of the second Class at the Expiration of the fourth Year, and of the third Class at the Expiration of the sixth Year, so that one third may be chosen every second Year; and if Vacancies happen by Resignation, or otherwise, during the Recess of the Legislature of any State, the Executive thereof may make temporary Appointments until the next Meeting of the Legislature, which shall then fill such Vacancies.

No Person shall be a Senator who shall not have attained to the Age of thirty Years, and been nine Years a Citizen of the United States, and who shall not, when elected, be an Inhabitant of that State for which he shall be chosen.

The Vice President of the United States shall be President of the Senate, but shall have no Vote, unless they be equally divided.

The Senate shall chuse their other Officers, and also a President pro tempore, in the Absence of the Vice President, or when he shall exercise the Office of President of the United States.

The Senate shall have the sole Power to try all Impeachments. When sitting for that Purpose, they shall be on Oath or Affirmation. When the President of the United States is tried, the Chief Justice shall preside: And no Person shall be convicted without the Concurrence of two thirds of the Members present.

Judgment in Cases of Impeachment shall not extend further than to removal from Office, and disqualification to hold and enjoy any Office of honor, Trust or Profit under the United States: but the Party convicted shall nevertheless be liable and subject to Indictment, Trial, Judgment and Punishment, according to Law.

The Times, Places and Manner of holding Elections for Senators and Representatives, shall be prescribed in each State by the Legislature thereof; but the Congress may at any time by Law make or alter such Regulations, except as to the Places of chusing Senators.

The Congress shall assemble at least once in every Year, and such Meeting shall *be on the first Monday in December*, unless they shall by Law appoint a different Day.

SECTION 5. Each House shall be the Judge of the Elections, Returns and Qualifications of its own Members, and a Majority of each shall constitute a Quorum to do Business; but a smaller Number may adjourn from day to day, and may be authorized to compel the Attendance of absent Members, in such Manner, and under such Penalties as each House may provide.

Each House may determine the Rules of its Proceedings, punish its Members for disorderly Behaviour, and, with the Concurrence of two thirds, expel a Member.

Each House shall keep a Journal of its Proceedings, and from time to time publish the same, excepting such Parts as may in their Judgment require Secrecy; and the Yeas and Nays of the Members of either House on any question shall, at the Desire of one fifth of those Present, be entered on the Journal.

Neither House, during the Session of Congress, shall, without the Consent of the other, adjourn for more than three days, nor to any other Place than that in which the two Houses shall be sitting.

SECTION 6. The Senators and Representatives shall receive a Compensation for their Services, to be ascertained by Law, and paid out of the Treasury of the United States. They shall in all Cases, except Treason, Felony and Breach of the Peace, be privileged from Arrest during their Attendance at the Session of their respective Houses, and in going to and returning from the same; and for any Speech or Debate in either House, they shall not be questioned in any other Place.

No Senator or Representative shall, during the Time for which he was elected, be appointed to any civil Office under the Authority of the United States, which shall have been created, or the Emoluments whereof shall have been encreased during such time; and no Person holding any Office under the United States, shall be a Member of either House during his Continuance in Office.

SECTION 7. All Bills for raising Revenue shall originate in the House of Representatives; but the Senate may propose or concur with Amendments as on other Bills.

Every Bill which shall have passed the House of Representatives and the Senate, shall, before it become a Law, be presented to the President of the United States: If he approve he shall sign it, but if not he shall return it, with his Objections to that House in which it shall have originated, who shall enter the Objections at large on their Journal, and proceed to reconsider it. If after such Reconsideration two thirds of that House shall agree to pass the Bill, it shall be sent, together with the Objections, to the other House, by which it shall likewise be reconsidered, and if approved by two thirds of that House, it shall become a Law. But in all such Cases the Votes of both Houses shall be determined by Yeas and Nays, and the Names of the Persons voting for and against the Bill shall be entered on the Journal of each House respectively. If any Bill shall not be returned by the President within ten Days (Sundays excepted) after it shall have been presented to him, the Same shall be a Law, in like Manner as if he had signed it, unless the Congress by their Adjournment prevent its Return, in which Case it shall not be a Law.

Every Order, Resolution, or Vote to which the Concurrence of the Senate and House of Representatives may be necessary (except on a question of Adjournment) shall be presented to the President of the United States; and before the Same shall take Effect, shall be approved by him, or being disapproved by him, shall be repassed by two thirds of the Senate and House of Representatives, according to the Rules and Limitations prescribed in the Case of a Bill.

SECTION 8. The Congress shall have Power To lay and collect Taxes, Duties, Imposts and Excises, to pay the Debts and provide for the common Defence and general Welfare of the United States; but all Duties, Imposts and Excises shall be uniform throughout the United States;

To borrow Money on the credit of the United States;

To regulate Commerce with foreign Nations, and among the several States, and with the Indian Tribes;

To establish an uniform Rule of Naturalization, and uniform Laws on the subject of Bankruptcies throughout the United States;

To coin Money, regulate the Value thereof, and of foreign Coin, and fix the Standard of Weights and Measures;

To provide for the Punishment of counterfeiting the Securities and current Coin of the United States;

To establish Post Offices and post Roads;

To promote the Progress of Science and useful Arts, by securing for limited Times to Authors and Inventors the exclusive Right to their respective Writings and Discoveries;

To constitute Tribunals inferior to the supreme Court;

To define and punish Piracies and Felonies committed on the high Seas, and Offences against the Law of Nations;

To declare War, grant Letters of Marque and Reprisal, and make Rules concerning Captures on Land and Water;

To raise and support Armies, but no Appropriation of Money to that Use shall be for a longer Term than two Years;

To provide and maintain a Navy;

To make Rules for the Government and Regulation of the land and naval Forces;

To provide for calling forth the Militia to execute the Laws of the Union, suppress Insurrections and repel Invasions;

To provide for organizing, arming, and disciplining, the Militia, and for governing such Part of them as may be employed in the Service of the United States, reserving to the States respectively, the Appointment of the Officers, and the Authority of training the Militia according to the discipline prescribed by Congress;

To exercise exclusive Legislation in all Cases whatsoever, over such District (not exceeding ten Miles square) as may, by Cession of particular States, and the Acceptance of Congress, become the Seat of the Government of the United States, and to exercise like Authority over all Places purchased by the Consent of the Legislature of the State in which the Same shall be, for the Erection of Forts, Magazines, Arsenals, dock-Yards, and other needful Buildings;—And

To make all Laws which shall be necessary and proper for carrying into Execution the foregoing Powers, and all other Powers vested by this Constitution in the Government of the United States, or in any Department or Officer thereof.

SECTION 9. The Migration or Importation of such Persons as any of the States now existing shall think proper to admit, shall not be prohibited by the Congress prior to the Year one thousand eight hundred and eight, but a Tax or duty may be imposed on such Importation, not exceeding ten dollars for each Person.

The Privilege of the Writ of Habeas Corpus shall not be suspended, unless when in Cases of Rebellion or Invasion the public Safety may require it.

No Bill of Attainder or ex post facto Law shall be passed.

No Capitation, or other direct, Tax shall be laid, unless in Proportion to the Census or enumeration herein before directed to be taken.

No Tax or Duty shall be laid on Articles exported from any State.

No Preference shall be given by any Regulation of Commerce or Revenue to the Ports of one State over those of another; nor shall Vessels bound to, or from, one State, be obliged to enter, clear, or pay Duties in another.

No Money shall be drawn from the Treasury, but in Consequence of Appropriations made by Law; and a regular Statement and Account of the Receipts and Expenditures of all public Money shall be published from time to time.

No Title of Nobility shall be granted by the United States: And no Person holding any Office of Profit or Trust under them, shall, without the Consent of the Congress, accept of any present, Emolument, Office, or Title, of any kind whatever, from any King, Prince, or foreign State.

SECTION 10. No State shall enter into any Treaty, Alliance, or Confederation; grant Letters of Marque and Reprisal; coin Money; emit Bills of Credit; make any Thing but gold and silver Coin a Tender in Payment of Debts; pass any Bill of Attainder, ex post facto Law, or Law impairing the Obligation of Contracts, or grant any Title of Nobility.

No State shall, without the Consent of the Congress, lay any Imposts or Duties on Imports or Exports, except what may be absolutely necessary for executing its inspection Laws: and the net Produce of all Duties and Imposts, laid by any State on Imports or Exports, shall be for the Use of the Treasury of the United States; and all such Laws shall be subject to the Revision and Control of the Congress.

No State shall, without the Consent of Congress, lay any Duty of Tonnage, keep Troops, or Ships of War in time of Peace, enter into any Agreement or Compact with another State, or with a foreign Power, or engage in War, unless actually invaded, or in such imminent Danger as will not admit of delay.

Article II

SECTION 1. The executive Power shall be vested in a President of the United States of America. He shall hold his Office during the Term of four Years, and, together with the Vice President, chosen for the same Term, be elected, as follows:

Each State shall appoint, in such Manner as the Legislature thereof may direct, a Number of Electors, equal to the whole Number of Senators and Representatives to which the State may be entitled in the Congress: but no Senator or Representative, or Person holding an Office of Trust or Profit under the United States, shall be appointed an Elector.

The Electors shall meet in their respective States, and vote by Ballot for two Persons, of whom one at least shall not be an Inhabitant of the same State with themselves. And they shall make a List of all the Persons voted for, and of the Number of Votes for each; which List they shall sign and certify, and transmit sealed to the Seat of the Government of the United States, directed to the President of the Senate. The President of the Senate shall, in the Presence of the Senate and House of Representatives, open all the Certificates, and the Votes shall then be counted. The Person having the greatest Number of Votes shall be the President, if such Number be a Majority of the whole Number of Electors appointed; and if there be more than one who have such Majority, and have an equal Number of Votes, then the House of Representatives shall immediately chuse by Ballot one of them for President; and if no Person have a Majority, then from the five highest on the List the said House shall in like Manner chuse the President. But in chusing the President, the Votes shall be taken by States, the Representatives from each State having one Vote; a quorum for this Purpose shall consist of a Member or Members from two thirds of the States, and a Majority of all the States shall be necessary to a Choice. In every Case, after the Choice of the President, the Person having the greatest Number of Votes of the Electors shall be the Vice President. But if there should remain two or more who have equal Votes, the Senate shall chuse from them by Ballot the Vice-President.

The Congress may determine the Time of chusing the Electors, and the Day on which they shall give their Votes; which Day shall be the same throughout the United States.

No Person except a natural born Citizen, or a Citizen of the United States, at the time of the Adoption of this Constitution, shall be eligible to the Office of President; neither shall any person be eligible to that Office who shall not have attained to the Age of thirty five Years, and been fourteen Years a Resident within the United States.

In Case of the Removal of the President from Office, or of his Death, Resignation, or Inability to discharge the Powers and Duties of the said Office, the Same shall devolve on the Vice President, and the Congress may by Law provide for the Case of Removal, Death, Resignation or Inability, both of the President and Vice President, declaring what Officer shall then act as President, and such Officer shall act accordingly, until the Disability be removed, or a President shall be elected.

The President shall, at stated Times, receive for his Services, a Compensation, which shall neither be encreased nor diminished during the Period for which he shall have been elected, and he shall not receive within that Period any other Emolument from the United States, or any of them.

Before he enter on the Execution of his Office, he shall take the following Oath or Affirmation:—"I do solemnly swear (or affirm) that I will faithfully execute the Office of President of the United States, and will to the best of my Ability, preserve, protect and defend the Constitution of the United States."

SECTION 2. The President shall be Commander in Chief of the Army and Navy of the United States, and of the Militia of the several States, when called into the actual Service of the United States; he may require the Opinion, in writing, of the principal Officer in each of the executive Departments, upon any Subject relating to the Duties of their respective Offices, and he shall have Power to Grant Reprieves and Pardons for Offences against the United States, except in Cases of Impeachment.

He shall have Power, by and with the Advice and Consent of the Senate, to make Treaties, provided two thirds of the Senators present concur; and he shall nominate, and by and with the Advice and Consent of the Senate, shall appoint Ambassadors, other public Ministers and Consuls, Judges of the supreme Court, and all other Officers of the United States, whose Appointments are not herein otherwise provided for, and which shall be established by Law: but the Congress may by Law vest the Appointment of such inferior Officers, as they think proper, in the President alone, in the Courts of Law, or in the Heads of Departments.

The President shall have Power to fill up all Vacancies that may happen during the Recess of the Senate, by granting Commissions which shall expire at the End of their next Session.

SECTION 3. He shall from time to time give to the Congress Information on the State of the Union, and recommend to their Consideration such Measures as he shall judge necessary and expedient; he may, on extraordinary Occasions, convene both Houses, or either of them, and in Case of Disagreement between them, with Respect to the Time of Adjournment, he may adjourn them to such Time as he shall think proper; he shall receive Ambassadors and other public Ministers; he shall take Care that the Laws be faithfully executed, and shall Commission all the Officers of the United States.

SECTION 4. The President, Vice President and all Civil Officers of the United States, shall be removed from Office on Impeachment for, and Conviction of, Treason, Bribery, or other high Crimes and Misdemeanors.

Article III

SECTION 1. The judicial Power of the United States, shall be vested in one supreme Court, and in such inferior Courts as the Congress may from time to time ordain and establish. The Judges, both of the supreme and inferior Courts, shall hold their Offices during good Behaviour, and shall, at stated Times, receive for their Services, a Compensation, which shall not be diminished during their Continuance in Office.

SECTION 2. The judicial Power shall extend to all Cases, in Law and Equity, arising under this Constitution, the Laws of the United States, and Treaties made, or which shall be made, under their Authority;—to all Cases affecting Ambassadors, other public ministers and Consuls;—to all Cases of admiralty and maritime Jurisdiction;—to Controversies to which the United States shall be a Party;—to Controversies between two or more States;—between a State and Citizens of another State;—between Citizens of different States;—between Citizens of the same State claiming Lands under Grants of different States, and between a State, or the Citizens thereof, and foreign States, Citizens or Subjects.

In all Cases affecting Ambassadors, other public Ministers and Consuls, and those in which a State shall be Party, the supreme Court shall have original Jurisdiction. In all the other Cases before mentioned, the supreme Court shall have appellate Jurisdiction, both as to Law and Fact, with such Exceptions, and under such Regulations as the Congress shall make.

The Trial of all Crimes, except in Cases of Impeachment, shall be by Jury; and such Trial shall be held in the State where the said Crimes shall have been committed; but when not committed within any State, the Trial shall be at such Place or Places as the Congress may by Law have directed.

SECTION 3. Treason against the United States, shall consist only in levying War against them, or in adhering to their Enemies, giving them Aid and Comfort. No Person shall be convicted of Treason unless on the Testimony of two Witnesses to the same overt Act, or on Confession in open Court.

The Congress shall have Power to declare the Punishment of Treason, but no Attainder of Treason shall work Corruption of Blood, or Forfeiture except during the Life of the Person attainted.

Article IV

SECTION 1. Full Faith and Credit shall be given in each State to the public Acts, Records, and judicial Proceedings of every other State. And the Congress may by general Laws prescribe the Manner in which such Acts, Records and Proceedings shall be proved, and the Effect thereof.

SECTION 2. The Citizens of each State shall be entitled to all Privileges and Immunities of Citizens in the several States.

A Person charged in any State with Treason, Felony, or other Crime, who shall flee from Justice, and be found in another State, shall on Demand of the executive Authority of the State from which he fled, be delivered up, to be removed to the State having Jurisdiction of the Crime.

No Person held to Service or Labour in one State, under the Laws thereof, escaping into another, shall, in Consequence of any Law or Regulation therein, be discharged from such Service or Labour, but shall be delivered up on Claim of the Party to whom such Service or Labour may be due.

SECTION 3. New States may be admitted by the Congress into this Union; but no new State shall be formed or erected within the Jurisdiction of any other State; nor any State be formed by the Junction of two or more States, or Parts of States, without the Consent of the Legislatures of the States concerned as well as of the Congress.

The Congress shall have Power to dispose of and make all needful Rules and Regulations respecting the Territory or other Property belonging to the United States; and nothing in this Constitution shall be so construed as to Prejudice any Claims of the United States, or of any particular State.

SECTION 4. The United States shall guarantee to every State in this Union a Republican Form of Government, and shall protect each of them against Invasion; and on Application of the Legislature, or of the Executive (when the Legislature cannot be convened) against domestic Violence.

Article V

The Congress, whenever two thirds of both Houses shall deem it necessary, shall propose Amendments to this Constitution, or, on the Application of the Legislatures of two thirds of the several States, shall call a Convention for proposing Amendments, which, in either Case, shall be valid to all Intents and Purposes, as Part of this Constitution, when ratified by the Legislatures of three fourths of the several States, or by Conventions in three fourths thereof, as the one or the other Mode of Ratification may be proposed by the Congress; Provided that no Amendment which may be made prior to the Year One thousand eight hundred and eight shall in any Manner affect the first and fourth Clauses in the Ninth Section of the first Article; and that no State, without its Consent, shall be deprived of its equal Suffrage in the Senate.

Article VI

All Debts contracted and Engagements entered into, before the Adoption of this Constitution, shall be as valid against the United States under this Constitution, as under the Confederation.

This Constitution, and the Laws of the United States which shall be made in Pursuance thereof; and all Treaties made, or which shall be made, under the Authority of the United States, shall be the supreme Law of the Land; and the Judges in every State shall be bound thereby, any Thing in the Constitution or Laws of any state to the Contrary notwithstanding.

The Senators and Representatives before mentioned, and the Members of the several State Legislatures, and all executive and judicial Officers, both of the United States and of the several States, shall be bound by Oath or Affirmation, to support this Constitution; but no religious Test shall ever be required as a Qualification to any Office or public Trust under the United States.

Article VII

The Ratification of the Conventions of nine States, shall be sufficient for the Establishment of this Constitution between the States so ratifying the Same.

2. Amendments to the Constitution

AMENDMENTS

Amendment I (1791)

Congress shall make no law respecting an establishment of religion, or prohibiting the free exercise thereof; or abridging the freedom of speech, or of the press; or the right of the people peaceably to assemble, and to petition the Government for a redress of grievances.

Amendment II (1791)

A well regulated Militia, being necessary to the security of a free State, the right of the people to keep and bear Arms, shall not be infringed.

Amendment III (1791)

No Soldier shall, in time of peace be quartered in any house, without the consent of the Owner, nor in time of war, but in a manner to be prescribed by law.

Amendment IV (1791)

The right of the people to be secure in their persons, houses, papers, and effects, against unreasonable searches and seizures, shall not be violated, and no Warrants shall issue, but upon probable cause, supported by Oath or affirmation, and particularly describing the place to be searched, and the persons or things to be seized.

Amendment V (1791)

No person shall be held to answer for a capital, or otherwise infamous crime, unless on a presentment or indictment of a Grand Jury, except in cases arising in the land or naval forces, or in the Militia, when in actual service in time of War or public danger; nor shall any person be subject for the same offence to be twice put in jeopardy of life or limb; nor shall be compelled in any criminal case to be a witness against himself, nor be deprived of life, liberty, or property, without due process of law; nor shall private property be taken for public use, without just compensation.

Amendment VI (1791)

In all criminal prosecutions, the accused shall enjoy the right to a speedy and public trial, by an impartial jury of the State and district wherein the crime shall have been committed, which district shall have been previously ascertained by law, and to be informed of the nature and cause of the accusation; to be confronted with the witnesses against him; to have compulsory process for obtaining witnesses in his favor, and to have the Assistance of Counsel for his defence.

Amendment VII (1791)

In Suits at common law, where the value in controversy shall exceed twenty dollars, the right of trial by jury shall be preserved, and no fact tried by a jury, shall be otherwise re-examined in any Court of the United States, than according to the rules of the common law.

Amendment VIII (1791)

Excessive bail shall not be required, nor excessive fines imposed, nor cruel and unusual punishments inflicted.

Amendment IX (1791)

The enumeration in the Constitution, of certain rights, shall not be construed to deny or disparage others retained by the people.

Amendment X (1791)

The powers not delegated to the United States by the Constitution, nor prohibited by it to the States, are reserved to the States respectively, or to the people.

Amendment XI (1795/1798)

The Judicial power of the United States shall not be construed to extend to any suit in law or equity, commenced or prosecuted against one of the United States by Citizens of another State, or by Citizens or Subjects of any Foreign State.

Amendment XII (1804)

The Electors shall meet in their respective states and vote by ballot for President and Vice-President, one of whom, at least, shall not be an inhabitant of the same state with them-selves; they shall name in their ballots the person voted for as President, and in distinct ballots the person voted for as Vice-President, and they shall make distinct lists of all persons voted for as President, and of all persons voted for as Vice-President, and of the number of votes for each, which lists they shall sign and certify, and transmit sealed to the seat of the government of the United States, directed to the President of the Senate;—The President of the Senate shall, in the presence of the Senate and House of Representatives, open all the certificates and the votes shall then be counted;—The person having the greatest Number of votes for President, shall be the President, if such number be a majority of the whole number of Electors appointed; and if no person have such majority, then from the persons having the highest numbers not exceeding three on the list of those voted for as President, the House of Representatives shall choose immediately, by ballot, the President. But in choosing the President, the votes shall be taken by states, the representation from each state having one vote; a quorum for this purpose shall consist of a member or members from two-thirds of the states, and a majority of all the states shall be necessary to a choice. And if the House of Representatives shall not choose a President whenever the right of choice shall devolve upon them, before the fourth day of March next following, then the Vice-President shall act as President, as in the case of the death or other constitutional disability of the President—The person having the greatest number of votes as Vice-President, shall be the Vice-President, if such number be a majority of the whole number of Electors appointed, and if no person have a majority, then from the two highest numbers on the list, the Senate shall choose the Vice-President; a quorum for the purpose shall consist of two-thirds of the whole number of Senators, and a majority of the whole number shall be necessary to a choice. But no person constitutionally ineligible to the office of President shall be eligible to that of Vice-President of the United States.

Amendment XIII (1865)

Section 1. Neither slavery nor involuntary servitude, except as a punishment for crime whereof the party shall have been duly convicted, shall exist within the United States, or any place subject to their jurisdiction.

Section 2. Congress shall have power to enforce this article by appropriate legislation.

Amendment XIV (1868)

SECTION 1. All persons born or naturalized in the United States and subject to the jurisdiction thereof, are citizens of the United States and of the State wherein they reside. No State shall make or enforce any law which shall abridge the privileges or immunities of citizens of the United States; nor shall any State deprive any person of life, liberty, or property, without due process of law; nor deny to any person within its jurisdiction the equal protection of the laws.

SECTION 2. Representatives shall be apportioned among the several States according to their respective numbers, counting the whole number of persons in each State, excluding Indians not taxed. But when the right to vote at any election for the choice of electors for President and Vice President of the United States, Representatives in Congress, the Executive and Judicial officers of a State, or the members of the Legislature thereof, is denied to any of the male inhabitants of such State, being twenty-one years of age, and citizens of the United States, or in any way abridged, except for participation in rebellion, or other crime, the basis of representation therein shall be reduced in the proportion which the number of such male citizens shall bear to the whole number of male citizens twenty-one years of age in such State.

SECTION 3. No person shall be a Senator or Representative in Congress, or elector of President and Vice President, or hold any office, civil or military, under the United States, or under any State, who, having previously taken an oath, as a member of Congress, or as an officer of the United States, or as a member of any State legislature, or as an executive or judicial officer of any State, to support the Constitution of the United States, shall have engaged in insurrection or rebellion against the same, or given aid or comfort to the enemies thereof. But Congress may by a vote of two-thirds of each House, remove such disability.

SECTION 4. The validity of the public debt of the United States, authorized by law, including debts incurred for payment of pensions and bounties for services in suppressing insurrection or rebellion, shall not be questioned. But neither the United States nor any State shall assume or pay any debt or obligation incurred in aid of insurrection or rebellion against the United States, or any claim for the loss or emancipation of any slave; but all such debts, obligations and claims shall be held illegal and void.

SECTION 5. The Congress shall have power to enforce, by appropriate legislation, the provisions of this article.

Amendment XV (1870)

SECTION 1. The right of citizens of the United States to vote shall not be denied or abridged by the United States or by any State on account of race, color, or previous condition of servitude.

SECTION 2. The Congress shall have power to enforce this article by appropriate legislation.

Amendment XVI (1913)

The Congress shall have power to lay and collect taxes on incomes, from whatever source derived, without apportionment among the several States, and without regard to any census or enumeration.

Amendment XVII (1913)

The Senate of the United States shall be composed of two Senators from each State, elected by the people thereof, for six years; and each Senator shall have one vote. The electors in each State shall have the qualifications requisite for electors of the most numerous branch of the State legislatures.

When vacancies happen in the representation of any State in the Senate, the executive authority of such State shall issue writs of election to fill such vacancies: Provided, That the legislature of any State may empower the executive thereof to make temporary appointments until the people fill the vacancies by election as the legislature may direct.

This amendment shall not be so construed as to affect the election or term of any Senator chosen before it becomes valid as part of the Constitution.

Amendment XVIII (1919)

SECTION 1. After one year from the ratification of this article the manufacture, sale, or transportation of intoxicating liquors within, the importation thereof into, or the exportation thereof from the United States and all territory subject to the jurisdiction thereof for beverage purposes is hereby prohibited.

SECTION 2. The Congress and the several States shall have concurrent power to enforce this article by appropriate legislation.

SECTION 3. This article shall be inoperative unless it shall have been ratified as an amendment to the Constitution by the legislatures of the several States, as provided in the Constitution, within seven years from the date of the submission hereof to the States by the Congress.

Amendment XIX (1920)

The right of citizens of the United States to vote shall not be denied or abridged by the United States or by any State on account of sex.

Congress shall have power to enforce this article by appropriate legislation.

Amendment XX (1933)

SECTION 1. The terms of the President and Vice President shall end at noon on the 20th day of January, and the terms of Senators and Representatives at noon on the 3d day of January, of the years in which such terms would have ended if this article had not been ratified; and the terms of their successors shall then begin.

SECTION 2. The Congress shall assemble at least once in every year, and such meeting shall begin at noon on the 3d day of January, unless they shall by law appoint a different day.

SECTION 3. If, at the time fixed for the beginning of the term of the President, the President elect shall have died, the Vice President elect shall become President. If a President shall not have been chosen before the time fixed for the beginning of his term, or if the President elect shall have failed to qualify, then the Vice President elect shall act as President until a President shall have qualified; and the Congress may by law provide for the case wherein neither a President elect nor a Vice President elect shall have qualified, declaring who shall then act as President, or the manner in which one who is to act shall be selected, and such person shall act accordingly until a President or Vice President shall have qualified.

SECTION 4. The Congress may by law provide for the case of the death of any of the persons from whom the House of Representatives may choose a President whenever the right of choice shall have devolved upon them, and for the case of the death of any of the persons from whom the Senate may choose a Vice President when-ever the right of choice shall have devolved upon them.

SECTION 5. Sections 1 and 2 shall take effect on the 15th day of October following the ratification of this article.

SECTION 6. This article shall be inoperative unless it shall have been ratified as an amendment to the Constitution by the legislatures of three-fourths of the several States within seven years from the date of its submission.

Amendment XXI (1933)

SECTION 1. The eighteenth article of amendment to the Constitution of the United States is hereby repealed.

SECTION 2. The transportation or importation into any State, Territory, or possession of the United States for delivery or use therein of intoxicating liquors, in violation of the laws thereof, is hereby prohibited.

SECTION 3. This article shall be inoperative unless it shall have been ratified as an amendment to the Constitution by conventions in the several States, as provided in the Constitution, within seven years from the date of the submission hereof to the States by the Congress.

Amendment XXII (1951)

SECTION 1. No person shall be elected to the office of the President more than twice, and no person who has held the office of President, or acted as President, for more than two years of a term to which some other person was elected President shall be elected to the office of the

President more than once. But this Article shall not apply to any person holding the office of President, when this Article was proposed by the Congress, and shall not prevent any person who may be holding the office of President, or acting as President, during the term within which this Article becomes operative from holding the office of President or acting as President during the remainder of such term.

SECTION 2. This article shall be inoperative unless it shall have been ratified as an amendment to the Constitution by the legislatures of three-fourths of the several States within seven years from the date of its submission to the States by the Congress.

Amendment XXIII (1961)

SECTION 1. The District constituting the seat of Government of the United States shall appoint in such manner as the Congress may direct:

A number of electors of President and Vice President equal to the whole number of Senators and Representatives in Congress to which the District would be entitled if it were a State, but in no event more than the least populous State; they shall be in addition to those appointed by the States, but they shall be considered, for the purposes of the election of President and Vice President, to be electors appointed by a State; and they shall meet in the District and perform such duties as provided by the twelfth article of amendment.

SECTION 2. The Congress shall have power to enforce this article by appropriate legislation.

Amendment XXIV (1964)

SECTION 1. The right of citizens of the United States to vote in any primary or other election for President or Vice President for electors for President or Vice President, or for Senator or Representative in Congress, shall not be denied or abridged by the United States or any State by reason of failure to pay any poll tax or other tax.

SECTION 2. The Congress shall have power to enforce this article by appropriate legislation.

Amendment XXV (1967)

SECTION 1. In case of the removal of the President from office or of his death or resignation, the Vice President shall become President.

SECTION 2. Whenever there is a vacancy in the office of the Vice President, the President shall nominate a Vice President who shall take office upon confirmation by a majority vote of both Houses of Congress.

SECTION 3. Whenever the President transmits to the President pro tempore of the Senate and the Speaker of the House of Representatives his written declaration that he is unable to discharge the powers and duties of his office, and until he transmits to them a written declaration to the contrary, such powers and duties shall be discharged by the Vice President as Acting President.

SECTION 4. Whenever the Vice President and a majority of either the principal officers of the executive departments or of such other body as Congress may by law provide, transmit to the President pro tempore of the Senate and the Speaker of the House of Representatives their written declaration that the President is unable to discharge the powers and duties of his office, the Vice President shall immediately assume the powers and duties of the office as Acting President.

Thereafter, when the President transmits to the President pro tempore of the Senate and the Speaker of the House of Representatives his written declaration that no inability exists, he shall resume the powers and duties of his office unless the Vice President and a majority of either the principal officers of the executive department or of such other body as Congress may by law provide, transmit within four days to the President pro tempore of the Senate and the Speaker of the House of Representatives their written declaration that the President is unable to discharge the powers and duties of his office. Thereupon Congress shall decide the issue, assembling within forty-eight hours for that purpose if not in session. If the Congress, within twenty-one days after receipt of the latter written declaration, or, if Congress is not in session, within twenty-one days after Congress is required to assemble, determines by two-thirds vote of both Houses that the President is unable to discharge the powers and duties of his office, the Vice President shall continue to discharge the same as Acting President; otherwise, the President shall resume the powers and duties of his office.

Amendment XXVI (1971)

SECTION 1. The right of citizens of the United States, who are eighteen years of age or older, to vote shall not be denied or abridged by the United States or by any State on account of age.

SECTION 2. The Congress shall have power to enforce this article by appropriate legislation.

Amendment XXVII (1992)

No law varying the compensation for the services of the Senators and Representatives shall take effect, until an election of Representatives shall have intervened.

3. Uniform Commercial Code, Article 2

UNIFORM COMMERCIAL CODE, ARTICLE 2
UCC ARTICLE 2 (2016)

SALES

UNIFORM COMMERCIAL CODE

ARTICLE 2 (2016)   **§ 2–101**

PART 7. REMEDIES

———

PART 1

SHORT TITLE, GENERAL CONSTRUCTION AND SUBJECT MATTER

§ 2–101. Short Title.

This Article shall be known and may be cited as Uniform Commercial Code—Sales.

Official Comment

This Article is a complete revision and modernization of the Uniform Sales Act which was promulgated by the National Conference of Commissioners on Uniform State Laws in 1906 and has been adopted in 34 states and Alaska, the District of Columbia and Hawaii.

The coverage of the present Article is much more extensive than that of the old Sales Act and extends to the various bodies of case law which have been developed both outside of and under the latter.

The arrangement of the present Article is in terms of contract for sale and the various steps of its performance. The legal consequences are stated as following directly from the contract and action taken under it without resorting to the idea of when property or title passed or was to pass as being the determining factor. The purpose is to avoid making practical issues between practical men turn upon the location of an intangible something, the passing of which no man can prove by evidence and to substitute for such abstractions proof of words and actions of a tangible character.

§ 2–102.   Scope; Certain Security and Other Transactions Excluded From This Article.

Unless the context otherwise requires, this Article applies to transactions in goods; it does not apply to any transaction which although in the form of an unconditional contract to sell or present sale is intended to operate only as a security transaction nor does this Article impair or repeal any statute regulating sales to consumers, farmers or other specified classes of buyers.

Official Comment

Prior Uniform Statutory Provision: Section 75, Uniform Sales Act.

Changes: Section 75 has been rephrased.

Purposes of Changes and New Matter: To make it clear that:

The Article leaves substantially unaffected the law relating to purchase money security such as conditional sale or chattel mortgage though it regulates the general sales aspects of such transactions. "Security transaction" is used in the same sense as in the Article on Secured Transactions (Article 9).

Cross Reference:

Article 9.

Definitional Cross References:

"Contract". Section 1–201.
"Contract for sale". Section 2–106.
"Present sale". Section 2–106.
"Sale". Section 2–106.

§ 2–103.   Definitions and Index of Definitions.

(1)   In this Article unless the context otherwise requires

(a)   "Buyer" means a person who buys or contracts to buy goods.

(b)   [Reserved.] ["Good faith" in the case of a merchant means honesty in fact and the observance of reasonable commercial standards of fair dealing in the trade.]

(c)   "Receipt" of goods means taking physical possession of them.

(d)   "Seller" means a person who sells or contracts to sell goods.

(2)   Other definitions applying to this Article or to specified Parts thereof, and the sections in which they appear are:

"Acceptance". Section 2–606.
"Banker's credit". Section 2–325.
"Between merchants". Section 2–104.
"Cancellation". Section 2–106(4).
"Commercial unit". Section 2–105.
"Confirmed credit". Section 2–325.
"Conforming to contract". Section 2–106.
"Contract for sale". Section 2–106.
"Cover". Section 2–712.
"Entrusting". Section 2–403.
"Financing agency". Section 2–104.
"Future goods". Section 2–105.
"Goods". Section 2–105.
"Identification". Section 2–501.
"Installment contract". Section 2–612.
"Letter of Credit". Section 2–325.
"Lot". Section 2–105.
"Merchant". Section 2–104.

"Overseas". Section 2–323.
"Person in position of seller". Section 2–707.
"Present sale". Section 2–106.
"Sale". Section 2–106.
"Sale on approval". Section 2–326.
"Sale or return". Section 2–326.
"Termination". Section 2–106.

(3)   "Control" as provided in Section 7–106 and the following definitions in other Articles apply to this Article:

"Check". Section 3–104.
"Consignee". Section 7–102.
"Consignor". Section 7–102.
"Consumer goods". Section 9–102.
"Dishonor". Section 3–502.
"Draft". Section 3–104.

(4)   In addition Article 1 contains general definitions and principles of construction and interpretation applicable throughout this Article.

As amended in 1994, 1999, and 2003.

Official Comment

Prior Uniform Statutory Provision: Subsection (1): Section 76, Uniform Sales Act.

Changes:

The definitions of "buyer" and "seller" have been slightly rephrased, the reference in Section 76 of the prior Act to "any legal successor in interest of such person" being omitted. The definition of "receipt" is new.

Purposes of Changes and New Matter:

1.   The phrase "any legal successor in interest of such person" has been eliminated since Section 2–210 of this Article, which limits some types of delegation of performance on assignment of a sales contract, makes it clear that not every such successor can be safely included in the definition. In every ordinary case, however, such successors are as of course included.

2.   "Receipt" must be distinguished from delivery particularly in regard to the problems arising out of shipment of goods, whether or not the contract calls for making delivery by way of documents of title, since the seller may frequently fulfill his obligations to "deliver" even though the buyer may never "receive" the goods. Delivery with respect to documents of title is defined in Article 1 and requires transfer of physical delivery of a tangible document of title and transfer of control of an electronic document of title. Otherwise the many divergent incidents of delivery are handled incident by incident.

Cross References:

Point 1: See Section 2–210 and Comment thereon.
Point 2: Section 1–201.

Definitional Cross Reference:

"Person". Section 1–201.

As amended in 2003.

§ 2–104.   Definitions: "Merchant"; "Between Merchants"; "Financing Agency".

(1)   "Merchant" means a person who deals in goods of the kind or otherwise by his occupation holds himself out as having knowledge or skill peculiar to the practices or goods involved in the transaction or to whom such knowledge or skill may be attributed by his employment of an agent or broker or other intermediary who by his occupation holds himself out as having such knowledge or skill.

UNIFORM COMMERCIAL CODE

(2) "Financing agency" means a bank, finance company or other person who in the ordinary course of business makes advances against goods or documents of title or who by arrangement with either the seller or the buyer intervenes in ordinary course to make or collect payment due or claimed under the contract for sale, as by purchasing or paying the seller's draft or making advances against it or by merely taking it for collection whether or not documents of title accompany or are associated with the draft. "Financing agency" includes also a bank or other person who similarly intervenes between persons who are in the position of seller and buyer in respect to the goods (Section 2–707).

(3) "Between merchants" means in any transaction with respect to which both parties are chargeable with the knowledge or skill of merchants.

As amended in 2003.

Official Comment

Prior Uniform Statutory Provision: None. But see Sections 15(2), (5), 16(c), 45(2) and 71, Uniform Sales Act, and Sections 35 and 37, Uniform Bills of Lading Act for examples of the policy expressly provided for in this Article.

Purposes:

1. This Article assumes that transactions between professionals in a given field require special and clear rules which may not apply to a casual or inexperienced seller or buyer. It thus adopts a policy of expressly stating rules applicable "between merchants" and "as against a merchant", wherever they are needed instead of making them depend upon the circumstances of each case as in the statutes cited above. This section lays the foundation of this policy by defining those who are to be regarded as professionals or "merchants" and by stating when a transaction is deemed to be "between merchants".

2. The term "merchant" as defined here roots in the "law merchant" concept of a professional in business. The professional status under the definition may be based upon specialized knowledge as to the goods, specialized knowledge as to business practices, or specialized knowledge as to both and which kind of specialized knowledge may be sufficient to establish the merchant status is indicated by the nature of the provisions.

The special provisions as to merchants appear only in this Article and they are of three kinds. Sections 2–201(2), 2–205, 2–207 and 2–209 dealing with the statute of frauds, firm offers, confirmatory memoranda and modification rest on normal business practices which are or ought to be typical of and familiar to any person in business. For purposes of these sections almost every person in business would, therefore, be deemed to be a "merchant" under the language "who . . . by his occupation holds himself out as having knowledge or skill peculiar to the practices . . . involved in the transaction . . ." since the practices involved in the transaction are non-specialized business practices such as answering mail. In this type of provision, banks or even universities, for example, well may be "merchants." But even these sections only apply to a merchant in his mercantile capacity; a lawyer or bank president buying fishing tackle for his own use is not a merchant.

On the other hand, in Section 2–314 on the warranty of merchantability, such warranty is implied only "if the seller is a merchant with respect to goods of that kind." Obviously this qualification restricts the implied warranty to a much smaller group than everyone who is engaged in business and requires a professional status as to particular kinds of goods. The exception in Section 2–402(2) for retention of possession by a merchant-seller falls in the same class; as does Section 2–403(2) on entrusting of possession to a merchant "who deals in goods of that kind".

A third group of sections includes 2–103(1)(b), which provides that in the case of a merchant "good faith" includes observance of reasonable commercial standards of fair dealing in the trade; 2–327(1)(c), 2–603 and 2–605, dealing with responsibilities of merchant buyers to follow seller's instructions, etc.; 2–509 on risk of loss, and 2–609 on adequate assurance of performance. This group of sections applies to persons who are merchants under either the "practices" or the "goods" aspect of the definition of merchant.

3. The "or to whom such knowledge or skill may be attributed by his employment of an agent or broker . . ." clause of the definition of merchant means that even persons such as universities, for example, can come within the definition of merchant if they have regular purchasing departments or business personnel who are familiar with business practices and who are equipped to take any action required.

Cross References:

Point 1: See Sections 1–102 and 1–203.

Point 2: See Sections 2–314, 2–315 and 2–320 to 2–325, of this Article, and Article 9.

Definitional Cross References:

"Bank". Section 1–201.
"Buyer". Section 2–103.
"Contract for sale". Section 2–106.
"Document of title". Section 1–201.
"Draft". Section 3–104.
"Goods". Section 2–105.
"Person". Section 1–201.
"Purchase". Section 1–201.
"Seller". Section 2–103.

§ 2–105. Definitions: Transferability; "Goods"; "Future" Goods; "Lot"; "Commercial Unit".

(1) "Goods" means all things (including specially manufactured goods) which are movable at the time of identification to the contract for sale other than the money in which the price is to be paid, investment securities (Article 8) and things in action. "Goods" also includes the unborn young of animals and growing crops and other identified things attached to realty as described in the section on goods to be severed from realty (Section 2–107).

(2) Goods must be both existing and identified before any interest in them can pass. Goods which are not both existing and identified are "future" goods. A purported present sale of future goods or of any interest therein operates as a contract to sell.

(3) There may be a sale of a part interest in existing identified goods.

(4) An undivided share in an identified bulk of fungible goods is sufficiently identified to be sold although the quantity of the bulk is not determined. Any agreed proportion of such a bulk or any quantity thereof agreed upon by number, weight or other measure may to the extent of the seller's interest in the bulk be sold to the buyer who then becomes an owner in common.

(5) "Lot" means a parcel or a single article which is the subject matter of a separate sale or delivery, whether or not it is sufficient to perform the contract.

(6) "Commercial unit" means such a unit of goods as by commercial usage is a single whole for purposes of sale and division of which materially impairs its character or value on the market or in use. A commercial unit may be a single article (as a machine) or a set of articles (as a suite of furniture or an assortment of sizes) or a quantity (as a bale, gross, or carload) or any other unit treated in use or in the relevant market as a single whole.

Official Comment

Prior Uniform Statutory Provision: Subsections (1), (2), (3) and (4)—Sections 5, 6 and 76, Uniform Sales Act; Subsections (5) and (6)—none.

Changes: Rewritten.

Purposes of Changes and New Matter:

1. Subsection (1) on "goods": The phraseology of the prior uniform statutory provision has been changed so that:

The definition of goods is based on the concept of movability and the term "chattels personal" is not used. It is not intended to deal with things which are not fairly identifiable as movables before the contract is performed.

Growing crops are included within the definition of goods since they are frequently intended for sale. The concept of "industrial" growing crops has been abandoned, for under modern practices fruit, perennial hay, nursery stock and the like must be brought within the scope of this Article. The young of animals are also included expressly in this definition since they, too, are frequently intended for sale and may be contracted for before birth. The period of gestation of domestic animals is such that the provisions of the section on identification can apply as in the case of crops to be planted. The reason of this definition also leads to the inclusion of a wool crop or the like as "goods" subject to identification under this Article.

The exclusion of "money in which the price is to be paid" from the definition of goods does not mean that foreign currency which is included in the definition of money may not be the subject matter of a sales transaction. Goods is intended to cover the sale of money when money is being treated as a commodity but not to include it when money is the medium of payment.

As to contracts to sell timber, minerals, or structures to be removed from the land Section 2-107(1) (Goods to be severed from Realty: recording) controls.

The use of the word "fixtures" is avoided in view of the diversity of definitions of that term. This Article in including within its scope "things attached to realty" adds the further test that they must be capable of severance without material harm thereto. As between the parties any identified things which fall within that definition become "goods" upon the making of the contract for sale.

"Investment securities" are expressly excluded from the coverage of this Article. It is not intended by this exclusion, however, to prevent the application of a particular section of this Article by analogy to securities (as was done with the Original Sales Act in *Agar v. Orda*, 264 N.Y. 248, 190 N.E. 479, 99 A.L.R. 269 (1934)) when the reason of that section makes such application sensible and the situation involved is not covered by the Article of this Act dealing specifically with such securities (Article 8).

2.   References to the fact that a contract for sale can extend to future or contingent goods and that ownership in common follows the sale of a part interest have been omitted here as obvious without need for expression; hence no inference to negate these principles should be drawn from their omission.

3.   Subsection (4) does not touch the question of how far an appropriation of a bulk of fungible goods may or may not satisfy the contract for sale.

4.   Subsections (5) and (6) on "lot" and "commercial unit" are introduced to aid in the phrasing of later sections.

5.   The question of when an identification of goods takes place is determined by the provisions of Section 2-501 and all that this section says is what kinds of goods may be the subject of a sale.

Cross References:

Point 1: Sections 2-107, 2-201, 2-501 and Article 8.
Point 5: Section 2-501.
See also Section 1-201.

Definitional Cross References:

"Buyer". Section 2-103.
"Contract". Section 1-201.
"Contract for sale". Section 2-106.
"Fungible". Section 1-201.
"Money". Section 1-201.
"Present sale". Section 2-106.
"Sale". Section 2-106.
"Seller". Section 2-103.

§ 2-106.   Definitions: "Contract"; "Agreement"; "Contract for Sale"; "Sale"; "Present Sale"; "Conforming" to Contract; "Termination"; "Cancellation".

(1)   In this Article unless the context otherwise requires "contract" and "agreement" are limited to those relating to the present or future sale of goods. "Contract for sale" includes both a present sale of goods and a contract to sell goods at a future time. A "sale" consists in the passing of title from the seller to the buyer for a price (Section 2-401). A "present sale" means a sale which is accomplished by the making of the contract.

(2)   Goods or conduct including any part of a performance are "conforming" or conform to the contract when they are in accordance with the obligations under the contract.

(3)   "Termination" occurs when either party pursuant to a power created by agreement or law puts an end to the contract otherwise than for its breach. On "termination" all obligations which are still executory on both sides are discharged but any right based on prior breach or performance survives.

(4)   "Cancellation" occurs when either party puts an end to the contract for breach by the other and its effect is the same as that of "termination" except that the cancelling party also retains any remedy for breach of the whole contract or any unperformed balance.

Official Comment

Prior Uniform Statutory Provision: Subsection (1)—Section 1(1) and (2), Uniform Sales Act; Subsection (2)—none, but subsection generally continues policy of Sections 11, 44 and 69, Uniform Sales Act; Subsections (3) and (4)—none.

Changes: Completely rewritten.

Purposes of Changes and New Matter:

1.   Subsection (1): "Contract for sale" is used as a general concept throughout this Article, but the rights of the parties do not vary according to whether the transaction is a present sale or a contract to sell unless the Article expressly so provides.

2.   Subsection (2): It is in general intended to continue the policy of requiring exact performance by the seller of his obligations as a condition to his right to require acceptance. However, the seller is in part safeguarded against surprise as a result of sudden technicality on the buyer's part by the provisions of Section 2–508 on seller's cure of improper tender or delivery. Moreover usage of trade frequently permits commercial leeways in performance and the language of the agreement itself must be read in the light of such custom or usage and also, prior course of dealing, and in a long term contract, the course of performance.

3.   Subsections (3) and (4): These subsections are intended to make clear the distinction carried forward throughout this Article between termination and cancellation.

Cross References:

Point 2: Sections 1–203, 1–205, 2–208 and 2–508.

Definitional Cross References:

"Agreement". Section 1–201.
"Buyer". Section 2–103.
"Contract". Section 1–201.
"Goods". Section 2–105.
"Party". Section 1–201.
"Remedy". Section 1–201.
"Rights". Section 1–201.
"Seller". Section 2–103.

§ 2–107.   Goods to Be Severed From Realty: Recording.

(1)   A contract for the sale of minerals or the like (including oil and gas) or a structure or its materials to be removed from realty is a contract for the sale of goods within this Article if they are to be severed by the seller but until severance a purported present sale thereof which is not effective as a transfer of an interest in land is effective only as a contract to sell.

(2)   A contract for the sale apart from the land of growing crops or other things attached to realty and capable of severance without material harm thereto but not described in subsection (1) or of timber to be cut is a contract for the sale of goods within this Article whether the subject matter is to be severed by the buyer or by the seller even though it forms part of the realty at the time of contracting, and the parties can by identification effect a present sale before severance.

(3)   The provisions of this section are subject to any third party rights provided by the law relating to realty records, and the contract for sale may be executed and recorded as a document transferring an

interest in land and shall then constitute notice to third parties of the buyer's rights under the contract for sale.

As amended in 1972.

Official Comment

Prior Uniform Statutory Provision: See Section 76, Uniform Sales Act on prior policy; Section 7, Uniform Conditional Sales Act.

Purposes:

1.   Subsection (1). Notice that this subsection applies only if the minerals or structures "are to be severed by the seller". If the buyer is to sever, such transactions are considered contracts affecting land and all problems of the Statute of Frauds and of the recording of land rights apply to them. Therefore, the Statute of Frauds section of this Article does not apply to such contracts though they must conform to the Statute of Frauds affecting the transfer of interests in land.

2.   Subsection (2). "Things attached" to the realty which can be severed without material harm are goods within this Article regardless of who is to effect the severance. The word "fixtures" has been avoided because of the diverse definitions of this term, the test of "severance without material harm" being substituted.

The provision in subsection (3) for recording such contracts is within the purview of this Article since it is a means of preserving the buyer's rights under the contract of sale.

3.   The security phases of things attached to or to become attached to realty are dealt with in the Article on Secured Transactions (Article 9) and it is to be noted that the definition of goods in that Article differs from the definition of goods in this Article.

However, both Articles treat as goods growing crops and also timber to be cut under a contract of severance.

Cross References:

Point 1: Section 2–201.
Point 2: Section 2–105.
Point 3: Article 9 and Section 9–102(a)(44).

Definitional Cross References:

"Buyer". Section 2–103.
"Contract". Section 1–201.
"Contract for sale". Section 2–106.
"Goods". Section 2–105.
"Party". Section 1–201.
"Present sale". Section 2–106.
"Rights". Section 1–201.
"Seller". Section 2–103.

PART 2

FORM, FORMATION AND READJUSTMENT OF CONTRACT

§ 2–201.   Formal Requirements; Statute of Frauds.

(1)   Except as otherwise provided in this section a contract for the sale of goods for the price of $500 or more is not enforceable by way of action or defense unless there is some writing sufficient to indicate that a contract for sale has been made between the parties and signed by the party against whom enforcement is sought or by his authorized agent or broker. A writing is not insufficient because it omits or incorrectly states a term agreed upon but the contract is not enforceable under this paragraph beyond the quantity of goods shown in such writing.

(2)   Between merchants if within a reasonable time a writing in confirmation of the contract and sufficient against the sender is received and the party receiving it has reason to know its contents, it satisfies the requirements of subsection (1) against such party unless written notice of objection to its contents is given within 10 days after it is received.

(3)   A contract which does not satisfy the requirements of subsection (1) but which is valid in other respects is enforceable

(a)   if the goods are to be specially manufactured for the buyer and are not suitable for sale to others in the ordinary course of the seller's business and the seller, before notice of repudiation is received and under circumstances which reasonably indicate that the goods are for the buyer, has made either a substantial beginning of their manufacture or commitments for their procurement; or

(b)   if the party against whom enforcement is sought admits in his pleading, testimony or otherwise in court that a contract for sale was made, but the contract is not enforceable under this provision beyond the quantity of goods admitted; or

(c)   with respect to goods for which payment has been made and accepted or which have been received and accepted (Section 2–606).

Official Comment

Prior Uniform Statutory Provision: Section 4, Uniform Sales Act (which was based on Section 17 of the Statute of 29 Charles II).

Changes: Completely rephrased; restricted to sale of goods. See also Sections 1–206, 8–319 and 9–203.

Purposes of Changes: The changed phraseology of this section is intended to make it clear that:

1.   The required writing need not contain all the material terms of the contract and such material terms as are stated need not be precisely stated. All that is required is that the writing afford a basis for believing that the offered oral evidence rests on a real transaction. It may be written in lead pencil on a scratch pad. It need not indicate which party is the buyer and which the seller. The only term which must appear is the quantity term which need not be accurately stated but recovery is limited to the amount stated. The price, time and place of payment or delivery, the general quality of the goods, or any particular warranties may all be omitted.

Special emphasis must be placed on the permissibility of omitting the price term in view of the insistence of some courts on the express inclusion of this term even where the parties have contracted on the basis of a published price list. In many valid contracts for sale the parties do not mention the price in express terms, the buyer being bound to pay and the seller to accept a reasonable price which the trier of the fact may well be trusted to determine. Again, frequently the price is not mentioned since the parties have based their agreement on a price list or catalogue known to both of them and this list serves as an efficient safeguard against perjury. Finally, "market" prices and valuations that are current in the vicinity constitute a similar check. Thus if the price is not stated in the memorandum it can normally be supplied without danger of fraud. Of course if the "price" consists of goods rather than money the quantity of goods must be stated.

Only three definite and invariable requirements as to the memorandum are made by this subsection. First, it must evidence a contract for the sale of goods; second, it must be "signed", a word which includes any authentication which identifies the party to be charged; and third, it must specify a quantity.

2.   "Partial performance" as a substitute for the required memorandum can validate the contract only for the goods which have been accepted or for which payment has been made and accepted.

Receipt and acceptance either of goods or of the price constitutes an unambiguous overt admission by both parties that a contract actually exists. If the court can make a just apportionment, therefore, the agreed price of any goods actually delivered can be recovered without a writing or, if the price has been paid, the seller can be forced to deliver an apportionable part of the goods. The overt actions of the parties make admissible evidence of the other terms of the contract necessary to a just apportionment. This is true even though the actions of the parties are not in themselves inconsistent with a different transaction such as a consignment for resale or a mere loan of money.

§ 2–202　　　　　　UNIFORM COMMERCIAL CODE

Part performance by the buyer requires the delivery of something by him that is accepted by the seller as such performance. Thus, part payment may be made by money or check, accepted by the seller. If the agreed price consists of goods or services, then they must also have been delivered and accepted.

3.　Between merchants, failure to answer a written confirmation of a contract within ten days of receipt is tantamount to a writing under subsection (2) and is sufficient against both parties under subsection (1). The only effect, however, is to take away from the party who fails to answer the defense of the Statute of Frauds; the burden of persuading the trier of fact that a contract was in fact made orally prior to the written confirmation is unaffected. Compare the effect of a failure to reply under Section 2–207.

4.　Failure to satisfy the requirements of this section does not render the contract void for all purposes, but merely prevents it from being judicially enforced in favor of a party to the contract. For example, a buyer who takes possession of goods as provided in an oral contract which the seller has not meanwhile repudiated, is not a trespasser. Nor would the Statute of Frauds provisions of this section be a defense to a third person who wrongfully induces a party to refuse to perform an oral contract, even though the injured party cannot maintain an action for damages against the party so refusing to perform.

5.　The requirement of "signing" is discussed in the comment to Section 1–201.

6.　It is not necessary that the writing be delivered to anybody. It need not be signed or authenticated by both parties but it is, of course, not sufficient against one who has not signed it. Prior to a dispute no one can determine which party's signing of the memorandum may be necessary but from the time of contracting each party should be aware that to him it is signing by the other which is important.

7.　If the making of a contract is admitted in court, either in a written pleading, by stipulation or by oral statement before the court, no additional writing is necessary for protection against fraud. Under this section it is no longer possible to admit the contract in court and still treat the Statute as a defense. However, the contract is not thus conclusively established. The admission so made by a party is itself evidential against him of the truth of the facts so admitted and of nothing more; as against the other party, it is not evidential at all.

Cross References:

See Sections 1–201, 2–202, 2–207, 2–209 and 2–304.

Definitional Cross References:

"Action". Section 1–201.
"Between merchants". Section 2–104.
"Buyer". Section 2–103.
"Contract". Section 1–201.
"Contract for sale". Section 2–106.
"Goods". Section 2–105.
"Notice". Section 1–201.
"Party". Section 1–201.
"Reasonable time". Section 1–204.
"Sale". Section 2–106.
"Seller". Section 2–103.

§ 2–202.　　Final Written Expression: Parol or Extrinsic Evidence.

Terms with respect to which the confirmatory memoranda of the parties agree or which are otherwise set forth in a writing intended by the parties as a final expression of their agreement with respect to such terms as are included therein may not be contradicted by evidence of any prior agreement or of a contemporaneous oral agreement but may be explained or supplemented

(a)　by course of performance, course of dealing, or usage of trade (Section 1–303); and

(b)　by evidence of consistent additional terms unless the court finds the writing to have been intended also as a complete and exclusive statement of the terms of the agreement.

Official Comment

Prior Uniform Statutory Provisions: None.

ARTICLE 2 (2016)   § 2–203

Purposes:

    1.   This section definitely rejects:

    (a)   Any assumption that because a writing has been worked out which is final on some matters, it is to be taken as including all the matters agreed upon;

    (b)   The premise that the language used has the meaning attributable to such language by rules of construction existing in the law rather than the meaning which arises out of the commercial context in which it was used; and

    (c)   The requirement that a condition precedent to the admissibility of the type of evidence specified in paragraph (a) is an original determination by the court that the language used is ambiguous.

    2.   Paragraph (a) makes admissible evidence of course of dealing, usage of trade and course of performance to explain or supplement the terms of any writing stating the agreement of the parties in order that the true understanding of the parties as to the agreement may be reached. Such writings are to be read on the assumption that the course of prior dealings between the parties and the usages of trade were taken for granted when the document was phrased. Unless carefully negated they have become an element of the meaning of the words used. Similarly, the course of actual performance by the parties is considered the best indication of what they intended the writing to mean.

    3.   Under paragraph (b) consistent additional terms, not reduced to writing, may be proved unless the court finds that the writing was intended by both parties as a complete and exclusive statement of all the terms. If the additional terms are such that, if agreed upon, they would certainly have been included in the document in the view of the court, then evidence of their alleged making must be kept from the trier of fact.

Cross References:

    Point 3: Sections 1–303, 2–207, 2–302 and 2–316.

Definitional Cross References:

    "Agreed" and "agreement". Section 1–201.
    "Course of dealing". Section 1–303.
    "Course of performance". Section 1–303.
    "Party". Section 1–201.
    "Term". Section 1–201.
    "Usage of trade". Section 1–303.
    "Written" and "writing". Section 1–201.

§ 2–203.   Seals Inoperative.

    The affixing of a seal to a writing evidencing a contract for sale or an offer to buy or sell goods does not constitute the writing a sealed instrument and the law with respect to sealed instruments does not apply to such a contract or offer.

Official Comment

Prior Uniform Statutory Provision: Section 3, Uniform Sales Act.

Changes: Portion pertaining to "seals" rewritten.

Purposes of Changes:

    1.   This section makes it clear that every effect of the seal which relates to "sealed instruments" as such is wiped out insofar as contracts for sale are concerned. However, the substantial effects of a seal, except extension of the period of limitations, may be had by appropriate drafting as in the case of firm offers (see Section 2–205).

    2.   This section leaves untouched any aspects of a seal which relate merely to signatures or to authentication of execution and the like. Thus, a statute providing that a purported signature gives prima facie evidence of its own authenticity or that a signature gives prima facie evidence of consideration is still applicable to sales transactions even though a seal may be held to be a signature within the meaning of such a statute. Similarly, the authorized affixing of a corporate seal bearing the corporate name to a contractual writing

purporting to be made by the corporation may have effect as a signature without any reference to the law of sealed instruments.

Cross Reference:

> Point 1: Section 2–205.

Definitional Cross References:

> "Contract for sale". Section 2–106.
> "Goods". Section 2–105.
> "Writing". Section 1–201.

§ 2–204.   Formation in General.

(1)   A contract for sale of goods may be made in any manner sufficient to show agreement, including conduct by both parties which recognizes the existence of such a contract.

(2)   An agreement sufficient to constitute a contract for sale may be found even though the moment of its making is undetermined.

(3)   Even though one or more terms are left open a contract for sale does not fail for indefiniteness if the parties have intended to make a contract and there is a reasonably certain basis for giving an appropriate remedy.

Official Comment

Prior Uniform Statutory Provision: Sections 1 and 3, Uniform Sales Act.

Changes: Completely rewritten by this and other sections of this Article.

Purposes of Changes:

Subsection (1) continues without change the basic policy of recognizing any manner of expression of agreement, oral, written or otherwise. The legal effect of such an agreement is, of course, qualified by other provisions of this Article.

Under subsection (1) appropriate conduct by the parties may be sufficient to establish an agreement. Subsection (2) is directed primarily to the situation where the interchanged correspondence does not disclose the exact point at which the deal was closed, but the actions of the parties indicate that a binding obligation has been undertaken.

Subsection (3) states the principle as to "open terms" underlying later sections of the Article. If the parties intend to enter into a binding agreement, this subsection recognizes that agreement as valid in law, despite missing terms, if there is any reasonably certain basis for granting a remedy. The test is not certainty as to what the parties were to do nor as to the exact amount of damages due the plaintiff. Nor is the fact that one or more terms are left to be agreed upon enough of itself to defeat an otherwise adequate agreement. Rather, commercial standards on the point of "indefiniteness" are intended to be applied, this Act making provision elsewhere for missing terms needed for performance, open price, remedies and the like.

The more terms the parties leave open, the less likely it is that they have intended to conclude a binding agreement, but their actions may be frequently conclusive on the matter despite the omissions.

Cross References:

> Subsection (1): Sections 1–103, 2–201 and 2–302.
> Subsection (2): Sections 2–205 through 2–209.
> Subsection (3): See Part 3.

Definitional Cross References:

> "Agreement". Section 1–201.
> "Contract". Section 1–201.
> "Contract for sale". Section 2–106.
> "Goods". Section 2–105.

"Party". Section 1–201.
"Remedy". Section 1–201.
"Term". Section 1–201.

§ 2–205.   Firm Offers.

An offer by a merchant to buy or sell goods in a signed writing which by its terms gives assurance that it will be held open is not revocable, for lack of consideration, during the time stated or if no time is stated for a reasonable time, but in no event may such period of irrevocability exceed three months; but any such term of assurance on a form supplied by the offeree must be separately signed by the offeror.

Official Comment

Prior Uniform Statutory Provision: Sections 1 and 3, Uniform Sales Act.

Changes: Completely rewritten by this and other sections of this Article.

Purposes of Changes:

1.   This section is intended to modify the former rule which required that "firm offers" be sustained by consideration in order to bind, and to require instead that they must merely be characterized as such and expressed in signed writings.

2.   The primary purpose of this section is to give effect to the deliberate intention of a merchant to make a current firm offer binding. The deliberation is shown in the case of an individualized document by the merchant's signature to the offer, and in the case of an offer included on a form supplied by the other party to the transaction by the separate signing of the particular clause which contains the offer. "Signed" here also includes authentication but the reasonableness of the authentication herein allowed must be determined in the light of the purpose of the section. The circumstances surrounding the signing may justify something less than a formal signature or initialing but typically the kind of authentication involved here would consist of a minimum of initialing of the clause involved. A handwritten memorandum on the writer's letterhead purporting in its terms to "confirm" a firm offer already made would be enough to satisfy this section, although not subscribed, since under the circumstances it could not be considered a memorandum of mere negotiation and it would adequately show its own authenticity. Similarly, an authorized telegram will suffice, and this is true even though the original draft contained only a typewritten signature. However, despite settled courses of dealing or usages of the trade whereby firm offers are made by oral communication and relied upon without more evidence, such offers remain revocable under this Article since authentication by a writing is the essence of this section.

3.   This section is intended to apply to current "firm" offers and not to long term options, and an outside time limit of three months during which such offers remain irrevocable has been set. The three month period during which firm offers remain irrevocable under this section need not be stated by days or by date. If the offer states that it is "guaranteed" or "firm" until the happening of a contingency which will occur within the three month period, it will remain irrevocable until that event. A promise made for a longer period will operate under this section to bind the offeror only for the first three months of the period but may of course be renewed. If supported by consideration it may continue for as long as the parties specify. This section deals only with the offer which is not supported by consideration.

4.   Protection is afforded against the inadvertent signing of a firm offer when contained in a form prepared by the offeree by requiring that such a clause be separately authenticated. If the offer clause is called to the offeror's attention and he separately authenticates it, he will be bound; Section 2–302 may operate, however, to prevent an unconscionable result which otherwise would flow from other terms appearing in the form.

5.   Safeguards are provided to offer relief in the case of material mistake by virtue of the requirement of good faith and the general law of mistake.

Cross References:

Point 1: Section 1–102.
Point 2: Section 1–102.
Point 3: Section 2–201.
Point 5: Section 2–302.

Definitional Cross References:

"Goods". Section 2–105.
"Merchant". Section 2–104.
"Signed". Section 1–201.
"Writing". Section 1–201.

§ 2–206. Offer and Acceptance in Formation of Contract.

(1)   Unless otherwise unambiguously indicated by the language or circumstances

(a)   an offer to make a contract shall be construed as inviting acceptance in any manner and by any medium reasonable in the circumstances;

(b)   an order or other offer to buy goods for prompt or current shipment shall be construed as inviting acceptance either by a prompt promise to ship or by the prompt or current shipment of conforming or non-conforming goods, but such a shipment of non-conforming goods does not constitute an acceptance if the seller seasonably notifies the buyer that the shipment is offered only as an accommodation to the buyer.

(2)   Where the beginning of a requested performance is a reasonable mode of acceptance an offeror who is not notified of acceptance within a reasonable time may treat the offer as having lapsed before acceptance.

Official Comment

Prior Uniform Statutory Provision: Sections 1 and 3, Uniform Sales Act.

Changes: Completely rewritten in this and other sections of this Article.

Purposes of Changes: To make it clear that:

1.   Any reasonable manner of acceptance is intended to be regarded as available unless the offeror has made quite clear that it will not be acceptable. Former technical rules as to acceptance, such as requiring that telegraphic offers be accepted by telegraphed acceptance, etc., are rejected and a criterion that the acceptance be "in any manner and by any medium reasonable under the circumstances," is substituted. This section is intended to remain flexible and its applicability to be enlarged as new media of communication develop or as the more time-saving present day media come into general use.

2.   Either shipment or a prompt promise to ship is made a proper means of acceptance of an offer looking to current shipment. In accordance with ordinary commercial understanding the section interprets an order looking to current shipment as allowing acceptance either by actual shipment or by a prompt promise to ship and rejects the artificial theory that only a single mode of acceptance is normally envisaged by an offer. This is true even though the language of the offer happens to be "ship at once" or the like. "Shipment" is here used in the same sense as in Section 2–504; it does not include the beginning of delivery by the seller's own truck or by messenger. But loading on the seller's own truck might be a beginning of performance under subsection (2).

3.   The beginning of performance by an offeree can be effective as acceptance so as to bind the offeror only if followed within a reasonable time by notice to the offeror. Such a beginning of performance must unambiguously express the offeree's intention to engage himself. For the protection of both parties it is essential that notice follow in due course to constitute acceptance. Nothing in this section however bars the possibility that under the common law performance begun may have an intermediate effect of temporarily barring revocation of the offer, or at the offeror's option, final effect in constituting acceptance.

4.   Subsection (1)(b) deals with the situation where a shipment made following an order is shown by a notification of shipment to be referable to that order but has a defect. Such a non-conforming shipment is normally to be understood as intended to close the bargain, even though it proves to have been at the same time a breach. However, the seller by stating that the shipment is non-conforming and is offered only as an accommodation to the buyer keeps the shipment or notification from operating as an acceptance.

Definitional Cross References:

"Buyer". Section 2–103.
"Conforming". Section 2–106.

"Contract". Section 1–201.
"Goods". Section 2–105.
"Notifies". Section 1–201.
"Reasonable time". Section 1–204.

§ 2–207.   Additional Terms in Acceptance or Confirmation.

(1)   A definite and seasonable expression of acceptance or a written confirmation which is sent within a reasonable time operates as an acceptance even though it states terms additional to or different from those offered or agreed upon, unless acceptance is expressly made conditional on assent to the additional or different terms.

(2)   The additional terms are to be construed as proposals for addition to the contract. Between merchants such terms become part of the contract unless:

(a)   the offer expressly limits acceptance to the terms of the offer;

(b)   they materially alter it; or

(c)   notification of objection to them has already been given or is given within a reasonable time after notice of them is received.

(3)   Conduct by both parties which recognizes the existence of a contract is sufficient to establish a contract for sale although the writings of the parties do not otherwise establish a contract. In such case the terms of the particular contract consist of those terms on which the writings of the parties agree, together with any supplementary terms incorporated under any other provisions of this Act.

Official Comment

Prior Uniform Statutory Provision: Sections 1 and 3, Uniform Sales Act.

Changes: Completely rewritten by this and other sections of this Article.

Purposes of Changes:

1.   This section is intended to deal with two typical situations. The one is the written confirmation, where an agreement has been reached either orally or by informal correspondence between the parties and is followed by one or both of the parties sending formal memoranda embodying the terms so far as agreed upon and adding terms not discussed. The other situation is offer and acceptance, in which a wire or letter expressed and intended as an acceptance or the closing of an agreement adds further minor suggestions or proposals such as "ship by Tuesday," "rush," "ship draft against bill of lading inspection allowed," or the like. A frequent example of the second situation is the exchange of printed purchase order and acceptance (sometimes called "acknowledgment") forms. Because the forms are oriented to the thinking of the respective drafting parties, the terms contained in them often do not correspond. Often the seller's form contains terms different from or additional to those set forth in the buyer's form. Nevertheless, the parties proceed with the transaction. [Comment 1 was amended in 1966.]

2.   Under this Article a proposed deal which in commercial understanding has in fact been closed is recognized as a contract. Therefore, any additional matter contained in the confirmation or in the acceptance falls within subsection (2) and must be regarded as a proposal for an added term unless the acceptance is made conditional on the acceptance of the additional or different terms. [Comment 2 was amended in 1966.]

3.   Whether or not additional or different terms will become part of the agreement depends upon the provisions of subsection (2). If they are such as materially to alter the original bargain, they will not be included unless expressly agreed to by the other party. If, however, they are terms which would not so change the bargain they will be incorporated unless notice of objection to them has already been given or is given within a reasonable time.

4.   Examples of typical clauses which would normally "materially alter" the contract and so result in surprise or hardship if incorporated without express awareness by the other party are: a clause negating such standard warranties as that of merchantability or fitness for a particular purpose in circumstances in which either warranty normally attaches; a clause requiring a guaranty of 90% or 100% deliveries in a case such as a contract by cannery, where the usage of the trade allows greater quantity leeways; a clause reserving to the

seller the power to cancel upon the buyer's failure to meet any invoice when due; a clause requiring that complaints be made in a time materially shorter than customary or reasonable.

5.   Examples of clauses which involve no element of unreasonable surprise and which therefore are to be incorporated in the contract unless notice of objection is seasonably given are: a clause setting forth and perhaps enlarging slightly upon the seller's exemption due to supervening causes beyond his control, similar to those covered by the provision of this Article on merchant's excuse by failure of presupposed conditions or a clause fixing in advance any reasonable formula of proration under such circumstances; a clause fixing a reasonable time for complaints within customary limits, or in the case of a purchase for sub-sale, providing for inspection by the sub-purchaser; a clause providing for interest on overdue invoices or fixing the seller's standard credit terms where they are within the range of trade practice and do not limit any credit bargained for; a clause limiting the right of rejection for defects which fall within the customary trade tolerances for acceptance "with adjustment" or otherwise limiting remedy in a reasonable manner (see Sections 2–718 and 2–719).

6.   If no answer is received within a reasonable time after additional terms are proposed, it is both fair and commercially sound to assume that their inclusion has been assented to. Where clauses on confirming forms sent by both parties conflict each party must be assumed to object to a clause of the other conflicting with one on the confirmation sent by himself. As a result the requirement that there be notice of objection which is found in subsection (2) is satisfied and the conflicting terms do not become a part of the contract. The contract then consists of the terms originally expressly agreed to, terms on which the confirmations agree, and terms supplied by this Act, including subsection (2). The written confirmation is also subject to Section 2–201. Under that section a failure to respond permits enforcement of a prior oral agreement; under this section a failure to respond permits additional terms to become part of the agreement. [Comment 6 was amended in 1966.]

7.   In many cases, as where goods are shipped, accepted and paid for before any dispute arises, there is no question whether a contract has been made. In such cases, where the writings of the parties do not establish a contract, it is not necessary to determine which act or document constituted the offer and which the acceptance. See Section 2–204. The only question is what terms are included in the contract, and subsection (3) furnishes the governing rule. [Comment 7 was added in 1966.]

Cross References:

See generally Section 2–302.
Point 5: Sections 2–513, 2–602, 2–607, 2–609, 2–612, 2–614, 2–615, 2–616, 2–718 and 2–719.
Point 6: Sections 1–102 and 2–104.

Definitional Cross References:

"Between merchants". Section 2–104.
"Contract". Section 1–201.
"Notification". Section 1–201.
"Reasonable time". Section 1–204.
"Seasonably". Section 1–204.
"Send". Section 1–201.
"Term". Section 1–201.
"Written". Section 1–201.

§ 2–208.   [Reserved.] [Course of Performance or Practical Construction.]

[(1)   Where the contract for sale involves repeated occasions for performance by either party with knowledge of the nature of the performance and opportunity for objection to it by the other, any course of performance accepted or acquiesced in without objection shall be relevant to determine the meaning of the agreement.

(2)   The express terms of the agreement and any such course of performance, as well as any course of dealing and usage of trade, shall be construed whenever reasonable as consistent with each other; but when such construction is unreasonable, express terms shall control course of performance and course of performance shall control both course of dealing and usage of trade (Section 1–205).

(3)   Subject to the provisions of the next section on modification and waiver, such course of performance shall be relevant to show a waiver or modification of any term inconsistent with such course of performance.

Official Comment

Prior Uniform Statutory Provision: No such general provision but concept of this section recognized by terms such as "course of dealing", "the circumstances of the case," "the conduct of the parties," etc., in Uniform Sales Act.

Purposes:

1.   The parties themselves know best what they have meant by their words of agreement and their action under that agreement is the best indication of what that meaning was. This section thus rounds out the set of factors which determines the meaning of the "agreement" and therefore also of the "unless otherwise agreed" qualification to various provisions of this Article.

2.   Under this section a course of performance is always relevant to determine the meaning of the agreement. Express mention of course of performance elsewhere in this Article carries no contrary implication when there is a failure to refer to it in other sections.

3.   Where it is difficult to determine whether a particular act merely sheds light on the meaning of the agreement or represents a waiver of a term of the agreement, the preference is in favor of "waiver" whenever such construction, plus the application of the provisions on the reinstatement of rights waived (see Section 2–209), is needed to preserve the flexible character of commercial contracts and to prevent surprise or other hardship.

4.   A single occasion of conduct does not fall within the language of this section but other sections such as the ones on silence after acceptance and failure to specify particular defects can affect the parties' rights on a single occasion (see Sections 2–605 and 2–607).]

Cross References:

Point 1: Section 1–201.
Point 2: Section 2–202.
Point 3: Sections 2–209, 2–601 and 2–607.
Point 4: Sections 2–605 and 2–607.

§ 2–209.   Modification, Rescission and Waiver.

(1)   An agreement modifying a contract within this Article needs no consideration to be binding.

(2)   A signed agreement which excludes modification or rescission except by a signed writing cannot be otherwise modified or rescinded, but except as between merchants such a requirement on a form supplied by the merchant must be separately signed by the other party.

(3)   The requirements of the statute of frauds section of this Article (Section 2–201) must be satisfied if the contract as modified is within its provisions.

(4)   Although an attempt at modification or rescission does not satisfy the requirements of subsection (2) or (3) it can operate as a waiver.

(5)   A party who has made a waiver affecting an executory portion of the contract may retract the waiver by reasonable notification received by the other party that strict performance will be required of any term waived, unless the retraction would be unjust in view of a material change of position in reliance on the waiver.

Official Comment

Prior Uniform Statutory Provision: Subsection (1)—Compare Section 1, Uniform Written Obligations Act; Subsections (2) to (5)—none.

Purposes of Changes and New Matter:

1.   This section seeks to protect and make effective all necessary and desirable modifications of sales contracts without regard to the technicalities which at present hamper such adjustments.

2.   Subsection (1) provides that an agreement modifying a sales contract needs no consideration to be binding.

However, modifications made thereunder must meet the test of good faith imposed by this Act. The effective use of bad faith to escape performance on the original contract terms is barred, and the extortion of a "modification" without legitimate commercial reason is ineffective as a violation of the duty of good faith. Nor can a mere technical consideration support a modification made in bad faith.

The test of "good faith" between merchants or as against merchants includes "observance of reasonable commercial standards of fair dealing in the trade" (Section 2–103), and may in some situations require an objectively demonstrable reason for seeking a modification. But such matters as a market shift which makes performance come to involve a loss may provide such a reason even though there is no such unforeseen difficulty as would make out a legal excuse from performance under Sections 2–615 and 2–616.

3.   Subsections (2) and (3) are intended to protect against false allegations of oral modifications. "Modification or rescission" includes abandonment or other change by mutual consent, contrary to the decision in *Green v. Doniger*, 300 N.Y. 238, 90 N.E.2d 56 (1949); it does not include unilateral "termination" or "cancellation" as defined in Section 2–106.

The Statute of Frauds provisions of this Article are expressly applied to modifications by subsection (3). Under those provisions the "delivery and acceptance" test is limited to the goods which have been accepted, that is, to the past. "Modification" for the future cannot therefore be conjured up by oral testimony if the price involved is $500.00 or more since such modification must be shown at least by an authenticated memo. And since a memo is limited in its effect to the quantity of goods set forth in it there is safeguard against oral evidence.

Subsection (2) permits the parties in effect to make their own Statute of Frauds as regards any future modification of the contract by giving effect to a clause in a signed agreement which expressly requires any modification to be by signed writing. But note that if a consumer is to be held to such a clause on a form supplied by a merchant it must be separately signed.

4.   Subsection (4) is intended, despite the provisions of subsections (2) and (3), to prevent contractual provisions excluding modification except by a signed writing from limiting in other respects the legal effect of the parties' actual later conduct. The effect of such conduct as a waiver is further regulated in subsection (5).

Cross References:

> Point 1: Section 1–203.
> Point 2: Sections 1–201, 1–203, 2–615 and 2–616.
> Point 3: Sections 2–106, 2–201 and 2–202.
> Point 4: Sections 2–202 and 2 208.

Definitional Cross References:

> "Agreement". Section 1–201.
> "Between merchants". Section 2–104.
> "Contract". Section 1–201.
> "Notification". Section 1–201.
> "Signed". Section 1–201.
> "Term". Section 1–201.
> "Writing". Section 1–201.

§ 2–210.   Delegation of Performance; Assignment of Rights.

(1)   A party may perform his duty through a delegate unless otherwise agreed or unless the other party has a substantial interest in having his original promisor perform or control the acts required by the contract. No delegation of performance relieves the party delegating of any duty to perform or any liability for breach.

(2)   Except as otherwise provided in Section 9–406, unless otherwise agreed, all rights of either seller or buyer can be assigned except where the assignment would materially change the duty of the other party, or increase materially the burden or risk imposed on him by his contract, or impair materially his chance of obtaining return performance. A right to damages for breach of the whole contract or a right arising out of the assignor's due performance of his entire obligation can be assigned despite agreement otherwise.

(3)   The creation, attachment, perfection, or enforcement of a security interest in the seller's interest under a contract is not a transfer that materially changes the duty of or increases materially the burden or risk imposed on the buyer or impairs materially the buyer's chance of obtaining return performance within the purview of subsection (2) unless, and then only to the extent that, enforcement actually results in a delegation of material performance of the seller. Even in that event, the creation, attachment, perfection, and enforcement of the security interest remain effective, but (i) the seller is liable to the buyer for damages caused by the delegation to the extent that the damages could not reasonably be prevented by the buyer, and (ii) a court having jurisdiction may grant other appropriate relief, including cancellation of the contract for sale or an injunction against enforcement of the security interest or consummation of the enforcement.

(4)   Unless the circumstances indicate the contrary a prohibition of assignment of "the contract" is to be construed as barring only the delegation to the assignee of the assignor's performance.

(5)   An assignment of "the contract" or of "all my rights under the contract" or an assignment in similar general terms is an assignment of rights and unless the language or the circumstances (as in an assignment for security) indicate the contrary, it is a delegation of performance of the duties of the assignor and its acceptance by the assignee constitutes a promise by him to perform those duties. This promise is enforceable by either the assignor or the other party to the original contract.

(6)   The other party may treat any assignment which delegates performance as creating reasonable grounds for insecurity and may without prejudice to his rights against the assignor demand assurances from the assignee (Section 2–609).

As amended in 1999.

Official Comment

Prior Uniform Statutory Provision: None.

Purposes:

1.   Generally, this section recognizes both delegation of performance and assignability as normal and permissible incidents of a contract for the sale of goods.

2.   Delegation of performance, either in conjunction with an assignment or otherwise, is provided for by subsection (1) where no substantial reason can be shown as to why the delegated performance will not be as satisfactory as personal performance.

3.   Under subsection (2) rights which are no longer executory such as a right to damages for breach may be assigned although the agreement prohibits assignment. In such cases no question of delegation of any performance is involved. Subsection (2) is subject to Section 9–406, which makes rights to payment for goods sold ("accounts"), whether or not earned, freely alienable notwithstanding a contrary agreement or rule of law.

4.   The nature of the contract or the circumstances of the case, however, may bar assignment of the contract even where delegation of performance is not involved. This Article and this section are intended to clarify this problem, particularly in cases dealing with output requirement and exclusive dealing contracts. In the first place the section on requirements and exclusive dealing removes from the construction of the original contract most of the "personal discretion" element by substituting the reasonably objective standard of good faith operation of the plant or business to be supplied. Secondly, the section on insecurity and assurances, which is specifically referred to in subsection (5) of this section, frees the other party from the doubts and uncertainty which may afflict him under an assignment of the character in question by permitting him to demand adequate assurance of due performance without which he may suspend his own performance. Subsection (5) is not in any way intended to limit the effect of the section on insecurity and assurances and the word "performance" includes

§ 2–301   **UNIFORM COMMERCIAL CODE**

the giving of orders under a requirements contract. Of course, in any case where a material personal discretion is sought to be transferred, effective assignment is barred by subsection (2).

5.   Subsection (4) lays down a general rule of construction distinguishing between a normal commercial assignment, which substitutes the assignee for the assignor both as to rights and duties, and a financing assignment in which only the assignor's rights are transferred.

This Article takes no position on the possibility of extending some recognition or power to the original parties to work out normal commercial readjustments of the contract in the case of financing assignments even after the original obligor has been notified of the assignment. This question is dealt with in the Article on Secured Transactions (Article 9).

6.   Subsection (5) recognizes that the non-assigning original party has a stake in the reliability of the person with whom he has closed the original contract, and is, therefore, entitled to due assurance that any delegated performance will be properly forthcoming.

7.   This section is not intended as a complete statement of the law of delegation and assignment but is limited to clarifying a few points doubtful under the case law. Particularly, neither this section nor this Article touches directly on such questions as the need or effect of notice of the assignment, the rights of successive assignees, or any question of the form of an assignment, either as between the parties or as against any third parties. Some of these questions are dealt with in Article 9.

Cross References:

Point 3: Articles 5 and 9.
Point 4: Sections 2–306 and 2–609.
Point 5: Article 9, Sections 9–402, 9–404, 9–405, and 9–406.
Point 7: Article 9.

Definitional Cross References:

"Agreement". Section 1–201.
"Buyer". Section 2–103.
"Contract". Section 1–201.
"Party". Section 1–201.
"Rights". Section 1–201.
"Seller". Section 2–103.
"Term". Section 1–201.

As amended in 1999.

PART 3

GENERAL OBLIGATION AND CONSTRUCTION OF CONTRACT

§ 2–301.   General Obligations of Parties.

The obligation of the seller is to transfer and deliver and that of the buyer is to accept and pay in accordance with the contract.

Official Comment

Prior Uniform Statutory Provision: Sections 11 and 41, Uniform Sales Act.

Changes: Rewritten.

Purposes of Changes:

This section uses the term "obligation" in contrast to the term "duty" in order to provide for the "condition" aspects of delivery and payment insofar as they are not modified by other sections of this Article such as those on cure of tender. It thus replaces not only the general provisions of the Uniform Sales Act on the parties' duties, but also the general provisions of that Act on the effect of conditions. In order to determine what is "in accordance with the contract" under this Article usage of trade, course of dealing and performance, and the general background of circumstances must be given due consideration in conjunction with the lay meaning of the words used to define the scope of the conditions and duties.

Cross References:

Section 1–106. See also Sections 1–205, 2–208, 2–209, 2–508 and 2–612.

Definitional Cross References:

"Buyer". Section 2–103.
"Contract". Section 1–201.
"Party". Section 1–201.
"Seller". Section 2–103.

§ 2–302.   Unconscionable Contract or Clause.

(1)   If the court as a matter of law finds the contract or any clause of the contract to have been unconscionable at the time it was made the court may refuse to enforce the contract, or it may enforce the remainder of the contract without the unconscionable clause, or it may so limit the application of any unconscionable clause as to avoid any unconscionable result.

(2)   When it is claimed or appears to the court that the contract or any clause thereof may be unconscionable the parties shall be afforded a reasonable opportunity to present evidence as to its commercial setting, purpose and effect to aid the court in making the determination.

Official Comment

Prior Uniform Statutory Provision: None.

Purposes:

1.   This section is intended to make it possible for the courts to police explicitly against the contracts or clauses which they find to be unconscionable. In the past such policing has been accomplished by adverse construction of language, by manipulation of the rules of offer and acceptance or by determinations that the clause is contrary to public policy or to the dominant purpose of the contract. This section is intended to allow the court to pass directly on the unconscionability of the contract or particular clause therein and to make a conclusion of law as to its unconscionability. The basic test is whether, in the light of the general commercial background and the commercial needs of the particular trade or case, the clauses involved are so one-sided as to be unconscionable under the circumstances existing at the time of the making of the contract. Subsection (2) makes it clear that it is proper for the court to hear evidence upon these questions. The principle is one of the prevention of oppression and unfair surprise (Cf. *Campbell Soup Co. v. Wentz*, 172 F.2d 80, 3d Cir. 1948) and not of disturbance of allocation of risks because of superior bargaining power. The underlying basis of this section is illustrated by the results in cases such as the following:

Kansas City Wholesale Grocery Co. v. Weber Packing Corporation, 93 Utah 414, 73 P.2d 1272 (1937), where a clause limiting time for complaints was held inapplicable to latent defects in a shipment of catsup which could be discovered only by microscopic analysis; *Hardy v. General Motors Acceptance Corporation*, 38 Ga.App. 463, 144 S.E. 327 (1928), holding that a disclaimer of warranty clause applied only to express warranties, thus letting in a fair implied warranty; *Andrews Bros. v. Singer & Co.* (1934 CA) 1 K.B. 17, holding that where a car with substantial mileage was delivered instead of a "new" car, a disclaimer of warranties, including those "implied," left unaffected an "express obligation" on the description, even though the Sale of Goods Act called such an implied warranty; *New Prague Flouring Mill Co. v. G. A. Spears*, 194 Iowa 417, 189 N.W. 815 (1922), holding that a clause permitting the seller, upon the buyer's failure to supply shipping instructions, to cancel, ship, or allow delivery date to be indefinitely postponed 30 days at a time by the inaction, does not indefinitely postpone the date of measuring damages for the buyer's breach, to the seller's advantage; and *Kansas Flour Mills Co. v. Dirks*, 100 Kan. 376, 164 P. 273 (1917), where under a similar clause in a rising market the court permitted the buyer to measure his damages for non-delivery at the end of only one 30 day postponement; *Green v. Arcos*, Ltd. (1931 CA) 47 T.L.R. 336, where a blanket clause prohibiting rejection of shipments by the buyer was restricted to apply to shipments where discrepancies represented merely mercantile variations; *Meyer v. Packard Cleveland Motor Co.*, 106 Ohio St. 328, 140 N.E. 118 (1922), in which the court held that a "waiver" of all agreements not specified did not preclude implied warranty of fitness of a rebuilt dump truck for ordinary use as

§ 2–303   UNIFORM COMMERCIAL CODE

a dump truck; *Austin Co. v. J. H. Tillman Co.*, 104 Or. 541, 209 P. 131 (1922), where a clause limiting the buyer's remedy to return was held to be applicable only if the seller had delivered a machine needed for a construction job which reasonably met the contract description; *Bekkevold v. Potts*, 173 Minn. 87, 216 N.W. 790, 59 A.L.R. 1164 (1927), refusing to allow warranty of fitness for purpose imposed by law to be negated by clause excluding all warranties "made" by the seller; *Robert A. Munroe & Co. v. Meyer* (1930) 2 K.B. 312, holding that the warranty of description overrides a clause reading "with all faults and defects" where adulterated meat not up to the contract description was delivered.

    2.   Under this section the court, in its discretion, may refuse to enforce the contract as a whole if it is permeated by the unconscionability, or it may strike any single clause or group of clauses which are so tainted or which are contrary to the essential purpose of the agreement, or it may simply limit unconscionable clauses so as to avoid unconscionable results.

    3.   The present section is addressed to the court, and the decision is to be made by it. The commercial evidence referred to in subsection (2) is for the court's consideration, not the jury's. Only the agreement which results from the court's action on these matters is to be submitted to the general triers of the facts.

Definitional Cross Reference:

    "Contract". Section 1–201.

§ 2–303.   Allocation or Division of Risks.

    Where this Article allocates a risk or a burden as between the parties "unless otherwise agreed", the agreement may not only shift the allocation but may also divide the risk or burden.

Official Comment

Prior Uniform Statutory Provision: None.

Purposes:

    1.   This section is intended to make it clear that the parties may modify or allocate "unless otherwise agreed" risks or burdens imposed by this Article as they desire, always subject, of course, to the provisions on unconscionability.

    Compare Section 1–102(4).

    2.   The risk or burden may be divided by the express terms of the agreement or by the attending circumstances, since under the definition of "agreement" in this Act the circumstances surrounding the transaction as well as the express language used by the parties enter into the meaning and substance of the agreement.

Cross References:

    Point 1: Sections 1–102, 2–302.
    Point 2: Section 1–201.

Definitional Cross References:

    "Party". Section 1–201.
    "Agreement". Section 1–201.

§ 2–304.   Price Payable in Money, Goods, Realty, or Otherwise.

    (1)   The price can be made payable in money or otherwise. If it is payable in whole or in part in goods each party is a seller of the goods which he is to transfer.

    (2)   Even though all or part of the price is payable in an interest in realty the transfer of the goods and the seller's obligations with reference to them are subject to this Article, but not the transfer of the interest in realty or the transferor's obligations in connection therewith.

Official Comment

Prior Uniform Statutory Provision: Subsections (2) and (3) of Section 9, Uniform Sales Act.

ARTICLE 2 (2016)   **§ 2–305**

Changes: Rewritten.

Purposes of Changes:

1.   This section corrects the phrasing of the Uniform Sales Act so as to avoid misconstruction and produce greater accuracy in commercial result. While it continues the essential intent and purpose of the Uniform Sales Act it rejects any purely verbalistic construction in disregard of the underlying reason of the provisions.

2.   Under subsection (1) the provisions of this Article are applicable to transactions where the "price" of goods is payable in something other than money. This does not mean, however, that this whole Article applies automatically and in its entirety simply because an agreed transfer of title to goods is not a gift. The basic purposes and reasons of the Article must always be considered in determining the applicability of any of its provisions.

3.   Subsection (2) lays down the general principle that when goods are to be exchanged for realty, the provisions of this Article apply only to those aspects of the transaction which concern the transfer of title to goods but do not affect the transfer of the realty since the detailed regulation of various particular contracts which fall outside the scope of this Article is left to the courts and other legislation. However, the complexities of these situations may be such that each must be analyzed in the light of the underlying reasons in order to determine the applicable principles. Local statutes dealing with realty are not to be lightly disregarded or altered by language of this Article. In contrast, this Article declares definite policies in regard to certain matters legitimately within its scope though concerned with real property situations, and in those instances the provisions of this Article control.

Cross References:

> Point 1: Section 1–102.
> Point 3: Sections 1–102, 1–103, 1–104 and 2–107.

Definitional Cross References:

> "Goods". Section 2–105.
> "Money". Section 1–201.
> "Party". Section 1–201.
> "Seller". Section 2–103.

§ 2–305.   Open Price Term.

(1)   The parties if they so intend can conclude a contract for sale even though the price is not settled. In such a case the price is a reasonable price at the time for delivery if

    (a)   nothing is said as to price; or

    (b)   the price is left to be agreed by the parties and they fail to agree; or

    (c)   the price is to be fixed in terms of some agreed market or other standard as set or recorded by a third person or agency and it is not so set or recorded.

(2)   A price to be fixed by the seller or by the buyer means a price for him to fix in good faith.

(3)   When a price left to be fixed otherwise than by agreement of the parties fails to be fixed through fault of one party the other may at his option treat the contract as cancelled or himself fix a reasonable price.

(4)   Where, however, the parties intend not to be bound unless the price be fixed or agreed and it is not fixed or agreed there is no contract. In such a case the buyer must return any goods already received or if unable so to do must pay their reasonable value at the time of delivery and the seller must return any portion of the price paid on account.

Official Comment

Prior Uniform Statutory Provision: Sections 9 and 10, Uniform Sales Act.

Changes: Completely rewritten.

Purposes of Changes:

1.   This section applies when the price term is left open on the making of an agreement which is nevertheless intended by the parties to be a binding agreement. This Article rejects in these instances the formula that "an agreement to agree is unenforceable" if the case falls within subsection (1) of this section, and rejects also defeating such agreements on the ground of "indefiniteness". Instead this Article recognizes the dominant intention of the parties to have the deal continue to be binding upon both. As to future performance, since this Article recognizes remedies such as cover (Section 2–712), resale (Section 2–706) and specific performance (Section 2–716) which go beyond any mere arithmetic as between contract price and market price, there is usually a "reasonably certain basis for granting an appropriate remedy for breach" so that the contract need not fail for indefiniteness.

2.   Under some circumstances the postponement of agreement on price will mean that no deal has really been concluded, and this is made express in the preamble of subsection (1) ("The parties *if they so intend*") and in subsection (4). Whether or not this is so is, in most cases, a question to be determined by the trier of fact.

3.   Subsection (2), dealing with the situation where the price is to be fixed by one party rejects the uncommercial idea that an agreement that the seller may fix the price means that he may fix any price he may wish by the express qualification that the price so fixed must be fixed in good faith. Good faith includes observance of reasonable commercial standards of fair dealing in the trade if the party is a merchant. (Section 2–103). But in the normal case a "posted price" or a future seller's or buyer's "given price," "price in effect," "market price," or the like satisfies the good faith requirement.

4.   The section recognizes that there may be cases in which a particular person's judgment is not chosen merely as a barometer or index of a fair price but is an essential condition to the parties' intent to make any contract at all. For example, the case where a known and trusted expert is to "value" a particular painting for which there is no market standard differs sharply from the situation where a named expert is to determine the grade of cotton, and the difference would support a finding that in the one the parties did not intend to make a binding agreement if that expert were unavailable whereas in the other they did so intend. Other circumstances would of course affect the validity of such a finding.

5.   Under subsection (3), wrongful interference by one party with any agreed machinery for price fixing in the contract may be treated by the other party as a repudiation justifying cancellation, or merely as a failure to take cooperative action thus shifting to the aggrieved party the reasonable leeway in fixing the price.

6.   Throughout the entire section, the purpose is to give effect to the agreement which has been made. That effect, however, is always conditioned by the requirement of good faith action which is made an inherent part of all contracts within this Act. (Section 1–203).

Cross References:

Point 1: Sections 2–204(3), 2–706, 2–712 and 2–716.
Point 3: Section 2–103.
Point 5: Sections 2–311 and 2–610.
Point 6: Section 1–203.

Definitional Cross References:

"Agreement". Section 1–201.
"Burden of establishing". Section 1–201.
"Buyer". Section 2–103.
"Cancellation". Section 2–106.
"Contract". Section 1–201.
"Contract for sale". Section 2–106.
"Fault". Section 1–201.
"Goods". Section 2–105.
"Party". Section 1–201.
"Receipt of goods". Section 2–103.
"Seller". Section 2–103.
"Term". Section 1–201.

§ 2–306.   Output, Requirements and Exclusive Dealings.

(1)   A term which measures the quantity by the output of the seller or the requirements of the buyer means such actual output or requirements as may occur in good faith, except that no quantity unreasonably disproportionate to any stated estimate or in the absence of a stated estimate to any normal or otherwise comparable prior output or requirements may be tendered or demanded.

(2)   A lawful agreement by either the seller or the buyer for exclusive dealing in the kind of goods concerned imposes unless otherwise agreed an obligation by the seller to use best efforts to supply the goods and by the buyer to use best efforts to promote their sale.

Official Comment

Prior Uniform Statutory Provision: None.

Purposes:

1.   Subsection (1) of this section, in regard to output and requirements, applies to this specific problem the general approach of this Act which requires the reading of commercial background and intent into the language of any agreement and demands good faith in the performance of that agreement. It applies to such contracts of nonproducing establishments such as dealers or distributors as well as to manufacturing concerns.

2.   Under this Article, a contract for output or requirements is not too indefinite since it is held to mean the actual good faith output or requirements of the particular party. Nor does such a contract lack mutuality of obligation since, under this section, the party who will determine quantity is required to operate his plant or conduct his business in good faith and according to commercial standards of fair dealing in the trade so that his output or requirements will approximate a reasonably foreseeable figure. Reasonable elasticity in the requirements is expressly envisaged by this section and good faith variations from prior requirements are permitted even when the variation may be such as to result in discontinuance. A shut-down by a requirements buyer for lack of orders might be permissible when a shut-down merely to curtail losses would not. The essential test is whether the party is acting in good faith. Similarly, a sudden expansion of the plant by which requirements are to be measured would not be included within the scope of the contract as made but normal expansion undertaken in good faith would be within the scope of this section. One of the factors in an expansion situation would be whether the market price had risen greatly in a case in which the requirements contract contained a fixed price. Reasonable variation of an extreme sort is exemplified in *Southwest Natural Gas Co. v. Oklahoma Portland Cement Co.*, 102 F.2d 630 (C.C.A.10, 1939). This Article takes no position as to whether a requirements contract is a provable claim in bankruptcy.

3.   If an estimate of output or requirements is included in the agreement, no quantity unreasonably disproportionate to it may be tendered or demanded. Any minimum or maximum set by the agreement shows a clear limit on the intended elasticity. In similar fashion, the agreed estimate is to be regarded as a center around which the parties intend the variation to occur.

4.   When an enterprise is sold, the question may arise whether the buyer is bound by an existing output or requirements contract. That question is outside the scope of this Article, and is to be determined on other principles of law. Assuming that the contract continues, the output or requirements in the hands of the new owner continue to be measured by the actual good faith output or requirements under the normal operation of the enterprise prior to sale. The sale itself is not grounds for sudden expansion or decrease.

5.   Subsection (2), on exclusive dealing, makes explicit the commercial rule embodied in this Act under which the parties to such contracts are held to have impliedly, even when not expressly, bound themselves to use reasonable diligence as well as good faith in their performance of the contract. Under such contracts the exclusive agent is required, although no express commitment has been made, to use reasonable effort and due diligence in the expansion of the market or the promotion of the product, as the case may be. The principal is expected under such a contract to refrain from supplying any other dealer or agent within the exclusive territory. An exclusive dealing agreement brings into play all of the good faith aspects of the output and requirement problems of subsection (1). It also raises questions of insecurity and right to adequate assurance under this Article.

Cross References:

Point 4: Section 2–210.
Point 5: Sections 1–203 and 2–609.

Definitional Cross References:

> "Agreement". Section 1–201.
> "Buyer". Section 2–103.
> "Contract for sale". Section 2–106.
> "Good faith". Section 1–201.
> "Goods". Section 2–105.
> "Party". Section 1–201.
> "Term". Section 1–201.
> "Seller". Section 2–103.

§ 2–307.　　Delivery in Single Lot or Several Lots.

Unless otherwise agreed all goods called for by a contract for sale must be tendered in a single delivery and payment is due only on such tender but where the circumstances give either party the right to make or demand delivery in lots the price if it can be apportioned may be demanded for each lot.

Official Comment

Prior Uniform Statutory Provision: Section 45(1), Uniform Sales Act.

Changes: Rewritten and expanded.

Purposes of Changes:

1.　　This section applies where the parties have not specifically agreed whether delivery and payment are to be by lots and generally continues the essential intent of original Act, Section 45(1) by assuming that the parties intended delivery to be in a single lot.

2.　　Where the actual agreement or the circumstances do not indicate otherwise, delivery in lots is not permitted under this section and the buyer is properly entitled to reject for a deficiency in the tender, subject to any privilege in the seller to cure the tender.

3.　　The "but" clause of this section goes to the case in which it is not commercially feasible to deliver or to receive the goods in a single lot as for example, where a contract calls for the shipment of ten carloads of coal and only three cars are available at a given time. Similarly, in a contract involving brick necessary to build a building the buyer's storage space may be limited so that it would be impossible to receive the entire amount of brick at once, or it may be necessary to assemble the goods as in the case of cattle on the range, or to mine them.

In such cases, a partial delivery is not subject to rejection for the defect in quantity alone, if the circumstances do not indicate a repudiation or default by the seller as to the expected balance or do not give the buyer ground for suspending his performance because of insecurity under the provisions of Section 2–609. However, in such cases the undelivered balance of goods under the contract must be forthcoming within a reasonable time and in a reasonable manner according to the policy of Section 2–503 on manner of tender of delivery. This is reinforced by the express provisions of Section 2–608 that if a lot has been accepted on the reasonable assumption that its nonconformity will be cured, the acceptance may be revoked if the cure does not seasonably occur. The section rejects the rule of *Kelly Construction Co. v. Hackensack Brick Co.*, 91 N.J.L. 585, 103 A. 417, 2 A.L.R. 685 (1918) and approves the result in *Lynn M. Ranger, Inc. v. Gildersleeve*, 106 Conn. 372, 138 A. 142 (1927) in which a contract was made for six carloads of coal then rolling from the mines and consigned to the seller but the seller agreed to divert the carloads to the buyer as soon as the car numbers became known to him. He arranged a diversion of two cars and then notified the buyer who then repudiated the contract. The seller was held to be entitled to his full remedy for the two cars diverted because simultaneous delivery of all of the cars was not contemplated by either party.

4.　　Where the circumstances indicate that a party has a right to delivery in lots, the price may be demanded for each lot if it is apportionable.

Cross References:

> Point 1: Section 1–201.
> Point 2: Sections 2–508 and 2–601.
> Point 3: Sections 2–503, 2–608 and 2–609.

Definitional Cross References:

> "Contract for sale". Section 2–106.
> "Goods". Section 2–105.
> "Lot". Section 2–105.
> "Party". Section 1–201.
> "Rights". Section 1–201.

§ 2–308.   Absence of Specified Place for Delivery.

Unless otherwise agreed

(a)   the place for delivery of goods is the seller's place of business or if he has none his residence; but

(b)   in a contract for sale of identified goods which to the knowledge of the parties at the time of contracting are in some other place, that place is the place for their delivery; and

(c)   documents of title may be delivered through customary banking channels.

Official Comment

Prior Uniform Statutory Provision: Paragraphs (a) and (b)—Section 43(1), Uniform Sales Act; Paragraph (c)—none.

Changes: Slight modification in language.

Purposes of Changes and New Matter:

1.   Paragraphs (a) and (b) provide for those noncommercial sales and for those occasional commercial sales where no place or means of delivery has been agreed upon by the parties. Where delivery by carrier is "required or authorized by the agreement", the seller's duties as to delivery of the goods are governed not by this section but by Section 2–504.

2.   Under paragraph (b) when the identified goods contracted for are known to both parties to be in some location other than the seller's place of business or residence, the parties are presumed to have intended that place to be the place of delivery. This paragraph also applies (unless, as would be normal, the circumstances show that delivery by way of documents is intended) to a bulk of goods in the possession of a bailee. In such a case, however, the seller has the additional obligation to procure the acknowledgment by the bailee of the buyer's right to possession.

3.   Where "customary banking channels" call only for due notification by the banker that the documents are available, leaving the buyer himself to see to the physical receipt of the goods, tender at the buyer's address is not required under paragraph (c). But that paragraph merely eliminates the possibility of a default by the seller if "customary banking channels" have been properly used in giving notice to the buyer. Where the bank has purchased a draft accompanied by or associated with documents or has undertaken its collection on behalf of the seller, Part 5 of Article 4 spells out its duties and relations to its customer. Where the documents move forward under a letter of credit the Article on Letters of Credit spells out the duties and relations between the bank, the seller and the buyer. Delivery in relationship to either tangible or electronic documents of title is defined in Article 1, Section 1–201.

4.   The rules of this section apply only "unless otherwise agreed." The surrounding circumstances, usage of trade, course of dealing and course of performance, as well as the express language of the parties, may constitute an "otherwise agreement".

Cross References:

> Point 1: Sections 2–504 and 2–505.
> Point 2: Section 2–503.
> Point 3: Section 2–512, Articles 4, Part 5, and 5.

Definitional Cross References:

> "Contract for sale". Section 2–106.
> "Delivery". Section 1–201.
> "Document of title". Section 1–201.

"Goods". Section 2–105.
"Party". Section 1–201.
"Seller". Section 2–103.

As amended in 2003.

§ 2–309.   Absence of Specific Time Provisions; Notice of Termination.

(1)   The time for shipment or delivery or any other action under a contract if not provided in this Article or agreed upon shall be a reasonable time.

(2)   Where the contract provides for successive performances but is indefinite in duration it is valid for a reasonable time but unless otherwise agreed may be terminated at any time by either party.

(3)   Termination of a contract by one party except on the happening of an agreed event requires that reasonable notification be received by the other party and an agreement dispensing with notification is invalid if its operation would be unconscionable.

Official Comment

Prior Uniform Statutory Provision: Subsection (1)—see Sections 43(2), 45(2), 47(1) and 48, Uniform Sales Act, for policy continued under this Article; Subsection (2)—none; Subsection (3)—none.

Changes: Completely different in scope.

Purposes of Changes and New Matter:

1.   Subsection (1) requires that all actions taken under a sales contract must be taken within a reasonable time where no time has been agreed upon. The reasonable time under this provision turns on the criteria as to "reasonable time" and on good faith and commercial standards set forth in Sections 1–203, 1–204 and 2–103. It thus depends upon what constitutes acceptable commercial conduct in view of the nature, purpose and circumstances of the action to be taken. Agreement as to a definite time, however, may be found in a term implied from the contractual circumstances, usage of trade or course of dealing or performance as well as in an express term. Such cases fall outside of this subsection since in them the time for action is "agreed" by usage.

2.   The time for payment, where not agreed upon, is related to the time for delivery; the particular problems which arise in connection with determining the appropriate time of payment and the time for any inspection before payment which is both allowed by law and demanded by the buyer are covered in Section 2–513.

3.   The facts in regard to shipment and delivery differ so widely as to make detailed provision for them in the text of this Article impracticable. The applicable principles, however, make it clear that surprise is to be avoided, good faith judgment is to be protected, and notice or negotiation to reduce the uncertainty to certainty is to be favored.

4.   When the time for delivery is left open, unreasonably early offers of or demands for delivery are intended to be read under this Article as expressions of desire or intention, requesting the assent or acquiescence of the other party, not as final positions which may amount without more to breach or to create breach by the other side. See Sections 2–207 and 2–609.

5.   The obligation of good faith under this Act requires reasonable notification before a contract may be treated as breached because a reasonable time for delivery or demand has expired. This operates both in the case of a contract originally indefinite as to time and of one subsequently made indefinite by waiver.

When both parties let an originally reasonable time go by in silence, the course of conduct under the contract may be viewed as enlarging the reasonable time for tender or demand of performance. The contract may be terminated by abandonment.

6.   Parties to a contract are not required in giving reasonable notification to fix, at peril of breach, a time which is in fact reasonable in the unforeseeable judgment of a later trier of fact. Effective communication of a proposed time limit calls for a response, so that failure to reply will make out acquiescence. Where objection is made, however, or if the demand is merely for information as to when goods will be delivered or will be ordered out, demand for assurances on the ground of insecurity may be made under this Article pending further

negotiations. Only when a party insists on undue delay or on rejection of the other party's reasonable proposal is there a question of flat breach under the present section.

7.   Subsection (2) applies a commercially reasonable view to resolve the conflict which has arisen in the cases as to contracts of indefinite duration. The "reasonable time" of duration appropriate to a given arrangement is limited by the circumstances. When the arrangement has been carried on by the parties over the years, the "reasonable time" can continue indefinitely and the contract will not terminate until notice.

8.   Subsection (3) recognizes that the application of principles of good faith and sound commercial practice normally call for such notification of the termination of a going contract relationship as will give the other party reasonable time to seek a substitute arrangement. An agreement dispensing with notification or limiting the time for the seeking of a substitute arrangement is, of course, valid under this subsection unless the results of putting it into operation would be the creation of an unconscionable state of affairs.

9.   Justifiable cancellation for breach is a remedy for breach and is not the kind of termination covered by the present subsection.

10.   The requirement of notification is dispensed with where the contract provides for termination on the happening of an "agreed event." "Event" is a term chosen here to contrast with "option" or the like.

Cross References:

Point 1: Sections 1–203, 1–204 and 2–103.
Point 2: Sections 2–320, 2–321, 2–504, and 2–511 through 2–514.
Point 5: Section 1–203.
Point 6: Section 2–609.
Point 7: Section 2–204.
Point 9: Sections 2–106, 2–318, 2–610 and 2–703.

Definitional Cross References:

"Agreement". Section 1–201.
"Contract". Section 1–201.
"Notification". Section 1–201.
"Party". Section 1–201.
"Reasonable time". Section 1–204.
"Termination". Section 2–106.

§ 2–310.   Open Time for Payment or Running of Credit; Authority to Ship Under Reservation.

Unless otherwise agreed

(a)   payment is due at the time and place at which the buyer is to receive the goods even though the place of shipment is the place of delivery; and

(b)   if the seller is authorized to send the goods he may ship them under reservation, and may tender the documents of title, but the buyer may inspect the goods after their arrival before payment is due unless such inspection is inconsistent with the terms of the contract (Section 2–513); and

(c)   if delivery is authorized and made by way of documents of title otherwise than by subsection (b) then payment is due regardless of where the goods are received (i) at the time and place at which the buyer is to receive delivery of the tangible documents or (ii) at the time the buyer is to receive delivery of the electronic documents and at the seller's place of business or if none, the seller's residence; and

(d)   where the seller is required or authorized to ship the goods on credit the credit period runs from the time of shipment but post-dating the invoice or delaying its dispatch will correspondingly delay the starting of the credit period.

As amended in 2003.

§ 2–310   UNIFORM COMMERCIAL CODE

Official Comment

Prior Uniform Statutory Provision: Sections 42 and 47(2), Uniform Sales Act.

Changes: Completely rewritten in this and other sections.

Purposes of Changes: This section is drawn to reflect modern business methods of dealing at a distance rather than face to face. Thus:

1.   Paragraph (a) provides that payment is due at the time and place "the buyer is to receive the goods" rather than at the point of delivery except in documentary shipment cases (paragraph (c)). This grants an opportunity for the exercise by the buyer of his preliminary right to inspection before paying even though under the delivery term the risk of loss may have previously passed to him or the running of the credit period has already started.

2.   Paragraph (b) while providing for inspection by the buyer before he pays, protects the seller. He is not required to give up possession of the goods until he has received payment, where no credit has been contemplated by the parties. The seller may collect through a bank by a sight draft against an order bill of lading "hold until arrival; inspection allowed." The obligations of the bank under such a provision are set forth in Part 5 of Article 4. Under subsection (c), in the absence of a credit term, the seller is permitted to ship under reservation and if he does payment is then due where and when the buyer is to receive delivery of the tangible documents of title. In the case of an electronic document of title, payment is due when the buyer is to receive delivery of the electronic document and at the seller's place of business, or if none, the seller's residence. Delivery as to documents of title is stated in Article 1, Section 1–201.

3.   Unless otherwise agreed, the place for the delivery of the documents and payment is the buyer's city but the time for payment is only after arrival of the goods, since under paragraph (b), and Sections 2–512 and 2–513 the buyer is under no duty to pay prior to inspection. Tender of a document of title requires that the seller be ready, willing and able to transfer possession of a tangible document of title or control of an electronic document of title to the buyer.

4.   Where the mode of shipment is such that goods must be unloaded immediately upon arrival, too rapidly to permit adequate inspection before receipt, the seller must be guided by the provisions of this Article on inspection which provide that if the seller wishes to demand payment before inspection, he must put an appropriate term into the contract. Even requiring payment against documents will not of itself have this desired result if the documents are to be held until the arrival of the goods. But under (b) and (c) if the terms are C.I.F., C.O.D., or cash against documents payment may be due before inspection.

5.   Paragraph (d) states the common commercial understanding that an agreed credit period runs from the time of shipment or from that dating of the invoice which is commonly recognized as a representation of the time of shipment. The provision concerning any delay in sending forth the invoice is included because such conduct results in depriving the buyer of his full notice and warning as to when he must be prepared to pay.

Cross References:

Generally: Part 5.
Point 1: Section 2–509.
Point 2: Sections 2–505, 2–511, 2–512, 2–513 and Article 4.
Point 3: Sections 2–308(b), 2–512 and 2–513.
Point 4: Section 2–513(3)(b).

Definitional Cross References:

"Buyer". Section 2–103.
"Delivery". Section 1–201.
"Document of title". Section 1–201.
"Goods". Section 2–105.
"Receipt of goods". Section 2–103.
"Seller". Section 2–103.
"Send". Section 1–201.
"Term". Section 1–201.

As amended in 2003.

§ 2–311.   Options and Cooperation Respecting Performance.

(1)   An agreement for sale which is otherwise sufficiently definite (subsection (3) of Section 2–204) to be a contract is not made invalid by the fact that it leaves particulars of performance to be specified by one of the parties. Any such specification must be made in good faith and within limits set by commercial reasonableness.

(2)   Unless otherwise agreed specifications relating to assortment of the goods are at the buyer's option and except as otherwise provided in subsections (1)(c) and (3) of Section 2–319 specifications or arrangements relating to shipment are at the seller's option.

(3)   Where such specification would materially affect the other party's performance but is not seasonably made or where one party's cooperation is necessary to the agreed performance of the other but is not seasonably forthcoming, the other party in addition to all other remedies

(a)   is excused for any resulting delay in his own performance; and

(b)   may also either proceed to perform in any reasonable manner or after the time for a material part of his own performance treat the failure to specify or to cooperate as a breach by failure to deliver or accept the goods.

Official Comment

Prior Uniform Statutory Provision: None.

Purposes:

1.   Subsection (1) permits the parties to leave certain detailed particulars of performance to be filled in by either of them without running the risk of having the contract invalidated for indefiniteness. The party to whom the agreement gives power to specify the missing details is required to exercise good faith and to act in accordance with commercial standards so that there is no surprise and the range of permissible variation is limited by what is commercially reasonable. The "agreement" which permits one party so to specify may be found as well in a course of dealing, usage of trade, or implication from circumstances as in explicit language used by the parties.

2.   Options as to assortment of goods or shipping arrangements are specifically reserved to the buyer and seller respectively under subsection (2) where no other arrangement has been made. This section rejects the test which mechanically and without regard to usage or the purpose of the option gave the option to the party "first under a duty to move" and applies instead a standard commercial interpretation to these circumstances. The "unless otherwise agreed" provision of this subsection covers not only express terms but the background and circumstances which enter into the agreement.

3.   Subsection (3) applies when the exercise of an option or cooperation by one party is necessary to or materially affects the other party's performance, but it is not seasonably forthcoming; the subsection relieves the other party from the necessity for performance or excuses his delay in performance as the case may be. The contract-keeping party may at his option under this subsection proceed to perform in any commercially reasonable manner rather than wait. In addition to the special remedies provided, this subsection also reserves "all other remedies". The remedy of particular importance in this connection is that provided for insecurity. Request may also be made pursuant to the obligation of good faith for a reasonable indication of the time and manner of performance for which a party is to hold himself ready.

4.   The remedy provided in subsection (3) is one which does not operate in the situation which falls within the scope of Section 2–614 on substituted performance. Where the failure to cooperate results from circumstances set forth in that Section, the other party is under a duty to proffer or demand (as the case may be) substitute performance as a condition to claiming rights against the noncooperating party.

Cross References:

Point 1: Sections 1–201, 2–204 and 1–203.
Point 3: Sections 1–203 and 2–609.
Point 4: Section 2–614.

Definitional Cross References:

"Agreement". Section 1–201.
"Buyer". Section 2–103.
"Contract for sale". Section 2–106.
"Goods". Section 2–105.
"Party". Section 1–201.
"Remedy". Section 1–201.
"Seasonably". Section 1–204.
"Seller". Section 2–103.

§ 2–312.   Warranty of Title and Against Infringement; Buyer's Obligation Against Infringement.

(1)   Subject to subsection (2) there is in a contract for sale a warranty by the seller that

(a)   the title conveyed shall be good, and its transfer rightful; and

(b)   the goods shall be delivered free from any security interest or other lien or encumbrance of which the buyer at the time of contracting has no knowledge.

(2)   A warranty under subsection (1) will be excluded or modified only by specific language or by circumstances which give the buyer reason to know that the person selling does not claim title in himself or that he is purporting to sell only such right or title as he or a third person may have.

(3)   Unless otherwise agreed a seller who is a merchant regularly dealing in goods of the kind warrants that the goods shall be delivered free of the rightful claim of any third person by way of infringement or the like but a buyer who furnishes specifications to the seller must hold the seller harmless against any such claim which arises out of compliance with the specifications.

Official Comment

Prior Uniform Statutory Provision: Section 13, Uniform Sales Act.

Changes: Completely rewritten, the provisions concerning infringement being new.

Purposes of Changes:

1.   Subsection (1) makes provision for a buyer's basic needs in respect to a title which he in good faith expects to acquire by his purchase, namely, that he receive a good, clean title transferred to him also in a rightful manner so that he will not be exposed to a lawsuit in order to protect it.

The warranty extends to a buyer whether or not the seller was in possession of the goods at the time the sale or contract to sell was made.

The warranty of quiet possession is abolished. Disturbance of quiet possession, although not mentioned specifically, is one way, among many, in which the breach of the warranty of title may be established.

The "knowledge" referred to in subsection 1(b) is actual knowledge as distinct from notice.

2.   The provisions of this Article requiring notification to the seller within a reasonable time after the buyer's discovery of a breach apply to notice of a breach of the warranty of title, where the seller's breach was innocent. However, if the seller's breach was in bad faith he cannot be permitted to claim that he has been misled or prejudiced by the delay in giving notice. In such case the "reasonable" time for notice should receive a very liberal interpretation. Whether the breach by the seller is in good or bad faith Section 2–725 provides that the cause of action accrues when the breach occurs. Under the provisions of that section the breach of the warranty of good title occurs when tender of delivery is made since the warranty is not one which extends to "future performance of the goods."

3.   When the goods are part of the seller's normal stock and are sold in his normal course of business, it is his duty to see that no claim of infringement of a patent or trademark by a third party will mar the buyer's title. A sale by a person other than a dealer, however, raises no implication in its circumstances of such a warranty. Nor is there such an implication when the buyer orders goods to be assembled, prepared or manufactured on his own specifications. If, in such a case, the resulting product infringes a patent or trademark,

the liability will run from buyer to seller. There is, under such circumstances, a tacit representation on the part of the buyer that the seller will be safe in manufacturing according to the specifications, and the buyer is under an obligation in good faith to indemnify him for any loss suffered.

4.   This section rejects the cases which recognize the principle that infringements violate the warranty of title but deny the buyer a remedy unless he has been expressly prevented from using the goods. Under this Article "eviction" is not a necessary condition to the buyer's remedy since the buyer's remedy arises immediately upon receipt of notice of infringement; it is merely one way of establishing the fact of breach.

5.   Subsection (2) recognizes that sales by sheriffs, executors, certain foreclosing lienors and persons similarly situated may be so out of the ordinary commercial course that their peculiar character is immediately apparent to the buyer and therefore no personal obligation is imposed upon the seller who is purporting to sell only an unknown or limited right. This subsection does not touch upon and leaves open all questions of restitution arising in such cases, when a unique article so sold is reclaimed by a third party as the rightful owner.

Foreclosure sales under Article 9 are another matter. Section 9–610 provides that a disposition of collateral under that section includes warranties such as those imposed by this section on a voluntary disposition of property of the kind involved. Consequently, unless properly excluded under subsection (2) or under the special provisions for exclusion in Section 9–610, a disposition under Section 9–610 of collateral consisting of goods includes the warranties imposed by subsection (1) and, if applicable, subsection (3).

6.   The warranty of subsection (1) is not designated as an "implied" warranty, and hence is not subject to Section 2–316(3). Disclaimer of the warranty of title is governed instead by subsection (2), which requires either specific language or the described circumstances.

Cross References:

> Point 1: Section 2–403.
> Point 2: Sections 2–607 and 2–725.
> Point 3: Section 1–203.
> Point 4: Sections 2–609 and 2–725.
> Point 6: Section 2–316.

Definitional Cross References:

> "Buyer". Section 2–103.
> "Contract for sale". Section 2–106.
> "Goods". Section 2–105.
> "Person". Section 1–201.
> "Right". Section 1–201.
> "Seller". Section 2–103.

As amended in 1999.

§ 2–313.   Express Warranties by Affirmation, Promise, Description, Sample.

(1)   Express warranties by the seller are created as follows:

(a)   Any affirmation of fact or promise made by the seller to the buyer which relates to the goods and becomes part of the basis of the bargain creates an express warranty that the goods shall conform to the affirmation or promise.

(b)   Any description of the goods which is made part of the basis of the bargain creates an express warranty that the goods shall conform to the description.

(c)   Any sample or model which is made part of the basis of the bargain creates an express warranty that the whole of the goods shall conform to the sample or model.

(2)   It is not necessary to the creation of an express warranty that the seller use formal words such as "warrant" or "guarantee" or that he have a specific intention to make a warranty, but an affirmation merely of the value of the goods or a statement purporting to be merely the seller's opinion or commendation of the goods does not create a warranty.

§ 2–313   UNIFORM COMMERCIAL CODE

Official Comment

Prior Uniform Statutory Provision: Sections 12, 14 and 16, Uniform Sales Act.

Changes: Rewritten.

Purposes of Changes: To consolidate and systematize basic principles with the result that:

1.   "Express" warranties rest on "dickered" aspects of the individual bargain, and go so clearly to the essence of that bargain that words of disclaimer in a form are repugnant to the basic dickered terms. "Implied" warranties rest so clearly on a common factual situation or set of conditions that no particular language or action is necessary to evidence them and they will arise in such a situation unless unmistakably negated.

This section reverts to the older case law insofar as the warranties of description and sample are designated "express" rather than "implied".

2.   Although this section is limited in its scope and direct purpose to warranties made by the seller to the buyer as part of a contract for sale, the warranty sections of this Article are not designed in any way to disturb those lines of case law growth which have recognized that warranties need not be confined either to sales contracts or to the direct parties to such a contract. They may arise in other appropriate circumstances such as in the case of bailments for hire, whether such bailment is itself the main contract or is merely a supplying of containers under a contract for the sale of their contents. The provisions of Section 2–318 on third party beneficiaries expressly recognize this case law development within one particular area. Beyond that, the matter is left to the case law with the intention that the policies of this Act may offer useful guidance in dealing with further cases as they arise.

3.   The present section deals with affirmations of fact by the seller, descriptions of the goods or exhibitions of samples, exactly as any other part of a negotiation which ends in a contract is dealt with. No specific intention to make a warranty is necessary if any of these factors is made part of the basis of the bargain. In actual practice affirmations of fact made by the seller about the goods during a bargain are regarded as part of the description of those goods; hence no particular reliance on such statements need be shown in order to weave them into the fabric of the agreement. Rather, any fact which is to take such affirmations, once made, out of the agreement requires clear affirmative proof. The issue normally is one of fact.

4.   In view of the principle that the whole purpose of the law of warranty is to determine what it is that the seller has in essence agreed to sell, the policy is adopted of those cases which refuse except in unusual circumstances to recognize a material deletion of the seller's obligation. Thus, a contract is normally a contract for a sale of something describable and described. A clause generally disclaiming "all warranties, express or implied" cannot reduce the seller's obligation with respect to such description and therefore cannot be given literal effect under Section 2–316.

This is not intended to mean that the parties, if they consciously desire, cannot make their own bargain as they wish. But in determining what they have agreed upon good faith is a factor and consideration should be given to the fact that the probability is small that a real price is intended to be exchanged for a pseudo-obligation.

5.   Paragraph (1)(b) makes specific some of the principles set forth above when a description of the goods is given by the seller.

A description need not be by words. Technical specifications, blueprints and the like can afford more exact description than mere language and if made part of the basis of the bargain goods must conform with them. Past deliveries may set the description of quality, either expressly or impliedly by course of dealing. Of course, all descriptions by merchants must be read against the applicable trade usages with the general rules as to merchantability resolving any doubts.

6.   The basic situation as to statements affecting the true essence of the bargain is no different when a sample or model is involved in the transaction. This section includes both a "sample" actually drawn from the bulk of goods which is the subject matter of the sale, and a "model" which is offered for inspection when the subject matter is not at hand and which has not been drawn from the bulk of the goods.

Although the underlying principles are unchanged, the facts are often ambiguous when something is shown as illustrative, rather than as a straight sample. In general, the presumption is that any sample or model just as any affirmation of fact is intended to become a basis of the bargain. But there is no escape from the question of fact. When the seller exhibits a sample purporting to be drawn from an existing bulk, good faith of course requires that the sample be fairly drawn. But in mercantile experience the mere exhibition of a "sample" does not of itself show whether it is merely intended to "suggest" or to "be" the character of the subject-matter of the contract. The question is whether the seller has so acted with reference to the sample as to make him responsible that the whole shall have at least the values shown by it. The circumstances aid in answering this question. If the sample has been drawn from an existing bulk, it must be regarded as describing values of the goods contracted for unless it is accompanied by an unmistakable denial of such responsibility. If, on the other hand, a model of merchandise not on hand is offered, the mercantile presumption that it has become a literal description of the subject matter is not so strong, and particularly so if modification on the buyer's initiative impairs any feature of the model.

7.   The precise time when words of description or affirmation are made or samples are shown is not material. The sole question is whether the language or samples or models are fairly to be regarded as part of the contract. If language is used after the closing of the deal (as when the buyer when taking delivery asks and receives an additional assurance), the warranty becomes a modification, and need not be supported by consideration if it is otherwise reasonable and in order (Section 2–209).

8.   Concerning affirmations of value or a seller's opinion or commendation under subsection (2), the basic question remains the same: What statements of the seller have in the circumstances and in objective judgment become part of the basis of the bargain? As indicated above, all of the statements of the seller do so unless good reason is shown to the contrary. The provisions of subsection (2) are included, however, since common experience discloses that some statements or predictions cannot fairly be viewed as entering into the bargain. Even as to false statements of value, however, the possibility is left open that a remedy may be provided by the law relating to fraud or misrepresentation.

Cross References:

> Point 1: Section 2–316.
> Point 2: Sections 1–102(3) and 2–318.
> Point 3: Section 2–316(2)(b).
> Point 4: Section 2–316.
> Point 5: Sections 1–205(4) and 2–314.
> Point 6: Section 2–316.
> Point 7: Section 2–209.
> Point 8: Section 1–103.

Definitional Cross References:

> "Buyer". Section 2–103.
> "Conforming". Section 2–106.
> "Goods". Section 2–105.
> "Seller". Section 2–103.

§ 2–314.   Implied Warranty: Merchantability; Usage of Trade.

(1)   Unless excluded or modified (Section 2–316), a warranty that the goods shall be merchantable is implied in a contract for their sale if the seller is a merchant with respect to goods of that kind. Under this section the serving for value of food or drink to be consumed either on the premises or elsewhere is a sale.

(2)   Goods to be merchantable must be at least such as

(a)   pass without objection in the trade under the contract description; and

(b)   in the case of fungible goods, are of fair average quality within the description; and

(c)   are fit for the ordinary purposes for which such goods are used; and

(d)   run, within the variations permitted by the agreement, of even kind, quality and quantity within each unit and among all units involved; and

(e)   are adequately contained, packaged, and labeled as the agreement may require; and

(f)   conform to the promise or affirmations of fact made on the container or label if any.

§ 2–314   UNIFORM COMMERCIAL CODE

(3)   Unless excluded or modified (Section 2–316) other implied warranties may arise from course of dealing or usage of trade.

Official Comment

Prior Uniform Statutory Provision: Section 15(2), Uniform Sales Act.

Changes: Completely rewritten.

Purposes of Changes: This section, drawn in view of the steadily developing case law on the subject, is intended to make it clear that:

1.   The seller's obligation applies to present sales as well as to contracts to sell subject to the effects of any examination of specific goods. (Subsection (2) of Section 2–316). Also, the warranty of merchantability applies to sales for use as well as to sales for resale.

2.   The question when the warranty is imposed turns basically on the meaning of the terms of the agreement as recognized in the trade. Goods delivered under an agreement made by a merchant in a given line of trade must be of a quality comparable to that generally acceptable in that line of trade under the description or other designation of the goods used in the agreement. The responsibility imposed rests on any merchant-seller, and the absence of the words "grower or manufacturer or not" which appeared in Section 15(2) of the Uniform Sales Act does not restrict the applicability of this section.

3.   A specific designation of goods by the buyer does not exclude the seller's obligation that they be fit for the general purposes appropriate to such goods. A contract for the sale of second-hand goods, however, involves only such obligation as is appropriate to such goods for that is their contract description. A person making an isolated sale of goods is not a "merchant" within the meaning of the full scope of this section and, thus, no warranty of merchantability would apply. His knowledge of any defects not apparent on inspection would, however, without need for express agreement and in keeping with the underlying reason of the present section and the provisions on good faith, impose an obligation that known material but hidden defects be fully disclosed.

4.   Although a seller may not be a "merchant" as to the goods in question, if he states generally that they are "guaranteed" the provisions of this section may furnish a guide to the content of the resulting express warranty. This has particular significance in the case of second-hand sales, and has further significance in limiting the effect of fine-print disclaimer clauses where their effect would be inconsistent with large-print assertions of "guarantee".

5.   The second sentence of subsection (1) covers the warranty with respect to food and drink. Serving food or drink for value is a sale, whether to be consumed on the premises or elsewhere. Cases to the contrary are rejected. The principal warranty is that stated in subsections (1) and (2)(c) of this section.

6.   Subsection (2) does not purport to exhaust the meaning of "merchantable" nor to negate any of its attributes not specifically mentioned in the text of the statute, but arising by usage of trade or through case law. The language used is "must be at least such as . . . ," and the intention is to leave open other possible attributes of merchantability.

7.   Paragraphs (a) and (b) of subsection (2) are to be read together. Both refer, as indicated above, to the standards of that line of the trade which fits the transaction and the seller's business. "Fair average" is a term directly appropriate to agricultural bulk products and means goods centering around the middle belt of quality, not the least or the worst that can be understood in the particular trade by the designation, but such as can pass "without objection." Of course a fair percentage of the least is permissible but the goods are not "fair average" if they are all of the least or worst quality possible under the description. In cases of doubt as to what quality is intended, the price at which a merchant closes a contract is an excellent index of the nature and scope of his obligation under the present section.

8.   Fitness for the ordinary purposes for which goods of the type are used is a fundamental concept of the present section and is covered in paragraph (c). As stated above, merchantability is also a part of the obligation owing to the purchaser for use. Correspondingly, protection, under this aspect of the warranty, of the person buying for resale to the ultimate consumer is equally necessary, and merchantable goods must therefore be "honestly" resalable in the normal course of business because they are what they purport to be.

9.   Paragraph (d) on evenness of kind, quality and quantity follows case law. But precautionary language has been added as a remainder of the frequent usages of trade which permit substantial variations both with and without an allowance or an obligation to replace the varying units.

10.   Paragraph (e) applies only where the nature of the goods and of the transaction require a certain type of container, package or label. Paragraph (f) applies, on the other hand, wherever there is a label or container on which representations are made, even though the original contract, either by express terms or usage of trade, may not have required either the labelling or the representation. This follows from the general obligation of good faith which requires that a buyer should not be placed in the position of reselling or using goods delivered under false representations appearing on the package or container. No problem of extra consideration arises in this connection since, under this Article, an obligation is imposed by the original contract not to deliver mislabeled articles, and the obligation is imposed where mercantile good faith so requires and without reference to the doctrine of consideration.

11.   Exclusion or modification of the warranty of merchantability, or of any part of it, is dealt with in the section to which the text of the present section makes explicit precautionary references. That section must be read with particular reference to its subsection (4) on limitation of remedies. The warranty of merchantability, wherever it is normal, is so commonly taken for granted that its exclusion from the contract is a matter threatening surprise and therefore requiring special precaution.

12.   Subsection (3) is to make explicit that usage of trade and course of dealing can create warranties and that they are implied rather than express warranties and thus subject to exclusion or modification under Section 2–316. A typical instance would be the obligation to provide pedigree papers to evidence conformity of the animal to the contract in the case of a pedigreed dog or blooded bull.

13.   In an action based on breach of warranty, it is of course necessary to show not only the existence of the warranty but the fact that the warranty was broken and that the breach of the warranty was the proximate cause of the loss sustained. In such an action an affirmative showing by the seller that the loss resulted from some action or event following his own delivery of the goods can operate as a defense. Equally, evidence indicating that the seller exercised care in the manufacture, processing or selection of the goods is relevant to the issue of whether the warranty was in fact broken. Action by the buyer following an examination of the goods which ought to have indicated the defect complained of can be shown as matter bearing on whether the breach itself was the cause of the injury.

Cross References:

> Point 1: Section 2–316.
> Point 3: Sections 1–203 and 2–104.
> Point 5: Section 2–315.
> Point 11: Section 2–316.
> Point 12: Sections 1–201, 1–205 and 2–316.

Definitional Cross References:

> "Agreement". Section 1–201.
> "Contract". Section 1–201.
> "Contract for sale". Section 2–106.
> "Goods". Section 2–105.
> "Merchant". Section 2–104.
> "Seller". Section 2–103.

§ 2–315.   Implied Warranty: Fitness for Particular Purpose.

Where the seller at the time of contracting has reason to know any particular purpose for which the goods are required and that the buyer is relying on the seller's skill or judgment to select or furnish suitable goods, there is unless excluded or modified under the next section an implied warranty that the goods shall be fit for such purpose.

Official Comment

Prior Uniform Statutory Provision: Section 15(1), (4), (5), Uniform Sales Act.

Changes: Rewritten.

§ 2–315   UNIFORM COMMERCIAL CODE

Purposes of Changes:

1. Whether or not this warranty arises in any individual case is basically a question of fact to be determined by the circumstances of the contracting. Under this section the buyer need not bring home to the seller actual knowledge of the particular purpose for which the goods are intended or of his reliance on the seller's skill and judgment, if the circumstances are such that the seller has reason to realize the purpose intended or that the reliance exists. The buyer, of course, must actually be relying on the seller.

2. A "particular purpose" differs from the ordinary purpose for which the goods are used in that it envisages a specific use by the buyer which is peculiar to the nature of his business whereas the ordinary purposes for which goods are used are those envisaged in the concept of merchantability and go to uses which are customarily made of the goods in question. For example, shoes are generally used for the purpose of walking upon ordinary ground, but a seller may know that a particular pair was selected to be used for climbing mountains.

A contract may of course include both a warranty of merchantability and one of fitness for a particular purpose.

The provisions of this Article on the cumulation and conflict of express and implied warranties must be considered on the question of inconsistency between or among warranties. In such a case any question of fact as to which warranty was intended by the parties to apply must be resolved in favor of the warranty of fitness for particular purpose as against all other warranties except where the buyer has taken upon himself the responsibility of furnishing the technical specifications.

3. In connection with the warranty of fitness for a particular purpose the provisions of this Article on the allocation or division of risks are particularly applicable in any transaction in which the purpose for which the goods are to be used combines requirements both as to the quality of the goods themselves and compliance with certain laws or regulations. How the risks are divided is a question of fact to be determined, where not expressly contained in the agreement, from the circumstances of contracting, usage of trade, course of performance and the like, matters which may constitute the "otherwise agreement" of the parties by which they may divide the risk or burden.

4. The absence from this section of the language used in the Uniform Sales Act in referring to the seller, "whether he be the grower or manufacturer or not," is not intended to impose any requirement that the seller be a grower or manufacturer. Although normally the warranty will arise only where the seller is a merchant with the appropriate "skill or judgment," it can arise as to non-merchants where this is justified by the particular circumstances.

5. The elimination of the "patent or other trade name" exception constitutes the major extension of the warranty of fitness which has been made by the cases and continued in this Article. Under the present section the existence of a patent or other trade name and the designation of the article by that name, or indeed in any other definite manner, is only one of the facts to be considered on the question of whether the buyer actually relied on the seller, but it is not of itself decisive of the issue. If the buyer himself is insisting on a particular brand he is not relying on the seller's skill and judgment and so no warranty results. But the mere fact that the article purchased has a particular patent or trade name is not sufficient to indicate nonreliance if the article has been recommended by the seller as adequate for the buyer's purposes.

6. The specific reference forward in the present section to the following section on exclusion or modification of warranties is to call attention to the possibility of eliminating the warranty in any given case. However it must be noted that under the following section the warranty of fitness for a particular purpose must be excluded or modified by a conspicuous writing.

Cross References:

Point 2: Sections 2–314 and 2–317.
Point 3: Section 2–303.
Point 6: Section 2–316.

Definitional Cross References:

"Buyer". Section 2–103.
"Goods". Section 2–105.
"Seller". Section 2–103.

§ 2–316.   Exclusion or Modification of Warranties.

(1)   Words or conduct relevant to the creation of an express warranty and words or conduct tending to negate or limit warranty shall be construed wherever reasonable as consistent with each other; but subject to the provisions of this Article on parol or extrinsic evidence (Section 2–202) negation or limitation is inoperative to the extent that such construction is unreasonable.

(2)   Subject to subsection (3), to exclude or modify the implied warranty of merchantability or any part of it the language must mention merchantability and in case of a writing must be conspicuous, and to exclude or modify any implied warranty of fitness the exclusion must be by a writing and conspicuous. Language to exclude all implied warranties of fitness is sufficient if it states, for example, that "There are no warranties which extend beyond the description on the face hereof."

(3)   Notwithstanding subsection (2)

(a)   unless the circumstances indicate otherwise, all implied warranties are excluded by expressions like "as is", "with all faults" or other language which in common understanding calls the buyer's attention to the exclusion of warranties and makes plain that there is no implied warranty; and

(b)   when the buyer before entering into the contract has examined the goods or the sample or model as fully as he desired or has refused to examine the goods there is no implied warranty with regard to defects which an examination ought in the circumstances to have revealed to him; and

(c)   an implied warranty can also be excluded or modified by course of dealing or course of performance or usage of trade.

(4)   Remedies for breach of warranty can be limited in accordance with the provisions of this Article on liquidation or limitation of damages and on contractual modification of remedy (Sections 2–718 and 2–719).

Official Comment

Prior Uniform Statutory Provision: None. See sections 15 and 71, Uniform Sales Act.

Purposes:

1.   This section is designed principally to deal with those frequent clauses in sales contracts which seek to exclude "all warranties, express or implied." It seeks to protect a buyer from unexpected and unbargained language of disclaimer by denying effect to such language when inconsistent with language of express warranty and permitting the exclusion of implied warranties only by conspicuous language or other circumstances which protect the buyer from surprise.

2.   The seller is protected under this Article against false allegations of oral warranties by its provisions on parol and extrinsic evidence and against unauthorized representations by the customary "lack of authority" clauses. This Article treats the limitation or avoidance of consequential damages as a matter of limiting remedies for breach, separate from the matter of creation of liability under a warranty. If no warranty exists, there is of course no problem of limiting remedies for breach of warranty. Under subsection (4) the question of limitation of remedy is governed by the sections referred to rather than by this section.

3.   Disclaimer of the implied warranty of merchantability is permitted under subsection (2), but with the safeguard that such disclaimers must mention merchantability and in case of a writing must be conspicuous.

4.   Unlike the implied warranty of merchantability, implied warranties of fitness for a particular purpose may be excluded by general language, but only if it is in writing and conspicuous.

5.   Subsection (2) presupposes that the implied warranty in question exists unless excluded or modified. Whether or not language of disclaimer satisfies the requirements of this section, such language may be relevant under other sections to the question whether the warranty was ever in fact created. Thus, unless the provisions of this Article on parol and extrinsic evidence prevent, oral language of disclaimer may raise issues of fact as to whether reliance by the buyer occurred and whether the seller had "reason to know" under the section on implied warranty of fitness for a particular purpose.

6.   The exceptions to the general rule set forth in paragraphs (a), (b) and (c) of subsection (3) are common factual situations in which the circumstances surrounding the transaction are in themselves sufficient to call the buyer's attention to the fact that no implied warranties are made or that a certain implied warranty is being excluded.

7.   Paragraph (a) of subsection (3) deals with general terms such as "as is," "as they stand," "with all faults," and the like. Such terms in ordinary commercial usage are understood to mean that the buyer takes the entire risk as to the quality of the goods involved. The terms covered by paragraph (a) are in fact merely a particularization of paragraph (c) which provides for exclusion or modification of implied warranties by usage of trade.

8.   Under paragraph (b) of subsection (3) warranties may be excluded or modified by the circumstances where the buyer examines the goods or a sample or model of them before entering into the contract. "Examination" as used in this paragraph is not synonymous with inspection before acceptance or at any other time after the contract has been made. It goes rather to the nature of the responsibility assumed by the seller at the time of the making of the contract. Of course if the buyer discovers the defect and uses the goods anyway, or if he unreasonably fails to examine the goods before he uses them, resulting injuries may be found to result from his own action rather than proximately from a breach of warranty. See Sections 2–314 and 2–715 and comments thereto.

In order to bring the transaction within the scope of "refused to examine" in paragraph (b), it is not sufficient that the goods are available for inspection. There must in addition be a demand by the seller that the buyer examine the goods fully. The seller by the demand puts the buyer on notice that he is assuming the risk of defects which the examination ought to reveal. The language "refused to examine" in this paragraph is intended to make clear the necessity for such demand.

Application of the doctrine of "caveat emptor" in all cases where the buyer examines the goods regardless of statements made by the seller is, however, rejected by this Article. Thus, if the offer of examination is accompanied by words as to their merchantability or specific attributes and the buyer indicates clearly that he is relying on those words rather than on his examination, they give rise to an "express" warranty. In such cases the question is one of fact as to whether a warranty of merchantability has been expressly incorporated in the agreement. Disclaimer of such an express warranty is governed by subsection (1) of the present section.

The particular buyer's skill and the normal method of examining goods in the circumstances determine what defects are excluded by the examination. A failure to notice defects which are obvious cannot excuse the buyer. However, an examination under circumstances which do not permit chemical or other testing of the goods would not exclude defects which could be ascertained only by such testing. Nor can latent defects be excluded by a simple examination. A professional buyer examining a product in his field will be held to have assumed the risk as to all defects which a professional in the field ought to observe, while a nonprofessional buyer will be held to have assumed the risk only for such defects as a layman might be expected to observe.

9.   The situation in which the buyer gives precise and complete specifications to the seller is not explicitly covered in this section, but this is a frequent circumstance by which the implied warranties may be excluded. The warranty of fitness for a particular purpose would not normally arise since in such a situation there is usually no reliance on the seller by the buyer. The warranty of merchantability in such a transaction, however, must be considered in connection with the next section on the cumulation and conflict of warranties. Under paragraph (c) of that section in case of such an inconsistency the implied warranty of merchantability is displaced by the express warranty that the goods will comply with the specifications. Thus, where the buyer gives detailed specifications as to the goods, neither of the implied warranties as to quality will normally apply to the transaction unless consistent with the specifications.

Cross References:

Point 2: Sections 2–202, 2–718 and 2–719.
Point 7: Sections 1–205 and 2–208.

Definitional Cross References:

"Agreement". Section 1–201.
"Buyer". Section 2–103.
"Contract". Section 1–201.
"Course of dealing". Section 1–205.

"Goods". Section 2–105.
"Remedy". Section 1–201.
"Seller". Section 2–103.
"Usage of trade". Section 1–205.

§ 2–317. Cumulation and Conflict of Warranties Express or Implied.

Warranties whether express or implied shall be construed as consistent with each other and as cumulative, but if such construction is unreasonable the intention of the parties shall determine which warranty is dominant. In ascertaining that intention the following rules apply:

(a) Exact or technical specifications displace an inconsistent sample or model or general language of description.

(b) A sample from an existing bulk displaces inconsistent general language of description.

(c) Express warranties displace inconsistent implied warranties other than an implied warranty of fitness for a particular purpose.

Official Comment

Prior Uniform Statutory Provision: On cumulation of warranties see Sections 14, 15, and 16, Uniform Sales Act.

Changes: Completely rewritten into one section.

Purposes of Changes:

1. The present section rests on the basic policy of this Article that no warranty is created except by some conduct (either affirmative action or failure to disclose) on the part of the seller. Therefore, all warranties are made cumulative unless this construction of the contract is impossible or unreasonable.

This Article thus follows the general policy of the Uniform Sales Act except that in case of the sale of an article by its patent or trade name the elimination of the warranty of fitness depends solely on whether the buyer has relied on the seller's skill and judgment; the use of the patent or trade name is but one factor in making this determination.

2. The rules of this section are designed to aid in determining the intention of the parties as to which of inconsistent warranties which have arisen from the circumstances of their transaction shall prevail. These rules of intention are to be applied only where factors making for an equitable estoppel of the seller do not exist and where he has in perfect good faith made warranties which later turn out to be inconsistent. To the extent that the seller has led the buyer to believe that all of the warranties can be performed, he is estopped from setting up any essential inconsistency as a defense.

3. The rules in subsections (a), (b) and (c) are designed to ascertain the intention of the parties by reference to the factor which probably claimed the attention of the parties in the first instance. These rules are not absolute but may be changed by evidence showing that the conditions which existed at the time of contracting make the construction called for by the section inconsistent or unreasonable.

Cross Reference:

Point 1: Section 2–315.

Definitional Cross Reference:

"Party". Section 1–201.

§ 2–318. Third Party Beneficiaries of Warranties Express or Implied.

Note: *If this Act is introduced in the Congress of the United States this section should be omitted. (States to select one alternative.)*

ALTERNATIVE A

A seller's warranty whether express or implied extends to any natural person who is in the family or household of his buyer or who is a guest in his home if it is reasonable to expect that such person may use, consume or be affected by the goods and who is injured in person by breach of the warranty. A seller may not exclude or limit the operation of this section.

ALTERNATIVE B

A seller's warranty whether express or implied extends to any natural person who may reasonably be expected to use, consume or be affected by the goods and who is injured in person by breach of the warranty. A seller may not exclude or limit the operation of this section.

ALTERNATIVE C

A seller's warranty whether express or implied extends to any person who may reasonably be expected to use, consume or be affected by the goods and who is injured by breach of the warranty. A seller may not exclude or limit the operation of this section with respect to injury to the person of an individual to whom the warranty extends.

As amended in 1966.

Official Comment

Prior Uniform Statutory Provision: None.

Purposes:

1.   The last sentence of this section does not mean that a seller is precluded from excluding or disclaiming a warranty which might otherwise arise in connection with the sale provided such exclusion or modification is permitted by Section 2-316. Nor does that sentence preclude the seller from limiting the remedies of his own buyer and of any beneficiaries, in any manner provided in Sections 2-718 or 2-719. To the extent that the contract of sale contains provisions under which warranties are excluded or modified, or remedies for breach are limited, such provisions are equally operative against beneficiaries of warranties under this section. What this last sentence forbids is exclusion of liability by the seller to the persons to whom the warranties which he has made to his buyer would extend under this section.

2.   The purpose of this section is to give certain beneficiaries the benefit of the same warranty which the buyer received in the contract of sale, thereby freeing any such beneficiaries from any technical rules as to "privity." It seeks to accomplish this purpose without any derogation of any right or remedy resting on negligence. It rests primarily upon the merchant-seller's warranty under this Article that the goods sold are merchantable and fit for the ordinary purposes for which such goods are used rather than the warranty of fitness for a particular purpose. Implicit in the section is that any beneficiary of a warranty may bring a direct action for breach of warranty against the seller whose warranty extends to him [As amended in 1966].

3.   The first alternative expressly includes as beneficiaries within its provisions the family, household and guests of the purchaser. Beyond this, the section in this form is neutral and is not intended to enlarge or restrict the developing case law on whether the seller's warranties, given to his buyer who resells, extend to other persons in the distributive chain.

The second alternative is designed for states where the case law has already developed further and for those that desire to expand the class of beneficiaries. The third alternative goes further, following the trend of modern decisions as indicated by Restatement of Torts 2d § 402A (Tentative Draft No. 10, 1965) in extending the rule beyond injuries to the person [As amended in 1966].

Cross References:

Point 1: Sections 2-316, 2-718 and 2-719.
Point 2: Section 2-314.

Definitional Cross References:

"Buyer". Section 2-103.
"Goods". Section 2-105.
"Seller". Section 2-103.

§ 2–319.   F.O.B. and F.A.S. Terms.

(1)   Unless otherwise agreed the term F.O.B. (which means "free on board") at a named place, even though used only in connection with the stated price, is a delivery term under which

(a)   when the term is F.O.B. the place of shipment, the seller must at that place ship the goods in the manner provided in this Article (Section 2–504) and bear the expense and risk of putting them into the possession of the carrier; or

(b)   when the term is F.O.B. the place of destination, the seller must at his own expense and risk transport the goods to that place and there tender delivery of them in the manner provided in this Article (Section 2–503);

(c)   when under either (a) or (b) the term is also F.O.B. vessel, car or other vehicle, the seller must in addition at his own expense and risk load the goods on board. If the term is F.O.B. vessel the buyer must name the vessel and in an appropriate case the seller must comply with the provisions of this Article on the form of bill of lading (Section 2–323).

(2)   Unless otherwise agreed the term F.A.S. vessel (which means "free alongside") at a named port, even though used only in connection with the stated price, is a delivery term under which the seller must

(a)   at his own expense and risk deliver the goods alongside the vessel in the manner usual in that port or on a dock designated and provided by the buyer; and

(b)   obtain and tender a receipt for the goods in exchange for which the carrier is under a duty to issue a bill of lading.

(3)   Unless otherwise agreed in any case falling within subsection (1)(a) or (c) or subsection (2) the buyer must seasonably give any needed instructions for making delivery, including when the term is F.A.S. or F.O.B. the loading berth of the vessel and in an appropriate case its name and sailing date. The seller may treat the failure of needed instructions as a failure of cooperation under this Article (Section 2–311). He may also at his option move the goods in any reasonable manner preparatory to delivery or shipment.

(4)   Under the term F.O.B. vessel or F.A.S. unless otherwise agreed the buyer must make payment against tender of the required documents and the seller may not tender nor the buyer demand delivery of the goods in substitution for the documents.

Official Comment

Prior Uniform Statutory Provision: None.

Purposes:

1.   This section is intended to negate the uncommercial line of decision which treats an "F.O.B." term as "merely a price term." The distinctions taken in subsection (1) handle most of the issues which have on occasion led to the unfortunate judicial language just referred to. Other matters which have led to sound results being based on unhappy language in regard to F.O.B. clauses are dealt with in this Act by Section 2–311(2) (seller's option re arrangements relating to shipment) and Sections 2–614 and 2–615 (substituted performance and seller's excuse).

2.   Subsection (1)(c) not only specifies the duties of a seller who engages to deliver "F.O.B. vessel," or the like, but ought to make clear that no agreement is soundly drawn when it looks to reshipment from San Francisco or New York, but speaks merely of "F.O.B." the place.

3.   The buyer's obligations stated in subsection (1)(c) and subsection (3) are, as shown in the text, obligations of cooperation. The last sentence of subsection (3) expressly, though perhaps unnecessarily, authorizes the seller, pending instructions, to go ahead with such preparatory moves as shipment from the interior to the named point of delivery. The sentence presupposes the usual case in which instructions "fail"; a prior repudiation by the buyer, giving notice that breach was intended, would remove the reason for the sentence, and would normally bring into play, instead, the second sentence of Section 2–704, which duly calls for lessening damages.

4.   The treatment of "F.O.B. vessel" in conjunction with F.A.S. fits, in regard to the need for payment against documents, with standard practice and case-law; but "F.O.B. vessel" is a term which by its very language makes express the need for an "on board" document. In this respect, that term is stricter than the ordinary overseas "shipment" contract (C.I.F., etc., Section 2–320).

Cross References:

Sections 2–311(3), 2–323, 2–503 and 2–504.

Definitional Cross References:

"Agreed". Section 1–201.
"Bill of lading". Section 1–201.
"Buyer". Section 2–103.
"Goods". Section 2–105.
"Seasonably". Section 1–204.
"Seller". Section 2–103.
"Term". Section 1–201.

§ 2–320.   C.I.F. and C. & F. Terms.

(1)   The term C.I.F. means that the price includes in a lump sum the cost of the goods and the insurance and freight to the named destination. The term C. & F. or C.F. means that the price so includes cost and freight to the named destination.

(2)   Unless otherwise agreed and even though used only in connection with the stated price and destination, the term C.I.F. destination or its equivalent requires the seller at his own expense and risk to

(a)   put the goods into the possession of a carrier at the port for shipment and obtain a negotiable bill or bills of lading covering the entire transportation to the named destination; and

(b)   load the goods and obtain a receipt from the carrier (which may be contained in the bill of lading) showing that the freight has been paid or provided for; and

(c)   obtain a policy or certificate of insurance, including any war risk insurance, of a kind and on terms then current at the port of shipment in the usual amount, in the currency of the contract, shown to cover the same goods covered by the bill of lading and providing for payment of loss to the order of the buyer or for the account of whom it may concern; but the seller may add to the price the amount of the premium for any such war risk insurance; and

(d)   prepare an invoice of the goods and procure any other documents required to effect shipment or to comply with the contract; and

(e)   forward and tender with commercial promptness all the documents in due form and with any indorsement necessary to perfect the buyer's rights.

(3)   Unless otherwise agreed the term C. & F. or its equivalent has the same effect and imposes upon the seller the same obligations and risks as a C.I.F. term except the obligation as to insurance.

(4)   Under the term C.I.F. or C. & F. unless otherwise agreed the buyer must make payment against tender of the required documents and the seller may not tender nor the buyer demand delivery of the goods in substitution for the documents.

Official Comment

Prior Uniform Statutory Provisions: None.

Purposes: To make it clear that:

1.   The C.I.F. contract is not a destination but a shipment contract with risk of subsequent loss or damage to the goods passing to the buyer upon shipment if the seller has properly performed all his obligations with respect to the goods. Delivery to the carrier is delivery to the buyer for purposes of risk and "title". Delivery of possession of the goods is accomplished by delivery of the bill of lading, and upon tender of the required documents the buyer must pay the agreed price without awaiting the arrival of the goods and if they have been

lost or damaged after proper shipment he must seek his remedy against the carrier or insurer. The buyer has no right of inspection prior to payment or acceptance of the documents.

2.   The seller's obligations remain the same even though the C.I.F. term is "used only in connection with the stated price and destination".

3.   The insurance stipulated by the C.I.F. term is for the buyer's benefit, to protect him against the risk of loss or damage to the goods in transit. A clause in a C.I.F. contract "insurance—for the account of sellers" should be viewed in its ordinary mercantile meaning that the sellers must pay for the insurance and not that it is intended to run to the seller's benefit.

4.   A bill of lading covering the entire transportation from the port of shipment is explicitly required but the provision on this point must be read in the light of its reason to assure the buyer of as full protection as the conditions of shipment reasonably permit, remembering always that this type of contract is designed to move the goods in the channels commercially available. To enable the buyer to deal with the goods while they are afloat the bill of lading must be one that covers only the quantity of goods called for by the contract. The buyer is not required to accept his part of the goods without a bill of lading because the latter covers a larger quantity, nor is he required to accept a bill of lading for the whole quantity under a stipulation to hold the excess for the owner. Although the buyer is not compelled to accept either goods or documents under such circumstances he may of course claim his rights in any goods which have been identified to his contract.

5.   The seller is given the option of paying or providing for the payment of freight. He has no option to ship "freight collect" unless the agreement so provides. The rule of the common law that the buyer need not pay the freight if the goods do not arrive is preserved.

Unless the shipment has been sent "freight collect" the buyer is entitled to receive documentary evidence that he is not obligated to pay the freight; the seller is therefore required to obtain a receipt "showing that the freight has been paid or provided for." The usual notation on the bill of lading that the freight has been prepaid is a sufficient receipt, as at common law. The phrase "provided for" is intended to cover the frequent situation in which the carrier extends credit to a shipper for the freight on successive shipments and receives periodical payments of the accrued freight charges from him.

6.   The requirement that unless otherwise agreed the seller must procure insurance "of a kind and on terms then current at the port for shipment in the usual amount, in the currency of the contract, sufficiently shown to cover the same goods covered by the bill of lading", applies to both marine and war risk insurance. As applied to marine insurance, it means such insurance as is usual or customary at the port for shipment with reference to the particular kind of goods involved, the character and equipment of the vessel, the route of the voyage, the port of destination and any other considerations that affect the risk. It is the substantial equivalent of the ordinary insurance in the particular trade and on the particular voyage and is subject to agreed specifications of type or extent of coverage. The language does not mean that the insurance must be adequate to cover all risks to which the goods may be subject in transit. There are some types of loss or damage that are not covered by the usual marine insurance and are excepted in bills of lading or in applicable statutes from the causes of loss or damage for which the carrier or the vessel is liable. Such risks must be borne by the buyer under this Article.

Insurance secured in compliance with a C.I.F. term must cover the entire transportation of the goods to the named destination.

7.   An additional obligation is imposed upon the seller in requiring him to procure customary war risk insurance at the buyer's expense. This changes the common law on the point. The seller is not required to assume the risk of including in the C.I.F. price the cost of such insurance, since it often fluctuates rapidly, but is required to treat it simply as a necessary for the buyer's account. What war risk insurance is "current" or usual turns on the standard forms of policy or rider in common use.

8.   The C.I.F. contract calls for insurance covering the value of the goods at the time and place of shipment and does not include any increase in market value during transit or any anticipated profit to the buyer on a sale by him.

The contract contemplates that before the goods arrive at their destination they may be sold again and again on C.I.F. terms and that the original policy of insurance and bill of lading will run with the interest in the goods by being transferred to each successive buyer. A buyer who becomes the seller in such an intermediate contract for sale does not thereby, if his sub-buyer knows the circumstances, undertake to insure the goods again at an increased price fixed in the new contract or to cover the increase in price by additional insurance, and his buyer may not reject the documents on the ground that the original policy does not cover such higher price. If such a sub-buyer desires additional insurance he must procure it for himself.

Where the seller exercises an option to ship "freight collect" and to credit the buyer with the freight against the C.I.F. price, the insurance need not cover the freight since the freight is not at the buyer's risk. On the other hand, where the seller prepays the freight upon shipping under a bill of lading requiring prepayment and providing that the freight shall be deemed earned and shall be retained by the carrier "ship and/or cargo lost or not lost," or using words of similar import, he must procure insurance that will cover the freight, because notwithstanding that the goods are lost in transit the buyer is bound to pay the freight as part of the C.I.F. price and will be unable to recover it back from the carrier.

9. Insurance "for the account of whom it may concern" is usual and sufficient. However, for a valid tender the policy of insurance must be one which can be disposed of together with the bill of lading and so must be "sufficiently shown to cover the same goods covered by the bill of lading". It must cover separately the quantity of goods called for by the buyer's contract and not merely insure his goods as part of a larger quantity in which others are interested, a case provided for in American mercantile practice by the use of negotiable certificates of insurance which are expressly authorized by this section. By usage these certificates are treated as the equivalent of separate policies and are good tender under C.I.F. contracts. The term "certificate of insurance", however, does not of itself include certificates or "cover notes" issued by the insurance broker and stating that the goods are covered by a policy. Their sufficiency as substitutes for policies will depend upon proof of an established usage or course of dealing. The present section rejects the English rule that not only brokers' certificates and "cover notes" but also certain forms of American insurance certificates are not the equivalent of policies and are not good tender under a C.I.F. contract.

The seller's failure to tender a proper insurance document is waived if the buyer refuses to make payment on other and untenable grounds at a time when proper insurance could have been obtained and tendered by the seller if timely objection had been made. Even a failure to insure on shipment may be cured by seasonable tender of a policy retroactive in effect; e.g., one insuring the goods "lost or not lost." The provisions of this Article on cure of improper tender and on waiver of buyer's objections by silence are applicable to insurance tenders under a C.I.F. term. Where there is no waiver by the buyer as described above, however, the fact that the goods arrive safely does not cure the seller's breach of his obligations to insure them and tender to the buyer a proper insurance document.

10. The seller's invoice of the goods shipped under a C.I.F. contract is regarded as a usual and necessary document upon which reliance may properly be placed. It is the document which evidences points of description, quality and the like which do not readily appear in other documents. This Article rejects those statements to the effect that the invoice is a usual but not a necessary document under a C.I.F. term.

11. The buyer needs all of the documents required under a C.I.F. contract, in due form and, if a tangible document of title, with necessary endorsements, so that before the goods arrive he may deal with them by negotiating the documents or may obtain prompt possession of the goods after their arrival. If the goods are lost or damaged in transit the documents are necessary to enable him promptly to assert his remedy against the carrier or insurer. The seller is therefore obligated to do what is mercantilely reasonable in the circumstances and should make every reasonable exertion to send forward the documents as soon as possible after the shipment. The requirement that the documents be forwarded with "commercial promptness" expresses a more urgent need for action than that suggested by the phrase "reasonable time".

12. Under a C.I.F. contract the buyer, as under the common law, must pay the price upon tender of the required documents without first inspecting the goods, but his payment in these circumstances does not constitute an acceptance of the goods nor does it impair his right of subsequent inspection or his options and remedies in the case of improper delivery. All remedies and rights for the seller's breach are reserved to him. The buyer must pay before inspection and assert his remedy against the seller afterward unless the nonconformity of the goods amounts to a real failure of consideration, since the purpose of choosing this form of contract is to give the seller protection against the buyer's unjustifiable rejection of the goods at a distant port of destination which would necessitate taking possession of the goods and suing the buyer there.

13. A valid C.I.F. contract may be made which requires part of the transportation to be made on land and part on the sea, as where the goods are to be brought by rail from an inland point to a seaport and thence transported by vessel to the named destination under a "through" or combination bill of lading issued by the railroad company. In such a case shipment by rail from the inland point within the contract period is a timely

ARTICLE 2 (2016)   § 2–321

shipment notwithstanding that the loading of the goods on the vessel is delayed by causes beyond the seller's control.

14.   Although subsection (2) stating the legal effects of the C.I.F. term is an "unless otherwise agreed" provision, the express language used in an agreement is frequently a precautionary, fuller statement of the normal C.I.F. terms and hence not intended as a departure or variation from them. Moreover, the dominant outlines of the C.I.F. term are so well understood commercially that any variation should, whenever reasonably possible, be read as falling within those dominant outlines rather than as destroying the whole meaning of a term which essentially indicates a contract for proper shipment rather than one for delivery at destination. Particularly careful consideration is necessary before a printed form or clause is construed to mean agreement otherwise and where a C.I.F. contract is prepared on a printed form designed for some other type of contract, the C.I.F. terms must prevail over printed clauses repugnant to them.

15.   Under subsection (4) the fact that the seller knows at the time of the tender of the documents that the goods have been lost in transit does not affect his rights if he has performed his contractual obligations. Similarly, the seller cannot perform under a C.I.F. term by purchasing and tendering landed goods.

16.   Under the C. & F. term, as under the C.I.F. term, title and risk of loss are intended to pass to the buyer on shipment. A stipulation in a C. & F. contract that the seller shall effect insurance on the goods and charge the buyer with the premium (in effect that he shall act as the buyer's agent for that purpose) is entirely in keeping with the pattern. On the other hand, it often happens that the buyer is in a more advantageous position than the seller to effect insurance on the goods or that he has in force an "open" or "floating" policy covering all shipments made by him or to him, in either of which events the C. & F. term is adequate without mention of insurance.

17.   It is to be remembered that in a French contract the term "C.A.F." does not mean "Cost and Freight" but has exactly the same meaning as the term "C.I.F." since it is merely the French equivalent of that term. The "A" does not stand for "and" but for "assurance" which means insurance.

Cross References:

> Point 4: Section 2–323.
> Point 6: Section 2–509(1)(a).
> Point 9: Sections 2–508 and 2–605(1)(a).
> Point 12: Sections 2–321(3), 2–512 and 2–513(3) and Article 5.

Definitional Cross References:

> "Bill of lading". Section 1–201.
> "Buyer". Section 2–103.
> "Contract". Section 1–201.
> "Goods". Section 2–105.
> "Rights". Section 1–201.
> "Seller". Section 2–103.
> "Term". Section 1–201.

As amended in 2003.

§ 2–321.   C.I.F. or C. & F.: "Net Landed Weights"; "Payment on Arrival"; Warranty of Condition on Arrival.

Under a contract containing a term C.I.F. or C. & F.

(1)   Where the price is based on or is to be adjusted according to "net landed weights", "delivered weights", "out turn" quantity or quality or the like, unless otherwise agreed the seller must reasonably estimate the price. The payment due on tender of the documents called for by the contract is the amount so estimated, but after final adjustment of the price a settlement must be made with commercial promptness.

(2)   An agreement described in subsection (1) or any warranty of quality or condition of the goods on arrival places upon the seller the risk of ordinary deterioration, shrinkage and the like in transportation

§ 2–322   UNIFORM COMMERCIAL CODE

but has no effect on the place or time of identification to the contract for sale or delivery or on the passing of the risk of loss.

(3)   Unless otherwise agreed where the contract provides for payment on or after arrival of the goods the seller must before payment allow such preliminary inspection as is feasible; but if the goods are lost delivery of the documents and payment are due when the goods should have arrived.

Official Comment

Prior Uniform Statutory Provision: None.

Purposes:

This section deals with two variations of the C.I.F. contract which have evolved in mercantile practice but are entirely consistent with the basic C.I.F. pattern. Subsections (1) and (2), which provide for a shift to the seller of the risk of quality and weight deterioration during shipment, are designed to conform the law to the best mercantile practice and usage without changing the legal consequences of the C.I.F. or C. & F. term as to the passing of marine risks to the buyer at the point of shipment. Subsection (3) provides that where under the contract documents are to be presented for payment after arrival of the goods, this amounts merely to a postponement of the payment under the C.I.F. contract and is not to be confused with the "no arrival, no sale" contract. If the goods are lost, delivery of the documents and payment against them are due when the goods should have arrived. The clause for payment on or after arrival is not to be construed as such a condition precedent to payment that if the goods are lost in transit the buyer need never pay and the seller must bear the loss.

Cross Reference:

Section 2–324.

Definitional Cross References:

"Agreement". Section 1–201.
"Contract". Section 1–201.
"Delivery". Section 1–201.
"Goods". Section 2–105.
"Seller". Section 2–103.
"Term". Section 1–201.

§ 2–322.   Delivery "Ex-Ship".

(1)   Unless otherwise agreed a term for delivery of goods "ex-ship" (which means from the carrying vessel) or in equivalent language is not restricted to a particular ship and requires delivery from a ship which has reached a place at the named port of destination where goods of the kind are usually discharged.

(2)   Under such a term unless otherwise agreed

(a)   the seller must discharge all liens arising out of the carriage and furnish the buyer with a direction which puts the carrier under a duty to deliver the goods; and

(b)   the risk of loss does not pass to the buyer until the goods leave the ship's tackle or are otherwise properly unloaded.

Official Comment

Prior Uniform Statutory Provision: None.

Purposes:

1.   The delivery term, "ex-ship", as between seller and buyer, is the reverse of the f.a.s. term covered.

2.   Delivery need not be made from any particular vessel under a clause calling for delivery "ex-ship", even though a vessel on which shipment is to be made originally is named in the contract, unless the agreement by appropriate language, restricts the clause to delivery from a named vessel.

ARTICLE 2 (2016)   § 2–323

3.   The appropriate place and manner of unloading at the port of destination depend upon the nature of the goods and the facilities and usages of the port.

4.   A contract fixing a price "ex-ship" with payment "cash against documents" calls only for such documents as are appropriate to the contract. Tender of a delivery order and of a receipt for the freight after the arrival of the carrying vessel is adequate. The seller is not required to tender a bill of lading as a document of title nor is he required to insure the goods for the buyer's benefit, as the goods are not at the buyer's risk during the voyage.

Cross Reference:

Point 1: Section 2–319(2).

Definitional Cross References:

"Buyer". Section 2–103.
"Goods". Section 2–105.
"Seller". Section 2–103.
"Term". Section 1–201.

§ 2–323.   Form of Bill of Lading Required in Overseas Shipment; "Overseas".

(1)   Where the contract contemplates overseas shipment and contains a term C.I.F. or C. & F. or F.O.B. vessel, the seller unless otherwise agreed must obtain a negotiable bill of lading stating that the goods have been loaded in board or, in the case of a term C.I.F. or C. & F., received for shipment.

(2)   Where in a case within subsection (1) a tangible bill of lading has been issued in a set of parts, unless otherwise agreed if the documents are not to be sent from abroad the buyer may demand tender of the full set; otherwise only one part of the bill of lading need be tendered. Even if the agreement expressly requires a full set

(a)   due tender of a single part is acceptable within the provisions of this Article on cure of improper delivery (subsection (1) of Section 2–508); and

(b)   even though the full set is demanded, if the documents are sent from abroad the person tendering an incomplete set may nevertheless require payment upon furnishing an indemnity which the buyer in good faith deems adequate.

(3)   A shipment by water or by air or a contract contemplating such shipment is "overseas" insofar as by usage of trade or agreement it is subject to the commercial, financing or shipping practices characteristic of international deep water commerce.

As amended in 2003.

Official Comment

Prior Uniform Statutory Provision: None.

Purposes:

1.   Subsection (1) follows the "American" rule that a regular bill of lading indicating delivery of the goods at the dock for shipment is sufficient, except under a term "F.O.B. vessel." See Section 2–319 and comment thereto.

2.   Subsection (2) deals with the problem of bills of lading covering deep water shipments, issued not as a single bill of lading but in a set of parts, each part referring to the other parts and the entire set constituting in commercial practice and at law a single bill of lading. Commercial practice in international commerce is to accept and pay against presentation of the first part of a set if the part is sent from overseas even though the contract of the buyer requires presentation of a full set of bills of lading provided adequate indemnity for the missing parts is forthcoming. In accord with the amendment to Section 7–304, bills of lading in a set are limited to tangible bills.

This subsection codifies that practice as between buyer and seller. Article 5 (Section 5–113) authorizes banks presenting drafts under letters of credit to give indemnities against the missing parts, and this subsection means that the buyer must accept and act on such indemnities if he in good faith deems them adequate. But

§ 2–324   **UNIFORM COMMERCIAL CODE**

neither this subsection nor Article 5 decides whether a bank which has issued a letter of credit is similarly bound. The issuing bank's obligation under a letter of credit is independent and depends on its own terms. See Article 5.

Cross References:

> Sections 2–508(2), 5–113.

Definitional Cross References:

> "Bill of lading". Section 1–201.
> "Buyer". Section 2–103.
> "Contract". Section 1–201.
> "Delivery". Section 1–201.
> "Financing agency". Section 2–104.
> "Person". Section 1–201.
> "Seller". Section 2–103.
> "Send". Section 1–201.
> "Term". Section 1–201.

As amended in 2003.

§ 2–324.   "No Arrival, No Sale" Term.

Under a term "no arrival, no sale" or terms of like meaning, unless otherwise agreed,

(a) the seller must properly ship conforming goods and if they arrive by any means he must tender them on arrival but he assumes no obligation that the goods will arrive unless he has caused the non-arrival; and

(b) where without fault of the seller the goods are in part lost or have so deteriorated as no longer to conform to the contract or arrive after the contract time, the buyer may proceed as if there had been casualty to identified goods (Section 2–613).

Official Comment

Prior Uniform Statutory Provision: None.

Purposes:

1.   The "no arrival, no sale" term in a "destination" overseas contract leaves risk of loss on the seller but gives him an exemption from liability for non-delivery. Both the nature of the case and the duty of good faith require that the seller must not interfere with the arrival of the goods in any way. If the circumstances impose upon him the responsibility for making or arranging the shipment, he must have a shipment made despite the exemption clause. Further, the shipment made must be a conforming one, for the exemption under a "no arrival, no sale" term applies only to the hazards of transportation and the goods must be proper in all other respects.

The reason of this section is that where the seller is reselling goods bought by him as shipped by another and this fact is known to the buyer, so that the seller is not under any obligation to make the shipment himself, the seller is entitled under the "no arrival, no sale" clause to exemption from payment of damages for non-delivery if the goods do not arrive or if the goods which actually arrive are non-conforming. This does not extend to sellers who arrange shipment by their own agents, in which case the clause is limited to casualty due to marine hazards. But sellers who make known that they are contracting only with respect to what will be delivered to them by parties over whom they assume no control are entitled to the full quantum of the exemption.

2.   The provisions of this Article on identification must be read together with the present section in order to bring the exemption into application. Until there is some designation of the goods in a particular shipment or on a particular ship as being those to which the contract refers there can be no application of an exemption for their non-arrival.

3.   The seller's duty to tender the agreed or declared goods if they do arrive is not impaired because of their delay in arrival or by their arrival after transshipment.

4.   The phrase "to arrive" is often employed in the same sense as "no arrival, no sale" and may then be given the same effect. But a "to arrive" term, added to a C.I.F. or C. & F. contract, does not have the full meaning given by this section to "no arrival, no sale". Such a "to arrive" term is usually intended to operate only to the extent that the risks are not covered by the agreed insurance and the loss or casualty is due to such uncovered hazards. In some instances the "to arrive" term may be regarded as a time of payment term, or, in the case of the reselling seller discussed in point 1 above, as negating responsibility for conformity of the goods, if they arrive, to any description which was based on his good faith belief of the quality. Whether this is the intention of the parties is a question of fact based on all the circumstances surrounding the resale and in case of ambiguity the rules of Sections 2–316 and 2–317 apply to preclude dishonor.

5.   Paragraph (b) applies where goods arrive impaired by damage or partial loss during transportation and makes the policy of this Article on casualty to identified goods applicable to such a situation. For the term cannot be regarded as intending to give the seller an unforeseen profit through casualty; it is intended only to protect him from loss due to causes beyond his control.

Cross References:

Point 1: Section 1–203.
Point 2: Section 2–501(a) and (c).
Point 5: Section 2–613.

Definitional Cross References:

"Buyer". Section 2–103.
"Conforming". Section 2–106.
"Contract". Section 1–201.
"Fault". Section 1–201.
"Goods". Section 2–105.
"Sale". Section 2–106.
"Seller". Section 2–103.
"Term". Section 1–201.

§ 2–325.   "Letter of Credit" Term; "Confirmed Credit".

(1)   Failure of the buyer seasonably to furnish an agreed letter of credit is a breach of the contract for sale.

(2)   The delivery to seller of a proper letter of credit suspends the buyer's obligation to pay. If the letter of credit is dishonored, the seller may on seasonable notification to the buyer require payment directly from him.

(3)   Unless otherwise agreed the term "letter of credit" or "banker's credit" in a contract for sale means an irrevocable credit issued by a financing agency of good repute and, where the shipment is overseas, of good international repute. The term "confirmed credit" means that the credit must also carry the direct obligation of such an agency which does business in the seller's financial market.

Official Comment

Prior Uniform Statutory Provision: None.

Purposes: To express the established commercial and banking understanding as to the meaning and effects of terms calling for "letters of credit" or "confirmed credit":

1.   Subsection (2) follows the general policy of this Article and Article 3 (Section 3–802) on conditional payment, under which payment by check or other short-term instrument is not ordinarily final as between the parties if the recipient duly presents the instrument and honor is refused. Thus the furnishing of a letter of credit does not substitute the financing agency's obligation for the buyer's, but the seller must first give the buyer reasonable notice of his intention to demand direct payment from him.

2.   Subsection (3) requires that the credit be irrevocable and be a prime credit as determined by the standing of the issuer. It is not necessary, unless otherwise agreed, that the credit be a negotiation credit; the seller can finance himself by an assignment of the proceeds under Section 5–116(2).

§ 2–326   UNIFORM COMMERCIAL CODE

3.   The definition of "confirmed credit" is drawn on the supposition that the credit is issued by a bank which is not doing direct business in the seller's financial market; there is no intention to require the obligation of two banks both local to the seller.

Cross References:

Sections 2–403, 2–511(3) and 3–802 and Article 5.

Definitional Cross References:

"Buyer". Section 2–103.
"Contract for sale". Section 2–106.
"Draft". Section 3–104.
"Financing agency". Section 2–104.
"Notifies". Section 1–201.
"Overseas". Section 2–323.
"Purchaser". Section 1–201.
"Seasonably". Section 1–204.
"Seller". Section 2–103.
"Term". Section 1–201.

§ 2–326.   Sale on Approval and Sale or Return; Rights of Creditors.

(1)   Unless otherwise agreed, if delivered goods may be returned by the buyer even though they conform to the contract, the transaction is

(a)   a "sale on approval" if the goods are delivered primarily for use, and

(b)   a "sale or return" if the goods are delivered primarily for resale.

(2)   Goods held on approval are not subject to the claims of the buyer's creditors until acceptance; goods held on sale or return are subject to such claims while in the buyer's possession.

(3)   Any "or return" term of a contract for sale is to be treated as a separate contract for sale within the statute of frauds section of this Article (Section 2–201) and as contradicting the sale aspect of the contract within the provisions of this Article on parol or extrinsic evidence (Section 2–202).

As amended in 1999.

Official Comment

Prior Uniform Statutory Provision: Section 19(3), Uniform Sales Act.

Changes: Completely rewritten in this and the succeeding section.

Purposes of Changes: To make it clear that:

1.   Both a "sale on approval" and a "sale or return" should be distinguished from other types of transactions with which they frequently have been confused. A "sale on approval," sometimes also called a sale "on trial" or "on satisfaction," deals with a contract under which the seller undertakes a risk in order to satisfy its prospective buyer with the appearance or performance of the goods that are sold. The goods are delivered to the proposed purchaser but they remain the property of the seller until the buyer accepts them. The price has already been agreed. The buyer's willingness to receive and test the goods is the consideration for the seller's engagement to deliver and sell. A "sale or return," on the other hand, typically is a sale to a merchant whose unwillingness to buy is overcome by the seller's engagement to take back the goods (or any commercial unit of goods) in lieu of payment if they fail to be resold. A sale or return is a present sale of goods which may be undone at the buyer's option. Accordingly, subsection (2) provides that goods delivered on approval are not subject to the prospective buyer's creditors until acceptance, and goods delivered in a sale or return are subject to the buyer's creditors while in the buyer's possession.

These two transactions are so strongly delineated in practice and in general understanding that every presumption runs against a delivery to a consumer being a "sale or return" and against a delivery to a merchant for resale being a "sale on approval."

2.   The right to return goods for failure to conform to the contract of sale does not make the transaction a "sale on approval" or "sale or return" and has nothing to do with this section or Section 2–327. This section is not concerned with remedies for breach of contract. It deals instead with a power given by the contract to turn back the goods even though they are wholly as warranted. This section nevertheless presupposes that a contract for sale is contemplated by the parties, although that contract may be of the particular character that this section addresses (i.e., a sale on approval or a sale or return).

If a buyer's obligation as a buyer is conditioned not on its personal approval but on the article's passing a described objective test, the risk of loss by casualty pending the test is properly the seller's and proper return is at its expense. On the point of "satisfaction" as meaning "reasonable satisfaction" when an industrial machine is involved, this Article takes no position.

3.   Subsection (3) resolves a conflict in the pre-UCC case law by recognizing that an "or return" provision is so definitely at odds with any ordinary contract for sale of goods that if a written agreement is involved the "or return" term must be contained in a written memorandum. The "or return" aspect of a sales contract must be treated as a separate contract under the Statute of Frauds section and as contradicting the sale insofar as questions of parol or extrinsic evidence are concerned.

4.   Certain true consignment transactions were dealt with in former Sections 2–326(3) and 9–114. These provisions have been deleted and have been replaced by new provisions in Article 9. See, e.g., Sections 9–109(a)(4); 9–103(d); 9–319.

Cross References:

Point 2: Article 9.
Point 3: Sections 2–201 and 2–202.

Definitional Cross References:

"Between merchants". Section 2–104.
"Buyer". Section 2–103.
"Conform". Section 2–106.
"Contract for sale". Section 2–106.
"Creditor". Section 1–201.
"Goods". Section 2–105.
"Sale". Section 2–106.
"Seller". Section 2–103.

As amended in 1999 and 2000.

§ 2–327.   Special Incidents of Sale on Approval and Sale or Return.

(1)   Under a sale on approval unless otherwise agreed

(a)   although the goods are identified to the contract the risk of loss and the title do not pass to the buyer until acceptance; and

(b)   use of the goods consistent with the purpose of trial is not acceptance but failure seasonably to notify the seller of election to return the goods is acceptance, and if the goods conform to the contract acceptance of any part is acceptance of the whole; and

(c)   after due notification of election to return, the return is at the seller's risk and expense but a merchant buyer must follow any reasonable instructions.

(2)   Under a sale or return unless otherwise agreed

(a)   the option to return extends to the whole or any commercial unit of the goods while in substantially their original condition, but must be exercised seasonably; and

(b)   the return is at the buyer's risk and expense.

Official Comment

Prior Uniform Statutory Provision: Section 19(3), Uniform Sales Act.

§ 2–328   **UNIFORM COMMERCIAL CODE**

Changes: Completely rewritten in preceding and this section.

Purposes of Changes: To make it clear that:

1.   In the case of a sale on approval:

If all of the goods involved conform to the contract, the buyer's acceptance of part of the goods constitutes acceptance of the whole. Acceptance of part falls outside the normal intent of the parties in the "on approval" situation and the policy of this Article allowing partial acceptance of a defective delivery has no application here. A case where a buyer takes home two dresses to select one commonly involves two distinct contracts; if not, it is covered by the words "unless otherwise agreed".

2.   In the case of a sale or return, the return of any unsold unit merely because it is unsold is the normal intent of the "sale or return" provision, and therefore the right to return for this reason alone is independent of any other action under the contract which would turn on wholly different considerations. On the other hand, where the return of goods is for breach, including return of items resold by the buyer and returned by the ultimate purchasers because of defects, the return procedure is governed not by the present section but by the provisions on the effects and revocation of acceptance.

3.   In the case of a sale on approval the risk rests on the seller until acceptance of the goods by the buyer, while in a sale or return the risk remains throughout on the buyer.

4.   Notice of election to return given by the buyer in a sale on approval is sufficient to relieve him of any further liability. Actual return by the buyer to the seller is required in the case of a sale or return contract. What constitutes due "giving" of notice, as required in "on approval" sales, is governed by the provisions on good faith and notice. "Seasonable" is used here as defined in Section 1–204. Nevertheless, the provisions of both this Article and of the contract on this point must be read with commercial reason and with full attention to good faith.

Cross References:

Point 1: Sections 2–501, 2–601 and 2–603.
Point 2: Sections 2–607 and 2–608.
Point 4: Sections 1–201 and 1–204.

Definitional Cross References:

"Agreed". Section 1–201.
"Buyer". Section 2–103.
"Commercial unit". Section 2–105.
"Conform". Section 2–106.
"Contract". Section 1–201.
"Goods". Section 2–105.
"Merchant". Section 2–104.
"Notifies". Section 1–201.
"Notification". Section 1–201.
"Sale on approval". Section 2–326.
"Sale or return". Section 2–326.
"Seasonably". Section 1–204.
"Seller". Section 2–103.

§ 2–328.   Sale by Auction.

(1)   In a sale by auction if goods are put up in lots each lot is the subject of a separate sale.

(2)   A sale by auction is complete when the auctioneer so announces by the fall of the hammer or in other customary manner. Where a bid is made while the hammer is falling in acceptance of a prior bid the auctioneer may in his discretion reopen the bidding or declare the goods sold under the bid on which the hammer was falling.

(3)   Such a sale is with reserve unless the goods are in explicit terms put up without reserve. In an auction with reserve the auctioneer may withdraw the goods at any time until he announces completion of

the sale. In an auction without reserve, after the auctioneer calls for bids on an article or lot, that article or lot cannot be withdrawn unless no bid is made within a reasonable time. In either case a bidder may retract his bid until the auctioneer's announcement of completion of the sale, but a bidder's retraction does not revive any previous bid.

(4)   If the auctioneer knowingly receives a bid on the seller's behalf or the seller makes or procures such a bid, and notice has not been given that liberty for such bidding is reserved, the buyer may at his option avoid the sale or take the goods at the price of the last good faith bid prior to the completion of the sale. This subsection shall not apply to any bid at a forced sale.

Official Comment

Prior Uniform Statutory Provision: Section 21, Uniform Sales Act.

Changes: Completely rewritten.

Purposes of Changes: To make it clear that:

1.   The auctioneer may in his discretion either reopen the bidding or close the sale on the bid on which the hammer was falling when a bid is made at that moment. The recognition of a bid of this kind by the auctioneer in his discretion does not mean a closing in favor of such a bidder, but only that the bid has been accepted as a continuation of the bidding. If recognized, such a bid discharges the bid on which the hammer was falling when it was made.

2.   An auction "with reserve" is the normal procedure. The crucial point, however, for determining the nature of an auction is the "putting up" of the goods. This Article accepts the view that the goods may be withdrawn before they are actually "put up," regardless of whether the auction is advertised as one without reserve, without liability on the part of the auction announcer to persons who are present. This is subject to any peculiar facts which might bring the case within the "firm offer" principle of this Article, but an offer to persons generally would require unmistakable language in order to fall within that section. The prior announcement of the nature of the auction either as with reserve or without reserve will, however, enter as an "explicit term" in the "putting up" of the goods and conduct thereafter must be governed accordingly. The present section continues the prior rule permitting withdrawal of bids in auctions both with and without reserve; and the rule is made explicit that the retraction of a bid does not revive a prior bid.

Cross Reference:

Point 2: Section 2–205.

Definitional Cross References:

"Buyer". Section 2–103.
"Good faith". Section 1–201.
"Goods". Section 2–105.
"Lot". Section 2–105.
"Notice". Section 1–201.
"Sale". Section 2–106.
"Seller". Section 2–103.

PART 4

TITLE, CREDITORS AND GOOD FAITH PURCHASERS

§ 2–401.   Passing of Title; Reservation for Security; Limited Application of This Section.

Each provision of this Article with regard to the rights, obligations and remedies of the seller, the buyer, purchasers or other third parties applies irrespective of title to the goods except where the provision refers to such title. Insofar as situations are not covered by the other provisions of this Article and matters concerning title become material the following rules apply:

(1) Title to goods cannot pass under a contract for sale prior to their identification to the contract (Section 2–501), and unless otherwise explicitly agreed the buyer acquires by their identification a special property as limited by this Act. Any retention or reservation by the seller of the title (property) in goods shipped or delivered to the buyer is limited in effect to a reservation of a security interest. Subject to these provisions and to the provisions of the Article on Secured Transactions (Article 9), title to goods passes from the seller to the buyer in any manner and on any conditions explicitly agreed on by the parties.

(2) Unless otherwise explicitly agreed title passes to the buyer at the time and place at which the seller completes his performance with reference to the physical delivery of the goods, despite any reservation of a security interest and even though a document of title is to be delivered at a different time or place; and in particular and despite any reservation of a security interest by the bill of lading

     (a) if the contract requires or authorizes the seller to send the goods to the buyer but does not require him to deliver them at destination, title passes to the buyer at the time and place of shipment; but

     (b) if the contract requires delivery at destination, title passes on tender there.

(3) Unless otherwise explicitly agreed where delivery is to be made without moving the goods,

     (a) if the seller is to deliver a tangible document of title, title passes at the time when and the place where he delivers such documents and if the seller is to deliver an electronic document of title, title passes when the seller delivers the document; or

     (b) if the goods are at the time of contracting already identified and no documents of title are to be delivered, title passes at the time and place of contracting.

(4) A rejection or other refusal by the buyer to receive or retain the goods, whether or not justified, or a justified revocation of acceptance revests title to the goods in the seller. Such revesting occurs by operation of law and is not a "sale".

As amended in 2003.

Official Comment

Prior Uniform Statutory Provision: See generally, Sections 17, 18, 19 and 20, Uniform Sales Act.

Purposes: To make it clear that:

1. This Article deals with the issues between seller and buyer in terms of step by step performance or non-performance under the contract for sale and not in terms of whether or not "title" to the goods has passed. That the rules of this section in no way alter the rights of either the buyer, seller or third parties declared elsewhere in the Article is made clear by the preamble of this section. This section, however, in no way intends to indicate which line of interpretation should be followed in cases where the applicability of "public" regulation depends upon a "sale" or upon location of "title" without further definition. The basic policy of this Article that known purpose and reason should govern interpretation cannot extend beyond the scope of its own provisions. It is therefore necessary to state what a "sale" is and when title passes under this Article in case the courts deem any public regulation to incorporate the defined term of the "private" law.

2. "Future" goods cannot be the subject of a present sale. Before title can pass the goods must be identified in the manner set forth in Section 2–501. The parties, however, have full liberty to arrange by specific terms for the passing of title to goods which are existing.

3. The "special property" of the buyer in goods identified to the contract is excluded from the definition of "security interest"; its incidents are defined in provisions of this Article such as those on the rights of the seller's creditors, on good faith purchase, on the buyer's right to goods on the seller's insolvency, and on the buyer's right to specific performance or replevin.

4. The factual situations in subsections (2) and (3) upon which passage of title turn actually base the test upon the time when the seller has finally committed himself in regard to specific goods. Thus in a "shipment" contract he commits himself by the act of making the shipment. If shipment is not contemplated subsection (3) turns on the seller's final commitment, i.e. the delivery of documents or the making of the contract. As to delivery of an electronic document of title, see definition of delivery in Article 1, Section 1–201.

This Article does not state a rule as to the place of title passage as to goods covered by an electronic document of title.

Cross References:

> Point 2: Sections 2–102, 2–501 and 2–502.
> Point 3: Sections 1–201, 2–402, 2–403, 2–502 and 2–716.

Definitional Cross References:

> "Agreement". Section 1–201.
> "Bill of lading". Section 1–201.
> "Buyer". Section 2–103.
> "Contract". Section 1–201.
> "Contract for sale". Section 2–106.
> "Delivery". Section 1–201.
> "Document of title". Section 1–201.
> "Good faith". Section 2–103.
> "Goods". Section 2–105.
> "Party". Section 1–201.
> "Purchaser". Section 1–201.
> "Receipt" of goods. Section 2–103.
> "Remedy". Section 1–201.
> "Rights". Section 1–201.
> "Sale". Section 2–106.
> "Security interest". Section 1–201.
> "Seller". Section 2–103.
> "Send". Section 1–201.

As amended in 2003.

§ 2–402.   Rights of Seller's Creditors Against Sold Goods.

(1)   Except as provided in subsections (2) and (3), rights of unsecured creditors of the seller with respect to goods which have been identified to a contract for sale are subject to the buyer's rights to recover the goods under this Article (Sections 2–502 and 2–716).

(2)   A creditor of the seller may treat a sale or an identification of goods to a contract for sale as void if as against him a retention of possession by the seller is fraudulent under any rule of law of the state where the goods are situated, except that retention of possession in good faith and current course of trade by a merchant-seller for a commercially reasonable time after a sale or identification is not fraudulent.

(3)   Nothing in this Article shall be deemed to impair the rights of creditors of the seller

(a)   under the provisions of the Article on Secured Transactions (Article 9); or

(b)   where identification to the contract or delivery is made not in current course of trade but in satisfaction of or as security for a pre-existing claim for money, security or the like and is made under circumstances which under any rule of law of the state where the goods are situated would apart from this Article constitute the transaction a fraudulent transfer or voidable preference.

Official Comment

Prior Uniform Statutory Provision: Subsection (2)—Section 26, Uniform Sales Act; Subsections (1) and (3)—none.

Changes: Rephrased.

Purposes of Changes and New Matter: To avoid confusion on ordinary issues between current sellers and buyers and issues in the field of preference and hindrance by making it clear that:

§ 2–403   UNIFORM COMMERCIAL CODE

    1.   Local law on questions of hindrance of creditors by the seller's retention of possession of the goods are outside the scope of this Article, but retention of possession in the current course of trade is legitimate. Transactions which fall within the law's policy against improper preferences are reserved from the protection of this Article.

    2.   The retention of possession of the goods by a merchant seller for a commercially reasonable time after a sale or identification in current course is exempted from attack as fraudulent. Similarly, the provisions of subsection (3) have no application to identification or delivery made in the current course of trade, as measured against general commercial understanding of what a "current" transaction is.

Definitional Cross References:

"Contract for sale". Section 2–106.
"Creditor". Section 1–201.
"Good faith". Section 2–103.
"Goods". Section 2–105.
"Merchant". Section 2–104.
"Money". Section 1–201.
"Reasonable time". Section 1–204.
"Rights". Section 1–201.
"Sale". Section 2–106.
"Seller". Section 2–103.

§ 2–403.   Power to Transfer; Good Faith Purchase of Goods; "Entrusting".

    (1)   A purchaser of goods acquires all title which his transferor had or had power to transfer except that a purchaser of a limited interest acquires rights only to the extent of the interest purchased. A person with voidable title has power to transfer a good title to a good faith purchaser for value. When goods have been delivered under a transaction of purchase the purchaser has such power even though

    (a)   the transferor was deceived as to the identity of the purchaser, or

    (b)   the delivery was in exchange for a check which is later dishonored, or

    (c)   it was agreed that the transaction was to be a "cash sale", or

    (d)   the delivery was procured through fraud punishable as larcenous under the criminal law.

    (2)   Any entrusting of possession of goods to a merchant who deals in goods of that kind gives him power to transfer all rights of the entruster to a buyer in ordinary course of business.

    (3)   "Entrusting" includes any delivery and any acquiescence in retention of possession regardless of any condition expressed between the parties to the delivery or acquiescence and regardless of whether the procurement of the entrusting or the possessor's disposition of the goods have been such as to be larcenous under the criminal law.

Official Comment

Prior Uniform Statutory Provision: Sections 20(4), 23, 24, 25, Uniform Sales Act; Section 9, especially 9(2), Uniform Trust Receipts Act; Section 9, Uniform Conditional Sales Act.

Changes: Consolidated and rewritten.

Purposes of Changes: To gather together a series of prior uniform statutory provisions and the case-law thereunder and to state a unified and simplified policy on good faith purchase of goods.

    1.   The basic policy of our law allowing transfer of such title as the transferor has is generally continued and expanded under subsection (1). In this respect the provisions of the section are applicable to a person taking by any form of "purchase" as defined by this Act. Moreover the policy of this Act expressly providing for the application of supplementary general principles of law to sales transactions wherever appropriate joins with the present section to continue unimpaired all rights acquired under the law of agency or of apparent agency or ownership or other estoppel, whether based on statutory provisions or on case law principles. The section also leaves unimpaired the powers given to selling factors under the earlier Factors Acts. In addition subsection (1)

provides specifically for the protection of the good faith purchaser for value in a number of specific situations which have been troublesome under prior law.

On the other hand, the contract of purchase is of course limited by its own terms as in a case of pledge for a limited amount or of sale of a fractional interest in goods.

2.   The many particular situations in which a buyer in ordinary course of business from a dealer has been protected against reservation of property or other hidden interest are gathered by subsections (2)–(4) into a single principle protecting persons who buy in ordinary course out of inventory. Consignors have no reason to complain, nor have lenders who hold a security interest in the inventory, since the very purpose of goods in inventory is to be turned into cash by sale.

The principle is extended in subsection (3) to fit with the abolition of the old law of "cash sale" by subsection (1)(c). It is also freed from any technicalities depending on the extended law of larceny; such extension of the concept of theft to include trick, particular types of fraud, and the like is for the purpose of helping conviction of the offender; it has no proper application to the long-standing policy of civil protection of buyers from persons guilty of such trick or fraud. Finally, the policy is extended, in the interest of simplicity and sense, to any entrusting by a bailor; this is in consonance with the explicit provisions of Section 7–205 on the powers of a warehouse who is also in the business of buying and selling fungible goods of the kind he stores. As to entrusting by a secured party, subsection (2) is limited by the more specific provisions of Section 9–320, which deny protection to a person buying farm products from a person engaged in farming operations.

3.   The definition of "buyer in ordinary course of business" (Section 1–201) is effective here and preserves the essence of the healthy limitations engrafted by the case-law on the older statutes. The older loose concept of good faith and wide definition of value combined to create apparent good faith purchasers in many situations in which the result outraged common sense; the court's solution was to protect the original title especially by use of "cash sale" or of over-technical construction of the enabling clauses of the statutes. But such rulings then turned into limitations on the proper protection of buyers in the ordinary market. Section 1–201(9) cuts down the category of buyer in ordinary course in such fashion as to take care of the results of the cases, but with no price either in confusion or in injustice to proper dealings in the normal market.

4.   Except as provided in subsection (1), the rights of purchasers other than buyers in ordinary course are left to the Articles on Secured Transactions, Documents of Title, and Bulk Sales.

Cross References:

Point 1: Sections 1–103 and 1–201.
Point 2: Sections 1–201, 2–402, 7–205 and 9–320.
Points 3 and 4: Sections 1–102, 1–201, 2–104, 2–707 and Articles 6, 7 and 9.

Definitional Cross References:

"Buyer in ordinary course of business". Section 1–201.
"Good faith". Sections 1–201 and 2–103.
"Goods". Section 2–105.
"Person". Section 1–201.
"Purchaser". Section 1–201.
"Signed". Section 1–201.
"Term". Section 1–201.
"Value". Section 1–201.

As amended in 2003.

PART 5

PERFORMANCE

§ 2–501.   Insurable Interest in Goods; Manner of Identification of Goods.

(1)   The buyer obtains a special property and an insurable interest in goods by identification of existing goods as goods to which the contract refers even though the goods so identified are non-

conforming and he has an option to return or reject them. Such identification can be made at any time and in any manner explicitly agreed to by the parties. In the absence of explicit agreement identification occurs

(a)   when the contract is made if it is for the sale of goods already existing and identified;

(b)   if the contract is for the sale of future goods other than those described in paragraph (c), when goods are shipped, marked or otherwise designated by the seller as goods to which the contract refers;

(c)   when the crops are planted or otherwise become growing crops or the young are conceived if the contract is for the sale of unborn young to be born within twelve months after contracting or for the sale of crops to be harvested within twelve months or the next normal harvest season after contracting whichever is longer.

(2)   The seller retains an insurable interest in goods so long as title to or any security interest in the goods remains in him and where the identification is by the seller alone he may until default or insolvency or notification to the buyer that the identification is final substitute other goods for those identified.

(3)   Nothing in this section impairs any insurable interest recognized under any other statute or rule of law.

Official Comment

Prior Uniform Statutory Provision: See Sections 17 and 19, Uniform Sales Act.

Purposes:

1.   The present section deals with the manner of identifying goods to the contract so that an insurable interest in the buyer and the rights set forth in the next section will accrue. Generally speaking, identification may be made in any manner "explicitly agreed to" by the parties. The rules of paragraphs (a), (b) and (c) apply only in the absence of such "explicit agreement".

2.   In the ordinary case identification of particular existing goods as goods to which the contract refers is unambiguous and may occur in one of many ways. It is possible, however, for the identification to be tentative or contingent. In view of the limited effect given to identification by this Article, the general policy is to resolve all doubts in favor of identification.

3.   The provision of this section as to "explicit agreement" clarifies the present confusion in the law of sales which has arisen from the fact that under prior uniform legislation all rules of presumption with reference to the passing of title or to appropriation (which in turn depended upon identification) were regarded as subject to the contrary intention of the parties or of the party appropriating. Such uncertainty is reduced to a minimum under this section by requiring "explicit agreement" of the parties before the rules of paragraphs (a), (b) and (c) are displaced—as they would be by a term giving the buyer power to select the goods. An "explicit" agreement, however, need not necessarily be found in the terms used in the particular transaction. Thus, where a usage of the trade has previously been made explicit by reduction to a standard set of "rules and regulations" currently incorporated by reference into the contracts of the parties, a relevant provision of those "rules and regulations" is "explicit" within the meaning of this section.

4.   In view of the limited function of identification there is no requirement in this section that the goods be in deliverable state or that all of the seller's duties with respect to the processing of the goods be completed in order that identification occur. For example, despite identification the risk of loss remains on the seller under the risk of loss provisions until completion of his duties as to the goods and all of his remedies remain dependent upon his not defaulting under the contract.

5.   Undivided shares in an identified fungible bulk, such as grain in an elevator or oil in a storage tank, can be sold. The mere making of the contract with reference to an undivided share in an identified fungible bulk is enough under subsection (a) to effect an identification if there is no explicit agreement otherwise. The seller's duty, however, to segregate and deliver according to the contract is not affected by such an identification but is controlled by other provisions of this Article.

6.   Identification of crops under paragraph (c) is made upon planting only if they are to be harvested within the year or within the next normal harvest season. The phrase "next normal harvest season" fairly

includes nursery stock raised for normally quick "harvest," but plainly excludes a "timber" crop to which the concept of a harvest "season" is inapplicable.

Paragraph (c) is also applicable to a crop of wool or the young of animals to be born within twelve months after contracting. The product of a lumbering, mining or fishing operation, though seasonal, is not within the concept of "growing". Identification under a contract for all or part of the output of such an operation can be effected early in the operation.

Cross References:

Point 1: Section 2–502.
Point 4: Sections 2–509, 2–510 and 2–703.
Point 5: Sections 2–105, 2–308, 2–503 and 2–509.
Point 6: Sections 2–105(1), 2–107(1) and 2–402.

Definitional Cross References:

"Agreement". Section 1–201.
"Contract". Section 1–201.
"Contract for sale". Section 2–106.
"Future goods". Section 2–105.
"Goods". Section 2–105.
"Notification". Section 1–201.
"Party". Section 1–201.
"Sale". Section 2–106.
"Security interest". Section 1–201.
"Seller". Section 2–103.

§ 2–502.   Buyer's Right to Goods on Seller's Repudiation, Failure to Deliver, or Insolvency.

(1)   Subject to subsections (2) and (3) and even though the goods have not been shipped a buyer who has paid a part or all of the price of goods in which he has a special property under the provisions of the immediately preceding section may on making and keeping good a tender of any unpaid portion of their price recover them from the seller if:

(a)   in the case of goods bought for personal, family, or household purposes, the seller repudiates or fails to deliver as required by the contract; or

(b)   in all cases, the seller becomes insolvent within ten days after receipt of the first installment on their price.

(2)   The buyer's right to recover the goods under subsection (1)(a) vests upon acquisition of a special property, even if the seller had not then repudiated or failed to deliver.

(3)   If the identification creating his special property has been made by the buyer he acquires the right to recover the goods only if they conform to the contract for sale.

As amended in 1999.

Official Comment

Prior Uniform Statutory Provision: Compare Sections 17, 18 and 19, Uniform Sales Act.

Purposes:

1.   This section gives an additional right to the buyer as a result of identification of the goods to the contract in the manner provided in Section 2–501. The buyer is given a right to recover the goods, conditioned upon making and keeping good a tender of any unpaid portion of the price, in two limited circumstances. First, the buyer may recover goods bought for personal, family, or household purposes if the seller repudiates the contract or fails to deliver the goods. Second, in any case, the buyer may recover the goods if the seller becomes insolvent within 10 days after the seller receives the first installment on their price. The buyer's right to recover

the goods under this section is an exception to the usual rule, under which the disappointed buyer must resort to an action to recover damages.

2.   The question of whether the buyer also acquires a security interest in identified goods and has rights to the goods when insolvency takes place after the ten-day period provided in this section depends upon compliance with the provisions of the Article on Secured Transactions (Article 9).

3.   Under subsection (2), the buyer's right to recover consumer goods under subsection (1)(a) vests upon acquisition of a special property, which occurs upon identification of the goods to the contract. See Section 2–501. Inasmuch as a secured party normally acquires no greater rights in its collateral that its debtor had or had power to convey, see Section 2–403(1) (first sentence), a buyer who acquires a right to recover under this section will take free of a security interest created by the seller if it attaches to the goods after the goods have been identified to the contract. The buyer will take free, even if the buyer does not buy in ordinary course and even if the security interest is perfected. Of course, to the extent that the buyer pays the price after the security interest attaches, the payments will constitute proceeds of the security interest.

4.   Subsection (3) is included to preclude the possibility of unjust enrichment, which would exist if the buyer were permitted to recover goods even though they were greatly superior in quality or quantity to that called for by the contract for sale.

Cross References:

Point 1: Sections 1–201 and 2–702.
Point 2: Article 9.

Definitional Cross References:

"Buyer". Section 2–103.
"Conform". Section 2–106.
"Contract for sale". Section 2–106.
"Goods". Section 2–105.
"Insolvent". Section 1–201.
"Rights". Section 1–201.
"Seller". Section 2–103.

As amended in 1999.

§ 2–503.   Manner of Seller's Tender of Delivery.

(1)   Tender of delivery requires that the seller put and hold conforming goods at the buyer's disposition and give the buyer any notification reasonably necessary to enable him to take delivery. The manner, time and place for tender are determined by the agreement and this Article, and in particular

(a)   tender must be at a reasonable hour, and if it is of goods they must be kept available for the period reasonably necessary to enable the buyer to take possession; but

(b)   unless otherwise agreed the buyer must furnish facilities reasonably suited to the receipt of the goods.

(2)   Where the case is within the next section respecting shipment tender requires that the seller comply with its provisions.

(3)   Where the seller is required to deliver at a particular destination tender requires that he comply with subsection (1) and also in any appropriate case tender documents as described in subsections (4) and (5) of this section.

(4)   Where goods are in the possession of a bailee and are to be delivered without being moved

(a)   tender requires that the seller either tender a negotiable document of title covering such goods or procure acknowledgment by the bailee of the buyer's right to possession of the goods; but

(b)   tender to the buyer of a non-negotiable document of title or of a record directing the bailee to deliver is sufficient tender unless the buyer seasonably objects, and except as otherwise

ARTICLE 2 (2016)   § 2–503

provided in Article 9 receipt by the bailee of notification of the buyer's rights fixes those rights as against the bailee and all third persons; but risk of loss of the goods and of any failure by the bailee to honor the non-negotiable document of title or to obey the direction remains on the seller until the buyer has had a reasonable time to present the document or direction, and a refusal by the bailee to honor the document or to obey the direction defeats the tender.

(5)   Where the contract requires the seller to deliver documents

(a)   he must tender all such documents in correct form, except as provided in this Article with respect to bills of lading in a set (subsection (2) of Section 2–323); and

(b)   tender through customary banking channels is sufficient and dishonor of a draft accompanying or associated with the documents constitutes non-acceptance or rejection.

As amended in 2003.

Official Comment

Prior Uniform Statutory Provision: See Sections 11, 19, 20, 43(3) and (4), 46 and 51, Uniform Sales Act.

Changes: The general policy of the above sections is continued and supplemented but subsection (3) changes the rule of prior section 19(5) as to what constitutes a "destination" contract and subsection (4) incorporates a minor correction as to tender of delivery of goods in the possession of a bailee.

Purposes of Changes:

1.   The major general rules governing the manner of proper or due tender of delivery are gathered in this section. The term "tender" is used in this Article in two different senses. In one sense it refers to "due tender" which contemplates an offer coupled with a present ability to fulfill all the conditions resting on the tendering party and must be followed by actual performance if the other party shows himself ready to proceed. Unless the context unmistakably indicates otherwise this is the meaning of "tender" in this Article and the occasional addition of the word "due" is only for clarity and emphasis. At other times it is used to refer to an offer of goods or documents under a contract as if in fulfillment of its conditions even though there is a defect when measured against the contract obligation. Used in either sense, however, "tender" connotes such performance by the tendering party as puts the other party in default if he fails to proceed in some manner. These concepts of tender would apply to tender of either tangible or electronic documents of title.

2.   The seller's general duty to tender and deliver is laid down in Section 2–301 and more particularly in Section 2–507. The seller's right to a receipt if he demands one and receipts are customary is governed by Section 1–205. Subsection (1) of the present section proceeds to set forth two primary requirements of tender: first, that the seller "put and hold conforming goods at the buyer's disposition" and, second, that he "give the buyer any notice reasonably necessary to enable him to take delivery."

In cases in which payment is due and demanded upon delivery the "buyer's disposition" is qualified by the seller's right to retain control of the goods until payment by the provision of this Article on delivery on condition. However, where the seller is demanding payment on delivery he must first allow the buyer to inspect the goods in order to avoid impairing his tender unless the contract for sale is on C.I.F., C.O.D., cash against documents or similar terms negating the privilege of inspection before payment.

In the case of contracts involving documents the seller can "put and hold conforming goods at the buyer's disposition" under subsection (1) by tendering documents which give the buyer complete control of the goods under the provisions of Article 7 on due negotiation.

3.   Under paragraph (a) of subsection (1) usage of the trade and the circumstances of the particular case determine what is a reasonable hour for tender and what constitutes a reasonable period of holding the goods available.

4.   The buyer must furnish reasonable facilities for the receipt of the goods tendered by the seller under subsection (1), paragraph (b). This obligation of the buyer is no part of the seller's tender.

5.   For the purposes of subsections (2) and (3) there is omitted from this Article the rule under prior uniform legislation that a term requiring the seller to pay the freight or cost of transportation to the buyer is equivalent to an agreement by the seller to deliver to the buyer or at an agreed destination. This omission is with the specific intention of negating the rule, for under this Article the "shipment" contract is regarded as the normal one and the "destination" contract as the variant type. The seller is not obligated to deliver at a named

destination and bear the concurrent risk of loss until arrival, unless he has specifically agreed so to deliver or the commercial understanding of the terms used by the parties contemplates such delivery.

6. Paragraph (a) of subsection (4) continues the rule of the prior uniform legislation as to acknowledgment by the bailee. Paragraph (b) of subsection (4) adopts the rule that between the buyer and the seller the risk of loss remains on the seller during a period reasonable for securing acknowledgment of the transfer from the bailee, while as against all other parties the buyer's rights are fixed as of the time the bailee receives notice of the transfer.

7. Under subsection (5) documents are never "required" except where there is an express contract term or it is plainly implicit in the peculiar circumstances of the case or in a usage of trade. Documents may, of course, be "authorized" although not required, but such cases are not within the scope of this subsection. When documents are required, there are three main requirements of this subsection: (1) "All": each required document is essential to a proper tender; (2) "Such": the documents must be the ones actually required by the contract in terms of source and substance; (3) "Correct form": All documents must be in correct form. These requirements apply to both tangible and electronic documents of title. When tender is made through customary banking channels, a draft may accompany or be associated with a document of title. The language has been broadened to allow for drafts to be associated with an electronic document of title. Compare Section 2–104(2) definition of financing agency.

When a prescribed document cannot be procured, a question of fact arises under the provision of this Article on substituted performance as to whether the agreed manner of delivery is actually commercially impracticable and whether the substitute is commercially reasonable.

Cross References:

Point 2: Sections 1–205, 2–301, 2–310, 2–507 and 2–513 and Article 7.
Point 5: Sections 2–308, 2–310 and 2–509.
Point 7: Section 2–614(1).

Specific matters involving tender are covered in many additional sections of this Article. See Sections 1–205, 2–301, 2–306 to 2–319, 2–321(3), 2–504, 2–507(2), 2–511(1), 2–513, 2–612 and 2–614.

Definitional Cross References:

"Agreement". Section 1–201.
"Bill of lading". Section 1–201.
"Buyer". Section 2–103.
"Conforming". Section 2–106.
"Contract". Section 1–201.
"Delivery". Section 1–201.
"Dishonor". Section 3–508.
"Document of title". Section 1–201.
"Draft". Section 3–104.
"Goods". Section 2–105.
"Notification". Section 1–201.
"Reasonable time". Section 1–204.
"Receipt" of goods. Section 2–103.
"Rights". Section 1–201.
"Seasonably". Section 1–204.
"Seller". Section 2–103.
"Written". Section 1–201.

As amended in 2003.

§ 2–504.   Shipment by Seller.

Where the seller is required or authorized to send the goods to the buyer and the contract does not require him to deliver them at a particular destination, then unless otherwise agreed he must

ARTICLE 2 (2016)   **§ 2–504**

(a) put the goods in the possession of such a carrier and make such a contract for their transportation as may be reasonable having regard to the nature of the goods and other circumstances of the case; and

(b) obtain and promptly deliver or tender in due form any document necessary to enable the buyer to obtain possession of the goods or otherwise required by the agreement or by usage of trade; and

(c) promptly notify the buyer of the shipment.

Failure to notify the buyer under paragraph (c) or to make a proper contract under paragraph (a) is a ground for rejection only if material delay or loss ensues.

Official Comment

Prior Uniform Statutory Provision: Section 46, Uniform Sales Act.

Changes: Rewritten.

Purposes of Changes: To continue the general policy of the prior uniform statutory provision while incorporating certain modifications with respect to the requirement that the contract with the carrier be made expressly on behalf of the buyer and as to the necessity of giving notice of the shipment to the buyer, so that:

1. The section is limited to "shipment" contracts as contrasted with "destination" contracts or contracts for delivery at the place where the goods are located. The general principles embodied in this section cover the special cases of F.O.B. point of shipment contracts and C.I.F. and C. & F. contracts. Under the preceding section on manner of tender of delivery, due tender by the seller requires that he comply with the requirements of this section in appropriate cases.

2. The contract to be made with the carrier under paragraph (a) must conform to all express terms of the agreement, subject to any substitution necessary because of failure of agreed facilities as provided in the later provision on substituted performance. However, under the policies of this Article on good faith and commercial standards and on buyer's rights on improper delivery, the requirements of explicit provisions must be read in terms of their commercial and not their literal meaning. This policy is made express with respect to bills of lading in a set in the provision of this Article on form of bills of lading required in overseas shipment.

3. In the absence of agreement, the provision of this Article on options and cooperation respecting performance gives the seller the choice of any reasonable carrier, routing and other arrangements. Whether or not the shipment is at the buyer's expense the seller must see to any arrangements, reasonable in the circumstances, such as refrigeration, watering of live stock, protection against cold, the sending along of any necessary help, selection of specialized cars and the like for paragraph (a) is intended to cover all necessary arrangements whether made by contract with the carrier or otherwise. There is, however, a proper relaxation of such requirements if the buyer is himself in a position to make the appropriate arrangements and the seller gives him reasonable notice of the need to do so. It is an improper contract under paragraph (a) for the seller to agree with the carrier to a limited valuation below the true value and thus cut off the buyer's opportunity to recover from the carrier in the event of loss, when the risk of shipment is placed on the buyer by his contract with the seller.

4. Both the language of paragraph (b) and the nature of the situation it concerns indicate that the requirement that the seller must obtain and deliver promptly to the buyer in due form any document necessary to enable him to obtain possession of the goods is intended to cumulate with the other duties of the seller such as those covered in paragraph (a).

In this connection, in the case of pool car shipments a delivery order furnished by the seller on the pool car consignee, or on the carrier for delivery out of a larger quantity, satisfies the requirements of paragraph (b) unless the contract requires some other form of document.

5. This Article, unlike the prior uniform statutory provision, makes it the seller's duty to notify the buyer of shipment in all cases. The consequences of his failure to do so, however, are limited in that the buyer may reject on this ground only where material delay or loss ensues.

A standard and acceptable manner of notification in open credit shipments is the sending of an invoice and in the case of documentary contracts is the prompt forwarding of the documents as under paragraph (b) of this section. It is also usual to send on a straight bill of lading but this is not necessary to the required notification.

§ 2-505   UNIFORM COMMERCIAL CODE

However, should such a document prove necessary or convenient to the buyer, as in the case of loss and claim against the carrier, good faith would require the seller to send it on request.

Frequently the agreement expressly requires prompt notification as by wire or cable. Such a term may be of the essence and the final clause of paragraph (c) does not prevent the parties from making this a particular ground for rejection. To have this vital and irreparable effect upon the seller's duties, such a term should be part of the "dickered" terms written in any "form," or should otherwise be called seasonably and sharply to the seller's attention.

6.   Generally, under the final sentence of the section, rejection by the buyer is justified only when the seller's dereliction as to any of the requirements of this section in fact is followed by material delay or damage. It rests on the seller, so far as concerns matters not within the peculiar knowledge of the buyer, to establish that his error has not been followed by events which justify rejection.

Cross References:

> Point 1: Sections 2–319, 2–320 and 2–503(2).
> Point 2: Sections 1–203, 2–323(2), 2–601 and 2–614(1).
> Point 3: Section 2–311(2).
> Point 5: Section 1–203.

Definitional Cross References:

> "Agreement". Section 1–201.
> "Buyer". Section 2–103.
> "Contract". Section 1–201.
> "Delivery". Section 1–201.
> "Goods". Section 2–105.
> "Notifies". Section 1–201.
> "Seller". Section 2–103.
> "Send". Section 1–201.
> "Usage of trade". Section 1–205.

§ 2–505.   Seller's Shipment Under Reservation.

(1)   Where the seller has identified goods to the contract by or before shipment:

(a)   his procurement of a negotiable bill of lading to his own order or otherwise reserves in him a security interest in the goods. His procurement of the bill to the order of a financing agency or of the buyer indicates in addition only the seller's expectation of transferring that interest to the person named.

(b)   a non-negotiable bill of lading to himself or his nominee reserves possession of the goods as security but except in a case of conditional delivery (subsection (2) of Section 2–507) a non-negotiable bill of lading naming the buyer as consignee reserves no security interest even though the seller retains possession or control of the bill of lading.

(2)   When shipment by the seller with reservation of a security interest is in violation of the contract for sale it constitutes an improper contract for transportation within the preceding section but impairs neither the rights given to the buyer by shipment and identification of the goods to the contract nor the seller's powers as a holder of a negotiable document of title.

As amended in 2003.

Official Comment

Prior Uniform Statutory Provision: Section 20(2), (3), (4), Uniform Sales Act.

Changes: Completely rephrased, the "powers" of the parties in cases of reservation being emphasized primarily rather than the "rightfulness" of reservation.

Purposes of Changes: To continue in general the policy of the prior uniform statutory provision with certain modifications of emphasis and language, so that:

ARTICLE 2 (2016)   § 2–505

1.   The security interest reserved to the seller under subsection (1) is restricted to securing payment or performance by the buyer and the seller is strictly limited in his disposition and control of the goods as against the buyer and third parties. Under this Article, the provision as to the passing of interest expressly applies "despite any reservation of security title" and also provides that the "rights, obligations and remedies" of the parties are not altered by the incidence of title generally. The security interest, therefore, must be regarded as a means given to the seller to enforce his rights against the buyer which is unaffected by and in turn does not affect the location of title generally. The rules set forth in subsection (1) are not to be altered by any apparent "contrary intent" of the parties as to passing of title, since the rights and remedies of the parties to the contract of sale, as defined in this Article, rest on the contract and its performance or breach and not on stereotyped presumptions as to the location of title.

This Article does not attempt to regulate local procedure in regard to the effective maintenance of the seller's security interest when the action is in replevin by the buyer against the carrier.

2.   Every shipment of identified goods under a negotiable bill of lading reserves a security interest in the seller under subsection (1) paragraph (a).

It is frequently convenient for the seller to make the bill of lading to the order of a nominee such as his agent at destination, the financing agency to which he expects to negotiate the document or the bank issuing a credit to him. In many instances, also, the buyer is made the order party. This Article does not deal directly with the question as to whether a bill of lading made out by the seller to the order of a nominee gives the carrier notice of any rights which the nominee may have so as to limit its freedom or obligation to honor the bill of lading in the hands of the seller as the original shipper if the expected negotiation fails. This is dealt with in the Article on Documents of Title (Article 7).

3.   A non-negotiable bill of lading taken to a party other than the buyer under subsection (1) paragraph (b) reserves possession of the goods as security in the seller but if he seeks to withhold the goods improperly the buyer can tender payment and recover them.

4.   In the case of a shipment by non-negotiable bill of lading taken to a buyer, the seller, under subsection (1) retains no security interest or possession as against the buyer and by the shipment he *de facto* loses control as against the carrier except where he rightfully and effectively stops delivery in transit. In cases in which the contract gives the seller the right to payment against delivery, the seller, by making an immediate demand for payment, can show that his delivery is conditional, but this does not prevent the buyer's power to transfer full title to a sub-buyer in ordinary course or other purchaser under Section 2–403.

5.   Under subsection (2) an improper reservation by the seller which would constitute a breach in no way impairs such of the buyer's rights as result from identification of the goods. The security title reserved by the seller under subsection (1) does not protect his retaining possession or control of the document or the goods for the purpose of exacting more than is due him under the contract.

Cross References:

Point 1: Section 1–201.
Point 2: Article 7.
Point 3: Sections 2–501(2) and 2–504.
Point 4: Sections 2–403, 2–507(2) and 2–705.
Point 5: Sections 2–310, 2–319(4), 2–320(4), 2–501 and 2–502 and Article 7.

Definitional Cross References:

"Bill of lading". Section 1–201.
"Buyer". Section 2–103.
"Consignee". Section 7–102.
"Contract". Section 1–201.
"Contract for sale". Section 2–106.
"Delivery". Section 1–201.
"Financing agency". Section 2–104.
"Goods". Section 2–105.
"Holder". Section 1–201.
"Person". Section 1–201.

"Security interest". Section 1–201.
"Seller". Section 2–103.

As amended in 2003.

§ 2–506.   Rights of Financing Agency.

(1)   A financing agency by paying or purchasing for value a draft which relates to a shipment of goods acquires to the extent of the payment or purchase and in addition to its own rights under the draft and any document of title securing it any rights of the shipper in the goods including the right to stop delivery and the shipper's right to have the draft honored by the buyer.

(2)   The right to reimbursement of a financing agency which has in good faith honored or purchased the draft under commitment to or authority from the buyer is not impaired by subsequent discovery of defects with reference to any relevant document which was apparently regular.

As amended in 2003.

Official Comment

Prior Uniform Statutory Provision: None.

Purposes:

1.   "Financing agency" is broadly defined in this Article to cover every normal instance in which a party aids or intervenes in the financing of a sales transaction. The term as used in subsection (1) is not in any sense intended as a limitation and covers any other appropriate situation which may arise outside the scope of the definition.

2.   "Paying" as used in subsection (1) is typified by the letter of credit, or "authority to pay" situation in which a banker, by arrangement with the buyer or other consignee, pays on his behalf a draft for the price of the goods. It is immaterial whether the draft is formally drawn on the party paying or his principal, whether it is a sight draft paid in cash or a time draft "paid" in the first instance by acceptance, or whether the payment is viewed as absolute or conditional. All of these cases constitute "payment" under this subsection. Similarly, "purchasing for value" is used to indicate the whole area of financing by the seller's banker, and the principle of subsection (1) is applicable without any niceties of distinction between "purchase," "discount," "advance against collection" or the like. But it is important to notice that the only right to have the draft honored that is acquired is that *against the buyer*; if any right against any one else is claimed it will have to be under some separate obligation of that other person. A letter of credit does not necessarily protect *purchasers* of drafts. See Article 5. And for the relations of the parties to documentary drafts see Part 5 of Article 4.

3.   Subsection (1) is made applicable to payments or advances against a draft which "relates to" a shipment of goods and this has been chosen as a term of maximum breadth. In particular the term is intended to cover the case of a draft against an invoice or against a delivery order. Further, it is unnecessary that there be an explicit assignment of the invoice attached to the draft to bring the transaction within the reason of this subsection.

4.   After shipment, "the rights of the shipper in the goods" are merely security rights and are subject to the buyer's right to force delivery upon tender of the price. The rights acquired by the financing agency are similarly limited and, moreover, if the agency fails to procure any outstanding negotiable document of title, it may find its exercise of these rights hampered or even defeated by the seller's disposition of the document to a third party. This section does not attempt to create any new rights in the financing agency against the carrier which would force the latter to honor a stop order from the agency, a stranger to the shipment, or any new rights against a holder to whom a document of title has been duly negotiated under Article 7.

5.   The deletion of the language "on its face" from subsection (2) is designed to accommodate electronic documents of title without changing the requirement of regularity of the document.

Cross References:

Point 1: Section 2–104(2) and Article 4.
Point 2: Part 5 of Article 4, and Article 5.
Point 4: Sections 2–501 and 2–502(1) and Article 7.

Definitional Cross References:

"Buyer". Section 2–103.
"Document of title". Section 1–201.
"Draft". Section 3–104.
"Financing agency". Section 2–104.
"Good faith". Section 2–103.
"Goods". Section 2–105.
"Honor". Section 1–201.
"Purchase". Section 1–201.
"Rights". Section 1–201.
"Value". Section 1–201.

As amended in 2003.

§ 2–507. Effect of Seller's Tender; Delivery on Condition.

(1)   Tender of delivery is a condition to the buyer's duty to accept the goods and, unless otherwise agreed, to his duty to pay for them. Tender entitles the seller to acceptance of the goods and to payment according to the contract.

(2)   Where payment is due and demanded on the delivery to the buyer of goods or documents of title, his right as against the seller to retain or dispose of them is conditional upon his making the payment due.

Official Comment

Prior Uniform Statutory Provision: See Sections 11, 41, 42 and 69, Uniform Sales Act.

Purposes:

1.   Subsection (1) continues the policies of the prior uniform statutory provisions with respect to tender and delivery by the seller. Under this Article the same rules in these matters are applied to present sales and to contracts for sale. But the provisions of this subsection must be read within the framework of the other sections of this Article which bear upon the question of delivery and payment.

2.   The "unless otherwise agreed" provision of subsection (1) is directed primarily to cases in which payment in advance has been promised or a letter of credit term has been included. Payment "according to the contract" contemplates immediate payment, payment at the end of an agreed credit term, payment by a time acceptance or the like. Under this Act, "contract" means the total obligation in law which results from the parties' agreement including the effect of this Article. In this context, therefore, there must be considered the effect in law of such provisions as those on means and manner of payment and on failure of agreed means and manner of payment.

3.   Subsection (2) deals with the effect of a conditional delivery by the seller and in such a situation makes the buyer's "right as against the seller" conditional upon payment. These words are used as words of limitation to conform with the policy set forth in the bona fide purchase sections of this Article. Should the seller after making such a conditional delivery fail to follow up his rights, the condition is waived. This subsection (2) codifies the cash seller's right of reclamation which is in the nature of a lien. There is no specific time limit for a cash seller to exercise the right of reclamation. However, the right will be defeated by delay causing prejudice to the buyer, waiver, estoppel, or ratification of the buyer's right to retain possession. Common law rules and precedents governing such principles are applicable (Section 1–103). If third parties are involved, Section 2–403(1) protects good faith purchasers. See PEB Commentary No. 1, dated March 10, 1990.

Cross References:

Point 1: Sections 2–310, 2–503, 2–511, 2–601 and 2–711 to 2–713.
Point 2: Sections 1–201, 2–511 and 2–614.
Point 3: Sections 2–401, 2–403, and 2–702(1)(b).

Definitional Cross References:

"Buyer". Section 2–103.
"Contract". Section 1–201.

§ 2-508   UNIFORM COMMERCIAL CODE

"Delivery". Section 1–201.
"Document of title". Section 1–201.
"Goods". Section 2–105.
"Rights". Section 1–201.
"Seller". Section 2–103.

As amended in 1990.

§ 2-508.   Cure by Seller of Improper Tender or Delivery; Replacement.

(1)   Where any tender or delivery by the seller is rejected because non-conforming and the time for performance has not yet expired, the seller may seasonably notify the buyer of his intention to cure and may then within the contract time make a conforming delivery.

(2)   Where the buyer rejects a non-conforming tender which the seller had reasonable grounds to believe would be acceptable with or without money allowance the seller may if he seasonably notifies the buyer have a further reasonable time to substitute a conforming tender.

Official Comment

Prior Uniform Statutory Provision: None.

Purposes:

1.   Subsection (1) permits a seller who has made a non-conforming tender in any case to make a conforming delivery within the contract time upon seasonable notification to the buyer. It applies even where the seller has taken back the non-conforming goods and refunded the purchase price. He may still make a good tender within the contract period. The closer, however, it is to the contract date, the greater is the necessity for extreme promptness on the seller's part in notifying of his intention to cure, if such notification is to be "seasonable" under this subsection.

The rule of this subsection, moreover, is qualified by its underlying reasons. Thus if, after contracting for June delivery, a buyer later makes known to the seller his need for shipment early in the month and the seller ships accordingly, the "contract time" has been cut down by the supervening modification and the time for cure of tender must be referred to this modified time term.

2.   Subsection (2) seeks to avoid injustice to the seller by reason of a surprise rejection by the buyer. However, the seller is not protected unless he had "reasonable grounds to believe" that the tender would be acceptable. Such reasonable grounds can lie in prior course of dealing, course of performance or usage of trade as well as in the particular circumstances surrounding the making of the contract. The seller is charged with commercial knowledge of any factors in a particular sales situation which require him to comply strictly with his obligations under the contract as, for example, strict conformity of documents in an overseas shipment or the sale of precision parts or chemicals for use in manufacture. Further, if the buyer gives notice either implicitly, as by a prior course of dealing involving rigorous inspections, or expressly, as by the deliberate inclusion of a "no replacement" clause in the contract, the seller is to be held to rigid compliance. If the clause appears in a "form" contract evidence that it is out of line with trade usage or the prior course of dealing and was not called to the seller's attention may be sufficient to show that the seller had reasonable grounds to believe that the tender would be acceptable.

3.   The words "a further reasonable time to substitute a conforming tender" are intended as words of limitation to protect the buyer. What is a "reasonable time" depends upon the attending circumstances. Compare Section 2–511 on the comparable case of a seller's surprise demand for legal tender.

4.   Existing trade usages permitting variations without rejection but with price allowance enter into the agreement itself as contractual limitations of remedy and are not covered by this section.

Cross References:

Point 2: Section 2–302.
Point 3: Section 2–511.
Point 4: Sections 1–205 and 2–721.

Definitional Cross References:

> "Buyer". Section 2–103.
> "Conforming". Section 2–106.
> "Contract". Section 1–201.
> "Money". Section 1–201.
> "Notifies". Section 1–201.
> "Reasonable time". Section 1–204.
> "Seasonably". Section 1–204.
> "Seller". Section 2–103.

§ 2–509.   Risk of Loss in the Absence of Breach.

(1)   Where the contract requires or authorizes the seller to ship the goods by carrier

(a)   if it does not require him to deliver them at a particular destination, the risk of loss passes to the buyer when the goods are duly delivered to the carrier even though the shipment is under reservation (Section 2–505); but

(b)   if it does require him to deliver them at a particular destination and the goods are there duly tendered while in the possession of the carrier, the risk of loss passes to the buyer when the goods are there duly so tendered as to enable the buyer to take delivery.

(2)   Where the goods are held by a bailee to be delivered without being moved, the risk of loss passes to the buyer

(a)   on his receipt of possession or control of a negotiable document of title covering the goods; or

(b)   on acknowledgment by the bailee of the buyer's right to possession of the goods; or

(c)   after his receipt of possession or control of a non-negotiable document of title or other direction to deliver in a record, as provided in subsection (4)(b) of Section 2–503.

(3)   In any case not within subsection (1) or (2), the risk of loss passes to the buyer on his receipt of the goods if the seller is a merchant; otherwise the risk passes to the buyer on tender of delivery.

(4)   The provisions of this section are subject to contrary agreement of the parties and to the provisions of this Article on sale on approval (Section 2–327) and on effect of breach on risk of loss (Section 2–510).

As amended in 2003.

Official Comment

Prior Uniform Statutory Provision: Section 22, Uniform Sales Act.

Changes: Rewritten, subsection (3) of this section modifying prior law.

Purposes of Changes: To make it clear that:

1.   The underlying theory of these sections on risk of loss is the adoption of the contractual approach rather than an arbitrary shifting of the risk with the "property" in the goods. The scope of the present section, therefore, is limited strictly to those cases where there has been no breach by the seller. Where for any reason his delivery or tender fails to conform to the contract, the present section does not apply and the situation is governed by the provisions on effect of breach on risk of loss.

2.   The provisions of subsection (1) apply where the contract "requires or authorizes" shipment of the goods. This language is intended to be construed parallel to comparable language in the section on shipment by seller. In order that the goods be "duly delivered to the carrier" under paragraph (a) a contract must be entered into with the carrier which will satisfy the requirements of the section on shipment by the seller and the delivery must be made under circumstances which will enable the seller to take any further steps necessary to a due tender. The underlying reason of this subsection does not require that the shipment be made after contracting, but where, for example, the seller buys the goods afloat and later diverts the shipment to the buyer, he must identify the goods to the contract before the risk of loss can pass. To transfer the risk it is enough that a proper shipment and a proper identification come to apply to the same goods although, aside from special agreement, the risk will not pass retroactively to the time of shipment in such a case.

§ 2–510   UNIFORM COMMERCIAL CODE

3.   Whether the contract involves delivery at the seller's place of business or at the situs of the goods, a merchant seller cannot transfer risk of loss and it remains upon him until actual receipt by the buyer, even though full payment has been made and the buyer has been notified that the goods are at his disposal. Protection is afforded him, in the event of breach by the buyer, under the next section.

The underlying theory of this rule is that a merchant who is to make physical delivery at his own place continues meanwhile to control the goods and can be expected to insure his interest in them. The buyer, on the other hand, has no control of the goods and it is extremely unlikely that he will carry insurance on goods not yet in his possession.

4.   Where the agreement provides for delivery of the goods as between the buyer and seller without removal from the physical possession of a bailee, the provisions on manner of tender of delivery apply on the point of transfer of risk. Due delivery of a negotiable document of title covering the goods or acknowledgment by the bailee that he holds for the buyer completes the "delivery" and passes the risk. See definition of delivery in Article 1, Section 1–201 and the definition of control in Article 7, Section 7–106.

5.   The provisions of this section are made subject by subsection (4) to the "contrary agreement" of the parties. This language is intended as the equivalent of the phrase "unless otherwise agreed" used more frequently throughout this Act. "Contrary" is in no way used as a word of limitation and the buyer and seller are left free to readjust their rights and risks as declared by this section in any manner agreeable to them. Contrary agreement can also be found in the circumstances of the case, a trade usage or practice, or a course of dealing or performance.

Cross References:

Point 1: Section 2–510(1).
Point 2: Sections 2–503 and 2–504.
Point 3: Sections 2–104, 2–503 and 2–510.
Point 4: Section 2–503(4).
Point 5: Section 1–201.

Definitional Cross References:

"Agreement". Section 1–201.
"Buyer". Section 2–103.
"Contract". Section 1–201.
"Delivery". Section 1–201.
"Document of title". Section 1–201.
"Goods". Section 2–105.
"Merchant". Section 2–104.
"Party". Section 1–201.
"Receipt" of goods. Section 2–103.
"Sale on approval". Section 2–326.
"Seller". Section 2–103.

As amended in 2003.

§ 2–510.   Effect of Breach on Risk of Loss.

(1)   Where a tender or delivery of goods so fails to conform to the contract as to give a right of rejection the risk of their loss remains on the seller until cure or acceptance.

(2)   Where the buyer rightfully revokes acceptance he may to the extent of any deficiency in his effective insurance coverage treat the risk of loss as having rested on the seller from the beginning.

(3)   Where the buyer as to conforming goods already identified to the contract for sale repudiates or is otherwise in breach before risk of their loss has passed to him, the seller may to the extent of any deficiency in his effective insurance coverage treat the risk of loss as resting on the buyer for a commercially reasonable time.

ARTICLE 2 (2016)   § 2–511

Official Comment

Prior Uniform Statutory Provision: None.

Purposes: To make clear that:

1.   Under subsection (1) the seller by his individual action cannot shift the risk of loss to the buyer unless his action conforms with all the conditions resting on him under the contract.

2.   The "cure" of defective tenders contemplated by subsection (1) applies only to those situations in which the seller makes changes in goods already tendered, such as repair, partial substitution, sorting out from an improper mixture and the like since "cure" by repossession and new tender has no effect on the risk of loss of the goods originally tendered. The seller's privilege of cure does not shift the risk, however, until the cure is completed.

Where defective documents are involved a cure of the defect by the seller or a waiver of the defects by the buyer will operate to shift the risk under this section. However, if the goods have been destroyed prior to the cure or the buyer is unaware of their destruction at the time he waives the defect in the documents, the risk of the loss must still be borne by the seller, for the risk shifts only at the time of cure, waiver of documentary defects or acceptance of the goods.

3.   In cases where there has been a breach of the contract, if the one in control of the goods is the aggrieved party, whatever loss or damage may prove to be uncovered by his insurance falls upon the contract breaker under subsections (2) and (3) rather than upon him. The word "effective" as applied to insurance coverage in those subsections is used to meet the case of supervening insolvency of the insurer. The "deficiency" referred to in the text means such deficiency in the insurance coverage as exists without subrogation. This section merely distributes the risk of loss as stated and is not intended to be disturbed by any subrogation of an insurer.

Cross Reference:

Section 2–509.

Definitional Cross References:

"Buyer". Section 2–103.
"Conform". Section 2–106.
"Contract for sale". Section 2–106.
"Goods". Section 2–105.
"Seller". Section 2–103.

§ 2–511.   Tender of Payment by Buyer; Payment by Check.

(1)   Unless otherwise agreed tender of payment is a condition to the seller's duty to tender and complete any delivery.

(2)   Tender of payment is sufficient when made by any means or in any manner current in the ordinary course of business unless the seller demands payment in legal tender and gives any extension of time reasonably necessary to procure it.

(3)   Subject to the provisions of this Act on the effect of an instrument on an obligation (Section 3–310), payment by check is conditional and is defeated as between the parties by dishonor of the check on due presentment.

As amended in 1994.

Official Comment

Prior Uniform Statutory Provision: Section 42, Uniform Sales Act.

Changes: Rewritten by this section and Section 2–507.

Purposes of Changes:

1.   The requirement of payment against delivery in subsection (1) is applicable to non-commercial sales generally and to ordinary sales at retail although it has no application to the great body of commercial contracts

which carry credit terms. Subsection (1) applies also to documentary contracts in general and to contracts which look to shipment by the seller but contain no term on time and manner of payment, in which situations the payment may, in proper case, be demanded against delivery of appropriate documents.

In the case of specific transactions such as C.O.D. sales or agreements providing for payment against documents, the provisions of this subsection must be considered in conjunction with the special sections of the Article dealing with such terms. The provision that tender of payment is a condition to the seller's duty to tender and complete "any delivery" integrates this section with the language and policy of the section on delivery in several lots which call for separate payment. Finally, attention should be directed to the provision on right to adequate assurance of performance which recognizes, even before the time for tender, an obligation on the buyer not to impair the seller's expectation of receiving payment in due course.

2.   Unless there is agreement otherwise the concurrence of the conditions as to tender of payment and tender of delivery requires their performance at a single place or time. This Article determines that place and time by determining in various other sections the place and time for tender of delivery under various circumstances and in particular types of transactions. The sections dealing with time and place of delivery together with the section on right to inspection of goods answer the subsidiary question as to when payment may be demanded before inspection by the buyer.

3.   The essence of the principle involved in subsection (2) is avoidance of commercial surprise at the time of performance. The section on substituted performance covers the peculiar case in which legal tender is not available to the commercial community.

4.   Subsection (3) is concerned with the rights and obligations as between the parties to a sales transaction when payment is made by check. This Article recognizes that the taking of a seemingly solvent party's check is commercially normal and proper and, if due diligence is exercised in collection, is not to be penalized in any way. The conditional character of the payment under this section refers only to the effect of the transaction "as between the parties" thereto and does not purport to cut into the law of "absolute" and "conditional" payment as applied to such other problems as the discharge of sureties or the responsibilities of a drawee bank which is at the same time an agent for collection.

The phrase "by check" includes not only the buyer's own but any check which does not effect a discharge under Article 3 (Section 3–802). Similarly the reason of this subsection should apply and the same result should be reached where the buyer "pays" by sight draft on a commercial firm which is financing him.

5.   Under subsection (3) payment by check is defeated if it is not honored upon due presentment. This corresponds to the provisions of article on Commercial Paper. (Section 3–802). But if the seller procures certification of the check instead of cashing it, the buyer is discharged. (Section 3–411).

6.   Where the instrument offered by the buyer is not a payment but a credit instrument such as a note or a check post-dated by even one day, the seller's acceptance of the instrument insofar as third parties are concerned, amounts to a delivery on credit and his remedies are set forth in the section on buyer's insolvency. As between the buyer and the seller, however, the matter turns on the present subsection and the section on conditional delivery and subsequent dishonor of the instrument gives the seller rights on it as well as for breach of the contract for sale.

Cross References:

Point 1: Sections 2–307, 2–310, 2–320, 2–325, 2–503, 2–513 and 2–609.
Point 2: Sections 2–307, 2–310, 2–319, 2–322, 2–503, 2–504 and 2–513.
Point 3: Section 2–614.
Point 5: Article 3, esp. Sections 3–802 and 3–411.
Point 6: Sections 2–507, 2–702, and Article 3.

Definitional Cross References:

"Buyer". Section 2–103.
"Check". Section 3–104.
"Dishonor". Section 3–508.
"Party". Section 1–201.
"Reasonable time". Section 1–204.
"Seller". Section 2–103.

§ 2–512.   Payment by Buyer Before Inspection.

(1)   Where the contract requires payment before inspection non-conformity of the goods does not excuse the buyer from so making payment unless

(a)   the non-conformity appears without inspection; or

(b)   despite tender of the required documents the circumstances would justify injunction against honor under this Act (Section 5–109(b)).

(2)   Payment pursuant to subsection (1) does not constitute an acceptance of goods or impair the buyer's right to inspect or any of his remedies.

As amended in 1995.

Official Comment

Prior Uniform Statutory Provision: None, but see Sections 47 and 49, Uniform Sales Act.

Purposes:

1.   Subsection (1) of the present section recognizes that the essence of a contract providing for payment before inspection is the intention of the parties to shift to the buyer the risks which would usually rest upon the seller. The basic nature of the transaction is thus preserved and the buyer is in most cases required to pay first and litigate as to any defects later.

2.   "Inspection" under this section is an inspection in a manner reasonable for detecting defects in goods whose surface appearance is satisfactory.

3.   Clause (a) of this subsection states an exception to the general rule based on common sense and normal commercial practice. The apparent non-conformity referred to is one which is evident in the mere process of taking delivery.

4.   Clause (b) is concerned with contracts for payment against documents and incorporates the general clarification and modification of the case law contained in the section on excuse of a financing agency. Section 5–109(b).

5.   Subsection (2) makes explicit the general policy of the Uniform Sales Act that the payment required before inspection in no way impairs the buyer's remedies or rights in the event of a default by the seller. The remedies preserved to the buyer are all of his remedies, which include as a matter of reason the remedy for total non-delivery after payment in advance.

The provision on performance or acceptance under reservation of rights does not apply to the situations contemplated here in which payment is made in due course under the contract and the buyer need not pay "under protest" or the like in order to preserve his rights as to defects discovered upon inspection.

6.   This section applies to cases in which the contract requires payment before inspection either by the express agreement of the parties or by reason of the effect in law of that contract. The present section must therefore be considered in conjunction with the provision on right to inspection of goods which sets forth the instances in which the buyer is not entitled to inspection before payment.

Cross References:

Point 4: Article 5.
Point 5: Section 1–207.
Point 6: Section 2–513(3).

Definitional Cross References:

"Buyer". Section 2–103.
"Conform". Section 2–106.
"Contract". Section 1–201.
"Financing agency". Section 2–104.
"Goods". Section 2–105.
"Remedy". Section 1–201.

"Rights". Section 1–201.

§ 2–513.   Buyer's Right to Inspection of Goods.

(1)   Unless otherwise agreed and subject to subsection (3), where goods are tendered or delivered or identified to the contract for sale, the buyer has a right before payment or acceptance to inspect them at any reasonable place and time and in any reasonable manner. When the seller is required or authorized to send the goods to the buyer, the inspection may be after their arrival.

(2)   Expenses of inspection must be borne by the buyer but may be recovered from the seller if the goods do not conform and are rejected.

(3)   Unless otherwise agreed and subject to the provisions of this Article on C.I.F. contracts (subsection (3) of Section 2–321), the buyer is not entitled to inspect the goods before payment of the price when the contract provides

(a)   for delivery "C.O.D." or on other like terms; or

(b)   for payment against documents of title, except where such payment is due only after the goods are to become available for inspection.

(4)   A place or method of inspection fixed by the parties is presumed to be exclusive but unless otherwise expressly agreed it does not postpone identification or shift the place for delivery or for passing the risk of loss. If compliance becomes impossible, inspection shall be as provided in this section unless the place or method fixed was clearly intended as an indispensable condition failure of which avoids the contract.

Official Comment

Prior Uniform Statutory Provisions: Section 47(2), (3), Uniform Sales Act.

Changes: Rewritten, Subsections (2) and (3) being new.

Purposes of Changes and New Matter: To correspond in substance with the prior uniform statutory provision and to incorporate in addition some of the results of the better case law so that:

1.   The buyer is entitled to inspect goods as provided in subsection (1) unless it has been otherwise agreed by the parties. The phrase "unless otherwise agreed" is intended principally to cover such situations as those outlined in subsections (3) and (4) and those in which the agreement of the parties negates inspection before tender of delivery. However, no agreement by the parties can displace the entire right of inspection except where the contract is simply for the sale of "this thing." Even in a sale of boxed goods "as is" inspection is a right of the buyer, since if the boxes prove to contain some other merchandise altogether the price can be recovered back; nor do the limitations of the provision on effect of acceptance apply in such a case.

2.   The buyer's right of inspection is available to him upon tender, delivery or appropriation of the goods with notice to him. Since inspection is available to him on tender, where payment is due against delivery he may, unless otherwise agreed, make his inspection before payment of the price. It is also available to him after receipt of the goods and so may be postponed after receipt for a reasonable time. Failure to inspect before payment does not impair the right to inspect after receipt of the goods unless the case falls within subsection (4) on agreed and exclusive inspection provisions. The right to inspect goods which have been appropriated with notice to the buyer holds whether or not the sale was by sample.

3.   The buyer may exercise his right of inspection at any reasonable time or place and in any reasonable manner. It is not necessary that he select the most appropriate time, place or manner to inspect or that his selection be the customary one in the trade or locality. Any reasonable time, place or manner is available to him and the reasonableness will be determined by trade usages, past practices between the parties and the other circumstances of the case.

The last sentence of subsection (1) makes it clear that the place of arrival of shipped goods is a reasonable place for their inspection.

4.   Expenses of an inspection made to satisfy the buyer of the seller's performance must be assumed by the buyer in the first instance. Since the rule provides merely for an allocation of expense there is no policy to prevent the parties from providing otherwise in the agreement. Where the buyer would normally bear the

expenses of the inspection but the goods are rightly rejected because of what the inspection reveals, demonstrable and reasonable costs of the inspection are part of his incidental damage caused by the seller's breach.

5.   In the case of payment against documents, subsection (3) requires payment before inspection, since shipping documents against which payment is to be made will commonly be tendered while the goods are still in transit. This Article recognizes no exception in any peculiar case in which the goods happen to arrive before the documents are tendered. However, where by the agreement payment is to await the arrival of the goods, inspection before payment becomes proper since the goods are then "available for inspection."

Where by the agreement the documents are to be tendered after arrival of the goods the buyer is entitled to inspect before payment since the goods are then "available for inspection". Proof of usage is not necessary to establish this right, but if inspection before payment is disputed the contrary must be established by usage or by an explicit contract term to that effect.

For the same reason, that the goods are available for inspection, a term calling for payment against storage documents or a delivery order does not normally bar the buyer's right to inspection before payment under subsection (3)(b). This result is reinforced by the buyer's right under subsection (1) to inspect goods which have been appropriated with notice to him.

6.   Under subsection (4) an agreed place or method of inspection is generally held to be intended as exclusive. However, where compliance with such an agreed inspection term becomes impossible, the question is basically one of intention. If the parties clearly intend that the method of inspection named is to be a necessary condition without which the entire deal is to fail, the contract is at an end if that method becomes impossible. On the other hand, if the parties merely seek to indicate a convenient and reliable method but do not intend to give up the deal in the event of its failure, any reasonable method of inspection may be substituted under this Article.

Since the purpose of an agreed place of inspection is only to make sure at that point whether or not the goods will be thrown back, the "exclusive" feature of the named place is satisfied under this Article if the buyer's failure to inspect there is held to be an acceptance with the knowledge of such defects as inspection would have revealed within the section on waiver of buyer's objections by failure to particularize. Revocation of the acceptance is limited to the situations stated in the section pertaining to that subject. The reasonable time within which to give notice of defects within the section on notice of breach begins to run from the point of the "acceptance."

7.   Clauses on time of inspection are commonly clauses which limit the time in which the buyer must inspect and give notice of defects. Such clauses are therefore governed by the section of this Article which requires that such a time limitation must be reasonable.

8.   Inspection under this Article is not to be regarded as a "condition precedent to the passing of title" so that risk until inspection remains on the seller. Under subsection (4) such an approach cannot be sustained. Issues between the buyer and seller are settled in this Article almost wholly by special provisions and not by the technical determination of the locus of the title. Thus "inspection as a condition to the passing of title" becomes a concept almost without meaning. However, in peculiar circumstances inspection may still have some of the consequences hitherto sought and obtained under that concept.

9.   "Inspection" under this section has to do with the buyer's check-up on whether the seller's performance is in accordance with a contract previously made and is not to be confused with the "examination" of the goods or of a sample or model of them at the time of contracting which may affect the warranties involved in the contract.

Cross References:

Generally: Sections 2–310(b), 2–321(3) and 2–606(1)(b).
Point 1: Section 2–607.
Point 2: Sections 2–501 and 2–502.
Point 4: Section 2–715.
Point 5: Section 2–321(3).
Point 6: Sections 2–606 to 2–608.
Point 7: Section 1–204.
Point 8: Comment to Section 2–401.
Point 9: Section 2–316(3)(b).

§ 2–514   UNIFORM COMMERCIAL CODE

Definitional Cross References:

"Buyer". Section 2–103.
"Conform". Section 2–106.
"Contract". Section 1–201.
"Contract for sale". Section 2–106.
"Document of title". Section 1–201.
"Goods". Section 2–105.
"Party". Section 1–201.
"Presumed". Section 1–201.
"Reasonable time". Section 1–204.
"Rights". Section 1–201.
"Seller". Section 2–103.
"Send". Section 1–201.
"Term". Section 1–201.

As amended in 2003.

§ 2–514.   When Documents Deliverable on Acceptance; When on Payment.

Unless otherwise agreed documents against which a draft is drawn are to be delivered to the drawee on acceptance of the draft if it is payable more than three days after presentment; otherwise, only on payment.

Official Comment

Prior Uniform Statutory Provision: Section 41, Uniform Bills of Lading Act.

Changes: Rewritten.

Purposes of Changes: To make the provision one of general application so that:

1.   It covers any document against which a draft may be drawn, whatever may be the form of the document, and applies to interpret the action of a seller or consignor insofar as it may affect the rights and duties of any buyer, consignee or financing agency concerned with the paper. Supplementary or corresponding provisions are found in Sections 4–503 and 5–112.

2.   An "arrival" draft is a sight draft within the purpose of this section.

Cross References:

Point 1: See Sections 2–502, 2–505(2), 2–507(2), 2–512, 2–513, 2–607 concerning protection of rights of buyer and seller, and 4–503 and 5–112 on delivery of documents.

Definitional Cross References:

"Delivery". Section 1–201.
"Draft". Section 3–104.

§ 2–515.   Preserving Evidence of Goods in Dispute.

In furtherance of the adjustment of any claim or dispute

(a)   either party on reasonable notification to the other and for the purpose of ascertaining the facts and preserving evidence has the right to inspect, test and sample the goods including such of them as may be in the possession or control of the other; and

(b)   the parties may agree to a third party inspection or survey to determine the conformity or condition of the goods and may agree that the findings shall be binding upon them in any subsequent litigation or adjustment.

Official Comment

Prior Uniform Statutory Provision: None.

ARTICLE 2 (2016)   **§ 2–601**

Purposes:

    1.   To meet certain serious problems which arise when there is a dispute as to the quality of the goods and thereby perhaps to aid the parties in reaching a settlement, and to further the use of devices which will promote certainty as to the condition of the goods, or at least aid in preserving evidence of their condition.

    2.   Under paragraph (a), to afford either party an opportunity for preserving evidence, whether or not agreement has been reached, and thereby to reduce uncertainty in any litigation and, in turn perhaps, to promote agreement.

    Paragraph (a) does not conflict with the provisions on the seller's right to resell rejected goods or the buyer's similar right. Apparent conflict between these provisions which will be suggested in certain circumstances is to be resolved by requiring prompt action by the parties. Nor does paragraph (a) impair the effect of a term for payment before inspection. Short of such defects as amount to fraud or substantial failure of consideration, non-conformity is neither an excuse nor a defense to an action for non-acceptance of documents. Normally, therefore, until the buyer has made payment, inspected and rejected the goods, there is no occasion or use for the rights under paragraph (a).

    3.   Under paragraph (b), to provide for third party inspection upon the agreement of the parties, thereby opening the door to amicable adjustments based upon the findings of such third parties.

    The use of the phrase "conformity or condition" makes it clear that the parties' agreement may range from a complete settlement of all aspects of the dispute by a third party to the use of a third party merely to determine and record the condition of the goods so that they can be resold or used to reduce the stake in controversy. "Conformity", at one end of the scale of possible issues, includes the whole question of interpretation of the agreement and its legal effect, the state of the goods in regard to quality and condition, whether any defects are due to factors which operate at the risk of the buyer, and the degree of non-conformity where that may be material. "Condition", at the other end of the scale, includes nothing but the degree of damage or deterioration which the goods show. Paragraph (b) is intended to reach any point in the gamut which the parties may agree upon.

    The principle of the section on reservation of rights reinforces this paragraph in simplifying such adjustments as the parties wish to make in partial settlement while reserving their rights as to any further points. Paragraph (b) also suggests the use of arbitration, where desired, of any points left open, but nothing in this section is intended to repeal or amend any statute governing arbitration. Where any question arises as to the extent of the parties' agreement under the paragraph, the presumption should be that it was meant to extend only to the relation between the contract description and the goods as delivered, since that is what a craftsman in the trade would normally be expected to report upon. Finally, a written and authenticated report of inspection or tests by a third party, whether or not sampling has been practicable, is entitled to be admitted as evidence under this Act, for it is a third party document.

Cross References:

    Point 2: Sections 2–513(3), 2–706 and 2–711(2) and Article 5.
    Point 3: Sections 1–202 and 1–207.

Definitional Cross References:

    "Conform". Section 2–106.
    "Goods". Section 2–105.
    "Notification". Section 1–201.
    "Party". Section 1–201.

PART 6

BREACH, REPUDIATION AND EXCUSE

§ 2–601.   **Buyer's Rights on Improper Delivery.**

    Subject to the provisions of this Article on breach in installment contracts (Section 2–612) and unless otherwise agreed under the sections on contractual limitations of remedy (Sections 2–718 and 2–719), if the goods or the tender of delivery fail in any respect to conform to the contract, the buyer may

   (a)   reject the whole; or

   (b)   accept the whole; or

   (c)   accept any commercial unit or units and reject the rest.

Official Comment

Prior Uniform Statutory Provision: No one general equivalent provision but numerous provisions, dealing with situations of non-conformity where buyer may accept or reject, including Sections 11, 44 and 69(1), Uniform Sales Act.

Changes: Partial acceptance in good faith is recognized and the buyer's remedies on the contract for breach of warranty and the like, where the buyer has returned the goods after transfer of title, are no longer barred.

Purposes of Changes: To make it clear that:

   1.   A buyer accepting a non-conforming tender is not penalized by the loss of any remedy otherwise open to him. This policy extends to cover and regulate the acceptance of a part of any lot improperly tendered in any case where the price can reasonably be apportioned. Partial acceptance is permitted whether the part of the goods accepted conforms or not. The only limitation on partial acceptance is that good faith and commercial reasonableness must be used to avoid undue impairment of the value of the remaining portion of the goods. This is the reason for the insistence on the "commercial unit" in paragraph (c). In this respect, the test is not only what unit has been the basis of contract, but whether the partial acceptance produces so materially adverse an effect on the remainder as to constitute bad faith.

   2.   Acceptance made with the knowledge of the other party is final. An original refusal to accept may be withdrawn by a later acceptance if the seller has indicated that he is holding the tender open. However, if the buyer attempts to accept, either in whole or in part, after his original rejection has caused the seller to arrange for other disposition of the goods, the buyer must answer for any ensuing damage since the next section provides that any exercise of ownership after rejection is wrongful as against the seller. Further, he is liable even though the seller may choose to treat his action as acceptance rather than conversion, since the damage flows from the misleading notice. Such arrangements for resale or other disposition of the goods by the seller must be viewed as within the normal contemplation of a buyer who has given notice of rejection. However, the buyer's attempts in good faith to dispose of defective goods where the seller has failed to give instructions within a reasonable time are not to be regarded as an acceptance.

Cross References:

   Sections 2–602(2)(a), 2–612, 2–718 and 2–719.

Definitional Cross References:

   "Buyer". Section 2–103.
   "Commercial unit". Section 2–105.
   "Conform". Section 2–106.
   "Contract". Section 1–201.
   "Goods". Section 2–105.
   "Installment contract". Section 2–612.
   "Rights". Section 1–201.

§ 2–602.   Manner and Effect of Rightful Rejection.

   (1)   Rejection of goods must be within a reasonable time after their delivery or tender. It is ineffective unless the buyer seasonably notifies the seller.

   (2)   Subject to the provisions of the two following sections on rejected goods (Sections 2–603 and 2–604),

   (a)   after rejection any exercise of ownership by the buyer with respect to any commercial unit is wrongful as against the seller; and

   (b)   if the buyer has before rejection taken physical possession of goods in which he does not have a security interest under the provisions of this Article (subsection (3) of Section 2–711), he is under a duty after rejection to hold them with reasonable care at the seller's disposition for a time sufficient to permit the seller to remove them; but

(c)   the buyer has no further obligations with regard to goods rightfully rejected.

(3)   The seller's rights with respect to goods wrongfully rejected are governed by the provisions of this Article on Seller's remedies in general (Section 2–703).

Official Comment

Prior Uniform Statutory Provision: Section 50, Uniform Sales Act.

Changes: Rewritten.

Purposes of Changes: To make it clear that:

1.   A tender or delivery of goods made pursuant to a contract of sale, even though wholly non-conforming, requires affirmative action by the buyer to avoid acceptance. Under subsection (1), therefore, the buyer is given a reasonable time to notify the seller of his rejection, but without such seasonable notification his rejection is ineffective. The sections of this Article dealing with inspection of goods must be read in connection with the buyer's reasonable time for action under this subsection. Contract provisions limiting the time for rejection fall within the rule of the section on "Time" and are effective if the time set gives the buyer a reasonable time for discovery of defects. What constitutes a due "notifying" of rejection by the buyer to the seller is defined in Section 1–201.

2.   Subsection (2) lays down the normal duties of the buyer upon rejection, which flow from the relationship of the parties. Beyond his duty to hold the goods with reasonable care for the buyer's [seller's] disposition, this section continues the policy of prior uniform legislation in generally relieving the buyer from any duties with respect to them, except when the circumstances impose the limited obligation of salvage upon him under the next section.

3.   The present section applies only to rightful rejection by the buyer. If the seller has made a tender which in all respects conforms to the contract, the buyer has a positive duty to accept and his failure to do so constitutes a "wrongful rejection" which gives the seller immediate remedies for breach. Subsection (3) is included here to emphasize the sharp distinction between the rejection of an improper tender and the non-acceptance which is a breach by the buyer.

4.   The provisions of this section are to be appropriately limited or modified when a negotiation is in process.

Cross References:

Point 1: Sections 1–201, 1–204(1) and (3), 2–512(2), 2–513(1) and 2–606(1)(b).
Point 2: Section 2–603(1).
Point 3: Section 2–703.

Definitional Cross References:

"Buyer". Section 2–103.
"Commercial unit". Section 2–105.
"Goods". Section 2–105.
"Merchant". Section 2–104.
"Notifies". Section 1–201.
"Reasonable time". Section 1–204.
"Remedy". Section 1–201.
"Rights". Section 1–201.
"Seasonably". Section 1–204.
"Security interest". Section 1–201.
"Seller". Section 2–103.

§ 2–603.   Merchant Buyer's Duties as to Rightfully Rejected Goods.

(1)   Subject to any security interest in the buyer (subsection (3) of Section 2–711), when the seller has no agent or place of business at the market of rejection a merchant buyer is under a duty after rejection of goods in his possession or control to follow any reasonable instructions received from the seller with respect to the goods and in the absence of such instructions to make reasonable efforts to sell them for the seller's account if they are perishable or threaten to decline in value speedily. Instructions are not reasonable if on demand indemnity for expenses is not forthcoming.

(2)   When the buyer sells goods under subsection (1), he is entitled to reimbursement from the seller or out of the proceeds for reasonable expenses of caring for and selling them, and if the expenses include no selling commission then to such commission as is usual in the trade or if there is none to a reasonable sum not exceeding ten per cent on the gross proceeds.

(3)   In complying with this section the buyer is held only to good faith and good faith conduct hereunder is neither acceptance nor conversion nor the basis of an action for damages.

Official Comment

Prior Uniform Statutory Provision: None.

Purposes:

1.   This section recognizes the duty imposed upon the merchant buyer by good faith and commercial practice to follow any reasonable instructions of the seller as to reshipping, storing, delivery to a third party, reselling or the like. Subsection (1) goes further and extends the duty to include the making of reasonable efforts to effect a salvage sale where the value of the goods is threatened and the seller's instructions do not arrive in time to prevent serious loss.

2.   The limitations on the buyer's duty to resell under subsection (1) are to be liberally construed. The buyer's duty to resell under this section arises from commercial necessity and thus is present only when the seller has "no agent or place of business at the market of rejection". A financing agency which is acting in behalf of the seller in handling the documents rejected by the buyer is sufficiently the seller's agent to lift the burden of salvage resale from the buyer. (See provisions of Sections 4–503 and 5–112 on bank's duties with respect to rejected documents.) The buyer's duty to resell is extended only to goods in his "possession or control", but these are intended as words of wide, rather than narrow, import. In effect, the measure of the buyer's "control" is whether he can practicably effect control without undue commercial burden.

3.   The explicit provisions for reimbursement and compensation to the buyer in subsection (2) are applicable and necessary only where he is not acting under instructions from the seller. As provided in subsection (1) the seller's instructions to be "reasonable" must on demand of the buyer include indemnity for expenses.

4.   Since this section makes the resale of perishable goods an affirmative duty in contrast to a mere right to sell as under the case law, subsection (3) makes it clear that the buyer is liable only for the exercise of good faith in determining whether the value of the goods is sufficiently threatened to justify a quick resale or whether he has waited a sufficient length of time for instructions, or what a reasonable means and place of resale is.

5.   A buyer who fails to make a salvage sale when his duty to do so under this section has arisen is subject to damages pursuant to the section on liberal administration of remedies.

Cross References:

Point 2: Sections 4–503 and 5–112.
Point 5: Section 1–106. Compare generally section 2–706.

Definitional Cross References:

"Buyer". Section 2–103.
"Good faith". Section 1–201.
"Goods". Section 2–105.
"Merchant". Section 2–104.
"Security interest". Section 1–201.
"Seller". Section 2–103.

ARTICLE 2 (2016)

§ 2–604

§ 2–604. Buyer's Options as to Salvage of Rightfully Rejected Goods.

Subject to the provisions of the immediately preceding section on perishables if the seller gives no instructions within a reasonable time after notification of rejection the buyer may store the rejected goods for the seller's account or reship them to him or resell them for the seller's account with reimbursement as provided in the preceding section. Such action is not acceptance or conversion.

Official Comment

Prior Uniform Statutory Provision: None.

Purposes:

The basic purpose of this section is twofold: on the one hand it aims at reducing the stake in dispute and on the other at avoiding the pinning of a technical "acceptance" on a buyer who has taken steps towards realization on or preservation of the goods in good faith. This section is essentially a salvage section and the buyer's right to act under it is conditioned upon (1) non-conformity of the goods, (2) due notification of rejection to the seller under the section on manner of rejection, and (3) the absence of any instructions from the seller which the merchant-buyer has a duty to follow under the preceding section.

This section is designed to accord all reasonable leeway to a rightfully rejecting buyer acting in good faith. The listing of what the buyer may do in the absence of instructions from the seller is intended to be not exhaustive but merely illustrative. This is not a "merchant's" section and the options are pure options given to merchant and nonmerchant buyers alike. The merchant-buyer, however, may in some instances be under a duty rather than an option to resell under the provisions of the preceding section.

Cross References:

Sections 2–602(1), and 2–603(1) and 2–706.

Definitional Cross References:

"Buyer". Section 2–103.
"Notification". Section 1–201.
"Reasonable time". Section 1–204.
"Seller". Section 2–103.

§ 2–605. Waiver of Buyer's Objections by Failure to Particularize.

(1) The buyer's failure to state in connection with rejection a particular defect which is ascertainable by reasonable inspection precludes him from relying on the unstated defect to justify rejection or to establish breach

(a) where the seller could have cured it if stated seasonably; or

(b) between merchants when the seller has after rejection made a request in writing for a full and final written statement of all defects on which the buyer proposes to rely.

(2) Payment against documents made without reservation of rights precludes recovery of the payment for defects apparent in the documents.

As amended in 2003.

Official Comment

Prior Uniform Statutory Provision: None.

Purposes:

1. The present section rests upon a policy of permitting the buyer to give a quick and informal notice of defects in a tender without penalizing him for omissions in his statement, while at the same time protecting a seller who is reasonably misled by the buyer's failure to state curable defects.

2. Where the defect in a tender is one which could have been cured by the seller, a buyer who merely rejects the delivery without stating his objections to it is probably acting in commercial bad faith and seeking to get out of a deal which has become unprofitable. Subsection (1)(a), following the general policy of this Article

§ 2–606   UNIFORM COMMERCIAL CODE

which looks to preserving the deal wherever possible, therefore insists that the seller's right to correct his tender in such circumstances be protected.

3.   When the time for cure is past, subsection (1)(b) makes it plain that a seller is entitled upon request to a final statement of objections upon which he can rely. What is needed is that he make clear to the buyer exactly what is being sought. A formal demand under paragraph (b) will be sufficient in the case of a merchant-buyer.

4.   Subsection (2) applies to the particular case of documents the same principle which the section on effects of acceptance applies to the case of goods. The matter is dealt with in this section in terms of "waiver" of objections rather than of right to revoke acceptance, partly to avoid any confusion with the problems of acceptance of goods and partly because defects in documents which are not taken as grounds for rejection are generally minor ones. The only defects concerned in the present subsection are defects in the documents which are apparent. This rule applies to both tangible and electronic documents of title. Where payment is required against the documents they must be inspected before payment, and the payment then constitutes acceptance of the documents. Under the section dealing with this problem, such acceptance of the documents does not constitute an acceptance of the goods or impair any options or remedies of the buyer for their improper delivery. Where the documents are delivered without requiring such contemporary action as payment from the buyer, the reason of the next section on what constitutes acceptance of goods, applies. Their acceptance by non-objection is therefore postponed until after a reasonable time for their inspection. In either situation, however, the buyer "waives" only the defects apparent in the documents.

Cross References:

Point 2: Section 2–508.
Point 4: Sections 2–512(2), 2–606(1)(b), 2–607(2).

Definitional Cross References:

"Between merchants". Section 2–104.
"Buyer". Section 2–103.
"Seasonably". Section 1–204.
"Seller". Section 2–103.
"Writing" and "written". Section 1–201.

As amended in 2003.

§ 2–606.   What Constitutes Acceptance of Goods.

(1)   Acceptance of goods occurs when the buyer

(a)   after a reasonable opportunity to inspect the goods signifies to the seller that the goods are conforming or that he will take or retain them in spite of their non-conformity; or

(b)   fails to make an effective rejection (subsection (1) of Section 2–602), but such acceptance does not occur until the buyer has had a reasonable opportunity to inspect them; or

(c)   does any act inconsistent with the seller's ownership; but if such act is wrongful as against the seller it is an acceptance only if ratified by him.

(2)   Acceptance of a part of any commercial unit is acceptance of that entire unit.

Official Comment

Prior Uniform Statutory Provision: Section 48, Uniform Sales Act.

Changes: Rewritten, the qualification in paragraph (c) and subsection (2) being new; otherwise the general policy of the prior legislation is continued.

Purposes of Changes and New Matter: To make it clear that:

1.   Under this Article "acceptance" as applied to goods means that the buyer, pursuant to the contract, takes particular goods which have been appropriated to the contract as his own, whether or not he is obligated to do so, and whether he does so by words, action, or silence when it is time to speak. If the goods conform to the contract, acceptance amounts only to the performance by the buyer of one part of his legal obligation.

ARTICLE 2 (2016) § 2–607

2. Under this Article acceptance of goods is always acceptance of identified goods which have been appropriated to the contract or are appropriated by the contract. There is no provision for "acceptance of title" apart from acceptance in general, since acceptance of title is not material under this Article to the detailed rights and duties of the parties. (See Section 2–401). The refinements of the older law between acceptance of goods and of title become unnecessary in view of the provisions of the sections on effect and revocation of acceptance, on effects of identification and on risk of loss, and those sections which free the seller's and buyer's remedies from the complications and confusions caused by the question of whether title has or has not passed to the buyer before breach.

3. Under paragraph (a), payment made after tender is always one circumstance tending to signify acceptance of the goods but in itself it can never be more than one circumstance and is not conclusive. Also, a conditional communication of acceptance always remains subject to its expressed conditions.

4. Under paragraph (c), any action taken by the buyer, which is inconsistent with his claim that he has rejected the goods, constitutes an acceptance. However, the provisions of paragraph (c) are subject to the sections dealing with rejection by the buyer which permit the buyer to take certain actions with respect to the goods pursuant to his options and duties imposed by those sections, without effecting an acceptance of the goods. The second clause of paragraph (c) modifies some of the prior case law and makes it clear that "acceptance" in law based on the wrongful act of the acceptor is acceptance only as against the wrongdoer and then only at the option of the party wronged.

In the same manner in which a buyer can bind himself, despite his insistence that he is rejecting or has rejected the goods, by an act inconsistent with the seller's ownership under paragraph (c), he can obligate himself by a communication of acceptance despite a prior rejection under paragraph (a). However, the sections on buyer's rights on improper delivery and on the effect of rightful rejection, make it clear that after he once rejects a tender, paragraph (a) does not operate in favor of the buyer unless the seller has re-tendered the goods or has taken affirmative action indicating that he is holding the tender open. See also Comment 2 to Section 2–601.

5. Subsection (2) supplements the policy of the section on buyer's rights on improper delivery, recognizing the validity of a partial acceptance but insisting that the buyer exercise this right only as to whole commercial units.

Cross References:

Point 2: Sections 2–401, 2–509, 2–510, 2–607, 2–608 and Part 7.
Point 4: Sections 2–601 through 2–604.
Point 5: Section 2–601.

Definitional Cross References:

"Buyer". Section 2–103.
"Commercial unit". Section 2–105.
"Goods". Section 2–105.
"Seller". Section 2–103.

§ 2–607. Effect of Acceptance; Notice of Breach; Burden of Establishing Breach After Acceptance; Notice of Claim or Litigation to Person Answerable Over.

(1) The buyer must pay at the contract rate for any goods accepted.

(2) Acceptance of goods by the buyer precludes rejection of the goods accepted and if made with knowledge of a non-conformity cannot be revoked because of it unless the acceptance was on the reasonable assumption that the non-conformity would be seasonably cured but acceptance does not of itself impair any other remedy provided by this Article for non-conformity.

(3) Where a tender has been accepted

(a) the buyer must within a reasonable time after he discovers or should have discovered any breach notify the seller of breach or be barred from any remedy; and

    (b) if the claim is one for infringement or the like (subsection (3) of Section 2–312) and the buyer is sued as a result of such a breach he must so notify the seller within a reasonable time after he receives notice of the litigation or be barred from any remedy over for liability established by the litigation.

    (4) The burden is on the buyer to establish any breach with respect to the goods accepted.

    (5) Where the buyer is sued for breach of a warranty or other obligation for which his seller is answerable over

    (a) he may give his seller written notice of the litigation. If the notice states that the seller may come in and defend and that if the seller does not do so he will be bound in any action against him by his buyer by any determination of fact common to the two litigations, then unless the seller after seasonable receipt of the notice does come in and defend he is so bound.

    (b) if the claim is one for infringement or the like (subsection (3) of Section 2–312) the original seller may demand in writing that his buyer turn over to him control of the litigation including settlement or else be barred from any remedy over and if he also agrees to bear all expense and to satisfy any adverse judgment, then unless the buyer after seasonable receipt of the demand does turn over control the buyer is so barred.

    (6) The provisions of subsections (3), (4) and (5) apply to any obligation of a buyer to hold the seller harmless against infringement or the like (subsection (3) of Section 2–312).

Official Comment

Prior Uniform Statutory Provision: Subsection (1)—Section 41, Uniform Sales Act; Subsections (2) and (3)—Sections 49 and 69, Uniform Sales Act.

Changes: Rewritten.

Purposes of Changes: To continue the prior basic policies with respect to acceptance of goods while making a number of minor though material changes in the interest of simplicity and commercial convenience so that:

    1. Under subsection (1), once the buyer accepts a tender the seller acquires a right to its price on the contract terms. In cases of partial acceptance, the price of any part accepted is, if possible, to be reasonably apportioned, using the type of apportionment familiar to the courts in quantum valebant cases, to be determined in terms of "the contract rate," which is the rate determined from the bargain in fact (the agreement) after the rules and policies of this Article have been brought to bear.

    2. Under subsection (2) acceptance of goods precludes their subsequent rejection. Any return of the goods thereafter must be by way of revocation of acceptance under the next section. Revocation is unavailable for a non-conformity known to the buyer at the time of acceptance, except where the buyer has accepted on the reasonable assumption that the non-conformity would be seasonably cured.

    3. All other remedies of the buyer remain unimpaired under subsection (2). This is intended to include the buyer's full rights with respect to future installments despite his acceptance of any earlier non-conforming installment.

    4. The time of notification is to be determined by applying commercial standards to a merchant buyer. "A reasonable time" for notification from a retail consumer is to be judged by different standards so that in his case it will be extended, for the rule of requiring notification is designed to defeat commercial bad faith, not to deprive a good faith consumer of his remedy.

    The content of the notification need merely be sufficient to let the seller know that the transaction is still troublesome and must be watched. There is no reason to require that the notification which saves the buyer's rights under this section must include a clear statement of all the objections that will be relied on by the buyer, as under the section covering statements of defects upon rejection (Section 2–605). Nor is there reason for requiring the notification to be a claim for damages or of any threatened litigation or other resort to a remedy. The notification which saves the buyer's rights under this Article need only be such as informs the seller that the transaction is claimed to involve a breach, and thus opens the way for normal settlement through negotiation.

    5. Under this Article various beneficiaries are given rights for injuries sustained by them because of the seller's breach of warranty. Such a beneficiary does not fall within the reason of the present section in regard to

discovery of defects and the giving of notice within a reasonable time after acceptance, since he has nothing to do with acceptance. However, the reason of this section does extend to requiring the beneficiary to notify the seller that an injury has occurred. What is said above, with regard to the extended time for reasonable notification from the lay consumer after the injury is also applicable here; but even a beneficiary can be properly held to the use of good faith in notifying, once he has had time to become aware of the legal situation.

6.   Subsection (4) unambiguously places the burden of proof to establish breach on the buyer after acceptance. However, this rule becomes one purely of procedure when the tender accepted was non-conforming and the buyer has given the seller notice of breach under subsection (3). For subsection (2) makes it clear that acceptance leaves unimpaired the buyer's right to be made whole, and that right can be exercised by the buyer not only by way of cross-claim for damages, but also by way of recoupment in diminution or extinction of the price.

7.   Subsections (3)(b) and (5)(b) give a warrantor against infringement an opportunity to defend or compromise third-party claims or be relieved of his liability. Subsection (5)(a) codifies for all warranties the practice of voucher to defend. Compare Section 3–803. Subsection (6) makes these provisions applicable to the buyer's liability for infringement under Section 2–312.

8.   All of the provisions of the present section are subject to any explicit reservation of rights.

Cross References:

Point 1: Section 1–201.
Point 2: Section 2–608.
Point 4: Sections 1–204 and 2–605.
Point 5: Section 2–318.
Point 6: Section 2–717.
Point 7: Sections 2–312 and 3–803.
Point 8: Section 1–207.

Definitional Cross References:

"Burden of establishing". Section 1–201.
"Buyer". Section 2–103.
"Conform". Section 2–106.
"Contract". Section 1–201.
"Goods". Section 2–105.
"Notifies". Section 1–201.
"Reasonable time". Section 1–204.
"Remedy". Section 1–201.
"Seasonably". Section 1–204.

§ 2–608.   Revocation of Acceptance in Whole or in Part.

(1)   The buyer may revoke his acceptance of a lot or commercial unit whose non-conformity substantially impairs its value to him if he has accepted it

(a)   on the reasonable assumption that its non-conformity would be cured and it has not been seasonably cured; or

(b)   without discovery of such non-conformity if his acceptance was reasonably induced either by the difficulty of discovery before acceptance or by the seller's assurances.

(2)   Revocation of acceptance must occur within a reasonable time after the buyer discovers or should have discovered the ground for it and before any substantial change in condition of the goods which is not caused by their own defects. It is not effective until the buyer notifies the seller of it.

(3)   A buyer who so revokes has the same rights and duties with regard to the goods involved as if he had rejected them.

Official Comment

Prior Uniform Statutory Provision: Section 69(1)(d), (3), (4) and (5), Uniform Sales Act.

Changes: Rewritten.

Purposes of Changes: To make it clear that:

1.   Although the prior basic policy is continued, the buyer is no longer required to elect between revocation of acceptance and recovery of damages for breach. Both are now available to him. The non-alternative character of the two remedies is stressed by the terms used in the present section. The section no longer speaks of "rescission," a term capable of ambiguous application either to transfer of title to the goods or to the contract of sale and susceptible also of confusion with cancellation for cause of an executed or executory portion of the contract. The remedy under this section is instead referred to simply as "revocation of acceptance" of goods tendered under a contract for sale and involves no suggestion of "election" of any sort.

2.   Revocation of acceptance is possible only where the non-conformity substantially impairs the value of the goods to the buyer. For this purpose the test is not what the seller had reason to know at the time of contracting; the question is whether the non-conformity is such as will in fact cause a substantial impairment of value to the buyer though the seller had no advance knowledge as to the buyer's particular circumstances.

3.   "Assurances" by the seller under paragraph (b) of subsection (1) can rest as well in the circumstances or in the contract as in explicit language used at the time of delivery. The reason for recognizing such assurances is that they induce the buyer to delay discovery. These are the only assurances involved in paragraph (b). Explicit assurances may be made either in good faith or bad faith. In either case any remedy accorded by this Article is available to the buyer under the section on remedies for fraud.

4.   Subsection (2) requires notification of revocation of acceptance within a reasonable time after discovery of the grounds for such revocation. Since this remedy will be generally resorted to only after attempts at adjustment have failed, the reasonable time period should extend in most cases beyond the time in which notification of breach must be given, beyond the time for discovery of non-conformity after acceptance and beyond the time for rejection after tender. The parties may by their agreement limit the time for notification under this section, but the same sanctions and considerations apply to such agreements as are discussed in the comment on manner and effect of rightful rejection.

5.   The content of the notice under subsection (2) is to be determined in this case as in others by considerations of good faith, prevention of surprise, and reasonable adjustment. More will generally be necessary than the mere notification of breach required under the preceding section. On the other hand the requirements of the section on waiver of buyer's objections do not apply here. The fact that quick notification of trouble is desirable affords good ground for being slow to bind a buyer by his first statement. Following the general policy of this Article, the requirements of the content of notification are less stringent in the case of a non-merchant buyer.

6.   Under subsection (2) the prior policy is continued of seeking substantial justice in regard to the condition of goods restored to the seller. Thus the buyer may not revoke his acceptance if the goods have materially deteriorated except by reason of their own defects. Worthless goods, however, need not be offered back and minor defects in the articles reoffered are to be disregarded.

7.   The policy of the section allowing partial acceptance is carried over into the present section and the buyer may revoke his acceptance, in appropriate cases, as to the entire lot or any commercial unit thereof.

Cross References:

Point 3: Section 2–721.
Point 4: Sections 1–204, 2–602 and 2–607.
Point 5: Sections 2–605 and 2–607.
Point 7: Section 2–601.

Definitional Cross References:

"Buyer". Section 2–103.
"Commercial unit". Section 2–105.
"Conform". Section 2–106.
"Goods". Section 2–105.
"Lot". Section 2–105.
"Notifies". Section 1–201.
"Reasonable time". Section 1–204.

"Rights". Section 1–201.
"Seasonably". Section 1–204.
"Seller". Section 2–103.

§ 2–609.   Right to Adequate Assurance of Performance.

(1)   A contract for sale imposes an obligation on each party that the other's expectation of receiving due performance will not be impaired. When reasonable grounds for insecurity arise with respect to the performance of either party the other may in writing demand adequate assurance of due performance and until he receives such assurance may if commercially reasonable suspend any performance for which he has not already received the agreed return.

(2)   Between merchants the reasonableness of grounds for insecurity and the adequacy of any assurance offered shall be determined according to commercial standards.

(3)   Acceptance of any improper delivery or payment does not prejudice the aggrieved party's right to demand adequate assurance of future performance.

(4)   After receipt of a justified demand failure to provide within a reasonable time not exceeding thirty days such assurance of due performance as is adequate under the circumstances of the particular case is a repudiation of the contract.

Official Comment

Prior Uniform Statutory Provision: See Sections 53, 54(1)(b), 55 and 63(2), Uniform Sales Act.

Purposes:

1.   The section rests on the recognition of the fact that the essential purpose of a contract between commercial men is actual performance and they do not bargain merely for a promise, or for a promise plus the right to win a lawsuit and that a continuing sense of reliance and security that the promised performance will be forthcoming when due, is an important feature of the bargain. If either the willingness or the ability of a party to perform declines materially between the time of contracting and the time for performance, the other party is threatened with the loss of a substantial part of what he has bargained for. A seller needs protection not merely against having to deliver on credit to a shaky buyer, but also against having to procure and manufacture the goods, perhaps turning down other customers. Once he has been given reason to believe that the buyer's performance has become uncertain, it is an undue hardship to force him to continue his own performance. Similarly, a buyer who believes that the seller's deliveries have become uncertain cannot safely wait for the due date of performance when he has been buying to assure himself of materials for his current manufacturing or to replenish his stock of merchandise.

2.   Three measures have been adopted to meet the needs of commercial men in such situations. First, the aggrieved party is permitted to suspend his own performance and any preparation therefor, with excuse for any resulting necessary delay, until the situation has been clarified. "Suspend performance" under this section means to hold up performance pending the outcome of the demand, and includes also the holding up of any preparatory action. This is the same principle which governs the ancient law of stoppage and seller's lien, and also of excuse of a buyer from prepayment if the seller's actions manifest that he cannot or will not perform. (Original Act, Section 63(2).)

Secondly, the aggrieved party is given the right to require adequate assurance that the other party's performance will be duly forthcoming. This principle is reflected in the familiar clauses permitting the seller to curtail deliveries if the buyer's credit becomes impaired, which when held within the limits of reasonableness and good faith actually express no more than the fair business meaning of any commercial contract.

Third, and finally, this section provides the means by which the aggrieved party may treat the contract as broken if his reasonable grounds for insecurity are not cleared up within a reasonable time. This is the principle underlying the law of anticipatory breach, whether by way of defective part performance or by repudiation. The present section merges these three principles of law and commercial practice into a single theory of general application to all sales agreements looking to future performance.

3.   Subsection (2) of the present section requires that "reasonable" grounds and "adequate" assurance as used in subsection (1) be defined by commercial rather than legal standards. The express reference to commercial standards carries no connotation that the obligation of good faith is not equally applicable here.

Under commercial standards and in accord with commercial practice, a ground for insecurity need not arise from or be directly related to the contract in question. The law as to "dependence" or "independence" of promises within a single contract does not control the application of the present section.

Thus a buyer who falls behind in "his account" with the seller, even though the items involved have to do with separate and legally distinct contracts, impairs the seller's expectation of due performance. Again, under the same test, a buyer who requires precision parts which he intends to use immediately upon delivery, may have reasonable grounds for insecurity if he discovers that his seller is making defective deliveries of such parts to other buyers with similar needs. Thus, too, in a situation such as arose in *Jay Dreher Corporation v. Delco Appliance Corporation*, 93 F.2d 275 (C.C.A.2, 1937), where a manufacturer gave a dealer an exclusive franchise for the sale of his product but on two or three occasions breached the exclusive dealing clause, although there was no default in orders, deliveries or payments under the separate sales contract between the parties, the aggrieved dealer would be entitled to suspend his performance of the contract for sale under the present section and to demand assurance that the exclusive dealing contract would be lived up to. There is no need for an explicit clause tying the exclusive franchise into the contract for the sale of goods since the situation itself ties the agreements together.

The nature of the sales contract enters also into the question of reasonableness. For example, a report from an apparently trustworthy source that the seller had shipped defective goods or was planning to ship them would normally give the buyer reasonable grounds for insecurity. But when the buyer has assumed the risk of payment before inspection of the goods, as in a sales contract on C.I.F. or similar cash against documents terms, that risk is not to be evaded by a demand for assurance. Therefore no ground for insecurity would exist under this section unless the report went to a ground which would excuse payment by the buyer.

4.   What constitutes "adequate" assurance of due performance is subject to the same test of factual conditions. For example, where the buyer can make use of a defective delivery, a mere promise by a seller of good repute that he is giving the matter his attention and that the defect will not be repeated, is normally sufficient. Under the same circumstances, however, a similar statement by a known corner-cutter might well be considered insufficient without the posting of a guaranty or, if so demanded by the buyer, a speedy replacement of the delivery involved. By the same token where a delivery has defects, even though easily curable, which interfere with easy use by the buyer, no verbal assurance can be deemed adequate which is not accompanied by replacement, repair, money-allowance, or other commercially reasonable cure.

A fact situation such as arose in *Corn Products Refining Co. v. Fasola*, 94 N.J.L. 181, 109 A. 505 (1920) offers illustration both of reasonable grounds for insecurity and "adequate" assurance. In that case a contract for the sale of oils on 30 days' credit, 2% off for payment within 10 days, provided that credit was to be extended to the buyer only if his financial responsibility was satisfactory to the seller. The buyer had been in the habit of taking advantage of the discount but at the same time that he failed to make his customary 10 day payment, the seller heard rumors, in fact false, that the buyer's financial condition was shaky. Thereupon, the seller demanded cash before shipment or security satisfactory to him. The buyer sent a good credit report from his banker, expressed willingness to make payments when due on the 30 day terms and insisted on further deliveries under the contract. Under this Article the rumors, although false, were enough to make the buyer's financial condition "unsatisfactory" to the seller under the contract clause. Moreover, the buyer's practice of taking the cash discounts is enough, apart from the contract clause, to lay a commercial foundation for suspicion when the practice is suddenly stopped. These matters, however, go only to the justification of the seller's demand for security, or his "reasonable grounds for insecurity".

The adequacy of the assurance given is not measured as in the type of "satisfaction" situation affected with intangibles, such as in personal service cases, cases involving a third party's judgment as final, or cases in which the whole contract is dependent on one party's satisfaction, as in a sale on approval. Here, the seller must exercise good faith and observe commercial standards. This Article thus approves the statement of the court in *James B. Berry's Sons Co. of Illinois v. Monark Gasoline & Oil Co., Inc.*, 32 F.2d 74 (C.C.A.8, 1929), that the seller's satisfaction under such a clause must be based upon reason and must not be arbitrary or capricious; and rejects the purely personal "good faith" test of the Corn Products Refining Co. case, which held that in the seller's sole judgment, if for *any* reason he was dissatisfied, he was entitled to revoke the credit. In the absence of the buyer's failure to take the 2% discount as was his custom, the banker's report given in that case would have been "adequate" assurance under this Act, regardless of the language of the "satisfaction" clause. However, the seller is reasonably entitled to feel insecure at a sudden expansion of the buyer's use of a credit term, and should be entitled either to security or to a satisfactory explanation.

The entire foregoing discussion as to adequacy of assurance by way of explanation is subject to qualification when repeated occasions for the application of this section arise. This Act recognizes that repeated delinquencies must be viewed as cumulative. On the other hand, commercial sense also requires that if repeated claims for assurance are made under this section, the basis for these claims must be increasingly obvious.

5.   A failure to provide adequate assurance of performance and thereby to re-establish the security of expectation, results in a breach only "by repudiation" under subsection (4). Therefore, the possibility is continued of retraction of the repudiation under the section dealing with that problem, unless the aggrieved party has acted on the breach in some manner.

The thirty day limit on the time to provide assurance is laid down to free the question of reasonable time from uncertainty in later litigation.

6.   Clauses seeking to give the protected party exceedingly wide powers to cancel or readjust the contract when ground for insecurity arises must be read against the fact that good faith is a part of the obligation of the contract and not subject to modification by agreement and includes, in the case of a merchant, the reasonable observance of commercial standards of fair dealing in the trade. Such clauses can thus be effective to enlarge the protection given by the present section to a certain extent, to fix the reasonable time within which requested assurance must be given, or to define adequacy of the assurance in any commercially reasonable fashion. But any clause seeking to set up arbitrary standards for action is ineffective under this Article. Acceleration clauses are treated similarly in the Articles on Commercial Paper and Secured Transactions.

Cross References:

Point 3: Section 1–203.
Point 5: Section 2–611.
Point 6: Sections 1–203 and 1–208 and Articles 3 and 9.

Definitional Cross References:

"Aggrieved party". Section 1–201.
"Between merchants". Section 2–104.
"Contract". Section 1–201.
"Contract for sale". Section 2–106.
"Party". Section 1–201.
"Reasonable time". Section 1–204
"Rights". Section 1–201.
"Writing". Section 1–201.

§ 2–610.   Anticipatory Repudiation.

When either party repudiates the contract with respect to a performance not yet due the loss of which will substantially impair the value of the contract to the other, the aggrieved party may

(a)   for a commercially reasonable time await performance by the repudiating party; or

(b)   resort to any remedy for breach (Section 2–703 or Section 2–711), even though he has notified the repudiating party that he would await the latter's performance and has urged retraction; and

(c)   in either case suspend his own performance or proceed in accordance with the provisions of this Article on the seller's right to identify goods to the contract notwithstanding breach or to salvage unfinished goods (Section 2–704).

Official Comment

Prior Uniform Statutory Provision: See Sections 63(2) and 65, Uniform Sales Act.

Purposes: To make it clear that:

1.   With the problem of insecurity taken care of by the preceding section and with provision being made in this Article as to the effect of a defective delivery under an installment contract, anticipatory repudiation centers upon an overt communication of intention or an action which renders performance impossible or demonstrates a clear determination not to continue with performance.

§ 2-611   UNIFORM COMMERCIAL CODE

Under the present section when such a repudiation substantially impairs the value of the contract, the aggrieved party may at any time resort to his remedies for breach, or he may suspend his own performance while he negotiates with, or awaits performance by, the other party. But if he awaits performance beyond a commercially reasonable time he cannot recover resulting damages which he should have avoided.

2.   It is not necessary for repudiation that performance be made literally and utterly impossible. Repudiation can result from action which reasonably indicates a rejection of the continuing obligation. And, a repudiation automatically results under the preceding section on insecurity when a party fails to provide adequate assurance of due future performance within thirty days after a justifiable demand therefor has been made. Under the language of this section, a demand by one or both parties for more than the contract calls for in the way of counter-performance is not in itself a repudiation nor does it invalidate a plain expression of desire for future performance. However, when under a fair reading it amounts to a statement of intention not to perform except on conditions which go beyond the contract, it becomes a repudiation.

3.   The test chosen to justify an aggrieved party's action under this section is the same as that in the section on breach in installment contracts—namely the substantial value of the contract. The most useful test of substantial value is to determine whether material inconvenience or injustice will result if the aggrieved party is forced to wait and receive an ultimate tender minus the part or aspect repudiated.

4.   After repudiation, the aggrieved party may immediately resort to any remedy he chooses provided he moves in good faith (see Section 1–203). Inaction and silence by the aggrieved party may leave the matter open but it cannot be regarded as misleading the repudiating party. Therefore the aggrieved party is left free to proceed at any time with his options under this section, unless he has taken some positive action which in good faith requires notification to the other party before the remedy is pursued.

Cross References:

Point 1: Sections 2–609 and 2–612.
Point 2: Section 2–609.
Point 3: Section 2–612.
Point 4: Section 1–203.

Definitional Cross References:

"Aggrieved party". Section 1–201.
"Contract". Section 1–201.
"Party". Section 1–201.
"Remedy". Section 1–201.

§ 2-611.   Retraction of Anticipatory Repudiation.

(1)   Until the repudiating party's next performance is due he can retract his repudiation unless the aggrieved party has since the repudiation cancelled or materially changed his position or otherwise indicated that he considers the repudiation final.

(2)   Retraction may be by any method which clearly indicates to the aggrieved party that the repudiating party intends to perform, but must include any assurance justifiably demanded under the provisions of this Article (Section 2–609).

(3)   Retraction reinstates the repudiating party's rights under the contract with due excuse and allowance to the aggrieved party for any delay occasioned by the repudiation.

Official Comment

Prior Uniform Statutory Provision: None.

Purposes: To make it clear that:

1.   The repudiating party's right to reinstate the contract is entirely dependent upon the action taken by the aggrieved party. If the latter has cancelled the contract or materially changed his position at any time after the repudiation, there can be no retraction under this section.

2.   Under subsection (2) an effective retraction must be accompanied by any assurances demanded under the section dealing with right to adequate assurance. A repudiation is of course sufficient to give reasonable

ground for insecurity and to warrant a request for assurance as an essential condition of the retraction. However, after a timely and unambiguous expression of retraction, a reasonable time for the assurance to be worked out should be allowed by the aggrieved party before cancellation.

Cross Reference:

Point 2: Section 2–609.

Definitional Cross References:

"Aggrieved party". Section 1–201.
"Cancellation". Section 2–106.
"Contract". Section 1–201.
"Party". Section 1–201.
"Rights". Section 1–201.

§ 2–612.   "Installment Contract"; Breach.

(1)   An "installment contract" is one which requires or authorizes the delivery of goods in separate lots to be separately accepted, even though the contract contains a clause "each delivery is a separate contract" or its equivalent.

(2)   The buyer may reject any installment which is non-conforming if the non-conformity substantially impairs the value of that installment and cannot be cured or if the non-conformity is a defect in the required documents; but if the non-conformity does not fall within subsection (3) and the seller gives adequate assurance of its cure the buyer must accept that installment.

(3)   Whenever non-conformity or default with respect to one or more installments substantially impairs the value of the whole contract there is a breach of the whole. But the aggrieved party reinstates the contract if he accepts a non-conforming installment without seasonably notifying of cancellation or if he brings an action with respect only to past installments or demands performance as to future installments.

Official Comment

Prior Uniform Statutory Provision: Section 45(2), Uniform Sales Act.

Changes: Rewritten.

Purposes of Changes: To continue prior law but to make explicit the more mercantile interpretation of many of the rules involved, so that:

1.   The definition of an installment contract is phrased more broadly in this Article so as to cover installment deliveries tacitly authorized by the circumstances or by the option of either party.

2.   In regard to the apportionment of the price for separate payment this Article applies the more liberal test of what can be apportioned rather than the test of what is clearly apportioned by the agreement. This Article also recognizes approximate calculation or apportionment of price subject to subsequent adjustment. A provision for separate payment for each lot delivered ordinarily means that the price is at least roughly calculable by units of quantity, but such a provision is not essential to an "installment contract." If separate acceptance of separate deliveries is contemplated, no generalized contrast between wholly "entire" and wholly "divisible" contracts has any standing under this Article.

3.   This Article rejects any approach which gives clauses such as "each delivery is a separate contract" their legalistically literal effect. Such contracts nonetheless call for installment deliveries. Even where a clause speaks of "a separate contract for all purposes", a commercial reading of the language under the section on good faith and commercial standards requires that the singleness of the document and the negotiation, together with the sense of the situation, prevail over any uncommercial and legalistic interpretation.

4.   One of the requirements for rejection under subsection (2) is non-conformity substantially impairing the value of the installment in question. However, an installment agreement may require accurate conformity in quality as a condition to the right to acceptance if the need for such conformity is made clear either by express provision or by the circumstances. In such a case the effect of the agreement is to define explicitly what amounts to substantial impairment of value impossible to cure. A clause requiring accurate compliance as a condition to

the right to acceptance must, however, have some basis in reason, must avoid imposing hardship by surprise and is subject to waiver or to displacement by practical construction.

Substantial impairment of the value of an installment can turn not only on the quality of the goods but also on such factors as time, quantity, assortment, and the like. It must be judged in terms of the normal or specifically known purposes of the contract. The defect in required documents refers to such matters as the absence of insurance documents under a C.I.F. contract, falsity of a bill of lading, or one failing to show shipment within the contract period or to the contract destination. Even in such cases, however, the provisions on cure of tender apply if appropriate documents are readily procurable.

5.   Under subsection (2) an installment delivery must be accepted if the non-conformity is curable and the seller gives adequate assurance of cure. Cure of non-conformity of an installment in the first instance can usually be afforded by an allowance against the price, or in the case of reasonable discrepancies in quantity either by a further delivery or a partial rejection. This Article requires reasonable action by a buyer in regard to discrepant delivery and good faith requires that the buyer make any reasonable minor outlay of time or money necessary to cure an overshipment by severing out an acceptable percentage thereof. The seller must take over a cure which involves any material burden; the buyer's obligation reaches only to cooperation. Adequate assurance for purposes of subsection (2) is measured by the same standards as under the section on right to adequate assurance of performance.

6.   Subsection (3) is designed to further the continuance of the contract in the absence of an overt cancellation. The question arising when an action is brought as to a single installment only is resolved by making such action waive the right to cancellation. This involves merely a defect in one or more installments, as contrasted with the situation where there is a true repudiation within the section on anticipatory repudiation. Whether the non-conformity in any given installment justifies cancellation as to the future depends, not on whether such non-conformity indicates an intent or likelihood that the future deliveries will also be defective, but whether the non-conformity substantially impairs the value of the whole contract. If only the seller's security in regard to future installments is impaired, he has the right to demand adequate assurances of proper future performance but has not an immediate right to cancel the entire contract. It is clear under this Article, however, that defects in prior installments are cumulative in effect, so that acceptance does not wash out the defect "waived." Prior policy is continued, putting the rule as to buyer's default on the same footing as that in regard to seller's default.

7.   Under the requirement of seasonable notification of cancellation under subsection (3), a buyer who accepts a non-conforming installment which substantially impairs the value of the entire contract should properly be permitted to withhold his decision as to whether or not to cancel pending a response from the seller as to his claim for cure or adjustment. Similarly, a seller may withhold a delivery pending payment for prior ones, at the same time delaying his decision as to cancellation. A reasonable time for notifying of cancellation, judged by commercial standard under the section on good faith, extends of course to include the time covered by any reasonable negotiation in good faith. However, during this period the defaulting party is entitled, on request, to know whether the contract is still in effect, before he can be required to perform further.

Cross References:

Point 2: Sections 2–307 and 2–607.
Point 3: Section 1–203.
Point 5: Sections 2–208 and 2–609.
Point 6: Section 2–610.

Definitional Cross References:

"Action". Section 1–201.
"Aggrieved party". Section 1–201.
"Buyer". Section 2–103.
"Cancellation". Section 2–106.
"Conform". Section 2–106.
"Contract". Section 1–201.
"Lot". Section 2–105.
"Notifies". Section 1–201.
"Seasonably". Section 1–204.

"Seller". Section 2–103.

§ 2–613.   Casualty to Identified Goods.

Where the contract requires for its performance goods identified when the contract is made, and the goods suffer casualty without fault of either party before the risk of loss passes to the buyer, or in a proper case under a "no arrival, no sale" term (Section 2–324) then

  (a)   if the loss is total the contract is avoided; and

  (b)   if the loss is partial or the goods have so deteriorated as no longer to conform to the contract the buyer may nevertheless demand inspection and at his option either treat the contract as avoided or accept the goods with due allowance from the contract price for the deterioration or the deficiency in quantity but without further right against the seller.

Official Comment

Prior Uniform Statutory Provision: Sections 7 and 8, Uniform Sales Act.

Changes: Rewritten, the basic policy being continued but the test of a "divisible" or "indivisible" sale or contract being abandoned in favor of adjustment in business terms.

Purposes of Changes:

1.   Where goods whose continued existence is presupposed by the agreement are destroyed without fault of either party, the buyer is relieved from his obligation but may at his option take the surviving goods at a fair adjustment. "Fault" is intended to include negligence and not merely wilful wrong. The buyer is expressly given the right to inspect the goods in order to determine whether he wishes to avoid the contract entirely or to take the goods with a price adjustment.

2.   The section applies whether the goods were already destroyed at the time of contracting without the knowledge of either party or whether they are destroyed subsequently but before the risk of loss passes to the buyer. Where under the agreement, including of course usage of trade, the risk has passed to the buyer before the casualty, the section has no application. Beyond this, the essential question in determining whether the rules of this section are to be applied is whether the seller has or has not undertaken the responsibility for the continued existence of the goods in proper condition through the time of agreed or expected delivery.

3.   The section on the term "no arrival, no sale" makes clear that delay in arrival, quite as much as physical change in the goods, gives the buyer the options set forth in this section.

Cross Reference:

Point 3: Section 2–324.

Definitional Cross References:

"Buyer". Section 2–103.
"Conform". Section 2–106.
"Contract". Section 1–201.
"Fault". Section 1–201.
"Goods". Section 2–105.
"Party". Section 1–201.
"Rights". Section 1–201.
"Seller". Section 2–103.

§ 2–614.   Substituted Performance.

(1)   Where without fault of either party the agreed berthing, loading, or unloading facilities fail or an agreed type of carrier becomes unavailable or the agreed manner of delivery otherwise becomes commercially impracticable but a commercially reasonable substitute is available, such substitute performance must be tendered and accepted.

(2)   If the agreed means or manner of payment fails because of domestic or foreign governmental regulation, the seller may withhold or stop delivery unless the buyer provides a means or manner of

payment which is commercially a substantial equivalent. If delivery has already been taken, payment by the means or in the manner provided by the regulation discharges the buyer's obligation unless the regulation is discriminatory, oppressive or predatory.

Official Comment

Prior Uniform Statutory Provision: None.

Purposes:

1.   Subsection (1) requires the tender of a commercially reasonable substituted performance where agreed to facilities have failed or become commercially impracticable. Under this Article, in the absence of specific agreement, the normal or usual facilities enter into the agreement either through the circumstances, usage of trade or prior course of dealing.

This section appears between Section 2–613 on casualty to identified goods and the next section on excuse by failure of presupposed conditions, both of which deal with excuse and complete avoidance of the contract where the occurrence or non-occurrence of a contingency which was a basic assumption of the contract makes the expected performance impossible. The distinction between the present section and those sections lies in whether the failure or impossibility of performance arises in connection with an incidental matter or goes to the very heart of the agreement. The differing lines of solution are contrasted in a comparison of *International Paper Co. v. Rockefeller*, 161 App.Div. 180, 146 N.Y.S. 371 (1914) and *Meyer v. Sullivan*, 40 Cal.App. 723, 181 P. 847 (1919). In the former case a contract for the sale of spruce to be cut from a particular tract of land was involved. When a fire destroyed the trees growing on that tract the seller was held excused since performance was impossible. In the latter case the contract called for delivery of wheat "f.o.b. Kosmos Steamer at Seattle." The war led to cancellation of that line's sailing schedule after space had been duly engaged and the buyer was held entitled to demand substituted delivery at the warehouse on the line's loading dock. Under this Article, of course, the seller would also be entitled, had the market gone the other way, to make a substituted tender in that manner.

There must, however, be a true commercial impracticability to excuse the agreed to performance and justify a substituted performance. When this is the case a reasonable substituted performance tendered by either party should excuse him from strict compliance with contract terms which do not go to the essence of the agreement.

2.   The substitution provided in this section as between buyer and seller does not carry over into the obligation of a financing agency under a letter of credit, since such an agency is entitled to performance which is plainly adequate on its face and without need to look into commercial evidence outside of the documents. See Article 5, especially Sections 5–102, 5–103, 5–109, 5–110, 5–114.

3.   Under subsection (2) where the contract is still executory on both sides, the seller is permitted to withdraw unless the buyer can provide him with a commercially equivalent return despite the governmental regulation. Where, however, only the debt for the price remains, a larger leeway is permitted. The buyer may pay in the manner provided by the regulation even though this may not be commercially equivalent provided that the regulation is not "discriminatory, oppressive or predatory."

Cross Reference:

Point 2: Article 5.

Definitional Cross References:

"Buyer". Section 2–103.
"Fault". Section 1–201.
"Party". Section 1–201.
"Seller". Section 2–103.

§ 2–615.   Excuse by Failure of Presupposed Conditions.

Except so far as a seller may have assumed a greater obligation and subject to the preceding section on substituted performance:

(a)   Delay in delivery or non-delivery in whole or in part by a seller who complies with paragraphs (b) and (c) is not a breach of his duty under a contract for sale if performance as agreed has been

ARTICLE 2 (2016)   § 2–615

made impracticable by the occurrence of a contingency the non-occurrence of which was a basic assumption on which the contract was made or by compliance in good faith with any applicable foreign or domestic governmental regulation or order whether or not it later proves to be invalid.

(b)   Where the causes mentioned in paragraph (a) affect only a part of the seller's capacity to perform, he must allocate production and deliveries among his customers but may at his option include regular customers not then under contract as well as his own requirements for further manufacture. He may so allocate in any manner which is fair and reasonable.

(c)   The seller must notify the buyer seasonably that there will be delay or non-delivery and, when allocation is required under paragraph (b), of the estimated quota thus made available for the buyer.

Official Comment

Prior Uniform Statutory Provision: None.

Purposes:

1.   This section excuses a seller from timely delivery of goods contracted for, where his performance has become commercially impracticable because of unforeseen supervening circumstances not within the contemplation of the parties at the time of contracting. The destruction of specific goods and the problem of the use of substituted performance on points other than delay or quantity, treated elsewhere in this Article, must be distinguished from the matter covered by this section.

2.   The present section deliberately refrains from any effort at an exhaustive expression of contingencies and is to be interpreted in all cases sought to be brought within its scope in terms of its underlying reason and purpose.

3.   The first test for excuse under this Article in terms of basic assumption is a familiar one. The additional test of commercial impracticability (as contrasted with "impossibility," "frustration of performance" or "frustration of the venture") has been adopted in order to call attention to the commercial character of the criterion chosen by this Article.

4.   Increased cost alone does not excuse performance unless the rise in cost is due to some unforeseen contingency which alters the essential nature of the performance. Neither is a rise or a collapse in the market in itself a justification, for that is exactly the type of business risk which business contracts made at fixed prices are intended to cover. But a severe shortage of raw materials or of supplies due to a contingency such as war, embargo, local crop failure, unforeseen shutdown of major sources of supply or the like, which either causes a marked increase in cost or altogether prevents the seller from securing supplies necessary to his performance, is within the contemplation of this section. (See *Ford & Sons, Ltd., v. Henry Leetham & Sons, Ltd.*, 21 Com.Cas. 55 (1915, K.B.D.).)

5.   Where a particular source of supply is exclusive under the agreement and fails through casualty, the present section applies rather than the provision on destruction or deterioration of specific goods. The same holds true where a particular source of supply is shown by the circumstances to have been contemplated or assumed by the parties at the time of contracting. (See *Davis Co. v. Hoffmann-LaRoche Chemical Works*, 178 App.Div. 855, 166 N.Y.S. 179 (1917) and *International Paper Co. v. Rockefeller*, 161 App.Div. 180, 146 N.Y.S. 371 (1914).) There is no excuse under this section, however, unless the seller has employed all due measures to assure himself that his source will not fail. (See *Canadian Industrial Alcohol Co., Ltd., v. Dunbar Molasses Co.*, 258 N.Y. 194, 179 N.E. 383, 80 A.L.R. 1173 (1932) and *Washington Mfg. Co. v. Midland Lumber Co.*, 113 Wash. 593, 194 P. 777 (1921).)

In the case of failure of production by an agreed source for causes beyond the seller's control, the seller should, if possible, be excused since production by an agreed source is without more a basic assumption of the contract. Such excuse should not result in relieving the defaulting supplier from liability nor in dropping into the seller's lap an unearned bonus of damages over. The flexible adjustment machinery of this Article provides the solution under the provision on the obligation of good faith. A condition to his making good the claim of excuse is the turning over to the buyer of his rights against the defaulting source of supply to the extent of the buyer's contract in relation to which excuse is being claimed.

6.   In situations in which neither sense nor justice is served by either answer when the issue is posed in flat terms of "excuse" or "no excuse," adjustment under the various provisions of this Article is necessary, especially the sections on good faith, on insecurity and assurance and on the reading of all provisions in the light of their purposes, and the general policy of this Act to use equitable principles in furtherance of commercial standards and good faith.

7.   The failure of conditions which go to convenience or collateral values rather than to the commercial practicability of the main performance does not amount to a complete excuse. However, good faith and the reason of the present section and of the preceding one may properly be held to justify and even to require any needed delay involved in a good faith inquiry seeking a readjustment of the contract terms to meet the new conditions.

8.   The provisions of this section are made subject to assumption of greater liability by agreement and such agreement is to be found not only in the expressed terms of the contract but in the circumstances surrounding the contracting, in trade usage and the like. Thus the exemptions of this section do not apply when the contingency in question is sufficiently foreshadowed at the time of contracting to be included among the business risks which are fairly to be regarded as part of the dickered terms, either consciously or as a matter of reasonable, commercial interpretation from the circumstances. (See *Madeirense Do Brasil, S.A. v. Stulman-Emrick Lumber Co.,* 147 F.2d 399 (C.C.A., 2 Cir., 1945).) The exemption otherwise present through usage of trade under the present section may also be expressly negated by the language of the agreement. Generally, express agreements as to exemptions designed to enlarge upon or supplant the provisions of this section are to be read in the light of mercantile sense and reason, for this section itself sets up the commercial standard for normal and reasonable interpretation and provides a minimum beyond which agreement may not go.

Agreement can also be made in regard to the consequences of exemption as laid down in paragraphs (b) and (c) and the next section on procedure on notice claiming excuse.

9.   The case of a farmer who has contracted to sell crops to be grown on designated land may be regarded as falling either within the section on casualty to identified goods or this section, and he may be excused, when there is a failure of the specific crop, either on the basis of the destruction of identified goods or because of the failure of a basic assumption of the contract.

Exemption of the buyer in the case of a "requirements" contract is covered by the "Output and Requirements" section both as to assumption and allocation of the relevant risks. But when a contract by a manufacturer to buy fuel or raw material makes no specific reference to a particular venture and no such reference may be drawn from the circumstances, commercial understanding views it as a general deal in the general market and not conditioned on any assumption of the continuing operation of the buyer's plant. Even when notice is given by the buyer that the supplies are needed to fill a specific contract of a normal commercial kind, commercial understanding does not see such a supply contract as conditioned on the continuance of the buyer's further contract for outlet. On the other hand, where the buyer's contract is in reasonable commercial understanding conditioned on a definite and specific venture or assumption as, for instance, a war procurement subcontract known to be based on a prime contract which is subject to termination, or a supply contract for a particular construction venture, the reason of the present section may well apply and entitle the buyer to the exemption.

10.   Following its basic policy of using commercial practicability as a test for excuse, this section recognizes as of equal significance either a foreign or domestic regulation and disregards any technical distinctions between "law," "regulation," "order" and the like. Nor does it make the present action of the seller depend upon the eventual judicial determination of the legality of the particular governmental action. The seller's good faith belief in the validity of the regulation is the test under this Article and the best evidence of his good faith is the general commercial acceptance of the regulation. However, governmental interference cannot excuse unless it truly "supervenes" in such a manner as to be beyond the seller's assumption of risk. And any action by the party claiming excuse which causes or colludes in inducing the governmental action preventing his performance would be in breach of good faith and would destroy his exemption.

11.   An excused seller must fulfill his contract to the extent which the supervening contingency permits, and if the situation is such that his customers are generally affected he must take account of all in supplying one. Subsections (a) and (b), therefore, explicitly permit in any proration a fair and reasonable attention to the needs of regular customers who are probably relying on spot orders for supplies. Customers at different stages of the manufacturing process may be fairly treated by including the seller's manufacturing requirements. A fortiori, the seller may also take account of contracts later in date than the one in question. The fact that such

spot orders may be closed at an advanced price causes no difficulty, since any allocation which exceeds normal past requirements will not be reasonable. However, good faith requires, when prices have advanced, that the seller exercise real care in making his allocations, and in case of doubt his contract customers should be favored and supplies prorated evenly among them regardless of price. Save for the extra care thus required by changes in the market, this section seeks to leave every reasonable business leeway to the seller.

Cross References:

Point 1: Sections 2–613 and 2–614.
Point 2: Section 1–102.
Point 5: Sections 1–203 and 2–613.
Point 6: Sections 1–102, 1–203 and 2–609.
Point 7: Section 2–614.
Point 8: Sections 1–201, 2–302 and 2–616.
Point 9: Sections 1–102, 2–306 and 2–613.

Definitional Cross References:

"Between merchants". Section 2–104.
"Buyer". Section 2–103.
"Contract". Section 1–201.
"Contract for sale". Section 2–106.
"Good faith". Section 1–201.
"Merchant". Section 2–104.
"Notifies". Section 1–201.
"Seasonably". Section 1–201.
"Seller". Section 2–103.

§ 2–616.   Procedure on Notice Claiming Excuse.

(1)   Where the buyer receives notification of a material or indefinite delay or an allocation justified under the preceding section he may by written notification to the seller as to any delivery concerned, and where the prospective deficiency substantially impairs the value of the whole contract under the provisions of this Article relating to breach of installment contracts (Section 2–612), then also as to the whole,

(a)   terminate and thereby discharge any unexecuted portion of the contract; or

(b)   modify the contract by agreeing to take his available quota in substitution.

(2)   If after receipt of such notification from the seller the buyer fails so to modify the contract within a reasonable time not exceeding thirty days the contract lapses with respect to any deliveries affected.

(3)   The provisions of this section may not be negated by agreement except in so far as the seller has assumed a greater obligation under the preceding section.

Official Comment

Prior Uniform Statutory Provision: None.

Purposes:

This section seeks to establish simple and workable machinery for providing certainty as to when a supervening and excusing contingency "excuses" the delay, "discharges" the contract, or may result in a waiver of the delay by the buyer. When the seller notifies, in accordance with the preceding section, claiming excuse, the buyer may acquiesce, in which case the contract is so modified. No consideration is necessary in a case of this kind to support such a modification. If the buyer does not elect so to modify the contract, he may terminate it and under subsection (2) his silence after receiving the seller's claim of excuse operates as such a termination. Subsection (3) denies effect to any contract clause made in advance of trouble which would require the buyer to stand ready to take delivery whenever the seller is excused from delivery by unforeseen circumstances.

§ 2–701   UNIFORM COMMERCIAL CODE

Cross References:

Point 1: Sections 2–209 and 2–615.

Definitional Cross References:

"Buyer". Section 2–103.
"Contract". Section 1–201.
"Installment contract". Section 2–612.
"Notification". Section 1–201.
"Reasonable time". Section 1–204.
"Seller". Section 2–103.
"Termination". Section 2–106.
"Written". Section 1–201.

PART 7

REMEDIES

§ 2–701.   Remedies for Breach of Collateral Contracts Not Impaired.

Remedies for breach of any obligation or promise collateral or ancillary to a contract for sale are not impaired by the provisions of this Article.

Official Comment

Prior Uniform Statutory Provision: None.

Purposes:

Whether a claim for breach of an obligation collateral to the contract for sale requires separate trial to avoid confusion of issues is beyond the scope of this Article; but contractual arrangements which as a business matter enter vitally into the contract should be considered a part thereof in so far as cross-claims or defenses are concerned.

Definitional Cross References:

"Contract for sale". Section 2–106.
"Remedy". Section 1–201.

§ 2–702.   Seller's Remedies on Discovery of Buyer's Insolvency.

(1)   Where the seller discovers the buyer to be insolvent he may refuse delivery except for cash including payment for all goods theretofore delivered under the contract, and stop delivery under this Article (Section 2–705).

(2)   Where the seller discovers that the buyer has received goods on credit while insolvent he may reclaim the goods upon demand made within ten days after the receipt, but if misrepresentation of solvency has been made to the particular seller in writing within three months before delivery the ten day limitation does not apply. Except as provided in this subsection the seller may not base a right to reclaim goods on the buyer's fraudulent or innocent misrepresentation of solvency or of intent to pay.

(3)   The seller's right to reclaim under subsection (2) is subject to the rights of a buyer in ordinary course or other good faith purchaser under this Article (Section 2–403). Successful reclamation of goods excludes all other remedies with respect to them.

As amended in 1966.

Official Comment

Prior Uniform Statutory Provision: Subsection (1)—Sections 53(1)(b), 54(1)(c) and 57, Uniform Sales Act; Subsection (2)—none; Subsection (3)—Section 76(3), Uniform Sales Act.

Changes: Rewritten, the protection given to a seller who has sold on credit and has delivered goods to the buyer immediately preceding his insolvency being extended.

Purposes of Changes and New Matter: To make it clear that:

1.   The seller's right to withhold the goods or to stop delivery except for cash when he discovers the buyer's insolvency is made explicit in subsection (1) regardless of the passage of title, and the concept of stoppage has been extended to include goods in the possession of any bailee who has not yet attorned to the buyer.

2.   Subsection (2) takes as its base line the proposition that any receipt of goods on credit by an insolvent buyer amounts to a tacit business misrepresentation of solvency and therefore is fraudulent as against the particular seller. This Article makes discovery of the buyer's insolvency and demand within a ten day period a condition of the right to reclaim goods on this ground. The ten day limitation period operates from the time of receipt of the goods.

An exception to this time limitation is made when a written misrepresentation of solvency has been made to the particular seller within three months prior to the delivery. To fall within the exception the statement of solvency must be in writing, addressed to the particular seller and dated within three months of the delivery.

3.   Because the right of the seller to reclaim goods under this section constitutes preferential treatment as against the buyer's other creditors, subsection (3) provides that such reclamation bars all his other remedies as to the goods involved.

As amended in 1966.

Cross References:

> Point 1: Sections 2–401 and 2–705.
> Compare Section 2–502.

Definitional Cross References:

> "Buyer". Section 2–103.
> "Buyer in ordinary course of business". Section 1–201.
> "Contract". Section 1–201.
> "Good faith". Section 1–201.
> "Goods". Section 2–105.
> "Insolvent". Section 1–201.
> "Person". Section 1–201.
> "Purchaser". Section 1–201.
> "Receipt" of goods. Section 2–103.
> "Remedy". Section 1–201.
> "Rights". Section 1–201.
> "Seller". Section 2–103.
> "Writing". Section 1–201.

§ 2–703.   Seller's Remedies in General.

Where the buyer wrongfully rejects or revokes acceptance of goods or fails to make a payment due on or before delivery or repudiates with respect to a part or the whole, then with respect to any goods directly affected and, if the breach is of the whole contract (Section 2–612), then also with respect to the whole undelivered balance, the aggrieved seller may

(a)   withhold delivery of such goods;

(b)   stop delivery by any bailee as hereafter provided (Section 2–705);

(c)   proceed under the next section respecting goods still unidentified to the contract;

(d)   resell and recover damages as hereafter provided (Section 2–706);

(e)   recover damages for non-acceptance (Section 2–708) or in a proper case the price (Section 2–709);

(f)   cancel.

Official Comment

Prior Uniform Statutory Provision: No comparable index section. See Section 53, Uniform Sales Act.

Purposes:

1.   This section is an index section which gathers together in one convenient place all of the various remedies open to a seller for any breach by the buyer. This Article rejects any doctrine of election of remedy as a fundamental policy and thus the remedies are essentially cumulative in nature and include all of the available remedies for breach. Whether the pursuit of one remedy bars another depends entirely on the facts of the individual case.

2.   The buyer's breach which occasions the use of the remedies under this section may involve only one lot or delivery of goods, or may involve all of the goods which are the subject matter of the particular contract. The right of the seller to pursue a remedy as to all the goods when the breach is as to only one or more lots is covered by the section on breach in installment contracts. The present section deals only with the remedies available after the goods involved in the breach have been determined by that section.

3.   In addition to the typical case of refusal to pay or default in payment, the language in the preamble, "fails to make a payment due," is intended to cover the dishonor of a check on due presentment, or the non-acceptance of a draft, and the failure to furnish an agreed letter of credit.

4.   It should also be noted that this Act requires its remedies to be liberally administered and provides that any right or obligation which it declares is enforceable by action unless a different effect is specifically prescribed (Section 1–106).

Cross References:

Point 2: Section 2–612.
Point 3: Section 2–325.
Point 4: Section 1–106.

Definitional Cross References:

"Aggrieved party". Section 1–201.
"Buyer". Section 2–103.
"Cancellation". Section 2–106.
"Contract". Section 1–201.
"Goods". Section 2–105.
"Remedy". Section 1–201.
"Seller". Section 2–103.

§ 2–704.   Seller's Right to Identify Goods to the Contract Notwithstanding Breach or to Salvage Unfinished Goods.

(1)   An aggrieved seller under the preceding section may

(a)   identify to the contract conforming goods not already identified if at the time he learned of the breach they are in his possession or control;

(b)   treat as the subject of resale goods which have demonstrably been intended for the particular contract even though those goods are unfinished.

(2)   Where the goods are unfinished an aggrieved seller may in the exercise of reasonable commercial judgment for the purposes of avoiding loss and of effective realization either complete the manufacture and wholly identify the goods to the contract or cease manufacture and resell for scrap or salvage value or proceed in any other reasonable manner.

ARTICLE 2 (2016)   § 2–705

Official Comment

Prior Uniform Statutory Provision: Sections 63(3) and 64(4), Uniform Sales Act.

Changes: Rewritten, the seller's rights being broadened.

Purposes of Changes:

1.   This section gives an aggrieved seller the right at the time of breach to identify to the contract any conforming finished goods, regardless of their resalability, and to use reasonable judgment as to completing unfinished goods. It thus makes the goods available for resale under the resale section, the seller's primary remedy, and in the special case in which resale is not practicable, allows the action for the price which would then be necessary to give the seller the value of his contract.

2.   Under this Article the seller is given express power to complete manufacture or procurement of goods for the contract unless the exercise of reasonable commercial judgment as to the facts as they appear at the time he learns of the breach makes it clear that such action will result in a material increase in damages. The burden is on the buyer to show the commercially unreasonable nature of the seller's action in completing manufacture.

Cross References:

Sections 2–703 and 2–706.

Definitional Cross References:

"Aggrieved party". Section 1–201.
"Conforming". Section 2–106.
"Contract". Section 1–201.
"Goods". Section 2–105.
"Rights". Section 1–201.
"Seller". Section 2–103.

§ 2–705.   Seller's Stoppage of Delivery in Transit or Otherwise.

(1)   The seller may stop delivery of goods in the possession of a carrier or other bailee when he discovers the buyer to be insolvent (Section 2–702) and may stop delivery of carload, truckload, planeload or larger shipments of express or freight when the buyer repudiates or fails to make a payment due before delivery or if for any other reason the seller has a right to withhold or reclaim the goods.

(2)   As against such buyer the seller may stop delivery until

(a)   receipt of the goods by the buyer; or

(b)   acknowledgment to the buyer by any bailee of the goods except a carrier that the bailee holds the goods for the buyer; or

(c)   such acknowledgment to the buyer by a carrier by reshipment or as a warehouseman; or

(d)   negotiation to the buyer of any negotiable document of title covering the goods.

(3)(a) To stop delivery the seller must so notify as to enable the bailee by reasonable diligence to prevent delivery of the goods.

(b)   After such notification the bailee must hold and deliver the goods according to the directions of the seller but the seller is liable to the bailee for any ensuing charges or damages.

(c)   If a negotiable document of title has been issued for goods the bailee is not obliged to obey a notification to stop until surrender of possession or control of the document.

(d)   A carrier who has issued a non-negotiable bill of lading is not obliged to obey a notification to stop received from a person other than the consignor.

As amended in 2003.

Official Comment

Prior Uniform Statutory Provision: Sections 57–59, Uniform Sales Act; see also Sections 12, 14 and 42, Uniform Bills of Lading Act and Sections 9, 11 and 49, Uniform Warehouse Receipts Act.

Changes: This section continues and develops the above sections of the Uniform Sales Act in the light of the other uniform statutory provisions noted.

Purposes: To make it clear that:

1.   Subsection (1) applies the stoppage principle to other bailees as well as carriers.

It also expands the remedy to cover the situations, in addition to buyer's insolvency, specified in the subsection. But since stoppage is a burden in any case to carriers, and might be a very heavy burden to them if it covered all small shipments in all these situations, the right to stop for reasons other than insolvency is limited to carload, truckload, planeload or larger shipments. The seller shipping to a buyer of doubtful credit can protect himself by shipping C.O.D.

Where stoppage occurs for insecurity it is merely a suspension of performance, and if assurances are duly forthcoming from the buyer the seller is not entitled to resell or divert.

Improper stoppage is a breach by the seller if it effectively interferes with the buyer's right to due tender under the section on manner of tender of delivery. However, if the bailee obeys an unjustified order to stop he may also be liable to the buyer. The measure of his obligation is dependent on the provisions of the Documents of Title Article (Section 7–303). Subsection 3(b) therefore gives him a right of indemnity as against the seller in such a case.

2.   "Receipt by the buyer" includes receipt by the buyer's designated representative, the subpurchaser, when shipment is made direct to him and the buyer himself never receives the goods. It is entirely proper under this Article that the seller, by making such direct shipment to the sub-purchaser, be regarded as acquiescing in the latter's purchase and as thus barred from stoppage of the goods as against him.

As between the buyer and the seller, the latter's right to stop the goods at any time until they reach the place of final delivery is recognized by this section.

Under subsection (3)(c) and (d), the carrier is under no duty to recognize the stop order of a person who is a stranger to the carrier's contract. But the seller's right as against the buyer to stop delivery remains, whether or not the carrier is obligated to recognize the stop order. If the carrier does obey it, the buyer cannot complain merely because of that circumstance; and the seller becomes obligated under subsection (3)(b) to pay the carrier any ensuing damages or charges.

3.   A diversion of a shipment is not a "reshipment" under subsection (2)(c) when it is merely an incident to the original contract of transportation. Nor is the procurement of "exchange bills" of lading which change only the name of the consignee to that of the buyer's local agent but do not alter the destination of a reshipment.

Acknowledgment by the carrier as a "warehouse" within the meaning of this Article requires a contract of a truly different character from the original shipment, a contract not in extension of transit but as a warehouse.

4.   Subsection (3)(c) makes the bailee's obedience of a notification to stop conditional upon the surrender of possession or control of any outstanding negotiable document.

5.   Any charges or losses incurred by the carrier in following the seller's orders, whether or not he was obligated to do so, fall to the seller's charge.

6.   After an effective stoppage under this section the seller's rights in the goods are the same as if he had never made a delivery.

Cross References:

Sections 2–702 and 2–703.
Point 1: Sections 2–503 and 2–609, and Article 7.
Point 2: Section 2–103 and Article 7.

Definitional Cross References:

"Buyer". Section 2–103.
"Contract for sale". Section 2–106.

"Document of title". Section 1–201.
"Goods". Section 2–105.
"Insolvent". Section 1–201.
"Notification". Section 1–201.
"Receipt" of goods. Section 2–103.
"Rights". Section 1–201.
"Seller". Section 2–103.

As amended in 2003.

§ 2–706. Seller's Resale Including Contract for Resale.

(1) Under the conditions stated in Section 2–703 on seller's remedies, the seller may resell the goods concerned or the undelivered balance thereof. Where the resale is made in good faith and in a commercially reasonable manner the seller may recover the difference between the resale price and the contract price together with any incidental damages allowed under the provisions of this Article (Section 2–710), but less expenses saved in consequence of the buyer's breach.

(2) Except as otherwise provided in subsection (3) or unless otherwise agreed resale may be at public or private sale including sale by way of one or more contracts to sell or of identification to an existing contract of the seller. Sale may be as a unit or in parcels and at any time and place and on any terms but every aspect of the sale including the method, manner, time, place and terms must be commercially reasonable. The resale must be reasonably identified as referring to the broken contract, but it is not necessary that the goods be in existence or that any or all of them have been identified to the contract before the breach.

(3) Where the resale is at private sale the seller must give the buyer reasonable notification of his intention to resell.

(4) Where the resale is at public sale

(a) only identified goods can be sold except where there is a recognized market for a public sale of futures in goods of the kind; and

(b) it must be made at a usual place or market for public sale if one is reasonably available and except in the case of goods which are perishable or threaten to decline in value speedily the seller must give the buyer reasonable notice of the time and place of the resale; and

(c) if the goods are not to be within the view of those attending the sale the notification of sale must state the place where the goods are located and provide for their reasonable inspection by prospective bidders; and

(d) the seller may buy.

(5) A purchaser who buys in good faith at a resale takes the goods free of any rights of the original buyer even though the seller fails to comply with one or more of the requirements of this section.

(6) The seller is not accountable to the buyer for any profit made on any resale. A person in the position of a seller (Section 2–707) or a buyer who has rightfully rejected or justifiably revoked acceptance must account for any excess over the amount of his security interest, as hereinafter defined (subsection (3) of Section 2–711).

Official Comment

Prior Uniform Statutory Provision: Section 60, Uniform Sales Act.

Changes: Rewritten.

Purposes of Changes: To simplify the prior statutory provision and to make it clear that:

1. The only condition precedent to the seller's right of resale under subsection (1) is a breach by the buyer within the section on the seller's remedies in general or insolvency. Other meticulous conditions and restrictions of the prior uniform statutory provision are disapproved by this Article and are replaced by

standards of commercial reasonableness. Under this section the seller may resell the goods after any breach by the buyer. Thus, an anticipatory repudiation by the buyer gives rise to any of the seller's remedies for breach, and to the right of resale. This principle is supplemented by subsection (2) which authorizes a resale of goods which are not in existence or were not identified to the contract before the breach.

2. In order to recover the damages prescribed in subsection (1) the seller must act "in good faith and in a commercially reasonable manner" in making the resale. This standard is intended to be more comprehensive than that of "reasonable care and judgment" established by the prior uniform statutory provision. Failure to act properly under this section deprives the seller of the measure of damages here provided and relegates him to that provided in Section 2–708.

Under this Article the seller resells by authority of law, in his own behalf, for his own benefit and for the purpose of fixing his damages. The theory of a seller's agency is thus rejected.

3. If the seller complies with the prescribed standard of duty in making the resale, he may recover from the buyer the damages provided for in subsection (1). Evidence of market or current prices at any particular time or place is relevant only on the question of whether the seller acted in a commercially reasonable manner in making the resale.

The distinction drawn by some courts between cases where the title had not passed to the buyer and the seller had resold as owner, and cases where the title had passed and the seller had resold by virtue of his lien on the goods, is rejected.

4. Subsection (2) frees the remedy of resale from legalistic restrictions and enables the seller to resell in accordance with reasonable commercial practices so as to realize as high a price as possible in the circumstances. By "public" sale is meant a sale by auction. A "private" sale may be effected by solicitation and negotiation conducted either directly or through a broker. In choosing between a public and private sale the character of the goods must be considered and relevant trade practices and usages must be observed.

5. Subsection (2) merely clarifies the common law rule that the time for resale is a reasonable time after the buyer's breach, by using the language "commercially reasonable." What is such a reasonable time depends upon the nature of the goods, the condition of the market and the other circumstances of the case; its length cannot be measured by any legal yardstick or divided into degrees. Where a seller contemplating resale receives a demand from the buyer for inspection under the section of preserving evidence of goods in dispute, the time for resale may be appropriately lengthened.

On the question of the place for resale, subsection (2) goes to the ultimate test, the commercial reasonableness of the seller's choice as to the place for an advantageous resale. This Article rejects the theory that the seller is required to resell at the agreed place for delivery and that a resale elsewhere can be permitted only in exceptional cases.

6. The purpose of subsection (2) being to enable the seller to dispose of the goods to the best advantage, he is permitted in making the resale to depart from the terms and conditions of the original contract for sale to any extent "commercially reasonable" in the circumstances.

7. The provision of subsection (2) that the goods need not be in existence to be resold applies when the buyer is guilty of anticipatory repudiation of a contract for future goods, before the goods or some of them have come into existence. In such a case the seller may exercise the right of resale and fix his damages by "one or more contracts to sell" the quantity of conforming future goods affected by the repudiation. The companion provision of subsection (2) that resale may be made although the goods were not identified to the contract prior to the buyer's breach, likewise contemplates an anticipatory repudiation by the buyer but occurring after the goods are in existence. If the goods so identified conform to the contract, their resale will fix the seller's damages quite as satisfactorily as if they had been identified before the breach.

8. Where the resale is to be by private sale, subsection (3) requires that reasonable notification of the seller's intention to resell must be given to the buyer. The length of notification of a private sale depends upon the urgency of the matter. Notification of the time and place of this type of sale is not required.

Subsection (4)(b) requires that the seller give the buyer reasonable notice of the time and place of a public resale so that he may have an opportunity to bid or to secure the attendance of other bidders. An exception is made in the case of goods "which are perishable or threaten to decline speedily in value."

9. Since there would be no reasonable prospect of competitive bidding elsewhere, subsection (4) requires that a public resale "must be made at a usual place or market for public sale if one is reasonably available;" i.e.,

a place or market which prospective bidders may reasonably be expected to attend. Such a market may still be "reasonably available" under this subsection, though at a considerable distance from the place where the goods are located. In such a case the expense of transporting the goods for resale is recoverable from the buyer as part of the seller's incidental damages under subsection (1). However, the question of availability is one of commercial reasonableness in the circumstances and if such "usual" place or market is not reasonably available, a duly advertised public resale may be held at another place if it is one which prospective bidders may reasonably be expected to attend, as distinguished from a place where there is no demand whatsoever for goods of the kind.

Paragraph (a) of subsection (4) qualifies the last sentence of subsection (2) with respect to resales of unidentified and future goods at public sale. If conforming goods are in existence the seller may identify them to the contract after the buyer's breach and then resell them at public sale. If the goods have not been identified, however, he may resell them at public sale only as "future" goods and only where there is a recognized market for public sale of futures in goods of the kind.

The provisions of paragraph (c) of subsection (4) are intended to permit intelligent bidding.

The provision of paragraph (d) of subsection (4) permitting the seller to bid and, of course, to become the purchaser, benefits the original buyer by tending to increase the resale price and thus decreasing the damages he will have to pay.

10.   This Article departs in subsection (5) from the prior uniform statutory provision in permitting a good faith purchaser at resale to take a good title as against the buyer even though the seller fails to comply with the requirements of this section.

11.   Under subsection (6), the seller retains profit, if any, without distinction based on whether or not he had a lien since this Article divorces the question of passage of title to the buyer from the seller's right of resale or the consequences of its exercise. On the other hand, where "a person in the position of a seller" or a buyer acting under the section on buyer's remedies, exercises his right of resale under the present section he does so only for the limited purpose of obtaining cash for his "security interest" in the goods. Once that purpose has been accomplished any excess in the resale price belongs to the seller to whom an accounting must be made as provided in the last sentence of subsection (6).

Cross References:

Point 1: Sections 2–610, 2–702 and 2–703.
Point 2: Section 1–201.
Point 3: Sections 2–708 and 2–710.
Point 4: Section 2–328.
Point 8: Section 2–104.
Point 9: Section 2–710.
Point 11: Sections 2–401, 2–707 and 2–711(3).

Definitional Cross References:

"Buyer". Section 2–103.
"Contract". Section 1–201.
"Contract for sale". Section 2–106.
"Good faith". Section 2–103.
"Goods". Section 2–105.
"Merchant". Section 2–104.
"Notification". Section 1–201.
"Person in position of seller". Section 2–707.
"Purchase". Section 1–201.
"Rights". Section 1–201.
"Sale". Section 2–106.
"Security interest". Section 1–201.
"Seller". Section 2–103.

§ 2–707.   "Person in the Position of a Seller".

(1)   A "person in the position of a seller" includes as against a principal an agent who has paid or become responsible for the price of goods on behalf of his principal or anyone who otherwise holds a security interest or other right in goods similar to that of a seller.

(2)   A person in the position of a seller may as provided in this Article withhold or stop delivery (Section 2–705) and resell (Section 2–706) and recover incidental damages (Section 2–710).

Official Comment

Prior Uniform Statutory Provision: Section 52(2), Uniform Sales Act.

Changes: Rewritten.

Purposes of Changes: To make it clear that:

In addition to following in general the prior uniform statutory provision, the case of a financing agency which has acquired documents by honoring a letter of credit for the buyer or by discounting a draft for the seller has been included in the term "a person in the position of a seller."

Cross Reference:

Article 5, Section 2–506.

Definitional Cross References:

"Consignee". Section 7–102.
"Consignor". Section 7–102.
"Goods". Section 2–105.
"Security interest". Section 1–201.
"Seller". Section 2–103.

§ 2–708.   Seller's Damages for Non-acceptance or Repudiation.

(1)   Subject to subsection (2) and to the provisions of this Article with respect to proof of market price (Section 2–723), the measure of damages for non-acceptance or repudiation by the buyer is the difference between the market price at the time and place for tender and the unpaid contract price together with any incidental damages provided in this Article (Section 2–710), but less expenses saved in consequence of the buyer's breach.

(2)   If the measure of damages provided in subsection (1) is inadequate to put the seller in as good a position as performance would have done then the measure of damages is the profit (including reasonable overhead) which the seller would have made from full performance by the buyer, together with any incidental damages provided in this Article (Section 2–710), due allowance for costs reasonably incurred and due credit for payments or proceeds of resale.

Official Comment

Prior Uniform Statutory Provision: Section 64, Uniform Sales Act.

Changes: Rewritten.

Purposes of Changes: To make it clear that:

1.   The prior uniform statutory provision is followed generally in setting the current market price at the time and place for tender as the standard by which damages for non-acceptance are to be determined. The time and place of tender is determined by reference to the section on manner of tender of delivery, and to the sections on the effect of such terms as FOB, FAS, CIF, C. & F., Ex Ship and No Arrival, No Sale.

In the event that there is no evidence available of the current market price at the time and place of tender, proof of a substitute market may be made under the section on determination and proof of market price. Furthermore, the section on the admissibility of market quotations is intended to ease materially the problem of providing competent evidence.

ARTICLE 2 (2016)   § 2–709

2.   The provision of this section permitting recovery of expected profit including reasonable overhead where the standard measure of damages is inadequate, together with the new requirement that price actions may be sustained only where resale is impractical, are designed to eliminate the unfair and economically wasteful results arising under the older law when fixed price articles were involved. This section permits the recovery of lost profits in all appropriate cases, which would include all standard priced goods. The normal measure there would be list price less cost to the dealer or list price less manufacturing cost to the manufacturer. It is not necessary to a recovery of "profit" to show a history of earnings, especially of a new venture is involved.

3.   In all cases the seller may recover incidental damages.

Cross References:

Point 1: Sections 2–319 through 2–324, 2–503, 2–723 and 2–724.
Point 2: Section 2–709.
Point 3: Section 2–710.

Definitional Cross References:

"Buyer". Section 2–103.
"Contract". Section 1–201.
"Seller". Section 2–103.

§ 2–709.   Action for the Price.

(1)   When the buyer fails to pay the price as it becomes due the seller may recover, together with any incidental damages under the next section, the price

(a)   of goods accepted or of conforming goods lost or damaged within a commercially reasonable time after risk of their loss has passed to the buyer; and

(b)   of goods identified to the contract if the seller is unable after reasonable effort to resell them at a reasonable price or the circumstances reasonably indicate that such effort will be unavailing.

(2)   Where the seller sues for the price he must hold for the buyer any goods which have been identified to the contract and are still in his control except that if resale becomes possible he may resell them at any time prior to the collection of the judgment. The net proceeds of any such resale must be credited to the buyer and payment of the judgment entitles him to any goods not resold.

(3)   After the buyer has wrongfully rejected or revoked acceptance of the goods or has failed to make a payment due or has repudiated (Section 2–610), a seller who is held not entitled to the price under this section shall nevertheless be awarded damages for non-acceptance under the preceding section.

Official Comment

Prior Uniform Statutory Provision: Section 63, Uniform Sales Act.

Changes: Rewritten, important commercially needed changes being incorporated.

Purposes of Changes: To make it clear that:

1.   Neither the passing of title to the goods nor the appointment of a day certain for payment is now material to a price action.

2.   The action for the price is now generally limited to those cases where resale of the goods is impracticable except where the buyer has accepted the goods or where they have been destroyed after risk of loss has passed to the buyer.

3.   This section substitutes an objective test by action for the former "not readily resalable" standard. An action for the price under subsection (1)(b) can be sustained only after a "reasonable effort to resell" the goods "at reasonable price" has actually been made or where the circumstances "reasonably indicate" that such an effort will be unavailing.

4.   If a buyer is in default not with respect to the price, but on an obligation to make an advance, the seller should recover not under this section for the price as such, but for the default in the collateral (though

§ 2–710   UNIFORM COMMERCIAL CODE

coincident) obligation to finance the seller. If the agreement between the parties contemplates that the buyer will acquire, on making the advance, a security interest in the goods, the buyer on making the advance has such an interest as soon as the seller has rights in the agreed collateral. See Section 9–204.

5.   "Goods accepted" by the buyer under subsection (1)(a) include only goods as to which there has been no justified revocation of acceptance, for such a revocation means that there has been a default by the seller which bars his rights under this section. "Goods lost or damaged" are covered by the section on risk of loss. "Goods identified to the contract" under subsection (1)(b) are covered by the section on identification and the section on identification notwithstanding breach.

6.   This section is intended to be exhaustive in its enumeration of cases where an action for the price lies.

7.   If the action for the price fails, the seller may nonetheless have proved a case entitling him to damages for non-acceptance. In such a situation, subsection (3) permits recovery of those damages in the same action.

Cross References:

> Point 4: Section 1–106.
> Point 5: Sections 2–501, 2–509, 2–510 and 2–704.
> Point 7: Section 2–708.

Definitional Cross References:

> "Action". Section 1–201.
> "Buyer". Section 2–103.
> "Conforming". Section 2–106.
> "Contract". Section 1–201.
> "Goods". Section 2–105.
> "Seller". Section 2–103.

§ 2–710.   Seller's Incidental Damages.

Incidental damages to an aggrieved seller include any commercially reasonable charges, expenses or commissions incurred in stopping delivery, in the transportation, care and custody of goods after the buyer's breach, in connection with return or resale of the goods or otherwise resulting from the breach.

Official Comment

Prior Uniform Statutory Provision: See Sections 64 and 70, Uniform Sales Act.

Purposes: To authorize reimbursement of the seller for expenses reasonably incurred by him as a result of the buyer's breach. The section sets forth the principal normal and necessary additional elements of damage flowing from the breach but intends to allow all commercially reasonable expenditures made by the seller.

Definitional Cross References:

> "Aggrieved party". Section 1–201.
> "Buyer". Section 2–103.
> "Goods". Section 2–105.
> "Seller". Section 2–103.

§ 2–711.   Buyer's Remedies in General; Buyer's Security Interest in Rejected Goods.

(1)   Where the seller fails to make delivery or repudiates or the buyer rightfully rejects or justifiably revokes acceptance then with respect to any goods involved, and with respect to the whole if the breach goes to the whole contract (Section 2–612), the buyer may cancel and whether or not he has done so may in addition to recovering so much of the price as has been paid

(a)   "cover" and have damages under the next section as to all the goods affected whether or not they have been identified to the contract; or

(b)   recover damages for non-delivery as provided in this Article (Section 2–713).

ARTICLE 2 (2016)   § 2–711

(2)   Where the seller fails to deliver or repudiates the buyer may also

(a)   if the goods have been identified recover them as provided in this Article (Section 2–502); or

(b)   in a proper case obtain specific performance or replevy the goods as provided in this Article (Section 2–716).

(3)   On rightful rejection or justifiable revocation of acceptance a buyer has a security interest in goods in his possession or control for any payments made on their price and any expenses reasonably incurred in their inspection, receipt, transportation, care and custody and may hold such goods and resell them in like manner as an aggrieved seller (Section 2–706).

Official Comment

Prior Uniform Statutory Provision: No comparable index section; Subsection (3)—Section 69(5), Uniform Sales Act.

Changes: The prior uniform statutory provision is generally continued and expanded in Subsection (3).

Purposes of Changes and New Matter:

1.   To index in this section the buyer's remedies, subsection (1) covering those remedies permitting the recovery of money damages, and subsection (2) covering those which permit reaching the goods themselves. The remedies listed here are those available to a buyer who has not accepted the goods or who has justifiably revoked his acceptance. The remedies available to a buyer with regard to goods finally accepted appear in the section dealing with breach in regard to accepted goods. The buyer's right to proceed as to all goods when the breach is as to only some of the goods is determined by the section on breach in installment contracts and by the section on partial acceptance.

Despite the seller's breach, proper retender of delivery under the section on cure of improper tender or replacement can effectively preclude the buyer's remedies under this section, except for any delay involved.

2.   To make it clear in subsection (3) that the buyer may hold and resell rejected goods if he has paid a part of the price or incurred expenses of the type specified. "Paid" as used here includes acceptance of a draft or other time negotiable instrument or the signing of a negotiable note. His freedom of resale is coextensive with that of a seller under this Article except that the buyer may not keep any profit resulting from the resale and is limited to retaining only the amount of the price paid and the costs involved in the inspection and handling of the goods. The buyer's security interest in the goods is intended to be limited to the items listed in subsection (3), and the buyer is not permitted to retain such funds as he might believe adequate for his damages. The buyer's right to cover, or to have damages for non-delivery, is not impaired by his exercise of his right of resale.

3.   It should also be noted that this Act requires its remedies to be liberally administered and provides that any right or obligation which it declares is enforceable by action unless a different effect is specifically prescribed (Section 1–106).

Cross References:

> Point 1: Sections 2–508, 2–601(c), 2–608, 2–612 and 2–714.
> Point 2: Section 2–706.
> Point 3: Section 1–106.

Definitional Cross References:

> "Aggrieved party". Section 1–201.
> "Buyer". Section 2–103.
> "Cancellation". Section 2–106.
> "Contract". Section 1–201.
> "Cover". Section 2–712.
> "Goods". Section 2–105.
> "Notifies". Section 1–201.
> "Receipt" of goods. Section 2–103.
> "Remedy". Section 1–201.
> "Security interest". Section 1–201.
> "Seller". Section 2–103.

§ 2–712.   "Cover"; Buyer's Procurement of Substitute Goods.

(1)   After a breach within the preceding section the buyer may "cover" by making in good faith and without unreasonable delay any reasonable purchase of or contract to purchase goods in substitution for those due from the seller.

(2)   The buyer may recover from the seller as damages the difference between the cost of cover and the contract price together with any incidental or consequential damages as hereinafter defined (Section 2–715), but less expenses saved in consequence of the seller's breach.

(3)   Failure of the buyer to effect cover within this section does not bar him from any other remedy.

Official Comment

Prior Uniform Statutory Provision: None.

Purposes:

1.   This section provides the buyer with a remedy aimed at enabling him to obtain the goods he needs thus meeting his essential need. This remedy is the buyer's equivalent of the seller's right to resell.

2.   The definition of "cover" under subsection (1) envisages a series of contracts or sales, as well as a single contract or sale; goods not identical with those involved but commercially usable as reasonable substitutes under the circumstances of the particular case; and contracts on credit or delivery terms differing from the contract in breach, but again reasonable under the circumstances. The test of proper cover is whether at the time and place the buyer acted in good faith and in a reasonable manner, and it is immaterial that hindsight may later prove that the method of cover used was not the cheapest or most effective.

The requirement that the buyer must cover "without unreasonable delay" is not intended to limit the time necessary for him to look around and decide as to how he may best effect cover. The test here is similar to that generally used in this Article as to reasonable time and seasonable action.

3.   Subsection (3) expresses the policy that cover is not a mandatory remedy for the buyer. The buyer is always free to choose between cover and damages for non-delivery under the next section.

However, this subsection must be read in conjunction with the section which limits the recovery of consequential damages to such as could not have been obviated by cover. Moreover, the operation of the section on specific performance of contracts for "unique" goods must be considered in this connection for availability of the goods to the particular buyer for his particular needs is the test for that remedy and inability to cover is made an express condition to the right of the buyer to replevy the goods.

4.   This section does not limit cover to merchants, in the first instance. It is the vital and important remedy for the consumer buyer as well. Both are free to use cover: the domestic or non-merchant consumer is required only to act in normal good faith while the merchant buyer must also observe all reasonable commercial standards of fair dealing in the trade, since this falls within the definition of good faith on his part.

Cross References:

Point 1: Section 2–706.
Point 2: Section 1–204.
Point 3: Sections 2–713, 2–715 and 2–716.
Point 4: Section 1–203.

Definitional Cross References:

"Buyer". Section 2–103.
"Contract". Section 1–201.
"Good faith". Section 2–103.
"Goods". Section 2–105.
"Purchase". Section 1–201.
"Remedy". Section 1–201.
"Seller". Section 2–103.

§ 2–713.   Buyer's Damages for Non-delivery or Repudiation.

(1)   Subject to the provisions of this Article with respect to proof of market price (Section 2–723), the measure of damages for non-delivery or repudiation by the seller is the difference between the market price at the time when the buyer learned of the breach and the contract price together with any incidental and consequential damages provided in this Article (Section 2–715), but less expenses saved in consequence of the seller's breach.

(2)   Market price is to be determined as of the place for tender or, in cases of rejection after arrival or revocation of acceptance, as of the place of arrival.

Official Comment

Prior Uniform Statutory Provision: Section 67(3), Uniform Sales Act.

Changes: Rewritten.

Purposes of Changes: To clarify the former rule so that:

1.   The general baseline adopted in this section uses as a yardstick the market in which the buyer would have obtained cover had he sought that relief. So the place for measuring damages is the place of tender (or the place of arrival if the goods are rejected or their acceptance is revoked after reaching their destination) and the crucial time is the time at which the buyer learns of the breach.

2.   The market or current price to be used in comparison with the contract price under this section is the price for goods of the same kind and in the same branch of trade.

3.   When the current market price under this section is difficult to prove the section on determination and proof of market price is available to permit a showing of a comparable market price or, where no market price is available, evidence of spot sale prices is proper. Where the unavailability of a market price is caused by a scarcity of goods of the type involved, a good case is normally made for specific performance under this Article. Such scarcity conditions, moreover, indicate that the price has risen and under the section providing for liberal administration of remedies, opinion evidence as to the value of the goods would be admissible in the absence of a market price and a liberal construction of allowable consequential damages should also result.

4.   This section carries forward the standard rule that the buyer must deduct from his damages any expenses saved as a result of the breach.

5.   The present section provides a remedy which is completely alternative to cover under the preceding section and applies only when and to the extent that the buyer has not covered.

Cross References:

Point 3: Sections 1–106, 2–716 and 2–723.
Point 5: Section 2–712.

Definitional Cross References:

"Buyer". Section 2–103.
"Contract". Section 1–201.
"Seller". Section 2–103.

§ 2–714.   Buyer's Damages for Breach in Regard to Accepted Goods.

(1)   Where the buyer has accepted goods and given notification (subsection (3) of Section 2–607) he may recover as damages for any non-conformity of tender the loss resulting in the ordinary course of events from the seller's breach as determined in any manner which is reasonable.

(2)   The measure of damages for breach of warranty is the difference at the time and place of acceptance between the value of the goods accepted and the value they would have had if they had been as warranted, unless special circumstances show proximate damages of a different amount.

(3)   In a proper case any incidental and consequential damages under the next section may also be recovered.

§ 2–715   UNIFORM COMMERCIAL CODE

Official Comment

Prior Uniform Statutory Provision: Section 69(6) and (7), Uniform Sales Act.

Changes: Rewritten.

Purposes of Changes:

1.   This section deals with the remedies available to the buyer after the goods have been accepted and the time for revocation of acceptance has gone by. In general this section adopts the rule of the prior uniform statutory provision for measuring damages where there has been a breach of warranty as to goods accepted, but goes further to lay down an explicit provision as to the time and place for determining the loss.

The section on deduction of damages from price provides an additional remedy for a buyer who still owes part of the purchase price, and frequently the two remedies will be available concurrently. The buyer's failure to notify of his claim under the section on effects of acceptance, however, operates to bar his remedies under either that section or the present section.

2.   The "non-conformity" referred to in subsection (1) includes not only breaches of warranties but also any failure of the seller to perform according to his obligations under the contract. In the case of such non-conformity, the buyer is permitted to recover for his loss "in any manner which is reasonable."

3.   Subsection (2) describes the usual, standard and reasonable method of ascertaining damages in the case of breach of warranty but it is not intended as an exclusive measure. It departs from the measure of damages for non-delivery in utilizing the place of acceptance rather than the place of tender. In some cases the two may coincide, as where the buyer signifies his acceptance upon the tender. If, however, the non-conformity is such as would justify revocation of acceptance, the time and place of acceptance under this section is determined as of the buyer's decision not to revoke.

4.   The incidental and consequential damages referred to in subsection (3), which will usually accompany an action brought under this section, are discussed in detail in the comment on the next section.

Cross References:

> Point 1: Compare Section 2–711; Sections 2–607 and 2–717.
> Point 2: Section 2–106.
> Point 3: Sections 2–608 and 2–713.
> Point 4: Section 2–715.

Definitional Cross References:

> "Buyer". Section 2–103.
> "Conform". Section 2–106.
> "Goods". Section 1–201.
> "Notification". Section 1–201.
> "Seller". Section 2–103.

§ 2–715.   Buyer's Incidental and Consequential Damages.

(1)   Incidental damages resulting from the seller's breach include expenses reasonably incurred in inspection, receipt, transportation and care and custody of goods rightfully rejected, any commercially reasonable charges, expenses or commissions in connection with effecting cover and any other reasonable expense incident to the delay or other breach.

(2)   Consequential damages resulting from the seller's breach include

(a)   any loss resulting from general or particular requirements and needs of which the seller at the time of contracting had reason to know and which could not reasonably be prevented by cover or otherwise; and

(b)   injury to person or property proximately resulting from any breach of warranty.

Official Comment

Prior Uniform Statutory Provisions: Subsection (2)(b)—Sections 69(7) and 70, Uniform Sales Act.

Changes: Rewritten.

Purposes of Changes and New Matter:

1.   Subsection (1) is intended to provide reimbursement for the buyer who incurs reasonable expenses in connection with the handling of rightfully rejected goods or goods whose acceptance may be justifiably revoked, or in connection with effecting cover where the breach of the contract lies in non-conformity or non-delivery of the goods. The incidental damages listed are not intended to be exhaustive but are merely illustrative of the typical kinds of incidental damage.

2.   Subsection (2) operates to allow the buyer, in an appropriate case, any consequential damages which are the result of the seller's breach. The "tacit agreement" test for the recovery of consequential damages is rejected. Although the older rule at common law which made the seller liable for all consequential damages of which he had "reason to know" in advance is followed, the liberality of that rule is modified by refusing to permit recovery unless the buyer could not reasonably have prevented the loss by cover or otherwise. Subparagraph (2) carries forward the provisions of the prior uniform statutory provision as to consequential damages resulting from breach of warranty, but modifies the rule by requiring first that the buyer attempt to minimize his damages in good faith, either by cover or otherwise.

3.   In the absence of excuse under the section on merchant's excuse by failure of presupposed conditions, the seller is liable for consequential damages in all cases where he had reason to know of the buyer's general or particular requirements at the time of contracting. It is not necessary that there be a conscious acceptance of an insurer's liability on the seller's part, nor is his obligation for consequential damages limited to cases in which he fails to use due effort in good faith.

Particular needs of the buyer must generally be made known to the seller while general needs must rarely be made known to charge the seller with knowledge.

Any seller who does not wish to take the risk of consequential damages has available the section on contractual limitation of remedy.

4.   The burden of proving the extent of loss incurred by way of consequential damage is on the buyer, but the section on liberal administration of remedies rejects any doctrine of certainty which requires almost mathematical precision in the proof of loss. Loss may be determined in any manner which is reasonable under the circumstances.

5.   Subsection (2)(b) states the usual rule as to breach of warranty, allowing recovery for injuries "proximately" resulting from the breach. Where the injury involved follows the use of goods without discovery of the defect causing the damage, the question of "proximate" cause turns on whether it was reasonable for the buyer to use the goods without such inspection as would have revealed the defects. If it was not reasonable for him to do so, or if he did in fact discover the defect prior to his use, the injury would not proximately result from the breach of warranty.

6.   In the case of sale of wares to one in the business of reselling them, resale is one of the requirements of which the seller has reason to know within the meaning of subsection (2)(a).

Cross References:

Point 1: Section 2–608.
Point 3: Sections 1–203, 2–615 and 2–719.
Point 4: Section 1–106.

Definitional Cross References:

"Cover". Section 2–712.
"Goods". Section 1–201.
"Person". Section 1–201.
"Receipt" of goods. Section 2–103.
"Seller". Section 2–103.

§ 2–716.   Buyer's Right to Specific Performance or Replevin.

(1)   Specific performance may be decreed where the goods are unique or in other proper circumstances.

§ 2-716   UNIFORM COMMERCIAL CODE

(2)   The decree for specific performance may include such terms and conditions as to payment of the price, damages, or other relief as the court may deem just.

(3)   The buyer has a right of replevin for goods identified to the contract if after reasonable effort he is unable to effect cover for such goods or the circumstances reasonably indicate that such effort will be unavailing or if the goods have been shipped under reservation and satisfaction of the security interest in them has been made or tendered. In the case of goods bought for personal, family, or household purposes, the buyer's right of replevin vests upon acquisition of a special property, even if the seller had not then repudiated or failed to deliver.

As amended in 1999.

Official Comment

Prior Uniform Statutory Provision: Section 68, Uniform Sales Act.

Changes: Rephrased.

Purposes of Changes: To make it clear that:

1.   The present section continues in general prior policy as to specific performance and injunction against breach. However, without intending to impair in any way the exercise of the court's sound discretion in the matter, this Article seeks to further a more liberal attitude than some courts have shown in connection with the specific performance of contracts of sale.

2.   In view of this Article's emphasis on the commercial feasibility of replacement, a new concept of what are "unique" goods is introduced under this section. Specific performance is no longer limited to goods which are already specific or ascertained at the time of contracting. The test of uniqueness under this section must be made in terms of the total situation which characterizes the contract. Output and requirements contracts involving a particular or peculiarly available source or market present today the typical commercial specific performance situation, as contrasted with contracts for the sale of heirlooms or priceless works of art which were usually involved in the older cases. However, uniqueness is not the sole basis of the remedy under this section for the relief may also be granted "in other proper circumstances" and inability to cover is strong evidence of "other proper circumstances".

3.   The legal remedy of replevin is given to the buyer in cases in which cover is reasonably unavailable and goods have been identified to the contract. This is in addition to the buyer's right to recover identified goods under Section 2-502. For consumer goods, the buyer's right to replevin vests upon the buyer's acquisition of a special property, which occurs upon identification of the goods to the contract. See Section 2-501. Inasmuch as a secured party normally acquires no greater rights in its collateral that its debtor had or had power to convey, see Section 2-403(1) (first sentence), a buyer who acquires a right of replevin under subsection (3) will take free of a security interest created by the seller if it attaches to the goods after the goods have been identified to the contract. The buyer will take free, even if the buyer does not buy in ordinary course and even if the security interest is perfected. Of course, to the extent that the buyer pays the price after the security interest attaches, the payments will constitute proceeds of the security interest.

4.   This section is intended to give the buyer rights to the goods comparable to the seller's rights to the price.

5.   If a negotiable document of title is outstanding, the buyer's right of replevin relates of course to the document not directly to the goods. See Article 7, especially Section 7-602.

Cross References:

> Point 3: Section 2-502.
> Point 4: Section 2-709.
> Point 5: Article 7.

Definitional Cross References:

> "Buyer". Section 2-103.
> "Goods". Section 1-201.
> "Rights". Section 1-201.

As amended in 1999.

§ 2–717. Deduction of Damages From the Price.

The buyer on notifying the seller of his intention to do so may deduct all or any part of the damages resulting from any breach of the contract from any part of the price still due under the same contract.

Official Comment

Prior Uniform Statutory Provision: See Section 69(1)(a), Uniform Sales Act.

Purposes:

1. This section permits the buyer to deduct from the price damages resulting from any breach by the seller and does not limit the relief to cases of breach of warranty as did the prior uniform statutory provision. To bring this provision into application the breach involved must be of the same contract under which the price in question is claimed to have been earned.

2. The buyer, however, must give notice of his intention to withhold all or part of the price if he wishes to avoid a default within the meaning of the section on insecurity and right to assurances. In conformity with the general policies of this Article, no formality of notice is required and any language which reasonably indicates the buyer's reason for holding up his payment is sufficient.

Cross Reference:

Point 2: Section 2–609.

Definitional Cross References:

"Buyer". Section 2–103.
"Notifies". Section 1–201.

§ 2–718. Liquidation or Limitation of Damages; Deposits.

(1) Damages for breach by either party may be liquidated in the agreement but only at an amount which is reasonable in the light of the anticipated or actual harm caused by the breach, the difficulties of proof of loss, and the inconvenience or nonfeasibility of otherwise obtaining an adequate remedy. A term fixing unreasonably large liquidated damages is void as a penalty.

(2) Where the seller justifiably withholds delivery of goods because of the buyer's breach, the buyer is entitled to restitution of any amount by which the sum of his payments exceeds

(a) the amount to which the seller is entitled by virtue of terms liquidating the seller's damages in accordance with subsection (1), or

(b) in the absence of such terms, twenty per cent of the value of the total performance for which the buyer is obligated under the contract or $500, whichever is smaller.

(3) The buyer's right to restitution under subsection (2) is subject to offset to the extent that the seller establishes

(a) a right to recover damages under the provisions of this Article other than subsection (1), and

(b) the amount or value of any benefits received by the buyer directly or indirectly by reason of the contract.

(4) Where a seller has received payment in goods their reasonable value or the proceeds of their resale shall be treated as payments for the purposes of subsection (2); but if the seller has notice of the buyer's breach before reselling goods received in part performance, his resale is subject to the conditions laid down in this Article on resale by an aggrieved seller (Section 2–706).

Official Comment

Prior Uniform Statutory Provision: None.

§ 2–719   UNIFORM COMMERCIAL CODE

Purposes:

1.   Under subsection (1) liquidated damage clauses are allowed where the amount involved is reasonable in the light of the circumstances of the case. The subsection sets forth explicitly the elements to be considered in determining the reasonableness of a liquidated damage clause. A term fixing unreasonably large liquidated damages is expressly made void as a penalty. An unreasonably small amount would be subject to similar criticism and might be stricken under the section on unconscionable contracts or clauses.

2.   Subsection (2) refuses to recognize a forfeiture unless the amount of the payment so forfeited represents a reasonable liquidation of damages as determined under subsection (1). A special exception is made in the case of small amounts (20% of the price or $500, whichever is smaller) deposited as security. No distinction is made between cases in which the payment is to be applied on the price and those in which it is intended as security for performance. Subsection (2) is applicable to any deposit or down or part payment. In the case of a deposit or turn in of goods resold before the breach, the amount actually received on the resale is to be viewed as the deposit rather than the amount allowed the buyer for the trade in. However, if the seller knows of the breach prior to the resale of the goods turned in, he must make reasonable efforts to realize their true value, and this is assured by requiring him to comply with the conditions laid down in the section on resale by an aggrieved seller.

Cross References:

Point 1: Section 2–302.
Point 2: Section 2–706.

Definitional Cross References:

"Aggrieved party". Section 1–201.
"Agreement". Section 1–201.
"Buyer". Section 2–103.
"Goods". Section 2–105.
"Notice". Section 1–201.
"Party". Section 1–201.
"Remedy". Section 1–201.
"Seller". Section 2–103.
"Term". Section 1–201.

§ 2–719.   Contractual Modification or Limitation of Remedy.

(1)   Subject to the provisions of subsections (2) and (3) of this section and of the preceding section on liquidation and limitation of damages,

(a)   the agreement may provide for remedies in addition to or in substitution for those provided in this Article and may limit or alter the measure of damages recoverable under this Article, as by limiting the buyer's remedies to return of the goods and repayment of the price or to repair and replacement of non-conforming goods or parts; and

(b)   resort to a remedy as provided is optional unless the remedy is expressly agreed to be exclusive, in which case it is the sole remedy.

(2)   Where circumstances cause an exclusive or limited remedy to fail of its essential purpose, remedy may be had as provided in this Act.

(3)   Consequential damages may be limited or excluded unless the limitation or exclusion is unconscionable. Limitation of consequential damages for injury to the person in the case of consumer goods is prima facie unconscionable but limitation of damages where the loss is commercial is not.

Official Comment

Prior Uniform Statutory Provision: None.

Purposes:

ARTICLE 2 (2016)   **§ 2–720**

1.   Under this section parties are left free to shape their remedies to their particular requirements and reasonable agreements limiting or modifying remedies are to be given effect.

However, it is of the very essence of a sales contract that at least minimum adequate remedies be available. If the parties intend to conclude a contract for sale within this Article they must accept the legal consequence that there be at least a fair quantum of remedy for breach of the obligations or duties outlined in the contract. Thus any clause purporting to modify or limit the remedial provisions of this Article in an unconscionable manner is subject to deletion and in that event the remedies made available by this Article are applicable as if the stricken clause had never existed. Similarly, under subsection (2), where an apparently fair and reasonable clause because of circumstances fails in its purpose or operates to deprive either party of the substantial value of the bargain, it must give way to the general remedy provisions of this Article.

2.   Subsection (1)(b) creates a presumption that clauses prescribing remedies are cumulative rather than exclusive. If the parties intend the term to describe the sole remedy under the contract, this must be clearly expressed.

3.   Subsection (3) recognizes the validity of clauses limiting or excluding consequential damages but makes it clear that they may not operate in an unconscionable manner. Actually such terms are merely an allocation of unknown or undeterminable risks. The seller in all cases is free to disclaim warranties in the manner provided in Section 2–316.

Cross References:

Point 1: Section 2–302.
Point 3: Section 2–316.

Definitional Cross References:

"Agreement". Section 1–201.
"Buyer". Section 2–103.
"Conforming". Section 2–106.
"Contract". Section 1–201.
"Goods". Section 2–105.
"Remedy". Section 1–201.
"Seller". Section 2–103.

§ 2–720.   Effect of "Cancellation" or "Rescission" on Claims for Antecedent Breach.

Unless the contrary intention clearly appears, expressions of "cancellation" or "rescission" of the contract or the like shall not be construed as a renunciation or discharge of any claim in damages for an antecedent breach.

Official Comment

Prior Uniform Statutory Provision: None.

Purpose:

This section is designed to safeguard a person holding a right of action from any unintentional loss of rights by the ill-advised use of such terms as "cancellation", "rescission", or the like. Once a party's rights have accrued they are not to be lightly impaired by concessions made in business decency and without intention to forego them. Therefore, unless the cancellation of a contract expressly declares that it is "without reservation of rights", or the like, it cannot be considered to be a renunciation under this section.

Cross Reference:

Section 1–107.

Definitional Cross References:

"Cancellation". Section 2–106.
"Contract". Section 1–201.

§ 2–721.   Remedies for Fraud.

Remedies for material misrepresentation or fraud include all remedies available under this Article for non-fraudulent breach. Neither rescission or a claim for rescission of the contract for sale nor rejection or return of the goods shall bar or be deemed inconsistent with a claim for damages or other remedy.

Official Comment

Prior Uniform Statutory Provision: None.

Purposes: To correct the situation by which remedies for fraud have been more circumscribed than the more modern and mercantile remedies for breach of warranty. Thus the remedies for fraud are extended by this section to coincide in scope with those for non-fraudulent breach. This section thus makes it clear that neither rescission of the contract for fraud nor rejection of the goods bars other remedies unless the circumstances of the case make the remedies incompatible.

Definitional Cross References:

"Contract for sale". Section 2–106.
"Goods". Section 1–201.
"Remedy". Section 1–201.

§ 2–722.   Who Can Sue Third Parties for Injury to Goods.

Where a third party so deals with goods which have been identified to a contract for sale as to cause actionable injury to a party to that contract

(a)   a right of action against the third party is in either party to the contract for sale who has title to or a security interest or a special property or an insurable interest in the goods; and if the goods have been destroyed or converted a right of action is also in the party who either bore the risk of loss under the contract for sale or has since the injury assumed that risk as against the other;

(b)   if at the time of the injury the party plaintiff did not bear the risk of loss as against the other party to the contract for sale and there is no arrangement between them for disposition of the recovery, his suit or settlement is, subject to his own interest, as a fiduciary for the other party to the contract;

(c)   either party may with the consent of the other sue for the benefit of whom it may concern.

Official Comment

Prior Uniform Statutory Provision: None.

Purposes: To adopt and extend somewhat the principle of the statutes which provide for suit by the real party in interest. The provisions of this section apply only after identification of the goods. Prior to that time only the seller has a right of action. During the period between identification and final acceptance (except in the case of revocation of acceptance) it is possible for both parties to have the right of action. Even after final acceptance both parties may have the right of action if the seller retains possession or otherwise retains an interest.

Definitional Cross References:

"Action". Section 1–201.
"Buyer". Section 2–103.
"Contract for sale". Section 2–106.
"Goods". Section 2–105.
"Party". Section 1–201.
"Rights". Section 1–201.
"Security interest". Section 1–201.

§ 2–723.   Proof of Market Price: Time and Place.

(1)   If an action based on anticipatory repudiation comes to trial before the time for performance with respect to some or all of the goods, any damages based on market price (Section 2–708 or Section 2–

ARTICLE 2 (2016)   § 2–724

713) shall be determined according to the price of such goods prevailing at the time when the aggrieved party learned of the repudiation.

(2)   If evidence of a price prevailing at the times or places described in this Article is not readily available the price prevailing within any reasonable time before or after the time described or at any other place which in commercial judgment or under usage of trade would serve as a reasonable substitute for the one described may be used, making any proper allowance for the cost of transporting the goods to or from such other place.

(3)   Evidence of a relevant price prevailing at a time or place other than the one described in this Article offered by one party is not admissible unless and until he has given the other party such notice as the court finds sufficient to prevent unfair surprise.

Official Comment

Prior Uniform Statutory Provision: None.

Purposes: To eliminate the most obvious difficulties arising in connection with the determination of market price, when that is stipulated as a measure of damages by some provision of this Article. Where the appropriate market price is not readily available the court is here granted reasonable leeway in receiving evidence of prices current in other comparable markets or at other times comparable to the one in question. In accordance with the general principle of this Article against surprise, however, a party intending to offer evidence of such a substitute price must give suitable notice to the other party.

This section is not intended to exclude the use of any other reasonable method of determining market price or of measuring damages if the circumstances of the case make this necessary.

Definitional Cross References:

"Action". Section 1–201.
"Aggrieved party". Section 1–201.
"Goods". Section 2–105.
"Notifies". Section 1–201.
"Party". Section 1–201.
"Reasonable time". Section 1–204.
"Usage of trade". Section 1–205.

§ 2–724.   Admissibility of Market Quotations.

Whenever the prevailing price or value of any goods regularly bought and sold in any established commodity market is in issue, reports in official publications or trade journals or in newspapers or periodicals of general circulation published as the reports of such market shall be admissible in evidence. The circumstances of the preparation of such a report may be shown to affect its weight but not its admissibility.

Official Comment

Prior Uniform Statutory Provision: None.

Purposes: To make market quotations admissible in evidence while providing for a challenge of the material by showing the circumstances of its preparation.

No explicit provision as to the weight to be given to market quotations is contained in this section, but such quotations, in the absence of compelling challenge, offer an adequate basis for a verdict.

Market quotations are made admissible when the price or value of goods traded "in any established market" is in issue. The reason of the section does not require that the market be closely organized in the manner of a produce exchange. It is sufficient if transactions in the commodity are frequent and open enough to make a market established by usage in which one price can be expected to affect another and in which an informed report of the range and trend of prices can be assumed to be reasonably accurate.

This section does not in any way intend to limit or negate the application of similar rules of admissibility to other material, whether by action of the courts or by statute. The purpose of the present section is to assure a minimum of mercantile administration in this important situation and not to limit any liberalizing trend in modern law.

Definitional Cross Reference:

"Goods". Section 2–105.

§ 2–725.   Statute of Limitations in Contracts for Sale.

(1)   An action for breach of any contract for sale must be commenced within four years after the cause of action has accrued. By the original agreement the parties may reduce the period of limitation to not less than one year but may not extend it.

(2)   A cause of action accrues when the breach occurs, regardless of the aggrieved party's lack of knowledge of the breach. A breach of warranty occurs when tender of delivery is made, except that where a warranty explicitly extends to future performance of the goods and discovery of the breach must await the time of such performance the cause of action accrues when the breach is or should have been discovered.

(3)   Where an action commenced within the time limited by subsection (1) is so terminated as to leave available a remedy by another action for the same breach such other action may be commenced after the expiration of the time limited and within six months after the termination of the first action unless the termination resulted from voluntary discontinuance or from dismissal for failure or neglect to prosecute.

(4)   This section does not alter the law on tolling of the statute of limitations nor does it apply to causes of action which have accrued before this Act becomes effective.

Official Comment

Prior Uniform Statutory Provision: None.

Purposes: To introduce a uniform statute of limitations for sales contracts, thus eliminating the jurisdictional variations and providing needed relief for concerns doing business on a nationwide scale whose contracts have heretofore been governed by several different periods of limitation depending upon the state in which the transaction occurred. This Article takes sales contracts out of the general laws limiting the time for commencing contractual actions and selects a four year period as the most appropriate to modern business practice. This is within the normal commercial record keeping period.

Subsection (1) permits the parties to reduce the period of limitation. The minimum period is set at one year. The parties may not, however, extend the statutory period.

Subsection (2), providing that the cause of action accrues when the breach occurs, states an exception where the warranty extends to future performance.

Subsection (3) states the saving provision included in many state statutes and permits an additional short period for bringing new actions, where suits begun within the four year period have been terminated so as to leave a remedy still available for the same breach.

Subsection (4) makes it clear that this Article does not purport to alter or modify in any respect the law on tolling of the Statute of Limitations as it now prevails in the various jurisdictions.

Definitional Cross References:

"Action". Section 1–201.
"Aggrieved party". Section 1–201.
"Agreement". Section 1–201.
"Contract for sale". Section 2–106.
"Goods". Section 2–105.
"Party". Section 1–201.
"Remedy". Section 1–201.
"Term". Section 1–201.
"Termination". Section 2–106.

4. Sarbanes-Oxley Act of 2002 (Selected Provisions)

SARBANES-OXLEY ACT OF 2002

[PUBLIC COMPANY ACCOUNTING REFORM AND INVESTOR PROTECTION ACT]
(Selected Provisions)

15 U.S.C. § 7201 – Definitions

Except as otherwise specifically provided in this Act, in this Act, the following definitions shall apply:

(1)APPROPRIATE STATE REGULATORY AUTHORITY

The term "appropriate State regulatory authority" means the State agency or other authority responsible for the licensure or other regulation of the practice of accounting in the State or States having jurisdiction over a registered public accounting firm or associated person thereof, with respect to the matter in question.

(2)AUDIT

The term "audit" means an examination of the financial statements of any issuer by an independent public accounting firm in accordance with the rules of the Board or the Commission (or, for the period preceding the adoption of applicable rules of the Board under section 7213 of this title, in accordance with then-applicable generally accepted auditing and related standards for such purposes), for the purpose of expressing an opinion on such statements.

(3)AUDIT COMMITTEE THE TERM "AUDIT COMMITTEE" MEANS—

(A)

a committee (or equivalent body) established by and amongst the board of directors of an issuer for the purpose of overseeing the accounting and financial reporting processes of the issuer and audits of the financial statements of the issuer; and

(B)

if no such committee exists with respect to an issuer, the entire board of directors of the issuer.

(4)AUDIT REPORT THE TERM "AUDIT REPORT" MEANS A DOCUMENT OR OTHER RECORD—

(A)

prepared following an audit performed for purposes of compliance by an issuer with the requirements of the securities laws; and

(B)in which a public accounting firm either—

(i)

sets forth the opinion of that firm regarding a financial statement, report, or other document; or

(ii)

asserts that no such opinion can be expressed.

(5)Board

The term "Board" means the Public Company Accounting Oversight Board established under section 7211 of this title.

(6)Commission

The term "Commission" means the Securities and Exchange Commission.

(7)Issuer

The term "issuer" means an issuer (as defined in section 78c of this title), the securities of which are registered under section 78l of this title, or that is required to file reports under section 78o(d) of this title, or that files or has filed a registration statement that has not yet become effective under the Securities Act of 1933 (15 U.S.C. 77a et seq.), and that it has not withdrawn.

(8)Non-audit services

The term "non-audit services" means any professional services provided to an issuer by a registered public accounting firm, other than those provided to an issuer in connection with an audit or a review of the financial statements of an issuer.

(9)Person associated with a public accounting firm

(A)In general The terms "person associated with a public accounting firm" (or with a "registered public accounting firm") and "associated person of a public accounting firm" (or of a "registered public accounting firm") mean any individual proprietor, partner, shareholder, principal, accountant, or other professional employee of a public accounting firm, or any other independent contractor or entity that, in connection with the preparation or issuance of any audit report—

(i)

shares in the profits of, or receives compensation in any other form from, that firm; or

(ii)

participates as agent or otherwise on behalf of such accounting firm in any activity of that firm.

(B)Exemption authority

The Board may, by rule, exempt persons engaged only in ministerial tasks from the definition in subparagraph (A), to the extent that the Board determines that any such exemption is consistent with the purposes of this Act, the public interest, or the protection of investors.

(C)Investigative and enforcement authority For purposes of sections 7202(c), 7211(c), 7 215, and 7217(c) of this title and the rules of the Board and Commission issued thereunder, except to the extent specifically excepted by such rules, the terms defined in subparagraph (A) shall include any person associated, seeking to become associated, or formerly associated with a public accounting firm, except that—

(i)

the authority to conduct an investigation of such person under section 7215(b) of this title shall apply only with respect to any act or practice, or omission to act, by the person while such person was associated or seeking to become associated with a registered public accounting firm; and (ii)the authority to commence a disciplinary proceeding under section 7215(c)(1) of this title, or impose sanctions under section 7215(c)(4) of this title, against such person shall apply only with respect to—

(I)

conduct occurring while such person was associated or seeking to become associated with a registered public accounting firm; or

(II)

non-cooperation, as described in section 7215(b)(3) of this title, with respect to a demand in a Board investigation for testimony, documents, or other information relating to a period when such person was associated or seeking to become associated with a registered public accounting firm.

(10)PROFESSIONAL STANDARDS THE TERM "PROFESSIONAL STANDARDS" MEANS—

(A) accounting principles that are—

(i)

established by the standard setting body described in section 19(b) of the Securities Act of 1933 [15 U.S.C. 77s(b)], or prescribed by the Commission under section 19(a) of that Act [15 U.S.C. 77s(a)] or section 78m(b) of this title; and

(ii)

relevant to audit reports for particular issuers, or dealt with in the quality control system of a particular registered public accounting firm; and

(B)auditing standards, standards for attestation engagements, quality control policies and procedures, ethical and competency standards, and independence standards (including rules implementing title II) that the Board or the Commission determines—

(i)

relate to the preparation or issuance of audit reports for issuers; and

(ii)

are established or adopted by the Board under section 7213(a) of this title, or are promulgated as rules of the Commission.

(11)PUBLIC ACCOUNTING FIRM THE TERM "PUBLIC ACCOUNTING FIRM" MEANS—

(A)

a proprietorship, partnership, incorporated association, corporation, limited liability company, limited liability partnership, or other legal entity that is engaged in the practice of public accounting or preparing or issuing audit reports; and

(B)

to the extent so designated by the rules of the Board, any associated person of any entity described in subparagraph (A).

(12)REGISTERED PUBLIC ACCOUNTING FIRM

The term "registered public accounting firm" means a public accounting firm registered with the Board in accordance with this Act.

(13)RULES OF THE BOARD

The term "rules of the Board" means the bylaws and rules of the Board (as submitted to, and approved, modified, or amended by the Commission, in accordance with section 7217 of this title), and those stated policies, practices, and interpretations of the Board that the Commission, by rule, may deem to be rules of the Board, as necessary or appropriate in the public interest or for the protection of investors.

(14)SECURITY

The term "security" has the same meaning as in section 78c(a) of this title.

(15)SECURITIES LAWS

The term "securities laws" means the provisions of law referred to in section 78c(a)(47) of this title and includes the rules, regulations, and orders issued by the Commission thereunder.

(16)STATE

The term "State" means any State of the United States, the District of Columbia, Puerto Rico, the Virgin Islands, or any other territory or possession of the United States.

(17)FOREIGN AUDITOR OVERSIGHT AUTHORITY

The term "foreign auditor oversight authority" means any governmental body or other entity empowered by a foreign government to conduct inspections of public accounting firms or otherwise to administer or enforce laws related to the regulation of public accounting firms.

15 U.S.C. § 7241 [Section 302] – Corporate Responsibility for Financial Reports

(a)REGULATIONS REQUIRED

The Commission shall, by rule, require, for each company filing periodic reports under section 78m(a) or 78o(d) of this title, that the principal executive officer or officers and the principal financial officer or officers, or persons performing similar functions, certify in each annual or quarterly report filed or submitted under either such section of this title that—

(1)

the signing officer has reviewed the report;

(2)

based on the officer's knowledge, the report does not contain any untrue statement of a material fact or omit to state a material fact necessary in order to make the statements made, in light of the circumstances under which such statements were made, not misleading;

(3)

based on such officer's knowledge, the financial statements, and other financial information included in the report, fairly present in all material respects the financial condition and results of operations of the issuer as of, and for, the periods presented in the report;

(4) the signing officers—

(A)

are responsible for establishing and maintaining internal controls;

(B)

have designed such internal controls to ensure that material information relating to the issuer and its consolidated subsidiaries is made known to such officers by others within those entities, particularly during the period in which the periodic reports are being prepared;

(C)

have evaluated the effectiveness of the issuer's internal controls as of a date within 90 days prior to the report; and

(D)

have presented in the report their conclusions about the effectiveness of their internal controls based on their evaluation as of that date;

(5) the signing officers have disclosed to the issuer's auditors and the audit committee of the board of directors (or persons fulfilling the equivalent function)—

(A)

all significant deficiencies in the design or operation of internal controls which could adversely affect the issuer's ability to record, process, summarize, and report financial data and have identified for the issuer's auditors any material weaknesses in internal controls; and

(B)

any fraud, whether or not material, that involves management or other employees who have a significant role in the issuer's internal controls; and

(6)

the signing officers have indicated in the report whether or not there were significant changes in internal controls or in other factors that could significantly affect internal controls subsequent to the date of their evaluation, including any corrective actions with regard to significant deficiencies and material weaknesses.

(b)Foreign reincorporations have no effect

Nothing in this section shall be interpreted or applied in any way to allow any issuer to lessen the legal force of the statement required under this section, by an issuer having reincorporated or having engaged in any other transaction that resulted in the transfer of the corporate domicile or offices of the issuer from inside the United States to outside of the United States.

(c)Deadline

The rules required by subsection (a) shall be effective not later than 30 days after July 30, 2002.

15 U.S.C. § 7242 [Section 303] – Improper Influence on Conduct of Audits

(a)Rules to prohibit

It shall be unlawful, in contravention of such rules or regulations as the Commission shall prescribe as necessary and appropriate in the public interest or for the protection of investors, for any officer or director of an issuer, or any other person acting under the direction thereof, to take any action to fraudulently influence, coerce, manipulate, or mislead any independent public or certified accountant engaged in the performance of an audit of the financial statements of that issuer for the purpose of rendering such financial statements materially misleading.

(b)ENFORCEMENT

In any civil proceeding, the Commission shall have exclusive authority to enforce this section and any rule or regulation issued under this section.

(c)NO PREEMPTION OF OTHER LAW

The provisions of subsection (a) shall be in addition to, and shall not supersede or preempt, any other provision of law or any rule or regulation issued thereunder.

(d)DEADLINE FOR RULEMAKING THE COMMISSION SHALL—

(1)

propose the rules or regulations required by this section, not later than 90 days after July 30, 2002; and

(2)

issue final rules or regulations required by this section, not later than 270 days after July 30, 2002.

15 U.S.C. § 7261 [Section 401] – Disclosure in Periodic Reports

(a)OMITTED

(b)COMMISSION RULES ON PRO FORMA FIGURES

Not later than 180 days after July 30, 2002, the Commission shall issue final rules providing that pro forma financial information included in any periodic or other report filed with the Commission pursuant to the securities laws, or in any public disclosure or press or other release, shall be presented in a manner that—

(1)

does not contain an untrue statement of a material fact or omit to state a material fact necessary in order to make the pro forma financial information, in light of the circumstances under which it is presented, not misleading; and

(2)

reconciles it with the financial condition and results of operations of the issuer under generally accepted accounting principles.

(c)STUDY AND REPORT ON SPECIAL PURPOSE ENTITIES

(1)Study required The Commission shall, not later than 1 year after the effective date of adoption of off-balance sheet disclosure rules required by section 78m(j) of this title, complete a study of filings by issuers and their disclosures to determine—

(A)

the extent of off-balance sheet transactions, including assets, liabilities, leases, losses, and the use of special purpose entities; and

(B)

whether generally accepted accounting rules result in financial statements of issuers reflecting the economics of such off-balance sheet transactions to investors in a transparent fashion.

(2)Report and recommendations Not later than 6 months after the date of completion of the study required by paragraph (1), the Commission shall submit a report to the President, the Committee on Banking, Housing, and Urban Affairs of the Senate, and the Committee on Financial Services of the House of Representatives, setting forth—

(A)

the amount or an estimate of the amount of off-balance sheet transactions, including assets, liabilities, leases, and losses of, and the use of special purpose entities by, issuers filing periodic reports pursuant to section 78m or 78o of this title;

(B)

the extent to which special purpose entities are used to facilitate off-balance sheet transactions;

(C)

whether generally accepted accounting principles or the rules of the Commission result in financial statements of issuers reflecting the economics of such transactions to investors in a transparent fashion;

(D)

whether generally accepted accounting principles specifically result in the consolidation of

special purpose entities sponsored by an issuer in cases in which the issuer has the majority of the risks and rewards of the special purpose entity; and

(E)

any recommendations of the Commission for improving the transparency and quality of reporting off-balance sheet transactions in the financial statements and disclosures required to be filed by an issuer with the Commission.

15 U.S.C. § 7262 [Section 404] – Management Assessment of Internal Controls

(a)Rules required

The Commission shall prescribe rules requiring each annual report required by section 78m(a) or 78o(d) of this title to contain an internal control report, which shall—

(1)

state the responsibility of management for establishing and maintaining an adequate internal control structure and procedures for financial reporting; and

(2)

contain an assessment, as of the end of the most recent fiscal year of the issuer, of the effectiveness of the internal control structure and procedures of the issuer for financial reporting.

(b)Internal control evaluation and reporting

With respect to the internal control assessment required by subsection (a), each registered public accounting firm that prepares or issues the audit report for the issuer, other than an issuer that is an emerging growth company (as defined in section 78c of this title), shall attest to, and report on, the assessment made by the management of the issuer. An attestation made under this subsection shall be made in accordance with standards for attestation engagements issued or adopted by the Board. Any such attestation shall not be the subject of a separate engagement.

(c)EXEMPTION FOR SMALLER ISSUERS

Subsection (b) shall not apply with respect to any audit report prepared for an issuer that is neither a "large accelerated filer" nor an "accelerated filer" as those terms are defined in Rule 12b–2 of the Commission (17 C.F.R. 240.12b–2).

18 U.S.C. § 1519 [Section 802] – Destruction, Alteration, or Falsification of Records in Federal Investigations and Bankruptcy

Whoever knowingly alters, destroys, mutilates, conceals, covers up, falsifies, or makes a false entry in any record, document, or tangible object with the intent to impede, obstruct, or influence the investigation or proper administration of any matter within the jurisdiction of any department or agency of the United States or any case filed under title 11, or in relation to or contemplation of any such matter or case, shall be fined under this title, imprisoned not more than 20 years, or both.

18 U.S.C. § 1350 [Section 906] – Corporate Responsibility for Financial Reports

(a)CERTIFICATION OF PERIODIC FINANCIAL REPORTS.—

Each periodic report containing financial statements filed by an issuer with the Securities Exchange Commission pursuant to section 13(a) or 15(d) of the Securities Exchange Act of 1934 (15 U.S.C. 78m(a) or 78o(d)) shall be accompanied by a written statement by the chief executive officer and chief financial officer (or equivalent thereof) of the issuer.

(b)CONTENT.—

The statement required under subsection (a) shall certify that the periodic report containing the financial statements fully complies with the requirements of section 13(a) or 15(d) of the Securities Exchange Act pf [sic] 1934 (15 U.S.C. 78m or 78o(d)) and that information contained in the periodic report fairly presents, in all material respects, the financial condition and results of operations of the issuer.

(c)CRIMINAL PENALTIES.—WHOEVER—

(1)

certifies any statement as set forth in subsections (a) and (b) of this section knowing that the periodic report accompanying the statement does not comport with all the requirements set forth in this section shall be fined not more than $1,000,000 or imprisoned not more than 10 years, or both; or

(2)

willfully certifies any statement as set forth in subsections (a) and (b) of this section knowing that the periodic report accompanying the statement does not comport with all the requirements set forth in this section shall be fined not more than $5,000,000, or imprisoned not more than 20 years, or both.

18 U.S.C. § 1513 [Section 1107] – Retaliating Against a Witness, Victim, or an Informant

(a)

(1)Whoever kills or attempts to kill another person with intent to retaliate against any person for—

(A)

the attendance of a witness or party at an official proceeding, or any testimony given or any record, document, or other object produced by a witness in an official proceeding; or

(B)

providing to a law enforcement officer any information relating to the commission or possible commission of a Federal offense or a violation of conditions of probation, supervised release, parole, or release pending judicial proceedings,

shall be punished as provided in paragraph (2).

(2)The punishment for an offense under this subsection is—

(A)

in the case of a killing, the punishment provided in sections 1111 and 1112; and

(B)

in the case of an attempt, imprisonment for not more than 30 years.

(b)Whoever knowingly engages in any conduct and thereby causes bodily injury to another person or damages the tangible property of another person, or threatens to do so, with intent to retaliate against any person for—

(1)

the attendance of a witness or party at an official proceeding, or any testimony given or any record, document, or other object produced by a witness in an official proceeding; or

(2)

any information relating to the commission or possible commission of a Federal offense or a violation of conditions of probation, supervised release, parole, or release pending judicial proceedings given by a person to a law enforcement officer;

or attempts to do so, shall be fined under this title or imprisoned not more than 20 years, or both.

(c)

If the retaliation occurred because of attendance at or testimony in a criminal case, the maximum term of imprisonment which may be imposed for the offense under this section shall be the higher of that otherwise provided by law or the maximum term that could have been imposed for any offense charged in such case.

(d)

There is extraterritorial Federal jurisdiction over an offense under this section.

(e)

Whoever knowingly, with the intent to retaliate, takes any action harmful to any person, including interference with the lawful employment or livelihood of any person, for providing to a law enforcement officer any truthful information relating to the commission or possible commission of any Federal offense, shall be fined under this title or imprisoned not more than 10 years, or both.

(f)

Whoever conspires to commit any offense under this section shall be subject to the same penalties as those prescribed for the offense the commission of which was the object of the conspiracy.

(g)

A prosecution under this section may be brought in the district in which the official proceeding (whether pending, about to be instituted, or completed) was intended to be affected, or in which the conduct constituting the alleged offense occurred.

5. Delaware General Corporate Law (Selected Provisions)

DELAWARE GENERAL CORPORATION LAW

(Selected Provisions)

§ 101 Incorporators; how corporation formed; purposes.

(a) Any person, partnership, association or corporation, singly or jointly with others, and without regard to such person's or entity's residence, domicile or state of incorporation, may incorporate or organize a corporation under this chapter by filing with the Division of Corporations in the Department of State a certificate of incorporation which shall be executed, acknowledged and filed in accordance with § 103 of this title.

(b) A corporation may be incorporated or organized under this chapter to conduct or promote any lawful business or purposes, except as may otherwise be provided by the Constitution or other law of this State.

(c) Corporations for constructing, maintaining and operating public utilities, whether in or outside of this State, may be organized under this chapter, but corporations for constructing, maintaining and operating public utilities within this State shall be subject to, in addition to this chapter, the special provisions and requirements of Title 26 applicable to such corporations.

§102 Contents of certificate of incorporation.

(a) The certificate of incorporation shall set forth:

(1) The name of the corporation, which (i) shall contain 1 of the words "association," "company," "corporation," "club," "foundation," "fund," "incorporated," "institute," "society," "union," "syndicate," or "limited," (or abbreviations thereof, with or without punctuation), or words (or abbreviations thereof, with or without punctuation) of like import of foreign countries or jurisdictions (provided they are written in roman characters or letters); provided, however, that the Division of Corporations in the Department of State may waive such requirement (unless it determines that such name is, or might otherwise appear to be, that of a natural person) if such corporation executes, acknowledges and files with the Secretary of State in accordance with § 103 of this title a certificate stating that its total assets, as defined in § 503(i) of this title, are not less than $10,000,000, or, in the sole discretion of the Division of Corporations in the Department of State, if the corporation is both a nonprofit nonstock corporation and an association of professionals, (ii) shall be such as to distinguish it upon the records in the office of the Division of Corporations in the Department of State from the names that are reserved on such records and from the names on such records of each other corporation, partner-

ship, limited partnership, limited liability company or statutory trust organized or registered as a domestic or foreign corporation, partnership, limited partnership, limited liability company or statutory trust under the laws of this State, except with the written consent of the person who has reserved such name or such other foreign corporation or domestic or foreign partnership, limited partnership, limited liability company or statutory trust, executed, acknowledged and filed with the Secretary of State in accordance with § 103 of this title, or except that, without prejudicing any rights of the person who has reserved such name or such other foreign corporation or domestic or foreign partnership, limited partnership, limited liability company or statutory trust, the Division of Corporations in the Department of State may waive such requirement if the corporation demonstrates to the satisfaction of the Secretary of State that the corporation or a predecessor entity previously has made substantial use of such name or a substantially similar name, that the corporation has made reasonable efforts to secure such written consent, and that such waiver is in the interest of the State, (iii) except as permitted by § 395 of this title, shall not contain the word "trust," and (iv) shall not contain the word "bank," or any variation thereof, except for the name of a bank reporting to and under the supervision of the State Bank Commissioner of this State or a subsidiary of a bank or savings association (as those terms are defined in the Federal Deposit Insurance Act, as amended, at 12 U.S.C. § 1813), or a corporation regulated under the Bank Holding Company Act of 1956, as amended, 12 U.S.C. § 1841 et seq., or the Home Owners' Loan Act, as amended, 12 U.S.C. § 1461 et seq.; provided, however, that this section shall not be construed to prevent the use of the word "bank," or any variation thereof, in a context clearly not purporting to refer to a banking business or otherwise likely to mislead the public about the nature of the business of the corporation or to lead to a pattern and practice of abuse that might cause harm to the interests of the public or the State as determined by the Division of Corporations in the Department of State;

(2) The address (which shall be stated in accordance with § 131(c) of this title) of the corporation's registered office in this State, and the name of its registered agent at such address;

(3) The nature of the business or purposes to be conducted or promoted. It shall be sufficient to state, either alone or with other businesses or purposes, that the purpose of the corporation is to engage in any lawful act or activity for which corporations may be organized under the General Corporation Law of Delaware, and by such statement all lawful acts and activities shall be within the purposes of the corporation, except for express limitations, if any;

(4) If the corporation is to be authorized to issue only 1 class of stock, the total

number of shares of stock which the corporation shall have authority to issue and the par value of each of such shares, or a statement that all such shares are to be without par value. If the corporation is to be authorized to issue more than 1 class of stock, the certificate of incorporation shall set forth the total number of shares of all classes of stock which the corporation shall have authority to issue and the number of shares of each class and shall specify each class the shares of which are to be without par value and each class the shares of which are to have par value and the par value of the shares of each such class. The certificate of incorporation shall also set forth a statement of the designations and the powers, preferences and rights, and the qualifications, limitations or restrictions thereof, which are permitted by § 151 of this title in respect of any class or classes of stock or any series of any class of stock of the corporation and the fixing of which by the certificate of incorporation is desired, and an express grant of such authority as it may then be desired to grant to the board of directors to fix by resolution or resolutions any thereof that may be desired but which shall not be fixed by the certificate of incorporation. The foregoing provisions of this paragraph shall not apply to nonstock corporations. In the case of nonstock corporations, the fact that they are not authorized to issue capital stock shall be stated in the certificate of incorporation. The conditions of membership, or other criteria for identifying members, of nonstock corporations shall likewise be stated in the certificate of incorporation or the bylaws. Nonstock corporations shall have members, but failure to have members shall not affect otherwise valid corporate acts or work a forfeiture or dissolution of the corporation. Nonstock corporations may provide for classes or groups of members having relative rights, powers and duties, and may make provision for the future creation of additional classes or groups of members having such relative rights, powers and duties as may from time to time be established, including rights, powers and duties senior to existing classes and groups of members. Except as otherwise provided in this chapter, nonstock corporations may also provide that any member or class or group of members shall have full, limited, or no voting rights or powers, including that any member or class or group of members shall have the right to vote on a specified transaction even if that member or class or group of members does not have the right to vote for the election of the members of the governing body of the corporation. Voting by members of a nonstock corporation may be on a per capita, number, financial interest, class, group, or any other basis set forth. The provisions referred to in the 3 preceding sentences may be set forth in the certificate of incorporation or the bylaws. If neither the certificate of incorporation nor the bylaws of a nonstock corporation state the conditions of membership, or other criteria for identifying members, the members of the corporation shall be deemed to be those entitled to vote for the election of the members of the governing body pursuant to the certificate of incorporation or bylaws of such corporation or otherwise until thereafter otherwise provided by the certificate of incorporation or the bylaws;

(5) The name and mailing address of the incorporator or incorporators;

(6) If the powers of the incorporator or incorporators are to terminate upon the filing of the certificate of incorporation, the names and mailing addresses of the persons who are to serve as directors until the first annual meeting of stockholders or until their successors are elected and qualify.

(b) In addition to the matters required to be set forth in the certificate of incorporation by subsection (a) of this section, the certificate of incorporation may also contain any or all of the following matters:

(1) Any provision for the management of the business and for the conduct of the affairs of the corporation, and any provision creating, defining, limiting and regulating the powers of the corporation, the directors, and the stockholders, or any class of the stockholders, or the governing body, members, or any class or group of members of a nonstock corporation; if such provisions are not contrary to the laws of this State. Any provision which is required or permitted by any section of this chapter to be stated in the bylaws may instead be stated in the certificate of incorporation;

(2) The following provisions, in haec verba, (i), for a corporation other than a nonstock corporation, viz:

"Whenever a compromise or arrangement is proposed between this corporation and its creditors or any class of them and/or between this corporation and its stockholders or any class of them, any court of equitable jurisdiction within the State of Delaware may, on the application in a summary way of this corporation or of any creditor or stockholder thereof or on the application of any receiver or receivers appointed for this corporation under § 291 of Title 8 of the Delaware Code or on the application of trustees in dissolution or of any receiver or receivers appointed for this corporation under § 279 of Title 8 of the Delaware Code order a meeting of the creditors or class of creditors, and/or of the stockholders or class of stockholders of this corporation, as the case may be, to be summoned in such manner as the said court directs. If a majority in number representing three fourths in value of the creditors or class of creditors, and/or of the stockholders or class of stockholders of this corporation, as the case may be, agree to any compromise or arrangement and to any reorganization of this corporation as consequence of such compromise or arrangement, the said compromise or arrangement and the said reorganization shall, if sanctioned by the court to which the said application has been made, be binding on all the creditors or class of creditors, and/or on all the stockholders or class of stockholders, of this corporation, as the case may be, and also on this corporation"; or

(ii), for a nonstock corporation, viz:

"Whenever a compromise or arrangement is proposed between this corporation and its creditors or any class of them and/or between this corporation and its members or any class of them, any court of equitable jurisdiction within the State of Delaware may, on the application in a summary way of this corporation or of any creditor or member thereof or on the application of any receiver or receivers appointed for this corporation under § 291 of Title 8 of the Delaware Code or on the application of trustees in dissolution or of any receiver or receivers appointed for this corporation under § 279 of Title 8 of the Delaware Code order a meeting of the creditors or class of creditors, and/ or of the members or class of members of this corporation, as the case may be, to be summoned in such manner as the said court directs. If a majority in number representing three fourths in value of the creditors or class of creditors, and/or of the members or class of members of this corporation, as the case may be, agree to any compromise or arrangement and to any reorganization of this corporation as consequence

of such compromise or arrangement, the said compromise or arrangement and the said reorganization shall, if sanctioned by the court to which the said application has been made, be binding on all the creditors or class of creditors, and/or on all the members or class of members, of this corporation, as the case may be, and also on this corporation";

(3) Such provisions as may be desired granting to the holders of the stock of the corporation, or the holders of any class or series of a class thereof, the preemptive right to subscribe to any or all additional issues of stock of the corporation of any or all classes or series thereof, or to any securities of the corporation convertible into such stock. No stockholder shall have any preemptive right to subscribe to an additional issue of stock or to any security convertible into such stock unless, and except to the extent that, such right is expressly granted to such stockholder in the certificate of incorporation. All such rights in existence on July 3, 1967, shall remain in existence unaffected by this paragraph unless and until changed or terminated by appropriate action which expressly provides for the change or termination;

(4) Provisions requiring for any corporate action, the vote of a larger portion of the stock or of any class or series thereof, or of any other securities having voting power, or a larger number of the directors, than is required by this chapter;

(5) A provision limiting the duration of the corporation's existence to a specified date; otherwise, the corporation shall have perpetual existence;

(6) A provision imposing personal liability for the debts of the corporation on its stockholders to a specified extent and upon specified conditions; otherwise, the stockholders of a corporation shall not be personally liable for the payment of the corporation's debts except as they may be liable by reason of their own conduct or acts;

(7) A provision eliminating or limiting the personal liability of a director to the corporation or its stockholders for monetary damages for breach of fiduciary duty as a director, provided that such provision shall not eliminate or limit the liability of a director: (i) For any breach of the director's duty of loyalty to the corporation or its stockholders; (ii) for acts or omissions not in good faith or which involve intentional misconduct or a knowing violation of law; (iii) under § 174 of this title; or (iv) for any transaction from which the director derived an improper personal benefit. No such provision shall eliminate or limit the liability of a director for any act or omission occurring prior to the date when such provision becomes effective. All references in this paragraph to a director shall also be deemed to refer to such other person or persons, if any, who, pursuant to a provision of the certificate of incorporation in accordance with § 141(a) of this title, exercise or perform any of the powers or duties otherwise conferred or imposed upon the board of directors by this title.

(c) It shall not be necessary to set forth in the certificate of incorporation any of the powers conferred on corporations by this chapter.

(d) Except for provisions included pursuant to paragraphs (a)(1), (a)(2), (a)(5), (a)(6), (b)(2), (b)(5), (b)(7) of this section, and provisions included pursuant to paragraph (a)(4) of this section specifying the classes, number of shares, and par value of shares a corporation other than a nonstock corporation is authorized to issue, any provision of the certificate of incorporation may be made dependent upon facts ascertainable outside such instrument, provided that the manner in which such facts shall operate upon the provision is clearly and explicitly set forth therein. The term "facts," as used in this subsection, includes, but is not limited to, the occurrence of any event, including a determination or action by any person or body, including the corporation.

(e) The exclusive right to the use of a name that is available for use by a domestic or foreign corporation may be reserved by or on behalf of:

(1) Any person intending to incorporate or organize a corporation with that name under this chapter or contemplating such incorporation or organization;

(2) Any domestic corporation or any foreign corporation qualified to do business in the State of Delaware, in either

case, intending to change its name or contemplating such a change;

(3) Any foreign corporation intending to qualify to do business in the State of Delaware and adopt that name or contemplating such qualification and adoption; and

(4) Any person intending to organize a foreign corporation and have it qualify to do business in the State of Delaware and adopt that name or contemplating such organization, qualification and adoption.

The reservation of a specified name may be made by filing with the Secretary of State an application, executed by the applicant, certifying that the reservation is made by or on behalf of a domestic corporation, foreign corporation or other person described in paragraphs (e)(1)-(4) of this section above, and specifying the name to be reserved and the name and address of the applicant. If the Secretary of State finds that the name is available for use by a domestic or foreign corporation, the Secretary shall reserve the name for the use of the applicant for a period of 120 days. The same applicant may renew for successive 120-day periods a reservation of a specified name by filing with the Secretary of State, prior to the expiration of such reservation (or renewal thereof), an application for renewal of such reservation, executed by the applicant, certifying that the reservation is renewed by or on behalf of a domestic corporation, foreign corporation or other person described in paragraphs (e)(1)-(4) of this section above and specifying

the name reservation to be renewed and the name and address of the applicant. The right to the exclusive use of a reserved name may be transferred to any other person by filing in the office of the Secretary of State a notice of the transfer, executed by the applicant for whom the name was reserved, specifying the name reservation to be transferred and the name and address of the transferee. The reservation of a specified name may be cancelled by filing with the Secretary of State a notice of cancellation, executed by the applicant or transferee, specifying the name reservation to be cancelled and the name and address of the applicant or transferee. Unless the Secretary of State finds that any application, application for renewal, notice of transfer, or notice of cancellation filed with the Secretary of State as required by this subsection does not conform to law, upon receipt of all filing fees required by law the Secretary of State shall prepare and return to the person who filed such instrument a copy of the filed instrument with a notation thereon of the action taken by the Secretary of State. A fee as set forth in § 391 of this title shall be paid at the time of the reservation of any name, at the time of the renewal of any such reservation and at the time of the filing of a notice of the transfer or cancellation of any such reservation.

(f) The certificate of incorporation may not contain any provision that would impose liability on a stockholder for the attorneys' fees or expenses of the corporation or any other party in connection with an internal corporate claim, as defined in § 115 of this title.

§ 106   Commencement of corporate existence.

Upon the filing with the Secretary of State of the certificate of incorporation, executed and acknowledged in accordance with § 103 of this title, the incorporator or incorporators who signed the certificate, and such incorporator's or incorporators' successors and assigns, shall, from the date of such filing, be and constitute a body corporate, by the name set forth in the certificate, subject to § 103(d) of this title and subject to dissolution or other termination of its existence as provided in this chapter.

§ 107 Powers of incorporators.

If the persons who are to serve as directors until the first annual meeting of stockholders have not been named in the certificate of incorporation, the incorporator or incorporators, until the directors are elected, shall manage the affairs of the corporation and may do whatever is necessary and proper to perfect the organization of the corporation, including the adoption of the original bylaws of the corporation and the election of directors.

§ 108 Organization meeting of incorporators or directors named in certificate of incorporation.

(a) After the filing of the certificate of incorporation an organization meeting of the incorporator or incorporators, or of the board of directors if the initial directors were named in the certificate of incorporation, shall be held, either within or without this State, at the call of a majority of the incorporators or directors, as the case may be, for the purposes of adopting bylaws, electing directors (if the meeting is of the incorporators) to serve or hold office until the first annual meeting of stockholders or until their successors are elected and qualify, electing officers if the meeting is of the directors, doing any other or further acts to perfect the organization of the corporation, and transacting such other business as may come before the meeting.

(b) The persons calling the meeting shall give to each other incorporator or director, as the case may be, at least 2 days' written notice thereof by any usual means of communication, which notice shall state the time, place and purposes of the meeting as fixed by the persons calling it. Notice of the meeting need not be given to anyone who attends the meeting or who signs a waiver of notice either before or after the meeting.

(c) Any action permitted to be taken at the organization meeting of the incorporators or directors, as the case may be, may be taken without a meeting if each incorporator or director, where there is more than 1, or the sole incorporator or director where there is only 1, signs an instrument which states the action so taken.

(d) If any incorporator is not available to act, then any person for whom or on whose behalf the incorporator was acting directly or indirectly as employee or agent, may take any action that such incorporator would have been authorized to take under this section or

§ 107 of this title; provided that any instrument signed by such other person, or any record of the proceedings of a meeting in which such person participated, shall state that such incorporator is not available and the reason therefor, that such incorporator was acting directly or indirectly as employee or agent for or on behalf of such person, and that such person's signature on such instrument or participation in such meeting is otherwise authorized and not wrongful.

§ 109 Bylaws.

(a) The original or other bylaws of a corporation may be adopted, amended or repealed by the incorporators, by the initial directors of a corporation other than a nonstock corporation or initial members of the governing body of a nonstock corporation if they were named in the certificate of incorporation, or, before a corporation other than a nonstock corporation has received any payment for any of its stock, by its board of directors. After a corporation other than a nonstock corporation has received any payment for any of its stock, the power to adopt, amend or repeal bylaws shall be in the stockholders entitled to vote. In the case of a nonstock corporation, the power to adopt, amend or repeal bylaws shall be in its members entitled to vote. Notwithstanding the foregoing, any corporation may, in its certificate of incorporation, confer the power to adopt, amend or repeal bylaws upon the directors or, in the case of a nonstock corporation, upon its governing body. The fact that such power has been so conferred upon the direc-

tors or governing body, as the case may be, shall not divest the stockholders or members of the power, nor limit their power to adopt, amend or repeal bylaws.

(b) The bylaws may contain any provision, not inconsistent with law or with the certificate of incorporation, relating to the business of the corporation, the conduct of its affairs, and its rights or powers or the rights or powers of its stockholders, directors, officers or employees. The bylaws may not contain any provision that would impose liability on a stockholder for the attorneys' fees or expenses of the corporation or any other party in connection with an internal corporate claim, as defined in § 115 of this title.

§ 121 General powers.

(a) In addition to the powers enumerated in § 122 of this title, every corporation, its officers, directors and stockholders shall possess and may exercise all the powers and privileges granted by this chapter or by any other law or by its certificate of incorporation, together with any powers incidental thereto, so far as such powers and privileges are necessary or convenient to the conduct, promotion or attainment of the business or purposes set forth in its certificate of incorporation.

(b) Every corporation shall be governed by the provisions and be subject to the restrictions and liabilities contained in this chapter.

§ 122 Specific powers.

Every corporation created under this chapter shall have power to:

(1) Have perpetual succession by its corporate name, unless a limited period of duration is stated in its certificate of incorporation;

(2) Sue and be sued in all courts and participate, as a party or otherwise, in any judicial, administrative, arbitrative or other proceeding, in its corporate name;

(3) Have a corporate seal, which may be altered at pleasure, and use the same by causing it or a facsimile thereof, to be impressed or affixed or in any other manner reproduced;

(4) Purchase, receive, take by grant, gift, devise, bequest or otherwise, lease, or otherwise acquire, own, hold, improve, employ, use and otherwise deal in and with real or personal property, or any interest therein, wherever situated, and to sell, convey, lease, exchange, transfer or otherwise dispose of, or mortgage or pledge, all or any of its property and assets, or any interest therein, wherever situated;

(5) Appoint such officers and agents as the business of the corporation requires and to pay or otherwise provide for them suitable compensation;

(6) Adopt, amend and repeal bylaws;

(7) Wind up and dissolve itself in the manner provided in this chapter;

(8) Conduct its business, carry on its operations and have offices and exercise its powers within or without this State;

(9) Make donations for the public welfare or for charitable, scientific or educational purposes, and in time of war or other national emergency in aid thereof;

(10) Be an incorporator, promoter or manager of other corporations of any type or kind;

(11) Participate with others in any corporation, partnership, limited partnership, joint venture or other association of any kind, or in any transaction, undertaking or arrangement which the participating corporation would have power to conduct by itself, whether or not such participation involves sharing or delegation of control with or to others;

(12) Transact any lawful business which the corporation's board of directors shall find to be in aid of governmental authority;

(13) Make contracts, including contracts of guaranty and suretyship, incur liabilities, borrow money at such rates of interest as the corporation may determine, issue its notes, bonds and other obligations, and secure any of its obligations by mortgage, pledge or other encumbrance of all or any of its property, franchises and income, and make contracts of guaranty and suretyship which are necessary or convenient to the conduct, promotion or attainment of the business of (a) a corporation all of the outstanding stock of which

is owned, directly or indirectly, by the contracting corporation, or (b) a corporation which owns, directly or indirectly, all of the outstanding stock of the contracting corporation, or (c) a corporation all of the outstanding stock of which is owned, directly or indirectly, by a corporation which owns, directly or indirectly, all of the outstanding stock of the contracting corporation, which contracts of guaranty and suretyship shall be deemed to be necessary or convenient to the conduct, promotion or attainment of the business of the contracting corporation, and make other contracts of guaranty and suretyship which are necessary or convenient to the conduct, promotion or attainment of the business of the contracting corporation;

(14) Lend money for its corporate purposes, invest and reinvest its funds, and take, hold and deal with real and personal property as security for the payment of funds so loaned or invested;

(15) Pay pensions and establish and carry out pension, profit sharing, stock option, stock purchase, stock bonus, retirement, benefit, incentive and compensation plans, trusts and provisions for any or all of its directors, officers and employees, and for any or all of the directors, officers and employees of its subsidiaries;

(16) Provide insurance for its benefit on the life of any of its directors, officers or employees, or on the life of any stockholder for the purpose of acquiring at such stock-

holder's death shares of its stock owned by such stockholder.

(17) Renounce, in its certificate of incorporation or by action of its board of directors, any interest or expectancy of the corporation in, or in being offered an opportunity to participate in, specified business opportunities or specified classes or categories of business opportunities that are presented to the corporation or 1 or more of its officers, directors or stockholders.

§ 124 Effect of lack of corporate capacity or power; ultra vires.

No act of a corporation and no conveyance or transfer of real or personal property to or by a corporation shall be invalid by reason of the fact that the corporation was without capacity or power to do such act or to make or receive such conveyance or transfer, but such lack of capacity or power may be asserted:

(1) In a proceeding by a stockholder against the corporation to enjoin the doing of any act or acts or the transfer of real or personal property by or to the corporation. If the unauthorized acts or transfer sought to be enjoined are being, or are to be, performed or made pursuant to any contract to which the corporation is a party, the court may, if all of the parties to the contract are parties to the proceeding and if it deems the same to be equitable, set aside and enjoin the performance of such contract, and in so doing may allow to the corporation or to the other parties to the contract, as the case may be, such

compensation as may be equitable for the loss or damage sustained by any of them which may result from the action of the court in setting aside and enjoining the performance of such contract, but anticipated profits to be derived from the performance of the contract shall not be awarded by the court as a loss or damage sustained;

(2) In a proceeding by the corporation, whether acting directly or through a receiver, trustee or other legal representative, or through stockholders in a representative suit, against an incumbent or former officer or director of the corporation, for loss or damage due to such incumbent or former officer's or director's unauthorized act;

(3) In a proceeding by the Attorney General to dissolve the corporation, or to enjoin the corporation from the transaction of unauthorized business.

§ 141 Board of directors; powers; number, qualifications, terms and quorum; committees; classes of directors; nonstock corporations; reliance upon books; action without meeting; removal.

(a) The business and affairs of every corporation organized under this chapter shall be managed by or under the direction of a board of directors, except as may be otherwise provided in this chapter or in its certificate of incorporation. If any such provision is made in the certificate of incorporation, the powers and duties conferred or imposed upon the board of directors by this chapter shall be exercised or performed to such extent and by such person or persons as shall be provided in the certificate of incorporation.

(b) The board of directors of a corporation shall consist of 1 or more members, each of whom shall be a natural person. The number of directors shall be fixed by, or in the manner provided in, the bylaws, unless the certificate of incorporation fixes the number of directors, in which case a change in the number of directors shall be made only by amendment of the certificate. Directors need not be stockholders unless so required by the certificate of incorporation or the bylaws. The certificate of incorporation or bylaws may prescribe other qualifications for directors. Each director shall hold office until such director's successor is elected and qualified or until such director's earlier resignation or removal. Any director may resign at any time upon notice given in writing or by electronic transmission to the corporation. A resignation is effective when the resignation is delivered unless the resignation specifies a later effective date or an effective date determined upon the happening of an event or events. A resignation which is conditioned upon the director failing to receive a specified vote for reelection as a director may provide that it is irrevocable. A majority of the total number of directors shall constitute a quorum for the transaction of business unless the certificate of incorporation or the bylaws require a greater number. Unless the certificate of incorporation provides otherwise, the bylaws may provide that a number less than a majority shall constitute a quorum which in no case shall be less than 1/3 of the total number of directors. The vote of the majority of the directors present at a meeting at which a quorum is present shall be the act of the board of directors unless the certificate of incorporation or the bylaws shall require a vote of a greater number.

(c)(1) All corporations incorporated prior to July 1, 1996, shall be governed by this paragraph (c)(1) of this section, provided that any such corporation may by a resolution adopted by a majority of the whole board elect to be governed by paragraph (c)(2) of this section, in which case this paragraph (c)(1) of this section shall not apply to such corporation. All corporations incorporated on or after July 1, 1996, shall be governed by paragraph (c)(2) of this section. The board of directors may, by resolution passed by a majority of the whole board, designate 1 or more committees, each committee to consist of 1 or more of the directors of the corporation. The board may designate 1 or more directors as alternate members of any committee, who may replace any absent or disqualified member at any meeting of the committee. The bylaws may provide that in the absence or disqualification of a member of a committee, the member or members present at any meeting and not disqualified from voting, whether or not the member or members present constitute a quorum, may unanimously appoint another member of the board of directors to act at the meeting in the place of any such absent or disqualified member. Any such committee, to the extent

provided in the resolution of the board of directors, or in the bylaws of the corporation, shall have and may exercise all the powers and authority of the board of directors in the management of the business and affairs of the corporation, and may authorize the seal of the corporation to be affixed to all papers which may require it; but no such committee shall have the power or authority in reference to amending the certificate of incorporation (except that a committee may, to the extent authorized in the resolution or resolutions providing for the issuance of shares of stock adopted by the board of directors as provided in § 151(a) of this title, fix the designations and any of the preferences or rights of such shares relating to dividends, redemption, dissolution, any distribution of assets of the corporation or the conversion into, or the exchange of such shares for, shares of any other class or classes or any other series of the same or any other class or classes of stock of the corporation or fix the number of shares of any series of stock or authorize the increase or decrease of the shares of any series), adopting an agreement of merger or consolidation under § 251, § 252, § 254, § 255, § 256, § 257, § 258, § 263 or § 264 of this title, recommending to the stockholders the sale, lease or exchange of all or substantially all of the corporation's property and assets, recommending to the stockholders a dissolution of the corporation or a revocation of a dissolution, or amending the bylaws of the corporation; and, unless the resolution, bylaws or certificate of incorporation expressly so provides, no such committee shall have the power or authority to declare a dividend, to authorize the issuance of stock or to adopt a certificate of ownership and merger pursuant to § 253 of this title.

(2) The board of directors may designate 1 or more committees, each committee to consist of 1 or more of the directors of the corporation. The board may designate 1 or more directors as alternate members of any committee, who may replace any absent or disqualified member at any meeting of the committee. The bylaws may provide that in the absence or disqualification of a member of a committee, the member or members present at any meeting and not disqualified from voting, whether or not such member or members constitute a quorum, may unanimously appoint another member of the board of directors to act at the meeting in the place of any such absent or disqualified member. Any such committee, to the extent provided in the resolution of the board of directors, or in the bylaws of the corporation, shall have and may exercise all the powers and authority of the board of directors in the management of the business and affairs of the corporation, and may authorize the seal of the corporation to be affixed to all papers which may require it; but no such committee shall have the power or authority in reference to the following matter: (i) approving or adopting, or recommending to the stockholders, any action or matter (other than the election or removal of directors) expressly required by this chapter to be submitted to stockholders

for approval or (ii) adopting, amending or repealing any bylaw of the corporation.

(3) Unless otherwise provided in the certificate of incorporation, the bylaws or the resolution of the board of directors designating the committee, a committee may create 1 or more subcommittees, each subcommittee to consist of 1 or more members of the committee, and delegate to a subcommittee any or all of the powers and authority of the committee. Except for references to committees and members of committees in subsection (c) of this section, every reference in this chapter to a committee of the board of directors or a member of a committee shall be deemed to include a reference to a subcommittee or member of a subcommittee.

(4) A majority of the directors then serving on a committee of the board of directors or on a subcommittee of a committee shall constitute a quorum for the transaction of business by the committee or subcommittee, unless the certificate of incorporation, the bylaws, a resolution of the board of directors or a resolution of a committee that created the subcommittee requires a greater or lesser number, provided that in no case shall a quorum be less than 1/3 of the directors then serving on the committee or subcommittee. The vote of the majority of the members of a committee or subcommittee present at a meeting at which a quorum is present shall be the act of the committee or subcommittee, unless the certificate of incorporation, the bylaws, a resolution of

the board of directors or a resolution of a committee that created the subcommittee requires a greater number.

(d) The directors of any corporation organized under this chapter may, by the certificate of incorporation or by an initial bylaw, or by a bylaw adopted by a vote of the stockholders, be divided into 1, 2 or 3 classes; the term of office of those of the first class to expire at the first annual meeting held after such classification becomes effective; of the second class 1 year thereafter; of the third class 2 years thereafter; and at each annual election held after such classification becomes effective, directors shall be chosen for a full term, as the case may be, to succeed those whose terms expire. The certificate of incorporation or bylaw provision dividing the directors into classes may authorize the board of directors to assign members of the board already in office to such classes at the time such classification becomes effective. The certificate of incorporation may confer upon holders of any class or series of stock the right to elect 1 or more directors who shall serve for such term, and have such voting powers as shall be stated in the certificate of incorporation. The terms of office and voting powers of the directors elected separately by the holders of any class or series of stock may be greater than or less than those of any other director or class of directors. In addition, the certificate of incorporation may confer upon 1 or more directors, whether or not elected separately by the holders of any class or series of stock, voting powers greater than or less than

those of other directors. Any such provision conferring greater or lesser voting power shall apply to voting in any committee, unless otherwise provided in the certificate of incorporation or bylaws. If the certificate of incorporation provides that 1 or more directors shall have more or less than 1 vote per director on any matter, every reference in this chapter to a majority or other proportion of the directors shall refer to a majority or other proportion of the votes of the directors.

(e) A member of the board of directors, or a member of any committee designated by the board of directors, shall, in the performance of such member's duties, be fully protected in relying in good faith upon the records of the corporation and upon such information, opinions, reports or statements presented to the corporation by any of the corporation's officers or employees, or committees of the board of directors, or by any other person as to matters the member reasonably believes are within such other person's professional or expert competence and who has been selected with reasonable care by or on behalf of the corporation.

(f) Unless otherwise restricted by the certificate of incorporation or bylaws, any action required or permitted to be taken at any meeting of the board of directors or of any committee thereof may be taken without a meeting if all members of the board or committee, as the case may be, consent thereto in writing, or by electronic transmission and the writing or writings or electronic transmission or transmissions are filed with the minutes of proceedings of the board, or committee. Such filing shall be in paper form if the minutes are maintained in paper form and shall be in electronic form if the minutes are maintained in electronic form. Any person (whether or not then a director) may provide, whether through instruction to an agent or otherwise, that a consent to action will be effective at a future time (including a time determined upon the happening of an event), no later than 60 days after such instruction is given or such provision is made and such consent shall be deemed to have been given for purposes of this subsection at such effective time so long as such person is then a director and did not revoke the consent prior to such time. Any such consent shall be revocable prior to its becoming effective.

(g) Unless otherwise restricted by the certificate of incorporation or bylaws, the board of directors of any corporation organized under this chapter may hold its meetings, and have an office or offices, outside of this State.

(h) Unless otherwise restricted by the certificate of incorporation or bylaws, the board of directors shall have the authority to fix the compensation of directors.

(i) Unless otherwise restricted by the certificate of incorporation or bylaws, members of the board of directors of any corporation, or any committee designated by the board, may participate in a meeting of such board, or committee by means of conference telephone or other communications equipment by means of which all persons participating in the meeting can hear each other, and participation in a meeting pursuant to this subsection shall constitute presence in person at the meeting.

(j) The certificate of incorporation of any nonstock corporation may provide that less than 1/3 of the members of the governing body may constitute a quorum thereof and may otherwise provide that the business and affairs of the corporation shall be managed in a manner different from that provided in this section. Except as may be otherwise provided by the certificate of incorporation, this section shall apply to such a corporation, and when so applied, all references to the board of directors, to members thereof, and to stockholders shall be deemed to refer to the governing body of the corporation, the members thereof and the members of the corporation, respectively; and all references to stock, capital stock, or shares thereof shall be deemed to refer to memberships of a nonprofit nonstock corporation and to membership interests of any other nonstock corporation.

(k) Any director or the entire board of directors may be removed, with or without cause, by the holders of a majority of the shares then entitled to vote at an election of directors, except as follows:

(1) Unless the certificate of incorporation otherwise provides, in the case of a corporation whose board is classified as

provided in subsection (d) of this section, stockholders may effect such removal only for cause; or

(2) In the case of a corporation having cumulative voting, if less than the entire board is to be removed, no director may be removed without cause if the votes cast against such director's removal would be sufficient to elect such director if then cumulatively voted at an election of the entire board of directors, or, if there be classes of directors, at an election of the class of directors of which such director is a part.

Whenever the holders of any class or series are entitled to elect 1 or more directors by the certificate of incorporation, this subsection shall apply, in respect to the removal without cause of a director or directors so elected, to the vote of the holders of the outstanding shares of that class or series and not to the vote of the outstanding shares as a whole.

§ 142 Officers; titles, duties, selection, term; failure to elect; vacancies.

(a) Every corporation organized under this chapter shall have such officers with such titles and duties as shall be stated in the bylaws or in a resolution of the board of directors which is not inconsistent with the bylaws and as may be necessary to enable it to sign instruments and stock certificates which comply with §§ 103(a)(2) and 158 of this title. One of the officers shall have the duty to record the proceedings of the meetings of the stockholders and directors

in a book to be kept for that purpose. Any number of offices may be held by the same person unless the certificate of incorporation or bylaws otherwise provide.

(b) Officers shall be chosen in such manner and shall hold their offices for such terms as are prescribed by the bylaws or determined by the board of directors or other governing body. Each officer shall hold office until such officer's successor is elected and qualified or until such officer's earlier resignation or removal. Any officer may resign at any time upon written notice to the corporation.

(c) The corporation may secure the fidelity of any or all of its officers or agents by bond or otherwise.

(d) A failure to elect officers shall not dissolve or otherwise affect the corporation.

(e) Any vacancy occurring in any office of the corporation by death, resignation, removal or otherwise, shall be filled as the bylaws provide. In the absence of such provision, the vacancy shall be filled by the board of directors or other governing body.

§ 152 Issuance of stock; lawful consideration; fully paid stock.

The consideration, as determined pursuant to § 153(a) and (b) of this title, for subscriptions to, or the purchase of, the capital stock to be issued by a corporation shall be paid in such form and in such manner as the board of directors shall determine. The board of directors may authorize capital stock to be issued for consideration consisting of cash, any tangible or intangible property or any benefit to the corporation, or any combination thereof. The resolution authorizing the issuance of capital stock may provide that any stock to be issued pursuant to such resolution may be issued in 1 or more transactions in such numbers and at such times as are set forth in or determined by or in the manner set forth in the resolution, which may include a determination or action by any person or body, including the corporation, provided the resolution fixes a maximum number of shares that may be issued pursuant to such resolution, a time period during which such shares may be issued and a minimum amount of consideration for which such shares may be issued. The board of directors may determine the amount of consideration for which shares may be issued by setting a minimum amount of consideration or approving a formula by which the amount or minimum amount of consideration is determined. The formula may include or be made dependent upon facts ascertainable outside the formula, provided the manner in which such facts shall operate upon the formula is clearly and expressly set forth in the formula or in the resolution approving the formula. In the absence of actual fraud in the transaction, the judgment of the directors as to the value of such consideration shall be conclusive. The capital stock so issued shall be deemed to be fully paid and nonassessable stock upon receipt by the corporation of such consideration; provided, however, nothing contained herein shall prevent the board of directors from issuing partly paid shares under § 156 of this title.

§ 211 Meetings of stockholders.

(a)(1) Meetings of stockholders may be held at such place, either within or without this State as may be designated by or in the manner provided in the certificate of incorporation or bylaws, or if not so designated, as determined by the board of directors. If, pursuant to this paragraph or the certificate of incorporation or the bylaws of the corporation, the board of directors is authorized to determine the place of a meeting of stockholders, the board of directors may, in its sole discretion, determine that the meeting shall not be held at any place, but may instead be held solely by means of remote communication as authorized by paragraph (a)(2) of this section.

(2) If authorized by the board of directors in its sole discretion, and subject to such guidelines and procedures as the board of directors may adopt, stockholders and proxyholders not physically present at a meeting of stockholders may, by means of remote communication:

a. Participate in a meeting of stockholders; and

b. Be deemed present in person and vote at a meeting of stockholders, whether such meeting is to be held at a designated place or solely by means of remote communication, provided that (i) the corporation shall implement reasonable measures to verify that each person deemed present and permitted to vote at the meeting by means of remote communication is a stockholder or proxyholder, (ii) the corporation shall implement reasonable measures to provide such stockholders and proxyholders a reasonable opportunity to participate in the meeting and to vote on matters submitted to the stockholders, including an opportunity to read or hear the proceedings of the meeting substantially concurrently with such proceedings, and (iii) if any stockholder or proxyholder votes or takes other action at the meeting by means of remote communication, a record of such vote or other action shall be maintained by the corporation.

(b) Unless directors are elected by written consent in lieu of an annual meeting as permitted by this subsection, an annual meeting of stockholders shall be held for the election of directors on a date and at a time designated by or in the manner provided in the bylaws. Stockholders may, unless the certificate of incorporation otherwise provides, act by written consent to elect directors; provided, however, that, if such consent is less than unanimous, such action by written consent may be in lieu of holding an annual meeting only if all of the directorships to which directors could be elected at an annual meeting held at the effective time of such action are vacant and are filled by such action. Any other proper business may be transacted at the annual meeting.

(c) A failure to hold the annual meeting at the designated time or to elect a sufficient number of directors to conduct the business of the corporation shall not affect otherwise valid corporate acts or work a forfeiture or dissolution of the corporation except as may be otherwise specifically provided in this chapter. If the annual meeting for election of directors is not held on the date designated therefor or action by written consent to elect directors in lieu of an annual meeting has not been taken, the directors shall cause the meeting to be held as soon as is convenient. If there be a failure to hold the annual meeting or to take action by written consent to elect directors in lieu of an annual meeting for a period of 30 days after the date designated for the annual meeting, or if no date has been designated, for a period of 13 months after the latest to occur of the organization of the corporation, its last annual meeting or the last action by written consent to elect directors in lieu of an annual meeting, the Court of Chancery may summarily order a meeting to be held upon the application of any stockholder or director. The shares of stock represented at such meeting, either in person or by proxy, and entitled to vote thereat, shall constitute a quorum for the purpose of such meeting, notwithstanding any provision of the certificate of incorporation or bylaws to the contrary. The Court of Chancery may issue such orders as may be appropriate, including, without limitation, orders designating the time and place of such meeting, the record date or dates for determination of stockholders entitled to notice of the meeting and to vote thereat, and the form of notice of such meeting.

(d) Special meetings of the stockholders may be called by the board of directors or by such person or persons as may be authorized by the certificate of incorporation or by the bylaws.

(e) All elections of directors shall be by written ballot unless otherwise provided in the certificate of incorporation; if authorized by the board of directors, such requirement of a written ballot shall be satisfied by a ballot submitted by electronic transmission, provided that any such electronic transmission must either set forth or be submitted with information from which it can be determined that the electronic transmission was authorized by the stockholder or proxy holder.

§ 212 Voting rights of stockholders; proxies; limitations.

(a) Unless otherwise provided in the certificate of incorporation and subject to § 213 of this title, each stockholder shall be entitled to 1 vote for each share of capital stock held by such stockholder. If the certificate of incorporation provides for more or less than 1 vote for any share, on any matter, every reference in this chapter to a majority or other proportion of stock, voting stock or shares shall refer to such majority or other proportion of the votes of such stock, voting stock or shares.

(b) Each stockholder entitled to vote at a meeting of stockholders or to express consent or dissent to corporate action in writing without a meeting may authorize another person or persons to act for such stockholder by proxy, but no such proxy shall be voted or acted upon after 3 years from its date, unless the proxy provides for a longer period.

(c) Without limiting the manner in which a stockholder may authorize another person or persons to act for such stockholder as proxy pursuant to subsection (b) of this section, the following shall constitute a valid means by which a stockholder may grant such authority:

(1) A stockholder may execute a writing authorizing another person or persons to act for such stockholder as proxy. Execution may be accomplished by the stockholder or such stockholder's authorized officer, director, employee or agent signing such writing or causing such person's signature to be affixed to such writing by any reasonable means including, but not limited to, by facsimile signature.

(2) A stockholder may authorize another person or persons to act for such stockholder as proxy by transmitting or authorizing the transmission of a telegram, cablegram, or other means of electronic transmission to the person who will be the holder of the proxy or to a proxy solicitation firm, proxy support service organization or like agent duly authorized by the person who will be the holder of the proxy to receive such transmission, provided that any such telegram, cablegram or other means of electronic transmission must either set forth or be submitted with information from which it can be determined that the telegram, cablegram or other electronic transmission was autho-

rized by the stockholder. If it is determined that such telegrams, cablegrams or other electronic transmissions are valid, the inspectors or, if there are no inspectors, such other persons making that determination shall specify the information upon which they relied.

(d) Any copy, facsimile telecommunication or other reliable reproduction of the writing or transmission created pursuant to subsection (c) of this section may be substituted or used in lieu of the original writing or transmission for any and all purposes for which the original writing or transmission could be used, provided that such copy, facsimile telecommunication or other reproduction shall be a complete reproduction of the entire original writing or transmission.

(e) A duly executed proxy shall be irrevocable if it states that it is irrevocable and if, and only as long as, it is coupled with an interest sufficient in law to support an irrevocable power. A proxy may be made irrevocable regardless of whether the interest with which it is coupled is an interest in the stock itself or an interest in the corporation generally.

§ 275 Dissolution generally; procedure.

(a) If it should be deemed advisable in the judgment of the board of directors of any corporation that it should be dissolved, the board, after the adoption of a resolution to that effect by a majority of the whole board at any meeting called for that purpose, shall cause notice of the adoption of the resolu-

tion and of a meeting of stockholders to take action upon the resolution to be mailed to each stockholder entitled to vote thereon as of the record date for determining the stockholders entitled to notice of the meeting.

(b) At the meeting a vote shall be taken upon the proposed dissolution. If a majority of the outstanding stock of the corporation entitled to vote thereon shall vote for the proposed dissolution, a certification of dissolution shall be filed with the Secretary of State pursuant to subsection (d) of this section.

(c) Dissolution of a corporation may also be authorized without action of the directors if all the stockholders entitled to vote thereon shall consent in writing and a certificate of dissolution shall be filed with the Secretary of State pursuant to subsection (d) of this section.

(d) If dissolution is authorized in accordance with this section, a certificate of dissolution shall be executed, acknowledged and filed, and shall become effective, in accordance with § 103 of this title. Such certificate of dissolution shall set forth:

(1) The name of the corporation;

(2) The date dissolution was authorized;

(3) That the dissolution has been authorized by the board of directors and stockholders of the corporation, in accordance with subsections (a) and (b) of this section, or that the dissolution has been authorized by all of the stockholders of the

corporation entitled to vote on a dissolution, in accordance with subsection (c) of this section;

(4) The names and addresses of the directors and officers of the corporation; and

(5) The date of filing of the corporation's original certificate of incorporation with the Secretary of State.

(e) The resolution authorizing a proposed dissolution may provide that notwithstanding authorization or consent to the proposed dissolution by the stockholders, or the members of a nonstock corporation pursuant to § 276 of this title, the board of directors or governing body may abandon such proposed dissolution without further action by the stockholders or members.

(f) Upon a certificate of dissolution becoming effective in accordance with § 103 of this title, the corporation shall be dissolved.

§ 342 Close corporation defined; contents of certificate of incorporation.

(a) A close corporation is a corporation organized under this chapter whose certificate of incorporation contains the provisions required by § 102 of this title and, in addition, provides that:

(1) All of the corporation's issued stock of all classes, exclusive of treasury shares, shall be represented by certificates and shall be held of record by not more than a specified number of persons, not exceeding 30; and

(2) All of the issued stock of all classes shall be subject to 1 or more of the restrictions on transfer permitted by § 202 of this title; and

(3) The corporation shall make no offering of any of its stock of any class which would constitute a "public offering" within the meaning of the United States Securities Act of 1933 [15 U.S.C. § 77a et seq.] as it may be amended from time to time.

(b) The certificate of incorporation of a close corporation may set forth the qualifications of stockholders, either by specifying classes of persons who shall be entitled to be holders of record of stock of any class, or by specifying classes of persons who shall not be entitled to be holders of stock of any class or both.

(c) For purposes of determining the number of holders of record of the stock of a close corporation, stock which is held in joint or common tenancy or by the entireties shall be treated as held by 1 stockholder.

§ 343 Formation of a close corporation.

A close corporation shall be formed in accordance with §§ 101, 102 and 103 of this title, except that:

(1) Its certificate of incorporation shall contain a heading stating the name of the corporation and that it is a close corporation; and

(2) Its certificate of incorporation shall contain the provisions required by § 342 of this title.

§ 351 Management by stockholders.

The certificate of incorporation of a close corporation may provide that the business of the corporation shall be managed by the stockholders of the corporation rather than by a board of directors. So long as this provision continues in effect:

(1) No meeting of stockholders need be called to elect directors;

(2) Unless the context clearly requires otherwise, the stockholders of the corporation shall be deemed to be directors for purposes of applying provisions of this chapter; and

(3) The stockholders of the corporation shall be subject to all liabilities of directors.

Such a provision may be inserted in the certificate of incorporation by amendment if all incorporators and subscribers or all holders of record of all of the outstanding stock, whether or not having voting power, authorize such a provision. An amendment to the certificate of incorporation to delete such a provision shall be adopted by a vote of the holders of a majority of all outstanding stock of the corporation, whether or not otherwise entitled to vote. If the certificate of incorporation contains a provision authorized by this section, the existence of such provision shall be noted conspicuously on the face or back of every stock certificate issued by such corporation.

§ 355 Stockholders' option to dissolve corporation.

(a) The certificate of incorporation of any close corporation may include a provision granting to any stockholder, or to the holders of any specified number or percentage of shares of any class of stock, an option to have the corporation dissolved at will or upon the occurrence of any specified event or contingency. Whenever any such option to dissolve is exercised, the stockholders exercising such option shall give written notice thereof to all other stockholders. After the expiration of 30 days following the sending of such notice, the dissolution of the corporation shall proceed as if the required number of stockholders having voting power had consented in writing to dissolution of the corporation as provided by § 228 of this title.

(b) If the certificate of incorporation as originally filed does not contain a provision authorized by subsection (a) of this section, the certificate may be amended to include such provision if adopted by the affirmative vote of the holders of all the outstanding stock, whether or not entitled to vote, unless the certificate of incorporation specifically authorizes such an amendment by a vote which shall be not less than 2/3 of all the outstanding stock whether or not entitled to vote.

(c) Each stock certificate in any corporation whose certificate of incorporation authorizes dissolution as permitted by this section shall conspicuously note on the face thereof the existence of the provision. Unless noted conspicuously on the face of the stock certificate, the provision is ineffective.

§ 362 Public benefit corporation defined; contents of certificate of incorporation.

(a) A "public benefit corporation" is a for-profit corporation organized under and subject to the requirements of this chapter that is intended to produce a public benefit or public benefits and to operate in a responsible and sustainable manner. To that end, a public benefit corporation shall be managed in a manner that balances the stockholders' pecuniary interests, the best interests of those materially affected by the corporation's conduct, and the public benefit or public benefits identified in its certificate of incorporation. In the certificate of incorporation, a public benefit corporation shall:

(1) Identify within its statement of business or purpose pursuant to § 102(a)(3) of this title 1 or more specific public benefits to be promoted by the corporation; and

(2) State within its heading that it is a public benefit corporation.

(b) "Public benefit" means a positive effect (or reduction of negative effects) on 1 or more categories of persons, entities, communities or interests (other than stockholders in their capacities as stockholders) including, but not limited to, effects of an artistic, charitable, cultural, economic, educational, environmental, literary, medical, religious, scientific or technological nature. "Public benefit provisions" means the provisions of

a certificate of incorporation contemplated by this subchapter.

(c) The name of the public benefit corporation may contain the words "public benefit corporation," or the abbreviation "P.B.C.," or the designation "PBC," which shall be deemed to satisfy the requirements of § 102(a)(l)(i) of this title. If the name does not contain such language, the corporation shall, prior to issuing unissued shares of stock or disposing of treasury shares, provide notice to any person to whom such stock is issued or who acquires such treasury shares that it is a public benefit corporation; provided that such notice need not be provided if the issuance or disposal is pursuant to an offering registered under the Securities Act of 1933 [15 U.S.C. § 77r et seq.] or if, at the time of issuance or disposal, the corporation has a class of securities that is registered under the Securities Exchange Act of 1934 [15 U.S.C. § 78a et seq.].

§ 365 Duties of directors.

(a) The board of directors shall manage or direct the business and affairs of the public benefit corporation in a manner that balances the pecuniary interests of the stockholders, the best interests of those materially affected by the corporation's conduct, and the specific public benefit or public benefits identified in its certificate of incorporation.

(b) A director of a public benefit corporation shall not, by virtue of the public benefit provisions or § 362(a) of this title, have any duty to any person on account of any interest of such person in the public benefit or public benefits identified in the certificate of incorporation or on account of any interest materially affected by the corporation's conduct and, with respect to a decision implicating the balance requirement in subsection (a) of this section, will be deemed to satisfy such director's fiduciary duties to stockholders and the corporation if such director's decision is both informed and disinterested and not such that no person of ordinary, sound judgment would approve.

(c) The certificate of incorporation of a public benefit corporation may include a provision that any disinterested failure to satisfy this section shall not, for the purposes of § 102(b)(7) or § 145 of this title, constitute an act or omission not in good faith, or a breach of the duty of loyalty.

§ 366 Periodic statements and third-party certification.

(a) A public benefit corporation shall include in every notice of a meeting of stockholders a statement to the effect that it is a public benefit corporation formed pursuant to this subchapter.

(b) A public benefit corporation shall no less than biennially provide its stockholders with a statement as to the corporation's promotion of the public benefit or public benefits identified in the certificate of incorporation and of the best interests of those materially affected by the corporation's conduct. The statement shall include:

(1) The objectives the board of directors has established to promote such public benefit or public benefits and interests;

(2) The standards the board of directors has adopted to measure the corporation's progress in promoting such public benefit or public benefits and interests;

(3) Objective factual information based on those standards regarding the corporation's success in meeting the objectives for promoting such public benefit or public benefits and interests; and

(4) An assessment of the corporation's success in meeting the objectives and promoting such public benefit or public benefits and interests.

(c) The certificate of incorporation or bylaws of a public benefit corporation may require that the corporation:

(1) Provide the statement described in subsection (b) of this section more frequently than biennially;

(2) Make the statement described in subsection (b) of this section available to the public; and/or

(3) Use a third-party standard in connection with and/or attain a periodic third-party certification addressing the corporation's promotion of the public benefit or public benefits identified in the certificate of incorporation and/or the best interests of those materially affected by the corporation's conduct.

6. JAMS Comprehensive Arbitration Rules & Procedures

JAMS COMPREHENSIVE ARBITRATION RULES & PROCEDURES (EFFECTIVE JULY 1, 2014)

(Reproduced by permission)

Rule 1. Scope of Rules

(a) The JAMS Comprehensive Arbitration Rules and Procedures ("Rules") govern binding Arbitrations of disputes or claims that are administered by JAMS and in which the Parties agree to use these Rules or, in the absence of such agreement, any disputed claim or counterclaim that exceeds $250,000, not including interest or attorneys' fees, unless other Rules are prescribed.

(b) The Parties shall be deemed to have made these Rules a part of their Arbitration agreement ("Agreement") whenever they have provided for Arbitration by JAMS under its Comprehensive Rules or for Arbitration by JAMS without specifying any particular JAMS Rules and the disputes or claims meet the criteria of the first paragraph of this Rule.

(c) The authority and duties of JAMS as prescribed in the Agreement of the Parties and in these Rules shall be carried out by the JAMS National Arbitration Committee ("NAC") or the office of JAMS General Counsel or their designees.

(d) JAMS may, in its discretion, assign the administration of an Arbitration to any of its Resolution Centers.

(e) The term "Party" as used in these Rules includes Parties to the Arbitration and their counsel or representatives.

(f) "Electronic filing" (e-file) means the electronic transmission of documents to and from JAMS and other Parties for the purpose of filing via the Internet. "Electronic service" (e-service) means the electronic transmission of documents via JAMS Electronic Filing System to a Party, attorney or representative under these Rules.

Rule 2. Party Self-Determination and Emergency Relief Procedures

(a) The Parties may agree on any procedures not specified herein or in lieu of these Rules that are consistent with the applicable law and JAMS policies (including, without limitation, Rules 15(i), 30 and 31). The Parties shall promptly notify JAMS of any such Party-agreed procedures and shall confirm such procedures in writing. The Party-agreed procedures shall be enforceable as if contained in these Rules.

(b) When an Arbitration Agreement provides that the Arbitration will be non-administered or administered by an entity other than JAMS and/or conducted in accordance with rules other than JAMS Rules, the Parties may subsequently agree to modify that Agreement to provide that the Arbitration will be administered by JAMS and/or conducted in accordance with JAMS Rules.

(c) Emergency Relief Procedures. These Emergency Relief Procedures are available in Arbitrations filed and served after July 1, 2014, and where not otherwise prohibited by law. Parties may agree to opt out of these Procedures in their Arbitration Agreement or by subsequent written agreement.

(i) A Party in need of emergency relief prior to the appointment of an Arbitrator may notify JAMS and all other Parties in writing of the relief sought and the basis for an Award of such relief. This Notice shall include an explanation of why such relief is needed on an expedited basis. Such Notice shall be given by facsimile, email or personal delivery. The Notice must include a statement certifying that all other Parties have been notified. If all other Parties have not been notified, the Notice shall include an explanation of the efforts made to notify such Parties.

(ii) JAMS shall promptly appoint an Emergency Arbitrator to rule on the emergency request. In most cases the appointment of an Emergency Arbitrator will be done within 24 hours of receipt of the request. The Emergency Arbitrator shall promptly disclose any circumstance likely, on the basis disclosed in the application, to affect the Arbitrator's ability to be impartial or independent. Any challenge to the appointment of the Emergency Arbitrator shall be made within 24 hours of the disclosures by the Emergency Arbitrator. JAMS will promptly review and decide any such challenge. JAMS' decision will be final.

(iii) Within two business days, or as soon as practicable thereafter, the Emergency Arbitrator shall establish a schedule for the consideration of the request for emergency relief. The schedule shall provide a reasonable opportunity for all Parties to be heard taking into account the nature of the relief sought. The Emergency Arbitrator has the authority to rule on his or her own jurisdiction and shall resolve any disputes with respect to the request for emergency relief.

(iv) The Emergency Arbitrator shall determine whether the Party seeking emergency relief has shown that immediate and irreparable loss or damage will result in the absence of emergency relief and whether the requesting Party is entitled to such relief. The Emergency Arbitrator shall enter an order or Award granting or denying the relief, as the case may be, and stating the reasons therefor.

(v) Any request to modify the Emergency Arbitrator's order or Award must be based on changed circumstances and may be made to the Emergency Arbitrator until such time as an Arbitrator or Arbitrators are appointed in accordance with the Parties' Agreement and JAMS' usual procedures. Thereafter, any request related to the relief granted or denied by the Emergency Arbitrator shall be determined by the Arbitrator(s) appointed in accordance with the Parties' Agreement and JAMS' usual procedures.

(vi) At the Emergency Arbitrator's discretion, any interim Award of emergency relief may be conditioned on the provision of adequate security by the Party seeking such relief.

Rule 3. Amendment of Rules

JAMS may amend these Rules without notice. The Rules in effect on the date of the commencement of an Arbitration (as defined in Rule 5) shall apply to that Arbitration, unless the Parties have agreed upon another version of the Rules.

Rule 4. Conflict with Law

If any of these Rules, or modification of these Rules agreed to by the Parties, is determined to be in conflict with a provision of applicable law, the provision of law will govern over the Rule in conflict, and no other Rule will be affected.

Rule 5. Commencing an Arbitration

(a) The Arbitration is deemed commenced when JAMS issues a Commencement Letter based upon the existence of one of the following:

(i) A post-dispute Arbitration Agreement fully executed by all Parties specifying JAMS administration or use of any JAMS Rules; or

(ii) A pre-dispute written contractual provision requiring the Parties to arbitrate the dispute or claim and specifying JAMS administration or use of any JAMS Rules or that the Parties agree shall be administered by JAMS; or

(iii) A written confirmation of an oral agreement of all Parties to participate in an Arbitration administered by JAMS or conducted pursuant to any JAMS Rules; or

(iv) The Respondent's failure to timely object to JAMS administration; or

(v) A copy of a court order compelling Arbitration at JAMS.

(b) The issuance of the Commencement Letter confirms that requirements for commencement have been met, that JAMS has received all payments required under the applicable fee schedule and that the Claimant has provided JAMS with contact information for all Parties along with evidence that the Demand for Arbitration has been served on all Parties.

(c) If a Party that is obligated to arbitrate in accordance with subparagraph (a) of this Rule fails to agree to participate in the Arbitration process, JAMS shall confirm in writing that Party's failure to respond or participate, and, pursuant to Rule 22(j), the Arbitrator, once appointed, shall schedule, and provide appropriate notice of, a Hearing or other opportunity for the Party demanding the Arbitration to demonstrate its entitlement to relief.

(d) The date of commencement of the Arbitration is the date of the Commencement Letter but is not intended to be applicable to any legal requirements such as the statute of limitations, any contractual limitations period or claims notice requirements. The term "commencement," as used in this Rule, is intended only to pertain to the operation of this and other Rules (such as Rules 3, 13(a), 17(a) and 31(a)).

Rule 6. Preliminary and Administrative Matters

(a) JAMS may convene, or the Parties may request, administrative conferences to discuss any procedural matter relating to the administration of the Arbitration.

(b) If no Arbitrator has yet been appointed, at the request of a Party and in the absence of Party agreement, JAMS may determine the location of the Hearing, subject to Arbitrator review. In determining the location of the Hearing, such factors as the subject matter of the dispute, the convenience of the Parties and witnesses, and the relative resources of the Parties shall be considered.

(c) If, at any time, any Party has failed to pay fees or expenses in full, JAMS may order the suspension or termination of the proceedings. JAMS may so inform the Parties in order that one of them may advance the required payment. If one Party advances the payment owed by a non-paying Party, the Arbitration shall proceed, and the Arbitrator may allocate the non-paying Party's share of such costs, in accordance with Rules 24(f) and 31(c). An administrative suspension shall toll any other time limits contained in these Rules or the Parties' Agreement.

(d) JAMS does not maintain an official record of documents filed in the Arbitration. If the Parties wish to have any documents returned to them, they must advise JAMS in writing within thirty (30) calendar days of the conclusion of the Arbitration. If special arrangements are required regarding file maintenance or document retention, they must be agreed to in writing, and JAMS reserves the right to impose an additional fee for such special arrangements. Documents that are submitted for e-filing are retained for thirty (30) calendar days following the conclusion of the Arbitration.

(e) Unless the Parties' Agreement or applicable law provides otherwise, JAMS, if it determines that the Arbitrations so filed have common issues of fact or law, may consolidate Arbitrations in the following instances:

(i) If a Party files more than one Arbitration with JAMS, JAMS may consolidate the Arbitrations into a single Arbitration.

(ii) Where a Demand or Demands for Arbitration is or are submitted naming Parties already involved in another Arbitration or Arbitrations pending under these Rules, JAMS may decide that the new case or cases shall be consolidated into one or more of the pending proceedings and referred to one of the Arbitrators or panels of Arbitrators already appointed.

(iii) Where a Demand or Demands for Arbitration is or are submitted naming Parties that are not identical to the Parties in the existing Arbitration or Arbitrations, JAMS may decide that the new case or cases shall be consolidated into one or more of the pending proceedings and referred to one of the Arbitrators or panels of Arbitrators already appointed.

When rendering its decision, JAMS will take into account all circumstances, including the links between the cases and the progress already made in the existing Arbitrations.

Unless applicable law provides otherwise, where JAMS decides to consolidate a proceeding into a pending Arbitration, the Parties to the consolidated case or cases will be deemed to have waived their right to designate an Arbitrator as well as any contractual provision with respect to the site of the Arbitration.

(f) Where a third party seeks to participate in an Arbitration already pending under these Rules or where a Party to an Arbitration under these Rules seeks to compel a third party to participate in a pending Arbitration, the Arbitrator shall determine such request, taking into account all circumstances he or she deems relevant and applicable.

Rule 7. Number and Neutrality of Arbitrators; Appointment and Authority of Chairperson

(a) The Arbitration shall be conducted by one neutral Arbitrator, unless all Parties agree otherwise. In these Rules, the term "Arbitrator" shall mean, as the context requires, the Arbitrator or the panel of Arbitrators in a tripartite Arbitration.

(b) In cases involving more than one Arbitrator, the Parties shall agree on, or, in the absence of agreement, JAMS shall designate, the Chairperson of the Arbitration Panel. If the Parties and the Arbitrators agree, a single member of the Arbitration Panel may, acting alone, decide discovery and procedural matters, including the conduct of hearings to receive documents and testimony from third parties who have been subpoenaed to produce documents.

(c) Where the Parties have agreed that each Party is to name one Arbitrator, the Arbitrators so named shall be neutral and independent of the appointing Party, unless the Parties have agreed that they shall be non-neutral.

Rule 8. Service

(a) The Arbitrator may at any time require electronic filing and service of documents in an Arbitration. If an Arbitrator requires electronic filing, the Parties shall maintain and regularly monitor a valid, usable and live email address for the receipt of all documents filed through JAMS Electronic Filing System. Any document filed electronically shall be considered as filed with JAMS when the transmission to JAMS Electronic Filing System is complete. Any document e-filed by 11:59 p.m. (of the sender's time zone) shall be deemed filed on that date. Upon completion of filing, JAMS Electronic Filing System shall issue a confirmation receipt that includes the date and time of receipt. The confirmation receipt shall serve as proof of filing.

(b) Every document filed with JAMS Electronic Filing System shall be deemed to have been signed by the Arbitrator, Case Manager, attorney or declarant who submits the document to JAMS Electronic Filing System, and shall bear the typed name, address and telephone number of a signing attorney. Documents containing signatures of third parties (i.e., unopposed motions, affidavits, stipulations, etc.) may also be filed electronically by indicating that the original signatures are maintained by the filing Party in paper format.

(c) Delivery of e-service documents through JAMS Electronic Filing System to other registered users shall be considered as valid and effective service and shall have the same legal effect as an original paper document. Recipients of e-service documents shall access their documents through JAMS Electronic Filing System. E-service shall be deemed complete when the Party initiating e-service completes the transmission of the electronic document(s) to JAMS Electronic Filing System for e-filing and/or e-service. Upon actual or constructive receipt of the electronic document(s) by the Party to be served, a Certificate of Electronic Service shall be issued by JAMS Electronic Filing System to the Party initiating e-service, and that Certificate shall serve as proof of service. Any Party who ignores or attempts to refuse e-service shall be deemed to have received the electronic document(s) 72 hours following the transmission of the electronic document(s) to JAMS Electronic Filing System.

(d) If an electronic filing or service does not occur because of (1) an error in the transmission of the document to JAMS Electronic Filing System or served Party that was unknown to the sending Party; (2) a failure to process the electronic document when received by JAMS Electronic Filing System; (3) the Party being erroneously excluded from the service list; or (4) other technical problems experienced by the filer, the Arbitrator or JAMS may, for good cause shown, permit the document to be filed *nunc pro tunc* to the date it was first attempted to be sent electronically. Or, in the case of service, the Party shall, absent extraordinary circumstances, be entitled to an order extending the date for any response or the period within which any right, duty or other act must be performed.

(e) For documents that are not filed electronically, service by a Party under these Rules is effected by providing one signed copy of the document to each Party and two copies in the case of a sole Arbitrator and four copies in the case of a tripartite panel to JAMS. Service may be made by hand-delivery, overnight delivery service or U.S. mail. Service by any of these means is considered effective upon the date of deposit of the document.

(f) In computing any period of time prescribed or allowed by these Rules for a Party to do some act within a prescribed period after the service of a notice or other paper on the Party and the notice or paper is served on the Party only by U.S. mail, three (3) calendar days shall be added to the prescribed period.

Rule 9. Notice of Claims

(a) Each Party shall afford all other Parties reasonable and timely notice of its claims, affirmative defenses or counterclaims. Any such notice shall include a short statement of its factual basis. No claim, remedy, counterclaim or affirmative defense will be considered by the Arbitrator in the absence of such prior notice to the other Parties, unless the Arbitrator determines that no Party has been unfairly prejudiced by such lack of formal notice or all Parties agree that such consideration is appropriate notwithstanding the lack of prior notice.

(b) Claimant's notice of claims is the Demand for Arbitration referenced in Rule 5. It shall include a statement of the remedies sought. The Demand for Arbitration may attach and incorporate a copy of a Complaint previously filed with a court. In the latter case, Claimant may accompany the Complaint with a copy of any Answer to that Complaint filed by any Respondent.

(c) Within fourteen (14) calendar days of service of the notice of claim, a Respondent may submit to JAMS and serve on other Parties a response and a statement of any affirmative defenses, including jurisdictional challenges, or counterclaims it may have.

(d) Within fourteen (14) calendar days of service of a counterclaim, a Claimant may submit to JAMS and serve on other Parties a response to such counterclaim and any affirmative defenses, including jurisdictional challenges, it may have.

(e) Any claim or counterclaim to which no response has been served will be deemed denied.

(f) Jurisdictional challenges under Rule 11 shall be deemed waived, unless asserted in a response to a Demand or counterclaim or promptly thereafter, when circumstances first suggest an issue of arbitrability.

Rule 10. Changes of Claims

After the filing of a claim and before the Arbitrator is appointed, any Party may make a new or different claim against a Party or any third party that is subject to Arbitration in the proceeding. Such claim shall be made in writing, filed with JAMS and served on the other Parties. Any response to the new claim shall be made within fourteen (14) calendar days after service of such claim. After the Arbitrator is appointed, no new or different claim may be submitted, except with the Arbitrator's approval. A Party may request a hearing on this issue. Each Party has the right to respond to any new or amended claim in accordance with Rule 9(c) or (d).

Rule 11. Interpretation of Rules and Jurisdictional Challenges

(a) Once appointed, the Arbitrator shall resolve disputes about the interpretation and applicability of these Rules and conduct of the Arbitration Hearing. The resolution of the issue by the Arbitrator shall be final.

(b) Jurisdictional and arbitrability disputes, including disputes over the formation, existence, validity, interpretation or scope of the agreement under which Arbitration is sought, and who are proper Parties to the Arbitration, shall be submitted to and ruled on by the Arbitrator. The Arbitrator has the authority to determine jurisdiction and arbitrability issues as a preliminary matter.

(c) Disputes concerning the appointment of the Arbitrator shall be resolved by JAMS.

(d) The Arbitrator may, upon a showing of good cause or *sua sponte*, when necessary to facilitate the Arbitration, extend any deadlines established in these Rules, provided that the time for rendering the Award may be altered only in accordance with Rules 22(i) or 24.

Rule 12. Representation

(a) The Parties, whether natural persons or legal entities such as corporations, LLCs or partnerships, may be represented by counsel or any other person of the Party's choice. Each Party shall give prompt written notice to the Case Manager and the other Parties of the name, address, telephone and fax numbers and email address of its representative. The representative of a Party may act on the Party's behalf in complying with these Rules.

(b) Changes in Representation. A Party shall give prompt written notice to the Case Manager and the other Parties of any change in its representation, including the name, address, telephone and fax numbers and email address of the new representative. Such notice shall state that the written consent of the former representative, if any, and of the new representative, has been obtained and shall state the effective date of the new representation.

Rule 13. Withdrawal from Arbitration

(a) No Party may terminate or withdraw from an Arbitration after the issuance of the Commencement Letter (see Rule 5), except by written agreement of all Parties to the Arbitration.

(b) A Party that asserts a claim or counterclaim may unilaterally withdraw that claim or counterclaim without prejudice by serving written notice on the other Parties and the Arbitrator. However, the opposing Parties may, within seven (7) calendar days of service of such notice, request that the Arbitrator condition the withdrawal upon such terms as he or she may direct.

Rule 14. Ex Parte Communications

(a) No Party may have any *ex parte* communication with a neutral Arbitrator, except as provided in section (b) of this Rule. The Arbitrator(s) may authorize any Party to communicate directly with the Arbitrator(s) by email or other written means as long as copies are simultaneously forwarded to the JAMS Case Manager and the other Parties.

(b) A Party may have *ex parte* communication with its appointed neutral or non-neutral Arbitrator as necessary to secure the Arbitrator's services and to assure the absence of conflicts, as well as in connection with the selection of the Chairperson of the arbitral panel.

(c) The Parties may agree to permit more extensive *ex parte* communication between a Party and a non-neutral Arbitrator. More extensive communication with a non-neutral Arbitrator may also be permitted by applicable law and rules of ethics.

Rule 15. Arbitrator Selection, Disclosures and Replacement

(a) Unless the Arbitrator has been previously selected by agreement of the Parties, JAMS may attempt to facilitate agreement among the Parties regarding selection of the Arbitrator.

(b) If the Parties do not agree on an Arbitrator, JAMS shall send the Parties a list of at least five (5) Arbitrator candidates in the case of a sole Arbitrator and ten (10) Arbitrator candidates in the case of a tripartite panel. JAMS shall also provide each Party with a brief description of the background and experience of each Arbitrator candidate. JAMS may replace any or all names on the list of Arbitrator candidates for reasonable cause at any time before the Parties have submitted their choice pursuant to subparagraph (c) below.

(c) Within seven (7) calendar days of service upon the Parties of the list of names, each Party may strike two (2) names in the case of a sole Arbitrator and three (3) names in the case of a tripartite panel, and shall rank the remaining Arbitrator candidates in order of preference. The remaining Arbitrator candidate with the highest composite ranking shall be appointed the Arbitrator. JAMS may grant a reasonable extension of the time to strike and rank the Arbitrator candidates to any Party without the consent of the other Parties.

(d) If this process does not yield an Arbitrator or a complete panel, JAMS shall designate the sole Arbitrator or as many members of the tripartite panel as are necessary to complete the panel.

(e) If a Party fails to respond to a list of Arbitrator candidates within seven (7) calendar days after its service, or fails to respond according to the instructions provided by JAMS, JAMS shall deem that Party to have accepted all of the Arbitrator candidates.

(f) Entities whose interests are not adverse with respect to the issues in dispute shall be treated as a single Party for purposes of the Arbitrator selection process. JAMS shall determine whether the interests between entities are adverse for purposes of Arbitrator selection, considering such factors as whether the entities are represented by the same attorney and whether the entities are presenting joint or separate positions at the Arbitration.

(g) If, for any reason, the Arbitrator who is selected is unable to fulfill the Arbitrator's duties, a successor Arbitrator shall be chosen in accordance with this Rule. If a member of a panel of Arbitrators becomes unable to fulfill his or her duties after the beginning of a Hearing but before the issuance of an Award, a new Arbitrator will be chosen in accordance with this Rule, unless, in the case of a tripartite panel, the Parties agree to proceed with the remaining two Arbitrators. JAMS will make the final determination as to whether an Arbitrator is unable to fulfill his or her duties, and that decision shall be final.

(h) Any disclosures regarding the selected Arbitrator shall be made as required by law or within ten (10) calendar days from the date of appointment. Such disclosures may be provided in electronic format, provided that JAMS will produce a hard copy to any Party that requests it. The Parties and their representatives shall disclose to JAMS any circumstance likely to give rise to justifiable doubt as to the Arbitrator's impartiality or independence, including any bias or any financial or personal interest in the result of the Arbitration or any past or present relationship with the Parties or their representatives. The obligation of the Arbitrator, the Parties and their representatives to make all required disclosures continues throughout the Arbitration process.

(i) At any time during the Arbitration process, a Party may challenge the continued service of an Arbitrator for cause. The challenge must be based upon information that was not available to the Parties at the time the Arbitrator was selected. A challenge for cause must be in writing and exchanged with opposing Parties, who may respond within seven (7) calendar days of service of the challenge. JAMS shall make the final determination as to such challenge. Such determination shall take into account the materiality of the facts and any prejudice to the Parties. That decision will be final.

(j) Where the Parties have agreed that a Party-appointed Arbitrator is to be non-neutral, that Party-appointed Arbitrator is not obliged to withdraw if requested to do so only by the Party who did not appoint that Arbitrator.

Rule 16. Preliminary Conference

At the request of any Party or at the direction of the Arbitrator, a Preliminary Conference shall be conducted with the Parties or their counsel or representatives. The Preliminary Conference may address any or all of the following subjects:

(a) The exchange of information in accordance with Rule 17 or otherwise;

(b) The schedule for discovery as permitted by the Rules, as agreed by the Parties or as required or authorized by applicable law;

(c) The pleadings of the Parties and any agreement to clarify or narrow the issues or structure the Arbitration Hearing;

(d) The scheduling of the Hearing and any pre-Hearing exchanges of information, exhibits, motions or briefs;

(e) The attendance of witnesses as contemplated by Rule 21;

(f) The scheduling of any dispositive motion pursuant to Rule 18;

(g) The premarking of exhibits, the preparation of joint exhibit lists and the resolution of the admissibility of exhibits;

(h) The form of the Award; and

(i) Such other matters as may be suggested by the Parties or the Arbitrator.

The Preliminary Conference may be conducted telephonically and may be resumed from time to time as warranted.

Rule 16.1. Application of Expedited Procedures

(a) If these Expedited Procedures are referenced in the Parties' agreement to arbitrate or are later agreed to by all Parties, they shall be applied by the Arbitrator.

(b) The Claimant or Respondent may opt into the Expedited Procedures. The Claimant may do so by indicating the election in the Demand for Arbitration. The Respondent may opt into the Expedited Procedures by so indicating in writing to JAMS with a copy to the Claimant served within fourteen (14) days of receipt of the Demand for Arbitration. If a Party opts into the Expedited

Procedures, the other side shall indicate within seven (7) calendar days of notice thereof whether it agrees to the Expedited Procedures.

(c) If one Party elects the Expedited Procedures and any other Party declines to agree to the Expedited Procedures, each Party shall have a client or client representative present at the first Preliminary Conference (which should, if feasible, be an in-person conference), unless excused by the Arbitrator for good cause.

Rule 16.2. Where Expedited Procedures Are Applicable

(a) The Arbitrator shall require compliance with Rule 17(a) prior to conducting the first Preliminary Conference. Each Party shall confirm in writing to the Arbitrator that it has so complied or shall indicate any limitations on full compliance and the reasons therefor.

(b) Document requests shall (1) be limited to documents that are directly relevant to the matters in dispute or to its outcome; (2) be reasonably restricted in terms of time frame, subject matter and persons or entities to which the requests pertain; and (3) not include broad phraseology such as "all documents directly or indirectly related to." The Requests shall not be encumbered with extensive "definitions" or "instructions." The Arbitrator may edit or limit the number of requests.

(c) E-Discovery shall be limited as follows:

(i) There shall be production of electronic documents only from sources used in the ordinary course of business. Absent a showing of compelling need, no such documents are required to be produced from backup servers, tapes or other media.

(ii) Absent a showing of compelling need, the production of electronic documents shall normally be made on the basis of generally available technology in a searchable format that is usable by the requesting Party and convenient and economical for the producing Party. Absent a showing of compelling need, the Parties need not produce metadata, with the exception of header fields for email correspondence.

(iii) The description of custodians from whom electronic documents may be collected should be narrowly tailored to include only those individuals whose electronic documents may reasonably be expected to contain evidence that is material to the dispute.

(iv) Where the costs and burdens of e-discovery are disproportionate to the nature of the dispute or to the amount in controversy, or to the relevance of the materials requested, the Arbitrator may either deny such requests or order disclosure on the condition that the requesting Party advance the reasonable cost of production to the other side, subject to the allocation of costs in the final Award.

(v) The Arbitrator may vary these Rules after discussion with the Parties at the Preliminary Conference.

(d) Depositions of percipient witnesses shall be limited as follows:

(i) The limitation of one discovery deposition per side (Rule 17(b)) shall be applied by the Arbitrator, unless it is determined, based on all relevant circumstances, that more depositions are warranted. The Arbitrator shall consider the amount in controversy, the complexity of the factual issues, the number of Parties and the diversity of their interests and whether any or all of the claims appear, on the basis of the pleadings, to have sufficient merit to justify the time and expense associated with the requested discovery.

(ii) The Arbitrator shall also consider the additional factors listed in the JAMS Recommended Arbitration Discovery Protocols for Domestic Commercial Cases.

(e) Expert depositions, if any, shall be limited as follows: Where written expert reports are produced to the other side in advance of the Hearing (Rule 17(a)), expert depositions may be conducted only by agreement of the Parties or by order of the Arbitrator for good cause shown.

(f) Discovery disputes shall be resolved on an expedited basis.

(i) Where there is a panel of three Arbitrators, the Parties are encouraged to agree, by rule or otherwise, that the Chair or another member of the panel is authorized to resolve discovery issues, acting alone.

(ii) Lengthy briefs on discovery matters should be avoided. In most cases, the submission of brief letters will sufficiently inform the Arbitrator with regard to the issues to be decided.

(iii) The Parties should meet and confer in good faith prior to presenting any issues for the Arbitrator's decision.

(iv) If disputes exist with respect to some issues, that should not delay the Parties' discovery on remaining issues.

(g) The Arbitrator shall set a discovery cutoff not to exceed seventy-five (75) calendar days after the Preliminary Conference for percipient discovery and not to exceed one hundred five (105) calendar days for expert discovery (if any). These dates may be extended by the Arbitrator for good cause shown.

(h) Dispositive motions (Rule 18) shall not be permitted, except as set forth in the JAMS Recommended Arbitration Discovery Protocols for Domestic Commercial Cases or unless the Parties agree to that procedure.

(i) The Hearing shall commence within sixty (60) calendar days after the cutoff for percipient discovery. Consecutive Hearing days shall be established unless otherwise agreed by the Parties or ordered by the Arbitrator. These dates may be extended by the Arbitrator for good cause shown.

(j) The Arbitrator may alter any of these Procedures for good cause.

Rule 17. Exchange of Information

(a) The Parties shall cooperate in good faith in the voluntary and informal exchange of all non-privileged documents and other information (including electronically stored information ("ESI")) relevant to the dispute or claim immediately after commencement of the Arbitration. They shall complete an initial exchange of all relevant, non-privileged documents, including, without limitation, copies of all documents in their possession or control on which they rely in support of their positions, and names of individuals whom they may call as witnesses at the Arbitration Hearing, within twenty-one (21) calendar days after all pleadings or notice of claims have been received. The Arbitrator may modify these obligations at the Preliminary Conference.

(b) Each Party may take one deposition of an opposing Party or of one individual under the control of the opposing Party. The Parties shall attempt to agree on the time, location and duration of the deposition. If the Parties do not agree, these issues shall be determined by the Arbitrator. The necessity of additional depositions shall be determined by the Arbitrator based upon the reasonable need for the requested information, the availability of other discovery options and the burdensomeness of the request on the opposing Parties and the witness.

(c) As they become aware of new documents or information, including experts who may be called upon to testify, all Parties continue to be obligated to provide relevant, non-privileged documents to supplement their identification of witnesses and experts and to honor any informal agreements or understandings between the Parties regarding documents or information to be exchanged. Documents that were not previously exchanged, or witnesses and experts that were not previously identified, may not be considered by the Arbitrator at the Hearing, unless agreed by the Parties or upon a showing of good cause.

(d) The Parties shall promptly notify JAMS when a dispute exists regarding discovery issues. A conference shall be arranged with the Arbitrator, either by telephone or in person, and the Arbitrator shall decide the dispute. With the written consent of all Parties, and in accordance with an agreed written procedure, the Arbitrator may appoint a special master to assist in resolving a discovery dispute.

Rule 18. Summary Disposition of a Claim or Issue

The Arbitrator may permit any Party to file a Motion for Summary Disposition of a particular claim or issue, either by agreement of all interested Parties or at the request of one Party, provided other interested Parties have reasonable notice to respond to the request.

Rule 19. Scheduling and Location of Hearing

(a) The Arbitrator, after consulting with the Parties that have appeared, shall determine the date, time and location of the Hearing. The Arbitrator and the Parties shall attempt to schedule consecutive Hearing days if more than one day is necessary.

(b) If a Party has failed to participate in the Arbitration process, the Arbitrator may set the Hearing without consulting with that Party. The non-participating Party shall be served with a Notice of Hearing at least thirty (30) calendar days prior to the scheduled date, unless the law of the relevant jurisdiction allows for, or the Parties have agreed to, shorter notice.

(c) The Arbitrator, in order to hear a third-party witness, or for the convenience of the Parties or the witnesses, may conduct the Hearing at any location. Any JAMS Resolution Center may be designated a Hearing location for purposes of the issuance of a subpoena or subpoena *duces tecum* to a third-party witness.

Rule 20. Pre-Hearing Submissions

(a) Except as set forth in any scheduling order that may be adopted, at least fourteen (14) calendar days before the Arbitration Hearing, the Parties shall file with JAMS and serve and exchange (1) a list of the witnesses they intend to call, including any experts; (2) a short description of the anticipated testimony of each such witness and an estimate of the length of the witness' direct testimony; (3) any written expert reports that may be introduced at the Arbitration Hearing; and (4) a list of all exhibits intended to be used at the Hearing. The Parties should exchange with each other copies of any such exhibits to the extent that they have not been previously exchanged. The Parties should pre-mark exhibits and shall attempt to resolve any disputes regarding the admissibility of exhibits prior to the Hearing.

(b) The Arbitrator may require that each Party submit a concise written statement of position, including summaries of the facts and evidence a Party intends to present, discussion of the applicable law and the basis for the requested Award or denial of relief sought. The statements, which may be in the form of a letter, shall be filed with JAMS and served upon the other Parties at least seven (7) calendar days before the Hearing date. Rebuttal statements or other pre-Hearing written submissions may be permitted or required at the discretion of the Arbitrator.

Rule 21. Securing Witnesses and Documents for the Arbitration Hearing

At the written request of a Party, all other Parties shall produce for the Arbitration Hearing all specified witnesses in their employ or under their control without need of subpoena. The Arbitrator may issue subpoenas for the attendance of witnesses or the production of documents either prior to or at the Hearing pursuant to this Rule or Rule 19(c). The subpoena or subpoena *duces tecum* shall be issued in accordance with the applicable law. Pre-issued subpoenas may be used in jurisdictions that permit them. In the event a Party or a subpoenaed person objects to the production of a witness or other evidence, the Party or subpoenaed person may file an objection with the Arbitrator, who shall promptly rule on the objection, weighing both the burden on the producing Party and witness and the need of the proponent for the witness or other evidence.

Rule 22. The Arbitration Hearing

(a) The Arbitrator will ordinarily conduct the Arbitration Hearing in the manner set forth in these Rules. The Arbitrator may vary these procedures if it is determined to be reasonable and appropriate to do so.

(b) The Arbitrator shall determine the order of proof, which will generally be similar to that of a court trial.

(c) The Arbitrator shall require witnesses to testify under oath if requested by any Party, or otherwise at the discretion of the Arbitrator.

(d) Strict conformity to the rules of evidence is not required, except that the Arbitrator shall apply applicable law relating to privileges and work product. The Arbitrator shall consider evidence that he or she finds relevant and material to the dispute, giving the evidence such weight as is appropriate. The Arbitrator may be guided in that determination by principles contained in the Federal Rules of Evidence or any other applicable rules of evidence. The Arbitrator may limit testimony to exclude evidence that would be immaterial or unduly repetitive, provided that all Parties are afforded the opportunity to present material and relevant evidence.

(e) The Arbitrator shall receive and consider relevant deposition testimony recorded by transcript or videotape, provided that the other Parties have had the opportunity to attend and cross-examine. The Arbitrator may in his or her discretion consider witness affidavits or other recorded testimony even if the other Parties have not had the opportunity to cross-examine, but will give that evidence only such weight as he or she deems appropriate.

(f) The Parties will not offer as evidence, and the Arbitrator shall neither admit into the record nor consider, prior settlement offers by the Parties or statements or recommendations made by a mediator or other person in connection with efforts to resolve the dispute being arbitrated, except to the extent that applicable law permits the admission of such evidence.

(g) The Hearing, or any portion thereof, may be conducted telephonically or videographically with the agreement of the Parties or at the discretion of the Arbitrator.

(h) When the Arbitrator determines that all relevant and material evidence and arguments have been presented, and any interim or partial Awards have been issued, the Arbitrator shall declare the Hearing closed. The Arbitrator may defer the closing of the Hearing until a date determined by the Arbitrator in order to permit the Parties to submit post-Hearing briefs, which may be in the form of a letter, and/or to make closing arguments. If post-Hearing briefs are to be submitted or closing arguments are to be made, the Hearing shall be deemed closed upon receipt by the Arbitrator of such briefs or at the conclusion of such closing arguments, whichever is later.

(i) At any time before the Award is rendered, the Arbitrator may, *sua sponte* or on application of a Party for good cause shown, reopen the Hearing. If the Hearing is reopened, the time to render the Award shall be calculated from the date the reopened Hearing is declared closed by the Arbitrator.

(j) The Arbitrator may proceed with the Hearing in the absence of a Party that, after receiving notice of the Hearing pursuant to Rule 19, fails to attend. The Arbitrator may not render an Award solely on the basis of the default or absence of the Party, but shall require any Party seeking relief to submit such evidence as the Arbitrator may require for the rendering of an Award. If the Arbitrator reasonably believes that a Party will not attend the Hearing, the Arbitrator may schedule the Hearing as a telephonic Hearing and may receive the evidence necessary to render an Award by affidavit. The notice of Hearing shall specify if it will be in person or telephonic.

(k) Any Party may arrange for a stenographic or other record to be made of the Hearing and shall inform the other Parties in advance of the Hearing.

(i) The requesting Party shall bear the cost of such stenographic record. If all other Parties agree to share the cost of the stenographic record, it shall be made available to the Arbitrator and may be used in the proceeding.

(ii) If there is no agreement to share the cost of the stenographic record, it may not be provided to the Arbitrator and may not be used in the proceeding, unless the Party arranging for the stenographic record agrees to provide access to the stenographic record either at no charge or on terms that are acceptable to the Parties and the reporting service.

(iii) If the Parties agree to the Optional Arbitration Appeal Procedure (Rule 34), they shall, if possible, ensure that a stenographic or other record is made of the Hearing and shall share the cost of that record.

(iv) The Parties may agree that the cost of the stenographic record shall or shall not be allocated by the Arbitrator in the Award.

Rule 23. Waiver of Hearing

The Parties may agree to waive the oral Hearing and submit the dispute to the Arbitrator for an Award based on written submissions and other evidence as the Parties may agree.

Rule 24. Awards

(a) The Arbitrator shall render a Final Award or a Partial Final Award within thirty (30) calendar days after the date of the close of the Hearing, as defined in Rule 22(h) or (i), or, if a Hearing has been waived, within thirty (30) calendar days after the receipt by the Arbitrator of all materials specified by the Parties, except (1) by the agreement of the Parties; (2) upon good cause for an extension of time to render the Award; or (3) as provided in Rule 22(i). The Arbitrator shall provide the Final Award or the Partial Final Award to JAMS for issuance in accordance with this Rule.

(b) Where a panel of Arbitrators has heard the dispute, the decision and Award of a majority of the panel shall constitute the Arbitration Award.

(c) In determining the merits of the dispute, the Arbitrator shall be guided by the rules of law agreed upon by the Parties. In the absence of such agreement, the Arbitrator shall be guided by the rules of law and equity that he or she deems to be most appropriate. The Arbitrator may grant any remedy or relief that is just and equitable and within the scope of the Parties' agreement, including, but not limited to, specific performance of a contract or any other equitable or legal remedy.

(d) In addition to a Final Award or Partial Final Award, the Arbitrator may make other decisions, including interim or partial rulings, orders and Awards.

(e) Interim Measures. The Arbitrator may grant whatever interim measures are deemed necessary, including injunctive relief and measures for the protection or conservation of property and disposition of disposable goods. Such interim measures may take the form of an interim or Partial Final Award, and the Arbitrator may require security for the costs of such measures. Any recourse by a Party to a court for interim or provisional relief shall not be deemed incompatible with the agreement to arbitrate or a waiver of the right to arbitrate.

(f) The Award of the Arbitrator may allocate Arbitration fees and Arbitrator compensation and expenses, unless such an allocation is expressly prohibited by the Parties' Agreement. (Such a prohibition may not limit the power of the Arbitrator to allocate Arbitration fees and Arbitrator compensation and expenses pursuant to Rule 31(c).)

(g) The Award of the Arbitrator may allocate attorneys' fees and expenses and interest (at such rate and from such date as the Arbitrator may deem appropriate) if provided by the Parties' Agreement or allowed by applicable law. When the Arbitrator is authorized to award attorneys' fees and must determine the reasonable amount of such fees, he or she may consider whether the failure of a Party to cooperate reasonably in the discovery process and/or comply with the Arbitrator's discovery orders caused delay to the proceeding or additional costs to the other Parties.

(h) The Award shall consist of a written statement signed by the Arbitrator regarding the disposition of each claim and the relief, if any, as to each claim. Unless all Parties agree otherwise, the Award shall also contain a concise written statement of the reasons for the Award.

(i) After the Award has been rendered, and provided the Parties have complied with Rule 31, the Award shall be issued by serving copies on the Parties. Service may be made by U.S. mail. It need not be sent certified or registered.

(j) Within seven (7) calendar days after service of a Partial Final Award or Final Award by JAMS, any Party may serve upon the other Parties and on JAMS a request that the Arbitrator correct any computational, typographical or other similar error in an Award (including the reallocation of fees pursuant to Rule 31(c) or on account of the effect of an offer to allow judgment), or the Arbitrator may *sua sponte* propose to correct such errors in an Award. A Party opposing such correction shall have seven (7) calendar days thereafter in which to file any objection. The Arbitrator may make any necessary and appropriate corrections to the Award within twenty-one (21) calendar days of receiving a request or fourteen (14) calendar days after his or her proposal to do so. The Arbitrator may extend the time within which to make corrections upon good cause. The corrected Award shall be served upon the Parties in the same manner as the Award.

(k) The Award is considered final, for purposes of either the Optional Arbitration Appeal Procedure pursuant to Rule 34 or a judicial proceeding to enforce, modify or vacate the Award pursuant to Rule 25, fourteen (14) calendar days after service is deemed effective if no request for a correction is made, or as of the effective date of service of a corrected Award.

Rule 25. Enforcement of the Award

Proceedings to enforce, confirm, modify or vacate an Award will be controlled by and conducted in conformity with the Federal Arbitration Act, 9 U.S.C. Sec 1, *et seq.*, or applicable state law. The Parties to an Arbitration under these Rules shall be deemed to have consented that judgment upon the Award may be entered in any court having jurisdiction thereof.

Rule 26. Confidentiality and Privacy

(a) JAMS and the Arbitrator shall maintain the confidential nature of the Arbitration proceeding and the Award, including the Hearing, except as necessary in connection with a judicial challenge to or enforcement of an Award, or unless otherwise required by law or judicial decision.

(b) The Arbitrator may issue orders to protect the confidentiality of proprietary information, trade secrets or other sensitive information.

(c) Subject to the discretion of the Arbitrator or agreement of the Parties, any person having a direct interest in the Arbitration may attend the Arbitration Hearing. The Arbitrator may exclude any non-Party from any part of a Hearing.

Rule 27. Waiver

(a) If a Party becomes aware of a violation of or failure to comply with these Rules and fails promptly to object in writing, the objection will be deemed waived, unless the Arbitrator determines that waiver will cause substantial injustice or hardship.

(b) If any Party becomes aware of information that could be the basis of a challenge for cause to the continued service of the Arbitrator, such challenge must be made promptly, in writing, to the Arbitrator or JAMS. Failure to do so shall constitute a waiver of any objection to continued service by the Arbitrator.

Rule 28. Settlement and Consent Award

(a) The Parties may agree, at any stage of the Arbitration process, to submit the case to JAMS for mediation. The JAMS mediator assigned to the case may not be the Arbitrator or a member of the Appeal Panel, unless the Parties so agree, pursuant to Rule 28(b).

(b) The Parties may agree to seek the assistance of the Arbitrator in reaching settlement. By their written agreement to submit the matter to the Arbitrator for settlement assistance, the Parties will be deemed to have agreed that the assistance of the Arbitrator in such settlement efforts will not disqualify the Arbitrator from continuing to serve as Arbitrator if settlement is not reached; nor shall such assistance be argued to a reviewing court as the basis for vacating or modifying an Award.

(c) If, at any stage of the Arbitration process, all Parties agree upon a settlement of the issues in dispute and request the Arbitrator to embody the agreement in a Consent Award, the Arbitrator shall comply with such request, unless the Arbitrator believes the terms of the agreement are illegal or undermine the integrity of the Arbitration process. If the Arbitrator is concerned about the possible consequences of the proposed Consent Award, he or she shall inform the Parties of that concern and may request additional specific information from the Parties regarding the proposed Consent Award. The Arbitrator may refuse to enter the proposed Consent Award and may withdraw from the case.

Rule 29. Sanctions

The Arbitrator may order appropriate sanctions for failure of a Party to comply with its obligations under any of these Rules or with an order of the Arbitrator. These sanctions may include, but are not limited to, assessment of Arbitration fees and Arbitrator compensation and expenses; assessment of any other costs occasioned by the actionable conduct, including reasonable attorneys' fees; exclusion of certain evidence; drawing adverse inferences; or, in extreme cases, determining an issue or issues submitted to Arbitration adversely to the Party that has failed to comply.

Rule 30. Disqualification of the Arbitrator as a Witness or Party and Exclusion of Liability

(a) The Parties may not call the Arbitrator, the Case Manager or any other JAMS employee or agent as a witness or as an expert in any pending or subsequent litigation or other proceeding involving the Parties and relating to the dispute that is the subject of the Arbitration. The Arbitrator, Case Manager and other JAMS employees and agents are also incompetent to testify as witnesses or experts in any such proceeding.

(b) The Parties shall defend and/or pay the cost (including any attorneys' fees) of defending the Arbitrator, Case Manager and/or JAMS from any subpoenas from outside parties arising from the Arbitration.

(c) The Parties agree that neither the Arbitrator, nor the Case Manager, nor JAMS is a necessary Party in any litigation or other proceeding relating to the Arbitration or the subject matter of the Arbitration, and neither the Arbitrator, nor the Case Manager, nor JAMS, including its employees or agents, shall be liable to any Party for any act or omission in connection with any Arbitration conducted under these Rules, including, but not limited to, any disqualification of or recusal by the Arbitrator.

Rule 31. Fees

(a) Each Party shall pay its *pro rata* share of JAMS fees and expenses as set forth in the JAMS fee schedule in effect at the time of the commencement of the Arbitration, unless the Parties agree on a different allocation of fees and expenses. JAMS› agreement to render services is jointly with the Party and the attorney or other representative of the Party in the Arbitration. The non-payment of fees may result in an administrative suspension of the case in accordance with Rule 6(c).

(b) JAMS requires that the Parties deposit the fees and expenses for the Arbitration from time to time during the course of the proceedings and prior to the Hearing. The Arbitrator may preclude a Party that has failed to deposit its *pro rata* or agreed-upon share of the fees and expenses from offering evidence of any affirmative claim at the Hearing.

(c) The Parties are jointly and severally liable for the payment of JAMS Arbitration fees and Arbitrator compensation and expenses. In the event that one Party has paid more than its share of such fees, compensation and expenses, the Arbitrator may award against any other Party any such fees, compensation and expenses that such Party owes with respect to the Arbitration.

(d) Entities whose interests are not adverse with respect to the issues in dispute shall be treated as a single Party for purposes of JAMS' assessment of fees. JAMS shall determine whether the interests between entities are adverse for purpose of fees, considering such factors as whether the entities are represented by the same attorney and whether the entities are presenting joint or separate positions at the Arbitration.

Rule 32. Bracketed (or High-Low) Arbitration Option

(a) At any time before the issuance of the Arbitration Award, the Parties may agree, in writing, on minimum and maximum amounts of damages that may be awarded on each claim or on all claims in the aggregate. The Parties shall promptly notify JAMS and provide to JAMS a copy of their written agreement setting forth the agreed-upon minimum and maximum amounts.

(b) JAMS shall not inform the Arbitrator of the agreement to proceed with this option or of the agreed-upon minimum and maximum levels without the consent of the Parties.

(c) The Arbitrator shall render the Award in accordance with Rule 24.

(d) In the event that the Award of the Arbitrator is between the agreed-upon minimum and maximum amounts, the Award shall become final as is. In the event that the Award is below the agreed-upon minimum amount, the final Award issued shall be corrected to reflect the agreed-upon minimum amount. In the event that the Award is above the agreed-upon maximum amount, the final Award issued shall be corrected to reflect the agreed-upon maximum amount.

Rule 33. Final Offer (or Baseball) Arbitration Option

(a) Upon agreement of the Parties to use the option set forth in this Rule, at least seven (7) calendar days before the Arbitration Hearing, the Parties shall exchange and provide to JAMS written proposals for the amount of money damages they would offer or demand, as applicable, and that they believe to be appropriate based on the standard set forth in Rule 24(c). JAMS shall promptly provide copies of the Parties' proposals to the Arbitrator, unless the Parties agree that they should not be provided to the Arbitrator. At any time prior to the close of the Arbitration Hearing, the Parties may exchange revised written proposals or demands, which shall supersede all prior proposals. The revised written proposals shall be provided to JAMS, which shall promptly provide them to the Arbitrator, unless the Parties agree otherwise.

(b) If the Arbitrator has been informed of the written proposals, in rendering the Award, the Arbitrator shall choose between the Parties' last proposals, selecting the proposal that the Arbitrator finds most reasonable and appropriate in light of the standard set forth in Rule 24(c). This provision modifies Rule 24(h) in that no written statement of reasons shall accompany the Award.

(c) If the Arbitrator has not been informed of the written proposals, the Arbitrator shall render the Award as if pursuant to Rule 24, except that the Award shall thereafter be corrected to conform to the closest of the last proposals and the closest of the last proposals will become the Award.

(d) Other than as provided herein, the provisions of Rule 24 shall be applicable.

Rule 34. Optional Arbitration Appeal Procedure

The Parties may agree at any time to the JAMS Optional Arbitration Appeal Procedure. All Parties must agree in writing for such procedure to be effective. Once a Party has agreed to the Optional Arbitration Appeal Procedure, it cannot unilaterally withdraw from it, unless it withdraws, pursuant to Rule 13, from the Arbitration.

7. Sample Corporate Bylaws (eBay, Inc.)

SAMPLE CORPORATE BYLAWS AMENDED AND RESTATED BYLAWS OF EBAY INC.

(a Delaware corporation)

eBay Inc. (the *"Corporation"*), pursuant to the provisions of Section 109 of the Delaware General Corporation Law, hereby adopts these Amended and Restated Bylaws, which restate, amend and supersede the bylaws of the Corporation, as previously amended and restated, in their entirety as described below:

ARTICLE I.

STOCKHOLDERS

SECTION 1.1: Place of Meetings. Meetings of the stockholders of the Corporation may be held at such place, either within or without the State of Delaware, as may be designated from time to time by the Board of Directors. The Board of Directors may, in its sole discretion, determine that the meeting shall not be held at any place, but may instead be held solely by means of remote communication as provided under the Delaware General Corporation Law.

SECTION 1.2: Annual Meetings. If required by applicable law, an annual meeting of stockholders shall be held for the election of directors at such date and time, as the Board of Directors shall each year fix. Any other proper business may be transacted at the annual meeting.

SECTION 1.3: Special Meetings.

(a) General. Special meetings of the stockholders, for any purpose or purposes described

in the notice of the meeting, may be called by (i) the Board of Directors pursuant to a resolution adopted by a majority of the total number of authorized directors (whether or not there exist any vacancies in previously authorized directorships at the time any such resolution is presented to the Board of Directors for adoption), (ii) the Chairman of the Board or (iii) the Chief Executive Officer of the Corporation, and shall be held at such place, if any, on such date, and at such time as they shall fix. Subject to the provisions of Section 1.3(b) and other applicable provisions of these bylaws, a special meeting of stockholders shall be called by the Secretary of the Corporation upon the written request (a *"Stockholder Requested Special Meeting"*) of one or more stockholders of record of the Corporation that together have continuously held, for their own account or on behalf of others, beneficial ownership of at least a twenty-five percent (25%) aggregate "net long position" of the outstanding common stock of the Corporation (the *"Requisite Percent"*) for at least thirty (30) days as of the date such request is delivered to the Corporation. For purposes of determining the Requisite Percent, "net long position" shall be determined with respect to each requesting holder in accordance with the definition thereof set forth in Rule 14e-4 under the Securities Exchange Act of 1934, as amended, and the rules and regulations thereunder (as so amended and inclusive of such rules and regulations, the *"Exchange Act"*); *provided* that (x) for purposes of such definition, (A) "the date that a tender offer is first publicly announced or otherwise made known by the bidder to the holders of the security to be acquired" shall be the date of the relevant Special Meeting Request, (B) the "highest tender offer price or stated amount of the consideration offered for the subject security" shall refer to the closing sales price of the Corporation's common stock on the NASDAQ Global Select Market (or any successor thereto) on such date (or, if such date is not a trading day, the next succeeding trading day), (C) the "person whose securities are the subject of the offer" shall refer to the Corporation, and (D) a "subject security" shall refer to the outstanding common stock of the Corporation; and (y) the net long position of such holder shall be reduced by the number of shares of common stock of the Corporation as to which such holder does not, or will not, have the right to vote or direct the vote at the special meeting or as to which such holder has entered into any derivative or other agreement, arrangement or understanding that hedges or transfers, in whole or in part, directly or indirectly, any of the economic consequences of ownership of such shares. Whether the requesting holders have complied with the requirements of this Article I and related provisions of the Bylaws shall be determined in good faith by the Board of Directors, which determina-

tion shall be conclusive and binding on the Corporation and the stockholders.

(b) Stockholder Requested Special Meetings. In order for a Stockholder Requested Special Meeting to be called, one or more requests for a special meeting (each, a *"Special Meeting Request,"* and collectively, the *"Special Meeting Requests"*) must be signed by the Requisite Percent of stockholders submitting such request and by each of the beneficial owners, if any, on whose behalf the Special Meeting Request is being made and must be delivered to the Secretary of the Corporation. The Special Meeting Request(s) shall be delivered to the Secretary of the Corporation at the principal executive offices of the Corporation by overnight express courier or registered mail, return receipt requested. Each Special Meeting Request shall (i) set forth a statement of the specific purpose(s) of the meeting and the matters proposed to be acted on at it, (ii) bear the date of signature of each such stockholder signing the Special Meeting Request, (iii) set forth (A) the name and address, as they appear in the Corporation's books, of each stockholder signing such request and the beneficial owners, if any, on whose behalf such request is made, and (B) the class, if applicable, and the number of shares of common stock of the Corporation that are owned of record and beneficially (within the meaning of Rule 13d-3 under the Exchange Act) by each such stockholder and the beneficial owners, if any, on whose behalf such request is made, (iv) include documentary evidence that the stockholders requesting the special meeting own the Requisite Percent as of the date on which the Special Meeting Request is delivered to the Secretary of the Corporation; *provided, however,* that if the stockholders are not the beneficial owners of the shares constituting all or part of the Requisite Percent, then to be valid, the Special Meeting Request must also include documentary evidence (or, if not simultaneously provided with the Special Meeting Request, such documentary evidence must be delivered to the Secretary of the Corporation within ten (10) days after the date on which the Special Meeting Request is delivered to the Secretary of the Corporation) that the beneficial owners on whose behalf the Special Meeting Request is made beneficially own such shares as of the date on which such Special Meeting Request is delivered to the Secretary of the Corporation, (v) an agreement by each of the stockholders requesting the special meeting and each beneficial owner, if any, on whose behalf the Special Meeting Request is being made to notify the Corporation promptly in the event of any decrease in the net long position held by such stockholder or beneficial owner following the delivery of such Special Meeting Request and prior to the special meeting and an acknowledgement that any such decrease shall be deemed to be a revocation of such Special Meeting Request by such stockholder or beneficial owner to the extent of such reduction, and (vi) contain the information required by Section 1.14 and Section 1.15, as applicable, provided that all references to "Proposing Person" in Section 1.14 and all references to "Nominating Person" in Section 1.15 shall, for purposes of this Section 1.3(b), mean (i) the stockholders of record making the Special Meeting Request, (ii) any beneficial owner or beneficial owners, if different, on whose behalf the Special Meeting Request is being made, and (iii) any affiliate or associate (each within the meaning of Rule 12b-2 under the Exchange Act for purposes of these Bylaws) of such stockholder or beneficial owner. Each stockholder making a Special Meeting Request and each beneficial owner, if any, on whose behalf the Special Meeting Request is being made is required to update the notice delivered pursuant to this Section 1.3(b) in accordance with Section 1.14(d) or Section 1.15(d), as applicable. Any requesting stockholder may revoke his, her or its Special Meeting Request at any time prior to the special meeting by written revocation delivered to the Secretary of the Corporation at the principal executive offices of the Corporation. If at any time after sixty (60) days following the earliest dated Special Meeting Request, the unrevoked (whether by specific written revocation by the stockholder or pursuant to clause (b)(v) of this Section 1.3) valid Special Meeting Requests represent in the aggregate less than the Requisite Percent, then the requesting stockholder(s) or beneficial owner(s) shall be deemed to have withdrawn such request (in connection with which the Board may cancel the meeting).

In determining whether a special meeting of stockholders has been requested by stockholders holding in the aggregate at least the Requisite Percent, multiple Special Meeting Requests delivered to the Secretary of the Corporation will be considered together only if (i) each Special Meeting Request identifies substantially the same purpose or purposes of the special meeting and substantially the same matters proposed to be acted on at the special meeting (in each case as determined in good faith by the Board of Directors), and (ii) such Special Meeting Requests have been delivered to the Secretary of the Corporation within sixty (60) days of the earliest dated Special Meeting Request.

(c) Calling of a Special Meeting. Except as provided in the next sentence, a special meeting requested by stockholders shall be held at such date, time and place within or without the State of Delaware as may be fixed by the Board of Directors; *provided, however*, that the date of any such special meeting shall be not more than ninety (90) days after the date on which valid Special Meeting Request(s) constituting the Requisite Percent are delivered to the Secretary of the Corporation (such date of delivery being the "*Delivery Date*"). Notwithstanding the foregoing, the Secretary of the Corporation shall not be required to call a special meeting of stockholders if (i) the Board of Directors calls an annual meeting of stockholders, or a special meeting of stockholders at which a Similar Item (as defined in this Section 1.3(c)) is to be presented pursuant to the notice of such meeting, in either case to be held not later than sixty (60) days after the Delivery Date; (ii) the Delivery Date

is during the period commencing ninety (90) days prior to the first anniversary of the date of the immediately preceding annual meeting and ending on the earlier of (A) the date of the next annual meeting and (B) thirty (30) days after the first anniversary of the date of the immediately preceding annual meeting; or (iii) the Special Meeting Request(s) (A) contain an identical or substantially similar item (as determined in good faith by the Board of Directors, a "*Similar Item*") to an item that was presented at any meeting of stockholders held not more than one hundred and twenty (120) days before the Delivery Date (and, for purposes of this clause (iii) the election of directors shall be deemed a "Similar Item" with respect to all items of business involving the election or removal of directors); (B) relate to an item of business that is not a proper subject for action by the stockholders under applicable law; (C) were made in a manner that involved a violation of Regulation 14A under the Exchange Act or other applicable law; or (D) do not comply with the provisions of this Section 1.3.

(d) Business Transacted at a Special Meeting. Business transacted at any Stockholder Requested Special Meeting shall be limited to the purpose or purposes stated in the Special Meeting Request(s) for such special meeting; *provided, however*, that nothing herein shall prohibit the Board of Directors from submitting additional matters to stockholders at any such special meeting pursuant to the Corporation's notice of meeting. If none of the stockholders who submitted a Special Meeting Request appears at or sends a duly authorized representative to the Stockholder Requested Special Meeting to present the matters to be presented for consideration that were specified in the Special Meeting Request, the corporation need not present such matters for a vote at such meeting.

SECTION 1.4: Notice of Meetings. Notice of all meetings of stockholders shall be given that shall state the place, if any, date and time of the meeting, the means of remote communications, if any, by which stockholders and proxy holders may be deemed to be present in person and vote at such meeting and, in the case of a special meeting, the purpose or purposes for which the meeting is called. Unless otherwise required by applicable law or the Certificate of Incorporation of the Corporation as currently in effect (the *"Certificate of Incorporation"*), such notice shall be given not less than ten (10) nor more than sixty (60) days before the date of the meeting to each stockholder entitled to vote at such meeting.

SECTION 1.5: Manner of Giving Notice; Affidavit of Notice.

(a) Notice of any meeting of stockholders, if mailed, is given when deposited in the United States mail, postage prepaid, directed to the stockholder at his, her or its address as it appears on the records of the Corporation.

(b) Except as otherwise prohibited by the Delaware General Corporation Law and without limiting the foregoing, any notice to stockholders given by the Corporation under

any provision of the Delaware General Corporation Law, the Certificate of Incorporation or these Bylaws shall be effective if given by a form of electronic transmission consented to (and not properly revoked by written notice to the Corporation) by the stockholder to whom the notice is given, to the extent such consent is required by the Delaware General Corporation Law. Any such consent shall be revocable by the stockholder by written notice to the Corporation. Any such consent shall be deemed revoked if (i) the Corporation is unable to deliver by electronic transmission two (2) consecutive notices given by the Corporation in accordance with such consent and (ii) such inability becomes known to the Secretary or an Assistant Secretary of the Corporation or to the transfer agent of the Corporation, or other person responsible for the giving of notice; *provided, however*, the inadvertent failure to treat such inability as a revocation shall not invalidate any meeting or other action. Any such notice shall be deemed given (i) if by facsimile telecommunication, when directed to a number at which the stockholder has consented to receive notice; (ii) if by electronic mail, when directed to an electronic mail address at which the stockholder has consented to receive notice; (iii) if by a posting on an electronic network together with separate notice to the stockholder of such specific posting, upon the later of (A) such posting and (B) the giving of such separate notice; and (iv) if by any other form of electronic transmission, when directed to the stockholder.

(c) For the purposes of these Bylaws, an *"electronic transmission"* means any form of communication, not directly involving the physical transmission of paper, that creates a record that may be retained, retrieved and reviewed by a recipient thereof, and that may be directly reproduced in paper form by such a recipient through an automated process.

(d) Except as otherwise prohibited under the Delaware General Corporation Law and without limiting the manner by which notice otherwise may be given to stockholders, any notice to stockholders given by the Corporation under any provision of the Delaware General Corporation Law, the Certificate of Incorporation or these Bylaws may be given by a single written notice to stockholders who share an address if consented to by the stockholders at that address to whom such notice is given. Such consent shall have been deemed to have been given if a stockholder fails to object in writing to the Corporation within sixty (60) days of having been given written notice by the Corporation of its intention to send the single notice in accordance with this Section 1.5(d). Any such consent shall be revocable by the stockholders by written notice to the Corporation.

(e) An affidavit of the Secretary or an Assistant Secretary of the Corporation or of the transfer agent or other agent of the Corporation that the notice has been given shall, in the absence of fraud, be *prima facie* evidence of the facts stated therein.

SECTION 1.6: Adjournments. Any meeting of stockholders may adjourn from time to time to reconvene at the same or another place, if any, or by means of remote communications, if any, by which stockholders and proxy holders may be deemed to be present in person and vote at such meeting, and notice need not be given of any such adjourned meeting if the place, if any, time and date thereof, and the means of remote communications, if any, by which stockholders and proxy holders may be deemed to be present in person and vote at such adjourned meeting are announced at the meeting at which the adjournment is taken; *provided, however,* that if the adjournment is for more than thirty (30) days, or if after the adjournment a new record date is fixed for the adjourned meeting, then a notice of the adjourned meeting shall be given to each stockholder of record entitled to vote at the meeting. At the adjourned meeting the Corporation may transact any business that might have been transacted at the original meeting.

SECTION 1.7: Quorum. At each meeting of stockholders the holders of a majority of the shares of stock entitled to vote at the meeting, present in person or represented by proxy, shall constitute a quorum for the transaction of business, except if otherwise required by applicable law. Where a separate vote by a class or classes or series is required, a majority of the shares of such class or classes or series then outstanding and entitled to vote present in person or by proxy shall constitute a quorum entitled to take action with respect to that vote on that matter. If a quorum shall fail to attend any meeting, the chairman of the meeting or the holders of a majority of the shares entitled to vote who are present, in person or by proxy, at the meeting may adjourn the meeting. Shares of the Corporation's stock belonging to the Corporation (or to another corporation, if a majority of the shares entitled to vote in the election of directors of such other corporation are held, directly or indirectly, by the Corporation), shall neither be entitled to vote nor be counted for quorum purposes; *provided, however*, that the foregoing shall not limit the right of the Corporation or any other corporation to vote any shares of the Corporation's stock held by it in a fiduciary capacity.

SECTION 1.8: Conduct of Business. Meetings of stockholders shall be presided over by such person as the Board of Directors may designate as chairman of the meeting, or, in the absence of such a person, the Chairman of the Board, or, in the absence of such person, the President of the Corporation, or, in the absence of such person, such person as may be chosen by the holders of a majority of the shares entitled to vote who are present, in person or by proxy, at the meeting. The Secretary of the Corporation shall act as secretary of the meeting, but in his or her absence the chairman of the meeting may appoint any person to act as secretary of the meeting. The Board of Directors shall be entitled to make such rules or regulations for the conduct of meetings of stockholders as it shall deem necessary, appropriate or convenient. Subject to such rules and regulations of the Board of Directors, if any, the chairman of the meeting shall have the right and authority to prescribe such rules, regulations and procedures and to do all such acts as, in the judgment of such chairman, are necessary, appropriate or convenient for the proper conduct of the meeting,

including, without limitation, adjourning the meeting if the chairman determines in his or her sole discretion that an adjournment is advisable, establishing an agenda or order of business for the meeting, rules and procedures for maintaining order at the meeting and the safety of those present, limitations on participation in the meeting to stockholders of record of the Corporation, their duly authorized and constituted proxies and such other persons as the chairman shall permit, restrictions on entry to the meeting after the time fixed for the commencement thereof, limitations on the time allotted to questions or comments by participants and regulation of the opening and closing of the polls for balloting and matters which are to be voted on by ballot.

SECTION 1.9: Voting; Proxies. Unless otherwise provided by law or the Certificate of Incorporation, each stockholder shall be entitled to one (1) vote for each share of stock held by such stockholder of record according to the records of the Corporation. The stockholders entitled to vote at any meeting of stockholders shall be determined in accordance with the provisions of Section 1.11 of these Bylaws, subject to Section 217 (relating to voting rights of fiduciaries, pledgors and joint owners of stock) and Section 218 (relating to voting trusts and other voting agreements) of the Delaware General Corporation Law. Each stockholder entitled to vote at a meeting of stockholders may authorize another person or persons to act for such stockholder by proxy. Such a proxy may be prepared, transmitted and delivered in any manner permitted by applicable law. Unless otherwise provided in the Certificate of Incorporation or a Certificate of Designation relating to a series of Preferred Stock, directors shall be elected as provided in Section 2.2 of these Bylaws. Unless otherwise provided by applicable law, the rules or regulations of any stock exchange applicable to the Corporation, the Certificate of Incorporation or these Bylaws, every matter other than the election of directors shall be decided by the affirmative vote of the holders of a majority in voting power of the shares of stock entitled to vote thereon that are present in person or represented by proxy at the meeting.

SECTION 1.10: [Intentionally Omitted.]

SECTION 1.11: Fixing Date for Determination of Stockholders of Record. In order that the Corporation may determine the stockholders entitled to notice of or to vote at any meeting of stockholders or any adjournment thereof or entitled to receive payment of any dividend or other distribution or allotment of any rights, or entitled to exercise any rights in respect of any change, conversion or exchange of stock or for the purpose of any other lawful action, the Board of Directors may fix, in advance, a record date, which (i) in the case of determination of stockholders entitled to vote at any meeting of stockholders or adjournment thereof, shall, unless otherwise required by law, not be more than sixty (60) nor less than ten (10) days before the date of such meeting, and (ii) in the case of any other action, shall not be more than sixty (60) days prior to any such other action. If no record date is fixed by the Board of Directors, then the record date shall be as provided by applicable law. A determination of stockholders of record entitled to notice of or to vote at a meeting of stockholders shall apply to any adjournment of the meeting; *provided, however,* that the Board of Directors may fix a new record date for the adjourned meeting.

SECTION 1.12: List of Stockholders Entitled to Vote. A complete list of stockholders entitled to vote at any meeting of stockholders, arranged in alphabetical order and showing the address of each stockholder and the number of shares registered in the name of each stockholder, shall be open to the examination of any stockholder, for any purpose germane to the meeting, for a period of at least ten (10) days prior to the meeting, (i) on a reasonably accessible electronic network, provided that the information required to gain access to such list is provided with the notice of the meeting, or (ii) during ordinary business hours, at the principal place of business of the Corporation. In the event that the Corporation determines to make the list available on an electronic network, the Corporation may take reasonable steps to ensure that such information is available only to the stockholders of the Corporation. If the meeting is to be held at a place, then the list shall be produced and kept at the time and place of the meeting during the whole time thereof and may be inspected by any stockholder who is present. If the meeting is to be held solely by means of remote communication, then the list shall also be open to the examination of any stockholder during the whole time of the meeting on a reasonably accessible electronic network, and the information required to access such list shall be provided with the notice of the meeting. Except as otherwise provided by law, such list shall be the only evidence as to who are the stockholders entitled to examine the list of stockholders required by this Section 1.12

or to vote in person or by proxy at any meeting of the stockholders. The Corporation shall not be required to include electronic mail addresses or other electronic contact information on such list.

SECTION 1.13: Inspectors of Elections.

(a) Applicability. Unless otherwise provided in the Corporation's Certificate of Incorporation or required by the Delaware General Corporation Law, the following provisions of this Section 1.13 shall apply only if and when the Corporation has a class of voting stock that is:

(i) listed on a national securities exchange;

(ii) authorized for quotation on an interdealer quotation system of a registered national securities association; or

(iii) held of record by more than 2,000 stockholders; in all other cases, observance of the provisions of this Section 1.13 shall be optional, and at the discretion of the Corporation.

(b) Appointment. The Corporation shall, in advance of any meeting of stockholders, appoint one or more inspectors of election to act at the meeting and make a written report thereof. The Corporation may designate one or more persons as alternate inspectors to replace any inspector who fails to act. If no inspector or alternate is able to act at a meeting of stockholders, the person presiding at the meeting shall appoint one or more inspectors to act at the meeting.

(c) Inspector's Oath. Each inspector of election, before entering upon the discharge of his or her duties, shall take and sign an oath faithfully to execute the duties of inspector with strict impartiality and according to the best of his or her ability.

(d) Duties of Inspectors. At a meeting of stockholders, the inspectors of election shall

(i) ascertain the number of shares outstanding and the voting power of each share;

(ii) determine the shares represented at a meeting and the validity of proxies and ballots;

(iii) count all votes and ballots;

(iv) determine and retain for a reasonable period of time a record of the disposition of any challenges made to any determination by the inspectors; and

(v) certify their determination of the number of shares represented at the meeting, and their count of all votes and ballots. The inspectors may appoint or retain other persons or entities to assist the inspectors in the performance of the duties of the inspectors.

(e) Opening and Closing of Polls. The date and time of the opening and the closing of the polls for each matter upon which the stockholders will vote at a meeting shall be announced by the inspectors at the meeting. No ballot, proxies or votes, nor any revocations thereof or changes thereto, shall be accepted by the inspectors after the closing of the polls unless the Court of Chancery upon application by a stockholder shall determine otherwise.

(f) Determinations. In determining the validity and counting of proxies and ballots, the inspectors shall be limited to an examination of the proxies, any envelopes submitted with those proxies, any information provided in connection with proxies in accordance with Section 211(e) or Section 212(c)(2) of the Delaware General Corporation Law, or any information provided pursuant to Section 211(a)(2)(B) (i) or (iii) of the Delaware General Corporation Law, ballots and the regular books and records of the Corporation, except that the inspectors may consider other reliable information for the limited purpose of reconciling proxies and ballots submitted by or on behalf of banks, brokers, their nominees or similar persons which represent more votes than the holder of a proxy is authorized by the record owner to cast or more votes than the stockholder holds of record. If the inspectors consider other reliable information for the limited purpose permitted herein, the inspectors at the time they make their certification of their determinations pursuant to this Section 1.13 shall specify the precise information considered by them, including the person or persons from whom they obtained the information, when the information was obtained, the means by which the information was obtained and the basis for

the inspectors' belief that such information is accurate and reliable.

SECTION 1.14: Notice of Stockholder Business to be Brought Before an Annual or Special Meeting.

(a) Business Properly Brought Before an Annual or Special Meeting. At an annual meeting of the stockholders, only such business shall be conducted as shall have been properly brought before the meeting. To be properly brought before an annual meeting, business must be

(i) brought before the meeting by the Corporation and specified in the notice of meeting given by or at the direction of the Board of Directors, (ii) brought before the meeting by or at the direction of the Board of Directors, or (iii) otherwise properly brought before the meeting by a stockholder who (A) was a stockholder of record (and, with respect to any beneficial owner, if different, on whose behalf such business is proposed, only if such beneficial owner was the beneficial owner of shares of the Corporation) both at the time of giving the notice provided for in this Section 1.14 and at the time of the meeting, (B) is entitled to vote at the meeting, and (C) has complied with this Section 1.14 as to such business. Except for proposals properly made in accordance with Rule 14a-8 under the Exchange Act, and included in the notice of meeting given by or at the direction of the Board of Directors, the foregoing clause (iii) shall be the exclusive means for a stockholder to propose business to be brought before an annual meeting of the stockholders. Stockholders shall not be permitted to propose business to be brought before a special meeting of the stockholders (other than pursuant to a Special Meeting Request in accordance with the requirements set forth in Section 1.3), and the only matters that may be brought before a special meeting are the matters specified in the Corporation's notice of meeting. Stockholders seeking to nominate persons for election to the Board must comply with Section 1.15 of these Bylaws, and this Section 1.14 shall not be applicable to nominations except as expressly provided in Section 1.15 of these Bylaws.

(b) Requirement of Timely Notice of Stockholder Business. Without qualification, for business to be properly brought before an annual meeting by a stockholder, the stockholder must (i) provide Timely Notice (as defined below) thereof in writing and in proper form to the Secretary of the Corporation and (ii) provide any updates or supplements to such notice at the times and in the forms required by this Section 1.14. To be timely, a stockholder's notice with respect to an annual meeting of stockholders must be delivered by overnight express courier or registered mail, return receipt requested, and received at, the principal executive offices of the Corporation not less than ninety (90) days nor more than one hundred twenty (120) days prior to the one year anniversary of the preceding year's annual meeting; *provided, however,* that if the date of the annual meeting is more

than thirty (30) days before or more than sixty (60) days after such anniversary date, notice by the stockholder to be timely must be so delivered, or mailed and received, not earlier than the one hundred twentieth (120th) day prior to such annual meeting and not later than the ninetieth (90th) day prior to such annual meeting or, if later, the tenth (10th) day following the day on which public disclosure of the date of such annual meeting was first made (such notice within such time periods, *"Timely Notice"*). In no event shall any adjournment or postponement of an annual meeting or the announcement thereof commence a new time period for the giving of Timely Notice as described above.

(c) Requirements for Proper Form of Stockholder Notice of Proposed Business. To be in proper form for purposes of this Section 1.14, a stockholder's notice to the Secretary shall set forth:

(i) Stockholder Information. As to each Proposing Person (as defined below), (A) the name and address of such Proposing Person (including, if applicable, the name and address that appear on the Corporation's books and records), (B) the class or series and number of shares of the Corporation that are, directly or indirectly, owned of record or beneficially owned (within the meaning of Rule 13d-3 under the Exchange Act) by such Proposing Person, except that such Proposing Person shall in all events be deemed to beneficially own any shares of any class or series of the Corporation as to which such Proposing Person has a right to acquire beneficial ownership at any time in the future and (C) representation whether such Proposing Person intends or is part of a group that intends (x) to deliver a proxy statement and/or form of proxy to holders of at least the percentage of the Corporation's outstanding stock required to approve or adopt the proposal or (y) otherwise to solicit proxies from stockholders in support of such proposal;

(ii) Information Regarding Disclosable Interests. As to each Proposing Person, (A) any derivative, swap or other transaction or series of transactions engaged in, directly or indirectly, by such Proposing Person, the purpose or effect of which is to give such Proposing Person economic risk similar to ownership of shares of any class or series of the Corporation, including due to the fact that the value of such derivative, swap or other transactions are determined by reference to the price, value or volatility of any shares of any class or series of the Corporation, or which derivative, swap or other transactions provide, directly or indirectly, the opportunity to profit from any increase in the price or value of shares of any class or series of the Corporation ("*Synthetic Equity Interests*"), which such Synthetic Equity Interests shall be disclosed without regard to whether (x) such derivative, swap or other transactions convey any voting rights in such shares to such Proposing Person, (y) the derivative, swap or other transactions are required to be, or are capable of being, settled through delivery of such shares or (z) such Proposing Person may

have entered into other transactions that hedge or mitigate the economic effect of such derivative, swap or other transactions, (B) any proxy (other than a revocable proxy or consent given in response to a solicitation made pursuant to, and in accordance with, Section 14(a) of the Exchange Act by way of a solicitation statement filed on Schedule 14A), agreement, arrangement, understanding or relationship pursuant to which such Proposing Person has or shares a right to vote any shares of any class or series of the Corporation, (C) any agreement, arrangement, understanding or relationship, including any repurchase or similar so-called "stock borrowing" agreement or arrangement, engaged in, directly or indirectly, by such Proposing Person, the purpose or effect of which is to mitigate loss to, reduce the economic risk (of ownership or otherwise) of shares of any class or series of the Corporation by, manage the risk of share price changes for, or increase or decrease the voting power of, such Proposing Person with respect to the shares of any class or series of the Corporation, or which provides, directly or indirectly, the opportunity to profit from any decrease in the price or value of the shares of any class or series of the Corporation ("*Short Interests*"), (D) any rights to dividends on the shares of any class or series of the Corporation owned beneficially by such Proposing Person that are separated or separable from the underlying shares of the Corporation, (E) any performance related fees (other than an asset based fee) that such Proposing Person is entitled to based on any increase or decrease in the price or value of shares of any class or series of the Corporation, or any Synthetic Equity Interests or Short Interests, if any, and (F) any other information relating to such Proposing Person that would be required to be disclosed in a proxy statement or other filing required to be made in connection with solicitations of proxies or consents by such Proposing Person in support of the business proposed to be brought before the meeting pursuant to Section 14(a) of the Exchange Act (the disclosures to be made pursuant to the foregoing clauses (A) through (F) are referred to as *"Disclosable Interests"*); *provided, however,* that Disclosable Interests shall not include any such disclosures with respect to the ordinary course business activities of any broker, dealer, commercial bank, trust company or other nominee who is a Proposing Person solely as a result of being the stockholder directed to prepare and submit the notice required by these Bylaws on behalf of a beneficial owner; and

(iii) Description of Proposed Business. As to each item of business the stockholder proposes to bring before the annual or special meeting, (A) a reasonably brief description of the business desired to be brought before the annual or special meeting, the reasons for conducting such business at the annual or special meeting and any material interest in such business of each Proposing Person, (B) the text of the proposal or business (including the text of any resolutions proposed for consideration), and (C) a reasonably detailed description of all agreements, arrangements and under-standings (x) between or among any of the Proposing Persons or (y) between or among any Proposing Person and any other person or entity (including their names) in connection with the proposal of such business by such stockholder.

(iv) Definition of Proposing Person. For purposes of this Section 1.14, the term *"Proposing Person"* shall mean (i) the stockholder providing the notice of business proposed to be brought before an annual or special meeting, (ii) the beneficial owner or beneficial owners, if different, on whose behalf the notice of the business proposed to be brought before the annual or special meeting is made, and (iii) any affiliate or associate of such stockholder or beneficial owner.

(d) Update and Supplement of Stockholder Notice of Proposed Business. A stockholder providing notice of business proposed to be brought before an annual or special meeting shall further update and supplement such notice, if necessary, so that the information provided or required to be provided in such notice pursuant to this Section 1.14 or in any Special Meeting Request delivered pursuant to Section 1.3(b) shall be true and correct as of the record date for the meeting and as of the date that is ten (10) business days prior to the meeting or any adjournment or postponement thereof, and such update and supplement shall be delivered to, or mailed and received by, the Secretary at the principal executive offices of the Corporation not later than five (5) business days after the record date for the meeting (in the case of the update and supplement required to be made as of the record date), and not later than eight (8) business days prior to the date of the meeting, or in the case of any adjournment or postponement thereof, eight (8) business days prior to the date of such adjournment or postponement.

(e) Business Not Properly Brought Before a Meeting. Notwithstanding anything in these Bylaws to the contrary, no business shall be conducted at an annual or special meeting except in accordance with this Section 1.14. The presiding officer of the meeting shall, if the facts warrant, determine that the business was not properly brought before the meeting in accordance with this Section 1.14, and if he or she should so determine, he or she shall so declare to the meeting and any such business not properly brought before the meeting shall not be transacted.

(f) Exchange Act Compliance. This Section 1.14 is expressly intended to apply to any business proposed to be brought before an annual or special meeting of stockholders other than any proposal made pursuant to Rule 14a-8 under the Exchange Act. In addition to the requirements of this Section 1.14 with respect to any business proposed to be brought before an annual or special meeting, each Proposing Person shall comply with all applicable requirements of the Exchange Act with respect to any such business. Nothing in this Section 1.14 shall be deemed to affect the rights of stockholders to request inclusion of proposals in the Corporation's proxy statement pursuant to Rule 14a-8 under the Exchange Act.

(g) Definition of Public Disclosure. For purposes of these Bylaws, *public disclosure* shall mean disclosure in a press release reported by a national news service or in a document publicly filed by the Corporation with the Securities and Exchange Commission pursuant to Sections 13, 14 or 15(d) of the Exchange Act.

SECTION 1.15: Nominations.

(a) Who May Make Nominations. Nominations of any person for election to the Board of Directors at an annual meeting or at a special meeting (but only if the election of directors is a matter specified in the notice of meeting given by or at the direction of the person calling such special meeting) may be made at such meeting only (i) by or at the direction of the Board of Directors, including by any committee or persons appointed by the Board of Directors, or (ii) by a stockholder who (A) was a stockholder of record (and, with respect to any beneficial owner, if different, on whose behalf such nomination is proposed to be made, only if such beneficial owner was the beneficial owner of shares of the Corporation) both at the time of giving the notice provided for in this Section 1.15 and at the time of the meeting, (B) is entitled to vote at the meeting, and (C) has complied with this Section 1.15 as to such nomination. The foregoing clause (ii) shall be the exclusive means for a stockholder to make any nomination of a person or persons for election to the Board of Directors at an annual meeting or special meeting (other than pursuant to a Special Meeting Request in accordance with the requirements set forth in Section 1.3).

(b) Requirement of Timely Notice of Stockholder Nominations. Without qualification, for a stockholder to make any nomination of a person or persons for election to the Board of Directors at an annual meeting, the stockholder must (i) provide Timely Notice (as defined in Section 1.14 of these Bylaws) thereof in writing and in proper form to the Secretary of the Corporation and (ii) provide any updates or supplements to such notice at the times and in the forms required by this Section 1.15. Without qualification, if the election of directors is a matter specified in the notice of meeting given by or at the direction of the person calling such special meeting, then for a stockholder to make any nomination of a person or persons for election to the Board of Directors at a special meeting, the stockholder must (i) provide timely notice thereof in writing and in proper form to the Secretary of the Corporation at the principal executive offices of the Corporation, and (ii) provide any updates or supplements to such notice at the times and in the forms required by this Section 1.15. To be timely, a stockholder's notice for nominations to be made at a special meeting (other than pursuant to a Special Meeting Request in accordance with the requirements set forth in Section 1.3) must be delivered to, or mailed and received at, the principal executive offices of the Corporation not earlier than the one hundred twentieth

(120th) day prior to such special meeting and not later than the ninetieth (90th) day prior to such special meeting or, if later, the tenth (10th) day following the day on which public disclosure (as defined in Section 1.14 of these Bylaws) of the date of such special meeting was first made. In no event shall any adjournment or postponement of an annual meeting or special meeting or the announcement thereof commence a new time period for the giving of a stockholder's notice as described above.

(c) Requirements for Proper Form of Notice of Stockholder Nominations. To be in proper form for purposes of this Section 1.15, a stockholder's notice to the Secretary shall set forth:

(i) Stockholder Information. As to each Nominating Person (as defined below), (A) the name and address of such Nominating Person (including, if applicable, the name and address that appear on the Corporation's books and records), (B) the class or series and number of shares of the Corporation that are, directly or indirectly, owned of record or beneficially owned (within the meaning of Rule 13d-3 under the Exchange Act) by such Nominating Person, except that such Nominating Person shall in all events be deemed to beneficially own any shares of any class or series of the Corporation as to which such Nominating Person has a right to acquire beneficial ownership at any time in the future and (C) a representation whether such Nominating Person intends or is part of a group that intends (x) to deliver a proxy statement and/or form of proxy to holders of at least the percentage of the Corporation's outstanding stock reasonably believed by the Nominating Person to be sufficient to elect the nominee or nominees proposed to be nominated by the Nominating Person;

(ii) Information Regarding Disclosable Interests. As to each Nominating Person, any Disclosable Interests (as defined in Section 1.14(c)(ii), except that for purposes of this Section 1.15 the term "Nominating Person" shall be substituted for the term "Proposing Person" in all places it appears in Section 1.14(c)(ii)), and the disclosure in clause (F) of Section 1.14(c)(ii) shall be made with respect to the election of directors at the meeting;

(iii) Information Regarding Proposed Nominees. As to each person whom a Nominating Person proposes to nominate for election as a director, (A) all information with respect to such proposed nominee that would be required to be set forth in a stockholder's notice pursuant to this Section 1.15 if such proposed nominee were a Nominating Person, (B) all information relating to such proposed nominee that is required to be disclosed in a proxy statement or other filings required to be made in connection with solicitations of proxies for election of directors in a contested election pursuant to Section 14(a) under the Exchange Act (including such proposed nominee's written consent to being named in the proxy statement as a nominee and to serving as a director if elected), (C) a description of all direct and indirect compensation and other

material monetary agreements, arrangements and understandings during the past three years, and any other material relationships, between or among any Nominating Person, on the one hand, and each proposed nominee, his or her respective affiliates and associates, on the other hand, including, without limitation, all information that would be required to be disclosed pursuant to Item 404 under Regulation S-K if such Nominating Person were the "registrant" for purposes of such rule and the proposed nominee were a director or executive officer of such registrant, and (D) a statement as to whether the proposed nominee, if elected, intends to tender, promptly following such person's election or re-election, an irrevocable resignation effective upon the occurrence of both (1) such person's failure to receive the required vote for re-election at the next meeting at which such person would face re-election and (2) acceptance of such resignation in accordance with Section 2.2 of these Bylaws and the Corporation's Governance Guidelines for the Board of Directors; and

(iv) Other Information to be Furnished by Proposed Nominees. The Corporation may require any proposed nominee to furnish such other information (A) as may reasonably be required by the Corporation to determine the eligibility of such proposed nominee to serve as an independent director of the Corporation in accordance with the Corporation's Governance Guidelines or (B) that could be material to a reasonable stockholder's understanding of the independence or lack of independence of such proposed nominee.

(v) Definition of Nominating Person. For purposes of this Section 1.15, the term "Nominating Person" shall mean (i) the stockholder providing the notice of the nomination proposed to be made at the meeting, (ii) the beneficial owner or beneficial owners, if different, on whose behalf the notice of the nomination proposed to be made at the meeting is made, and (iii) any affiliate or associate of such stockholder or beneficial owner.

(d) Update and Supplement of Stockholder Notice of Nominations. A stockholder providing notice of any nomination proposed to be made at a meeting shall further update and supplement such notice, if necessary, so that the information provided or required to be provided in such notice pursuant to this Section 1.15 or in any Special Meeting Request delivered pursuant to Section 1.3(b) shall be true and correct as of the record date for the meeting and as of the date that is ten (10) business days prior to the meeting or any adjournment or postponement thereof, and such update and supplement shall be delivered to, or mailed and received by, the Secretary at the principal executive offices of the Corporation not later than five (5) business days after the record date for the meeting (in the case of the update and supplement required to be made as of the record date), and not later than eight (8) business days prior to the date of the meeting, or in the case of any adjournment

or postponement thereof, eight (8) business days prior to the date of such adjournment or postponement.

(e) Defective Nominations. Notwithstanding anything in these Bylaws to the contrary, no person shall be eligible for election as a director of the Corporation unless nominated in accordance with this Section 1.15. The presiding officer at the meeting shall, if the facts warrant, determine that a nomination was not properly made in accordance with this Section 1.15, and if he or she should so determine, he or she shall so declare such determination to the meeting and the defective nomination shall be disregarded.

(f) Compliance with Exchange Act. In addition to the requirements of this Section 1.15 with respect to any nomination proposed to be made at a meeting, each Nominating Person shall comply with all applicable requirements of the Exchange Act with respect to any such nominations.

ARTICLE II.

BOARD OF DIRECTORS

SECTION 2.1: Number; Qualifications. The Board of Directors shall consist of one or more members. The initial number of directors shall be five (5), and thereafter shall be fixed from time to time by resolution of the Board of Directors. No decrease in the authorized number of directors constituting the Board of Directors shall shorten the term of any incumbent director. Directors need not be stockholders of the Corporation.

SECTION 2.2: Election.

(a) The directors shall be elected as provided in the Certificate of Incorporation.

(b) Each director to be elected by the stockholders of the Corporation shall be elected by the affirmative vote of a majority of the votes cast with respect to such director by the shares represented and entitled to vote therefor at a meeting of the stockholders for the election of directors at which a quorum is present (an *Election Meeting*); *provided, however,* that if the Board of Directors determines that the number of nominees exceeds the number of directors to be elected at such meeting (a *Contested Election*), and the Board of Directors has not rescinded such determination by the date that is twenty (20) days prior to the date of the Election Meeting as initially announced, each of the directors to be elected at the Election Meeting shall be elected by the affirmative vote of a plurality of the votes cast by the shares represented and entitled to vote at such meeting with respect to the election of such director. For purposes of this Section 2.2, a *majority of the votes cast* means that the number of votes cast "for" a candidate for director exceeds the number of votes cast "against" that director. In an election other than a Contested Election, stockholders will be given the choice to cast votes "for" or "against" the election of directors or to "abstain" from such vote and shall not have the ability to cast any other vote with respect to such election of directors. In a Contested Election, stockholders will be given the choice to cast "for" or "withhold" votes for the election of directors and shall not have the ability to cast any other vote with respect to such election of directors. In the event an Election Meeting involves the election of directors by separate votes by class or classes or series, the determination as to whether an election constitutes a Contested Election shall be made on a class by class or series by series basis, as applicable.

(c) In the event one or more incumbent directors (each, a *Subject Director*) fails to receive the affirmative vote of a majority of the votes cast at an Election Meeting at which there was no Contested Election, either (i) the Corporate Governance and Nominating Committee or (ii) if one or more of the members of the Corporate Governance and Nominating Committee is a Subject Director or the Board of Directors determines that any decision to be made with respect to a Subject Director should be made by a committee other than the Corporate Governance and Nominating Committee, a committee consisting solely of independent directors (as determined in accordance with any stock exchange rules and regulations applicable to the Corporation and any additional criteria set forth in the Corporation's Governance Guidelines for the Board of Directors or Corporate Governance and Nominating Committee Charter, as applicable) who are not Subject Directors (the committee described in clause (i) or (ii) of this sentence, the *Committee*) will make a determination as to whether to accept or reject any previously tendered

Resignations (as defined below), or whether other action should be taken (including whether to request that a Subject Director resign from the Board of Directors if no Resignation had been tendered prior to the relevant Election Meeting). The Committee will act with respect to any Subject Directors within ninety (90) days from the date of the certification of the election results and shall notify the Subject Directors of its decision. The Committee may consider all factors it considers relevant, including any stated reasons for "against" votes, whether the underlying cause or causes of the "against" votes are curable, the relationship between such causes and the actions of such Subject Director, the factors, if any, set forth in the Corporation's Governance Guidelines for the Board of Directors or other policies that are to be considered by the Corporate Governance and Nominating Committee in evaluating potential candidates for the Board of Directors as such criteria relate to such Subject Director, the length of service of such Subject Director, the size and holding period of such Subject Director's stock ownership in the Corporation, and such Subject Director's contributions to the Corporation. Subject Directors shall not participate in the deliberation or decision(s) of the Committee. The Corporation shall publicly disclose the decision(s) of the Committee in a Current Report on Form 8-K filed with the Securities and Exchange Commission. Notwithstanding the foregoing, if the result of accepting all tendered Resignations then pending and requesting resignations from incumbent directors who

did not submit a Resignation prior to the relevant Election Meeting, would be that the Corporation would have fewer than three (3) directors who were in office before the election of directors, the Committee may determine to extend such ninety (90)-day period by an additional ninety (90) days if it determines that such an extension is in the best interests of the Corporation and its stockholders. For purposes of this Section 2.2, a "*Resignation*" is an irrevocable resignation submitted by an incumbent director nominated for re-election prior to the relevant Election Meeting that will become effective upon the occurrence of both (i) the failure to receive the affirmative vote of a majority of the votes cast at an Election Meeting at which there was no Contested Election and (ii) acceptance of such resignation by the Committee.

(d) If a Subject Director's tendered Resignation is not accepted by the Committee or such Subject Director does not otherwise submit his or her resignation to the Board of Directors, such director shall continue to serve until his or her successor is duly elected, or his or her earlier resignation or removal pursuant to Section 2.3. If a Subject Director's Resignation is accepted by the Committee pursuant to this Section 2.2, or if a nominee for director is not elected and the nominee is not an incumbent director, then the Board of Directors, in its sole discretion, may fill any resulting vacancy pursuant to the provisions of Section 2.3 or decrease the size of the Board of Directors pursuant to the provisions of Section 2.1 of these Bylaws.

SECTION 2.3: Resignation; Removal; Vacancies. Subject to the provisions of the Certificate of Incorporation, each director shall serve until his or her successor is duly elected and qualified, or until his or her earlier death, resignation, retirement or removal from service as a director. Any director may resign at any time upon notice given in writing or by electronic transmission to the Corporation. Subject to the rights of any holders of Preferred Stock then outstanding and the Certificate of Incorporation:

(i) (A) prior to the third annual meeting of stockholders following the effectiveness of the Amended and Restated Certificate of Incorporation that declassifies the Board of Directors (the "*Declassification Amendment*"), any director or the entire Board of Directors may be removed, only for cause, by the holders of a majority of the shares then entitled to vote at an election of directors and (B) after the third annual meeting of stockholders following the effectiveness of the Declassification Amendment, the holders of a majority of the shares entitled to vote in an election of directors may remove any director or the entire Board of Directors with or without cause, and

(ii) any vacancy occurring in the Board of Directors for any reason, and any newly created directorship resulting from any increase in the authorized number of directors to be elected by all stockholders having the right to vote as a single class, shall be filled only by a majority of the directors then in office, although less than a quorum, or by a sole remaining director.

SECTION 2.4: Regular Meetings. Regular meetings of the Board of Directors may be held at such places, within or without the State of Delaware, and at such times as the Board of Directors may from time to time determine. Notice of regular meetings need not be given if the date, times and places thereof are fixed by resolution of the Board of Directors.

SECTION 2.5: Special Meetings. Special meetings of the Board of Directors may be called by the Chairman of the Board, the Chief Executive Officer or a majority of the members of the Board of Directors then in office and may be held at any time, date or place, within or without the State of Delaware, as the person or persons calling the meeting shall fix. Notice of the time, date and place of such meeting shall be given, orally or in writing, by the person or persons calling the meeting to all directors at least four (4) days before the meeting if the notice is mailed, or at least twenty-four (24) hours before the meeting if such notice is given by telephone, hand delivery, overnight express courier, facsimile, electronic mail or other electronic transmission. Unless otherwise indicated in the notice, any and all business may be transacted at a special meeting. The notice shall be deemed given

(i) in the case of hand delivery or notice by telephone, when received by the director to whom notice is to be given or by any person accepting such notice on behalf of such director,

(ii) in the case of delivery by mail, upon deposit in the United States mail, postage prepaid, directed to the director to whom notice is being given at such director's address as it appears on the records of the Corporation,

(iii) in the case of delivery by overnight express courier, on the first business day after such notice is dispatched, and

(iv) in the case of delivery via facsimile, electronic mail or other electronic transmission, when sent to the director to whom notice is to be given or by any person accepting such notice on behalf of such director at such director's facsimile number or electronic mail address, as the case may be, as it appears on the Corporation's records.

SECTION 2.6: Telephonic Meetings Permitted. Members of the Board of Directors, or any committee of the Board of Directors, may participate in a meeting of the Board of Directors or such committee by means of conference telephone or similar communications equipment by means of which all persons participating in the meeting can hear each other, and participation in a meeting pursuant to conference telephone or similar communications equipment shall constitute presence in person at such meeting.

SECTION 2.7: Quorum; Vote Required for Action. At all meetings of the Board of Directors a majority of the total number of authorized directors shall constitute a quorum for the transaction of business. Except as otherwise provided herein or in the Certificate of Incorporation, or required by law, the vote of a majority of the directors present at a meeting at which a quorum is present shall be the act of the Board of Directors. If a quorum is not present at any meeting of the Board of Directors, then the directors present thereat may adjourn the meeting from time to time, without notice other than announcement at the meeting, until a quorum is present.

SECTION 2.8: Chairman of the Board. The Board of Directors shall have the power to elect the Chairman of the Board from among the members of the Board of Directors. The Chairman of the Board shall have the power to preside at all meetings of the Board of Directors and shall have such other powers and duties as provided in these Bylaws and as the Board of Directors may from time to time prescribe.

SECTION 2.9: Organization. Meetings of the Board of Directors shall be presided over by the Chairman of the Board, or in his or her absence by the Chief Executive Officer, or in his or her absence by a chairman chosen at the meeting. The Secretary shall act as secretary of the meeting, but in his or her absence the chairman of the meeting may appoint any person to act as secretary of the meeting.

SECTION 2.10: Written Action by Directors. Any action required or permitted to be taken at any meeting of the Board of Directors, or of any committee thereof, may be taken without a meeting if all members of the Board or such committee, as the case may be, consent thereto in writing, or by electronic transmission and the writing or writings or electronic transmission or transmissions are filed with the minutes of proceedings of the Board or committee, respectively. Such filing shall be in paper form if the minutes are maintained in paper form and shall be in electronic form if the minutes are maintained in electronic form.

SECTION 2.11: Powers. The Board of Directors may, except as otherwise required by law or the Certificate of Incorporation, exercise all such powers and do all such acts and things as may be exercised or done by the Corporation.

SECTION 2.12: Compensation of Directors. Directors, as such, may receive, pursuant to a resolution of the Board of Directors, fees and other compensation for their services as directors, including without limitation their services as members of committees of the Board of Directors.

ARTICLE III.

COMMITTEES

SECTION 3.1: Committees. The Board of Directors may, by resolution passed by a majority of the authorized number of directors, designate one or more committees, each committee to consist of one or more of the directors of the Corporation. The Board may designate one or more directors as alternate members of any committee, who may replace any absent or disqualified member at any meeting of the committee. In the absence or disqualification of a member of the committee, the member or members thereof present at any meeting of such committee who are not disqualified from voting, whether or not he, she or they constitute a quorum, may unanimously appoint another member of the Board of Directors to act at the meeting in place of any such absent or disqualified member. Any such committee, to the extent provided in a resolution of the Board of Directors, shall have and may exercise all the powers and authority of the Board of Directors in the management of the business and affairs of the Corporation and may authorize the seal of the Corporation to be affixed to all papers that may require it; but no such committee shall have power or authority in reference to the following matters: (i) approving or adopting, or recommending to the stockholders, any action or matter (other than the election or removal of directors) expressly required by the Delaware General Corporation Law to be submitted to stockholders for approval, or (ii) adopting, amending or repealing any Bylaw of the Corporation.

SECTION 3.2: Committee Rules. Unless the Board of Directors otherwise provides, each committee designated by the Board of Directors may make, alter and repeal rules for the conduct of its business. In the absence of such rules each committee shall conduct its business in the same manner as the Board of Directors conducts its business pursuant to Article II of these Bylaws.

ARTICLE IV.

OFFICERS

SECTION 4.1: Generally. The officers of the Corporation shall consist of a Chief Executive Officer and/or a President, one or more Vice Presidents, a Secretary, a Treasurer and such other officers, including a Chief Financial Officer, as may from time to time be appointed by the Board of Directors. All officers shall be elected by the Board of Directors; *provided, however,* that the Board of Directors may empower the Chief Executive Officer of the Corporation to appoint officers other than the Chief Executive Officer, the President, the Chief Financial Officer or the

Treasurer. Each officer shall hold office until his or her successor is elected and qualified or until his or her earlier resignation or removal. Any number of offices may be held by the same person. Any officer may resign at any time upon written notice to the Corporation. Any vacancy occurring in any office of the Corporation by death, resignation, removal or otherwise may be filled by the Board of Directors.

SECTION 4.2: Chief Executive Officer. Subject to the control of the Board of Directors and such supervisory powers, if any, as may be given by the Board of Directors, the powers and duties of the Chief Executive Officer of the Corporation are:

  (a) To act as the general manager and, subject to the control of the Board of Directors, to have general supervision, direction and control of the business and affairs of the Corporation;

  (b) To preside at all meetings of the stockholders;

  (c) To call meetings of the stockholders to be held at such times and, subject to the limitations prescribed by law or by these Bylaws, at such places as he or she shall deem proper; and

  (d) To affix the signature of the Corporation to all deeds, conveyances, mortgages, guarantees, leases, obligations, bonds, certificates and other papers and instruments in writing which have been authorized by the Board of Directors or which, in the judgment of the Chief Executive Officer, should be executed on behalf of the Corporation; to

sign certificates for shares of stock of the Corporation; and, subject to the direction of the Board of Directors, to have general charge of the property of the Corporation and to supervise and control all officers, agents and employees of the Corporation.

The President shall be the Chief Executive Officer of the Corporation unless the Board of Directors shall designate another officer to be the Chief Executive Officer. If there is no President, and the Board of Directors has not designated any other officer to be the Chief Executive Officer, then the Chairman of the Board shall be the Chief Executive Officer.

SECTION 4.3: President. The President shall be the Chief Executive Officer of the Corporation unless the Board of Directors shall have designated another officer as the Chief Executive Officer of the Corporation. Subject to the provisions of these Bylaws and to the direction of the Board of Directors, and subject to the supervisory powers of the Chief Executive Officer (if the Chief Executive Officer is an officer other than the President), and subject to such supervisory powers and authority as may be given by the Board of Directors to the Chairman of the Board, and/or to any other officer, the President shall have the responsibility for the general management and the control of the business and affairs of the Corporation and the general supervision and direction of all of the officers, employees and agents of the Corporation (other than the Chief Executive Officer, if the Chief Executive Officer is an officer other than the President) and shall perform all duties and have all powers that are commonly incident to the office of President or that are delegated to the President by the Board of Directors.

SECTION 4.4: Vice President. Each Vice President shall have all such powers and duties as are commonly incident to the office of Vice President, or that are delegated to him or her by the Board of Directors or the Chief Executive Officer. A Vice President may be designated by the Board to perform the duties and exercise the powers of the Chief Executive Officer in the event of the Chief Executive Officer's absence or disability.

SECTION 4.5: Chief Financial Officer. Subject to the direction of the Board of Directors and the President, the Chief Financial Officer shall perform all duties and have all powers that are commonly incident to the office of chief financial officer.

SECTION 4.6: Treasurer. The Treasurer shall have custody of all monies and securities of the Corporation. The Treasurer shall make such disbursements of the funds of the Corporation as are authorized and shall render from time to time an account of all such transactions. The Treasurer shall also perform such other duties and have such other powers as are commonly incident to the office of Treasurer, or as the Board of Directors or the President may from time to time prescribe.

SECTION 4.7: Secretary. The Secretary shall issue or cause to be issued all authorized notices for, and shall keep, or cause to be kept, minutes of all meetings of the stockholders and the Board of Directors. The Secretary shall have charge of the corporate minute books and similar records and shall perform such other duties and have

such other powers as are commonly incident to the office of Secretary, or as the Board of Directors or the President may from time to time prescribe.

SECTION 4.8: Delegation of Authority. The Board of Directors may from time to time delegate the powers or duties of any officer to any other officers or agents, notwithstanding any provision hereof.

SECTION 4.9: Removal. Any officer of the Corporation shall serve at the pleasure of the Board of Directors and may be removed at any time, with or without cause, by the Board of Directors. Such removal shall be without prejudice to the contractual rights of such officer, if any, with the Corporation.

ARTICLE V.

STOCK

SECTION 5.1: Certificates. The shares of the Corporation shall be represented by certificates, provided that the Board of Directors may provide by resolution or resolutions that some or all of any or all classes or series of the Corporation's stock shall be uncertificated shares. Any such resolution shall not apply to shares represented by a certificate until such certificate is surrendered to the Corporation. Every holder of stock represented by certificates shall be entitled to have a certificate signed by or in the name of the Corporation by the Chairman or Vice-Chairman of the Board of Directors, or the President or a Vice President, and by the Treasurer or an Assistant Treasurer, or the Secretary or an Assistant Secretary, of the Corporation, representing the number of shares registered in certificate form. Any or all of the signatures on the certificate may be a facsimile.

SECTION 5.2: Lost, Stolen or Destroyed Stock Certificates; Issuance of New Certificates or Uncertificated Shares. The Corporation may issue a new certificate of stock or uncertificated shares in the place of any certificate previously issued by it, alleged to have been lost, stolen or destroyed, and the Corporation may require the owner of the lost, stolen or destroyed certificate, or such owner's legal representative, to agree to indemnify the Corporation and/or to give the Corporation a bond sufficient to indemnify it, against any claim that may be made against it on account of the alleged loss, theft or destruction of any such certificate or the issuance of such new certificate or uncertificated shares.

SECTION 5.3: Other Regulations. The issue, transfer, conversion and registration of stock certificates or uncertificated shares shall be governed by such other regulations as the Board of Directors may establish.

ARTICLE VI.

INDEMNIFICATION

SECTION 6.1: Indemnification of Officers and Directors. Each person who was or is made a party to, or is threatened to be made a party to, or is involved in any action, suit or proceeding, whether civil, criminal, administrative or investigative (a "*proceeding*"), by reason of the fact that he or she (or a person of whom he or she is the legal representative), is or was a director or officer of the Corporation or a Reincorpo-

rated Predecessor (as defined below) or is or was serving at the request of the Corporation or a Reincorporated Predecessor (as defined below) as a director, officer or employee of another corporation, or of a partnership, joint venture, trust or other enterprise, including service with respect to employee benefit plans (each such director, officer or employee, a "*Covered Person*"), shall be indemnified and held harmless by the Corporation to the fullest extent permitted by the Delaware General Corporation Law, against all expenses, liability and loss (including attorneys' fees, judgments, fines, ERISA excise taxes and penalties and amounts paid or to be paid in settlement) reasonably incurred or suffered by such person in connection therewith; *provided, however*, that the Corporation shall indemnify any such Covered Person seeking indemnity in connection with a proceeding (or part thereof) initiated by such Covered Person only if such proceeding (or part thereof) was authorized by the Board of Directors of the Corporation. As used herein, the term "*Reincorporated Predecessor*" means a corporation that is merged with and into the Corporation in a statutory merger where (a) the Corporation is the surviving corporation of such merger; (b) the primary purpose of such merger is to change the corporate domicile of the Reincorporated Predecessor to Delaware.

SECTION 6.2: Advance of Expenses. The Corporation shall pay all expenses (including attorneys' fees) incurred by a Covered Person in defending any such proceeding as they are incurred in advance of its final disposition; *provided, however*, that if the Delaware General Corporation Law then so requires, the payment of such expenses incurred by a Covered

Person in advance of the final disposition of such proceeding shall be made only upon delivery to the Corporation of an undertaking, by or on behalf of such Covered Person, to repay all amounts so advanced if it should be determined ultimately that such Covered Person is not entitled to be indemnified under this Article VI or otherwise; and provided, further, that the Corporation shall not be required to advance any expenses to a Covered Person against whom the Corporation directly brings a claim, in a proceeding, alleging that such person has breached his or her duty of loyalty to the Corporation, committed an act or omission not in good faith or that involves intentional misconduct or a knowing violation of law, or derived an improper personal benefit from a transaction.

SECTION 6.3: Non-Exclusivity of Rights. The rights conferred on any person in this Article VI shall not be exclusive of any other right that such person may have or hereafter acquire under any statute, provision of the Certificate of Incorporation, Bylaw, agreement, vote or consent of stockholders or disinterested directors, or otherwise. Additionally, nothing in this Article VI shall limit the ability of the Corporation, in its discretion, to indemnify or advance expenses to persons whom the Corporation is not obligated to indemnify or advance expenses pursuant to this Article VI. The Board of Directors of the Corporation shall have the power to delegate to such officer or other person as the Board of Directors shall specify the determination of whether indemnification shall be given to any person pursuant to this Section 6.3.

SECTION 6.4: Indemnification Contracts. The Board of Directors is authorized to cause the Corporation to enter into indemnification contracts with any director, officer, employee or agent of the Corporation, or any person serving at the request of the Corporation as a director, officer, employee or agent of another corporation, partnership, joint venture, trust or other enterprise, including employee benefit plans, providing indemnification rights to such person. Such rights may be greater than those provided in this Article VI.

SECTION 6.5: Continuation of Indemnification. The rights to indemnification and to advancement of expenses provided by, or granted pursuant to, this Article VI shall continue notwithstanding that the person has ceased to be a Covered Person and shall inure to the benefit of his or her estate, heirs, executors, administrators, legatees and distributees; *provided, however,* that the Corporation shall indemnify any such person seeking indemnity in connection with a proceeding (or part thereof) initiated by such person only if such proceeding (or part thereof) was authorized by the Board of Directors of the Corporation.

SECTION 6.6: Effect of Amendment or Repeal. The provisions of this Article VI shall constitute a contract between the Corporation, on the one hand, and, on the other hand, each individual who serves or has served as a Covered Person (whether before or after the adoption of these Bylaws), in consideration of such person's performance of such services, and pursuant to this Article VI, the Corporation intends to be legally bound to each such current or former Covered Person. With respect to current and former Covered Persons, the rights conferred under this Article VI are present contractual rights and such rights are fully vested, and shall be deemed to have vested fully, immediately upon adoption of these Bylaws. With respect to any Covered Persons who commence service following adoption of these bylaws, the rights conferred under this Article VI shall be present contractual rights, and such rights shall fully vest, and be deemed to have vested fully, immediately upon such Covered Person's service in the capacity which is subject to the benefits of this Article VI.

ARTICLE VII.

NOTICES

SECTION 7.1: Notice.

(a) General. Except as otherwise specifically provided herein or required by law, all notices required to be given pursuant to these Bylaws shall be in writing and may in every instance be effectively given by hand delivery (including use of a delivery service), by depositing such notice in the mail, postage prepaid, or by sending such notice by prepaid overnight express courier or facsimile. Any such notice shall be addressed to the person to whom notice is to be given at such person's address or facsimile number, as the case may be, as it appears on the records of the Corporation. The notice shall be deemed given

(i) in the case of hand delivery, when received by the person to whom notice is to be given or by any person accepting such notice on behalf of such person;

(ii) in the case of delivery by mail, upon deposit in the United States mail, postage prepaid, directed to the person to whom notice is being given at such person's address as it appears on the records of the Corporation;

(iii) in the case of delivery by overnight express courier, on the first business day after such notice is dispatched; and

(iv) in the case of delivery via facsimile, when directed to the person to whom notice is to be given or by any person accepting such notice on behalf of such person.

SECTION 7.2: Waiver of Notice. Whenever notice is required to be given under any provision of these Bylaws, a written waiver of notice, signed by the person entitled to notice, or a waiver by electronic transmission by the person entitled to notice, whether before or after the time stated therein, shall be deemed equivalent to notice. Attendance of a person at a meeting shall constitute a waiver of notice of such meeting, except when the person attends a meeting for the express purpose of objecting at the beginning of the meeting to the transaction of any business because the meeting is not lawfully called or convened. Neither the business to be transacted at, nor the purpose of, any regular or special meeting of the stockholders, directors or members of a committee of directors need be specified in any written waiver of notice or any waiver by electronic transmission.

ARTICLE VIII.

INTERESTED DIRECTORS

SECTION 8.1: Interested Directors; Quorum. No contract or transaction between the Corporation and one or more of its directors or officers, or between the Corporation and any other corporation, partnership, association or other organization in which one or more of its directors or officers are directors or officers, or have a financial interest, shall be void or voidable solely for this reason, or solely because the director or officer is present at or participates in the meeting of the Board of Directors or committee thereof that authorizes the contract or transaction, or solely because his, her or their votes are counted for such purpose, if:

(i) the material facts as to his, her or their relationship or interest and as to the contract or transaction are disclosed or are known to the Board of Directors or the committee, and the Board of Directors or committee in good faith authorizes the contract or transaction by the affirmative votes of a majority of the disinterested directors, even though the disinterested directors be less than a quorum;

(ii) the material facts as to his, her or their relationship or interest and as to the contract or transaction are disclosed or are known to the stockholders entitled to vote thereon, and the contract or transaction is specifically approved in good faith by vote of the stockholders; or

(iii) the contract or transaction is fair as to the Corporation as of the time it is authorized, approved or ratified by the Board of Directors, a committee thereof, or the stockholders. Common or interested directors may be counted in determining the presence of a quorum at a meeting of the Board of Directors or of a committee which authorizes the contract or transaction.

ARTICLE IX.

MISCELLANEOUS

SECTION 9.1: Fiscal Year. The fiscal year of the Corporation shall be determined by resolution of the Board of Directors.

SECTION 9.2: Seal. The Board of Directors may provide for a corporate seal, which shall have the name of the Corporation inscribed thereon and shall otherwise be in such form as may be approved from time to time by the Board of Directors.

SECTION 9.3: Form of Records. Any records maintained by the Corporation in the regular course of its business, including its stock ledger, books of account and minute books, may be kept on, or by means of, or be in the form of, any information storage device or method provided that the records so kept can be converted into clearly legible paper form within a reasonable time. The Corporation shall so convert any records so kept upon the request of any person entitled to inspect such records pursuant to any provision of the Delaware General Corporation Law.

SECTION 9.4: Reliance Upon Books and Records. A member of the Board of Directors, or a member of any committee designated by the Board of Directors shall, in the performance of his or her duties, be fully protected in relying in good faith upon records of the Corporation and upon such information, opinions, reports or statements presented to the Corporation by any of the Corporation's officers or employees, or committees of the Board of Directors, or by any other person as to matters the member reasonably believes are within such other person's professional or expert competence and who has been selected with reasonable care by or on behalf of the Corporation.

SECTION 9.5: Certificate of Incorporation Governs. In the event of any conflict between the provisions of the Corporation's Certificate of Incorporation and Bylaws, the provisions of the Certificate of Incorporation shall govern.

SECTION 9.6: Severability. If any provision of these Bylaws shall be held to be invalid, illegal, unenforceable or in conflict with the provisions of the Corporation's Certificate of Incorporation, then such provision shall nonetheless be enforced to the maximum extent possible consistent with such holding and the remaining provisions of these Bylaws (including without limitation, all portions of any section of these Bylaws containing any such provision held to be invalid, illegal, unenforceable or in conflict with the Certificate of Incorporation, that are not themselves invalid, illegal, unenforceable or in conflict with the Certificate of Incorporation) shall remain in full force and effect.

ARTICLE X.

AMENDMENT

SECTION 10.1: Amendments. Subject to Section 6.6 of these Bylaws, stockholders of the Corporation holding at least a majority of the Corporation's outstanding voting stock shall have the power to adopt, amend or repeal Bylaws. To the extent provided in the Corporation's Certificate of Incorporation, the Board of Directors of the Corporation shall also have the power to adopt, amend or repeal Bylaws of the Corporation.

CERTIFICATION OF BYLAWS OF EBAY INC.

(a Delaware Corporation)

KNOW ALL BY THESE PRESENTS:

I, Michael R. Jacobson, certify that I am Secretary of eBay Inc., a Delaware corporation (the "*Company*"), that I am duly authorized to make and deliver this certification, that the attached Bylaws are a true and correct copy of the Bylaws of the Company in effect as of the date of this certificate.

Dated: April 27, 2012

/s/ Michael R. Jacobson
Michael R. Jacobson, Secretary

8. Business Law Glossary

BUSINESS LAW GLOSSARY

Abatement: Reduction.

Abnormal use: A defense to products liability actions by which a defendant argues it is not responsible for harm caused by the product because the plaintiff used the product for an unforeseeable purpose.

Acceptance: Agreeing to the terms of an offer.

Accord and satisfaction: Accepting performance, or a substitute for performance, as adequate.

Acquisition: Gaining of possession or control over a company.

Actual authority: The powers actually granted to an agent by the principal.

Actual malice: The standard of proof required of public figures in a defamation case. The public figure must show that the defendant knew the statement was false or acted with reckless disregard as to whether the statement was false or not.

Actus reus: Latin for "guilty act." Actions that constitute a crime when done with the appropriate state of mind (*actus reus*).

Adjudication: The exercise of judicial power by an administrative agency. Adjudication usually deals with disputes between the agency and individuals or business entities.

Ad litem: "For the purposes of the suit."

Administrative Procedure Act: The federal law that establishes the procedure for rulemaking and adjudication by federal administrative agencies.

Affidavit: A written statement of facts given under oath.

Agent: A person who is authorized to act for another person.

Alternative dispute resolution: Any means of settling disputes without litigation.

Amendatory: Supplemental, additional.

Answer: A written pleading filed by a defendant to respond to a complaint filed by a plaintiff in a lawsuit.

Antenuptial agreements: A pre-marital contract in which the parties agree on issues like the disposition of property after death or dissolution of the marriage.

Anticipatory breach: Informing a party that a contract will be breached before the breach takes place.

Apparent Authority: The reasonable assumption that an agent is allowed to act for a principal under given circumstances.

Appellant: The party who files an appeal of a court decision.

Appellee: The party responding to an appeal filed by the other party.

Arbitration: A method of alternative dispute resolution in which the parties present their case to one or more neutral parties, called arbitrators, who issue a binding decision on the parties.

Arbitration clause: A clause in a written agreement requiring the parties to resolve disputes between them through the arbitration process.

Arraignment: A court proceeding calling a party to court to answer a criminal charge.

Articles of incorporation: The document filed with the state for the formation of a corporation.

Articles of organization: The document filed with the state for the formation of a limited liability company.

Assumption of risk: A defense to tort liability in which a defendant argues it is not liable because the plaintiff knew and accepted the risks of an activity.

Attenuate: To lessen or weaken.

At-will employment: An employment relationship under which the employer or employee may end the relationship at any time.

Authentication: Formal proof of a security agreement, such as a signed document.

Author: In copyright law, the creator of a copyrightable work.

Automatic stay: An order from the Bankruptcy Court that stops all collection efforts against a debtor. The automatic stay goes into effect as soon as a bankruptcy case is filed.

Award: The final decision of the arbitrator in an arbitration proceeding.

Beyond a reasonable doubt: Standard of proof for a criminal conviction. "Reasonable doubt" is when jurors are not convinced of the defendant's guilt, or when they believe there is a reasonable possibility that the defendant is not guilty.

Binding mediation: A method of alternative dispute resolution in which the parties attempt mediation, but if they do not reach an agreement, they agree to follow a binding decision issued by the mediator.

Board of directors: Individuals elected to act as representatives of shareholders in running a corporation.

Board of governors: Individuals elected to act as representatives of members in running a limited liability company.

Bona fide occupational qualification: An employment qualification, related to an essential job duty, that employers may consider in making decisions about hiring and retention of employees.

Bond: A written promise to pay money. In securities law, long-term, interest bearing debt instruments, backed by the assets of the issuer.

Brief: A written legal argument submitted to the court.

Burden of proof: The amount of proof needed to prove one's case.

By-laws: The rules and regulations adopted to govern the operation of a corporation.

Cabinet: The most senior appointed officers of the executive branch of government, nominated by the President and confirmed by the Senate.

Capacity: The legal ability to make a contract.

Capitation: A tax levy that is a fixed sum per person, without regard to any other factors.

Cartel: A combination of sellers or producers of a product who join together to control production or price.

Causation: The causing or producing of an effect.

Cause of action: Fact(s) that enable a party to bring legal action against another party.

Cause-in-fact: The action that caused an injured party's injury. It is also referred to as but-for causation.

C corporation: A corporation that is subject to the federal corporate income tax. All for-profit corporations are C corporations, unless they qualify as an S corporation.

Certification mark: A type of trademark that certifies some characteristic of a product, such as the place of origin, method of manufacture, quality, or material.

Certiorari: A higher court's acceptance of a case from a lower court for review.

Chancellor: The judge presiding over a court of chancery, or equity.

Civil claim: A lawsuit to remedy a private wrong

Civil penalty: A fine assessed for a violation of a statute or regulation. A civil penalty is not considered to be punishment for a crime.

Class action: A lawsuit in which a single person or a small group of people represents the interests of a larger group.

Collateral: Property or goods used to guarantee payment of an obligation.

Collective bargaining: The process through which unions negotiate terms of employment with employers on behalf of the employees.

Collective bargaining agreement: The agreed-upon contract between union employees and the employer.

Collective mark: A type of trademark that shows membership in a group, or that identifies the goods or services offered by the members of the group.

Common carrier: A business that offers its services to the public for transportation of people, goods, or messages.

Common law: Law developed through court decisions over time rather than through constitutions or codes.

Common market: A geographic group of countries that seek to eliminate trade barriers among themselves and promote free movement of capital and labor within the member countries.

Comparative negligence: A doctrine under which a plaintiff's recovery of damages may be reduced by the amount of negligence attributed to the plaintiff.

Compensatory damages: A sum of money awarded to the injured party in a lawsuit to compensate for expenses incurred as a result of the injuries.

Complaint: The first document filed with a court by a party that claims legal rights against another party.

Concealment: The act of refraining from disclosure, especially an act by which one prevents or hinders the discovery of something.

Conflagration: A great destructive burning or fire.

Consideration: A bargained for exchange; a legal detriment.

Constitutionality: Whether a law or government action agrees with the Constitution.

Consumer product: For purposes of the Fair Packaging and Labeling Act, a product customarily produced or distributed for sale through retail sales for consumption by individuals, or use by individuals for personal care or household services.

Contributory negligence: A doctrine under which a plaintiff may be barred from recovering damages because the plaintiff was partially at fault for the accident or injury.

Convention: In international law, an agreement among several nations.

Convicted: Being found guilty of a crime.

Conviction: The declaration of guilt for a criminal charge.

Cooperative federalism: The collective cooperative interaction of state, local, and federal governments to solve common problems.

Corporate promoter: A person who solicits investors for a corporation before it is formed.

Corporation: A legal entity formed under the laws of a state to do business.

Counterclaim: A claim asserted by the defendant against the plaintiff in a lawsuit.

Counteroffer: A response to an offer that proposes different or additional terms.

Court of Exchequer: A trial level court which existed until 1873. Its jurisdiction was subsequently turned over to the Exchequer Division and then the Queen's Bench Division of the High Court of Justice.

Creditor: A person who owes money. In bankruptcy law, the "debtor" is the person or entity that files a bankruptcy petition.

Cross examination: Examination of a witness that has already testified in a court proceeding, conducted by the other side.

Crowdfunding: Funding a project or venture by soliciting money from a large number of people, usually via internet solicitation.

Customs duty: A tax paid on imported items based on the country of origin and the item's description.

Customs union: A free trade area that also adopts a common external tariff.

Damages: Money compensation awarded to the injured party in a lawsuit.

Debenture: A bond backed only by the general credit and financial reputation of the company issuing the bond.

Debtor in possession: A Chapter 11 bankruptcy debtor over the term of the Chapter 11 process.

Debtor: A person to whom money is owed. In bankruptcy law, a "creditor" has or may have a claim against the debtor's property.

Deed: A document that evidences a transfer of real estate. All transfers or conveyances of real estate must be in writing.

Defamation: A false statement that damages the other party's reputation.

Default judgment: A binding judgment entered by a court if the defendant does not respond to the plaintiff's complaint.

Defendant: The party accused in a legal action. The party who responds to a lawsuit initiated by another party; the defendant is the party whom the plaintiff alleges engaged in a tort.

De minimis: Small, or trivial. From the Latin maxim *de minimis non curat lex* (the law does not concern itself with trifles).

Demurrer: A demurrer is a means of attacking a party's pleading. In essence, the attacker argues that the pleading need not be answered because it is insufficient or defective in some manner. There are a variety of different demurrers, some of which are still recognized. The modem equivalent of a general demurrer is a request for dismissal under Federal Rule of Civil Procedure 12 (b) (6). A request under 12

(b) (6) alleges that the opposing party fails to state a claim for which relief can be granted.

Deposition: The process of receiving and recording the sworn testimony of a party or witness during discovery.

Derivative work: A work based on another work. Examples of derivative works include adaptations or sequels.

Design defect: A defect in the design of the product that makes the product dangerous or useless.

Detour: An agent's minor deviation from the principal's business for personal reasons.

Direct examination: Examination of a witness by the party that called the witness to testify

Directed verdict: A ruling in a lawsuit entered by the trial judge after a determination that a reasonable jury could not reach a different conclusion.

Disability insurance: A type of insurance providing income protection to individuals who become disabled and cannot work for a long period of time.

Discharge: A debt is discharged when the debtor is no longer liable for paying it.

Discovery: The process by which the parties to a lawsuit obtain information from each other and from witnesses.

Disparate impact: The effect of a neutral practice that is non-discriminatory in intention, but disproportionately affects individuals of a protected class.

Disparate treatment: Intentional, unequal treatment of an employee on the basis of a protected class by an employer.

Disposable income: Income to a bankrupt debtor that is beyond what the debtor needs for the maintenance or support of herself and her dependents or for payments to operate her business.

Diversity jurisdiction: A federal court case with parties from different states or with a foreign party

Divestiture: A court order to a defendant to rid itself of property, securities, or other assets to prevent a monopoly or restraint of trade.

Dividends: The distribution of profits to shareholders or members.

Document requests: A written request for documents, electronically stored information, or other items issued during discovery to an opposing party.

Durable power of attorney: A power of attorney that remains effective even if the principal becomes incapacitated.

Duress: 1. Inducing an agreement by means of a threat or wrongful act. 2. Threats of harm or other pressure that force a person to commit a criminal act against his will.

Easement: The right to use or cross land, without the right to possess the land.

Economic strikers: Striking union workers seeking to obtain an economic benefit for the workers.

Electronically stored information (ESI): Data or information that is stored in electronic format, including documents, emails, voice mails, tweets, blogs, social media posts, files, and other records.

Elements: The parts of a crime or legal action that must be proven.

Employee: A person working for another person or a business firm for pay.

Employee benefits: Non-cash compensation and services provided to employees by employers.

Enacted laws: Laws adopted by a legislative or administrative body

Enumerated powers: Specific identified powers reserved only for the federal government.

Exclusionary Rule: A rule that prohibits illegally obtained evidence from being used in court.

Execution: An order allowing the seizure another person's property to enforce a money judgment.

Executory contracts: An agreement that is not yet fully performed on both sides.

Exempt: Protected from being taken by creditors, unless the owner agrees. State and federal law both list certain items of real and personal property that are exempt.

Expectation damages: The monetary value of the benefit that would have been received if the contract had been performed as agreed.

Express authority: Actions and tasks that the principal specifically assigns to an agent.

Family and medical leave: An unpaid leave from work taken by an employee for family and medical reasons.

Federal question jurisdiction: A case with alleged violations of the U.S. Constitution, federal laws, or federal treaties.

Federal Register: A daily publication containing documents and orders issued by Executive Branch agencies.

Federalism: A governmental system that shares power between national and state governments

Felony: A crime punishable by a sentence of incarceration for more than one year, or by death.

Fiduciary/fiduciary duty: A fiduciary is a person required to act for the benefit of another person. A fiduciary owes the other person the duties of good faith, trust, confidence, and candor.

Fifth Amendment privilege: The rule set out in the Fifth Amendment to the U.S. Constitution that no person "shall be compelled in any criminal case to be a witness against himself." The privilege applies in any type of proceeding, so that a person may decline to answer questions if her answer could lead to criminal charges.

First sale: A defense to an action for copyright and patent infringement. A person who lawfully acquires a copyright or patent protected item may resell that item without violating the copyright or patent.

Foreseeability: The foreseeability of the consequences of a defendant's actions depend on the balancing between the likelihood of risk and the magnitude of damages flowing therefrom.

Franchise: A franchise is a type of agreement that lets one party have access to another's proprietary knowledge, processes, and trademarks in order to sell a product or provide a service.

Fraudulent misrepresentation: A false statement made with the intention to induce the other person's reliance on the statement.

Free trade area: Countries that negotiate a free trade agreement to reduce or eliminate customs duties and other trade barriers between themselves.

Frolic: An agent's significant deviation from the principal's business for personal reasons.

Full warranty: Under the Magnuson-Moss Warranty Act, a warranty that obliges the seller of a product to remedy a defective product within a reasonable time. If the defect cannot be remedied after a reasonable number of attempts, the seller must replace it, or refund the price paid.

General damages: The harm that normally flows form a breach of contract.

General partner: In a limited partnership, the party who operates the business.

General warranty deed: A deed that guarantees that the grantor of real estate has good title to the property.

Grand jury: A panel of citizens who examine accusations in a criminal case to determine if the case should go forward.

Grantor: A person who transfer ownership of property to another.

Habeas corpus: A proceeding brought to challenge the legality of a person's confinement.

Health care power of attorney: A power of attorney that allows another to make health care decisions when the principal is unable to make those choices.

Homicide: The taking of another person's life.

Identification: A collector must disclose that he is trying to collect a debt when contacting the debtor.

Implied authority: The agent's power to do whatever is necessary to accomplish specific responsibilities assigned by the principal.

Incontestable: A trademark that is immune from legal challenge to its validity.

Indemnification: Reimbursing another party for financial losses or damages, or an agreement to indemnify against losses or damages.

Indemnify: To insure or secure another party against a future loss or liability.

Independent contractors: Workers with a high level of independence who are in business for themselves.

In forma pauperis: "In the manner of a pauper"; being excused from paying court costs and fees.

Injunction: A court order for a party to do or not to do a specific thing.

Insider trading: A corporate insider's use of nonpublic information to trade the shares of a company.

Insolvent: Inability to pay debts as they become due.

Intentional interference with contractual relations: The tort that occurs when a person intentionally harms the plaintiff's contractual or business relationship.

Intentional interference with prospective economic advantage: The tort that occurs when a person intentionally harms the plaintiff's business relationship that was likely to have economic benefit for the plaintiff.

Intentional tort: A civil wrong causing harm to another that results from a party's intentional act.

Interrogatories: A written set of questions served by a party to a lawsuit to an opposing party during discovery. The responding party prepares written answers under oath.

Invasion: An encroachment upon the rights of another.

Issue of first impression: Refers to the first time a question of law is considered for determination by a court.

Joint and several liability: Liability that applies both to a group and to the individual members of the group personally.

Joint tenants: Two or more co-owners of real estate who take an undivided interest in the property. A joint tenant may not sell his interest in the property without the permission of the other joint tenant.

Judgment notwithstanding the verdict (JNOV): A judgment entered by the trial judge which reverses a jury verdict because the judge finds that there was no factual basis for the verdict or it was contrary to law.

Judicial arbitration: Arbitration that is required by a statute, court, court rule, or regulation, but is not binding on the parties.

Judicial review: A court's review of an administrative agency's factual or legal findings.

Jurisdiction: 1. The legal power to hear a case. 2. The geographic territory over which authority is exercised (such as, a state or county).

Labor certification: A statement from the Department of Labor indicating that there are insufficient U.S. workers who are qualified and available to perform a particular job, and that employment of a foreign worker for the job will not negatively affect U.S. workers.

Labor union: An organized association of workers in the same trade that is formed for the purpose of representing the members' interests regarding wages, benefits, and working conditions.

Landlord: A person who leases real estate to another.

Last clear chance: A doctrine usually associated with negligence law which places liability for an injury on the person with the last opportunity to avoid the accident by exercising reasonable care; it is not applied in every jurisdiction.

Lease: A contract giving a person or company the right to occupy real estate for a limited time.

Levy: The act of taking property to satisfy a judgment.

Libel: A written false statement that damages another person's reputation.

Lien: A claim on someone else's property that is made to enforce a debt.

Lien creditor: A person who claims a lien on someone else's property.

Limitation of liability: A contract clause which restricts the amount of damages a party may recover from the other party in the event of a lawsuit.

Limited liability company: A hybrid business organization that combines the liability protection for owners of a corporation, with the pass-through taxation of a partnership. Identified by the initials "LLC."

Limited liability partnership: A partnership in which partners are not personally liable for partnership debts or obligations. Identified by the initials "LLP."

Limited partners: A partner in a limited partnership who receives a share of the profits, but whose personal liability for partnership debts is limited to her investment in the limited partnership.

Limited partnership: A type of partnership in which one or more of the partners (the limited partners) is liable only to the extent of the amount of money that he has invested.

Limited warranty: Under the Magnuson-Moss Warranty Act, a warranty that does not meet the requirements of a full warranty. Limited warranties must be clearly labelled as "limited."

Limited warranty deed: A deed that guarantees that nothing the grantor has done while she owned the property affects the title to the property.

Liquidated damages: A contract clause that specifies a predetermined amount of money that must be paid as damages if a party breaches the contract.

Litigation: The process of resolving a dispute through a lawsuit initiated in the court system.

Living will: A document that shows a person's choices for end-of-life care when he is unable to indicate those preferences.

Lockout: A temporary work stoppage implemented by the employer.

Long-arm statute: A statute providing for jurisdiction over a nonresident defendant who has had contacts with the territory in which the statute is in effect.

Manufacturing defect: A product defect that occurs in the manufacturing process due to poor workmanship or poor quality materials.

Material breach: A breach of contract that deprives the non-breaching party of the value of the contract.

Material misrepresentation: A misrepresentation of a fact that would induce a reasonable person to make an agreement.

Maternity leave: A period of absence from work for a female employee for the purpose of giving birth and taking care of an infant child.

Mediation: A method of alternative dispute resolution in which the parties work with a neutral third party, a mediator, in an attempt to reach a settlement.

Mediation-arbitration: A method of alternative dispute resolution in which the parties attempt to mediate the case, and if they do not resolve the dispute, the dispute is then submitted to arbitration.

Medicaid: A federal-state cooperative program providing medical care to low-income individuals. The program is administered by the states in compliance with federal criteria, and is funded jointly by the state and federal governments.

Member: The owner, or one of the owners, of a limited liability company.

Mens rea: Latin for "guilty mind." The mental state of a person committing the criminal act (*actus reus*).

Merchant: Under Article 2 of the U.C.C., a person who regularly deals in goods of a kind.

Merger: The combining or uniting of two companies.

Metadata: Information about electronic files describing how, when, and by whom a particular set of data was collected, and how the data is formatted.

Minimum contacts: A nonresident defendant's forum-state connections, such as business activity or actions foreseeably leading to business activity, that are substantial enough to bring the defendant within the forum-state court's personal jurisdiction without offending traditional notions of fair play and substantial justice.

Minimum wage: The lowest wage permitted by law to be paid to workers.

Mini-trial: A method of alternative dispute resolution in which the parties present their arguments to a third party who issues an advisory opinion.

Minor breach: A breach of contract that allows the non-breaching party to have the benefits of the agreement.

Misclassification: When an employer incorrectly classifies an employee as an independent contractor.

Misdemeanor: A crime punishable by a fine or imprisonment of no more than one year.

Misrepresentation: The act of making a false or misleading statement about something, usually with the intent to deceive.

Modification: A defense to products liability by which the defendant argues it should not be liable for the defective product because the plaintiff modified the product.

Monopoly: Control over a market by one company or individual.

Moral rights: The right to be identified as the author of a copyrighted work, and the right to prevent unauthorized publication, display, modification, or distortion of a work. Moral rights are recognized mostly in European law.

Mortgage: The use of real estate as collateral for a debt.

Motion to dismiss: A party's request to end a legal action.

Motion: A request to the judge to make a decision on an issue in a lawsuit.

Navigable waters: A body of water used, or capable of being used, for commerce. The term includes the tributaries of such bodies of water.

Necessity: A defense to a criminal charge that says that the defendant acted in an emergency situation not of her own creation to prevent a harm greater than the harm caused by her actions.

Negligence: The failure to act as a reasonably prudent person would act in the same circumstances.

Negligence per se: A doctrine under which negligence is proven through the defendant's violation of a statute or regulation designed to prevent the type of injury that occurred.

Negotiation: A method of alternative dispute resolution in which the parties, either with or without their attorneys, work to reach a resolution.

Nolle prosequi: A formal declaration that a prosecutor or plaintiff will "no longer prosecute" a particular case.

Non-profit corporation: A business organization formed to serve some public purpose, rather than to make a profit for investors.

Note: An unconditional written promise to pay money.

Nuisance: A condition, activity, or situation that interferes with the use or enjoyment of a person's property.

Offer: A proposal to make a contract.

Offeree: The person to whom an offer is made.

Offeror: The person who makes an offer.

Office action: An examiner's communication with the applicant for a patent, usually giving reasons why the application is denied.

Operating agreement: The rules and regulations adopted to govern the operation of a limited liability company.

Option contract: Agreement that allows a party to buy something for a given price at a later date.

Oral argument: Spoken presentation of arguments to the appeals court by attorneys for the parties appearing in person.

OSHA: The Occupational Safety and Health Administration, which implements and enforces workplace safety rules.

Overtime pay: Additional compensation paid to workers for hours worked in excess of forty hours per week.

Parol evidence: Oral or verbal evidence. In contract law, "parol evidence" refers to evidence of agreements outside of the written agreement. Parol evidence is generally not admissible when it would alter or contradict the terms of a written agreement.

Partnership: An association of two or more persons for the purpose of carrying on a business for profit.

Party: Plaintiff or defendant in a court case

Paternity leave: An absence from work provided to male employees upon the birth of a child.

Perfection: Filing of a security interest paperwork with the government to provide notice of the creditor's right to the security.

Personal jurisdiction: Power of a court over the defendant in a case.

Personal property: Any property other than real estate. Also called "personalty."

Petition: In bankruptcy law, the documents that ask the court for relief under the Bankruptcy Act.

Piercing the corporate veil: The legal process by which corporate shareholders or LLC members may be held liable for the debts or obligations of a corporation or LLC.

Plaintiff: The party who files a complaint to initiate a lawsuit against another party; the injured party who seeks compensation from a tortfeasor.

Plea agreement: Agreement in a criminal case between prosecutor and defendant by which defendant agrees to plead guilty to a particular charge in return for some deal from the prosecutor.

Pleadings: Documents filed with the court by the parties to a lawsuit. Pleadings include the complaint, answer, and counterclaims.

Ponzi scheme: A fraudulent investment scheme in which money contributed by investors is used to pay people who made a prior investment. Usually, money is not invested in any revenue-producing enterprise, or if it is, the enterprise does not generate expected revenue.

Power of attorney: A document by which a principal gives an agent authority to perform specified acts on behalf of the principal.

Precedent: An earlier court decision regarded as a guide to be considered in similar, subsequent cases

Preemption: The principle that federal law can supersede state law or regulation.

Preponderance of the evidence: More than half of the evidence

Principal: A person who authorizes another to act on her behalf.

Probable cause: An objective and fact-based belief that a person has committed a crime or that there is evidence of a crime in a specific place.

Probation: A criminal sentence in which the defendant is not imprisoned, but is allowed to remain free, subject to certain conditions.

Product misuse: A defense to products liability in which the defendant argues the plaintiff used the product for an abnormal purpose.

Products liability: A manufacturer or seller's liability for a defective product created by the manufacturer and sold to the public.

Prosecutor: A public official who starts legal proceedings against another, usually for a crime.

Protected class: A personal characteristic that cannot be targeted for discrimination.

Proximate cause: The main or legal cause of an injury. The type of cause which in the natural and continuous sequence unbroken by any new independent cause produces an event, and without which the injury would not have occurred.

Public benefit corporation: A corporation that has a public or social purpose in addition to the purpose of earning a profit for shareholders.

Public domain: Work that cannot be copyrighted. An old copyright may have expired, or the author or owner of the work has made an explicit designation that the work is public domain. The term also refers to U.S. Government works that cannot be copyrighted.

Publicly-traded companies: A company whose stock is freely traded among members of the general public.

Puffery: Minor exaggeration of fact when selling goods.

Punitive damages: A sum of money awarded to the injured party in a lawsuit to punish the wrongdoer for his actions.

Purchase money security interests: A security interest in property that is purchased by means of the debt, such as a car purchase loan secured by the car itself.

Pyramid scheme: Business model based on making payments to members for enrolling new members, instead of providing a return on investment or products and services.

Quantum meruit: An equitable doctrine that allows a party to recover the actual value of goods and services rendered, even in the absence of an enforceable contract. The goal is to prevent unjust enrichment of a party.

Quitclaim deed: A deed that gives the grantee all of the grantor's interest in property. A quitclaim deed does not guarantee title.

Ratify: Accepting or confirming a prior act.

Real estate: Land, structures permanently attached to land, and legal interests in land.

Reasonable accommodation: A modification or adjustment to enable people with disabilities to perform job duties.

Reasonable person: The legal standard by which a person's conduct is measured in a negligence action. A party must act as a reasonable person would act in the same circumstances.

Receiver: A person appointed by a bankruptcy court to oversee a business.

Redeem/redemption: A foreclosed mortgage may be redeemed and the borrower may regain rights to the property if the borrower pays the full amount of the balance on the mortgage.

Reformation: Rewriting a contract to conform to the terms of the parties' agreement.

Reliance: Dependence or trust by a person, especially when combined with action based on that dependence or trust.

Reliance damages: The amount that the non-breaching party spent to perform the contract, in reliance on the other party's performance.

Remand: The result when an appellate court sends a case back to the trial court for further proceedings.

Renunciation: Termination of an agency agreement by the agent.

Replevin: A court order, or writ, deciding who is entitled to physical possession of particular personal property. Replevin does not decide who the legal owner of the property is, only who is entitled to possess it.

Requests for admission: A written set of questions or statements served by a party to a lawsuit on an opposing party or witness during discovery in an effort to determine agreed-upon facts. The responding party must deny or admit each statement in writing.

Res ipsa loquitur: A principle by which negligence may be presumed where the defendant had exclusive control of the situation and it is the type of incident that would not normally occur without negligence on the defendant's part.

Rescission: Cancellation of an agreement. The parties to the agreement are put back to where they were before the contract was made.

Restitution: Payment to a victim in compensation for a loss. Restitution is usually ordered as a part of a civil or criminal penalty.

Restitution damages: Damages awarded when there was no legally enforceable contract.

Reversionary interest: An interest in real estate that will give the holder ownership of the property in the future, when a certain event happens.

Revocation: Termination of an agency agreement by the principal.

Right to work laws: Laws prohibiting agreements between employers and unions that require workers to join the union or pay union dues or fees.

Rule absolute: A rule which commands that an order be forthwith enforced.

Sarbanes-Oxley Act: A federal law that protects investors from fraudulent accounting practices.

Scope of authority: The amount of power granted to an agent under a specific agency agreement.

Scope of employment: An act of a servant done with the intention to perform it as a part of or incident to a service on account of which he is employed.

S corporation: A corporation that meets certain qualifications and that has chosen to be taxed as a partnership.

Secondary meaning: A special meaning that attaches to a descriptive mark through use and advertising.

Security: An instrument that evidences an ownership right in a company, such as stock, or that is evidence of a debt or obligation (bonds, debentures, or notes).

Separation of powers: Giving legislative, executive, and judicial powers of government to separate bodies of the government.

Servicemark: Something that is used to identify the source or origin of services. Some of the things that may be a servicemark include words, sounds, symbols, devices, logos, or phrases.

Severance agreement: A contract between an employer and employee detailing the rights and responsibilities of both parties after job termination.

Share: One of a number of equal parts into which the stock of a corporation is divided.

Shareholder: The owner of all or part of a corporation.

Sherman Act: A federal statute, passed in 1890, that prohibits direct or indirect interference with the freely competitive interstate production and distribution of goods. This Act was amended by the Clayton Act in 1914.

Sick leave: An absence from work when an employee is sick.

Slander: A spoken false statement that damages another person's reputation.

Sole proprietorship: An unincorporated business owned entirely by one person.

Special damages: Damages that occur due to the special circumstances of a particular contract.

Specific performance: An order from the court to do what the contract obligates the person to do.

Springing power of attorney: A power of attorney that becomes effective when the principal becomes incapacitated (it "springs" into effect).

Stare decisis: The doctrine that requires a court to follow earlier judicial decisions when the same points arise again.

Statute of Frauds: A law that states that certain types of contract are not enforceable unless they are in writing.

Statutes: Written laws passed by a legislative body.

Statutory damages: Damages that are fixed by statute. They are awarded without considering what the actual loss was.

Stayed sentence: A sentence that the court imposes, but delays the requirement that the defendant comply with it immediately. For example, a stayed prison sentence will allow the defendant to remain free as long as he remains law abiding and complies with the conditions of probation.

Stock: A proportional part of the capital of a corporation. Stock grants its owner the right to vote on the management of the corporation.

Strict Liability: 1. The imposition of liability on a party without a showing of fault. 2. In criminal law, a crime that does not have require proof of a guilty state of mind.

Strike: A collective effort of union employees to refuse to work in order to persuade the employer to negotiate or accept contract terms.

Subject matter jurisdiction: The authority of a court to decide a case of a particular type.

Sufficient contacts: Enough connection between a non-resident defendant with the state where a legal case is filed to give that court personal jurisdiction over that defendant.

Summary judgment: A judgment entered by the court deciding the case in favor of one party or the other based on application of the law to the available evidence, but without a full trial. Summary judgment is granted only when there is no genuine issue of material fact.

Summary jury trial: A method of alternative dispute resolution in which the parties engage in a short mock trial and a jury issues a non-binding verdict. The purpose is to encourage the parties to settle the case based on the verdict result.

Supreme court: The highest appellate court in a jurisdiction. In New York, the state trial court.

Suspended sentence: A criminal sentence that the defendant is not required to serve immediately.

Tenant: A person who rents real estate from another.

Tenants in common: Two or more co-owners of real estate who take an undivided interest in the property. A tenant in common may sell her interest in the property without the permission of the other tenant.

Termination: When an employee is fired from his or her job.

Title VII: A section of the Civil Rights Act of 1964 prohibiting employment discrimination on the basis of sex, race, color, national origin, and religion.

Tort: A lawsuit brought by an injured party seeking compensation from the party who performed an act that caused the harm.

Tortfeasor: An individual who commits a wrongful act that injures another person.

Trade libel: A defamatory statement about the quality of a business's services or products. It is also referred to as product disparagement.

Trademark: Something that is used to identify the source or origin of goods. Some of the things that may be a trademark include words, sounds, symbols, devices, logos, or phrases.

Trade name: The name under which a business operates.

Transferred intent: Shifting intent from the crime the defendant originally intended to commit to the crime that actually was committed.

Trap and trace device: means to capture the origination and routing information for email messages.

Trespass: An unlawful act against the person or property of another. The term is usually used to mean entry onto another person's property without the permission of the owner.

Trustee: A person appointed to hold or manage property for another. In bankruptcy law, a person appointed to oversee the case.

Ultra vires: An action outside the legal ability of an entity to perform.

Uncodified law: Rules taken from custom and precedent rather than statutes.

Unemployment compensation: Insurance benefits paid by the government to individuals who are out of work.

Unfair labor practice strikers: Union workers who are striking to protest an unfair labor practice by the employer.

Unlawful detainer: A type of legal action claiming that a tenant no longer has the right to remain on a property.

Unsecured: A debt is unsecured if there is no collateral guaranteeing the debt. Most credit cards are unsecured.

Validation notice: A notice to a debtor from a collector providing information on the debt, including the total and the creditor, as well as how to contest the debt.

Venue: The residence of defendant or place where most events leading to a legal claim took place.

Vested right: A right that is unconditional, that cannot be taken away from a party.

Vicarious liability: A principal's legal responsibility for the action or inaction of its agent while the agent was working on behalf of the principal.

Voir dire: The process of questioning potential jurors to determine if they are qualified to serve on the jury.

Warrant: Written authority to conduct a search or to seize property or arrest a person.

Warranty: A promise or guarantee to a consumer.

Warranty of merchantability: A promise from the manufacturer that the product is in good working order and can safely be used for the purposes stated on the label.

Well-pleaded complaint: An original or initial pleading that sufficiently sets forth a claim for relief—by including the grounds for the court's jurisdiction, the basis for the relief claimed, and a demand for judgment—so that a defendant may draft an answer that is responsive to the issues presented. A well-pleaded complaint must raise a controlling issue of federal law for a federal court to have federal-question jurisdiction over the lawsuit.

Whistleblower: An employee who reports her employer's wrongdoing to the government or to law enforcement.

Work for hire: A work that was either created by an employee within the scope of her employment, or that was commissioned for a special purpose with the written agreement that it would be work-for-hire. Copyright for a work-for-hire automatically vests in the employer or person who commissioned the work.

Work permit: Authorization from U.S. Citizenship and Immigration Services allowing individuals living in the United States under non-work visas to work in the U.S.

Workers' compensation: A type of insurance providing benefits to employees who are injured on the job.

Writ of certiorari: Permission to have a case heard by the U.S. Supreme Court that is given by the Court in response to a petition by the appealing party.

Writ of error: An order by an appellate court directing the trial court to produce the record of the case it is reviewing.

Writ of mandamus: A writ requiring a lower court or government official to perform some duty or act.

INDEX